# Human Resource Management

## GAINING A COMPETITIVE ADVANTAGE

# Human Resource Management

## GAINING A COMPETITIVE ADVANTAGE 12e

**RAYMOND A. NOE**
*The Ohio State University*

**JOHN R. HOLLENBECK**
*Michigan State University*

**BARRY GERHART**
*University of Wisconsin–Madison*

**PATRICK M. WRIGHT**
*University of South Carolina*

McGraw Hill

HUMAN RESOURCE MANAGEMENT: GAINING A COMPETITIVE ADVANTAGE, TWELFTH EDITION

Published by McGraw-Hill Education, 2 Penn Plaza, New York, NY 10121. Copyright © 2021 by McGraw-Hill Education. All rights reserved. Printed in the United States of America. Previous editions © 2019, 2017, and 2015. No part of this publication may be reproduced or distributed in any form or by any means, or stored in a database or retrieval system, without the prior written consent of McGraw-Hill Education, including, but not limited to, in any network or other electronic storage or transmission, or broadcast for distance learning.

Some ancillaries, including electronic and print components, may not be available to customers outside the United States.

This book is printed on acid-free paper.

1 2 3 4 5 6 7 8 9 0 LWI 24 23 22 21 20

ISBN 978-1-260-26257-5 (bound edition)
MHID 1-260-26257-X (bound edition)

ISBN 978-1-260-78076-5 (loose-leaf edition)
MHID 1-260-78076-7 (loose-leaf edition)

Portfolio Manager: *Peter Jurmu*
Product Developer: *Kelsey Darin*
Executive Marketing Manager: *Debbie Clare*
Content Project Managers: *Maria McGreal; Bruce Gin; Karen Jozefowicz*
Buyer: *Susan K. Culbertson*
Design: *Matt Diamond*
Content Licensing Specialists: *Shawntel Schmitt*
Cover Image: *©Monkey Business Images/Shutterstock*
Compositor: *Aptara®, Inc.*

All credits appearing on page or at the end of the book are considered to be an extension of the copyright page.

**Library of Congress Cataloging-in-Publication Data**

Names: Noe, Raymond A., author. | Hollenbeck, John R., author. | Gerhart, Barry A., author.
Title: Human resource management : gaining a competitive advantage / Raymond A. Noe, The Ohio State University, John R. Hollenbeck, Michigan State University, Barry Gerhart, University of Wisconsin-Madison, Patrick M. Wright, University of South Carolina.
Description: Twelfth Edition. | Dubuque : McGraw-Hill Education, 2020. | Revised edition of Human resource management, 2016.
Identifiers: LCCN 2019044777 (print) | LCCN 2019044778 (ebook) | ISBN 9781260262575 (hardcover) | ISBN 9781260780765 (spiral bound) | ISBN 9781260780758 (ebook) | ISBN 9781260780734 (ebook other)
Subjects: LCSH: Personnel management—United States.
Classification: LCC HF5549.2.U5 N64 2020 (print) | LCC HF5549.2.U5 (ebook) | DDC 658.3—dc23
LC record available at https://lccn.loc.gov/2019044777
LC ebook record available at https://lccn.loc.gov/2019044778

The Internet addresses listed in the text were accurate at the time of publication. The inclusion of a website does not indicate an endorsement by the authors or McGraw-Hill Education, and McGraw-Hill Education does not guarantee the accuracy of the information presented at these sites.

mheducation.com/highered

# ABOUT THE AUTHORS

**RAYMOND A. NOE** is the Robert and Anne Hoyt Designated Professor of Management at The Ohio State University. He was previously a professor in the Department of Management at Michigan State University and the Industrial Relations Center of the Carlson School of Management, University of Minnesota. He received his BS in psychology from The Ohio State University and his MA and PhD in psychology from Michigan State University. Professor Noe conducts research and teaches undergraduate as well as MBA and PhD students in human resource management, managerial skills, quantitative methods, human resource information systems, training, employee development, performance management, and organizational behavior. He has published over 70 articles and invited chapters and authored, co-authored or edited seven books covering a variety of topics in training and development (training needs, trainee motivation, informal learning, autonomous learning, mentoring), human resource management (recruiting), and organizational behavior (psychological contracts, teams, work, and family). Professor Noe has received awards for his teaching and research excellence, including the Ernest J. McCormick Award for Distinguished Early Career Contribution from the Society for Industrial and Organizational Psychology. He is also a fellow of the Society of Industrial and Organizational Psychology and American Psychological Association.

**JOHN R. HOLLENBECK** holds the positions of University Distinguished Professor at Michigan State University and Eli Broad Professor of Management at the Eli Broad Graduate School of Business Administration. Dr. Hollenbeck received his PhD in Management from New York University in 1984. He served as the acting editor at *Organizational Behavior and Human Decision Processes* in 1995, the associate editor of *Decision Sciences* from 1999 to 2004, and the editor of *Personnel Psychology* from 1996 to 2002. He has published over 90 articles and book chapters on the topics of team decision making and work motivation. According to the Web of Science, this body of work has been cited over 6,000 times by other researchers. Dr. Hollenbeck has been awarded fellowship status in both the Academy of Management and the American Psychological Association, and was recognized with the Career Achievement Award by the HR Division of the Academy of Management (2011), the Distinguished Service Contributions Award (2014), and the Early Career Award by the Society of Industrial and Organizational Psychology (1992). At Michigan State, Dr. Hollenbeck has won several teaching awards including the Michigan State Distinguished Faculty Award, the Michigan State Teacher-Scholar Award, and the Broad MBA Most Outstanding Faculty Member.

**BARRY GERHART** is Professor of Management and Human Resources and the Bruce R. Ellig Distinguished Chair in Pay and Organizational Effectiveness, Wisconsin School of Business, University of Wisconsin-Madison. He has served as department chair at Cornell and Vanderbilt, as well as department chair, senior associate dean, and as interim Albert O. Nicholas Dean at Wisconsin. His research interests include compensation, human resource/human capital strategy, international human resources, and employee retention. Professor Gerhart received his BS in psychology from Bowling Green State University and his PhD in Industrial Relations from the University of Wisconsin-Madison. He has co-authored two books in the area of compensation. Professor Gerhart is a past recipient of the Heneman Career Achievement Award, the Thomas A. Mahoney Mentoring Award (for his work with doctoral students), the Scholarly Achievement Award, and (twice) the International Human Resource Management Scholarly Research Award, all from the Human Resources Division, Academy of Management. He has also received the Michael R. Losey Excellence in Human Resource Research Award, a career achievement award from the Society for Human Resource Management. Professor Gerhart has been elected as a Fellow of the Academy of Management, the American Psychological Association, and the Society for Industrial and Organizational Psychology.

**PATRICK M. WRIGHT** is Thomas C. Vandiver Bicentennial Chair and the Director of the Center for Executive Succession in the Darla Moore School of Business at the University of South Carolina. Prior to joining USC, he served on the faculties at Cornell University, Texas A&M University, and the University of Notre Dame. Professor Wright teaches, conducts research, and consults in the area of strategic human resource management (SHRM), particularly focusing on how firms use people as a source of competitive advantage and the changing nature of the chief HR officer (CHRO) role. He is the faculty leader for the Cornell ILR Executive Education/NAHR program, "The Chief HR Officer: Strategies for Success," aimed at developing potential successors to the CHRO role. He served as the lead editor on the recently released book, *The Chief HR Officer: Defining the New Role of Human Resource Leaders*, published by Wiley. Professor Wright has published more than 60 research articles in journals as well as more than 20 chapters in books and edited volumes. He recently served as the editor at the *Journal of Management*, has co-edited a special issue of *Research in Personnel and Human Resources Management* titled "Strategic Human Resource Management in the 21st Century," and guest edited a special issue of *Human Resource Management Review* titled "Research in Strategic HRM for the 21st Century." He currently serves as a member on the Board of Directors for the Society for Human Resource Management and the National Academy of Human Resources. He is a former board member of HRPS, SHRM Foundation, and World at Work (formerly American Compensation Association). He has been named a Fellow in the National Academy of Human Resources and the Academy of Management, has won SHRM's Michael Losey Award for HR Research and the AOM HR Division's Herb Heneman Career Achievement Award, and from 2011 to 2018, he has been named by *HRM Magazine* as one of the 20 "Most Influential Thought Leaders in HR."

# PREFACE

Our intent is to provide students with the background to be successful HRM professionals, to manage human resources effectively, and to be knowledgeable consumers of HRM products. Managers must be able to identify effective HRM practices to purchase these services from a consultant, to work with the HRM department, or to design and implement them personally. *Human Resources Management: Gaining a Competitive Advantage,* 12th edition, emphasizes how a manager can more effectively manage human resources and highlights important issues in current HRM practice.

*Human Resources Management: Gaining a Competitive Advantage* represents a valuable approach to teaching human resource management for several reasons:

- The text draws from the diverse research, teaching, and consulting experiences of four authors who have taught human resource management to undergraduates, traditional day MBA students as a required and elective course, and more experienced managers and professional employees in weekend and evening MBA programs. The teamwork approach gives a depth and breadth to the coverage that is not found in other texts.
- Human resource management is viewed as critical to the success of a business. The text emphasizes how the HRM function, as well as the management of human resources, can help companies gain a competitive advantage.
- The book discusses current issues such as artificial intelligence and robotics, use of nontraditional employment relationships, big data, talent management, diversity, and the employee experience, all of which have a major impact on business and HRM practice.
- Strategic human resource management is introduced early in the book and integrated throughout.
- Examples of how new technologies are being used to improve the efficiency and effectiveness of HRM practices are provided throughout.
- We provide examples of how companies are evaluating HRM practices to determine their value.

## Organization

*Human Resource Management: Gaining a Competitive Advantage,* 12th edition, includes an introductory chapter (Chapter 1) and five parts.

Chapter 1 provides a detailed discussion of the global, economic, sustainability, and technology challenges that influence companies' abilities to successfully meet the needs of shareholders, customers, employees, and other stakeholders. We discuss how the management of human resources can help companies meet the competitive challenges.

Part One includes a discussion of the environmental forces that companies face in attempting to capitalize on their human resources as a means to gain competitive advantage. The environmental forces include the strategic direction of the business, the legal environment, and the type of work performed and physical arrangement of the work.

A key focus of Chapter 2, on strategic human resource management, is to highlight the role that staffing, performance management, training and development, and compensation play in different types of business strategies.

A key focus of Chapter 3, on the legal environment, is to enhance managers' understanding of laws related to sexual harassment, affirmative action, and accommodations for disabled employees. The various types of discrimination and ways they have been interpreted by the courts are discussed.

Chapter 4, on analysis and design of work, emphasizes how work systems can improve company competitiveness by alleviating job stress and by improving employees' motivation and satisfaction with their jobs.

Part Two deals with the acquisition and preparation of human resources, including human resource planning and recruitment, selection, and training.

Chapter 5, on human resource planning and recruitment, illustrates the process of developing a human resource plan. Also, the strengths and weaknesses of staffing options such as outsourcing, use of contingent workers, and downsizing are discussed. Strategies for recruiting talented employees are emphasized.

Chapter 6, on selection and placement, emphasizes ways to minimize errors in employee selection and placement to improve the company's competitive position. Selection method standards such as validity and reliability are discussed in easily understandable terms without compromising the technical complexity of these issues. The chapter discusses selection methods such as interviews and various types of tests (including personality, honesty, and drug tests) and compares them on measures of validity, reliability, utility, and legality.

Chapter 7 discusses the components of effective training systems and the manager's role in determining employees' readiness for training, creating a positive learning environment, and ensuring that training is used on the job. The advantages and disadvantages of different training methods are described, such as e-learning, serious games, microlearning, virtual reality and augmented reality, and mobile training.

Part Three explores how companies can determine the value of employees and capitalize on their talents through retention and development strategies.

Chapter 8, on performance management, discusses the evolution of performance management systems to a more continuous process that encourages setting short and long term goals, frequent performance conversations between managers and their employees, and peer feedback. The chapter examines the strengths and weaknesses of performance management methods that use ratings, objectives, or behaviors.

Chapter 9, on employee development, introduces the student to how assessment, job experiences, formal courses, and mentoring relationships are used to develop employees.

Chapter 10, on retention and separation, discusses how managers can maximize employee productivity and satisfaction to avoid absenteeism and turnover. The chapter emphasizes the use of employee surveys to monitor job and organizational characteristics that affect satisfaction and subsequently retention.

Part Four covers rewarding and compensating human resources, including designing pay structures (Chapter 11), recognizing individual contributions (Chapter 12), and providing benefits (Chapter 13).

Here we explore how managers should decide the pay rate for different jobs, given the company's compensation strategy and the worth of jobs. The advantages and disadvantages of merit pay, gainsharing, and skill-based pay are discussed. The benefits chapter highlights the different types of employer-provided benefits and discusses how benefit costs can be contained. International comparisons of compensation and benefit practices are provided.

Part Five covers special topics in human resource management, including labor-management relations, international HRM, and strategically managing the HRM function.

Chapter 14, on collective bargaining and labor relations, focuses on traditional issues in labor-management relations, such as union structure and membership, the organizing process, and contract negotiations; it also discusses new union agendas and less adversarial approaches to labor-management relations.

Chapter 15 discusses social and political changes, such as Brexit, on global human resource management. Selecting, preparing, and rewarding employees for foreign assignments is also discussed.

The text concludes with Chapter 16, which emphasizes how HRM practices should be aligned to help the company meet its business objectives. The chapter emphasizes that the HRM function needs to have a customer focus to be effective.

# Features

The chapter openers, in-text boxes, and end-of-chapter materials provide questions that provide students the opportunity to discuss and apply HR concepts to a broad range of issues including strategic human resource management, HR in small businesses, helping companies achieve sustainability through environment, social, and governance practices, adopting and using technology, adapting to globalization, and ethics and integrity. This should make the HR classroom more interactive and increase students' understanding of the concepts and their application.

- **Enter the World of Business chapter-opening vignettes** provide relevant examples of real business problems or issues that provide background for the issues discussed in the chapter.
- **Video Conversations with Chief HR Officers (CHROs)**, created by the Center for Executive Succession at the Darla Moore School of Business, University of South Carolina, feature video conversations with CHROs from top organizations such as Accenture, Bank of America, Boeing, GE, HP, Merck, and others are tied in to pertinent chapters. In addition, the videos are featured in Connect, along with questions related to chapter content.
- **Evidence-Based HR sections** highlight an evidence-based approach to HR management and focuses on people, employees, and human capital.
- **Competing through Environmental, Social, and Governance Practices boxes** show how organizations can engage in HR practices to make a profit without sacrificing the resources of its employees, the community, or the environment.
- **Competing through Globalization boxes** focus on how companies use HR practices to improve their ability to compete in international markets and prepare employees for global assignments.
- **Competing through Technology boxes** highlight how organizations are using social networking, artificial intelligence, robotics, human resource information systems, cloud computing, dashboards, and other tools to enhance the efficiency and effectiveness of HR practices, employees, and the workplace.
- **Integrity in Action boxes** highlight the good (and bad) HR-related decisions made by company leaders and managers that either reinforce (or undermine) the importance of ethical behavior in the company.
- **A Look Back segments**, at the end of the chapter, encourage students to recall the chapter's opening vignettes and apply what they have just learned to questions about them.

- **Self-Assessment Exercises**, at the end of each chapter, provide a brief exercise for students to complete and evaluate their own skills related to topics covered in the chapter. In addition, the self-assessments are featured in Connect.
- **Managing People cases** look at incidents and real companies and encourage students to critically evaluate each problem and apply the chapter contents.
- **Exercising Strategy cases** pose strategic questions based on real-life practices.
- **HR in Small Business cases** highlight HR issues and practices in entrepreneurial, family-owned, and emerging businesses. Questions provoke students to think critically about "people practices" in small businesses.

# New Features and Content Changes in This Edition

All examples, figures, and statistics have been updated to incorporate the most recently published human resource data. Each chapter was revised to include current examples, research results, and relevant topical coverage. All of the Exercising Strategy, Managing People, and HR in Small Business end-of-chapter cases are either new or updated. Following are the highlights for each chapter:

## Chapter 1

**New Opening Vignette:** Describes how HR practices have evolved at IBM as the company increasingly emphasizes cloud-based services, artificial intelligence (AI) based products, and blockchaining (a security system for bitcoin and cryptocurrencies).

**New Boxes:**
- Practices of Microsoft, Apple, Gap, and Mars contribute to sustainability by delivering positive results for local and global communities.
- Sanfoli's efforts to advance women into top management positions and the metrics they are using to track their progress.
- Under Armour's change of employee reimbursement practices to avoid contributing to a work culture where sexual harassment is encouraged or tolerated.
- Cisco providing jobs for persons with disabilities around the world.
- Human and robots working together at Dynamic Group.

**New Text Material:**
- Advantages of having an HR professional and an HR department rather than relying on a manager.
- Examples of how the top HR professionals interact with the CEO and help align HR practices with business strategy and contribute to business goals: Honeywell and Lawson.
- How Sonic Automotive uses big data to help determine which training programs have a positive ROI and are helping to meet the company's strategic goals.
- Updated median salaries for HR professionals.
- Competing through Sustainability has been renamed Competing through Environmental, Social, and Governance Practices to reflect business emphasis on sustainability through "the triple bottom line"—the simultaneous delivery of positive results for people, planet and profit.
- Discussion of environmental, social, and governance (ESG) practices with an example from Goldman Sachs.

- Economy data, labor force statistics, occupational and job growth projections, skill shortages, working at home, immigration, world economy and emerging markets.
- How HR practices at Hilton Worldwide help the company deal with change by contributing to agility example.
- Employee experience and its relationship to employee engagement (SunTrust example).
- Employee value proposition (EVP) (Dell example).
- Mastercard's talent management practices.
- Automattic's use of remote work.
- Ingersoll Rand Plc and Ultra Machining Company efforts to retain older employees by offering them shorter work hours.
- Detailed discussion of characteristics of Generation Z.
- How EY's human resource practices meet Millennials and Generation Z employees' workplace needs.
- Sylvan Gardens Landscape had to cancel contract because it could not hire enough workers due to the low level of unemployment and higher demand for visas under the H-2B season worker visa program.
- The increased awareness of sexual assault and harassment in the workplace due to the #MeToo movement.
- Data security and protection is now required for company's who handle the data of an individual in the European Union due to the General Data Protection Regulation which took effect in May 2018.
- How tariffs are affecting RelianceCM's business
- Artificial intelligence and robots.
- Potential ways that automation will affect work activities and jobs.
- Use of robots at Just Born, Beehex, Mercedes-Benz, and in masonry work.

## Chapter 2

**New Opening Vignette:** Explores why one of the world's most admired and successful companies eventually failed.

**New Boxes:**
- The complexities and potential of corporate/government espionage.
- The mistakes in analyzing big data and how this impacted firms' plans for the "gig" economy.
- Technology is responsible for Honda's shift from producing everything in-house to using suppliers.
- The importance of CEOs hiring and building a strong team of employees.

**New Text Material:**
- New sections on talent, culture, and aligning strategy, talent, and culture with a figure to show that these are all aligned around customer value.

## Chapter 3

**New Opening Vignette:** Uses Harvard as a platform to discuss a number of issues regarding discrimination and equal employment opportunity law.

**New Boxes:**
- Nike's history of a negative culture and its commitment to eliminating this negativity.
- Some victims of sexual harassment who file a complaint experience retaliation from their firms.

- #MeToo is a global and widespread movement.
- Toyota uses exoskeletons to lower risk of worker injury.

**New Text Material:**
- Updated data on age discrimination complaints.
- Updated data on religious discrimination complaints.
- Updated data on sexual harassment complaints.
- Updated data on disability complaints.
- New section on Gender Equity in pay and representation.
- Updated data on injuries, illnesses, and fatalities in the workplace.

## Chapter 4

**New Opening Vignette:** Analyzes the role of robots in the workforce, illustrating how advanced technology changes the nature of jobs more than the number of jobs in the economy.

**New Boxes:**
- China's 2025 initiative aimed at becoming the world's #1 producer of industrial robots.
- The re-emergence of a deadly chemical to work production processes that everyone believed was totally eliminated.
- The reasons behind the increased role of interpersonal skills in the job requirements list for software programmers.
- The introduction of unsafe work practices by foreign companies into automobile parts factories in the southern United States.
- The impact of extreme clean air standards on worker productivity in a traditional manufacturing environment.

**New Text Material:**
- How Toyota's 2017 strategic decision to stop producing sedans, like the Camry and Avalon, in favor of SUV's and pickups affected HRM practices related to how work needed to be designed.
- Why Apple's decision to not manufacture a single phone in the United States makes sense in terms of profits and job creation.
- How Smart Helmets now allow specialists working remotely to see and hear the physical machinery they need to manipulate using local workers hands.
- How and why Pfizer reorganized its organizational structure in order to promote greater innovation.
- How and why the job creation surge in 2017–2018 made people rethink the notion that we are moving to a "gig" economy.

## Chapter 5

**New Opening Vignette:** Examines how more restrictive immigration policies regarding immigrants and refugees are creating labor shortages in the areas of agriculture and meat processing.

**New Boxes:**
- Robotic technology still relies very heavily on human intervention using call centers as an example.
- Limits on H1-B visas in the United States are creating competitive disadvantages compared with Canada in the field of high tech.

- The Trade Adjustment Assistance (TAA) program provides money for training to U.S. workers when their jobs move overseas.
- The increased aggressiveness of workplace raids conducted by Immigration and Customs Enforcement (ICE) office is breaking up families and local communities.
- Recent evidence shows that immigration results in a loss of U.S. jobs in the short term, but in the long term, results in large job gains for the country.

**New Text Material:**
- Qualcomm used leading indicators and forecasting to avoid a labor surplus that would have been caused by failures at Samsung–one of their primary customers.
- Improvements in technology reduce the need for workers when manufacturing jobs that moved overseas move back to the United States.
- Changes in American eating habits related to restaurants is causing a shortage of labor for cooks, where turnover rates have soared to 100% in some regions.
- Low cost, online degree programs in the field of law have created a vast over-supply of unemployable lawyers.
- Deloitte is addressing a potential brain drain caused by the imminent retirement of a large cadre of workers.

## Chapter 6

**New Opening Vignette:** Discusses how Uber's business model relies on relaxed personnel vetting processes relative to more traditional taxi companies, and how scandals due to Uber's failure to conduct routine background checks now threatens that business model.

**New Boxes:**
- How and why Saudi Arabia is changing its staffing model for business within the kingdom and how these business practices are challenging cultural norms.
- The role of artificial intelligence applications in changing how organizations make team staffing decisions to promote team chemistry.
- An examination of controversies regarding Harvard's alleged discrimination against Asian Americans and the role of "personality" as a tool to discriminate.
- How some organizations in the hospitality industry are at the forefront of getting former opioid addicts back into the labor pool.
- How Github used blind evaluations of written code to reduce discrimination against women who were applying for jobs in the software industry.

**New Text Material:**
- How the current labor shortage is reducing organizations' ability to rigorously screen potential applicants, and the sometime disastrous results of this.
- How organizations in the tech industry use well-funded public competitions to find and recruit the most talent programmers.
- How recent legal challenges against employers such as Texas Roadhouse and Abercrombie and Fitch make reference to "customer preference" a losing legal argument.
- Why the different business models of Amazon, Google, Intel, and Github require workers with very different skills and why they rarely compete for the same people when staffing.
- How employers can prevent illegal discrimination against pregnant employees, using UPS's recent experience as a salient example.
- How the legalization of marijuana in many states is changing the landscape related to drug testing in different industries.

## Chapter 7

**New Opening Vignette:** Highlights how AT&T is staying competitive by using training to develop employees skills for their current job and future career.

**New Boxes:**
- Tyson Foods offers training opportunities for immigrant employees to help them both in the in the workplace and in their nonwork lives.
- Campari Group's language training program.
- Community and company partnerships develop skills using apprenticeships.
- Aristocrat Technologies customizes training using artificial intelligence.
- Edwards Jones' evaluation of sales training program.

**New Text Material:**
- Moneris helps employees obtain the skills and knowledge needed to meet customers payment needs by accessing the company's learning and development portal.
- McDonald's needs assessment to examine the relevance of current training topics and the effectiveness of training methods.
- Methods that H&H Castings and KLA-Tencor used to conduct needs assessment.
- Microlearning or training delivered in small pieces or chunks designed to engage trainees, motivate them to learn, and help facilitate retention.
- Example of microlearning at Nationwide Mutual Insurance.
- Avande Synaptics' use of a searchable YouTube channel to support training.
- How GE Power uses an app to support knowledge sharing.
- How Gales Residential and CVS get learners actively involved and help to ensure transfer of training.
- Data on use of different training methods.
- Farmer's use of videos in training.
- Aggreko's use of an app to deliver training materials and videos.
- On-the-job training at Nomad Communications Solutions.
- Farmers Insurance's use of virtual reality to train claims adjusters.
- Augmented reality (AR).
- Argo's use of AR.
- Use of games in training at Deloitte and University of North Carolina.
- Use of MOOC at World Bank.
- Blended learning at Anthem Inc.
- Learning management systems at Ferguson Enterprises and Gukenheimer.
- Verizon's use of training outcomes to evaluate its Sales Leadership Academy (SLA).
- Verizon's ROI for customer service training.
- Employee repatriation efforts at Monsanto Company, Asurion, and L'Oreal.
- Unconscious bias and unconscious bias training programs.
- The actions Rockwell Automation, National Life Group, and Blackstone Group are taking to manage diversity.
- Onboarding at Forum Credit Union and Bazaarvoice.

## Chapter 8

**New Opening Vignette:** Discusses Patagonia's transition from traditional performance management system to a continuous performance management system emphasizing frequent performance conversations, annual goals and quarterly stretch goals, and encouraging employees to seek feedback.

**New Boxes:**

- How Bluejeans, a global company with employees working in virtual teams, uses a 360-degree feedback process for performance management.
- How Wells Fargo's overreliance on managing performance using rewards linked to goals cheated its customers and damaged the company's reputation.
- Feedback model that PennStation East Coast Subs gives managers to help them provide employees with timely and actionable feedback.
- IBM's, Goldman Sachs', and Uber's use of apps in the performance management process.
- How Kronos's upward feedback system influenced employees intentions to stay with the company.

**New Text Material:**

- Differences in performance measures used for exempt compared to non-exempt employees.
- Google's performance management system includes objectives and key results (OKRs) for the entire company, as well as at the team, managerial, and employee levels.
- The continuous performance management process and how it compares to the traditional performance management process.
- Reasons why companies are adopting a continuous performance management process.
- How Facebook and Procter & Gamble adopted some of the features of continuous performance management systems into their current appraisal systems.
- Purposes of performance management: strategic, administrative, developmental, communication, organizational maintenance, and documentation.
- How GE's new performance management system supports the company's strategic direction.
- Additional implications of fairness for performance management process.
- Analysis Group's use of self-appraisals in performance management.
- Hospitals' use of monitoring of behaviors such as doctors and nurses hand-washing to reduce infections and improve patient care.
- Inaccuracy of systems monitoring work hours leads to lawsuits against American Airlines and Krogers.
- Research results showing how calibration meetings affected changes in performance ratings and employees and managers reactions to them.
- One way to avoid overly personalizing employees poor performance is to focus on the situation (where the problem behavior occurred), specific behaviors that occurred in the situation, and the results of the behavior for peers, customers, and if appropriate, for themselves.

# Chapter 9

**New Opening Vignette:** Shows how Vi, a company that operates residential communities for older adults, invests in employee development to attract and retain talented employees who in turn provide high-quality services to residents.

**New Boxes:**

- Verizon Wireless, Discover Financial Services, Taco Bell, and Disney pay the costs of formal education employees need to obtain a job or advance in their careers.
- General Motors' and Cardinal Health's use of software to match mentors and protégés in contrast with PayPal's face-to-face approach.

- West Monroe Partners help employees develop in ways that demonstrate social responsibility to its stakeholders.
- How Mondelez International use of challenging international job experiences for employee development also contribute to sustainability through helping local communities.

**New Text Material:**
- Kate Cole's career path from waitress to group president exemplifies a protean career.
- Miami Children's Health System's use of projects to develop and retain Millennial employees.
- CarMax provides employees with a Career Conversation Guide, including competency self-assessment that helps them take ownership of their development.
- IBM uses AI to provide employees with personalized recommendations about job openings based on data from their résumé, assessments, and the type of work that excites them.
- GE uses an app to increase the effectiveness of development conversations between employees and their managers.
- Procter & Gamble's promotion from within policy is supported by development plans completed by every employee.
- 3M's and Penn Station EastCoast Subs' career management and development systems.
- Telus International's development programs for employees at different career stages.
- NBA leadership development programs.
- TELUS employees attend an MBA program customized to the company and industry leadership and strategy issues.
- Guckenheimer's use of DiSC for managers to understand their communications style.
- CHG Healthcare's and Lupin's use of 360-degree feedback.
- H&M's and Haskell's use of job rotation for employee development.
- Use of promotions at PepsiCo.
- Sabbaticals at Morris Financial Concepts and Edelman Financial Services.
- General Mills' and Prudential's support for employees to take volunteer assignment in local communities and abroad.
- Mentoring programs at Cisco Systems and Michigan Medical.
- U.S. Government Accountability Office's use of orientation and mentor training.
- Benefits of UnitedHealthcare's reverse mentoring program for Millennial mentor and more senior manager protégé.
- Role of coaches at PwC Coaching as part of managers role at Procter & Gamble.
- Coaching improves employees skills and performance especially when an internal coach is used (manager who has been trained in coaching).
- Data on women in executive positions.
- How companies are engaging men to consider their role in creating a workplace that allows both men and women to contribute and maximize their potential.
- Use the 9-box grid but actively manage employees to help them improve.
- Difficulties in following the succession planning process and how companies are changing their process to address them.
- Succession planning at ITU AbsorbTech.

## Chapter 10

**New Opening Vignette:** Discusses how "pass the trash" policies related to sexual harassment claims at Google led 20,000 employees to stage a mass protest and what this means for HR going forward when it comes to handling such complaints.

**New Boxes:**
- The concept of "flexicurity" and the challenges confronting France as it tries to rewrite its labor code to be more business-friendly.
- How the culture at Uber, as operationalized via its sour guiding values, needed to be over-hauled due to numerous scandals that were enabled by those values.
- How new technology related to "predictive scheduling" is being used by Walmart to limit last-minute changes to employee's work schedules.
- 2018 was the first year that large corporations had to report the ratio of their CEO's pay to the median worker pay in a public format, and we describe what this revealed and how people reacted.
- New evidence from rigorous experimental research suggests that past evidence regarding the positive effect of employee wellness programs is inflated.

**New Text Material:**
- How, rather than being the champion for employees, HR was often the villain when it came to handling sexual harassment charges at some large companies.
- How Microsoft's recent experience with employees trying to establish a collective bargaining unit informs the rules related to what constitutes "wrongful discharge."
- How recent legislation is challenging the use of "non-compete" contracts and what this means for employee retention programs.
- New rules for Employee Assistance Programs when it comes to testing for and treating people with certain legal prescription drugs.
- How and why organizations like IBM are moving away from programs that allow employees to work off site and, instead, are placing a renewed emphasis on co-location.

## Chapter 11

**New Opening Vignette:** Looks at how companies such as Walmart, Amazon, Starbucks, and CVS are increasing pay levels and offering new benefits such as paid family leave to help them compete for workers in the face of low unemployment rates (and correspondingly high rates of employee turnover) to help them attract and retain talent to improve their customer experience and business strategy execution. It also talks about how some companies are automating to reduce their dependence on employees.

**New Boxes:**
- How automobile production has shifted to low labor cost countries over time.
- How Tesla has had to reduce labor costs to control the costs of its cars.
- How Amazon is using automation and technology to reduce hiring of workers.
- Why an increasing number of companies do not ask applicants about their salary histories.
- How some companies are helping their lower-income employees deal with financial "precarity" (income insecurity), including helping these employees be less vulnerable to high interest short-term loans.
- Why companies like Foxconn (which assembles Apple products like the iPhone) are looking beyond China for other production locations and how they balance labor costs, production costs, and the need to be close to customers in deciding where to locate.

**New Text Material:**
- New examples of how much different companies (including airlines and professional baseball teams) spend on labor costs.

- Updated examples of pay differences, including by job type, across countries.
- Updated data on international worker productivity differences.
- Updated data on executive pay and how it compares to employee pay.
- Update on change in salary test under the Fair Labor Standards Act.
- Regulatory challenges for employers in using workers in the sharing and gig economy.
- The search for lower fees in the wealth management industry and how that affects investment advisor compensation.

## Chapter 12

**New Opening Vignette:** Examines how U.S. companies are balancing the goal of avoiding increases to fixed labor costs (salaries and benefits) by using bonuses against the effectiveness of salaries and benefits in attracting and retaining workers in the current low unemployment rate environment.

**New Boxes:**
- How financial services firms are increasingly relying on social media and automation to compete.
- How Japanese companies are increasingly competing head to head for workers by paying for performance (rather than seniority, the tradition).
- How Royal Dutch Shell is using pay for performance incentives to better achieve carbon emissions control targets.
- How Novartis is modifying its pay for performance strategy in an effort to reward employees not only for achieving financial goals, but holding them responsible for how such goals are achieved.

**New Text Material:**
- How pay for performance incentives "went wrong" at Wells Fargo and Volkswagen.
- A new example of a balanced scorecard (from Tenet Healthcare).
- Streamlined exhibit on the key features of different pay for performance programs.
- New discussion on the importance of not confusing pay for performance (which takes many forms and is pervasive) with individual incentives (which are rare).
- How pay for performance "down under" at Australia and New Zealand Banking Group also "went wrong" and how it is working to fix it.

## Chapter 13

**New Opening Vignette:** Discusses why balancing work and family in high tech, finance, and consulting is becoming increasingly necessary to attract and retain top talent and how Millennials "speaking up" about their views on this matter have contributed to such changes.

**New Boxes:**
- Why employers like Fiat Chrysler are providing health care, sometimes for free, directly to their employees.
- How companies are forming alliances and using technology (including big data and telemedicine) to control costs and improve quality of health care for their employees.
- How the worker experience depends on whether they are employees or contractors (gig workers).
- How employers are improving expatriate access to health care, including through telemedicine and apps, and how this helps deal with different health care systems and language barriers.

**New Text Material:**
- Updates on benefits costs and benefits coverage generally.
- Updates on how companies differentiate themselves by using unique benefits.
- Update on the number and percentage of people without health insurance in the United States.
- Update on how hours worked continues to be higher in the United States than in other advanced economies.
- New return on investment data for employee wellness programs.
- How companies are working to control health care costs by reducing emergency room visits.
- How some companies have evaluated the return on investment to new paid family leave policies.
- New data on which benefits communication methods employers find to be most effective.
- Update on the employer mandate under the Affordable Care Act.
- How some employers are controlling health care costs by passing more costs on to workers while others are using big data or improving access to more efficient care delivery.

## Chapter 14

**New Opening Vignette:** Describes how the airline, JetBlue, although nonunion for two decades, has recently had its pilots unionize and may be facing similar unionization by other employee groups. Additionally, considers the implications of this new unionization for costs and operating income.

**New Boxes:**
- Update on the Alliance for Bangladesh Worker Safety in the garment industry.
- Update on nontraditional representation for nonunion employees at Uber in New York City, including a new minimum hourly wage.
- How employees use social media apps for union organizing efforts at Walmart and other companies (and how Walmart has now responded with its own app).
- President Macron's attempt to bring labor reform to France and the unique challenges he faces in doing so.

**New Text Material:**
- Updated data on unionization levels in the United States and the largest labor unions.
- Updates on unfair labor practice rates and related indicators of employer resistance to union organizing efforts.
- New exhibit on employer actions to support versus resist union organization efforts.
- New section on legal protection for concerted activity by workers.
- Update on how the new presidential administration will affect NLRB rulings that influence success of union organizing efforts.
- Update of exhibit on when teams or employee participation may be illegal.
- Update on work stoppages (e.g., strikes) and the number of workers involved.
- Updates on union-nonunion differences in wages and benefits.
- Challenges faced by foreign companies operating in the United States.
- Updates on international differences in union membership and coverage.
- Comparison of labor-management relations at Verizon, Kaiser Permanente, and Boeing.

## Chapter 15

**New Opening Vignette:** Discusses how firms are hesitant to locate operations in China and are now looking to diversify the geographic locations within their supply chains.

**New Boxes:**
- How Amazon's international expansion, particularly in China, creates ethical issues.
- How the fastest growing and highest paying jobs in the future will require "Hybrid Skills."
- A scandal in South Korea highlights the complexities about the intersection of entertainment, business, and law enforcement.
- How companies are dealing with the obstacles that stand in the way of maximizing the use of green energy.

**New Text Material:**
- Updated discussion of the European Union/Brexit and the U.S.–Mexico–Canada Free Trade Agreement as developments impact global business.
- Expanded discussion about the importance or unimportance of culture in the Evidence-Based HR box.
- Updated table of *Fortune*'s global largest companies.
- Updated hourly compensation costs across countries.
- Updated information on world's costliest cities.
- New example of an expatriate balance sheet from Abbvie.

## Chapter 16

**New Opening Vignette:** Discusses Wells Fargo's troubles after the scandal of creating fake customer accounts and the departure of two CEOs in two years.

**New Boxes:**
- New technologies are changing the way firms hire and conduct interviews.
- How IKEA's presence in India require HR to acquire, train, and motivate their employees.
- The ways in which an effective CHRO would have been helpful in managing the behavior of CBS's former CEO, Leslie Moonves.
- How Environmental, Social, and Governance Practices is becoming a key focus of HR officers.

**New Text Material:**
- Discussion about the use of AI and bots in HR.
- Discussion of how Hershey has created a predictive analytics program to predict potential turnover.

## Acknowledgments

As this book enters its 12th edition, it is important to acknowledge those who started it all. The first edition of this book would not have been possible if not for the entrepreneurial spirit of two individuals. Bill Schoof, president of Austen Press, gave us the resources and had the confidence that four unproven textbook writers could provide a new perspective for teaching human resource management. John Weimiester, our editor for many of editions, worked diligently to get the author team to consider new features to incorporate into the book to keep it interesting and help students learn about HRM. He supported us all along the journey. The succcess and longevity of textbooks goes far beyond the skills of the author team. For this edition we were grateful to work with a fantastic group of editors, developers, and project managers. We want to thank Peter Jurmu for encouraging us to consider new features and keep the book fresh by introducing current HRM research and effective contemporary practices. Kudos go to Kelsey Darin for all of her efforts in identifying and helping us place the videos that are new to this edition. Michelle Houston worked diligently on this and other editions of the book to ensure that our writing was understandable. We thank Debbie Clare for her ideas on how to best highlight the features of this edition. Last but not least, Maria McGreal kept the revision on schedule; gently prodded us when needed; and helped make sense of our sometimes cryptic directions, incomplete sentences, and misplaced paragraphs.

We would also like to thank the professors who gave of their time to review the text and attend focus groups throughout the life of the product. Their helpful comments and suggestions have greatly helped to enhance this learning program:

Vondra Armstrong
*Pulaski Technical College*

Richard Arvey
*National University of Singapore*

Steve Ash
*University of Akron*

Carlson Austin
*South Carolina State University*

Janice Baldwin
*The University of Texas at Arlington*

Alison Barber
*Michigan State University*

Kathleen Barnes
*University of Wisconsin, Superior*

Brian Bartel
*Mid-State Technical College*

James E. Bartlett, II
*University of South Carolina-Columbia*

Ron Beaulieu
*Central Michigan University*

Joan Benek-Rivera
*University of Pennsylvania-Bloomsburg*

Philip Benson
*New Mexico State University*

Nancy Bereman
*Wichita State University*

Chris Berger
*Purdue University*

Carol Bibly
*Triton College*

Angela Boston
*University of Texas at Arlington*

Wendy Boswell
*Texas A&M University*

Sarah Bowman
*Idaho State University*

Charles Braun
*University of Kentucky*

James Browne
*University of Southern Colorado*

Ronald Brownie
*Purdue University-North Central*

Jon Bryan
*Bridgewater State College*

David Calland
*Liberty University*

Gerald Calvasina
*Southern Utah University*

Stacy Campbell
*Kennesaw State University*

Martin Carrigan
*University of Findlay*

Georgia Chao
*Michigan State University*

Fay Cocchiara
*Arkansas State University*

LeAnne Coder
*Western Kentucky University*

Walter Coleman
*Florida Southern College*

Mary Connerley
*Virginia Tech University*

Donna Cooke
*Florida Atlantic University-Davis*

Craig Cowles
*Bridgewater State College*

Susie Cox
*McNeese State University*

Michael Crant
*University of Notre Dame*

Shaun W. Davenport
*High Point University*

Shannon Davis
*North Carolina State University*

Roger Dean
*Washington & Lee University*

John Delery
*University of Arkansas*

Fred Dorn
*University of Mississippi*

Jennifer Dose
*Messiah College*

Tom Dougherty
*University of Missouri*

Berrin Erdogan
*Portland State University*

Angela Farrar
*University of Nevada–Las Vegas*

Dan Farrell
*Western Michigan University*

Dyanne Ferk
*University of Illinois–Springfield*

Anne Fiedler
*Nova Southeastern University*

Robert Figler
*University of Akron*

Louis Firenze
*Northwood University*

Art Fischer
*Pittsburgh State University*

Barry Friedman
*State University of New York at Oswego*

Cynthia Fukami
*University of Denver*

Daniel J. Gallagher
*University of Illinois–Springfield*

Donald G. Gardner
*University of Colorado at Colorado Springs*

Bonnie Fox Garrity
*D'Youville College*

David Gerth
*Nashville State Community College*

Sonia Goltz
*Michigan Technological University*

Bob Graham
*Sacred Heart University*

Terri Griffith
*Washington University*

Ken Gross
*University of Oklahoma–Norman*

John Hannon
*University at Buffalo*

Bob Hatfield
*Indiana University*

Alan Heffner
*James Monroe Center*

Fred Heidrich
*Black Hills State University*

Rob Heneman
*Ohio State University*

Gary Hensel
*McHenry County College*

Kim Hester
*Arkansas State University*

Nancy Higgins
*Montgomery College–Rockville*

Michael Hill
*University of Georgia*

Wayne Hockwater
*Florida State University*

Fred Hughes
*Faulkner University*

Ning Hou
*St. Cloud State University*

Denise Tanguay Hoyer
*Eastern Michigan University*

Natalie J. Hunter
*Portland State University*

Julie Indvik
*California State University, Chico*

Sanford Jacoby
*University of California–Los Angeles*

Frank Jeffries
*University of Alaska–Anchorage*

Roy Johnson
*Iowa State University*

Gwen Jones
*Fairleigh Dickinson University*

Gwendolyn Jones
*University of Akron*

Hank Karp
*Hampton University*

Gundars Kaupins
*Boise State University*

Marianne Koch
*University of Oregon*

James Kolacek
*Palm Beach Atlantic University*

Tom Kolenko
*Kennesaw State College*

Elias Konwufine
*Keiser University*

Beth Koufteros
*Texas A&M University*

Ken Kovach
*George Mason University*

Chalmer Labig
*Oklahoma State University*

Patricia Lanier
*University of Louisiana at Lafayette*

Vonda Laughlin
*Carson-Newman College*

Helen LaVan
*DePaul University*

Renee Lerche
*University of Michigan*

Nancy Boyd Lillie
*University of North Texas*

Beth A. Livingston
*Cornell University*

Karen Locke
*William & Mary*

Michael Dane Loflin
*York Technical College*

Susan Madsen
*Utah Valley University*

Larry Mainstone
*Valparaiso University*

Ann-Marie Majeskey
*Mount Olive College*

Liz Malatestinic
*Indiana University*

Patricia Martina
*University of Texas-San Antonio*

Nicholas Mathys
*DePaul University*

Lisa McConnell
*Oklahoma State University*

Liliana Meneses
*University of Maryland University College*

Jessica Methot
*Rutgers University*

Angela Miles
*North Carolina A&T State University*

Stuart Milne
*Georgia Institute of Technology*

Barbara Minsky
*Troy University*

Kelly Mollica
*University of Memphis*

Jim Morgan
*California State University-Chico*

Pamela Mulvey
*Olney Central College Lake Land College*

Gary Murray
*Rose State College*

David M. Nemi
*Niagara County Community College*

Millicent Nelson
*Middle Tennessee State University*

Lam Nguyen
*Palm Beach State College*

Nhung Nguyen
*Towson University*

Thomas J. Norman
*California State University-Dominguez Hills*

Cheri Ostroff
*Teachers College Columbia*

Teresa Palmer
*Illinois State University*

Robert Paul
*Kansas State University*

Tracy Porter
*Cleveland State University*

Gregory Quinet
*Southern Polytechnic State University*

Sam Rabinowitz
*Rutgers University*

David Rahn
*California State University-Chico*

Jude Rathburn
*University of Wisconsin-Milwaukee*

Katherine Ready
*University of Wisconsin*

Herbert Ricardo
*Indian River State College*

Mike Ritchie
*University of South Carolina*

Gwen Rivkin
*Cardinal Stritch University*

Mark Roehling
*Michigan State University*

Mary Ellen Rosetti
*Hudson Valley Community College*

Craig J. Russell
*University of Oklahoma*

Sarah Sanders-Smith
*Purdue University-North Central*

Miyako Schanely
*Jefferson Community College*

Robert Schappe
*University of Michigan-Dearborn*

Jack Schoenfelder
*Ivy Tech Community College*

Machelle K. Schroeder
*University of Wisconsin-Platteville*

Joshua Schwarz
*Miami University-Ohio*

Pat Setlik
*Harper College*

Christina Shalley
*Georgia Tech*

Richard Shuey
*Thomas More College*

Richard Simpson
*University of Utah*

Romila Singh
*University of Wisconsin-Milwaukee*

Erika Engel Small
*Coastal Carolina University*

Mark Smith
*Mississippi Gulf Coast Community College-Gulfport*

Scott Snell
*University of Virginia*

Kris Sperstad
*Chippewa Valley Technical College*

Howard Stanger
*Canisius College*

Carol S. Steinhaus
*Northern Michigan University*

Gary Stroud
*Franklin University*

Cynthia Sutton
*Indiana University-South Bend*

Peg Thomas
*Pennsylvania State University-Behrend*

Steven L. Thomas
*Missouri State University*

Tom Timmerman
*Tennessee Technology University*

George Tompson
*University of Tampa*

J. Bruce Tracey
*Cornell University*

K. J. Tullis
*University of Central Oklahoma*

Dan Turban
*University of Missouri-Columbia*

Linda Turner
*Morrisville State College*

Linda Urbanski
*University of Toledo*

William Van Lente
*Alliant International University*

Charles Vance
*Loyola Marymount University*

John Varlaro
*Johnson & Wales University*

Kim Wade
*Washington State University*

Sheng Wang
*University of Nevada-Las Vegas*

Renee Warning
*University of Central Oklahoma*

Bruce Western
*Western Illinois University*

Lynn Wilson
*Saint Leo University*

Jenell Wittmer
*University of Toledo*

George Whaley
*San Jose State University*

Steve Woods
*University of Baltimore*

Lin Xiu
*University of Minnesota-Duluth*

Daniel Yazak
*Montana State University-Billings*

Ryan D. Zimmerman
*Texas A&M University*

Finally, we would like to thank the reviewers of the 11th edition for their thoughtful feedback:

Amy Banta
*Central Michigan University*

Brian Chupp
*Purdue University*

Paul Davis
*Cornell University*

Todd Harris
*Bridgewater State University*

Julia Levashina
*Kent State University*

Matt Lozykowski
*Kent State University*

Chris McChesney
*Indian River State College*

Edward Meda
*University of Texas-Dallas*

Liana Passantino
*Michigan State University*

Gang Wang
*Florida State University*

**Raymond A. Noe**
**John R. Hollenbeck**
**Barry Gerhart**
**Patrick M. Wright**

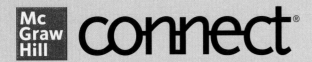

## You're in the driver's seat.

Want to build your own course? No problem. Prefer to use our turnkey, prebuilt course? Easy. Want to make changes throughout the semester? Sure. And you'll save time with Connect's auto-grading too.

# 65%
## Less Time Grading

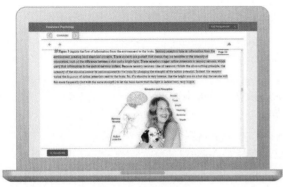

Laptop: McGraw-Hill; Woman/dog: George Doyle/Getty Images

## They'll thank you for it.

Adaptive study resources like SmartBook® 2.0 help your students be better prepared in less time. You can transform your class time from dull definitions to dynamic debates. Find out more about the powerful personalized learning experience available in SmartBook 2.0 at **www.mheducation.com/highered/connect/smartbook**

## Make it simple, make it affordable.

Connect makes it easy with seamless integration using any of the major Learning Management Systems— Blackboard®, Canvas, and D2L, among others—to let you organize your course in one convenient location. Give your students access to digital materials at a discount with our inclusive access program. Ask your McGraw-Hill representative for more information.

Padlock: Jobalou/Getty Images

## Solutions for your challenges.

A product isn't a solution. Real solutions are affordable, reliable, and come with training and ongoing support when you need it and how you want it. Our Customer Experience Group can also help you troubleshoot tech problems— although Connect's 99% uptime means you might not need to call them. See for yourself at **status.mheducation.com**

Checkmark: Jobalou/Getty Images

SUPPORT AT every step

## Effective, efficient studying.

Connect helps you be more productive with your study time and get better grades using tools like SmartBook 2.0, which highlights key concepts and creates a personalized study plan. Connect sets you up for success, so you walk into class with confidence and walk out with better grades.

## Study anytime, anywhere.

Download the free ReadAnywhere app and access your online eBook or SmartBook 2.0 assignments when it's convenient, even if you're offline. And since the app automatically syncs with your eBook and SmartBook 2.0 assignments in Connect, all of your work is available every time you open it. Find out more at **www.mheducation.com/readanywhere**

> *"I really liked this app—it made it easy to study when you don't have your text-book in front of you."*
>
> - Jordan Cunningham, Eastern Washington University

Calendar: owattaphotos/Getty Images

## No surprises.

The Connect Calendar and Reports tools keep you on track with the work you need to get done and your assignment scores. Life gets busy; Connect tools help you keep learning through it all.

## Learning for everyone.

McGraw-Hill works directly with Accessibility Services Departments and faculty to meet the learning needs of all students. Please contact your Accessibility Services office and ask them to email accessibility@mheducation.com, or visit **www.mheducation.com/about/accessibility** for more information.

# BRIEF CONTENTS

# CONTENTS

**PART 2
Acquisition and Preparation of
Human Resources  196**

5  **Human Resource Planning and Recruitment  196**

6  **Selection and Placement  234**

# Human Resource Management

## GAINING A COMPETITIVE ADVANTAGE

# Human Resource Management: Gaining a Competitive Advantage

## ┌─ LEARNING OBJECTIVES ─

*After reading this chapter, you should be able to:*

**LO 1-1**   Discuss the roles and activities of a company's human resource management function. *page 5*

**LO 1-2**   Discuss the implications of the economy, the makeup of the labor force, and ethics for company sustainability. *page 17*

**LO 1-3**   Discuss how human resource management affects a company's balanced scorecard. *page 29*

**LO 1-4**   Discuss what companies should do to compete in the global marketplace. *page 46*

**LO 1-5**   Identify how social networking, artificial intelligence, and robotics are influencing human resource management. *page 50*

**LO 1-6**   Describe how automation using artificial intelligence and robotics has the potential to change jobs. *page 51*

**LO 1-7**   Discuss human resource management practices that support high-performance work systems. *page 52*

**LO 1-8**   Provide a brief description of human resource management practices. *page 55*

## The Evolution of HRM Practices at IBM

IBM has moved from a business that primarily focused on manufacturing and selling computer hardware and managing clients on-site data centers to becoming a key player in cloud-based services, artificial intelligence–based products, and block-chaining (a security system for Bitcoin and cryptocurrencies). In the 2000s, IBM's revenue declined for 22 consecutive quarters as it made the transition. Today, more than 50% of IBM's revenue comes from business they entered in the 2000s, and 50% of its employees have joined the company in the last five years. The business focus at IBM today is speed, innovation, and a focus on the client experience.

To attract and retain talented employees, to support change, and to facilitate the creative and innovative thinking that IBM needed to transition to new businesses required adopting new HRM practices. To do so, IBM's chief human resource officer, Diane Gherson worked collaboratively with employees, managers, HR staff, and technical experts, listened to their ideas, asked questions, and was open to new ideas and different perspectives. She also had to find leaders who would support the implementation of new HRM practices. For example, IBM's new performance management system known as Checkpoint provides managers and employees with an app they can use to provide and receive feedback on a timely and more continuous basis. This allows employees and managers to change behaviors and modify performance goals in "real-time" due to business or team needs rather than waiting for their mid year or annual review when it is too late. Checkpoint was based on the ideas and suggestions of more than 100,000 IBM employees who now use blogs to comment on what they like about Checkpoint and how it can be improved.

Innovative products and services often result from employees with diverse backgrounds working together. Recognizing this, as well as wanting to be an inclusive employer, IBM has taken several steps to develop a pipeline of skilled and diverse tech employees. The company's New Collar program helps identify and hire individuals from nontraditional backgrounds who have the potential to master technical skills but might otherwise get ignored because they don't have the necessary education background, such as a college education. In 2017 15% of IBM's hires in the United States came from the New Collar program. IBM provides opportunities for women who have not been working for an extended period of time to develop the skills needed for tech jobs. The company has also been recognized for its efforts in hiring graduates of historically black colleges and universities.

Many of the new HR practices involve using state-of-the art AI applications and data analytics. IBM's traditional learning management system provided many training and development opportunities. The new system still does but it is customized to match employees' interests and needs. AI is used to review employees' skills, current position, and career path and to provide personal learning recommendations including specific courses, webinars, YouTube videos, and TED talks. Learning opportunities are organized on the learning management system by channels, similar to what you have experienced on Netflix or Amazon. Employees can get answers to their questions about the learning opportunities by accessing a live-chat adviser. They can also see how their peers have evaluated the various learning opportunities. Since the redesign of the learning management system, employees are using it over one-third more than in previous years and course completion rates have increased. IBM's Blue Matching tool helps employees identify new opportunities within the company. It identifies jobs that match employees

*CONTINUED*

skills, experiences, current location where they work or their location preferences, and historical job performance. IBM estimates Blue Matching saved the company more than $100 million by reducing turnover and improving productivity.

Effective leadership is an important ingredient for a successful business transformation. IBM identified 36 characteristics that its leaders need to help employees navigate the business transformation. IBM's leaders are involved in 360-degree feedback assessment that identifies their strengths and opportunities for improvement in leadership characteristics. Coaches are provided to the leaders to help them improve in the areas they need to develop. This initiative is especially important for support leaders who are responsible for business units undergoing significant change.

SOURCES: Based on A. McIlvaine, "Transforming Big Blue," *Human Resource Executive* (October 2018), pp. 14–16; L. Burrell, "Co-Creating the Employee Experience," *Harvard Business Review* (March–April 2018), pp. 54–58; O. Louissaint, "Diversity Without Inclusion Is a Missed Opportunity," *TD* (December 2018), pp. 32–37; T. Bingham and P. Galagan, "AI is Coming for Everyone," *TD* (December 2018), pp. 26–31.

# Introduction

**Competitiveness**
A company's ability to maintain and gain market share in its industry.

IBM illustrates the key role that human resource management plays in determining the survival, effectiveness, and competitiveness of U.S. businesses. **Competitiveness** refers to a company's ability to maintain and gain market share in its industry. IBM's human resource management practices are helping support the company's business strategy and provide services the customer values. The value of a product or service is determined by its quality and how closely the product fits customer needs.

Competitiveness is related to company effectiveness, which is determined by whether the company satisfies the needs of stakeholders (groups affected by business practices). Important stakeholders include stockholders, who want a return on their investment; customers, who want a high-quality product or service; and employees, who desire interesting work and reasonable compensation for their services. The community, which wants the company to contribute to activities and projects and minimize pollution of the environment, is also an important stakeholder. Companies that do not meet stakeholders' needs are unlikely to have a competitive advantage over other firms in their industry.

**Human resource management (HRM)**
The policies, practices, and systems that influence employees' behavior, attitudes, and performances.

**Human resource management (HRM)** refers to the policies, practices, and systems that influence employees' behavior, attitudes, and performance. Many companies refer to HRM as involving "people practices." Figure 1.1 emphasizes that there are several

**Figure 1.1**
Human Resource Management Practices

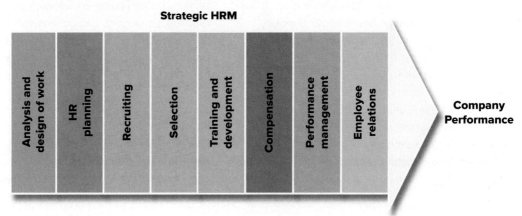

**Strategic HRM**

Analysis and design of work · HR planning · Recruiting · Selection · Training and development · Compensation · Performance management · Employee relations → **Company Performance**

important HRM practices. The strategy underlying these practices needs to be considered to maximize their influence on company performance. As the figure shows, HRM practices include analyzing and designing work, determining human resource needs (HR planning), attracting potential employees (recruiting), choosing employees (selection), teaching employees how to perform their jobs and preparing them for the future (training and development), rewarding employees (compensation), evaluating their performance (performance management), and creating a positive work environment (employee relations). The HRM practices discussed in this chapter's opening highlighted how effective HRM practices support business goals and objectives. That is, effective HRM practices are strategic! Effective HRM has been shown to enhance company performance by contributing to employee and customer satisfaction, innovation, productivity, and development of a favorable reputation in the firm's community.[1]

We begin by discussing the roles and skills that a human resource management department and/or managers need for any company to be competitive. The second section of the chapter identifies the competitive challenges that U.S. companies currently face, which influence their ability to meet the needs of shareholders, customers, employees, and other stakeholders. We discuss how these competitive challenges are influencing HRM. The chapter concludes by highlighting the HRM practices covered in this book and the ways they help companies compete.

# What Responsibilities and Roles Do HR Departments Perform?

Table 1.1 shows the responsibilities of human resource departments. How much should companies budget for HR and how many HR professionals should a company employ? One study estimates that HR budgets on average are $2,936 per employee.[2]

High-impact HR teams have one staff person per 64 employees, spend more than the average HR budget per employee ($4,434 on average per employee), and employ a higher percentage of HR specialists than more compliance-driven and basic HR organizations.

High-impact HR functions are more integrated with the business and skilled at helping managers in attracting, building, engaging, and retaining talented employees. They can adapt quickly to business needs and workforce changes, identify and promote talent from within the company, and are continuously trying to identify what motivates employees to help them grow and develop. Also, high-impact HR functions ensure that they are continuously building the talent and skills of HR professionals necessary to help the company meet new competitive challenges. The greater cost-per-employee of high-impact HR functions is offset by the greater savings resulting from reduced turnover and increased levels of employee engagement.

The HR department is solely responsible for outplacement, labor law compliance, record keeping, testing, unemployment compensation, and some aspects of benefits administration. The HR department is most likely to collaborate with other company functions on employment interviewing, performance management and discipline, and efforts to improve quality and productivity. Large companies are more likely than small ones to employ HR specialists, with benefits specialists being the most prevalent. Other common specializations include recruitment, compensation, and training and development.[3]

Many different roles and responsibilities can be performed by the HR department, depending on the size of the company, the characteristics of the workforce, the industry, and the value system of company management. The HR department may take full responsibility for human resource activities in some companies, whereas in others it

**LO 1-1**

Discuss the roles and activities of a company's human resource management function.

**Table 1.1**
Responsibilities of HR Departments

| FUNCTION | RESPONSIBILITIES |
|---|---|
| Analysis and design of work | Job analysis, work analysis, job descriptions |
| Recruitment and selection | Recruiting, posting job descriptions, interviewing, testing, coordinating use of temporary employees |
| Training and development | Orientation, skills training, development programs, career development |
| Performance management | Performance measures, preparation and administration of performance appraisals, feedback and coaching, discipline |
| Compensation and benefits | Wage and salary administration, incentive pay, insurance, vacation, retirement plans, profit sharing, health and wellness, stock plans |
| Employee relations/labor relations | Attitude surveys, employee handbooks, labor law compliance, relocation and outplacement services |
| Personnel policies | Policy creation, policy communications |
| Employee data and information systems | Record keeping, HR information systems, workforce analytics, social media, intranet and Internet access |
| Legal compliance | Policies to ensure lawful behavior; safety inspections, accessibility accommodations, privacy policies, ethics |
| Support for business strategy | Human resource planning and forecasting, talent management, change management, organization development |

SOURCES: Based on Bureau of Labor Statistics, U.S. Department of Labor, "Human Resources Specialists," *Occupational Outlook Handbook*, from www.bls.gov/ooh/business-and-financial/human-resources-specialists.htm, accessed February 17, 2019; SHRM-BNA Survey No. 66, "Policy and Practice Forum: Human Resource Activities, Budgets, and Staffs, 2000–2001," *Bulletin to Management*, Bureau of National Affairs Policy and Practice Series, June 28, 2001 (Washington, DC: Bureau of National Affairs).

may share the roles and responsibilities with managers of other departments such as finance, operations, or information technology. In some companies the HR department advises top-level management; in others the HR department may make decisions regarding staffing, training, and compensation after top managers have decided relevant business issues.

Some companies that want managers to have more accountability for employees believe that traditional HR departments are unnecessary because they inhibit innovation by creating unnecessary and inefficient policies and procedures.[4] In these companies, important payroll, benefits, and other HR processes are automated or outsourced. Also, at smaller companies HR responsibilities are often handled by the owner. They do so for many possible reasons, including not wanting to incur the costs of having an HR manager or outsourcing HR services and being unwilling or unable to delegate HR responsibilities or share information with others. However, there are many advantages to having HR professionals and an HR department. Managers often lack the specialized knowledge necessary to understand employment laws and how to identify potential employees, determine skills and salaries for positions, and develop current employees. HR professionals can create systems to avoid legal liability, counsel employees, and coach managers on how to identify, retain, and develop talent. For example, the owner of a marketing company hired an HR professional after she realized the downside of trying to handle HR responsibilities herself.[5] She handled recruiting, hiring, payroll, and other HR responsibilities, but this took her away from the time she could spend growing the business and resulted in a decrease in company revenues. Also, she recognized that to grow the business, she needed

**Figure 1.2**

HR as a Business with Three Product Lines

**Administrative Services and Transactions:**
Compensation, hiring, and staffing
- Emphasis: Resource efficiency and service quality

**Business Partner Services:**
Developing effective HR systems and helping implement business plans, talent management
- Emphasis: Knowing the business and exercising influence—problem solving, designing effective systems to ensure needed competencies

**Strategic Partner:**
Contributing to business strategy based on considerations of human capital, business capabilities, readiness, and developing HR practices as strategic differentiators
- Emphasis: Knowledge of HR and of the business, competition, the market, and business strategies

SOURCE: Adapted from Figure 1, "HR Product Lines" in E. E. Lawler, "From Human Resource Management to Organizational Effectiveness," *Human Resource Management* 44 (2005), pp. 165–69.

an HR professional who knew more about how to identify and find the most qualified candidates to fill open positions at her company.

One way to think about the roles and responsibilities of HR departments is to consider HR as a business within the company with three product lines. Figure 1.2 shows the three product lines of HR. The first product line, administrative services and transactions, is the traditional product that HR has historically provided. The newer HR products—business partner services and the strategic partner role—are the HR functions that top managers want HR to deliver.

To ensure that HR is business focused, Walgreens's HR professionals are paired with functional leaders.[6] The HR field organization works to develop strategic talent plans for each business and helps implement important initiatives such as succession planning, change management, organizational design, and culture and leadership development. The HR director at TAMKO Building Products Inc. helped align the company's HR function to business needs.[7] She noticed that inexperienced HR professionals were spending too much time on transactional duties such as payroll and benefits administration. She wanted them to focus on supplying managers with skilled, well-trained employees and meaningful data. She revised their training to ensure that they understood the industry and the skills that the company needed for continued success. She urged her staff to be proactive (rather than reactive) about offering HR solutions to help managers avoid or solve workplace problems. The team responded by identifying and implementing a new time-and-attendance tracking system, a virtual onboarding and orientation process, and a leadership development program.

## Strategic Role of the HRM Function

The amount of time that the human resource management function devotes to administrative tasks is decreasing, and its roles as a strategic business partner, change agent, and employee advocate are increasing.[8] HR managers face two important challenges: shifting their focus from current operations to strategies for the future and preparing non-HR managers to develop and implement HR practices.[9] To ensure that HRM contributes to the company's competitive advantage, many HR departments are organized on the basis of a shared service model. The shared service model can help control costs and improve the business relevance and timeliness of HR practices. A **shared service model** is a way to organize the HR function that includes centers of expertise or excellence, service centers, and business partners.[10] Centers of expertise or excellence include HR specialists in areas such as staffing or training who provide their services companywide. Service centers are a central place for administrative and transactional tasks such as enrolling in training programs or changing benefits that employees and managers can access online. Business partners are HR staff members who work with business-unit managers on strategic issues such as creating new compensation plans or development programs for preparing high-level managers. Walgreens provides employee relations, recruiting, and HR data services through a shared services team.[11] Walgreens introduced a website, myHR, that employees can access to get answers to their questions about benefits, HR policies, and talent management. It provides confidential personalized information that is easy for employees to access. We will discuss the shared service model in more detail in Chapter 16.

**Shared service model**
A way to organize the HR function that includes centers of expertise or excellence, service centers, and business partners.

The role of HRM in administration is decreasing as technology is used for many administrative purposes, such as managing employee records and allowing employees to get information about and enroll in training, benefits, and other programs. The availability of the Internet has decreased the HRM role in maintaining records and providing self-service to employees.[12] **Self-service** refers to giving employees online access to, or apps that provide, information about HR issues such as training, benefits, compensation, and contracts; enrolling online in programs and services; and completing online attitude surveys. The shift to self-service means that HR can focus more time on consulting with managers on important employee issues and less time on day-to-day transactional tasks. For example, U.S. Bancorp implemented the PeopleSoft human capital management system, which allows managers to review or approve basic personnel actions such as terminations, relocations, and salary changes.[13] As managers became more comfortable with the system, they were given control over transactions such as approving bonuses, reviewing résumés, and evaluating job candidates. Managers were initially resistant to take on duties that previously were handled by HR staff, but they accepted the change because it enabled them to execute transactions more quickly and gave them more access to workforce data they could use for decision making. HR professionals now have more time to work with managers on ensuring the right employee development plans are in place, evaluating workforce needs due to retirements or growth, and ensuring their organizational structures are efficient and effective.

**Self-service**
Giving employees online access to human resources information.

Many companies are also contracting with HR service providers to conduct important but administrative HR functions such as payroll processing, as well as to provide expertise in strategically important practice areas such as recruiting. **Outsourcing** refers to the practice of having another company (a vendor, third party, or consultant) provide services. The most commonly outsourced activities include those related to benefits administration (e.g., flexible spending accounts, health plan eligibility status), relocation, and payroll. The major reasons that company executives choose to outsource HR practices include cost savings, increased ability to recruit and manage talent, improved HR service quality, and protection of the company from potential lawsuits by standardizing processes such as selection and recruitment.[14] ADP, Hewitt, IBM, and Accenture are examples of leading outsource providers.

**Outsourcing**
An organization's use of an outside organization for a broad set of services.

Goodyear Tire and Rubber Company reenergized its recruitment and hiring practices through outsourcing recruiting practices.[15] The recruiting outsource provider worked with the company to understand its culture, its history, and its employees' recruitment experiences. The recruiting outsourcing service provider was able to help Goodyear streamline the recruiting process by providing hiring managers with online access to create new job requisitions, providing interview feedback, scheduling interviews, generating customized job offer letters, and gaining a real-time perspective on job candidates' progress in the recruitment process. Goodyear recognized several benefits from outsourcing recruitment, including improving the timeliness of job offers, increasing the diversity and quality of new hires, and reducing turnover.

Traditionally, the HRM department (also known as "personnel" or "employee relations") was primarily an administrative expert and employee advocate. The department took care of employee problems, made sure employees were paid correctly, administered labor contracts, and avoided legal problems. The HRM department ensured that employee-related issues did not interfere with the manufacturing or sales of products or services. Human resource management was primarily reactive; that is, HR issues were a concern only if they directly affected the business. That still remains the case in many companies that have yet to recognize the competitive value of HRM, or among HR professionals who lack the competencies and skills or understanding needed to anticipate problems and contribute to the business strategy. However, other companies believe that HRM is important for business success and therefore have expanded the role of HRM as a change agent and strategic partner.

A discussion group of company HR directors and academic thought-leaders reported that increasingly HR professionals are expected to lead efforts focused on talent management and performance management in order to create the global workforces that companies need to be successful.[16] HR professionals have to be able to use and analyze data to make a business case for ideas and problem solutions. In many companies, top HR managers report directly to the CEO, president, or board of directors to answer questions about how people strategies drive value for the company. For example, the vice president of human resources for Lawson Products, a company that distributes industrial maintenance and repair products, meets weekly with the operations committee which includes the CEO, chief financial officer, general legal council, and company vice presidents.[17] She also has monthly meetings with the CEO and is involved in Lawson's annual budgeting process and strategy meetings.

This also means that HR professionals have to be prepared to use their people management skills across the business. For example, the top business executives at Honeywell International gave its chief HR executive the responsibility for leading a cost-cutting strategy.[18] To do so the HR executive worked with business leaders from finance and other departments to identify more than 100 ways to cut costs and gain efficiencies in operations. Because of his success leading the cost-cutting strategy he was given the responsibility of managing Honeywell's procurement business, which has more than 100,000 employees and earned more than $40 billion in revenue for the company. He still had to perform his regular duties managing HR and communications. He found his HR skills useful for developing strategies to recruit and train managers to run the procurement operation. After a corporate reorganization he lost his procurement responsibilities but was given a new role in security management.

Consider how HRM has supported the business at Juniper Networks and Abbott.[19] Juniper Networks, a networking technology company that had become successful by introducing a new router, was a major innovator in the computer network industry. But Juniper found that, despite its success, it needed to reinvent its business strategy and grow. To help reinvent its business strategy and structure, Juniper's HR team had conversations with 150 senior company leaders, including the company chairman, and 100 other managers located around the world. During these conversations, the HR team asked the leader or manager questions about important environmental challenges facing Juniper, how the challenges affected the leader's or manager's team, what most excited them about Juniper's business strategy and execution of that strategy, and key business concerns. The conversations helped identify that Juniper had too many business priorities, leaders tended to avoid conflict, and work was overly complex, making it difficult to provide customers with the best solutions. As a result of the conversations, product lines have been streamlined and the company adopted a simpler and more integrated business structure. For example, across the company, any decision can be made by six people.

Abbott spun off a new company, AbbVie, which focused on pharmaceutical research and development, while keeping consumer-oriented health care products such as Ensure nutrition shakes. Spin-offs are new companies that are created from the parent company with a specialized focus on one aspect of the business market. They are expected to be worth more as independent businesses than as part of a larger business. Human resource issues such as retaining talent, making sure employees are enthusiastic and motivated, and making sure employees are in the right roles in the new company are important for the success of spin-offs. The chief human resource officer (CHRO) for AbbVie, who worked for Abbott, was faced with the challenging and complex assignment of helping to get the new company established. Specifically, he worked with other executives to create the new organizational structure, logo, and branding campaign. Also, he worked on people issues such as making sure the reasons for the spin-off were communicated, to reduce employees' fear and anxiety; deciding which employees would join the new company and determining their job assignments; and developing a new compensation and benefits plan.

Table 1.2 provides several questions that managers can use to determine if HRM is playing a strategic role in the business. If these questions have not been considered, it is highly unlikely that (1) the company is prepared to deal with competitive challenges or (2) HRM is being used strategically to help a company gain a competitive advantage. The bottom line for evaluating the relationship between HRM and the business strategy is to consider this question: "What is HRM doing to ensure that the right people with the right skills are doing the right things in the jobs that are important for the execution of the business strategy?"[20] We will discuss strategic HRM in more detail in Chapter 2.

Consider how the structure and responsibilities of HR departments are changing to ensure that they have a strategic role. One strategic area of emphasis in many companies is improving the employee and customer experience. Airbnb recognizes that the employee experience is critical for keeping employees happy and committed to the company. Happier employees are more likely to work hard to satisfy customers, which helps the company grow and prosper.[21] To maximize the employee experience, Airbnb combined three separate HR groups (talent, recruiting, and "Ground Control") into one group. Airbnb's top HR officer's title is chief

**Table 1.2**

Questions to Ask: Is HRM Playing a Strategic Role in the Business?

1. What is HRM doing to provide value-added services to internal clients?
2. Do the actions of HRM support and align with business priorities?
3. How are you measuring the effectiveness of HRM?
4. How can we reinvest in employees?
5. What HRM strategy will we use to get the business from point A to point B?
6. From an HRM perspective, what should we be doing to improve our marketplace position?
7. What's the best change we can make to prepare for the future?
8. Do we react to business problems or anticipate them in advance?

SOURCES: Based on D. Ulrich, D. Kryscynski, M. Ulrich, and W. Brockbank, *Victory Through Organization* (New York: McGraw-Hill Education, 2017);  P. Wright, *Human Resource Strategy: Adapting to the Age of Globalization* (Alexandria, VA: Society for Human Resource Management Foundation, 2008).

employee experience officer (CEEO). At Airbnb, human resources involves marketing, communications, real estate, and social responsibility, in addition to traditional HR functions. The CEEO's responsibilities go beyond the traditional HR functions such as talent management, and compensation to include workplace design and facilities, food, global citizenship, and the network of community managers who interact daily with Airbnb employees. For example, Airbnb's airy, open workplace includes small lockers for employees to charge their devices, which provides more room for a conference room, couches, nap spaces, communal tables, and small spaces for employees to have conversations with their peers. Numerous cafes are available where employees can eat or collaborate on projects. Also, human resources helps employees give back to the communities where Airbnb operates by encouraging four hours a month of individual volunteering as well as by participating in larger events such as painting a homeless shelter or cooking meals for hospital patients' families.

At Adobe, the chief human resource officer is also the company's first chief customer service officer who oversees all of the functions related to the customer experience.[22] She has been working on tying pay and bonuses more closely to measures related to servicing and building customer relations rather than to traditional measures like sales. The goal is to make sure every employee has an incentive based on the customer's experience. Employees can access examples of what they can do to improve the customer experience on Adobe's intranet. Online or physical listening stations have been provided to employees so they can hear conversations with Adobe customers to understand what they like or don't like about Adobe's products.

HRM may be the most important lever for companies to gain a competitive advantage over both domestic and foreign competitors. We believe this is because HRM practices are directly related to companies' success in meeting competitive challenges. These challenges and their implications for HRM are discussed later in the chapter.

## DEMONSTRATING THE STRATEGIC VALUE OF HRM: HR ANALYTICS AND EVIDENCE-BASED HR

For HRM to contribute to business goals, there is increasing recognition that data must be used to answer questions such as "Which practices are effective?" and "Which practices are cost effective?" and to project the outcomes of changes in practices on employees' attitudes, behavior, and company profits and costs. This helps show that time and money invested in HR programs are worthwhile and that human resources is as important to the business as finance, marketing, and accounting. **Evidence-based HR** refers to the demonstration that HR practices have a positive influence on the company's bottom line or key stakeholders (employees, customers, community, shareholders). Evidence-based HR requires the use of HR or workforce analytics. **HR or workforce analytics** refers to the practice of using quantitative methods and scientific methods to analyze data (often big data) to understand the role of talent in executing the business strategy and achieving business goals.[23]

**Big data** refers to information merged from HR databases, corporate financial statements, employee surveys, and other data sources to make evidence-based HR decisions and show that HR practices influence the organization's bottom line, including profits and costs.[24] Several companies have used workforce analytics to analyze big data to help improve HR practices.[25] Google was one of the first companies to use analytics to improve its workforce. Google created algorithms or equations to identify which job candidates were most likely to succeed. It also produced algorithms to review applications that were rejected. This helped Google hire engineers who its normal application screening process would have missed.

Sonic Automotive, an automobile retailer, uses big data to help determine which training programs have a positive ROI and are helping to meet the company's strategic goals.

**Evidence-based HR**
Demonstrating that HR practices have a positive influence on the company's bottom line or key stakeholders (employees, customers, community, shareholders).

**HR or workforce analytics**
The practice of using data from HR databases and other data sources to make evidence-based HR decisions.

**Big data**
Information merged from a variety of sources, including HR databases, corporate financial statements, and employee surveys, to make evidence-based HR decisions and show that HR practices can influence the organization's bottom line.

Big data is used for several purposes. Sonic University tracks the usage rates of its hundreds of learning modules by individual learner. A recruiting dashboard provides information about the number of applicants for a position, applicants screened and interviewed, and open and filled positions. This information can be used by its training team to identify who is struggling to find candidates and fill positions, which may suggest they need training in the recruiting tools and processes the company uses. Data from new hire and exit surveys have been used to identify managers who need training in coaching skills.

Credit Suisse has a department of HR analysts who specialize in using workforce data to help reduce turnover. This can provide substantial cost savings to the company. For example, if the turnover rate for the company's 46,600 employees could be reduced by 1% per year, it could save $100 million! Each year, eight different pieces of data, including employees' performance ratings, their bosses' performance ratings, their yearly changes in compensation, and the length of time they have been in a job without a promotion, are used to identify who is likely to leave. The analysis provides reports for managers showing the turnover risk of their employees, which they can use to decide how to prevent them from leaving. For example, managers can use this information to recommend a raise, a promotion, or access to development training or opportunities for high-performing employees they don't want to lose.

Because evidence-based HR and analytics are important for showing the value of HR practices and how they contribute to business strategy and goals, throughout each chapter of the book we provide examples of companies' use of workforce analytics to make evidenced-based HR decisions or to evaluate HR practices.

## THE HRM PROFESSION: POSITIONS AND JOBS

There are many different types of jobs in the HRM profession. Table 1.3 shows various HRM positions and their salaries. A survey conducted by the Society for Human Resource Management (SHRM), to better understand what HR professionals do, found that the primary activities involve performing the HR generalist role (providing a wide range of HR services); fewer HR professionals are involved in the HR function at the executive level of the company, training and development, HR consulting, and administrative activities.[26] Projections suggest that overall employment in HR-related positions is expected to grow by 9% between 2014 and 2024, faster than the average for all occupations in the United States.[27]

Salaries for HR professionals vary according to position, level of experience, training, location, and firm size. As you can see from Table 1.3, some positions involve work in specialized areas of HRM, like recruiting, training, or labor and industrial relations. HR generalists usually make between $49,000 and $63,000 depending on their experience and education level. HR generalists perform a wide range of activities including recruiting, selection, training, labor relations, and benefits administration. HR specialists work in one specific functional area such as training or compensation. Although HR generalists tend to be found in smaller companies, many mid- to large-size companies employ HR generalists at the plant or business levels and HR specialists at the corporate, product, or regional levels. Most HR professionals chose human resources as a career because they found it appealing, they wanted to work with people, or they were asked by chance to perform HR tasks and responsibilities.[28]

Visit your instructor's Connect® course and access your eBook to view this video.

**"HR is literally the core to every organization."**
—Johnny C. Taylor Jr.,
President and CEO, SHRM

Source: Video produced for the Center for Executive Succession in the Darla Moore School of Business at the University of South Carolina by Coal Powered Filmworks

| POSITION | SALARY |
|---|---|
| Chief human resource officer (CHRO) | $238,710 |
| Global HR manager | 127,800 |
| Management development manager | 123,543 |
| Health and safety manager | 102,162 |
| Employee benefits manager | 100,901 |
| HR manager | 102,162 |
| Mid-level labor relations specialist | 89,030 |
| Campus recruiter | 68,590 |
| Entry-level HRIS specialist | 56,590 |
| HR generalist | 55,283 |
| Entry-level compensation analyst | 59,855 |
| Entry-level employee training specialist | 40,590 |

**Table 1.3**
Median Salaries for
HRM Positions

SOURCE: Based on data from Salary.com, www1.salary.com, accessed February 13, 2019.

## EDUCATION AND EXPERIENCE

The HR profession will likely continue to be in transition in the near future.[29] A large number of HR professionals who will be retiring soon have held mainly administrative roles with little previous formal education in HRM. As is currently the case for many HR professionals, the new generation of HR professionals will likely have a four-year college degree and many will have completed a graduate HR degree. Business is typically the field of study (human resources or industrial relations), although some HR professionals have degrees in the social sciences (economics or psychology), the humanities, or law. Those who have completed graduate work have master's degrees in HRM, business management, industrial organizational psychology, or a similar field. Human resource professionals can be expected to have both strategic and tactical roles. For example, a senior HR role will likely involve developing and supporting the company culture, employee recruitment, retention and engagement, succession planning, and designing the company's overall HR strategy. Junior HR roles will handle all of the transactions related to paperwork, benefits and payroll administration, answering employee questions, and data management.

Professional certification demonstrating that an individual has gained foundational knowledge in human resources is available through the Human Resources Certification Institute (HRCI) or SHRM.[30] Only 12% of U.S. HR professionals hold certification. One reason for the low level of certification is that many companies value education and/or experience more than certification when hiring for HR positions. As a result, professional certification in HRM is less common than membership in professional associations. A well-rounded educational background will likely serve a person well in an HRM position. As one HR professional noted, "One of the biggest misconceptions is that it is all warm and fuzzy communications with the workers. Or that it is creative and involved in making a more congenial atmosphere for people at work. Actually it is both of those some of the time, but most of the time it is a big mountain of paperwork which calls on a myriad of skills besides the 'people' type. It is law, accounting, philosophy, and logic as well as psychology, spirituality, tolerance, and humility."[31]

## COMPETENCIES AND BEHAVIORS

Many experts acknowledge that top-level HR professionals are generalists who have expertise in benefits, compensation, and labor relations and focus on important issues such as employee engagement and managing company culture.[32] However, they lack business acumen, the expertise in relating human resources to real-world business needs. That is, they don't know how key decisions are made and are unable to determine why employees or parts of the company fail to meet performance goals. This is congruent with the belief of companies' top HR leaders that developing the skills of professionals working in human resources is an urgent need.[33] Less than 10% of HR leaders believe that their functional teams have the skills needed to help companies meet their current competitive challenges. Consider the requirements that Netflix wanted when it was looking for a new HR director.[34] Netflix wanted someone who puts business first, customers second, and talent third. It did not want a change agent, organizational development practitioner, an SHRM certificate, or a people person. HR professionals should consider themselves as business people, not morale boosters. They need to be able to consider key questions, such as "What's good for the company?" "How do we communicate that to employees?" and "How can we help every employee understand what is meant by high performance?"

HR professionals need to have the nine competencies shown in Figure 1.3. These are the most recent competencies developed by SHRM, based on a literature review, input from over 1,200 HR professionals, and a survey of over 32,000 respondents.[35] The full version of the competency model, which can be found on the SHRM website (**www .shrm.org**), provides more detailed information on the competencies, behaviors, and standards for proficiency for HR professionals at entry, mid, senior, and executive career stages. Demonstrating these competencies can help HR professionals show managers that they are capable of helping the HR function create value, contribute to the business strategy, and shape the company culture. They also help the HR department effectively and efficiently provide the three HR products discussed earlier and shown in Figure 1.2. These competencies and behaviors show that although the level of expertise required may vary by career level, all HR professionals need to have a working knowledge of strategic business management, HR planning, development, compensation and benefits, risk management (safety, quality, etc.), labor relations, HR technology, evidence-based decision making, and global human resources. HR professionals need to be able to interact and coach employees and managers, yet engage in ethical practice through maintaining confidentiality and acting with integrity. Providing support for the usefulness and validity of the SHRM competency model, research shows that HR professionals who have a higher level of proficiency on the SHRM competencies do perform better in their jobs.[36]

Many top-level managers and HR professionals believe that the best way to develop employees who have the competencies needed to be effective in an HR role is to train them or ensure they have on-the-job experiences that help them understand the business and the role of HRM in it. For example, an HR leader at Rivermark Community Credit Union developed skills in reading and interpreting financial data by spending time with the CFO.[37] This has allowed her to contribute more in senior-level leader meetings.

Both Garden City Group and General Motors use job experiences for ensuring that current and aspiring HR professionals have the competencies they need to meet both employees and managers needs.[38] Also, these opportunities help build relationships both in the HR department and across locations. Garden City rotates HR professionals through each of its office locations and encourages its staff to shadow other HR professionals working in different functional areas. To develop future HR leaders General Motors has two specialized HR career paths: a manufacturing path and a corporate path. In the manufacturing path, employees who already work for General Motors but want to work in HR spend a year each working in labor relations, as a business partner, and in a production group. Similarly, the corporate path offered for HR interns include a labor relations assignment as well as a year assignment in global compensation and benefits

**Figure 1.3**

Competencies and Example Behaviors for HR Professionals

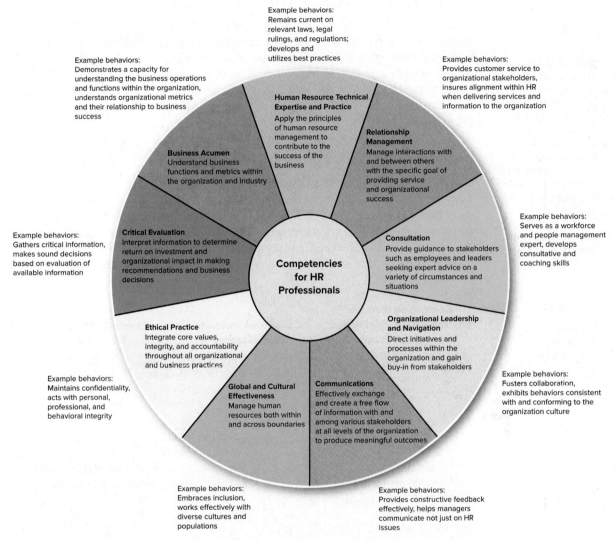

SOURCE: Based on SHRM Competency Model, Society for Human Resource Management, 2012, www.shrm.org, accessed February 9, 2017.

and either talent acquisition or talent management. Participants in both career paths are matched with mentors who can provide personal insight and advice. Also, participants in both tracks have opportunities to attend training, presentations from speakers outside the company, and forums with senior leaders.

The primary professional organization for HRM is the Society for Human Resource Management. SHRM is the world's largest HRM association, with more than 300,000 professional and student members throughout the world. If you are interested in human resources, you should join SHRM. The organization provides education and information services, conferences and seminars, government and media representation, certification, and online services and publications (such as *HR Magazine*). You can visit SHRM's website at **www.shrm.org**.

# Competitive Challenges Influencing Human Resource Management

Three competitive challenges that companies now face will increase the importance of human resource management practices: the challenge of sustainability, the global challenge, and the technology challenge. These challenges are shown in Figure 1.4.

As you will see in the following discussion, these competitive challenges are directly linked to the HR challenges that companies are facing, including developing, attracting, and retaining talented employees; finding employees with the necessary skills; and breaking down cultural barriers to create a global company.[39]

## COMPETING THROUGH ENVIRONMENTAL, SOCIAL, AND GOVERNANCE (ESG) PRACTICES

**Sustainability** refers to the company's ability to meet its needs without sacrificing the ability of future generations to meet their needs.[40] This includes the ability to deal with economic and social changes, practice environmental responsibility, engage in responsible and ethical business practices, provide high-quality products and services, and put in place methods to determine if the company is meeting stakeholders' needs. The results of

**Sustainability**
The ability of a company to make a profit without sacrificing the resources of its employees, the community, or the environment. Based on an approach to organizational decision making that considers the long-term impact of strategies on stakeholders (e.g., employees, shareholders, suppliers, community).

**Figure 1.4**

Competitive Challenges Influencing U.S. Companies

| Competing through Environmental, Social, and Governance Practices | Competing through Globalization | Competing through Technology |
|---|---|---|
| • Deal with the workforce and employment implications of the economy<br>• Understand and enhance the value of intangible assets and human capital<br>• Meet the needs of stakeholders: shareholders, customers, employees, and the community<br>• Emphasize customer service and quality<br>• Recognize and capitalize on the demographics and diversity of the workforce<br>• Deal with legal and ethical issues | • Enter international markets<br>• Consider offshore and/or reshoring jobs | • Consider social networking<br>• Use HRIS, mobile devices, cloud computing, and HR dashboards<br>• Consider High-performance work systems and virtual teams<br>• Consider the role of artificial intelligence and robotics |

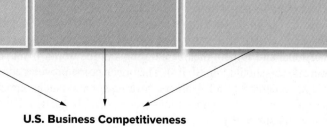

**U.S. Business Competitiveness**

companies focus on sustainability is often referred to "the triple bottom line"—the simultaneous delivery of positive results for people, planet, and profit.

To positively influence the "triple bottom line," companies need to focus on environment, social, and governance (ERG) practices. ESG practices should be part of a company's business model to help gain a competitive advantage and reduce legal risks.[41] Environment practices include a company's use of energy, physical resources such as water and natural gas, and the waste and pollution it generates. Social practices relate to the company's relationships with other businesses and the communities in which it operates. Governance practices includes the company's relationship with its stakeholders. **Stakeholders** refers to shareholders, the community, customers, employees, and all of the other parties that have an interest in seeing that the company succeeds. In fact, companies stakeholders are increasingly paying attention to its ESG practices.[42] Shareholders and potential investors consider ESG practices as a potential source for competitive advantage. For current and potential employees, customers, and consumers, ESG practices help create a positive impression of the company and its products and services. Many companies such as Goldman Sachs publish a yearly report highlighting their ESG practices and accomplishments. For example, one of Goldman Sachs accomplishments was related to clean energy.[43] The firm entered into an agreement with NextEra Energy Resources that will enable the development of a new wind project providing renewable energy. The wind project will reduce the use of 200,000 greenhouse gas emissions each year. Another accomplishment was providing $10 million to Sixup, an organization that provides college loans to gifted youth from low income families that would not normally qualify for loans.

From an HR perspective, this means creating HR systems and engaging in practices that create the skills, motivation, values, and culture that help the company and ensure long-term benefits for the organization's stakeholders. If company HR or other practices have an adverse impact on ESG factors, stakeholders will usually pursue lawsuits and financial compensation. For example, Volkswagen's paid billions of dollars to cover the costs of its emissions scandal that polluted the environment.

> **Stakeholders**
> The various interest groups who have relationships with and, consequently, whose interests are tied to the organization (e.g., employees, suppliers, customers, shareholders, community).

## Deal with the Workforce and Employment Implications of the Economy

The economy has important implications for HRM. Some key statistics about the economy and the workforce are shown in Table 1.4, and we will discuss their implications in greater

> **LO 1-2**
> Discuss the implications of the economy, the makeup of the labor force, and ethics for company sustainability.

**Table 1.4**
Highlights of Employment Projections to 2026

- The labor force is projected to increase by 11.5 million, reaching approximately 168 million.
- Today, 93% of U.S. jobs are nonagriculture wage and salary jobs: 12% are in goods-producing industries (mining, construction, manufacturing); 81% are in service-providing industries; and 1.3% in agriculture, forestry, fishing, and hunting. The distribution of jobs across industries is projected to be similar in 2026.
- 46.5 million job openings are expected, with more than three-fourths resulting from the need to replace workers who retire or leave an occupation.
- The median age of the workforce will increase to 42.3 years, the highest ever recorded.
- Health care support and practitioner occupations are projected to be the fastest-growing occupational groups and contribute the most new jobs (one out of four new jobs).

SOURCES: Bureau of Labor Statistics, U.S. Department of Labor, "Employment Projections: 2016–2026," News Release, October 24, 2017, from www.bls.gov/emp, accessed January 5, 2019; Bureau of Labor Statistics, U.S. Department of Labor, "Employment Projections, Table 3.4, Civilian Labor Force by Age, Sex, Race, and Ethnicity 1996, 2006, 2016, and Projected 2026," from www.bls.gov, accessed January 5, 2019; T. Alan Lacey, Mitra Toossi, Kevin S. Dubina, and Andrea B. Gensler, "Projections Overview and Highlights, 2016–26," *Monthly Labor Review*, U.S. Bureau of Labor Statistics, October 2017, from www.bls.gov, accessed January 5, 2019.

detail. These include the structure of the economy, aging of the workforce, and growth in professional and service occupations. Growth in professional and service occupations means that skill demands for jobs have changed, with knowledge becoming more valuable. Not only have skill demands changed, but remaining competitive in a global economy requires demanding work hours and changes in traditional employment patterns. The creation of new jobs, aging employees leaving the workforce, slow population growth, and a lack of employees who have the skills needed to perform the high-demand jobs means that companies need to give more attention to HR practices that influence their ability to attract and retain employees.

Today, the U.S. economy is thriving.[44] The stock market has reached record highs: The Dow Jones Industrial Average exceeded 20,000 in 2018. Annual growth in economic output is close to 3%. Based on their confidence in the economy, many U.S. businesses are adding jobs and expanding. The labor market is at or close to full employment, with an historically low employment rate that has reached below 4%. For some workers, wages have increased as the economy grew, unemployment dropped, and companies experienced labor shortages. For example, pay for workers in retail jobs rose 3.8% in the second quarter of 2018. Skilled job candidates in high-demand fields such as information technology received competing offers with increasing pay. Regardless of wage growth, because the consumer-price inflation remains low, workers lose less of what they earned due to the rising costs of goods and services. It is important to recognize that regardless of the current economic cycle, HRM practices have been shown to positively contribute to a company's performance. For example, companies that used more selective staffing and training before the economic recession of 2009 outproduced and had better performance than competitors before the recession and recovered more quickly.[45]

However, there are several threats to economic growth.[46] The Federal Reserve is faced with the challenge of how much to raise interest rates to avoid inflation or stimulating a recession when unemployment rates and economic growth move back toward their historical levels. President Trump has imposed tariffs on imports from China to try to reduce the U.S. trade deficit, which has been blamed on unfair trading practices. The U.S. trade deficit, which was over $502 billion in 2016, represented the largest deficit in four years. China has retaliated by placing tariffs on U.S. imports. President Trump is also renegotiating the North American Free Trade Agreement (NAFTA) with Canada and Mexico. The U.S. trade deficit means that the United States imports more products than it exports to the rest of the world. President Trump believes that taking actions on trade will continue to stimulate economic growth and support U.S. jobs, especially for working-class Americans. However, the relationship among trade, economic growth, and employment is complex, and it is influenced by factors such as currency exchange rates and government spending and taxation. In fact, the United States has had trade deficits during periods of economic expansion and recession, and under high and low employment. The impact of the U.S.-China trade war are being felt in many companies but especially in small businesses.[47] For example, the prices of trailers that Smokey Mountain Trailers in Tennessee purchases to sell to consumers have increased as much as 7% because of tariffs on steel and aluminum. This means the company has to either absorb the costs itself or increase prices, which may reduce demand for its trailers. For Byers Steel, a family-owned Ohio company with 130 employees, tariffs on Chinese steel increased sales 30% from last year. But Byers is not making planned investments in systems that would improve product quality, productivity, and employee safety because of uncertainty about the future of U.S. trade policy and the long-term effects of tariffs.

One of the implications of the current economy with low unemployment rates is that companies are unable to find employees with the skills they need to expand their operations, replace retiring employees, or keep up with increased demands for their products and services.[48] Also, valuable high-performing employees may be looking to change jobs for higher wages or better career opportunities.

***Labor Force and Employment Characteristics.*** Table 1.4 highlights employment projections to 2026. Our discussion of employment projections is based on the work done by the U.S. Bureau of Labor Statistics.[49] Population is the most important factor in determining the size and composition of the labor force. The labor force is expected to grow to almost 168 million by 2026. The size of the labor force will increase, but it is growing more slowly than in previous decades primarily because of the declining growth rate of the population. The labor force will continue to age with more people from the Baby Boomer generation (born between 1946 and 1964) entering retirement age or having already left the workforce.

Because the U.S. population is expected to become increasingly diverse, so is the U.S. workforce. The growth rate of women in the labor force will be faster than the growth rate for men. Immigration is an important force in population and workforce growth and diversity. Traditionally, Hispanic and Asian men have high labor force participation. All racial and ethnic groups, except non-Hispanic whites, are expected to grow by 2026; the share of non-Hispanic whites is expected to decline. With the fastest population growth of all racial and ethnic groups, Hispanics are projected to make up nearly 20% of the labor force (the diversity and aging of the workforce is discussed in more detail later in this chapter).

The importance of the service sector in the U.S. economy is emphasized by considering industry and occupational employment rates and future projections. In all, 80% of jobs are in the service sector. Currently, the largest percentages of jobs are found in health care and social assistance, leisure and hospitality, state and local government, professional and business services, and retail trade. Health care support and practitioner occupations are projected to be the fastest-growing occupational groups and contribute the most new jobs (one out of four new jobs) from 2016 to 2026. All other occupations are expected to add jobs between 2016 and 2026 except for production and forestry, farming, and fishing.[50]

Table 1.5 provides examples of the largest percentage growths in jobs from 2016 to 2026. Of the 30 fastest-growing occupations, 16 are in health care and related occupations (such as home health care aid, personal care aids, physicians assistants, and nurse practitioners). Other occupations in the top 30 are energy related or in computer and information technology. The growth in health care reflects the inpatient and outpatient medical care that is needed for the aging U.S. population. Computer occupations are expected to see job growth as the demand increases for artificial intelligence, robots, and other technologies. The expected increase in energy prices will drive growth for energy occupations, especially those related to oil and gas extraction and solar power.

All major occupations are projected to gain jobs between 2016 and 2026 except production occupations, and farming, fishery, and forestry. Six industries are projected to have decreases in employment—manufacturing; federal government; agriculture; forestry, fishing, and hunting; information; and utilities. This loss of jobs and workers is due to several factors including technological improvements, which means fewer workers are needed; global competition; industry consolidation; cost-cutting and more efficient work processes; and a decrease in the number of workers who want to work in these occupations.

Education plays an important role in meeting occupational or job requirements and in employee earnings.[51] A minimum level of education is not required for approximately 31% of U.S. jobs. But, 22% of jobs require some form of training such as a certificate or license. Further, 11 of the 15 fastest-growing occupations require some level of postsecondary education and have higher median weekly earnings than the national average. Today, the median weekly earnings for jobs requiring a high school diploma is $730, compared to $802 for those who have some college but no degree, $862 for an associate degree,

**Table 1.5**

Examples of the Fastest-Growing Occupations

| OCCUPATION | EMPLOYMENT CHANGE 2016–2026 | | MOST SIGNIFICANT EDUCATION OR TRAINING | MEDIAN ANNUAL WAGES, MAY 2016 |
|---|---|---|---|---|
| | NUMBER (TO NEAREST THOUSANDS) | PERCENT | | |
| Solar photovoltaic installers | 12 | 105 | High school diploma or equivalent | $39,240 |
| Wind turbine service technicians | 6 | 96 | Postsecondary nondegree; long-term, on-the-job training | $52,260 |
| Home health aids | 431 | 47 | High school diploma or equivalent; short-term, on-the-job training | $22,600 |
| Personal care aids | 778 | 39 | High school diploma or equivalent; short-term, on-the-job training | $21,920 |
| Physician assistants | 40 | 37 | Master's degree | $101,480 |
| Nurse practitioners | 56 | 36 | Master's degree | $100,910 |
| Statisticians | 13 | 34 | Master's degree | $80,500 |
| Physical therapy assistants | 27 | 31 | Associate's degree | $56,610 |
| Software developers, applications | 255 | 31 | Bachelor's degree | $100,080 |
| Mathematicians | 1 | 30 | Master's degree | $105,810 |

SOURCE: Based on Bureau of Labor Statistics, U.S. Department of Labor, "Employment Projections: 2016–2026," News Release, October 24, 2017, from www.bls.gov/emp, accessed February 9, 2019.

$1,198 for a bachelor's degree, and $1,884 for a professional degree. The discrepancy in earnings is expected to continue in the future.

The low unemployment rate and business growth has resulted in employers in many industries, such as construction and manufacturing and particularly small businesses, having difficulty finding qualified workers. Unskilled, assembly line work is being replaced with advanced manufacturing jobs that require hard-to-find computer, information technology, or other technical knowledge and skills. In many of today's jobs, especially those in the service sector, routine tasks have been automated or outsourced. Kyocera SGS Precision Tools, an Ohio company, has half the employees it had 20 years ago but produces twice as much due to computer-assisted manufacturing tools and higher-skilled employees.[52] The company is struggling to find maintenance technicians with the electrical and mechanical skills needed to keep equipment running.

Several studies illustrate the skills deficit that U.S. companies are experiencing.[53] Skills deficits are not limited to any one business sector, industry, or job. Nearly half of CEOs of U.S. businesses believe that a significant skills gap exists that will result in loss of business, loss of revenue, decreased customer satisfaction, or a delay in new products or services. The Manufacturing Institute found that 80% of manufacturers report a moderate or serious shortage of qualified applicants for skilled and highly skilled production positions. One estimate is that 60% of manufacturing job openings in the next 10 years are likely to be unfilled due to the lack of employees with the necessary skills. The Organisation for

Economic Co-operation and Development (OECD) found that the United States ranked 28 out of 35 countries in math and 16 out of 35 countries in problem solving. But skills deficits are not just a problem facing U.S. companies. They are occurring around the world. For example, in Italy and Spain nearly 3 out of 10 adults perform at or below the lowest proficiency level in literacy and numerical ability. One study found that, regardless of their education level, only half the companies surveyed rated new employees as adequately prepared for work.

There is especially a shortage of employees with STEM skills. **STEM skills** refer to skills in science, technology, engineering, and math. Many available workers also lack "soft skills," including the ability to communicate clearly, take the initiative, problem solve, get along with peers, and interact with customers.[54] Further, the variety and customization of products and services many companies offer require employees to be creative and good problem solvers. Also, continuous innovation requires the ability to learn.

This shortage of qualified workers means that employers are faced with the undesirable option of leaving jobs unfilled, which can limit their production and growth. Companies in most industries, including hospitality, retail, and manufacturing, are having problems attracting, finding, and retaining talented employees with the skills they need. Many are relying on HRM practices including staffing, compensation, training, and development as part of the solution.[55] For example, companies are recruiting, hiring, and accommodating individuals with disabilities who have traditionally been overlooked or not considered for employment. Both SAP and Microsoft are finding that workers with autism are detail-oriented and analytical, which makes them successful in software-testing positions. Companies are also seeking workers who may have retired from their previous job or left their career. Goldman Sachs's Returnship program provides eight paid weeks of training and mentoring for individuals who have taken a career break of longer than two years. Of the 350 people who have completed the program, about half have found permanent employment at Goldman Sachs. Also, companies are reviewing minimum education and experience requirements and lowering or dropping them for some jobs, which helps fill open positions faster. Hasbro divided four marketing jobs, which it previously designed for business-school graduates with MBAs, into eight lower-level positions with no college requirement. The lower level positions involve more routine activities supporting higher-level staff in the division. Amazon raised the minimum wage it pays to all U.S. employees to $15 per hour.

To avoid losing employees who otherwise might leave for a better career opportunity, Walmart has made a two-year investment of over $2.7 billion to increase workers' wages as well as provide additional training. Walmart's training for both new and experienced associates is designed to provide them with the interpersonal and business skills they need to be successful, share possible career paths they might pursue, help them understand the retail business model, and explain the reasons for the job tasks they are asked to perform. One of the steps being taken by the hotel industry is to offer tuition assistance to attract, retain, and prepare new employees for managerial roles. The American Hotel & Lodging Association and Pearson PLC are testing a new program for hotel industry employees that will cover the cost of a two-year online associate's degree and a significant portion of the cost of a bachelor's degree. Ten companies, including Red Roof Inns and Wyndham Hotels and Resorts, with a total of 50,000 employees are participating in the program.

Some companies are even extending training beyond their current workforce to ensure they have employees available in the future.[56] GW Plastics, based in Vermont, provides high school students with for-credit classes in advanced manufacturing at its plant. The company also has a scholarship program that pays for the cost of tuition and provides a paid internship for students earning a degree in mechanical engineering technology at Vermont Technical College.

**STEM skills**
Science, technology, engineering, and math skills that U.S. employers need and value, but employees lack.

## Understand and Enhance the Value Placed on Intangible Assets and Human Capital

Today more and more companies are interested in using intangible assets and human capital as a way to gain an advantage over competitors. A company's value includes three types of assets that are critical for the company to provide goods and services: financial assets (cash and securities), physical assets (property, plant, equipment), and intangible assets. Table 1.6 provides examples of intangible assets. **Intangible assets** include human capital, customer capital, social capital, and intellectual capital. Intangible assets are equally or even more valuable than financial and physical assets, but they are difficult to duplicate or imitate.[57] By one estimate, up to 75% of the source of value in a company is in intangible assets.[58]

Intangible assets have been shown to be responsible for a company's competitive advantage. Human resource management practices such as training, selection, performance management, and compensation have a direct influence on human and social capital through influencing customer service, work-related know-how and competence, and work relationships.

Blue Apron, a company that delivers the fresh ingredients and cooking instructions its customers need to prepare delicious meals, puts a great deal of effort into developing human capital, social capital, and customer capital.[59] Blue Apron hosts a wine happy hour that brings customers together to help build friendships, facilitate networking, and introduce wines the company is selling that month as part of its meal delivery subscription. Full-time employees attend an annual camping trip, which often involves visiting a farm to see where its ingredients are grown. Blue Apron provides leadership training

**Intangible assets**
A type of company asset that includes human capital, customer capital, social capital, and intellectual capital.

**Table 1.6**
Examples of Intangible Assets

| |
|---|
| Human capital |
| • Tacit knowledge |
| • Education |
| • Work-related know-how |
| • Work-related competence |
| Customer capital |
| • Customer relationships |
| • Brands |
| • Customer loyalty |
| • Distribution channels |
| Social capital |
| • Corporate culture |
| • Management philosophy |
| • Management practices |
| • Informal networking systems |
| • Coaching/mentoring relationships |
| Intellectual capital |
| • Patents |
| • Copyrights |
| • Trade secrets |
| • Intellectual property |

SOURCES: Based on L. Weatherly, *Human Capital: The Elusive Asset* (Alexandria, VA: SHRM Research Quarterly, 2003); E. Holton and S. Naquin, "New Metrics for Employee Development," *Performance Improvement Quarterly* 17 (2004), pp. 56–80; M. Huselid, B. Becker, and R. Beatty, *The Workforce Scorecard* (Boston: Harvard University Press, 2005).

programs for every level of manager within the company. The training programs focus on how managers want to develop as leaders, how they can help their employees develop, and how to lead across the organization.

Intangible assets have been shown to be related to a company's financial performance, productivity, and innovation.[60] The American Society for Training and Development found that companies that invested the most in training and development had a shareholder return 86% higher than companies in the bottom half and 46% higher than the market average.

One way companies try to increase intangible assets is through attracting, developing, and retaining knowledge workers. **Knowledge workers** are employees who contribute to the company not through manual labor, but through what they know about customers or a specialized body of knowledge. Employees cannot simply be ordered to perform tasks; they must share knowledge and collaborate on solutions. Knowledge workers contribute specialized knowledge that their managers may not have, such as information about customers. Managers depend on them to share information. Knowledge workers have many job opportunities. If they choose, they can leave a company and take their knowledge to a competitor. Knowledge workers are in demand because companies need their skills, and the jobs requiring them are growing (see Table 1.5).

**Knowledge workers**
Employees who own the intellectual means of producing a product or service.

***Emphasize Empowerment and Continuous Learning.*** To completely benefit from employees' knowledge requires a management style that focuses on developing and empowering employees. **Empowering** means giving employees responsibility and authority to make decisions regarding all aspects of product development or customer service.[61] Employees are then held accountable for products and services; in return, they share the rewards and losses of the results. For empowerment to be successful, managers must be trained to link employees to resources within and outside the company (people, websites, etc.), help employees interact with their fellow employees and managers throughout the company, and ensure that employees are updated on important issues and cooperate with each other. Employees must also be trained to understand how to use the Web, e-mail, and other tools for communicating, collecting, and sharing information.

**Empowering**
Giving employees the responsibility and authority to make decisions.

As more companies become knowledge-based, it's important that they promote continuous learning at the employee, team, and company levels. A **learning organization** embraces a culture of lifelong learning, enabling all employees to continually acquire and share knowledge. Improvements in product or service quality do not stop when formal training is completed.[62] Employees need to have the financial, time, and content resources (courses, experiences, development opportunities) available to increase their knowledge. Managers take an active role in identifying training needs and helping to ensure that employees use training in their work. Also, employees should be actively encouraged to identify problems, make decisions, continuously experiment, and improve.

**Learning organization**
An organization whose employees are continuously attempting to learn new things and apply what they have learned to improve product or service quality.

Keller Williams Realty, which focuses on buying and selling residential and commercial real estate, emphasizes continuous learning both to attract new real estate agents and to help all agents boost their sales, which means the company makes profits and they earn more money.[63] Learning is accessible for agents anywhere and anytime via KW Connect, a learning platform that includes all of the company's training programs and materials, as well as user-generated content from top real-estate professionals. For example, KW Connect includes videos, audio files, and links, a feature that allows learners to follow top executives and agents and receive notifications when they post new content, a question-and-answer forum, user ratings and comments for all content that helps identify the best ideas, and a searchable calendar that allows agents to sign up for over 250,000 instructor-led training classes. Top agents provide videos explaining how they deal with common real estate challenges. Office managers can create custom content for new agents or other groups.

**Change**
The adoption of a new idea or behavior by a company.

*Adapt to Change.* **Change** refers to the adoption of a new idea or behavior by a company. Technological advances, changes in the workforce or government regulations, globalization, and new competitors are among the many factors that require companies to change. Change is inevitable in companies as products, companies, and entire industries experience shorter life cycles.[64]

**Agility**
Companies and their employees ability to anticipate and cause change, adapt to it, and take specific actions to support change.

HRM plays an important role in helping companies and their employees manage change through becoming more agile. **Agility** refers to anticipating and causing, adapting, and taking specific actions to support change.[65] For example, Hilton Worldwide was faced with the business challenge of adopting technology to create operational efficiency and engage with its hotel guests from when they book their stay to when they check out.[66] More than 80,000 front-desk staff and managers in 4,400 hotels needed to become familiar with Digital Check-in, an app that customers can use to make reservations, choose their room, and check in with their mobile devices. To make the change successful, Hilton relied on training. Hilton used a training approach that includes short games, job aids, and quick reference guides available using a computer or smartphone. This approach gave employees convenient access to the training and made learning fun. As a result, employees were motivated to complete the training which helped ease the transition to the customer-driven check-in system and led to more satisfied guests.

Change has also played a major role in reshaping the employment relationship.[67] New or emergent business strategies that result from these changes cause companies to merge, acquire new companies, grow, and in some cases downsize and restructure. This has resulted in changes in the employment relationship. Companies demand excellent customer service and high productivity levels. Employees are expected to take more responsibility for their own careers, from seeking training to balancing work and family. In exchange for top performance and working longer hours without job security, employees want companies to provide flexible work schedules, comfortable working conditions, more autonomy in accomplishing work, training and development opportunities, and financial incentives based on how the company performs. Employees realize that companies cannot provide employment security, so they want employability—that is, they want their company to provide training and job experiences to help ensure that employees can find other employment opportunities. The HRM challenge is how to build a committed, productive workforce in economic conditions that offer opportunity for financial success but can also quickly turn sour, making every employee expendable.

**Employee engagement**
The degree to which employees are fully involved in their work and the strength of their job and company commitment.

*Maximize Employee Engagement.* **Employee engagement** refers to the degree to which employees are fully involved in their work and the strength of their commitment to their job and the company.[68] How do we know if an employee is engaged? An engaged employee is passionate about his or her work, is committed to the company and its mission, and works hard to contribute. Engagement survey results show that only 34% of U.S. employees are engaged in their work, 53% are not engaged, and 13% are actively disengaged.[69] Actively disengaged employees cost the United States billions of dollars every year in lost productivity.

Perhaps the best way to understand engagement is to consider how companies measure employee engagement. Companies measure employees' engagement levels with attitude or opinion surveys. Although the types of questions asked on these surveys vary from company to company, research suggests the questions generally measure 10 common themes shown in Table 1.7. As you probably realize after reviewing the themes shown in Table 1.7, employees' engagement is influenced by how managers treat employees as well

**Table 1.7**
Common Themes
of Employee
Engagement

Pride in employer
Satisfaction with employer
Satisfaction with the job
Opportunity to perform challenging work
Recognition and positive feedback for contributions
Personal support from manager
Effort above and beyond the minimum
Understanding the link between one's job and the company's mission
Prospects for future growth with the company
Intention to stay with the company

SOURCES: Based on R. Vance, *Employee Engagement and Commitment* (Alexandria, VA: Society for Human Resource Management, 2006); T. Lytle, "The Engagement Challenge," *HR Magazine*, October 2016, pp. 52–58.

as HR practices such as recruiting, selection, training and development, performance management, work design, and compensation.

Many companies are moving beyond a narrow focus on employee engagement to focus instead on creating a positive employee experience.[70] **Employee experience** refers to everything that influences employees daily life both inside and outside of the workplace. The employee experience is influenced by the company culture, emotional experience, opportunities for personal growth, and the physical work space.[71] Some of the factors that contribute to a positive employee experience include doing important work that contributes to a larger purpose, open and honest company leaders, flexible work schedules, and availability of private and social work spaces. Also, use of technology such as apps to improve productivity, collaboration, and well-being, clear and transparent performance goals, receiving recognition, and a fair and inclusive environment all contribute to a positive employee experience.

For example, SunTrust, a banking and financial services company, has strived to create a positive employee experience in several different ways.[72] SunTrust's company mission to help clients and communities achieve financial well-being was extended to its employees. The online financial fitness money management program it offers for clients is now offered to employees. The program covers topics including debt management, insurance, buying or renting a home, and budgeting. Employees who are participating in the program receive a paid day off so they have the time to develop a will or set up a budget. Each employee who completes the program receives $1,000 from SunTrust for their personal emergency management fund. Survey results after the program showed that almost three-quarters of program participants took actions to improve their credit score and more than half reported less financial stress. SunTrust has also introduced some initiatives directly in response to the results of its engagement survey that showed employees wanted more flexible work options and schedules to reduce commuting time and better work–life balance. SunTrust opened co-working sites in several cities where its offices are located. SunTrust also expanded its maternity and parental leave. Birth moms get 10 weeks of paid leave they can choose to take on a week-by-week basis. Six weeks of paid parental leave are available for fathers, domestic partners, and adoptive parents.

To attract and retain talented employees, companies often use an employee value proposition (EVP) to communicate the experience that employees can expect. An **employee value proposition (EVP)** is a strategic statement that communicates the company values, how they affect employees, and how the employee experience reflects the values.[73] For example, Dell's EVP emphasizes an entrepreneurial culture, the freedom to develop a

**Employee experience**
Everything that influences employees daily life both inside and outside of the workplace.

**Employee value proposition (EVP)**
A strategic statement that communicates the company values, how they affect employees, and how the employee experience reflects the values.

career within or across functions, diversity and inclusion, and a commitment to community and the environment.

**Talent management**
Attracting, retaining, developing, and motivating highly skilled employees and managers.

*Manage Talent.*   **Talent management** refers to the systematic planned strategic effort by a company to use bundles of HRM practices—including acquiring and assessing employees, learning and development, performance management, and compensation—to attract, retain, develop, and motivate highly skilled employees and managers. This means recognizing that all HR practices are interrelated, are aligned with business needs, and help the organization manage talent to meet business goals. For example, at Qualcomm, a San Diego company, talent management is organized around core values that emphasize recruiting smart, motivated employees and creating a work environment that allows them to innovate, execute, partner, and lead.[74] When Qualcomm wanted to introduce technology for its performance management process, HR generalists worked together with organizational development and information technology specialists to ensure that what employees were being evaluated on (performance management) and what employees were paid and rewarded for (compensation and rewards) were aligned. Managers were trained to use the performance management system and now focus on identifying employee skills gaps to identify opportunities to improve performance.

Opportunities for career growth, learning, and development, and performing exciting and challenging work are some of the most important factors in determining employees' engagement and commitment to their current employer.[75] High-achieving employees may be looking to leave companies if they do not feel they have adequate opportunities to develop or move to positions in which they can best utilize their skills.

Consider how Mastercard and BNSF manage talent.[76] Mastercard emphasizes promoting its current employees. It provides employees with job rotation opportunities to develop their skills, career paths, and an online tool they can use to research jobs and their skill requirements. BNSF, the largest freight railroad in North America, recognizes that developing and promoting talent from within the company is critical for business success because of the technical nature of the work, the complicated operating environment, and the company's desire to maintain its strong culture. BNSF uses programs and processes to develop its internal talent, including an internship and management training program that starts with college and graduate school hires, regular department-level discussions of top talent and talent movement, and development plans matched to each employees' development needs and desired career path. The emphasis on talent has paid off: 38% of the company's top talent received a development move or promotion and 96% of its top 500 leadership positions have been filled with internal talent.

**Nontraditional employment**
Includes the use of independent contractors, freelancers, on-call workers, temporary workers, and contract company workers.

**Gig economy**
Companies who rely primarily on nontraditional employment to meet service and product demands.

*Consider Nontraditional Employment and the Gig Economy.*   More companies are moving away the traditional employment model based on full-time workers to increasingly rely on nontraditional employment. **Nontraditional employment** includes the use of independent contractors, freelancers, on-call workers, temporary workers, and contract company workers. Studies estimate that between 20% and 35% of the total U.S. workforce is engaged in nontraditional employment, including those who have a full-time job (what is called "moonlighting").[77] Companies that rely primarily on nontraditional employment to meet service and product demands are competing in the **gig economy**.[78] Although many companies will continue to rely on a traditional employment model using full- and part-time employees, 40% believe they will use a nontraditional model (independent contractors, project-based or freelance need-based work) in the next decade.

What does nontraditional employment look like? Often, a website or mobile app is used to assign work, and the worker sets his or her own schedule. Because these workers do not work for a company, they do not have taxes withheld from their earnings, they do not have to receive minimum wage or overtime pay, and they are not eligible for worker's compensation and unemployment insurance. Examples of companies that rely on the gig economy include transportation services Uber and Lyft and food-delivery services such as Caviar. Nontraditional employment has advantages and disadvantages for both individuals and employers.[79]

More workers in nontraditional employment relationships are choosing these arrangements. Nontraditional employment can benefit both individuals and employers. More and more individuals don't want to be attached to any one company. They want the flexibility to work when and where they choose. They may want to work fewer hours to better balance work and family responsibilities. Also, individuals who have been downsized may choose nontraditional employment while they are seeking full-time employment. From the company perspective, it is easier to add temporary employees when they are needed and easier to terminate their employment when they are not needed. Part-time workers can be a valuable source of skills that current employees may not have and are needed for a specific project that has a set completion date. Part-time workers can be less expensive than permanent employees because they do not receive employer health benefits or participate in pension plans. Employing part-time workers such as interns allows the company to determine if the worker meets performance requirements and fits in with the company culture, and if so, the company may then decide to offer the employee a permanent position. For example, Ammacore's workers install cabling and perform electronic troubleshooting for the company's clients.[80] Ammacore uses a third-party vendor to screen and verify credentials of technicians it uses. A community manager communicates with the technicians before, during, and after a project to ensure they have the information they need. Using a service provided by the third-party vendor, the company rates the technicians' timeliness, performance, and reliability. The technicians rate Ammacore on the timeliness of the payment for their services and communication during the project. Technicians who perform well receive small bonuses. Ammacore depends on receiving good ratings from technicians to attract talented technicians. Some technology companies such as Honeywell have relied on crowdsourcing using services such as Topcoder and Amazon's Mechanical Turk to find scientists and software engineers who have the skills not found in the company's employees to solve problems, create apps, or write code. Alphabet Inc., the parent company of Google, has equal numbers of full-time and temporary and contract workers who test self-driving cars, manage projects, review legal documents, and do other jobs. Nontraditional employment also has potential disadvantages. These include concerns about work quality, inability to maintain the company culture or team environment, and legal liability.[81]

***Provide Flexibility to Help Employees Meet Work and Life Demands.*** The globalization of the world economy and the development of e-commerce have made the notion of a 40-hour work week obsolete. Survey results show that 46% of employees work more than 45 hours per week.[82] As a result, companies need to be staffed 24 hours a day, seven days a week. Employees in manufacturing environments and service call centers are being asked to move from 8- to 12-hour days or to work afternoon or midnight shifts. Similarly, professional employees face long hours and work demands that spill over into their personal lives. Notebook computers, smartphones, and smartwatches bombard employees with information and work demands. In the car, on vacation, on planes, and even in the bathroom, employees can be interrupted by work demands. More demanding work results in greater employee stress, less satisfied employees, loss of productivity, and higher turnover—all of which are costly for companies.

One study found that because of work demands 75% of employees report not having enough time for their children, and 61% report not having enough time for their husbands or wives. However, only half of employees in the United States strongly agree that they have the flexibility they need to successfully manage their work and personal or family lives.[83] Many companies are recognizing the benefits that can be gained by both the company and employees through providing flexible work schedules, allowing work-at-home arrangements, protecting employees' free time, and more productively using employees' work time.[84] The benefits include the ability to have an advantage in attracting and retaining talented employees, reduced stress resulting in healthier employees, and a rested workforce that can maximize the use of their skills. It is estimated that 43% of employees do most or all of their work from home, meaning they spend time working in a location away from their peers.[85] Employees in managerial, business, and financial operations and professional occupations are most likely to do some or all of their work at home.

For example, at Automattic, almost all work is done remotely.[86] Automattic, which provides a content management system that is used on websites, has over 500 employees working in more than 50 countries. The company is selling its office in San Francisco because so few employees work there. Instead employees rely on several tools including Slack, Zoom, and its own internal discussion board for documenting work, having discussions, and videoconferencing. The use of these tools means that everyone can access and search internal communications, creating feelings of transparency and inclusion. At Dell, 58% of its employees work remotely, especially in jobs involving business support functions such as HR, legal, data science, and marketing

The use of nontraditional work employment and work-at-home has resulted in the development of co-working sites or shared offices where diverse workers such as designers, artists, freelancers, consultants, and other independent contractors pay a daily or monthly fee for a guaranteed work space.[87] Co-working sites are equipped with desks, Internet, and conferences rooms, and some even provide couches for relaxing and free coffee and beer. Co-working sites help independent contractors and employees who work at home, travel, or telecommute and who have feelings of isolation, enabling them to collaborate and interact, providing a more professional working atmosphere than coffee shops, and helping to decrease traffic and pollution.

### Meet the Needs of Stakeholders: Shareholders, Customers, Employees, and Community

As we mentioned earlier, company effectiveness and competitiveness are determined by whether the company satisfies the needs of stakeholders. Stakeholders include stockholders (who want a return on their investment), customers (who want a high-quality product or service), and employees (who desire interesting work and reasonable compensation for their services). The community, which wants the company to contribute to activities and projects and minimize pollution of the environment, is also an important stakeholder.

**Balanced scorecard**
A means of performance measurement that gives managers a chance to look at their company from the perspectives of internal and external customers, employees, and shareholders.

***Demonstrate Performance to Stakeholders: The Balanced Scorecard.*** The **balanced scorecard** gives managers an indication of the performance of a company based on the degree to which stakeholder needs are satisfied; it depicts the company from the perspective of internal and external customers, employees, and shareholders.[88] The balanced scorecard is important because it brings together most of the features that a company needs to focus on to be competitive. These include being customer-focused, improving quality, emphasizing teamwork, reducing new product and service development times, and managing for the long term.

The balanced scorecard differs from traditional measures of company performance by emphasizing that the critical indicators chosen are based on the company's business strategy and competitive demands. Companies need to customize their balanced scorecards based on different market situations, products, and competitive environments.

**Table 1.8**
The Balanced Scorecard

| PERSPECTIVE | QUESTIONS ANSWERED | EXAMPLES OF CRITICAL BUSINESS INDICATORS | EXAMPLES OF CRITICAL HR INDICATORS |
|---|---|---|---|
| Customer | How do customers see us? | Time, quality, performance, service, cost | Employee satisfaction with HR department services Employee perceptions of the company as an employer |
| Internal | What must we excel at? | Processes that influence customer satisfaction, availability of information on service and/or manufacturing processes | Training costs per employee, turnover rates, time to fill open positions |
| Innovation and learning | Can we continue to improve and create value? | Improve operating efficiency, launch new products, continuous improvement, empowering of workforce, employee satisfaction | Employee/skills competency levels, engagement survey results, change management capability |
| Financial | How do we look to shareholders? | Profitability, growth, shareholder value | Compensation and benefits per employee, turnover costs, profit per employee, revenue per employee |

SOURCES: Based on K. Thompson and N. Mathys, "The Aligned Balanced Scorecard," *Organizational Dynamics* 37 (2008), pp. 378–393; B. Becker, M. Huselid, and D. Ulrich, *The HR Scorecard: Linking People, Strategy, and Performance* (Boston: Harvard Business School Press, 2001).

The balanced scorecard should be used to (1) link human resource management activities to the company's business strategy and (2) evaluate the extent to which the HRM function is helping the company meet its strategic objectives. Communicating the scorecard to employees gives them a framework that helps them see the company's goals and strategies, how these goals and strategies are measured, and how they influence the critical indicators. Measures of HRM practices primarily relate to productivity, people, and process.[89] Productivity measures involve determining output per employee (such as revenue per employee). Measuring people includes assessing employees' behavior, attitudes, or knowledge. Process measures focus on assessing employees' satisfaction with people systems within the company. People systems can include the performance management system, the compensation and benefits system, and the development system. To show that HRM activities contribute to a company's competitive advantage, managers need to consider the questions shown in Table 1.8 and be able to identify critical indicators or metrics related to human resources. As shown in the last column of Table 1.8, critical indicators of HR practices primarily relate to people, productivity, and process.

For example, at ConocoPhillips, the balanced scorecard for top executives includes costs, health and safety, production, and resource replacement.[90] ConocoPhillips has also developed scorecards for operational-level activities such as safety. Some physicians employed by OhioHealth, a hospital system, receive up to 10% of their pay based on a balanced scorecard consisting of quality, service, financial performance, and employee engagement.[91]

*Demonstrate Social Responsibility.* Increasingly, companies are recognizing that social responsibility can help boost a company's image with customers, gain access to new markets, and help attract and retain talented employees. Companies thus try to meet shareholder and general public demands that they be more socially, ethically, and environmentally

**LO 1-3**
Discuss how human resource management affects a company's balanced scorecard.

## Socially Responsible Programs Boost the Returns to All Stakeholders

Sustainability is an important part of many companies' business strategy. Apple has participated in the ConnectED initiative, pledging $100 million of teaching and learning solutions to more than 100 under-served schools across the country. Apple provides an iPad to every student, a Mac and iPad to every teacher, and an Apple TV to every classroom. In Kenya, Microsoft partnered with M-KOPA Solar to connect homes to solar power for the first time, using the Microsoft Cloud as a pay-as-you-go model that helps households living on less than $2 a day establish a credit history. Microsoft has also been a leader in advancing measures to defend and protect technology from cyberattacks by criminal organizations and rogue states around the world. Microsoft and 34 other technology firms, including Intuit, Facebook, Dell, and SAP, helped develop a Cybersecurity Tech Accord in which they pledge to advance online security around the world.

The Gap is working to improve the lives of garment workers as a member of the Alliance for Bangladesh Worker Safety. The Alliance provides fire safety training for workers and managers and a toll-free confidential hotline for garment workers to share their concerns about the workplace. The Gap is also committed to act on climate change through setting a goal of cutting the carbon footprint of its global facilities in half by the end of 2020.

The Mars Ambassador Program provides employees with the opportunity to share their expertise and develop skills by spending up to six weeks supporting projects managed by organizations such as the Rainforest Alliance or the World Wildlife Federation or working with local communities. For example, one Mars Ambassador team spent a week in Puerto Rico rebuilding an animal shelter. The local community benefited by being able to provide better care and quality of life for the animals. The employees learned how to work as a team in a challenging situation. Another team worked with students in Bucharest, Romania, to design and implement an energy audit for their school, which resulted in cost savings and energy conservation.

### DISCUSSION QUESTION

1. How does a company's sustainability efforts help the company attract, retain, and develop employees? Explain your answer.

SOURCES: www.apple.com, accessed February 10, 2019; "Taking Action: 1.3+ Million Workers Trained," from www.gap.com, accessed February 10, 2019; "Dawn of a New Era in Safety: Accelerating Progress in the Alliance's Final Year," Alliance for Bangladesh Worker Safety Annual Report (November 2017) from http://www.bangladeshworkersafety.org, accessed February 10, 2019.; "Microsoft 2018 Corporate Social Responsibility Report," from www.micrsoft.com, accessed February 10, 2019; B. Smith, "34 Companies Stand Up For Tech Security With Cyber Accord," April 17, 2018, from https://blogs.microsoft.com, accessed February 10, 2019; D. Moss, "One Sweet Job," *HR Magazine*, October 2016, pp. 43–45; "Mars Ambassador Program," www.mars.com, accessed February 5, 2019.

responsible. For example, Johnson & Johnson is actively involved in improving health care for pregnant women and their unborn children. mMitra, a mobile messaging program, sends vital health information to expectant and new mothers living in low-income urban communities in India—positively impacting the lives of millions of women and their children.[92] The Competing through Environmental, Social, and Governance Practices box highlights the sustainable business practices of several companies.

### Emphasize Customer Service and Quality

Companies' customers judge quality and performance. As a result, customer excellence requires attention to product and service features as well as to interactions with customers. Customer-driven excellence includes understanding what the customer wants and anticipating future needs. Customer-driven excellence includes reducing defects and errors, meeting specifications, and reducing complaints. How the company recovers from defects and errors is also important for retaining and attracting customers.

Due to increased availability of knowledge and competition, consumers are very knowledgeable and expect excellent service. This presents a challenge for employees who interact with customers. The way in which clerks, sales staff, front-desk personnel, and service providers interact with customers influences a company's reputation and financial performance. Employees need product knowledge and service skills, and they need to be clear about the types of decisions they can make when dealing with customers.

To compete in today's economy, whether on a local or global level, companies need to provide a quality product or service. If companies do not adhere to quality standards, their ability to sell their product or service to vendors, suppliers, or customers will be restricted. Some countries even have quality standards that companies must meet to conduct business there. **Total quality management (TQM)** is a companywide effort to continuously improve the way people, machines, and systems accomplish work.[93] Core values of TQM include the following:[94]

- Methods and processes are designed to meet the needs of internal and external customers.
- Every employee in the company receives training in quality.
- Quality is designed into a product or service so that errors are prevented from occurring rather than being detected and corrected.
- The company promotes cooperation with vendors, suppliers, and customers to improve quality and hold down costs.
- Managers measure progress with feedback based on data.

**Total quality management (TQM)**
A cooperative form of doing business that relies on the talents and capabilities of both labor and management to continually improve quality and productivity.

*Malcolm Baldrige National Quality Award.* One way that companies can improve the quality of their products or services is through competing for the **Malcolm Baldrige National Quality Award** or gaining certification in the **ISO 9000:2015** standards. The Baldrige award, created by public law, is the highest level of national recognition for quality that a U.S. company can receive. To become eligible for the Baldrige, a company must complete a detailed application that consists of basic information about the firm as well as an in-depth presentation of how it addresses specific criteria related to quality improvement.[95] The categories and point values for the Baldrige Award are found in Table 1.9. The award is not given for specific products or services. Organizations can compete for the Baldrige Award in one of several categories, including manufacturing, service, small business, education, health care, and nonprofit. The Baldrige Award is given annually in each of the categories with a total limit each year of 18 awards. All applicants for the Baldrige Award undergo a rigorous examination process that takes from 300 to 1,000 hours. Applications are reviewed by an independent board of about 400 examiners who come primarily from the private sector. One of the major benefits of applying for the Baldrige Award is the feedback report from the examining team noting the company's strengths and areas for improvement.[96]

The Baldrige Award winners usually excel at HR practices. For example, consider Don Chalmers Ford, a 2016 small business award winner.[97] Don Chalmers Ford is an independent Ford Motor automobile dealer with 182 employees in Rio Rancho, New Mexico. Don Chalmers has been nationally recognized by Ford Motors for customer satisfaction and market share 13 times over the past 17 years. This has been accomplished by only 4% of U.S. Ford dealerships. In the past four years, its dealership profits increased by 13%, exceeding Ford's national dealership benchmark by over 8%. In addition to analyzing its service and sales processes on a daily, weekly, and monthly basis to identify opportunities

**Malcolm Baldrige National Quality Award**
An award established in 1987 to promote quality awareness, to recognize quality achievements of U.S. companies, and to publicize successful quality strategies.

**ISO 9000:2015**
A family of standards developed by the International Organization for Standardization that includes 20 requirements for dealing with such issues as how to establish quality standards and document work processes.

**Table 1.9**
Categories and Point Values for the Malcolm Baldrige National Quality Award Examination

| | |
|---|---|
| **Leadership** | **120** |
| How senior executives create and sustain vision, values, and mission; promote legal and ethical behavior; create a sustainable company; and communicate with and engage the workforce. | |
| **Measurement, Analysis, and Knowledge Management** | **90** |
| How the company selects, gathers, analyzes, uses, manages, and improves its data, information, and knowledge assets | |
| **Strategic** | **85** |
| How the company sets strategic direction, how it determines action plans, how it changes strategy and action plans if required, and how it measures progress | |
| **Workforce** | **85** |
| How the company develops and utilizes the workforce to achieve high performance; how the company engages, manages, and develops the potential of the workforce in alignment with company goals | |
| **Operations** | **85** |
| How the company designs, manages, and improves work systems and work processes to deliver customer value and achieve company success and sustainability | |
| **Results** | **450** |
| How the company performs and improves in key business areas (product, service, and supply quality; productivity; operational effectiveness and related financial indicators; environmental, legal, and regulatory compliance); the company's level of ethical and social responsibility | |
| **Customer** | **85** |
| The company's knowledge of the customer, customer service systems, current and potential customer concerns, and customer satisfaction and engagement | |
| **Total Points** | **1,000** |

SOURCE: Based on National Institute of Standards and Technology (NIST), "2017–2018 Criteria for Performance Excellence and Point Values," Baldridge Excellence Framework, January 2017, www.nist.gov/baldridge.

for improvement, Don Chalmers's HR practices support the dealership's commitment to quality. To retain sales consultants, new employees are mentored by senior leaders to ensure they understand the business strategy and that their role is aligned with the company's core values. This resulted in a 71% employee retention rate in 2015, which is 45% higher than the national average for Ford's non-luxury-brand dealerships. To help meet the needs of its diverse workforce, Don Chalmers provides a free on-site wellness clinic staffed with a nurse practitioner for employees and their families. To engage employees, Don Chalmers management provides employees with monthly status reports on its operations and business plans, and the senior leadership team regularly discusses customer satisfaction and provides performance feedback. Employees are encouraged to submit ideas for improvement, and senior leaders review, discuss, and implement them.

***ISO (International Organization for Standardization) 9000 Standards.*** ISO (International Organization for Standardization), a network of national standards institutes including 160 countries with a central governing body in Geneva, Switzerland, is the world's largest developer and publisher of international standards.[98] The ISO develops standards related to management, as well as a wide variety of other areas including education, music, ships, and even the protection of children. ISO standards are voluntary, though countries may decide to adopt ISO standards in their regulations, in which case they may become a requirement to compete in the market.

The ISO 9000 is a family of standards related to quality (ISO 9000, ISO 9001, ISO 9004, and ISO 19011). The ISO 9000 quality standards address what the company does to meet regulatory requirements and the customer's quality requirements while striving to improve customer satisfaction and continuous improvement. The standards represent an international consensus on quality management practices. ISO 9000:2015 (2015 is the most recent version) has been adopted as the quality standard in nearly 170 countries, meaning that companies have to follow the standards to conduct business in those countries. The quality management standards of the ISO 9000 are based on eight quality management principles, including customer focus, leadership, employee engagement, a process approach, a systems approach to management, continuous improvement, using facts to make decisions, and establishing mutually beneficial relationships with suppliers. ISO 9001:2008 is the most comprehensive standard because it provides a set of requirements for a quality management system for all organizations both private and public. The ISO 9001:2015 has been implemented by over 1 million organizations around the world. ISO 9004 provides a guide for companies that want to improve.

Why are standards useful? Customers may want to check that the product they ordered from a supplier meets the purpose for which it is required. One of the most efficient ways to do this is when the specifications of the product have been defined in an International Standard. That way, both supplier and customer are on the same wavelength, even if they are based in different countries, because they are both using the same references. Many products require testing for conformance with specifications or compliance with safety or other regulations before they can be put on many markets. In addition, national legislation may require such testing to be carried out by independent bodies, particularly when the products concerned have health or environmental implications. One example of an ISO standard is on the back cover of this book and nearly every other book. On the back cover is something called an ISBN. ISBN stands for International Standard Book Number. Publishers and booksellers are very familiar with ISBNs because they are the method through which books are ordered and bought. Try buying a book on the Internet, and you will soon learn the value of the ISBN—there is a unique number for the book you want! And it is based on an ISO standard.

*Six Sigma.* In addition to competing for quality awards and seeking ISO certification, many companies are using the Six Sigma process and lean thinking. The **Six Sigma process** refers to a process of measuring, analyzing, improving, and then controlling processes once they have been brought within the narrow Six Sigma quality tolerances or standards. The objective of Six Sigma is to create a total business focus on serving the customer, that is, to deliver what customers really want when they want it. Six Sigma involves highly trained employees known as Champions, Master Black Belts, Black Belts, and Green Belts who lead and teach teams that are focusing on an ever-growing number of quality projects. The quality projects focus on improving efficiency and reducing errors in products and services. The Six Sigma quality initiative has produced more than $5 billion in benefits for General Electric. For example, introducing the Six Sigma quality initiative at GE meant going from approximately 35,000 defects per million operations (which is average for most companies, including GE) to fewer than four defects per million in every element of every process GE businesses perform—from manufacturing a locomotive part to servicing a jet engine, or reinventing radiation technology used in health care.[99]

**Six Sigma process**
A system of measuring, analyzing, improving, and controlling processes once they meet quality standards.

**Lean thinking**

A way to do more with less effort, equipment space, and time, but still provide customers what they need and want.

*Lean Thinking and Process Improvement.* Training is an important component of quality programs because it teaches employees statistical process control and how to engage in "lean thinking." **Lean thinking** is a way to do more with less effort, time, equipment, and space, but still provide customers what they need and want. Part of lean thinking includes training workers in new skills or how to apply old skills in new ways so that they can quickly take over new responsibilities or use new skills to help fill customer orders. CenturyLink is a telecommunications company that provides communications and data services to residential, business, governmental, and wholesale customers.[100] CenturyLink's lean initiative includes training employees to identify and reduce unneeded steps in business processes. The training includes lectures, activities, business process mapping analysis, and development of cross-functional projects focused on reducing waste. As a result, the time to complete the processes that have been part of the cross-functional projects has been reduced by 45 minutes, thereby saving money and reducing frustrations experienced by employees and customers.

In addition to developing products or providing services that meet customer needs, one of the most important ways to improve customer satisfaction is to improve the quality of employees' work experiences. Research shows that satisfied employees are more likely to provide high-quality customer service. Customers who receive high-quality service are more likely to be repeat customers. As Table 1.10 shows, companies that are recognized as

**Table 1.10**

Examples of HR Practices That Enhance Customer Service

**Wegmans**
Has given $100 million in scholarships to more than 32,000 employees. Senior managers sit side-by-side with employees, listening in on phones in the company's call center.

**Asana**
Gives employees a $10,000 allowance for computers and office décor, which employees can use to purchase mini-refrigerators, headphones, and ergonomic chairs. Asana also offers free yoga classes and in-house chefs prepare and serve three meals every day.

**Google**
Provides employees with food service, fitness centers, bicycle repairs, and napping pods.

**Unilever**
The Agile Working Program allows employees to work any hours, anywhere they want. Office cubicles have been replaced with collaborative work spaces with small, shared work pods. The new work areas are designed to provide a comfortable environment by including televisions, foosball tables, and treadmills.

**Delaware North Companies**
Uses tests that assess job candidates' personality and work styles to ensure they have the friendliness, curiosity, and ability to multitask, which customer service representatives need to help customers plan vacations.

**Cadillac**
Performance of repair technicians is carefully monitored to ensure they are not repeating mistakes in repairs. Dealers who maintain good customer service ratings based on customer surveys receive cash rewards.

**Ricoh USA**
Service employees participate in several training programs focused on communication skills and listening skills, telephone etiquette, and technical printing technologies. The programs are delivered via e-learning, face-to-face, and virtual instruction.

SOURCES: Based on Ricoh USA, Inc., "Services Team Annual Recognition Program," *Training*, January/February 2017, pp. 98–99; "Learn and Grow," www.wegmans.com, accessed March 1, 2017; www.asana.com, accessed Match 1, 2017; L. Weber, "To Get a Job, New Hires Are Put to the Test," *Wall Street Journal*, April 15, 2015, pp. A1, A10; R. Feintzeig, "Meet Silicon Valley's Little Elves," *Wall Street Journal*, November 21, 2014, pp. A1, A10; W. Bunch, "Unleashing the Workforce," *Human Resource Executive*, November 2012, pp. 14–17; J. McGregor, "Customer Service Champs," *Bloomberg Businessweek*, March 5, 2007, pp. 52–64.

providing elite customer service emphasize state-of-the-art HR practices, including rigorous employee selection, employee loyalty, training, and keeping employees satisfied by offering generous benefits.

## Recognize and Capitalize on the Demographics and Diversity of the Workforce

A company's performance on the balanced scorecard is influenced by the characteristics of its labor force. The labor force of current employees is often referred to as the **internal labor force**. Employers identify and select new employees from the external labor market through recruiting and selection. The **external labor market** includes persons actively seeking employment. As a result, the skills and motivation of a company's internal labor force are influenced by the composition of the available labor market (the external labor market). The skills and motivation of a company's internal labor force determine the need for training and development practices and the effectiveness of the company's compensation and reward systems.

**Internal labor force**
Labor force of current employees.

**External labor market**
Persons outside the firm who are actively seeking employment.

Important changes in the demographics and diversity of the workforce are projected. First, the average age of the workforce will increase. Second, the workforce will become more diverse in terms of gender, race, and generations. Third, immigration will continue to affect the size and diversity of the workforce.

*Aging of the Workforce.*   The labor force will continue to age, and the proportion of workers age 55 and older will grow from 23% to 25% by 2026.[101] The median age of the labor force in 2026, 42.3 years, will be the highest ever recorded. Figure 1.5 compares the distribution of the age of the workforce in 2016 to that projected for 2026. The labor force participation of those 55 years and older is expected to grow because older individuals are leading healthier and longer lives than in the past, providing the opportunity to work more years; the high cost of health insurance and decrease in health benefits causes many employees to keep working to keep their employer-based insurance or to return to work after retirement to obtain health insurance through their employer; and the trend toward pension plans based on individuals' contributions to them rather than years of service provides an incentive for older employees to continue working. The aging labor force means companies are likely to employ a growing share of older workers—many in their second or third career. Older people want to work, and many say they plan a working retirement. Despite myths to the contrary, worker performance and learning are not adversely affected by aging.[102] Older employees are willing and able to learn new technology.

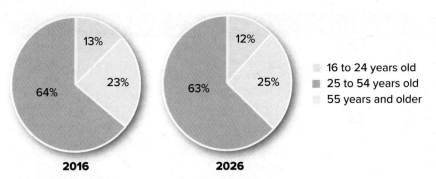

**Figure 1.5**

Comparison of the Age Distribution of the 2016 and 2026 Labor Forces

16 to 24 years old
25 to 54 years old
55 years and older

SOURCE: Bureau of Labor Statistics, U.S. Department of Labor, "Employment projections: 2016–2026," News Release, October 24, 2017, from www.bls.gov/emp, accessed January 5, 2019.

An emerging trend is for qualified older workers to ask to work part time or for only a few months at a time as a means to transition to retirement. Employees and companies are redefining the meaning of retirement to include second careers as well as part-time and temporary work assignments. An aging workforce means that employers will increasingly face HRM issues such as career plateauing, retirement planning, and retraining older workers to avoid skill obsolescence. Companies will struggle with how to control the rising costs of benefits and health care. Companies face competing challenges with older workers. Companies will have to ensure that older workers are not discriminated against in hiring, training, and workforce reduction decisions. At the same time, companies will want to encourage retirement and make it financially and psychologically acceptable.

Many companies are offering special programs to capitalize on older employees' skills and accommodate their needs.[103] Both Ingersoll Rand Plc and Ultra Machining Company are trying to retain older employees by offering them shorter work hours. CVS/pharmacy has stores in every region of the United States. CVS created its Snowbirds Program to allow older employees to move among locations according to their preferences. This is especially important for older employees who spend winters in the southern states and summer in the northern states. Over 1,000 employees, including retail clerks, pharmacists, and managers, have participated in the program.

Scripps Health has equipped patient rooms with lifts to help all employees, but especially older workers, provide assistance to move patients from beds to wheelchairs, help them to sit up, and change their position in bed. The National Institutes of Health (NIH) has two phased-retirement programs that allow employees to choose to gradually transition to retirement by reducing hours or a trial-retirement program that allows retirees to return to work within one year of retiring in case they decide they aren't ready to leave the workforce. This helps ease their transition out of the job and workplace but provides them time to share their knowledge and help train other employees to take their jobs.

***The Multigenerational Workforce.*** Because employees are working longer, the workforce now has five generations, each one with unique characteristics and characteristics similar to the others. Table 1.11 shows the year born, nicknames, and ages represented for each generation. Consider some of the attributes that are believed to characterize each generation.[104] For example, Generation Z, born after 1995, have started to graduate from college and are already part of the workforce. With Baby Boomers retiring, Generation Z will have many job and career opportunities. They are digital natives, more attached to mobile phones and tablets for learning and connecting with others than are Millennials. Generation Z may be more entrepreneurial than other generations, more competitive with others, interested in meaningful work but want financial stability. Generation Z wants a work environment in which they can get instant communications and access to answers.

**Table 1.11**
Generations in the Workforce

| YEAR BORN | GENERATION | AGES |
|---|---|---|
| 1925–45 | Traditionalists Silent Generation | >74 |
| 1946–64 | Baby Boomers | 55–74 |
| 1965–80 | Generation X | 39–54 |
| 1981–95 | Millennials Generation Y Echo Boomers | 24–38 |
| 1996 | Generation Z | <23 |

Diversity is the norm for Generation Z and they want to get involved in political and social movements and make a difference.

Millennials grew up with diversity in their schools and were coached, praised, and encouraged for participation rather than accomplishment by their Baby Boomer parents. Millennials are characterized as being optimistic, willing to work and learn, eager to please, self-reliant, globally aware, and valuing of diversity and teamwork. They are also believed to have high levels of self-esteem. Millennials are a highly educated and technologically connected group who approach the workplace with the mentality, "What's in it for me?" They are the generation most likely to switch jobs and be on the lookout for new opportunities. Millennials want to understand how they fit in with their jobs, teams, and companies. They look for work that fuels their sense of purpose and makes them feel important. They do not feel close ties to their jobs or the brands to which they give their money.

Generation Xers grew up during a time when the divorce rate doubled, the number of women working outside the home increased, and the personal computer was invented. They were often left on their own after school (latchkey kids). They value skepticism, informality, and practicality; seek work–life balance; and dislike close supervision. They tend to be impatient and cynical. They have experienced change all of their lives (in terms of parents, homes, and cities).

Baby Boomers, the "Me" generation, marched against the "establishment" for equal rights and an end to the Vietnam War. They value social conscientiousness and independence. They are competitive, hard working, and concerned with the fair treatment of all employees. They are often considered to be workaholics and rigid in conforming to rules.

Traditionalists grew up during the Great Depression and lived during World War II. They tend to value frugality, are patriotic and loyal, adhere to rules, are loyal to employers, and take responsibility and sacrifice for the good of the company.

Members of each generation may have misperceptions of each other, causing tensions and misunderstanding in the workplace.[105] For example, Generation Xers who will be managing Generation Z employees may become irritated by having to answer Generation Z employees' questions about why they are expected to perform a job a certain way, and by their employees' preference for instant feedback and praise when they get work completed. Millennials may think Generation X managers are bitter, jaded, abrasive, uninterested in them, and poor delegators. In turn, their Generation X managers consider Millennials too needy for attention, demanding, and overly self-confident. Millennials might believe that Baby Boomers are too rigid and follow company rules too closely. They believe employees in the older generations have been too slow in adopting social media tools and overvalue tenure rather than knowledge and performance. Traditionalists and Baby Boomers believe that Millennials don't have a strong work ethic because they are too concerned with work–life balance. Also, members of the younger generations may resent Baby Boomers and Traditionalists who are working longer before retiring, blocking promotions and career moves.

Although generational differences likely exist, members of the same generation are no more alike than members of the same gender or race. This means that you should be cautious in attributing differences in employee behaviors and attitudes to generational differences or expecting all employees of a generation to have similar values. Research suggests that the generations of employees have similarities as well as differences.[106] Although differences in work ethic have been found among Baby Boomers, Generation Xers, and Millennials, Millennial employees are more similar than different from other generations in their work beliefs, job values, and gender beliefs. Most employees view work as a means to more fully use their skills and abilities, meet their interests, and allow them to live a desirable lifestyle. They also value work–life balance, meaning flexible work policies are necessary to allow them to choose where and when work is performed.

**Figure 1.6**

The U.S. Workforce, 2026

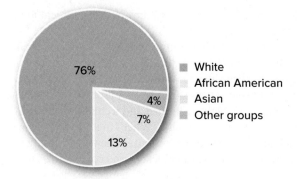

- White
- African American
- Asian
- Other groups

76%

4%

7%

13%

SOURCE: Bureau of Labor Statistics, U.S. Department of Labor, "Employment Projections: 2016–2026," News Release, October 24, 2017, from www.bls.gov/emp, accessed January 5, 2019.

EY, the accounting and professional services company formerly known as Ernst and Young, is taking actions to meet Millennials and Generation Z employees' needs for constant technology-aided learning, job flexibility, more frequent feedback, and opportunities to develop high-demand skills.[107] EY's performance evaluation system provides opportunities for managers and teams to have daily digital conversations. In the EY Badges program, employees can earn credentials for demonstrating mastery in high-demand skills related to artificial intelligence and robotics. Badges can also be earned by publishing a paper, helping colleagues, or volunteering in the community. EY employees can publicly demonstrate their accomplishments by posting the badges they earn on their Facebook or LinkedIn pages. These actions help EY attract and retain talented Millennials and Generation Z employees.

*A Workforce of Mixed Gender, Race, and Nationality.* As Figure 1.6 shows, by 2026 the workforce is expected to be 76% white, 13% African American, 7% Asian, and 4% other ethnic or cultural groups, which includes individuals of multiple racial origin, American Indian, Alaskan Native, or Native Hawaiian and other Pacific Islanders.[108] Between 2016 and 2026, the U.S. labor force will continue to grow more ethnically and racially diverse due to immigration, increased participation of minorities in the workforce, and higher minority fertility rates. For example, between 2016 and 2026, the projected annual growth rates are higher for Hispanics (2.7%) and Asians (2.5%) than for African Americans and other groups. By 2026, 53% of the labor force will be men and 47% will be women.

Immigration contributes to the diversity of the U.S. population and workforce. Many U.S. industries, including high-technology, meatpacking, construction, farming, and service, rely on immigrants to perform jobs requiring physical labor or skills not readily available in the U.S. workforce. Although a common belief is that most immigrants have rudimentary skills, the percentage of highly skilled immigrants now exceeds the percentage of low-skilled immigrants.

There is an ongoing debate in the U.S. government about the role of both legal and illegal immigration in terrorism and the reduction of job opportunities for U.S. citizens. Over 40 million people living in the United States were born in other countries, and approximately an equal number have a foreign-born parent. More than 1 million immigrants come to the United States each year, and 4 out of 10 are relatives of U.S. citizens.[109] Mexico, China, and Cuba are the leading countries of birth for lawful permanent residents or "green card" recipients, who may live and work anywhere in the United States. Another 12% come on work-related visas, some of which are available only for workers with exceptional qualifications in science, business, or the arts. The U.S. government also provides temporary visas to a limited number of highly educated workers, allowing them to work in the country for a set period of time but not to remain as immigrants. The permissible number of refugees allowed to be admitted to the United States (85,000) has been reached each year since 2016. This includes refugees (persecuted persons) from Democratic Republic of the Congo, Burma, Iraq, Somalia, and Syria. Once they pass screening and are resettled in the United States, they are eligible for employment.

One key question is what is the proper amount of legal immigration into the United States that is needed to meet our economic needs? One study suggests that immigrants have helped the U.S. economy over the long term and have had little impact on wages or employment levels of U.S.-born employees.[110] In recent years, Immigration and Customs Enforcement (ICE) has focused its efforts on auditing employers to ensure they are not employing undocumented immigrants. The focus on identifying and deporting illegal immigrants is likely to continue with the added involvement of state and local law enforcement.[111] Regardless, many companies would face severe hardship if they were forced to no longer rely on immigrants. Visas for immigrant workers are either in short supply or, if they are available, difficult to obtain.[112] Difficulties in obtaining visas coupled with the low unemployment rate means that many employers are struggling to fill both full-time and seasonal skilled and unskilled jobs.[113] For example, Sylvan Gardens Landscape had to cancel $80,000 in landscaping contracts because it couldn't hire enough workers due to the low level of unemployment and higher demand for visas under the H-2B seasonal worker visa program.[114] The company applied for eight visas but received none. The H-2B visa program permits 66,000 workers every 12 months, but in the first three-quarters of 2018, U.S. employers requested 167,000 visas. The U.S. Congress did not allow exemptions for returning foreign workers that it had allowed in other years with low levels of unemployment, and the Department of Homeland Security opted to add only 15,000 visas of the 69,000 it was authorized to issue. Thousands of Mexican workers and other immigrants are needed to pick citrus crops in Florida and work in restaurants such as Tacoliscious in San Francisco. Apple, Google, and other high-tech companies rely on the U.S. visa program to provide foreign employees with specialized skills needed to design software and new products, skills in short supply among U.S. workers.

The implications of the changing labor market for managing human resources are far-reaching. Managing diversity involves many different activities, including creating an organizational culture that values diversity, ensuring that HRM systems are bias-free, facilitating higher career involvement of women, promoting knowledge and acceptance of cultural differences, ensuring involvement in education both within and outside the company, and dealing with employees' resistance to diversity.[115] Table 1.12 presents ways that managing cultural diversity can provide a competitive advantage. How diversity issues are managed has implications for creativity, problem solving, retaining good employees, and developing markets for the firm's products and services. To successfully manage a diverse workforce, managers must develop a new set of skills, including the following:

1. Communicating effectively with employees from a variety of cultural backgrounds
2. Coaching and developing employees of different ages, educational backgrounds, ethnicities, physical abilities, and races
3. Providing performance feedback based on objective outcomes rather than values and stereotypes that work against women, minorities, and disabled persons by prejudging these persons' abilities and talents
4. Creating a work environment that makes it comfortable for employees of all backgrounds to be creative and innovative
5. Recognizing and responding to generational issues[116]

**Table 1.12**
How Managing Cultural Diversity Can Provide a Competitive Advantage

| | | |
|---|---|---|
| 1. | Cost argument | As organizations become more diverse, the cost of a poor job in integrating workers will increase. Those who handle this well will thus create cost advantages over those who don't. |
| 2. | Employee attraction and retention argument | Companies develop reputations on favorability as prospective employers for women and ethnic minorities. Those with the best reputations for managing diversity will win the competition for talent. As the labor pool shrinks and changes composition, this edge will become increasingly important. |
| 3. | Marketing argument | The insight and cultural sensitivity that diverse employees bring to the marketing effort should help the company enter new markets and develop products and services for diverse populations. |
| 4. | Creativity argument | Diversity of perspectives and less emphasis on conformity to norms of the past improves the level of creativity. |
| 5. | Problem-solving argument | Heterogeneity in decisions and problem-solving groups potentially produces better decisions through a wider range of perspectives and more thorough critical analysis of issues. |
| 6. | System flexibility argument | Greater flexibility to react to changes in customer preferences and tastes (i.e., reactions should be faster and cost less). |

SOURCES: A. C. Homan, C. Buengeler, R. A. Eckhoff, W. P. van Ginkel, and S. C. Voelpel. "The Interplay of Diversity Training and Diversity Beliefs on Team Creativity in Nationality Diverse Teams," *Journal of Applied Psychology* 100 (2015), pp. 1456–67; M. E. Mor Barak, *Managing Diversity: Toward a Globally Inclusive Workplace*, 3rd ed. (Thousand Oaks, CA: Sage, 2013); T. H. Cox and S. Blake, "Managing Cultural Diversity: Implications for Organizational Competitiveness," *Academy of Management Executive*, 5 (1991), pp. 45–56; N. Lockwood, *Workplace Diversity: Leveraging the Power of Difference for Competitive Advantage* (Alexandria, VA: Society for Human Resource Management, 2005).

Diversity is important for tapping all employees' creative, cultural, and communication skills and using those skills to provide a competitive advantage as shown in Table 1.12.

Consider Microsoft's approach to diversity, which focuses on its employees, culture, suppliers, and customers.[117] To find the best and brightest employees, Microsoft has expanded the universities, conferences, and events from which it recruits new employees, to include the National Society of Black MBAs, the National Society of Hispanic MBAs, Out and Equal, and Recruit Military Expo. To support universities' and high schools' information technology curriculum and to develop opportunities for women and minorities, the company has formed partnerships with traditionally women's schools, historically black colleges and universities, and Hispanic-serving institutions. Also, through its DigiGirlz program and Blacks at Microsoft Minority Student Day, the company exposes diverse high school students to the high-tech work world. A diverse culture is supported in several ways. Current employees can participate in resource groups including those for parents, Asians, Blacks, Hispanics and Latinos, women, the LBGTQ community, and the physically challenged. Training courses on topics such as managing diversity, how to build an inclusive culture, and understanding unconscious bias are available for all employees and managers. Microsoft offers flexible work policies to help employees balance work and life. These include resource and referral services as well as generous maternity and paternity leave policies. On the customer side, Microsoft has spent more than $2 billion with suppliers that are minority, women, or veteran owned, or owned by persons with disabilities. Also, Microsoft is developing technology that contributes to diversity by removing barriers between people. For example, the Kinect Sign Language Translator eliminates communication barriers by enabling speech-to–sign language translation.

The bottom line is that to gain a competitive advantage, companies must harness the power of the diverse workforce. These practices are needed not only to meet employee needs but also to reduce turnover costs and ensure that customers receive the best service possible. The implication of diversity for HR practices will be highlighted throughout this book. For example, from a staffing perspective, it is important to ensure that tests used to select employees are not biased against minority groups. From a work-design perspective, employees need flexible schedules that allow them to meet nonwork needs. From a training perspective, it is clear that all employees need to be made aware of the potential damaging effects of stereotypes. From a compensation perspective, new benefits such as elder care and day care need to be included in reward systems to accommodate the needs of a diverse workforce. The Evidence-Based HR box highlights the value of development programs specifically designed to prepare women for key leadership roles.

# EVIDENCE-BASED HR

Sanfoli, a global health care company with over 100,000 employees, recognized that in its different business lines women were well represented. However, significantly fewer women than men were in top-management roles. Sanfoli's diversity and inclusion, talent management, and workforce planning functions conducted an internal and external analysis. Internally, they were able to identify the level where women's advancement in the company stalled. They also identified that there was a lack of focus on considering women for key leadership roles during the company's succession planning process. Externally, they benchmarked what other companies were doing to help women reach high level positions. Based on their analysis ELEVATE was designed. ELEVATE is offered to women leaders in senior-level positions across all business lines who are nominated to attend based on the company's talent review process. Groups of 20 to 25 women attend the six-month program together. ELEVATE participants take courses designed to develop leadership skills and complete a six-month action learning project involving working on a business problem in a small team that has a senior-level sponsor and a project coach. They also receive personal coaching from a senior executive who helps them reflect on and apply what they have learned from participating in the program. Participants' managers are also invited to some of the executive coaching sessions to understand how to facilitate the participants' continued development after they leave the program.

So far, 80 women have completed the program and 60% have received promotions or new roles. Qualitative data suggest that as a result of the program women who have completed the program consider themselves better leaders. They also interact with the other participants providing peer coaching and support after they graduate from the program. For now ELEVATE focuses on women, but Sanfoli hopes to develop a similar program for other groups of employees, such as women of color, who are underrepresented in management or executive positions.

SOURCE: Based on C. Patel, "Sanfoli's ELEVATE Program Supports Women Leaders," January 8, 2018, from www.massbio.org, accessed February 17, 2019; J. London, "ELEVATE: Sanfoli's Leadership Development Program," May 9, 2017, from www.diversitybestpractices.com, accessed Februrary 17, 2019.

## Consider Legal and Ethical Issues

*Legal Issues.* There will likely be development and debate of new and current employ-ment laws and regulations, as well as increased emphasis on enforcing specific aspects of current laws and regulations such as those related to immigrant employment.[118] There are likely to be more challenges of sex and race discrimination because of lack of access to training and development opportunities that are needed for promotions to better-paying jobs or higher-level management positions. Eliminating discrimination against veterans and people with disabilities, especially among federal contractors, is likely. This is especially likely due to the expanded definition of disability under the Americans with Disabilities Act to include cancer, diabetes, epilepsy, and intellectual disabilities.

The increased awareness of sexual assault and harassment in the workplace due to the #MeToo movement will continue. The phrase "Me Too" originated in 2006 from Tarana Burke who had personally experienced sexual assault and wanted to help other women survivors.[119] The brave women who overcame their fear and embarrassment to speak out about these incidents helped spur the #MeToo movement. The #MeToo movement gave millions of women worldwide the chance to publicly share their experi-ences of sexual assault or harassment on social media. Today, we have a greater aware-ness of sexual harassment and violence toward women because of incidents involving high-profile men in sports, media, entertainment, and business. Employees, like those at Google who staged a series of walkouts to protest what they feel promotes and pro-tects individuals who engage in sexual harassment, are becoming more vocal in insisting change is necessary.[120] As a result, companies are reviewing their policies and practices to ensure they are not either ignoring or somehow encouraging sexual harassment or assault in the workplace. We are also likely to see increased scrutiny of the scope of arbitration agreements that employees voluntarily sign when they are hired prohibiting them from suing the company for a variety of employment-related claims including sexual harassment.[121]

As a result of the growing gig economy, more legal challenges related to whether work-ers are misclassified as independent contractors rather than full-time employees (who are eligible for overtime pay, unemployment, and worker's compensation) are likely. Such a case was brought against ride-sharing services Uber and Lyft in California and Massachusetts and settled out of court, but cases in other states are likely.[122] However, given the current political environment, it is also possible that government regulations might loosen the distinction between full-time employment and independent contractors, creating a middle ground that could, for example, allow companies to contribute to employees' health care costs without having to pay for overtime.

Universal health care coverage will continue to be debated in Congress. The plan they decide on will affect the availability of health care for employees, the conditions and dependents that will be covered, and out-of-pocket charges and employer costs. Regardless, in their efforts to reduce employee health care insurance costs, companies will continue to offer incentives for employees to participate in wellness programs and provide penalties if they do not. Wellness programs typically include smoking cessation, exercise, dieting, and submitting to biometric screening tests (e.g., blood tests) to detect illness or risk of illness such as heart attacks. However, wellness programs are coming under scrutiny. The Equal Employment Opportunity Commission has issued preliminary rules about when the penalties or rewards related to participating in wellness programs are too extreme and may violate the Americans with Disabilities Act.

Under the Trump administration, immigration will continue to come under increased scrutiny, to protect both national security and American jobs. Scrutiny of companies that employ unlawful immigrants or abuse laborers will face significant penalties. Companies can face criminal charges if immigration and customs officials can show that they knowingly employed undocumented and illegal immigrants. The number of company audits conducted by ICE has increased over the past several years, resulting in over $10 million in fines.

The number of workers eligible to enter the United States under different visa programs may be reconsidered, and employers may have to pay a fine or tariff for employing foreign workers. Bans on immigration from countries suspected of harboring terrorists are possible. Legislation affecting immigration will be fiercely debated because of its potential impact on business and the diversity of the United Sates. For example, leaders in many companies, but especially those in technology industries such as Apple, Microsoft, and Facebook, have been the most vocal to criticize legislation intended to reduce the possibility of terrorist attacks by banning people from seven Muslim-majority countries (Iran, Iraq, Libya, Somalia, Sudan, Syria, and Yemen) from entering the United States.[123] Their criticisms are based on their personal perspective, business needs, and business values. The leaders personally believe that immigration has always played and will continue to play an important role in the United States. Many businesses, even those not necessarily in the technology industry, need skilled foreign talent to fill engineering roles, help design innovative products and services, and create new business start-ups. Finally, most companies, such as Coca-Cola and Ford Motors, have core values that include respect for all people and commitment to diversity and inclusion that run counter to the ban.

The publication of classified documents by WikiLeaks, Wall Street insider trading probes, and data breaches of employee data have resulted in companies more carefully scrutinizing data-security practices and increased concerns about protecting intellectual property. For example, a Boeing employee who could not format a spreadsheet sent it to his spouse for help, causing a security breach that could have exposed ID numbers, accounting codes, and Social Security numbers for 36,000 employees.[124] In fact, data security and protection is now required for company's that handle the data of an individual in the European Union due to the General Data Protection Regulation, which took effect in May of 2018.[125] Similar types of regulations and laws are likely to be considered at a state level in the United States. Data-security and privacy concerns will likely influence HR practices related to performance management, such as the use of electronic monitoring and surveillance of knowledge workers. We may see more litigation related to employee privacy rights and intellectual property rights as a result of companies terminating employees or taking disciplinary action against them for data-security breaches, discussing employment practices using social media, or sharing or stealing intellectual property for personal gain. Also, issues regarding the confidentiality and security of employees' health care information will receive more attention as companies provide employees with wearables (such as Fitbits) and apps as part of wellness initiatives to track what they eat and drink, their heart rate, and physical activity. Employers who provide employees with wearables as part of wellness programs are not allowed by health privacy laws to view any single employee's health statistics.

*Ethical Issues.* Many organizations have engaged in serious ethical misconduct, including Equifax (failure to notify investors and customers of a data breach), Wells Fargo (employees created fake credit card accounts), and Takata (installed faulty airbags). Many decisions related to managing human resources are characterized by uncertainty. **Ethics** can be considered the fundamental principles of right and wrong by which employees and companies interact.[126] These principles should be considered in making business decisions and interacting with clients and customers. Ethical, successful companies can be

**Ethics**
The fundamental principles of right and wrong by which employees and companies interact.

**Figure 1.7**

Principles of Ethical Companies

characterized by four principles shown in Figure 1.7.[127] First, in their relationships with customers, vendors, and clients, these companies emphasize mutual benefits. Second, employees assume responsibility for the actions of the company. Third, such companies have a sense of purpose or vision that employees value and use in their day-to-day work. Finally, they emphasize fairness; that is, another person's interests count as much as their own. HR and business decisions should be ethical, but that is not always the case. A recent survey of employees found that only 21% believe they work in a company with a strong ethical culture.[128] This probably helps explain public perception of business ethics: 32% rated business executives' honesty and ethics standards as low or very low.[129] It is important to note that *ethics* refers to behavior that is not clearly right or wrong. *Compliance* means that the company is not violating legal regulations. But a company can be compliant and still have employees engaging in unethical practices.

The **Sarbanes-Oxley Act of 2002** sets strict rules for corporate behavior and sets heavy fines and prison terms for noncompliance: Organizations are spending millions of dollars each year to comply with regulations under the Sarbanes-Oxley Act, which imposes criminal penalties for corporate governing and accounting lapses, including retaliation against whistle-blowers who report violations of Securities and Exchange Commission (SEC) rules.[130] Due to Sarbanes-Oxley and SEC regulations that impose stricter standards for disclosing executive pay, corporate boards are paying more attention to executive pay as well as issues such as leadership development and succession planning.[131] This has resulted in an increase in the number of HR executives and individuals with HR expertise who are being asked to serve on corporate boards to provide data and analysis. For example, a CEO or chief financial officer (CFO) who falsely represents company finances may be fined up to $1 million and/or imprisoned for up to 10 years. The penalty for willful violations is up to $5 million and/or 20 years of imprisonment. Sarbanes-Oxley requires CEOs and CFOs to certify corporate financial reports, prohibits personal loans to officers and directors, and prohibits insider trading during pension fund blackout periods.[132] A "blackout" is any period of more than three consecutive business days during which the company temporarily stops 50% or more of company plan participants or beneficiaries from

**Sarbanes-Oxley Act of 2002**

A congressional act passed in response to illegal and unethical behavior by managers and executives. The act sets stricter rules for business, especially related to accounting practices—including requiring more open and consistent disclosure of financial data and the CEO's assurance that the data are completely accurate—and provisions that affect the employee– employer relationship (e.g., development of a code of conduct for senior financial officers).

acquiring, selling, or transferring an interest in any of the company's equity securities in the pension plan. The law also requires retention of all documents relevant to a government investigation. Because of the burden it places on companies the Sarbanes-Oxley Act will be carefully scrutinized, and perhaps changed by Congress or President Trump.

Sarbanes-Oxley has a number of provisions that directly affect the employer–employee relationship.[133] Whistle-blowers are individuals who have turned in the company or one or more of its officers for an illegal act. The act prohibits retaliation against whistle-blowers and government informants. The act also requires that publicly traded companies disclose whether they have a code of ethics.[134] Other federal guidelines such as the Federal Acquisition Regulation also require or provide incentives to encourage all businesses to adopt codes of conduct, train employees on these codes, and create effective ways to audit and report ethical and unethical behavior. This means that companies, with human resources taking the lead, should develop codes of conduct that clearly define ethics and professional responsibility. HR professionals, along with other top-level managers, usually play a key role in helping conduct ethics audits, develop ethical codes of conduct, and respond to ethics violations. Guidelines for disciplinary actions for employees guilty of unethical behavior and conduct need to be developed. Managers and employees will need to be trained on ethics policies to ensure that business processes and procedures are correctly followed. HR professionals will need to document the fact that employees have received these policies and have attended training to ensure their compliance with the law. Because of the potential liability for retaliation in the context of discrimination and harassment, policies should include assurances that an employee will not be retaliated against for making a complaint or for serving as a witness. Executive compensation programs will need to be monitored to ensure that the program is in compliance with provisions related to personal loans and the sale of pension funds during blackout periods.

Consider the policies and practices that companies are using to help ensure an ethical workplace.[135] Dimension Data's employees participate in a half-day ethics program discussing how they would respond to different ethical dilemmas that occur at work. Southern Company invited a convicted felon to speak to employees about how a good person can violate ethics. Before his conviction, which resulted in a five-year prison term, the felon was CFO for a health care company. Eaton Corporation includes its ethics principles on its website. Examples of the company's principles include obeying the law, avoiding conflicts of interest, acting with integrity, protecting assets and information, and respecting human rights. Eaton Corporation's employees receive regular training on how to apply ethical principles to their daily work. The Global Ethics and Compliance Office provides ethics training programs and communications designed to ensure that Eaton's ethics and values are integrated into its business practices on a consistent basis around the world. Xerox conducts regular ethics surveys, which ask employees if they have experienced an ethics violation. To receive promotions, managers are expected to take an active role in supporting Xerox's ethics strategy. Managers review their previous year's performance, create action plans as to how they plan to improve the ethics policy (such as with more training or better communications), and are expected to chair their local ethics committee. All employees are encouraged to report ethics violations or questions to the ethics office; they can do so face-to-face, using an ethics hotline, or by sending them to an e-mail address. Xerox's high ethical standards have won it recognition as one of the world's most ethical companies. This has helped Xerox to recruit high-quality employees, especially in global locations where business decisions are not transparent to employees and ethics are frequently violated.

Human resource managers must satisfy three basic standards for their practices to be considered ethical.[136] First, HRM practices must result in the greatest good for the largest number of people. Second, employment practices must respect basic human rights of

# INTEGRITY IN ACTION

## Under Armour Strives to Avoid a #MeToo Moment

Under Armour, headquartered in Baltimore, Maryland, is one of the leading companies in the sports apparel industry. You may have seen the Under Armour logo on the uniforms worn by players on college and university or professional sports teams. You may even own Under Armour t-shirts, shorts, or athletic shoes. Under Armour has over 14,000 employees and generates several billion dollars in annual revenue. Women make up a sizable proportion of Under Armour's workforce and are well-represented in high-level managerial positions.

Recently, to make good on the company's commitment to diversity, inclusive leadership, and an innovative and respectful culture, Under Armour reviewed and changed several company policies and practices. It had been a long-standing practice for Under Armour company executives and employees to go alone or take athletes and other VIPs to strip clubs after corporate and sporting events.

A strip club with nude dancers located close to Under Armour headquarters was a popular place to visit. Under Armour's new policy no longer allows employees to charge visits to strip clubs on corporate credit cards. Company event managers often invited female employees to large events the company hosted (and sometimes attended by CEO Kevin Plank) based on the extent to which their physical attractiveness would interest athletes, public officials, and other VIP guests. Some employees and guests who attended an annual party CEO Kevin Plank held at his horse farm in Maryland before the Preakness Stakes horse race voiced concerns when the party included scantily clad go-go dancers. The party was not held in 2018.

In addition to the previous policies and practices, Under Armour has had several incidents in recent years suggesting that the company was not paying enough attention to the possibility that the work culture was toxic for women. For example, Under Armour's co-founder gave up his role as chief product officer after it was revealed that he had violated company policy by having a romantic relationship with a female subordinate. Kevin Plank's brother left the company in 2012 under allegations of sexual misconduct. Additionally, some female employees have complained that they don't believe they have a fair chance of being promoted, and several women in leadership positions have left the company.

### DISCUSSION QUESTION

1. Do you think that changing the policies and practices will help Under Armour attract and retain talented women? Explain.

SOURCES: Based on K. Safdar, "Under Armour Ends Strip Club Perk," *Wall Street Journal*, November 6, 2018, pp. B1, B5; "About Under Armour," from www .underarmour.com, accessed February 9, 2018; E. Sherman, "Under Armour's Latest Decision to Stop Spending on Strip Clubs Is an Example of Corporate 'Me-Too' Tone Deafness," www.inc.com, November 6, 2018, accessed February 9, 2019.

privacy, due process, consent, and free speech. Third, managers must treat employees and customers equitably and fairly.

To call attention to the important role of legal issues and ethics in the workplace, throughout the book we include Integrity in Action boxes that highlight the good (and bad) decisions related to legal and ethical HR practices made by company leaders and managers. The Integrity in Action box in this chapter highlights how Under Armour is trying to create a work culture that does not condone sexual harassment.

**LO 1-4**
Discuss what companies should do to compete in the global marketplace.

## COMPETING THROUGH GLOBALIZATION

Every business must be prepared to deal with the global economy. Companies are finding that to survive they must compete in international markets as well as fend off foreign corporations' attempts to gain ground in the United States. To meet these challenges,

U.S. businesses must develop global markets, use their practices to improve global competitiveness, and better prepare employees for global assignments.

Globalization is not limited to any particular sector of the economy, product market, or company size.[137] Companies without international operations may buy or use goods that have been produced overseas, hire employees with diverse backgrounds, or compete with foreign-owned companies operating within the United States.

Businesses around the world are attempting to increase their competitiveness and value by increasing their global presence, often through mergers and acquisitions.

### Entering International Markets

Companies compete in international markets by exporting their products overseas, building manufacturing facilities or service centers in other countries, entering into alliances, acquiring, or merging with foreign companies, and engaging in e-commerce. One estimate is that 80% of the world's economy is based in emerging markets that include China, India, and Russia, some of the largest and most populated countries in the world.[138] Other counties that are considered emerging markets include Brazil, Colombia, Chile, Poland, and Indonesia. To be considered an emerging market, countries need to have a growing middle class, strong infrastructure, business-friendly regulations, and acceptance of outside investment. Although emerging markets are attractive from an economic perspective, they are often plagued by political instability, natural disasters, and rapidly changing food and oil prices. There is a rising global demand for good and services in emerging markets. For example, one projection is that emerging markets will account for two-thirds of the world's manufacturing products by 2025 including cars, building products, and machinery.

China is an emerging market with the most growth.[139] For example, consider that China represents one-third of the global market for luxury goods and 40% of the global market for textile and clothing consumption. China is the largest market for automobiles and smartphones in the world (there were 444 million shipments of smartphones in 2017). Consider how some companies are expanding their business globally into China and other emerging markets.[140] Amazon and Alibaba host millions of third-party sellers. McDonald's has more than 30,000 restaurants in more than 30 countries. Starbucks has more than 26,000 stores in 75 countries. PepsiCo has introduced potato chips to markets such as Thailand and India providing flavors such as hot chili squid and magic masala that appeal to local tastes. German brands Audi, BMW, and Mercedes-Benz are the top-selling luxury brands in China, but U.S. automakers are trying to take away some of their market share. General Motors opened a Cadillac factory in Shanghai, its first plant built to support the brand in China. The plant can produce more than 150,000 Cadillacs each year. Anticipating demand for electric cars in China, Tesla and Volkswagen AG are building plants in Shanghai to make electric vehicles.

Global companies are struggling to find and retain talented employees, especially in emerging markets, because the demand for them exceeds the supply. Also, companies often place successful U.S. managers in charge of overseas operations, but these managers lack the cultural understanding necessary to attract, motivate, and retain talented employees. To cope with these problems, companies are taking actions to better prepare their managers and their families for overseas assignments and to ensure that training and development opportunities are available for global employees. Cross-cultural training prepares employees and their families to understand the culture and norms of the country they are being relocated to and to return to their home country after the assignment. Cross-cultural training is discussed in Chapter 7. For example, McDonald's has designated Russia as its high-growth market, with more than a dozen restaurants in Siberian towns and plans to open more.[141] When a new McDonald's opened in Tomsk, it served 6,000 customers in the first day of operations. McDonald's global sales in 2016 were the strongest in five years, while the U.S. market was struggling. To train future managers in store operations, leadership, and staff management skills needed for global expansion to be successful, McDonald's has seven Hamburger Universities in the United States and abroad, including campuses in Oak Brook, Illinois; Sydney; Munich; London; Tokyo; São Paulo; and Shanghai. All provide training materials and tools in different languages and cultures. At Boeing, the aerospace company with employees in more than 20 countries, employees and their families going on an international assignment are provided with one-on-one cultural sensitivity training and orientation. Boeing also provides "lunch and learn" cultural talks and rotation programs that allow overseas staff to work up to nine months in the United States.[142]

The Competing through Globalization box shows how Cisco is providing opportunities for individuals with disabilities around the world to obtain jobs and start their careers. Cisco benefits by gaining a new source of talented employees.

### Offshoring and Reshoring

**Offshoring** refers to the exporting of jobs from developed countries, such as the United States, to other countries where labor and other costs are lower. India, Canada, China, Russia, Mexico, Brazil, and the Philippines are some of the destination countries for offshored jobs. **Reshoring**, or the return of jobs to the United States, is becoming more common. Whether to offshore or reshore is a complex decision based on a number of factors including labor and shipping costs, the availability of a skilled workforce, and potential supply chain disruptions due to natural disasters and political instability. Also considered are quality concerns, local standards for safety, health, and working conditions, tariffs imposed on imported products, and customer preference for U.S.-made products.[143]

For example, Hanes brands has added workers to a plant in North Carolina.[144] Socks are knitted there and then sent to a plant in El Salvador that sews, dyes, and packages the socks. Although El Salvador has the advantage on labor costs, electricity costs in North Carolina are much lower. Also, having plants in both places provides a backup in case of problems. Peds Legwear also makes socks in North Carolina, allowing the company to avoid import taxes, cut shipping costs, and respond faster to shifts in demand. Plus, selling socks made in the United States was a major reason Walmart contracted with the company. Due to proposed tariffs on Chinese imports, the president of RelianceCM, a small contract electronic manufacturer in Oregon, expects his customers to move production to a Chinese manufacturer because of higher material costs.[145] The Chinese company would use identical components as RelianceCM but won't have the added cost of a 25% tariff. RelianceCM fears that it will no longer be able to compete, endangering the jobs of its 30 employees.

## COMPETING THROUGH TECHNOLOGY

Technology has reshaped the way we play, shop, communicate, and plan our lives, and where and how we work. Consider these statistics: Roughly 84% of U.S. households have a computer (desktop, laptop, tablet, or smartphone) and 75% have Internet access. Some 60% visit Google during the week, and 43% have a Facebook page.[146] Most of us (especially Americans) are so attached to our smartphones for access to apps, social media, and the Internet that the devices are with us day and night: 41% check their phone a few

**Offshoring**
A special case of outsourcing, in which the jobs that move leave one country and go to another.

**Reshoring**
Moving jobs from overseas to the United States.

## Cisco Provides Jobs for Persons with Disabilities around the World

The World Bank group estimates that 15% of the world's population, representing 1 billion people, have some form of disability. In the United States alone, the unemployment rate for persons with disabilities is slightly below 10%, more than double that for persons without a disability. However, most disabled individuals are educated, motivated, and want to work and have the high-demand skills that companies are seeking. However, many persons with disabilities face hiring biases, transportation challenges, and difficulties using technology that keep them from getting jobs and pursuing their career.

Cisco's LifeChanger Program uses the company's voice, video, and collaboration technologies to help employees with disabilities navigate the hiring process and succeed on the job. The program is the result of Cisco working together with other technology companies, government and state agencies that focus on issues facing persons with disabilities, and its own employee volunteers. Cisco has tried out the program in its operations in California, India, and Brazil. One of the issues that Cisco has faced is that many potential employees had most of the interpersonal skills needed to be successful, but they lacked some key technical abilities and had never worked in a corporate environment. To overcome these obstacles to employment, Cisco provided six months training in technical and relationship-building skills.

Individuals who are hired can use Cisco's technologies to help them perform their work. Also, they are paired with mentors from Cisco's employee resource group for employees with disabilities known as the Connected Disabilities Awareness Network. This resource group also works with employees managers to help them better understand the needs of employees with disabilities and their career goals and aspirations.

Since 2015, Cisco has hired approximately 100 persons around the world through the LifeChanger program. The program has been successful so far. Employees hired through this program have higher retention rates, lower absenteeism, and over two times higher productivity compared to their peers without disabilities. The program is helping Cisco increase the diversity of its workforce and develop a great source of talent. Cisco plans to expand the program to its other operations to make it a key part of its global practices.

### DISCUSSION QUESTION

1. What concerns do you think managers have about hiring persons with disabilities? Which HRM practices would you recommend that managers consider to help alleviate their concerns?

SOURCES: Based on C. Patton, "Chance to Succeed," *Human Resource Executive*, September 2018, pp. 20–22; "Cisco LifeChanger," from www.cisco.com, accessed February 10, 2019; "Cisco Project LifeChanger," from www.diversityjournal.com, February 27, 2017, accessed February 10, 2019; "Cisco 2018 Corporate Social Responsibility Report," from www.cisco.com, accessed February 10, 2019; "Disability Inclusion," from www.worldbank.org, accessed February 10, 2018.

---

times each hour, and 40% report they would feel significant anxiety if their smartphone went missing for a day. Using Facebook, Twitter, LinkedIn, and other social networking tools available on the Internet and accessed through smartphones, notebooks, or personal computers, companies can connect with job candidates and employers can connect with friends, family, and co-workers.

Artificial intelligence (AI) and robotics are transforming how we live and work.[147] Artificial intelligence has provided us with personal assistants such as Apple's Siri or Amazon's Alexa that we can give orders to, such as to make a purchase, play your favorite music, or turn on your kitchen light.[148]

## Consider Applications of Social Networking, Artificial Intelligence, and Robotics

**LO 1-5**
Identify how social networking, artificial intelligence, and robotics are influencing human resource management.

Advances in sophisticated technology along with reduced costs for the technology are changing many aspects of human resource management. Specifically, companies are using or considering using social networking, artificial intelligence, and robotics.

*Social Networking.* Technological advances in electronics and communications software have made possible mobile technology such as personal digital assistants (PDAs), iPads, and iPods and enhanced the Internet by developing enhanced capability for social networking. **Social networking** refers to websites such as Facebook, Twitter, and LinkedIn, as

**Social networking**
Websites and blogs that facilitate interactions between people.

well as wikis and blogs that facilitate interactions between people usually around shared interests. In general, social networking facilitates communication, decentralized decision making, and collaboration.[149] Social networking can be useful for connecting to customers. It is also valuable for busy employees to share knowledge and ideas and receive feedback, recognition, mentoring, and coaching from their peers and managers with whom they may not have much time to interact face-to-face on a daily basis. Companies can also use social networking for identifying and connecting with potential job candidates.

Despite the potential advantages of social networking, many companies are uncertain whether they should embrace it.[150] They fear that social networking will result in employees wasting time or offending or harassing their co-workers. Other companies believe that the benefits of using social networking for HR practices and allowing employees to access social networks at work outweigh the risks. They trust employees to use social networking productively and are proactive in developing policies about personal use and training employees about privacy settings and social network etiquette. They realize that employees will likely check their Twitter, Facebook, or LinkedIn accounts but ignore it unless it is interfering with completing their work. In some ways, social networking has become the electronic substitute for daydreaming at one's desk or walking to the break room to socialize with co-workers.

**Artificial intelligence**
Technology that can think like a human.

*Artificial Intelligence and Robotics.* **Artificial intelligence** is a technology that simulates human thinking. It works through queries that allow it to learn from data over time so that it can identify trends and patterns that influence future searches and suggestions. Due to advances in AI and robotics, the use of automation to perform work previously done by employees is expected to increase quickly in the next decade. One survey found that robots and AI are currently doing 12% of work, but respondents report that their use will increase to 22% in just the next three years![151] Over 60% of companies today do not use automation to complete work; rather, they use it to support employees in their work by helping to avoid mistakes and errors and perform tasks that can be automated, freeing employees time for more important high-value work. Table 1.13 highlights some of the ways automation might affect work.

**Table 1.13**
The Potential Impact of Automation on Work

By 2030, 15% of the global workforce representing over 400 million workers could be potentially displaced by the adoption of automation. Three percent (75 million) of workers will need to change their occupation.

By 2030, up to one-third of the workforce in the United States and Germany, and nearly 50% in Japan, may need to learn new skills and find jobs in new occupations.

SOURCE: Based on J. Manyika, S. Lund, M. Chui, J. Bughin, J. Woetzel, P. Batra, R. Ko, and S. Sanghvi, "Jobs Lost, Jobs Gained: Workforce Transitions in a Time of Automation," McKinsey Global Institute, December 2017, from www.mckinsey.com, accessed February 6, 2019.

The use of AI and robots can affect jobs in several different ways. One way is that they can provide skills that are difficult to find.[152] For example, bricklaying contractors are unable to find enough bricklayers. But a semi-automated mason (SAM) can help perform some, but not all, of the human mason's tasks. SAM can't read blueprints, lay brick on corners or curves, and other workers have to load and refill its mortar and brick and clean up the joints on the bricks it lays. SAM helps alleviate the shortage of bricklayers but at a cost of $400,000 each.

Another way robots can affect jobs is to perform some job tasks previously completed by employees. These could include tasks that the robot can perform with equal if not more precision and consistency than humans (such as some forms of surgery), tasks that are potentially harmful to humans (e.g., painting and welding robots) and simple, repetitive tasks, which enable employees to spend more time on higher-value tasks. Robots (known as "cobots") can also work collaboratively with humans.[153] For example, BeeHex Inc. is building 3-D food printers that can decorate cookies or cakes. This means that pastry chefs can devote their time and energy to developing new flavors of cookies rather than spending their time icing dozens of cookies the same way. Humans still need to monitor the robots to ensure they are performing as expected, provide necessary maintenance, and refine their skills through reprogramming. Robots with highly sensitive "hands" can pick up Peeps on Just Born's production line enabling it to speed up production, or at a retail clothing store locate and deliver merchandise to shoppers they have ordered online. At the Mercedes-Benz automobile plant in South Carolina, a robot arm that acts like an extension of a human limb gives employees the needed strength to pick up and place heavy parts.

Finally, robots may eliminate some jobs.[154] Jobs involving physical activities in predictable environments such as operating equipment and machinery and preparing food are likely to be automated. Also, jobs that involve collecting and processing data that occur in banking, finance, accounting, and legal work (such as preparing mortgages and computing taxes) can be done more efficiently and effectively through automation. For example, one study of Ohio employees found that almost half of their jobs are likely to be automated in the future, including cashiers, truck drivers, fast-food workers, warehouse laborers, bookkeepers, accountants, and auditing clerks.[155] This would result in the loss of 2.5 million jobs due to automation. However, there are several activities where automation cannot replace human performance including jobs where work activities are unpredictable, involve managing other people, exercising creativity, applying expertise, and social interactions such as in jobs like plumbers, child care workers, artists, performers, builders, engineers, and scientists.

Automation using AI and robotics is impacting human resource practices.[156] About one-third of human resource functions have started to change their activities to prepare for increases in automation by identifying new skill requirements and matching talent to them. Twenty-five percent are planning to identify skill gaps in the future. However, 38% report they are unprepared to identify how to reskill employees whose jobs are affected by automation. The Competing through Technology box highlights the benefits of employees and robots working together at Dynamic Group.

## Consider High-Performance Work Systems and Virtual Teams

The use of AI, robots, and other technology to automate work provides the opportunity to create high-performance work systems. **High-performance work systems** maximize the fit between the company's social system (employees) and its technical system.[157] For example, computer-integrated manufacturing uses robots and computers to automate the manufacturing process. The computer allows the production of different products simply by reprogramming the computer. As a result, laborer, material handler, operator/assembler, and maintenance jobs may be merged into one position. Computer-integrated manufacturing requires employees to monitor equipment and troubleshoot problems with

## COMPETING THROUGH TECHNOLOGY

### Humans and Robots Can Make a Great Team

Dynamic Group is a manufacturer specializing in providing molded injection parts for the electronics of medical, electronics, and technology industries. Before Dynamic Group started using robots, it took four employees to work an injection press to make catheter tubes. One employee inserted the catheter tubes into a frame while another set the frame on the mold, inserted it into the injection press, and then removed it. A third employee removed the finished tubes from the frame and cut away any excess plastic that remained. The fourth employee inspected the finished catheter tube. Now, using the robot the entire process takes less than 45 seconds. One employee is needed to examine the finished catheters and insert tubes into frames.

The employee and the robot work collaboratively. The robot is easy to move and reprogram and is a safe working companion (if it hits someone it stops working without causing injury). The robot paid for itself within two months by increasing the efficiency of the injection press and eliminating scrap. Productivity actually decreased at first when the robot was installed because employees enjoyed watching it work. The chief executive of Dynamic Group believes that manufacturing systems in the future will work alone through taking raw materials and transforming them into products. He believes such a system will create more (not less) jobs and allow the company's machine operators to use their knowledge to help program the robots to do

the work more efficiently and effectively rather than personally perform the work. As a result, the operators can put more effort into coming up with more creative and innovative ways to make products.

**DISCUSSION QUESTIONS**

1. Do you think that robots will ultimately replace humans in many jobs? Why or why not?
2. What skills will employees need to work side by side with robots?

SOURCES: Based on "About Us", from www .dynamicgroup.com, accessed February 6, 2019; A. Nusca, "Humans vs. Robots: How to Thrive in an Automated Workplace," *Fortune*, June 30, 2017, from www.fortune.com, accessed February 6, 2019; K. Tingley, "Learning to Love Our Robot Co-Workers," *The New York Times*, February 23, 2017, from www .nytimes.com, accessed April 15, 2018; "Working with Robots: The Future of Collaboration," from www.siemens.com, accessed April 15, 2018.

---

**LO 1-7**
Discuss human resource management practices that support high-performance work systems.

sophisticated equipment, share information with other employees, and understand the relationships between all components of the manufacturing process.[158]

Human resource management practices that support high-performance work systems are shown in Table 1.14. The HRM practices involved include employee selection, work design, training, compensation, and performance management. These practices are designed to give employees skills, incentives, knowledge, and autonomy. Research studies suggest that high-performance work practices are usually associated with increases in productivity and long-term financial performance.[159] Research also suggests that it is more effective to improve HRM practices as a whole, rather than focus on one or two isolated practices (such as the pay system or selection system).[160] There may be a best HRM system, but whatever the company does, the practices must be aligned with each other and be consistent with the system if they are to positively affect company performance.[161] We will discuss this alignment in more detail in Chapters 2 and 16.

Employees often have responsibility for hiring and firing team members and can make decisions that influence profits. As a result, employees must be trained in principles of employee selection, quality, and customer service. They need to understand financial data so that they can see the link between their performance and company performance.

**Table 1.14**
How HRM Practices
Support High-
Performance Work
Systems

| Staffing | • Employees participate in selecting new employees, for example, peer interviews. |
|---|---|
| Work design | • Employees understand how their jobs contribute to the finished product or service. |
| | • Employees participate in planning changes in equipment, layout, and work methods. |
| | • Work may be organized in teams. |
| | • Job rotation is used to develop skills. |
| | • Equipment and work processes are structured and technology is used to encourage flexibility and interaction between employees. |
| | • Work design allows employees to use a variety of skills. |
| | • Decentralized decision making, reduced status distinctions, information sharing. |
| | • Increased safety. |
| Training | • Ongoing training emphasized and rewarded. |
| | • Training in finance and quality control methods. |
| Compensation | • Team-based performance pay. |
| | • Part of compensation may be based on company or division financial performance. |
| Performance management | • Employees receive performance feedback and are actively involved in the performance improvement process. |

SOURCES: Based on K. Birdi, C. Clegy, M. Patterson, A. Robinson, C. Stride, T. Wall, and S. Wood, "The Impact of Human Resource and Operational Management Practices on Company Productivity: A Longitudinal Study," *Personnel Psychology* 61 (2008), pp. 467–501; A. Zacharatos, J. Barling, and R. Iverson, "High Performance Work Systems and Occupational Safety," *Journal of Applied Psychology* 90 (2005), pp. 77–93; S. Way, "High Performance Work Systems and Intermediate Indicators of Performance within the U.S. Small Business Sector," *Journal of Management* 28 (2002), pp. 765–85; M. A. Huselid, "The Impact of Human Resource Management Practices on Turnover, Productivity, and Corporate Financial Performance," *Academy of Management Journal* 38 (1995), pp. 635–72.

In high-performance work systems, previously established boundaries between managers and employees, employees and customers, employees and vendors, and the various functions within the company are abandoned. Employees, managers, vendors, customers, and suppliers work together to improve service and product quality and to create new products and services. Line employees are trained in multiple jobs, communicate directly with suppliers and customers, and interact frequently with engineers, quality experts, and employees from other functions.

Consider how HRM practices support high-performance work systems at HindlePower.[162] HindlePower is a manufacturer of battery chargers. Most of HindlePower's 80 employees work in the factory as assemblers. There is no time clock. Employees do not need to punch in or out and there are no rules for time off. Employees don't abuse the policy—hours in the factory consistently reach 97% to 100% of full time. Hindle established a program called the Professional Manufacturing Team, which pairs training with employee involvement in designing more efficient processes. The training includes 25 to 30 courses customized for each production line. Employees are responsible for completing all of the courses, and when they do they are designated as a manufacturing professional. Employees are also involved in decisions that go beyond training. For example, employees redesigned a production line resulting in an additional 150,000 units produced per week.

Besides changing the way that products are built or services are provided within companies, technology has allowed companies to form partnerships with one or more other companies. **Virtual teams** refer to teams that are separated by time, geographic distance, culture, and/or organizational boundaries and that rely almost exclusively on technology (e-mail, Internet, videoconferencing) to interact and complete their projects. Virtual teams can be formed within one company whose facilities are scattered throughout the country or the world. A company may also use virtual teams in partnerships with suppliers or competitors to pull together the necessary talent to complete a project or speed the delivery of a product to the marketplace. For example, Art & Logic software developers all work remotely from across the United States and Canada from home offices, rented office space, or at a co-working facility.[163] Their clients represent a diverse set of industries, including education, aerospace, music technology, consumer electronics, entertainment, and financial services. The project teams work on the most unusual and difficult problems, which developers at other companies have failed to solve. Art & Logic tries to accommodate the unique schedule and work-style requirements of its developers, but its work is highly collaborative within project teams. Every project consists of at least a project manager/developer and has a maximum of five to seven developers. Teams use Google Apps for Business for sharing documents and communicating (both within the team and with clients).

### Use HRIS, Mobile Devices, Cloud Computing, and HR Dashboards

Companies continue to use human resource information systems to store large quantities of employee data including personal information, training records, skills, compensation rates, absence records, and benefits usages and costs. A **human resource information system (HRIS)** is a computer system used to acquire, store, retrieve, and distribute information related to a company's human resources.[164] An HRIS can support strategic decision making, help the company avoid lawsuits, provide data for evaluating policies and programs, and support day-to-day HR decisions. Hilton Worldwide is giving managers access to talent data so that they can integrate it with business data to make more effective and strategic decisions about talent and performance.[165] This allows managers to perform workforce planning by seeing the gaps between workforce projections and available supply of staff or projected turnover and modeling different scenarios.

**Mobile devices** refer to smartphones and tablet computers. Mobile devices are increasingly being used to provide employees with anytime, anywhere access to HR applications and other work-related information. For example, at Rackspace, employees can use their devices to check their pay stubs, bonus reports, and time cards, and share knowledge.[166] At Biogen, salespersons can access e-learning modules on their tablets. PepsiCo has a mobile-accessible career site. In the first year of using the recruitment app, the company found 150 job candidates who started an employment application each month.

"Cloud computing" allows companies to lease software and hardware. **Cloud computing** refers to a computing system that provides information technology infrastructure over a network in a self-service, modifiable, and on-demand model.[167] In fact, many companies have moved their HRIS to the cloud or are considering doing so in the next few years.[168] Clouds can be delivered on-demand via the Internet (public cloud) or restricted to use by a single company (private cloud). Cloud computing gives companies and their employees access to applications and information from

**Virtual teams**
Teams that are separated by time, geographic distance, culture, and/or organizational boundaries and rely exclusively on technology for interaction between team members.

**Human resource information system (HRIS)**
A system used to acquire, store, manipulate, analyze, retrieve, and distribute information related to human resources.

**Mobile devices**
Equipment such as smartphones and tablet computers that provide employees with anytime, anywhere access to HR applications and other work-related information.

**Cloud computing**
A computing system that provides information technology infrastructure over a network in a self-service, modifiable, and on-demand model.

mobile devices rather than relying solely on personal computers. It also allows groups to work together in new ways, can make employees more productive by allowing them to more easily share documents and information, and provides greater access to large company databases. This means that tools for conducting workforce analytics using metrics on turnover, absenteeism, and performance, as well as social media and collaboration tools such as Twitter, blogs, Google documents, and YouTube videos will be more easily accessible and available for use. Cloud computing also can make it easier for employees to access training programs from a variety of vendors and educational institutions. Siemens has a cloud computing system for its more than 400,000 employees who work in 190 countries. This allowed Siemens to standardize its global recruitment and development processes into a single system using the cloud.[169]

More sophisticated systems extend management applications to decision making in areas such as compensation and performance management. Managers can schedule job interviews or performance appraisals, guided by the system to provide the necessary information and follow every step called for by the procedure.[170] One of the most important uses of Internet technology is the development of HR dashboards. An **HR dashboard** is a series of indicators or metrics that managers and employees have access to on the company intranet or HRIS. The HR dashboard provides access to important HR metrics for conducting workforce analytics. HR dashboards are important for determining the value of HR practices and how they contribute to business goals. As a result, the use of dashboards is critical for evidence-based HR discussed earlier in the chapter. For example, Cisco Systems views building talent as a priority, so it has added to its dashboard of people measures a metric to track how many people move and the reasons why.[171] This allows Cisco to identify divisions that are developing new talent.

**HR dashboard**
HR metrics such as productivity and absenteeism that are accessible by employees and managers through the company intranet or human resource information system.

# Meeting Competitive Challenges through HRM Practices

We have discussed the sustainability, globalization, and technology challenges U.S. companies are facing. We have emphasized that management of human resources plays a critical role in determining companies' success in meeting these challenges. HRM practices have not traditionally been seen as providing economic value to the company. Economic value is usually associated with equipment, technology, and facilities. However, HRM practices have been shown to be valuable. Compensation, staffing, training and development, performance management, and other HRM practices are investments that directly affect employees' motivation and ability to provide products and services that are valued by customers. Research has shown that companies that attempt to increase their competitiveness by investing in new technology and becoming involved in the quality movement also invest in state-of-the-art staffing, training, and compensation practices.[172] Figure 1.8 shows examples of HRM practices that help companies deal with the three challenges. For example, to meet the environmental, social, and governance challenge, companies need to identify through their selection processes whether prospective employees value customer relations and have the levels of interpersonal skills necessary to work with fellow employees in teams. To meet all three challenges, companies need to capitalize on the diversity of values, abilities, and perspectives that employees bring to the workplace.

**LO 1-8**
Provide a brief description of human resource management practices.

**Figure 1.8**

Examples of How HRM Practices Can Help Companies Meet Competitive Challenges

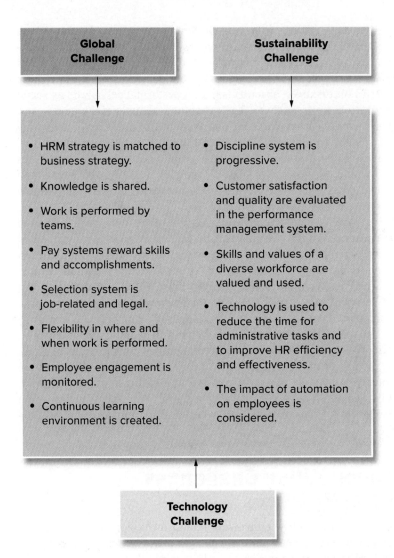

HRM practices that help companies deal with the competitive challenges can be grouped into the four dimensions shown in Figure 1.9. These dimensions include the human resource environment, acquiring and preparing human resources, assessment and development of human resources, and compensating human resources. In addition, some companies have special issues related to labor–management relations, international human resource management, and managing the human resource function.

**Figure 1.9**

Major Dimensions of HRM Practices Contributing to Company Competitiveness

**Dimensions of HRM Practices**

| Managing the human resource environment | Acquiring and preparing human resources | Assessment and development of human resources | Compensating human resources | Competitiveness |

## MANAGING THE HUMAN RESOURCE ENVIRONMENT

Managing internal and external environmental factors allows employees to make the greatest possible contribution to company productivity and competitiveness. Creating a positive environment for human resources involves the following:

- Linking HRM practices to the company's business objectives—that is, strategic human resource management
- Ensuring that HRM practices comply with federal, state, and local laws
- Designing work that motivates and satisfies employees as well as maximizes customer service, quality, and productivity

## ACQUIRING AND PREPARING HUMAN RESOURCES

Customer needs for new products or services influence the number and type of employees that businesses need to be successful. Terminations, promotions, and retirements also influence human resource requirements. Managers need to predict the number and type of employees needed to meet customer demands for products and services. Managers must also identify current or potential employees who can successfully deliver products and services. This area of HRM deals with the following:

- Identifying human resource requirements—that is, human resource planning, recruiting employees, and selecting employees
- Training employees to have the skills needed to perform their jobs

## ASSESSMENT AND DEVELOPMENT OF HUMAN RESOURCES

Managers need to ensure that employees have the necessary skills to perform current and future jobs. As we discussed earlier, because of new technology and the quality movement, many companies are redesigning work so that it is performed by teams. As a result, managers and employees may need to develop new skills to succeed in a team environment. Companies need to create a work environment that supports employees' work and nonwork activities. This area of HRM addresses the following:

- Measuring employees' performance
- Preparing employees for future work roles and identifying employees' work interests, goals, values, and other career issues
- Creating an employment relationship and work environment that benefits both the company and the employee

## COMPENSATING HUMAN RESOURCES

Besides interesting work, pay and benefits are the most important incentives that companies can offer employees in exchange for contributing to productivity, quality, and customer service. Also, pay and benefits are used to reward employees' membership in the company and attract new employees. The positive influence of new work designs, new technology, and the quality movement on productivity can be damaged if employees are not satisfied with the level of pay and benefits or believe pay and benefits are unfairly distributed. This area of HRM includes the following:

- Creating pay systems
- Rewarding employee contributions
- Providing employees with benefits

## SPECIAL ISSUES

In some companies, employees are represented by a labor union. Managing human resources in a union environment requires knowledge of specific laws, contract administration, and the collective bargaining process.

**Table 1.15**
Topics Covered in
This Book

Part One   The Human Resource Environment
  1   Human Resource Management: Gaining a Competitive Advantage
  2   Strategic Human Resource Management
  3   The Legal Environment: Equal Employment Opportunity and Safety
  4   The Analysis and Design of Work
Part Two   Acquisition and Preparation of Human Resources
  5   Human Resource Planning and Recruitment
  6   Selection and Placement
  7   Training
Part Three   Assessment and Development of Human Resources
  8   Performance Management
  9   Employee Development
  10   Employee Separation and Retention
Part Four   Compensation of Human Resources
  11   Pay Structure Decisions
  12   Recognizing Employee Contributions with Pay
  13   Employee Benefits
Part Five   Special Topics in Human Resource Management
  14   Collective Bargaining and Labor Relations
  15   Managing Human Resources Globally
  16   Strategically Managing the HRM Function

Many companies are globally expanding their business through joint ventures, mergers, acquisitions, and establishing new operations. Successful global expansion depends on the extent to which HRM practices are aligned with cultural factors as well as management of employees sent to work in another country. Human resource management practices must contribute to organizational effectiveness.

Human resource management practices of both managers and the human resource function must be aligned and contribute to the company's strategic goals. The final chapter of the book explains how to effectively integrate human resource management practices.

## Organization of This Book

The topics in this book are organized according to the four areas of human resource management and special issues. Table 1.15 lists the chapters covered in the book.

The content of each chapter is based on academic research and examples of effective company practices. Each chapter includes examples of how the HRM practice covered in the chapter helps a company gain a competitive advantage by addressing sustainability, global, and technological challenges. Also, each chapter includes an example of a company that demonstrates how HR practices add value (evidence-based HR).

 ## A LOOK BACK

### HRM at IBM

IBM underwent a significant change in its business, moving from an emphasis on computer hardware and onsite management of clients data to a focus today on cloud computing, AI, and blockchain technologies.

## QUESTIONS

1. Do IBM's HRM practices support and align with the business priorities? Explain your answer.
2. Which of the competencies needed by HR professionals were the most important for IBM's chief human resource officer to manage the process of changing its HRM practices?
3. Would IBM's HR practices be effective in other industries such as manufacturing or health care? Explain

## SUMMARY

This chapter introduced the roles and activities of a company's human resource management function and emphasized that effective management of human resources can contribute to a company's business strategy and competitive advantage. Human resources can be viewed as having three product lines: administrative services, business partner services, and strategic services. To successfully manage human resources, individuals need personal credibility, business knowledge, understanding of the business strategy, technology knowledge, and the ability to deliver HR services. Human resource management practices should be evidence-based, that is, based on data showing the relationship between the practice and business outcomes related to key company stakeholders (customers, shareholders, employees, community). In addition to contributing to a company's business strategy, HR practices are important for helping companies deal with environmental, social, and governance (ESG) challenges, global challenges, and technology challenges. The ESG challenges are related to the economy, the characteristics and expectations of the labor force, how and where work is done, the value placed on intangible assets and human capital, and meeting stakeholder needs (ethical practices, high-quality products

and services, return to shareholders, and social responsibility). Global challenges include entering international markets, immigration, and offshoring. Technology challenges include using new technologies to support flexible and virtual work arrangements; high-performance work systems; and implementing and using social networks, wearables, human resource information systems, mobile devices, and considering the role of artificial intelligence and robotics on jobs.

The chapter concludes by showing how the book is organized. The book includes five topical areas: the human resource environment (strategic HRM, legal, analysis and design of work), acquisition and preparation of human resources (HR planning and recruitment, selection, training), assessment and development of human resources (performance management, development, separation and retention), compensation of human resources (pay structures, recognizing employee contributions with pay, benefits), and special topics (collective bargaining and labor relations, managing human resources globally, and strategically managing the HR function). All of the topical areas are important for companies to deal with the competitive challenges and contribute to business strategy.

## KEY TERMS

Competitiveness, 4
Human resource management (HRM), 4
Shared service model, 8
Self-service, 8
Outsourcing, 8
Evidence-based HR, 11
HR or workforce analytics, 11
Big data, 11
Sustainability, 16
Stakeholders, 17
STEM skills, 21
Intangible assets, 22
Knowledge workers, 23
Empowering, 23
Learning organization, 23

Change, 24
Agility, 24
Employee engagement, 24
Employee experience, 25
Employee value proposition (EVP), 25
Talent management, 26
Nontraditional employment, 26
Gig economy, 26
Balanced scorecard, 28
Total quality management (TQM), 31
Malcolm Baldrige National Quality
    Award, 31
ISO 9000:2015, 31
Six Sigma process, 33
Lean thinking, 34

Internal labor force, 35
External labor market, 35
Ethics, 43
Sarbanes-Oxley Act of 2002, 44
Offshoring, 48
Reshoring, 48
Social networking, 50
Artificial intelligence, 50
High-performance work systems, 51
Virtual teams, 54
Human resource information
    system (HRIS), 54
Mobile devices, 54
Cloud computing, 54
HR dashboard, 55

# DISCUSSION QUESTIONS

1. Traditionally, human resource management practices were developed and administered by the company's human resource department. Some companies are abandoning or don't have HR departments. Why is this occurring? Is it a good idea for companies not to have an HR department or HR professionals? Explain your position.

2. Staffing, training, compensation, and performance management are important HRM functions. How can each of these functions help companies succeed in meeting the environmental, social, and governance challenge, the global challenge, and the technology challenge?

3. What are intangible assets? How are they influenced by HRM practices?

4. What is evidence-based HR? Why might an HR department resist becoming evidence based?

5. What types of big data would you collect and analyze to understand why an employer was experiencing a high turnover rate?

6. Which HR practices can benefit by the use of social collaboration tools like Twitter and Facebook? Identify the HR practices and explain the benefits gained.

7. Do you agree with the statement "Employee engagement is something companies should be concerned about only if they are making money"? Explain.

8. How does employee engagement relate to the employee experience? Explain.

9. This book covers four HRM practice areas: managing the human resource environment, acquiring and preparing human resources, assessment and development of human resources, and compensating human resources. Which area do you believe contributes most to helping a company gain a competitive advantage? Which area do you believe contributes the least? Why?

10. What is the balanced scorecard? Identify the four perspectives included in the balanced scorecard. How can HRM practices influence the four perspectives?

11. Is HRM becoming more strategic? Explain your answer.

12. What is sustainability? How can HR practices help a company become more socially and environmentally conscious?

13. Explain the implications of each of the following labor force trends for HRM: (1) aging workforce, (2) diverse workforce, (3) skill deficiencies.

14. What role do HRM practices play in a business decision to expand internationally?

15. What might a quality goal and high-performance work systems have in common in terms of HRM practices?

16. What disadvantages might result from outsourcing HRM practices? From employee self-service? From increased line manager involvement in designing and using HR practices?

17. What factors should a company consider before reshoring? What are the advantages and disadvantages of reshoring?

18. Discuss the different ways automation using AI and robots can affect jobs.

# SELF-ASSESSMENT EXERCISE

**Mc Graw Hill connect®**
**Also assignable in Connect.**

## Do You Have What It Takes to Work in HR?

*Instructions:* Read each statement and circle *yes* or *no*.

Yes No 1. I have leadership and management skills I have developed through prior job experiences, extracurricular activities, community service, or other noncourse activities.

Yes No 2. I have excellent communications, dispute resolution, and interpersonal skills.

Yes No 3. I can demonstrate an understanding of the fundamentals of running a business and making a profit.

Yes No 4. I can use spreadsheets and the Internet, and I am familiar with information systems technology.

Yes No 5. I can work effectively with people of different cultural backgrounds.

Yes No 6. I have expertise in more than one area of human resource management.

Yes No 7. I have a willingness to learn.

Yes No 8. I listen to issues before reacting with solutions.

Yes No 9. I can collect and analyze data for business solutions.

Yes No 10. I am a good team member.

Yes No 11. I have knowledge of local and global economic trends.

Yes No 12. I demonstrate accountability for my actions.

*Scoring:* The greater the number of yes answers, the better prepared you are to work as an HR professional. For questions you answered *no*, you should seek courses and experiences to change your answers to *yes*—and better prepare yourself for a career in HR!

SOURCES: Based on B. E. Kaufman, "What Companies Want from HR Graduates," *HR Magazine*, September 1994; SHRM Elements for HR Success Competency Model, 2012, from www.shrm.org, March 21, 2012.

# EXERCISING STRATEGY

## Publix: HR Practices Result in Happy Employees and Customers

Publix is a leader in the supermarket industry. As the largest employee-owned grocery store chain in the United States, Publix employs over 190,000 people in the Southeast, with over 1,200 store locations, nine distribution centers, and 11 manufacturing facilities. Publix is a great place to work and to shop. Publix has been recognized as one of *Fortune* magazine's "100 Best Companies to Work For" for 21 consecutive years and as one of *Fortune*'s "100 Best Workplaces for Millennials." The company has also received numerous awards for customer service and satisfaction and has been named as one of America's favorite grocery stores. Publix's mission is to be the world's premier quality food retailer. Publix strives to do so through its commitment to providing customers with value; its intolerance of waste; its dedication to the dignity, value, and employment security of its associates; its devotion to stewardship for stockholders; and its involvement in the communities in which Publix stores operate.

Publix employees are extremely loyal. The average store manager has been with Publix for more than 25 years, and over 44,000 associates have been with the company for more than 10 years. Its voluntary turnover rate is 5%, compared to the retail industry average of 65%. Other supermarket chains such as Whole Foods and Safeway have recently laid off employees, but Publix has never laid off an employee in its history. In fact, rather than closing or consolidating stores, as its competitors have done, Publix continues to grow through opening new stores.

What accounts for Publix's business success and makes it a great place to work? Its human resource management practices play an important role in ensuring that employees are satisfied and motivated at work and committed to the company. Publix values diversity because of the new ideas and perspectives that can come from associates from different, backgrounds, cultures, abilities, ethnicities, gender, and ages. For example, 25% of associates are 50 years or older, including many over 90 years of age. Because it is a company priority to attract and hire a diverse workforce, Publix emphasizes a more general job requirement: the desire to serve others. They do so to avoid discouraging potential employees who have limited experience or education due to their background. Also, once they are hired Publix helps associates gain the skills they need for their current job as well as identify and move along their career path. Computers are located in offices and breakrooms of every store to make it easy for associates to access training courses. Associates receive training on standards for customer service, cleanliness, safety, teamwork, merchandising, waste intolerance, and a drug-free work environment. Publix has a generous tuition reimbursement program that supports employees who want to earn a college degree to expand their career opportunities. Supporting employees' development and career growth is the Publix policy to promote from within to fill all store manager positions and most department manager positions. Publix does this to ensure that managers are aware of company standards, best practices, and culture. Any current associate interested in moving into a management role can register their interest by completing what is called an ROI. The ROI helps managers understand associates' career ambitions and match their skills to job openings. Typically, more than 60,000 associates complete ROIs each year, with more than 9,500 promoted into positions leading to management and 2,100 promoted into management positions. Associates who become managers must move to a different store than the one in which they worked. This practice ensures that management talent is spread across the company, and it also helps employees create new personal and professional networks.

Another management practice is to give associates the opportunity to become an owner of Publix. Any associate who stays with Publix for more than a year and works more than 1,000 hours is granted shares of company stock that are worth between 8% and 12% of their annual pay. Once in the plan, they can buy additional stock through a paycheck deduction. From 1974 through 2015, the stock has provided an average annual return of nearly 17%.

Beyond holding stock, being a true owner requires an understanding of how you are doing and receiving rewards for your accomplishments. Publix makes sure its associates receive frequent feedback, and good performance is linked to raises. New employees have "check-ins" with their manager every 30, 60, and 90 days. After six months, associates qualify for their first raise and are eligible for future raises every six months. Full- and part-time associates receive an annual holiday bonus, which is uncommon in the retail industry. Full-time associates receive two weeks' pay, and salaried associates receive a full month's pay. Finally, Publix supports its associates' efforts to give back to the communities where they live and work. Publix and its associates contribute more than $36 million a year and hours of volunteer work to charitable organizations such as the United Way, Special Olympics, March of Dimes, Children's Miracle Network, and Food for All.

### QUESTIONS

1. Which of Publix's HR practices do you think are most important for its success? Why?
2. Could promotion from within have disadvantages for Publix? Explain why.
3. Do Publix's HR practices give it an advantage over its competitors? Why or why not?

SOURCES: Based on www.corporatepublix.com, accessed February 8, 2019; M. Bush and S. Lewis-Kulin, "100 Best Companies to Work For: Publix Supermarkets," *Fortune*, March 1, 2018, p. 65; M. Turner, "Publix' and Wegman's Named America's Favorite Grocery Stores," from www.forbes.com, January 18, 2018, accessed February 8, 2019; C. Tkaczyk, "My Five Days of Bleeding Green," *Fortune*, March 15, 2016, pp. 166–76; "Publix Super Markets Inc.," http://reviews.greatplacetowork.com/publix-super-markets-inc, accessed February 8, 2017.

## MANAGING PEOPLE

### Zappos Faces Competitive Challenges

Zappos, based in Las Vegas, is an online retailer with the initial goal of trying to be the best website for buying shoes by offering a wide variety of brands, styles, colors, sizes, and widths. Zappos has over 1,500 employees and carries more than 1,000 brands. The Zappos.com brand has grown to offer shoes, handbags, eyewear, watches, and accessories for online purchase. The company's goal is to provide the best service online, not just in shoes but in any product category. Zappos believes that the speed with which a customer receives an online purchase plays a critical role in how that customer thinks about shopping online again in the future, so the company is focusing on making sure the items get delivered to its customers as quickly as possible.

Zappos CEO Tony Hsieh has shaped the company's customer-service-focused culture, brand, and business strategy around 10 core values:

Deliver WOW through service.
Embrace and drive change.
Create fun and a little weirdness.
Be adventurous, creative, and open-minded.
Pursue growth and learning.
Build open and honest relationships with communication.
Build a positive team and family spirit.
Do more with less.
Be passionate and determined.
Be humble.

"Deliver WOW through service" means that call center employees need to provide excellent customer service. Call center employees encourage callers to order more than one size or color because shipping and return shipping is free. They are also encouraged to use their imaginations to meet customer needs.

Zappos has received many awards for its workplace culture and practices, including being frequently recognized in *Fortune* magazine's annual rankings of the "100 Best Companies to Work For." The job of human resources at Zappos is more than just a rule enforcer. HR's job is to protect the culture and to educate employees. HR focuses on interactions with managers and employees to understand what they need from HR (HR is even invited to attend work teams' happy hours). Zappos's employment practices help perpetuate its company culture. Only about 1 out of 100 applicants passes a hiring process that is equally weighted on job skills and on the potential to work in Zappos's culture. Some managers at Zappos believe that if you want to get a job the most important value to demonstrate is "be humble" including a focus on "we" instead of "I." Job candidates are interviewed for cultural fit and a willingness to change and learn. For example, they observe whether job candidates talk at lunch with others or just the person they think is making the hiring decision. The HR team uses unusual interview questions—such as, "How weird are you?" and "What's your theme song?"—to find employees who are creative and have strong individuality. Zappos provides free lunch in the cafeteria (cold cuts) and a full-time life coach (employees have to sit on a red velvet throne to complain), managers are encouraged to spend time with employees outside of the office, and any employee can reward another employee a $50 bonus for good performance. Call center employees can use an online scheduling tool that allows them to set their own hours, and they can earn more pay if they work during hours with greater customer demand. Most of the over 1,500 employees at Zappos are hourly. Every new hire undergoes four weeks of training, during which the company culture must be committed to memory, and spends two weeks dealing with customers by working the telephones. New recruits are offered $3,000 to leave the company during training to weed out individuals who will not be happy working at the company. Zappos provides free breakfast, lunch, snacks, coffee, tea, and vending machine snacks. Employees participate in more than 25 parades every year. Work is characterized by constant change; a loud, open office environment; and team interactions. Employees at Zappos move around. For example, call center employees can bid for different shifts every month.

To reinforce the importance of the 10 core values, Zappos's performance management system asks managers to evaluate how well employees' behaviors demonstrate the core values such as being humble or expressing their personalities. To evaluate task performance, managers are asked to regularly provide employees with status reports on such things as how much time they spend on the telephone with customers. The status reports and evaluations of the core values are informational or used to identify training needs. Zappos also believes in helping others understand what inspired the company culture. The company created the Zappos.com library, which provides a collection of books about creating a passion for customer service, products, and local communities. These books can be found in the front lobby of Zappos offices and are widely read and discussed by company employees.

Corporate culture is more than a set of values, and it is maintained by a complex web of human interactions. At Zappos, the liberal use of social media including blogs and Twitter facilitates the network that links employees with one another and with the company's customers. Zappos takes the pulse of the organization monthly, measuring the health of the culture with a happiness survey. Employees respond to such unlikely questions as whether they believe that the company has a higher purpose than profits, whether their own role has meaning, whether they feel in control of their career path, whether they consider their co-workers to be like family and friends, and whether they are happy in their jobs. Results from the survey are broken down by department, and opportunities for development are identified and acted upon. For example, when it was clear from the survey that one department had veered off course and felt isolated from the rest of the organization, a program was instituted that enabled individuals in the group to learn more about how integral their work was. To keep the company vibrant, CEO Tony Hsieh spent $350 million to develop a neighborhood in downtown Las Vegas, which is the home of Zappos.com's new headquarters. Hsieh wants to provide employees with a great place to work as well as to live and socialize.

Zappos embraces a management philosophy, holocracy, which gives employees the freedom and responsibility to decide how to get their work done and eliminated people managers. Hsieh's intent was to allow employees to act more like entrepreneurs and help stimulate new ideas, bring their full selves to work, and have a purpose beyond making money, all of which he believes will benefit the business. Employees work in teams or "circles" rather than as individuals, and team membership can change. However, employees are finding the new management system confusing and requires them to spend more time in meetings. Also, they wonder how they will earn raises and advance their careers without management jobs. In all, 210 employees found the new philosophy so dissatisfying that they took three months of severance pay and left the company. Zappos is changing its recruitment process to ensure that its new hires are comfortable with holocracy's self-management style.

Despite this setback, other companies are trying to learn from Zappos's practices. Zappos Insights is a department within Zappos created to share the Zappos culture with other companies. Zappos Insights provides programs about building a culture (3-Day Culture Camp), its WOW service philosophy (School of WOW), the power of a coaching-based culture (Coaching Event), how the HR function protects the culture and how its programs support it (People Academy), and custom programs. The cost to attend these programs ranges from $2,000 to $6,000 for each attendee.

## QUESTIONS

1. Zappos seems to be well-positioned to have a competitive advantage over other online retailers. What challenges discussed in Chapter 1 pose the biggest threat to Zappos's ability to maintain and enhance its competitive position? How can HRM practices help Zappos meet these challenges?
2. Do you think that employees of Zappos have high levels of engagement? Why?
3. Which of Zappos's 10 core values do you believe that HR practices can influence the most? The least? Why? For each of the core values, identify the HR practices that are related to it. Explain how the HR practices you identified are related to the core values.
4. How might the change to the holocracy management style undermine Zappos's core values and cause employees to have lower levels of engagement?

SOURCES: Based on S. Heathfield, "Find Out How Zappos Reinforces Its Culture," September 21, 2018, from www.thebalancecareers.com, accessed Februray 13, 2019; www.zappos.com, accessed February 13, 2019; E. Bernstein, J. Bunch, N. Canner, and M. Lee, "Beyond the Holocracy Hype," *Harvard Business Review*, July/August 2016, pp. 38–49; J. Reingold, "The Zappos Experiment," *Fortune*, March 15, 2016, pp. 206–14; "Zappos Insights," www.zapposinsights.com, accessed March 1, 2017; D. Richard, "At Zappos, Culture Pays," *Strategy + Business*, August 2010, p. 60, www.strategybusiness.com, accessed March 25, 2013; K. Gurchick, "Delivering HR at Zappos," *HR Magazine*, June 2011; R. Pyrillis, "The Reviews Are In," *Workforce Management*, May 2011, pp. 20–25; J. O'Brien, "Zappos Knows How to Kick It," *Fortune*, February 2, 2009, pp. 55–66; R. Silverman, "Going Bossless Backfires at Zappos," *Wall Street Journal*, May 21, 2015, pp. A1, A10.

# HR IN SMALL BUSINESS

## Network Is the Key to HRM at 1Collision

The typical auto body shop used to be a small, independent business that dealt directly with car owners or the local claims adjuster at an owner's insurance company. Today, however, more shops are part of a chain or join a network of shops. One reason is that insurers prefer to direct work to a few companies, rather than many small shops. Another is that a larger organization can support shops with functions such as human resource management. In fact, the two advantages build on each other: Joining a successful network brings in more business, which requires more employees, which requires more sophisticated HR practices.

Milwaukee-based 1Collision Network has seized on these opportunities by emphasizing HRM along with marketing to consumers and insurance companies. The more than 40 shops that have joined 1Collision Network use its online software to carry out the tasks of signing up new employees and enrolling all employees in benefits such as health insurance and retirement savings plans.

Jim Keller, 1Collision's president, says many shops find recruiting new employees to be a particular challenge. The network has employees who work full time on providing shops with support for recruiting qualified technicians.

The network also supports performance management and training. It works with an outside service provider to apply key performance indicators, using them to identify areas in which coaching can help the shop improve. For training, 1Collision works with equipment suppliers to identify training requirements and necessary certifications. Then 1Collision makes arrangements to have the instruction delivered to the shops in its network. The network also promotes learning through peer meetings in which the shops share lessons from experience.

## QUESTIONS

1. Give examples of 1Collision's HRM professionals providing the competencies of (a) HR technical expertise and (b) critical evaluation.
2. How might HRM support from the 1Collision Network make an auto body shop more competitive than if it relied on the shop manager to handle human resource management? In other words, how might this support contribute to business success?

SOURCES: 1Collision Network, "Body Shop Partners," http://1collision.com, accessed March 8, 2018; Brian Albright, "Strength in Numbers," *Auto Body Repair Network*, October 2015, pp. 36–38; Stacey Phillips, "Growing Trend of Collision Repair Networks Led to Formation of 1Collision Network," *Autobody News*, September 14, 2015, http://www.autobodynews.com.

# NOTES

1. J. T. Delaney and M. A. Huselid, "The Impact of Human Resource Management Practices on Perceptions of Organizational Performance," *Academy of Management Journal* 39 (1996), pp. 949–69; R. E. Ployhart, J. A. Weekley, and J. Ramsey, "The Consequences of Human Resources Stocks and Flows: A Longitudinal Examination of Unit Service Orientation and Unit Effectiveness," *Academy of Management Journal* 52 (2009), pp. 996–1015; Y. Kim and R. E. Ployhart, "The Effects of Staffing and Training on Firm Productivity and Profit Growth before, during, and after the Great Recession" *Journal of Applied Psychology* 99 (2014), pp. 361–89; R. Ployhart and T. Moliterno, "Emergence of the Human Capital Resource: A Multilevel Model," *Academy of Management Review* 36 (2011), pp. 127–50; B. Campbell, R. Coff, and D. Kryscynski, "Rethinking Sustained Competitive Advantage from Human Capital," *Academy of Management Review* 37 (2010), pp. 376–395: T. Crook, S. Todd, J. Combs, D. Woehr, and D. Ketchen, Jr., "Does Human Capital Matter? A Meta-Analysis of the Relationship between Human Capital and Firm Performance," *Journal of Applied Psychology* 96 (2011), pp. 443–56.
2. K. O'Leonard, "A Breed Apart," *Human Resource Executive*, January/February 2015, p. 38.
3. SHRM-BNA Survey No. 66, "Policy and Practice Forum: Human Resources Activities, Budgets, and Staffs: 2000–2001," *Bulletin to Management,* Bureau of National Affairs Policy and Practice Series, June 28, 2001 (Washington, DC: Bureau of National Affairs); Bureau of Labor Statistics, U.S. Department of Labor, "Human Resources Specialists," *Occupational Outlook Handbook, 2016–17 Edition,* https://www.bls.gov/ooh/business-and-financial/human-resources-specialists.htm, accessed February 9, 2017.
4. L. Weber and R. Feintzeig, "Is It a Dream or a Drag? Companies without HR," *Wall Street Journal*, March 9, 2014, pp. B1, B7; Henneman, "Is HR at Its Breaking Point?"
5. J. Rosenberg, "Don't DIY: Business Owners Delegate Human Resources Tasks" *USA Today* (August 6, 2018).
6. G. Tucker, "HR at the Corner of People and Strategy," *HR Magazine*, May 2014, pp. 42–44.
7. R. Zeidner, "Rebuilding HR," *HR Magazine*, May 2015, pp. 26–34.
8. A. Halcrow, "Survey Shows HRM in Transition," *Workforce*, June 1998, pp. 73–80; J. Laabs, "Why HR Can't Win Today," *Workforce*, May 1998, pp. 62–74; C. Cole, "Kodak Snapshots," *Workforce*, June 2000, pp. 65–72; W. Ruona and S. Gibson, "The Making of Twenty-First Century HR: An Analysis of the Convergence of HRM, HRD, and OD," *Human Resource Management* 43 (2004), pp. 49–66.
9. J. Bersin, "What's in Store for HR in 2015," *HR Magazine*, January/February 2015, pp. 32–51; T. Starner, "An HR Exodus," *HR Executive*, May 2014, p. 13; T. Henneman, "Is HR at Its Breaking Point?" *Workforce Management*, April 2013, pp. 28–32; C. Gibson, I. Ziskin, and J. Boudreau, "What Is the Future of HR?" *Workforce*, January 2014, pp. 30–33, 48; M. McGraw, "What's Keeping HR Up at Night," *Human Resource Executive*, September 2013, pp. 32–36.
10. R. Grossman, "Saving Shared Services," *HR Magazine*, September 2010, pp. 26–31.
11. Tucker, "HR at the Corner of People and Strategy."
12. S. Greengard, "Building a Self-Service Culture That Works," *Workforce*, July 1998, pp. 60–64.
13. D. Zielinski, "Making the Most of Manager Self-Service," *HR Magazine*, December 2013, pp. 51–55.
14. K. Kramer, "Industrial-Organizational (I-O) Psychology's Contribution to Strategic Human Resources Outsourcing (HRO): How Can We Shape the Future of HR?" *The Industrial-Organizational Psychologist*, January 2011, pp. 13–20.
15. B. Roberts, "Outsourcing in Turbulent Times," *HR Magazine*, November 2009, pp. 42–47; The Right Thing, "The Goodyear Tire and Rubber Company Discovers Key to Successful Outsourcing Partnerships," *Workforce Management*, March 2011, p. S2.
16. D. Ulrich, D. Kryscynski, M. Ulrich, and W. Brockbank, *Victory Through Organization* (New York: McGraw-Hill Education, 2017); P. Cappelli and A. Tavis, "HR Goes Agile," *Harvard Business Review,* March/April 2018, pp. 47–53; Society for Human Resource Management, "Future Insights: Top Ten Trends Affecting the Workplace and the HR Profession According to SHRM Special Expertise Panels," 2016, www.shrm.org, accessed February 14, 2017.

17. T. Lee and D. Wilkie, "Are You Practicing the HR Your CEO Wants?" *HR Magazine,* November/December 2018, pp. 40–48.

18. W. Bunch, "Breaking Down Boundaries," *Human Resource Executive,* October 2018, pp. 10–12.

19. J. Boudreau and S. Rice, "Bright, Shiny Objects and the Future of HR," *Harvard Business Review,* July/August 2015, pp. 72–78; W. Bunch, "Split Decision," *Human Resource Executive,* September 2015, pp. 14–16.

20. D. Ulrich, D. Kryscynski, M. Ulrich, and W. Brockbank, *Victory Through Organization* (New York: McGraw-Hill Education, 2017); S. Milligan, "HR 2025: Reach New Heights By Becoming A Trusted Advisor," *HR Magazine,* November/December 2018, pp. 30–38; T. Lee and D. Wilke, "Are You Practicing What Your CEO Wants?" *HR Magazine,* November/December 2018, pp. 41–48; P. Wright, *Human Resource Strategy: Adapting to the Age of Globalization* (Alexandria, VA: Society for Human Resource Management Foundation, 2008).

21. W. Bunch, "The (Other) Airbnb Experience," *Human Resource Executive,* July/August 2016, pp. 14–16; J. Meister and K. Mulcahy, *The Future Workplace Experience* (New York: McGraw-Hill, 2017).

22. W. Bunch, "Extending the Experience," *Human Resource Executive,* July/August 2018, pp. 12–14.

23. M. Huselid, "The Science and Practice of Workforce Analytics: Introduction to the Special Issue," *Human Resource Management* 57 (2018), pp. 679–684.

24. J. Ramirez, "The Anticipators," *Human Resource Executive,* May 2016, pp. 14–17; E. Frauenheim, "Numbers Game," *Workforce Management,* March 2011, pp. 20–21; P. Gallagher, "Rethinking HR," *Human Resource Executive,* September 2, 2009, pp. 1, 18–23.

25. L. Freifeld, "Sonic Automotive's Drive for Innovation," *training,* January/February 2018, pp. 34–36; C. Fleck, "An Algorithm for Success," *HR Magazine,* June 2016, pp. 130–35.

26. L. Claus and J. Collison, *The Maturing Profession of Human Resources: Worldwide and Regional View* (Alexandria, VA: Society for Human Resource Management, 2005).

27. Bureau of Labor Statistics, U.S. Department of Labor, *Occupational Outlook Handbook, 2016–17 Edition,* "Human Resources Specialists," www.bls.gov/ooh/business-and-financial/human-resources-specialists.htm, accessed February 9, 2017.

28. A. Devers, "10 Reasons I Love Being An HR Professional," February 10, 2015 from https://workology.com, accessed February 14, 2019; M. Breitfelder and D. Dowling, "Why Did We Ever Go Into HR," *Harvard Business Review,* July/August 2008, pp. 39–43; E. Krell, "Become a Master of Expertise and Credibility," *HR Magazine,* May 2010, pp. 53–63.

29. T. Starner, "An HR Exodus," *HR Executive,* May 2014, p. 13.

30. S. Greengard, "The Debate over HR Credentials," *Workforce,* June 2016, pp. 40–43, 48.

31. J. Wiscombe, "Your Wonderful, Terrible HR Life," *Workforce,* June 2001, pp. 32–38.

32. R. Charan, "It's Time to Split HR," *Harvard Business Review,* July/August 2014, p. 34; Henneman, "Is HR at Its Breaking Point?"

33. D. Ulrich, D. Kryscynski, M. Ulrich, and W. Brockbank, "Competencies for HR Professionals Who Deliver Outcomes," *Employment Relations Today* 44 (2017), pp. 37–44; D. Ulrich, D. Kryscynski, M. Ulrich, and W. Brockbank, *Victory Through Organization* (New York: McGraw-Hill Education, 2017); P. Cappelli, "Why We Love to Hate HR . . . and What HR Can Do about It," *Harvard Business Review,* July/August 2015, pp. 54–61.

34. P. McCord, "How Netflix Reinvented HR," *Harvard Business Review,* January/February 2014, pp. 71–76; Henneman, "Is HR at Its Breaking Point?"

35. Society for Human Resource Management, SHRM Elements for HR Success Competency Model, www.shrm.org, accessed March 21, 2012; R. Zeidner, "Rebuilding HR," *HR Magazine,* May 2015, pp. 26–34.

36. K. Strobel, "Competency Proficiency Predicts Better Job Performance," *HR Magazine,* October 2014, p. 67.

37. Zeidner, "Rebuilding HR."

38. J. Arnold, "Building Strength through Cross-Training," *HR Magazine,* April 2017, pp. 50–55.

39. K. Frasch, "Engagement Still Keeping HR Awake," *Human Resource Executive,* April 2016, p. 21; J. Benz et al., "Happy New HR: Nine Thought Leaders Map Out Everything You Need to Know and Do in 2016 and Beyond," *HR Magazine,* December 2015/January 2016, pp. 28–44; M. McGraw, *"Engagement Is Still the Issue," Human Resource Executive,* March 2017, p. 36.

40. E. Cohen, S. Taylor, and M. Muller-Camen, *HRM's Role in Corporate Social and Environmental Sustainability* (Alexandria, VA: SHRM Foundation, 2012); WCED, *Our Common Future* (Oxford: Oxford University Press, 1987), A. A. Savitz, *The Triple Bottom Line* (San Francisco: Jossey-Bass, 2006); S. Hart and S. Milstein, "Creating Sustainable Value," *Academy of Management Executive* 17 (2003), pp. 56–67.

41. "What Is ESG (Environmental, Social, and Governance)?" from https://corporatefinanceinstitute.com, accessed February 14, 2019; E. Cohen, S. Taylor, and M. Muller-Camen, *HRM's Role in Corporate Social and Environmental Responsibility"* (Alexandria, VA: Society for Human Resource Management Foundation, 2012).

42. "ESG and the Role of the Chief Human Resources Officer," 2018 HR Policy Association (working draft).

43. "Purpose & Progress: 2017 Environmental, Social, & Governance Report," from www.goldmansachs.com, accessed February 21, 2019.

44. "99 Months and Counting, U.S. Job Machine Keeps Cranking," *Wall Street Journal,* January 5/6, 2019, p. A10; E. Morath, "Record Job Run Powers On," *Wall Street Journal,* February 2/3, 2019, pp. A1, A2; A. Ramkumar, "Stocks Post Best January in Thirty Years," *Wall Street Journal,* February 1, 2019, pp. A1, A2; J. Hilsenrath, "Booming Economy Powers Growth . . .," *Wall Street Journal,* December 19, 2018, pp. R1, R2.

45. Y. Kim and R. E. Ployhart, "The Effects of Staffing and Training on Firm Productivity and Profit Growth Before, During, and After the Great Recession," *Journal of Applied Psychology* 99 (2014), pp. 361–389.

46. L. Weber, "CEOs Say Recession Is Top Worry for 2019," January 16, 2019, from www.wsj.com, accessed February 12, 2019; J. Lahart, "How to Spot a Recession," *Wall Street Journal,* December 31, 2018, from www.wsj.com accessed February 12, 2019; A. Otani, "US Stocks Face Rocky Path in 2019," *Wall Street Journal,* January 2, 2019, p. R12; G. Ip, "Low Jobless Rate Confronts the Fed," *Wall Street Journal,* March 23, 2018, p. A6.

47. R. Simon, "Tariffs Unsettle Small Companies," *Wall Street Journal,* August 7, 2018, pp. A1, A8; R. Simon, "Steelmakers' Fortunes Diverge," *Wall Street Journal,* February 11, 2019, pp. A1, A8.

48. E. Morath, "Employers Feel Pinch of Robust Job Market," *Wall Street Journal,* September 12, 2018, p. A3; E. Morath and J. Smith, "Jobs Go Unfilled as the Economy Expands," *Wall Street Journal,* August 8, 2018, p. A2; D. Cameron, "Defense

Industry Scrambles to Find Skilled Workers," *Wall Street Journal,* December 31, 2018, p. B3.

49. Bureau of Labor Statistics, U.S. Department of Labor, "Employment Projections: 2016–2026," News Release, October 24, 2017, from www.bls.gov/emp, accessed January 5, 2019; Bureau of Labor Statistics, U.S. Department of Labor, "Employment Projections, Table 3.4, Civilian Labor Force by Age, Sex, Race, and Ethnicity 1996, 2006, 2016, and Projected 2026," from www.bls.gov, accessed January 5, 2019; T. Alan Lacey, Mitra Toossi, Kevin S. Dubina, and Andrea B. Gensler, "Projections Overview and Highlights, 2016–26," Monthly Labor Review, U.S. Bureau of Labor Statistics, October 2017, from www.bls.gov, accessed January 5, 2019.

50. Based on Bureau of Labor Statistics, U.S. Department of Labor, "Employment Projections: 2016–2026," News Release, October 24, 2017, from www.bls.gov/emp, accessed January 5, 2019.

51. Bureau of Labor Statistics, "Employment Projections: Earnings and Unemployment Rates by Educational Attainment, 2018," www.bls.gov/emp/tables/unemployment-earnings-education .htm, accessed August, 14, 2019; Bureau of Labor Statistics, "Occupational Requirements Survey Summary," February 21, 2019, from www.bls.gov/ors, accessed August 14, 2019.

52. J. Sparshott, "Job Training Ramps Up at Smaller Firms," *Wall Street Journal,* February 3, 2017, p. A2.

53. Organisation for Economic Co-operation and Development (OECD), "Survey of Adult Skills," from http://skills.oecd.org, accessed February 12, 2019; Organisation for Economic Co-operation and Development (OECD), "Skills for Jobs" (U.S. Note, September 2018) from https://www .oecdskillsforjobsdatabase.org, accessed February 12, 2019; Deloitte Development LLC, "Upskilling Manufacturing: How Technology Is Disrupting America's Industrial Labor Force," in The Skills Gap in U.S. Manufacturing: 2015 and Beyond, www .pwc.com, accessed February 14, 2017; Meinert, "Manufacturing Magnets"; "Good to Grow: 2014 US CEO Survey"; P. Gaul, "Nearly Half of U.S. Executives Are Concerned About Skills Gap," T+D (February 2014), p. 18; "2014 Accenture Manufacturing Skills & Training Study," from www .themanufacturinginstitute.org, accessed March 2, 2015; and "Survey of Adult Skills," www.manufacturinginstitute.org, accessed February 14, 2017.

54. L. Weber, "The Hybrid Skills That Tomorrow's Jobs Will Require," *Wall Street Journal,* January 22, 2019, p. R14.

55. D. Eng, "Where Autism Workers Thrive," *Fortune,* July 1, 2018, pp. 38–39; K. Gee, "Employers Eager to Try a New Policy: 'No Experience Necessary,'" July 28, 2018 from www.wsj.com, accessed February 15, 2019; P. Coy, "Companies Give Worker Training Another Try," *Bloomberg Businessweek,* October 28, 2018, pp. 36–37. V. Salama and V. Fuhrmans, "Firms Vow to Train Millions of Workers," *Wall Street Journal,* July 20, 2018, p. A3; L. Stevens, "Amazon to Lift Wages to $15 An Hour," *Wall Street Journal,* October 3, 2018, pp. A1, A9; D. Harrison and E. Morath, "More Employees Say I Quit," *Wall Street Journal,* July 5, 2018, pp. A1, A2; E. Morath, "Wages Rise As Hiring Accelerates," *Wall Street Journal,* November 3-4, 2018, pp. A1, A2; V. Fuhrmans, "Hotels, Pearson Team for Tuition Program," *Wall Street Journal,* March 1, 2018, p. B6; D. Stafford, "Inside Wal-Mart's New Training Sessions: Trying to Adapt to Retail Landscape Changes," from www.chicagotribune.com/ business, accessed June 6, 2017; B. Sozzi, "Walmart's New Secret Weapon for Success: Big Bonuses and Vital Training for Employees," *The Street,* October 17, 2016, accessed from www .thestreet.com, January 23, 2018; "Opportunities to Build a Career," from https://corporate.walmart.com/opportunity, accessed January 23, 2018; and K. King-Sumner, "Walmart Invests in Employees with Training Academy," *The Republic,* November 14, 2016, from https://www.azcentral.com/ story/money/business/jobs/2016/11/14/walmart-invests-employees-training-academy/93792526/, accessed January 23, 2018; S. Emling, "Good News for Job Seekers Over Fifty," April 4, 2018 from www.aarp.org, accessed February 15, 2019; "2019 Goldman Sachs Returnship Program," from www .goldmansachs.com, accessed February 15, 2019.

56. R. Simon, "Recruiting Workers Involves More Work," *Wall Street Journal* (February 22, 2018), p. B4.

57. J. Barney, *Gaining and Sustaining a Competitive Advantage* (Upper Saddle River, NJ: Prentice Hall, 2002).

58. L. Weatherly, *Human Capital: The Elusive Asset* (Alexandria, VA: SHRM Research Quarterly, 2003).

59. G. Tucker, "HR in the Age of Disruption," *HR Magazine,* September 2016, pp. 68–73.

60. L. Bassi, J. Ludwig, D. McMurrer, and M. Van Buren, *Profiting from Learning: Do Firms' Investments in Education and Training Pay Off?* (Alexandria, VA: American Society for Training and Development, September 2000); S. Sung and J. Choi, "Do Organizations Spend Wisely on Employees? Effects of Training and Development Investments on Learning and Innovation in Organizations," *Journal of Organizational Behavior* 35 (2014), pp. 393–412; H. Aguinis and K. Kraiger, "Benefits of Training and Development for Individuals, Teams, Organizations, and Society," *Annual Review of Psychology* 60 (2009), pp. 451–74.

61. T. J. Atchison, "The Employment Relationship: Untied or Re-Tied," *Academy of Management Executive* 5 (1991), pp. 52–62.

62. D. Senge, "The Learning Organization Made Plain and Simple," *Training and Development Journal,* October 1991, pp. 37–44.

63. L. Freifeld, "Keller Williams Realty's View from the Top," *Training,* January/February 2017, pp. 26–30.

64. *SHRM Workplace Forecast* (Alexandria, VA: Society for Human Resource Management, 2013).

65. K. Oakes, "The 3A's of Organizational Agility," *Human Resource Executive,* July/August 2018, pp. 22–23.

66. J. Salopek, "No Vacancy," *TD* (October 2016), pp. 38–40.

67. J. O'Toole and E. Lawler III, *The New American Workplace* (New York: Palgrave McMillan, 2006); R. Hoffman, B. Casnocha, and C. Yeh, "Tours of Duty: The New Employer-Employee Compact," *Harvard Business Review,* June 2013, pp. 48–58.

68. R. Vance, *Employee Engagement and Commitment* (Alexandria, VA: Society for Human Resource Management, 2006).

69. J. Harter, "Employee Engagement on the Rise in the U.S.," August 26, 2018 from https://news.gallup.com, accessed February 6, 2019.

70. J. Meister and K. Mulchay, "The Future Workplace Experience"; J. Meister, "The Employee Experience Is the Future of Work: 10 HR Trends for 2017," January 5, 2017 from www.forbes.com; Deloitte Development LLC, "The Employee Experience: 2017 Deloitte Global Human Capital Trends," http://marketing .bersin.com, accessed February 8, 2019.

71. Meister and Mulchay, "The Future Workplace Experience"; Deloitte Development LLC, "The Employee Experience: 2017 Deloitte Global Human Capital Trends," http://marketing .bersin.com, accessed February 8, 2019.

72. M. Ciccarelli, "Are You Delivering a Great Employee Experience?" *Human Resource Executive,* November 2018, pp. 43–44.

73. J. Cook-Ramirez, "A Promising Proposition," *Human Resource Executive,* June 2018, pp. 10–12.

74. M. Ciccarelli, "Keeping the Keepers," *Human Resource Executive*, January/February 2011, pp. 1, 20-23.

75. P. Cappelli, "Talent Management for the Twenty-First Century," *Harvard Business Review*, March 2008, pp. 74-81; "Towers Watson 2014 Global Talent Management and Rewards Study," *HR Magazine*, April 2015, p. 54.

76. S. Shellenbarger, "Why Perks No Longer Cut It for Workers," *Wall Street Journal,* December 4, 2018, p. R9; M. Weinstein, "BNSF Railway Is on the Right Training Track," *Training,* January/February 2017, pp. 42-44.

77. Freelancers Union & Elance-oDesk, "Freelancing in America: 2016," www.freelancersunion.org, accessed February 15, 2017; Bureau of Labor Statistics, "Contingent and Alternative Employment Arrangements, February 2005," www.bls.gov, accessed February 28, 2017.

78. A. Sussman and J. Zumbrun, "'Gig' Economy Spreads Broadly," *Wall Street Journal,* March 26, 2016, pp. A1, A2; Bloomberg BNA, "The Gig Economy: HR's Role in Navigating the On-Demand Workforce," January 2016, https://www.bna.com/gig-economy-hrs-m57982067661/.

79. J. Wald, "The Benefits or Lack Thereof of the 'Gig'," *Workforce,* August 2016, pp. 22-25.

80. L. Weber, "The End of Employees," *Wall Street Journal,* February 3, 2017, pp. A1, A10; A. McIlvaine, "The Contingent Quandary," *Human Resource Executive,* November 2015, pp. 14-16.

81. E. Frauenheim, "Creating a New Contingent Culture," *Workforce Management,* August 2012, pp. 34-39.

82. Gallup, "Work and Workplace," August 3-7, 2016, www.gallup.com, accessed February 17, 2017.

83. C. Patton, "On the Frontier of Flexibility," *Human Resource Executive*, May 2, 2009, pp. 48-51.

84. A. Fox, "Achieving Integration," *HR Magazine*, April 2011, pp. 42-47; P. Marinova, "Who Works from Home and When," February 28, 2013, www.cnn.com; C. Suddath, "Work-from-Home Truths, Half-Truths, and Myths," *Bloomberg Businessweek*, March 4-March 10, 2013, p. 75; R. Silverman and Q. Fottrell, "The Home Office in the Spotlight," *Wall Street Journal*, February 27, 2013, p. B6; N. Shah, "More Americans Working from Home Remotely," *Wall Street Journal*, April 6, 2013, p. A3.

85. A. Mann and A. Atkins, "America's Coming Workplace: Home Alone," March 15, 2017 from http://news.gallup.com/businessjournal/206033/america-coming-workplace-home-alone.aspx, accessed January 6, 2018; Bureau of Labor Statistics, "American Time Use Survey," June 24, 2016, from www.bls.gov/tus, accessed February 17, 2017; and Gallup, "Work and Workplace," August 3-7, 2016, from www.gallup.com, accessed February 17, 2017.

86. C. Mims, "More Workers Have Out-of-Office Experience," *Wall Street Journal,* June 5, 2017, pp. B1, B4.

87. R. Feintzeig, "WeWork Courts More Corporate Clients," *Wall Street Journal,* August 16, 2016, pp. B1, B2; A. Fox, "At Work in 2020," *HR Magazine,* January 2010, pp. 18-23.

88. R. S. Kaplan and D. P. Norton, "The Balanced Scorecard—Measures That Drive Performance," *Harvard Business Review*, January-February 1992, pp. 71-79; R. S. Kaplan and D. P. Norton, "Putting the Balanced Scorecard to Work," *Harvard Business Review*, September/October 1993, pp. 134-47.

89. S. Bates, "The Metrics Maze," *HR Magazine*, December 2003, pp. 50-55; D. Ulrich, "Measuring Human Resources: An Overview of Practice and a Prescription for Results," *Human Resource Management* 36 (1997), pp. 303-20.

90. SAS Institute, "Customer Success: SAS Helps ConocoPhillips Norway Focus on Performance and Control Costs," www.sas.com, accessed April 24, 2012.

91. B. Sutherly, "Doctor Pay Still Based on Volume," *The Columbus Dispatch*, March 24, 2013, pp. A1, A9.

92. Johnson & Johnson, "2017 Health for Humanity Report," from https://www.jnj.com/caring/citizenship-sustainability, accessed February 10, 2019.

93. J. R. Jablonski, *Implementing Total Quality Management: An Overview* (San Diego: Pfeiffer, 1991).

94. R. Hodgetts, F. Luthans, and S. Lee, "New Paradigm Organizations: From Total Quality to Learning World-Class," *Organizational Dynamics*, Winter 1994, pp. 5-19.

95. National Institute of Standards and Technology (NIST), Baldrige Performance Excellence Program, "Baldrige Frequently Asked Questions," www.nist.gov/baldrige, accessed April 8, 2011.

96. A. Pomeroy, "Winners and Learners," *HR Magazine*, April 2006, pp. 62-67.

97. National Institute of Standards and Technology, "Don Chalmers Ford, Malcolm Baldrige National Quality Award 2016 Award Recipient, Small Business," November 17, 2016, www.nist.gov/baldrige/don-chalmers-ford, accessed February 13, 2017.

98. "About ISO", "Quality Management Principles," "ISO 9000 Family-Quality Management," International Organization for Standardization, www.iso.org, accessed March 23, 2018.

99. General Electric Company website, "What Is Six Sigma?" www.ge.com, accessed February 13, 2017; Shmula, "GE and Six Sigma: The Beginning of a Beautiful Relationship," www.shmula.com, accessed March 1, 2017.

100. "Best Practices & Outstanding Training Initiatives: CenturyLink Lean Applied to Business Process Program," *Training,* March/April 2019, p. 83.

101. T. Alan Lacey, Mitra Toossi, Kevin S. Dubina, and Andrea B. Gensler, "Projections Overview and Highlights, 2016-26," Monthly Labor Review, U.S. Bureau of Labor Statistics, October 2017, from www.bls.gov, accessed February 5, 2019.

102. S. Milligan, "Wisdom of the Ages," *HR Magazine*, November 2014, pp. 22-27; C. Paullin, *The Aging Workforce: Leveraging the Talents of Mature Employees* (Alexandria, VA: The SHRM Foundation, 2014); N. Lockwood, *The Aging Workforce* (Alexandria, VA: Society for Human Resource Management, 2003).

103. C. Hymowitz, "Seventy Is the New Sixty-Five," *Bloomberg Businessweek,* October 1, 2018, pp. 43-44; R. Simon, "Booming Job Market Can't Fill Retirement Shortfall," *Wall Street Journal,* December 24, 2018, pp. A1, A9; J. Ramirez, "Betting on Older Workers," *Human Resource Executive,* June 16, 2016, pp. 14-16; Milligan, "Wisdom of the Ages"; V. Giang, "The Fifty Best Employers for Older Workers," *Business Insider*, accessed April 14, 2015, www.businessinsider.com; S. Hewlett, L. Sherbin, and K. Sumberg, "How Gen Y & Boomers Will Reshape Your Agenda," *Harvard Business Review*, July/August 2009, pp. 71-76.

104. J. Miller, "10 Things You Need to Know About Gen Z," *HR Magazine,* November/December 2018, pp. 50-56; J. Adamy, "Your New Workers are Gen Z - Get Ready," *Wall Street Journal,* September 7, 2018, pp. A1, A9; S. Gale, "What HR Leaders Need to Know About Generation Z," *Workforce,* September/October 2018, p. 10; A. Adkins, "What Millennials Want from Work and Life," www.gallup.com, May 11, 2016, accessed February 20, 2017; S. Gale, "Forget Millennials: Are You Ready for Generation Z?" *Chief Learning Officer,* July 2015, pp. 38-48; K. Tyler, "New Kids on the Block," *HR Magazine*, October 2013, pp. 35-40; Milligan, "Wisdom of the Ages"; Hewlett, Sherbin,

and Sumberg, "How Gen Y & Boomers Will Reshape Your Agenda"; A. Fox, "Mixing It Up," *HR Magazine*, May 2011, pp. 22–27; K. Ball and G. Gotsill, *Surviving the Baby Boomer Exodus* (Boston, MA: Cengage, 2011).

105. J. Meriac, D. Woehr, and C. Banister, "Generational Differences in Work Ethic: An Examination of Measurement Equivalence across Three Cohorts," *Journal of Business and Psychology*, 25 (2010), pp. 315–24; K. Real, A. Mitnick, and W. Maloney, "More Similar than Different: Millennials in the U.S. Building Trades," *Journal of Business and Psychology*, 25 (2010), pp. 303–13.

106. T. Lennon, "Managing a Multi-generational Workforce: The Myths vs. the Realities," 2015, www.haygroup.com, accessed February 20, 2017; S. Lyons and L. Kuron, "Generational Differences in the Workplace: A Review of the Evidence and Directions for Future Research," *Journal of Organizational Behavior* 35 (2013), pp. 139–57; J. Deal, D. Altman, and S. Rogelberg, "Millennials at Work: What We Know and What We Need to Do (If Anything)," *Journal of Business and Psychology*, 25 (2010), pp. 191–99.

107. W. Bunch, "Fixed on the Future," *Human Resources Executive,* December 2017, pp. 32–33.

108. Bureau of Labor Statistics, U.S. Department of Labor, "Employment projections: 2016–2026," News Release, October 24, 2017, from www.bls.gov/emp, accessed January 5, 2019; Bureau of Labor Statistics, U.S. Department of Labor, "Employment projections, Table 3.4, Civilian Labor Force by Age, Sex, Race, and Ethnicity 1996, 2006, 2016, and Projected 2026," from www.bls.gov, accessed January 5, 2019.

109. K. Witsman, "U.S. Lawful Permanent Residents: 2017," *Annual Flow Report*, August 2018, U.S. Department of Homeland Security, Office of Immigration Statistics, www.dhs.gov, accessed February 5, 2019; and N. Mossaad and R. Baugh, "Refugees and Asylees: 2016," *Annual Flow Report*, January 2018, U.S. Department of Homeland Security, Office of Immigration Statistics, www.dhs.gov, accessed February 5, 2019.

110. J. Sparshott, "Immigration Study Sees More Pros Than Cons," *Wall Street Journal*, September 23, 2016, p. A2; National Academies of Science, Engineering, and Medicine, *The Economic and Fiscal Consequences of Immigration* (Washington, DC: National Academies Press, 2016).

111. J. Ramirez, "ICE Ramps Up Employer Audits," *Human Resource Executive,* July/August 2018, p. 8; L. Meckler, "U.S. Sets Hard Line on Illegal Immigrants," *Wall Street Journal,* February 22, 2017, pp. A1, A6.

112. "Import Food or Labor?" *Bloomberg Businessweek*, June 11, 2018, p. 6.

113. L. Meckler, "H-1B's Future Causes Rift," *Wall Street Journal,* February 10, 2017, p. B4; M. Trottman, "Clash Erupts over Seasonal-Worker Visas," *Wall Street Journal,* February, 26, 2016, p. A3; L. Meckler and L. Stevens, "White House Takes on Working Visas," *Wall Street Journal,* February 1, 2017; M. Jordan and S. Perez, "Employers' Lament: Too Few Immigrants," *Wall Street Journal*, November 25, 2016, pp. A1, A9.

114. S. Raice, "Seasonal Businesses Feel the Burn," *Wall Street Journal*, August 27, 2018, p. A3.

115. B. Groysberg and K. Connolly, "Great Leaders Who Make the Mix Work," *Harvard Business Review*, September 2013, pp. 68–76; K. Jones, E. King, J. Nelson, D. Geller, and L. Bowes-Sperry, "Beyond the Business Case: The Ethical Perspective on Diversity Training," *Human Resource Management*, January–February 2013, pp. 55–74; T. H. Cox and S. Blake, "Managing Cultural Diversity: Implications for Organizational Competitiveness," *The Executive* 5 (1991), pp. 45–56.

116. Groysberg and Connolly, "Great Leaders Who Make the Mix Work"; M. Loden and J. B. Rosener, *Workforce America!* (Homewood, IL: Business One Irwin, 1991); N. Lockwood, *Workplace Diversity: Leveraging the Power of Difference for Competitive Advantage* (Alexandria, VA: Society for Human Resource Management, 2005).

117. L. McIntyre, "Diversity and Inclusion Update: The Journey Continues," November 14, 2018, from https://blogs.microsoft.com, accessed Februray 5, 2019; "Global Diversity and Inclusion, Inside Microsoft," www.microsoft.com, accessed February 5, 2019: J. Robinson, "Culture-Change Agents," *Human Resource Executive,* September 16, 2016, pp. 10–12.

118. S. Sipek, "Wearing Your Health on Your Sleeve," *Workforce*, August 2014, p. 16; C. Donham, "Legal Considerations," *Workforce*, August 2014, p. 47; L. Weber, "EEOC Issues Proposal for Wellness Programs," *Wall Street Journal*, April 17, 2015, p. B5; M. Mihelich, "Sacred Ground for Lawsuits," *Workforce*, April 2014, pp. 18–19; J. Hyman, "Any Headway on Headware?" *Workforce*, November 2013, p. 27; M. Mihelich, "The Expanded Definition of Disability," *Workforce*, February 2014, pp. 20–21; J. Palazzolo, "Family-Leave Lawsuits Take Off," *Wall Street Journal*, August 9–10, 2014, p. A3; R. Grossman, "No Federal Regulatory Relief in Sight," *HR Magazine*, February 2013, pp. 24–25.

119. Associated Press, "'Silence Breakers' Named *Time Magazine*'s Person of the Year," December 6, 2017, from www.chicagotribune.com, accessed February 8, 2019; Chicago Tribune Staff and K. Hawbaker, "#MeToo: A Timeline of Events," from www.chicagotribune.com, accessed February 8, 2019.

120. D. MacMillian, E. Minaya, and M. Sun, "Google Workers Walk Out in Protest," *Wall Street Journal,* November 2, 2018, pp. B1, B4.

121. M. Abelson, "Welcome to Arbitration Hell," *Bloomberg Businessweek,* January 28, 2019, pp. 45–49;

122. L. Weber, "Uber Settlement with Drivers Meets Dissent," *Wall Street Journal,* June 2, 2016, p. B3; C. Duhigg, "How Trump Might Become a Workplace Disrupter," *New York Times,* February 22, 2017.

123. S. Jakab, C. Grant, and D. Gallagher, "Why Travel Curb Irks Executives," *Wall Street Journal,* January 31, 2017, p. B12; J. Nicas, "Executives Say Move Hurts High Tech Workers," *Wall Street Journal,* January 30, 2017, p. A4; D. Paletta and N. Hong, "Migrant Order Faces New Challenges," *Wall Street Journal,* January 31, 2017, pp. A1, A5.

124. A. Wright, "Boeing Insider Data Breach Serves as Reminder for HR," www.shrm.org, accessed March 10, 2017.

125. A. Burjek, "All Eyes On You," *Workforce,* October 2018, pp. 22–26; P. Brans, "Do You Need to Comply With GDPR?" from www.cisco.com, accessed February 10, 2019.

126. M. Pastin, *The Hard Problems of Management: Gaining the Ethics Edge* (San Francisco: Jossey-Bass, 1986); T. Thomas, J. Schermerhorn, Jr., and J. Dienhart, "Strategic Leadership of Ethical Behavior in Business," *Academy of Management Executive* 18 (2004), pp. 56–66.

127. T. Thomas, J. Schermerhorn, Jr., and J. Dienhart, "Strategic Leadership of Ethical Behavior in Business," *Academy of Management Executive* 18 (2004), pp. 56–66; T. Agovino, "Make Ethics Your Guide," *HR Magazine,* November/December 2018, pp. 60–65; J. Robinson, "Balancing Act," *Human Resource Executive,* December 2016, pp. 14–16.

128. Ethics and Compliance Initiative from www.ethics.org, accessed February 15, 2018; T. Agovino, "Make Ethics Your Guide," *HR Magazine,* November/December 2018, pp. 60–65.

129. Gallup, "Honesty/Ethics in Professions," December 2015, www.gallup.com, accessed February 20, 2017.

130. K. Gurchiek, "Sarbanes-Oxley Compliance Costs Rising," *HR Magazine*, January 2005, pp. 29, 33.

131. R. Grossman, "HR and the Board," *HR Magazine*, January 2007, pp. 52–58.

132. J. Segal, "The 'Joy' of Uncooking," *HR Magazine* 47 (2002).

133. D. Buss, "Corporate Compasses," *HR Magazine* 49 (2004), pp. 126–32.

134. E. Krell, "How to Conduct an Ethics Audit," *HR Magazine*, April 2010, pp. 48–50.

135. "Global Ethics & Compliance," www.eaton.com, accessed February 20, 2017; D. Meinert, "Creating an Ethical Culture," *HR Magazine*, April 2014, pp. 22–27; A. McIlvaine, "Ethical Champions," *Human Resource Executive*, November 2014, pp. 14–16.

136. G. F. Cavanaugh, D. Moberg, and M. Velasquez, "The Ethics of Organizational Politics," *Academy of Management Review* 6 (1981), pp. 363–74.

137. McKinsey & Company, "Globalization in Transition: The Future of Trade and Value Chains," January 2019, from www.mckinsey .com, accessed February 10, 2019.

138. A. Straders, "What Are Emerging Markets? Characteristics and List in 2019," December 31, 2018, from www.thestreet.com, accessed February 7, 2019; McKinsey & Company, "Globalization in Transition: The Future of Trade and Value Chains," January 2019, from www.mckinsey.com, accessed February 10, 2019.

139. McKinsey & Company, "Globalization in Transition: The Future of Trade and Value Chains," January 2019, from www.mckinsey .com, accessed February 10, 2019.

140. McKinsey & Company, "Globalization in Transition: The Future of Trade and Value Chains," January 2019, from www.mckinsey .com, accessed February 10, 2019; T. Moss, "Drop in China Car Sales Idles Foreign Firms' Plants," *Wall Street Journal*, December 26, 2018, pp. A1–A2; B. Einhorn, "Can Lincoln and Caddy Find Fans in China?" *Bloomberg Businessweek*, April 7, 2016, pp. 21–22.

141. J. Marson, "McDonald's Puts Down Stakes in Siberia," *Wall Street Journal*, January 24, 2017, p. B6.

142. R. Chebium, "A Common Language: Training across Borders," *HR Magazine*, January/ February 2015, pp. 52–58.

143. J. Hagerty and M. Magnier, "Companies Tiptoe Back Toward 'Made in America,'" *Wall Street Journal*, January 14, 2015, pp. A1, A12; J. Schramm, "Offshoring," *Workplace Visions* 2 (Alexandria, VA: Society for Human Resource Management, 2004); P. Babcock, "America's Newest Export: White Collar Jobs," *HR Magazine* 49 (4) 2004, pp. 50–57.

144. J. Hagerty, "Decimated U.S. Industry Pulls Up Its Socks," *Wall Street Journal*, December 26, 2014, p. B6.

145. R. Simon, "Tariffs Unsettle Small Companies," *Wall Street Journal*, August 7, 2018, pp. A1, A8.

146. U.S. Census Bureau, "Census Bureau's American Community Survey Provides New State and Local Income, Poverty, Health Insurance Statistics," www.census.gov, accessed February 27, 2015; L. Morales, "Nearly Half of Americans Are Frequent Internet Users," January 2, 2009, www.gallup.com; L. Morales, "Google and Facebook Users, Skew Young, Affluent and Educated," February 17, 2011, www.gallup.com; F. Newport, "Most US Smartphone Owners Check Phone at Least Hourly," July 9, 2015, www.gallup.com; and L. Saad, "Nearly Half of Smartphone Users Can't Imagine Life without It," July 13, 2015, www.gallup.com, accessed February 20, 2017.

147. W. Cascio and R. Montealegre, "How Technology Is Changing Work and Organizations," *Annual Review of Organizational Psychology and Organizational Behavior*, 3 (2016), pp. 349–75; J. Bersin, "Transformative Tech: A Disruptive Year Ahead," *HR Magazine*, February 2017, pp. 29–36; G. Colvin, "In the Future, Will There Be Any Work Left for People to Do?" *Fortune*, June 2, 2014; T. Aeppel, "Jobs and the Clever Robot," *Wall Street Journal*, February 25, 2015, pp. A1, A10.

148. S. Gale, "Ready or Not, the Future Is Now," *Chief Learning Officer*, March 2017, pp. 20–21; J. Stern, "Alexa, Stop Bringing Chaos to Anyone with a Similar Name," *Wall Street Journal*, January 27, 2016, pp. A1, A8;

149. L. McFarland and R. Ployhart, "Social Media: A Contextual Framework to Guide Research and Practice," *Journal of Applied Psychology* 100 (2015), pp. 1653–77; D. Robb, "Cultivating Connections," *HR Magazine*, September 2014, pp. 65–66; M. McGraw, "Managing the Message," *Human Resource Executive*, December 2014, pp. 16–18; P. Brotherson, "Social Networks Enhance Employee Learning," *T + D*, April 2011, pp. 18–19; M. Derven, "Social Networking: A Frame for Development," *T + D*, July 2009, pp. 58–63; M. Weinstein, "Are You Linked In?" *Training*, September/October, 2010, pp. 30–33.

150. C. Goodman, "Employers Wrestle with Social-Media Policies," *The Columbus Dispatch*, January 30, 2011, p. D3.

151. Willis Towers Watson, "The Future of Work: Debunking Myths and Navigating Realities," 2018, from www.willistowerswatson .com, accessed February 6, 2019.

152. Q. Bui and R. Kisby, "Brick after Brick," *The Columbus Dispatch*, March 12, 2018, pp. C1, C5.

153. H. Wilson and P. Daugherty, "Collaborative Intelligence: Humans and AI are Joining Forces," *Harvard Business Review*, July/August 2018, pp. 114–123; J. Neumann, "Zara Turns to Robots for In-Store Pickup," *Wall Street Journal*, March 6, 2018, p. B4; D. Hernandez, "Robots' Hands Are Given the Human Touch," *Wall Street Journal*, March 12, 2018, p. R2.

154. C. Mims, "Where Robots Will Soon Rule," *Wall Street Journal*, February 8/9, 2019, p. B4; J. Manyika, S. Lund, M. Chui, J. Bughin, J. Woetzel, P. Batra, R. Ko, and S. Sanghvi, "What the Future of Work Will Mean for Jobs, Skills, and Wages," November 2017, from www.mckinsey.com, accessed April 12, 2018.

155. M. Williams and D. Caruso, "Some Jobs On the Way Out," *The Columbus Dispatch*, February 6, 2018, pp. A1, A8.

156. Willis Towers Watson, "The Future of Work: Debunking Myths and Navigating Realities," 2018, from www.willistowerswatson .com, accessed February 6, 2019.

157. J. A. Neal and C. L. Tromley, "From Incremental Change to Retrofit: Creating High-Performance Work Systems," *Academy of Management Executive* 9 (1995), pp. 42–54.

158. K. A. Miller, *Retraining the American Workforce* (Reading, MA: Addison-Wesley, 1989).

159. M. A. Huselid, "The Impact of Human Resource Management Practices on Turnover, Productivity, and Corporate Financial Performance," *Academy of Management Journal* 38 (1995), pp. 635–72; U.S. Dept. of Labor, *High-Performance Work Practices and Firm Performance* (Washington, DC: U.S. Government Printing Office, 1993); J. Combs, Y. Liu, A. Hall, and D. Ketchen, "How Much Do High-Performance Work Practices Matter? A Meta-Analysis of Their Effects on Organizational Performance," *Personnel Psychology* 59 (2006), pp. 501–28.

160. B. Becker and M. A. Huselid, "High-Performance Work Systems and Firm Performance: A Synthesis of Research and Managerial Implications," in *Research in Personnel and Human Resource Management* 16, ed. G. R. Ferris (Stamford, CT: JAI Press, 1998), pp. 53–101; A. Zacharatos, J. Barling, and R. Iverson,

"High Performance Work Systems and Occupational Safety," *Journal of Applied Psychology* 90 (2005), pp. 77–93.

161. B. Becker and B. Gerhart, "The Impact of Human Resource Management on Organizational Performance: Progress and Prospects," *Academy of Management Journal* 39 (1996), pp. 779–801.

162. Company website, www.hindlepowerinc.com, accessed February 6, 2019; P. Fehrenbach, "HindlePower's Pro Shop: Greatness Within," *Industry Week*, June 3, 2014; ProQuest eLibrary, http://elibrary.bigchalk.com; J. Juski, "The Value of Labor," *Industry Week*, November 2013, pp. 24–26; A. Wlazelek, "HindlePower Inc.: Manufacturing without a Time Clock," *Morning Call* (Lehigh Valley, PA), March 4, 2013, http://articles.mcall.com.

163. B. Reynolds, "Twenty-Six Companies That Thrive on Remote Work," *Flex Jobs*, www.flexjobs.com, accessed February 5, 2019; company website, www.artandlogic.com, accessed February 5, 2019; "Working at Art & Logic," www.artandlogic.com/careers, accessed February 5, 2019.

164. M. J. Kavanaugh, H. G. Guetal, and S. I. Tannenbaum, *Human Resource Information Systems: Development and Application* (Boston: PWS-Kent, 1990).

165. A. Abbatiello, "The Digital Override," *Workforce*, May 2014, pp. 36–39.

166. D. Zielinski, "The Mobilization of HR Tech," *HR Magazine*, February 2014, pp. 30–36.

167. A. McAfee, "What Every CEO Needs to Know about the Cloud," *Harvard Business Review*, November 2011, pp. 124–132; B. Roberts, "The Grand Convergence," *HR Magazine*, October 2011, pp. 39–46; M. Paino, "All Generations Learn in the Cloud," *Chief Learning Officer*, September 28, 2011, http://blog.clomedia.com, accessed October 11, 2011.

168. "HR Heads to the Cloud," *Human Resource Executive,* September 2016, p. 16.

169. M. Charney, "Five Reasons Why Cloud Computing Matters for Recruitment and Hiring," *Monster.com*, http://hiring.monster.com, accessed May 17, 2015; D. Shane, "A Human Giant," *Information Age*, accessed May 17, 2015, http://www.information-age.com.

170. L. Weatherly, "HR Technology: Leveraging the Shift to Self-Service," *HR Magazine*, March 2005.

171. N. Lockwood, *Maximizing Human Capital: Demonstrating HR Value with Key Performance Indicators* (Alexandria, VA: SHRM Research Quarterly, 2006).

172. S. A. Snell and J. W. Dean, "Integrated Manufacturing and Human Resource Management: A Human Capital Perspective," *Academy of Management Journal* 35 (1992), pp. 467–504; M. A. Youndt, S. Snell, J. W. Dean Jr., and D. P. Lepak, "Human Resource Management, Manufacturing Strategy, and Firm Performance," *Academy of Management Journal* 39 (1996), pp. 836–66.

CHAPTER

# 2 Strategic Human Resource Management

## ⌐ LEARNING OBJECTIVES ¬

*After reading this chapter, you should be able to:*

**LO 2-1**  Describe the differences between strategy formulation and strategy implementation. *page 76*

**LO 2-2**  List the components of the strategic management process. *page 77*

**LO 2-3**  Discuss the role of the HRM function in strategy formulation. *page 79*

**LO 2-4**  Describe the linkages between HRM and strategy formulation. *page 80*

**LO 2-5**  Discuss the more popular typologies of generic strategies and the various HRM practices associated with each. *page 86*

**LO 2-6**  Describe the different HRM issues and practices associated with various directional strategies. *page 97*

# ENTER THE WORLD OF BUSINESS

## GE: The Fall of an Iconic Company

General Electric (GE), the company founded by Thomas Edison and which former CEO Jack Welch turned into one of the world's most admired companies, seemingly possessed an inability to fail . . . until it did. Previously one of the most financially successful companies, GE's stock price went from just under $33 in 2016 to less than $9 at the beginning of 2019. In addition, the company once known for its strong dividend payouts to shareholders reduced its dividend to 1 cent. Finally, the company once known for being a leadership factory that produced CEOs for companies like Home Depot, 3M, and Boeing, ended up firing internally promoted CEO John Flannery after 14 months and brought in outsider Larry Culp.

What caused this fall? Poor strategic and financial decisions. Strategically, GE had long been powered by GE capital, what could at one time have been considered the nation's seventh largest bank, lending to a vast variety of businesses and providing a revenue and profit stream that could cover losses in other areas of the conglomerate. However, in an effort to get out of the regulatory constraints following the financial collapse in 2009, CEO Jeff Immelt sought to sell GE capital, partly to fund acquiring French industrial conglomerate Alstom SA. Additionally, when GE spun off its insurance business as Genworth Financial, it agreed to cover any losses stemming from its long-term-care insurance, that is, expenses like assisted living and nursing homes. However, these losses quickly mounted to between $3 and $6 billion. Finally, the acquisition of Alstom was a

Jonathan Weiss/Shutterstock

means to create scale within the power business, but the result was that GE's power business grew just at a time when the industry was shrinking.

It seems that at the core of this was a culture within GE that led few to question or push back on strategic decisions. While after the fact it became clear that many within GE disagreed with these decisions, the culture had become described as "Success Theatre" that rewarded those that did not rock the boat and applauded the CEO's decisions. However, these poor decisions led to trouble, and as the company cut costs and sold businesses, talent began to flee for more stable companies. The story of GE provides a platform for discussing strategic human resource management, and, in particular, how firms need to create alignment between strategy, culture, and people.

SOURCE: Gryta, T. and Mann, T. (Dec 14, 2018), "GE Powered the American Century—Then It Burned Out," https://www.wsj.com/articles/ge-powered-the-american-centurythen-it-burned-out-11544796010, accessed December 14, 2018.

# Introduction

As the GE example illustrates, business organizations exist in an environment of competition. They can use a number of resources to compete with other companies. These resources are physical (such as plant, equipment, technology, and geographic location), organizational (the structure; planning, controlling, and coordinating systems; and group relations), and human (the experience, skill, and intelligence of employees). It is these resources under the control of the company that provide competitive advantage.[1]

The goal of strategic management in an organization is to deploy and allocate resources in a way that gives it a competitive advantage. As you can see, two of the three classes of resources (organizational and human) are directly tied to the human resource management function. As Chapter 1 pointed out, the role of human resource management is to ensure that a company's human resources provide a competitive advantage. Chapter 1 also pointed out some of the major competitive challenges that companies face today. These challenges require companies to take a proactive, strategic approach in the marketplace.

To be maximally effective, the HRM function must be integrally involved in the company's strategic management process.[2] This means that human resource managers should (1) have input into the strategic plan, both in terms of people-related issues and in terms of the ability of the human resource pool to implement particular strategic alternatives; (2) have specific knowledge of the organization's strategic goals; (3) know what types of employee skills, behaviors, and attitudes are needed to support the strategic plan; and (4) develop programs to ensure that employees have those skills, behaviors, and attitudes.

We begin this chapter by discussing the concepts of business models and strategy and by depicting the strategic management process. Then, we discuss the levels of integration between the HRM function and the strategic management process in strategy formulation. Next, we explore the role of culture and talent as critical levers in the strategy implementation process. Then we review some of the more common strategic models and, within the context of these models, discuss the various types of employee skills, behaviors, and attitudes, and the ways HRM practices aid in implementing the strategic plan. Finally, we discuss the role of HR in creating competitive advantage.

Visit your instructor's Connect® course and access your eBook to view this video.

"As an HR professional, you have to be able to understand how the HR initiatives impact the business."
—Tim Hourigan,
Executive Vice President, Human Resources, The Home Depot

Source: Video produced for the Center for Executive Succession in the Darla Moore School of Business at the University of South Carolina by Coal Powered Filmworks

# What Is a Business Model?

A business model is a story of how the firm will create value for customers and, more important, how it will do so profitably. We often hear or read of companies that have "transformed their business model" in one way or another, but what that means is not always clear. To understand this, we need to grasp a few basic accounting concepts.

First, fixed costs are generally considered the costs that are incurred regardless of the number of units produced. For instance, if you are producing widgets in a factory, you have the rent you pay for the factory, depreciation of the machines, the utilities, the property taxes, and so on. In addition, you generally have a set number of employees who work a set number of hours with a specified level of benefits, and although you might be able to vary these over time, on a regular basis you pay the same total labor costs whether your factory runs at 70% capacity or 95% capacity.

Second, you have a number of variable costs, which are those costs that vary directly with the units produced. For instance, all of the materials that go into the widget might cost a total of $10, which means that you have to charge at least $10 per widget, or you cannot even cover the variable costs of production.

Third is the concept of "contribution margins," or margins. Margins are the difference between what you charge for your product and the variable costs of that product. They are called contribution margins because they are what contributes to your ability to cover your fixed costs. So, for instance, if you charged $15 for each widget, your contribution margin would be $5 ($15 price – $10 variable cost).

Fourth, the gross margin is the total amount of margin you made and is calculated as the number of units sold times the contribution margin. If you sold 1,000,000 units, your gross margin would then be $5,000,000. Did you make a profit? That depends. Profit refers to what is left after you have paid your variable costs and your fixed costs. If your gross margin was $5,000,000, and your fixed costs were $6,000,000, then you lost $1,000,000.

## GM'S ATTEMPT TO SURVIVE

Let's look at how a business model plays out with the recent challenges faced by General Motors (GM). Critics of GM talk about the fact that GM has higher labor costs than its foreign competitors. This is true, but misleading. GM's average hourly wage for its existing workforce is reasonably competitive. However, the two aspects that make GM uncompetitive are its benefit costs (in particular, health care) and, most important, the cost of its legacy workforce.

A legacy workforce describes the former workers (i.e., those no longer working for the company) to whom the firm still owes financial obligations. GM and the United Automobile Workers (UAW) union have negotiated contracts over the years that provide substantial retirement benefits for former GM workers. In particular, retired GM workers have defined benefit plans that guarantee a certain percentage of their final (preretirement) salary as a pension payment as long as they live; in addition, the company pays for their health insurance. The contract specifies that workers are entitled to retire at full pension after 30 years of service.

This might have seemed sustainable when the projections were that GM would continue growing its sales and margins. However, since the 1970s, foreign competitors have been eating away at GM's market share to the extent that GM's former 50% of the market has shrunk to closer to 20%. Since the 2008 economic crisis, the market itself has been shrinking, leaving GM with a decreasing percentage of a decreasing market. For instance, in December of 2005, GM sold 26% of the cars in the global market, but by 2015 that market share had shrunk to 11.2%.[3] Thus, in addition to the legacy workforce, GM had a significant number of plants with thousands of employees that were completely unnecessary, given the volume of cars GM can produce and sell.[4]

If you look at Figure 2.1, you'll see that the solid lines represent the old GM business model, which was based on projections that GM would be able to sell 4 million units at a reasonably high margin, and thus completely cover its fixed costs to make a strong profit. However, the reality was that its products didn't sell at the higher prices, so to try to sell 4 million vehicles, GM offered discounts, which cut into its margins. When GM ended up selling only 3.5 million vehicles, and those were sold at a lower margin, the company could not cover its fixed costs, resulting in a $9 billion loss in 2008 (this is illustrated by the dotted blue line in the figure). So, when GM refers to the "redesigned business model," what it is referring to is a significant reduction in fixed costs (through closing plants and cutting workers) to get the fixed-cost base low enough (the dotted brown line) to remain profitable while selling fewer cars at lower margins (again, the dotted blue line).

**Figure 2.1**

An Illustration of a Business Model for GM

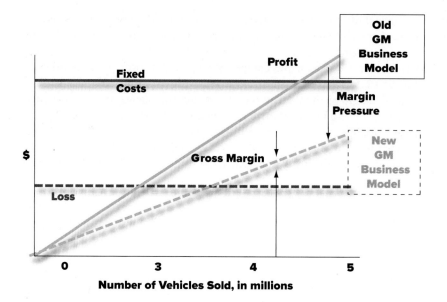

One can easily see how, given the large component that labor costs are to most companies, reference to business models almost inevitably leads to discussions of labor costs. These can be the high cost associated with current unionized employees in developed countries within North America or Europe or, in some cases, the high costs associated with a legacy workforce. For instance, the Big Three automakers have huge numbers of retired or laid-off workers for whom they still have the liability of paying pensions and health care benefits. This is a significant component of their fixed-cost base, which makes it difficult for them to compete with other automakers that either have fewer retirees to cover or have no comparable costs because their home governments provide pensions and health care. In fact, this changing business model at GM has driven it to locate more manufacturing outside of the United States.

# What Is Strategic Management?

**LO 2-1**

Describe the differences between strategy formulation and strategy implementation.

Many authors have noted that in today's competitive market, organizations must engage in strategic planning to survive and prosper. Strategy comes from the Greek word *strategos,* which has its roots in military language. It refers to a general's grand design behind a war or battle. In fact, *Webster's New American Dictionary* defines *strategy* as the "skillful employment and coordination of tactics" and as "artful planning and management."

Strategic management is a process, an approach to addressing the competitive challenges an organization faces. It can be thought of as managing the "pattern or plan that integrates an organization's major goals, policies, and action sequences into a cohesive whole."[5] These strategies can be either the generic approach to competing or the specific adjustments and actions taken to deal with a particular situation.

First, business organizations engage in generic strategies that often fit into some strategic type. One example is "cost, differentiation, or focus."[6] Another is "defender, analyzer, prospector, or reactor."[7] Different organizations within the same industry often have different generic strategies. These generic strategy types describe the consistent way the company attempts to position itself relative to competitors.

However, a generic strategy is only a small part of strategic management. The second aspect of strategic management is the process of developing strategies for achieving the company's goals in light of its current environment. Thus, business organizations engage in generic strategies, but they also make choices about such things as how to scare off competitors, how to keep competitors weaker, how to react to and influence pending legislation, how to deal with various stakeholders and special interest groups, how to lower production costs, how to raise revenues, what technology to implement, and how many and what types of people to employ. Each of these decisions may present competitive challenges that have to be considered.

Strategic management is more than a collection of strategic types. It is a process for analyzing a company's competitive situation, developing the company's strategic goals, and devising a plan of action and allocation of resources (human, organizational, and physical) that will increase the likelihood of achieving those goals. This kind of strategic approach should be emphasized in human resource management. HR managers should be trained to identify the competitive issues the company faces with regard to human resources and think strategically about how to respond.

**Strategic human resource management (SHRM)** can be thought of as "the pattern of planned human resource deployments and activities intended to enable an organization to achieve its goals."[8] For example, many firms have developed integrated manufacturing systems such as advanced manufacturing technology, just-in-time inventory control, and total quality management in an effort to increase their competitive position. However, these systems must be run by people. SHRM in these cases entails assessing the employee skills required to run these systems and engaging in HRM practices, such as selection and training, that develop these skills in employees.[9] To take a strategic approach to HRM, we must first understand the role of HRM in the strategic management process.

**Strategic human resource management (SHRM)**
A pattern of planned human resource deployments and activities intended to enable an organization to achieve its goals.

## COMPONENTS OF THE STRATEGIC MANAGEMENT PROCESS

The strategic management process has two distinct yet interdependent phases: strategy formulation and strategy implementation. During **strategy formulation**, the strategic planning groups decide on a strategic direction by defining the company's mission and goals, its external opportunities and threats, and its internal strengths and weaknesses. They then generate various strategic alternatives and compare those alternatives' ability to achieve the company's mission and goals. During **strategy implementation**, the organization follows through on the chosen strategy. This consists of structuring the organization, allocating resources, ensuring that the firm has skilled employees in place, and developing reward systems that align employee behavior with the organization's strategic goals. Both of these strategic management phases must be performed effectively. This process does not happen sequentially. As we will discuss later with regard to emergent strategies, this process entails a constant cycling of information and decision making. Figure 2.2 presents the strategic management process.

In recent years organizations have recognized that the success of the strategic management process depends largely on the extent to which the HRM function is involved.[10]

**LO 2-2**
List the components of the strategic management process.

**Strategy formulation**
The process of deciding on a strategic direction by defining a company's mission and goals, its external opportunities and threats, and its internal strengths and weaknesses.

## LINKAGE BETWEEN HRM AND THE STRATEGIC MANAGEMENT PROCESS

The strategic choice really consists of answering questions about competition—that is, how the firm will compete to achieve its mission and goals. These decisions consist of

**Strategy implementation**
The process of devising structures and allocating resources to enact the strategy a company has chosen.

Figure 2.2
A Model of the Strategic Management Process

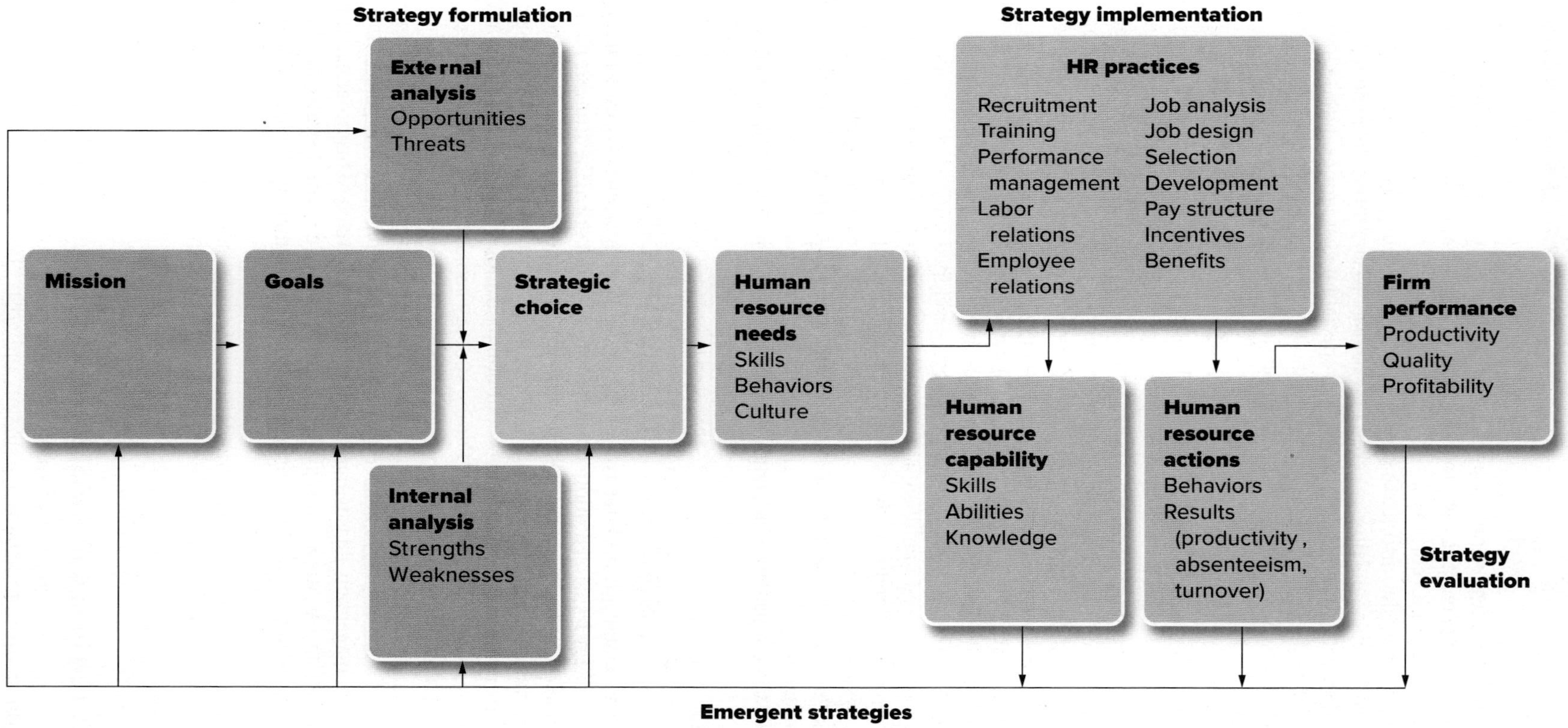

**Strategy formulation**

**Mission**

**Goals**

**External analysis**
Opportunities
Threats

**Internal analysis**
Strengths
Weaknesses

**Strategic choice**

**Human resource needs**
Skills
Behaviors
Culture

**Strategy implementation**

**HR practices**

Recruitment
Training
Performance management
Labor relations
Employee relations

Job analysis
Job design
Selection
Development
Pay structure
Incentives
Benefits

**Human resource capability**
Skills
Abilities
Knowledge

**Human resource actions**
Behaviors
Results (productivity, absenteeism, turnover)

**Firm performance**
Productivity
Quality
Profitability

**Strategy evaluation**

**Emergent strategies**

**Figure 2.3**
Strategy—Decisions
about Competition

1. Where to compete?
    In what market or markets (industries, products, etc.) will we compete?
2. How to compete?
    On what criterion or differentiating characteristic(s) will we compete? Cost?
    Quality? Reliability? Delivery?
3. With what will we compete?
    What resources will allow us to beat our competition?
    How will we acquire, develop, and deploy those resources to compete?

addressing the issues of where to compete, how to compete, and with what to compete, which are described in Figure 2.3.

Although these decisions are all important, strategic decision makers often pay less attention to the "with what will we compete" issue, resulting in poor strategic decisions. For example, PepsiCo in the 1980s acquired the fast-food chains of Kentucky Fried Chicken, Taco Bell, and Pizza Hut ("where to compete" decisions) in an effort to increase its customer base. However, it failed to adequately recognize the differences between its existing workforce (mostly professionals) and that of the fast-food industry (lower-skilled people and high schoolers) as well as its ability to manage such a workforce. This was one reason that PepsiCo, in 1998, spun off the fast-food chains. In essence, it had made a decision about where to compete without fully understanding what resources would be needed to compete in that market.

Boeing illustrates how failing to address the "with what" issue resulted in problems in its "how to compete" decisions. When the aerospace firm's consumer products division entered into a price war with Airbus Industrie, it was forced to move away from its traditional customer service strategy toward emphasizing cost reduction.[11] The strategy was a success on the sales end as Boeing received large numbers of orders for aircraft from firms such as Delta, Continental, Southwest, and Singapore Airlines. However, it had recently gone through a large workforce reduction (thus, it didn't have enough people to fill the orders) and did not have the production technology to enable the necessary increase in productivity. The result of this failure to address "with what will we compete" in making a decision about how to compete resulted in the firm's inability to meet delivery deadlines and the ensuing penalties it had to pay to its customers. The end result is that after all the travails, for the first time in the history of the industry, Airbus sold more planes than Boeing in 2003. Luckily, Boeing was able to overcome this stumble, in large part because of a number of stumbles on the part of its chief rival, Airbus. However, Boeing has faced difficulties as its new Dreamliner was grounded because of fires starting in the wiring.

## ROLE OF HRM IN STRATEGY FORMULATION

As the preceding examples illustrate, often the "with what will we compete" question presents ideal avenues for HRM to influence the strategic management process. This might be through either limiting strategic options or forcing thoughtfulness among the executive team regarding how and at what cost the firm might gain or develop the human resources (people) necessary for such a strategy to be successful. For example, HRM executives at PepsiCo could have noted that the firm had no expertise in managing the workforce of fast-food restaurants. The limiting role would have been for these

**LO 2-3**
Discuss the role of the HRM function in strategy formulation.

**Figure 2.4**

Linkages of Strategic Planning and HRM

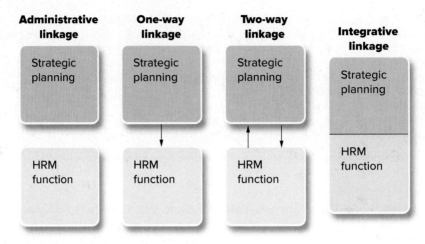

SOURCE: Adapted from K. Golden and V. Ramanujam, "Between a Dream and a Nightmare: On the Integration of the Human Resource Function and the Strategic Business Planning Process," *Human Resource Management* 24 (1985), pp. 429–51.

executives to argue against the acquisition because of this lack of resources. Alternatively, they might have influenced the decision by educating top executives as to the costs (of hiring, training, and so on) associated with gaining people who had the right skills to manage such a workforce.

A firm's strategic management decision-making process usually takes place at its top levels, with a strategic planning group consisting of the chief executive officer, the chief financial officer, the president, and various vice presidents. However, each component of the process involves people-related business issues. Therefore, the HRM function needs to be involved in each of those components. One recent study of 115 strategic business units within *Fortune* 500 corporations found that 49 to 69% of the companies had some link between HRM and the strategic planning process.[12] However, the level of linkage varied, and it is important to understand these different levels.

Four levels of integration seem to exist between the HRM function and the strategic management function: administrative linkage, one-way linkage, two-way linkage, and integrative linkage.[13] These levels of linkage will be discussed in relation to the different components of strategic management. The linkages are illustrated in Figure 2.4.

### Administrative Linkage

**LO 2-4**

Describe the linkages between HRM and strategy formulation.

In administrative linkage (the lowest level of integration), the HRM function's attention is focused on day-to-day activities. The HRM executive has no time or opportunity to take a strategic outlook toward HRM issues. The company's strategic business planning function exists without any input from the HRM department. Thus, in this level of integration, the HRM department is completely divorced from any component of the strategic management process in both strategy formulation and strategy implementation. The department simply engages in administrative work unrelated to the company's core business needs.

### One-Way Linkage

In one-way linkage, the firm's strategic business planning function develops the strategic plan and then informs the HRM function of the plan. Early in the history of SHRM, people believed this level of integration constituted strategic HRM—that is, the role of the

HRM function is to design systems and/or programs that implement the strategic plan. Although one-way linkage does recognize the importance of human resources in implementing the strategic plan, it precludes the company from considering human resource issues while formulating the strategic plan. This level of integration often leads to strategic plans that the company cannot successfully implement.

### Two-Way Linkage

Two-way linkage allows for consideration of human resource issues during the strategy formulation process. This integration occurs in three sequential steps. First, the strategic planning team informs the HRM function of the various strategies the company is considering. Then HRM executives analyze the human resource implications of the various strategies, presenting the results of this analysis to the strategic planning team. Finally, after the strategic decision has been made, the strategic plan is passed on to the HRM executive, who develops programs to implement it. The strategic planning function and the HRM function are interdependent in two-way linkage.

### Integrative Linkage

Integrative linkage is dynamic and multifaceted, based on continuing rather than sequential interaction. In most cases the HRM executive is an integral member of the senior management team. Rather than using an iterative process of information exchange, companies with integrative linkage have their HRM functions built in to the strategy formulation and implementation processes. It is this role that we will discuss throughout the rest of this chapter.

Thus, in strategic HRM, the HRM function is involved in both strategy formulation and strategy implementation. The HRM executive gives strategic planners information about the company's human resource capabilities, and these capabilities are usually a direct function of the HRM practices.[14] This information about human resource capabilities helps top managers choose the best strategy because they can consider how well each strategic alternative would be implemented. Once the strategic choice has been determined, the role of HRM changes to the development and alignment of HRM practices that will give the company employees having the necessary skills to implement the strategy.[15] In addition, HRM practices must be designed to elicit actions from employees in the company.[16] One recent study found that strategic HR functions were positively related to firm performance, but only when those firms had structures and systems in place to leverage the input of their employees.[17] In the next two sections of this chapter, we show how HRM can provide a competitive advantage in the strategic management process.

# Strategy Formulation

Five major components of the strategic management process are relevant to strategy formulation.[18] These components are depicted in Figure 2.5. The first component is the organization's mission. The mission is a statement of the organization's reason for being; it usually specifies the customers served, the needs satisfied and/or the values received by the customers, and the technology used. The mission statement is often accompanied by a statement of a company's vision and/or values. For example, Table 2.1 illustrates the mission and values of Merck & Co., Inc.

An organization's **goals** are what it hopes to achieve in the medium- to long-term future; they reflect how the mission will be operationalized. The overarching goal of

**Goals**
What an organization hopes to achieve in the medium- to long-term future.

**Figure 2.5**
Strategy Formulation

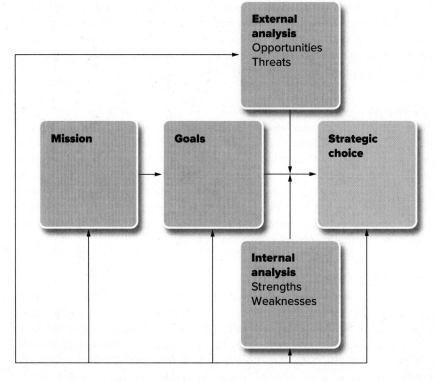

SOURCE: Adapted from K. Golden and V. Ramanujam, "Between a Dream and a Nightmare," *Human Resource Management* 24 (1985), pp. 429–51.

**Table 2.1**
Merck & Co.'s
Mission and Values

| MISSION STATEMENT |
| --- |
| To discover, develop and provide innovative products and services that save and improve lives around the world. |
| **Values:** |
| **Improving Life** |
| We embrace our quest to tackle health challenges because we are inspired by the differences we can make in the lives of people around the world. |
| **Ethics and Integrity** |
| We are committed to the highest standards of ethics and integrity. |
| We are responsible to our customers, to Merck employees, to the environments we inhabit, and to the societies we serve worldwide. |
| **Innovation** |
| We are dedicated to the highest level of scientific excellence. |
| We strive to identify the most critical needs of consumers and customers, and through continuous innovation we challenge ourselves to meet those needs. |
| **Access to Health** |
| We aspire to improve the health and wellness of people around the world by expanding access to our medicines and vaccines. |
| **Diversity and Teamwork** |
| Our ability to excel depends on the integrity, knowledge, imagination, skill, diversity and teamwork of our employees. |

SOURCE: Courtesy of Merck.

## The Potential for Corporate/Government Espionage?

Huawei Technologies is part of a large Chinese corporation with a huge presence in the telecommunications industry. While the company has displayed tremendous business success within the industry, non-Chinese governments have begun to question whether or not the company is truly just a Chinese multinational, or if it is being used by the Chinese government for more suspicious purposes.

This was only exacerbated recently when Polish authorities charged a Huawei employee and a former Polish security official with espionage. The former security official had top secret clearances, giving him access to extremely sensitive information. For instance, he had access to communications with Poland's allies such as the United States and NATO. Huawei immediately fired the employee saying that his actions were entirely unrelated to his employment with the company.

This comes on the heels of a number of countries, such as the United States, seeking to preclude Huawei from gaining contracts to build out 5G technologies. These countries fear that the 5G networks could allow the Chinese government to gain access to communications and essentially spy on Americans. In addition, the founder's daughter, Meng Wanzhou, was recently detained in Vancouver to potentially be extradited to the United States. She is alleged to have helped Huawei defraud banks by finding ways to do business with Iran in spite of U.S. sanctions.

### DISCUSSION QUESTIONS

1. Do you think that Huawei might be working with the Chinese government to engage in some type of espionage? Why or why not?
2. How can multinational companies ensure that they maintain a pure business focus, and not get involved in cross-country governmental issues?

SOURCE: B. Pancevski and N. Ojewska, "Polish Ex-Security Official Charged with Spying for China During Government Service," *Wall Street Journal*, January 15, 2019, from https://www.wsj.com/articles/polish-ex-security-official-charged-with-spying-for-china-during-government-service-11547575221, accessed January 18, 2019; N. Khan, D. Strumpf, and W. Fan, "The Public Face of Huawi's Global Fight," *Wall Street Journal*, January 19, 2019, from https://www.wsj.com/articles/the-public-face-of-huaweis-global-fight-11547874008?mod=hp_lead_pos5, accessed January 19, 2019.

most profit-making companies in the United States is to maximize stockholder wealth. But companies have to set other long-term goals in order to maximize stockholder wealth.

**External analysis** consists of examining the organization's operating environment to identify the strategic opportunities and threats. Examples of opportunities are customer markets that are not being served, technological advances that can aid the company, and labor pools that have not been tapped. Threats include potential labor shortages, new competitors entering the market, pending legislation that might adversely affect the company, and competitors' technological innovations. Currently, most companies use what is known as PESTEL analysis. This entails focusing on the trends likely to impact the firm or the industry in six areas: Political, Economic, Socio-Cultural, Technological, Environmental, and Legal. The Competing through Globalization box describes how the political and legal implications of the fear of corporate espionage are restricting Chinese company Huawei's expansion potential.

**Internal analysis** attempts to identify the organization's strengths and weaknesses. It focuses on the quantity and quality of resources available to the organization—financial, capital, technological, and human resources. Organizations have to honestly and accurately assess each resource to decide whether it is a strength or a weakness. Many companies today examine their strengths and weaknesses through value chain analysis.

**External analysis**
Examining the organization's operating environment to identify strategic opportunities and threats.

**Internal analysis**
The process of examining an organization's strengths and weaknesses.

**Table 2.2**
SWOT Analysis for
Google Inc.

| STRENGTHS | WEAKNESSES |
|---|---|
| Expanding liquidity | Issues with Chinese government |
| Operational efficiency | Dependence on advertising segment |
| Broad range of services portfolio | Losses at YouTube |

| OPPORTUNITIES | THREATS |
|---|---|
| Growing demand for online video | Weak economic outlook |
| Growth in Internet advertising market | Invalid clicks |
| Inorganic growth | Microsoft–Yahoo! deal |

SOURCE: GlobalData.

This entails breaking the firm's entire process from R&D to after-sales service into sets of "capabilities." Then, these capabilities can be examined for which currently or potentially provides a competitive advantage. We will explore this more later in the chapter with regard to identifying talent.

External analysis and internal analysis combined constitute what has come to be called the SWOT (strengths, weaknesses, opportunities, threats) analysis. Table 2.2 shows an example of a SWOT analysis for Google. After going through the SWOT analysis, the strategic planning team has all the information it needs to generate a number of strategic alternatives. The strategic managers compare the ability of each alternative to attain the organization's strategic goals; then they make their **strategic choice**. The strategic choice is the organization's strategy; it describes the ways the organization will attempt to fulfill its mission and achieve its long-term goals.

**Strategic choice**
The organization's strategy; the ways an organization will attempt to fulfill its mission and achieve its long-term goals.

Many of the opportunities and threats in the external environment are people related. With fewer and fewer highly qualified individuals entering the labor market, organizations compete not just for customers but also for employees. It is HRM's role to keep close tabs on the external environment for HR–related opportunities and threats, especially those directly related to the HRM function: potential labor shortages, competitor wage rates, government regulations affecting employment, and so on. For example, as discussed in Chapter 1, U.S. companies are finding that more and more high school graduates lack the basic skills needed to work, which is one source of the "human capital shortage."[19] However, not recognizing this environmental threat, many companies have encouraged the exit of older, more skilled workers while hiring less skilled younger workers who require basic skills training.[20]

In addition, many firms over-reacted to the threat that the nature of work was going to change dramatically with the rise of the gig economy. The Integrity in Action box describes how the economists who originally forecast this have now corrected themselves to suggest that the move toward the gig economy was due to a bad economy, not because people wanted to work that way.

An analysis of a company's internal strengths and weaknesses also requires input from the HRM function. Today companies are increasingly realizing that their human resources are one of their most important assets. A company's failure to consider the strengths and weaknesses of its workforce may result in choosing strategies it is not capable of pursuing.[21] However, some research has demonstrated that few companies have achieved this level of linkage.[22] For example, one company chose a strategy of cost reduction through technological improvements. It built a plant designed around a

# INTEGRITY IN ACTION

## Coming Clean on the Hype Regarding the "Gig" Economy

It's hard to admit you made a mistake, and if you're a well-known academic researcher, it is even harder. But two economists who had foretold the rise in the gig economy recently admitted that their projections were based on bad data.

For the past five-plus years, the field of HR has worried over the rise of the gig economy, that is, the idea that instead of people wanting to work in full-time positions for an organization, they would rather work with a series of "gigs" with multiple employers. Numerous warnings went out about how firms would need to restructure their design of work to manage "gig" rather than full-time employees. A lot of the "sky is falling" rhetoric stemmed from economists Alan Krueger and Lawrence Katz, who developed their own methodology for assessing the U.S. labor market.

Their 2015 survey found a jump of as much as five percentage points in workers in alternative work arrangements.

While they noted that much of this rise was due to Uber, they still expressed warnings about the rise of workers wanting to work in "gig" roles. However, now they noted that their numbers vastly overestimated the phenomenon. "After sifting through the new evidence," Mr. Krueger said, "Larry Katz and I now conclude that there was a modest rise in the share of the workforce in nontraditional jobs over the last decade—probably on the order of one to two percentage points, instead of the five percentage point rise we originally reported."

Because 2015 was a time where economic growth had been stagnant and unemployment rather high, they now recognize that many just viewed this as an opportunity for workers to experiment with gig work. This does not mean that gig work will not be higher in the future than it was in the past, but it does suggest that earlier warnings about this being the future of work may have been overstated.

### DISCUSSION QUESTIONS

1. Do you think that the percentage of workers that want to work "gig" jobs will continue to grow, or do most workers really want to work for a single organization?
2. How important do you think it is for researchers to be willing to admit when they made a mistake? Why?

SOURCE: J. Zumbrun, "How Estimates of the Gig Economy Went Wrong," *Wall Street Journal*, January 8, 2019, from https://www.wsj.com/articles/how-estimates-of-the-gig-economy-went-wrong-11546857000?mod=hp_lead_pos4.

computer-integrated manufacturing system with statistical process controls. Although this choice may seem like a good one, the company soon learned otherwise. It discovered that its employees could not operate the new equipment because 25% of the workforce was functionally illiterate.[23]

Thus, with an integrative linkage, strategic planners consider all the people-related business issues before making a strategic choice. These issues are identified with regard to the mission, goals, strengths, weaknesses, opportunities, and threats, leading the strategic planning team to make a more intelligent strategic choice. Although this process does not guarantee success, companies that address these issues are more likely to make choices that will ultimately succeed.

Recent research has supported the need to have HRM executives integrally involved in strategy formulation. One study of U.S. petrochemical refineries found that the level of HRM involvement was positively related to the refinery manager's evaluation of the effectiveness of the HRM function.[24] A second study of manufacturing firms found that HRM involvement was highest when top managers viewed employees as a strategic asset and associated them with reduced turnover.[25] However, both studies found that HRM involvement was unrelated to operating unit financial performance.

Research has indicated that few companies have fully integrated HRM into the strategy formulation process.[26] As we've mentioned before, companies are beginning to recognize that in an intensely competitive environment, managing human resources strategically can provide a competitive advantage. Thus, companies at the administrative linkage level will either become more integrated or face extinction. In addition, companies will move toward becoming integratively linked in an effort to manage human resources strategically.

It is of utmost importance that all people-related business issues be considered during strategy formulation. These issues are identified in the HRM function. Mechanisms or structures for integrating the HRM function into strategy formulation may help the strategic planning team make the most effective strategic choice. Once that strategic choice is determined, HRM must take an active role in implementing it. This role will be discussed in the next section.

# Strategy Implementation

**LO 2-5**
Discuss the more popular typologies of generic strategies and the various HRM practices associated with each.

After an organization has chosen its strategy, it has to execute that strategy—make it come to life in its day-to-day workings. The strategy a company pursues dictates certain HR needs. For a company to have a good strategy foundation, certain tasks must be accomplished in pursuit of the company's goals, individuals must possess certain skills to perform those tasks, and these individuals must be motivated to perform their skills effectively.

The basic premise behind strategy implementation is that "an organization has a variety of structural forms and organizational processes to choose from when implementing a given strategy," and these choices make an economic difference.[27] Five important variables determine success in strategy implementation: organizational structure; task design; the selection, training, and development of people; reward systems; and types of information and information systems.

As we see in Figure 2.6, HRM has primary responsibility for three of these five implementation variables: task, people, and reward systems. In addition, HRM can directly affect the two remaining variables: structure and information and decision processes. First, for the strategy to be successfully implemented, the tasks must be designed and grouped into jobs in a way that is efficient and effective.[28] In Chapter 4 we will examine

**Figure 2.6**
Variables to Be Considered in Strategy Implementation

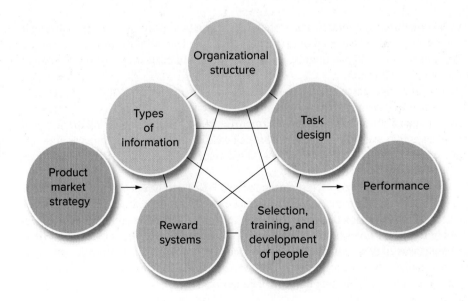

how this can be done through the processes of job analysis and job design. Second, the HRM function must ensure that the organization is staffed with people who have the necessary knowledge, skill, and ability to perform their part in implementing the strategy. This goal is achieved primarily through recruitment, selection and placement, training, development, and career management—topics covered in Chapters 5, 6, 7, and 9. In addition, the HRM function must develop performance management and reward systems that lead employees to work for and support the strategic plan. The specific types of performance management systems are covered in Chapter 8, and the many issues involved in developing reward systems are discussed in Chapters 11, 12, and 13. In other words, the role of the HRM function becomes one of (1) ensuring that the company has the proper number of employees with the levels and types of skills required by the strategic plan[29] and (2) developing "control" systems that ensure that those employees are acting in ways that promote the achievement of the goals specified in the strategic plan.[30]

As we explore how firms implement their strategies, we need to address two of the major components: culture and talent.

## ORGANIZATIONAL CULTURE

Organizational culture can be defined as ". . . a complex set of values, beliefs, assumptions, and symbols that define the way in which a firm conducts its business."[31] Thus culture helps to define its relevant stakeholders (employees, customers, suppliers, and competitors) and how it interacts with them. You experience organizational culture whenever you go shopping at a store, have dinner at a restaurant, or stay in a hotel. The interactions you have with the employees in these settings reflect the values and beliefs regarding how the organizations wants to deal with you, the customer. Recent scandals such as creating fake customer accounts at Wells Fargo or sex-based discrimination at Uber have considerably damaged those firms' reputations, driving increased focus on culture for both CEOs and boards. Culture has moved up to becoming the number 3–ranked deliverable demanded by CEOs according to a recent survey of chief HR officers.[32] In addition, the National Academy of Corporate Directors recently developed a report for board members. These scandals, while representing the consequences of a dysfunctional culture, do not adequately represent the full potential for culture to help drive organizational success.

Earlier we noted that one of the key questions in strategy is "how we compete" in terms of the value that we offer to customers. Because culture helps define how the firm interacts with customers, when cultural values align with the customer value, the firm has a better chance of actually delivering that customer value.[33] If a firm such as Marriott tries to differentiate itself through customer service, it will do so much more effectively if service represents one of the most important and well-defined cultural values.

In addition, "with what do we compete" represents another strategic question focused on the people, technologies, and processes that create the capability to deliver that value to customers. Culture serves as the conduit to help attract and retain the right people for these capabilities, as well as guide their behavior to help maximally deliver the customer value.

Leading HR Guru Dave Ulrich argues that effective cultures are the ones where the values internally relate directly to the value that customers seek from that company.[34] For example, he notes a negative *New York Times* story about Amazon's practices (some of which, if true, are unethical), and the demanding, rigorous, and driven culture. He then asks why people buy from Amazon, and they cite the low cost, predictable short time frame for delivery, and ease of working with them. Making his point, he asks his audience what type of culture Amazon needs to provide those valued outcomes to their customers. Obviously Amazon needs a needs a culture of discipline, standardization, and rigor and precision in order to meet the expectations customers have that cause them to want to buy from Amazon rather than somewhere else.

So, in order for firms to be maximally effective and efficient, both their strategy and their culture need to be aligned with regard to the value that they will provide to customers.

## TALENT

Before going too far, it is important to define what we mean by talent. *Talent* is a term thrown around quite a bit, but one that illustrates the problem of people using the same vocabulary, but different dictionaries. For instance, some firms view talent as the current and future leaders in the company. Others view talent widely as anyone who can have a positive impact on the firm's performance. Finally, some firms view talent as those individuals who can have a disproportionate (either positive or negative) impact on the firm. While all of these definitions are valid, we are going to emphasize the latter one as a means of providing a clearer approach to how a strategic approach to HR can be implemented.

Early on in the field of strategic HRM, many authors sought to develop typologies for what kinds of HR practices might be associated with different strategies. However, more recent attempts to link HR to strategy have focused on integrating the strategy, capabilities, and people through an understanding the value chain of an organization. This entails identifying where a firm seeks to create the greatest value, and the talent necessary to do so. Remember that earlier in this chapter we referred to the major strategic questions as being "Where do we compete?" "How do we compete?" and "With what do we compete?" Linking talent and strategy entails focusing on integrating the "how" and "with what" questions.

The value chain is a model that breaks up all of the different parts of the organization into a variety of capabilities such as research and development (R&D), supply chain, manufacturing, distribution, and service (as shown in Figure 2.7). The first step for decision makers is to determine where in the value chain they seek to create the most value for customers. Remember earlier in the chapter when we referred to the question of "How do we compete?" in terms of what differentiates our product or service in a way that makes customers want to buy from us, rather than our competitors. To link that discussion to this one, if a firm seeks to provide value through innovation, then that means that firm must be world class in its R&D capability. If the firm seeks to be the lowest cost, then it might need to be world class in either its supply chain or manufacturing capabilities. Again, this links the "how" question to the "with what do we compete" question by understanding the

**Figure 2.7**

Supply Chain, Manufacturing, Distribution, and Service

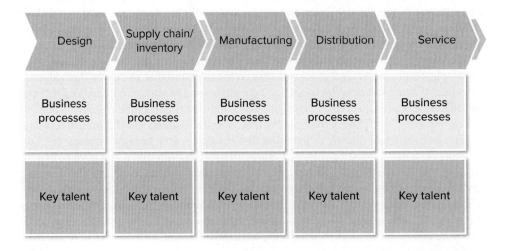

## COMPETING THROUGH TECHNOLOGY

### Technology Forces Honda to "Buy" Capabilities

Honda has distinguished itself as one of the most successful global automobile companies. Much of its success stems from having built a reputation for applying its core competence, engineering capability in building engines, across a variety of industries including motorcycles, lawn mowers, and recreational vehicles. Since its founding in the 1960s, the company has prided itself on designing almost all of the technologies that go into a Honda product, and this has become part of the Honda culture. In fact, founder Sochiro Honda was once quoted as saying, "We refuse to depend on anyone else."

However, change is in the works. With the rapid expansion of a variety of technologies such as sensing systems and electric engines, all automakers struggle to keep up with the potential technologies that can make cars safer and more efficient. Honda simply does not have the size to continue to try to create everything in-house. They now purchase an off-the-shelf driving sensing system from Robert Bosch GmbH. Most surprising given their historic competence in engines, they currently partner with Hitachi Ltd. on the development of an electric motor in a joint venture where the latter has the majority stake.

Yuji Yasui, chief engineer for autonomous vehicles, describes the current mindset at Honda as,

"Car makers focus on developing some things, suppliers on others. We haven't changed. What changed is that it is inefficient for Honda to do everything ourselves."

#### DISCUSSION QUESTION

1. Why do companies have to rely on other companies for technologies that might be central to their product? How would they make the decision as to building something in-house versus buying it from others?

SOURCE: S. McLain, "Honda Took Pride in Doing Everything Itself: The Cost of Technology Made That Impossible," *Wall Street Journal*, August 5, 2018, from https://www.wsj.com/articles/honda-took-pride-in-doing-everything-itself-the-cost-of-technology-made-that-impossible-1533484840.

capabilities necessary to provide the strategic value to customers. For instance, most readers of this book would love to own a Tesla. Elon Musk's company has been able to design beautiful electric automobiles. However, it has not been able to make money because it currently does not possess sufficient capability to actually manufacture the cars. In fact, some are beginning to suggest that, like Apple, Tesla would be better off outsourcing the manufacturing of the cars to a company better at manufacturing, and let Tesla focus on innovating in the technological design.[35] The Competing through Technology box describes how Honda has had to buy capabilities from other companies because it simply could not build them internally in a way that would allow them to compete.

Next, because capabilities are made up of the combination of people, systems, and processes, firms need to identify which key talent pools (jobs or job families) must be world class in order to build or maintain that capability. Note that while all employees are inherently valuable and their performance is necessary for the firm to succeed, certain employees provide more strategic value. The former need to be good, but the latter need to be among the best. Lucien Alziari, the chief HR officer at Prudential refers to this as knowing which employee groups need to be world class versus those for which "good is good enough." For instance, if a firm seeks to build innovation capability, then it needs the best R&D scientists or the best software developers working within great business processes and equipped with the best technological systems. While its manufacturing group needs to be good, because that capability does not differentiate the firm, for them good talent is good enough. Thus, companies like Apple seek to hire great software developers to create the operating systems that are easy for customers to use, but as noted above, they outsource their manufacturing to other firms.

**Figure 2.8**

Best of All Worlds Is
When the Strategy,
Culture, and Talent
Are Completely
Aligned around
Customer Value

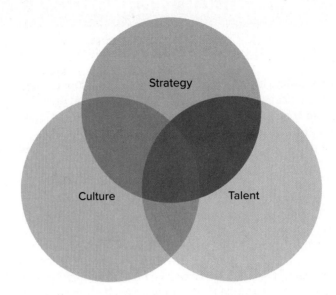

This approach treats "talent" as being those that comprise the key groups of employees that are critical to driving value in the part of the value chain that is responsible for driving value to the customer. Again, keep in mind, one of the key strategic questions revolves around choosing what value the firm will offer to customers that will make customers want to buy from them. As we saw in the previous section, one key aspect of culture has to be ensuring that the cultural values align with the value offered to customers. Finally, we think about talent by defining the groups most important to the capabilities from which the value to customers is generated. Thus, the best of all worlds is when the strategy, culture, and talent are completely aligned around customer value, as illustrated in Figure 2.8.

In essence, this is what has been referred to as the "vertical alignment" of HR with strategy. Vertical alignment means that the HR practices and processes are aimed at addressing the strategic needs of the business. But the link between strategy and HR practices is primarily through people. This means strategically managing the "talent" as previously described, but also managing the larger workforce to be aligned around how the company seeks to create value for customers. For instance, as IBM moved from being a manufacturer of personal computers to being a fully integrated service provider, the types of people it needed changed significantly. Instead of employing thousands of workers in manufacturing or assembly plants, IBM increasingly needed software engineers to help write new "middleware" programs, and an army of consultants who could help their corporate customers to implement these systems. In addition, as IBM increasingly differentiated itself as being the "integrated solutions" provider (meaning it could sell the hardware, software, consulting, and service for a company's entire information technology needs), employees needed a new mindset that emphasized cooperating across different business divisions rather than running independently. IBM's more recent transformation into the "smarter planet" increasingly relies on the use of big data to provide insights. Thus, with each change in strategy comes a change in the kinds of skills, employees, and behaviors required to execute that strategy effectively.

How does the HRM function implement strategy through getting the right talent and supporting the right culture? As Figure 2.9 shows, it is through administering HRM practices: job analysis and design, recruitment, selection systems, training and development programs, performance management systems, reward systems, and labor relations programs. The details of each of these HRM practices are the focus of the rest of this book.

**Figure 2.9**
Strategy Implementation

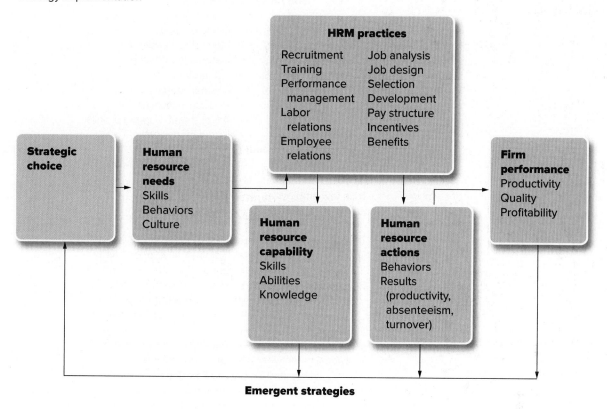

**HRM practices**

| Recruitment | Job analysis |
| Training | Job design |
| Performance | Selection |
| management | Development |
| Labor | Pay structure |
| relations | Incentives |
| Employee | Benefits |
| relations | |

**Strategic choice**

**Human resource needs**
Skills
Behaviors
Culture

**Human resource capability**
Skills
Abilities
Knowledge

**Human resource actions**
Behaviors
Results
(productivity, absenteeism, turnover)

**Firm performance**
Productivity
Quality
Profitability

**Emergent strategies**

However, at this point it is important to present a general overview of the HRM practices and their role in strategy implementation. We then discuss the various strategies companies pursue and the types of HRM systems congruent with those strategies. First we focus on how the strategic types are implemented; then we discuss the HRM practices associated with various directional strategies.

## HRM PRACTICES

The HRM function can be thought of as having six menus of HRM practices, from which companies can choose the ones most appropriate for implementing their strategy. Each of these menus refers to a particular functional area of HRM: job analysis and design; recruitment and selection; training and development; performance management; pay structure, incentives, and benefits; and labor and employee relations.[36] These menus are presented in Table 2.3.

### Job Analysis and Design

Companies produce a given product or service (or set of products or services), and the manufacture of these products requires that a number of tasks be performed. These tasks are grouped together to form jobs. **Job analysis** is the process of getting detailed information about jobs. **Job design** addresses what tasks should be grouped into a particular job. The way that jobs are designed should have an important tie to the strategy of an

**Job analysis**
The process of getting detailed information about jobs.

**Job design**
The process of defining the way work will be performed and the tasks that will be required in a given job.

**Table 2.3**
Menu of HRM
Practice Options

| Job Analysis and Design | | |
|---|---|---|
| Few tasks | ↔ | Many tasks |
| Simple tasks | ↔ | Complex tasks |
| Few skills required | ↔ | Many skills required |
| Specific job descriptions | ↔ | General job descriptions |
| **Recruitment and Selection** | | |
| External sources | ↔ | Internal sources |
| Limited socialization | ↔ | Extensive socialization |
| Assessment of specific skills | ↔ | Assessment of general skills |
| Narrow career paths | ↔ | Broad career paths |
| **Training and Development** | | |
| Focus on current job skills | ↔ | Focus on future job skills |
| Individual orientation | ↔ | Group orientation |
| Train few employees | ↔ | Train all employees |
| Spontaneous, unplanned | ↔ | Planned, systematic |
| **Performance Management** | | |
| Behavioral criteria | ↔ | Results criteria |
| Developmental orientation | ↔ | Administrative orientation |
| Short-term criteria | ↔ | Long-term criteria |
| Individual orientation | ↔ | Group orientation |
| **Pay Structure, Incentives, and Benefits** | | |
| Pay weighted toward salary and benefits | ↔ | Pay weighted toward incentives |
| Short-term incentives | ↔ | Long-term incentives |
| Emphasis on internal equity | ↔ | Emphasis on external equity |
| Individual incentives | ↔ | Group incentives |
| **Labor and Employee Relations** | | |
| Collective bargaining | ↔ | Individual bargaining |
| Top-down decision making | ↔ | Participation in decision making |
| Formal due process | ↔ | No due process |
| View employees as expense | ↔ | View employees as assets |

SOURCES: Adapted from R. S. Schuler and S. F. Jackson, "Linking Competitive Strategies with Human Resource Management Practices," *Academy of Management Executive* 1 (1987), pp. 207–19; and C. Fisher, L. Schoenfeldt, and B. Shaw, *Human Resource Management*, 2nd ed. (Boston: Houghton Mifflin, 1992).

organization because the strategy requires either new and different tasks or different ways of performing the same tasks. In addition, because many strategies entail the introduction of new technologies, this affects the way that work is performed.[37]

In general, jobs can vary from having a narrow range of tasks (most of which are simplified and require a limited range of skills) to having a broad array of complex tasks requiring multiple skills. In the past, the narrow design of jobs has been used to increase efficiency, while the broad design of jobs has been associated with efforts to increase innovation. However, with the advent of total quality management (TQM) methods and a variety of employee involvement programs such as quality circles, many jobs are moving toward the broader end of the spectrum.[38]

## Employee Recruitment and Selection

**Recruitment** is the process through which the organization seeks applicants for potential employment. **Selection** refers to the process by which it attempts to identify applicants with the necessary knowledge, skills, abilities, and other characteristics that will help the

**Recruitment**
The process of seeking applicants for potential employment.

**Selection**
The process by which an organization attempts to identify applicants with the necessary knowledge, skills, abilities, and other characteristics that will help it achieve its goals.

company achieve its goals. Companies engaging in different strategies need different types and numbers of employees. Thus, the strategy a company is pursuing will have a direct impact on the types of employees that it seeks to recruit and select.[39]

## Employee Training and Development

A number of skills are instilled in employees through training and development. **Training** refers to a planned effort to facilitate the learning of job-related knowledge, skills, and behavior by employees. **Development** involves acquiring knowledge, skills, and behavior that improve employees' ability to meet the challenges of a variety of existing jobs or jobs that do not yet exist. Changes in strategies often require changes in the types, levels, and mixes of skills. Thus, the acquisition of strategy-related skills is an essential element of the implementation of strategy. For example, many companies have recently emphasized quality in their products, engaging in TQM programs. These programs require extensive training of all employees in the TQM philosophy, methods, and often other skills that ensure quality.[40]

Through recruitment, selection, training, and development, companies can obtain a pool of human resources capable of implementing a given strategy.[41]

## Performance Management

**Performance management** is used to ensure that employees' activities and outcomes are congruent with the organization's objectives. It entails specifying those activities and outcomes that will result in the firm successfully implementing the strategy. For example, companies that are "steady state" (not diversified) tend to have evaluation systems that call for subjective performance assessments of managers. This stems from the fact that those above the first-level managers in the hierarchy have extensive knowledge about how the work should be performed. By contrast, diversified companies are more likely to use quantitative measures of performance to evaluate managers because top managers have less knowledge about how work should be performed by those below them in the hierarchy.[42]

Similarly, executives who have extensive knowledge of the behaviors that lead to effective performance use performance management systems that focus on the behaviors of their subordinate managers. However, when executives are unclear about the specific behaviors that lead to effective performance, they tend to focus on evaluating the objective performance results of their subordinate managers.[43]

An example of how performance management can be aligned with strategy is provided in Figure 2.10. This comes from a firm in the health care industry whose strategy

**Training**
A planned effort to facilitate the learning of job-related knowledge, skills, and behavior by employees.

**Development**
The acquisition of knowledge, skills, and behaviors that improve an employee's ability to meet changes in job requirements and in client and customer demands.

**Performance management**
The means through which managers ensure that employees' activities and outcomes are congruent with the organization's goals.

## Figure 2.10

Percentage of Objectives Identified in Individual Performance Plans That Are Tied to Each Strategic Imperative

| Strategic Imperative | Business A | Business B | International | Investment | Finance | Legal | IT | HR&S | Enterprise |
|---|---|---|---|---|---|---|---|---|---|
| Achieve superior medical performance | 10.5% | 12.5% | 2.7% | 7.6% | 3.1% | 2.7% | 11.4% | 2.1% | 10.0% |
| Effectively serve our customers | 24.7% | 27.2% | 36.7% | 12.2% | 10.3% | 27.2% | 18.9% | 19.5% | 23.7% |
| Create great products and services | 5.6% | 6.1% | 10.1% | 9.8% | 5.0% | 10.1% | 15.3% | 8.9% | 6.9% |
| Create a winning environment | 27.7% | 29.7% | 30.1% | 29.9% | 30.3% | 33.7% | 22.4% | 39.4% | 27.7% |
| Establish a cost advantage | 31.5% | 24.5% | 20.5% | 40.5% | 51.3% | 26.3% | 32% | 30.0% | 31.7% |
| Total | 100% | 100% | 100% | 100% | 100% | 100% | 100% | 100% | 100% |

consisted of five "strategic imperatives," or things that the company was trying to accomplish. In this company all individuals set performance objectives each year, and each of their objectives had to be tied to at least one of the strategic imperatives. The senior VP of HR used the firm's technology system to examine the extent to which each business unit or function was focused on each of the imperatives. The figure illustrates the percentage of objectives that were tied to each imperative across the different units. This analysis allowed the company to determine if the mix of objectives was right enterprisewide as well as within each business unit or function.

### Pay Structure, Incentives, and Benefits

The pay system has an important role in implementing strategies. First, a high level of pay and/or benefits relative to that of competitors can ensure that the company attracts and retains high-quality employees, but this might have a negative impact on the company's overall labor costs.[44] Second, by tying pay to performance, the company can elicit specific activities and levels of performance from employees.

In a study of how compensation practices are tied to strategies, researchers examined 33 high-tech and 72 traditional companies. They classified them by whether they were in a growth stage (greater than 20% inflation-adjusted increases in annual sales) or a maturity stage. They found that high-tech companies in the growth stage used compensation systems that were highly geared toward incentive pay, with a lower percentage of total pay devoted to salary and benefits. By contrast, compensation systems among mature companies (both high-tech and traditional) devoted a lower percentage of total pay to incentives and a higher percentage to benefits.[45]

### Labor and Employee Relations

Whether companies are unionized or not, the general approach to relations with employees can strongly affect their potential for gaining competitive advantage.

Companies can choose to treat employees as an asset that requires investment of resources or as an expense to be minimized.[46] They have to make choices about how much employees can and should participate in decision making, what rights employees have, and what the company's responsibility is to them. The approach a company takes in making these decisions can result in it either successfully achieving its short- and long-term goals or ceasing to exist.

Recent research has begun to examine how companies develop sets of HRM practices that maximize performance and productivity. For example, one study of automobile assembly plants around the world found that plants that exhibited both high productivity and high quality used "HRM best practices," such as heavy emphasis on recruitment and hiring, compensation tied to performance, low levels of status differentiation, high levels of training for both new and experienced employees, and employee participation through structures such as work teams and problem-solving groups.[47] Another study found that HRM systems composed of selection testing, training, contingent pay, performance appraisal, attitude surveys, employee participation, and information sharing resulted in higher levels of productivity and corporate financial performance, as well as lower employee turnover.[48] Finally, a recent study found that companies identified as some of the "best places to work" had higher financial performances than a set of matched companies that did not make the list.[49] Similar results have also been observed in a number of other studies.[50]

In addition to the relationship between HR practices and performance in general, in today's fast-changing environment, businesses have to change quickly, requiring changes in employees' skills and behaviors. In one study the researchers found that the flexibility of HR practices, employee skills, and employee behaviors were all positively related to the firm's financial performance, but only the skill flexibility was related to cost efficiency.[51] Although these relationships are promising, the causal direction has not yet been proven. For instance, effective HR practices should help firms perform better, but it is also true that highly profitable firms can invest more in HR practices.[52] The research seems to indicate that although the relationship between practices and performance is consistently positive, we should not go too far out on a limb arguing that increasing the use of HRM practices will automatically result in increased profitability.[53]

## STRATEGIC TYPES

As we discussed earlier, companies can be classified by the generic strategies they pursue. These generic "strategies" are not what we mean by a strategic plan. They are merely similarities in the ways companies seek to compete in their industries. Various typologies have been offered, but we focus on the two generic strategies proposed by Michael Porter of Harvard Business School: cost and differentiation.[54]

According to Porter, competitive advantage stems from a company's being able to create value in its production process. Value can be created in one of two ways. First, value can be created by reducing costs. Second, value can be created by differentiating a product or service in such a way that it allows the company to charge a premium price relative to its competitors. This leads to two basic strategies. According to Porter, the "overall cost leadership" strategy focuses on becoming the lowest cost producer in an industry. This strategy is achieved by constructing efficient large-scale facilities, by reducing costs through capitalizing on the experience curve, and by controlling overhead costs and costs in such areas as research and development, service, sales force, and advertising. This strategy provides above-average returns within an industry, and it tends to bar other firms' entry into the industry because the firm can lower its prices below competitors' costs.

The "differentiation" strategy, according to Porter, attempts to create the impression that the company's product or service is different from that of others in the industry. The perceived differentiation can come from creating a brand image, from technology, from offering unique features, or from unique customer service. If a company succeeds in differentiating its product, it will achieve above-average returns, and the differentiation may protect it from price sensitivity. For instance, Dell Computer Company built its reputation on providing the lowest cost computers through leveraging its supply chain and direct selling model. However, recently they have seen share eroding as the consumer market grows and HP has offered more differentiated, stylish-looking computers sold through retail outlets where customers can touch and feel them. In addition, Apple has differentiated itself through its own operating system that integrates well with peripheral devices such as the iPad and iPhone. In both cases, these companies can charge a premium (albeit higher for Apple) over Dell's pricing.[55]

## HRM NEEDS IN STRATEGIC TYPES

Although all of the strategic types require competent people in a generic sense, each of the strategies also requires different types of employees with different types of behaviors and attitudes. As we noted earlier, different strategies require employees with specific skills. They also require these employees to exhibit different "role behaviors."[56] **Role behaviors** are the behaviors required of an individual in his or her role as a jobholder in a social work environment. These role behaviors vary on a number of dimensions. Additionally, different role behaviors are required by the different strategies. For example, companies engaged in a cost strategy require employees to have a high concern for quantity and a short-term focus, to be comfortable with stability, and to be risk averse.

**Role behaviors**
Behaviors that are required of an individual in his or her role as a jobholder in a social work environment.

These employees are expected to exhibit role behaviors that are relatively repetitive and performed independently or autonomously.

Thus, companies engaged in cost strategies, because of the focus on efficient production, tend to specifically define the skills they require and invest in training employees in these skill areas. They also rely on behavioral performance management systems with a large performance-based compensation component. These companies promote internally and develop internally consistent pay systems with high pay differentials between superiors and subordinates. They seek efficiency through worker participation, soliciting employees' ideas on how to achieve more efficient production.

By contrast, employees in companies with a differentiation strategy need to be highly creative and cooperative; to have only a moderate concern for quantity, a long-term focus, and a tolerance for ambiguity; and to be risk takers. Employees in these companies are expected to exhibit role behaviors that include cooperating with others, developing new ideas, and taking a balanced approach to process and results.

Thus, differentiation companies will seek to generate more creativity through broadly defined jobs with general job descriptions. They may recruit more from outside, engage in limited socialization of newcomers, and provide broader career paths. Training and development activities focus on cooperation. The compensation system is geared toward external equity, as it is heavily driven by recruiting needs. These companies develop results-based performance management systems and divisional–corporate performance evaluations to encourage risk taking on the part of managers.[57] The Evidence-Based HR box describes some of the most recent research comparing commitment- versus control-oriented HRM systems.

# EVIDENCE-BASED HR

## Commitment versus Control or Commitment *Plus* Control?

A study of HRM among steel mini-mills in the United States found that mills pursuing different strategies used different systems of HRM. Mills seeking cost leadership tended to use control-oriented HRM systems that were characterized by high centralization, low participation, low training, low wages, low benefits, and highly contingent pay, whereas differentiator mills used "commitment" HRM systems, characterized as the opposite on each of those dimensions. A later study from the same sample revealed that the mills with the commitment systems had higher productivity, lower scrap rates, and lower employee turnover than those with the control systems.

However, more recent research suggests that the commitment versus control distinction might be mistaken. One study found that adding control practices (disciplinary procedures, monitoring employees, etc.) explained additional variance in firm performance. Another study found that the highest performance was observed among firms that had implemented both commitment and control practices.

SOURCES: Z. Su and P. Wright, "Human Resource Management System and Firm Performance: A Study Based on the Chinese Context," *International Journal of Human Resource Management*, 23(10), 2012, pp. 2065–86; Z. Su, P. Wright, and M. Ulrich, "Beyond the SHRM Paradigm: Four Approaches to Governing Employees," *Journal of Management*, (in press) DOI: 10.1177/0149206315618011.

## DIRECTIONAL STRATEGIES

As discussed earlier in this chapter, strategic typologies are useful for classifying the ways different organizations seek to compete within an industry. However, it is also necessary to understand how increasing size (growth) or decreasing it (downsizing) affects the HRM function. For example, the top-management team might decide that they need to invest more in product development or to diversify as a means for growth. With these types of strategies, it is more useful for the HRM function to aid in evaluating the feasibility of the various alternatives and to develop programs that support the strategic choice.

Companies have used four possible categories of directional strategies to meet objectives.[58] Strategies emphasizing market share or operating costs are considered "concentration" strategies. With this type of strategy, a company attempts to focus on what it does best within its established markets and can be thought of as "sticking to its knitting." Strategies focusing on market development, product development, innovation, or joint ventures make up the "internal growth" strategy. Companies with an internal growth strategy channel their resources toward building on existing strengths. Those attempting to integrate vertically or horizontally or to diversify are exhibiting an **external growth strategy**, usually through mergers or acquisitions. This strategy attempts to expand a company's resources or to strengthen its market position through acquiring or creating new businesses. Finally, a "divestment," or downsizing, strategy is one made up of retrenchment, divestitures, or liquidation. These strategies are observed among companies facing serious economic difficulties and seeking to pare down their operations. The human resource implications of each of these strategies are quite different.

**LO 2-6**
Describe the different HRM issues and practices associated with various directional strategies.

**External growth strategy**
An emphasis on acquiring vendors and suppliers or buying businesses that allow a company to expand into new markets.

### Concentration Strategies

**Concentration strategies** require that the company maintain the current skills that exist in the organization. This requires that training programs provide a means of keeping those skills sharp among people in the organization and that compensation programs focus on retaining people who have those skills. Appraisals in this strategy tend to be more behavioral because the environment is more certain, and the behaviors necessary for effective performance tend to be established through extensive experience.

**Concentration strategy**
A strategy focusing on increasing market share, reducing costs, or creating and maintaining a market niche for products and services.

### Internal Growth Strategies

**Internal growth strategies** present unique staffing problems. Growth requires that a company constantly hire, transfer, and promote individuals, and expansion into different markets may change the necessary skills that prospective employees must have. In addition, appraisals often consist of a combination of behaviors and results. The behavioral appraisal emphasis stems from the knowledge of effective behaviors in a particular product market, and the results appraisals focus on achieving growth goals. Compensation packages are heavily weighted toward incentives for achieving growth goals. Training needs differ depending on the way the company attempts to grow internally. For example, if the organization seeks to expand its markets, training will focus on knowledge of each market, particularly when the company is expanding into international markets. By contrast, when the company is seeking innovation or product development, training will be of a more technical nature, as well as focusing on interpersonal skills such as team building. Joint ventures require extensive training in conflict resolution techniques because of the problems associated with combining people from two distinct organizational cultures.

**Internal growth strategy**
A focus on new market and product development, innovation, and joint ventures.

## Mergers and Acquisitions

Increasingly, we see both consolidation within industries and mergers across industries. For example, Procter & Gamble's acquisition of Gillette represented a consolidation, or a reduction in the number of firms within the industry. By contrast, Citicorp's merger with Travelers Group to form Citigroup represented firms from different industries (pure financial services and insurance) combining to change the dynamics within both. Whatever the type, one thing is for sure—mergers and acquisitions are on the increase, and HRM needs to be involved.[59] In addition, these mergers more frequently consist of global mega-mergers, in spite of some warnings that these might not be effective.

According to a report by the Conference Board, "people issues" may be one of the major reasons that mergers do not always live up to expectations. Some companies now heavily weigh firm cultures before embarking on a merger or acquisition. For example, prior to acquiring Value Rx, executives at Express Scripts Inc. interviewed senior executives and middle managers at the potential target firm in order to get a sense of its culture.[60] In spite of this, fewer than one-third of the HRM executives surveyed said that they had a major influence in how mergers are planned, yet 80% of them said that people issues have a significant impact after the deals are finalized.[61]

In addition to the desirability of HRM playing a role in evaluating a merger opportunity, HRM certainly has a role in the actual implementation of a merger or acquisition. Training in conflict resolution is also necessary when companies engage in an external growth strategy. All the options for external growth consist of acquiring or developing new businesses, and these businesses often have distinct cultures. Thus, many HRM programs face problems in integrating and standardizing practices across the company's businesses. The relative value of standardizing practices across businesses must be weighed against the unique environmental requirements of each business and the extent of desired integration of the two firms. For example, with regard to pay practices, a company may desire a consistent internal wage structure to maintain employee perceptions of equity in the larger organization. In a recent new business developed by IBM, the employees pressured the company to maintain the same wage structure as IBM's main operation. However, some businesses may function in environments where pay practices are driven heavily by market forces. Requiring these businesses to adhere to pay practices in other environments may result in an ineffective wage structure.

## Downsizing

**Downsizing**
The planned elimination of large numbers of personnel, designed to enhance organizational effectiveness.

Of increasing importance to organizations in today's competitive environment is HRM's role in **downsizing**, or "rightsizing." The number of organizations undergoing downsizing increased significantly from the third to the fourth quarter of 2008, and although this trend has slowed, layoffs are still significant (see Figure 2.11).[62] In fact, some of these layoffs were due to outright bankruptcies because firms simply did not have sustainable business models. In addition, even as the economy has grown, layoffs continue in companies that face challenging environments. For instance, by partway through 2016, Macy's announced 4,350 job cuts, Microsoft 4,700 job cuts, Intel 12,000 job cuts, Halliburton 15,200 job cuts, and Walmart 17,500 job cuts.[63] A recent review of the downsizing literature noted that downsizing tends to fall short of meeting

**Figure 2.11**

Layoff Events and Separations 2009–2013

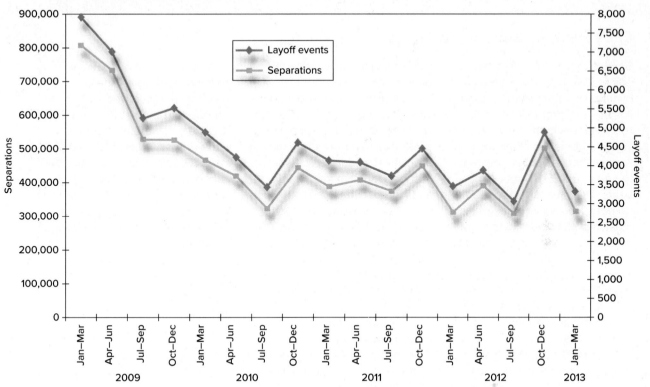

SOURCE: U.S. Department of Labor, Bureau of Labor Statistics, "Mass Layoffs Summary," May 13, 2013, www.bls.gov/
news.release/mslo.nr0.htm.

companies' financial and organizational objectives, and has negative effects on employee morale and productivity.[64]

One would have great difficulty ignoring the massive "war for talent" that went on during the late 1990s, particularly with the notable dot-com craze. Firms during this time sought to become "employers of choice," to establish "employment brands," and to develop "employee value propositions" as ways to ensure that they would be able to attract and retain talented employees. The Competing through Environmental, Social, and Governance Practices box describes the results of a survey of over 400 CEOs around the globe, and how they focus on talent and culture as critical parts of their job.

The dynamic economic conditions requiring firms to constantly churn their workforces means that one important question facing firms is, How can we develop a reputation as an employer of choice, and engage employees to the goals of the firm, while laying off a significant portion of our workforce? How firms answer this question will determine how they can compete by meeting the stakeholder needs of their employees.

In spite of the increasing frequency of downsizing, research reveals that it is far from universally successful for achieving the goals of increased productivity and increased

profitability. For example, Table 2.4 illustrates the results of a survey conducted by the American Management Association (AMA), indicating that only about one-third of the companies that went through downsizing actually achieved their goal of increased profits. Another survey by the AMA found that over two-thirds of the companies that downsize repeat the effort a year later.[65] Also, research by the consulting firm Mitchell & Company found that companies that downsized during the 1980s lagged the industry average stock price in 1991.[66] Thus, it is important to understand the best ways of managing downsizings, particularly from the standpoint of HRM.

Downsizing presents a number of challenges and opportunities for HRM.[67] In terms of challenges, the HRM function must "surgically" reduce the workforce by cutting only the workers who are less valuable in their performance. Achieving this is difficult because the best workers are most able (and often willing) to find alternative employment and may leave voluntarily prior to any layoff. For example, in 1992 General Motors and the UAW agreed to an early retirement program for individuals between the ages of 51 and 65 who had been employed for 10 or more years. The program provided those who agreed to retire their full pension benefits, even if they obtained employment elsewhere, and as much as $13,000 toward the purchase of a GM car.[68] As mentioned earlier in the chapter, this is part of GM's labor cost problem.

| DESIRED OUTCOME | PERCENTAGE THAT ACHIEVED DESIRED RESULT |
|---|---|
| Reduced expenses | 46% |
| Increased profits | 32 |
| Improved cash flow | 24 |
| Increased profits | 22 |
| Increased return on investment | 21 |
| Increased competitive advantage | 19 |
| Reduced bureaucracy | 17 |
| Improved decision making | 14 |
| Increased customer satisfaction | 14 |
| Increased sales | 13 |
| Increased market share | 12 |
| Improved product quality | 9 |
| Technological advances | 9 |
| Increased innovation | 7 |
| Avoidance of a takeover | 6 |

**Table 2.4**
Effects of Downsizing on Desired Outcomes

SOURCES: From *Wall Street Journal* by News Corporation; Dow Jones & Co, June 6, 1991.

Early retirement programs, although humane, essentially reduce the workforce with a "grenade" approach. This type of reduction does not distinguish between good and poor performers but rather eliminates an entire group of employees. In fact, recent research indicates that when companies downsize by offering early retirement programs, they usually end up rehiring to replace essential talent within a year. Often the company does not achieve its cost-cutting goals because it spends 50 to 150% of the departing employees' salaries in hiring and retraining new workers.[69]

Another HRM challenge is to boost the morale of employees who remain after the reduction; this topic is discussed in greater detail in Chapter 5. Survivors may feel guilt over keeping their jobs when their friends have been laid off, or they may envy their friends who have retired with attractive severance and pension benefits. Their reduced satisfaction with and commitment to the organization may interfere with work performance. Thus, the HRM function must maintain open communication with remaining employees to build their trust and commitment rather than withholding information.[70] All employees should be informed of the purpose of the downsizing, the costs to be cut, the duration of the downsizing, and the strategies to be pursued. In addition, companies going through downsizing often develop compensation programs that tie the individual's compensation to the company's success. Employee ownership programs often result from downsizing, and gainsharing plans such as the Scanlon plan (discussed in Chapter 12) as a way to incent employees to cut costs because it will benefit them monetarily.

In spite of these challenges, downsizing provides opportunities for HRM. First, it often allows the company to "get rid of dead wood" and make way for fresh ideas. In addition, downsizing is often a unique opportunity to change an organization's culture. In firms characterized by antagonistic labor–management relations, downsizing can force the parties to cooperate and to develop new, positive relationships.[71] Finally, downsizing can demonstrate to top-management decision makers the value of the company's human resources to its ultimate success. The role of HRM is to effectively manage the process in a way that makes this value undeniable. We discuss the implications of downsizing as a labor force management strategy in Chapter 5.

## STRATEGY EVALUATION AND CONTROL

A final component to the strategic management process is that of strategy evaluation and control. Thus far we have focused on the planning and implementation of strategy. However, it is extremely important for the firm to constantly monitor the effectiveness of both the strategy and the implementation process. This monitoring makes it possible for the company to identify problem areas and either revise existing structures and strategies or devise new ones. In this process we see emergent strategies appear as well as the critical nature of human resources in competitive advantage.

# The Role of Human Resources in Providing Strategic Competitive Advantage

Thus far we have presented the strategic management process as including a step-by-step procedure by which HRM issues are raised prior to deciding on a strategy and then HRM practices are developed to implement that strategy. However, human resources can provide a strategic competitive advantage in two additional ways: through emergent strategies and through enhancing competitiveness.

## EMERGENT STRATEGIES

Having discussed the process of strategic management, we also must distinguish between intended strategies and emergent strategies. Most people think of strategies as being proactive, rational decisions aimed toward some predetermined goal. The view of strategy we have presented thus far in the chapter focuses on intended strategies. Intended strategies are the result of the rational decision-making process used by top managers as they develop a strategic plan. This is consistent with the definition of *strategy* as "the pattern or plan that integrates an organization's major goals, policies, and action sequences into a cohesive whole."[72] The idea of emergent strategies is evidenced by the feedback loop in Figure 2.2.

Most strategies that companies espouse are intended strategies. For example, when Howard Schultz founded Starbucks, he had the idea of creating a third place (between work and home) where people could enjoy traditional Italian-style coffee. He knew that the smell of the coffee and the deeper, darker, stronger taste would attract a new set of customers to enjoy coffee the way he thought it should be enjoyed. This worked, but as Starbucks grew, customers began asking if they could have nonfat milk in their lattes, or if they could get flavor shots in their coffees. Schultz swore that such things would essentially pollute the coffee and refused to offer them. Finally, after repeated requests from his store managers who kept hearing customers demanding such things, Schultz finally relented.[73]

Emergent strategies, by contrast, consist of the strategies that evolve from the grassroots of the organization and can be thought of as what organizations actually do, as opposed to what they intend to do. Strategy can also be thought of as "a pattern in a stream of decisions or actions."[74] For example, when Honda Motor Company first entered the U.S. market with its 250-cc and 350-cc motorcycles in 1959, it believed that no market existed for its smaller 50-cc bike. However, the sales on the larger motorcycles were sluggish, and Japanese executives running errands around Los Angeles on Honda 50s attracted a lot of attention, including that of a buyer with Sears, Roebuck. Honda found a previously undiscovered market as well as a new distribution outlet (general retailers) that it had not planned on. This emergent strategy gave Honda a 50% market share by 1964.[75]

The distinction between intended and emergent strategies has important implications for human resource management.[76] The new focus on strategic HRM has tended to focus primarily on intended strategies. Thus, HRM's role has been seen as identifying for top management the people-related business issues relevant to strategy formulation and then developing HRM systems that aid in the implementation of the strategic plan.

However, most emergent strategies are identified by those lower in the organizational hierarchy. It is often the rank-and-file employees who provide ideas for new markets, new products, and new strategies. HRM plays an important role in facilitating communication throughout the organization, and it is this communication that allows for effective emergent strategies to make their way up to top management. For example, Starbucks' Frappuccino was a drink invented by one of the store employees in California; Starbucks leaders (including Schultz) thought it was a terrible idea. They fought it in a number of meetings, but the employee kept getting more and more information supporting her case for how much customers seemed to like it. The leaders finally gave the go-ahead to begin producing it, and it has become a $1 billion a year product, and one that has contributed to the Starbucks brand.[77]

## ENHANCING FIRM COMPETITIVENESS

A related way in which human resources can be a source of competitive advantage is through developing a human capital pool that gives the company the unique ability to adapt to an ever-changing environment. Recently managers have become interested in the idea of a "learning organization," in which people continually expand their capacity to achieve the results they desire.[78] This requires the company to be in a constant state of learning through monitoring the environment, assimilating information, making decisions, and flexibly restructuring to compete in that environment. Companies that develop such learning capability have a competitive advantage. Although certain organizational information-processing systems can be an aid, ultimately the people (human capital) who make up the company provide the raw materials in a learning organization.[79]

Thus, the role of human resources in competitive advantage should continue to increase because of the fast-paced change characterizing today's business environment. It is becoming increasingly clear that even as U.S. automakers have improved the quality of their cars to compete with the Japanese, these competitors have developed such flexible and adaptable manufacturing systems that they can respond to customer needs more quickly.[80] This flexibility of the manufacturing process allows the emergent strategy to come directly from the marketplace by determining and responding to the exact mix of customer desires. It requires, however, that the company have people in place who have the skills to similarly adapt quickly.[81] As former Starbucks CEO Howard Schultz says, "If people relate to the company they work for, if they form an emotional tie to it and buy into its dreams, they will pour their heart into making it better. When employees have self-esteem and self-respect they can contribute so much more; to their company, to their family, to the world."[82] This statement exemplifies the increasing importance of human resources in developing and maintaining competitive advantage.[83]

## A LOOK BACK

### GE's Challenges Going Forward

As this chapter has shown, firms need to clearly link their strategies, cultures, and people. Strategies define where, how, and with what firms will compete. Culture defines the shared norms regarding appropriate behaviors and can encourage behavior that supports the strategy. People execute strategies and culture can attract and guide them.

While GE was known for years as being the role model for other companies, it drifted over time. Part of the strategy entailed being the best in any industry, and if they were not the best, the business leader was to fix it, close it, or sell it. This strategy was supported by a highly disciplined and competitive culture that attracted and retained bright and ambitious people. However, as the strategy drifted and the culture evolved into one that seemed to reinforce conformity. GE's struggles seemingly stem from a culture that stifled dissent. The lack of dissent led the company into a series of strategic decisions that ended up putting the company at risk. The current financial situation threatens their ability to attract and retain talent. John Flannery took over as CEO in 2017, inheriting a series of difficult challenges. As much as he tried to deal with them, the winds blew too strongly against him, and he was fired 14 months after assuming the helm. He was replace by Larry Culp, a board member who has served as the CEO of Danaher Corporation. Sadly, the company that was known for building the greatest leaders had to hire its next CEO from outside.

### QUESTIONS

1. What do you think might have led GE to make poor strategic decisions? How might an HR executive influence those decisions to be better?
2. How important do you think culture is to the success of a business? In what ways can getting culture right contribute to the business and getting it wrong hurt the business?
3. Why do you think talent or people are critical to business success? In what ways do they need to be aligned to strategy?

## SUMMARY

A strategic approach to human resource management seeks to proactively provide a competitive advantage through the company's most important asset: its human resources. Although human resources are the most important asset, they are also usually the single largest controllable cost within the firm's business model. The HRM function needs to be integrally involved in the formulation of strategy to identify the people-related business issues the company faces. Once the strategy has been determined, HRM has a profound impact on the implementation of the plan by developing and aligning HRM practices that ensure that the company has motivated employees with the necessary skills. Finally, the emerging strategic role of the HRM function requires that HR professionals in the future develop business, professional–technical, change management, and integration competencies. As you will see more clearly in later chapters, this strategic approach requires more than simply developing a valid selection procedure or state-of-the-art performance management systems. Only through these competencies can the HR professional take a strategic approach to human resource management.

## KEY TERMS

Strategic human resource management (SHRM), 77
Strategy formulation, 77
Strategy implementation, 77
Goals, 81
External analysis, 83
Internal analysis, 83

Strategic choice, 84
Job analysis, 91
Job design, 91
Recruitment, 92
Selection, 92
Training, 93
Development, 93

Performance management, 93
Role behaviors, 95
External growth strategy, 97
Concentration strategy, 97
Internal growth strategy, 97
Downsizing, 98

# DISCUSSION QUESTIONS

1. Pick one of your university's major sports teams (like football or basketball). How would you characterize that team's generic strategy? How does the composition of the team members (in terms of size, speed, ability, and so on) relate to that strategy? What are the strengths and weaknesses of the team? How do they dictate the team's generic strategy and its approach to a particular game?
2. Do you think that it is easier to tie human resources to the strategic management process in large or in small organizations? Why?
3. Consider one of the organizations you have been affiliated with. What are some examples of human resource practices that were consistent with that organization's

strategy? What are examples of practices that were inconsistent with its strategy?
4. How can strategic management within the HRM department ensure that HRM plays an effective role in the company's strategic management process?
5. What types of specific skills (such as knowledge of financial accounting methods) do you think HR professionals will need in order to have the business, professional–technical, change management, and integrative competencies necessary in the future? Where can you develop each of these skills?
6. What are some of the key environmental variables that you see changing in the business world today? What impact will those changes have on the HRM function in organizations?

# SELF-ASSESSMENT EXERCISE

**McGraw Hill connect**

Also assignable in Connect.

Think of a company you have worked for, or find an annual report for a company you are interested in working for. (Many companies post their annual reports on their website.) Then answer the following questions.

### QUESTIONS

1. How has the company been affected by the trends discussed in this chapter?
2. Does the company use the HR practices recommended in this chapter?
3. What else should the company do to deal with the challenges posed by the trends discussed in this chapter?

# EXERCISING STRATEGY

## Amazon: From Digital to Brick-and-Mortar?

Amazon.com's Internet-based business model created havoc in the retail industry. Beginning with selling books online, then music, then just about anything, the company cut into traditional retailers' markets and margins. Built on a business model that created profits through selling high volume at a low margin, and doing so with very little physical assets, it quickly became the 800-pound gorilla every retailer had to face. Those that have survived have done so by trying to develop their own online presence while maintaining their brick-and-mortar operations.

Now Amazon is attacking them on their traditional turf: the brick-and-mortar store. The company recently unveiled a grocery store called "Amazon Go." The plans are to open more than 2,000 of these grocery stores, which would put them on par with Kroger Co., which has around 2,800 locations in 35 states. These stores will be multi-functioning, with curbside pickup capability, in-store shopping, and even delivery.

One potential format would be like a convenience store, but one that eliminates checkouts, cash registers, and lines.

Customers scan their phones upon entering the store, and using artificial intelligence–powered technology, Amazon can determine what customers took from the shelves, charge them for the items, and send a receipt. Another format would resemble the traditional 30,000- to 40,000-square-foot grocery store where customers pick the fresh selections they like and also order other items via touch-screen to be delivered later.

### QUESTIONS

1. The chapter mentions that Amazon's culture has been described as quite difficult. Do you think the culture will need to change with this store format? If so, how, and if not, why not?
2. What will be the implications of Amazon's foray into brick-and-mortar stores for the talent that they will need?

SOURCE: L. Stevens and S. Khadeeja, "Amazon Working on Several Grocery Store Formats, Could Open More Than 2,000 Locations," *Wall Street Journal*, December 5, 2016, https://www.wsj.com/articles/amazon-grocery-store-concept-to-open-in-seattle-in-early-2017-1480959119.

## MANAGING PEOPLE

### How Should Dell Respond to the HP Challenge?

Dell Computers was founded by Michael Dell in his college dormitory room. It quickly became one of the fastest growing businesses in history, an almost unparalleled success story. By 2005 Dell had become the largest manufacturer of PCs, primarily focusing on the B2B market. This was achieved by creating a "Direct" model that allowed companies to buy customized computers directly from Dell, cutting out the margins previously captured by middlemen such as CDW. The creation of Dell's "Premier Pages" website made it easy for corporate customers to easily place orders for large numbers of computers configured exactly as they wanted. The direct model also allowed Dell to better manage its supply chain, reducing both the inventory of components as well as finished products.

However, by 2007 HP had surpassed Dell in PC sales. After having tried to imitate the Dell model, in 2005 HP hired Todd Bradley to turn the business around. Instead of fighting Dell in Internet and phone sales where Dell was strong, Mr. Bradley decided to focus on its strength, retail stores, where Dell was completely absent, and where individual customers, the fastest growing segment, made most of their purchases. He noted that PCs "aren't just a commodity that you run out and buy on the Internet. People are going to want to touch it and feel it and understand how it connects." He also began advertising campaigns using celebrities such as hip-hop mogul Jay-Z to talk about how they used their HP laptops.

In talking with retailers, he found that they complained about late and incomplete deliveries. So, he focused on fixing the logistical problems and consolidated 30 manufacturing plants into 23. This enabled HP to reduce both the time and cost of building PCs, and reduce late deliveries by 30%. HP's margins grew to 4.8% in the second quarter of 2007 from 3.6% a year earlier while Dell's fell to 6.5% from 6.7% a year earlier.

Finally, he built better relationships with the retailers. He pushed products such as touch-screen PCs that would garner attention from customers. He also helped retailers to design products exclusive to their stores, enabling them to differentiate their products from competitors. He worked with them to be able to create customized imprints. For instance, working with Best Buy, HP created a silver and white laptop, softer colors aimed at female customers.

Thus, in 2007 Dell gave up its title as the largest producer of PCs. In addition, as the consumer market continued to grow at a much faster rate than the corporate market, Dell was ill-positioned to reverse this trend.

### QUESTIONS

1. What are the major competitive and strategic challenges Dell needs to deal with if it is to regain a position of strength within the industry?
2. What can HR do to help Dell re-establish its position as the leader in PCs? Assume you just got on the elevator with Michael Dell and want to explain how HR will aid him in regaining its pre-eminent position. What will you tell him in the 1 to 2 minutes you have?

SOURCE: C. Lawton, "How HP Regained Its Lead over Dell," *Wall Street Journal*, June 4, 2007, from http://online.wsj.com/article_print/SB1180092117687623314.

## HR IN SMALL BUSINESS

### Radio Flyer Rolls Forward

The mid-2000s were a difficult time for Radio Flyer, a private business famous for its little red wagons. After spending hundreds of thousands of dollars to develop what they hoped was a hit, managers realized their idea wouldn't fly, so they killed it. And in the same year, management decided the company could no longer afford to build wagons in the United States.

First, the development flop: Thomas Schlegel, vice president for product development, thought he had a winner with an idea for a collapsible wagon to be called Fold 2 Go Wagon. It would be a fun product that parents could fold up and toss into the back of a minivan for a trip to the park or other outings. The problem was, a collapsing toy that children sit inside is difficult to make both functional and safe. The costs were excessive.

When Schlegel ended the project, he feared his reputation might suffer as well. But CEO Robert Pasin assured Schlegel that failure was acceptable as long as the company could learn from it. The value placed on learning became something that Schlegel capitalized on as his team applied what they learned to the development of a new success, the Twist Trike and a new model of its wagons called the Ultimate Family Wagon. Furthermore, Pasin expanded that one experience into a teaching opportunity. He invites new employees to join him for breakfasts, during which he recalls the incident as a way to reinforce the company's commitment to innovation and learning.

The story of Radio Flyer's need to outsource manufacturing has what some might see as a less-happy ending. Looking at the numbers, management determined that it would have to close its factory in Chicago and lay off about half of its workforce. Manufacturing moved to a factory in China. Pasin describes the effort as "an incredibly difficult time."

The company's effort with its remaining U.S. employees focused on building morale. These efforts include creating ideas for employees to have fun and pursue their passions, with events such as the Radio Flyer Olympics, during which employees compete in silly contests like tricycle races. More seriously, teams of employees tackle issues that they care about. The wellness committee put together a cash benefit that pays employees up to $300 for participating in health-related activities such as weight-loss counseling or running races. Another committee brought together employees concerned about the environment. They assembled a campaign aimed at persuading employees to reduce their carbon footprint.

In caring for the U.S. employees, Radio Flyer hasn't forgotten the ones in China. The company tries to maintain similar levels of benefits and engagement among the four dozen employees in its China office.

## QUESTIONS

1. How could a human resource manager help Radio Flyer get the maximum benefit from the motivational efforts described in this case?
2. Do you think outsourcing would be harder on employees in a small company such as Radio Flyer than in a large corporation? Why or why not? How could HRM help to smooth the transition?
3. What additional developments described in this chapter could help Radio Flyer live out the high value it places on learning and innovation?

SOURCES: Company website, www.radioflyer.com, accessed May 24, 2015; "Best Places to Work 2015 in Chicago: #7 Radio Flyer," *Crain's Chicago Business*, www .chicagobusiness.com, accessed May 24, 2015; J. Scanlon, "Radio Flyer Learns from a Crash," *Bloomberg Businessweek*, www.businessweek.com, accessed May 24, 2015.

## NOTES

1. J. Barney, "Firm Resources and Sustained Competitive Advantage," *Journal of Management* 17 (1991), pp. 99–120.
2. L. Dyer, "Strategic Human Resource Management and Planning," in *Research in Personnel and Human Resources Management,* ed. K. Rowland and G. Ferris (Greenwich, CT: JAI Press, 1985), pp. 1–30.
3. J. Parashar, "Why Is General Motors' Global Market Share Falling?" March 15, 2016, from http://marketrealist.com/2016/03/ general-motors-global-market-share-falling/
4. P. Ingrassia, "GM's Plan: Subsidize Our 48-Year-Old Retirees," *Wall Street Journal,* February 19, 2009, http://online.wsj.com/ article/SB123500874299418721.html; S. Terlep and N. King, "Bondholders Say GM's Plan Fails to Tackle Issues," *Wall Street Journal,* February 19, 2009, http://online.wsj.com/article/ SB123500467245718075.html?mod=testMod.
5. J. Quinn, *Strategies for Change: Logical Incrementalism* (Homewood, IL: Richard D. Irwin, 1980).
6. M. Porter, *Competitive Strategy: Techniques for Analyzing Industries and Competitors* (New York: Free Press, 1980).
7. R. Miles and C. Snow, *Organizational Strategy, Structure, and Process* (New York: McGraw-Hill, 1978).
8. P. Wright and G. McMahan, "Theoretical Perspectives for Strategic Human Resource Management," *Journal of Management* 18 (1992), pp. 295–320.
9. D. Guest, "Human Resource Management, Corporate Performance and Employee Well-Being: Building the Worker into HRM," *Journal of Industrial Relations* 44 (2002), pp. 335–58; B. Becker, M. Huselid, P. Pinckus, and M. Spratt, "HR as a Source of Shareholder Value: Research and Recommendations," *Human Resource Management* 36 (1997), pp. 39–47.
10. P. Boxall and J. Purcell, *Strategy and Human Resource Management* (Basingstoke, Hants, U.K.: Palgrave MacMillan, 2003).
11. F. Biddle and J. Helyar, "Behind Boeing's Woes: Chunky Assembly Line, Price War with Airbus," *Wall Street Journal,* April 24, 1998, pp. A1, A16.
12. K. Martell and S. Carroll, "How Strategic Is HRM?" *Human Resource Management* 34 (1995), pp. 253–67.
13. K. Golden and V. Ramanujam, "Between a Dream and a Nightmare: On the Integration of the Human Resource Function and the Strategic Business Planning Process," *Human Resource Management* 24 (1985), pp. 429–51.
14. P. Wright, B. Dunford, and S. Snell, "Contributions of the Resource-Based View of the Firm to the Field of Strategic HRM: Convergence of Two Fields," *Journal of Management* 27 (2001), pp. 701–21.
15. J. Purcell, N. Kinnie, S. Hutchinson, B. Rayton, and J. Swart, *Understanding the People and Performance Link: Unlocking the Black Box* (London: CIPD, 2003).
16. P. M. Wright, T. Gardner, and L. Moynihan, "The Impact of Human Resource Practices on Business Unit Operating and Financial Performance," *Human Resource Management Journal* 13, no. 3 (2003), pp. 21–36.
17. H. Kim and K. Sung-Choon, "Strategic HR Functions and Firm Performance: The Moderating Effects of High-Involvement Work Practices," *Asia Pacific Journal of Management* 30, no. 1 (2013), pp. 91–113.
18. C. Hill and G. Jones, *Strategic Management Theory: An Integrated Approach* (Boston: Houghton Mifflin, 1989).
19. W. Johnston and A. Packer, *Workforce 2000: Work and Workers for the Twenty-First Century* (Indianapolis, IN: Hudson Institute, 1987).
20. "Labor Letter," *Wall Street Journal,* December 15, 1992, p. A1.
21. P. Wright, G. McMahan, and A. McWilliams, "Human Resources and Sustained Competitive Advantage: A Resource-Based

Perspective," *International Journal of Human Resource Management* 5 (1994), pp. 301-26.

22. P. Buller, "Successful Partnerships: HR and Strategic Planning at Eight Top Firms," *Organizational Dynamics* 17 (1988), pp. 27-42.

23. M. Hitt, R. Hoskisson, and J. Harrison, "Strategic Competitiveness in the 1990s: Challenges and Opportunities for U.S. Executives," *The Executive* 5 (May 1991), pp. 7-22.

24. P. Wright, G. McMahan, B. McCormick, and S. Sherman, "Strategy, Core Competence, and HR Involvement as Determinants of HR Effectiveness and Refinery Performance." Paper presented at the 1996 International Federation of Scholarly Associations in Management, Paris, France.

25. N. Bennett, D. Ketchen, and E. Schultz, "Antecedents and Consequences of Human Resource Integration with Strategic Decision Making." Paper presented at the 1995 Academy of Management Meeting, Vancouver, BC, Canada.

26. Golden and Ramanujam, "Between a Dream and a Nightmare."

27. J. Galbraith and R. Kazanjian, *Strategy Implementation: Structure, Systems, and Process* (St. Paul, MN: West, 1986).

28. B. Schneider and A. Konz, "Strategic Job Analysis," *Human Resource Management* 27 (1989), pp. 51-64.

29. P. Wright and S. Snell, "Toward an Integrative View of Strategic Human Resource Management," *Human Resource Management Review* 1 (1991), pp. 203-25.

30. S. Snell, "Control Theory in Strategic Human Resource Management: The Mediating Effect of Administrative Information," *Academy of Management Journal* 35 (1992), pp. 292-327.

31. J. Barney, "Organizational Culture: Can It Be a Source of Sustained Competitive Advantage?" *The Academy of Management Review* 11, no. 3 (1986), pp. 656-665.

32. P. Wright, A. Nyberg, S. Essman, and D. Schepker, "The Chief HR Officer: Exploring the Counselor, Confidante, and Coach Role," 2018, from https://sc.edu/study/colleges_schools/moore/documents/center_for_executive_succession/chro_survey_2018_report_1.pdf

33. D. Ulrich and W. Brockbank, "Take Your Culture to New Heights," *Your Workplace* 18, no. 3 (2016), pp. 27-32.

34. D. Ulrich, "Culture Is not Enough: Get the Right Culture," *LinkedIn*, May 23, 2017, from https://www.linkedin.com/pulse/culture-enoughget-right-dave-ulrich/ accessed January 1, 2019.

35. J. Stoll, "Tesla Should Pull an Apple: Leave Production Hell to Other People," *Wall Street Journal*, January 25, 2019, from https://www.wsj.com/articles/tesla-should-pull-an-apple-leave-production-hell-to-other-people-11548435605?mod=hp_lead_pos8 accessed January 25, 2019.

36. R. Schuler, "Personnel and Human Resource Management Choices and Organizational Strategy," in *Readings in Personnel and Human Resource Management*, 3rd ed., ed. R. Schuler, S. Youngblood, and V. Huber (St. Paul, MN: West, 1988).

37. J. Dean and S. Snell, "Integrated Manufacturing and Job Design: Moderating Effects of Organizational Inertia," *Academy of Management Journal* 34 (1991), pp. 776-804.

38. E. Lawler, *The Ultimate Advantage: Creating the High Involvement Organization* (San Francisco: Jossey-Bass, 1992).

39. J. Olian and S. Rynes, "Organizational Staffing: Integrating Practice with Strategy," *Industrial Relations* 23 (1984), pp. 170-83.

40. G. Smith, "Quality: Small and Midsize Companies Seize the Challenge—Not a Moment Too Soon," *Bloomberg Businessweek*, November 30, 1992, pp. 66-75.

41. J. Kerr and E. Jackofsky, "Aligning Managers with Strategies: Management Development versus Selection," *Strategic Management Journal* 10 (1989), pp. 157-70.

42. J. Kerr, "Strategic Control through Performance Appraisal and Rewards," *Human Resource Planning* 11 (1988), pp. 215-23.

43. Snell, "Control Theory in Strategic Human Resource Management."

44. B. Gerhart and G. Milkovich, "Employee Compensation: Research and Practice," in *Handbook of Industrial and Organizational Psychology,* 2nd ed., ed. M. Dunnette and L. Hough (Palo Alto, CA: Consulting Psychologists Press, 1992), pp. 481-569.

45. D. Balkin and L. Gomez-Mejia, "Toward a Contingency Theory of Compensation Strategy," *Strategic Management Journal* 8 (1987), pp. 169-82.

46. S. Cronshaw and R. Alexander, "One Answer to the Demand for Accountability: Selection Utility as an Investment Decision," *Organizational Behavior and Human Decision Processes* 35 (1986), pp. 102-18.

47. P. MacDuffie, "Human Resource Bundles and Manufacturing Performance: Organizational Logic and Flexible Production Systems in the World Auto Industry," *Industrial and Labor Relations Review* 48 (1995), pp. 197-221; P. McGraw, "A Hard Drive to the Top," *U.S. News & World Report* 118 (1995), pp. 43-44.

48. M. Huselid, "The Impact of Human Resource Management Practices on Turnover, Productivity, and Corporate Financial Performance," *Academy of Management Journal* 38 (1995), pp. 635-72.

49. B. Fulmer, B. Gerhart, and K. Scott, "Are the 100 Best Better? An Empirical Investigation of the Relationship between Being a 'Great Place to Work' and Firm Performance," *Personnel Psychology* 56 (2003), pp. 965-93.

50. J. E. Delery and D. H. Doty, "Modes of Theorizing in Strategic Human Resource Management: Tests of Universalistic, Contingency and Configurational Performance Predictions," *Academy of Management Journal* 39 (1996), pp. 802-83; D. Guest, J. Michie, N. Conway, and M. Sheehan, "Human Resource Management and Corporate Performance in the UK," *British Journal of Industrial Relations* 41 (2003), pp. 291-314; J. Guthrie, "High Involvement Work Practices, Turnover, and Productivity: Evidence from New Zealand," *Academy of Management Journal* 44 (2001), pp. 180-192; J. Harter, F. Schmidt, and T. Hayes, "Business-Unit-Level Relationship between Employee Satisfaction, Employee Engagement, and Business Outcomes: A Meta-analysis," *Journal of Applied Psychology* 87 (2002), pp. 268-79; Watson Wyatt, Worldwide, "Human Capital Index®: Human Capital as a Lead Indicator of Shareholder Value" (2002).

51. M. Bhattacharya, D. Gibson, and H. Doty, "The Effects of Flexibility in Employee Skills, Employee Behaviors, and Human Resource Practices on Firm Performance," *Journal of Management* 31 (2005), pp. 622-40.

52. D. Guest, J. Michie, N. Conway, and M. Sheehan, "Human Resource Management and Corporate Performance in the UK," *British Journal of Industrial Relations* 41 (2003), pp. 291-314; P. Wright, T. Gardner, L. Moynihan, and M. Allen, "The HR-Performance Relationship: Examining Causal Direction," *Personnel Psychology* 58 (2005), pp. 409-76.

53. P. Wright, *No Strategy: Adaptive to the Age of Globalization* (Arlington, VA: SHRM Foundation, 2008).

54. M. Porter, *Competitive Advantage* (New York: Free Press, 1985).

55. C. Lawton, "How HP Reclaimed Its PC Lead over Dell," June 2007; "Can Dell's Turnaround Strategy Keep HP at Bay?" September 2007, *Knowledge@Wharton*, http://knowledge.wharton.upenn.edu/article.cfm?articleid51799.

56. R. Schuler and S. Jackson, "Linking Competitive Strategies with Human Resource Management Practices," *Academy of Management Executive* 1 (1987), pp. 207-19.

57. Z. Su, and P. Wright, "Human Resource Management System and Firm Performance: A Study Based on the Chinese Context," *International Journal of Human Resource Management* 23, no. 10

(2012), pp. 2065–86. Z. Su, P. Wright, and M. Ulrich, "Beyond the SHRM Paradigm: Four Approaches to Governing Employees," *Journal of Management,* (in press) DOI: 10.1177/0149206315618011

58. A. Thompson and A. Strickland, *Strategy Formulation and Implementation: Tasks of the General Manager,* 3rd ed. (Plano, TX: BPI, 1986).

59. J. Schmidt, *Making Mergers Work: The Strategic Importance of People* (Arlington, VA: SHRM Foundation, 2003).

60. G. Fairclough, "Business Bulletin," *Wall Street Journal,* March 5, 1998, p. A1.

61. P. Sebastian, "Business Bulletin," *Wall Street Journal,* October 2, 1997, p. A1.

62. U.S. Department of Labor, Bureau of Labor Statistics, "Mass Layoffs Summary," May 13, 2013, www.bls.gov/news.release/mslo.nr0.htm.

63. Challenger, Gray, and Christmas, "2016 July Job Cut Report: Cuts Jump 19 Percent to 45,346," https://www.challengergray.com/press/press-releases/2016-july-job-cut-report-cuts-jump-19-percent-45346.

64. M. Hansson, and F. Gandolfi, "Causes and Consequences of Downsizing: Towards an Integrative Framework," *Journal of Management & Organization* 17, no. 4 (2010), pp. 498–521.

65. S. Pearlstein, "Corporate Cutback Yet to Pay Off," *Washington Post,* January 4, 1994, p. B6.

66. K. Cameron, "Guest Editor's Note: Investigating Organizational Downsizing—Fundamental Issues," *Human Resource Management* 33 (1994), pp. 183–88.

67. W. Cascio, *Responsible Restructuring: Creative and Profitable Alternatives to Layoffs* (San Francisco: Berrett-Koehler, 2002).

68. N. Templin, "UAW to Unveil Pact on Slashing GM's Payroll," *Wall Street Journal,* December 15, 1992, p. A3.

69. J. Lopez, "Managing: Early-Retirement Offers Lead to Renewed Hiring," *Wall Street Journal,* January 26, 1993, p. B1.

70. A. Church, "Organizational Downsizing: What Is the Role of the Practitioner?" *Industrial–Organizational Psychologist* 33, no. 1 (1995), pp. 63–74.

71. N. Templin, "A Decisive Response to Crisis Brought Ford Enhanced Productivity," *Wall Street Journal,* December 15, 1992, p. A1.

72. Quinn, *Strategies for Change.*

73. H. Schultz and D. Yang, *Pour Your Heart Into It* (New York: Hyperion, 1987).

74. R. Pascale, "Perspectives on Strategy: The Real Story behind Honda's Success," *California Management Review* 26 (1984), pp. 47–72.

75. Templin, "A Decisive Response to Crisis."

76. P. Wright and S. Snell, "Toward a Unifying Framework for Exploring Fit and Flexibility in Strategic Human Resource Management," *Academy of Management Review* 23, no. 4 (1998), pp. 756–72.

77. H. Behar, *It's Not about the Coffee: Lessons for Putting People First from a Life at Starbucks* (New York: Penguin Group, 2007).

78. T. Stewart, "Brace for Japan's Hot New Strategy," *Fortune,* September 21, 1992, pp. 62–76.

79. B. Dunford, P. Wright, and S. Snell, "Contributions of the Resource-Based View of the Firm to the Field of Strategic HRM: Convergence of Two Fields," *Journal of Management* 27 (2001), pp. 701–21.

80. C. Snow and S. Snell, *Staffing as Strategy,* vol. 4 of *Personnel Selection* (San Francisco: Jossey-Bass, 1992).

81. T. Batten, "Education Key to Prosperity—Report," *Houston Chronicle,* September 7, 1992, p. 1B.

82. Schultz and Yang, *Pour Your Heart Into It.*

83. G. McMahan, University of Texas at Arlington, personal communications.

# 3

# The Legal Environment: Equal Employment Opportunity and Safety

## ⌐ LEARNING OBJECTIVES ¬

*After reading this chapter, you should be able to:*

**LO 3-1** Identify the three branches of government and the role each plays in influencing the legal environment of human resource management. *page 112*

**LO 3-2** List the major federal laws that require equal employment opportunity and the protections provided by each of these laws. *page 114*

**LO 3-3** Discuss the roles, responsibilities, and requirements of the federal agencies responsible for enforcing equal employment opportunity laws. *page 121*

**LO 3-4** Identify the three theories of discrimination under Title VII of the Civil Rights Act and apply these theories to different discrimination situations. *page 124*

**LO 3-5** Identify behavior that constitutes sexual harassment, and list things that an organization can do to eliminate or minimize it. *page 137*

**LO 3-6** Discuss the legal issues involved with preferential treatment programs. *page 140*

**LO 3-7** Identify the major provisions of the Occupational Safety and Health Act (1970) and the rights of employees that are guaranteed by this act. *page 145*

# ENTER THE WORLD OF BUSINESS

## Does Harvard Discriminate in Undergraduate Admissions?

As you know, academic institutions rightfully seek to bring in a diverse set of students. They know that having people from diverse backgrounds in class with one another, interacting with one another, and building relationships with one another provides the atmosphere for the students to learn about and appreciate others' perspectives. In addition, because they are "academic" institutions, they want to make sure that they bring in students with the qualifications to succeed in the university setting. Sometimes these two goals compete such that academic qualifications may be downplayed in order to increase diversity.

For example, Harvard was recently sued by Asian Americans who claimed that they had been discriminated against in the admissions process, a case that, as of the writing of this chapter, had recently been heard by the Supreme Court. Harvard uses a number of different criteria for its admissions decisions including an "academic index" (using things like test scores and high school GPA) along with additional criteria such as an "extracurricular" rating, "athletic" rating, and ratings by two teachers and a school counselor. However, the main issue revolves around the "personal" rating made by the admissions group (there is also a personal rating made by alumni). The plaintiffs argue that the admissions group gives lower personal ratings to Asian Americans to offset the higher academic ratings these applicants have. Harvard argues that it uses multiple criteria, and that when examining the final outcomes, there is no discrimination. They also argue that using only the academic rating would result in cutting their African American and Hispanic admits by half.

This case provides a unique platform for discussing a number of issues regarding equal employment opportunity law, particularly in what types of statistics support that an organization is or is not discriminating against an individual or a particular group. In this chapter we will discuss the basic framework of employment law in the United States, and provide a number of examples to illustrate how the legal framework applies to organizational decision making.

SOURCE: A. Harticollis, "Does Harvard Admissions Discriminate?" *The New York Times*, October 15, 2018, https://www.nytimes.com/2018/10/15/us/harvard-affirmative-action-asian-americans.html, accessed January 2, 2019.

# Introduction

In Chapter 1, we discussed the environment of the human resource management function, and we noted that several environmental factors affect an organization's HRM function. One is the legal environment, particularly the laws affecting the management of people. As the potential troubles at Oracle suggest, legal issues can cause serious problems for a company's success and survival. In this chapter, we first present an overview of the U.S. legal system, noting the different legislative bodies, regulatory agencies, and judicial bodies that determine the legality of certain HRM practices. We then discuss the major laws and executive orders that govern these practices.

One point to make clear at the outset is that managers often want a list of "dos and don'ts" that will keep them out of legal trouble. They rely on rules such as "Don't ever ask a female applicant if she is married" without understanding the "why" behind these rules.

Clearly, certain practices are illegal or inadvisable, and this chapter will provide some valuable tips for avoiding discrimination lawsuits. However, such lists are not compatible with a strategic approach to HRM and are certainly not the route to developing a competitive advantage. They are simply mechanical reactions to the situations. Our goal is to provide an understanding of how the legislative, regulatory, and judicial systems work to define equal employment opportunity law. Armed with this understanding, a manager is better prepared to manage people within the limits imposed by the legal system. Doing so effectively is a source of competitive advantage. Doing so ineffectively results in competitive disadvantage. Rather than viewing the legal system as a constraint, firms that embrace the concept of diversity can often find that they are able to leverage the differences among people as a tremendous competitive tool.

# The Legal System in the United States

**LO 3-1**

Identify the three branches of government and the role each plays in influencing the legal environment of human resource management.

The foundation for the U.S. legal system is set forth in the U.S. Constitution, which affects HRM in two ways. First, it delineates a citizen's constitutional rights, on which the government cannot impinge.[1] Most individuals are aware of the Bill of Rights, the first 10 amendments to the Constitution; but other amendments, such as the Fourteenth Amendment, also influence HRM practices. The Fourteenth Amendment, called the equal protection clause, states that all individuals are entitled to equal protection under the law.

Second, the Constitution established three major governing bodies: the legislative, executive, and judicial branches. The Constitution explicitly defines the roles and responsibilities of each of these branches. Each branch has its own areas of authority, but these areas have often overlapped, and the borders between the branches are often blurred.

## LEGISLATIVE BRANCH

The legislative branch of the federal government consists of the House of Representatives and the Senate. These bodies develop laws that govern many HRM activities. Most of the laws stem from a perceived societal need. For example, during the civil rights movement of the early 1960s, the legislative branch moved to ensure that various minority groups received equal opportunities in many areas of life. One of these areas was employment, and thus Congress enacted Title VII of the Civil Rights Act. Similar perceived societal needs have brought about labor laws such as the Occupational Safety and Health Act, the Employee Retirement Income Security Act, the Age Discrimination in Employment Act, and, more recently, the Americans with Disabilities Act of 1990 and the Civil Rights Act of 1991.

## EXECUTIVE BRANCH

The executive branch consists of the president of the United States and the many regulatory agencies the president oversees. Although the legislative branch passes the laws, the executive branch affects these laws in many ways. First, the president can propose bills to Congress that, if passed, would become laws. Second, the president has the power to veto any law passed by Congress, thus ensuring that few laws are passed without presidential approval—which allows the president to influence how laws are written.

Third, the regulatory agencies, under the authority of the president, have responsibility for enforcing the laws. Thus, a president can influence what types of violations are pursued. For example, many laws affecting employment discrimination are enforced by the Equal Employment Opportunity Commission under the Department of Justice. During President Jimmy Carter's administration, the Department of Justice brought a lawsuit against the Birmingham, Alabama, fire department for not having enough black firefighters. This suit resulted in a consent decree that required blacks to receive preferential treatment in hiring and promotion decisions. Two years later, during Ronald Reagan's administration, the Department of Justice sided with white firefighters in a lawsuit against the city of Birmingham, alleging that the preferential treatment required by the consent decree discriminated against white firefighters.[2]

Fourth, the president can issue executive orders, which sometimes regulate the activities of organizations that have contracts with the federal government. For example, Executive Order 11246, signed by President Lyndon Johnson, required all federal contractors and subcontractors to engage in affirmative action programs designed to hire and promote women and minorities within their organizations. Fifth, the president can influence the Supreme Court to interpret laws in certain ways. When particularly sensitive cases come before the Court, the attorney general's office, representing the executive branch, argues for certain preferred outcomes. For example, one court case involved a white female schoolteacher who was laid off from her job in favor of retaining a black schoolteacher with equal seniority and performance with the reason given as "diversity." The white woman filed a lawsuit in federal court and the George H. W. Bush administration filed a brief on her behalf, arguing that diversity was not a legitimate reason to use race in decision making. She won in federal court, and the school district appealed. The Bill Clinton administration, having been elected in the meantime, filed a brief on behalf of the school district, arguing that diversity was a legitimate defense.

Finally, the president appoints all the judges in the federal judicial system, subject to approval from the legislative branch. This affects the interpretation of many laws.

## JUDICIAL BRANCH

The judicial branch consists of the federal court system, which is made up of three levels. The first level consists of the U.S. District Courts and quasi-judicial administrative agencies. The district courts hear cases involving alleged violations of federal laws. The quasi-judicial agencies, such as the National Labor Relations Board (or NLRB, which is actually an arm of the executive branch, but serves a judicial function), hear cases regarding their particular jurisdictions (in the NLRB's case, disputes between unions and management). If neither party to a suit is satisfied with the decision of the court at this level, the parties can appeal the decision to the U.S. Courts of Appeals. These courts were originally set up to ease the Supreme Court's caseload, so appeals generally go from the federal trial level to one of the 13 appellate courts before they can be heard by the highest level, the Supreme Court. The Supreme Court must grant certiorari before hearing an appealed case. However, this is not usually granted unless two appellate courts have come to differing decisions on the same point of law or if the case deals with an important interpretation of constitutional law.

The Supreme Court serves as the court of final appeal. Decisions made by the Supreme Court are binding; they can be overturned only through legislation. For example, Congress, dissatisfied with the Supreme Court's decisions in certain cases such as *Wards Cove Packing v. Atonio*, overturned those decisions through the Civil Rights Act of 1991.[3]

Having described the legal system that affects the management of human resources, we now explore some laws that regulate HRM activities, particularly equal employment opportunity laws. We first discuss the major laws that mandate equal employment opportunity in the United States. Then we examine the agencies involved in enforcing these laws. This leads us into an examination of the four theories of discrimination, with a discussion of some relevant court cases. Finally, we explore some equal employment opportunity issues facing today's managers.

# Equal Employment Opportunity

**LO 3-2**
List the major federal laws that require equal employment opportunity and the protections provided by each of these laws.

**Equal employment opportunity (EEO)**
The government's attempt to ensure that all individuals have an equal opportunity for employment, regardless of race, color, religion, sex, age, disability, or national origin.

**Equal employment opportunity (EEO)** refers to the government's attempt to ensure that all individuals have an equal chance for employment, regardless of race, color, religion, sex, age, disability, or national origin. To accomplish this, the federal government has used constitutional amendments, legislation, and executive orders, as well as the court decisions that interpret these laws. (However, equal employment laws are not the same in all countries.) The major EEO laws we discuss are summarized in Table 3.1.

## CONSTITUTIONAL AMENDMENTS

### Thirteenth Amendment

The Thirteenth Amendment of the Constitution abolished slavery in the United States. Though one might be hard-pressed to cite an example of race-based slavery in the United States today, the Thirteenth Amendment has been applied in cases where the discrimination involved the "badges" (symbols) and "incidents" of slavery.

### Fourteenth Amendment

The Fourteenth Amendment forbids the states from taking life, liberty, or property without due process of law and prevents the states from denying equal protection of the laws. Passed immediately after the Civil War, this amendment originally applied only to discrimination against blacks. It was soon broadened to protect other groups such as immigrants and Asian Americans, and more recently it has been applied to the protection of whites in allegations of reverse discrimination. In *Bakke v. California Board of Regents*, Alan Bakke alleged that he had been discriminated against in the selection of entrants to the University of California at Davis medical school.[4] The university had set aside 16 of the available 100 places for "disadvantaged" applicants who were members of racial minority groups. Under this quota system, Bakke was able to compete for only 84 positions, whereas a minority applicant was able to compete for all 100. The Court ruled in favor of Bakke, noting that this quota system had violated white individuals' right to equal protection under the law.

One important point regarding the Fourteenth Amendment is that it is applicable only to "state actions." This means that only the decisions or actions of the government or of private groups whose activities are deemed state actions can be construed as violations of the Fourteenth Amendment. Thus, one could file a claim under the Fourteenth Amendment if one were fired from a state university (a government organization) but not if one were fired by a private employer.

## CONGRESSIONAL LEGISLATION

### Reconstruction Civil Rights Acts (1866 and 1871)

The Thirteenth Amendment eradicated slavery in the United States, and the Reconstruction Civil Rights Acts were attempts to further this goal. The Civil Rights Act passed in 1866 was later broken into two statutes. Section 1982 granted all persons the same property rights as white citizens. Section 1981 granted other rights, including the right to enter into and enforce contracts. Courts have interpreted Section 1981 as granting individuals the right to make and enforce employment contracts. The Civil Rights Act of 1871 granted all citizens the right to sue in federal court if they felt they had been deprived of some civil right. Although these laws might seem outdated, they are still used because they allow the plaintiff to recover both compensatory and punitive damages.

**Table 3.1**
Summary of Major EEO Laws and Regulations

| ACT | REQUIREMENTS | COVERS | ENFORCEMENT AGENCY |
|---|---|---|---|
| Thirteenth Amendment | Abolished slavery | All individuals | Court system |
| Fourteenth Amendment | Provides equal protection for all citizens and requires due process in state action | State actions (e.g., decisions of government organizations) | Court system |
| Civil Rights Acts (CRAs) of 1866 and 1871 (as amended) | Grants all citizens the right to make, perform, modify, and terminate contracts and enjoy all benefits, terms, and conditions of the contractual relationship | All individuals | Court system |
| Equal Pay Act of 1963 | Requires that men and women performing equal jobs receive equal pay | Employers engaged in interstate commerce | Equal Employment Opportunity Commission (EEOC) |
| Title VII of the CRA of 1964 | Forbids discrimination based on race, color, religion, sex, or national origin | Employers with 15 or more employees working 20 or more weeks per year; labor unions; and employment agencies | EEOC |
| Age Discrimination in Employment Act of 1967 | Prohibits discrimination in employment against individuals 40 years of age and older | Employers with 15 or more employees working 20 or more weeks per year; labor unions; employment agencies; federal government | EEOC |
| Rehabilitation Act of 1973 | Requires affirmative action in the employment of individuals with disabilities | Government agencies; federal contractors and subcontractors with contracts greater than $2,500 | Office of Federal Contract Compliance Programs (OFCCP) |
| Vietnam Veteran's Readjustment Assistance Act of 1974 | Prohibits discrimination against veterans | Employers with federal contracts greater than $100,000 | OFCCP |
| Pregnancy Discrimination Act | Prohibits discrimination on the basis of pregnancy, childbirth, or related medical conditions | Employers with more than 15 employees | EEOC |
| Americans with Disabilities Act of 1990 | Prohibits discrimination against individuals with disabilities | Employers with more than 15 employees | EEOC |
| Civil Rights Act of 1991 | Prohibits discrimination (same as Title VII) | Same as Title VII, plus applies Section 1981 to employment discrimination cases | EEOC |
| Executive Order 11246 | Requires affirmative action in hiring women and minorities | Federal contractors and subcontractors with contracts greater than $10,000 | OFCCP |
| Executive Order 11478 | Requires the federal government base its employment policies on merit and fitness, not race, color, sex, religion, or national origin | Federal contractors and subcontractors with contracts greater than $10,000 | U.S. Office of Personnel Management (OPM) |

In fact, these laws came to the forefront in a Supreme Court case: *Patterson v. McLean Credit Union.*[5] The plaintiff had filed a discrimination complaint under Section 1981 for racial harassment. After being hired by McLean Credit Union, Patterson failed to receive any promotions or pay raises while she was employed there. She was also told that "blacks work slower than whites." Thus, she had grounds to prove discrimination and filed suit under Section 1981, arguing that she had been discriminated against in the making and enforcement of an employment contract. The Supreme Court ruled that this situation did not fall under Section 1981 because it did not involve the making and enforcement of contracts. However, the Civil Rights Act of 1991 amended this act to include the making, performance, modification, and termination of contracts, as well as all benefits, privileges, terms, and conditions of the contractual relationship.

### Equal Pay Act of 1963

The Equal Pay Act, an amendment to the Fair Labor Standards Act, requires that men and women in the same organization who are doing equal work must be paid equally. The act defines *equal* in terms of skill, effort, responsibility, and working conditions. However, the act allows for reasons why men and women performing the same job might be paid differently. If the pay differences are the result of differences in seniority, merit, quantity or quality of production, or any factor other than sex (such as shift differentials or training programs), then differences are legally allowable.

### Title VII of the Civil Rights Act of 1964

Title VII is the major legislation regulating equal employment opportunity in the United States. It was a direct result of the civil rights movement of the early 1960s, led by such individuals as Dr. Martin Luther King Jr. To ensure that employment opportunities would be based on character or ability rather than on race, Congress wrote and passed Title VII, which President Lyndon Johnson signed into law.

Title VII states that it is illegal for an employer to "(1) fail or refuse to hire or discharge any individual, or otherwise discriminate against any individual with respect to his compensation, terms, conditions, or privileges of employment because of such individual's race, color, religion, sex, or national origin, or (2) to limit, segregate, or classify his employees or applicants for employment in any way that would deprive or tend to deprive any individual of employment opportunities or otherwise adversely affect his status as an employee because of such individual's race, color, religion, sex, or national origin." The act applies to organizations with 15 or more employees working 20 or more weeks a year that are involved in interstate commerce, as well as state and local governments, employment agencies, and labor organizations. The Competing through Environmental, Social, and Governance Practices box describes how a number of women have complained that they were discriminated against at Nike.

### Age Discrimination in Employment Act of 1967

Passed in 1967 and amended in 1986, the Age Discrimination in Employment Act (ADEA) prohibits discrimination against employees over the age of 40. The act almost exactly mirrors Title VII in terms of its substantive provisions and the procedures to be followed in pursuing a case.[6] As with Title VII, the Equal Employment Opportunity Commission (EEOC) is responsible for enforcing this act.

The ADEA was designed to protect older employees when a firm reduces its workforce through layoffs. By targeting older employees, who tend to have higher pay, a firm can substantially cut labor costs. Recently, firms have often offered early retirement incentives,

# COMPETING THROUGH ENVIRONMENTAL, SOCIAL, AND GOVERNANCE PRACTICES

## A Cultural Challenge at Nike

Nike stands atop the sportswear apparel industry. Since its founding, the company has developed a strongly competitive culture, consistent with the competitiveness of athletics. While their culture has significantly contributed to the firm's success, it also may have resulted in some not-so-successful outcomes.

In 2018 the company went through a management shakeup in response to a number of complaints of discrimination against women in pay and promotions, as well as a culture that could best be described as a "boys club." Some Nike employees say that the culture has existed for years. For instance, at a global sports marketing meeting in 2002, after the last night's dinner a bus with a few dozen employees pulled up to a strip club. Lordana Ranza, who was on the bus, said only four people did not go into the club: three women and a man. "At the end of the day you need to

survive. You don't say 'this is bad,' you just think it and try to find a way to work around it."

The problems stemmed from the top of the organization. Two high-level executives, one of whom observers believed would be the next CEO, seemingly wielded inordinate power over promotions, and favored their male friends over women. In addition, when women were promoted, they were subjected to a much more rigorous vetting process. Both leaders were ousted in the shakeup.

However, more troubling, the head of HR seemed to be part of the problem. A few years ago an investigation was conducted in response to employees complaining that he was demeaning and condescending. He agreed to seek counseling and told others that his behavior needed to change. Then last year a second investigation of him was sparked by allegations that he was creating

a hostile work environment. A few months later he was encouraged to retire.

Nike clearly recognizes the past problems and has begun to rectify them. At least 11 executives left the firm as part of the purge. In addition, Nike has announced that it will raise the pay of 7,000 employees after an analysis of its compensation practices. Clearly Nike has realized the potentially negative components of culture and seeks to eliminate those and build the positive aspects of its culture.

### DISCUSSION QUESTION

1. What additional steps do you think Nike needs to do to eliminate the negative aspects of its culture while maintaining the positive aspects?

SOURCE: S. German and J. Lublin, "Inside Nike, a Boys-Club Culture and Flawed HR," *Wall Street Journal*, March 31, 2018, from www .wsj.com/article/inside-nike-a-boys-club-culture-and-flawed-hr-1522509975R.

a possible violation of the act because of the focus on older employees. Early retirement incentives require employees to sign an agreement waiving their rights to sue under the ADEA. Courts have tended to uphold the use of early retirement incentives and waivers as long as the individuals were not coerced into signing the agreements, the agreements were presented in a way that the employees could understand, and the employees were given enough time to make a decision.[7]

However, age discrimination complaints make up a large percentage of the complaints filed with the EEOC, and the number of complaints continues to grow whenever the economy is slow. For example, as we see in Figure 3.1, the number of cases increased during the early 1990s, when many firms were downsizing, but then decreased as the economy expanded. The number of complaints increased again as the economy began slowing in 2000 and with the recession in 2008. These trends often stem from firms seeking to lay off older (and thus higher-paid) employees when they are downsizing.

**Figure 3.1**

Age Discrimination Complaints, 1991–2017

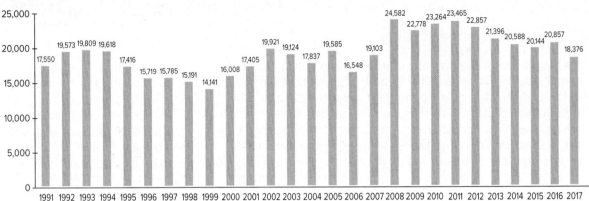

SOURCE: Equal Employment Opportunity Commission, "Age Discrimination in Employment Act (Charges Filed with EEOC)," https://www.eeoc.gov/eeoc/statistics/enforcement/adea.cfm.

These cases can be costly; most are settled out of court, but such settlements run from $50,000 to $400,000 per employee.[8] In one case, Schering-Plough Corporation fired 35-year employee Fred Maiorino after he twice failed to accept an early retirement offer made to all sales representatives. After hearing testimony that Maiorino's boss had plastered his file with negative paperwork aimed at firing him, rather than trying to help him improve his performance, the jurors unanimously decided he had been discriminated against because of his age. They awarded him $435,000 in compensatory damages and $8 million in punitive damages.[9]

### Rehabilitation Act of 1973

The Rehabilitation Act covers executive agencies and contractors and subcontractors that receive more than $2,500 annually from the federal government. It requires them to engage in affirmative action for individuals with disabilities. Congress designed this act to encourage employers to actively recruit qualified individuals with disabilities and to make reasonable accommodations to allow them to become active members of the labor market. The Employment Standards Administration of the Department of Labor enforces this act.

### Vietnam Era Veteran's Readjustment Assistance Act of 1974

Similar to the Rehabilitation Act, the Vietnam Veteran's Readjustment Assistance Act requires federal contractors and subcontractors to take affirmative action toward employing Vietnam veterans (those serving between August 5, 1964, and May 7, 1975). In addition, in 1994 (and amended in 2005) the Uniformed Services Employment and Reemployment Act was passed to prohibit discrimination against veterans, and while both acts cover more than disabilities, they are both aimed at increasing employment opportunities for veterans with disabilities. The Office of Federal Contract Compliance Programs (OFCCP), discussed later in this chapter, has authority to enforce these acts.

### Pregnancy Discrimination Act

The Pregnancy Discrimination Act is an amendment to Title VII of the Civil Rights Act of 1964. It makes illegal discrimination on the basis of pregnancy, childbirth, or related medical conditions as a form of unlawful sex discrimination. An employer cannot refuse to hire a pregnant woman because of her pregnancy; a pregnancy-related condition; or the prejudices of co-workers, clients, or customers. For instance, in a recent court case, the retail store Motherhood Maternity, a Philadelphia-based maternity clothes retailer, settled a pregnancy discrimination and retaliation lawsuit brought by the EEOC. The EEOC had charged that the company refused to hire qualified female applicants because they were pregnant. As a result of the settlement, Motherhood Maternity agreed to a three-year consent decree requiring them to pay plaintiffs $375,000, adopt and distribute an antidiscrimination policy specifically prohibiting discrimination on the basis of pregnancy, train its Florida employees on the new policy, post a notice of resolution of the lawsuit, and provide twice-a-year reports to the EEOC on any pregnancy discrimination complaints.[10]

In addition, regarding pregnancy and maternity leave, employers may not single out pregnancy-related conditions for special procedures to determine an employee's ability to work, and if an employee is temporarily unable to perform during her pregnancy, the employer must treat her the same as any temporarily disabled employees. The act also requires that any health insurance must cover expenses for pregnancy-related conditions on the same basis as costs for other medical conditions. Finally, pregnancy-related benefits cannot be limited to married employees, and if an employer provides any benefits to workers on leave, they must also provide the same benefits for those on leave for pregnancy-related conditions.

Recently the EEOC filed suit against HCS Medical Staffing Inc. for allegedly discriminating against a pregnant employee and then firing her while she was on maternity leave. According to the EEOC's suit, owner Charles Sisson engaged in escalating negative comments about the upcoming maternity leave of HCS bookkeeper Roxy Leger. He allegedly insisted that Leger's pregnancy was a joke, described her maternity leave as "vacation," and insisted that maternity leave should be no longer than two days. Sisson then allegedly terminated Leger, who had no prior negative comments on her work performance, seven days after she gave birth by cesarean section.[11]

## Civil Rights Act of 1991
The Civil Rights Act of 1991 (CRA 1991) amends Title VII of the Civil Rights Act of 1964, Section 1981 of the Civil Rights Act of 1866, the Americans with Disabilities Act, and the Age Discrimination in Employment Act of 1967. One major change in EEO law under CRA 1991 has been the addition of compensatory and punitive damages in cases of discrimination under Title VII and the Americans with Disabilities Act. Before CRA 1991, Title VII limited damage claims to equitable relief such as back pay, lost benefits, front pay in some cases, and attorneys' fees and costs. CRA 1991 allows compensatory and punitive damages when intentional or reckless discrimination is proven. Compensatory damages include such things as future pecuniary loss, emotional pain, suffering, and loss of enjoyment of life. Punitive damages are meant to discourage employers from discriminating by providing for payments to the plaintiff beyond the actual damages suffered.

Recognizing that one or a few discrimination cases could put an organization out of business, thus adversely affecting many innocent employees, Congress has put limits on the amount of punitive damages. Table 3.2 depicts these limits. As can be seen, damages range from $50,000 to $300,000 per violation, depending on the size of the organization. Punitive damages are available only if the employer intentionally discriminated against the plaintiff(s) or if the employer discriminated with malice or reckless indifference to the employee's federally protected rights. These damages are excluded for an employment practice held to be unlawful because of its disparate impact.[12]

**Table 3.2**
Maximum Punitive
Damages Allowed
under the Civil Rights
Act of 1991

| EMPLOYER SIZE | DAMAGE LIMIT |
|---|---|
| 14 to 100 employees | $ 50,000 |
| 101 to 200 employees | 50,000 |
| 201 to 500 employees | 200,000 |
| More than 500 employees | 300,000 |

The addition of damages to CRA 1991 has had two immediate effects. First, by increasing the potential payoff for a successful discrimination suit, it has increased the number of suits filed against businesses. Second, organizations are now more likely to grant all employees an equal opportunity for employment, regardless of their race, sex, religion, or national origin. Many organizations have felt the need to make the composition of their workforce mirror the general population to avoid costly lawsuits. This act adds a financial incentive for doing so.

## Americans with Disabilities Act of 1990

Americans with
Disabilities Act
(ADA)
A 1990 act prohibiting
individuals with
disabilities from being
discriminated against
in the workplace.

One of the most far-reaching acts concerning the management of human resources is the **Americans with Disabilities Act (ADA)**. This act protects individuals with disabilities from being discriminated against in the workplace. It prohibits discrimination based on disability in all employment practices such as job application procedures, hiring, firing, promotions, compensation, and training—in addition to other employment activities such as advertising, recruitment, tenure, layoff, leave, and fringe benefits. We will cover its various stipulations individually.

The ADA defines a disability as a physical or mental impairment that substantially limits one or more major life activities, a record of having such an impairment, or being regarded as having such an impairment. The first part of the definition refers to individuals who have serious disabilities—such as epilepsy, blindness, deafness, or paralysis—that affect their ability to perform major life activities such as walking, seeing, performing manual tasks, learning, caring for oneself, and working. The second part refers to individuals who have a history of disability, such as someone who has had cancer but is currently in remission, someone with a history of mental illness, and someone with a history of heart disease. The third part of the definition, "being regarded as having a disability," refers, for example, to an individual who is severely disfigured and is denied employment because an employer fears negative reactions from others.[13]

Thus, the ADA covers specific physiological disabilities such as cosmetic disfigurement and anatomical loss affecting the neurological, musculoskeletal, sensory, respiratory, cardiovascular, reproductive, digestive, genitourinary, hemic, or lymphatic systems. In addition, it covers mental and psychological disorders such as intellectual disability, organic brain syndrome, emotional or mental illness, and learning disabilities. However, conditions such as obesity, substance abuse, eye and hair color, and lefthandedness are not covered.[14]

In addition, the Americans with Disabilities Act Amendments Act (ADAAA), effective January 1, 2009, broadened the scope of who is considered to be an individual with a disability. It states that the definition of disability should be broadly construed and that the "question of whether an individual's impairment is a disability under the ADA should not demand extensive analysis." The Supreme Court had interpreted the term "substantially limited" in a major life activity to require the individual to be "significantly restricted," but the ADAAA states that this is too high a standard and directs the EEOC to revise its regulations to set a lower standard. Also, regarding the term "regarded as disabled," previously employers could avoid liability by showing that the impairment did not substantially limit a major life activity. However, the ADAAA states that an employee can prove he or she was subjected to an illegal act "because of an actual or perceived physical or mental impairment whether or not the impairment limits or is perceived to limit a major life activity." In fact, in response to the ADAAA, the EEOC has clarified and somewhat redefined *disability*. According to their most recent guidelines, a disability is defined along three so-called prongs: a physical or mental impairment that "substantially limits one or more major life activity"; a record or past history of such an impairment; and/or being "regarded as" having a disability by an employer whether you have one or not, usually in terms of hiring, firing, or demotion. In essence, a person is considered disabled not only if he or she cannot *do* something but also if he or she has a medical condition, whether or not it impairs functioning.[15]

## EXECUTIVE ORDERS

Executive orders are directives issued and amended unilaterally by the president. These orders do not require congressional approval, yet they have the force of law. Two executive orders directly affect HRM.

### Executive Order 11246

President Johnson issued this executive order, which prohibits discrimination based on race, color, religion, sex, and national origin. Unlike Title VII, this order applies only to federal contractors and subcontractors. Employers receiving more than $10,000 from the federal government must take affirmative action to ensure against discrimination, and those with contracts greater than $50,000 must develop a written affirmative action plan for each of their establishments within 120 days of the beginning of the contract. The OFCCP enforces this executive order.

Although this order requires contractors to take affirmative action, many companies seek, on their own, to develop more diverse workforces. When they do so, they are proud to broadcast this. However, creating a diverse workforce is often difficult, particularly in the science, technology, engineering, and mathematics (STEM) fields.

### Executive Order 11478

President Richard Nixon issued Executive Order 11478, which requires the federal government to base all its employment policies on merit and fitness, and specifies that race, color, sex, religion, and national origin should not be considered. (The U.S. Office of Personnel Management is in charge of enforcement.) The order also extends to all contractors and subcontractors doing $10,000 worth of business with the federal government. (The relevant government agencies are responsible for ensuring that contractors and subcontractors comply with the order.)

# Enforcement of Equal Employment Opportunity

**LO 3-3**
Discuss the roles, responsibilities, and requirements of the federal agencies responsible for enforcing equal employment opportunity laws.

As discussed previously, the executive branch of the federal government bears most of the responsibility for enforcing all EEO laws passed by the legislative branch. In addition, the executive branch must enforce the executive orders issued by the president. The two

**Equal Employment Opportunity Commission (EEOC)** The government commission established to ensure that all individuals have an equal opportunity for employment, regardless of race, color, religion, sex, age, disability, or national origin.

agencies responsible for the enforcement of these laws and executive orders are the **Equal Employment Opportunity Commission (EEOC)** and the Office of Federal Contract Compliance Programs, respectively.

## EQUAL EMPLOYMENT OPPORTUNITY COMMISSION (EEOC)

An independent federal agency, the EEOC is responsible for enforcing most of the EEO laws, such as Title VII, the Equal Pay Act, and the Americans with Disabilities Act. The EEOC has three major responsibilities: investigating and resolving discrimination complaints, gathering information, and issuing guidelines.

### Investigation and Resolution

Individuals who feel they have been discriminated against must file a complaint with the EEOC or a similar state agency within 180 days of the incident. Failure to file a complaint within the 180 days results in the case being dismissed immediately, with certain exceptions, such as the enactment of a seniority system that has an intentionally discriminatory purpose. For instance, the Lilly Ledbetter Fair Pay Act signed by President Barack Obama was crafted in direct response to the 180-day window. Ledbetter had been an area manager at the Goodyear Tire and Rubber plant in Alabama from 1979 to 1998, during which time she received lower raises than male employees. The differences were such that by the end of her career she was making $6,700 less per year than her male counterparts, and because pension payments were related to the salary at the time of retirement, she received smaller pension payments. When she filed the lawsuit, the Supreme Court ruled that the illegal acts were the pay raise decisions themselves (which fell far outside the 180-day window); Ledbetter wanted to argue that every time she received a pension check lower than her peers it served as an act of discrimination. Thus, Congress passed the act specifying that an "illegal act" occurs when (1) a discriminatory compensation decision is adopted; (2) an employee becomes subject to the decision; or (3) an employee is affected by its application, including each time compensation is paid.

Once the complaint is filed, the EEOC takes responsibility for investigating the claim of discrimination. The complainant must give the EEOC 60 days to investigate the complaint. If the EEOC either does not believe the complaint to be valid or fails to complete the investigation, the complainant may sue in federal court. If the EEOC determines that discrimination has taken place, its representatives will attempt to provide a reconciliation between the two parties without burdening the court system with a lawsuit. Sometimes the EEOC enters into a consent decree with the discriminating organization. This decree is an agreement between the agency and the organization that the organization will cease certain discriminatory practices and possibly institute additional affirmative action practices to rectify its history of discrimination.

If the EEOC cannot come to an agreement with the organization, it has two options. First, it can issue a "right to sue" letter to the alleged victim, which certifies that the agency has investigated and found validity in the victim's allegations. Second, although less likely, the agency may aid the alleged victim in bringing suit in federal court.

### Information Gathering

The EEOC also plays a role in monitoring the hiring practices of organizations. Each year, organizations with 100 or more employees must file a report (EEO-1) with the EEOC that provides the number of women and minorities employed in nine different job categories. The EEOC computer analyzes these reports to identify patterns of discrimination that can then be attacked through class-action suits.

## Issuance of Guidelines

A third responsibility of the EEOC is to issue guidelines that help employers determine when their decisions are violations of the laws enforced by the EEOC. These guidelines are not laws themselves, but the courts give great deference to them when hearing employment discrimination cases.

For example, the *Uniform Guidelines on Employee Selection Procedures* is a set of guidelines issued by the EEOC, the Department of Labor, the Department of Justice, and the U.S. Civil Service Commission.[16] This document provides guidance on the ways an organization should develop and administer selection systems so as not to violate Title VII. The courts often refer to the *Uniform Guidelines* to determine whether a company has engaged in discriminatory conduct or to determine the validity of the procedures it used to validate a selection system. Another example: Since the passage of the ADA, employers have been somewhat confused about the act's implications for their hiring procedures. Therefore, the EEOC issued guidelines in the *Federal Register* that provided more detailed information regarding what the agency will consider legal and illegal employment practices concerning disabled individuals. Although companies are well advised to follow these guidelines, it is possible that courts will interpret the ADA differently from the EEOC. Thus, through the issuance of guidelines, the EEOC gives employers directions for making employment decisions that do not conflict with existing laws.

## OFFICE OF FEDERAL CONTRACT COMPLIANCE PROGRAMS (OFCCP)

The OFCCP is the agency responsible for enforcing the executive orders that cover companies doing business with the federal government. Businesses with contracts for more than $50,000 cannot discriminate in employment based on race, color, religion, national origin, or sex, and they must have a written affirmative action plan on file.

These plans have three basic components.[17] First, the **utilization analysis** compares the race, sex, and ethnic composition of the employer's workforce with that of the available labor supply. For each job group, the employer must identify the percentage of its workforce with a given characteristic (e.g., female) and identify the percentage of workers in the relevant labor market with that characteristic. If the percentage in the employer's workforce is much less than the percentage in the comparison group, then that minority group is considered to be "underutilized."

Second, the employer must develop specific **goals and timetables** for achieving balance in the workforce concerning these characteristics (particularly where underutilization exists). Goals and timetables specify the percentage of women and minorities that the employer seeks to have in each job group and the date by which that percentage is to be attained. These are not to be viewed as quotas, which entail setting aside a specific number of positions to be filled only by members of the protected class. Goals and timetables are much more flexible, requiring only that the employer have specific goals and take steps to achieve those goals. In fact, one study that examined companies with the goal of increasing black employment found that only 10% of them actually achieved their goals. Although this may sound discouragingly low, it is important to note that these companies increased their black employment more than companies that set no such goals.[18]

Third, employers with federal contracts must develop a list of **action steps** they will take toward attaining their goals to reduce underutilization. The company's CEO must make it clear to the entire organization that the company is committed to reducing underutilization, and all management levels must be involved in the planning process. For example, organizations can communicate job openings to women and minorities through publishing the company's affirmative action policy, recruiting at predominantly

**Utilization analysis**
A comparison of the race, sex, and ethnic composition of an employer's workforce with that of the available labor supply.

**Goals and timetables**
The part of a written affirmative action plan that specifies the percentage of women and minorities that an employer seeks to have in each job group and the date by which that percentage is to be attained.

**Action steps**
The part of a written affirmative action plan that specifies what an employer plans to do to reduce underutilization of protected groups.

female or minority schools, participating in programs designed to increase employment opportunities for underemployed groups, and removing unnecessary barriers to employment. Organizations must also take affirmative steps toward hiring Vietnam veterans and individuals with disabilities.

The OFCCP annually audits government contractors to ensure that they actively pursue the goals in their plans. These audits consist of (1) examining the company's affirmative action plan and (2) conducting on-site visits to examine how individual employees perceive the company's affirmative action policies. If the OFCCP finds that the contractors or subcontractors are not complying with the executive order, then its representatives may notify the EEOC (if there is evidence that Title VII has been violated), advise the Department of Justice to institute criminal proceedings, request that the secretary of labor cancel or suspend any current contracts, and forbid the firm from bidding on future contracts. This last penalty, called debarment, is the OFCCP's most potent weapon.

Having discussed the major laws defining equal employment opportunity and the agencies that enforce these laws, we now address the various types of discrimination and the ways these forms of discrimination have been interpreted by the courts in a number of cases.

# Types of Discrimination

**LO 3-4**
Identify the three theories of discrimination under Title VII of the Civil Rights Act and apply these theories to different discrimination situations.

How would you know if you had been discriminated against? Assume that you have applied for a job and were not hired. How do you know if the organization decided not to hire you because you are unqualified, because you are less qualified than the individual ultimately hired, or simply because the person in charge of the hiring decision "didn't like your type"? Discrimination is a multifaceted issue. It is often not easy to determine the extent to which unfair discrimination affects an employer's decisions.

Legal scholars have identified three theories of discrimination: disparate treatment, disparate impact, and reasonable accommodation. In addition, there is protection for those participating in discrimination cases or opposing discriminatory actions. In the act, these theories are stated in very general terms. However, the court system has defined and delineated these theories through the cases brought before it. A comparison of the theories of discrimination is given in Table 3.3.

## DISPARATE TREATMENT

**Disparate treatment**
A theory of discrimination based on different treatment given to individuals because of their race, color, religion, sex, national origin, age, or disability status.

**Disparate treatment** exists when individuals in similar situations are treated differently and the different treatment is based on the individual's race, color, religion, sex, national origin, age, or disability status. If two people with the same qualifications apply for a job and the employer decides whom to hire based on one individual's race, the individual not hired is a victim of disparate treatment. In a disparate treatment case, the plaintiff must prove that there was a discriminatory motive—that is, that the employer intended to discriminate.

Whenever individuals are treated differently because of their race, sex, or the like, there is disparate treatment. For example, if a company fails to hire women with school-age children (claiming the women will be frequently absent) but hires men with school-age children, the applicants are being treated differently based on sex. Another example would be an employer who checks the references and investigates the conviction records of minority applicants but does not do so for white applicants. Why are managers advised not to ask about marital status? Because in most cases, a manager will either ask only the female applicants or, if the manager asks both males and females, he or she will make different

**Table 3.3**

Comparison of Discrimination Theories

| | TYPES OF DISCRIMINATION | | |
| --- | --- | --- | --- |
| | DISPARATE TREATMENT | DISPARATE IMPACT | REASONABLE ACCOMMODATION |
| Show intent? | Yes | No | Yes |
| Show intent? | Individual is a member of a protected group, was qualified for the job, and was turned down for the job, and the job remained open | Statistical disparity in the effects of a facially neutral employment practice | Individual has a belief or disability, provided the employer with notice (request to accommodate), and was adversely affected by a failure to be accommodated |
| Employer's defense | Produce a legitimate, nondiscriminatory reason for the employment decision or show bona fide occupational qualification (BFOQ) | Prove that the employment practice bears a manifest relationship with job performance | Job-relatedness and business necessity, undue hardship, or direct threat to health or safety |
| Plaintiff's rebuttal | Reason offered was merely a "pretext" for discrimination | Alternative procedures exist that meet the employer's goal without having disparate impact | |
| Monetary damages | Compensatory and punitive damages | Equitable relief (e.g., back pay) | Compensatory and punitive damages (if discrimination was intentional or employer failed to show good-faith efforts to accommodate) |

assumptions about females (such as "She will have to move if her husband gets a job elsewhere") and males (such as "He's very stable"). In all these examples, notice that (1) people are being treated differently and (2) there is an actual intent to treat them differently.[19]

For instance, the Timken Company agreed to a $120,000 settlement over a sex and disability discrimination suit. In 2007, Carmen Halloran applied for a full-time position at Timken, after having worked at the facility as a part-time process associate for four years. The EEOC alleged that the company refused to hire Halloran because managers believed that Halloran, who is the mother of a disabled child, would be unable to work full time and care for her disabled child. They also alleged that this decision was based on an unfounded gender stereotype that the mother of a disabled child would necessarily be the primary caregiver because they did hire men with disabled children. "The EEOC is committed to fighting discrimination in the workplace," said Lynette A. Barnes, regional attorney for the EEOC's Charlotte District Office. "Employers must be careful not to apply stereotypes against women based on perceptions that they must always be the primary caregivers and therefore are unreliable employees."[20]

To understand how disparate treatment is applied in the law, let's look at how an actual court case, filed under disparate treatment, would proceed.

### The Plaintiff's Burden

As in any legal case, the plaintiff has the burden of proving that the defendant has committed an illegal act. This is the idea of a *prima facie* case. In a disparate treatment case, the plaintiff meets the prima facie burden by showing four things:

1. The plaintiff belongs to a protected group.
2. The plaintiff applied for and was qualified for the job.
3. Despite possessing the qualifications, the plaintiff was rejected.
4. After the plaintiff was rejected, the position remained open and the employer continued to seek applicants with similar qualifications, or the position was filled by someone with similar qualifications.

Although these four elements may seem easy to prove, it is important to note that what the court is trying to do is rule out the most obvious reasons for rejecting the plaintiff's claim (for example, the plaintiff did not apply or was not qualified, or the position was already filled or had been eliminated). If these alternative explanations are ruled out, the court assumes that the hiring decision was based on a discriminatory motive.

### The Defendant's Rebuttal

Once the plaintiff has made the prima facie case for discrimination, the burden shifts to the defendant. The burden is different depending on whether the prima facie case presents only circumstantial evidence (there is no direct evidence of discrimination such as a formal policy to discriminate, but rather discriminatory intent must be inferred) or direct evidence (a formal policy of discrimination for some perceived legitimate reason). In cases of circumstantial evidence, the defendant simply must produce a legitimate, nondiscriminatory reason, such as that, although the plaintiff was qualified, the individual hired was more qualified.

However, in cases where direct evidence exists, such as a formal policy of hiring only women for waitress jobs because the business is aimed at catering to male customers, then the defendant is more likely to offer a different defense. This defense argues that, for this job, a factor such as sex or religion was a **bona fide occupational qualification (BFOQ)**. For example, if one were hiring an individual to hand out towels in a women's locker room, being a woman might be a BFOQ. However, there are very few cases in which sex qualifies as a BFOQ, and in these cases it must be a necessary, rather than simply a preferred, characteristic of the job.

*UAW v. Johnson Controls, Inc.*, illustrates the difficulty in using a BFOQ as a defense.[21] Johnson Controls, a manufacturer of car batteries, had instituted a "fetal protection" policy that excluded women of childbearing age from a number of jobs in which they would be exposed to lead, which can cause birth defects in children. The company argued that sex was a BFOQ essential to maintaining a safe workplace. The Supreme Court did not uphold the company's policy, arguing that BFOQs are limited to policies that are directly related to a worker's ability to do the job.

Interestingly, some factors are by no means off-limits when it comes to discrimination. For instance, a survey by *Newsweek* of 202 hiring managers revealed that almost 60% said that qualified, yet unattractive, applicants face a harder time getting hired. In addition, two-thirds believe that managers hesitate before hiring qualified, but overweight, candidates.[22]

### The Plaintiff's Rebuttal

If the defendant provides a legitimate, nondiscriminatory reason for its employment decision, the burden shifts back to the plaintiff. The plaintiff must now show that the reason

**Bona fide occupational qualification (BFOQ)** A job qualification based on race, sex, religion, and so on that an employer asserts is a necessary qualification for the job.

offered by the defendant was not in fact the reason for its decision but merely a "pretext" or excuse for its actual discriminatory decision. This could entail providing evidence that white applicants with similar qualifications to the plaintiff have often been hired while black applicants with similar qualifications were all rejected. To illustrate disparate treatment, let's look at the first major case dealing with disparate treatment, *McDonnell Douglas Corp. v. Green*.

This Supreme Court case was the first to delineate the four criteria for a prima facie case of discrimination. From 1956 to 1964, Green had been an employee at McDonnell Douglas, a manufacturing plant in St. Louis, Missouri, that employed about 30,000 people. In 1964, he was laid off during a general workforce reduction. While unemployed, he participated in some activities that the company undoubtedly frowned upon: a "lock-in," where he and others placed a chain and padlock on the front door of a building to prevent the employees from leaving; and a "stall-in," where a group of employees stalled their cars at the gates of the plant so that no one could enter or leave the parking lot. About three weeks after the lock-in, McDonnell Douglas advertised for qualified mechanics, Green's trade, and he reapplied. When the company rejected his application, he sued, arguing that the company didn't hire him because of his race and because of his persistent involvement in the civil rights movement.

In making his prima facie case, Green had no problem showing that he was a member of a protected group, that he had applied for and was qualified for the job (having already worked in the job), that he was rejected, and that the company continued to advertise the position. The company's defense was that the plaintiff was not hired because he participated in the lock-in and the stall-in. In other words, the company was merely refusing to hire a troublemaker.

The plaintiff responded that the company's stated reason for not hiring him was a pretext for discrimination. He pointed out that white employees who had participated in the same activities (the lock-in and the stall-in) were rehired, whereas he was not. The court found in favor of the plaintiff.

This case illustrates how similarly situated individuals (white and black) can be treated differently (whites were hired back whereas blacks were not) with the differences in treatment based on race. As we will discuss later, most plaintiffs bring cases of sexual harassment under this theory of discrimination, sexual harassment being a situation in which individuals are treated differently because of their sex.

## Mixed-Motive Cases

In a mixed-motive case, the defendant acknowledges that some discriminatory motive existed but argues that the same hiring decision would have been reached even without the discriminatory motive. In *Hopkins v. Price Waterhouse*, Ann Hopkins was an accountant who had applied for partnership in her firm. Although she had brought in a large amount of business and had received high praise from her clients, she was turned down for a partnership on two separate occasions. In her performance reviews, she had been told to adopt more feminine dress and speech and received many other comments that suggested gender-based stereotypes. In court, the company admitted that a sex-based stereotype existed but argued that it would have come to the same decision (not promoted Hopkins) even if the stereotype had not existed.

One of the main questions that came out of this case was, Who has the burden of proof? Does the plaintiff have to prove that a different decision would have been made (that Hopkins would have been promoted) in the absence of the discriminatory motive? Or does the defendant have to prove that the same decision would have been made?

According to CRA 1991, if the plaintiff demonstrates that race, sex, color, religion, or national origin was a motivating factor for any employment practice, the prima facie burden has been met, and the burden of proof is on the employer to demonstrate that the same decision would have been made even if the discriminatory motive had not been present. If the employer can do this, the plaintiff cannot collect compensatory or punitive damages. However, the court may order the employer to quit using the discriminatory motive in its future employment decisions. The Evidence-Based HR box describes how weight discrimination impacts people with obesity.

## EVIDENCE-BASED HR

### A Large Discrimination Problem

Weight discrimination, that is, making decisions based on negative stereotypes about people who are perceived as overweight, is not illegal and has been described as the last acceptable form of discrimination. A recent study used experts to rate male and female CEOs regarding their weight. These ratings suggested that 5 to 22% of top female CEOs in the United States are overweight and approximately 5% are obese, and that 45 to 61% of male CEOs are overweight and approximately 5% are obese. Compared to the general U.S. population, overweight and obese women are significantly underrepresented among top female CEOs. Compared to the population, these results show that overweight and obese female CEOs are underrepresented, overweight male CEOs are overrepresented, and obese male CEOs are underrepresented. In other words, weight discrimination occurs at the highest levels in organizations, and it impacts women more negatively than men.

SOURCE: Patricia V. Roehling, Mark V. Roehling, Jeffrey D. Vandlen, Justin Blazek, William C. Guy, "Weight Discrimination and the Glass Ceiling Effect among Top US CEOs," *Equal Opportunities International*, 28, no. 2 (2009), pp. 179–196.

## DISPARATE IMPACT

**Disparate impact**
A theory of discrimination based on facially neutral employment practices that disproportionately exclude a protected group from employment opportunities.

The second type of discrimination is called **disparate impact**. It occurs when a facially neutral employment practice disproportionately excludes a protected group from employment opportunities. A facially neutral employment practice is one that lacks obvious discriminatory content yet affects one group to a greater extent than other groups, such as an employment test. Although the Supreme Court inferred disparate impact from Title VII in the *Griggs v. Duke Power* case (discussed later in this section), it has since been codified into the Civil Rights Act of 1991.

There is an important distinction between disparate impact and disparate treatment discrimination. For there to be discrimination under disparate treatment, there has to be intentional discrimination. Under disparate impact, intent is irrelevant. The important criterion is that the consequences of the employment practice are discriminatory.

For example, if, for some practical reason, you hired individuals based on their height, you may not have intended to discriminate against anyone, yet using height would have a disproportionate impact on certain protected groups. Women tend to be shorter than men, so fewer women will be hired. Certain ethnic groups, such as those of Asian ancestry, also tend to be shorter than those of European ancestry. Thus, your facially neutral employment practice will have a disparate impact on certain protected groups.

This is not to imply that simply because a selection practice has disparate impact, it is necessarily illegal. Some characteristics (such as height) are not equally distributed across race and gender groups; however, the important question is whether the characteristic is related to successful performance on the job. To help you understand how disparate impact works, let's look at a court proceeding involving a disparate impact claim.

## The Plaintiff's Burden

In a disparate impact case, the plaintiff must make the prima facie case by showing that the employment practice in question disproportionately affects a protected group relative to the majority group. To illustrate this theory, let's assume that you are a manager who has 60 positions to fill. Your applicant pool has 80 white and 40 black applicants. You use a test that selects 48 of the white and 12 of the black applicants. Is this a disparate impact? Two alternative quantitative analyses are often used to determine whether a test has adverse impact.

The **four-fifths rule** states that a test has disparate impact if the hiring rate for the minority group is less than four-fifths (or 80%) of the hiring rate for the majority group. Applying this analysis to the preceding example, we would first calculate the hiring rates for each group:

$$\text{Whites} = 48/80 = 60\%$$
$$\text{Blacks} = 12/40 = 30\%$$

Then we would compare the hiring rate of the minority group (30%) with that of the majority group (60%). Using the four-fifths rule, we would determine that the test has adverse impact if the hiring rate of the minority group is less than 80% of the hiring rate of the majority group. Because it is less (i.e., 30%/60% = 50%, which is less than 80%), we would conclude that the test has adverse impact. The four-fifths rule is used as a rule of thumb by the EEOC in determining adverse impact.

The **standard deviation rule** uses actual probability distributions to determine adverse impact. This analysis uses the difference between the expected representation (or hiring rates) for minority groups and the actual representation (or hiring rate) to determine whether the difference between these two values is greater than would occur by chance. Thus, in our example, 33% (40 of 120) of the applicants were blacks, so one would expect 33% (20 of 60) of those hired to be black. However, only 12 black applicants were hired. To determine if the difference between the expected representation and the actual representation is greater than we would expect by chance, we calculate the standard deviation (which, you might remember from your statistics class, is the standard deviation in a binomial distribution):

$$\sqrt{\text{Number hired} \times \frac{\text{Number of minority applicants}}{\text{Number of total applicants}} \times \frac{\text{Number of nonminority applicants}}{\text{Number of total applicants}}}$$

or in this case:

$$\sqrt{60 \times \frac{40}{120} \times \frac{80}{120}} = 3.6$$

If the difference between the actual representation and the expected representation (20 − 12 = 8 in this case) of blacks is greater than 2 standard deviations (2 × 3.6 = 7.2

**Four-fifths rule**
A rule that states that an employment test has disparate impact if the hiring rate for a minority group is less than four-fifths, or 80%, of the hiring rate for the majority group.

**Standard deviation rule**
A rule used to analyze employment tests to determine disparate impact; it uses the difference between the expected representation for minority groups and the actual representation to determine whether the difference between the two is greater than would occur by chance.

in this case), we would conclude that the test had adverse impact against blacks, because we would expect this result less than 1 time in 20 if the test were equally difficult for both whites and blacks.

The *Wards Cove Packing Co. v. Atonio* case involved an interesting use of statistics. The plaintiffs showed that the jobs in the cannery (lower-paying jobs) were filled primarily with minority applicants (in this case, American Eskimos). However, only a small percentage of the noncannery jobs (those with higher pay) were filled by minorities. The plaintiffs argued that this statistical disparity in the racial makeup of the cannery and noncannery jobs was proof of discrimination. The federal district, appellate, and Supreme Courts all found for the defendant, stating that this disparity was not proof of discrimination.

Once the plaintiff has demonstrated adverse impact, he or she has met the burden of a prima facie case of discrimination.[23]

### Defendant's Rebuttal

According to CRA 1991, once the plaintiff has made a prima facie case, the burden of proof shifts to the defendant, who must show that the employment practice is a "business necessity." This is accomplished by showing that the practice bears a relationship with some legitimate employer goal. With respect to job selection, this relationship is demonstrated by showing the job relatedness of the test, usually by reporting a validity study of some type, to be discussed in Chapter 6. For now, suffice it to say that the employer shows that the test scores are significantly correlated with measures of job performance.

Measures of job performance used in validation studies can include such things as objective measures of output, supervisor ratings of job performance, and success in training.[24] Normally, performance appraisal ratings are used, but these ratings must be valid for the court to accept the validation results. For example, in *Albemarle Paper v. Moody*, the employer demonstrated that the selection battery predicted performance (measured with supervisors' overall rankings of employees) in only some of the 13 occupational groups in which it was used. In this case, the court was especially critical of the supervisory ratings used as the measure of job performance. The court stated, "There is no way of knowing precisely what criteria of job performance the supervisors were considering."[25]

### Plaintiff's Rebuttal

If the employer shows that the employment practice is the result of some business necessity, the plaintiff's last resort is to argue that other employment practices could sufficiently meet the employer's goal without adverse impact. Thus, if a plaintiff can demonstrate that selection tests other than the one used by the employer exist, do not have adverse impact, and correlate with job performance as highly as the employer's test, then the defendant can be found guilty of discrimination. Many cases deal with standardized tests of cognitive ability, so it is important to examine alternatives to these tests that have less adverse impact while still meeting the employer's goal. At least two separate studies reviewing alternative selection devices such as interviews, biographical data, assessment centers, and work sample tests have concluded that none of them met both criteria.[26] It seems that when the employment practice in question is a standardized test of cognitive ability, plaintiffs will have a difficult time rebutting the defendant's rebuttal.

To illustrate how this process works, let's look at the *Griggs v. Duke Power* case.[27] Following the passage of Title VII, Duke Power instituted a new system for making selection and promotion decisions. The system required either a high school diploma or a

| | BASELINE | | EXPANDED | |
|---|---|---|---|---|
| | ADMIT RATE | FOUR-FIFTHS | ADMIT RATE | FOUR-FIFTHS |
| White | 4.20 | 0.95 | 8.00 | 0.74* |
| Hispanic | 5.30 | 0.75* | 7.00 | 0.84 |
| African American | 6.50 | 0.62* | 8.60 | 0.68* |
| Asian | 4.00 | | 5.90 | |
| Total | 4.50 | 0.89 | 7.30 | 0.80 |

**Table 3.4**
Harvard Admit Rates by Racial/Ethnic Group

*Admit rate for Asian Americans less than 80% of the compared group

passing score on two professionally developed tests (the Wonderlic Personnel Test and the Bennett Mechanical Comprehension Test). A passing score was set so that it would be equal to the national median for high school graduates who had taken the tests.

The plaintiffs met their prima facie burden showing that both the high school diploma requirement and the test battery had adverse impacts on blacks. According to the 1960 census, 34% of white males had high school diplomas, compared with only 12% of black males. Similarly, 58% of white males passed the test battery, whereas only 6% of blacks passed.

Duke Power was unable to defend its use of these employment practices. A company vice president testified that the company had not studied the relationship between these employment practices and the employees' ability to perform the job. In addition, employees already on the job who did not have high school diplomas and had never taken the tests were performing satisfactorily. Thus, Duke Power lost the case.

It is interesting to note that the court recognized that the company had not intended to discriminate, mentioning that the company was making special efforts to help undereducated employees through financing two-thirds of the cost of tuition for high school training. This illustrates the importance of the consequences, as opposed to the motivation, in determining discrimination under the disparate impact theory.

The Harvard story at the beginning of this chapter provides a great opportunity to explore how plaintiffs use statistics in a disparate impact case.

The plaintiff's expert witness used two data sets to make the case that Harvard was discriminating. One was the "baseline" set that excluded athletes, legacies, and early decision applicants, and the "expanded" set included all those applicants as well. Table 3.4 shows the admit rates for each group, with the four-fifths rule applied to each group relative to Asian Americans.

On the other hand, the defendant, Harvard, argues that the share of the different groups in the applicant pool is very similar to the share of each group in those students admitted. This can be seen in the numbers in Table 3.5.

| | SHARE OF APPLICANTS | SHARE OF ADMITS |
|---|---|---|
| White | 40.3 | 37.6 |
| Hispanic | 12.8 | 14.9 |
| African American | 11.0 | 15.8 |
| Asian | 28.3 | 24.9 |

**Table 3.5**
Comparison of the Pool of Harvard's Applicants to Admits by Racial/Ethnic Groups

So, as you can see, the different sides in a disparate impact case use the statistics that support their case.

## PATTERN AND PRACTICE

In class-action pattern and practice lawsuits, plaintiffs attempt to show three things. First, they show some statistical disparities between the composition of some group within the company compared to some other relevant group. For instance, in a discrimination case brought against Walmart (*Dukes v. Walmart*), the plaintiff's lawyers pointed to two comparative statistics as evidence of discrimination. First, they compared the female representation in the nonmanagerial (63.4%) and managerial (33.6%) employee groups. They also compared the female representation in the managerial group (again, 33.6%) with that in their top 20 competitors (56.5%). They also calculated that hourly female workers were paid, on average, $1,100 less per year than men and salaried women received $14,500 less. However, Walmart disputed the list of comparison companies, arguing that if a broader group were used, reflecting Walmart's wide geographic footprint and variety of products offered, it did not differ from that group. The company also argued that if it had claimed its highest-level hourly wage supervisors as "managers" on its EEO-1 forms, as many of the comparison companies do, the entire disparity disappeared. Walmart also noted that of the applicants for managerial positions, only 15% were female, and of those promoted, 18% were female. Finally, regarding pay, Walmart's experts suggested that the plaintiff's pay comparisons did not account for crucial factors such as the number of hours worked or whether the work was night-shift work, which pays more. Their analyses suggested that when pay was compared at the department level, where pay decisions are determined, 92.8% of all stores showed no statistically significant pay disparities, and that of the remainder, 5.2% showed disparities favoring men whereas 2.0% showed disparities favoring women.

Second, plaintiffs try to show that individual acts of intentional discrimination suggest that the statistical disparity is a function of the employer's larger culture. In the *Dukes* case, the plaintiffs argued that at Monday morning meetings of high-level Sam's Club executives, female store employees were referred to as "Janie Q's," and that this continued even after a woman executive complained that she found the term demeaning.

Finally, plaintiffs usually try to make the case that the promotion and/or pay procedures leave too much discretion to managers, providing the avenue through which their unconscious biases can play a part. In the *Dukes* case, the plaintiffs brought in expert witnesses to argue that the performance management processes were extremely subjective, and that male managers have subconscious tendencies to favor male over female employees.

## REASONABLE ACCOMMODATION

**Reasonable accommodation**
Making facilities readily accessible to and usable by individuals with disabilities.

**Reasonable accommodation** presents a relatively new theory of discrimination. It began with regard to religious discrimination but has been both expanded and popularized with the passage of the ADA. Reasonable accommodation differs from the other two theories in that rather than simply requiring an employer to refrain from some action, reasonable accommodation places a special obligation on an employer to affirmatively do something to accommodate an individual's disability or religion. This theory is violated when an employer fails to make reasonable accommodation, where that is required, to a qualified person with a disability or to a person's religious observation and/or practices.

### Religion and Accommodation

Often individuals with strong religious beliefs find that some observations and practices of their religion come into direct conflict with their work duties. For example,

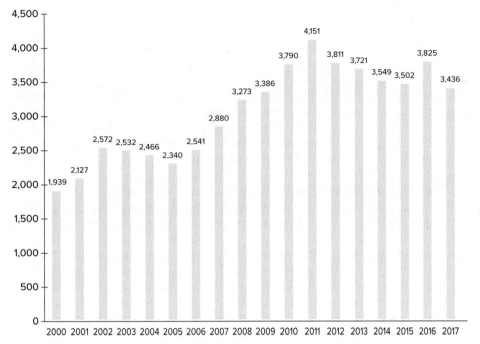

**Figure 3.2**

Religious Discrimination Complaints, 2000–2017

SOURCE: Equal Employment Opportunity Commission, "Religion-Based Charges (Charges Filed with EEOC)," https://www.eeoc.gov/eeoc/statistics/enforcement/religion.cfm.

some religions forbid individuals from working on the sabbath day when the employer schedules them for work. Others might have beliefs that preclude them from shaving, which might conflict with a company's dress code. Although Title VII forbids discrimination on the basis of religion, just like race or sex, religion also receives special treatment requiring employers to exercise an affirmative duty to accommodate individuals' religious beliefs and practices. As Figure 3.2 shows, the number of religious discrimination complaints has dropped consistently over the past few years but began to rise again in 2016.

In cases of religious discrimination, an employee's burden is to demonstrate that he or she has a legitimate religious belief and provided the employer with notice of the need to accommodate the religious practice, and that adverse consequences occurred due to the employer's failure to accommodate. In such cases, the employer's major defense is to assert that to accommodate the employee would require an undue hardship.

Examples of reasonably accommodating a person's religious obligations might include redesigning work schedules (most often accommodating those who cannot work on their sabbath), providing alternative testing dates for applicants, not requiring union membership and/or allowing payment of "charitable contributions" in lieu of union dues, or altering certain dress or grooming requirements. Although an employer is required to make a reasonable accommodation, it need not be the one that is requested by the employee.[28]

In one case, Walmart agreed to settle with a former employee who alleged that he was forced to quit in 1993 after refusing to work on Sunday. Walmart agreed to pay the former employee unspecified damages, to instruct managers on employees' rights to have their religious beliefs accommodated, and to prepare a computer-based manual describing employees' rights and religious harassment.[29]

Following the 9/11 terrorist attacks, a number of cases sprang up with regard to discrimination against Muslims, partly accounting for the significant increase in religious discrimination complaints in 2002. In one case, the EEOC and Electrolux Group settled a religious accommodation case brought by Muslim workers from Somalia. The Islamic faith requires Muslims to offer five prayers a day, with two of these prayers offered within restricted time periods (early morning and sunset). Muslim employees alleged that they were disciplined for using an unscheduled break traditionally offered to line employees on an as-needed basis to observe their sunset prayer. Electrolux worked with the EEOC to respect the needs of its Muslim workers without creating a business hardship by affording them with an opportunity to observe their sunset prayer.[30]

Religion and accommodation also bring up the question of what to do when different rights collide. For instance, John Nemecek had been a respected business professor at Spring Arbor University for 15 years, when administrators at the evangelical college in Michigan began to take issue with some of his behavior. After he began wearing earrings and makeup and asking friends to call him "Julie," Nemecek found himself demoted and then fired because his womanly appearance violated "Christian behavior." In 2004, a doctor diagnosed Nemecek with a "gender identity disorder," in which a person identifies with a gender different from the one assigned at birth based on physical characteristics. Soon after, the school began taking away some of his responsibilities, and then issued him a contract revoking his dean's post, reassigning him to a non-tenure-track role in which he would work from home, teaching online. It also required him not to wear any makeup or female clothing or to display any outward signs of femininity when visiting campus. Gayle Beebe, the university's president, said, "We felt through a job reassignment we could give him the space to work on this issue." Nemecek signed the contract but then violated it by showing up on campus with earrings and makeup on four separate occasions. Nemecek filed a complaint with the EEOC, and the university then declined to renew his contract. Nemecek, whose Baptist church also asked him to leave the congregation, said of the university, "Essentially, they're saying they can define who is a Christian. I don't agree that our biology determines our gender."[31]

## Disability and Accommodation

As stated earlier, the ADA made discrimination against individuals with disabilities illegal. However, the act itself states that the employer is obligated not just to refrain from discriminating but also to take affirmative steps to accommodate individuals who are protected under the act.

Under disability claims, the plaintiff must show that she or he is a qualified applicant with a disability and that adverse action was taken by a covered entity. The employer's defense then depends on whether the decision was made without regard to the disability or in light of the disability. For example, if the employer argues that the plaintiff is not qualified, then it has met the burden, and the question of reasonable accommodation becomes irrelevant.

If, however, the decision was made "in light of" the disability, then the question becomes one of whether the person could perform adequately with a reasonable accommodation. This leads to three potential defenses. First, the employer could allege job relatedness or business necessity through demonstrating, for example, that it is using a test that assesses ability to perform essential job functions. However, the question then arises of whether the applicant could perform the essential job functions with a reasonable accommodation. Second, the employer could claim an undue hardship to accommodate the individual. In essence, this argues that the accommodation necessary is an action entailing significant difficulty or expense. Finally, the employer could argue that the individual with the disability might pose a direct threat to his or her own or others' health or safety in the workplace. This requires examining the duration of the risk, the nature and severity of potential harm, the probability of the harm occurring, and the imminence of the potential harm. For instance, Walmart was sued by one of its employees, a fitting room attendant who had cerebral palsy and was confined to a wheelchair. The employee requested to use a grabber and a shopping cart to help her pick up and hold clothes. However, a manager prevented her from using both and then implemented progressive discipline, ending in the attendant's termination.[32]

What are some examples of reasonable accommodation with regard to disabilities? First, an employer might provide readily accessible facilities such as ramps and/or elevators for disabled individuals to enter the workplace. Second, job restructuring might include eliminating marginal tasks, shifting these tasks to other employees, redesigning job procedures, or altering work schedules. Third, an employer might reassign a disabled employee to a job with essential job functions he or she could perform. Fourth, an employer might accommodate applicants for employment who must take tests by providing alternative testing formats, providing readers, or providing additional time for taking the test. Fifth, readers, interpreters, or technology to offer reading assistance might be given to a disabled employee. Sixth, an employer could allow employees to provide their own accommodation such as bringing a guide dog to work.[33] Most accommodations are inexpensive. A study by Sears, Roebuck & Co. found that 69% of all accommodations cost nothing; 29% cost less than $1,000; and only 3% cost more than $1,000.[34] The Evidence-Based HR box describes how technological advances may have a discriminatory impact on people with disabilities.

# EVIDENCE-BASED HR

As information technology becomes more and more ubiquitous in the workplace, some researchers have begun to explore the implications for people with disabilities. Researchers at the Yang-Tan Institute on Employment and Disability at Cornell University recently reviewed the accessibility of 10 job boards and 31 corporate e-recruiting websites using Bobby 3.2, a software program designed to check for errors that cause accessibility concerns. They found that none of the job boards and only a small minority of the e-recruiting sites met the Bobby standards.

In phase 2 of the study, the researchers surveyed 813 HR professionals who were members of the Society for Human Resource Management (SHRM). Between 16% and 46% of the HR professionals were familiar with six of the most common assistive technologies to adapt computers for disabled individuals (screen magnifiers, speech recognition software, video captioning, Braille readers/displays, screen readers, guidelines for web design). In addition, only 1 in 10 said they knew that their firm had evaluated the websites for accessibility to people with disabilities.

This study indicates that, although firms may not have any intention of discriminating against people with disabilities, the rapid expansion of information technology combined with an inattention to and/or lack of education regarding accessibility issues may lead them to do so unintentionally.

SOURCE: S. Bruyere, S. Erickson, and S. VanLooy, "Information Technology and the Workplace: Implications for Persons with Disabilities," *Disability Studies Quarterly* 25, no. 2 (2005), www.dsq-sds.org.

# Retaliation for Participation and Opposition

Suppose you overhear a supervisor in your workplace telling someone that he refuses to hire women because he knows they are just not cut out for the job. Believing this to be illegal discrimination, you face a dilemma. Should you come forward and report this statement? Or if someone else files a lawsuit for gender discrimination, should you testify on behalf of the plaintiff? What happens if your employer threatens to fire you if you do anything?

Title VII of the Civil Rights Act of 1964 protects you. It states that employers cannot retaliate against employees for either "opposing" a perceived illegal employment practice or "participating in a proceeding" related to an alleged illegal employment practice. Opposition refers to expressing to someone through proper channels that you believe that an illegal employment act has taken place or is taking place. Participation refers to actually testifying in an investigation, hearing, or court proceeding regarding an illegal employment act. Clearly, the purpose of this provision is to protect employees from employers' threats and other forms of intimidation aimed at discouraging the employees from bringing to light acts they believe to be illegal.

The EEOC filed suit against Dillard's, a major department store chain, for firing a business manager as retaliation for filing a discrimination charge. In 2008, Shontel Mayfield filed a charge with the EEOC in which she alleged that Dillard's management had discriminated against her because of her race. She had begun working for Dillard's in July 2001 and earned a promotion to business manager of the Estee Lauder counter in 2006. However, in September 2008, Mayfield complied with a Jefferson County, Texas, mandatory evacuation order and evacuated the area in advance of Hurricane Ike. She returned to Jefferson County consistent with the directives of the county's "disaster declarations." After Mayfield returned to work, she was told that she was being fired for the stated reason of "excessive absenteeism." On her termination paperwork, she was accused of having "failed to maintain verbal communication concerning her absences with either the store manager or the operations manager." Yet telephone records showed that Mayfield placed numerous calls to Dillard's "disaster recovery" number, as well as to the cellular telephones of the store manager and the operations manager during the evacuation period.[35]

These cases can be extremely costly for companies because they are alleging acts of intentional discrimination, and therefore plaintiffs are entitled to punitive damages. For example, a 41-year-old former Allstate employee who claimed that a company official told her that the company wanted a "younger and cuter" image was awarded $2.8 million in damages by an Oregon jury. The jury concluded that the employee was forced out of the company for opposing age discrimination against other employees.[36]

In one case, Target Corporation agreed to pay $775,000 to a group of black workers who charged that, at one store, the company condoned a racially hostile work environment exemplified by inappropriate comments and verbal berating based on race. When one of the black employees objected to this treatment, he was allegedly retaliated against, forcing him to resign.[37]

This does not mean that employees have an unlimited right to talk about how racist or sexist their employers are. The courts tend to frown on employees whose activities result in a poor public image for the company unless those employees had attempted to use the organization's internal channels—approaching one's manager, raising the issue with the HRM department, and so on—before going public.

In today's environment, firms face cell phones as the greatest whistle-blower. Millions of people have seen video of the forcible removal of United Airlines passenger David Dao. The Integrity in Action box describes how the large number of retaliation complaints filed with the EEOC might indicate problems in a company's culture.

# INTEGRITY IN ACTION

## Retaliation as an Indicator of Culture

The #MeToo movement has helped to shed light on the sad state of sexual harassment in the workplace. The movement initially resulted in victims of harassment feeling more emboldened to come out and talk about the harassment they had experienced. The hope of the movement was that as more and more people willingly talked about it, more and more victims would feel empowered to file complaints, either within their organizations or with the EEOC. As can be seen in Figure 3.3, it does seem that more sexual harassment charges have been filed with the EEOC. However, at what cost?

While more victims come forward, it seems they do so at increased risk of retaliation.

An analysis of all the charges filed with the EEOC between 2012 and 2016 found that over two-thirds of those filing charges claimed that they were retaliated against for doing so. In addition, almost all of those ultimately left their jobs, either by being fired or finding the environment so uncomfortable that they left voluntarily.

For instance, when Laurie West internally reported lewd and inappropriate behavior by her boss, she was assigned to a new supervisor. However, she alleges that her marketing budget was then cut, creating difficulty in performing her job as a sales rep. She was fired four days after she filed a complaint with the EEOC.

Certainly, smart firms seek to create a culture where sexual harassment is considered completely unacceptable. However, what does it say about a culture that punishes the victims, rather than the perpetrators of such behavior?

### DISCUSSION QUESTIONS

1. How can firms seek to create a culture that protects employees from sexual harassment?
2. What should firms do when victims allege retaliation for reporting sexual harassment?

SOURCE: L. Weber, "After #MeToo, Those Who Report Harassment Risk Retaliation," *Wall Street Journal*, December 12, 2019 from https://www.wsj.com/articles/after-metoo-those-who-report-harassment-still-risk-retaliation-11544643939, accessed 1/19/2019.

# Current Issues Regarding Diversity and Equal Employment Opportunity

Because of recent changes in the labor market, most organizations' demographic compositions are becoming increasingly diverse. A study by the Hudson Institute projected that 85% of the new entrants into the U.S. labor force over the next decade will be females and minorities.[38] Integrating these groups into organizations made up predominantly of able-bodied white males will bring attention to important issues like sexual harassment, affirmative action, and the "reasonable accommodation" of employees with disabilities.

**LO 3-5**
Identify behavior that constitutes sexual harassment, and list things that an organization can do to eliminate or minimize it.

## SEXUAL HARASSMENT

A number of recent allegations of sexual harassment have made it into the news. For instance, now-retired Uber CEO Travis Kalanick announced that Uber will begin an "urgent investigation" following a former female engineer's blog post alleging systemic sexual harassment. The engineer, Susan Fowler, says her manager propositioned her for sex during her first day on the job. When she complained, she was told he would not be punished because he was a "high performer" and this was his first offense. However, she later spoke to other women whom the manager had also propositioned and each of them had been told it was his "first offense." Kalanick has instructed Uber's chief HR officer to conduct the investigation because "what's described here is abhorrent & against everything we believe in."[39]

**Figure 3.3**

Charges Alleging
Sexual Harassment,
2010–2018

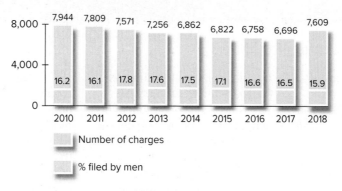

SOURCE: Charges Alleging Sex-Based Harassment (Charges filed with Equal Employment Opportunity Commission) FY 2010 - FY 2018, https://www.eeoc.gov/eeoc/statistics/enforcement/sexual_harassment_new.cfm.

In spite of the big headlines, the number of sexual harassment charges filed steadily decreased since 2010. However, largely due to the #MeToo movement, 2018 saw a significant uptick in claims, as we see in Figure 3.3.

Sexual harassment refers to unwelcome sexual advances (see Table 3.6). It can take place in two basic ways. "Quid pro quo" harassment occurs when some kind of benefit (or punishment) is made contingent on the employee's submitting (or not submitting) to sexual advances, such as the situation with Uber. For example, a male manager tells his female secretary that if she has sex with him, he will help her get promoted, or he threatens to fire her if she fails to do so; these are clearly cases of quid pro quo sexual harassment.

The *Bundy v. Jackson* case illustrates quid pro quo sexual harassment.[40] Sandra Bundy was a personnel clerk with the District of Columbia Department of Corrections. She received repeated sexual propositions from Delbert Jackson, who was at the time a fellow employee (although he later became the director of the agency). She later began to receive propositions from two of her supervisors: Arthur Burton and James Gainey. When she raised the issue with their supervisor, Lawrence Swain, he dismissed her complaints, telling her that "any man in his right mind would want to rape you," and asked her to begin a sexual relationship with him. When Bundy became eligible for a promotion, she was passed over because of her "inadequate work performance," although she had never been told that her work performance was unsatisfactory. The U.S. Court of Appeals found that Bundy had been discriminated against because of her sex, thereby extending the idea of discrimination to sexual harassment.

**Table 3.6**

EEOC Definition of
Sexual Harassment

| Unwelcome sexual advances, requests for sexual favors, and other verbal or physical contact of a sexual nature constitute sexual harassment when |
| --- |
| 1. Submission to such conduct is made either explicitly or implicitly a term or condition of an individual's employment, |
| 2. Submission to or rejection of such conduct by an individual is used as the basis for employment decisions affecting such individual, or |
| 3. Such conduct has the purpose or effect of unreasonably interfering with an individual's work performance or creating an intimidating, hostile, or offensive working environment. |

SOURCE: EEOC guideline based on the Civil Rights Act of 1964, Title VII.

A more subtle, and possibly more pervasive, form of sexual harassment is a "hostile working environment." This occurs when someone's behavior in the workplace creates an environment that makes it difficult for someone of a particular sex to work. Many plaintiffs in sexual harassment lawsuits have alleged that men ran their fingers through the plaintiffs' hair, made suggestive remarks, and physically assaulted them by touching their intimate body parts. Other examples include having pictures of naked women posted in the workplace, using offensive sexually explicit language, or using sex-related jokes or innuendos in conversations.[41]

For instance, in the aforementioned situation at Uber, the engineer claimed that a manager bought leather jackets for more than 120 men but not six women because there were not enough to get a similar bulk discount. Fowler was told that "if we wanted leather jackets, we women needed to find jackets that were the same price as the bulk-order price of the men's jackets."

When she threatened to go to HR, her manager threatened to fire her. "I told him that was illegal, and he replied that he had been a manager for a long time, he knew what was illegal, and threatening to fire me for reporting things to HR was not illegal." When she reported the situation to HR, the managers there told her retaliation is illegal, but then they did nothing in response to the threat.[42]

These types of behaviors are actionable under Title VII because they treat individuals differently based on their sex. In addition, although most harassment cases involve male-on-female harassment, any individual can be harassed. For example, male employees at Jenny Craig alleged that they were sexually harassed, and a federal jury found that a male employee had been sexually harassed by his male boss.[43]

In another example, Ron Clark Ford of Amarillo, Texas, agreed to pay $140,000 to six male plaintiffs who alleged that they and others were subjected to a sexually hostile work environment and different treatment by male managers because of their gender. Evidence gathered showed that the men were subjected to lewd, inappropriate comments of a sexual nature, and had their genitals and buttocks grabbed against their will by their male managers. The defendants argued that the conduct was "harmless horseplay."[44]

Finally, Babies 'R' Us agreed to pay $205,000 to resolve a same-sex suit. The lawsuit alleged that Andres Vasquez was subjected to a sexually hostile working environment and was the target of unwelcome and derogatory comments as well as behavior that mocked him because he did not conform to societal stereotypes of how a male should appear or behave.[45]

Sexual harassment charge filings with the EEOC by men increased to 16.6% of all filings in 2016, up from 10% of filings in 1994. Although the commission does not track same-sex, male-on-male charges, anecdotal evidence shows that most harassment allegations by men are against other men.

There are three critical issues in these cases. First, the plaintiff cannot have "invited or incited" the advances. Often the plaintiff's sexual history, whether she or he wears provocative clothing, and whether she or he engages in sexually explicit conversations are used to prove or disprove that the advance was unwelcome. However, in the absence of substantial evidence that the plaintiff invited the behavior, courts usually lean toward assuming that sexual advances do not belong in the workplace and thus are unwelcome. In *Meritor Savings Bank v. Vinson*, Mechelle Vinson claimed that during the four years she worked at a bank she was continually harassed by the bank's vice president, who repeatedly asked her to have sex with him (she eventually agreed) and sexually assaulted her.[46] The Supreme Court ruled that the victim's voluntary participation in sexual relations was not the major issue, saying that the focus of the case was on whether the vice president's advances were unwelcome.

A second critical issue is that the harassment must have been severe enough to alter the terms, conditions, and privileges of employment. Although it has not yet been consistently applied, many courts have used the "reasonable woman" standard in determining the severity or pervasiveness of the harassment. This consists of assessing whether a reasonable woman, faced with the same situation, would have reacted similarly. The reasonable woman standard recognizes that behavior that might be considered appropriate by a man (like off-color jokes) might not be considered appropriate by a woman.

The third issue is that the courts must determine whether the organization is liable for the actions of its employees. In doing so, the court usually examines two things. First, did the employer know about, or should he or she have known about, the harassment? Second, did the employer act to stop the behavior? If the employer knew about it and the behavior did not stop, the court usually decides that the employer did not act appropriately to stop it.

Sexual harassment suits can be quite costly for companies. For instance, Aaron's Inc., the furniture rental company, faced a sexual harassment suit filed by a female employee who claimed that her manager groped her, exposed himself to her, and sexually assaulted her. She contacted a company harassment hotline but was never called back. She also alleged that she was denied a promotion for complaining about the alleged assault. In 2011, a jury awarded the employee $95 million, a significant sum given that Aaron's profits had been $118 million the previous year.[47]

To ensure a workplace free from sexual harassment, organizations can follow some important steps. First, the organization can develop a policy statement that makes it clear that sexual harassment will not be tolerated in the workplace. Second, all employees, new and old, can be trained to identify inappropriate workplace behavior. Third, the organization can develop a mechanism for reporting sexual harassment that encourages people to speak out. Fourth, management can prepare to take prompt disciplinary action against those who commit sexual harassment as well as appropriate action to protect the victims of sexual harassment.[48] The Competing through Globalization box describes how the #MeToo movement, which began in the United States, has spread across the globe.

## AFFIRMATIVE ACTION AND REVERSE DISCRIMINATION

**LO 3-6**
Discuss the legal issues involved with preferential treatment programs.

Few people would disagree that having a diverse workforce in terms of race and gender is a desirable goal, if all individuals have the necessary qualifications. In fact, many organizations today are concerned with developing and managing diversity. To eliminate discrimination in the workplace, many organizations have affirmative action programs to increase minority representation. Affirmative action was originally conceived as a way of taking extra effort to attract and retain minority employees. This was typically done by extensively recruiting minorities on college campuses, advertising in minority-oriented publications, and providing educational and training opportunities to minorities.[49] However, over the years, many organizations have resorted to quota-like hiring to ensure that their workforce composition mirrors that of the labor market. Sometimes these organizations act voluntarily; in other cases, the quotas are imposed by the courts or by the EEOC. Whatever the impetus for these hiring practices, many white and/or male individuals have fought against them, alleging what is called reverse discrimination.

An example of an imposed quota program is found at the fire department in Birmingham, Alabama. Having admitted a history of discriminating against blacks, the department entered into a consent decree with the EEOC to hold 50% of positions at all levels in the fire department open for minorities, even though minorities made up only 28% of the relevant labor market. The result was that some white applicants were denied employment or promotion in favor of black applicants who scored lower on a selection battery. The federal court

## #MeToo Goes Global

Tarana Burke founded the Me Too movement in 2006 as a way to help victims of sexual assault gain access to the resources they needed to heal from their tragic experiences. Then, in 2017 after revelations of Harvey Weinstein's abuse of actresses became public, actress Alyssa Milano posted on Twitter that women who had been sexually harassed should post Me Too to create a community of assault and harassment survivors, and the #MeToo went viral.

Since that founding in the United States, the #MeToo movement has gone global. For instance:

- In the United Kingdom, a number of politicians have been accused of sexual harassment. Following accusations, Michael Fallon was pressured to resign as defense secretary, and Damian Green, the de facto deputy prime minister, was forced to step down.

- In South Korea, regional governor and presidential contender An Hee-jung, resigned after his secretary accused him of raping her on business trips. Although he was recently found not guilty of sexual assault, prosecutors said they would appeal. In addition, An did issue an apology following the verdict.

- In Israel, David Keyes left his post as Prime Minister Benjamin Netanyahu's spokesman after a New York City politician, Julia Salazar, accused him of sexually assaulting her. Keyes denied the allegations, but he was forced to resign after more than a dozen other women came forward.

- A number of journalists in India have been put on leave pending investigations for allegations of sexual harassment. The political editor of the *Hindustan Times* was stripped of his management responsibilities until an investigation is completed. Also, a top editor of *The Times of India* was put on leave after seven women accused him of explicit messages, unwanted touching, and sexual propositions.

### DISCUSSION QUESTIONS

1. Do you think that the #MeToo movement is just a temporary fad or is it a lasting change in society?
2. What things do you think an organization needs to do to eliminate sexual harassment?

SOURCES: K. Adam and W. Booth, "A Year after It Began, Has #MeToo Become a Global Movement?" *Washington Post*, October 5, 2018, from https://www.washingtonpost.com/world/a-year-after-it-began-has-metoo-become-a-global-movement/2018/10/05/1fc0929e-c71a-11e8-9c0f-2ffaf6d422aa_story.html?noredirect=on&utm_term=.9f210a9282c0; V. Goel, A. Venkatraman, K. Schultz, "After a Long Wait, India's #MeToo Movement Suddenly Takes Off," *The New York Times*, October 8, 2018, from https://www.nytimes.com/2018/10/09/world/asia/india-sexual-harassment-me-too-bollywood.html.

found that the city's use of the inflexible hiring formula violated federal civil rights law and the constitutional guarantee of equal protection. The appellate court agreed, and the Supreme Court refused to hear the case, thus making the decision final.

*Ricci v. DeStefano* is another case that was appealed to the Supreme Court regarding the potential for reverse discrimination based on a situation in New Haven, Connecticut. In this case, a professional consulting firm developed a firefighter test specifically eliminating questions that had adverse impact against minority members (based on pilot study testing). However, when the test was given, no blacks made the promotion list, so the city simply ignored the test and promoted no one. White and Hispanic firefighters who would have been on the promotion list sued, stating that the failure to use the test results discriminated against them because of their race. The district and appellate courts ruled that because no blacks were promoted either (because there were no promotions), there had been no discrimination.

The entire issue of affirmative action should evoke considerable attention and debate over the next few years. Although most individuals support the idea of diversity, few argue for the kinds of quotas that have to some extent resulted from the present legal climate. In fact, one survey revealed that only 16% of the respondents favored affirmative action with quotas, 46% favored it without quotas, and 28% opposed all affirmative action programs. One study found that people favor affirmative action when it is operationalized as recruitment, training, and attention to applicant qualifications but oppose it when it consists of discrimination, quotas, and preferential treatment.[50]

## OUTCOMES OF THE AMERICANS WITH DISABILITIES ACT

The ADA was passed with the laudable goals of providing employment opportunities for the truly disabled who, in the absence of legislation, were unable to find employment. Certainly, some individuals with disabilities have found employment as a result of its passage. However, as often occurs with legislation, the impact is not necessarily what was intended. First, there has been increased litigation. The EEOC reports that since 2010 an average of over 26,000 complaints have been filed each year. Approximately 50% of the complaints filed have been found to be without reasonable cause. For example, in one case a company fired an employee for stealing from other employees and bringing a loaded gun to work. The fired employee sued for reinstatement under the ADA, claiming that he was the victim of a mental illness and thus should be considered disabled.[51]

A second problem is that the kinds of cases being filed are not based on the rights that Congress intended to protect. Although the act was passed because of the belief that discrimination against individuals with disabilities occurred in the failure to hire them, 52.2% of the claims deal with firings, 28.9% with failure to make reasonable accommodation, and 12.5% with harassment. Only 9.4% of the complaints allege a failure to hire or rehire.[52] In addition, although the act was passed to protect people with major disabilities such as blindness, deafness, lost limbs, or paralysis, these disabilities combined account for a small minority of the disabilities claimed. As we see in Table 3.7, the biggest disability category is "other," meaning that the plaintiff claims a disability that is not one of the 35 types of impairment listed in the EEOC charge data system. The second largest category is "being regarded as disabled" accounting for 13.4% of all charges, followed by "back impairment" claims at 8.8%. As an example, a fired employee sued IBM asking for $5 million in damages for violation of the Americans with Disabilities Act. The employee had been fired for spending hours at work visiting adult chat rooms on his computer. He alleged that his addiction to sex and the Internet stemmed from trauma experienced by seeing a friend killed in 1969 during an army patrol in Vietnam.[53]

Finally, the act does not appear to have had its anticipated impact on the employment of Americans with disabilities. According to the Bureau of Labor Statistics, only 17.5% of people with disabilities are employed, compared to 65% of the general population.[54,55]

For these reasons, Congress has explored the possibility of amending the act to more narrowly define the term *disability*.[56] The debate continues regarding the effectiveness of the ADA.

## GENDER EQUITY

We discussed the Equal Pay Act earlier in the chapter, and some more of the legal issues regarding pay will be discussed in Chapter 11. However, one recent development in organizations deals with gender equity. Gender equity has two main areas of emphasis: equity in pay and equity in representation.

In terms of pay equity, in response to social trends, many organizations are taking the initiative to determine if pay inequities exist in their organizations. Consistent with the

**Table 3.7**

Sample of Complaints Filed under the ADA

| | 2000 | 2001 | 2002 | 2003 | 2004 | 2005 | 2006 | 2007 | 2008 | 2009 | 2010 | 2011 | 2012 | 2013 | 2014 | 2015 | 2016 | 2017 |
|---|---|---|---|---|---|---|---|---|---|---|---|---|---|---|---|---|---|---|
| Number of complaints | 15,864 | 16,470 | 15,964 | 15,377 | 15,576 | 14,893 | 15,575 | 17,734 | 19,453 | 21,451 | 25,165 | 25,742 | 26,379 | 25,957 | 25,369 | 26,968 | 28,073 | 26,838 |
| Percentage dealing with*: | | | | | | | | | | | | | | | | | | |
| Asthma | 2.0% | 1.6% | 1.6% | 1.6% | 1.5% | 1.6% | 1.7% | 1.0% | 1.7% | 1.6% | 1.7% | 1.9% | 1.6% | 1.5% | 1.4% | 1.3% | 1.2% | 1.3% |
| Orthopedic and structural impairment | 10.2 | 9.3 | 9.5 | 8.6 | 8.0 | 8.4 | 8.1 | 8.3 | 9.3 | 9.9 | 9.7 | 8.2 | 8.9 | 8.7 | 8.8 | 8.2 | 7.9 | 7.1 |
| Cancer | 2.7 | 2.8 | 2.9 | 2.9 | 2.8 | 2.7 | 3.2 | 3.3 | 3.6 | 3.7 | 3.9 | 4.4 | 4.4 | 4.7 | 4.4 | 3.4 | 3.2 | 3.2 |
| Diabetes | 4.1 | 4.3 | 4.7 | 4.8 | 4.7 | 4.5 | 4.8 | 5.1 | 5.6 | 5.5 | 5.4 | 4.6 | 4.2 | 4.7 | 5.0 | 4.2 | 4.1 | 4.3 |
| Hearing | 3.1 | 2.9 | 3.2 | 3.1 | 3.4 | 3.2 | 3.3 | 3.0 | 3.3 | 3.3 | 3.1 | 3.2 | 3.4 | 3.4 | 3.7 | 3.1 | 2.7 | 2.6 |
| Vision | 2.3 | 2.3 | 2.6 | 2.6 | 2.5 | 2.3 | 2.3 | 2.5 | 2.6 | 2.2 | 2.3 | 2.5 | 2.4 | 2.4 | 2.2 | 2.0 | 1.9 | 1.6 |
| Heart | 3.3 | 3.6 | 4.0 | 3.7 | 3.5 | 3.3 | 3.4 | 3.7 | 3.8 | 3.8 | 4.2 | 4.0 | 3.7 | 4.0 | 3.9 | 3.1 | 3.0 | 3.0 |
| Regarded as disabled | 13.7 | 12.8 | 13.7 | 16.8 | 18.2 | 17.4 | 17.2 | 17.7 | 16.7 | 14.1 | 12.8 | 13.0 | 13.1 | 13.8 | 13.4 | 10.8 | 10.5 | 11.0 |
| Drug addiction | 0.6 | 0.5 | 0.6 | 0.6 | 0.5 | 0.3 | 0.5 | 0.5 | 0.7 | 0.6 | 0.5 | 0.5 | 0.5 | 0.4 | 0.3 | 0.5 | 0.5 | 0.4 |
| Anxiety | 3.4 | 3.4 | 4.1 | 3.5 | 2.4 | 2.2 | 2.2 | 2.8 | 4.5 | 5.3 | 5.3 | 4.5 | 5.1 | 5.5 | 5.8 | 7.2 | 7.6 | 8.2 |
| Depression | 6.5 | 6.1 | 6.7 | 6.3 | 2.9 | 5.4 | 6.6 | 5.5 | 6.1 | 6.5 | 6.3 | 6.6 | 6.8 | 6.3 | 6.4 | 6.8 | 6.9 | 7.0 |
| Other | 22.2 | 22.3 | 23.7 | 18.1 | 12.3 | 14.7 | 15.7 | 16.4 | 20.2 | 24.4 | 26.3 | 28.2 | 29.4 | 29.4 | 30.5 | 35.4 | 35.5 | 36.9 |

*Not all complaints are listed.

SOURCE: Equal Employment Opportunity Commission, "ADA Charge Data by Impairment/Bases—Receipts," www.eeoc.gov, accessed May 26, 2019.

requirements of the Equal Pay Act, they analyze the pay of all employees (at this point, usually beginning in the United States) and use all of the relevant determinants of pay (e.g., job, location, performance, tenure in the job, education, etc.) and then determine if any employees' pay falls outside the expected range. For instance, at a recent professional society meeting, one chief HR officer told how she was proud to report to her CEO that their analysis found 99.2% of their company's employees were found to be in range. She said "He looked at me and said 'I don't want to work for a company where only 99.2% of the employees have fair pay. Do you?' So we immediately went out and made corrections for the 0.8% who fell outside their projected range."

Companies can often have pay equity in all jobs, but not have equity in representation at the highest levels of the organization. For example, research by McKinsey finds that women represent 48% of entry-level professionals, 29% of vice presidents, and only 23% of c-suite executives. Thus, even if a company pays equitably in each job, but has very few women in the highest-paying jobs, they do not have true equity. Thus, many firms seek to increase the representation of women in top jobs. For instance, the Paradigm for Parity is a consortium of companies that have committed to achieving overall gender pay equity, both within jobs and representation across jobs, by the year 2030.

## LGBT ISSUES

Society, in general, and most large businesses have developed much more inclusive attitudes toward lesbian, gay, bisexual, transgender, and queer (LGBTQ) individuals. Most large companies state that they do not discriminate on the basis of sexual orientation, and many have opened up benefit packages to same-sex partners of their employees, even prior to the *Obergefell* Supreme Court decision legalizing same-sex marriage. However, the state of employment law has not completely caught up yet.

The Equality Act of 2017 was proposed in Congress after earlier versions failed to pass. The act would amend Title VII of the Civil Rights Act (along with some other federal laws) to include sexual orientation and gender identity as protected categories. However, the legislation is unlikely to pass in the foreseeable future. Thus, much of the activity surrounding these protections has been through the court system, making the argument that sexual orientation should be covered by Title VII. For instance, in a recent case heard by the Seventh Circuit Court of Appeals, Kimberly Hively alleged that she was not hired full time and was dismissed from her part-time teaching role at Ivy Tech because she is a lesbian. In essence, she argued that the application of stereotypes such as those regarding the sex of a person's partner are illegal sex discrimination.

In an 8-3 decision, the Seventh Circuit agreed with this logic. One of the concurring judges, Diane Wood, wrote, "Any discomfort, disapproval, or job decision based on the fact that the complainant—woman or man—dresses differently, speaks differently, or dates or marries a same-sex partner, is a reaction purely and simply based on sex. That means that it falls within Title VII's prohibition against sex discrimination." However, the Seventh Circuit's Diane Sykes argued in her dissenting opinion that this does not qualify as sex discrimination: "We are not authorized to infuse the text with a new or unconventional meaning or to update it to respond to changed social, economic, or political conditions. . . . It's understandable that the court is impatient to protect lesbians and gay men from workplace discrimination without waiting for Congress to act. Legislative change is arduous and can be slow to come. But we're not authorized to amend Title VII by interpretation." Because the Eleventh Circuit Court, in a similar case, concluded that sexual orientation did not qualify for protection as sex discrimination, it appears that the issue remains unresolved until either Congress passes a law or the Supreme Court rules in a way that clarifies whether or not sexual orientation and gender identity are protected categories.[57]

# Employee Safety

LO 3-7
Identify the major provisions of the Occupational Safety and Health Act (1970) and the rights of employees that are guaranteed by this act.

In March 2005, officials at the BP refinery in Texas City, Texas, were aware that repairs needed to be done on some of the equipment in an octane-boosting processing unit. On March 23, knowing that some of the key alarms were not working, managers authorized a start-up of the unit. The start-up resulted in the deadliest petrochemical accident in 15 years, killing 15 people and injuring an additional 170.[58]

Like equal employment opportunity, employee safety is regulated by both the federal and state governments. However, to fully maximize the safety and health of workers, employers need to go well beyond the letter of the law and embrace its spirit. With this in mind, we first spell out the specific protections guaranteed by federal legislation and then discuss various kinds of safety awareness programs that attempt to reinforce these standards.

## THE OCCUPATIONAL SAFETY AND HEALTH ACT (OSHA)

Although concern for worker safety would seem to be a universal societal goal, the **Occupational Safety and Health Act (OSHA)**—the most comprehensive legislation regarding worker safety—did not emerge in the United States until the early 1970s. At that time, there were roughly 15,000 work-related fatalities every year.

OSHA authorized the federal government to establish and enforce occupational safety and health standards for all places of employment engaging in interstate commerce. The responsibility for inspecting employers, applying the standards, and levying fines was assigned to the Department of Labor. The Department of Health and Human Services was assigned responsibility for conducting research to determine the criteria for specific operations or occupations and for training employers to comply with the act. Much of this research is conducted by the National Institute for Occupational Safety and Health (NIOSH).

**Occupational Safety and Health Act (OSHA)**
The 1970 law that authorizes the federal government to establish and enforce occupational safety and health standards for all places of employment engaging in interstate commerce.

### Employee Rights under OSHA

The main provision of OSHA states that each employer has a general duty to furnish each employee a place of employment free from recognized hazards that cause or are likely to cause death or serious physical harm. This is referred to as the **general duty clause**. Some specific rights granted to workers under this act are listed in Table 3.8. The Department of Labor recognizes many specific types of hazards, and employers are required to comply with all the occupational safety and health standards published by NIOSH.

**General duty clause**
The provision of the Occupational Safety and Health Act that states an employer has an overall obligation to furnish employees with a place of employment free from recognized hazards.

**Table 3.8**
Rights Granted to Workers under the Occupational Safety and Health Act

Employees have the right to
1. Work in safe and healthful workplaces;
2. Know about hazardous chemicals in their workplaces;
3. Receive information about injuries and illnesses in their workplaces;
4. Complain or request hazard correction from their employers;
5. Receive training about workplace hazards;
6. Examine hazard exposure and medical records;
7. File a complaint with OSHA;
8. Participate in an OSHA inspection; and
9. Be free from retaliation for exercising rights.

SOURCE: "Employee's Role & Rights Under the OSH Act," *Lion Technology*, 2013, https://www.lion.com/lion-news/june-2013/employees-role-rights-under-the-osh-act.

OSHA is responsible for inspecting businesses, applying safety and health standards, and levying fines for violations. OSHA regulations prohibit notifying employers of inspections in advance.

SOURCE: OSHA, www.OSHA.gov.

A recent example is the development of OSHA standards for occupational exposure to blood-borne pathogens such as the AIDS virus. These standards identify 24 affected industrial sectors, encompassing 500,000 establishments and 5.6 million workers. Among other features, these standards require employers to develop an exposure control plan (ECP). An ECP must include a list of jobs whose incumbents might be exposed to blood, methods for implementing precautions in these jobs, postexposure follow-up plans, and procedures for evaluating incidents in which workers are accidentally infected.

Although NIOSH publishes numerous standards, regulators clearly cannot anticipate all possible hazards that could occur in the workplace. Thus, the general duty clause requires employers to be constantly alert for potential sources of harm in the workplace (as defined by the standards of a reasonably prudent person) and to correct them. For example, managers at Amoco's Joliet, Illinois, plant realized that over the years some employees had created undocumented shortcuts and built them into their process for handling flammable materials. These changes appeared to be labor saving but created a problem: Workers did not have uniform procedures for dealing with flammable products. This became an urgent issue because many of the experienced workers were reaching retirement age, and the plant was in danger of losing critical technical expertise. To solve this problem, the plant adopted a training program that met all the standards required by OSHA. That is, it conducted a needs analysis highlighting each task new employees had to learn and then documented these processes in written guidelines. New employees were given hands-on training with the new procedures and were then certified in writing by their supervisor. A computer tracking system was installed to monitor who was handling flammable materials, and this system immediately identified anyone who was not certified. The plant met requirements for both ISO 9000 standards and OSHA regulations and continues to use the same model for safety training in other areas of the plant.[59]

Many companies have also explored the use of technologies as a way to increase occupational safety and health. The Competing through Technology box describes one new technology that can reduce repetitive motion injuries and help others to better perform jobs requiring grip strength.

## OSHA Inspections

OSHA inspections are conducted by specially trained agents of the Department of Labor called compliance officers. These inspections usually follow a tight "script." Typically, the compliance officer shows up unannounced. For obvious reasons, OSHA's regulations prohibit advance notice of inspections. The officer, after presenting credentials, tells the employer the reasons for the inspection and describes, in a general way, the procedures necessary to conduct the investigation.

An OSHA inspection has four major components. First, the compliance officer reviews the employer's records of deaths, injuries, and illnesses. OSHA requires this kind of record keeping from all firms with 11 or more full- or part-time employees. Second, the officer, typically accompanied by a representative of the employer (and perhaps by a representative of the employees), conducts a "walkaround" tour of the employer's premises. On this tour, the officer notes any conditions that may violate specific

### Iron Man in the Workplace

A number of manufacturing jobs require motions that are repetitive, and sometimes physically demanding. For instance checking the welds on the Toyota RAV4 as it goes down the assembly line requires ultrasonic testing requiring workers to raise their arms over their heads with a testing device. This type of repetitive motion can cause injuries and lower productivity.

However, Toyota recently began using "exoskeletons" to make these jobs physically easier on the workers. The devices help to transfer weight from the arms to the hips using a series of pulleys and cables. When the worker raises his or her arms, the exoskeleton takes the pressure off the arms, acting as a counterweight. As the worker lowers his or her arms, the system slowly releases.

An 11-year veteran of the plant describes using the exoskeleton: "It's so futuristic, you just look at it and you kind of laugh because you don't know what it is. But once you get used to it, it's just like a piece of you."

Toyota has been using exoskeletons in its Woodstock plant, but plans to expand its use to other plants. Health and Safety Manager Marc Duplessis says "We identified risks of working overhead as a primary factor and contributor to injuries, so we tried to find ways to eliminate those risks, and the exoskeleton fit the bill quite well."

**DISCUSSION QUESTIONS**
1. Do you think firms should do this for business (i.e., higher productivity) or ethical reasons (safety and health of employees)?
2. What other areas or kinds of jobs do you think might be targets for exoskeletons?

SOURCE: L. Kamping-Carder, "Industrial Exoskeletons Give Workers a Lift," *Wall Street Journal*, January 17, 2018, from https://www.wsj.com/articles/industrial-exoskeletons-give-workers-a-lift-11547730001, accessed January 18, 2019.

published standards or the less specific general duty clause. The third component of the inspection, employee interviews, may take place during the tour. At this time, any person who is aware of a violation can bring it to the attention of the officer. Finally, in a closing conference, the compliance officer discusses the findings with the employer, noting any violations. The employer is given a reasonable time frame in which to correct these violations. If any violation represents imminent danger (that is, could cause serious injury or death before being eliminated through the normal enforcement procedures), the officer may, through the Department of Labor, seek a restraining order from a U.S. district court. Such an order compels the employer to correct the problem immediately.

### Citations and Penalties

If a compliance officer believes that a violation has occurred, he or she issues a citation to the employer that specifies the exact practice or situation that violates the act. The employer is required to post this citation in a prominent place near the location of the violation—even if the employer intends to contest it. Nonserious violations may be assessed up to $7,000 for each incident, but this penalty may be adjusted downward if the employer has no prior history of violations or if the employer has made a good-faith effort to comply with the act. Serious violations of the act or willful, repeated violations may be fined up to $70,000 per incident. Fines for safety violations are never levied against the employees themselves. The assumption is that safety is primarily the responsibility of the employer, who needs to work with employees to ensure that they use safe working procedures.

**Table 3.9**
Workplace Illnesses
and Injuries

| NONFATAL INJURIES AND ILLNESSES, PRIVATE INDUSTRY | FATAL WORK-RELATED INJURIES |
|---|---|
| Total recordable cases: 2.8 million in 2017 | Total fatal injuries (all sectors): 5,147 in 2017 |
| Cases involving days away from work: 882,730 in 2017 | Roadway incidents (all sectors): 2,077 in 2017 |
| Median days away from work: 8 in 2017 | Falls, slips, trips (all sectors): 887 in 2017 |
| Cases involving sprains, strains, tears: 34,110 in 2017 | Homicides (all sectors): 458 in 2017 |
| Cases involving injuries to the back: 148,780 in 2017 | |
| Cases involving falls, slips, trips: 227,760 in 2017 | |

SOURCE: Bureau of Labor Statistics, www.bls.gov.

In addition to these civil penalties, criminal penalties may also be assessed for willful violations that kill an employee. Fines can go as high as $20,000, and the employer or agents of the employer can be imprisoned. Criminal charges can also be brought against anyone who falsifies records that are subject to OSHA inspection or anyone who gives advance notice of an OSHA inspection without permission from the Department of Labor.

### The Effect of OSHA

OSHA has been unquestionably successful in raising the level of awareness of occupational safety. Table 3.9 presents recent data on occupational injuries and illnesses. Yet legislation alone cannot solve all the problems of work site safety.[60] Many industrial accidents are a product of unsafe behaviors, not unsafe working conditions. Because the act does not directly regulate employee behavior, little behavior change can be expected unless employees are convinced of the standards' importance.[61] This has been recognized by labor leaders. For example, Lynn Williams, then president of the United Steelworkers, noted, "We can't count on government. We can't count on employers. We must rely on ourselves to bring about the safety and health of our workers."[62]

Because conforming to the statute alone does not necessarily guarantee safety, many employers go beyond the letter of the law. In the next section we examine various kinds of employer-initiated safety awareness programs that comply with OSHA requirements or, in some cases, exceed them.

### SAFETY AWARENESS PROGRAMS

**Safety awareness programs**
Employer programs that attempt to instill symbolic and substantive changes in the organization's emphasis on safety.

**Safety awareness programs** go beyond compliance with OSHA and attempt to instill symbolic and substantive changes in the organization's emphasis on safety. These programs typically focus either on specific jobs and job elements or on specific types of injuries or disabilities. A safety awareness program has three primary components: identifying and communicating hazards, reinforcing safe practices, and promoting safety internationally.

## Identifying and Communicating Job Hazards

Employees, supervisors, and other knowledgeable sources need to sit down and discuss potential problems related to safety. The **job hazard analysis technique** is one means of accomplishing this.[63] With this technique, each job is broken down into basic elements, and each of these is rated for its potential for harm or injury. If there is consensus that some job element has high hazard potential, this element is isolated and potential technological or behavioral changes are considered.

Another means of isolating unsafe job elements is to study past accidents. The **technic of operations review (TOR)** is an analysis methodology that helps managers determine which specific element of a job led to a past accident.[64] The first step in a TOR analysis is to establish the facts surrounding the incident. To accomplish this, all members of the work group involved in the accident give their initial impressions of what happened. The group must then, through group discussion, reach a consensus on the single, systematic failure that most contributed to the incident as well as two or three major secondary factors that contributed to it.

An analysis of jobs at Burger King, for example, revealed that certain jobs required employees to walk across wet or slippery surfaces, which led to many falls. Specific corrective action was taken based on analysis of where people were falling and what conditions led to these falls. Now Burger King provides mats at critical locations and has generally upgraded its floor maintenance. The company also makes slip-resistant shoes available to employees in certain job categories.[65]

Communication of an employee's risk should take advantage of several media. Direct verbal supervisory contact is important for its saliency and immediacy. Written memos are important because they help establish a "paper trail" that can later document a history of concern regarding the job hazard. Posters, especially those placed near the hazard, serve as a constant reminder, reinforcing other messages.

In communicating risk, it is important to recognize two distinct audiences. Sometimes relatively young or inexperienced workers need special attention. Research by the National Safety Council indicates that 40% of all accidents happen to individuals in the 20 to 29 age group and that 48% of all accidents happen to workers during their first year on the job.[66] The employer's primary concern with respect to this group is to inform them. However, the employer must not overlook experienced workers. Here the key concern is to remind them. Research indicates that long-term exposure to and familiarity with a specific threat lead to complacency.[67] Experienced employees need retraining to jar them from complacency about the real dangers associated with their work. This is especially the case if the hazard in question poses a greater threat to older employees. For example, falling off a ladder is a greater threat to older workers than to younger ones. More than 20% of such falls lead to a fatality for workers in the 55 to 65 age group, compared with just 10% for all other workers.[68] Although most of this discussion has focused on workplace safety, technology has increasingly enabled and encouraged workers to work at home off the clock.

**Job hazard analysis technique**
A breakdown of each job into basic elements, each of which is rated for its potential for harm or injury.

**Technic of operations review (TOR)**
Method of determining safety problems via an analysis of past accidents.

## Reinforcing Safe Practices

One common technique for reinforcing safe practices is implementing a safety incentive program to reward workers for their support and commitment to safety goals. Initially, programs are set up to focus on improving short-term monthly or quarterly goals or to encourage safety suggestions. These short-term goals are later expanded to include more wide-ranging, long-term goals. Prizes are typically distributed in highly public forums (like annual meetings or events). These prizes usually consist of merchandise

**Table 3.10**

A 10-Step Program for Reducing Eye-Related Injuries

1. Conduct an eye hazard job analysis.
2. Test all employees' vision to establish a baseline.
3. Select protective eyewear designed for specific operations.
4. Establish a 100% behavioral compliance program for eyewear.
5. Ensure that eyewear is properly fitted.
6. Train employees in emergency procedures.
7. Conduct ongoing education programs regarding eye care.
8. Continually review accident prevention strategies.
9. Provide management support.
10. Establish written policies detailing sanctions and rewards for specific results.

SOURCE: From T. W. Turrif, "NSPB Suggests 10-Step Program to Prevent Eye Injury," *Occupational Health and Safety* 60 (1991), pp. 62–66. Copyright © Media Inc. Reprinted with permission.

rather than cash because merchandise represents a lasting symbol of achievement. A good deal of evidence suggests that such programs are effective in reducing injuries and their cost.[69]

Whereas the safety awareness programs just described focus primarily on the job, other programs focus on specific injuries or disabilities. Lower back disability (LBD), for example, is a major problem that afflicts many employees. LBD accounts for approximately 25% of all workdays lost, costing firms nearly $30 billion a year.[70] Human resource managers can take many steps to prevent LBD and rehabilitate those who are already afflicted. Eye injuries are another target of safety awareness programs. The National Society to Prevent Blindness estimated that 1,000 eye injuries occur every day in occupational settings.[71] A 10-step program to reduce eye injuries is outlined in Table 3.10. Similar guidelines can be found for everything from chemical burns to electrocution to injuries caused by boiler explosions.[72]

### Promoting Safety Internationally

Given the increasing focus on international management, organizations also need to consider how to best ensure the safety of people regardless of the nation in which they operate. Cultural differences may make this more difficult than it seems. For example, a study examined the impact of one standardized corporation-wide safety policy on employees in three different countries: the United States, France, and Argentina. The results of this study indicated that the same policy was interpreted differently because of cultural differences. The individualistic, control-oriented culture of the United States stressed the role of top management in ensuring safety in a top-down fashion. However, this policy failed to work in Argentina, where the collectivist culture made employees feel that safety was everyone's joint concern; therefore, programs needed to be defined from the bottom up.[73]

At the beginning of this section, we discussed a horrific accident at BP's Texas City refinery. After examining the causes of the explosion, the U.S. Chemical Safety and Hazard Investigation Board asked BP to set up an independent panel that would focus on overseeing radical changes in BP's safety procedures. This panel was tasked with investigating the safety culture at BP along with the procedures for inspecting equipment and reporting near-miss accidents. The panel's charter is not just to oversee the Texas City refinery, but also to look at the safety practices in refineries that BP has acquired over the years.[74]

## A LOOK BACK

### Discrimination at Harvard?

So, does Harvard admissions illegally discriminate against Asian American applicants? Those on the plaintiff's side of the issue point to the fact that Asian American applicants with the same or higher academic ratings have a much lower likelihood of being admitted compared to other racial groups. Those on the defendant's side of the issue note that in the end, the percentage of Asian American students admitted reflects the percentage of those who applied. The Supreme Court will soon rule on this case providing guidance for a number of organizations regarding how to best build diverse student bodies (or workforces) in a way that treats all groups fairly.

## SUMMARY

Viewing employees as a source of competitive advantage results in dealing with them in ways that are ethical and legal as well as providing a safe workplace. An organization's legal environment—especially the laws regarding equal employment opportunity and safety—has a particularly strong effect on its HRM function. HRM is concerned with the management of people, and government is concerned with protecting individuals. One of HRM's major challenges, therefore, is to perform its function within the legal constraints imposed by the government. Given the multimillion-dollar settlements resulting from violations of EEO laws (and the moral requirement to treat people fairly regardless of their sex or race) as well as the penalties for violating OSHA, HR and line managers need a good understanding of the legal requirements and prohibitions in order to manage their businesses in ways that are sound, both financially and ethically. Organizations that do so effectively will definitely have a competitive advantage.

## KEY TERMS

Equal employment opportunity
  (EEO), 114
Americans with Disabilities
  Act (ADA), 120
Equal Employment Opportunity
  Commission (EEOC), 122
Utilization analysis, 123
Goals and timetables, 123

Action steps, 123
Disparate treatment, 124
Bona fide occupational qualification
  (BFOQ), 126
Disparate impact, 128
Four-fifths rule, 129
Standard deviation rule, 129
Reasonable accommodation, 132

Occupational Safety and Health
  Act (OSHA), 145
General duty clause, 145
Safety awareness programs, 148
Job hazard analysis
  technique, 149
Technic of operations review
  (TOR), 149

## DISCUSSION QUESTIONS

1. Disparate impact theory was originally created by the court in the *Griggs* case before finally being codified by Congress 20 years later in the Civil Rights Act of 1991. Given the system of law in the United States, from what branch of government should theories of discrimination develop?

2. Disparate impact analysis (the four-fifths rule, standard deviation analysis) is used in employment discrimination cases. The National Assessment of Education Progress conducted by the U.S. Department of Education found that among those aged 21 to 25, (1) 60% of whites, 40% of Hispanics, and 25% of blacks could locate

information in a news article or almanac; (2) 25% of whites, 7% of Hispanics, and 3% of blacks could decipher a bus schedule; and (3) 44% of whites, 20% of Hispanics, and 8% of blacks could correctly determine the change they were due from the purchase of a two-item restaurant meal. Do these tasks (locating information in a news article, deciphering a bus schedule, and determining correct change) have adverse impact? What are the implications?

3. Many companies have dress codes that require men to wear suits and women to wear dresses. Is this discriminatory according to disparate treatment theory? Why or why not?

4. Cognitive ability tests seem to be the most valid selection devices available for hiring employees, yet they also have adverse impact against blacks and Hispanics. Given the validity and adverse impact, and considering that race norming is illegal under the Civil Rights Act of 1991, what would you say in response to a recommendation that such tests be used for hiring?

5. How might the ADA's reasonable accommodation requirement affect workers such as law enforcement officers and firefighters?

6. The reasonable woman standard recognizes that women have different ideas than men of what constitutes appropriate behavior. What are the implications of this distinction? Do you think it is a good or bad idea to make this distinction?

7. Employers' major complaint about the ADA is that the costs of making reasonable accommodations will reduce their ability to compete with businesses (especially foreign ones) that do not face these requirements. Is this a legitimate concern? How should employers and society weigh the costs and benefits of the ADA?

8. Many people have suggested that OSHA penalties are too weak and misdirected (aimed at employers rather than employees) to have any significant impact on employee safety. Do you think that OSHA-related sanctions need to be strengthened, or are existing penalties sufficient? Defend your answer.

# SELF-ASSESSMENT EXERCISE

Also assignable in Connect.

Take the following self-assessment quiz. For each statement, circle T if the statement is true or F if the statement is false.

## WHAT DO YOU KNOW ABOUT SEXUAL HARASSMENT?

1. A man cannot be the victim of sexual harassment.   T   F
2. The harasser can only be the victim's manager or a manager in another work area.   T   F
3. Sexual harassment charges can be filed only by the person who directly experiences the harassment.   T   F

4. The best way to discourage sexual harassment is to have a policy that discourages employees from dating each other.   T   F
5. Sexual harassment is not a form of sex discrimination. T   F
6. After receiving a sexual harassment complaint, the employer should let the situation cool off before investigating the complaint.   T   F
7. Sexual harassment is illegal only if it results in the victim being laid off or receiving lower pay.   T   F

# EXERCISING STRATEGY

## Discrimination at Oracle?

The U.S. Department of Labor recently filed suit against Oracle Corp., alleging that the company is discriminating in pay and hiring practices. Interestingly, the discrimination they allege is in favor of whites for pay, and Asians in hiring.

As a government contractor with millions of dollars in contracts, Oracle faces significant risks if it is found guilty. Government contractors are prohibited from discriminating in any employment decision on the basis of race, color, sex, sexual orientation or gender identity, or national origin and are required to take affirmative actions with regard to these characteristics. The government alleges

that Oracle prefers hiring Asians over non-Asians in its product development and other technical jobs. At the same time, the government alleges that Oracle pays Caucasian male employees more than female, African American, and Asian employees.

Oracle, not surprisingly, denies the claim. An Oracle spokeswoman stated, "Oracle values diversity and inclusion, and is a responsible equal opportunity and affirmative action employer. Our hiring and pay decisions are nondiscriminatory and made based on legitimate business factors including experience and merit."

So who is correct? The government relies on statistical analyses showing differences in average pay or hiring rates. Oracle claims those differences are due to legitimate business factors. So, how will this case play out?

Interestingly, we may never know. The case was brought by the Obama administration's Labor Department near the end of his term. Oracle allegedly refused to comply with a number of requests for employment and pay data, delaying the process. Now that the Trump administration has taken over, no one knows whether or not the new Labor Department appointees will want to continue the case.

## QUESTIONS

1. Do you think that Oracle is discriminating? Why or why not?
2. What type of data would tell you whether or not Oracle is discriminating?

SOURCE: A. Steele and S. Green, "U.S. Sues Oracle, Alleging Salary and Hiring Discrimination," *Wall Street Journal*, January 18, 2017, https://www.wsj.com/articles/u-s-sues-oracle-alleging-salary-and-hiring-discrimination-1484768488.

# MANAGING PEOPLE

## Uber Life after Kalanick?

Earlier in the chapter we referred to the challenge Uber faced in response to a former female engineer's blog alleging that Uber had created a very discriminatory and sexist environment. However, that may have been the least of Uber's problems.

Earlier in 2017 CEO Travis Kalanick was caught on video berating an Uber driver. Kalanick attempted to minimize this public relations disaster by confessing that he needed to "grow up" and get "leadership help." He was seeking to hire a chief operating officer (COO) to provide such leadership and help manage the company. However, after interviewing a number of potential COO's, Uber was unsuccessful at hiring one, in part because many did not find the proposition of reporting to Kalanick appealing. Many said they would not take the job if Kalanick remained as CEO.

This vacancy created an even greater executive-level staffing challenge as Uber had lost some of its most important executives over the previous year. The leaders of operations, marketing, finance, communications, and self-driving car development had all left either through resignation or firing. In fact, Jeff Jones had been hired away from his chief marketing officer role at Target to become president of ride-sharing. However, Jones left after six months saying in a written statement "that the beliefs and approach to leadership that

have guided my career are inconsistent with what I saw and experienced at Uber."

In June 2017 the board of directors at Uber asked for and received Kalanick's resignation as CEO. He will remain on the board because of his significant holdings of Uber's stock, but will no longer exert any operational control over the organization.

So, now Uber has no CEO, no CFO, no COO, and a number of other c-suite jobs vacant. In addition, the recent Covington report chastised Uber for creating an extremely dysfunctional culture.

## QUESTIONS

1. Do you think CEO's should be fired for not having a good leadership style, even if the company seems to be performing well? Why or why not?
2. Given the large number of problems facing Uber, what should the focus be on solving first, second, and third?

SOURCES: G. Bensinger and M. Farrell, "How Uber Backers Orchestrated Kalanick's Ouster as CEO," *Wall Street Journal*, June 21, 2017, https://www.wsj.com/articles/how-uber-backers-orchestrated-kalanicks-ouster-as-ceo-1498090688; G. Bensinger, "Uber's President of Ride-Sharing Jeff Jones Resigns," *Wall Street Journal*, March 20, 2017,://www.wsj.com/articles/uber-president-of-ride-sharing-jeff-jones-resigns-1489961810.

# HR IN SMALL BUSINESS

## Company Fails Fair-Employment Test

Companies have to comply with federal as well as state and local laws. One company that didn't was Professional Neurological Services (PNS), which was cited by the Chicago Commission on Human Relations when it discriminated against an employee because she is a parent. Chicago is one of a few cities that prohibit this type of discrimination.

The difficulties began for employee Dena Lockwood as soon as she was interviewing for a sales position with PNS. The interviewer noticed that Lockwood made a reference to her children, and he asked her if her responsibilities as a parent would "prevent her from working 70 hours a week." Lockwood said no, but the job offer she received suggests that the interviewer had his doubts. According to Lockwood's later complaint, female sales reps without children routinely were paid a $45,000 base salary plus a 10% commission. Lockwood was offered $25,000 plus the 10% commission. Lockwood negotiated and eventually accepted $45,000 plus 5%, with a promise to increase the commission rate to 10% when she reached sales of $300,000. She was also offered five vacation days a year; when she objected, she was told not to worry.

Lockwood worked hard and eventually reached her sales goal. Then the company raised the requirement for the higher commission rate, and the situation took a turn for the worse. Lockwood's daughter woke up one morning with pink-eye, a highly contagious ailment. Lockwood called in to reschedule a meeting for that day, but her manager told her not to bother; she was being fired. When Lockwood asked why, the manager said "it just wasn't working out."

She went to the Chicago Human Relations Commission for help. The commission investigated and could find no evidence of performance-related problems that would justify her dismissal. Instead, the commission found that Lockwood was a victim of "blatant" discrimination against employees with children and awarded her $213,000 plus attorney's fees—a hefty fine for a company with fewer than 50 employees. PNS stated that it would appeal the decision.

## QUESTIONS

1. Why do you think "parental discrimination" was the grounds for this complaint instead of a federally protected class? Could you make a case for discrimination on the basis of sex? Why or why not?
2. How could Professional Neurological Services have avoided this problem?
3. Imagine that the company has called you in to help it hold down human resources costs, including costs of lawsuits such as this one. What advice would you give? How can the company avoid discrimination and still build an efficient workforce?

SOURCES: Courtney Rubin, "Single Mother Wins $200,000 in Job Bias Case," *Inc.*, January 25, 2010; and Ameet Sachdev, "She Took a Day Off to Care for Sick Child, Got Fired," *Chicago Tribune*, January 24, 2010, NewsBank, http://infoweb.newsbank.com.

# NOTES

1. J. Ledvinka, *Federal Regulation of Personnel and Human Resource Management* (Boston: Kent, 1982).
2. *Martin v. Wilks*, 49 FEP Cases 1641 (1989).
3. *Wards Cove Packing Co. v. Atonio*, FEPC 1519 (1989).
4. *Bakke v. Regents of the University of California*, 17 FEPC 1000 (1978).
5. *Patterson v. McLean Credit Union*, 49 FEPC 1814 (1987).
6. J. Friedman and G. Strickler, *The Law of Employment Discrimination: Cases and Materials*, 2nd ed. (Mineola, NY: Foundation Press, 1987).
7. "Labor Letter," *Wall Street Journal*, August 25, 1987, p. 1.
8. J. Woo, "Ex-Workers Hit Back with Age-Bias Suits," *Wall Street Journal*, December 8, 1992, p. B1.
9. W. Carley, "Salesman's Treatment Raises Bias Questions at Schering-Plough," *Wall Street Journal*, May 31, 1995, p. A1.
10. Equal Employment Opportunity Commission, "Maternity Store Giant to Pay $375,000 to Settle EEOC Pregnancy Discrimination and Retaliation Lawsuit," January 8, 2017, www.eeoc.gov/press/1-8-07.html.
11. Equal Employment Opportunity Commission, "EEOC Sues Milwaukee Medical Staffing Agency for Pregnancy Discrimination," April 27, 2011, www.eeoc.gov/eeoc/newsroom/release/4-27-11b.cfm.
12. Special feature issue: "The New Civil Rights Act of 1991 and What It Means to Employers," *Employment Law Update* 6 (December 1991), pp. 1–12.
13. "ADA: The Final Regulations (Title I): A Lawyer's Dream/An Employer's Nightmare," *Employment Law Update* 16, no. 9 (1991), p. 1.
14. "ADA Supervisor Training Program: A Must for Any Supervisor Conducting a Legal Job Interview," *Employment Law Update* 7, no. 6 (1992), pp. 1–6.
15. https://www.eeoc.gov/eeoc/history/35th/thelaw/ada.html.
16. Equal Employment Opportunity Commission, "Uniform Guidelines on Employee Selection Procedures," *Federal Register* 43 (1978), pp. 38290–315.
17. Ledvinka, *Federal Regulation of Personnel.*
18. R. Pear, "The Cabinet Searches for Consensus on Affirmative Action," *New York Times*, October 27, 1985, p. E5.
19. *McDonnell Douglas v. Green*, 411 U.S. 972 (1973).
20. Equal Employment Opportunity Commission, "The Timken Company to Pay $120,000 to Settle EEOC Gender and Disability Discrimination Suit," April 29, 2011, www.eeoc.gov/eeoc/newsroom/release/4-29-11.cfm.
21. *UAW v. Johnson Controls, Inc.* 499 U.S. 187 (1991).
22. M. O'Brien, "Ugly People Need Not Apply?" *HR Executive*, September 16, 2010, p. 12.
23. Special feature issue: "The New Civil Rights Act of 1991," pp. 1–6.
24. *Washington v. Davis*, 12 FEP 1415 (1976).
25. *Albemarle Paper Company v. Moody*, 10 FEP 1181 (1975).
26. R. Reilly and G. Chao, "Validity and Fairness of Some Alternative Employee Selection Procedures," *Personnel Psychology* 35 (1982), pp. 1–63; J. Hunter and R. Hunter, "Validity and Utility of Alternative Predictors of Job Performance," *Psychological Bulletin* 96 (1984), pp. 72–98.
27. *Griggs v. Duke Power Company*, 401 U.S. 424 (1971).
28. B. Lindeman and P. Grossman, *Employment Discrimination Law* (Washington, DC: BNA Books, 1996).
29. M. Jacobs, "Workers' Religious Beliefs May Get New Attention," *Wall Street Journal*, August 22, 1995, pp. B1, B8.
30. Equal Employment Opportunity Commission, "EEOC and Electrolux Reach Voluntary Resolution in Class Religious Accommodation Case," September 24, 2003, www.eeoc.gov/press/9-24-03.
31. S. Sataline, "Who's Wrong When Rights Collide?" *Wall Street Journal*, March 6, 2007, p. B1.

32. "Manager's Failure to Accommodate Creates Liability for Store," *Disability Compliance Bulletin*, January 15, 2009.

33. Lindeman and Grossman, *Employment Discrimination Law*.

34. J. Reno and D. Thornburgh, "ADA—Not a Disabling Mandate," *Wall Street Journal*, July 26, 1995, p. A12.

35. Equal Employment Opportunity Commission, "Dillard's Sued by EEOC for Retaliation," April 28, 2011, www.eeoc.gov/eeoc/news-room/release/4-28-11.cfm.

36. Woo, "Ex-Workers Hit Back."

37. Equal Employment Opportunity Commission, "Target Corp. to Pay $775,000 for Racial Harassment: EEC Settles Suit for Class of African American Employees; Remedial Relief Included," January 26, 2007, www.eeoc.gov/press/1-26-07.html.

38. W. Johnston and A. Packer, *Workforce 2000* (Indianapolis, IN: Hudson Institute, 1987).

39. G. Toppo, "Uber CEO Calls for Investigation of Sexual Harassment Claims," *USA Today*, from http://www.usatoday.com/story/tech/2017/02/19/uber-ceo-investigation-sexual-harassment/98142146/, accessed February 20, 2017.

40. *Bundy v. Jackson*, 641 F.2d 934, 24 FEP 1155 (D.C. Cir., 1981).

41. L. A. Graf and M. Hemmasi, "Risqué Humor: How It Really Affects the Workplace," *HR Magazine*, November 1995, pp. 64–69.

42. G. Toppo, "Uber CEO Calls for Investigation of Sexual Harassment Claims," *USA Today*, from http://www.usatoday.com/story/tech/2017/02/19/uber-ceo-investigation-sexual-harassment/98142146/, accessed February 20, 2017.

43. B. Carton, "At Jenny Craig, Men Are Ones Who Claim Sex Discrimination," *Wall Street Journal*, November 29, 1995, p. A1; "Male-on-Male Harassment Suit Won," *Houston Chronicle*, August 12, 1995, p. 21A.

44. Equal Employment Opportunity Commission, "Texas Car Dealership to Pay $140,000 to Settle Same-Sex Harassment Suit by EEOC," October 28, 2002, www.eeoc.gov/press/10-28-02.

45. Equal Employment Opportunity Commission, "Babies 'R' Us to Pay $205,000, Implement Training Due to Same-Sex Harassment of Male Employee," January 15, 2003, www.eeoc.gov/press/1-15-03.

46. *Meritor Savings Bank v. Vinson* 477 U.S. 57 (1986).

47. R. Patrick, "Verdict: Jury Awards $95 Million in Fairview Heights Sex Harassment Suit," *St. Louis Post-Dispatch*, June 10, 2011, www.stltoday.com/news/local/crime-and-courts/jury-awards-million-in-fairview-heights-sex-harassment-suit/article_6f46fa47-3a8b-5266-b094-b95910d51c46.html.

48. R. Paetzold and A. O'Leary-Kelly, "The Implications of U.S. Supreme Court and Circuit Court Decisions for Hostile Environment Sexual Harassment Cases," in *Sexual Harassment: Perspectives, Frontiers, and Strategies*, ed. M. Stockdale (Beverly Hills, CA: Sage); R. B. McAfee and D. L. Deadrick, "Teach Employees to Just Say 'No'!" *HR Magazine*, February 1996, pp. 586–89.

49. C. Murray, "The Legacy of the 60's," *Commentary*, July 1992, pp. 23–30.

50. D. Kravitz and J. Platania, "Attitudes and Beliefs about Affirmative Action: Effects of Target and of Respondent Sex and Ethnicity," *Journal of Applied Psychology* 78 (1993), pp. 928–38.

51. J. Mathews, "Rash of Unintended Lawsuits Follows Passage of Disabilities Act," *Houston Chronicle*, May 16, 1995, p. 15A.

52. C. Bell, "What the First ADA Cases Tell Us," *SHRM Legal Report* (Winter 1995), pp. 4–7.

53. J. Fitzgerald, "Chatty IBMer Booted," *New York Post*, February 18, 2007.

54. https://www.bls.gov/news.release/disabl.nr0.htm

55. National Organization on Disability, *2006 Annual Report*, www.nod.org.

56. K. Mills, "Disabilities Act: A Help, or a Needless Hassle," *B/CS Eagle*, August 23, 1995, p. A7.

57. Tarm, M. (April 5, 2017) Gay Rights Organizations Hail Court Ruling as "Game Changer". USNews and World Report. https://www.usnews.com/news/business/articles/2017-04-05/gay-rights-organizations-hail-court-ruling-as-game-changer.

58. C. Cummins and T. Herrick, "Investigators Fault BP for More Lapses in Refinery Safety," *Wall Street Journal*, August 18, 2005, p. A3.

59. V. F. Estrada, "Are Your Factory Workers Know-It-All?" *Personnel Journal*, September 1995, pp. 128–34.

60. R. L. Simison, "Safety Last," *Wall Street Journal*, March 18, 1986, p. 1.

61. J. Roughton, "Managing a Safety Program through Job Hazard Analysis," *Professional Safety* 37 (1992), pp. 28–31.

62. M. A. Verespec, "OSHA Reform Fails Again," *Industry Week*, November 2, 1992, p. 36.

63. R. G. Hallock and D. A. Weaver, "Controlling Losses and Enhancing Management Systems with TOR Analysis," *Professional Safety* 35 (1990), pp. 24–26.

64. H. Herbstman, "Controlling Losses the Burger King Way," *Risk Management* 37 (1990), pp. 22–30.

65. L. Bryan, "An Ounce of Prevention for Workplace Accidents," *Training and Development Journal* 44 (1990), pp. 101–2.

66. J. F. Mangan, "Hazard Communications: Safety in Knowledge," *Best's Review* 92 (1991), pp. 84–88.

67. T. Markus, "How to Set Up a Safety Awareness Program," *Supervision* 51 (1990), pp. 14–16.

68. J. Agnew and A. J. Saruda, "Age and Fatal Work-Related Falls," *Human Factors* 35 (1994), pp. 731–36.

69. R. King, "Active Safety Programs, Education Can Help Prevent Back Injuries," *Occupational Health and Safety* 60 (1991), pp. 49–52.

70. J. R. Hollenbeck, D. R. Ilgen, and S. M. Crampton, "Lower Back Disability in Occupational Settings: A Review of the Literature from a Human Resource Management View," *Personnel Psychology* 45 (1992), pp. 247–78.

71. T. W. Turriff, "NSPB Suggests 10-Step Program to Prevent Eye Injury," *Occupational Health and Safety* 60 (1991), pp. 62–66.

72. D. Hanson, "Chemical Plant Safety: OSHA Rule Addresses Industry Concerns," *Chemical and Engineering News* 70 (1992), pp. 4–5; K. Broscheit and K. Sawyer, "Safety Exhibit Teaches Customers and Employees about Electricity," *Transmission and Distribution* 43 (1992), pp. 174–79; R. Schuch, "Good Training Is Key to Avoiding Boiler Explosions," *National Underwriter* 95 (1992), pp. 21–22.

73. M. Janssens, J. M. Brett, and F. J. Smith, "Confirmatory Cross-Cultural Research: Testing the Viability of a Corporation-wide Safety Policy," *Academy of Management Journal* 38 (1995), pp. 364–82.

74. Cummins and Herrick, "Investigators Fault BP."

# 4 The Analysis and Design of Work

---

## LEARNING OBJECTIVES

*After reading this chapter, you should be able to:*

**LO 4-1** Analyze an organization's structure and work-flow process, identifying the output, activities, and inputs in the production of a product or service. *page 161*

**LO 4-2** Understand the importance of job analysis for line managers and strategic human resource managers. *page 175*

**LO 4-3** Choose the right job analysis technique for a variety of human resource activities. *page 181*

**LO 4-4** Identify the tasks performed and the skills required in a given job. *page 183*

**LO 4-5** Understand the different approaches to job design. *page 184*

**LO 4-6** Comprehend the trade-offs among the various approaches to designing jobs. *page 184*

# ENTER THE WORLD OF BUSINESS

## The Workerless Economy: The Future That Never Arrives

In 1964, due to the rise of automation at that time, a group of scientists sent a letter to then President Lyndon Johnson stating that a "cybernation revolution" was creating an ever-expanding threat to workers. Their concern was that robots would replace almost all human workers and that the country was going to be confronted with a huge cohort of unemployed citizens who would have no means to support themselves. Jump ahead to 2017, and one sees that on the one hand, technological advances in robotic technology have indeed greatly expanded over the last 50 years, and robots are doing more tasks and more varied tasks than ever before. However, in July 2018, the jobless rate in the U.S. economy stood at an all-time low, both for skilled and unskilled workers, and most employers were experiencing labor shortages across the board.

In order to reconcile how this 50-year-old prediction could be both right and wrong at the same time, one needs to understand how automation often winds up complementing, and not replacing the need for human workers. For example, in the home-building industry, modern manufacturing technology has increasingly used robots to build modular housing units. These robots work indoors, off-site, and out of harsh weather conditions in order to create "Lego-like pieces of homes that are then transported and assembled on site. By the time these components reach the work site, the home is already 60% complete. Although one might fear that this would eliminate a large number of jobs, in fact, people at the factories work side by side with the robots. As one builder notes, "robots can cut the hole, but somebody still has to put the electrical boxes and pipes in the right place." Indeed, the jobs that are automated tend to the most tedious and disliked jobs in the industry such as boring holes, nailing boards, and fastening metal to metal.

This makes sense for construction, but what about the trucks that transport these products? Won't trucks become automated and driverless? Well, again yes and no. On the one hand, artificial intelligence systems are being developed for big rigs that make them largely self-driving on the highways. As any trucker will tell you, this is the most boring, unhealthy, mindless, and dangerous aspect of the work. However, planning the trip, getting the truck loaded and to the highway, and then off the highway to local roads and the end destination is still the work of a real live person. Moreover, even when on the highways, dozens of people (some older and nearing retirement) sit at a central headquarters minding arrays of monitors, each tracking live-feeds off the dashboard from three to five trucks, as they barrel down the interstate. At the end of the day, all of these workers go home to their own homes and families, avoiding weeks of sleeping on the road in their own trucks.

Alright, but all of these people have to stop for lunch right? What about the low-skill jobs in the fast-food industry—aren't they going away? On the one hand, self-serve kiosks and large

*CONTINUED*

157

industrial dishwashers have taken over many tasks once performed by real people. In fact, there is even a new robot name "flippy" that can place burgers on the grill, flip them at the right time, and then place them on a bun when they are perfectly cooked. However, rather than totally eliminating human workers, all of this automation frees them to focus on table service, food delivery, and more craftlike work (salads and specialty items), and eliminates the least desirable aspects of the work.

Clearly, predicting the future is difficult, and there may come a time when robots take over all of our tasks, not just the tasks people dislike. However, in the face of one of the lowest levels of unemployment in our lifetimes, it seems like that day may be far off, at least, much farther off than they thought back in 1964.

SOURCES: P. Coy, "The Robots Are Coming: But You Still Need to Work," *Bloomberg Businessweek*, June 26, 2017, pp. 8–10; E. Morath, "Jobless Rates for Hispanic and Black Workers Fall to Historic Lows," *The Wall Street Journal Online*, July 10, 2017; P. Ghopal and H. Perlberg, "Robots Will Build Your Next House," *Bloomberg Businessweek*, April 24, 2017, pp 43–45; M. Chafkin and J. Eidelson, "Changing Lanes," *Bloomberg Businessweek*, June 26, 2017, pp. 60–65; J. Jargon and E. Morath, "Short of Workers, Fast Food Restaurants Turn to Robots," *The Wall Street Journal Online*, June 25, 2018.

# Introduction

In Chapter 2, we discussed the processes of strategy formulation and strategy implementation. Strategy formulation is the process by which a company decides how it will compete in the marketplace; this is often the energizing and guiding force for everything it does. Strategy implementation is the way the strategic plan gets carried out in activities of organizational members. We noted five important components in the strategy implementation process, three of which are directly related to the human resource management function and one of which we will discuss in this chapter: the task or job.

For example, in the vignette that opened this chapter, it is clear that one choice an organization needs to make is how to distribute various tasks to robots versus humans. For example, organizations that compete on quality and differentiation may lean toward keeping the 'human touch" in the delivery of some service, but firms competing on cost may shift work toward robots. The strategic decision may also rest on the external environment, in the sense that organizations may react to labor shortages like the one we witnessed in 2018 with a shift from humans to robots. As John Fernald, an economist with the Federal Reserve Bank notes, "you can meet demand for a while by hiring more workers, but with an unemployment rate of 3.8%, eventually you are going to run out of easy-to-find" employees.[1]

Many central aspects of strategy formulation address how the work gets done, in terms of individual job design as well as the design of organizational structures that link individual jobs to each other and the organization as a whole. The way a firm competes can have a profound impact on the way jobs are designed and how they are linked via organizational structure. In turn, the fit between the company's structure and environment can have a major impact on the firm's competitive success.

If a company decides to compete on cost, and hence hire low-cost offshore labor, the jobs have to be designed so that they can be performed by minimally skilled people who will require little training. The organization in this case needs to have a centralized structure so that low-level workers are not forced into making too many decisions and the workers should work independently to prevent errors from cascading through the system. In contrast, if the organization is going to compete by differentiating its product, and hence hiring high-wage labor, it has to design the jobs in a different way.

For example, when shoe manufacturers in Portugal saw that they were losing sales to cheaper Chinese competitors, they completely revamped their work processes to emphasize higher quality shoes that would support higher prices. Well-trained and well-paid employees worked with expensive, state-of-the-art technology like high-speed waterjet cutters to produce small batches of high-end shoes that were sold to luxury designers. Portuguese shoes are now second only to those made in Italy when it comes to export price—$32 a pair, compared to $4 for China.[2]

Throughout this chapter, we provide examples of the kinds of decisions that need to be made with regard to how organizations should be structured and to the jobs that exist within these organizations, so that you can learn how these choices affect a number of outcomes. This includes not just quantity and quality of production, but also outcomes like coordination; innovation; and worker attraction, motivation, and retention. In many cases, there are trade-offs associated with the choices, and the more you know about these trade-offs, the better decisions you can make in terms of making your team or organization more competitive.

It should be clear from the outset of this chapter that there is no "one best way" to design jobs and structure organizations. The organization needs to create a fit between its environment, competitive strategy, and philosophy, on the one hand, and its jobs and organizational design, on the other. Failing to design effective organizations and jobs has important implications for competitiveness. Many years ago, some people believed that the difference between U.S. auto producers and their foreign competitors could be traced to American workers; however, when companies like Toyota and Honda came into the United States and demonstrated clearly that they could run profitable car companies with American workers, the focus shifted to processes and organization. In some cases, the work processes that were imported into the United States were far better than what existed in traditional U.S. firms in terms of efficiency. In other cases, however, as the Competing through Environmental, Social, and Governance Practices box shows, the processes imported achieved efficiency gains at the cost of worker safety.[3]

This chapter discusses the analysis and design of work and, in doing so, lays out considerations involved in making informed decisions about how to create and link jobs. The chapter is divided into three sections, the first of which deals with "big picture" issues related to work-flow analysis and organizational structure. The remaining two sections deal with more specific, lower level issues related to job analysis and job design.

The fields of job analysis and job design have extensive overlap, yet in the past they have been treated differently. Job analysis has focused on analyzing existing jobs to gather information for other HRM practices such as selection, training, performance appraisal, and compensation. Job design, by contrast, has focused on redesigning existing jobs to make them more efficient or more motivating to jobholders. Thus, job design has had a more proactive orientation toward changing the job, whereas job analysis has had a passive, information-gathering orientation.

## COMPETING THROUGH ENVIRONMENTAL, SOCIAL, AND GOVERNANCE PRACTICES

### Creating Jobs and Injuries in the American South

"This brings shame on your reputation. American consumers are not going to want to buy cars stained with the blood of American workers." This was the stern warning that David Michaels, Director of the Occupational Safety and Health (OSHA), gave to top-level executives at Hyundai Motor Company and Kia Motors Company after showing them some startling statistics. All of these numbers pertained to serious safety violations and injuries that were occurring at U.S. plants that supplied parts to the giant automakers. Most of the plants were located in Southern states such as Alabama, and the statistics were unpleasant. For example, workers at auto supplies plants located in Alabama were 50% more likely to be injured compared to the industry as a whole, and over 50% of those injuries could be traced to Korean-owned plants.

Southern states originally opened their arms to non-U.S. manufacturers when they moved into the region in the 1990s, and the partnership seemed like a win–win proposition for all. Companies like Hyundai and Kia created thousands of new jobs for American workers, and in return, the companies received favorable tax treatment and access to a large labor force that had a strong work ethic and that

was largely nonunionized. This workforce was clearly a source of advantage for these firms when it came to competing against U.S. companies, many of which are located in the Northern states. Twenty years later, however, many of these states are reconsidering the bargain they struck due to the fear that the harsh working conditions often found in Asian sweatshops are also being imported into the American South.

For example, Reco Allen took a custodian's job at the Matsu Alabama plant at just $9 an hour, specifically avoiding higher paid jobs due to his fear of the machinery. His only training basically consisted of where to find the mop and pail. Still, despite this, on one evening after a 12-hour shift, he was ordered to work a metal pressing machine when the employee who regularly did that job failed to show up for work. Unfortunately, the machine malfunctioned and when Allen tried to fix it, it kicked back on and the press slammed down on both of his arms. It took emergency crews over an hour to free Allen, all the while his arms were burning and crushed inside the press. Subsequent investigations into Matsu revealed that this was far from an isolated incident. The evidence showed that the plant had routinely forced untrained

employees to operate dangerous machines that were often producing at a rate that exceeded the manufacturer's recommendations.

To be fair, most of the problems that OSHA was able to document did not directly point to the large automakers themselves. The safety records for workers at Hyundai and Kia themselves are not worse than the industry as a whole. However, OSHA felt that the large companies were pressuring their smaller suppliers, who were operating with small margins and competing against Asian and Mexican plants, to hit quotas that were impossible to achieve without bending the rules. The sustainability of this practice is highly questionable, and now many employees who once worked with companies that supplied Hyundai and Kia have quit and taken their skills to American-owned auto plant suppliers. One such employee was Cordney Crutcher, who left Matsu and joined a U.S. plant whose workers were represented by the United Auto Workers. Crutcher notes that "They teach you the right way. They don't throw you to the wolves."

**DISCUSSION QUESTIONS**

1. Most local governments and politicians are driven to bring jobs into their districts. What can be done at the

*CONTINUED*

local level or the national level to attract employers, but at the same time protect taxpayers and the local labor force?

2. Are the financial penalties that are administered by OSHA enough to deter employers from engaging in unsafe work practices, and if not, what else can be done to protect employees and better inform them of the risks associated with specific employers?

SOURCES: P. Waldman, "Don't Let the Monster Eat You Up," *Bloomberg Businessweek*, April 2, 2017, pp. 46–51; K. Bo-gyung. "U.S. Authorities Warn Hyundai, Kia Motors Over Worker Safety," *The Korea Herald Online*, January 16, 2017; J. Little, "Auburn Auto Parts Supplier for Hyundai, Kia Fined 106,020 for Safety Violations," *Opelika-Auburn News Online*, September 29, 2018.

# Work-Flow Analysis and Organization Structure

*Work-flow design* is the process of analyzing the tasks necessary for the production of a product or service, prior to allocating and assigning these tasks to a particular job category or person. Only after we thoroughly understand work-flow design can we make informed decisions regarding how to initially bundle various tasks into discrete jobs that can be executed by a single person.

*Organization structure* refers to the relatively stable and formal network of vertical and horizontal interconnections among jobs that constitute the organization. Only after we understand how one job relates to those above (supervisors), below (subordinates), and at the same level in different functional areas (marketing versus production) can we make informed decisions about how to redesign or improve jobs to benefit the entire organization.

Finally, work-flow design and organization structure have to be understood in the context of how an organization has decided to compete. Both work-flow design and organization structure can be leveraged to gain competitive advantage for the firm, but how one does this depends on the firm's strategy and its competitive environment.

**LO 4-1**

Analyze an organization's structure and work-flow process, identifying the output, activities, and inputs in the production of a product or service.

## WORK-FLOW ANALYSIS

All organizations need to identify the outputs of work, to specify the quality and quantity standards for those outputs, and to analyze the processes and inputs necessary for producing outputs that meet the quality standards. This conception of the work-flow process is useful because it provides a means for the manager to understand all the tasks required to produce a number of high-quality products as well as the skills necessary to perform those tasks. This work-flow process is depicted in Figure 4.1.

### Analyzing Work Outputs

Every work unit—whether a department, a team, or an individual—seeks to produce some output that others can use. An output is the product of a work unit and this is often an identifiable object such as a jet engine blade, a forklift, or a football jersey. Strategically, an organization may decide to change its outputs, and this will have downstream consequences for all the rest of the workflow. For example, in 2017, Toyota came to the conclusion that it was producing too many sedans like the Camry and Avalon, and that it was missing the boat when it came to SUVs and roomier pickups that more consumers were demanding. It decided to close this gap relative to the market by shifting its output—at the cost of over $80 million in downstream workflow costs.[4] An output is not always a

**Figure 4.1**

Developing a Work–Unit Activity Analysis

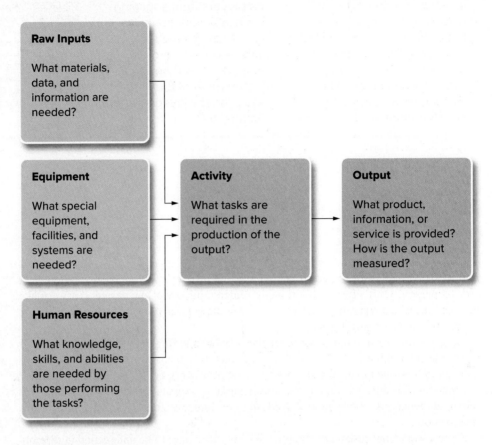

**Raw Inputs**

What materials, data, and information are needed?

**Equipment**

What special equipment, facilities, and systems are needed?

**Activity**

What tasks are required in the production of the output?

**Output**

What product, information, or service is provided? How is the output measured?

**Human Resources**

What knowledge, skills, and abilities are needed by those performing the tasks?

physical product, however, and can also be a service, such as an airline that transports you to some destination, a housecleaning service that maintains your house, or a babysitter who watches over your children.

We often picture an organization only in terms of the product that it produces, and then we focus on that product as the output. Merely identifying an output or set of outputs is not sufficient. Once these outputs have been identified, it is necessary to specify standards for the quantity or quality of these outputs. In many cases, the number and nature of the outputs chosen create challenges for how to efficiently process the inputs in order to generate the outputs. Strategically, a service company needs to decide how many different services it is going to provide, and again, this has downstream implications for the rest of the workflow. For example, recently McDonald's restaurants added many new items to its menus, including oatmeal, snack wraps, and lattes in order to appeal to a wider array of consumers. In fact, the number of menu items at McDonald's swelled to 121 items in 2014, compared to just 85 in 2007. Not surprisingly, this results in slower service, and McDonald's also recorded its worst speed-of-performance metrics that same year. Managers often referred to the McWrap specifically as a "showstopper" that required many of the workers to look up a series of instructions in order to execute a single order.[5]

Once the output or service has been chosen, the organization has to decide whether they are going to focus on producing the whole product or service or just one or two parts of it. For example, although many politicians focus on the value of creating manufacturing jobs, research actually shows that organizations derive far more return on investment from jobs that precede or follow the manufacturing process. That is, the best value and highest wages are associated with the research, development, and design that occurs before manufacturing, as well as branding, sales service, and support that occurs after manufacturing. This is sometimes referred to as "the smile curve," and the base of the smile in this case is manufacturing and the jobs associated with it.

For example, when it comes to a product like an iPhone, Apple designs the product, and then sells and services it, but it does not manufacture a single phone. This is a wise decision because manufacturing accounts for only 3% of the phone's cost, and the remaining 97% of the costs are a result of design, sales, and service. Thus, a company like Apple enjoyed a net income of 21% of revenue in 2016 and its shares traded at 18 times earnings. Compare this to Han Hoi Precision Company who manufactures the iPhone in China. They report net income of 3% of revenue and its shares trade at 12 times earnings. The strategic decision to focus on design, sales, and service, rather than manufacturing, allows Apple to create 80,000 jobs in the United States alone with plans to expand to 100,000 jobs by 2020.[6]

## Analyzing Work Processes

Once the outputs of the work unit have been identified, it is possible to examine the work processes used to generate the output. The work processes are the activities that members of a work unit engage in to produce a given output. Every process consists of operating procedures that specify how things should be done at each stage of the development of the product. These procedures include all the tasks that must be performed in the production of the output. The tasks are usually broken down into those performed by each person in the work unit. Of course, in many situations where the work that needs to be done is highly complex, no single individual is likely to have all the required skills. In these situations, the work may be assigned to a team. Team-based job design is becoming increasingly popular in contemporary organizations. In addition to providing a wider set of skills, team members can back each other up, share work when any member becomes overloaded, and catch each other's errors.

For example, although the job of driving a truck used to be an individual job, increasingly teams of drivers are assigned to trucks in order to keep the big rigs—which reflect a major capital investment—moving 24 hours a day. U.S. regulations limit the number of hours truck drivers can operate to 11 hours a day, but by swapping drivers at the end of a shift, teams can carry goods more than twice the distance than can be accomplished by drivers working alone.[7]

The use of teams can also be seen in the field of medicine, where team-based care is increasingly becoming the norm. Rather than a single one-on-one doctor–patient relationship, many medical services are delivered by a team that might include a nurse practitioner, a physician's assistant, a clinical pharmacist, and a variety of technicians who work alongside the primary physician. Part of this is a result of the increased workload created by the Affordable Care Act as well as the decreased number of general practitioners minted by medical schools. As noted by Kirsten Meisinger, a supervising physician who oversees an 11-person team, "I can't possibly do everything that needs to be done for all of our patients as a single human being."[8] Having all the work reside within a single patient-focused team also eliminates depersonalized "hand-offs" from one separate functional unit to another—one of the major sources of errors in traditionally structured hospitals. Avoiding errors attributed to faulty work procedures is critical because routine medical errors are the third leading cause of death in the United States, trailing only heart disease and cancer.[9]

There is a great deal of value in studying work-flow processes and this is best illustrated when private equity groups come in and buy a failing company at a low price, revamp the

ProStockStudio/Shutterstock

This job may look tedious or possibly even uninteresting. Considering how to engage employees in seeing the benefits of their work outside of the lab is an important way to motivate them through their day.

work-flow process, and then sell the company again at a higher price. Private equity groups employ efficiency experts who try to wring out every ounce of waste in production operations. When efficiency experts first visit a company, they are looking for three different kinds of waste: (1) movement that creates no value, (2) the overburdening of specific people or machines, and (3) inconsistent production that creates excessive inventories. Typically armed with stopwatches, clipboards, and flowcharts, efficiency experts prowl the manufacturing floor for waste that would not be detected by most managers. More often than not, this leads to a reduction in headcount because improved procedures dramatically streamline operations. As Justin Hillenbrand, an executive at Monomoy Capital Partners, notes, "You could have the best CEO in the world, but in a manufacturing company, profits are made on the floor."[10]

Organizations often work hard to minimize overstaffing via lean production techniques. *Lean production* refers to processes developed in Japan, but then adopted worldwide, emphasizing manufacturing goods with a minimum amount of time, materials, money—and most important—people. Lean production tries to leverage technology, along with small numbers of flexible, well-trained, and skilled personnel in order to produce more custom-based products at less cost. This can be contrasted with more traditional "batch work" methods, where large groups of low-skilled employees churn out long runs of identical mass products that are stored in inventories for later sale. In lean production systems, there are fewer employees to begin with, and the skill levels of those employees are so high that the opportunity to cuts costs by laying off employees is simply less viable.

Indeed, a paradox of the most recent recession was how small many of the layoffs in the manufacturing sector of the economy were given the huge drop in production levels. For example, 14 months into the recession of 2000, manufacturers cut 9.5% of their employees in response to a *2% cut* in production. In contrast, in 2009, the same 9.5% of employees were laid off in response to a *12% cut* in production. If the same ratio of job cuts to production cuts from the year 2000 held in the year 2009, this would have resulted in an astounding layoff rate of over 50% of manufacturing employees. Many observers have attributed the lower "job cut–to–production cut" ratio in the most recent recession to the use of job redesign initiatives that emphasize lean production over more traditional approaches.

Although lean design is great for employers, it is not always great for workers. For example, one side effect of this increased level of efficiency is that when the economy bounces back, there is much less new hiring. This can leave a permanent dent in the number of U.S. manufacturing jobs because many of those jobs never come back due to more efficient design of work processes.[11]

## Analyzing Work Inputs

The final stage in work-flow analysis is to identify the inputs used in the development of the work unit's product. As shown in Figure 4.1, these inputs can be broken down into the raw materials, equipment, and human skills needed to perform the tasks. *Raw materials* consist of the materials that will be converted into the work unit's product.

Organizations that try to increase efficiency via lean production techniques often try to minimize the stockpile of inputs via "just-in-time" inventory control procedures. Indeed, in some cases, inventories are being abandoned altogether, and companies at the edge of the lean production process do not even manufacture any products until customers place an order for them. For example, surgical device maker CONMED used to forecast demand for its products one to two months ahead, and when those forecasts turned out to be inaccurate it would either lose sales or stockpile inventories. Today, because the length of time it takes to produce its devices has decreased from six weeks to 48 hours, it does not even manufacture any products that are not already sold. The impact of this can be seen at CONMED's plant in Utica, New York, where a $93,000 inventory that used to take up 3,300 square feet on the factory floor has been all but eliminated. This allowed the company to take back lost sales from Chinese competitors that, despite their lower labor costs, face the costs of long lead times, inventory pile-ups, quality problems, and transportation costs. As David Johnson, vice president for global operations at CONMED notes, "If more U.S. companies deploy these job design methods we can compete with anybody and still provide security to our workforce."[12]

However, there are also downsides to "just-in-time" inventory management practices. Specifically, the efficiency gained from maintaining an inventory measured in days rather than weeks creates a lack of flexibility. An example of this can be seen in the aftermath of the earthquake that struck northern Japan in 2011. This region of Japan was home to a number of suppliers who had to unexpectedly halt all production overnight on March 22. This disruption rippled through the entire global economy that relied on "just-in-time" practices when organizations as varied as Boeing, General Motors, John Deere, Hewlett-Packard, and Dell had to halt their own production lines after running out of inputs. As one analyst noted, "If supply is disrupted in this situation, there's nowhere to get inputs."[13]

*Equipment* refers to the technology and machinery necessary to transform raw materials into the product. In general, the amount of money that an organization invests in equipment is calculated in terms of the amount of "capital spending per worker," and some labor economists in the United States are concerned that this form of investment has not kept pace with what is needed to compete against international competition. For example, 2016 marked the seventh year in a row that the U.S. economy showed no growth in capital spending per worker, and not coincidentally, this year also witnessed a severe drop in worker productivity. This metric climbed in 2017 and 2018, however, and many analysts attribute this to the large tax breaks that were granted to employers in 2016.[14] Companies had a lot of money on their hands, all of a sudden, and due to the labor shortage could not spend all of this on labor. Still, even though investment went up, some lamented the rather small size of these investments relative to the largess that was distributed in tax cuts. Moreover, as the Competing through Globalization box illustrates, one of the United States major competitors, China, has made it a national priority to increase their level of capital investment.

### Made in China 2025

In the vignette that opened this chapter, we discussed how robots were changing the nature of work for the people that work alongside them in the United States. Although the impact of this kind of technology seems far reaching in this country, when it comes to robots, the United States actually lags most other industrialized nations in terms of "robots per 10,000 workers"—at 176. This is far behind the world leader, South Korea, at 531, and also trails Singapore, Japan, Germany, Sweden, Taiwan, and Denmark. However, the use of robots in the Untied States is still three times higher than China, who is still below 50 when it comes to this metric. But that may be changing.

Historically, China's competitive advantage was borne in a labor force that was very large, not very picky about the nature of the work, and willing to work for far less money than the rest of the industrialized world. Larger societal forces in the Middle Kingdom, however, are threatening this former advantage. In particular, the "one child policy" has resulted in a reduction in the rate of population growth, and thus, reduced the supply of labor. This labor force is also aging, and the next generation of Chinese workers is less interested in doing repetitive work, under difficult working conditions, at low pay. Thus, the government is trying to make the transition from its

past to its future with a thrust into robotics called "Made in China 2025." The goal of this program is to increase the share of homemade robots from 30 to 50%, and quadruple the number of robots per 10,000 workers.

On the one hand, this is a lofty goal given the current state of affairs because most Chinese robot makers currently buy most of their parts and components from Japan and the United States. In some cases, Chinese robotic firms have imported components from industry leaders like Seimens AG or Fanuc, put them in a robot shell with an arm, and then placed a Chinese label on them. Still, it would be unwise to underestimate the potential for growth in this context. China's leaders see this as a global strategic move to dominate emerging markets for autonomous vehicle and digitally connected appliances and homes. They have also tactically focused on automated warehousing and logistics, because China still employs thousands of warehouse workers, as well as truck and motorcycle deliverymen to move products from place to place. The vision is to replace all of this with domestically produced drones and driverless vehicles that will deliver packages to far flung and remote rural regions.

The government is committed to this strategy, and new entrants into this market will be

offered subsidies, tax waivers, and rent-free land, which could help jump-start new ventures. Already, the country's development bank is working with China's industry ministry to provide $43.9 billion of financing for major projects. As one industry analyst has noted, "fair or unfair, you can expect Chinese companies to get a lot of preferential treatment and funding because they actually have a comprehensive plan to get there."

### DISCUSSION QUESTIONS

1. How in this example does the nature of a country's workforce shape strategic plans related to robots and technological investment?

2. In this example, the Chinese Government is clearly supporting companies and steering them to a specific strategy. In the United States, there is a general philosophy that suggests that the government should not get involved in business decisions and instead, let the markets decide where businesses should invest. Which of those two strategies do you think best in the short term versus the long term?

SOURCES: D. Roberts, R. Chang, and T. Black, "China's Robot Revolution," *Bloomberg Businessweek*, May 1 2017, pp. 34–34.; N. Kahn, "Inside China's Factory of the Future," *The Wall Street Journal Online*, August 25, 2018; K. Bradshear, "A Robot Revolution: This Time in China," *The New York Times Online*, May 12, 2017.

Cutting-edge equipment can boost productivity in many ways, but as we saw in our opening vignette, new technology often improves how humans work; it does not necessarily eliminate jobs. For example, new augmented reality helmets allow the wearer of the device to electronically relay exactly what he or she is seeing and hearing to another worker who has needed expertise, but may not be on site. Thus, in the past, when it came to repairing a broken turbine in Malaysia, Baker Hughes traditionally would fly a five-person specialized crew from the United States to Asia—a process that was time consuming and expensive. Today, however, the specialized crew never leaves town and instead, can work remotely with local workers who become their eyes and ears on the ground. Smart helmets such as these also allow older, highly experienced workers who may not be able to physically get to dangerous or remote locations to stay on the job—thus preserving their human capital for their employers. As noted by Shell's vice president of HR, Aliso Choong, "with these technologies, it is more about the people than the hardware."[15]

Another example of how technology improves, rather than replaces, human operators can be seen with the software program "Orion," that drastically improves the efficiency of truck drivers and delivery personnel working for UPS. In terms of competitive advantage and disadvantage, UPS competes directly with FedEx, but unlike FedEx, who employs a private contractor model and delivers mainly to businesses, UPS manages a high-wage union workforce who delivers mainly to widely scattered households. The problem with planning the best route each day for all these scattered customers, however, is that there are literally more than a billion options. If one were to leave each driver to his or her own discretion in how to plan their route, there would be very wide variability in their decisions, and the odds that any one of them might come up with the optimal path is zero.

This is where the computer program "Orion" comes in. Orion is a 1,000-page algorithm that tries to mathematically determine the optimal route for making those 120 stops every day for UPS drivers. Working like a GPS system on steroids, Orion constantly updates a driver's schedule and automatically vectors the vehicle based on two criteria; optimum efficiency and consistency. This latter criterion, consistency, is one of the features that make Orion different from most purely mathematical optimizing programs. The program recognizes that both human operators and customers place a great deal of value on consistency, and thus, sacrifices some degree of pure efficiency in order to create a comfortable routine in terms of delivery times and routes.[16]

Of course, sometimes a work-flow analysis points to the fact that employees are using some specific piece of equipment too much. For example, cardiac telemetry is performed with equipment that lets a clinician monitor the heart for abnormal rhythms. At Christiana Care hospitals, administrators knew that these machines were being used by many physicians even when it was not considered necessary. To reduce routine use of this machine, the electronic ordering system was redesigned so that physicians could not order the tests by simply checking a box. A physician could still override the system and "write it in," but he or she had to take this one extra step. The results a year later showed that use of telemetry fell by 70%, costs were reduced by over $13,000, and there was no negative effect on patients. Nader Najafi, the University of California at San Francisco professor who led the study, noted, "It is remarkable to achieve such a substantial reduction in the use of such a resource without significantly increased adverse outcomes."[17]

The final input in the work-flow process is the *human skills* and efforts necessary to perform the tasks. Obviously, the human skills consist of the workers available to the company. Generally speaking, in terms of human skills, work should be delegated to the lowest-cost employee who can do the work well, and in some cases this principle is violated when too much emphasis is placed on reducing headcount. For example, the U.S. economy wiped out over 1 million office and administrative support positions in the last 10 years. Although this might seem a reasonable place to cut costs, does it really make financial sense to have c-suite executives booking their own travel, completing routine paperwork, loading toner into the copier, and screening 500 e-mails a day, 400 of which are spam? For an executive making $1 million a year, an $80,000 assistant needs to increase that person's productivity by only 8% for the company to break even.[18]

## ORGANIZATION STRUCTURE

Whereas work-flow design provides a longitudinal overview of the dynamic relationships by which inputs are converted into outputs, organization structure provides a cross-sectional overview of the static relationships between individuals and units that create the outputs. Organization structure is typically displayed via organizational charts that convey both vertical reporting relationships and horizontal functional responsibilities.

### Dimensions of Structure

**Centralization**
The degree to which decision-making authority resides at the top of the organizational chart.

**Departmentalization**
The degree to which work units are grouped based on functional similarity or similarity of work flow.

Two of the most critical dimensions of organization structure are centralization and departmentalization. **Centralization** refers to the degree to which decision-making authority resides at the top of the organizational chart as opposed to being distributed throughout lower levels (in which case authority is *decentralized*). **Departmentalization** refers to the degree to which work units are grouped based on functional similarity or similarity of work flow.

For example, a school of business could be organized around functional similarity so that there would be a marketing department, a finance department, and an accounting department, and faculty within these specialized departments would each teach their area of expertise to all kinds of students. Alternatively, one could organize the same school around work-flow similarity, so that there would be an undergraduate unit, a graduate unit, and an executive development unit. Each of these units would have its own marketing, finance, and accounting professors who taught only their own respective students and not those of the other units.

### Structural Configurations

Although there are an infinite number of ways to combine centralization and departmentalization, two common configurations of organization structure tend to emerge in organizations. The first type, referred to as a *functional structure*, is shown in Figure 4.2. A functional structure, as the name implies, employs a functional departmentalization scheme with relatively high levels of centralization. High levels of centralization tend to go naturally with functional departmentalization because individual units in the structures are so specialized that members of the unit may have a weak conceptualization of the overall organization mission. Thus, they tend to identify with their department and cannot always be relied on to make decisions that are in the best interests of the organization as a whole. In addition, the opportunity for finger pointing and conflict between subunits that fundamentally do not understand the work that other subunits do creates the need for a centralized decision-making mechanism to manage potential disputes.[19]

**Figure 4.2**

The Functional Structure

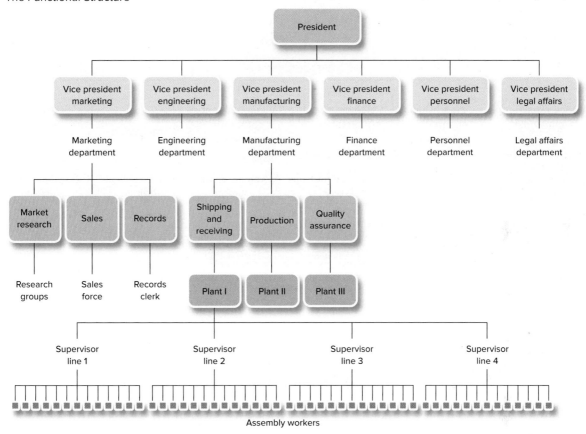

SOURCE: Adapted from J. A. Wagner and J. R. Hollenbeck, *Organizational Behavior: Securing Competitive Advantage*, 3rd ed. (New York: Prentice Hall, 1998).

Alternatively, a second common configuration is a *divisional structure*, three examples of which are shown in Figures 4.3, 4.4, and 4.5. Divisional structures combine a divisional departmentalization scheme with relatively low levels of centralization. Units in these structures act almost like separate, self-sufficient, semi-autonomous organizations. The organization shown in Figure 4.3 is divisionally organized around different products, the organization shown in Figure 4.4 is divisionally organized around geographic regions, and the organization shown in Figure 4.5 is divisionally organized around different clients. A real-world example of this can be seen at the pharmaceutical giant Pfizer that recently re-organized to create three separate divisions, one devoted to research and innovative medicines, a second one devoted to over-the-counter consumer sales of products like Advil and Centrum, and a third devoted to established prescription medicines such as Lipitor and Viagra.[20]

## Variations in an Organization's Structure

Regardless of how subunits are formed, many organizations try to keep the size of each subunit small enough that people within the subunit feel like they can make a difference and feel connected to others. People within very large subunits experience reduced feelings of individual accountability and motivation, which hinders organizational performance.

**Figure 4.3**

Divisional Structure: Product Structure

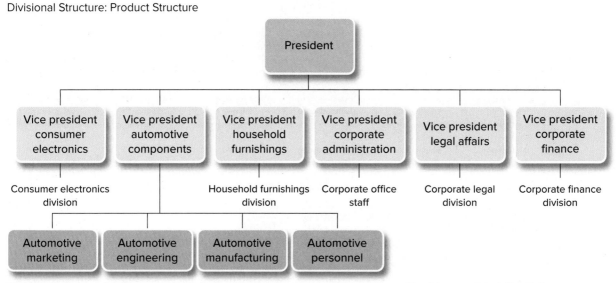

SOURCE: Adapted from J. A. Wagner and J. R. Hollenbeck, *Organizational Behavior: Securing Competitive Advantage*, 3rd ed. (New York: Prentice Hall, 1998).

**Figure 4.4**

Divisional Structure: Geographic Structure

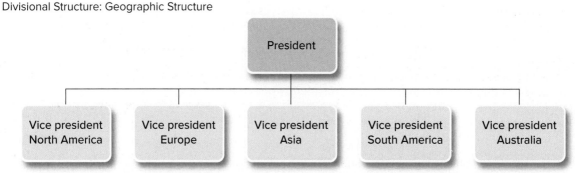

SOURCE: Adapted from J. A. Wagner and J. R. Hollenbeck, *Organizational Behavior: Securing Competitive Advantage*, 3rd ed. (New York: Prentice Hall, 1998).

**Figure 4.5**

Divisional Structure: Client Structure

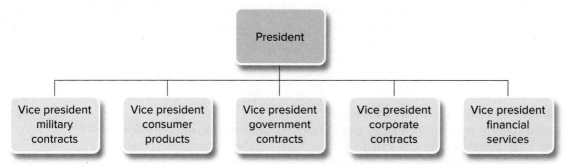

SOURCE: Adapted from J. A. Wagner and J. R. Hollenbeck, *Organizational Behavior: Securing Competitive Advantage*, 3rd ed. (New York: Prentice Hall, 1998).

Research suggests that these types of problems start to manifest themselves once a group exceeds 150 people; hence, many organizations try to limit subunits to this specific size. For example, W.L. Gore and Associates, the company that makes Gore-Tex and other innovative materials, typically will break up a division once its size exceeds this number, splitting it in two and opening a new physical office.[21]

Because of their work-flow focus, their semi-autonomous nature, and their proximity to a homogeneous consumer base, divisional structures tend to be more flexible and innovative. They can detect and exploit opportunities in their respective consumer bases faster than the more centralized functionally structured organizations. Indeed, because decision making in functional structures occurs at a level far from the shop floor or customer interface, there can sometimes be a disconnect between the perceived needs of those working on the front lines and upper management. For example, earlier we noted how the expansion of menus at McDonald's was causing problems for franchise owners. As one owner noted, "If more of the corporate people would spend their lunch hour and work the line and in the kitchen, we wouldn't be in the position we're in today. They kept expanding the menu; we knew this was only making the problem worse."[22]

By contrast, it is also the case that some strategic decisions made at corporate headquarters are more informed by wider trends in the industry that may not be recognizable by those on the front lines. For example, back at McDonald's, the local operators offered stiff resistance to the decision to offer "all-day breakfast" because, again, this was expanding the menu.[23] However, that decision was based on wide-ranging market surveys conducted at the corporate level, and that program turned out to be a huge success for all.[24] All of this again points to the fact that there is no one best way to design the organization's structure and that the key is to make sure the structure is aligned with the competitive strategy.

In fact, when highly functional structures that are really built for efficiency and cost containment try to compete via speed and flexibility, serious problems can ensue. This is perfectly illustrated in the "fast-fashion" industry. Historically, retailers launched new styles at the beginning of each season, and it often took a full year for a design concept to go from the drawing board to the store floor. Although last-minute changes could be made, these were typically costly and cut into margins at a rate that offset the value of the change. However, chains such as H&M and Zara are rewriting the rules of the fashion industry and increasingly introducing new styles every month as part of the push for "fast fashion."[25]

The only problem with this practice, however, is that many people feel that it can be accomplished only via the exploitation of workers in small, emerging, third-world labor markets. It might not seem like such a major request to shift an order from 20,000 blue blouses to 10,000 blue blouses and 10,000 red blouses. However, quick shifts in operations like this, when not accompanied by changes in order delivery dates, cause plant managers in emerging economies to pump up worker hours and take shortcuts with maintenance that create major safety issues. These problems have surfaced most clearly in Bangladesh, a country that has been at the forefront of the fast-fashion industry after surging wages in China sent retailers looking for cheaper and more accommodating manufacturers.[26]

In some extreme cases, divisional structures may be so decentralized that some small divisions may not even be supervised by a formal manager, and the employees may self-manage. For example, Valve Corporation, a video-game producer located in Bellevue, Washington, touts itself as a "boss-free" company where decisions regarding hiring, firing, and pay are made by the employees themselves, who are organized into teams. The teams tend to vote on most decisions, or in some cases, due to experience or expertise, one or two people will emerge as leaders for specific projects. Typically this type of leadership emergence occurs in a way that is supported by the team. As one employee notes,

"It absolutely is less efficient up front, but once you have the organization behind it, the buy-in and the execution happen quickly."[27]

Zappos, the Amazon-owned shoe retailer, also employs what it calls a "bossless" company, and its experience too suggests that this nontraditional structure requires a great deal of time to learn. The orientation program at Zappos that teaches new employees the self-motivation and collaboration skills needed to be successful at the company takes four weeks, that is, unless you are late on the first day, in which case you are fired on the spot.[28]

Although flexible, divisional structures are not very efficient because of the redundancy associated with each group carrying its own functional specialists. Also, divisional structures can "self-cannibalize" if the gains achieved in one unit come at the expense of another unit. For example, iPhone's and iPads are managed by different divisions at Apple, and although the iPhone is certainly a very successful product, the folks over at iPad realized very quickly that iPhones were affecting their sales in a very negative way.[29]

Similarly, many retailers house in-store sales and e-commerce sales in different divisions and then find that there e-commerce sales wind up killing their in-store sales. This is exactly what happened at Nordstrom's during the holiday season in 2016 when in-store sales were crushed, in part, due to the increased sales that were being generated online. As one industry analyst has noted, "most retailers haven't yet figured out how to grow and maintain brick and mortar profitability while trying to keep up with the likes of Amazon in today's increasingly digital environment."[30]

Decentralized and divisional structures can also create problems if the stand-alone divisions start making decisions that are overly risky or out of line with the organization's larger goals. This can be particularly problematic when the organization is trying to manage a universal brand image with demands for standardized practices across many far-flung units. For example, Chipotle Mexican Grill had a winning formula for luring customers and investors with promise of healthy fast food, achieved in an environmentally sustainable manner. At the core of its business strategy was the decentralized nature of decision making where franchise managers had the freedom to make their own decisions regarding local sourcing of ingredients. Unlike national burger chains such as McDonald's and Burger King that rely on a small number of huge beef and potato suppliers chosen by corporate headquarters, Chipotle's 2,000 restaurants rely on decentralized supply chain decisions that involved hundreds of small, local independent farmers. This was a distinguishing element of its competitive strategy and it was one of the main factors that made Chipotle a darling of the "farm-to-table" segment of the market.

All of this changed, however, in June 2017 when the organization was upended by a breakout of *E. coli* bacterial poisoning at many of its restaurants—the second major incident in two years. Typically, outbreaks such as this are isolated incidents, but when one chain is struck in so many different regions at the same time, customers and investors begin to think that something is systematically going wrong. Many came to believe that the decentralized nature of the decisions regarding ingredients was simply too loose when it came to strict quality control. Sales dropped by 16% soon after the outbreaks, and the stock price closed 22% lower in the wake of the scandal. As one industry analyst noted, "this strikes deeper at their brand, because so much of their story is based on the quality of their ingredients."[31]

Another example of divisions not making decisions that are in the best interests of the company as a whole can be seen at Procter & Gamble (P&G), where each separate division had been given control over its own research and development budget. During tough economic times, each separate unit began to reduce expenditures on R&D in an effort to tighten their budgets and meet short-term profit goals. The cumulative effect of all of these short-term independent decisions was that, as a company, P&G was under-investing in R&D, and a dearth of new and innovative products harmed the company's long-term competitiveness. Then-CEO Bob McDonald stepped in and centralized the R&D function so that the majority of researchers worked in a single unit and reported to a single authority, Jorge Mesquita. The hope was to leverage the research talent that was spread across the divisions and consolidate them into a single unit focused on more radical breakthroughs rather than incremental innovations.[32]

Alternatively, functional structures are very efficient, with little redundancy across units, and they provide little opportunity for self-cannibalization or for rogue units running wild. Also, although the higher level of oversight in centralized structures tends to reduce the number of errors made by lower-level workers, when errors do occur in overly centralized systems, they tend to cascade through the system as a whole more quickly and can, therefore, be more debilitating. For example, nowhere was this more evident than in the 2014 recall of 2.7 million General Motor (GM) vehicles due to failures in the ignition system that resulted in the deaths and injuries of more than 500 customers and financial losses of over $400 million.

There were two specific problems associated with the structure of GM that helped contribute to the ignition system disaster. First, the structure created functional silos where people who worked on one aspect of the cars rarely spoke to people who worked in other functional areas. For example, the switch problem was, in part, a result of a single engineer who redesigned a faulty part, but failed to renumber it. Because it was not renumbered, when the part moved down through the line through other divisions, those divisions all thought they were working on the original part. Then, when reports of cars stalling began rolling in, this was treated as a customer satisfaction problem, not a safety issue or a design flaw. Thus, the personnel that were monitoring customer satisfaction never talked to the personnel in design who were not even aware of the problem until it was too late.

A second problem with GM's structure was that it was not at all clear who had decision-making authority for different decisions, and people at lower levels of the organization were reluctant to take responsibility for problems or pass bad news up the organizational chart. An external investigation of the incident conducted by the U.S. Attorney General's Office revealed that many people were aware of the problem as far back as 2001, but these individuals either said nothing or pointed the finger of blame at other units, and so no one actually did anything to solve the problem. In fact, when the Attorney General's Office asked one worker who knew about the problem if "fixing the problem was part of your job description," the person simply answered "No." The report from the Attorney General's Office specifically noted that "no single person owned any decision related to the ignition switch problem."[33]

In contrast to divisional structures, functional structures are most appropriate in stable, predictable environments, where demand for resources can be well anticipated and coordination requirements between jobs can be refined and standardized over consistent repetitions of activity. This type of structure also helps support organizations that compete on cost, because efficiency is central to making this strategy work. Divisional structures are most appropriate in unstable, unpredictable environments, where it is difficult to anticipate demands for resources, and coordination requirements between jobs are not consistent over time. This type of structure also helps support organizations that compete on differentiation or innovation, because flexible responsiveness is central to making this strategy work.

Of course, designing an organizational structure is not an either–or proposition, and some research suggests that "middle-of-the-road" options that combine functional and divisional elements are often best. For example, most organizations take a "mixed" approach to how they structure the HR function. Typically, there is a subunit called a shared service center that is highly centralized and handles all the major routine transactional tasks such as payroll. There is also a center of excellence subunit that houses specialized expertise in the area of training or labor relations, which is centralized but separate from the shared service center. Finally, there is a third decentralized subunit that acts as business partner to other subunit leaders on talent management or succession planning. This three-pronged structure has elements that strive to achieve efficiency when it comes to routine tasks, specialization when it comes to complex tasks, and flexibility when it comes to supporting each separate business unit.[34]

### Structure and the Nature of Jobs

Finally, moving from big-picture issues to lower-level specifics, the type of organization structure also has implications for the design of jobs. Jobs in functional structures need to be narrow and highly specialized. Workers in these structures (even middle managers) tend to have little decision-making authority or responsibility for managing coordination between themselves and others. In contrast, the steel producer Nucor is structured divisionally; production at its 30 minimill plants has doubled almost every two years, and profit margins have pushed beyond 10% largely because of its flat, divisional structure. At Nucor, individual plant managers have wide autonomy in how to design work at their own mills. Nucor plants sometimes compete against each other, but the CEO makes sure that the competition is healthy and that best practices are distributed throughout the organization as fast as possible, preventing any long-term sustainable advantage to any one plant. Moreover, the profit sharing plan that makes up the largest part of people's pay operates at the organizational level, which also promotes collaboration among managers who want to make sure that every plant is successful.[35]

Nucor employs just four levels of management and operates a headquarters of just 66 people, compared to one of its competitors, U.S. Steel, which has over 20 levels and 1,200 people at its headquarters. This gives Nucor a long-term sustainable competitive advantage, which it has held for close to 25 years. Many expect this competitive advantage to grow even more in the future, because Nucor is one of the firms that has been helped out the most when it comes to the new tariffs that the U.S. government imposed on foreign steel producers in 2018.[36]

The choice of structure also has implications for people who would assume the jobs created in functional versus divisional structures. For example, managers of functional structures often need to be specialists with deep experience in a narrow topic area. For example, because patents for well-established drugs run out after a set time period, a company like Eli Lilly can survive only by inventing new products before the time bomb represented by their older drugs goes off. Faced with the prospect of losing the patent on its $5 billion a year schizophrenia medication, Zyprexa, this company restructured operations in a functional direction in order to create new products more quickly and efficiently. For example, all persons who were responsible for converting molecules into medicine were taken out of their home departments and placed under one roof in the new Development Center for Excellence.

This group of intensely focused specialists, who were all working together for the first time, came up with an innovative new method for launching and testing drugs. This group took a formerly sequential two-stage process for determining general effectiveness and then the optimal dosage, and converted it into a single-stage process in which multiple dose levels were tested all at once and compared to each other. This process shaved 14 months off the process of developing a new drug for diabetes and was then generalized to other therapeutic causes.[37]

# Job Analysis

**Job analysis** refers to the process of getting detailed information about jobs. It is important for organizations to understand and match job requirements and people to achieve high-quality performance. This is particularly true in today's competitive marketplace.

## THE IMPORTANCE OF JOB ANALYSIS FOR HR SPECIALISTS

Job analysis is the building block of everything that human resource managers do. Almost every human resource management program requires some type of information that is gleaned from job analysis: work redesign, human resource planning, selection, training and development, performance appraisal, career planning, and job evaluation.

### Work Redesign

As previously discussed, job analysis and job design are interrelated. Often a firm will seek to redesign work to make it more efficient or effective. To redesign the work, detailed information about the existing job(s) must be available. In addition, redesigning a job will, in fact, be similar to analyzing a job that does not yet exist.

### Human Resource Planning

In human resource planning, managers analyze an organization's human resource needs in a dynamic environment and develop activities that enable a firm to adapt to change. This planning process requires accurate information about the levels of skill required in various jobs to ensure that enough individuals are available in the organization to meet the human resource needs of the strategic plan.

### Selection

Human resource selection identifies the most qualified applicants for employment. To identify which applicants are most qualified, it is first necessary to determine the tasks that will be performed by the individual hired and the knowledge, skills, and abilities the individual must have to perform the job effectively. This information is gained through job analysis.

### Training and Development

Almost every employee hired by an organization will require training. Some training programs may be more extensive than others, but all require the trainer to have identified the tasks performed in the job to ensure that the training will prepare individuals to perform their jobs effectively.

### Performance Appraisal

Performance appraisal deals with getting information about how well each employee is performing in order to reward those who are effective, improve the performance of those who are ineffective, or provide a written justification for why the poor performer should be disciplined. Through job analysis, the organization can identify the behaviors and results that distinguish effective performance from ineffective performance.

**LO 4-2**
Understand the importance of job analysis for line managers and strategic human resource managers.

**Job analysis**
The process of getting detailed information about jobs.

### Career Planning

Career planning entails matching an individual's skills and aspirations with opportunities that are or may become available in the organization. This matching process requires that those in charge of career planning know the skill requirements of the various jobs. This allows them to guide individuals into jobs in which they will succeed and be satisfied.

### Job Evaluation

The process of job evaluation involves assessing the relative dollar value of each job to the organization to set up internally equitable pay structures. If pay structures are not equitable, employees will be dissatisfied and quit, or they will not see the benefits of striving for promotions. To put dollar values on jobs, it is necessary to get information about different jobs to determine which jobs deserve higher pay than others.

## THE IMPORTANCE OF JOB ANALYSIS TO LINE MANAGERS

Job analysis is clearly important to the HR department's various activities, but why it is important to line managers may not be as clear. There are many reasons. First, managers must have detailed information about all the jobs in their work group to understand the work-flow process. Second, managers need to understand the job requirements to make intelligent hiring decisions. Very seldom do employees get hired by the HR department without a manager's input. Third, a manager is responsible for ensuring that each individual is performing satisfactorily (or better). This requires the manager to evaluate how well each person is performing and to provide feedback to those whose performance needs improvement. Finally, it is also the manager's responsibility to ensure that work is being done safely, know where potential hazards might manifest themselves, and create a climate where people feel free to interrupt the production process if dangerous conditions exist.

For example, in 2016, Donald Blankenship, the CEO of Massey Energy Company, was fined $250,000 and sentenced to a year in prison for conspiring to violate federal safety standards when it came to running mining operations. Prosecutors in this case argued that Blankenship created a culture at the organization that placed financial performance ahead of safety standards and that this contributed to the deaths of 29 miners after an explosion in the Upper Big Branch Mine in Appalachia.[38]

In contrast, some observers were shocked when Alcoa's new CEO Paul O'Neill's opening remarks at his first shareholders' meeting were focused on pointing out the nearest emergency exits in the building. However, O'Neill's emphasis on safety and work processes actually ended up making him one of the best CEOs in history. After he took over at Alcoa, O'Neill changed reporting procedures so that any time an employee got hurt, the department head in that unit had to develop a plan detailing how work processes were going to be changed to make sure the same accident did not happen again. Executives who failed to embrace this new standard routine were fired. As a result of this new policy, each department head had to become intimately familiar with work processes, which ultimately led to many conversations with lower-level workers who had great ideas not only for shoring up safety but also for streamlining work flow. Eventually, even as safety was improving, costs came down, quality went up, and productivity skyrocketed.[39]

Of course, one problem with trying to make job analysis fulfill so many different purposes is that the best job analysis for one objective may not be the best job analysis for another. For example, a job description that is based on a job analysis performed for recruitment purposes needs to be short and attract attention to applicants who may not spend a great deal of time reading an advertisement. In contrast, a job description that is based on a job analysis used as part of a performance management program needs to be detailed enough to tease out the strengths and weaknesses of a job incumbent who may have been observed over a full year. Thus, a company may perform multiple job analyses for a single job or derive multiple job descriptions from a single job analysis. Sodexo USA, a food and facilities management company, does exactly this and has "dual documents" for over 900 different jobs.[40]

## JOB ANALYSIS INFORMATION
### Nature of Information

Two types of information are most useful in job analysis: job descriptions and job specifications. A **job description** is a list of the tasks, duties, and responsibilities (TDRs) that a job entails. TDRs are observable actions. For example, a clerical job requires the jobholder to type. If you were to observe someone in that position for a day, you would certainly see some typing. When a manager attempts to evaluate job performance, it is most important to have detailed information about the work performed in the job (that is, the TDRs). This makes it possible to determine how well an individual is meeting each job requirement. Table 4.1 shows a sample job description. On the one hand, job descriptions need to be written broadly because overly restrictive descriptions make it easy for someone to claim that some important task, perhaps unforeseen, "is not my job." On the other hand, lack of specificity can result in disagreement and conflict between people about the essential elements of what the job entails.[41] Thus, it is critical

**Job description**
A list of the tasks, duties, and responsibilities (TDRs) that a job entails.

**Table 4.1**
A Sample Job Description

Job Title: Maintenance Mechanic
**General Description of Job:** General maintenance and repair of all equipment used in the operations of a particular district. Includes the servicing of company vehicles, shop equipment, and machinery used on job sites.
1. *Essential Duty (40%): Maintenance of Equipment*—Tasks: Keep a log of all maintenance performed on equipment. Replace parts and fluids according to maintenance schedule. Regularly check gauges and loads for deviances that may indicate problems with equipment. Perform nonroutine maintenance as required. May involve limited supervision and training of operators performing maintenance.
2. *Essential Duty (40%): Repair of Equipment*—Tasks: Requires inspection of equipment and a recommendation that a piece be scrapped or repaired. If equipment is to be repaired, mechanic will take whatever steps are necessary to return the piece to working order. This may include a partial or total rebuilding of the piece using various hand tools and equipment. Will primarily involve the overhaul and troubleshooting of diesel engines and hydraulic equipment.
3. *Essential Duty (10%): Testing and Approval*—Tasks: Ensure that all required maintenance and repair has been performed and that it was performed according to manufacturer specifications. Approve or reject equipment as being ready for use on a job.
4. *Essential Duty (10%): Maintain Stock*—Tasks: Maintain inventory of parts needed for the maintenance and repair of equipment. Responsible for ordering satisfactory parts and supplies at the lowest possible cost.
*Nonessential Functions*
Other duties as assigned.

 McGraw Hill **connect**

Visit your instructor's Connect® course and access your eBook to view this video.

"We are looking at those work systems in the back of the restaurant in terms of where to use potential automation that actually elevates the experience of the employee and makes it a better place to work."

—Scott A. Weisberg,
Former Chief People Officer, The Wendy's Company

Source: Video produced for the Center for Executive Succession in the Darla Moore School of Business at the University of South Carolina by Coal Powered Filmworks

to strike an effective balance between breadth and specificity when constructing job descriptions.

A **job specification** is a list of the knowledge, skills, abilities, and other characteristics (KSAOs) that an individual must have to perform the job. *Knowledge* refers to factual or procedural information that is necessary for successfully performing a task. A *skill* is an individual's level of proficiency at performing a particular task. *Ability* refers to a more general enduring capability that an individual possesses. Finally, *other characteristics* might be personality traits such as one's achievement motivation or persistence. Thus, KSAOs are characteristics of people that are not directly observable; they are observable only when individuals are carrying out the TDRs of the job. If someone applied for the clerical job mentioned earlier, you could not simply look at the individual to determine whether he or she possessed typing skills. However, if you were to observe that individual typing something, you could assess the level of typing skill. When a manager is attempting to fill a position, it is important to have accurate information about the characteristics a successful jobholder must have. This requires focusing on the KSAOs of each applicant, and as shown in the Competing through Technology box, not be driven by inaccurate stereotypes.

**Job specification**
A list of the knowledge, skills, abilities, and other characteristics (KSAOs) that an individual must have to perform a job.

## Sources of Job Analysis Information

In performing the job analysis, one question that often arises is, Who should be responsible for providing the job analysis information? Whatever job analysis method you choose, the process of job analysis entails obtaining information from people familiar with the job. We refer to these people as *subject-matter experts* because they possess deep knowledge of the job.

In general, it will be useful to go to the job incumbent to get the most accurate information about what is actually done on the job. This is especially the case when it is difficult to monitor the person who does the job. The ratings of multiple job incumbents that are doing the same job do not always agree, however, especially if the job is complex and does not involve standardized equipment or tight scripts for customer contact.[42] Thus, you will also want to ask others familiar with the job, such as supervisors, to look over the information generated by the job incumbent. This serves as a check to determine whether what is being done is congruent with what is supposed to be done in the job.

Job incumbents are also useful when one is trying to assess the informal social network that exists within the formal organizational structure. That is, although the formal organizational structure suggests who *should* be talking to whom from a top-down normative perspective, an analysis of a company's social structure shows who *really* is talking to whom from a bottom-up descriptive perspective. In fact, one example of the growing field of business analytics deals with people analytic programs that show who is talking to whom on a day-to-day basis via self-report surveys or e-mail trails or from data derived from wearable sensors.

In many cases, social networks develop due to limitations in the formal structure when people realize they need to interact with some person in a way that was not anticipated by a formal organizational designer. Once alerted to this need, formal planners may wish to reconfigure the formal structure to reflect the needs identified by the informal, emergent

# COMPETING THROUGH TECHNOLOGY

## Not Wanted: Lone Genius Nerd

Because job specifications drive so much of a firm's hiring and eventual culture, it is critical that the company avoid inaccurate stereotypes. Increasingly, one such stereotype can be found in technology companies that are rejecting what Claire Cain Miller calls "the lone, genius, nerd" archetype that has been so prevalent in the industry. On the one hand, programming can indeed be a solo activity in computer science courses where people first learn the skills, as well as entry-level jobs where those newly learned skills are applied in a highly routine nature. In addition, almost all of the well-known programming competitions that help identify geniuses, such as Google Code Jam or Facebook Hacker Cup, do pit individuals against individuals on short-term tasks that can be solved by individuals working alone.

However, real-life tech firms competing in labor markets and product markets need a more varied set of skills. On the labor market side, tech firms need to attract the best talent, and for many people, any job description that smacks of social isolation is an immediate turn-off. In addition, hyper-competitive cultures that penalize and disparage cooperative people produce a self-reinforcing cycle that creates a hostile work environment that drives those people from the work even if they were once attracted to it.

More importantly, however, once one gets beyond entry-level positions, a close analysis of the work shows that it demands high levels of collaboration, often as part of diverse teams. Large projects demand the skills of many technical specialists who have mastered deep and complex skills within narrow disciplines, rather than "jacks of all trades" who possess generic problem-solving skills. As Tracy Cho, a software engineer at Pinterest notes, "when building a big software system, you can have dozens or hundreds or thousands of engineers all working on the same code base, and everything still has to work together." The notion that any one person working alone could build a large software system is simply untenable regardless of how many ACM-ICPC International Collegiate Programming Contests the individual has won. Eventually, just coming up with innovative solutions may not be enough if one is unable to convince their leader or the team or investors of their genius.

On the product market side, tech firms also need to attract and retain workers who are grounded in the real world and can take the customer's perspective. Programmers need to anticipate how large groups of diverse people are likely to react to various products or product upgrades in order to generate sales. Nathan Ensmenger, a renowned historian of the software industry notes that, "the failure rate for software development is enormous, but it almost never means that the code doesn't work. Instead, the code doesn't solve the problem that actually exists or it imagines a user completely different from actual users." For example, although Google Glass was a remarkable achievement when it comes to embedding a large amount of computing power in a pair of glasses, it was not clear that anyone other than a loner genius would want to wear them on a regular basis. People who are regularly engaged with others realized immediately that the product violated the need to protect others' privacy. This was not a failure of imagination or problem-solving skills, but rather a failure of perspective-taking when it came to a pair of glasses.

### DISCUSSION QUESTIONS

1. In what ways have stereotypes regarding the job requirements for tech workers limited opportunities for otherwise qualified workers in terms of demographic diversity? Is there still a place in the world of work for loners, and what kind of jobs might legitimately promote that trait as a requirement?
2. Can you think of other jobs totally outside the tech industry where the job specifications may be based on inaccurate stereotypes in a similar way, and thus limit both organizational performance and individual opportunity?

SOURCES: C. Cain Miller, "Tech's Damaging Myth of the Loner, Genius Nerd," *The New York Times Online*, August 12, 2017; D. Wakabayashi, "Google Fires Engineer for Divisive Memo," *The New York Times Online*, August 7, 2017; L. Bradford, "Six Soft Skills That Technical Employees Need to Thrive," *Forbes Online*, August 26, 2017.

**Figure 4.6**

Social Network within an Organization

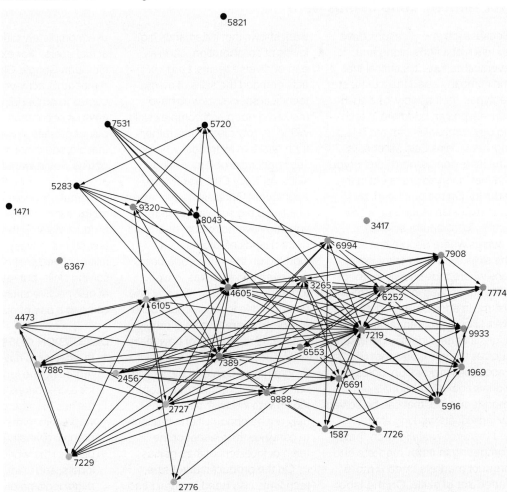

social structure.[43] For example, Figure 4.6 shows a social network among the division leaders within an organization that produces scientific equipment. In this figure, the blue dots represent engineers engaged in production, the green dots represent scientists engaged in design, the black dots represent administrative support personnel, and the red dots represent the top management team. The lines in this figure denote who frequently interacts with whom on a face-to-face basis.

Unlike formal structures designed in a top-down fashion that tend to embrace symmetry and balance, social networks are much more organic and seemingly chaotic. These pictures are an important supplement to the formal organizational chart, however, because they often point out individuals who are more central to the organization than one might think given their job description and the formal chart.[44] In Figure 4.6, individuals like 4605, 7219, 2727, and 7389 are important "boundary spanners" across the units, whereas 3417, 2776, 1471, and 6367 do not even seem closely tied to members of their own units. It is easy for organizations to underestimate the importance of these informal boundary spanners, and the loss of any one of these individuals is likely to have a much more negative impact on the organization than the loss of individuals who are social outliers.

For these and many other reasons, organizations are increasingly complementing depictions of their formal structure with depictions of these informal structures, and these pictures may not just rely on self-reports.[45] Bluetooth signals coming from wearable sensors can accomplish the same goal, and indeed, the social network depicted in Figure 4.6 was based on data from wearable sensors and not self-reports.[46] By relying on relational data captured automatically and continuously via this technology, one can obtain monthly, weekly, and even daily social network depictions that, due to their organic nature, are more volatile than formal organizational charts. In many cases, informal structures arise as adaptations to problems with formal structures, and over time, the formal structure may be changed so that it conforms more closely to the informal structure.

In contrast to cases where some communication link develops between people in order to meet a legitimate need to get the job done, a close examination of the social network in other cases uncovers individuals who over-communicate for no good reason related to the work and, hence, waste their time and the time of others. For example, one company that analyzed its e-mail communications found one executive who generated so many e-mails that it took the equivalent of 10 people working full time just to read the e-mails sent by this one person. An analysis of these e-mails suggested that few of the people who were being sent the communications really needed e-mails from this person to do their job. An intervention directed at "fixing" this part of the social network increased the efficiency of a large number of people.[47]

One conclusion that can be drawn from this research is that incumbents may provide the most accurate estimates of the actual time spent performing job tasks, and who really has to talk to whom. However, supervisors may be a more accurate source of information about the importance of job duties. Incumbents also seem more accurate in terms of assessing safety-related risk factors associated with various aspects of work, and in general, the farther one moves up the organizational hierarchy, the less accurate the risk assessments.[48]

Although job incumbents and supervisors are the most obvious and frequently used sources of job analysis information, other sources, such as customers, can be helpful, particularly for service jobs. However, because they lack training in evaluations and assessment, customers can sometimes show racial bias or sex bias when evaluating the nature of the work.[49] Finally, when it comes to analyzing skill levels, external job analysts who have more experience rating a wide range of jobs may be the best source.[50]

## JOB ANALYSIS METHODS

There are various methods for analyzing jobs and no "one best way." In this section, we discuss two methods for analyzing jobs: the Position Analysis Questionnaire (PAQ) and the Occupational Information Network (O*NET). Although most managers may not have time to use each of these techniques in the exact manner suggested, the two provide some anchors for thinking about broad approaches, task-focused approaches, and person-oriented approaches to conducting job analysis.

**LO 4-3**
Choose the right job analysis technique for a variety of human resource activities.

### Position Analysis Questionnaire (PAQ)

We lead off this section with the PAQ because this is one of the broadest and most well-researched instruments for analyzing jobs. Moreover, its emphasis on inputs, processes, relationships, and outputs is consistent with the work-flow analysis approach discussed at the beginning of this chapter (Figure 4.1).

The PAQ is a standardized job analysis questionnaire containing 194 items.[51] These items represent work behaviors, work conditions, and job characteristics that can be generalized across a wide variety of jobs. They are organized into six sections:

1. *Information input*—Where and how a worker gets information needed to perform the job.
2. *Mental processes*—The reasoning, decision-making, planning, and information-processing activities that are involved in performing the job.
3. *Work output*—The physical activities, tools, and devices used by the worker to perform the job.
4. *Relationships with other persons*—The relationships with other people required in performing the job.
5. *Job context*—The physical and social contexts where the work is performed.
6. *Other characteristics*—The activities, conditions, and characteristics other than those previously described that are relevant to the job.

The job analyst is asked to determine whether each item applies to the job being analyzed. The analyst then rates the item on six scales: extent of use, amount of time, importance to the job, possibility of occurrence, applicability, and special code (special rating scales used with a particular item). These ratings are submitted to the PAQ headquarters, where a computer program generates a report regarding the job's scores on the job dimensions.

Research has indicated that the PAQ measures 12 overall dimensions of jobs (listed in Table 4.2) and that a given job's scores on these dimensions can be very useful. The PAQ database has linked scores on certain dimensions to scores on subtests of the General Aptitude Test Battery (GATB). Thus, knowing the dimension scores provides some guidance regarding the types of abilities that are necessary to perform the job. Obviously, this technique provides information about the work performed in a format that allows for comparisons across jobs, whether those jobs are similar or dissimilar. Another advantage of the PAQ is that it covers the work context as well as inputs, outputs, and processes.

Knowledge of work context is important because in many cases, one can predict absenteeism and turnover from the nature of the surroundings in which the work takes place, and some people are more resilient than others when it comes to dealing with adverse environments. For example, one aspect of the work environment that is being reconsidered is the use of open office plans that eliminate private offices and

**Table 4.2**
Overall Dimensions of the Position Analysis Questionnaire

Decision/communication/general responsibilities
Clerical/related activities
Technical/related activities
Service/related activities
Regular day schedule versus other work schedules
Routine/repetitive work activities
Environmental awareness
General physical activities
Supervising/coordinating other personnel
Public/customer/related contact activities
Unpleasant/hazardous/demanding environment
Nontypical work schedules

place employees in larger more public spaces. The hope was that this kind of office design would spur collaboration and creativity, but in many instances, due to the need to concentrate, many employees would put on head phones and never look up from their cubicle that was often "redecorated" in ways that would preclude people seeing one another.[52]

There was also the hope that open office designs would promote a more egalitarian environment because upper-level managers often resided in the same space, and were more accessible relative to when they were in a big private office. But again, these plans backfired because many workers were stressed out by having their supervisors around constantly. In addition, the upper-level managers also required privacy for many of their tasks, and when they left their "open space" for "communal private space" to meet in private, this fueled needless speculation and rumors. Thus, for a host of reasons, when it comes to work surroundings, many companies are returning to private offices.[53]

### The Occupational Information Network (O*NET)

The *Dictionary of Occupational Titles* (DOT) was born during the 1930s and served as a vehicle for helping the new public employment system link the demand for skills and the supply of skills in the U.S. workforce. Although this system served the country well for more than 60 years, it became clear to officials at the U.S. Department of Labor that jobs in the new economy were so qualitatively different from jobs in the old economy that the DOT no longer served its purpose. Technological changes in the nature of work, global competition, and a shift from stable, fixed manufacturing jobs to a more flexible, dynamic, service-based economy were quickly making the system obsolete.[54]

For all these reasons, the Department of Labor abandoned the DOT in 1998 and developed an entirely new system for classifying jobs referred to as the Occupational Information Network, or O*NET. Instead of relying on fixed job titles and narrow task descriptions, the O*NET uses a common language that generalizes across jobs to describe the abilities, work styles, work activities, and work context required for various occupations that are more broadly defined (e.g., instead of the 12,000 jobs in the DOT, the O*NET describes only 1,000 occupations).[55]

Reviews of the O*NET have praised it for its breadth and scope in terms of covering the wide variety of work reflected in the U.S. economy; however, it has also been criticized for the fact that many of its different sections are poorly coordinated and redundant and that many sections are laced with jargon that is difficult for nonspecialists to understand.[56]

Still, the O*NET is a valuable source of information, especially for job seekers who are unfamiliar with the requirements associated with certain jobs. For example, the O*NET seems particularly well suited to describing the literacy requirements associated with alternative jobs. Thus, individuals who want to improve their ability to find employment can obtain from the O*NET relatively accurate information about what jobs they are qualified for given their current literacy level. They can also see how much their literacy skills would have to improve if they wanted to apply for higher-level jobs characterized by higher levels of complexity.[57]

### DYNAMIC ELEMENTS OF JOB ANALYSIS

Although we tend to view jobs as static and stable, in fact, jobs tend to change and evolve over time. Those who occupy or manage the jobs often make minor, cumulative adjustments to the job that try to match either changing conditions in the environment or personal preferences for how to conduct the work. Indeed, although there are

**LO 4-4**
Identify the tasks performed and the skills required in a given job.

numerous sources for error in the job analysis process, most inaccuracy is likely to result from job descriptions simply being outdated. For this reason, in addition to statically defining the job, the job analysis process must also detect changes in the nature of jobs.

For example, although working in a nursing home has always been a stressful occupation mentally, changes over time in the nature of the patients has dramatically increased requirements related to pure physical strength. The percentage of morbidly obese patients has increased from less than 15% in 2000 to over 25% in 2015, which has led to an unprecedented spike in staff injuries related to heavy lifting because, in many cases, this aspect of the job was not reflected in outdated job descriptions.[58]

Indeed, in today's world of rapidly changing products and markets, some people have begun to question whether the concept of "the job" is simply a social artifact that has outlived its usefulness. The belief is that traditional "jobs" will be replaced by "gigs" where workers all act as private contractors. Instead of being "W-2" employees working for an employer, each worker will be a freelancer and part of some part-time work arrangement. Although this vision of the future may be true for Uber drivers, Task Rabbit contributors, and some employees on the fringe of the high-tech industry, recent statistics from the Bureau of Labor Statistics suggests that the percentage of U.S. workers that would be categorized as being part of "alternative work arrangements" is small (10%) and has actually decreased in the last decade.[59] In particular, as the labor market tightened up in 2018, it began to appear that so-called gig jobs were just a temporary resort that workers turned to after the previous recession left many out of traditional jobs.

# Job Design

So far we have approached the issue of managing work in a passive way, focusing only on understanding what gets done, how it gets done, and the skills required to get it done. Although this is necessary, it is a very static view of jobs, in that jobs must already exist and that they are already assumed to be structured in the one best way. However, a manager may often be faced with a situation in which the work unit does not yet exist, requiring jobs within the work unit to be designed from scratch. Sometimes work loads within an existing work unit are increased, or work-group size is decreased while the same work load is required. Finally, sometimes the work is not being performed in the most efficient manner. In these cases, a manager may decide to change the way that work is done in order for the work unit to perform more effectively and efficiently. This requires redesigning the existing jobs.

**Job design**
The process of defining the way work will be performed and the tasks that will be required in a given job.

**Job redesign**
The process of changing the tasks or the way work is performed in an existing job.

**Job design** is the process of defining how work will be performed and the tasks that will be required in a given job. **Job redesign** refers to changing the tasks or the way work is performed in an existing job. To effectively design jobs, one must thoroughly understand the job as it exists (through job analysis) and its place in the larger work unit's work-flow process (work-flow analysis). Having a detailed knowledge of the tasks performed in the work unit and in the job, a manager then has many alternative ways to design a job. This can be done most effectively through understanding the trade-offs between certain design approaches.

Research has identified four basic approaches that have been used among the various disciplines (such as psychology, management, engineering, and ergonomics) that have dealt with job design issues.[60] All jobs can be characterized in terms of how they fare according to each approach; thus a manager needs to understand the trade-offs of emphasizing one approach over another. The Work Design Questionnaire (WDQ), a specific instrument that reliably measures these and other job design characteristics, is available for use by companies wishing to comprehensively assess their jobs on these dimensions.[61]

## MECHANISTIC APPROACH

The mechanistic approach has roots in classical industrial engineering. The focus of the mechanistic approach is identifying the simplest way to structure work that maximizes efficiency. This most often entails reducing the complexity of the work to provide more human resource efficiency—that is, making the work so simple that anyone can be trained quickly and easily to perform it. This approach focuses on designing jobs around the concepts of task specialization, skill simplification, and repetition. For example at Chili's Restaurants, cooks used to cut up vegetables, meats, and other ingredients as part of preparing a meal. To increase efficiency, the organization decided to break this job into two smaller parts: one job, called "prep cook," involves coming in the morning to cut up the ingredients, and the second job, "line cook," involves using these prepared ingredients to assemble the final meal.[62]

*Scientific management* was one of the earliest and best-known statements of the mechanistic approach.[63] According to this approach, productivity could be maximized by taking a scientific approach to the process of designing jobs. Scientific management first sought to identify the "one best way" to perform the job. Once the best way to perform the work is identified, workers should be selected based on their ability to do the job, they should be trained in the standard "one best way" to perform the job, and they should be offered monetary incentives to motivate them to work at their highest capacity.

The scientific management approach was built upon in later years, resulting in a mechanistic approach that calls for jobs to be designed so that they are very simple. By designing jobs in this way, the organization reduces its need for high-ability individuals and thus becomes less dependent on individual workers. Individuals are easily replaceable—that is, a new employee can be trained to perform the job quickly and inexpensively.

Many jobs structured this way are performed in developing countries where there is a large supply of low-skilled labor and relatively lax legal guidelines regarding safety standards.[64] For example, manufacturing silicon chips involves a process that exposes workers to a large number of carcinogens that are regulated less heavily in Asia than in the United States; hence, chip production has largely moved overseas.[65] Unfortunately, as can be seen in the Integrity in Action box, what was learned about how to protect workers from many of these carcinogens did not make the trip when those jobs were relocated.

In some cases, jobs designed via mechanistic practices result in work that is so simple that a child could do it, and this is exactly what can happen in some undeveloped countries. This can lead to a backlash against companies that benefit from this unethical practice, and increasingly, organizations are taking the lead in preventing these kinds of practices. For example, when it learned that Uzbekistan cotton growers were using child labor to pick their crops, Walmart used its power to force them to abandon this practice. Working with other large U.S. retailers, Walmart took the lead to create the first system for tracking where cotton came from and organized a boycott against Uzbekistan, which quickly acquiesced to the corporate giant's pressure, freeing the children to return to school.[66]

# INTEGRITY IN ACTION

## Toxic Killer Comes Back from the Dead

It was considered one of the greatest achievements in public health at the time. A lone health and safety worker at Digital Electronics Corporation, a computer chip plant in Hudson, Massachusetts, noticed a strange pattern of data at the facility that suggested that women there were experiencing miscarriages at a rate that far exceeded the expected rate in the population. Industry experts were very skeptical of the small sample study and challenged the initial findings. Eventually, two separate and much larger studies, funded by the industry, were conducted. One of the studies was conducted by scientists at the University of California at Davis who examined 14 different facilities operated by different companies, and one by John Hopkins University that focused on only one large producer: IBM.

Despite the fact that the two studies were completely independent and examined totally different sets of workers at different chip-making facilities, the results were identical both in terms of showing unusual evidence of miscarriages (in addition to birth defects) at these facilities, as well as the specific source of the problem—a group of toxic chemicals called ethylene glycol ethers (EGEs). Faced with evidence from three independent studies, leaders within the industry jointly agreed to totally eliminate EGEs from chip-production processes in the United States in 1992. Even though safer alternatives to EGE were more expensive, less effective, and less abundant, the ethical costs associated with exposing women to this hazard far outweighed the financial considerations. EGEs were gone forever—until they weren't.

Over 20 years later, a South Korean epidemiologist named Kim Myoung-hee working within a Samsung Electronics plant also noticed an anomaly. Two young women working side-by-side at the plant both died from a rare form of leukemia within a six-month time period. The odds of developing this rare form of leukemia were 3 out of 100,000 and thus, to discover this in two people sitting at the same workstation was too high to discount. Myoung-hee began a quiet investigation into the problem as Samsung and other electronic producers discovered more and more cases similar to the one that first captured her attention. At first, she discounted EGEs as the culprit because every study she ever read regarding EGEs noted that EGEs had been banned from the industry. However, an examination of random samples taken from drums of chemicals obtained from Samsung and SK Hynix, another large South Korean chip manufacturer, revealed that there were traces of EGE in 60% of the drums.

Chip makers originally denied the accusations and aggressively fought the victims in court, often in ways that relied on nontransparency. They claimed that their production processes were trade secrets and that settlements to other victims were covered by nondisclosure agreements—a claim actually supported by South Korean Commerce Ministry. Ultimately, however, more research, as well as a groundswell of support for the victims from South Korean citizens and politicians, forced change. Accusations that the industry simply shifted exposure from U.S. workers to Korean workers were simply too widespread to deny. By 2018, Samsung had changed its tune and a spokesperson for the company noted that "we have been working to help out former semi-conductor employees and their families who have endured the hardship and heartache." Hopefully, EGEs will be gone forever—again.

### DISCUSSION QUESTIONS

1. Although the computer chip manufacturing industry left the United States long ago, in what way are U.S. authorities in the industry responsible for ensuring that what was learned in this country regarding worker safety is exported along with the jobs?

2. Everyone who owns a computer or a cell phone is a consumer of the types of computer chips manufactured by Samsung. What can each of us do as concerned consumers to ensure that the products we love are not manufactured in a way that harms unsuspecting workers?

SOURCES: C. Simpson, "The Price of a Digital World," *Bloomberg Businessweek*, June 19, 2017, pp. 58–65; S. Jong-a, "Samsung Finds Unlikely Ally in Stance on Worker Safety," *Financial Times Online*, July 2, 2018; E. Jeong, "Samsung Agrees to Compensation Deal Over Chip Worker Deaths, Illnesses," *The Wall Street Journal Online*, July 24, 2018.

## MOTIVATIONAL APPROACH

The motivational approach to job design has roots in organizational psychology and management literature and, in many ways, emerged as a reaction to mechanistic approaches to job design. It focuses on the job characteristics that affect psychological meaning and motivational potential, and it views attitudinal variables (such as satisfaction) as the most important outcomes of job design. The prescriptions of the motivational approach focus on increasing the meaningfulness of jobs through such interventions as job enlargement and job enrichment.

A model of how job design affects employee reactions is the Job Characteristics Model.[67] According to this model, jobs can be described in terms of five characteristics. *Skill variety* is the extent to which the job requires a variety of skills to carry out the tasks. *Task identity* is the degree to which a job requires completing a "whole" piece of work from beginning to end. *Autonomy* is the degree to which the job allows an individual to make decisions about the way the work will be carried out. *Feedback* is the extent to which a person receives, from the work itself, clear information about performance effectiveness. *Task significance* is the extent to which the job has an important impact on the lives of other people. Although all five characteristics are important, the belief that the task is significant because performing it well leads to outcomes one values may be the most critical motivational aspect of work. This can often be enhanced by making it clear to the worker how his or her job affects other people, whether they be customers, co-workers, or society in general.

For example, working in a call center trying to drum up contributions to a university's scholarship fund is boring, routine work that, more often than not, leads to rejection for employees. However, one experiment conducted in this setting found that after introducing the workers to scholarship recipients whose lives were changed by their awards, productivity among the call center team increased over 150%.[68] Helping workers see the meaningfulness of their jobs can be very motivational, and it is easy to lose this "line of sight" on a day-to-day basis if it is not reinforced.

Indeed, the term "job gentrification" has been coined to capture the fact that many well-educated workers, who struggle to see meaning in their work, have reverted to taking many formerly "nonprofessional" jobs like bartender, barber, and butcher. These jobs have a hands-on aspect to them where one works directly with customers on a day-to-day basis and, hence, can see people appreciate their work. When executed as part of job gentrification, these jobs have a distinct "performance" element to the work that differentiates it from how the job is traditionally performed. For example, a trendy whole animal butcher produces products and attracts clients that are willing to pay a premium for those products, which differ from what one sees at their local grocery store chain.[69]

## BIOLOGICAL APPROACH

The biological approach to job design comes primarily from the sciences of biomechanics (i.e., the study of body movements), work physiology, and occupational medicine, and it is usually referred to as *ergonomics*. **Ergonomics** is concerned with examining the interface between individuals' physiological characteristics and the physical work environment. The goal of this approach is to minimize physical strain on the worker by structuring the physical work environment around the way the human body works. It therefore focuses on outcomes such as physical fatigue, aches and pains, and health complaints. Any job that creates a significant number of injuries is a target for ergonomic redesign.

The biological approach has been applied in redesigning equipment used in jobs that are physically demanding. Such redesign is often aimed at reducing the physical demands

**Ergonomics**
The interface between individuals' physiological characteristics and the physical work environment.

of certain jobs so that anyone can perform them. In addition, many biological interventions focus on redesigning machines and technology, such as adjusting the height of the computer keyboard to minimize occupational illnesses (like carpal tunnel syndrome). The design of chairs and desks to fit posture requirements is very important in many office jobs and is another example of the biological approach to job design.

Although providing comfortable, ergonomically designed chairs is certainly laudable, recent research suggests that getting employees out of their chairs is also critically important when it comes to health outcomes. That is, the evidence is becoming increasingly clear that merely sitting for long periods can be damaging to employees. From an evolutionary perspective, the human body was designed to move, and long stretches of sedentary behavior are at odds with this design. For example, people who are above the mean in "time spent sitting" have a 24% greater risk of developing colon cancer, a 32% higher risk of endometrial cancer, and a 21% increased risk of lung cancer, even when one controls for the amount of physical exercise that people get when they are not sitting. Thus, office redesign programs that involve the introduction of treadmill desks or stand-up desks are becoming increasingly common elements of design, and some organizations are trying to make standing, rather than sitting, the default position for performing jobs.[70]

However, too much time standing can also be problematic when it comes to ergonomics. That is, recent evidence suggests that standing too long causes people to lean in odd directions that result in musculature problems, back problems, foot problems, carotid artery disease, and even varicose veins. Ergonomic science is now honing in on the precise formula for mixing sitting, standing, and light activity while at work for a standard eight-hour day. The current evidence suggests that the best mix includes two to four hours of standing and roughly 15 episodes of light activity (two minutes) spread throughout the day. Still, few workers are able to maintain the discipline required for this balance without some technical aid, such as sensors to remind them when to do what for how long a period.[71]

Although most ergonomic research focuses on highly visible aspects of the work environment and how workers interact with their equipment, as the Evidenced-Base HR box shows, recent research on less visible aspects of one's work context can also have a large impact on performance.

# EVIDENCE-BASED HR

Although it is obvious that all workers need air, you might not think that subtle differences in air quality within the range typically found in standard offices can have a major impact on performance, however, the evidence suggests otherwise. Research conducted at the Syracuse Center for Excellence, an organization focused on "green technologies" was interested in seeing how air quality, quantified via a metric called volatile organic compounds (VOC) impacted cognitive functioning. VOC represents the amount of toxic by-products of common office products floating through the air, and there are official standards for this metric published by OSHA.

In this research, participants were randomly assigned to three conditions. The "standard condition" blew air into the workspace that mirrored exactly what would be found in the average work office in a large city. The level of VOC in this condition was well within the recommended range and did not in any way present a threat to research participants according to these standards. The "green condition"

*CONTINUED*

increased the ventilation in the same space by 50% and the third condition, "enhanced green," increased the ventilation by 100%.

Observing workers over the course of six days, they documented that performance on a battery of standardized cognitive tests increased by 61% in the "green condition," and 100% in the "enhanced green" condition relative to the standard condition. There are very few jobs where performance increases of this magnitude would not pay for themselves when it comes to just turning up the fans.

SOURCE: T. Deangelis, "Healthy Buildings, Productive People," *Monitor on Psychology*, May, 2017, pp. 40–45.

In addition to the direct effects of these kinds of interventions on worker well-being, such programs also have a positive psychological effect on workers by emphasizing an organizational climate that values safety and health. That is, in addition to changes in design, some organizations try to instill a safety culture by giving each and every employee the power to report, or better yet, stop any worker who engages in unsafe behavior. At Chevron, for example, any worker within its headquarters office in San Ramon, California, can halt an activity he or she deems unsafe by taking out a small white "stop work" card. Thus, in terms of decision-making authority, each person has the power to identify and correct safety lapses regardless of where they reside on the formal organizational chart.[72] Indeed, in workplaces where safety is a major concern—such as working on a nuclear submarine—there may be hundreds of rules that new employees have to memorize prior to being able to start on the job.[73]

Unfortunately, not all organizations necessarily share the same culture committed to employee health and well-being. For example, in 2018, workers in the Venezuela oil industry were leaving their jobs at such a high rate that the government placed a limit on the behavior at "five resignations a day." Due to hyper-inflation in the economy, effective salary rates were cut to a level where the workers could not even feed themselves because food inflation surpassed 2,500% in one month alone. Workers doing heavy physical labor need to consume roughly 3,600 calories a day, however, in many regions in Venezuela they were down to just 400 calories a day. In one facility, 12 malnourished workers collapsed in one day and had to be taken off drilling platforms for treatment. After 500 workers quit in just one month at one prominent facility, the government cracked down and issued the "five resignations a day" policy, backed up by threats to imprison any "traitors to the homeland" who quit without permission.[74]

## PERCEPTUAL–MOTOR APPROACH

The perceptual–motor approach to job design has roots in human-factors literature. Whereas the biological approach focuses on physical capabilities and limitations, the perceptual–motor approach focuses on human mental capabilities and limitations. The goal is to design jobs in a way that ensures they do not exceed people's mental capabilities and limitations. This approach generally tries to improve reliability, safety, and user reactions by designing jobs to reduce their information-processing requirements. In designing jobs, one looks at the least capable worker and then constructs job requirements that an individual of that ability level could meet. Similar to the mechanistic approach, this approach generally decreases the job's cognitive demands.

Recent changes in technological capacities hold the promise of helping to reduce job demands and errors, but in some cases, these developments have made the problem worse. The term "absence presence" has been coined to refer to the reduced attentive state that one might experience when simultaneously interacting with multiple media. For example, someone might be talking on a cell phone while driving a car, or surfing the Internet while attending a business meeting, or checking e-mail while preparing a presentation. In all these cases, the new technology serves as a source of distraction from the primary task, reducing performance and increasing the opportunities for errors.[75] In this case, the source of distraction is mental, not physical. Hence, ergonomic interventions aimed at reducing physical barriers are likely to be largely ineffective. For example, holding a stressful conversation while driving in heavy traffic is dangerous regardless of whether one is using a "hands-free" device or not. It is the mental strain, not the physical challenge, that makes this a hazardous activity.[76]

Unfortunately, in the information age, there is a temptation to push more and more information at employees to the point that it can actually detract from performance. For example, in the airline industry, new handheld devices given to flight attendants provide sweeping amounts of information regarding each and every passenger far beyond what you might expect. Part of this is to promote customer service, and hence, a picture of a birthday cake comes up for any passenger whose recorded birthdate matches that date on the calendar. The handheld also tells the staff whether or not the person's experiences on their last five flights were good or bad in terms of on-time arrival and how well their connecting flight looks this time. Finally, the device also tells the attendant whether or not the passenger has been disruptive or caused problems in the past, and hence needs to be watched carefully. When one multiplies all this new information times the number of passengers, the mental calculations that one has to go through to make sure some customers will think their privacy is being invaded in the pursuit of customer service may well crowd out more important duties related to keeping the cabin safe.[77]

## A LOOK BACK

### Revisiting Robots, Humans and Effective Job Design

This chapter opened with a vignette that illustrated how the increased use of robots at work is not necessarily eliminating jobs, but instead, drastically changing the nature of work done by humans in organizational work contexts. We also showed throughout the chapter numerous methods and examples of how organizations can effectively design work and create jobs where duties are clear, the work is meaningful, and workers are protected from unsafe conditions.

#### QUESTIONS

1. The analysis of workflow design traditionally starts at the end of the process, with the final product or service that is to be rendered. If an employer wants to commit to processes that highlight the purchase of robots, how could the process of workflow design play out and how might the results be different than if the organization was committing to processes that were aimed at hiring more people?

2. Although there are advantages and disadvantages to different structural configurations, why might it be more difficult to change one's structure in some directions than others?

3. Many ways of reducing the cost of getting jobs done often come at some price to workers who have to do those jobs. What can be done to promote a more humane and sustainable workforce in all corners of the world? Does the competitive nature of product or labor markets mean that "nice guys always finish last?"

# SUMMARY

The analysis and design of work is one of the most important components to developing and maintaining a competitive advantage. Strategy implementation is virtually impossible without thorough attention devoted to work-flow analysis, job analysis, and job design. Managers need to understand the entire work-flow process in their work unit to ensure that the process maximizes efficiency and effectiveness. To understand this process, managers also must have clear, detailed information about the jobs that exist in the work unit, and the way to gain this information is through job analysis. Equipped with an understanding of the work-flow process and the existing job, managers can redesign jobs to ensure that the work unit is able to achieve its goals while individuals within the unit benefit from the various work outcome dimensions such as motivation, satisfaction, safety, health, and achievement. This is one key to competitive advantage.

# KEY TERMS

Centralization, 168
Departmentalization, 168
Job analysis, 175

Job description, 177
Job specification, 178
Job design, 184

Job redesign, 184
Ergonomics, 187

# DISCUSSION QUESTIONS

1. Assume you are the manager of a fast-food restaurant. What are the outputs of your work unit? What are the activities required to produce those outputs? What are the inputs?
2. Based on Question 1, consider the cashier's job. What are the outputs, activities, and inputs for that job?
3. Consider the "job" of college student. Perform a job analysis on this job. What are the tasks required in the job? What are the knowledge, skills, and abilities necessary to perform those tasks? What environmental trends or shocks (like computers) might change the job, and how would that change the skill requirements?
4. Discuss how the following trends are changing the skill requirements for managerial jobs in the United States:

(a) increasing use of computers and (b) increasing international competition.
5. Why is it important for a manager to be able to conduct a job analysis? What are the negative outcomes that would result from not understanding the jobs of those reporting to the manager?
6. What are the trade-offs between the different approaches to job design? Which approach do you think should be weighted most heavily when designing jobs?
7. For the cashier job in Question 2, which approach to job design was most influential in designing that job? In the context of the total work-flow process of the restaurant, how would you redesign the job to more heavily emphasize each of the other approaches?

# SELF-ASSESSMENT EXERCISE

Also assignable in Connect.

The chapter described how the Department of Labor's Occupational Information Network (O*NET) can help employers. The system was also designed to help job seekers. To see if you think this new system meets the goal of promoting "the effective education, training, counseling, and employment needs of the American workforce," visit O*NET's website at https://www.onetonline.org/.

Look up the listing for your current job or dream job. List the skills identified for that job. For each skill, evaluate how well your own experiences and abilities enable you to match the job requirements.

## EXERCISING STRATEGY

### Growing Old Together in Japan

At Osaka Machine Tool, one piece of equipment, the Spiramatic Jigmill Horizontal Boring Mill, made by the DeVlieg Machine Company in Michigan over 50 years ago, is still in operation. This one piece of equipment is emblematic of the decaying equipment infrastructure in Japan that many believe is holding back the country's national competitive strategy when it comes to manufacturing. As noted by one of Japan's chief economic analysts, Toshihiro Nagahama, "facilities and equipment getting creaky isn't good for our economy and Japanese companies are falling behind our foreign rivals."

The average age of facilities and equipment in Japan is over 15 years and according to a 2016 survey conducted by the Bank of Japan, manufacturers in that country only plan to increase capital spending by 1%. Many years of economic stagnation and deflation in Japan prompted companies to restrain from domestic spending on equipment, and even when the economy started to turn around, companies used those profits to invest in shifting production to facilities outside of Japan where labor costs were lower. Over the years, this failure to reinvest in local manufacturing has taken a toll on the country's manufacturing infrastructure.

Moreover, the aging of Japan's equipment is made even more problematic by its aging workforce. Japan is already home to world's oldest manufacturing workforce, with over 12% of factory workers over 65 years of age. The average age of company owners is also at an all-time high of 59.2 years old, versus 54 years in 1990. Many of these owners operate small

companies that serve as suppliers to larger companies like Toyota, Nissan, Canon, and Panasonic, and about two-thirds of them lack any formal succession plan for when the proprietors retire or pass on. In 2016, over 25,000 Japanese firms shut down voluntarily by owners who could not find successors. This translates into a trickle-up effect that could ripple through the economy when these companies have to seek overseas contractors, which results in a further hollowing out these industries. This is definitely the case at Osaka Machine Tool, where there is only one employee at the company old enough to even operate the Spiramatic—the company's 70-year-old chairman, Katumi Takata, who plans on retiring at the end the year.

#### QUESTIONS

1. How does this example illustrate the trade-offs that have to be made between short-term versus long-term strategy and investment at both the organizational level and the national level?
2. Ironically, although the average age of Japan's equipment is very high, that country is also home to many advanced robotic factories. How might investments in robotic technology be leveraged to change Japan's competitive position in the world?

SOURCES: K. Ujikane and M. Horie, "In Japan, Older Workers Work Older Machines," *Bloomberg Businessweek*, April 21, 2015, pp. 21–22; E. Warnock, "Numbers of Japanese Elders in Workforce Soars," *Wall Street Journal*, November 28, 2016, www.wsj.com; "Japan's Aging Population has Business Owners Struggling to Find Successors," *Reuters Online*, October 3, 2016.

## MANAGING PEOPLE

### New Organizational Structures: Teeming with Teams

"Years ago, people just kind of did their tasks in front of them. Work was much more about what I did to accomplish something. Now it's much more about who did I work with so we could accomplish things together." These are the word of Hugh Welsh, an executive for the North American branch of Royal DSM, a global science-based company active in the areas of health and nutrition. Welsh is the general counsel for Royal DSM, however, he holds several other job titles in the company, and across his many roles, he has over 100 direct and indirect employees who report to him.

Welsh is not alone, in this regard, because organizations are increasingly organizing work around teams that create many more opportunities and challenges when it comes to managing workplace relationships. A recent survey of 7,000 managers from over 130 countries conducted by Deloitte Consulting indicates that over half of the companies

surveyed had either restructured work around teams or were in the process of doing so. The goal of this revolutionary change in the nature of work is to break down former functional silos and increase speed of operations by creating cross-discipline teams that manage their own group processes with a minimum amount of hierarchical micro-management. John Chambers, CEO of electronics firms Cisco notes this need for speed arguing that "we compete against market transitions, not competitors, and transitions that used to take seven years now take one or two."

However, as anyone who ever worked in agriculture can tell you, silos have their uses, and the same Deloitte survey also indicates that only 20% of managers feel they have the teamwork skills necessary to coordinate and motivate all the members of all the teams of which they are a part. Indeed, not everyone has the teamwork skills necessary to work effectively in these kinds of organizations even when the structure of inter-team relationships is clear. More critically, however, only 12% of managers working in team-based structures feel they have a solid understanding of all the social networks embedded in their organization. The fluid nature of these loose networks makes them hard to understand even for people with strong interpersonal skills, and the process of directly linking people with specialized talents to every team that needs them runs the risk of creating role overload that prevents any work from being done.

Organizations moving to team-based structure are finding that creating the right balance between effective and timely collaboration, on the one hand, with the ability to still execute one's primary job, on the other hand, is easy to mishandle. Hugh Welsh's skills as a general counsel makes him potentially valuable to many different teams, but he notes that during a recent trip to the company's headquarters in the Netherlands, he scrambled from one meeting to the next, mainly making "token appearances" at each before rushing off to more meetings. "I said to myself, 'what the hell am I doing? This is crazy. I'm not making meaningful contributions to the business.'"

## QUESTIONS

1. If an employer wants to commit to processes that highlight the role of effective collaboration and teamwork, how could the process of workflow design play out and how might the results be different than if the organization was committing to processes that were aimed at promoting individual autonomy?
2. If an organization is moving from a more traditional, functional bureaucratic work structure to one that is team-based, what downstream implications does this have for personnel selection, training, and pay? Are some workers going to be resistant to such changes, and if so, how can HR help overcome this resistance?

SOURCES: R. Feintzeig, "So Busy at Work, No Time to Do the Job," *Wall Street Journal*, June 28, 2016, www.wsj.com; P. Schumpeter, "Team Spirit," *The Economist*, March 23, 2016; C. Duhigg, "How to Build a Perfect Team," *Wall Street Journal*, February 28, 2016, www.wsj.com.

# HR IN SMALL BUSINESS

## Blink UX Takes a Hard Look at Work Design

The main human resource challenge that faced Blink UX was related to the company's small size. As a research and digital-product design firm specializing in user experience (UX), Blink offers meaningful work to talented professionals. Its employees—researchers and designers with master's and doctorate degrees—enable the firm's client businesses to improve how they interact with their customers online. But with only a few dozen employees, the Seattle-based firm offered limited opportunities for career growth. Blink's founder and CEO, Karen Clark Cole, tried to hire people who would stay and contribute until retirement, but employees would leave after a few years when they saw no opportunities for advancement.

Clark Cole took a hard look at the way work was structured. Employees were assigned to project teams. Project directors controlled the decisions related to their projects, which sometimes caused team members to focus more on satisfying their director. The director was left to ensure that the team focused on clients' needs.

Though this setup had allowed Blink to build an expanding client base and great reputation, Clark Cole realized it was holding back the full potential of her firm's people. So she eliminated the lines of authority; now each employee takes responsibility for satisfying clients. Employees also are asked to choose specialty areas in which to become experts. A team called the GROW group (with rotating membership) meets each week to assign employees to fill roles on projects, aiming to ensure employees get assigned to roles that will help them develop their careers as well as use their areas of expertise to provide great service and creative solutions.

Yet another round of change is in the works. After several years of rapid growth in revenues, Blink UX is preparing to expand into several new branch offices. As Clark Cole ramps up the hiring process to staff those offices, she needs to be careful that new employees can function well in a culture that values learning, flexibility, and the ability to take the perspective of others, including clients and end users.

## QUESTIONS

1. As described, is Blink UX's redesigned approach to teamwork an example of a structure based on function or one based on customers? How well does this structure fit the company's goals for employee empowerment?
2. Does the example of job redesign at Blink UX sound most like an example of job enlargement, job rotation, or job enrichment? Explain your answer.

SOURCES: "America's Best Small Companies 2016: Blink UX," *Forbes*, http://www.forbes.com; Karen Clark Cole, "Blink UX Named One of *Forbes* Magazine's Best Small Companies in America!" Blink UX blog, February 4, 2016, http://blinkux.com; Adam Worcester, "For Blink's Karen Clark Cole, UX Is a Tidal Wave of Opportunity," *BizWomen*, December 1, 2015, http://www.bizjournals.com; Amber Johnson, "Creating a Business That's Optimized for Personal Growth and a Thriving Culture: Blink UX," blog of the Benedictine University Center for Values-Driven Leadership, March 13, 2014, http://www.cvdl.org.

## NOTES

1.  B. Casselman, "Robots? Training? Factories Tackle the Productivity Puzzle," *The New York Times Online*, June 25, 2018.

2.  N. Leiber, "Portuguese Shoemakers Get Fancy," *Bloomberg Businessweek*, September 7, 2015, pp. 45-46.

3.  B. Snavely, "Fiat Chrysler Returns to $101.2 Million Profit in Q1," *USA Today*, April 29, 2015, www.usatoday.com.

4.  J. Lippert, "Remodeling a Sedan Plant for the SUV Era," *Bloomberg Businessweek*, July 3, 2017, pp. 18-19.

5.  J. Jargon, "McDonald's Menu Problem: It's Supersized," *Wall Street Journal*, December 3, 2014.

6.  M. Schuman, "Smiles Aren't Factory Made," *Bloomberg Businessweek*, June 12, 2017, pp. 8-10.

7.  L. Chao, "Trucker Teams Drive to the Rescue of Online Shipping," *Wall Street Journal*, December 26, 2015, www.wsj.com.

8.  L. Landro, "The Doctor's Team Will See You Now," *Wall Street Journal*, February 17, 2014.

9.  J. Christensen, "Medical Errors May Be the Third Leading Cause of Death in the U.S.," *CNN.com*, May 3, 2016.

10. B. Greeley, "We're from Private Equity and We're Here to Help," *Bloomberg Businessweek*, April 30, 2012, pp. 55-59.

11. E. Porter, "The Mirage of a Return to Manufacturing Greatness," *New York Times*, April 26, 2016, https://www.nytimes.com/2016/04/27/business/economy/the-mirage-of-a-return-to-manufacturing-greatness.html.

12. P. Engardio, "Lean and Mean Gets Extreme," *Bloomberg Businessweek*, March 23, 2009, pp. 60-62.

13. T. Black, "Downsides of Just-in-Time Inventory," *Bloomberg Businessweek*, March 28, 2011, pp. 17-18.

14. J. Fox, "Businesses Are Investing More in 2018; But It Is No Boom," *Bloomberg Businessweek Online*, July 26, 2018.

15. M. Vinn, "Goggles with a Work Crew Inside," *Bloomberg Businessweek*, April 2, 2018, pp. 30-31.

16. Rosenbush and L. Stevens, "At UPS, the Algorithm Is the Driver," *The Wall Street Journal Online*, February 16, 2015.

17. J. Whalen, "Hospitals Cut Costs by Getting Doctors to Stick to Guidelines," *Wall Street Journal*, September, 22, 2014.

18. S. Kolhatkar, "Where Have All the Secretaries Gone?" *Bloomberg Businessweek*, April 8, 2013, pp. 67-69.

19. S. Grobart, "Hooray for Hierarchy," *Bloomberg Businessweek*, January 14, 2013, p. 74.

20. E. Court, "Two Huge Drugmakers Are Spinning Off Iconic Brands," *Business Insider Online*, December 20, 2018.

21. D. Bennett, "The Dunbar Number," *Bloomberg Businessweek*, January 10, 2013, pp. 53-56.

22. B. Gruley and L. Patton, "The Franchises Are Not Lovin' It," *Bloomberg Businessweek*, September 16, 2015, pp. 64-69.

23. J. Chung, "The Franchises Are Not Lovin' It," *Bloomberg Businessweek*, September 16, 2015, pp. 64-69.

24. J. Jargon, "All Day Breakfast Is a Pick-Me-Up for McDonald's," *Wall Street Journal*, www.wsj.com, January 25, 2016.

25. K. Akter, "The Bloodshed Behind Our Cheap Clothes," *CNN.com*, May 3, 2013.

26. M. M. Uddin, "Deadly Costs of 'Fast Fashion,'" *Textile Today Online*, December 19, 2017.

27. R. E. Silverman, "Who's the Boss? There Isn't One," *Wall Street Journal*, June 13, 2012.

28. R. Greenfield, "The Future Is Bossless," *Bloomberg Businessweek*, December, 7, 2016, p. 63.

29. K. Marco, "Apple's Product Cannibalization Means Cook Might Eat His Own Words," *Forbes Online*, April 30, 2015.

30. T. Ryan, "Are Chains Cannibalizing Their Own In-Store Sales with E-Commerce," *Retail Wire Online*, May 7, 2017.

31. J. Jargon, "Over 100 Report Being Sickened at Chipotle," *The Wall Street Journal Online*, June 20, 2017.

32. J. E. Ellis, "At P&G, the Innovation Well Runs Dry," *Bloomberg Businessweek*, September 12, 2012, pp. 24-26.

33. P. Valdez-Dalpena and T. Yellin, "Steps to a Recall Nightmare," CNN.money.com, May 21, 2014.

34. T. Henneman, "Is HR at Its Breaking Point," *Workforce Management*, April 2013, pp. 28-33.

35. J. W. Miller, "Steel Firms in U.S. Strive to Fight with Imports," *The Wall Street Journal Online*, June 17, 2015

36. J. Tankersley, "Steel Giants with Ties to Trump Officials Block Tariff Relief to Hundreds of Firms," *The New York Times Online*, August 5, 2018.

37. A. Weintraub and M. Tirrell, "Eli Lilly's Drug Assembly Line," *Bloomberg Businessweek*, February 25, 2010, pp. 34-35.

38. A. Blinder, "Donald Blankenship Sentenced to a Year in Prison in Mine Safety Case," *New York Times*, April 6, 2016, https://www.nytimes.com/2016/04/07/us/donald-blankenship-sentenced-to-a-year-in-prison-in-mine-safety-case.html.

39. M. Rosenwald, "Bound by Habit," *Bloomberg Businessweek*, March 19, 2012, pp. 106-7.

40. L. Weber, "Help Wanted—on Writing Job Descriptions," *Wall Street Journal*, October 2, 2013.

41. E. C. Dierdorf and F. P. Morgeson, "Effects of Descriptor Specificity and Observability on Incumbent Work Analysis Ratings," *Personnel Psychology* 62 (2009), pp. 601-28.

42. P. Lievens, J. I. Sanchez, D. Bartram, and A. Brown, "Lack of Consensus among Competency Ratings of the Same Occupation: Noise or Substance," *Journal of Applied Psychology* 95 (2010), pp. 562-71.

43. C. Mims, "In 'People Analytics,' You're Not a Human, You're a Data Point," *Wall Street Journal*, February 16, 2015.

44. J. R. Hollenbeck and B. Jamieson, "Human Capital, Social Capital, and Social Network Analysis: Implications for Strategic Human Resource Management," *Academy of Management Perspectives,* 29 (2015), pp. 370-385.

45. R. McMillan, "Social Networking Comes (at Last) to the Workplace," *Wall Street Journal*, March 14, 2016, www.wsj.com.

46. J. Matusik, R. Heidl, J. R., Hollenbeck, A. Yu, H. W. Lee, and M. Howe, "Wearable Bluetooth Sensors for Capturing Relational Variables and Temporal Variability in Relationships: A Construct Validation Study," *Journal of Applied Psychology,* 2019.

47. S. Shellenbarger, "Stop Wasting Everyone's Time," *Wall Street Journal*, December 2, 2014.

48. A. K. Weyman, "Investigating the Influence of Organizational Role on Perceptions of Risk in Deep Coal Mines," *Journal of Applied Psychology* 88 (2003), pp. 404-12.

49. A. C. Feldberg and T. Kim, "How Companies Can Identify Racial and Gender Bias in Their Customer Service," *Harvard Business Review Online*, May 28, 2018.

50. L. E. Baranowski and L. E. Anderson, "Examining Rater Source Variation in Work Behavior to KSA Linkages," *Personnel Psychology* 58 (2005), pp. 1041-54.

51. E. McCormick and R. Jeannerette, "The Position Analysis Questionnaire," in *The Job Analysis Handbook for Business, Industry, and Government* (New York: Wiley, 1988), pp. 880-901.

52. J. McGregor, "Open Office Plans Are as Bad as You Thought," *The Washington Post Online*, July 18, 2018.

53. V. Fuhrmans, "CEO's Want Their Office Back," *The Wall Street Journal Online*, May 22, 2017.

54. N. G. Peterson, M. D. Mumford, W. C. Borman, P. R. Jeanneret, and E. A. Fleishman, *An Occupational Information System for the 21st Century: The Development of O\*NET* (Washington, DC: American Psychological Association, 1999).

55. N. G. Peterson, M. D. Mumford, W. C. Borman, P. R. Jeanneret, E. A. Fleishman, K. Y. Levin, M. A. Campion, M. S. Mayfield, F. P. Morgenson, K. Pearlman, M. K. Gowing, A. R. Lancaster, M. B. Silver, and D. M. Dye, "Understanding Work Using the Occupational Information Network (O\*NET): Implications for Practice and Research," *Personnel Psychology* 54 (2001), pp. 451–92.

56. M. J. Handle, "The O\*NET Content Model: Strengths and Limitations," *Journal of Labour Market Research*, February 23, 2016, 157–176.

57. C. C. Lapolice, G. W. Carter, and J. W. Johnson, "Linking O\*NET Descriptors to Occupational Literacy Requirements Using Job Component Validation," *Personnel Psychology* 61 (2008), pp. 405–441.

58. S. Varney, "Rising Obesity Rates Put Strain on Nursing Homes," *New York Times*, December 14, 2015, https://www.nytimes.com/2015/12/15/health/rising-obesity-rates-put-strain-on-nursing-homes.html.

59. B. Casselman, "Maybe the Gig Economy Isn't Reshaping Work After All," *The New York Times Online,* June 7, 2018.

60. M. Campion and P. Thayer, "Development and Field Evaluation of an Interdisciplinary Measure of Job Design," *Journal of Applied Psychology* 70 (1985), pp. 29–34.

61. F. P. Morgeson and S. E. Humphrey, "The Work Design Questionnaire (WDQ): Developing and Validating a Comprehensive Measure for Assessing Job Design and the Nature of Work," *Journal of Applied Psychology* 91 (2006), pp. 1312–39.

62. J. Jargon, "Chili's Feels Heat to Pare Costs," *Wall Street Journal*, January 28, 2011, pp. B8.

63. F. Taylor, *The Principles of Scientific Management* (New York: W. W. Norton, 1967) (originally published in 1911 by Harper & Brothers).

64. C. Blattman and S. Dercon, "Do Sweatshops Lift Workers Out of Poverty?" *The New York Times Online*, April 28, 2017.

65. Simpson, "Samsung's War at Home," *Bloomberg Businessweek*, April 10, 2014, pp. 60–65.

66. M. Gunther, "Wal-Mart: A Bully Benefactor," CNNMoney.com, December 5, 2008, p. 1.

67. R. Hackman and G. Oldham, *Work Redesign* (Boston: Addison-Wesley, 1980).

68. B. Schwartz, "Rethinking Work," *New York Times*, August 28, 2015, https://www.nytimes.com/2015/08/30/opinion/sunday/rethinking-work.html.

69. L. Weber, "Why Old-Timey Jobs Are Hot Again," *The Wall Street Journal Online*, June 6, 2017.

70. A. Park, "Stand Up for Yourself," *Time*, September 8, 2014, pp. 22–23.

71. C. Paddock, "Prolonged Standing Can Cause Health Problems Too," *Medical News Today Online*, July 15, 2015.

72. R. Feintzieg and A. Berzon, "Safety Cops Patrol the Office for High Heels," *Wall Street Journal*, July 27, 2014.

73. J. E. Barnes, "Life on a Navy Sub Relies on Rules: Some Dead Serious, Others Completely Ridiculous," *Wall Street Journal*, May 1, 2014.

74. F. Zerpa, "Too Hungry to Pump Oil," *Bloomberg Businessweek*, March 5, 2018, pp. 38–39.

75. D. K. Berman, "Technology Has Us So Plugged into Data, We Have Turned Off," *Wall Street Journal*, November 10, 2003, pp. A1–A2.

76. M. Beck, "What Cocktail Parties Teach Us," *Wall Street Journal*, April 22, 2012.

77. S. McCartney, "What the Airlines Knows About the Guy in Seat 14C," *The Wall Street Journal Online*, June 20, 2018."

CHAPTER

# 5 Human Resource Planning and Recruitment

## LEARNING OBJECTIVES

*After reading this chapter, you should be able to:*

**LO 5-1**  Discuss how to align a company's strategic direction with its human resource planning. *page 199*

**LO 5-2**  Determine the labor demand for workers in various job categories. *page 200*

**LO 5-3**  Discuss the advantages and disadvantages of various ways of eliminating a labor surplus and avoiding a labor shortage. *page 202*

**LO 5-4**  Describe the various recruitment policies that organizations adopt to make job vacancies more attractive. *page 219*

**LO 5-5**  List the various sources from which job applicants can be drawn, their relative advantages and disadvantages, and the methods for evaluating them. *page 222*

**LO 5-6**  Explain the recruiter's role in the recruitment process, the limits the recruiter faces, and the opportunities available. *page 227*

## Labor Force Drop Outs: Not Employed and Yet—Not Unemployed

"Business' number one problem is finding qualified workers. At the current pace of job growth, if sustained this problem is set to get much worse." These are the words of Mark Zandi, the chief economic officer for Moody's Analytics discussing the U.S. economy. With unemployment rates at close to 3% across the nation, organizations from all industries and regions are scrambling to find employees, often competing against each other by raising wages. This is a great outcome for qualified workers, but in some low margin businesses, it is difficult to pass these higher costs onto the customer, and thus, this becomes an existential threat. Still, it is useful to remember that the unemployment rate is a ratio, where the number of unemployed people is in the numerator, and the labor force participation rate is in the denominator. This is critical to remember because if someone decides to stop looking for work, they are no longer unemployed, but they are not really employed either.

For example, in Utah, where the unemployment rate is actually lower than the national average, a full 32% of the adult population was not looking for work in 2018. This is not an isolated case, and reflects a broader national trend of people who have stopped looking for work—a trend that has been attributed to four causes. First, unlike past generations of American workers who migrated from one region of the country to another when employment patterns changed, this cohort of potential employees has tended to stay put—right where they are. For example, a large portion of the job growth has occurred in dynamic urban centers like New York, Los Angeles, and Chicago, but many rural workers are not willing to move to those locations, and instead just stop looking for work. Second, even in many rural areas such as those surrounding Ames, Iowa, or Portland, Maine,

employers who are struggling to find help attribute this to the unattractive nature of the jobs. For example, Ron Gibson, owner of a dairy farm that has been in his family for five generations, is at risk for bankruptcy because no one is willing to apply for the jobs his industry offers. As he admits, "the work is dirty, stinky and hard—it is not the kind of work that we teach our young people to do."

In other cases, people who are not participating in the labor force are unemployable because they cannot pass a drug test. The United States is currently facing an unprecedented opioid epidemic, and close to 3 million potential U.S. workers have become unemployable due their addiction to pain killers. For example, in Jonestown, Pennsylvania, when Bill Polacek tried to hire 50 welders, he interviewed 400 people to get the pool down to 100 qualified applicants, but then found that a full 50% of those qualified workers could not pass a drug test. Drug testing is mandated by federal law for any occupation that is considered "safety sensitive," and in some industries such as construction and mining, close to 20% of applicants cannot pass a drug test.

Finally, although it is small consolation, at least Mr. Polacek could find 100 qualified workers. By far, the biggest factor causing unemployability is the lack of fit between the skills some people have, and the skills demanded in today's world of work. Chauncy Lennon, the head of workforce development at JPMorgan Chase notes that today's manufacturing jobs demand "specialized training and certifications, and you cannot just show up at a plant after high school and get hired any longer." Many states provide skills training and these programs can be highly successful. For example, the KentuckianaWorks program has trained over 1,000 people who went on to successfully launch

*CONTINUED*

new careers, however, programs such as these are tough and intense. Classes start at 8 a.m. and run to 5 p.m. with tests every Friday. Regrettably, half of those who start this program fail to stick it out until the end, thus remaining largely unemployable.

SOURCES: B. Appelbaum, "Lack of Workers, Not Work, Weighs on the Nation's Economy," *The New York Times Online*, May 22, 2017; J. Smialek, "Where the Jobs Are," *Bloomberg Businessweek*, March 19, 2018, pp. 38–43; A. MacGillis, "Stay or Leave?" *Bloomberg Businessweek*, May 28, 2018; J. Smialek, "Why the Fed Cares About America's Opioid Crisis," *Bloomberg Businessweek*, July 31, 2017; C. Hymowitz, "Training Day," *Bloomberg Businessweek*, March 20, pp. 18–19.

# Introduction

Human resource managers are at the forefront of the worldwide war for competitive advantage. Organizations need to find the best set of workers for meeting their strategic objectives, attract those workers to their companies, and then get them to stay long enough to obtain some return on their investment. As our opening vignette shows, the failure to secure a sufficient supply of domestic labor is crippling certain companies. Throughout this chapter, we will highlight other job categories where the demand for labor is outstripping the supply and what employers are trying to do to secure the workers they need. We will also examine occupations characterized by an over-supply of labor and what workers can do to make sure that the talents they develop fit the needs of the current labor market. Employers who are able to tap in to the best pool of talent for executing their own unique competitive strategy gain a competitive advantage over their rivals that is often sustainable for a long period.

The purpose of this chapter is to examine factors that influence the supply and demand for labor and, in particular, to focus on what HR managers can do in terms of planning and executing policies that give their firms competitive advantage in a dynamic environment. Although our focus is at the firm level, nations also compete in labor markets, and when a country begins to see most of its human talent emigrate, this type of "brain drain" can have a devastating impact on national competitiveness. For example, in Iran, 40% of the top graduates in undergraduate science and technology programs leave the country to attend graduate school in Europe and the United States, and then, upon matriculation, 90% never return to Iran.[1] Similarly, when a large number of very high-profile Western-trained economists left important policy-making positions in India to return to the United States in 2018, many wondered if political pressures within India were making it hostile to its best and brightest citizens.[2] Thus, the war for talent takes place at both the organizational level and the national level, and later in this chapter we will highlight some of the countries that are winning and losing this war.

Two of the major ways that societal trends and events affect employers are through (1) consumer markets, which affect the demand for goods and services, and (2) labor markets, which affect the supply of people to produce goods and services. In some cases, the market might be characterized by a labor shortage. In other cases, there might be a surplus of labor. Reconciling the difference between the supply and demand for labor presents a challenge for organizations, and how they address this challenge will affect their overall competitiveness.

There are three keys to effectively utilizing labor markets to one's competitive advantage. First, companies must have a clear idea of their current configuration of human resources. In particular, they need to know the strengths and weaknesses of their present stock of employees. Second, organizations must know where they are going in the future and be aware of how their present configuration of human resources relates to the configuration that will be needed. Third, where there are discrepancies between the present configuration and the configuration required for the future, organizations need programs that will address these discrepancies.

This chapter looks at tools and technologies that can help an organization develop and implement effective strategies for leveraging labor market "threats" into opportunities to gain competitive advantage. In the first half of the chapter, we lay out the steps that go into developing and implementing an HR plan. Through each section, we focus especially on recent trends and practices that can have a major impact on the firm's bottom line and overall reputation. In the second half of the chapter, we familiarize you with the process by which individuals find and choose jobs and the role of personnel recruitment in reaching these individuals and shaping their choices.

# The Human Resource Planning Process

An overview of human resource planning is depicted in Figure 5.1. The process consists of forecasting, goal setting and strategic planning, and program implementation and evaluation. We discuss each of these stages in the next sections of this chapter.

## FORECASTING

The first step in the planning process is **forecasting**, as shown in the top portion of Figure 5.1. In personnel forecasting, the HR manager attempts to ascertain the supply of and demand for various types of human resources. The primary goal is to predict areas within the organization where there will be future labor shortages or surpluses.

Forecasting, on both the supply and demand sides, can use either statistical methods or judgmental methods. Statistical methods are excellent for capturing historic trends in a company's demand for labor, and under the right conditions they give predictions that are much more precise than those that could be achieved through subjective judgments of a human forecaster. However, many important events that occur in the labor market have no historical precedent; hence, statistical methods that work from historical trends are of little use in such cases. With no historical precedent, one must rely on the pooled subjective judgments of experts, and their "best guesses" might be the only source from which to make inferences about the future. Typically, because of the complementary strengths and weaknesses of the two methods, companies that engage in human resource planning use a balanced approach.

**LO 5-1**
Discuss how to align a company's strategic direction with its human resource planning.

**forecasting**
The attempts to determine the supply of and demand for various types of human resources to predict areas within the organization where there will be future labor shortages or surpluses.

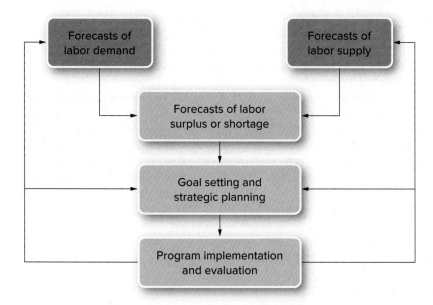

**Figure 5.1**
Overview of the Human Resource Planning Process

Mc Graw Hill **connect**

Visit your instructor's Connect® course and access your eBook to view this video.

"How do we think about making sure this company has access to the right skills and capabilities to grow a company for the future?"

—Heidi B. Capozzi,
Senior VP, Human Resources, The Boeing Company

Source: Video produced for the Center for Executive Succession in the Darla Moore School of Business at the University of South Carolina by Coal Powered Filmworks

**LO 5-2**
Determine the labor demand for workers in various job categories.

**Leading indicator**
An objective measure that accurately predicts future labor demand.

An example of the forecasting process can be seen at Qualcomm, one of the world's biggest suppliers of chips for mobile phones. Qualcomm products handle cellular communications and computing in smartphones, and although one might think there is a never-ending demand for these types of chips, Qualcomm's analysis of the market in 2015 suggested that there was going to be an over-supply of its product in the future. Samsung was the biggest buyer for Qualcomm's chips; however, Samsung's share of the cell phone market was shrinking, causing future collateral damage at Qualcomm. In addition, smaller upstarts like MediaTek were cutting into Qualcomm's share of the market, and then Samsung announced it was going to start manufacturing its own chips for its new phone. According to Qualcomm's forecast, the company was likely to produce far too many chips for the market if it failed to take preventive steps, one of which included a workforce reduction of 155 people.[3]

## Determining Labor Demand

Typically, demand forecasts are developed around specific job categories or skill areas relevant to the organization's current and future state. Once the job categories or skills are identified, the planner needs to seek information that will help predict whether the need for people with those skills or in that job category will increase or decrease in the future. For example, due to the aging population in the United States, elder care is one of the fast-growing industries; thus, there is likely to be a high demand for workers with skills that suit this work.

In contrast, the demand for appraisers in the housing industry will experience a drop in demand due to big data and computing advances that allow online companies like Zillow and Redfin to precisely estimate a house's value without human intervention. Once large mortgage companies like Freddie Mac became comfortable using computer estimates, as one industry analyst put it, "the future for appraisers in the residential market for doing mortgage work is coming to an end.[4]

Organizations differ in the sophistication with which labor demand forecasts are derived. At the most sophisticated level, an organization might have statistical models that predict labor demand for the next year given relatively objective statistics on leading indicators from the previous year. A **leading indicator** is an objective measure that accurately predicts future labor demand.

For example, although the relationship between oil prices and demand for rig workers is well known, the drop in oil prices in 2015, attributed to the rapid growth of the fracking industry, came as a surprise to many. Hence, over 100,000 workers had to be laid off when this industry confronted an unanticipated change in demand.[5] Then, when the industry made a comeback in 2017, rather than hire back all of the workers, many firms in the industry turned to labor-saving automation that largely replaced the "roustabouts" who, in the past, performed the task of connecting hundreds of drill pipes. Drilling sites that used to employ 20 workers can now can be managed with 5, and the 15 jobs eliminated will probably never come back. As one manager noted, "It used to be that you had a toolbox full of wrenches and tubing benders, but now, your main tool is a laptop."[6]

Similarly, statistics suggest a strong increase in the numbers of people eating out at U.S. restaurants, relative to the past. This has led to an increase in the demand for cooks at high-end restaurants, as well as for managers of low-level fast-food chains. In December 2016, the unemployment rate was at 4.7%, a 10-year low. This led to a turnover rate among restaurant workers that exceeded 100% a year. Gregg Flynn, CEO of Flynn Restaurant Group, which runs Taco Bell, Applebee's, and Panera Bread Company, spoke for many in this industry when he noted, "It's as hard as it's ever been to attract and retain great people."[7]

Statistical planning models are useful when there is a long, stable history that can be used to reliably detect relationships among variables. However, these models almost always have to be complemented by subjective judgments of people who have expertise in the area. There are simply too many one-time changes that have to be considered that cannot be captured accurately in statistical models. For example, only a decade ago, no one would have heard the job title "cloud computing engineer," yet this is projected to be one of the fast-growing areas when it comes to the demand for labor in the future. Thus, there are no historical data for a job like this. Experts in this area rely instead on subjective judgments; hence, Robert Patrick, vice president for marketing at Hewlett-Packard, confidently predicts that "the clouds skill gap is the single biggest barrier to the future adoption of cloud infrastructures."[8]

### Determining Labor Supply

Once a company has projected labor demand, it needs to get an indicator of the firm's labor supply. Determining the internal labor supply calls for a detailed analysis of how many people are currently in various job categories (or who have specific skills) within the company. This analysis is then modified to reflect changes in the near future caused by retirements, promotions, transfers, voluntary turnover, and terminations.

As in the case of labor demand, projections for labor supply can be derived either from historical statistical models or through judgmental techniques. One type of statistical procedure that can be employed for this purpose involves transitional matrices. **Transitional matrices** show the proportion (or number) of employees in different job categories at different times. Typically these matrices show how many people move in one year from one state (outside the organization) or job category to another state or job category.

Table 5.1 shows a transitional matrix for a hypothetical manufacturer, focusing on seven job categories. Although these matrices look imposing at first, they are easy to read and use in determining the internal labor supply. A matrix like the one in this table can be read in two ways. First, we can read the rows to answer the question "Where did people in

**Transitional matrix** A matrix showing the proportion or number of employees in different job categories at different times.

**Table 5.1**
A Hypothetical Transitional Matrix for an Auto Parts Manufacturer

| 2016 | 2019 | | | | | | | |
|---|---|---|---|---|---|---|---|---|
| | (1) | (2) | (3) | (4) | (5) | (6) | (7) | (8) |
| (1) Sales manager | .95 | | | | | | | .05 |
| (2) Sales representative | .05 | .60 | | | | | | .35 |
| (3) Sales apprentice | | .20 | .50 | | | | | .30 |
| (4) Assistant plant manager | | | | .90 | .05 | | | .05 |
| (5) Production manager | | | | .10 | .75 | | | .15 |
| (6) Production assembler | | | | | .10 | .80 | | .10 |
| (7) Clerical | | | | | | | .70 | .30 |
| (8) Not in organization | .00 | .20 | .50 | .00 | .10 | .20 | .30 | |

this job category in 2016 go by 2019?" For example, 70% of those in the clerical job category (row 7) in 2016 were still in this job category in 2019, and the remaining 30% had left the organization. For the production assembler job category (row 6), 80% of those in this position in 2016 were still there in 2019. Of the remaining 20%, half (10%) were promoted to the production manager job category, and the other half (10%) left the organization.

A transitional matrix can also be read from top to bottom (in the columns) to answer the question "Where did the people in this job category in 2019 come from (i.e., where were they in 2016)?" Again, starting with the clerical job (column 7), 70% of the 2019 clerical positions were filled by people who were also in this position in 2016, and the remaining 30% were external hires (they were not part of the organization in 2016). In the production assembler job category (column 6), 80% of those occupying this job in 2019 occupied the same job in 2016, and the other 20% were external hires.

Matrices such as these are extremely useful for charting historical trends in the company's supply of labor. More important, if conditions remain somewhat constant, they can also be used to plan for the future. For example, if we believe that we are going to have a surplus of labor in the production assembler job category in the next three years, then we see that by simply initiating a freeze on external hires, the ranks of this position will be depleted by 20% on their own. Similarly, if we believe that we will have a labor shortage in the area of sales representatives, the matrix informs us that we may want to (1) decrease the amount of voluntary turnover in this position, since 35% of those in this category leave every three years, (2) speed the training of those in the sales apprentice job category so that they can be promoted more quickly than in the past, and/or (3) expand external recruitment of individuals for this job category, since the usual 20% of job incumbents drawn from this source may not be sufficient to meet future needs.

## Determining Labor Surplus or Shortage

**LO 5-3**
Discuss the advantages and disadvantages of various ways of eliminating a labor surplus and avoiding a labor shortage.

Once forecasts for labor demand and supply are known, the planner can compare the figures to ascertain whether there will be a labor shortage or labor surplus for the respective job categories. When this is determined, the organization can determine what it is going to do about these potential problems. For example, in the construction industry in 2015, a shortage of skilled laborers meant that many real estate developers had to cut back on building plans or had these plans delayed an inordinate amount of time because of the inability to find workers with specific skills. In Denver, Shea Homes had plans and funding to build 325 homes but could not execute these plans because the company could not find workers to fit and install cabinets, as well as heating, ventilation, and air conditioning installers.[9]

This problem was compounded in 2017 when tighter rules on immigration cut the number of workers in the home-building trades even further. Many of those employed in the construction trades are immigrants, including 50% of drywall and ceiling tile installers, 40% of roofers, and 60% of plasterers and stucco workers. Svenda Gudell, the chief economist at real estate tracker Zillow noted, "When you ask builders, 'why aren't you building more?' labor shortages are at the top of their list."[10]

In contrast to construction workers, the Bureau of Labor Statistics estimates that during the decade ending in 2020, the U.S. economy will create roughly 70,000 lawyer positions, while U.S. law schools are matriculating over 25,000 graduates a year. This translates into a labor surplus of 180,000 lawyers with little or nothing to do.[11] Some observers have noted that smaller, private, and less reputable law schools have contributed to this problem. Kyle McEntee, executive director of the advocacy group Law School Transparency notes, "People are not being helped by going to these schools. The debt is really high, bar passage rates are poor and employment opportunities are horrendous."[12]

Determining the underlying reason for the shortage or surplus is also important, because this will have implications down the line when it comes to addressing the problem. For example, in some cases, stereotypes about the job may be needlessly restricting the supply of potential workers. In Japan, for instance, working in the auto industry was traditionally not viewed as "women's work," however, when confronted with critical labor shortages due to an aging domestic population, companies like Honda, Nissan, and Toyota started to hire many more women.[13] In contrast, in the United States, chronic labor shortages in the field of nursing, a job that is traditionally considered "women's work," has prompted employers to hire more male nurses. Ironically, many of these men moving into nursing were transitioning from jobs in the U.S. auto industry when they were displaced by robots or other forms of technology.[14]

## GOAL SETTING AND STRATEGIC PLANNING

The second step in human resource planning is goal setting and strategic planning, as shown in the middle of Figure 5.1. The purpose of setting specific quantitative goals is to focus attention on the problem and provide a benchmark for determining the relative success of any programs aimed at redressing a pending labor shortage or surplus. The goals should come directly from the analysis of labor supply and demand and should include a specific figure for what should happen with the job category or skill area and a specific timetable for when results should be achieved.

Once these goals are established, the firm needs to choose from the many different strategies available for redressing labor shortages and surpluses. Table 5.2 shows some of the options for an HR planner seeking to reduce a labor surplus. Table 5.3 shows some options available to the same planner intent on avoiding a labor shortage.

| OPTION | SPEED | HUMAN SUFFERING |
|---|---|---|
| 1. Downsizing | Fast | High |
| 2. Pay reductions | Fast | High |
| 3. Demotions | Fast | High |
| 4. Transfers | Fast | Moderate |
| 5. Work sharing | Fast | Moderate |
| 6. Hiring freeze | Slow | Low |
| 7. Natural attrition | Slow | Low |
| 8. Early retirement | Slow | Low |
| 9. Retraining | Slow | Low |

**Table 5.2** Options for Reducing an Expected Labor Surplus

| OPTION | SPEED | REVOCABILITY |
|---|---|---|
| 1. Overtime | Fast | High |
| 2. Temporary employees | Fast | High |
| 3. Outsourcing | Fast | High |
| 4. Retrained transfers | Slow | High |
| 5. Turnover reductions | Slow | Moderate |
| 6. New external hires | Slow | Low |
| 7. Technological innovation | Slow | Low |

**Table 5.3** Options for Avoiding an Expected Labor Shortage

This stage is critical because the many options available to the planner differ widely in their expense, speed, effectiveness, amount of human suffering, and revocability (how easily the change can be undone). For example, if the organization can anticipate a labor surplus far enough in advance, it may be able to freeze hiring and then just let natural attrition adjust the size of the labor force. If successful, an organization may be able to avoid layoffs altogether, so that no one has to lose a job. Similarly, with enough advance warning, if an organization can anticipate a labor shortage for some job category like "welder," then it might be able to work with a local community college to provide scholarships to students who are willing to learn those skills in return for committing to work for that employer in the future.

Unfortunately for many workers, in the past decade the typical organizational response to a surplus of labor has been downsizing, which is fast but high in human suffering. The human suffering caused by downsizing has both an immediate and a long-term element. In the short term, the lack of pay, benefits, and meaningful work has negative implications for financial, physical, and psychological aspects of individuals, causing bankruptcies, illnesses, and depression. Then, even if one can survive these immediate problems, in the long term, an extended bout of unemployment (e.g., lasting over six months) can stigmatize the individual, thus reducing future opportunities. In particular, in job categories where skills are perishable and need to be updated continually, many laid-off workers will take any work within their area—even unpaid volunteer work—to prevent a gap in their employment history.[15] However, as we noted in the vignette that opened this chapter, after very long periods of unemployment, people may give up looking for work altogether.

In contrast, the typical organizational response to a labor shortage has been either hiring temporary employees or outsourcing, responses that are fast and high in revocability. Given the pervasiveness of these choices, we will devote special subsections of this chapter to each of these options.

## Downsizing

**Downsizing**
The planned elimination of large numbers of personnel, designed to enhance organizational effectiveness.

We define **downsizing** as the planned elimination of large numbers of personnel designed to enhance organizational effectiveness. Although one tends to think of downsizing as something that a company turns to in times of recession or when facing bouts of poor performance, in fact, many companies that are doing quite well still downsize their workforce regularly for strategic reasons. For example, although Microsoft was doing fine in 2014, it still laid off 18,000 workers in the phone and tablet divisions after the purchase of Nokia left the company with a surplus of workers in those areas.[16] Similarly, Hewlett-Packard cut 16,000 jobs that same year and used the roughly $1 billion in savings to invest more heavily in cloud computing services.[17]

Surveys indicate three major reasons that organizations engage in downsizing. First, many organizations are looking to reduce costs, and because labor costs represent a big part of a company's total costs, this is an attractive place to start.

An example of this can be seen in 2017 as Boeing announced plans to downsize to cut costs. John Hamilton, the company's vice president of engineering noted, "We continue to operate in an environment characterized by fewer sales opportunities and tough competition, and the decision to reduce the number of 777 jets underscores that environment and what we need to do to help Boeing win."[18] This is a clear example of projections of reduced sales triggering cost-cutting downsizing moves.

Second, in some organizations, the introduction of new technologies or robots reduces the need for a large number of employees. This places the focus of competition on who can produce the best robots, and when it comes to this battle, Japanese manufacturers seem to be far ahead of their rivals. Japanese companies such as Fanuc and Kawasaki Heavy Industries produce over 50% of the world's working robots.[19]

Although not employing robots per se, General Electric's new battery manufacturing plant in Schenectady, New York, shows how new technology can reduce jobs. The entire 200,000-square-foot facility requires only 370 workers, only 200 of which are actually on the shop floor. The plant manager runs the entire operation, including lights, heat, inventory, purchasing, and maintenance from an iPad that is linked to wireless sensors embedded in the batteries themselves. As Prescott Logan, the general manager of the plant, states, "It is not about low cost labor but high technology. We are listening directly to what our batteries are telling us and then thinking about ways to monetize that."[20] In general, new technologies often displace some workers, and as shown in the Competing through Technology box shows, in today's modern world, a small number of highly skilled workers can do the work that in previous generations required hundreds of low-skilled laborers.

Third, many firms downsized for economic reasons by changing the location where they do business. Some of this shift was from one region of the United States to another—in particular, many organizations moved from the Northeast, the Midwest, and California to the South and the mountain regions of the West. In other cases, jobs moved from one country to another, resulting in downsizing in the country that exports the jobs. For example, most garment jobs left the United States over 20 years ago, but in the intervening period, these same jobs have moved over and over again, from India to China to Bangladesh and now, most recently, to Africa. In addition to the lure of low worker wages ($20 a month), Africa is able to produce its own cotton, and its expanse of open space allows companies to build single-level plants that are cheaper and safer relative to the multilevel structures in Bangladesh.[21]

Although downsizing has an immediate effect on costs, much of the evidence suggests that it has negative effects on long-term organizational effectiveness, especially for some types of firms. Thus, it is important to understand what goes into an effective versus an ineffective downsizing campaign. There seem to be a number of reasons for the failure of most downsizing efforts to live up to expectations in terms of enhancing firm performance. First, although the initial cost savings are a short-term plus, the long-term effects of an improperly managed downsizing effort can be negative. Downsizing not only leads to a loss of talent, but in many cases it also disrupts the social networks needed to promote creativity and flexibility.[22] For example, many observers have attributed the slow public health response to the Ebola outbreak in 2014 to cuts made at local agencies. City, county, and state health departments cut 60,000 jobs in the six-year period from 2008 to 2014, which included the elimination of programs that might have prevented health care workers like those in Dallas from catching the disease from their own patients. Reversing this process in an area that relies on skilled employees is difficult. As one industry expert noted, "You may be able to buy equipment quickly but you can't buy trained personnel quickly."[23]

Second, many downsizing campaigns let go of people who turn out to be irreplaceable assets. In fact, one survey indicated that in 80% of the cases, firms wind up replacing some of the very people who were let go. In other cases, firms bring back the specific people who were let go, often at a higher salary. In fact, the term *boomerang employee* has been coined to refer to this increasingly used source of recruits. Several companies such as Procter & Gamble, JCPenney, Nike, PepsiCo, and Toys "R" Us have tapped former executives to lead their management team. These individuals come in knowing the company well, but they also bring a new perspective achieved by having success at some other venture. More than a traditional outsider, boomerang executives have a sense of what changes will and will not take hold at their old company.[24]

## Automation: Effects on the Quantity and Quality of Jobs

A trip around the world can show how automation both drastically decreases the number of employees to produce a given product, and at the same time, increases the quality of the jobs for the employees that remain in terms of the nature of work, the security of work, and the safety of work. For example, in the 1960s a traditional mill would require 1,000 employees to produce 500,000 tons of steel. However in 2018, a steel mill in Donawitz, Austria, produces the same output with just 14 employees. Blue-collar jobs in a traditional steel mill required a great deal of hard, physical, manual labor next to blazing hot blast furnaces, but at the Donawitz facility, all that work has been automated. The work that remains looks more like a video game, where workers sit in clean, quiet control rooms perched above all the fray, monitoring the movement and processing of molten iron ore via a bank of computer screens. When asked what steel production is going to look like in the future, plant manager Wolfgang Eder notes that "it is impossible to predict, but the positive thing is, the jobs surviving in the long run will be really attractive."

In addition to enhancing the nature of the work, automation has also radically improved job security. Traditionally, jobs in the manufacturing industry were subject to the whims of supply and demand, and workers were accustomed to being laid off and then reinstated over and over again. In 2018, however, layoffs in the United States hit a 50-year low, and most of this could be traced to enhanced stability in the manufacturing sector of the economy. In Detroit, Michigan, for example, PVS Chemical Company has stabilized employment at roughly 800 employees, and has not laid anyone off despite ebbs of demand for its products. CEO David Nicholson notes that, "we have become much more careful about letting people go. Most manufacturing jobs today are technology jobs, and it takes a long time to train someone for the role—and thus—you're reluctant to let them go for short-term slowdowns."

Finally, in terms of enhanced safety, an examination of the Rotterdam shipyards reveals how automation is increasing safety and reducing injuries. In the past, the work of the "stevedores," the local name given to dockworkers, was back-breaking labor that often resulted in a whole host of injuries. Whether due to accidents or just declining physical capacity, most stevedores struggled to work past the age of 45, when they were then either dismissed or placed on permanent disability. Today, the ports are automated and cargo is loaded and unloaded remotely, moved from place to place via driverless vehicles. The threat of injuries is greatly reduced because where in the past, you had a large number of men physically moving heavy containers, you now find one 22-year-old woman with perfect eye-hand coordination orchestrating workflow.

Although this type of automation is great when it comes to creating jobs that are more attractive, secure, and safe, the downside is that it obviously displaces a lot of workers such as the "stevedores." Still, as we noted in the opener to Chapter 4, unemployment in Western societies was hitting record lows in 2018 and, as we noted in the opener of this chapter, many displaced people were simply adapting and moving on to other jobs. People that, due to lack of ability or lack of motivation, were not able to adapt, probably just dropped out of the workforce, which means they are no longer counted as unemployed.

### DISCUSSION QUESTIONS

1. How does the introduction of automation single out certain subpopulations when it comes to securing and holding a job?
2. What can HR professionals, as well as local and federal governments, do to protect these subpopulations? How can employers design jobs like the ones currently dominating the AI field that are more interesting for workers?

SOURCES: T. Biesheuval, "500,000 Tons of Steel. 14 Jobs," *Bloomberg Businessweek*, January 26, 2017, pp. 16–17; S. Nunn, "Layoffs Just Reached a Half-Century Low," *The Wall Street Journal Online*, September 6, 2018; E. Morath, "Factory Workers Don't Get Laid Off Like They Did before the Recession," *The Wall Street Journal Online*, July 10, 2018; "Blame Automation, Not Immigration," *Bloomberg Businessweek*, March 6, 2017, pp. 30–33.

A third reason downsizing efforts often fail is that employees who survive the purges often become narrow minded, self-absorbed, and low in organizational commitment.[25] Motivation levels drop off because any hope of future promotions—or even a future—with the company dies out. Many employees also start looking for alternative employment opportunities.[26] The negative publicity associated with a downsizing campaign can also hurt the company's image in the labor market, making it more difficult to recruit employees later. Especially in an age of text messaging and social media, the once-private practice of laying off employees is becoming increasingly transparent, and any organizational mistake that gets made in the process is likely to become highly public.

The key to a successful downsizing effort is to avoid indiscriminate across-the-board reductions, and instead perform surgical strategic cuts that not only reduce costs but also improve the firm's competitive position. For example, at the State University of New York, $50 million was saved across the system via a series of cuts that consolidated many senior administrative positions. The same practice cut $70 million at the University of California at Berkeley, and $5 million at the University of Kansas. These cuts were specifically targeted at "administrative bloat" revealed by research that showed that the number of employees hired by colleges to administer people and programs rose 50% faster than the number of professors in the preceding 12 years. The size of the instructional and research staff was left as is, and the evidence suggests that student outcomes were not affected at all by such cuts.[27]

## Early Retirement Programs and Buyouts

Another popular means of reducing a labor surplus is to offer an early retirement program. As shown in Figure 5.2, the average age of the U.S. workforce is increasing. Although many Baby Boomers are approaching traditional retirement age, early indications are that this group has no intention of retiring any time soon.[28] Indeed, 40% of Americans who are 65 and older still work, and many of those individuals had actually retired in the past. Several forces fuel the drawing out of older workers' careers.

First, some of this is driven by finances and the failure to adequately plan for the future. Many workers because they fear Social Security will be cut, and many have skimpy employer-sponsored pensions that may not be able to cover their expenses. Second, many

**Figure 5.2**

Aging of the U.S.
Population,
2000–2020

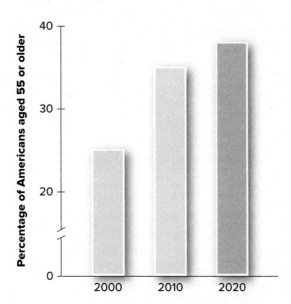

people who "unretired" did so because they were bored or missed the meaningful social interaction associated with working with others.[29] Third, the improved health of older people in general, in combination with the decreased physical labor in many jobs, has made working longer a viable option. Fourth, age discrimination legislation and the outlawing of mandatory retirement ages have created constraints on organizations' ability to unilaterally deal with an aging workforce. For example, the EEOC is currently investigating IBM for age discrimination related to thousands of terminations that, according to leaked internal documents, were aimed at correcting the "seniority mix" at the company.[30]

In contrast to what we see at IBM, other employers are increasingly concerned about losing the wealth of experience that older workers bring to their companies and try to keep them employed. Although historically Baby Boomers made up the largest share of the U.S. population and Generation X made up the largest share of the workforce, in 2016, for the first time, both of these generational groups trailed Millennials on both of these statistics. Organizations such as Deloitte Consulting are trying to keep older workers on board longer in order to help train the next generation of leaders. Deloitte forecasts that, in just a few years, there will be no Baby Boomers left in its leadership ranks. To prevent the permanent loss of implicit knowledge embodied in these workers, Deloitte pairs them with Millennial managers to create synergistic pairs that are greater than the sum of their parts. As one participant in this program noted, "Millennials bring data and analytics but boomers have experience that they can rely on when the data isn't sufficient."[31]

Although an older workforce has some clear advantages for employers in terms of experience and stability, it also poses problems. First, older workers are sometimes more costly than younger workers because of their higher seniority, higher medical costs, and higher pension contributions. Second, because older workers typically occupy the highest ranking jobs, they sometimes block the advancement of younger workers. This is frustrating for the younger workers and leaves the organization in a perilous position whenever the older workers decide to retire.

In the face of such demographic pressures, many employers try to induce voluntary attrition among their older workers through early retirement incentive programs. For example, at Toyota's plant in Georgetown, Kentucky, veteran workers earn $26 an hour, compared to $16 an hour for new hires. In an effort to shift the workforce from high-paid to low-paid workers, Toyota offered retirement incentives to 2,000 workers at the plant. Each worker could get a lump-sum payment equal to two weeks of pay for every year of service, up to a maximum of 25 years, plus eight weeks' additional pay. In return for taking the buyout, workers would agree to retire on a fixed schedule that prevents all the workers from retiring at once.[32] Although these programs do induce attrition among some older workers, to a large extent, such programs' success is contingent on accurate forecasting and it is easy for employers to overestimate or underestimate the number of people that will respond to various incentives.

### Temporary Workers and Independent Contractors

Whereas downsizing has been a popular method for reducing a labor surplus, hiring temporary workers and outsourcing have been the most widespread means of eliminating a labor shortage. The number of temporary employees in the United States swelled from 4.5 million in 1997 to 28 million in 2014.[33] Temporary employment afforded firms the flexibility needed to operate efficiently in the face of swings in the demand for goods and services. In fact, a surge in temporary employment often preceded a jump in permanent hiring and was often a leading indicator that the economy was expanding. However, that no longer seems to be the case. Employers today seem to appreciate the flexibility that comes with hiring temporary employees and like being able to match quick changes in consumer demands for products and services with quick changes in the supply of labor.

In addition to flexibility, hiring temporary workers offers several other advantages. For one, the use of temporary workers frees the firm from many administrative tasks and financial burdens associated with being the "employer of record." Second, small companies that cannot afford their own testing programs often get employees who have been tested by a temporary agency. Third, many temporary agencies train employees before sending them to employers, which reduces training costs and eases the transition for both the temporary worker and the company. Finally, because the temporary worker has little experience in the host firm, the person brings an objective perspective to the organization's problems and procedures that is sometimes valuable.

Steven Berkenfeld, an investment banker who specializes in this area, sums up the feeling of many employers when he says that, when it comes to needing more labor, the key questions are, "Can I automate it? If not, can I outsource it? If not, can I give it to an independent contractor?"[34] Few jobs make it through that obstacle course, and for many contemporary organizations, hiring a real employee is the last resort.

It is useful to distinguish between temporary workers, who are part of a large employment agency and are more or less rented by the primary employer, and independent contract workers, who are more or less freelancers and not part of any organization. Independent contractors are unattached individuals who agree to do specific tasks for specific time periods as part of a written contract between the worker and the employer. Rather than shifting the burden to be the "employer of record" from the employer to a temporary agency, in this case, virtually all the burden associated with this distinction falls on the worker himself or herself.

There has been an unprecedented increase in the use of contract workers like this in recent years, fueled in part by the ability of mobile apps to link employers to workers without the need to go through any other intermediary. In addition, the demonstrated success associated with this business model achieved by companies like Uber, Instacart, TaskRabbit, and Handy have made this option even more attractive to employers, and the number of individuals working as part of this form of employment grew by 10 million people from 2005 to 2015.[35]

Although many individuals prefer the autonomy, freedom, and flexibility associated with being an independent contractor, for many workers, this option is chosen only as a last resort. Independent contracting jobs rarely provide any job security, health benefits, or retirement support, and many of the jobs are poorly paid. In Spain, over 90% of the job growth in that country experienced in the 2012–2015 period was attributed to such jobs, often referred to as *trabajo basura*, or "garbage work."[36]

Governments and labor organizations in both the United States and the European Union have been worried about this trend in employment and are studying ways to help protect workers who are part of such arrangements.[37] In the meantime, Uber recently agreed to settle a class-action lawsuit for $84 million brought by its drivers, who argued that they were misclassified as independent contractors. Uber also agreed to give drivers more warning before being deactivated and that they could no longer block drivers who turned down rides too frequently.[38]

## Outsourcing and Offshoring

Whereas a temporary employee can be brought in to manage a single job, in other cases a firm may be interested in getting a much broader set of services performed by an outside organization; this is called **outsourcing**. Outsourcing is a logical choice when a firm simply does not have certain expertise and is not willing to invest time and effort into

**Outsourcing**
An organization's use of an outside organization for a broad set of services.

developing it. For example, rather than hire an MBA full time, some companies may decide just to "rent one" for a short, specific project. In fact, a group of Harvard MBAs started a new firm called HourlyNerd to meet just this growing need. Businesses pay $75–$100 an hour for specific one-time tasks like pricing a new product or valuating a business that requires a short dose of expertise.[39]

Similarly, in the area of research and development, generic labs have sprung up that allow companies to perform experiments and product testing that may require expensive equipment that is better to rent than own. For example, Emerald Therapeutics provides these kinds of services for small pharmaceutical companies that may have big ideas but limited infrastructure to test such ideas. Emerald rents out both its expensive machinery and talented technicians, thus essentially creating a virtual research and development division for a small company that could never develop this capacity internally.[40]

Ironically, companies increasingly outsource many of their HRM tasks to outside vendors that specialize in efficiently performing many of the more routine administrative tasks associated with this function. Cost savings in this area are easily obtained because rather than purchase and maintain their own specialized hardware and software, as well as specialized staff to support such systems, companies can time-share the facilities and expertise of a firm that focuses on this technology. HR outsourcing firms often focus on health care or financial/retirement programs because these areas are subject to heavy government regulation. These regulations are often changing and demand a great deal of paperwork that is best left to experts who focus single-mindedly on these tasks.[41] The hope is that this frees up HR managers to focus on more strategic issues.

In other cases, outsourcing is aimed at simply reducing costs by hiring less expensive labor to do the work, and, more often than not, this means moving the work outside the country. **Offshoring** is a special case of outsourcing, in which the jobs that move leave one country and go to another. This kind of job migration has always taken place; however, rapid technological changes have made the current trends in this area unprecedented. Offshoring is controversial because although it may help a company's bottom line, it harms many citizens who lose their jobs and then look to their government for relief.

**Offshoring**
A special case of outsourcing, in which the jobs that move leave one country and go to another.

For example, the United States has lost over 5 million manufacturing jobs to China since the mid-1990s, and a great deal of political pressure is being placed on companies to "reshore" this work.[42] For example, Walmart created a program called the Reshoring Initiative that had a goal of spending $250 billion over 10 years on domestically produced goods. On the one hand, this program was successful, in that it did shift production away from China and back to the United States. However, when this production came back to the United States, much of the work was automated; thus, far fewer jobs were created relative to those lost originally.[43] Most experts believe that the only way to achieve a significant increase in the number of new jobs for workers displaced by offshoring is through retraining, although as the Competing through Globalization box shows, other approaches, like tariffs, have been tried.

This political pressure regarding outsourcing may seem problematic for U.S. employers, but still, if effectively managed, firms that offshore certain aspects of work gain an undeniable competitive advantage over their rivals. Ignoring this source of advantage is self-defeating and akin to putting one's head in the sand. For example, Levi-Strauss tried for years to compete against other low-cost jeans manufacturers who offshored their labor. However, after years of one plant shutdown after another, the firm finally gave up and closed down all of its U.S. manufacturing plants. The move, which many people saw as inevitable, was long overdue, and had it been made earlier, the company might have been able to avoid losing over $20 million.[44]

When making the decision to offshore some product or service, organizations should consider several critical factors. Many companies that failed to look before they leaped onto the

### Picking Winners and Losers in the Trade War

Every war has winners and losers, and this is just as true when it comes to trade wars as it is when war is waged with armed forces. In 2018, tariffs installed by the U.S. government launched one such trade war, and it did not take too long to see who would win and who would lose as a result of the ongoing battles. In some cases, entire industries stood to win. For example, aluminum manufacturers in the United States and the workers they employed were clearly winners. As recently as 2000, the United States was home to 23 aluminum smelters, but that number dropped to just 6 in 2018. In addition, whereas the United States produces 67% of its own steel, it imports 85% of its aluminum, thus, U.S.-based aluminum companies had close to a monopoly on domestic supply. Michael Bless, CEO of Century Aluminum, celebrated the trade war, noting that "our country was within months of seeing an entire industry disappear."

In contrast, other industries, like the soybean industry, were clearly losers. In retaliation for the moves made by the United States, China placed a tariff on soybeans that crippled the entire industry. Prior to the tariffs, China was the number one importer of U.S. soybeans, worth over $13 million annually. That figure dropped by 94%, however, after the tariffs were imposed. Arthur Companies, a firm that operates six grain elevators in North Dakota, began piling up beans in an open field behind the fully packed grain silos. At one point, the 1 million bushels of soybeans that constituted the pile created the largest hill in the county. As noted by Greg Gebeke, a farmer who works 5,000 acres near the Arthur Company silos notes, "I am trying to follow and figure out who the winners are in this tariff war. I know who one of the losers—and that's us."

In other industries, some businesses within the industry win and other businesses in the same industry lose. Ironically, when it comes to the automobile industry, U.S. companies like General Motors (GM) that moved production overseas to China benefit, whereas foreign companies that opened plants in the United States suffer. That is, GM sells a large number of cars in China, but virtually all of the cars that it sells in that market are built in China. Thus, when China slapped a 40% tariff on U.S. automobiles, GM was totally unaffected. In contrast, companies like BMW and Daimler that built huge plants in the southern United States—employing thousands of American workers—were subject to the tariffs when it came to exporting to China. Half of those jobs were supported by exports. Porsche AG, who built no plants in the United States was overjoyed at this state of affairs, and their CEO noted that "This is a favorable situation for us because the products from manufacturers in the U.S. are becoming far less competitive."

Finally, when it comes to their win and loss record, some companies are 1 and 1 when it comes to tariffs. For example, Harley Davidson is clearly hurt by the current tariffs for two reasons. First, the cost of Harley's raw supplies has sky-rocketed—especially steel and aluminum. This adds to their costs. Second, due to declining U.S. sales, Harley has become a net exporter to other countries—especially China. Thus, the tariffs detract from revenues. Although it is small consolation, at least Harley can reflect with fondness on the good old days when they were beneficiaries of tariffs. In 1983, in order to protect U.S. motorcycle producers from Japanese competitors like Honda and Kawasaki, President Ronald Reagan put a 10-fold tariff on imported bikes coming from Japan. Apparently, what goes around, comes around when it comes to cycles.

#### DISCUSSION QUESTIONS

1. In what sense is a tariff like a tax, and in what way does their implementation implicitly reflect tax policy?
2. Might the short-term losses attributable to tariffs possibly be offset by longer-term gains when it comes to re-establishing free trade?

SOURCES: M. Philips and J. Deaux, "The Metal That Started Trump's Trade War," *Bloomberg Businessweek Online*, September 27, 2018; B. Appelbaum, "Their Soybeans Piling Up, Farmers Hope Trade War Ends before Beans Rot," *The New York Times Online*, November 5, 2018; W. Boston, "What the Tariff Battle Means for Auto Plants in South Carolina," *The Wall Street Journal Online*, June 10, 2018; J. D. Stoll, "Harley-Davidson Is Fighting the Trade Wars on Two Fronts," *The Wall Street Journal Online*, June 25, 2018.

offshoring bandwagon have been disappointed by their results. Quality control problems, security violations, and poor customer service experiences have in many cases wiped out all the cost savings attributed to lower wages, and more. For example, in 2014, meat supplier OSI Group Inc., a main supplier of beef and chicken to restaurants such as McDonald's, Yum Brands, and Burger King, was fined when inspectors discovered that meat processed in Shanghai, China, was repackaged and sold long after the legally mandated sell-by dates. Sheldon Lavin, the CEO of the company, had to go public after this incident and stated, "I will not try to defend or explain it. It was terribly wrong, and I am appalled that it ever happened in a company that I own." This incident threatened the long-term relationship between OSI and the many restaurants that it supplied, and in some cases, those relationships came to an end.[45]

As another example, much of the computer software work that U.S. companies once sent to India is now being executed by domestic companies, many of which have popped up in the former industrial Midwest. For example, Nexient, a domestic software outsourcing company, has lured business customers that were frustrated by the problems associated with navigating time zones, language, and culture associated with outsourcing tech work to India. The company is headquartered in the Midwest, rather than the traditional East or West Coast hub because of the availability of local talent that wants to stay in the region where the cost of living is lower. Although, the cost of their workers is still two or three times what the same worker would cost in India, this is far less than the eight-fold differences one saw 10 years ago. Moreover, this central location makes it easy for the company to fly representatives to the sites where they are working to increase valuable face-to-face interactions. Indeed, this business model has been so successful that now, Indian outsourcing giants such as Infosys are making plans to open their own shops in the U.S. Midwest.[46]

### Immigration

If one cannot take the work overseas, but still wishes to tap into less-expensive global talent to fill a labor shortage, then one might simply bring foreign workers into the country. Immigration has always been a vital part of the American economy, and many foreign workers are happy to leave their homes and pursue their own American dream.[47] However, entrance of foreign workers into the United States to fill jobs is federally regulated, so there are limits to what can be accomplished here. Because immigration is a complex and controversial topic both for HR professionals and people in general, we will examine these issues closely, focusing first on low skills jobs that are regulated with H2-A visas, and then high skill jobs that are regulated with H1-B visas.

### A Close Look at H2-A Visas

First, when it comes to low-skill jobs, the U.S. government provides H2-A visas that allow foreign workers into this country to do seasonal work, mostly in agriculture. Employers in this sector of the economy are desperate for this labor because these jobs are dirty, hot, low paid, and no American citizen has any interest in doing this work.[48] Much of the work is also difficult to automate, and although mechanization has made inroads when it comes to processing corn, rice, soybean, and wheat, other high-value crops such as fruits and berries require human labor.

Because of the high demand for this labor, employers' applications for H2-A visas have tripled between 2011 and 2018.[49] Unlike H1-A visas, there are no caps on H2-A visas, but despite this, many employers find the process expensive and unreliable. It is also very time-consuming, sometimes taking close to four weeks to process, which defeats the purpose when it comes to time-sensitive seasonal produce. Finally, for many employers, the demand for this labor is not technically seasonal. Dairy farmers, meat processors, and construction companies all find it impossible to recruit American citizens for some jobs, but the work they offer proceeds year-round.

Because the H2-A process fails to meet the needs of employers, these organizations often turn to undocumented workers who are in the United States illegally. These workers are illegal because they do not have visas or green cards that would make them permanent residents of the United States, and hence, they are not eligible to work in this country. Now, one might ask, why don't these illegal workers just go through the process of getting their green cards—or better yet—become full-fledged U.S. citizens?

This seemingly obvious solution breaks down when one realizes that this process can take up to three or four years and requires hiring an immigration lawyer that can cost over $25,000. This is a price that is typically beyond the reach of farm laborers. Moreover, because undocumented workers entered the United States illegally (often dragged into the country when they were children), the last step of this process is to leave the United States, and then re-enter legally once their paperwork is all set. Most undocumented workers in the United States are over 35 years of age and have families in this country that they are afraid to leave. They are terrified to take this last step, worried that they may never make it back if something is wrong in the paperwork—which is legally technical and hard to understand and check yourself.

Because of the difficulties employers find with H2-A visas and the difficulties undocumented workers have getting green cards—and the fact that crops will quickly rot if not processed—this results in a situation where employers in these industries pretty much "knowingly" hire undocumented workers. In fact, over 50% of the labor in agriculture and meat processing is done by workers who are in the country illegally.

So, you might say, why not crack down on the employers who are hiring these workers? Indeed, this was what the U.S. government did in 2011 when it initiated the E-Verify program that required employers to check the legal status of all hires, filling out an I-9 Form for each employee. Employers who failed to secure I-9 Forms were subject to financial penalties for failure to comply. Problem solved, right?

Well, although the E-Verify program looked like a perfect solution to the problem of undocumented workers on paper, there were two problems when this was put in practice. First, the rules of the program were written up in a way that required the government to prove the employer "knew" that some worker was undocumented. This spawned a cottage industry of fake I-9 Forms and other documents that employers, who desperately needed the workers, were more than willing to examine with a closed eye. This allowed them to say, "it looked good to me—I did not know" when pressed by the government. Second, they were never really pressed by the government. The E-Verify program was never strongly enforced, and an undercover investigation revealed that in most states; no one even knew who was responsible for enforcing the program. As one labor economist noted, "lawmakers got all the political benefits of supporting immigration enforcement without the cost of hurting their local businesses."[50]

This might be considered a highly cynical and imperfect solution, but still, it is a solution right? Well, yes, until 2017 and 2018 when the government decided to actually enforce the program. The Immigration and Custom Enforcement (ICE) started launching unannounced raids on employers, who were very ill-prepared for the onslaught. Employers were not ready for these raids for two reasons. First, they had grown used to ignoring the I-9 Form. Second, unannounced raids were technically not legal either. ICE referred to the raids as "audits," which are clearly part of their jurisdiction. However, the audits actually required the government to provide employers with a three-day "Notice of Inspection," in order to get their paperwork in order. ICE often skipped this step.[51] With federal authorities now actually taking them to task, local employers turned to their state governments, and as shown in the Integrity in Action box, many states came to the aid of their employers, setting up a war between federal and state authorities.

## Local Authorities Defy Federal Changes in Enforcement

Jorge Garcia was smuggled into the United States when he was 10 years old. Bit by bit and piece by piece, Garcia built a life in this country, and 30 years later, he was a married father of two. Garcia supported his family by working for the last 15 years for a landscaping company operating out of Lincoln Park, Michigan. He had no criminal record and was never arrested. Thus, it came as more than a surprise when he was separated from his family, taken into custody by Immigration and Customs Enforcement (ICE), and deported to Mexico, a country that he did not even remember. U.S. Human Rights Activists and some state politicians were shocked at this, with one noting that, "I don't see the justice in this. For a man who cares deeply and supports his family, obeys the law, pays taxes, and has a history of helping others, I think the federal government acted cruelly to this person."

Indeed, there have been recent changes in federal policy regarding undocumented workers without criminal records that has created some degree of separation between federal and local authorities (states and cities) when it comes to prosecuting undocumented workers. In the past, both federal and local authorities were in agreement that the priority for deportation needed to focus on undocumented workers who committed serious or violent crimes. In fact, ICE employees, state officials,

and city authorities often worked closely within the immigrant community to help identify and arrest serious criminals in their midst. In return, the authorities did not prosecute people whose only crime was illegal entry. However, due to an Executive Order passed in 2017, federal authorities changed their focus, and expanded deportation processes to all undocumented workers regardless of their criminal history.

Many states and municipalities disagreed with this change in focus, however, because of the unfairness of the process when it came to "proportionality" of crime and punishment in cases such as Jorge Garcia. In addition, they were also concerned with the economic ramifications for local employers who could not survive (and pay taxes) in many states and cities without hiring undocumented workers. For example, in California, a full 10% of the workforce (1.75 million people) is undocumented, and the state cannot function without these workers. As former ICE Director, Doris Meisser notes, "in communities such as this, the local politics gets hot and heavy" because local employers need these workers and local retailers need these customers.

Indeed, one of the battles between federal and state agencies on this issue was waged at 7-Eleven stores in California precisely because this was where many undocumented people

both work and shop. On the one side, the federal government told employers that they had to comply with ICE agents who raided the stores. At the same time, state authorities told employers they had to demand search warrants, emphasizing that it was a crime to provide ICE any information on people not covered by the warrant. As usual, businesses were caught in the crossfire. Most employers did not know how to read a search warrant and they were totally confused about what they should and should not do in this situation. Whether because of their own ethical values or their own economic needs, in the end, most of the employers complied with their state authorities rather than the federal authorities. As Ms. Meisser concluded, "when your laws don't align with the market, then the market is always going to win."

### DISCUSSION QUESTIONS

1. How does this war between the federal government and state government when it comes to immigration wind up harming all workers and citizens?

2. How might comprehensive revisions to the immigration policy and practices related to H1-A and H1-B visas solve these problems for both federal and state authorities? What is the moral responsibility of employers for ensuring that they are not harboring

*CONTINUED*

illegal workers who pose a threat to their communities?

3. Some "sanctuary cities," such as Los Angeles and Austin, refuse to enforce federal laws that they feel target nondangerous undocumented people living in their communities. What are the ethical implications of these cities refusing to enforce federal laws?

SOURCES: D. Hawkins, "A Michigan Father, Too Old for DACA, Is Deported after 30 Years in the U.S.," *The Washington Post Online*, January 16, 2018; L. Etter and D. Rafieyan, "ICE Agents Go from Advocate to Adversary," *Bloomberg Businessweek*, August 6, 2017, pp. 30–31; N. Malas, "California Employers in a Bind Over Immigration Enforcement," *The Wall Street Journal Online*, February 13, 2018; N. Kitroeff, "Workplace Raids Signal Shifting Tactics in Immigration Fight," *The New York Times Online*, January 15, 2018.

## A Close Look at H1-B Visas

Although the state of affairs when it comes to low-skilled workers and the H2-A visa may seem a little confused, one might hope that the situation is a little clearer when it comes to high-skill workers regulated by the H1-B visa program, because that is where the money is when it comes to wages and products. Let's see.

First, unlike the H2-A program, the H1-B program is capped and employers are limited to roughly 85,000 visas a year. Typically, three times as many applications come in for these visas and they are awarded on a lottery basis. Although some of the visas go to universities, the vast majority wind up going to the tech industry. These are highly paid jobs (average salaries of $125,000) that the U.S. government tries to protect and reserve for American workers, however, tech companies claim that American universities are not producing enough workers with skills in Science, Technology, Engineering, and Math (STEM) to meet their needs.

Thus, the industry is constantly lobbying for a larger number of H1-B visas. The tech companies argue that rather than taking jobs, each immigrant they hire instead of an American actually winds up creating five jobs for American workers.[52] These efforts often pay off, as in 2013 when a new immigration bill was approved that provided access to a green card for any foreign worker in a job with an advanced degree in STEM.[53]

More recently, however, people outside the tech industry have pushed back on these arguments, and one survey conducted in 2016, showed that 80% of Americans wanted to see more restrictions on high-skilled foreign workers.[54] In addition, many have suggested that not all the visas actually wind up going to highly skilled people, especially when the big tech companies like Microsoft, Facebook, eBay, Apple, and Amazon.com file applications for smaller companies where they outsource work. Salaries for these jobs are lower ($60,000 is the lower limit for H1-B Visa) and an estimated 90% of them do not require advanced degrees or training.[55] Arguments like this have motivated the government to tighten rules on the program, and some of suggested that it be ended altogether.[56]

Employer reactions to this pushback have been widely varied. On the one hand, some of the major players in the outsourcing field such as Infosys have announced that they are going to open up facilities in the United States, hiring as many as 10,000 new workers.[57] This is surprising because the company was laying off thousands of workers in India at the same time.[58] In contrast, other employers moved their jobs from the United States to Canada where they felt immigration policies were more supportive.[59] As one Microsoft executive noted when they expanded their operations in Vancouver, "the U.S. Laws clearly did not meet our needs, and thus we had [to] look other places."[60]

Finally, before leaving the topic of immigration, we should also note that some employers are turning to a new supply of labor from outside the United States—refugees—to solve their chronic labor shortage problems. In contrast to immigrants, U.S. regulations allow refugees to work as soon as they arrive in the country. Over the years, the share of immigrant labor in Midwest slaughterhouses has grown to 35%, many of which come from Somalia. At the higher end of the labor pool, some refugees are well trained, and it is not uncommon for some individuals who worked as doctors in their own country, to work in areas like nursing in the United States, where there are chronic labor shortages.[61] Starbucks also recently announced that they will hire 10,000 refugees worldwide citing their outstanding work ethic and drive for self-improvement.[62]

However, this strategy is also in peril because in 2017 the United States placed restrictions on refugees entering the country, cutting this supply of labor in half. Clearly, there is a need for comprehensive immigration reform in the United States, but until that day arrives, HR professionals and employers need to stay acutely tuned to day-to-day developments on this front when it comes to managing both H2-A visas, H1-B visas, undocumented workers, and refugees. Although the difficulties associated with increasing globalization and softening borders are many, as the Evidence-Based HR box shows, the difficulties associated with isolation may be even worse.

## EVIDENCE-BASED HR

The thought of globalization scares some workers and citizens because of its uncertain impact on domestic jobs. With this as a starting point, one might ask, what is the downside of just rejecting globalization and sealing oneself off from the world? Although the United Kingdom's (UK) experience with Brexit is hardly an experiment in totally sealing oneself off from the world, it does shed light on what happens when a country limits its options—and the evidence is pretty clear—you lose jobs for sure.

*Brexit* is the term used to describe the United Kingdom's departure from the European Union (EU), and the sucking sound that citizens of London heard after this move was the mass exodus of jobs from that city to Central and Eastern Europe. For example, Poland lured over 30,000 former British jobs to their country by offering its customers unfettered access to the European Union. In the financial industry alone, Goldman Sachs moved 3,000 jobs from London to Warsaw and JPMorgan moved 2,500 jobs from the British capital to Krakow. AT&T and Hewlett-Packard went a slightly different direction, moving their jobs to Prague and Budapest, respectively. In total, economists estimate a loss of 17% of the existing jobs in London that could be traced to Brexit.

SOURCE: Z. Simon, "In Europe, Brain Drain Flows the Other Way," *Bloomberg Businessweek*, April 3, 2017, pp. 16–18.

### Altering Pay and Hours

Companies facing a shortage of labor may be reluctant to hire new full-time or part-time employees. Under some conditions, these firms may have the option of trying to garner more hours out of the existing labor force. Despite having to pay workers time-and-a-half for overtime production, employers see this as preferable to hiring and training new employees—especially if they are concerned that current demand for products or services may not extend to the future. Also, for a short time at least, many workers enjoy the added compensation.

However, over extended periods, employees experience stress and frustration from being overworked in this manner. Historically, in the United States, overtime pay was granted only to hourly workers or workers earning less than $24,000 a year, but a law passed in 2016 expanded overtime pay to any worker earning less than $50,000 a year. This significantly increased the number of workers eligible for overtime pay and was aimed primarily at employers who might be misclassifying exempt workers in an attempt to avoid paying overtime.[63]

In the face of a labor surplus, organizations can sometimes avoid layoffs if they can get their employees to take pay cuts. In general, wages tend to be "sticky" in the sense that employers are reluctant to cut someone's pay, and the data suggest that this holds true even during economic recessions.[64] During economic expansions and labor shortages, it is almost impossible to lower wages, at least in the private sector. The U.S. government did institute a pay freeze for federal employees, however, in 2018, despite the unprecedented labor shortage. The move was an attempt to stamp down on spending in a context where worker mobility opportunities might be less for public employees relative to those in the private sector.[65]

Alternatively, one can avoid layoffs and hold the pay rate constant but reduce the number of hours of all the workers. For example, when business at the Bristol, Rhode Island, plastics manufacturer Saint-Gobain slowed in 2012, none of the workers were laid off, but many had their hours cut by 40%. This would have resulted in a major cut in pay for the workers, except for a state government program that helped Saint-Gobain pay 70% of the lost wages in return for the company keeping the workers on the payroll. The state would have wound up paying a similar amount in unemployment compensation, but this program allowed the company to hold on to experienced employees for when the economy turned around. These kinds of "work share" programs have always been popular in Europe but are now starting to be seen in the United States.[66]

When a cut in hours is targeted at salaried workers rather than hourly workers, this is called a *furlough*. For example, in 2016, roughly 10,000 workers at Honeywell were furloughed for one week. The program was an attempt to reduce costs necessary because of slow economic growth and decreased U.S. defense spending.[67] Furloughs are perceived as a good strategy to use when the employer has an immediate need to conserve money and protect cash flow, but also believes that need will be short term and the employees involved have skills that make them hard to replace in the long term.[68]

Furloughs are controversial because, unlike most hourly workers who go home after the assembly line stops running, the work of most white-collar professionals simply piles up when they leave the office for extended periods of time. Furloughs are also controversial because they hit higher-paid employees harder than lower-paid employees, and if these pay differences were a result of some type of pay-for-performance system, this means that the best employees take the biggest hit.

## PROGRAM IMPLEMENTATION AND EVALUATION

The programs developed in the strategic planning stage of the process are put into practice in the program-implementation stage, shown at the bottom of Figure 5.1. A critical aspect of program implementation is to make sure that some individual is held accountable for achieving the stated goals and has the necessary authority and resources to accomplish this goal. It is also important to have regular progress reports on the implementation to be sure that all programs are in place by specified times and that the early returns from these programs are in line with projections. The final step in the planning process is to evaluate the results. This evaluation consists of comparing results to goals, as well as an "after-action-review" of what worked or failed to work when it came to accomplishing goals.

## THE SPECIAL CASE OF AFFIRMATIVE ACTION PLANNING

Human resource planning is an important function that should be applied to an organization's entire labor force. It is also important to plan for various subgroups within the labor force. For example, affirmative action plans forecast and monitor the proportion of various protected group members, such as women and minorities, that are in various job categories and career tracks. The proportion of workers in these subgroups can then be compared with the proportion that each subgroup represents in the relevant labor market. This type of comparison is called a **workforce utilization review**. This process can be used to determine whether there is any subgroup whose proportion in the relevant labor market is substantially different from the proportion in the job category.

**Workforce utilization review**
A comparison of the proportion of workers in protected subgroups with the proportion that each subgroup represents in the relevant labor market.

If such an analysis indicates that some group—for example, African Americans—makes up 35% of the relevant labor market for a job category but that this same group constitutes only 5% of the actual incumbents in that job category in that organization, then this is evidence of underutilization. Evidence exactly like this was recently discovered in the banking industry, where EEOC statistics showed that African Americans held only 5% of the positions at several of the major banks, despite reflecting 15% of the overall population.

In his annual letter to shareholders in 2017, Jamie Dimon, CEO of JP Morgan Chase and Company, frankly admitted that "there is one area in particular where we simply have not met the standards we have set for ourselves—and that is increasing African American talent in the firm." This was a frank assessment and shareholders were initially impressed—until they were shown that he made the exact same statement in the 2016 letter. Still, the bank did make a $5 million investment toward improving diversity, much of which was channeled into scholarships that have an impact much further down the line.[69]

Evidence for underutilization can also be found in many areas of high tech. For example, only 15% of software engineers in Silicon Valley are women, a proportion that is far short of their general participation rate.[70] The proportion is even lower for African Americans, who represent just 1% of software engineers versus a 13% general participation rate. These figures would support the inference that these groups are underutilized, and many firms are trying to respond to this situation. For example, Google has sent several workers to predominantly African American colleges like Howard University to help cultivate future coders.[71]

These kinds of affirmative action programs are often controversial because many non-minorities see them as unfair. However, when the evidence provided from a workforce utilization review makes it clear that a specific minority group has been historically underrepresented because of past discrimination, and that increasing the level of representation will benefit workforce diversity and competitiveness, then these kinds of programs are easier to justify to all involved. Organizations need to realize, however, that affirmative action plans need to be complemented with communication programs that clearly spell out the needs and benefits that these programs bring to the organization and the larger society.[72]

# The Human Resource Recruitment Process

As the first half of this chapter shows, it is difficult to always anticipate exactly how many (if any) new employees will have to be hired in a given year in a given job category. The role of human resource recruitment is to build a supply of potential new hires that the organization can draw on if the need arises. Thus, **human resource recruitment** is defined as any practice or activity carried on by the organization with the primary purpose of identifying and attracting potential employees. It thus creates a buffer between planning and actual selection of new employees, which is the topic of our next chapter.

The goal of the recruiting is not simply to generate large numbers of applicants. If the process generates a sea of unqualified applicants, the organization will incur great expense in personnel selection, but few vacancies will actually be filled. This problem of generating too many applicants is often promulgated by the use of wide-reaching technologies like the Internet to reach people.

The goal of personnel recruitment is not to finely discriminate among reasonably qualified applicants, either. Recruiting new personnel and selecting new personnel are both complex processes. Organizations explicitly trying to do both at the same time will probably not do either well. For example, research suggests that applicants apparently remember less information about the recruiting organization after dual-purpose interviews.[73]

In general, as shown in Figure 5.3, all companies have to make decisions in three areas of recruiting: (1) personnel policies, which affect the kinds of jobs the company has to offer; (2) recruitment sources used to solicit applicants, which affect the kinds of people who apply; and (3) the characteristics and behaviors of the recruiter. These, in turn, influence both the nature of the vacancies and the nature of the people applying for jobs in a way that shapes job choice decisions.

**Human resource recruitment**
The practice or activity carried on by the organization with the primary purpose of identifying and attracting potential employees.

## PERSONNEL POLICIES

*Personnel policies* is a generic term we use to refer to organizational decisions that affect the nature of the vacancies for which people are recruited. If the research on recruitment makes one thing clear, it is that characteristics of the vacancy are more important than recruiters or recruiting sources when it comes to predicting job choice.

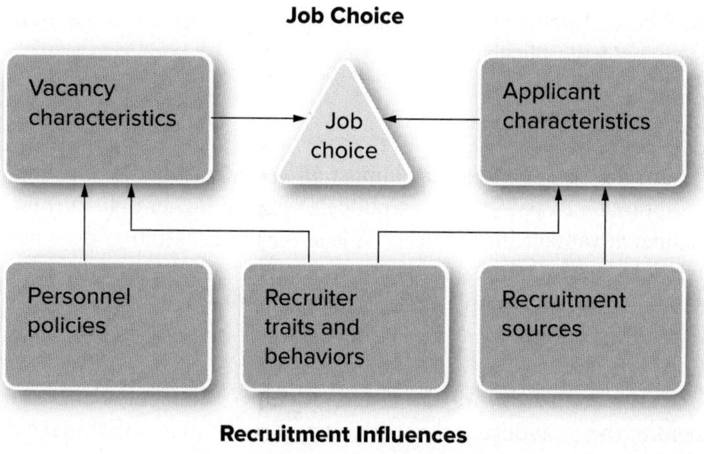

**LO 5-4**
Describe the various recruitment policies that organizations adopt to make job vacancies more attractive.

**Job Choice**

**Recruitment Influences**

**Figure 5.3**
Overview of the Individual Job Choice–Organizational Recruitment Process

## Internal versus External Recruiting: Job Security

One desirable feature of a vacancy is that it provides ample opportunity for advancement and promotion. One organizational policy that affects this is the degree to which the company "promotes from within"—that is, recruits for upper-level vacancies internally rather than externally. Promote-from-within policies make it clear to applicants that there are opportunities for advancement within the company. These opportunities spring not just from the first vacancy but from the vacancy created when a person in the company fills that vacancy.

For example, Optimove is a software company that creates products that support the automation of personalized customer retention marketing focused mainly on the gaming industry. CEO Pini Yakuel has relied almost exclusively on promotion-from-within policies that attempt to commit the worker to the organization and vice versa. Yakuel notes that "the big advantage is that these people know the company in all its particulars from top to bottom, and it's a strength that an outside manager will need time and extra skills to match."[74]

Although these programs are popular with employees because they increase job security and promotion opportunities, there are two downsides. First, this type of program sometimes upsets current managers of employees who are recruited away. Many of these employees are top performers in their current units, and some managers bristle at the loss of these individuals.[75] Second, bringing in recruits from external sources often helps spur creativity and innovation that might not originate from insiders who have grown accustomed to routine work processes. For example, in 2016, Carnival Cruise Line changed its recruiting procedures from hiring industry insiders to bringing in employees who had close to zero experience with cruises. Although these novices do have to be surrounded by some experts in the area, they often came up with new and lucrative ideas, such as volunteer public service cruises where social-conscious passengers got off the boat and helped local villages build housing. This was a new niche in the market that no one steeped in cruise culture was likely to see.[76]

**Due process policies**
Policies by which a company formally lays out the steps an employee can take to appeal a termination decision.

In addition to using promote-from-within policies and internal recruiting sources, employers can promote perceptions of job security and long-term commitment to the organization through due process policies. **Due process policies** formally lay out the steps an employee can take to appeal a termination decision. Organizational recruiting materials that emphasize due process, rights of appeal, and grievance mechanisms send a message that job security is high; employment-at-will policies suggest the opposite. **Employment-at-will policies** state that either party in the employment relationship can terminate that relationship at any time, regardless of cause. Companies that do not have employment-at-will provisions typically have extensive due process policies. Research indicates that job applicants find companies with due process policies more attractive than companies with employment-at-will policies.[77]

**Employment-at-will policies**
Policies stating that either an employer or an employee can terminate the employment relationship at any time, regardless of cause.

## Extrinsic and Intrinsic Rewards

Because pay is an important job characteristic for almost all applicants, companies that take a "lead-the-market" approach to pay—that is, a policy of paying higher-than-current-market wages—have a distinct advantage in recruiting. A lead-the-market strategy does not just mean that the organizations raise wages relative to what they have done in the past; instead, they raise wages faster than the competition. When pay rates are already rising, as was the case in 2015, when the average pay rate was rising 2.5% a year, this requires moves larger than the going rate of change.[78]

In some cases, high pay may be the only way to attract people to some jobs. For example, in the drilling segment of the oil industry, the work takes place in places that make it extremely difficult to recruit workers. The work is dirty, physically demanding, and temperatures at work sites like the Permian Basin in Texas hover well above 100 degrees. There is not a single shade tree anywhere in sight, and the nearest market, restaurant, or bar is hours away. Most workers are forced to live in alcohol-free dormitories for weeks on end away from their families. Still, as one employee aptly notes, "if you don't have a college education, where else are you going to make 100,000 a year?"[79]

Pay can also make up for a job's less desirable features—for example, paying higher wages to employees who have to work midnight shifts. These kinds of specific shift differentials and other forms of more generic compensating differentials will be discussed in more detail in later chapters that focus on compensation strategies. We note here that "lead" policies make any given vacancy more attractive to applicants.

There are limits to what can be done in terms of using pay to attract people to certain jobs, however. For example, the U.S. Army cannot compete on pay, because as General Michael Rochelle, then head of army recruiting, noted, "We can't get started down a slippery slope where we are depending on money to lure people in. The reality is that while we have to remain at least competitive, we're never going to be able to pay as much as the private sector." To offset this disadvantage in extrinsic financial rewards, the army has to rely on more intrinsic rewards related to patriotism and personal growth opportunities that people associate with military service.

For example, because cyberwar is an increasingly large element within the field of national defense, the military needs coders and software engineers that are already in high demand in the private sector. Although the military cannot match pay with the private sector, it can leverage intrinsic motivation related to serving one's country and learning new skills. Many of the military's cyber warriors are "homegrown" and trained specialists who come from other jobs such as mechanics.[80]

## Image Advertising

Organizations often advertise specific vacancies (discussed in the next section). Sometimes, however, organizations advertise just to promote themselves as a good place to work in general. Image advertising is particularly important for companies in highly competitive labor markets that perceive themselves as having a bad image. For example, recent events that hurt the images of companies such as at Facebook (privacy breeches), Wells Fargo (defrauding customers), and Uber (hostile work environment) triggered advertising campaigns aimed not just at customers, but also at future potential employees in an attempt to minimize the damage. These apology campaigns included print, digital, and billboard ads, as well as television commercials airing during major events like the NBA playoffs. Although companies have always made mistakes, in the past those seeking forgiveness would simply print an apology letter in a national newspapers, but that no longer seems to cut it.[81]

Even though it does not provide information about any specific job, image advertising is often effective because job applicants develop ideas about the general reputation of the firm (i.e., its brand image), and then this spills over to influence their expectations about the nature of specific jobs or careers at the organization. These perceptions then influence the degree to which the person feels attracted to the organization, especially if there appears to be a good fit between the traits of the applicant and the traits that describe the organization.[82] Applicants seem particularly sensitive to issues of diversity and inclusion in these types of advertisements; hence, organizations that advertise their image need to ensure that the actors in their advertisements reflect the broad nature of the labor market constituencies to which they are trying to appeal, in terms of race, gender, and culture.

## RECRUITMENT SOURCES

The sources from which a company recruits potential employees are a critical aspect of its overall recruitment strategy. The type of person who is likely to respond to a job advertised on the Internet may be different from the type of person who responds to an ad in the classified section of a local newspaper. In this section, we examine the different sources from which recruits can be drawn, highlighting the advantages and disadvantages of each.

### Internal versus External Sources

We discussed internal versus external sources of recruits earlier in this chapter and focused on the positive effects that internal recruiting can have on recruits' perceptions of job security. We discuss this issue again here but with a focus on how using internal sources affects the kinds of people who are recruited.

In general, relying on internal sources offers a company several advantages. First, it generates a sample of applicants who are well known to the firm. Second, these applicants are relatively knowledgeable about the company's vacancies, which minimizes the possibility of inflated expectations about the job. Third, it is generally cheaper and faster to fill vacancies internally. Finally, inside hires often outperform outsiders, especially when it comes to filling jobs at the top end of the hierarchy.

When one examines what happens at the top of the organization, the evidence is quite clear that outsiders often struggle to adapt to their new role. For example, when it comes to tenure, CEOs hired from outside the company average four years prior to departing, compared to five years for insiders. In addition, when it comes to being forced out, 35% of outsider CEOs get ousted after less than three years, compared to 19% for insiders. Finally, in terms of return on investment, companies with an internally hired CEO outperformed those headed by an outsider by 4.4%.[83]

With all these advantages, you might ask why any organization would ever employ external recruiting methods. There are several good reasons why organizations might decide to recruit externally. First, for entry-level positions and perhaps even for some specialized upper-level positions, there may not be any internal recruits from which to draw. Second, bringing in outsiders may expose the organization to new ideas or new ways of doing business. Using only internal recruitment can result in a workforce whose members all think alike and who therefore may be poorly suited to innovation. Finally, recruiting from outside sources is a good way to strengthen one's own company and weaken one's competitors at the same time. In fact, having one's employees "poached" by another company can be so devastating that companies go to great lengths, perhaps even illegal or unethical lengths, to prevent this from happening.

For example, in the constant war for talent in Silicon Valley, poaching the best programmers away from one's competition is a common strategy, and "cold calling" is the central tactic employed to execute that strategy. *Cold calling* refers to the practice in which recruiters from one company call an employee of some other company who has the skills they need and try to get that person to switch sides. Thus, rather than search for new employees among those that do not have jobs and are looking for work, cold callers search the pool of people who have jobs and are not looking for work. Obviously, to move a person who is basically happy and not looking for work costs money, and this can lead to bidding wars that drive up salaries and employers' costs.

### Direct Applicants and Referrals

**Direct applicants**
People who apply for a job vacancy without prompting from the organization.

**Referrals**
People who are prompted to apply for a job by someone within the organization.

**Direct applicants** are people who apply for a vacancy without prompting from the organization. **Referrals** are people who are prompted to apply by someone within the organization. These two sources of recruits share some characteristics that make them excellent sources from which to draw.

First, many direct applicants are to some extent already "sold" on the organization. Most of them have done some homework and concluded that there is enough fit between themselves and the vacancy to warrant their submitting an application. This process is called *self-selection*. A form of aided self-selection occurs with referrals. Many job seekers look to friends, relatives, and acquaintances to help find employment, and evoking these social networks can greatly aid the job search process for both the job seeker and the organization. Current employees (who are knowledgeable of both the vacancy and the person they are referring) do their homework and conclude that there is a fit between the person and the vacancy; they then sell the person on the job. In terms of motivating employee referrals, generally, employees receive from $250 for entry-level positions to more than $25,000 for top executives, with the most common bonus falling between $1,000 and $2,500.[84]

In the war for talent, some employers who try to entice one new employee from a competitor will often try to leverage that one person to try to entice even more people away. The term *liftout* has been coined for this practice of trying to recruit a whole team of people. The team chemistry and coordination that often takes years to build is already in place after a liftout, and this kind of speed provides competitive advantage. Of course, having a whole team lifted out of your organization is devastating, because customers are frequently the next to leave, following the talent rather than standing pat; hence, firms have to work hard to make sure they can retain their critical teams.

## Electronic Recruiting

There are many ways to employ the Internet and social media to recruit employees, and increasingly organizations are refining their use of this medium. Obviously, one of the easiest ways to get into "e-cruiting" is to simply use the organization's own website to solicit applications. By using their own website, organizations can highly tune their recruitment message and focus on specific people. For example, the interactive nature of this medium allows individuals to fill out surveys that describe what they are looking for and what they have to offer the organization. These surveys can be "graded" immediately, and recruits can be given direct feedback about how well they are matched for the organization. The value of steering recruits to company websites is so high that many employers will pay to have their sites rise to the top of the list in particular search engines when certain terms are entered.

Of course, smaller and less well-known organizations may not attract any attention to their own websites; thus, for them this is not a good option. A second way for organizations to use the Web is to interact with the large, well-known job boards sites such as Craigslist, Monster.com, or LinkedIn. These sites attract a vast array of applicants, who submit standardized résumés that can be searched electronically using key terms. Applicants can also search for companies in a similar fashion.

Each of these sites has its advantages and disadvantages. Since it is the most widely used, ads on Monster.com are viewed by thousands of potential applicants, but if not properly written, ads here can generate a large number of poorly qualified applicants. Craigslist is better for local ads focused on freelancers or part-time workers, but some users complain that it is too unregulated and susceptible to fake ads or scams that try to rip off applicants. LinkedIn is good for professionals and allows you to link into existing social networks; however, most of the people on this site already have jobs, and hence they may be costly to recruit.[85]

Social networking sites such as Facebook are yet another avenue for employers to reach out to younger workers in their own environments. Facebook does not allow employers to create pages as members, but it does allow them to purchase pages in order to create what is called a "sponsored group." Unlike more formal media, the conversations held here are very informal and serve as an easy first step for potential recruits to take in their relationship with the company. The downside is that the privacy of those conversations, cannot be always be guaranteed, and the ability to prevent applicants or other organizations from commenting on your ads may make it difficult to control your image.

However, it is critical to make sure that advertisements on outlets like Facebook do not discriminate based on age. Advertisements aimed at recruiting employees are qualitatively different from advertisements aimed at consumers. Target segmentation is a best practice when it comes to consumers, but a potentially illegal practice when used with employees. For example, one recent undercover investigation found that dozens of companies who bought Facebook ads aimed their messages to potential workers within limited age ranges. Applicants who were over 40 years of age could not even access the ads, which is a clear violation of the Age Discrimination Act.[86]

### Public and Private Employment Agencies

The Social Security Act of 1935 requires that everyone receiving unemployment compensation be registered with a local state employment office. These state employment offices work with the United States Employment Service (USES) to try to ensure that unemployed individuals eventually get off state aid and back on employer payrolls. To accomplish this, agencies collect information from the unemployed about their skills and experiences.

Employers can register their job vacancies with their local state employment office, and the agency will attempt to find someone suitable using its computerized inventory of local unemployed individuals. The agency makes referrals to the organization at no charge, and these individuals can be interviewed or tested by the employer for potential vacancies. Because of certain legislative mandates, state unemployment offices often have specialized "desks" for minorities, handicapped individuals, and Vietnam-era veterans. Thus, this is an excellent source for employers who feel they are currently underutilizing any of these subgroups.

Many states go far beyond just supporting their residents with public employment agencies. Some states engage in the kind of image advertising that we discussed earlier with respect to private employers. For example, Wisconsin launched a $1 million campaign in 2017 aimed directly at Chicago residents in an effort to get them to move to the Badger State. Like many other states in the Midwest, Wisconsin is experiencing a labor shortage attributable to an aging population, few immigrants, and low birth rates. The ads tried to emphasize quality of life issues that made living in Wisconsin cheaper, easier, and more fun than living in Chicago.[87] In addition to competing with other states for employees, as the Competing through Environmental, Social, and Governance Practices box shows, states also compete, perhaps too heatedly, when attracting employers.

Public employment agencies serve primarily the blue-collar labor market; private employment agencies perform much the same service for the white-collar labor market. Unlike public agencies, however, private employment agencies charge the organization for the referrals. Another difference between private and public employment agencies is that one doesn't have to be unemployed to use a private employment agency. One special type of private employment agency is the so-called executive search firm. These agencies are often referred to as *headhunters* because, unlike the other sources we have examined, they operate almost exclusively with people who are currently employed. Dealing with executive search firms is sometimes a sensitive process because executives may not want to advertise their availability for fear of their current employer's reaction.

## Economic Development: Tales of Regret, Renegotiation, and Rejection

States and local communities often lust for large employers to come into their region and bring the types of high-paying jobs that help politicians get re-elected. However, in some cases, the treasure that is given to employers in order to open up shop in a state may place such a burden on the local community that it is unsustainable after the deal is signed. In general, there has been a great deal of variance in the experiences of different local communities, some of which questions whether the bare-knuckle brawl between the states for jobs is always worth fighting.

For example, many consider the experience of the state of Ohio's seduction of Amazon .com a tale of regret. The state's private economic development agency, JobsOhio, gave Amazon $17 million in state tax incentives, $1.5 million in cash, as well as a 15-year waiver on property taxes to open a warehouse in Licking County. Once the plant was in full operational mode, however, local officials quickly came to realize that the costs associated with servicing the facility were not offset by any property tax revenue. The fire department alone would sometimes respond to three calls a day at the million-square-foot facility, the cost of which was eventually picked up by local taxpayers who were forced to pay a $6.5 million property tax

levy in order to keep the department on life support.

In Racine, Wisconsin, the decision by Foxconn to open up a new plant to produce large-screen TVs was initially celebrated but quickly turned to an opportunity for reappraisal as the project moved from conception to construction. The state originally pledged $3 billion in tax subsidies, reinforced by another $800 million from local authorities, in return for what they believed was going to be a 22 million-square-foot liquid-crystal, large screen, display-panel plant that would hire 13,000 factory workers. However, shortly after announcing the deal, Foxconn changed the plan from building large screens to small screens, a change that requires a smaller site and investment. Also, interviews with prospective employees seemed to suggest that most of the jobs were going to involve highly skilled engineering jobs rather than factory jobs. The supply of highly skilled engineering jobs in Wisconsin is much smaller than the supply for factory jobs, and it appeared that Foxconn could only meet its demand for skilled labor by bringing Chinese workers to Wisconsin. Fortunately, unlike what was the case in Ohio, the Wisconsin deal includes "performance-based incentives" that would rescind the state's offers if Foxconn fails to hit hiring, wage, and investment

targets, making this a story of potential ongoing renegotiation.

In contrast, the story of Tyson Foods' attempt to open up a new plant in Tonganoxie, Kansas, is ultimately a story of outright rejection. Although Tyson originally thought that its plan to build a huge, 320 million-square-foot chicken-processing plant in the town (supported by the state's Governor Sam Brownback) would be welcomed with open arms, instead a local grassroots movement in the community arose to block the deal. Residents objected to the plant, arguing that it would place too much stress on local roads and waterways. In addition, most residents in the community already had jobs, and were opposed to the influx of hundreds of outsiders into the town who were merely coming because they were attracted to the low-skill, low-wage jobs it created. Eventually, the Leavenworth County's Board of Commissioners rescinded their decision to open the plant.

Similarly, New York City also rejected the offer of Amazon to build a headquarters facility in Long Island City, citing similar problems to those that arouse back in Lick County, Ohio.

### DISCUSSION QUESTIONS

1. In many cases, the overly lucrative offers made by states to lure employers are attributable to states competing with other states.

*CONTINUED*

How does this competition within the nation affect overall national competitiveness when it comes to competing in the global economy? How does this potential "race-to-the-bottom" affect citizens of some states, especially when one considers that the politicians that struck these bargains may be long gone well after the effects are still in place?

2. What other steps might the government take to help individuals find new work when they are displaced by foreign trade?

SOURCES: M. Frazier, "Amazon Gets a Good Deal in Ohio," *Bloomberg Businessweek*, October 30, 2017; A. Carr, "Another Glorious Day in Trump's Manufacturing Paradise," *Bloomberg Businessweek*, February 11, 2019, pp. 54–61; "How Tyson's Chicken Plant Became a Turkey," *Bloomberg Businessweek*, October 16, 2017, pp. 17–19; A.J. Yale, "Amazon Backs Out of HQ Deal in New York City," *Forbes Online*, February 14, 2019.

### Colleges and Universities

Most colleges and universities have placement services that seek to help their graduates obtain employment. Indeed, on-campus interviewing is the most important source of recruits for entry-level professional and managerial vacancies. Organizations tend to focus especially on colleges that have strong reputations in areas for which they have critical needs (chemical engineering, public accounting, or the like). For example, colleges with strong reputations in the areas of science, technology, engineering, and mathematics (STEM) have been inundated with employers desperate to find workers with these skills. Research estimates that the demand for these workers is going to rise 15% between now and 2022, and this source of talent is critical particularly given the limit on H1-B visas that we dicsussed earlier.[88]

Many employers have found that to effectively compete for the best students, they need to do more than just sign up prospective graduates for interview slots. One of the best ways to establish a stronger presence on a campus is with a college internship program. These kinds of programs allow an organization to get early access to potential applicants and to assess their capacities directly. These programs also allow applicants to gain first-hand experience with the employer, so that both parties can make well-informed choices about fit with relatively low costs and commitment.[89]

Employers trying to lure college talent also find that programs that help students pay off their college loans are powerful tools. The Federal Reserve Bank estimates that there is $1.5 trillion in student debt that needs to be paid off, and increasingly hiring organizations are willing to take on some of the debt in return for a commitment from the student. For example, Abbott Laboratories will set aside an additional 5% of a new hires salary in a 401(k)-like investment if the employee is willing to place 2% of their salary in the same vehicle. Abbott hires over 1,000 college students every year, and the tax implications of this program make it much cheaper than raising salaries, while still highly attractive to students.[90]

In some of the toughest labor markets, employers have bypassed colleges and gone straight to high schools. Online coding tutorials and collaborative Web communities have made it possible for many high school students to develop their own applications well before they reach the age to go to college. If these apps become successful, then the coder who created them immediately draws attention from recruiters. For example, Facebook recruited Michael Saymen when he was just 16 years old after learning that the game he built using Facebook's development tools had attracted more than 500,000 players.[91]

### Evaluating the Quality of a Source

Because there are few rules about the quality of a given source for a given vacancy, it is generally a good idea for employers to monitor the quality of all their recruitment sources. One means of accomplishing this is to develop and compare yield ratios for each source.

**Table 5.4**

Hypothetical Yield Ratios for Five Recruitment Sources

| | RECRUITING SOURCE | | | | |
|---|---|---|---|---|---|
| | LOCAL UNIVERSITY | RENOWNED UNIVERSITY | EMPLOYEE REFERRALS | NEWSPAPER ADS | EXECUTIVE SEARCH FIRMS |
| Résumés generated | 200 | 400 | 50 | 500 | 20 |
| Interview offers accepted | 175 | 100 | 45 | 400 | 20 |
| Yield ratio | 87% | 25% | 90% | 80% | 100% |
| Applicants judged acceptable | 100 | 95 | 40 | 50 | 19 |
| Yield ratio | 57% | 95% | 89% | 12% | 95% |
| Accept employment offers | 90 | 10 | 35 | 25 | 15 |
| Yield ratio | 90% | 11% | 88% | 50% | 79% |
| Cumulative yield ratio | 90/200 | 10/400 | 35/50 | 25/500 | 15/20 |
| | 45% | 3% | 70% | 5% | 75% |
| Cost | $30,000 | $50,000 | $15,000 | $20,000 | $90,000 |
| Cost per hire | $333 | $5,000 | $428 | $800 | $6,000 |

Yield ratios express the percentage of applicants who successfully move from one stage of the recruitment and selection process to the next. Comparing yield ratios for different sources helps determine which is best or most efficient for the type of vacancy being investigated.

Table 5.4 shows hypothetical yield ratios and cost-per-hire data for five recruitment sources. For the job vacancies generated by this company, the best two sources of recruits are local universities and employee referral programs. Newspaper ads generate the largest number of recruits, but relatively few of these are qualified for the position. Recruiting at nationally renowned universities generates highly qualified applicants, but relatively few of them ultimately accept positions. Finally, executive search firms generate a small list of highly qualified, interested applicants, but this is an expensive source compared with other alternatives.

## RECRUITERS

The last part of the model presented in Figure 5.3 that we will discuss is the recruiter. Many applicants approach the recruiter with some degree of skepticism. Knowing that it is the recruiter's job to sell them on a vacancy, some applicants may discount what the recruiter says relative to what they have heard from other sources (like friends, magazine articles, and professors). For these and other reasons, recruiters' characteristics and behaviors seem to have less impact on applicants' job choices than we might expect.

Most organizations use both HR specialists and line managers when it comes to working with applicants. The HR specialist is an expert on employment at the company as a whole, and the line manager is best for sharing details about the exact nature of the work. Two traits stand out with applicants' reactions to either type of recruiter. The first is "warmth," which reflects the degree to which the recruiter seems to care about the applicant and is enthusiastic about her potential to contribute to the company.

**LO 5-6**

Explain the recruiter's role in the recruitment process, the limits the recruiter faces, and the opportunities available.

The second characteristic could be called "informativeness." In general, applicants respond more positively to recruiters who are perceived as warm and informative. In addition, timing seems to play a role as well, in the sense that recruiters have a bigger impact early in the job search process, but then give way to job and organizational characteristics when it comes down to the applicant's final decision.[92]

Perhaps the most well-researched aspect of recruiting deals with the level of realism that the recruiter incorporates into his message. Because the recruiter's job is to attract candidates, there is some pressure to exaggerate the positive features of the vacancy while downplaying the negative features. Applicants are highly sensitive to negative information. However, if the recruiter goes too far in a positive direction, the candidate can be misled and lured into taking the job under false pretenses.

Many studies have looked at the capacity of "realistic job previews" to circumvent this problem and help minimize early job turnover. On the whole, the research indicates that realistic job previews do lower expectations and can help reduce future turnover in the workforce. Certainly, the idea that one can go overboard in selling a vacancy to a recruit has merit.[93] However, the belief that informing people about the negative characteristics of the job will totally "inoculate" them to such characteristics seems unwarranted, based on the research conducted to date. Thus, we return to the conclusion that an organization's decisions about personnel policies that directly affect the job's attributes (pay, security, advancement opportunities, and so on) will probably be more important than recruiter traits and behaviors in affecting job choice.

## A LOOK BACK

### Addressing Labor Shortages and Surpluses: Exploring Your Options

We opened this chapter with a story of how domestic labor shortages in the United States, caused by a variety of factors, are so severe that many employers face an existential threat. We also saw showed how some companies are relying on enhanced training, outsourcing, automation, immigration, and offshoring of work in stay competitive and survive. There are advantages and disadvantages to recruiting workers from different sources, and we highlighted the strengths and weaknesses of alternative methods for addressing a labor shortage or a labor surplus.

**QUESTIONS**

1. Discuss the advantages and disadvantages of hiring local workers versus off-shoring versus bringing in immigrant labor? How does the nature of the product market affect what you might do in the labor market?
2. Assume you are a well-established company that, instead of facing a labor shortage, was now facing a labor surplus in some job category. Why might it be in your best interest to use some method other than layoffs to reduce this surplus, and why are your options a function of how well you did in terms of forecasting labor demand and supply?
3. Discuss the advantages and disadvantages of promoting workers from within your own firm versus going outside the firm to bring in external hires. How does the nature of the business situation affect this decision?

## SUMMARY

Human resource planning uses labor supply and demand forecasts to anticipate labor shortages and surpluses. It also entails programs that can be utilized to reduce a labor surplus (such as downsizing and early retirement programs) and eliminate a labor shortage (like bringing in temporary workers or expanding overtime). When done well, human resource planning can enhance the success of the organization while minimizing the human suffering resulting from poorly anticipated labor surpluses or shortages. Human resource recruiting is a buffer activity that creates an applicant pool that the organization can draw from in the event of a labor shortage

that is to be filled with new hires. Organizational recruitment programs affect applications through personnel policies (such as promote-from-within policies or due process provisions) that affect the attributes of the vacancies themselves. They can also impact the nature of people who apply for positions by using different recruitment sources (like recruiting from universities versus advertising in newspapers). Finally, organizations can use recruiters to influence individuals' perceptions of jobs (eliminating misconceptions, clarifying uncertainties) or perceptions of themselves (changing their valences for various work outcomes).

## KEY TERMS

Forecasting, 199
Leading indicator, 200
Transitional matrix, 201
Downsizing, 204

Outsourcing, 209
Offshoring, 210
Workforce utilization review, 218
Human resource recruitment, 219

Due process policies, 220
Employment-at-will policies, 220
Direct applicants, 222
Referrals, 222

## DISCUSSION QUESTIONS

1. Discuss the effects that an impending labor shortage might have on the following three subfunctions of human resource management: selection and placement, training and career development, and compensation and benefits. Which subfunction might be affected most heavily? In what ways might these groups develop joint cooperative programs to avert a labor shortage?
2. Discuss the costs and benefits associated with statistical versus judgmental forecasts for labor demand and labor supply. Under what conditions might either of these techniques be infeasible? Under what conditions might both be feasible, but one more desirable than the other?
3. Some companies have detailed affirmative action plans, complete with goals and timetables, for women and minorities, and yet have no formal human resource plan for the organization as a whole. Why might this be the

case? If you were a human resource specialist interviewing with this company for an open position, what would this practice imply for the role of the human resource manager in that company?
4. Recruiting people for jobs that entail international assignments is increasingly important for many companies. Where might one go to look for individuals interested in these types of assignments? How might recruiting practices aimed at these people differ from those one might apply to the "average" recruit?
5. Discuss the relative merits of internal versus external recruitment. What types of business strategies might best be supported by recruiting externally, and what types might call for internal recruitment? What factors might lead a firm to decide to switch from internal to external recruitment or vice versa?

## SELF-ASSESSMENT EXERCISE

Also assignable in Connect.

Most employers have to evaluate hundreds of résumés each week. If you want your résumé to have a good chance of being read by prospective employers, you must invest time

and energy not only in its content but also in its appearance. Review your résumé and answer yes or no to each of the following questions.

1. Does it avoid typos and grammatical errors?
2. Does it avoid using personal pronouns (such as I and me)?
3. Does it clearly identify what you have done and accomplished?
4. Does it highlight your accomplishments rather than your duties?
5. Does it exceed two pages in length?
6. Does it have correct contact information?
7. Does it have an employment objective that is specific and focuses on the employer's needs as well as your own?
8. Does it have at least one-inch margins?
9. Does it use a maximum of two typefaces or fonts?
10. Does it use bullet points to emphasize your skills and accomplishments?
11. Does it avoid use of underlining?
12. Is the presentation consistent? (Example: If you use all caps for the name of your most recent workplace, do you do that for previous workplaces as well?)

The more "yes" answers you gave, the more likely your résumé will attract an employer's attention and get you a job interview!

# EXERCISING STRATEGY

## America's Got Talent: But Still Needs More H1-B Visas

Although the war for talent is often focused on companies, the battle for the world's best workers also takes place at the national level, and countries need to decide how to compete in this space. For example, in the global war for talent, one measure of success is the number of Nobel Prizes awarded to citizens from different countries. Four countries are clearly winning in this war; however, these countries are increasingly accomplishing this via immigrants rather than native-born citizens. Specifically, over 30% of Nobel Prizes awarded in the last 30 years have gone to immigrants, and more than 50% of those went to immigrants working in the United States. Indeed, over 50% of U.S. startups worth over $1 billion were founded by an immigrant. Although trailing the United States on this metric, Great Britain, Australia, and Canada are the other three clear winners in this competition, whereas India, China, and the Philippines are the clearest losers when it comes to this international brain drain.

The United States's ability to maintain this status, however, is increasingly threatened by strategic changes in immigration policies that may restrict the flow of talent into the country. When it comes to highly skilled workers, the H1-B is critical because it allows highly skilled workers in areas where there are shortages of labor to work in the country for three years.

Recent changes in immigration policies and a shortage of such visas, however, are leaving human resource managers in high-tech fields struggling to fill critical jobs. This, plus the general perception that the United States is increasingly unfriendly toward foreign workers is considered a major threat to employers such as Google, Amazon, Microsoft, and Facebook who alone employ over 100,000 people who are part of the H1-B program. Facebook CEO Mark Zuckerberg spoke for many in the industry when he stated that "we need to keep this country safe, but we should do that by focusing on people who actually pose a threat."

### QUESTIONS

1. How does the increased difficulty of working in the United States create exploitable opportunities for countries like India, China, and the Philippines when it comes to plugging their brain drain?
2. What can a country like the United States do to decrease its reliance on immigration to fill high-tech jobs?

SOURCES: A. Creighton, "Four Nations Are Winning the Global War for Talent," *The Wall Street Journal Online*, www.wsj.com, October 18, 2016; M. Jordan, "Demand for H1-B Skilled Worker Visas Forces Agency into Lottery," *The Wall Street Journal Online*, www.wsj.com, April 7, 2016; E. Huet and G. DeVynck, "America's Got No Talent," *Bloomberg Businessweek*, November 21, 2016, pp 32–33; "Google Criticizes Impact on Staff of Trump Immigration Order," *The Wall Street Journal Online*, www.wsj.com, January 28, 2017.

# MANAGING PEOPLE

## Biting the Hand That Feeds You?

California's central valley is home to some of the nation's most fertile farmland. Over 6 million people live in the area, and the fields bring in $35 billion a year in revenue. It is a bustling region in a state that provides the United States with more of its food than any other state. However, in 2016, large portions of the annual crop rotted in the fields due to the inability of employers to find workers to harvest the wide variety of produce grown in the valley. In general, California's agricultural economy reported lost production across the board of 8 to 10% that year, and some individual growers lost over 25% of their crop due to labor shortages caused by crackdowns on illegal workers from Mexico.

Further east, meat producers in the Midwest also experienced similar problems with labor shortages that limited production. Already burned by hiring illegal immigrants in prior years, only to watch them be deported, meat producers changed their strategy 10 years ago, and turned to a new supply of labor—refugees—to solve their chronic labor shortage problem. U.S. regulations allow refugees to work as soon as they arrive in the country and over the years, the share of immigrant labor in Midwest slaughterhouses has grown to 35% many of which come from Somalia. However, this strategy was upended in 2017 when U.S. policy placed restriction on refugees entering the country, cutting this supply of labor in half. Like produce, meat is a commodity that needs to be processed in a timely fashion, and thus labor shortages also threaten the viability of this segment of the economy, worth $29 billion.

The common element to the problems plaguing these two industries is that the nature of the work is so undesirable that no native-born Americans would be willing to take these jobs. The work is very physically demanding and conducted in either the scorching hot sun or within freezing ice coolers at very low pay. However, the strategy of relying on illegal workers and refugees to plug this labor gap is becoming increasingly untenable, leaving the human resource management professionals in these industries struggling to meet the demand for labor.

H2-A visas are temporary visas issued strictly to farmworkers, and back in California, employers are trying to get the government to raise the number of H2-As but they are running into stiff political opposition. This has also been the experience of large meat producers who have been unable to get relief from the limits on refugees, many of which come from predominantly Muslim countries. Joseph Pezzini, COO of Ocean Mist farms, notes that when it comes to feeding the nation, "labor has always been an important part of what we do, but there were other resources issues that would take center stage like safety or water. But now the highest priority issue is the availability of labor"

**QUESTIONS**

1. What are some alternatives to the use of immigrants and refugees when it comes to addressing a labor shortage for jobs that are unattractive to U.S. workers?
2. One response to labor shortages is to raise pay. Why is this option seemingly "off-the-table" when it comes to agriculture jobs versus manufacturing jobs?

SOURCES: C. Dickerson and J. Medina, "California Farmers Backed Trump, but Now Fear Losing Field Workers," *The New York Times Online*, February 9, 2017; K. Gee and J. Bunge, "Tighter Refugee Rules Seen Squeezing Meat Companies," *The Wall Street Journal Online*, www.wsj.com, January 28, 2017; "Big Meat Braces for a Labor Shortage," *Bloomberg Businessweek*, February 8, 2017, pp. 19–21; I. Brat, "On U.S. Farms, Fewer Hands for the Harvest," *The Wall Street Journal Online*, www.wsj.com, August 12, 2015.

# HR IN SMALL BUSINESS

## For Personal Financial Advisors, a Small Staffing Plan with a Big Impact

Robert J. Reed has been a financial planner since 1978 and received his certified financial planner designation in 1981. In 1999, he hired Lucy Banquer, a former legal secretary, to work as his assistant and the only employee at his firm, Personal Financial Advisors LLC in Covington, Louisiana. At that point, human resource planning wasn't on Reed's radar at all.

But around 2005, Reed began to act on a desire to have a more complete plan for his firm's growth. He determined that he wanted the business to grow from about $400,000 in annual revenues to become a million-dollar firm by 2012. That was a realistic goal, but not one he could achieve with only the support of Banquer. Although Banquer does an excellent job of fielding client phone calls and answering questions, Reed needed to bring in more financial expertise to serve more clients.

Typically, a financial-planning firm like Reed's expands by hiring an entry-level advisor to handle routine tasks while learning on the job until he or she can take on clients independently. But Reed didn't simply take the usual path; he considered what role he wanted for himself in his firm as it grew.

Reed realized that the part he excelled at and loved most was managing the investments, not the presentations to clients, and that he wanted the firm to grow in a way that would free more time for him to spend with his family, not expand his hours to supervise others. As Reed defined the scope of his own desired job, he clarified what he wanted from his next employee: a certified financial planner who had experience plus an interest in all the planning and advising tasks *except* investment management.

With that strategy in mind, Reed began the search for another planner to work with him. After about eight months of recruiting, Reed met Lauren Gadkowski, who was running her own advisory firm in Boston but preparing to relocate to Baton Rouge to be with her future husband, Lee Lindsay. Reed wanted his new financial planner to operate independently, so he agreed to the idea of her office being in Baton Rouge, about a 45-minute drive from his, and he let her determine how often she would need to visit the Covington office.

Reed stuck to his plan: Lauren Lindsay quickly began working with Reed's larger clients and introduced herself as their main contact with the firm. After sitting in on a few meetings to satisfy himself that he had made a good hiring decision, Reed shifted his efforts to managing the investments. About 10% of the clients indicated they would prefer to maintain their working relationship with Reed. Lindsay took over the remaining 90% as well as the new clients she has brought into the firm since joining it.

Reed's decision to focus on investment management has paid off for Personal Financial Advisors, giving the firm better-than-average performance on its investments even as revenues have climbed. And with Lindsay on board to handle client contact, Reed became able to follow the more traditional path to further growth by hiring an associate financial planner, David Hutchinson, in 2008. In contrast to Lindsay, Hutchinson is still preparing to become a certified financial planner, but he has an educational background in financial planning and experience as an investment broker.

## QUESTIONS

1. Is a company ever too small to need to engage in human resource planning? Why or why not? Discuss whether you think Robert Reed planned his hiring strategy at an appropriate time in the firm's growth.
2. Using Table 5.3, review the options for avoiding a labor shortage, and discuss how well the options besides new hires could have worked as ways for Reed to reach his goals for growth. As you do so, consider qualities of a financial-planning business that might be relevant (for example, direct client contact and the need for confidentiality).
3. Suppose that when Reed was seeking to hire a certified financial planner, he asked you for advice on where to recruit this person. Which sources would you suggest, and why?

SOURCES: Angie Herbers, "Letting Go," *Investment Advisor*, June 2009, pp. 96–97; Personal Financial Advisors, "Why Choose Us?", corporate website, http://www.mypfa.com.

# NOTES

1. G. Motevalli, "Iran's Latest Headache: A Brain Drain," *Bloomberg Businessweek*, May 18, 2014, pp. 18–19.
2. S. Dume, "Gita Gopinath and India's Brain Drain," *The Wall Street Journal Online*, October 4, 2018.
3. D. Clark and C. Dulaney, "Qualcomm to Cut 15% of Workforce," *Wall Street Journal*, July 22, 2015.
4. J. Light, "Mamas, Don't Let Your Babies Grow Up to Be Appraisers," *Bloomberg Businessweek*, July 17, 2017, pp. 29–30.
5. D. Molinski, "Oil Layoffs Hit 100,000 and Counting," *Wall Street Journal*, April 14, 2015.
6. D. Wethe, "Drilling Is Back, What about the Workers?" *Bloomberg Businessweek,* January 30, 2017, pp. 14–15.
7. L. Patton, "The Latest Shortage: Fast-Food Workers," *Bloomberg Businessweek*, January 16, 2017.
8. G. Beach, "The Dog Fight for Tech Talent," *Wall Street Journal*, August 18, 2014, http://blogs.wsj.com.
9. K. Hudson, "Labor Shortage Bests Home Builders," *Wall Street Journal*, May 1, 2014.
10. C. Kirkham, "Trump Immigration Rules Likely to Exacerbate Home Builders' Labor Shortfall," *Wall Street Journal*, www.wsj.com, January 28, 2017.
11. P. M. Barrett, "Big Law: The Future," *Bloomberg Businessweek*, May 2, 2013, pp. 53–58.
12. N. Scheiber, "An Expensive Law Degree and Nowhere to Use It," *New York Times,* June 17, 2016.
13. N. Sano, K. Inoue, and J. Clenfield, "Why Japan's Automakers Are Finally Recruiting Women," *Bloomberg Businessweek*, May 21, 2018, pp. 17–18.
14. C. C. Miller and R. Fremson, "Forget about Stigma: Male Nurses Explain Why Nursing Is a Job of the Future for Men," *The New York Times Online*, January 4, 2018.
15. T. R. Homan and Z. Tracer, "The Long-Term Jobless Are Being Left Behind," *Bloomberg Businessweek*, August 9, 2010, pp. 53–54.
16. S. Ovide, "Microsoft to Cut Up to 18,000 Jobs," *Wall Street Journal*, July 17, 2014.
17. S. E. Ante, "H-P Slashes up to 16,000 More Jobs," *Wall Street Journal*, May 22, 2014.
18. D. Gates, "Boeing Plans Buyouts, Layoffs for Engineers in First of Three Cuts for 2017," *Seattle Times*, January 10, 2017.
19. B. Bremner, "Japan Releases a Robot Revolution," *Bloomberg Businessweek*, May 28, 2015.
20. R. Foroohar and B. Shaparito, "Made in the USA," *Time*, April 11, 2013, pp. 22–29.
21. C. Passareillo and S. Kapner, "Search for Ever Cheaper Garment Factories Leads to Africa," *Wall Street Journal*, July 8, 2015.
22. T. Amabile and R. Conti, "Changes in the Work Environment for Creativity During Downsizing," *Academy of Management Journal* 42 (2017), pp. 1203–25.
23. J. Tozzi and B. Greeley, "Making It Up as We Go," *Bloomberg Businessweek*, October 26, 2014, pp. 27–28.
24. J. S. Lublin, "How to Be a Good Boss—The Second Time Around," *Wall Street Journal*, January 9, 2014.
25. A. Mishra and G. M. Spreitzer, "Explaining How Survivors Respond to Downsizing: The Roles of Trust, Empowerment, Justice, and Work Design," *Academy of Management Review*, 2017, pp. 617–36.
26. C. O. Trevor and A. J. Nyberg, "Keeping Your Headcount When All About You Are Losing Theirs: Downsizing, Voluntary Turnover Rates, and the Moderating Role of HR Practices," *Academy of Management Journal* 51 (2008), pp. 259–76.
27. D. Belkin, "Colleges Trim Staffing Bloat," *Wall Street Journal*, December 25, 2013.
28. J. Marquez, "The Would-Be Retirees," *Workforce Management*, November 3, 2008, pp. 24–28.
29. C. Hymowitz, "Me, Retire?" *Bloomberg Businessweek*, October 2, 2017, pp. 47–48.
30. G. De Vynck, "IBM's Retirement Plan," *Bloomberg Businessweek*, September 24, 2018, pp. 23–25.
31. J. Green, "Chowing Down on Boomers' Brains," *Bloomberg Businessweek*, January 21, 2016, pp. 19–20.
32. M. Ramsey, "Toyota Offers U.S. Workers Retirement Incentives," *Wall Street Journal*, November 30, 2012.
33. M. Zuckerman, "The Full-Time Scandal of Part-Time America," *Wall Street Journal*, July 13, 2014.
34. L. Weber, "The End of Employees," *Wall Street Journal*, February 7, 2017.
35. N. Irwin, "With 'Gigs' Instead of Jobs, Workers Bear New Burdens," *New York Times*, March 31, 2016.

36. C. Matlack and N. Leiber, "Empleado Ymiserable," *Bloomberg Businessweek,* July 4, 2015.

37. J. Eidelson, "Unionize Me," *Bloomberg Businessweek,* January 16, 2017.

38. S. Riordan, "An Uber Shakedown," *Wall Street Journal,* April 24, 2016.

39. E. Zlomek, "Why Hire an MBA When You Can Rent One," *Bloomberg Businessweek,* October 24, 2013, pp. 60-62.

40. A. Vance, "Emerald Therapeutics: Biotech Lab for Hire," *Bloomberg Businessweek,* July 3, 2014.

41. E. Newcomer, "This Time, It's HR Getting Fired," *Bloomberg Businessweek,* May 21, 2015.

42. N. E. Boudette, "Ford Criticized by Trump, Cancels Plans to Build Mexican Plant," *New York Times,* January 3, 2017.

43. S. Pettypiece, "This Owl Won't Save American Jobs," *Bloomberg Businessweek,* July 26. 2016, pp. 14-15.

44. P. McDougall, "Bored of the USA?: 'Made in America' Jeans Maker Levi Strauss to Move 500 Jobs Offshore," *International Business Times,* November 13, 2014.

45. L. Burkitt and J. Bunge, "Meat Supplier's CEO Apologizes for China Unit," *Wall Street Journal,* July 23, 2014.

46. S. Lohr, "Hot Spot for Tech Outsourcing: The United States," *The New York Times Online,* July 30, 2017.

47. K. Weise, "Send Us Your Educated Masses," *Bloomberg Businessweek,* May 23, 2013, p. 30.

48. R. Johnson, "Import Food—or Labor," *Bloomberg Businessweek,* June 11, 2018, p. 6

49. M. Jamriso, "I Need More Mexicans," *Bloomberg Businessweek,* June 26, 2017, pp. 26-27

50. M. Newkirk "The South's Pretend War on Immigration," *Bloomberg Businessweek,* August 27, 2018, pp. 36-37

51. J. A. Mackenzie, "Cold as ICE," *Workforce,* August, 2018, pp. 20-21.

52. M. L. Slaughter, "How America Loses a Job Every 43 Seconds," *Wall Street Journal,* March 25, 2014.

53. P. Coy, "An Inconvenient Myth about Free Trade," *Bloomberg Businessweek,* May 31, 2016, p. 6-7.

54. P. Coy, "An Inconvenient Myth About Free Trade," *Bloomberg Businessweek,* May 1, 2016, p. 6-7.

55. J. Brustein, "The Secret Way Silicon Valley Uses the H1-B Visa Program," *Bloomberg Businessweek,* June 6, 2017, pp. 26-28

56. M. D. Shear, "Planned Trump Order Will Discourage Hiring of Low-Wage Foreign Workers," *The New York Times Online,* April 18, 2017.

57. M. V. Rafter, "Hiring and the H1-B Visa," *Workforce,* September 2017, pp. 44-48.

58. E. Shine and S. Rastello, "Laid Off Indian High Tech Workers Blame Trump," *Bloomberg Businessweek,* May 23, 2017, pp. 14-15.

59. K. Weise and S. Rai, "The American Dream Leads to Canada," *Bloomberg Businessweek,* April 23, 2018.

60. K. Weise, "How to Hack a Visa Limit," *Bloomberg Businessweek,* June 1, 2014.

61. P. Shulman, "Why Refugee Doctors Become Taxi Drivers," *CNN Online,* August 9, 2017.

62. A. Betts, "The Data Driven Argument for Putting Refugees Back to Work," *Bloomberg Businessweek,* July 31, 2017, p. 68.

63. D. J. Boudreaux and L. Palagashilivi, "Working Overtime to Avoid the Truth," *Wall Street Journal,* April 7, 2016.

64. B. Greeley, "The Incredible Stickiness of Wages," *Bloomberg Businessweek,* April 10, 2015.

65. K. Davidson, "Trump Says He Will Eliminate Pay Raises for Federal Employees Next Year," *The Wall Street Journal Online,* August 30, 2018.

66. L. Woellert, "Half the Hours, Most of the Pay," *Bloomberg Businessweek,* January 31, 2013, pp. 23-24.

67. R. Randazza, "Honeywell Employees Told to Take Furloughs," *Arizona Republic,* May 25, 2016.

68. C. Tuna, "Weighing Furlough vs. Layoff," *Wall Street Journal,* April 13, 2009, p. B6.

69. M. Abelson and J. Holman, "Black Executives Are Losing Ground at Some Big Banks," *Bloomberg Businessweek,* July 31, 2017, pp. 25-27.

70. C. Suddath, "Girl Code," *Bloomberg Businessweek,* May 13, 2015.

71. V. Vara, "Why Doesn't Silicon Valley Hire Black Coders," *Bloomberg Businessweek,* January 21, 2016, pp. 40-45.

72. I. Hideg and J. L. Michela, "Overcoming Negative Reactions of Nonbeneficiaries of Employment Equity: The Effect of Participation in Policy Formulation," *Journal of Applied Psychology* 96 (2013), pp. 363-76.

73. A. E. Barber, J. R. Hollenbeck, S. L. Tower, and J. M. Phillips, "The Effects of Interview Focus on Recruitment Effectiveness: A Field Experiment," *Journal of Applied Psychology* 79 (1994), pp. 886-96.

74. P. Yakuel, "Why Promoting from Within Works," *Forbes Online,* June 20, 2018.

75. R. E. Silverman and L. Weber, "An Inside Job: More Firms Opt to Recruit from Within," *Wall Street Journal,* May 29, 2012.

76. C. Palmeri, "Carnival Rocks the Boat," *Bloomberg Businessweek,* November 12, 2015, pp. 22-23.

77. C. M. Harold, B. C. Holtz, B. K. Griepentrog, L. M. Brewer, and S. M. Marsh, "Investigating the Effects of Applicant Justice Perceptions on Job Offer Acceptance," *Personnel Psychology,* 69 (2016), pp. 199-227.

78. J. Smialek and R. Miller, "Wages Bounce Back," *Bloomberg Businessweek,* November 12, 2015, pp. 16-18.

79. R. Adams-Heard, "Heat and Dust, But Also Free Wi-Fi," *Bloomberg Businessweek,* August 13, 2018, pp. 34-35.

80. J. Robertson and M. Riley, "Drop and Give Me 20 Lines of Code," *Bloomberg Businessweek,* July 9, 2015.

81. S. Vranica, "'I'm Sorry' Gets More Expensive for Wells, Uber and Facebook," *The Wall Street Journal Online,* May 30, 2018.

82. B. W. Swider, R. D. Zimmerman, and M. R. Barrick, "Searching for the Right Fit: Development of Person-Organization Fit Perceptions during the Recruitment Process," *Journal of Applied Psychology* 100 (2015), pp. 880-93.

83. L. Kwoh, "Chief Executives Hired Internally Outlast, Outperform Their Rivals," *Wall Street Journal,* May 29, 2012.

84. R. Muerer, "Employee Referrals Remain Top Source for Recruits," *Society for Human Resource Management Online,* June 22, 2017.

85. S. Edwards, "The Pros and Cons of Popular Job Sites," *Inc. Online,* May 24, 2016.

86. J. Larson, "These Are the Job Ads You Can't See on Facebook If You're Older," *The New York Times Online,* December 19, 2017.

87. M. DeFour, "WEDC Launches $1 Million Advertising Campaign in Chicago," *Madison State Journal Online,* January 10, 2018.

88. M. V. Rafter, "Recruiting Down to a Science," *Workforce,* January 2016, pp. 36-39.

89. H. Zhao and R. C. Liden, "Internship: A Recruitment and Selection Perspective," *Journal of Applied Psychology* 96 (2011), pp. 221-29.

90. T. P. Chen, "Companies Lure New Workers with College Coaching, Student Debt Repayment," *The Wall Street Journal Online,* October 3, 2018.

91. S. Frier, "OMG, Best Summer Ever," *Bloomberg Businessweek,* July 20, 2014, pp. 31-32.

92. K. L. Uggerslev, N. E. Fassina, and D. Kraichy, "Recruiting through the Stages: A Meta-Analytic Test of Predictors of Applicant Attraction at Different Stages of the Recruiting Process," *Personnel Psychology* 65 (2012), pp. 597-660.

93. J. Sabel, "Four Types of Realistic Job Previews That Engage Qualified Candidates," *Glassdoor for Employers Online,* April 3, 2018.

# 6 Selection and Placement

## ⌐ LEARNING OBJECTIVES ¬

*After reading this chapter, you should be able to:*

**LO 6-1**  Establish the basic scientific properties of personnel selection methods, including reliability, validity, and generalizability. *page 237*

**LO 6-2**  Discuss how the particular characteristics of a job, an organization, or an applicant affect the utility of any test. *page 246*

**LO 6-3**  Describe the government's role in personnel selection decisions, particularly in the areas of constitutional law, federal laws, executive orders, and judicial precedent. *page 248*

**LO 6-4**  List the common methods used in selecting human resources. *page 254*

**LO 6-5**  Describe the degree to which each of the common methods used in selecting human resources meets the demands of reliability, validity, generalizability, utility, and legality. *page 254*

## When Strangers Meet in a World with No Background Checks

Most people growing up were probably told by their parents to "never accept a ride from a stranger." In today's age of ride-sharing apps, that advice probably seems quaint. Still, although quaint, it may also be tragically true. Ride-sharing companies exploded on the scene only very recently and quickly gained a major competitive advantage over traditional taxis and limousine services for a number of factors. One of the big factors was their hiring model, because unlike traditional driver services where employees had to undergo background checks (that included fingerprint records validated by state authorities), ride-sharing companies were allowed to skip this step. These checks are expensive and time consuming, sometimes taking over two weeks. By escaping this part of the regulatory process, companies like Uber were able to hire drivers cheaper, faster, and more flexibly relative to the competition. As one industry analyst noted, "Taxis and limos are still required to abide by the old more stringent rules, but with Uber, it's a free for all. It's become the Wild West."

There are now questions as to whether this source of competitive advantage is going to be sustainable, however. Recent evidence suggests that Uber was routinely hiring convicted criminals and exposing its customers to risks that they could not possible imagine. For example, a simple search on the Internet—a technology we can assume Uber is aware of—would have revealed to the company that Talal Chammout should never have been hired. He had been convicted of shooting a person, hitting his wife with a crowbar, hiring a hitman, and even attempting to smuggle in a rocket launcher as part of a terrorist plot. The young woman who stepped into his car one night was blithely unaware of this and was totally unprepared when he followed her into her apartment and sexually assaulted her.

Chammout won't be driving for Uber for the next 25 years while he serves his sentence in a federal prison, but regrettably, he is not an isolated case. Investigations into Uber drivers have revealed that the company hired thousands of convicted felons. There have been over 100 cases in just the last four years where Uber drivers were arrested for murder, sexual assault, or first degree assault. Although the company has policies that bar drivers from carrying firearms in their vehicles, it is impossible for them to enforce that policy. In order to protect themselves from the total strangers they pick up, many Uber drivers are packing heat—in many cases with unregistered firearms. In fact, the only aspect of Uber's selection practices that might be worse than their hiring standards and enforcement is that they actively lobbied local governments to protect this source of competitive advantage. In many cases, state and city lawmakers would pass bills that were written with language provided by lobbyists for the ride-sharing industry. As Saika Chen, an attorney who specializes in ride-sharing laws notes, "Lobbying is nothing new, but this is lobbying on steroids."

The sustainability of this form of competitive advantage is now being challenged, however, with lawsuits filed from both harmed passengers and state law enforcement agencies. For example, Uber was recently fined over $25 million by the District Attorneys from San Francisco and Los Angeles. Colorado's Public Utility Service fined Uber over $4 million for a "failure to protect public safety." Many other local jurisdictions, like sharks smelling blood in the water, are considering similar actions against what they see as a vulnerable and deep-pocketed potential defendant. Time will tell if Uber can withstand all of this pressure and survive, but the verdict

*CONTINUED*

is already in on its CEO, Travis Kalanick. He was forced to leave the company he founded due to the hostile culture he tolerated when it came to employees. Well, at least with respect to his own employees, perhaps he knew who he was dealing with.

SOURCES: C. Devine, N. Black, D. Girffin, and C. Roberts, "Thousands of Criminals Were Cleared to Be Uber Drivers, Here's How the Rideshare Companies Fought Harder Checks," *CNN Online*, June 1, 2018; R. Ellis and S. Jones, "Uber Driver Held after Fatal Shooting of Passenger in Denver," *CNN Online*, June 2, 2018; "Uber Embraces Major Reforms as Travis Kalanick, the CEO Steps Away," *The New York Times Online*, June 13, 2017.

# Introduction

Any organization that intends to compete through people must take the utmost care with how it chooses organizational members. These decisions have a critical impact on the organization's ability to compete, as well as on each and every job applicant's life. Organizations have to strive to make sure that the decisions they make with respect to who gets accepted or rejected for jobs promote the best interests of the company and are fair to all parties involved. Poorly informed decisions like the ones we saw at the beginning of this chapter harm everyone who comes into contact with such organizations.

Although the vignette that opened this chapter focused on Uber, similar concerns apply to job applicants who go on to commit other crimes. For example, the terrorist who killed 49 people in an Orlando nightclub, Omar Mateen, had been hired by the global security firm G4S, which issued him one of the weapons used in the fatal attack. G4S blamed this hiring decision on "a clerical error." The question then becomes whether one would trust their security needs to a company that would make such an egregious mistake with an otherwise simple background check.[1]

Many organizations seem to have forgotten how important it is to maintain hiring standards, especially when confronted with the labor shortages like we have witnessed in the last few years. For example, in 2018, many companies reacted to labor shortages by hiring people sight unseen. Applicants would call in a number and be interviewed on the phone, believing that if the phone call went well; they would get an onsite interview. Instead, most were hired right on the spot and told when and where to show up for work. This was so unprecedented that it raised concerns even among job applicants. In fact, when Jamari Powell was hired at Macy's after just a 20-minute phone interview, she noted that, "It was a little weird. It kind of feels like a scam almost."[2]

Selecting the best talent is critical to the competitiveness of organizations and nations. Innovation and economic growth are fueled by people, and the firms or countries that bring in the best people will be the ones that compete most successfully. For example, the United States has always tried to be a magnet for talent from other countries, and this country grew economically powerful due to the contributions of people who have emigrated from other countries. In contrast, the recent evidence suggests that Russia is losing its edge when it comes to keeping young talent in the country. The number of people emigrating from Russia and the former Soviet Union states jumped from 14,000 to 56,000 in just the last four years. Recent public demonstrations in Moscow and other Russian cities in protest of corruption have been the largest rallies ever seen, and most of the protesters were college students that represent the country's future.[3]

The purpose of this chapter is to familiarize you with ways to minimize errors in employee selection and placement and, in doing so, improve your company's competitive position when it comes to hiring winners. We focus first on five standards that any selection method should meet. Then we evaluate several common selection methods that meet those standards and discuss how these may be used to prevent companies from hiring low performing, dubious characters that may harm the firm's reputation.

# Selection Method Standards

Personnel selection is the process by which companies decide who will or will not be allowed into organizations. Several generic standards should be met in any selection process. We focus on five: (1) reliability, (2) validity, (3) generalizability, (4) utility, and (5) legality. The first four build off each other in the sense that the preceding standard is often necessary but not sufficient for the one that follows. This is less the case with legal standards. However, a thorough understanding of the first four standards helps us understand the rationale underlying many legal standards.

## RELIABILITY

Much of the work in personnel selection involves measuring characteristics of people to determine who will be accepted for job openings. For example, we might be interested in applicants' physical characteristics (like strength or endurance), their cognitive abilities (such as spatial memory or verbal reasoning), or aspects of their personality (like their decisiveness or integrity). Many people have inaccurate stereotypes about how these kinds of characteristics may be related to factors such as race, sex, age, or ethnic background; therefore, we need to get past these stereotypes and measure the actual attributes directly.[4] For example, with respect to jobs in the field of public safety, research employing fake résumés sent to employers found that white applicants with a criminal background were more likely to be hired than African American applicants with no criminal record but identical on all other attributes.[5]

One key standard for any measuring device is its reliability. We define **reliability** as the degree to which a measure is free from random error. If a measure of some supposedly stable characteristic such as intelligence is reliable, then the score a person receives based on that measure will be consistent over time and in different contexts.

**Reliability**
The consistency of a performance measure; the degree to which a performance measure is free from random error.

### Estimating the Reliability of Measurement

Most measurement in personnel selection deals with complex characteristics like intelligence, integrity, and leadership ability. However, to appreciate some of the complexities in measuring people, we will consider something concrete in discussing these concepts: the measurement of height. For example, if we were measuring an applicant's height, we might start by using a 12-inch ruler. Let's say the first person we measure turns out to be 6 feet, $1\frac{1}{4}$ inches tall. It would not be surprising to find out that someone else measuring the same person a second time, perhaps an hour later, found this applicant's height to be 6 feet, $\frac{3}{4}$ inches. The same applicant, measured a third time, maybe the next day, might be measured at 6 feet, $1\frac{1}{2}$ inches tall.

As this example makes clear, even though the person's height is a stable characteristic, we get slightly different results each time he is assessed. This means that each time the person is assessed, we must be making slight errors. If we used a measure of height that was not as reliable as a ruler—for example, guessing someone's height after seeing her walk across the room—we might see an even greater amount of unreliability in the measure. Thus *reliability* refers to the measuring instrument (a ruler versus a visual guess) rather than to the characteristic itself.

We can estimate reliability in several different ways, and because most of these rely on computing a correlation coefficient, we will briefly describe and illustrate this statistic. The *correlation coefficient* is a measure of the degree to which two sets of numbers are related. The correlation coefficient expresses the strength of the relationship in numerical form. A perfect positive relationship (as one set of numbers goes up, so does the other) equals $+1.0$; a perfect negative relationship (as one goes up, the other goes down) equals $-1.0$. When there is no relationship between the sets of numbers, the correlation equals $0.00$.

Although the actual calculation of this statistic goes beyond the scope of this book, it will be useful for us to conceptually examine the nature of the correlation coefficient and what this means in personnel selection contexts.

When assessing the reliability of a measure, for example, we might be interested in knowing how scores on the measure at one time relate to scores on the same measure at another time. Obviously, if the characteristic we are measuring is supposedly stable (like intelligence or integrity) and the time period is short, this relationship should be strong. If it were weak, then the measure would be inconsistent—hence, unreliable. This is called assessing *test–retest reliability*. Note that the time period between measurements is important when it comes to interpreting test–retest reliability. The assumption is that the characteristic being measured is not changing; hence, any change from Time 1 to Time 2 is treated as an error. When the time period becomes too long, this increases the chance that the characteristic itself is changing. For example, if one is measuring personality traits, the evidence suggests that people become more conscientious, more introverted, and more emotionally stable as they get older. These are not age stereotypes but rather scientifically documented facts about the instability of certain personality traits over extended periods of time.[6]

Plotting the two sets of numbers on a two-dimensional graph often helps us to appreciate the meaning of various levels of the correlation coefficient. Figure 6.1, for example, examines the relationship between student scholastic aptitude in one's junior and senior years in high school, where aptitude for college is measured in three ways: (1) via scores on the SAT (formerly known as the Scholastic Aptitude Test), (2) via ratings from a high school counselor on a 1-to-100 scale, and (3) via tossing dice. In this plot, each number on the graphs represents a person whose scholastic aptitude is assessed twice (in the junior and senior years), so in Figure 6.1a, 1 represents a person who scored 1580 on the SAT in the junior year and 1500 in the senior year; 20 represents a person who scored 480 in the junior year and 620 in the senior year.

Figure 6.1a shows a very strong relationship between SAT scores across the two years. This relationship is not perfect in that the scores changed from one year to the next but

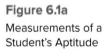

**Figure 6.1a**

Measurements of a Student's Aptitude

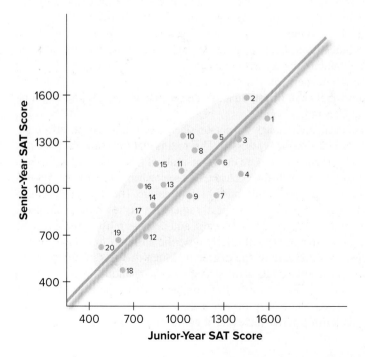

**Figure 6.1b**

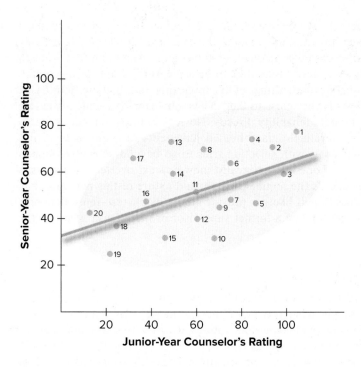

not by a great deal. Turning to Figure 6.1b, we see that the relationship between the high school counselors' ratings across the two years, while still positive, is not as strong. That is, the counselors' ratings of individual students' aptitudes for college are less consistent over the two years than are the students' test scores. This might be attributable to the fact the counselor's rating during the junior year was based on a smaller number of observations relative to the ratings made during senior year. Finally, Figure 6.1c shows a

**Figure 6.1c**

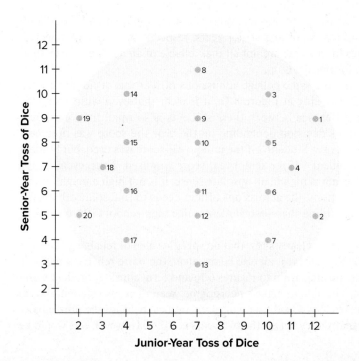

worst-case scenario, where the students' aptitudes are assessed by tossing two six-sided dice. As you would expect, the random nature of the dice means that there is virtually no relationship between scores taken in one year and scores taken the next. Although no one would seriously consider tossing dice to be a measure of aptitude, research shows that the correlation of overall ratings of job applicants' suitability for jobs based on unstructured interviews is very close to 0.00. Thus, one cannot assume a measure is reliable without checking its reliability directly. Novices in measurement are often surprised at exactly how unreliable many human judgments turn out to be. Thus, much of the science that deals with selection tries to go beyond subjective human judgments. So for example, if one wants to really know how extroverted a person is, a sociometric badge that records the number, length, and nature of this person's communication patterns across time is likely to provide more reliable test–retest data relative to the subjective perceptions of a former supervisor or interviewer who met the person just once.[7]

## Standards for Reliability

Regardless of what characteristic we are measuring, we want highly reliable measures. Thus, in the previous example, when it comes to measuring students' aptitudes for college, the SAT is more reliable than counselors' ratings, which in turn are more reliable than tossing dice. But in an absolute sense, how high is high enough—0.50, 0.70, 0.90? This is a difficult question to answer specifically because the required reliability depends in part on the nature of the decision being made about the people being measured.

For example, let's assume some college admissions officer was considering several students depicted in Figures 6.1a and 6.1b. Turning first to Figure 6.1b, assume the admissions officer was deciding between Student 1 and Student 20. For this decision, the 0.50 reliability of the ratings is high enough because the difference between the two students' counselors' ratings is so large that one would make the same decision for admissions regardless of the year in which the rating was taken. That is, Student 1 (with scores of 100 and 80 in the junior and senior years, respectively) is always admitted and Student 20 (with scores of 12 and 42 for junior and senior years, respectively) is always rejected. Thus, although the ratings in this case are not all that reliable in an absolute sense, their reliability is high enough for this decision.

By contrast, let's assume the same college admissions officer was deciding between Student 1 and Student 2. Looking at Figure 6.1a, it is clear that even with the highly reliable SAT scores, the difference between these students is so small that one would make a different admissions decision depending on the year the score was obtained. Student 1 would be selected over Student 2 if the junior-year score was used, but Student 2 would be chosen over Student 1 if the senior-year score was used. Thus, even though the reliability of the SAT exam is high in an absolute sense, it is not high enough for this decision. Under these conditions, the admissions officer needs to find some other basis for making the decision regarding these two students (like high school GPA or rank in graduating class).

Although these two scenarios clearly show that no specific value of reliability is always acceptable, they also demonstrate why, all else being equal, the more reliable a measure is, the better. For example, turning again to Figures 6.1a and 6.1b, consider Student 9 and Student 14. One would not be able to make a decision between these two students based on scholastic aptitude scores if assessed via counselors' ratings, because the unreliability in the ratings is so large that scores across the two years conflict. However, one would be able to base the decision on scholastic aptitude scores if assessed via the SAT, because the reliability of the SAT scores is so high that scores across the two years point to the same conclusion.

## VALIDITY

We define **validity** as the extent to which performance on the measure is related to performance on the job. A measure must be reliable if it is to have any validity. By contrast, we can reliably measure many characteristics (like height) that may have no relationship to whether someone can perform a job. For this reason, reliability is a necessary but insufficient condition for validity.

### Criterion-Related Validation

One way of establishing the validity of a selection method is to show that there is an empirical association between scores on the selection measure and scores for job performance. If there is a substantial correlation between test scores and job-performance scores, **criterion-related validity** has been established. For example, Figure 6.2 shows the relationship between 2014 scores on the SAT and 2015 freshman grade point average (GPA). In this example, there is roughly a 0.50 correlation between the SAT and GPA. This 0.50 is referred to as a *validity coefficient*. Note that we have used the correlation coefficient to assess both reliability and validity, which may seem somewhat confusing. The key distinction is that the correlation reflects a reliability estimate when we are attempting to assess the same characteristic twice (such as SAT scores in the junior and senior years), but the correlation coefficient reflects a validity coefficient when we are attempting to relate one characteristic (SAT) to performance on some task (GPA).

Criterion-related validity studies come in two varieties. **Predictive validation** seeks to establish an empirical relationship between test scores taken *prior* to being hired

**Validity**
The extent to which a performance measure assesses all the relevant—and only the relevant—aspects of job performance.

**Criterion-related validity**
A method of establishing the validity of a personnel selection method by showing a substantial correlation between test scores and job-performance scores.

**Predictive validation**
A criterion-related validity study that seeks to establish an empirical relationship between applicants' test scores and their eventual performance on the job.

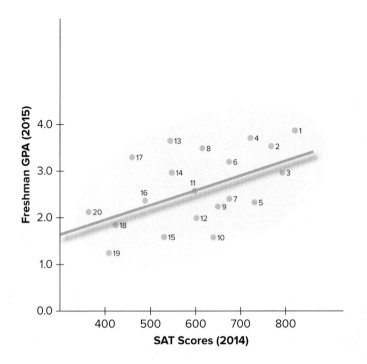

**Figure 6.2**

Relationship between 2014 SAT Scores and 2015 Freshman GPA

**Concurrent validation**
A criterion-related validity study in which a test is administered to all the people currently in a job and then incumbents' scores are correlated with existing measures of their performance on the job.

and eventual performance on the job. Because of the time and effort required to conduct a predictive validation study, many employers are tempted to use a different design. **Concurrent validation** assesses the validity of a test by administering it to people already on the job and then correlating test scores with existing measures of each person's performance. For example, the testing company Infor measures 39 behavioral, cognitive, and cultural traits among job applicants and then compares their scores on those dimensions with the top performers in the company. The assumption is that if high performers in the company score high on any trait, then the company should use scores on this trait to screen new hires.[8] Figure 6.3 compares the two types of validation study.

Despite the extra effort and time needed for predictive validation, it is superior to concurrent validation for a number of reasons. First, job applicants (because they are seeking work) are typically more motivated to perform well on the tests than are current employees (who already have jobs). Thus, job applicants are more tempted to fake responses in order to look good relative to current jobholders. Second, current

**Figure 6.3**

Graphic Depiction of Concurrent and Predictive Validation Designs

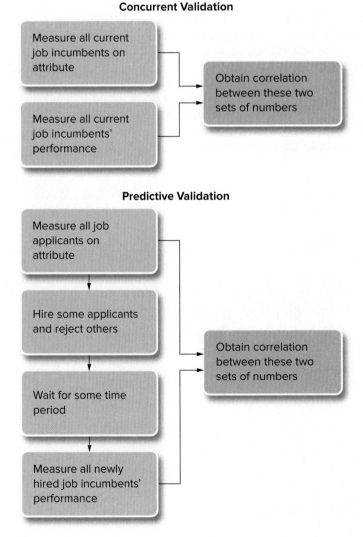

| SAMPLE SIZE | REQUIRED CORRELATION |
|---|---|
| 5 | 0.75 |
| 10 | 0.58 |
| 20 | 0.42 |
| 40 | 0.30 |
| 80 | 0.21 |
| 100 | 0.19 |

**Table 6.1**
Required Level of
Correlation to
Reach Statistical
Significance as a
Function of
Sample Size

employees have learned many things on the job that job applicants have not yet learned. Therefore, the correlation between test scores and job performance for current employees may not be the same as the correlation between test scores and job performance for less knowledgeable job applicants. Thus, although concurrent studies can sometimes help one to anticipate the results of predictive studies, they do not serve as substitutes.

Obviously, we would like our measures to be high in validity; but as with the reliability standard, we must also ask, how high is high enough? When trying to determine how much validity is enough, one typically has to turn to tests of statistical significance. A test of statistical significance answers the question, "Assuming that there is no true relationship between the predictor and the criterion, what are the odds of seeing a relationship this strong by chance alone?" If these odds are very low, then one might infer that the results from the test were in fact predicting future job performance.

Table 6.1 shows how big a correlation between a selection measure and a measure of job performance needs to be to achieve statistical significance at a level of 0.05 (that is, there is only a 5 out of 100 chance that one could get a correlation this big by chance alone). Although it is generally true that bigger correlations are better, the size of the sample on which the correlation is based plays a large role as well. Because many of the selection methods we examine in the second half of this chapter generate correlations in the 0.20s and 0.30s, we often need samples of 80 to 90 people. A validation study with a small sample (such as 20 people) is almost doomed to failure from the start.

Advances in the ability to process big data via cloud-based analytics is greatly expanding the ability to find valid predictors of future job performance. For example, in the past, when it came to staffing its call centers, Xerox Corporation always looked for applicants who had done the job before. This seemed like a reasonable approach to take until the company assessed the empirical relationship between experience, on the one hand, and performance and turnover, on the other hand, and learned that experience did not matter at all. Instead, what really separated winners and losers in this occupation was their personality. People who were creative tended to perform well and stay on the job for a long time, whereas those who were inquisitive tended to struggle with the job and leave well before the company ever recouped its $5,000 investment in training.

Xerox now leaves all hiring for its nearly 500,000 call center jobs to a computer software algorithm that tirelessly looks for links between responses to personality items and a highly specific set of job outcomes. The program was developed by Evolv Inc., and rather than relying on interviewer judgments that might be subject to personal biases, the Evolv program puts applicants through a battery of tests and personality items, then tracks their outcomes at the company over time. The algorithm is continually adjusting itself with the accumulation of ever more data, all in an effort to develop a statistical model that describes the ideal call center employee.[9]

Evolv is just one player in an expanding industry that seeks to use big data to help companies find and retain the best employees. Globally, spending on this sort of talent management software rose 15% in just one year to an estimated value of $3.8 billion, and the competition for this business is intense. Indeed, as the Competing through Technology box shows, the competition in this business involves not just hiring the right person, but assembling a number of "right persons" into a team. This is important because organizations are increasingly structured in teams, and many organizations are often disappointed when a set of individuals who all look great on paper and when working alone, fall apart or become problems when working interdependently with others.[10] Indeed, some have suggested that organizations should recruit only intact teams, rather than individuals who are then assembled into arbitrary teams.[11]

### Content Validation

When sample sizes are small, an alternative test validation strategy, content validation, can be used. Although criterion-related validity is established by empirical means, content validity is achieved primarily through a process of expert judgment. **Content validation** is performed by demonstrating that the questions or problems posed by the test are a representative sample of the kinds of situations or problems that occur on the job. A test that is content valid exposes the job applicant to situations that are likely to occur on the job, and then tests whether the applicant currently has sufficient knowledge, skills, or abilities to handle such situations.

Many of the new simulations that organizations are using are essentially computer-based role-playing games, where applicants play the role of the job incumbent, confronting the exact types of people and problems real-live job incumbents would face. The simulations are just like traditional role-playing games (e.g., *The Sims*), and the applicant's reactions and behaviors are scored to see how well they match with what one would expect from the ideal employee. For example, if one is considering applicants for a wait staff job at a restaurant, the game *Wasabi Waiter*, designed by Knack.it, allows the employer to watch how the applicant responds to finicky customers, uppity receptionists, emotionally unstable chefs, and other predictably challenging situations that are likely to take place in a busy establishment.[12]

Because the content of these tests so closely parallels the content of the job, one can safely make inferences from one to the other. For example, in the field of computer programming, employers see the skills needed to win international software code problem-solving competitions as highly related to the skills necessary to perform well on the job. For those who are unaware of the fast-growing sport of computer programming, an important warning—these contests do not make for riveting television.

In most of the contests, roughly two dozen competitors who worked their way to the finals by topping thousand of others in preliminary events online, rarely move from their workstation as they work through five standardized puzzles that have to be solved quickly with code that is as efficient as possible. Still, many employers study the results from these events looking to hire both winners and runner-ups because they view this as a highly valid work sample test. As Vladimir Novakovski, vice president for engineering at Addepar, a software provider in the investment industry notes that, "Every time I hire someone who is good in these contexts, they have crushed the job. They tend to be fast, accurate, and into getting things done."[13] If there is any problem with this source of recruits, it is that some of the competitors are so good and make so much money in the contests, they have no interest in applying for a full-time job.[14]

**Content validation**
A test-validation strategy performed by demonstrating that the items, questions, or problems posed by a test are a representative sample of the kinds of situations or problems that occur on the job.

## One Part Personality plus One Part AI: The Formula for Team Chemistry

The 2004 U.S. Men's Basketball Team was composed of some of the greatest players of all time, including LeBron James, Dwayne Wade, Tim Duncan, Allen Iverson, Carmello Anthony, and Stephon Marbury. The coaching staff was also renowned for their past success and included Larry Brown, Greg Popovich, and Roy Williams. Rarely has this amount of individual talent ever been assembled on one team and never has a team with this much individual talent so underachieved. The 2004 version of the Dream Team turned out to be a nightmare that lost three games, coming away with nothing more than a Bronze Medal in a sport that was invented in their country.

Clearly, although personnel selection can never ignore talent at the individual level, organizations increasingly employ team-based structures, and thus, there is an urgent need to go beyond the individual level and consider the team as a separate object in and of itself. That is, HR staffing specialists need to learn when and where a collection of individuals will come together to be greater than—or less than—the sum of their parts. Some companies are turning to artificial intelligence (AI) solutions to solve this problem. For example,

Nexus AI is a Chicago-based firm that composes teams for companies as part of a two-stage process.

The first stage matches individual's skills and abilities with the job requirements associated with the functional role that a person will play. This is very standard HR, and there are many tech companies that can provide a similar service. However, Nexus does not stop there and, after recommending a large slate of potential people to fill potential roles based on abilities, then goes on to a second stage that determines the right mix of individuals based upon their personalities. The AI solution begins at Time 1 with a set of general principles based upon past research. Then, after every project, the team is evaluated by peers and supervisors, and the AI tracks these responses. Over time the AI begins to learn what mix of personality traits is best for different types of team projects, thus going beyond past research.

Nexus also tracks workforce utilization parameters to make sure that the AI algorithm is not learning and incorporating the biases inherent in the human judgments into its algorithm. For example, an earlier foray into AI and personnel selection at Amazon learned the hard way

that performance evaluations were biased against female applicants in some job categories. The AI learned the exact same prejudice like a precocious child and then incorporated it into decisions that had adverse impacts on women. In another case, the data revealed that workers from two zip code areas tended to have lower performance evaluations relative to others. The AI quickly picked up this fact and used it to discriminate against people from that zip code—who turned out to be primarily African Americans. Thus, in HR contexts, preventing artificial discrimination is just as important as leveraging artificial intelligence.

### DISCUSSION QUESTIONS

1. How does the evolution to team-based structures change the equation when it comes to personnel selection and placement?

2. In what ways are AI analytic solutions similar to—and different from—traditional criterion-related validation approaches?

SOURCES: A. Chowdhry, "How Nexus A.I. is Helping Companies Discover Untapped Talent," *Forbes Online*, November 13, 2017; J. Davis, "Can AI Really Build Effective Teams?" *HR Daily Advisor Online*, April 17, 2018; J. McGregor, "Why Robots Aren't Going to Make the Call on Hiring Anytime Soon," *The Washington Post Online*, October 11, 2018.

The ability to use content validation in small-sample settings makes it generally more applicable than criterion-related validation. However, content validation has two limitations. First, one assumption behind content validation is that the person who is to be hired must have the knowledge, skills, or abilities at the time he or she is hired. Second, because subjective judgment plays such a large role in content validation, it is critical to minimize the amount of inference involved on the part of judges. Thus, the judges' ratings need to be made with respect to relatively concrete and observable behaviors.

## GENERALIZABILITY

It was once believed, for example, that validity coefficients were situationally specific—that is, the level of correlation between test and performance varied as one went from one organization to another, even though the jobs studied seemed to be identical. Subsequent research has indicated that this is largely false. Rather, tests tend to show similar levels of correlation even across jobs that are only somewhat similar (at least for tests of intelligence and cognitive ability). Correlations with these kinds of tests change as one goes across widely different kinds of jobs, however. Specifically, the more complex the job, the higher the validity of many tests. It was also believed that tests showed differential subgroup validity, which meant that the validity coefficient for any test–job performance pair was different for people of different races or genders. This belief was also refuted by subsequent research, and, in general, one finds very similar levels of correlations across different groups of people.[15]

Because the evidence suggests that test validity often extends across situations and subgroups, *validity generalization* stands as an alternative for validating selection methods for companies that cannot employ criterion-related or content validation. Validity generalization is a three-step process. First, the company provides evidence from previous criterion-related validity studies conducted in other situations that shows that a specific test (such as a test of emotional stability) is a valid predictor for a specific job (like nurse at a large hospital). Second, the company provides evidence from a job analysis to document that the job it is trying to fill (nurse at a small hospital) is similar to the job already validated elsewhere (nurse at a large hospital). Finally, if the company can show that it uses a test that is the same as or similar to that used in the validated setting, then one can "generalize" the validity from the first context (large hospital) to the new context (small hospital).

## UTILITY

**Utility** is the degree to which the information provided by selection methods enhances the bottom-line effectiveness of the organization. In general, the more reliable, valid, and generalizable the selection method is, the more utility it will have. However, many characteristics of particular selection contexts enhance or detract from the usefulness of given selection methods, even when reliability, validity, and generalizability are held constant.

Figures 6.4a and 6.4b, for example, show two different scenarios where the correlation between a measure of extroversion and the amount of sales revenue generated by a sample of sales representatives is the same for two different companies: Company A and Company B. Although the correlation between the measure of extroversion and sales is the same, Company B derives much more utility or practical benefit from the measure. That is, as indicated by the arrows proceeding out of the boxes (which indicate the people selected), the average sales revenue of the three people selected by Company B (Figure 6.4b) is $850,000, compared to $780,000 from the three people selected by Company A (Figure 6.4a).

The major difference between these two companies is that Company B generated twice as many applicants as Company A. This means that the selection ratio (the percentage of people selected relative to the total number of people tested) is quite low for Company B (3/20) relative to Company A (3/10). Thus, the people selected by Company B have higher amounts of extroversion than those selected by Company A; therefore, Company

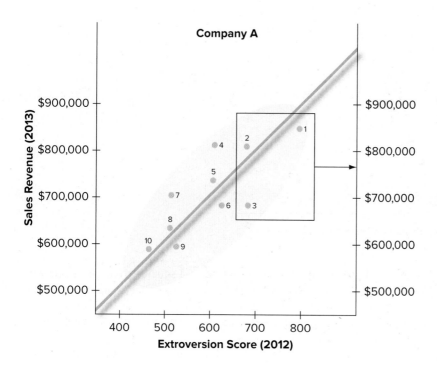

**Figure 6.4a**
Utility of Selecting on Extroversion Scores When Selection Ratio Is High

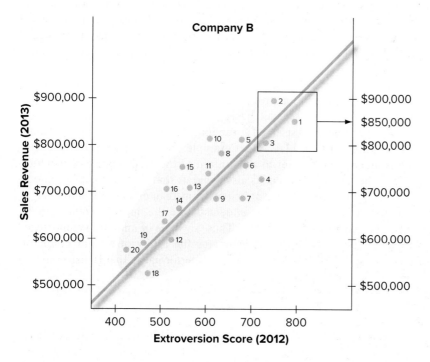

**Figure 6.4b**
Utility of Selecting on Extroversion Scores When Selection Ratio Is Low

B takes better advantage of the relationship between extroversion and sales. Thus, the utility of any test generally increases as the selection ratio decreases, as long as the additional costs of recruiting and testing are not excessive.

The utility of a test also depends upon the distribution of the trait or the performance metric. Most individual differences take on the form of a *normal distribution*. In

**Figure 6.5**

Comparing a Normal Distribution (Red Curve) to a Power Law (Blue Shading)

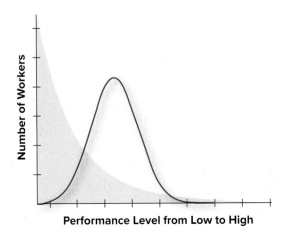

other words, most people are in the middle, followed by a smaller group of people who are a little bit above or below the mean, followed by an even smaller group of outliers far above and below the mean. This belief in the normal distribution has traditionally been extended to people's beliefs about job performance, even though little evidence has been collected to test this belief.

However, a study examining over 600,000 entertainers, politicians, amateur athletes, professional athletes, and scientists has challenged this idea and instead suggests that job performance follows a *power law distribution*. Figure 6.5 shows how a distribution that follows a power law differs dramatically from a normal distribution, in the sense that there are few high performers and a large group of potentially poor performers.[16]

The implication of these findings for utility analysis is important because it implies that the dollar value of a "highly productive worker" (e.g., someone who is one standard deviation above the mean, perhaps selected based upon a validated test) and an "average worker" (e.g., at the mean, perhaps selected at random) is much greater than one would expect if the distribution were normal. As an example, a scientist with the "average" publication rate is much, much closer to the bottom of the performance distribution than he or she is to the top. These findings also suggests that the use of dichotomous, success versus failure criteria (e.g., above or below the median or some arbitrary cut-off score) for evaluating performance may far underestimate the huge difference among people, all of whom might be above the mean. Thus, any type of minimum competency cut-off used to score success vastly underestimates the utility of a valid predictor. Overall, a test has much more utility when it predicts performance that is distributed as a power law.[17]

## LEGALITY

**LO 6-3**
Describe the government's role in personnel selection decisions, particularly in the areas of constitutional law, federal laws, executive orders, and judicial precedent.

The final standard to which any selection method should adhere is *legality*. All selection methods should conform to existing laws and existing legal precedents. For example, Kentucky Fried Chicken requires its workers to wear slacks and was charged with discrimination when it refused to allow Sheila Silver, a Pentecostal Christian, to wear a long dress at work, which was what her religion required. In a similar case, with a different religion, the New York City Police Department was charged with violating the religious rights of a Muslim officer whose religion-required beard violated the department's appearance code.[18] These are hardly isolated incidents in the sense that cases based on religious discrimination have skyrocketed recently. According to the Equal Employment Opportunity Commission (EEOC), in 2013 alone, over 3,700 religious discrimination claims were brought against employers.[19] In both of these cases, the court upheld the religious beliefs of the job applicant against requirements posed by the employer.

Employers who are taken to court for illegal discrimination experience high costs associated with litigation, settlements, and awards, and also suffer potential damage to their social reputations as good employers, making recruitment and growth more difficult. This is exactly what happened to Chick-fil-A. Even though the firm had never been charged with any form of employment discrimination, when the president of the company made disparaging comments regarding gay marriage in 2012, there was an immediate negative backlash against "hate chicken" that harmed sales.

Even worse, it threatened the company's expansion plans and strategy to move into northern and urban areas. The mayor of Boston went so far as to send a letter to the company urging it to back down from plans to locate in Boston, and he was quoted in the *Boston Herald* saying that "he would make it very difficult" for the restaurant to come to town. Chicago mayor Rahm Emanuel chimed in and stated that "Chick-fil-A's values are not Chicago's values," and protest movements in New York City and San Francisco were organized to oppose expansion into those areas. All of this happened even though no one ever presented any evidence or even charged the company with discriminating against gay customers or job applicants.[20]

## Federal Legislation

Three federal laws form the basis for a majority of the suits filed by job applicants: the Civil Rights Act of 1991, the Age Discrimination in Employment Act of 1967, and the Americans with Disabilities Act of 1990 (all discussed in Chapter 3).

*Civil Rights Act of 1991.* An extension of the Civil Rights Act of 1964, the Civil Rights Act of 1991 protects individuals from discrimination based on race, color, sex, religion, and national origin with respect to hiring as well as compensation and working conditions.

This act defines employers' explicit obligation to establish the business necessity of any neutral-appearing selection method that has had adverse impact on groups specified by the law. This is typically done by showing that the test has significant criterion-related or content validity. If the employer cannot show such a difference, which the research suggests will be difficult, then the process may be ruled illegal. Ironically, for example, the Consumer Finance Protection Bureau (CFPB) that was created as part of the Dodd-Frank Act, which regulates banks and financial institutions to specifically prevent discrimination in loan practices, discovered that its own promotion policies created adverse impact. An investigation into the CFPB's promotion policies found that 21% of the agency's white employees received the highest performance rating compared with just 10% of the African American employees and 9% of Hispanic employees. Since this rating was used to make promotion decisions, it became a neutral-appearing employment practice that created adverse impact and thus had to be justified.[21]

Many other employers, if challenged, could find themselves with similar problems because the statistics at CFBP actually mirror the statistics for employers as a whole. Investigations into employers believed to be unfairly discriminating against African American candidates will often send résumés from fictitious applicants whose credentials are exactly the same except for race. Studies show that white applicants in these studies are 33% more likely to be hired than the identically qualified black candidate, which is pure evidence of bias.[22]

Similar data was assembled in the banking industry, and a class action suit was filed against Goldman Sachs, accusing the firm of discriminating against women. This is a tough industry for female employees; no woman has ever run a major New York bank, and less than 20% of executive and senior managers at Citigroup, JPMorgan Chase, and Goldman Sachs are women.[23] In the case against Goldman, Christina Chen-Oster and her legal team were able to document how the percentage of women at each transition level (e.g., from regional director to vice president, and then vice president to managing director) got smaller and smaller.[24] This is the kind of evidence that "shifts the burden of proof" to the employer (i.e., Goldman Sachs), to prove that these promotion decisions were based on a business necessity.

The Civil Rights Act of 1991 allows the individual filing the complaint to have a jury decide whether he or she may recover punitive damages (in addition to lost wages and benefits) for emotional injuries caused by the discrimination. This can generate large financial settlements as well as poor public relations that can hinder the organization's ability to compete.

Finally, the 1991 act explicitly prohibits the granting of preferential treatment to minority groups. Preferential treatment is often attractive because many of the most valid methods for screening people, especially cognitive ability tests and work sample tests, often are high in adverse impact.[25] For example, although software coding sport competitions help organizations uncover talented programmers, almost all of the tournament champions tend to be white males. Thus, there is somewhat of a trade-off in terms of selecting the highest scorers on validated tests, on the one hand, and creating diversity in the workforce, on the other hand.[26]

One potential way to "have your cake and eat it too" is to simply rank the scores of different races or gender groups within their own groups, and then take perhaps the top 10% of scorers from each group, instead of the top 10% that would be obtained if one ignored race or gender. Many observers feel that this practice is justified because it levels the playing field in a context where bias works against African Americans. However, the 1991 act specifically outlaws this practice (sometimes referred to as *race norming*). Some believe that race norming is just reverse discrimination and gives preferential treatment—rather than equal treatment—to minorities, and thus this practice has been challenged in court.

Two specific Supreme Court cases show that policies that may be construed as promoting preferential treatment will not stand up in court. In the first case, voters in the state of Michigan backed an initiative that made it illegal to engage in affirmative action for minorities when it came to admissions to Michigan colleges. Because the majority of voters in this state were white, this initiative was challenged because of legal precedents that protect minorities from being targeted for unfair treatment through the political process. That is, taken to an extreme, if a majority of members of a state were white, it would not be permissible for them to support a ballot initiative that would prevent minorities from attending college at all, since doing so would be patently unfair. The challenge to the Michigan initiative claimed that its effect was close to this extreme, but the challenge was struck down by the Supreme Court, which decided that the electorate was acting within its rights.[27] The Court did not necessarily say that affirmative action was illegal in this case, but rather that it was fair for the general electorate to impose its will this way, which leaves colleges that are trying to promote diversity scrambling for other alternatives, one of which was adopted at the University of Texas.[28]

The Supreme Court case that involved the University of Texas illustrates how difficult it can be to achieve diversity goals while still upholding merit-based selection and avoiding perceptions of reverse discrimination. Specifically, in order to increase the percentage of African American and Hispanic students in the UT system, the school made it a policy to accept the top 10% of the graduating class of every high school. Because many high schools in Texas tend to be segregated by race and ethnicity, this policy worked somewhat like race norming in ensuring that members of every group found their way into college, but it was not explicitly race norming.[29]

To push the diversity gains even further, though, the admissions officers at UT noted that many African American students in affluent suburban schools often were rejected for admission, even though they had higher test scores than African American students from urban schools. When the school tried to reach out and accept those students, however, this policy was challenged. In 2016, a divided Supreme Court upheld the legality of the UT affirmative action program. Writing for the 4–3 majority, Justice Anthony Kennedy stated that "the university is entitled considerable deference in defining the type of institution it wished to be, including intangible characteristics, such as student body diversity that might be central to the university's identity and educational mission.[30]

Whereas the issue at the heart of the UT case dealt with the underrepresentation of African American students, a separate issue deals with what to do when neutral-appearing selection methods create a situation where some minority group might exceed its representation in the general population. For example, as shown in the Competing through Environmental, Social, and Governance Practices box shows, admitting a percentage of Asian American students that reflects their percentage in the population actually holds them back.

Rather than employing race norming, employers can partially achieve both goals of maximizing predicted future performance and diversity in several ways. First, aggressive recruiting of members of protected groups allows an employer to generate a larger pool of protected group members, and, by being highly selective within this larger group, the scores of admitted applicants will more closely match those of all the other groups.[31] Second, as we will see later in this chapter, different selection methods have different degrees of adverse impact, and multistage selection batteries that use different methods at different stages can also help.[32]

Finally, one common approach that does not seem to work is to abandon the kinds of compliance-driven, evidenced-based workforce utilization reviews discussed in Chapter 5, in favor of softer, "inclusion" initiatives that express the generic value of diversity but fail to document goals and timetables statistically. Some organizations treat diversity more like a marketing campaign than an HR initiative, and it is not uncommon to see companies that won awards for their "inclusion programs," such as Texaco and Bank of America, also later convicted of illegal discrimination. Some have noted that there is an almost complete overlap of the lists of the top 50 companies for inclusion and the top 50 companies for advertising expenditures, and the need to complement style with substance cannot be overlooked in this critical area.[33] The simple truth is that the best predictors of whether a firm becomes truly diverse and avoids litigation is whether (1) there is a specific person (e.g., a diversity compliance officer) whose sole job is to monitor hiring statistics, (2) this person has the power to change hiring practices, and (3) this person is held strictly accountable in his or her own performance appraisal for achieving quantifiable results.[34]

*Age Discrimination in Employment Act of 1967.* Court interpretations of the Age Discrimination in Employment Act mirror those of the Civil Rights Act, in that if any neutral-appearing practice happens to have adverse impact on those over age 40, then the burden of proof shifts to the employer, who must show business necessity to avoid a guilty verdict. This act outlaws almost all "mandatory retirement" programs (company policies that dictate that everyone who reaches a set age must retire).

## According to Harvard: "Asian-Americans Have Bad Personalities"

Although the Asian American population in the United States has more than doubled in the last 30 years, the percentage of Asian Americans admitted to Harvard in 2017 was the same as it was in 1980. This is despite the fact than when it comes to almost all the published factors that the institution claims to use in selection (standardized test scores, grade point average, extracurricular activities, ratings from high school teachers, and personal essays), as a group, Asian Americans outperform Caucasians, Hispanics, and African Americans. In fact, based upon the objective evidence, if one just made selection decisions based on these factors, the Asian American acceptance rate would be 43% versus the 19% that it was in 2017. There is only one factor where Asian Americans perform poorly, and this factor alone costs them the 24% of the positions they might have otherwise earned—the dreaded "personal score."

The "personal score" rating used at Harvard purportedly captures the student's "likability, helpfulness, courage, kindness, positive personality, and respectability." This subjective judgment, often rendered by an admissions officer who has never met the student, has a devastating impact on Asian American students—especially those who would otherwise score highly on the rest of the selection battery. Asian American students who would be in the top 10% of applicants on everything other than the personal score get a "2" on a 5-point scale more than 20% of the time. One can find "2" ratings for other groups of students, but for Caucasians, these low ratings are predominantly found in the 60th to 70th percentile, and in the 70th to 80th percentile for Hispanics, and the 80th to 90th percentile for African Americans. Thus, the personal score becomes a knock-out factor for Asians who would have been selected otherwise, but has no effect on other groups because the poorly rated students would not have been admitted anyway.

Does Harvard really believe that Asian Americans have bad personalities? After all, the Dean of Admissions at the Massachusetts Institute for Technology did call one Korean American student who was denied admission in his institution, "just another texture-less math grind." Still, although the potential for stereotypes does seem to play a part in this process, many others see this case as part of a much larger battle against affirmative action. Specifically, current law does allow schools and employers to use race as a "plus factor" in a "holistic process" that includes all the other factors that go into a selection battery. However, the law precludes strict quotas in favor of one group or caps that work against one group. Critics of Harvard's admission process argue that the personal score is just a flexible, seemingly innocuous, and—most importantly—legal mechanism that can be used to cap Asian American admissions far below 43%.

Thus, some believe that Harvard is regulating admission rates in such a way that its population is representative of the larger diversity in United States. Indeed, Harvard does seem to be achieving this goal, but some question if this will be sustainable. Currently, the admission rate for Asian Americans mirrors their percentage of the U.S. population, and the same is true for Caucasians, Hispanics, and African Americans. Although this may seem fair, for the roughly 20% of Asian Americans who would have otherwise been admitted, this may seem unfair, and especially harsh, when it is falsely attributed to their bad personalities. When the principle of Stuyvesant High School in New York, a school for gifted children that is over 70% Asian American, was informed of these statistics when she was on the witness stand during a

*CONTINUED*

federal lawsuit where this is all playing out, she actually broke down and started crying. When asked why she was crying she stated, "because these numbers make it seem like there's discrimination and I love these kids, and I know how hard they work. So these all just look like numbers to you guys, but I see their faces." Apparently, when she looks into the faces of her students, she does not see the same "texture-less math grinds" that others see.

SOURCES: K. Benner, "Asian-American Students Suing Harvard over Affirmative Action Win Justice Department Support," *The New York Times Online*, August 30, 2018; N. Corn and N. Hong, "Justice Department Says Harvard Hurts Asian-Americans' Admission Prospects With 'Personal Rating,'" *The Wall Street Journal Online*, August 30, 2018; K. Reilly, "With Harvard on Trial, So Is Affirmative Action," *Bloomberg Businessweek*, October 29, 2018; W. Yang, "Harvard Is Wrong That Asians Have Terrible Personalities," *The New York Times Online*, June 25, 2018.

For example, the Texas Roadhouse restaurant company was sued for discrimination based on this law. Whereas 20% of servers nationally are over the age of 40, this was true for less than 2% of Texas Roadhouse employees. The suit was brought by a 40-year-old woman who applied for a job at a Texas Roadhouse restaurant in Palm Bay, Florida, and was told there were no openings. A few days later, she learned that one of her daughter's friends interviewed after she did and got a job offer. Despite this incident and the larger data on underutilization, the chain defended its action by stating that it needed younger workers to reflect its brand image and attract more customers.[35] This appeal to brand image and customer preference has a long history as a "business necessity" defense, but it rarely seems to prevail in court.[36]

***Americans with Disabilities Act (ADA) of 1990.*** The ADA protects individuals with physical and mental disabilities (or with a history of the same), and requires that employers make "reasonable accommodation" to disabled individuals whose handicaps may prevent them from performing essential functions of the job as currently designed. "Reasonable accommodation" could include restructuring jobs, modifying work schedules, making facilities accessible, providing readers, or modifying equipment. The ADA does not require an organization to hire someone whose disability prevents him or her from performing either critical or routine aspects of the job, nor does it require accommodations that would cause "undue hardship."

There is some degree of political pressure to increase the hiring of disabled workers, and in 2014, the Department of Labor issued new rules aimed at government contractors that decreed they should set a goal of having 7% of their workforce be composed of disabled employees. Thus, if you are applying for a job with a government contractor, you need to check a box that asks whether or not you are disabled. The ruling was controversial because many disabled workers, especially those with nonobvious physical impairments or mental impairments, are unlikely to check that box. This means that some employers may be meeting the goal but are not able to show it because of applicants' reluctance to check the box.[37]

One source of disabled workers that employers are increasingly tapping in to is the pool of Gulf War–era veterans. This pool of potential workers was once highly underutilized by employers and experienced an unemployment rate well over 30%. That proportion has since dropped to less than 10%.

Although part of the drop is attributable to a general improvement in the labor market, some of it is also due to the heroic efforts of programs like the Wounded Warrior Project, which seeks to help disabled veterans find jobs in the private sector. This group helps veterans translate how skills and job categories in the military match civilian jobs.[38] For example, the skills of a "medic" in the military vary from case to case, and effectively entering the civilian medical industry at the right spot requires help communicating the similarities and differences between the two domains. This group also led efforts to reclassify the idiosyncratic codes for technical skills used in the military to the codes used by the Department of Labor's O*NET system (see Chapter 4 for a description of O*NET). This made it much easier for veterans to translate their skills into terms more broadly used in the private sector.[39]

**LO 6-4**
List the common methods used in selecting human resources.

**LO 6-5**
Describe the degree to which each of the common methods used in selecting human resources meets the demands of reliability, validity, generalizability, utility, and legality.

Visit your instructor's Connect® course and access your eBook to view this video.

"Its really about understanding whether or not they'll fit into an organization. Things like behavioral interviews are really important."

—Jim Duffy, Executive Vice President and Chief Human Resources Officer, CIT Group, Inc.

Source: Video produced for the Center for Executive Succession in the Darla Moore School of Business at the University of South Carolina by Coal Powered Filmworks

# Types of Selection Methods

In the first half of this chapter, we laid out the five standards by which to judge selection measures. In this half of the chapter, we examine the common selection methods used in various organizations and discuss their advantages and disadvantages in terms of these standards.

## INTERVIEWS

A selection interview is a dialogue initiated by one or more persons to gather information and evaluate the qualifications of an applicant for employment. The selection interview is the most widespread selection method employed in organizations, and there have been literally hundreds of studies examining their effectiveness.[40]

Unfortunately, the long history of research on the employment interview suggests that, without proper care, it can be unreliable, low in validity, and biased against a number of different groups. Moreover, interviews are relatively costly because they require at least one person to interview another person, and these people are often in different locations. Finally, in terms of legality, the subjectivity embodied in the process, as well as the opportunity for unconscious bias effects, often makes applicants upset, particularly if they fail to get a job after being asked apparently irrelevant questions. In the end, subjective selection methods like the interview must be validated by traditional criterion-related or content-validation procedures if they show any degree of adverse impact.

Fortunately, more recent research has pointed to a number of concrete steps that one can employ to increase the utility of the personnel selection interview. First, HR staff should keep the interview structured, standardized, and focused on accomplishing a small number of goals. That is, they should plan to come out of each interview with quantitative ratings on a small number of dimensions that are observable (like interpersonal style or ability to express oneself) and avoid ratings of abilities that may be better measured by tests (like intelligence). In addition to coming out of the interview with quantitative ratings, interviewers should also have a structured note-taking system that will aid recall when it comes to justifying the ratings. Finally, overall judgments of applicants should be left until the very end of the process, because implicit, first impression biases often cloud initial interpersonal reactions.[41]

Selection interviews should be focused totally on rating and ranking applicants, and even though it may be tempting to accomplish other goals like recruiting the candidate, this temptation needs to be resisted.[42] As we saw in Chapter 5, recruitment interviews should be kept separate from selection interviews because these types of dual-purpose interviews tend to fail on both scores. Then, after a sufficient amount of time to obtain performance evaluation data, interviewers should get normative feedback on which of the employees that they selected performed well versus poorly so that they can learn from past experience.[43]

When it comes to content, interviewers should ask questions dealing with specific situations that are likely to arise on the job, and use the responses to determine what the person is likely to do in those situations. These types of **situational interview** items have been shown to have high predictive validity.[44] Situational judgment items come in two varieties, as shown in Table 6.2.

Some items are "experience-based" and require the applicant to reveal an experience he or she had in the past when confronting the situation. So for example, both Amazon and Google were recruiting thousands of experienced software engineers for their new headquarters, but the experience they were looking for differed. In interviews, Amazon was looking for software engineers that had experience in coding languages like C+ and Java, whereas Google needed people with experience in Linus and Python.[45]

In contrast, some items are "future oriented." That is, although the idea that asking one about his or her past experience would seem obvious, unlike Amazon and Google,

**Situational interview**
An interview procedure where applicants are confronted with specific issues, questions, or problems that are likely to arise on the job.

## Table 6.2
Examples of Experience-Based and Future-Oriented Situational Interview Items

| **Experience-based** | |
|---|---|
| Motivating employees | "Think about an instance when you had to motivate an employee to perform a task that he or she disliked but that you needed to have done. How did you handle that situation?" |
| Resolving conflict | "What was the biggest difference of opinion you ever had with a co-worker? How did you resolve that situation?" |
| Overcoming resistance to change | "What was the hardest change you ever had to bring about in a past job, and what did you do to get the people around you to change their thoughts or behaviors?" |
| **Future-oriented** | |
| Motivating employees | "Suppose you were working with an employee who you knew greatly disliked performing a particular task. You needed to get this task completed, however, and this person was the only one available to do it. What would you do to motivate that person?" |
| Resolving conflict | "Imagine that you and a co-worker disagree about the best way to handle an absenteeism problem with another member of your team. How would you resolve that situation?" |
| Overcoming resistance to change | "Suppose you had an idea for a change in work procedures that would enhance quality, but some members of your work group were hesitant to make the change. What would you do in that situation?" |

companies like Intel and Github care more about the applicant's potential future rather than their past. These companies are willing to hire self-taught programmers or programmers that attended coding boot camps, even if they have never practiced those skills on a real job.[46] Organizations that employ future-oriented items tend to emphasize on-the-job training specifically focused on their own needs rather than years of past experience meeting some other employers' needs.

These examples show the competitive dynamics associated with HR activities, in the sense that one can compete by emphasizing experience, paying higher wages, and have reduced training needs, or on the other hand, compete by de-emphasizing experience, paying lower wages, but increasing training budgets and socialization expenses. This is critical because as we noted earlier, due to recent labor shortage, more companies are moving to a "no experience necessary" model.

In fact, between 2012 and 2017, the percentage of employers who required three years' experience dropped from 30% to 20%, a move that opens up employment opportunities for 1.2 million people. Companies with a "no experience necessary" policy need to have interviewers who are skilled at recognizing an applicant's potential for growth and fit with the company's culture. As Greg Pryor, the vice president of HR at Workday Inc. notes, "this puts a huge responsibility on the company because the burden of proof moves from the candidate to the interviewer."[47] Indeed, perhaps for this reason, research suggests that although both types of items can show validity, experience-based items often outperform future-oriented ones.[48]

It is also important to use multiple interviewers who are trained to avoid many of the subjective errors that can result when one human being is asked to rate another. For example, at Google, there were definite concerns with demographic similarity bias in interviews, because their own analysis of local data was suggesting that managers were hiring people who seemed just like them. To eliminate this problem, Google now compiles elaborate files for each candidate, and then has all interviews conducted by groups rather than individuals. Laszlo Bock, then vice president for Google's People Operations, noted that "we do everything to minimize the authority and power of the lone manager in making hiring decisions that are going to affect the entire company."[49]

Indeed, many have suggested that one of the major causes of the large number of sexual harassment claims registered in the field of security brokerage is that the broker, who is usually male, makes hiring and compensation decisions regarding female administrative assistants by himself with no input from the firm's HR staff. These individual brokers, however, are not sole proprietors, but rather employees themselves, so this practice is being curtailed at many of the largest companies.[50]

Many companies find that a good way to get "multiple eyes" on an applicant is to conduct digitally taped interviews, and then send the digitized files (rather than the applicants) around from place to place. Some employers find that the lack of true interaction that can take place in videos limits their value; hence, the use of face-to-face interactive technology like Skype to conduct virtual interviews over long distance.[51]

Digital Vision/Getty Images

When more than one person is able to interview a candidate for a position, there is significant advantage in removing any errors or biases that a single individual might make in choosing the correct person for the job. In today's technological world, it is becoming easier for multiple people to give their input in an interview by watching a video recording or listening via conference call if they cannot be there in person.

## REFERENCES, APPLICATION BLANKS, AND BACKGROUND CHECKS

Except in extreme cases, nearly all employers use some method for getting background information on applicants before an interview. This information can be solicited from the people who know the candidate through reference checks.

The evidence on the reliability and validity of reference checks suggests that these are, at best, weak predictors of future success on the job. The main reason for this low validity is that the evaluations supplied in most reference letters are so positive that it is hard to differentiate applicants. This problem with reference letters has two causes. First, the applicant usually gets to choose who writes the letter and can thus choose only those writers who think the highest of her abilities. Second, because letter writers can never be sure who will read the letters, they may justifiably fear that supplying damaging information about someone could come back to haunt them. Thus, it is clearly not in the past employers' interest to reveal too much information beyond job title and years of service.

Another problem with reference checks is that applicants do not always tell the truth when it comes to listing their references. In fact, 30% of the companies that check references find false or misleading references on applications. Michael Erwin, a career advisor at CareerBuilder, notes, "For some reason, people think companies aren't going to check their references and therefore they think they can get away with all sorts of fabrications." In reality, 80% of companies do in fact check references prior to offering someone an interview or prior to making an offer.[52]

In addition to outside references, employers can also collect background information from the applicants themselves. The low cost of obtaining such information significantly enhances its utility, especially when the information is used in conjunction with a well-designed, follow-up interview that complements, rather than duplicates, the biographical information bank.

One of the most important elements of biographical information deals with educational background. Indeed, providing background information on one's education is probably one of the few things that a written résumé is still good for in this day and age. In some cases, employers are looking for specialized educational backgrounds reflected in functional degrees such as business or nursing or engineering, but in other cases, employers are just looking for critical-thinking and problem-solving skills that might be associated with any college degree.[53]

This focus on education is attributed to the nature of the economy, which increasingly demands people with high levels of education. Indeed, it is ironic that despite relatively high levels of employment, many employers find it impossible to find people with the skills they need.[54] The term *education gap* has been coined to capture the difference between the average years of education required in a job listing in a given area, and the average years of education in that same area. For the nation as a whole, the education gap runs at about 5%, but in some cities, like Las Vegas, the gap exceeds 10%. Areas that have larger education gaps experience much higher rates of unemployment and are usually the last to show signs of job recovery during an economic expansion.[55]

Again, as with the interview, the biggest concern with the use of biographical data is that applicants who supply the information may be motivated to misrepresent themselves. Some research suggests that over 80% of job applications contain some misleading or false information; so again, hiring sight unseen is a very risky proposition.[56] For example, investigators found that Timothy Loehmann, the police officer who shot Tamir Rice, an innocent 14-year-old boy in Cleveland, had falsified his application hiding several past terminations for overly aggressive behavior. This resulted in a $6 million wrongful death lawsuit that might have been prevented with a more thorough background check.[57]

To prevent embarrassing episodes, many employers hire outside companies to do background checks on employees. For example, Steve Masiello applied for a position coaching basketball at the University of South Florida, a routine background check revealed that he had lied on his application when he stated that he had earned a degree in communications from the University of Kentucky in 2000. This came as an embarrassment to Masiello's current employer, Manhattan College, which also required a college degree for any top coaching position but apparently never checked on this when they hired Masiello.[58] A similar failure to conduct a routine background check was partially to blame for the 2015 jailbreak at the Clinton Correctional Facility in New York, where an employee helped two convicted murderers escape.[59] An investigation in the wake of this incident revealed widespread lapses and failures to conduct adequate background checks at the prison.[60]

## PHYSICAL ABILITY TESTS

Although automation and other advances in technology have eliminated or modified many physically demanding occupational tasks, many jobs still require certain physical abilities or psychomotor abilities. In these cases, tests of physical abilities may be relevant not only to predicting performance but also to predicting occupational injuries and disabilities.[61] There are seven classes of tests in this area: ones that evaluate (1) muscular tension, (2) muscular power, (3) muscular endurance, (4) cardiovascular endurance, (5) flexibility, (6) balance, and (7) coordination.[62]

The criterion-related validities for these kinds of tests for certain jobs, such as firefighting, are quite strong.[63] Unfortunately, these tests, particularly the strength tests, are likely to have an adverse impact on some applicants with disabilities and many female applicants. For example, roughly two-thirds of all males score higher than the highest-scoring female on muscular tension tests.[64] This difference between the sexes in physical strength was once used to legally bar women from certain jobs in the military; however, this is no longer the case, and all jobs within the U.S. military were opened up to women in 2015.[65]

There are two key questions to ask in deciding whether to use these kinds of tests. First, is the physical ability essential to performing the job, and is it mentioned prominently enough in the job description? Neither the Civil Rights Act nor the ADA requires employers to hire individuals who cannot perform essential job functions, and both accept a written job description as evidence of the essential functions of the job. Second, is there a probability that failure to adequately perform the job would result in some risk to the safety or health of the applicant, co-workers, or clients? The "direct threat" clause of the ADA makes it clear that adverse impact against those with disabilities is warranted under such conditions.

Invoking this clause can sometimes cause controversy, as in 2014, when United Parcel Service (UPS) cited this clause to support the decision to fire a pregnant worker because she could not lift packages weighing more than 20 pounds. UPS was sued, because it routinely made accommodations for injured employees, and the same woman who was fired for being pregnant would have been accommodated had she hurt her back at work. The company tried to argue that pregnant women were being treated the same way as men who were injured *outside* of work.[66] UPS eventually settled out of court and eliminated this policy, probably as much for public relations reasons as for any other factor related to business necessity.[67]

An important lesson to learn from litigation that involves terminating pregnant women (or placing them on unpaid leave) is that letters from medical personnel to companies need to be very specific when it comes to laying out what duties can and cannot be performed at different stages of the pregnancy. Form letters or letters that are too general in nature are often interpreted in the least favorable light for the employee by employers looking to save money or reduce their exposure to risk.[68]

## COGNITIVE ABILITY TESTS

**Cognitive ability tests** differentiate individuals based on their mental rather than physical capacities. Cognitive ability has many different facets, although we will focus only on three dominant ones. **Verbal comprehension** refers to a person's capacity to understand and use written and spoken language. **Quantitative ability** concerns the speed and accuracy with which one can solve arithmetic problems of all kinds. **Reasoning ability**, a broader concept, refers to a person's capacity to invent solutions to many diverse problems.

Some jobs require only one or two of these facets of cognitive ability. Under these conditions, maintaining the separation among the facets is appropriate. However, many jobs that are high in complexity require most, if not all, of the facets; hence, one general test is often as good as many tests of separate facets. Highly reliable commercial tests measuring these kinds of abilities are widely available, and they are generally valid predictors of job performance in many different kinds of contexts, including widely different countries.[69] For example, in sales, based on the results of studies he ran on hundreds of salespeople and hundreds of applicants for sales positions, Wharton Professor Adam Grant concluded that "cognitive ability was more than five times more powerful than emotional intelligence when it came to performance." The results from his research suggested that an employee with high cognitive ability generated annual revenue of over $195,000, compared with $159,000 for those with moderate cognitive ability and $109,000 for those with low cognitive ability.[70] The validity of these kinds of tests is slightly related to the complexity of the job, however, in that one sees higher criterion-related validation for complex jobs than for simple jobs.

One of the major drawbacks to these tests is that they typically have adverse impact on some minority groups. Indeed, the size of the differences is so large that some observers have advocated abandoning these types of tests for making decisions regarding who will be accepted for certain schools or jobs. This is somewhat ironic in that these standardized tests were originally designed to be anti-elitist and to help identify talented individuals who may not be high in socioeconomic status but were still very bright by objective standards. However, over time, the tests have become a major hurdle to many disadvantaged groups by restricting their college opportunities and thus are now perceived as elitist due to their adverse impact on minorities.[71]

The notion of race norming, mentioned earlier, was born of the desire to use these high-utility tests in a manner that avoided adverse impact. Although race norming was made illegal by amendments to the Civil Rights Act, some people have advocated the use of banding both to achieve the benefits of testing and to minimize its adverse impact. The concept of *banding* suggests that similar groups of people whose scores differ by only a small amount all be treated as having the same score. Then, within any band, preferential treatment is given to minorities. Most observers feel preferential treatment of minorities is acceptable when scores are tied, and banding simply broadens the definition of what constitutes a tied score. Like race norming, banding is controversial, especially if the bands are set too wide.[72]

As with all the selection measures we have seen so far, a concern is that applicants may be tempted to cheat in order to score well on whatever instrument is used to make

**Cognitive ability tests**
Tests that include three dimensions: verbal comprehension, quantitative ability, and reasoning ability.

**Verbal comprehension**
Refers to a person's capacity to understand and use written and spoken language.

**Quantitative ability**
Refers to the speed and accuracy with which one can solve arithmetic problems of all kinds.

**Reasoning ability**
Refers to a person's capacity to invent solutions to many diverse problems.

selection decisions. Cheating on tests is hardly a new phenomenon, however. What is new is the degree to which the use of computerized testing and social networking has changed the nature and scope of cheating. The term *question harvesting* has been coined to capture the process whereby test takers use advanced technology to download questions or capture images of questions with digital cameras or other devices while taking a test, and then transmit the content of the test wirelessly to people outside the testing facility, who then post the questions for future test takers.[73] Cheating scandals such as these become particularly controversial when allegations are based on nationality. For example, the evidence of wrongdoing with respect to test scores reported from China and South Korea grew so large in 2014 that the Educational Testing Service withheld the scores for applicants from these countries until all the allegations could be sorted out.[74]

## PERSONALITY INVENTORIES

Whereas ability tests attempt to categorize individuals relative to what they can do, personality measures tend to categorize individuals by what they are like. The number of firms employing personality tests as screens has ballooned over the years, from just 26% in 2000 to just under 60% in 2014.[75] Research suggests that there are five major dimensions of personality, known as the "Big Five": (1) extroversion, (2) adjustment, (3) agreeableness, (4) conscientiousness, and (5) openness to experience. Table 6.3 lists each of these with a corresponding list of adjectives that fit each dimension.

Although it is possible to find reliable, commercially available measures of each of these traits, the evidence for their validity and generalizability is mixed at best.[76] For example, conscientiousness, which captures the concepts of self-regulation and self-motivation, is one of the few factors that displays any validity across a number of different job categories, and many real-world managers rate this as one of the most important characteristics they look for in employees. People who are high in conscientiousness tend to show very good self-control when pursuing work goals and are especially adept at overcoming challenges and obstacles, relative to people low in this trait.[77] In contrast, lack of conscientiousness among employees creates a number of difficulties for employers, some of which are shown in the Competing through Globalization box.

Instead of showing strong direct and positive correlations with future performance across all jobs, the validity coefficients associated with personality measures tend to be job specific. For example, extroverts tend to excel in jobs likes sales or politics

**Table 6.3**
The Five Major Dimensions of Personality Inventories

| | | |
|---|---|---|
| 1. | Extroversion | Sociable, gregarious, assertive, talkative, expressive |
| 2. | Adjustment | Emotionally stable, nondepressed, secure, content |
| 3. | Agreeableness | Courteous, trusting, good-natured, tolerant, cooperative, forgiving |
| 4. | Conscientiousness | Dependable, organized, persevering, thorough, achievement-oriented |
| 5. | Openness to experience | Curious, imaginative, artistically sensitive, broad-minded, playful |

## Phantom Hires Haunt Saudi Change Efforts

The business model for the "old Saudi Arabia"—and hence employers working in the region—was relatively simple. The Kingdom generated huge sums of money from oil, a non–labor intense industry, and staffed both low-skilled and high-skilled jobs with foreign workers. Saudi citizens were basically offered a deal where they were provided free health care, education, and utilities, as well as public-sector jobs, in return for not challenging the royal family's absolute authority. The rulers of the country basically created a "nanny state" where citizens were sheltered from cradle to grave when it came to working in more competitive and demanding private-sector jobs. Although it would be unfair to suggest that all Saudi's lack conscientiousness, this was a culture where lack of this trait was not always totally debilitating. However, all of that is now changing, and the country's new Crown Prince Mohammed bin Salmon, often referred to as "MBS," launched a program called "Saudization" that aims to move his citizens from the public payroll to private payrolls.

There were several forces that were driving this change effort. First, lower worldwide demand for Saudi oil was putting a dent in the country's treasury, which made it harder for the royal family to hold up their part of the deal. Second, most of the money that the government paid to Saudi citizens was spent outside the country. The state needed people to spend more of that money at home and, hence, expand local businesses. Finally due to the strict Islamic culture within Saudi Arabia, where beheadings are not unusual and women are not allowed to work, it was always difficult to recruit skilled workers from more liberal Western cultures. This problem was only intensified in 2018 after the brazen dismemberment and murder of *Washington Post* journalist Jamal Khashoggi that sent thousands of Western employees for the exits. In the wake of all these developments, Saudization was the only answer. As one analyst noted, "the old Saudi Arabia business model is not viable—the country was going to collapse."

In order to help his citizens make the transition, the Crown Prince authorized a set of hiring quotas. Most of these quotas were targeted at low-skill jobs because, although MBS eventually wants to make inroads into solar power, high-tech, and entertainment industries, few Saudis have the skills that are required for jobs in these industries. Thus, the quotas were aimed at bakeries, electronic shops, furniture stores, and jewelry stores and demanded that all workers in such establishments be Saudis. The only problem with this approach, however, was that most Saudi citizens were either not qualified for this work or, if they were qualified, were unwilling to do it. As the owner of the Osool jewelry (a 25-store chain) complained, "this is gold, it cannot just be handled and sold by anyone. There are not enough trained and qualified young Saudis. Or they quit due to long hours."

When confronted with terrorizing raids on their businesses, however, the employers needed to do something, and so many turned to "phantom worker programs." Employers would hire and register Saudi citizens, put them on the payroll, but agree that the person hired would never actually show up for work. As the owner of Osool states, "We have their names, they are registered, but they don't work." Phantom workers add to the employer's cost, but clearly provide no value other than to prevent one from being fined or imprisoned. The combination of increased expenses and fears of raids prompted many employers to leave the country. This, ironically, places even more urgency on Saudization and the process of becoming more self-sufficient when it comes to hiring Saudi workers.

*CONTINUED*

**DISCUSSION QUESTIONS**

1. How does the unique nature of Saudi culture make it difficult to change the rules of engagement for workers like the ones seen here?

2. What aspects of Saudi politics make it easier to change the rules of engagement for these workers?

3. In the end, which of these two forces are likely to win out and why?

SOURCES: M. Rashad and S. Kalin, "Saudi Arabia Needs 1.2 Million Jobs by 2022 to Hit Unemployment Target," *Reuters Online*, April 25, 2018; M. Stancati and D. Abdulaziz, "Saudi Arabia's Economic Revamp Means More Jobs for Saudis—If Only They Wanted Them," *The Wall Street Journal Online*, June 19, 2018; J. Northam, "Saudi Arabian Businesses Struggle with Rule to Replace Foreign Workers With Locals," *NPR Online*, May 28, 2018; "Mobily Penalized in Saudi Arabia for Not Hiring Enough Nationals," *Bloomberg Businessweek Online*, October 8, 2018.

because these jobs demand gregariousness and assertiveness, two of the central features shared by all extroverts. In contrast, introverts are better at studying and working in isolation, and hence they are best at jobs like accountant or research scientist because these jobs demand patience and vigilance. Extroverts tend to enjoy working in team-oriented environments more than introverts, but this does not always spill over into performance differences for engaging in teamwork.[78] Both extroverts and introverts can become effective leaders, although they achieve effectiveness in different ways. Extroverts tend to be top-down, autocratic and charismatic leaders who motivate followers by getting them emotionally engaged. In contrast, effective introverted leaders tend to be more bottom-up, participative leaders who listen to empowered employees and then engineer reward structures so that people are working toward their own self-interests.[79]

One important element of staffing in team-based structures, however, relates to how the selection of one team member influences the requirements associated with other team members.[80] In some cases, organizations might try to select people who have similar values and personality traits in order to create a strong team culture. When there is a strong team culture, everyone shares the same views and traits, promoting harmony and cohesiveness.[81] In other cases, people putting together a team go out of their way to make sure that the people on the team have different values and personalities. The hope here is that a diversity of opinion promotes internal debate and creativity. For example, at Pinterest, programming teams are put together one person at a time, and each new person added to the team is evaluated and selected based on some unique trait or perspective they might bring to the team that is not already there.[82]

The concept of "emotional intelligence" is also important in team contexts and has been used to describe people who are especially effective in fluid and socially intensive contexts. Emotional intelligence is traditionally conceived of as having five aspects: (1) self-awareness (knowledge of one's strengths and weaknesses), (2) self-regulation (the ability to keep disruptive emotions in check), (3) self-motivation (the ability to motivate oneself and persevere in the face of obstacles), (4) empathy (the ability to sense and read emotions in others), and (5) social skills (the ability to manage the emotions of other people).[83] Relative to standard measures of ability and personality, there has not been a great deal of scientific research on emotional intelligence, and critics have raised both theoretical and empirical questions about the construct itself. Theoretically, some critics have argued that the construct is overly broad and confuses aspects of perception, ability, and temperament that are best conceptualized as separate processes.[84] Empirically, the data seem to suggest that if one holds constant the scores on the variables captured by the five-factor model of personality and scores on tests of cognitive ability, there is little, if any, added predictive power attributable to emotional intelligence.[85]

Regardless of the nature of the context, the validity for almost all of the Big Five factors in terms of predicting job performance also seems to be higher when the scores are not obtained from the applicant but are instead taken from other people.[86] The lower validity associated with self-reports of personality can be traced to three factors. First, people sometimes lack insight into what their own personalities are actually like (or how they are perceived by others), so their scores are inaccurate or unreliable.

Second, people's personalities sometimes vary across different contexts. Thus, someone may be very conscientious when it comes to social activities such as planning a family wedding or a fraternity party, but less conscientious when it comes to doing a paid job. Thus, contextualized measures that add the term "at work" to standard personality items often perform better as predictors than standard noncontextualized measures. On average, "contextualizing" measures on personality tests in this manner can boost their average validity coefficient from around 0.10 to 0.25.[87]

A third factor that also limits the validity of personality items is that, unlike cognitive ability scores, applicants find it easier to fake traits by providing socially desirable responses to questions. That is, research suggests that when people fill out these inventories when applying for a job, their scores on conscientiousness and emotional stability are much higher relative to when they are just filling out the same questionnaires anonymously for research purposes.[88] Also, if people fail a personality test and then take the same test again in the future, their scores seem to increase dramatically.[89]

Several steps can be used to try to reduce faking. For example, if employers simply warn applicants that they are going to cross-check the applicants' self-ratings with other people, this seems to reduce faking.[90] Also, the degree to which people can fake various personality traits is enhanced with questionnaires, and one sees much less faking of traits when interviewers are assessing the characteristics.[91] All of this reinforces the idea that it is better to obtain this information from people other than the job applicant, and that it is better to use this information to reject low scorers but not necessarily hire all higher scorers on the basis of self-reports alone.

Finally, technologies are now being developed to create objective measures of traits from "digital traces" that people leave on the world. For example, software has been developed to track people's "likes and dislikes" on Facebook and then link these to the traits captured by the Big Five framework. Research shows that computer algorithms that process these data can generate an estimated score on the five traits that converges with self-reports better than what can be obtained from co-workers, friends, or even close relatives. In a different comprehensive study, researchers tracked the frequency of use, social interaction, and news consumption recorded on digital platforms for a sample of over 20,000 individuals across 20 countries. The findings showed that extroversion, agreeableness, and conscientiousness were all positively related to different types of social media use, whereas emotional stability and openness were negatively related to the same traces.[92]

## WORK SAMPLES

Work-sample tests attempt to simulate the job in a pre-hiring context to observe how the applicant performs in the simulated job. For example, at Compose Inc., a cloud-based storage firm in California, all applicants are brought in on one day to work on "mock projects" that simulate the actual work. The identities of the applicants are kept secret, and those making the hiring decision make it based solely on the work produced without ever meeting the candidates personally or studying their résumés.[93] Thus, as the Evidence-Based HR box shows, this type of blind test can enhance validity while reducing adverse impact.

# EVIDENCE-BASED HR

The evidence is crystal clear that hiring practices in some areas of high tech can have an adverse impact on female applicants. Although in the 1980s tech jobs were evenly split between the genders, in 2017, only 15% of software engineers working in Silicon Valley were women. Based upon the shifting burden of proof model that we discussed earlier in this chapter, the question then becomes, is this really a business necessity or are employers unfairly discriminating against women?

One empirical answer to this question comes from companies that "mask" the identity of work samples provided by men and women when it comes to writing software code. For example, at Github, the company had computer scientists analyze the acceptability of code written by anonymous women versus women whose identities were clearly shown. The results showed the experts rated roughly 70% of the code acceptable when it was written by a man or when the developer's gender was unknown, but only 60% when it was clearly written by a woman. Thus, the evidence seems to suggest that there is bias at work when it comes to evaluating women for coding jobs.

SOURCE: C. Suddath, "Girl Code," *Bloomberg Businessweek*, May 14, 2015; K. Zaleski, "Job Interviews without Gender," *The New York Times*, January 6, 2018.

The degree of fidelity in work samples can vary greatly. In some cases, applicants respond to a set of standardized hypothetical case studies and role-play how they would react to certain situations.[94] Often these standardized role-plays employ interactive video technology to create "virtual job auditions."[95] Simulations involving video-based role-plays seem to be more engaging and display higher levels of predictive validity relative to paper-and-pencil approaches.[96] In other cases, the job applicants are brought to the employers' location and perform the job for a short time period as part of a "job tryout."[97]

In some cases, as we saw earlier, employers will sponsor competitions in which contestants (who at this point are not even considered job applicants) vie for attention by going head-to-head in solving certain job-related problems.[98] These sorts of competitions have been common in some industries like architecture and fashion design, but their use is spreading across many other business contexts. These competitions tend to be cost effective in generating a lot of interest, and some have attracted as many as 1,000 contestants who bring their talents to bear on specific problems faced by the employing organization.

Competitions are particularly well-suited for assessing and "discovering" young people who may not have extended track records or portfolios to evaluate. For example, "hackathons," that is, competitions between computer programmers, were once held only on campuses with college students. Today, however, these contests are increasingly being won by high school dropouts who bypassed college altogether to focus exclusively on programming and application development using Web-based tools generally accessible to a wider audience.[99]

With all these advantages of work-sample tests come two drawbacks. First, by their very nature the tests are job specific, so generalizability is low. Second, partly because a new test has to be developed for each job and partly because of their nonstandardized formats, these tests are relatively expensive to develop. It is much more cost effective to purchase a commercially available cognitive ability test that can be used for a number of different job categories within the company than to develop a test for each job.

In the area of managerial selection, work-sample tests are typically the cornerstone in assessment centers. Generically, the term **assessment center** is used to describe a wide variety of specific selection programs that employ multiple selection methods to rate either applicants or job incumbents on their managerial potential. Someone attending an assessment center would typically experience work-sample tests such as an in-basket test and several tests of more general abilities and personality. Because assessment centers employ multiple selection methods, their criterion-related validity tends to be quite high.

Assessment centers seem to tap a number of different characteristics, but problem-solving ability and interpersonal skills stand out as probably the two most important skills tapped via this method.[100] However, many observers have argued that it is the exercises themselves—through their value as work samples—that explain why assessment centers have such high criterion-related validity, rather than their ability to tap generic underlying traits and skills.[101]

**Assessment center**
A process in which multiple raters evaluate employees' performance on a number of exercises.

## HONESTY TESTS AND DRUG TESTS

Many problems that confront society also exist within organizations, which has led to the development of honesty tests and drug-use tests. Many companies formerly employed polygraph tests, or lie detectors, to evaluate job applicants, but this changed with the passage of the Polygraph Act in 1988. This act banned the use of polygraphs in employment screening for most organizations. However, it did not eliminate the problem of theft by employees. As a result, the paper-and-pencil honesty-testing industry was born.

Paper-and-pencil honesty tests come in a number of different forms. Some directly emphasize questions dealing with past theft admissions or associations with people who stole from employers. Other items are less direct and tap more basic traits such as social conformity, conscientiousness, or emotional stability.[102] A large-scale independent review of validity studies suggests they can predict both theft and other disruptive behaviors. However, the reported correlations tend to be much higher when the research studies were conducted by test publishers who market the tests, relative to outside, objective parties with a less obvious conflict of interest. Thus, it is always a good idea for organizations to check the predictive accuracy of these kinds of tests for themselves and not rely solely on the results reported by test publishers.[103]

As is the case with measures of personality, some people are concerned that people confronting an honesty test can fake their way to a passing score. The evidence suggests that people instructed to fake their way to a high score (indicating honesty) can do so. However, it is not clear that this affects the validity of the predictions made using such tests. That is, it seems that despite this built-in bias, scores on the test still predict future theft. Thus, the effect of the faking bias is not large enough to detract from the test's validity.[104]

As with theft, there is a growing perception of the problems caused by drug use among employees. There are two societal trends in the United States that have heightened the need for such tests. First, there is an opioid epidemic that continues to spread across the country, with a record 72,000 drug overdose deaths estimated in 2017. As you might expect, much of the fallout is increasingly spilling over to the workplace—especially construction sites, factories, warehouses, and back offices. At least 217 workers died from an unintentional drug or alcohol overdose while at work in 2016, up 32% from 2015, according to the Bureau of Labor Statistics.[105] Workplace overdose deaths have been increasing by 25% or more a year since 2010. Those numbers don't include the many more overdoses that don't end in death or accidents that are only caused partly by drug impairment. Getting former addicts back on the job is dangerous and difficult, and as the Integrity in Action box shows, may require charitable contributions.

# INTEGRITY IN ACTION

## Serving Up Soup, Rehabilitation, and Compassion

Columbia Boiler, a manufacturer of galvanized containers in Youngstown, Ohio, provides well-paid jobs that offer full benefits, even though many of the jobs do not even require a high school diploma. The company is doing well; however, it loses over $200,000 worth of business each month due to a shortage of workers. Where does that business go? According to Michael Sherwin, the CEO of Boiler, "our main competitor in Germany can get things done more quickly because they have a better labor pool." One might ask, "What does it mean to have a 'better labor pool' when the jobs don't even require a high school education?" The answer is: a labor pool that can pass a drug test. Over 25% of applicants to Boiler fail drug tests. This company's experience is far from extraordinary, but rather representative of a broader national problem that is only getting worse.

The opioid epidemic is part of the culprit in this case, and this has been true for several years. However, increasingly, new laws that allow for the recreational use of marijuana have greatly expanded the number of failed drug tests across the country. Seven states in the United States allowed for the recreational use of marijuana in 2017, and in 2018 three more states—Michigan, Utah, and Missouri—joined their ranks. Still, even though it may be fine for the government to ignore someone's drug use, this

is much more difficult for employers. For example, back at Columbia Boiler, Sherwin notes that "the lightest product we make is 1,500 pounds and some go up to 250,000 pounds. If something goes wrong, it won't hurt our workers. It'll kill them." Any such incident such as this would trigger an investigation, and a drug test cannot discriminate whether a worker was doing drugs at work or at home. This subtle distinction could be easily lost on a judge or jury in a wrongful death suit.

Although few would argue that current drug use is a legitimate knock-out factor when it comes to employment, an additional question arises with respect to what to do with former users or addicts who can pass a test today but, given the evidence for recidivism, may not be able to pass a test tomorrow? Ironically, one of the industries that is most susceptible to hiring workers with drug problems—the restaurant industry—is also one where some of the most innovative "rehabilitation and re-employment initiatives" are being forged.

For example, Rob and Diane Perez founded a restaurant called DV8 that hires only workers who are in treatment for opioid and related addictions. In fact, beyond just hiring these workers, the restaurant makes this unique personnel selection strategy the center of their business model. The name DV8 itself highlights the goal of helping the

workers change the paths of their lives. Customers are attracted to the eatery because of the delicious food, but also because it makes them feel good about supporting some of the local folks in the community who are trying to rebuild their lives. In fact, the restaurant was opened with a $300,000 gift from local charities and philanthropists and works hand in hand with local rehabilitation centers in a joint effort to strengthen the community. In terms of product differentiation, one customer expressed it best when she admitted that "you wouldn't pay $4 for a cinnamon roll anywhere else, but I don't mind paying a little extra to help people get back on their feet."

### DISCUSSION QUESTIONS

1. Do you believe the local experiment described here could be replicated on a national scale, where one sees a whole restaurant chain buily upon this "dual-purpose" business venture?

2. Can you think of other industries other than hospitality that might also be suited—or suited better—for this unique business model that blends charity with commerce?

SOURCE: N. D. Schwartz, "Economy Needs Workers, but Drug Tests Take a Toll," *The New York Times Online*, July 24, 2017; K. McLaughlin and N. V. Osipova, "A Reckoning with the Dark Side of the Restaurant Industry," *The Wall Street Journal Online*, November 12, 2018; P. Krishna, "A Restaurant Takes on the Opioid Crisis, One Worker at a Time," *The New York Times Online*, July 10, 2018.

As mentioned previously, a second change in the United States that employers need to recognize is the shifting legal status of marijuana in many states. Marijuana is currently legal for medicinal and recreational use in many states, and some employers are backing off requirements associated with marijuana when they can—but not all can. Drug testing is mandated by federal law for many occupations classified as "safety sensitive" jobs regulated by the Transportation Department such as truck drivers, pilots, ship captains, and train engineers. The number of people who tested positive for illegal drugs was less than in 2% in 2002, but is now over 5%.[106] Moreover, this rate is higher in certain occupations and regions of the country. The rate for those working in the mining industry and construction industry is 18% and the states of Colorado and Washington show the highest in the nation. Indeed, Jesse Russow, owner of Avalanche Roofing and Exteriors in Colorado Springs, states that "to find a roofer or painter who can pass a drug test is unheard of."[107]

Ironically, one employer that may back off testing for marijuana is the Federal Bureau of Investigation (FBI), which noticed that many of the young applicants best skilled for tracking down cyber crimes also have a history of marijuana use. In fact, the acting director of the FBI suggested in 2014 the agency may have to loosen its no-tolerance policy for marijuana in order to attract this talent, noting that "I have to hire a great workforce to compete with cyber criminals and some of the best kids want to smoke weed on the way to the interview."[108] Thus, the quest for deriving competitive advantage from one's workforce sometimes takes odd twists.

## A LOOK BACK

### Validation and Personnel Selection: Strangers No More

The decisions that organizations make regarding who is going to be part of the organization and who is going to be turned away are some of the most important decisions that the firm will make. As we saw in our opening vignette focusing on Uber, these decisions impact the performance and reputation of the company and its executives, as well as the lives of job applicants and the people they engage with as part of their jobs. The importance of these decisions means that they have to be based upon procedures that have been empirically validated and not left to idiosyncratic judgments of untrained individuals who may be confronting a labor shortage in the jobs they are trying to fill and thus subject to making hasty, ill-informed decisions. This chapter has summarized a large and varied set of tactics that firms can use to make the right hiring decisions when it comes to the selection process.

#### QUESTIONS

1. Based on this chapter, what are the best methods of obtaining information about job applicants and how might these have been used at Uber to prevent many of the problems they created?

2. What are the best characteristics to look for in applicants, and how does this depend on the nature of the job? How does the unique nature of jobs at ride-sharing companies like Uber affect selection methods?

3. If you could use only two of the methods described in this chapter and could assess only two of the characteristics discussed, which would you choose, and why?

# SUMMARY

In this chapter, we examined the five critical standards with which all personnel selection methods should conform: reliability, validity, generalizability, utility, and legality. We also looked at nine different selection methods currently used in organizations and evaluated each with respect to these five standards. Table 6.4 summarizes these selection methods and can be used as a guide in deciding which test to use for a specific purpose. Although we discussed each type of test individually, it is important to note in closing that there is no need to use only one type of test for any one job. Indeed, managerial assessment centers use many different forms of tests over a two- or three-day period to learn as much as possible about candidates for important executive positions. As a result, highly accurate predictions are often made, and the validity associated with the judicious use of multiple tests is higher than that for tests used in isolation.

# KEY TERMS

Reliability, 237
Validity, 241
Criterion-related validity, 241
Predictive validation, 241
Concurrent validation, 242

Content validation, 244
Utility, 246
Situational interview, 255
Cognitive ability tests, 259

Verbal comprehension, 259
Quantitative ability, 259
Reasoning ability, 259
Assessment center, 265

# DISCUSSION QUESTIONS

1. We examined nine different types of selection methods in this chapter. Assume that you were just rejected for a job based on one of these methods. Obviously, you might be disappointed and angry regardless of what method was used to make this decision, but can you think of two or three methods that might leave you most distressed? In general, why might the acceptability of the test to applicants be an important standard to add to the five we discussed in this chapter?

2. Video-recording applicants in interviews is becoming an increasingly popular means of getting multiple assessments of that individual from different perspectives. Can you think of some reasons why video-recording interviews might also be useful in evaluating the interviewer? What would you look for in an interviewer if you were evaluating one on video?

3. Distinguish between concurrent and predictive validation designs, and discuss why the latter is preferred over the former. Examine each of the nine selection methods discussed in this chapter and determine which of these would have their validity most and least affected by the type of validation design employed.

4. Some observers have speculated that, in addition to increasing the validity of decisions, employing rigorous selection methods has symbolic value for organizations. What message is sent to applicants about the organization through hiring practices, and how might this message be reinforced by recruitment programs that occur before selection and by training programs that occur after selection?

# SELF-ASSESSMENT EXERCISE

Also assignable in Connect.

Reviews of research about personality have identified five common aspects of personality, referred to as the Big Five personality traits. Find out which are your most prominent traits. Read each of the following statements, marking "Yes" if it describes you and "No" if it does not.

1. In conversations, I tend to do most of the talking.
2. Often people look to me to make decisions.
3. I am a very active person.
4. I usually seem to be in a hurry.
5. I am dominant, forceful, and assertive.
6. I have a very active imagination.
7. I have an active fantasy life.
8. How I feel about things is important to me.
9. I find it easy to feel myself what others are feeling.

**Table 6.4**
A Summary of Personnel Selection Methods

| METHOD | RELIABILITY | VALIDITY | GENERALIZABILITY | UTILITY | LEGALITY |
|---|---|---|---|---|---|
| Interviews | Low when unstructured and when assessing nonobservable traits | Low if unstructured and nonbehavioral | Low | Low, especially because of expense | Low because of subjectivity and potential interviewer bias; also, lack of validity makes job-relatedness low |
| Reference checks | Low, especially when obtained from letters | Low because of lack of range in evaluations | Low | Low, although not expensive to obtain | Those writing letters may be concerned with charges of libel |
| Biographical information | High test–retest, especially for verifiable information | High criterion-related validity; low in content validity | Usually job specific, but have been successfully developed for many job types | High; inexpensive way to collect vast amounts of potentially relevant data | May have adverse impact; thus often develop separate scoring keys based on sex or race |
| Physical ability tests | High | Moderate criterion-related validity; high content validity for some jobs | Low; pertain only to physically demanding jobs | Moderate for some physical jobs; may prevent expensive injuries and disability | Often have adverse impact on women and people with disabilities; need to establish job-relatedness |
| Cognitive ability tests | High | Moderate criterion-related validity; content validation inappropriate | High; predictive for most jobs, although best for complex jobs | High; low cost and wide application across diverse jobs in companies | Often have adverse impact on race, especially for African Americans, though decreasing over time |
| Personality inventories | High | Low to moderate criterion-related validity for most traits; content validation inappropriate | Low; few traits predictive for many jobs, except conscientiousness | Low, although inexpensive for jobs where specific traits are relevant | Low because of cultural and sex differences on most traits, and low job-relatedness in general |
| Work-sample tests | High | High criterion and content validity | Usually job specific, but have been successfully developed for many job types | High, despite the relatively high cost to develop | High because of low adverse impact and high job-relatedness |
| Honesty tests | Insufficient independent evidence | Insufficient independent evidence | Insufficient independent evidence | Insufficient independent evidence | Insufficient history of litigation, but will undergo scrutiny |
| Drug tests | High | High | High | Expensive, but may yield high payoffs for health-related costs | May be challenged on invasion-of-privacy grounds |

10. I think it's interesting to learn and develop new hobbies.
11. My first reaction is to trust people.
12. I believe that most persons are basically well intentioned.
13. I'm not crafty or shy.
14. I'd rather not talk about myself and my accomplishments.
15. I'd rather praise others than be praised myself.
16. I come into situations being fully prepared.
17. I pride myself on my sound judgment.
18. I have a lot of self-discipline.
19. I try to do jobs carefully so that they don't have to be done again.
20. I like to keep everything in place so that I know where it is.
21. I enjoy performing under pressure.
22. I am seldom sad or depressed.
23. I'm an even-tempered person.
24. I am levelheaded in emergencies.
25. I feel I am capable of coping with most of my problems.

The statements are grouped into categories. Statements 1–5 describe extroversion; 6–10, openness to experience; 11–15, agreeableness; 16–20, conscientiousness; and 21–25, emotional stability. The more times you wrote "Yes" for the statements in a category, the more likely you are to have the associated trait.

# EXERCISING STRATEGY

## Employers Unite to Fight "Religious Freedom" Bills

Almost all organizations that care about ethics have a mission statement and a value statement that they adhere to with religious fervor when it comes to executing their strategy. However, in some contexts this comes into conflict with legislation that, in an effort to protect freedom of religion, contradicts those values. For example, across the United States a large number of states have introduced "religious freedom bills" that allow employers to discriminate against lesbian, gay, bisexual, and transgender (LGBT) applicants and employees. The argument is that the practices engaged by LGBT individuals run counter to the religious beliefs held by some business owners, and that the values of the LGBT community should not be forced on those employers.

Indiana was one of the first states to pass a religious freedom bill, and although that bill was later repealed, it sparked numerous other similar efforts in other regions. According to the Bureau of Labor Statistics, anti-gay discrimination is legal in 28 states that, as a whole, comprise over 50% of the workforce. There are also over 200 new bills under consideration in 33 states that are considered hostile to gay and transgender individuals, according to Human Rights Campaign (HRC).

Many employers who view that this legislation runs counter to their own values are collaborating and fighting to strike down or prevent future laws. In the beginning, employers took a divide and conquer strategy to this battle, where different companies led in different regions. For example, Eli Lilly and Salesforce spearheaded efforts in Indiana, Disney has led efforts in Georgia, and MGM Resorts has focused on Mississippi, all because they had substantial operations in those regions. However, now, a more integrated approach is being adopted so that companies do not have to take a reactive, "whack-a-mole" approach to impending legislation. As one of the employers stated, "Equality is a core value, and where we see negative legislation we have to take a stand. We want to be a spark for other to get involved in areas and states that are considering these types of legislation."

### QUESTIONS

1. How can one reconcile the religious values espoused by some business owners with the values of LGBT employees or is this strictly a zero-sum game?
2. Why is the effort to thwart religious freedom bills primarily sponsored by large employers, and is there any way to reconcile the values of large employers and small employers on this issue?
3. What does "reasonable accommodation" mean in the personnel selection context, and how does one test for what is "reasonable"?

SOURCES: J. Green and Tim Higgens, "LGBT Inc.," *Bloomberg Businessweek*, April 27, 2016, pp. 26–28; J. Eidelson, "Sweet Cakes with a Bitter Aftertaste," *Bloomberg Businessweek*, May 30, 2016, pp. 29–30; J. Green, "At Work and Out of the Closet in the Heartland," *Bloomberg Businessweek*, March 6, 2017, pp. 22–23.

# MANAGING PEOPLE

## Policing Hiring Practices in the Field of Law Enforcement

William Melendez had quite a long criminal record—for a policeman. Melendez worked as part of the police force in Garden City, Michigan. In his 15 years as an officer there, he was involved in over a dozen lawsuits alleging a variety of forms of misconduct including the use of excessive force, planting evidence, making arrests without probable cause, and wrongful death. In one 1996 case, Melendez shot an unarmed motorist who he had made lie down by the side of the road during a traffic stop. The city settled with the deceased man's family for $1 million in a plea deal that allowed Melendez to avoid prison. Although this was all in the public record, it did not stop Melendez from landing a new job in Inkster, Michigan, a few years later, where in 2016 he was arrested again when video released showing him drag a man who ran a stop light out of his car and beat him unconscious. The City of Inkster, like Garden City, also settled out of court, awarding the beaten motorist $1.4 million.

In the wake of recent controversies like this, as well as other nationally publicized police brutality cases in New York City, Baltimore, Chicago, Seattle, and Ferguson, Missouri, many are beginning to ask questions about how police officers are selected and why some "bad apples" are allowed to move from one jurisdiction to another despite clearly questionable past employment histories. Indeed, a recent study conducted by the *Wall Street Journal* followed the cases of roughly 3,500 officers who lost their jobs due to arrests or convictions for seven years and found that over 10% of this group was still working in law enforcement.

Part of this can be traced to the difficulty of finding people willing to do this dangerous work, as well as the difficulty associated with obtaining the information needed to make better decisions. Although some states have formal decertification lists containing the names of officers who were fired for criminal acts, some do not. Moreover, the decertification process varies widely between states that have such lists. The State of Georgia, for example, decertified close to 6,000 officers in the last nine years, whereas the State of Pennsylvania decertified less than 30 over the same time period. Finally, although it may seem remarkable, there is no national registry that aggregates this state level data that one could search when making a hiring decision, which allows decertified cops to move from state to state.

The lack of standardization and subjective nature of selection decisions in law enforcement is now a focus of national scrutiny. After the killing of Michael Brown in Ferguson, a commission was created to collect, maintain, and distribute decertification data to all states. The goal is to make it easier for those making hiring decisions to isolate those with troubled pasts and keep them off the streets. For this information to be useful, however, it has to be combined with the creation of a different culture that will promote the use of that information. When Gregory Gaskin, the Inkster Police Chief who hired William Melendez was asked about whether he read the pre-hiring background investigation dealing with the applicant's background, he simply responded, "Well, I read it, but as far as significance, I didn't think much of it."

## QUESTIONS

1. How is the nature of police work qualitatively different from most jobs, and what can be done to help organizations share information about their own hiring experiences?
2. Why might former police officers whose employment had been terminated be better suited than most job incumbents when it comes to avoiding detection?

SOURCES: L. Radnofsky, Z. Elinson, J. R. Emshwiller, and G. Fields, "Why Some Problem Cops Don't Lose Their Badges," *The Wall Street Journal Online*, December 30, 2016; "Police Balance Crime Fighting with Protecting Citizen's Rights," *The Wall Street Journal Online*, June 14, 2015; F. Speilman, "Emanual Opens the Door to Relaxing Police Hiring Standards," *The Chicago Sun Times Online*, December 14, 2016.

## HR IN SMALL BUSINESS

### Kinaxis Chooses Sales Reps with Personality

Kinaxis, a software company headquartered in Ottawa, Ontario, sells to clients around the world. Its specialty is software for supply chain management—all the processes and relationships through which companies obtain supplies as needed and get their products to customers on time and at minimal cost. This is a sophisticated type of product, tailored to a company's specific needs. Therefore, Kinaxis depends on salespeople who understand how businesses work, who listen carefully to identify needs, and who provide excellent customer service to maintain long-term business relationships.

Recently, Bob Dolan, vice president for sales at Kinaxis, needed to hire a sales team to serve clients in North America. The company had just one salesperson serving the continent, and Dolan wanted to add four more. He received about 100 résumés and wanted to select from these.

He started by reviewing the résumés against job requirements and selected 20 candidates for a first round of interviews. The interview process helped Dolan cut the list of candidates in half, so he needed another way to narrow his options.

Dolan decided his next step would be personality testing. He hired a firm called Opus Productivity Solutions to administer a test called PDP ProScan to the remaining 10 candidates. In addition, Dolan himself took the test and had his current sales rep do the same. The existing salesperson was doing an excellent job, so the results of his test could help Dolan and Opus pinpoint the characteristics of someone likely to succeed in sales at Kinaxis. Based on analysis of all the results, Opus created a benchmark of traits associated with success in the job.

Representatives from Opus also discussed the test results with each candidate, giving each one a chance to disagree with the scores. No one did. Dolan observed that all the candidates scored high in assertiveness and extroversion—not surprising for people in sales. In addition, two of them scored above the benchmark in conformity and below the benchmark in dominance. Those results suggested to Dolan that these candidates might be so eager to please that they would be quick to give in to whatever customers requested—a pattern that could become costly for the company. Dolan eliminated those two candidates.

That meant Dolan still had eight candidates to fill four positions. He asked each one to give him the names of major accounts he or she had signed up in the previous two years. Four candidates were able to come up with three or four large clients. Those were the candidates Dolan hired.

Since then, Dolan says his experience with personality testing has only reinforced his belief that this selection method helps Kinaxis identify the best candidates. For example, one sales rep had scored low on "pace," indicating that the individual might lack the patience needed for the slow cycles required to close a sale of a complex software system. Dolan hoped the issue could be overcome if he provided

enough coaching, but in fact, the sales rep sometimes behaved impatiently, annoying prospects. After three years of trying to help him grow into the job, Dolan laid him off.

The company's commitment to careful selection is expressed on its website: "As a growing and determined company, we're always looking for people eager to push the limits of each day of what's possible." Kinaxis was recently named one of Canada's top employers for young people.

## QUESTIONS

1. What selection methods did Bob Dolan use for hiring salespeople? Did he go about using these methods in the best order? What, if anything, would you change about the order of the methods used?
2. What were the advantages to Kinaxis of using personality tests to help select sales representatives? What were the disadvantages?
3. Given the information gathered from the selection methods, what process did Dolan use to make his selection decision? What improvements can you recommend to this process for decisions to hire sales reps in the future?

SOURCES: Susan Greco, "Personality Testing for Sales Recruits," *Inc.*, March 1, 2009; Kinaxis website, Corporate Overview and Careers pages, www.kinaxis.com.

# NOTES

1. K. Maher, "Security Firm That Employed Orlando Killer Says It Made 'Clerical Error' in Evaluation Documents," *Wall Street Journal*, June 19, 2016.
2. C. Cutter, "Yes, You're Hired; No We Do Not Need to Meet You," *The Wall Street Journal Online*, November 15, 2018.
3. Z. Nemtsova, "Young, Liberal and Russian," *The New York Times Online*, September 23, 2018.
4. D. Nishi, "Tackling Stereotypes before Your Job Interview," *Wall Street Journal*, August 2, 2014.
5. P. Coy, "Will the Jobs Boom End Too Soon," *Bloomberg Businessweek*, December 3, 2015, p. 15.
6. E. Bernstein, "Personality Research Says Change in Major Traits Occurs Naturally," *Wall Street Journal*, April 22, 2014.
7. B. Weber, "Gender Bias by the Numbers," *Bloomberg Businessweek*, January 30, 2014.
8. E. Gray, "Do You Understand Why Stars Twinkle?" *Time*, June 22, 2015.
9. J. Walker, "Meet the New Boss: Big Data," *Wall Street Journal*, September 20, 2012.
10. J. Diamond, "Baseball Tackles Workplace Mystery: How to Build team Chemistry," *The Wall Street Journal Online*, July 12, 2017.
11. S. Finklestein, "Why Companies Should Hire Teams, Not Individuals," *The Wall Street Journal Online*, October 29, 2017.
12. A. Ito, "Hiring in the Age of Big Data," *Bloomberg Businessweek*, November 13, 2013, pp. 40–41.
13. B. Poucher, "Behind the Scenes at The International Collegiate Programming Contest" *Forbes*, July 1, 2016.
14. L. Chapman, "Hacking the Need for a Full Time Job," *Bloomberg Businessweek*, April 10, 2017, pp. 33–34.
15. F. Schmidt, H. Le, I. S. Oh, and J. Shaffer, "General Mental Ability, Job Performance, and Red Herrings: Responses to Osterman, Hauser, and Schmitt," *Academy of Management Perspectives* 21 (2007), pp. 64–76.
16. H. Aguinis, H. Y. Ji, and H. Joo, "Gender Productivity Gap Among Star Performers in STEM and Other Scientific Fields," *Journal of Applied Psychology*, 2018.
17. E. O'Boyle and H. Aguinis, "The Best and the Rest: Revisiting the Norm of Normality of Individual Performance," *Personnel Psychology* 65 (2012), pp. 79–119.
18. A. Southall, "Muslim Officer Sues New York Police Department over No Beard Policy," *New York Times*, June 22, 2016.
19. M. Mihelich, "Sacred Grounds—for Lawsuits," *Workforce*, April 2014, pp. 18–19.
20. D. Bennett, "Deep Fried Civil War," *Bloomberg Businessweek*, August 2, 2012, pp. 62–64.
21. R. L. Lubin, "When 'Disparate Impact' Bites Back," *Wall Street Journal*, March 9, 2014.
22. J. Simons, "For Black Applicants, the Hiring Market Hasn't Changed Much in 25 Years," *The Wall Street Journal Online*, October 3, 2017
23. J. Holman and M. Abelson, "Will a Woman Ever Get a Shot at Leading Goldman?" *Bloomberg Businessweek*, March 19, 2018, p. 33.
24. D. Lawrence and M. Abelson, "Women vs. Wall Street," *Bloomberg Businessweek*, May 7, 2018, pp. 44–49.
25. P. Roth, P. Bobko, L. McFarland, and M. Buster, "Work Sample Tests in Personnel Selection: A Meta-analysis of Black-White Differences in Overall Exercise Scores," *Personnel Psychology* 61 (2008), pp. 637–61.

26. R. E. Ployhart and B. C. Holtz, "The Diversity-Validity Dilemma: Strategies for Reducing Racioethnic and Sex Group Differences and Adverse Impact in Selection," *Personnel Psychology* 61 (2008), pp. 153–72.

27. J. Bravin, "Supreme Court Upholds Michigan's Affirmative Action Ban," *Wall Street Journal*, April 22, 2014.

28. T. Lewin, "Colleges Seek New Paths to Diversity after Court Ruling," *New York Times*, April 22, 2014.

29. E. Zlomik, "An End Run around Affirmative Action Bans," *Bloomberg Businessweek*, April 23, 2012, p. 52.

30. J. Bravin, "Supreme Court Upholds Affirmative Action in University Admissions," *Wall Street Journal*, June 23, 2016.

31. D. A. Newman and J. S. Lyon, "Recruitment Efforts to Reduce Adverse Impact: Targeted Recruiting for Personality, Cognitive Ability and Diversity," *Journal of Applied Psychology* 94 (2009), pp. 298–317.

32. D. M. Finch, B. D. Edwards, and J. C. Wallace, "Multistage Selection Strategies: Simulating the Effects of Adverse Impact and Expected Performance for Various Predictor Combinations," *Journal of Applied Psychology* 94 (2009), pp. 318–40.

33. F. Hanson, "Diversity of a Different Color," *Workforce Management*, June 2010, pp. 21–24.

34. L. T. Cullen, "The Diversity Delusion," *Time*, May 2007, p. 45.

35. P. G. Lee, "No Place for Old Waiters at Texas Roadhouse," *Bloomberg Businessweek*, September 28, 2015, pp. 23–24.

36. C. A. Liptak, "Muslim Denied Job over Head Scarf Wins in Supreme Court," *Wall Street Journal*, June 1, 2015.

37. L. Weber, "Are You Disabled? Your Boss Needs to Know," *Wall Street Journal*, March 18, 2014.

38. P. Aulino, "Skills Translation Critical for Hiring Veterans," *Bloomberg Businessweek Online,* September 20, 2017.

39. M. Phillips, "From War Zone to Workplace," *Bloomberg Businessweek*, November 25, 2015, pp. 18–19.

40. R. A. Posthuma, F. R. Morgeson, and M. A. Campion, "Beyond Employment Interview Validity: A Comprehensive Narrative Review of Recent Research and Trends over Time," *Personnel Psychology* 55 (2002), pp. 1–81.

41. S. Shellenbarger, "The Mistakes You Make in a Meeting's First Milliseconds," *The Wall Street Journal Online*, January 30, 2018.

42. A. Wilhelmy, M. Kleinmann, C. J. Konig, K. G. Melchers, and D. M. Truxillo, "How and Why Do Interviewers Try to Make Impressions on Applicants? A Qualitative Study," *Journal of Applied Psychology* 101 (2016), pp. 313–32.

43. C. J. Hartwell and M. A. Campion, "Getting on the Same Page: The Effect of Normative Feedback Interventions on Structured Interview Ratings," *Journal of Applied Psychology* 101 (2016), pp. 757–78.

44. M. A. McDaniel, F. P. Morgeson, E. B. Finnegan, M. A. Campion, and E. P. Braverman, "Use of Situational Judgment Tests to Predict Job Performance: A Clarification of the Literature," *Journal of Applied Psychology* 86 (2001), pp. 730–40.

45. E. Monath and L. Weber, "Amazon, Google, Poised for Race to Hire Software Developers," *The Wall Street Journal Online*, November 13, 2018.

46. K. Gee, "Employers Eager to Hire Try a New Policy 'No Experience Necessary,'" *The Wall Street Journal Online*, July 29, 2018.

47. L. Dixon, "What's More Important When Hiring: Future Potential or Past Performance," *Talent Economy*, June 5, 2017.

48. A. P. J. Ellis, B. J. West, A. M. Ryan, and R. P. DeShon, "The Use of Impression Management Tactics in Structured Interviews: A Function of Question Type?" *Journal of Applied Psychology* 87 (2002), pp. 1200–8.

49. A. Bryant, "Google's Quest to Build a Better Boss," *New York Times*, March 12, 2011, p. C1.

50. C. Willmer, "Harrassment at the Broker's Office," *Bloomberg Businessweek,* March 21, 2018, pp. 26–27.

51. A. Dizik, "Wooing Job Recruiters with Video Resumes," *Wall Street Journal*, May 2010, p. D4.

52. C. Suddath, "Imaginary Friends," *Bloomberg Businessweek*, January 21, 2013, p. 66.

53. M. Korn, "Wealth of Waste? Rethinking the Value of a Business Major," *Wall Street Journal*, April 5, 2012.

54. V. L. Chien and J. Berman, "Companies Are Hiring, Just Not You," *Bloomberg Businessweek*, August 15, 2011, pp. 10–11.

55. C. Dougherty, "Gap Hurts Job Hunters," *Wall Street Journal*, August 29, 2012.

56. S. F. Gale, "Passing the Stress Test," *Workforce*, August, 2017.

57. S. Johnson, "Officer Fired After Tamir Rice Shooting Probe," *CNN Online,* May 30, 2017.

58. K. Darcy, "Manhattan: Steve Masiello on Leave," *ESPN*, March 26, 2014.

59. R. Sanchez, G. Botelho, and F. Karimi, "New York Prison Employee Arraigned for Allegedly Helping Killers Escape," *CNN*, June 12, 2015, www.cnn.com.

60. M. Schwirtz and M. Winerip, "Warning Signs Overlooked in Hiring for New York City Jails," *New York Times*, January 15, 2015.

61. M. Barnekow-Bergkvist, U. Aasa, K. A. Angquist, and H. Johansson, "Prediction of Development of Fatigue during a Simulated Ambulance Work Task from Physical Performance Tests," *Ergonomics* 47 (2004), pp. 1238–50.

62. D. Lechner, "The Value of Physical Ability Testing," *Risk Management*, December 1, 2016

63. N. D. Henderson, "Predicting Long-Term Firefighter Performance from Measures of Cognitive Ability and Physical Ability Measures," *Personnel Psychology* 63 (2010), pp. 999–1039.

64. J. Hogan, "Physical Abilities," in *Handbook of Industrial & Organizational Psychology*, 2nd ed., ed. M. D. Dunnette and L. M. Hough (Palo Alto, CA: Consulting Psychologists Press, 1991).

65. M. Rosenbert and D. Phillips, "All Combat Roles Now Open to Women, Defense Secretary Says," *New York Times*, December 3, 2015.

66. N. Kitroeff and J. Silver-Greenberg, "Pregnancy Discrimination Is Rampant Inside America's Biggest Companies," *The New York Times Online*, June 15, 2018.

67. Editorial Board, "Women Who Work," *New York Times*, November 30, 2014.

68. C. St. Louis, "Doctor's Notes for Pregnant Employees Can Backfire, Experts Warn," *New York Times*, July 8, 2015.

69. J. F. Salagado, N. Anderson, S. Moscoso, C. Bertua, and F. De Fruyt, "International Validity Generalization of GMA and Cognitive Abilities: A European Community Meta-Analysis," *Personnel Psychology* 56 (2003), pp. 573–605.

70. S. Lebowitz, "Science Says IQ May Be the Best Predictor of Your Potential to Excel at Work—and No One Wants to Hear It," *Business Insider*, October 8, 2017.

71. P. Coy, "The SAT Is Elitist, Unfair, Out of Date, or All of the Above," *Bloomberg Businessweek*, October 7, 2013.

72. M. A. Campion, J. L. Outtz, S. Zedeck, F. S. Schmidt, J. E. Kehoe, K. R. Murphy, and R. M. Guion, "The Controversy over Score Banding in Personnel Selection: Answers to 10 Key Questions," *Personnel Psychology* 54 (2001), pp. 149–85.

73. C. McWhirter, "High Tech Cheaters Pose Test Threat," *Wall Street Journal*, June 10, 2013.

74. E. Barber, "Chinese and South Korean SAT Students Face Nervous Wait after Scores Delayed," *Time*, October 30, 2014.

75. L. Weber, "Today's Personality Tests Raise the Bar for Job Seekers," *Wall Street Journal*, April 14, 2015.

76. F. P. Morgeson, M. A. Campion, R. L. Dipboye, J. R. Hollenbeck, K. R. Murphy, and N. Schmitt, "Reconsidering the Use of Personality Tests in Personnel Selection Contexts," *Personnel Psychology* 60 (2007), pp. 683–729.

77. L. Winerman, "What Sets High Achievers Apart?" *Monitor on Psychology*, December 2013, pp. 28–31.

78. R. Pyrillis, "Searching for Solace," *Workforce*, November, 2014, pp. 41–43.

79. B. Walsh, "The Upside of Being an Introvert (and Why Extroverts Are Over-Rated)," *Time*, February 6, 2012, pp. 40–45.

80. S. E. Humphrey, J. R. Hollenbeck, C. J. Meyer, and D. R. Ilgen, "Trait Configurations in Self-Managed Teams: A Conceptual Examination of the Use of Seeding for Maximizing and Minimizing Trait Variance in Teams," *Journal of Applied Psychology* 92 (2007), pp. 885–92.

81. A. Hedger, "Employee Screening: Common Challenges, Smart Solutions," *Workforce Management*, March 17, 2008, pp. 39–46.

82. E. Huet, "In the Land of the Blind Hire," *Bloomberg Businessweek*, January 23, 2017, pp. 27–28.

83. D. Goleman, "Sometimes, EQ Is More Important Than IQ," *CNN.com*, January 14, 2005, p. 1.

84. R. D. Roberts, G. Mathews, and M. Zeidner, "Emotional Intelligence: Muddling through Theory and Measurement," *Industrial and Organizational Psychology* 3 (2010), pp. 140–44.

85. D. L. Joseph and D. A. Newman, "Emotional Intelligence: An Integrative Meta-analysis and Cascading Model," *Journal of Applied Psychology* 95 (2010), pp. 54–78.

86. J. M. Hunthausen, D. M. Truxillo, T. N. Bauer, and L. B. Hammer, "A Field Study of Frame of Reference Effects on Personality Test Validity," *Journal of Applied Psychology* 88 (2003), pp. 545–51.

87. J. A. Shaffer and J. E. Postlewaite, "A Matter of Context: A Meta-analytic Investigation of the Relative Validity of Contextualized and Non-contextualized Personality Measures," *Personnel Psychology*, 65 (2012), pp. 445–494.

88. S. A. Birkland, T. M. Manson, J. L. Kisamore, M. T. Brannick, and M. A. Smith, "Faking on Personality Measures," *International Journal of Selection and Assessment* 14 (December 2006), pp. 317–35.

89. J. P. Hausknecht, "Candidate Persistence and Personality Test Practice Effects: Implications for Staffing System Management," *Personnel Psychology* 63 (2010), pp. 299–324.

90. N. L. Vasilopoulos, J. M. Cucina, and J. M. McElreath, "Do Warnings of Response Verification Moderate the Relationship between Personality and Cognitive Ability?" *Journal of Applied Psychology* 90 (2005), pp. 306–22.

91. C. H. Van Iddekinge, P. H. Raymark, and P. L. Roth, "Assessing Personality with a Structured Employment Interview: Construct-Related Validity and Susceptibility to Response Inflation," *Journal of Applied Psychology* 90 (2005), pp. 536–52.

92. G. Zuniga, T. Deihl, B. Huber and J. Liu, "Personality Traits and Social Media Use in 20 Countries: How Personality Relates to Frequency of Social Media Use, Social Media News Use, and Social Media Use for Social Interaction," *Cyber-Psychology, Behavior and Social Networking* 20 (2017), pp. 540–552.

93. R. Feintzeig, "The Boss Doesn't Want Your Resume," *Wall Street Journal*, January 5, 2016.

94. C. Palmeri, "Putting Managers to the Test," *Bloomberg Businessweek*, November 20, 2006, p. 82.

95. C. Winkler, "Job Tryouts Go Virtual: Online Job Simulations Provide Sophisticated Candidate Assessments," *HR Magazine*, September 2006, pp. 10–15.

96. M. S. Christian, B. D. Edwards, and J. C. Bradley, "Situational Judgment Tests: Constructs Assessed and a Meta-analysis of Their Criterion-Related Validities," *Personnel Psychology* 63 (2010), pp. 83–117.

97. E. White, "Walk a Mile in My Shoes," *Wall Street Journal*, January 16, 2006, p. B3.

98. B. Spindle, "The Thrill of Victory in Welding, Baking and Bricklaying," *The Wall Street Journal Online*, October 29, 2017.

99. S. Leckhart, "The Hackathon Fast Track, From Campus to Silicon Valley," *New York Times*, April 6, 2015.

100. T. Oliver, P. Hausdorf, F. Lievens, and P. Conlon, "Interpersonal Dynamics in Assessment Center Exercises: Effects of Role Player Portrayed Disposition," *Journal of Management* 42 (2016), pp. 1992–2017.

101. D. J. Jackson, G. Michaelides, C. Dewberry, and Y. J. Kim, "Everything That You Have Ever Been Told about Assessment Center Ratings Is Confounded," *Journal of Applied Psychology* 101 (2016), pp. 976–994.

102. A. Furnham, "Can You Really Test Someone for Integrity," *Forbes*, August 11, 2015.

103. C. H. Van Iddekinge, P. L. Roth, P. H. Raymark, and H. N. Odle-Dusseau, "The Criterion-Related Validity of Integrity Tests: An Updated Meta-analysis," *Journal of Applied Psychology*, 97 (2012), pp. 499–530.

104. M. R. Cunningham, D. T. Wong, and A. P. Barbee, "Self-Presentation Dynamics on Overt Integrity Tests: Experimental Studies of the Reid Report," *Journal of Applied Psychology* 79 (1994), pp. 643–58.

105. J. Gold, "Workers Overdose on the Job, and Employers Struggle to Respond," *The New York Times Online*, September 21, 2018.

106. L. Weber, "More American Workers Are Testing Positive for Drugs," *The Wall Street Journal Online*, May 16, 2017.

107. J. Calmes, "Hiring Hurdle: Finding Workers Who Can Pass a Drug Test," *The New York Times Online*, May 17, 2016.

108. C. Levinson, "Comey: FBI 'Grappling' with Hiring Policy Concerning Marijuana," *Wall Street Journal*, May 20, 2014.

┌─ **LEARNING OBJECTIVES** ──────────────────────────────

*After reading this chapter, you should be able to:*

**LO 7-1**   Discuss how training, informal learning, and knowledge management can contribute to continuous learning and companies' business strategy. *page 279*

**LO 7-2**   Explain the role of the manager in identifying training needs and supporting training on the job. *page 281*

**LO 7-3**   Conduct a needs assessment. *page 283*

**LO 7-4**   Evaluate employees' readiness for training. *page 289*

**LO 7-5**   Discuss the strengths and weaknesses of presentation, hands-on, and group training methods. *page 295*

**LO 7-6**   Explain the potential advantages of e-learning for training. *page 303*

**LO 7-7**   Design a training session to maximize learning. *page 309*

**LO 7-8**   Choose appropriate evaluation design and training outcomes based on the training objectives and evaluation purpose. *page 310*

**LO 7-9**   Design a cross-cultural preparation program. *page 313*

**LO 7-10**  Develop a program for effectively managing diversity. *page 317*

## AT&T: Staying Competitive by Helping Employees Update Their Skills and Careers

AT&T is well-known for its work in building the telephone infrastructure in the United States. But as the telecommunications industry moves from cables and landlines to smartphones, the Internet, and the cloud, AT&T is having to reinvent itself to survive. This not only means investing in wireless technology but also in developing its employees' technical skills in areas such as cloud-based computing and coding. This is especially important because employees with these skills are in short supply and high demand from many other employers such as Amazon and Google.

To get the skills the company needs, AT&T has invested more than $250 million in employee training and development. AT&T wants to encourage all of its employees to develop their skills for future job opportunities. An online portal called Career Intelligence lets workers see what jobs are available, the skills required for each, the potential salary range, and whether that particular area is projected to grow or shrink in the years ahead. In short, it gives them a roadmap to get from where they are today to where the company needs them to be in the future. To do so, AT&T provides employees with many different options they can use to learn and develop their careers. For example, an online self-service platform provides career profile, career intelligence, and job simulation tools. The career profile tool evaluates employees' skills and competencies, experience, and educational credentials. It provides a development profile that employees can use to find open positions across AT&T's business units that match their interests, preferences, and skills and links them to resources for developing competencies they may need. The career intelligence tool helps employees make informed career decisions by providing data on hiring trends within the company and profiles of different jobs that include salary range and number of current employees holding the job. The simulation tool provides employees with situations they may actually encounter in a job and asks them to assess their preference for working in such jobs. This helps employees identify whether they fit a job on the basis of the type of work they like to do.

Using the information they gain from these tools, other employees, and discussions with their managers, employees have several options for developing their skills. These include online and face-to-face courses; 6- to 12-month nanodegree programs in high-demand specialties such as software engineering, coding, Web development, and data analytics offered by massive open online course (MOOC) provider Udacity; and online master's degree programs in computer science, with tuition costs subsidized by AT&T.

AT&T is also taking steps to encourage employees to develop a more contemporary mindset about their career and to encourage them to engage in continuous learning. To do so, AT&T is replacing traditional career paths—which emphasize a ladder of career progression through advancing in one's role and job title, with increasing importance and scope of responsibilities—with career lattices, which encourage career paths involving lateral, cross-functional, and even downward moves that require employees to stretch their skill sets and develop cross-functional knowledge. This helps change employees' mindsets from assuming the company is responsible for their development to one in which they take charge of their own career through actively seeking new roles and experiences.

So far, AT&T's investment is paying off. In the first six months of 2016, employees who had been retrained filled half of the technology management positions and received slightly less than 50% of all promotions. AT&T has seen a 40% reduction in

*CONTINUED*

product-development cycle time and increased time to revenue by over 30%. By 2020, AT&T wants to have trained 100,000 employees with the skills they need for new technology jobs ensuring they have the workforce needed to compete in the next century.

SOURCES: Based on M. Mancini, "AT&T: Continuously Dialing Up the Learning Evolution," *Chief Learning Officer*, June 2017, pp. 40–41; J. Donovan and C. Benko, "AT&T's Talent Overall," *Harvard Business Review*, October 2016, pp. 69–73; C. Anthony, "Three Keys to Our Culture," *Fortune*, January 1, 2018, p. 32; S. Caminiti "AT&T's $1 Billion Gambit: Retraining Nearly Half Its Workforce for Jobs of the Future," March 13, 2018, from www.CNBC.com, accessed December 31, 2018.

# Introduction

As the chapter opener shows, training contributes to AT&T's competitive advantage by ensuring that its employees have the skills they need to succeed in their current jobs and develop for future positions. From AT&T's perspective, training is strategic because it leads to its ability to provide up-to-date technology and services to customers, attract and retain high-quality employees, and generate positive revenues. AT&T recognizes that there is stiff competition in the technology services business—success requires smart, motivated employees.

Why is the emphasis on strategic training important? Companies are in business to make money, and every business function is under pressure to show how it contributes to business success or it may face spending cuts and even outsourcing. To contribute to a company's success, training activities should help the company achieve its business strategy. (Consider how AT&T's training reduced product development cycle time and increased time to revenue.)

There is both a direct and an indirect link between training and business strategy and goals. Training can help employees develop skills needed to perform their jobs, which directly affects the business. Giving employees opportunities to learn and develop creates a positive work environment, which supports the business strategy by attracting talented employees as well as motivating and retaining current employees.

Why do AT&T and many other companies believe that an investment in training can help them gain a competitive advantage? Training can

- Increase employees' knowledge of foreign competitors and cultures, which is critical for success in foreign markets.
- Help ensure that employees have the basic skills needed to work with new technology, such as robots and computer-assisted manufacturing processes.
- Help employees understand how to work effectively in teams to contribute to product and service quality.
- Ensure that the company's culture emphasizes innovation, creativity, and learning.
- Ensure employment security by providing new ways for employees to contribute to the company when their jobs change, their interests change, or their skills become obsolete.
- Prepare employees to accept and work more effectively with each other, particularly with minorities and women.[1]

In this chapter, we emphasize the conditions through which training practices can help companies gain competitive advantage and how managers can contribute to effective training and other learning initiatives. We begin by discussing a systematic and effective approach to training design. Next, we review training methods and training evaluation. The chapter concludes with a discussion of special training issues including cross-cultural preparation, managing diversity, and orienting and socializing employees.

# Training: Its Role in Continuous Learning and Competitive Advantage

As we discussed in Chapter 1, intangible assets, including human capital, customer capital, social capital, and intellectual capital, help companies gain competitive advantage. Recognizing that formal training, informal learning, and knowledge management are important for the development of intangible assets, many companies now consider training one part of a larger emphasis on continuous learning. Figure 7.1 shows that formal training and development, informal learning, and knowledge management are the key features of a continuous learning philosophy that focuses on performance and supports the business strategy. **Continuous learning** refers to a learning system that requires employees to understand the entire work system; they are expected to acquire new skills, apply them on the job, and share what they have learned with other employees.[2]

**Training** refers to a planned effort by a company to facilitate employees' learning of job-related competencies, knowledge, skills, and behaviors. The goal of training is for employees to master the knowledge, skills, and behaviors emphasized in training and apply them to their day-to-day activities. Traditionally, companies have relied on formal training through a course, a program, or an event to teach employees the knowledge, skills, and behaviors they need to successfully perform their jobs. **Formal training** refers to training and development programs, courses, and events that are developed and organized by the company. Typically employees are required to attend or complete these programs, which can include face-to-face training programs (such as instructor-led courses) as well as online programs. U.S. companies make substantial investments in formal training. One estimate is that U.S. organizations spend over $70 billion on formal employee training and development.[3] We will discuss employee development in Chapter 9.

Despite companies' significant investments in formal training and development activities, informal learning is also important for facilitating knowledge and skill acquisition.[4] **Informal learning** refers to learning that is learner initiated, involves action and doing, is motivated by an intent to develop, and does not occur in a formal learning setting.[5] Informal learning occurs without an instructor, and its breadth, depth, and timing are

## Figure 7.1

Key Features of Continuous Learning

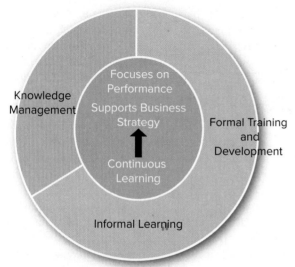

**LO 7-1**
Discuss how training, informal learning, and knowledge management can contribute to continuous learning and companies' business strategy.

**Continuous learning**
A learning system that requires employees to understand the entire work process and expects them to acquire new skills, apply them on the job, and share what they have learned with other employees.

**Training**
A planned effort to facilitate the learning of job-related knowledge, skills, and behavior by employees.

**Formal training**
Training and development programs and courses that are developed and organized by the company.

**Informal learning**
Learning that is learner initiated, involves action and doing, is motivated by an intent to develop, and does not occur in a formal learning setting.

controlled by the employee. It occurs on an as-needed basis and may involve an employee learning alone or through face-to-face or technology-aided social interactions. Informal learning can occur through many different ways, including casual unplanned interactions with peers, e-mail, informal mentoring, or company-developed or publicly available social networking websites such as Twitter or Facebook. The application of social media from a marketing strategy to a learning strategy and the availability of Web 2.0 technologies such as social networks, microblogs, and wikis give employees easy access to social learning through collaboration and sharing with one or two or more people.[6] One estimate is that informal learning may account for up to 75% of learning within organizations.

Both formal training and informal learning contribute to the development of intangible assets but especially human capital. Human capital includes knowledge (know what), advanced skills (know how), system understanding and creativity (know why), as well as motivation to deliver high-quality products and services (care why).[7] One reason informal learning may be especially important is that it may lead to the effective development of *tacit* knowledge, which can be contrasted with *explicit* knowledge.[8] **Explicit knowledge** refers to knowledge that is well documented, easily articulated, and easily transferred from person to person. Examples of explicit knowledge include processes, checklists, flowcharts, formulas, and definitions. Explicit knowledge tends to be the primary focus of formal training. **Tacit knowledge** refers to personal knowledge based on individual experiences that make it difficult to codify. It is best acquired through informal learning. The characteristics of the formal training environment may limit the extent to which tacit knowledge can be acquired, such as the relatively short duration of classroom or online training and limited opportunities for practice. Thus, informal learning is central to the development of tacit knowledge. Well-designed formal training programs can help employees acquire explicit knowledge. But to acquire tacit knowledge employees need to interact with peers, colleagues, and experts and have learning experiences that are not usually found in formal training. Informal learning does not replace formal training. Formal training is still needed to prepare employees for their jobs and help them progress to future positions. Informal learning complements training by helping employees gain tacit knowledge that formal training cannot provide.

**Knowledge management** refers to the process of enhancing company performance by designing and implementing tools, processes, systems, structures, and cultures to improve the creation, sharing, and use of knowledge.[9] Knowledge management contributes to informal learning.

Moneris is a Canadian company that provides payment processing and supporting technologies.[10] Its business customers have precise and sometimes complex payment needs. To help obtain the skills and knowledge needed to meet customers payment needs employees can access resources by topic such as leadership development, sales, payment industry news, and general business skills using the company's learning and development portal. After completing a training course, trainees can use the portal to share best practices and what they have learned. Employees can also post questions on a discussion board. This helps encourage employees to learn outside the boundaries of training courses by collaborating and networking with peers and experts.

It is important for all aspects of continuous learning, including formal training and development, informal learning, and knowledge management, to contribute to and support the business strategy. Continuous learning needs to address performance issues that lead to improved business results. To do so requires that the emphasis on continuous learning aligns with the business strategy; has visible support from senior managers and involves leaders as instructors and teachers; creates a culture or work environment that encourages learning; provides a wide range of learning opportunities including training,

**Explicit knowledge**
Knowledge that is well documented and easily transferred to other persons.

**Tacit knowledge**
Knowledge based on personal experience that is difficult to codify.

**Knowledge management**
The process of enhancing company performance by designing and using tools, systems, and cultures to improve creation, sharing, and use of knowledge.

informal learning, knowledge management, and employee development; uses traditional methods and innovative technologies to design and deliver learning; and measures the effectiveness and overall business impact of learning.[11]

Consider how Jiffy Lube embraces a continuous learning philosophy that supports the business strategy.[12] Jiffy Lube's strategic goals focus on developing growth opportunities for franchisees and providing a world-class customer experience. Jiffy Lube's customer value proposition is that every driver deserves to be free from the anxiety of keeping his or her vehicle in excellent shape. This requires that service technicians be knowledgeable about and able to provide high-quality and necessary services to drivers. At Jiffy Lube this means that service technicians need to be trained and certified. Training is provided through Jiffy Lube University (JLU). Its estimated that employees participated in more than 2 million learning hours in the previous two years. Learning for employees and franchisees is offered using face-to-face and virtual instruction, as well as online self-paced modules. JLU evaluates the success of learning efforts many ways, including through learner feedback, franchisee surveys, the number of training courses completed, earned certifications, and customer service scores from mystery shoppers.

Jiffy Lube recognizes the value of continuous learning and informal learning. Recently, every employee, including the company president, was required to complete courses at JLU plus spend at least one day at a Jiffy Lube service center. The courses included orientation and safety and training for the courtesy technician, upper bay technician, customer service advisor, and team lead positions. To help further service center employees' careers, JLU offers courses they can take to earn up to 25 hours of college credit at trade schools and colleges and universities. Learners and managers can access an online roadmap, which shows how training is helping them advance their careers. Also, recognizing that its service center employees typically are 18–25 year olds who are actively involved in social media, Jiffy Lube provides video cameras so that store employees can capture best practices and ideas. These videos have focused on customer service, team building, operational excellence, and safety. Jiffy Lube trainers edit the videos and make them available to all employees on YouTube.

# Designing Effective Formal Training Activities

A key characteristic of training activities that contribute to competitiveness is that they are designed according to the training design process.[13] **Training design process** refers to a systematic approach for developing training programs. Instructional System Design (ISD) and the ADDIE model (analysis, design, development, implementation, evaluation) are two specific types of training design processes you may know. Figure 7.2 presents the six stages of this process, which emphasizes that effective training practices involve more than just choosing the most popular or colorful training method.

The first stage is to assess needs to determine if training is needed. Stage 2 involves ensuring that employees have the readiness for training and that they have the motivation and basic skills to master training content. Stage 3 addresses whether the training session (or the learning environment) has the factors necessary for learning to occur. Stage 4 focuses on ensuring that trainees apply the content of training to their jobs. This requires support from managers and peers for the use of training content on the job as well as getting the employee to understand how to take personal responsibility for skill improvement. Stage 5 involves choosing a training method. As we will see in this chapter, a variety

**LO 7-2**
Explain the role of the manager in identifying training needs and supporting training on the job.

**Training design process**
A systematic approach for developing training programs.

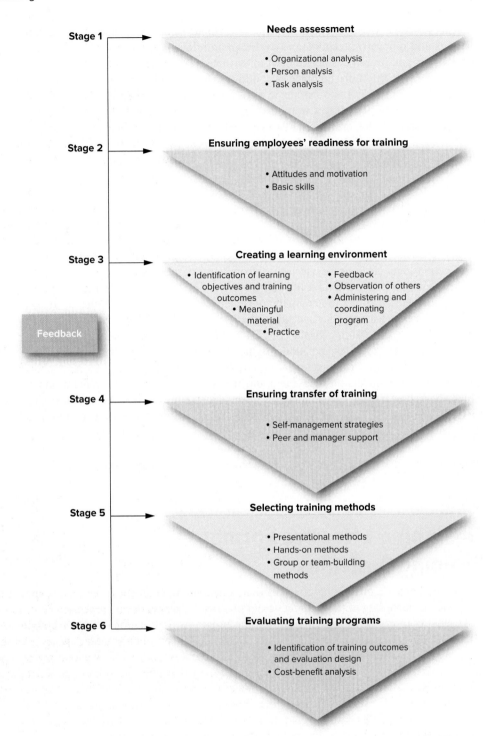

**Figure 7.2**
The Training Process

of training methods are available ranging from traditional on-the-job training to newer technologies such as social media. The key is to choose a training method that will provide the appropriate learning environment to achieve the training objectives. Stage 6 is evaluation—that is, determining whether training achieved the desired learning outcomes and/or financial objectives.

The training design process should be systematic yet flexible enough to adapt to business needs. Different steps may be completed simultaneously. Also, feedback from each stage in the process can be useful for the other stages. For example, if transfer of training is difficult, then the learning environment should overemphasize practice and feedback. Keep in mind that designing training unsystematically will reduce the benefits that can be realized. For example, choosing a training method before determining training needs or ensuring employees' readiness for training increases the risk that the method chosen will not be the most effective one for meeting training needs. Also, training may not even be necessary and may result in a waste of time and money. Employees may have the knowledge, skills, or behavior they need but simply not be motivated to use them. In the next several sections, we discuss important aspects of the training design process.

## NEEDS ASSESSMENT

The first step in the instructional design process, **needs assessment**, refers to the process used to determine if training is necessary. Figure 7.3 shows the causes and outcomes resulting from needs assessment. As the figure illustrates, many different "pressure points" suggest that training is necessary. These pressure points include performance problems, new technology, internal or external customer requests for training, job redesign, new legislation, changes in customer preferences, new products, or employees' lack of basic skills as well as support for the company's business strategy (e.g., growth, global business expansion). Training is not always the correct solution to a pressure point. Consider, for example, a delivery truck driver whose job is to deliver anesthetic gases to medical facilities. The driver mistakenly hooks up the supply line of a mild anesthetic to the supply line of a hospital's oxygen system, contaminating the hospital's oxygen supply. Why did the driver make this mistake, which is clearly a performance problem? The driver may have done this because of a lack of knowledge about the appropriate line hookup for the anesthetic, anger over a requested salary increase that his manager recently denied, or mislabeled valves for connecting the gas supply. Only the lack of knowledge can be addressed by training. The other pressure points require addressing issues related to the consequence of good performance (pay system) or the design of the work environment.

**LO 7-3**
Conduct a needs assessment.

**Needs assessment**
The process used to determine if training is necessary.

**Figure 7.3**
The Needs Assessment Process

*Reasons or "pressure points"*   What is the context?   *Outcomes*

- Legislation
- Lack of basic skills
- Poor performance
- New technology
- Customer requests
- New products
- Higher performance standards
- New jobs
- Business growth or contraction
- Global business expansion

Organization analysis
Task analysis
Person analysis

In what do they need training?

Who needs training?

- What trainees need to learn
- Who receives training
- Type of training
- Frequency of training
- Buy-versus-build training decision
- Training versus other HR options such as selection or job redesign
- How training should be evaluated

Needs assessment typically involves organizational analysis, person analysis, and task analysis.[14] Organizational analysis considers the context in which training will occur. That is, **organizational analysis** involves determining the business appropriateness of training, given the company's business strategy, its resources available for training, and support by managers and peers for training activities.

Person analysis helps identify who needs training. **Person analysis** involves (1) determining whether performance deficiencies result from a lack of knowledge, skills, or abilities (a training issue) or from a motivational or work-design problem; (2) identifying who needs training; and (3) determining employees' readiness for training. **Task analysis** includes identifying the important tasks and knowledge, skills, and behaviors that need to be emphasized in training for employees to complete their tasks.

In practice, organizational analysis, person analysis, and task analysis are usually not conducted in any specific order. However, because organizational analysis is concerned with identifying whether training fits with the company's strategic objectives and whether the company wants to devote time and money to training, it is usually conducted first. Person analysis and task analysis are often conducted at the same time because it can be difficult to determine whether performance deficiencies are a training problem without understanding the tasks and the work environment.

What outcomes result from a needs assessment? As shown in Figure 7.3, needs assessment shows who needs training and what trainees need to learn, including the tasks in which they need to be trained plus knowledge, skill, behavior, or other job requirements. Needs assessment helps determine whether the company will purchase training from a vendor or consultant or develop training using internal resources.

McDonald's conducted a needs assessment to examine the relevance of current training topics and the effectiveness of training methods.[15] The chief learning officer and her team examined employees' backgrounds including education level, gender, language, age, and generation to get a better understanding of trainees. They gathered data about the frequency of use of training online content and its accessibility. Also, they reviewed the responsibilities, tasks, and leadership skills for each job to ensure that they were supported by training classes and curriculum. The needs assessment showed that although more trainees were Millennials and Generation Z the way that training was delivered did not meet their needs or expectations. As a result, they created a shorter training curriculum that was more accessible using smartphones, computers, and tablets.

## Organizational Analysis

Three factors need to be considered before choosing training as the solution to any pressure point: the support of managers and peers for training activities, the company's strategy, and the training resources available.

***Support of Managers and Peers.*** Various studies have found that peer and manager support for training is critical. The key factors for success are a positive attitude among peers and managers about participation in training activities; managers' and peers' willingness to tell trainees how they can more effectively use knowledge, skills, or behaviors learned in training on the job; and the availability of opportunities for the trainees to use training content in their jobs.[16] If peers' and managers' attitudes and behaviors are not supportive, then employees are not likely to apply training content to their jobs.

***Company Strategy.*** In Chapter 2, we discussed the importance of business strategy for a company to gain a competitive advantage, and earlier in this chapter we discussed how Jiffy Lube relies on learning to support the company's mission and strategy. As Figure 7.1

---

**Organizational analysis**
A process for determining the business appropriateness of training.

**Person analysis**
A process for determining whether employees need training, who needs training, and whether employees are ready for training.

**Task analysis**
The process of identifying the tasks, knowledge, skills, and behaviors that need to be emphasized in training.

| STRATEGIC TRAINING AND DEVELOPMENT INITIATIVES | IMPLICATIONS |
|---|---|
| Improve customer service | • Ensure that employees have product and service knowledge.<br>• Ensure that employees have skills needed to interact with customers.<br>• Ensure that employees understand their roles and decision-making authority. |
| Improve employee engagement | • Ensure that employees have opportunities to develop.<br>• Ensure that employees understand career opportunities and personal growth opportunities.<br>• Ensure that training and development addresses employees' needs in current job as well as growth opportunities. |
| Enhance innovation and creativity | • Capture insight and information from knowledgeable employees.<br>• Logically organize and store information.<br>• Provide methods to make information available (e.g., resource guides, websites).<br>• Dedicate physical space to encourage teamwork, collaboration, creativity, and knowledge sharing. |
| Growth in global markets | • Prepare high-potential managers to take over global leadership positions.<br>• Prepare expatriates to function cross-culturally.<br>• Train local workforce in company culture. |

**Table 7.1**

Examples of Strategic Initiatives and Their Implications for Training Practices

SOURCE: Based on S. Tannenbaum, "A Strategic View of Organizational Training and Learning," in *Creating, Implementing and Managing Effective Training and Development*, ed. K. Kraiger (San Francisco: Jossey-Bass, 2002), pp. 10–52.

highlights, training should help companies achieve their business strategy. Table 7.1 shows possible strategic initiatives and their implications for training practices.

It is important to identify the prevailing business strategy and goals to ensure that (1) the company allocates enough of its budget to training, (2) employees receive training on relevant topics, and (3) employees get the right amount of training.[17] Consider how training at Genpact supports the business.[18] At Genpact, a business service provider, metrics are used to show how training and development contributes to the company's growth, profit margins, capability building, and transformational goals. For example, a program developed for the sales force to help improve their effectiveness at generating clients resulted in a 34% increase in service bookings. Another program designed to develop internal skills for positions that were difficult to hire new employees resulted in a $9 million in savings.

The Integrity in Action box highlights how Tyson Foods is using training to help employees improve their life and workplace skills.

***Training Resources.*** The company must determine whether it has the budget, time, and expertise for training. For example, if the company is installing computer-based manufacturing equipment in one of its plants, it has three possible strategies to have computer-literate employees. First, the company can use technical experts on staff to train all affected employees. Second, the company may decide that it is more cost

# INTEGRITY IN ACTION

## At Tyson Foods Learning Goes beyond Job Responsibilities

Tyson Foods is the second largest processor of chicken, beef, and pork in the world. Its values include operating with integrity, being faith-friendly and inclusive, serving as stewards of resources, and providing a safe work environment. In the early 2000s, Tyson was charged with illegal immigration practices, including smuggling unauthorized immigrants from Mexican to work on processing lines. Tyson was subsequently cleared of these charges and now follows federal immigration guidelines, such as auditing immigration documents to ensure that immigrant employees are legally in the country. Further, Tyson provides training opportunities for immigrant employees to help them both in the workplace and in their nonwork lives. The training includes topics such as how to understand work-specific vocabulary (such as *forklift* and *pallet*) as well as how to rent an apartment, schedule doctor's appointments, and interact with their children's teachers.

The program known as Upward Academy was launched in 2016 in Tyson Foods' first processing plant in in Springdale,

Arkansas, a community consisting largely of immigrants who came to America seeking a better life. Several hundred employees signed up to participate. Now Upward Academy has more than 1,000 participants in 27 facilities in Arkansas, Missouri, Texas, and North Carolina. Expansion will continue over the next several years to cover the entire company.

In partnership with local community organizations, Upward Academy provides team members with important life skills by offering free and accessible classes in English as a Second Language (ESL), General Educational Development (GED), citizenship, and other essential life and workplace skills. Driver education, computer literacy, and financial literacy classes have been offered at some locations. Classes are held before and after plant shifts with some in early morning and others later at night. Tyson also offers health care and back-to-school events for Upward Academy participants' children.

The results of the program have been encouraging. Retention rates of Upward Academy participants are higher than those who do not participate,

and over half of participants realized a gain in their education level. Over 80% of program participants report they have improved their communication skills and are happier at work, and 77% report they feel greater loyalty to Tyson as an employer. In addition to being good for the business, the program has positively impacted participants' lives outside of work. As one participant reported, "It changes my life in a big way, mostly at home, where I will be able to assist my daughter with her homework. I want to set an example on how important education is in her life."

### DISCUSSION QUESTION

1. Do you think companies take the responsibility (and absorb the costs) for providing employees with knowledge and skill training outside of the scope of their job such as financial and computer literacy? Explain.

SOURCE: Based on S. Gale, "Moving on Up(ward)", *Chief Learning Officer*, September 2018, pp. 52–53; "Tyson Foods' Workforce Education Initiative Continues to Expand," April 19, 2018, https://www.tysonfoods.com/, accessed January 7, 2019; T. Henderson, "E-Verify Immigrant Job Screening Is a Game Of Chicken, Politics and State Laws," April 27, 2018, from www.huffingtonpost.com, accessed January 7, 2019.

effective to identify computer-literate employees by using tests and work samples and replace or reassign employees who lack the necessary skills. Third, if it lacks time or expertise, the company may decide to purchase training from an outside consultant or organization.

Table 7.2 provides examples of questions to ask vendors and consultants to help evaluate whether they can meet the company's training needs.

**Table 7.2**
Questions to Ask Vendors and Consultants

- How do your products and services fit our needs?
- How much and what type of experience does your company have in designing and delivering training?
- What are the qualifications and experiences of your staff?
- Can you provide demonstrations or examples of training programs you have developed?
- Can you provide references from clients for whom you worked?
- What evidence do you have that your programs work?
- How long will it take to develop the training program?
- How much will your services cost?
- What instructional design methods do you use?
- What about recurring costs, such as those related to administering, updating, and maintaining the training program?
- Do you provide technical support?

SOURCES: Adapted from R. Zemke and J. Armstrong, "Evaluating Multimedia Developers," *Training*, November 1996, pp. 33–38; B. Chapman, "How to Create the Ideal RFP," *Training*, January 2004, pp. 40–43; M. Weinstein, "What Vendors Wished You Knew," *Training*, February 2010, pp. 122–125.

## Person Analysis

Person analysis helps the manager identify whether training is appropriate and which employees need training. In certain situations, such as the introduction of a new technology or service, all employees may need training. However, when managers, customers, or employees identify a problem (usually as a result of a performance deficiency), it is often unclear whether training is the solution.

A major pressure point for training is poor or substandard performance—that is, when a gap exists between employees' current performance and their expected performance. Poor performance is indicated by customer complaints, low performance ratings, or on-the-job accidents or unsafe behavior. Another potential indicator of the need for training is if the job changes so that current performance levels need improvement or employees must complete new tasks.

For managers to determine if training is needed to address a performance problem, they must analyze characteristics of the performer, input, output, consequences, and feedback.[19] This can be done by assessing whether

1. The performance problem is important and has the potential to cost the company a significant amount of money from lost productivity or customers.
2. Employees do not know how to perform effectively. Perhaps they received little or no previous training or the training was ineffective (person characteristics).
3. Employees cannot demonstrate the correct knowledge or behavior. Perhaps they were trained but they infrequently or never used the training content (knowledge, skills, etc.) on the job (input problem).
4. Performance expectations are clear (input) and there are no obstacles to performance such as faulty tools or equipment (output).
5. There are positive consequences for good performance, whereas poor performance is not rewarded. For example, if employees are dissatisfied with their compensation, their peers or a union may encourage them to slow down their pace of work (consequences).
6. Employees receive timely, relevant, accurate, constructive, and specific feedback about their performance (feedback).
7. Other solutions such as job redesign or transferring employees to other jobs are too expensive or unrealistic.

If employees lack the knowledge and skill to perform and the other factors are satisfactory, then training is likely the effective solution. If employees have the knowledge and skill to perform, but input, output, consequences, or feedback are inadequate, then training may not be the best solution. For example, if poor performance results from faulty equipment, training cannot solve this problem, but repairing the equipment will. If poor performance results from a lack of feedback, then employees may not need training, but their managers may need training on how to give performance feedback.

## Task Analysis

A task analysis identifies the conditions in which tasks are performed. The conditions include identifying equipment and the environment the employee works in, time constraints (deadlines), safety considerations, or performance standards. Task analysis results in a description of work activities, including tasks performed by the employee and the knowledge, skills, and abilities required to successfully complete the tasks. A *job* is a specific position requiring the completion of specific tasks. A *task* is a statement of an employee's work activity in a specific job. The four steps in a task analysis are (1) identifying the job(s) to be analyzed; (2) developing a list of tasks performed on the job; (3) validating or confirming the tasks; and (4) identifying the knowledge, skills, abilities, and other factors (e.g., equipment, working conditions) needed to successfully perform each task.[20]

For example, consider how H&H Castings and KLA-Tencor conducted needs assessment.[21] Employees in the melt department at H&H Castings have a demanding and potentially dangerous job that requires them to pour hot aluminum into casting molds. To reduce the risks of accidents and improve new employee training, H&H Castings analyzed melt department employees job tasks to identify the procedures needed to complete them. To identify the tasks and procedures employees wore eye-tracking glasses as they worked. A computer connected to the eye-tracking glasses recorded what the employee was looking at while working. As a result, a detailed and precise view of how the employees completed the tasks was provided. The perspective obtained from the eye-tracking glasses was used to create videos that are used for training new employees as well as identifying changes in work processes that could be made to make the mold-pouring process more safe and efficient.

KLA-Tencor supplies process controls and equipment to the semiconductor industry. KLA-Tencor service engineers need to diagnose and repair its customers' complex machines that use advanced laser, optical, and robotic technologies. The engineers need to gain proficiency in their current skills as well as add new skills to keep pace with new technology used in the company's equipment. This is critical for KLA-Tencor to quickly solve equipment problems, which if unresolved, can result in millions of dollars of lost revenue for its customers. Providing effective service is critical for the company to keep current customers and develop new business. In fact, one of the company's values is "indispensable" (the other values are perseverance; drive to be better; high-performance teams; and honest, forthright, and consistent).

KLA-Tencor uses a skills management process (the "right people, right knowledge" process) to monitor its workforce skills and use this information to change its training programs. The process involves developing a task list, training on the task, practicing on-the-job training to gain certification, and conducting an annual skills assessment. To conduct the skills assessment, KLA-Tencor sent a survey to all of its more than 1,000 service engineers. For each task, the engineers were asked to rate their capability of doing the task on a scale from "I don't know how" to "I can teach it to others." Also, they were asked to evaluate how frequently they performed the task, from "never" to "more than two times per year." Based on their responses, they were assigned a training task. More than 200 courses were created to train the engineers. To ensure that the training was completed, both engineers and their managers were held accountable. This helped the company to achieve a 95% completion rate within one year after training was assigned. The skills assessment data were also used to identify gaps in current training, resulting in more than 2,000 changes in courses and certification programs. The skills assessment is done annually to ensure that service engineers' skills keep up to date with new technology and products.

## ENSURING EMPLOYEES' READINESS FOR TRAINING

The second stage in the training design process is to evaluate whether employees are ready for training. **Readiness for training** refers to employee characteristics that provide employees with the desire, energy, and focus necessary to learn from training. The desire, energy, and focus is referred to as **motivation to learn**.[22] Various research studies have shown that motivation to learn is related to knowledge gain, behavior change, or skill acquisition in training programs.[23] Table 7.3 presents factors that influence motivation to learn and the actions that strengthen them. Motivation to learn influences mastery of all types of training content, including knowledge, behavior, and skills. Managers need to ensure that employees' motivation to learn is as high as possible. They can do this by ensuring employees' self-efficacy; understanding the benefits of training; being aware of training needs, career interests, and goals; understanding work environment characteristics; and ensuring employees' basic skill levels.

## CREATING A LEARNING ENVIRONMENT

Learning permanently changes behavior. For employees to acquire knowledge and skills in the training program and apply this information in their jobs, the training program must include specific learning principles. Educational and industrial psychologists and instructional design specialists have identified several conditions under which employees learn best.[24] Table 7.4 shows the events that should take place for learning to occur in the training program and their implications for instruction.

Many companies are designing training according to principles of microlearning to get employees more actively involved in learning and facilitate their recall of what they learned. **Microlearning** refers to training delivered in small pieces or chunks designed to engage trainees, motivate them to learn, and help facilitate retention.[25] The chunks of learning are presented using videos or games that are typically five to eight minutes long. Microlearning is used to replace longer training courses with one or several short courses. It is also being used to reinforce or supplement formal training (send quizzes after training, share short pieces of training content before the program to generate excitement), and create just-in-time learning content. The primary benefits of microlearning for learners focus on time, that is, they can access learning when it is convenient for them and learning does not take a lot of time and they can access learning on-the-job when they need it.[26] Also, trainees progress in games or simulations can be tracked and reported, microlearning content can be linked together based on topic or skills. The primary barrier for effective microlearning is that trainees are not held accountable for learning.

Consider how several companies are creating a positive learning environment using a variety of training methods.[27] Nationwide Mutual Insurance Company created the Cohort Learning Program for its new associates who answer customer service calls. The Cohort Learning Program replaced traditional lecture with small and large group discussions and activities that encourage problem solving to ensure application of knowledge. Four to six member groups consist of individuals with different levels of experience and personality types. Each associate is responsible for creating their own learning plan and for identifying knowledge and skills they need to review and practice. Activities and scenarios

**LO 7-4**
Evaluate employees' readiness for training.

**Readiness for training**
Employee characteristics that provide them with the desire, energy, and focus necessary to learn from training.

**Motivation to learn**
The desire of the trainee to learn the content of a training program.

**Microlearning**
Training delivered in small pieces or chunks designed to engage trainees, motivate them to learn, and help facilitate retention.

**Table 7.3**
Factors That Influence Motivation to Learn

| FACTOR | DESCRIPTION | ACTIONS TO ENHANCE OR IMPROVE |
|---|---|---|
| Self-efficacy | Employee belief that they can successfully learn the content of the training program | Show employees their peers' training success.<br>Communicate that the purpose of training is to improve, not identify, area of incompetence.<br>Communicate purpose and activities involved in training. Emphasize that learning is under their personal control. |
| Benefits or consequences of training | Job-related, personal, career benefits that can result from attending training | Communicate realistic short- and long-term benefits from training. |
| Awareness of training needs | Knowledge of skill strengths and weaknesses | Communicate why they were asked to attend the training program.<br>Share performance appraisal information.<br>Encourage trainees to complete self-evaluation of all strengths and weaknesses.<br>Give employees input on the choice of training to attend. |
| Work environment | Proper tools and equipment, materials, supplies, budget time; managers' and peers' willingness to provide feedback and reinforce use of training content | Give employees opportunities to practice skills and apply them to their work.<br>Encourage employees to provide feedback to each other.<br>Encourage trainees to share training experiences and situations where use of training content was beneficial.<br>Acknowledge use of training content in their work.<br>Provide resources necessary for training content to be used in their work. |
| Basic skills | Cognitive ability, reading and writing skills | Ensure trainees have prerequisite skills needed for understanding and learning training content. Provide remedial training.<br>Use video or other visual training methods.<br>Modify training program to meet trainees' basic skill levels. |
| Goal orientation | Goals held by employees in a learning situation | Create a learning goal orientation by deemphasizing competition between trainees; allow trainees to make errors and to experiment with new knowledge, skills, and behavior during training; and set learning goals. |
| Conscientiousness | Tendency to be reliable, hardworking, self-disciplined, and persistent | Communicate need for learning. |

SOURCES: Based on J. Colquitt, J. LePine, and R. Noe, "Toward an Integrative Theory of Training Motivation: A Meta-Analytic Path Analysis of 20 Years of Research," *Journal of Applied Psychology* 85 (2000), pp. 678–707; R. Noe and J. Colquitt, "Planning for Impact Training: Principles of Training Effectiveness," in K. Kraiger (ed.), *Creating, Implementing, and Managing Effective Training and Development* (San Francisco: Jossey-Bass, 2002), pp. 53–79.

simulate actual call experiences. Associates have to solve problems and provide customers with solutions. Knowledge and skill assessments are used to provide associates with feedback about their learning. Also, trainers and peers provide face-to-face feedback during the group activities. Evaluation of the associates who completed the Cohort Learning Program compared to those who received traditional lecture-based classroom training showed that they had an average of a 72-second decrease in call hold time, and average 49-second decrease in time handling each call which resulted in a yearly cost savings of

**Table 7.4**
Conditions for Learning and Their Importance

| CONDITIONS FOR LEARNING | IMPORTANCE AND APPLICATION TO TRAINING |
|---|---|
| Need to know why they should learn | Employees need to understand the purpose or objectives of the training program to help them understand why they need training and what they are expected to accomplish. |
| Meaningful training content | Motivation to learn is enhanced when training is related to helping learner (such as related to current job tasks, problems, enhancing skills, or dealing with jobs or company changes). The training context should be similar to the work environment. |
| Opportunities for practice | Trainees need to demonstrate what is learned (knowledge, skill, behavior) to become more comfortable using it and to commit it to memory. Let trainees choose their practice strategy. |
| Feedback | Feedback helps learners to modify behavior or skill, or to use knowledge to meet objectives. Video, other trainees, and the trainer are useful feedback sources. |
| Observe, experience, and interact with training content, other learners, and the instructor | Adults learn best by doing. They can gain new perspectives and insights by working with others and can learn by observing the actions of models or by sharing experiences with each other in communities of practice or through social networking. Interacting with and manipulating content through reading or using tools that allow for building ideas and solving problems, such as worksheets and online interactions, is helpful. |
| Good program coordination and administration | Eliminate distractions that could interfere with learning, such as cell phone calls. Make sure the room is properly organized, comfortable, and appropriate for the training method (e.g., movable seating for team exercises). Trainees should receive announcements of the purpose of training, place, hour, and any pretraining materials such as cases or readings. |
| Commit training content to memory | Facilitate recall of training content after training. Examples include using concept maps showing relationships among ideas, using multiple types of review (writing, drawing, role-plays), teaching key words, providing a visual image, or asking trainees to reflect on what they learned. Limit instruction to manageable units or chunks that don't exceed memory limits; review and practice over multiple days (overlearning). Use short quizzes or other activities to help trainees retrieve what they learned and emphasize its importance. |

SOURCES: Based on R. M. Gagne, "Learning Processes and Instruction," *Training Research Journal* 1 (1995/1996), pp. 17–28; M. Knowles, *The Adult Learner*, 4th ed. (Houston: Gulf, 1990); A. Bandura, *Social Foundations of Thought and Action* (Englewood Cliffs, NJ: Prentice Hall, 1986); E. A. Locke and G. D. Latham, *A Theory of Goal Setting and Task Performance* (Englewood Cliffs, NJ: Prentice Hall, 1990); B. Mager, *Preparing Instructional Objectives*, 2nd ed. (Belmont, CA: Lake, 1984); B.J. Smith and B. L. Delahaye, *How to Be an Effective Trainer*, 2nd ed. (New York: Wiley, 1987); K. A. Smith-Jentsch, F. G. Jentsch, S. C. Payne, and E. Salas, "Can Pretraining Experience Explain Individual Differences in Learning?" *Journal of Applied Psychology* 81 (1996), pp. 110–16; H. Nuriddin, "Building the Right Interaction," *T + D*, March 2011, pp. 32–35; R. Feloni, "This Simple Daily Exercise Boosts Employee Performance," *Business Insider India*, www.businessinsider.in.com; G. Di Stefano, F. Gino, G. Pisano, and B. Staats, "Learning by Thinking: How Reflection Aids Performance," Harvard Business School Working Paper, 14-093 (March 25, 2014); M. Plater, "Three Trends Shaping Learning," *Chief Learning Officer*, June 2014, pp. 44–47; A. Kohn, "Use It or Lose It," *T + D*, February 2015, pp. 56–61; J. Karpicke and Henry Roediger III, "The Critical Importance of Retrieval for Learning," *Science*, February 2008, pp. 966–68; A. Paul, "Microlearning 101," *HR Magazine*, May 2016, pp. 6–42; M. Cole, "Microlearning: Delivering Bite-Sized Knowledge" (Alexandria, VA: Association for Talent Development, 2017).

over $63,000. Trainees at Avenade have access to minicourses that include topics like design thinking and leading the self. The courses are organized into either a progressive series or as pathways in which courses of related content can be taken in any order. All of the minicourses include learner guides, activities, reflection prompts, and an interactive discussion board. Trainees reactions to the minicourses were positive. They felt that the minicourses allowed them to fit learning into their busy schedules.

## ENSURING TRANSFER OF TRAINING

**Transfer of training**
The use of knowledge, skills, and behaviors learned in training on the job.

**Transfer of training** refers to on-the-job use of knowledge, skills, and behaviors learned in training. As Figure 7.4 shows, transfer of training is influenced by manager support, peer support, opportunity to use learned capabilities, technology support, and self-management skills. As we discussed earlier, learning is influenced by the learning environment (such as meaningfulness of the material and opportunities for practice and feedback) and employees' readiness for training (e.g., their self-efficacy and basic skill level). If no learning occurs in the training program, transfer is unlikely.

### Manager Support

**Manager support**
The degree to which trainees' managers emphasize the importance of attending training programs and stress the application of training content to the job.

**Action plan**
A document summarizing what the trainee and manager will do to ensure that training transfers to the job.

**Manager support** refers to the degree to which trainees' managers (1) emphasize the importance of attending training programs and (2) stress the application of training content to the job. Table 7.5 shows what managers should do to support training.

The greater the level of manager support, the more likely that transfer of training will occur.[28] The basic level of support that a manager should provide is acceptance, that is, allowing trainees to attend training. The highest level of support is to participate in training as an instructor (teaching in the program). Managers who serve as instructors are more likely to provide lower-level support functions such as reinforcing use of newly learned capabilities, discussing progress with trainees, and providing opportunities to practice. Managers can also facilitate transfer through use of action plans. An **action plan** is a written document that includes the steps that the trainee and manager will take to ensure that training transfers to the job. The action plan includes (1) a goal identifying what training content will be used and how it will be used (project, problem); (2) strategies for reaching the goal, including resources needed; (3) strategies for getting feedback (such as meetings with the manager); and (4) expected outcome (what will be different?). The action plan includes a schedule of specific dates and times when the manager and trainee agree to meet to discuss the progress being made in using learned capabilities on the job.

To help ensure learning and transfer of training, Western Union's Guide.Performance .Succeed (GPS) program requires leaders to get involved in helping to develop their employees' skills by setting clear expectations, providing regular real-time feedback, and holding their employees and themselves accountable for meeting talent development goals.[29] At Sonic Automotive, an automotive retailer, after trainees complete interactive instructor-led training, they are asked to identify an opportunity to use their new skills at their store. Their action plan has to be developed within 7 days and implemented within 45 days.[30]

At a minimum, special sessions should be scheduled with managers to explain the purpose of the training and to set expectations that they will encourage attendance at the

**Figure 7.4**
Work Environment Characteristics Influencing Transfer of Training

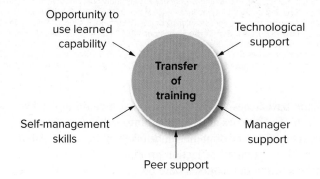

**Table 7.5**
How Managers Can Support Training

- Understand the content of the training.
- Know how training relates to what you need employees to do.
- In performance appraisals, evaluate employees on how they apply training to their jobs.
- Support employees' use of training when they return to work.
- Ensure that employees have the equipment and technology needed to use training.
- Prior to training, discuss with employees how they plan to use training.
- Recognize newly trained employees who use training content.
- Give employees release time from their work to attend training.
- Explain to employees why they have been asked to attend training.
- Give employees feedback related to skills or behavior they are trying to develop.
- If possible, be a trainer.

SOURCES: Based on S. Bailey, "The Answer to Transfer," *Chief Learning Officer*, November 2014, pp. 33–41; R. Hewes, "Step by Step," *T + D*, February 2014, pp. 56–61; R. Bates, "Managers as Transfer Agents," in E. Holton III and T. Baldwin (eds.), *Improving Learning Transfer in Organizations* (San Francisco: Jossey-Bass, 2003), pp. 243–70; A. Rossett, "That Was a Great Class, but . . .," *Training and Development*, July 1997, p. 21.

training session, provide practice opportunities, reinforce use of training, and follow up with employees to determine their progress in using newly acquired capabilities.

## Peer Support

Transfer of training can also be enhanced by creating a support network among the trainees.[31] A **support network** is a group of two or more trainees who agree to meet and discuss their progress in using learned capabilities on the job. This could involve face-to-face meetings or communications via e-mail, Twitter, or other social networking tools. For example, the learning team at New York Community Bancorp Inc. developed a blog that includes frequently asked questions and scenarios along with their responses, comments, and requests to follow-up.[32] Employees are encouraged to use the blog to ask for help or share best practices with their peers.

**Support network**
Trainees who meet to discuss their progress in using learned capabilities on the job.

Websites or electronic newsletters might be used to show how trainees are dealing with transfer of training issues. Available to all trainees, the newsletter or website might feature interviews with trainees who were successful in using new skills or provide tips for using new skills. Managers may also provide trainees with a mentor—a more experienced employee who previously attended the same training program. The mentor, who may be a peer, can provide advice and support (such as how to find opportunities to use the learned capabilities).

## Opportunity to Use Learned Capabilities

Opportunity to use learned capabilities **(opportunity to perform)** refers to the extent to which the trainee is provided with or actively seeks experience with newly learned knowledge, skills, and behaviors from the training program.[33] Opportunity to perform is influenced by both the work environment and trainee motivation. One way trainees can use learned capabilities is through assigned work experiences (problems or tasks) that require their use. The trainees' manager usually plays a key role in determining work assignments. Opportunity to perform is also influenced by the degree to which trainees take personal responsibility to actively seek out assignments that allow them to use newly acquired capabilities. Trainees given many opportunities to use training content on the job are more likely to maintain learned capabilities than trainees given few opportunities.[34]

**Opportunity to perform**
The trainee is provided with or actively seeks experience using newly learned knowledge, skills, or behavior.

## Technological Support: Performance Support and Knowledge Management Systems

**Performance support systems** are computer applications that can provide, as requested, skills training, information access, and expert advice.[35] Performance support may be used to enhance transfer of training by giving trainees an electronic information source that they can refer to as needed as they attempt to apply learned capabilities on the job.

For example, Synaptics provides touch-enabled products for computers, smartphones, and automobiles.[36] The company found that because employees' knowledge wasn't documented they often were solving the same or similar problems multiple times. To store and give employees better access to knowledge Synaptics developed a searchable YouTube channel. A few months after the YouTube channel was introduced, over six hundred videos were created, shared, and watched by employees across the company's various locations.

As discussed earlier in the chapter, many companies are using knowledge management systems to improve the creation, sharing, and use of knowledge. GE used an app to help integrate and encourage knowledge sharing between employees at GE Power and employees of Alstom's power business which was acquired.[37] The app matched employees with similar skills, education, and experiences, provided them with collaborative spaces where they could virtually interact, and suggested discussion topics.

Knowledge management systems often include communities of practice. **Communities of practice** are groups of employees who work together, learn from each other, and develop a common understanding of how to get work accomplished. Tata Consultancy Services, a global information technology services, consulting, and business services organization provides employees with communities of practice on its social collaboration platform.[38] The communities include Eminence, for sharing new ideas, success stories, and trends in technology; Learners Enablers community, where employees share their expertise and availability to help others; and Culturesque, which offers cultural quizzes on countries where the company does business.

## Self-Management Skills

Training programs should prepare employees to self-manage their use of new skills and behaviors on the job.[39] Specifically, within the training program, trainees should set goals for using skills or behaviors on the job, identify conditions under which they might fail to use them, identify the positive and negative consequences of using them, and monitor their use of them. Also, trainees need to understand that it is natural to encounter difficulty in trying to use skills on the job; relapses into old behavior and skill patterns do not indicate that trainees should give up. Finally, because peers and supervisors on the job may be unable to reward trainees using new behaviors or to provide feedback automatically, trainees need to create their own reward system and ask peers and managers for feedback.

As you should have realized by now, learning and transfer of training are closely related. If training does not facilitate learning there is nothing to transfer to the job. Similarly, if employees do learn, transfer of training will not occur if the work environment does not support or actively discourages applying what was learned.

Consider how Gales Residential and CVS get learners actively involved and help to ensure transfer of training.[40] The leadership development program at Gables Residential, a real estate company, focuses on developing self-awareness and skills in coaching and managing high-performance teams. Each month following a training session, a training and development manager meets with each participant to discuss what they learned and provide coaching and support to encourage them to further develop their skills. CVS Health, a health and medical services company you may know because of their retail pharmacies, provides 10-minute learning snippets which include fun activities, games, visuals, and quizzes to support formal training. Employees can access the learning snippets anytime after they complete training. The learning snippets are designed to help trainees retain what they have learned.

## SELECTING TRAINING METHODS

A number of different methods can help employees acquire new knowledge, skills, and behaviors. Figure 7.5 provides an overview of the use of training methods across companies of all sizes. The instructor-led classroom remains the most frequently used training method. However, the use of online learning, mobile learning, social learning, and blended learning (i.e., a combination of approaches) for training continues to increase. Expectations are that this trend with continue.

One estimate is that nearly 40% of executives plan to use tablets such as the iPad in their new training and development initiatives.[41] These devices are expected to be used for learning and performance support but also for coaching and mentoring employees, mobile gaming, and microblogging (e.g., Twitter).

Regardless of the training method, for training to be effective it needs to be based on the training design model shown in Figure 7.2. Needs assessment, a positive learning environment, and transfer of training are critical for training program effectiveness. The Competing through Globalization box shows how globalization affects the choice of training methods.

### Presentation Methods

**Presentation methods** refer to methods in which trainees are passive recipients of information. Presentation methods include traditional classroom instruction, distance learning, and audiovisual training. They can include the use of personal computers, smartphones, and tablet computers such as iPads. These methods are ideal for presenting new facts, information, different philosophies, and alternative problem-solving solutions or processes.

**Percentage of training hours delivered by each method**

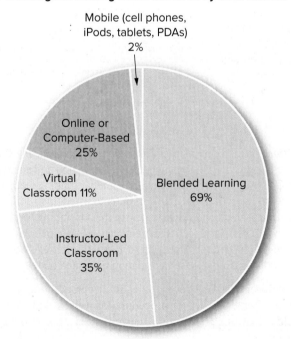

**LO 7-5**
Discuss the strengths and weaknesses of presentation, hands-on, and group training methods.

**Presentation methods**
Training methods in which trainees are passive recipients of information.

**Figure 7.5**
Overview of Use of Training Methods
SOURCE: "2018 Training Industry Report," *training*, November/December 2018, pp. 18–31.

### Campari Group's Spirited Language Training

Language barriers can be a problem even though the English language is typically used when conducting business across borders. Providing employees working globally with language training is difficult because it requires time, practice, and a knowledgeable instructor. Language training also needs to determine and build on employees' proficiency levels and to ensure they are exposed to language and phrases that they will use in their jobs.

Campari Group, the company known for its adult beverages—including Campari, an aperitif, along with Grand Marnier, Skyy Vodka, and Wild Turkey bourbon—has 4,000 employees located around the world. Campari found that its English language program wasn't meeting employees' needs for gaining English proficiency, so it decided to develop a new one through partnering with Voxy, a provider of English proficiency training. Typically, English proficiency training programs use formal scripts and vocabulary lessons tiered based on learners' demonstrated competency, which tends to make them less realistic and meaningful for learners.

Campari's new language training program uses authentic conversations to teach language. The program includes both self-paced lessons and live virtual classes that include business conversations learners are likely to experience at work. Before learners begin the training, they are asked to complete a survey used to determine their current English language proficiency, identify what they want to gain from the class, and identify the type of content they like to read. This information is used to provide customized training content that is appropriate for each learner's current ability and interests. For example, one learner lIked to read foodie magazines and articles about world news, so those types of articles were included in her lessons.

The virtual classes include a live instructor but also give learners the opportunity to practice their speaking skills through interacting with others in the class. To keep learners engaged in the class, the course includes a leaderboard that publicly displays their class performance, and trainers send learners news articles on the importance of English proficiency for career growth and tips for studying English. Evaluation of the program has shown that learners liked the program and their English proficiency levels had increased from beginners to intermediate level.

#### DISCUSSION QUESTION

1. Which conditions for learning emphasized in Campari's new language training program have contributed to its effectiveness? Explain how they have contributed.

SOURCES: Based on S. Gale, "The Language of Business," *Chief Learning Officer*, January/February 2019, pp. 60–61; "Case Study: Campari" from https://learn.voxy.com/campari-case-study, accessed January 7, 2019.

***Instructor-Led Classroom Instruction.*** Classroom instruction typically involves having the trainer lecture a group. In many cases, the lecture is supplemented with question-and-answer periods, discussion, or case studies. Classroom instruction remains a popular training method despite new technologies such as interactive video and computer-assisted instruction. Traditional classroom instruction is one of the least expensive, least time-consuming ways to present information on a specific topic to many trainees. The more active participation, job-related examples, and exercises that the instructor can build in to traditional classroom instruction, the more likely trainees will learn and use the information presented on the job.

***Distance Learning.*** Distance learning is used by geographically dispersed companies to provide information about new products, policies, or procedures as well as skills training and expert lectures to field locations.[42] Distance learning features two-way communications between people.[43] First, it can include teleconferencing. **Teleconferencing** refers to synchronous exchange of audio, video, and/or text between two or more individuals or groups at two or more locations. Trainees attend programs in facilities in which they can communicate with trainers (who are at another location) and other trainees using the telephone or personal computer. Second, distance learning can include a virtual classroom. A third type of distance learning also includes individualized, personal computer–based training.[44] Employees participate in training anywhere they have access to a personal computer. This can also include **webcasting**, which involves face-to-face instruction provided online through live broadcasts. Course material, including video, can be distributed using the company's intranet. Trainers and trainees interact using e-mail, bulletin boards, and conferencing systems. Distance learning can also allow trainees to respond to questions posed during the training program using a keypad.

Distance learning usually includes a link so that trainees viewing the presentation can call in questions and comments to the trainer. Also, satellite networks allow companies to link up with industry-specific and educational courses for which employees receive college credit and job certification.

An advantage of distance learning is that the company can save on travel costs. It also allows employees in geographically dispersed sites to receive training from experts who would not otherwise be available to visit each location. For example, for training its tax professionals, EY combines e-learning with a virtual classroom (described in more detail later in the chapter) and face-to-face instruction.[45] The virtual classroom courses are 30 minutes long. In the first 10 minutes, online polling is used to test participants' understanding of key concepts covered in the e-learning course. The trainer is encouraged to help clarify any key concepts that the participants don't understand. Following the polling, participants work in five- or six-person virtual teams on case studies. Next, participants attend the live, face-to-face class in which they complete income tax returns using EY's processes and technology.

The major disadvantage of distance learning is the potential for lack of interaction between the trainer and the audience. To help ensure that distance learning is effective, a high degree of interaction between trainees and the trainer is necessary.[46] That's why establishing a communications link between employees and the trainer is important. Also, on-site instructors or facilitators should be available to answer questions and moderate question-and-answer sessions.

*Audiovisual Training.* Audiovisual training includes the use of overheads, slides, and video. It has been used for improving communication skills, interviewing skills, and customer service skills and for illustrating how procedures (such as welding) should be followed. Learners may not be required to attend a class. They can work independently, using materials in workbooks or on the Internet. PowerPoint or other presentation software and video or audio clips can also be used to show learning points, real-life experiences, and examples. Consider how Farmers Insurance uses videos as part of its employee training to improve the customer experience.[47] Farmers Insurance uses 16 videos that are two to three minutes long. Employees observe actual customer interactions, identify their responsibilities, and determine what they could do to improve the customer's experience. Managers are provided with a guide for each video. The guide provide tips on how to discuss the key points and reinforce learning after employees complete a video.

Audiovisual training can easily be made available on desktop computers, smartphones, and tablet computers. These devices allow users to access the materials at any time or place.

Onoky Photography/SuperStock

**Teleconferencing**
Synchronous exchange of audio, video, or text between individuals or groups at two or more locations.

**Webcasting**
Classroom instruction provided online via live broadcasts.

Mobile technology is useful not only for entertainment but also for employees who travel and need to be in touch with the office. Smartphones, tablets, and other digital devices also give employees the ability to listen to and participate in training programs at their leisure.

They also allow instruction to include video clips, podcasts, charts and diagrams, learning points, and lectures. This helps facilitate learning by appealing to a variety of the users' senses and by both communicating and demonstrating knowledge, skills, and behaviors.

For example, Aggreko, a power generation supplier, created a mobile app that employees can use to connect with and share pictures and video with each other.[48] All training handouts and handbooks that were printed are now digital, which means they can be accessed as-needed on the job. The app can also be used to post pre- and post-training discussion questions. More than 300 courses can be accessed by employees who are located around the world.

The use of audiovisual training has a number of advantages. First, users have control over the presentation. They can review, slow down, or speed up the lesson, which permits flexibility in customizing the session depending on trainees' expertise. Second, trainees can be exposed to equipment, problems, and events that cannot be demonstrated easily in a classroom. Another advantage is that learners get a consistent presentation.

Most problems from these methods result from having too much content for the trainee to learn, overuse of humor or music, and drama that distracts from the key learning points.[49]

## Hands-On Methods

**Hands-on methods**
Training methods that require the trainee to be actively involved in learning.

**Hands-on methods** are training methods that require the trainee to be actively involved in learning. Hands-on methods include on-the-job training, simulations, business games and case studies, behavior modeling, interactive video, and Web-based training. These methods are ideal for developing specific skills, understanding how skills and behaviors can be transferred to the job, experiencing all aspects of completing a task, and dealing with interpersonal issues that arise on the job.

**On-the-job training (OJT)**
Peers or managers training new or inexperienced employees who learn the job by observation, understanding, and imitation.

*On-the-Job Training.* **On-the-job training (OJT)** refers to new or inexperienced employees learning through observing peers or managers performing the job and trying to imitate their behavior. OJT can be useful for training newly hired employees, upgrading experienced employees' skills when new technology is introduced, cross-training employees within a department or work unit, and orienting transferred or promoted employees to their new jobs.

OJT takes various forms, including apprenticeships and internships (discussed later in this section). OJT is an attractive training method because, compared to other methods, it needs less investment in time or money for materials, trainers' salaries, or instructional design. Managers or peers who are job knowledge experts are used as instructors. OJT must be structured to be effective. Table 7.6 shows the principles of structured OJT.

For example, at Nomad Communications Solutions, a company that builds and equips disaster response trailers, each task in the manufacturing process is assigned to an employee expert who breaks ever step into simple, easy-to-understand language.[50] The expert works alongside every new employee explaining the steps needed to complete their assigned task. The expert repeats steps that appear confusing to the new employee and asks questions to ensure that the employee understands what they are doing and are able to remember the steps.

**Apprenticeship**
A work-study training method with both on-the-job and classroom training.

**Apprenticeship** is a work-study training method with both OJT and classroom training. To qualify as a registered apprenticeship program under state or federal guidelines, at least 144 hours of classroom instruction and 2,000 hours, or one year, of on-the-job experience are required.[51] Apprenticeships can be sponsored by individual companies or by groups of companies cooperating with a union. The majority of apprenticeship programs are in the skilled trades, such as plumbing, carpentry, electrical work, and bricklaying.

**Table 7.6**
Principles of On-the-Job Training

| PREPARING FOR INSTRUCTION |
| --- |

1. Break down the job into important steps.
2. Prepare the necessary equipment, materials, and supplies.
3. Decide how much time you will devote to OJT and when you expect the employees to be competent in skill areas.

| ACTUAL INSTRUCTION |
| --- |

1. Tell the trainees the objective of the task and ask them to watch you demonstrate it.
2. Show the trainees how to do it without saying anything.
3. Explain the key points or behaviors. (Write out the key points for the trainees, if possible.)
4. Show the trainees how to do it again.
5. Have the trainees do one or more single parts of the task and praise them for correct reproduction (optional).
6. Have the trainees do the entire task and praise them for correct reproduction.
7. If mistakes are made, have the trainees practice until accurate reproduction is achieved.
8. Praise the trainees for their success in learning the task.

SOURCES: Based on W. J. Rothwell and H. C. Kazanas, "Planned OJT Is Productive OJT," *Training and Development Journal*, October 1990, pp. 53–55; P. J. Decker and B. R. Nathan, *Behavior Modeling Training* (New York: Praeger Scientific, 1985).

The hours and weeks that must be devoted to completing specific skill units are clearly defined. OJT involves assisting a certified tradesperson (a journeyman) at the work site. The on-the-job training portion of the apprenticeship follows the guidelines for effective on-the-job training.[52]

A major advantage of apprenticeship programs is that learners can earn pay while they learn. This is important because programs can last several years. Learners' wages usually increase automatically as their skills improve. Also, apprenticeships are usually effective learning experiences because they involve learning why and how a task is performed in classroom instruction provided by local trade schools, high schools, or community colleges. Apprenticeships also usually result in full-time employment for trainees when the program is completed. From the company's perspective, apprenticeship programs meet specific business needs and help to attract talented employees. The Competing through Environmental, Social, and Governance Practices box shows how employers, communities, and educational institutions are partnering to develop apprenticeships.

There are several potential disadvantages of apprenticeship programs. One is that there is no guarantee that jobs will be available when the program is completed. Another disadvantage is that employers may not hire apprentices because they believe apprentices are narrowly trained in one occupation or with one company, and program graduates may have only company-specific skills and may be unable to acquire new skills or adapt their skills to changes in the workplace.

An **internship** is on-the-job learning sponsored by an educational institution or is part of an academic program. Students are placed in paid positions where they can gain experiences related to their area of study. For example, Ford, Whirlpool, and Rolls-Royce use

**Internship**
On-the-job learning sponsored by an educational institution, or part of an academic program.

interns in human resources and engineering positions. If interns perform well, many companies offer them full-time positions after they complete their studies.

**Simulation**

A training method that represents a real-life situation, allowing trainees to see the outcomes of their decisions in an artificial environment.

***Simulations.*** A **simulation** is a training method that represents a real-life situation, with trainees' decisions resulting in outcomes that mirror what would happen if they were on the job. Simulations, which allow trainees to see the impact of their decisions in an artificial, risk-free environment, are used to teach production and process skills as well as management and interpersonal skills. Simulations are used for training pilots, cable installers, and call center employees.

IBM uses a simulation to train security teams how to handle cyberattacks.[53] The staging area is similar to a flight simulator but with room for two dozen people. Video panels cover the front wall and racks of computer servers located below the floor simulate the data stream of a company's network. One simulation involves a phishing e-mail sent to an HR representative. The hackers took data before the information technology crew could determine the source of the computer breach. After news of the breach leaked to the press, U.S. government agencies started an investigation. As the simulation developed, the security team discovered that the hackers had also changed the company's financial data before its quarterly report. Security teams have to learn to deal with the pressure the breach created, identify what was stolen, take steps to notify the appropriate persons and agencies, and secure the breach.

One way to enhance simulations is through virtual reality. **Virtual reality** is a computer-based technology that provides trainees with a three-dimensional (3-D) learning experience. Using specialized equipment or viewing the virtual model on the computer screen, trainees move through the simulated environment and interact with its components.[54] Technology is used to stimulate multiple senses of the trainee.[55] Devices relay information from the environment to the senses. For example, audio interfaces, gloves that provide a sense of touch, treadmills, or motion platforms are used to create a realistic, artificial environment. Devices also communicate information about the trainee's movements to a computer. These devices allow the trainee to experience the perception of actually being in a particular environment.

Claims adjusters at Farmers Insurance have to be trained on how to inspect homes that have been damaged in earthquakes, floods, tornadoes, and other disasters.[56] Farmers is using virtual reality to create different scenarios that are impossible to simulate in the company's existing training program. Farmers worked with a VR developer to create a VR two-story home that's suffered water damage. Each scenario, which takes about 15 minutes to complete, appears randomly so that water leaks appear in different places for each trainee. Trainees working in the home have access to a digital tool that lets them tag problem toilets or hot water heaters. They can even use a "fake" iPad to call a plumber or contact the insurance agent when they feel they have identified all of the problems. The prospective claims adjusters are scored based on the problems they identify and the appropriateness of the action they take. The virtual training experience can be broadcast to a classroom where other claims adjusters can watch their fellow trainees perform live. The VR sessions can also be recorded and employees can access them to review the session.

As you can see from the examples, simulations can be effective for several reasons.[57] First, trainees can use them on their desktop, eliminating the need to travel to a central training location. Second, simulations are meaningful, get trainees involved in learning, and are emotionally engaging (they can even be fun). This helps increase employees' willingness to practice, retain, and improve their skills. Third, simulators provide a consistent message of what needs to be learned; trainees can work at their own pace; and, compared to face-to-face instruction, simulators can incorporate more situations or problems that a trainee might encounter. Fourth, simulations can safely put employees in situations that would be dangerous in the real world. Fifth, simulations have been found to result in positive outcomes such as training being completed in a shorter time compared to traditional training courses, and providing a positive return on investment. Disadvantages of simulations include their cost and need for constant updating. This is because simulators must have elements identical to those found in the work environment. The simulator needs to respond exactly as the equipment (or customer) would under the conditioned response given by the trainee.[58]

*Augmented Reality.* **Augmented reality (AR)** allows trainees see the physical world around them but their view includes virtual media.[59] AR brings digital elements into the physical world to enhance the information and context that people experience. The major

**Virtual reality**
Computer-based technology that provides trainees with a three-dimensional learning experience. Trainees operate in a simulated environment that responds to their behaviors and reactions.

**Augmented reality (AR)**
A training method in which trainees see the physical world around them but their view includes virtual media.

difference between AR and virtual reality is that the physical reality is always present in AR. That is, AR provides information that supplements the real world the employee is working in while virtual reality creates an entirely artificial environment that the employee trains in.

For example, employees building tractors and other farm equipment at Argo, an agricultural equipment manufacturer, wear smart glasses that enable them to request information by varying their field of vision or through voice commands.[60] The smart glasses also serve as their safety goggles. AR has contributed to the efficiency and effectiveness of employees training. Each employee at Arco has to know how to perform three jobs. Using AR for training has reduced the training time to 30 to 40 days for a new hire to learn multiple jobs from the previous 50 to 90 days to learn only one job. Also, the quality of new hires work has improved. AR has also helped reduce training costs. Employees previously used tablets that each cost $3,000 and often were broken when employees dropped them as they tried to assemble and inspect equipment. Each pair of smart glasses cost $1,500 and none have been broken.

***Games and Case Studies.***  Games that require trainees to gather information, analyze it, and make decisions as well as case studies (situations that trainees study and discuss) are used primarily for management skill development.

Games can be played face-to-face or accessed through apps or notebook computers. **Serious games** refer to games in which the training content is turned into a game but has business objectives.[61] *Gamification* means that game-based strategies are applied to e-learning programs. Games enhance learning by providing a fun way to learn, use leaderboards to increase learners' motivation by capitalizing on their competitiveness, and incorporate levels that require learners to demonstrate they are competent in prerequisite knowledge and skills (by achieving certain scores) before learning more challenging knowledge and skills.

Games stimulate learning because participants are actively involved and they mimic the competitive nature of business. The types of decisions that participants make in games include all aspects of management practice, including labor relations (such as agreement in contract negotiations), marketing (the price to charge for a new product), and finance (financing the purchase of new technology). A realistic game or case may stimulate more learning than presentation methods (such as classroom instruction) because it is more meaningful.

Consider how Deloitte and University of North Carolina are using games in training.[62] At Deloitte, DLearn training courses can involve several different types of games. The games are interactive and played either individually or within teams. Mini-games featuring a buzzer and a bonus wheel can be used to ask trainees questions, and they gain points for correct answers. Another type of game allows instructors to develop cases that require teams of trainees to make decisions. Based on trainees answers the game can branch off to different paths, varying the points the teams earn based on the quality of their decisions. Instructors can use leaderboards to display points trainees earn playing the games as well as to award trainees badges for participation in class discussion boards and completing courses. Each trainee has a personal profile including the badges they have earned, which they can share with others.

A team of nurse educators from University of North Carolina Chapel Hill used a game, Friday Night at the ER, to improve the collaboration between nurses, physicians, and other health professionals who work in rural county hospital emergency rooms. Needs assessment showed that the professional staff working in these emergency rooms felt the greatest training need was for improved communications and collaboration to deliver better patient care. The game challenges players to help manage a hospital during a typical day. Each player performs a role that is different from, yet dependent on players in other hospital roles.

**Serious games**
Games in which the training content is turned into a game but has business objectives.

Each session of the game concludes with the opportunity for players to reflect on and discuss what they learned and to make plans to apply what they learned in their real hospital roles.

There are many sources of case studies, including Harvard Business School and the Darden Business School at University of Virginia. Cases may be especially appropriate for developing higher-order intellectual skills such as analysis, synthesis, and evaluation. These skills are often required by managers, physicians, and other professional employees. Cases also help trainees develop the willingness to take risks given uncertain outcomes, based on their analysis of the situation. To use cases effectively, the learning environment must let trainees prepare and discuss their case analyses. Also, face-to-face or electronic communication among trainees must be arranged. Because trainee involvement is critical for the effectiveness of the case method, learners must be willing and able to analyze the case and then communicate and defend their positions.

*Behavior Modeling.*  Research suggests that behavior modeling is one of the most effective techniques for teaching interpersonal skills.[63] Each training session, which typically lasts four hours, focuses on one interpersonal skill, such as coaching or communicating ideas. Each session presents the rationale behind key behaviors, a video of a model performing key behaviors, practice opportunities using role-playing, evaluation of a model's performance in the video, and a planning session devoted to understanding how the key behaviors can be used on the job. In the practice sessions, trainees get feedback regarding how closely their behavior matches the key behaviors demonstrated by the model. The role-playing and modeled performance are based on actual incidents in the employment setting in which the trainee needs to demonstrate success.

*E-Learning.*  **E-learning**, *computer-based training, online learning*, and *Web-based training* refer to instruction and delivery of training by computer through the Internet or the Web.[64] To enhance learning, these training methods can include and integrate the following into instruction: text; interaction using simulations and games; video; collaboration using blogs, wikis, and social networks; and hyperlinks to additional resources. In some types of computer-based training, content is provided using standalone software with no connection to the Internet. Trainees can still interact with the training content, answer questions, and choose responses regarding how they would behave in certain situations, but they cannot collaborate with other learners.

Online learning, e-learning, and Web-based training all include delivery of instruction using the Internet or Web. The training program can be accessed using a password through the public Internet or the company's private intranet. There are many potential features that can be included in online learning to help trainees learn and transfer training to their jobs. For example, online programs that use video may make it an interactive experience for trainees. That is, trainees watch the video and have the opportunity to use the keyboard or touch the screen to answer questions, respond with how they would act in certain situations, or identify the steps they would take to solve a problem. Interactive video is especially valuable for helping trainees learn technical or interpersonal skills.

For example, e-learning offered by the U.S. Office of Disease Prevention and Health Promotion uses modeling through simulated conversations and interactions with patients to train health care providers how to provide high-quality patient care.[65] They can take on different roles such as a busy nurse working as a pain management professional at her practice. Trainees can make choices about how to respond to patients' questions, get feedback on their choice, and learn from their mistakes.

Effective e-learning is grounded on a thorough needs assessment and complete learning objectives. **Repurposing** refers to directly translating an instructor-led, face-to-face training program online. Online learning that merely repurposes an ineffective training

**E-learning**
Instruction and delivery of training by computers through the Internet or company intranet.

**LO 7-6**
Explain the potential advantages of e-learning for training.

**Repurposing**
Directly translating instructor-led training online.

program will remain ineffective. Unfortunately, in their haste to develop online learning, many companies are repurposing bad training. The best e-learning combines the advantages of the Internet with the principles of a good learning environment. Effective online learning takes advantage of the Web's dynamic nature and ability to use many positive learning features, including linking to other training sites and content through the use of hyperlinks, and allowing the trainee to collaborate with other learners. Online learning also gives the learner control over the pace of learning, exercises, and the use of links to other material and peer and expert networks. Online learning allows activities typically led by the instructor (presentations, visuals, slides), trainees (discussion, questions), and group interaction (discussion of application of training content) to be incorporated into training without trainees or the instructor having to be physically present in a training room. Effective online learning gives trainees meaningful content, relevant examples, and the ability to apply content to work problems and issues. Also, trainees can practice and receive feedback through problems, exercises, assignments, and tests.

**Massive open online courses (MOOCs)**
Online learning designed to enroll large numbers of learners who have access to the Internet and composed of interactive coursework including video lectures, discussion groups, wikis, and assessment quizzes.

Massive open online courses (MOOCs) are a new type of e-learning. **Massive open online courses (MOOCs)** is learning that is designed to enroll a large number of learners (massive); is free and accessible to anyone with an Internet connection (open); takes place online using videos of lectures, interactive course work including discussion groups, and wikis (online); and has specific start and completion dates, quizzes and assessment, and exams (courses).[66] MOOCs cover a wide variety of subject matter, including chemistry, math, physics, computer science, philosophy, mythology, health policy, cardiac arrest and resuscitation, and even poetry.

Popular providers of MOOCs include Coursera, edX (nonprofit founded by Harvard and MIT), and Udacity (a for-profit company founded by a Stanford University Research professor and founder of Google X Labs). The courses are often developed in partnership with colleges and universities and by private companies. For example, Udacity and AT&T created MOOC courses for nanodegrees, which provide AT&T's programmers with the opportunity to take a series of courses that prepare them for high-technology specializations such as software engineering, coding, or Web development. The World Bank developed a four-week MOOC for its clients to learn how to secure financing to achieve sustainable development goals, including eliminating hunger, achieving gender equality, and providing high-quality education and clean water.[67] The MOOC is taught by five World Bank instructors, government officials, and private-sector experts. Fifty thousand participants from several hundred countries signed up for the course. The MOOC provided learners with the opportunity to talk to each other as well as listen to presentations. As a final course project, participants were asked to identify a development problem in their community and propose a financing solution based on what they learned in the course. This resulted in over 1,000 digital artifacts that could subsequently be used for developing financing solutions.

MOOCs have several advantages and disadvantages.[68] Their low cost, accessibility, and wide range of topics make them attractive to learners. They include many features that facilitate learning and transfer: Learning is interactive, learner controlled, involves social interaction, and emphasizes application. Learning happens through engaging short lectures combined with interaction with course materials, other students, and the instructor. It emphasizes applying knowledge and skills using role-plays, cases, and projects. It is semisynchronous, meaning learners receive the same assignments, video lectures, readings, quizzes, and discussions, but they can complete the coursework on their own time. Also, many MOOCs offer college credit or certificates of completion, which provide incentives for learning and formal acknowledgement. However, despite claims that MOOCs will revolutionize training and education, they have significant disadvantages. Those who enroll in

MOOCs tend to interact with them less over time, dropping off after the first two weeks of the course; course completion rates are low (10–20%), and most students who complete the courses don't take the credential exam. MOOCs may also be inappropriate for courses where synchronous or real-time collaboration or interaction is needed. Surprisingly, only 5% of employees receive financial support from their companies for enrolling in MOOCs. However, providing employees with financial support for MOOCs does payoff. Employees who receive financial support have higher course completion rates and are less likely to look for job opportunities outside of their current employer.[69]

Many companies are using tablets such as the iPad for training because of their ease of use, colorful easy-to-read display, ability to connect to the Web, access to social media, and availability of powerful apps. Apps are primarily being used to supplement training, manage the path or sequence of training, and help employees maintain training records.[70] For example, PwC provides employees with an app that enables them to access course materials, complete course prerequisites, and access materials on an as-needed basis.[71] More than 9,000 pieces of content were accessed and more than 36,000 hours of learning were completed by employees on their mobile devices.

The Competing through Technology box highlights how artificial intelligence is being used to adapt training based on the trainees current level of skills or knowledge.

*Blended Learning.* Many companies are moving to a hybrid, or blended, learning approach because of the limitations of e-learning related to technology (e.g., insufficient bandwidth, lack of high-speed Web connections), trainee preferences for face-to-face contact with instructors and other learners, and employees' inability to find unscheduled time during their workday to devote to learning from their desktops. **Blended learning** refers to combining technology methods, such as e-learning, simulations, or social media, with face-to-face instruction, for delivery of learning content and instruction. Anthem Inc., a health insurance provider, transitioned from face-to-face learning for its associates to online training that provides learners with more control and the ability to learn from a coach and their peers.[72] Anthem Health Guide (AHG) is a consumer product that helps them better understand and use their benefits. AHG Flipped Classroom training begins with a video chat orientation where trainers introduce learners to the learning objectives, training agenda, and the technology that will be used. The training content is then delivered face-to-face using videos, games, group activities, role-plays, and providing individualized coaching. Also, a social collaboration site on the company intranet provides learners with the opportunity to interact with trainers and other learners.

**Blended learning**
Delivering content and instruction with a combination of technology-based and face-to-face methods.

*Learning Management Systems.* A **learning management system (LMS)** refers to a technology platform that can be used to automate the administration, development, and delivery of all of a company's training programs. An LMS can provide employees, managers, and trainers with the ability to manage, deliver, and track learning activities.[73] LMSs are becoming more popular for several reasons. An LMS can help companies reduce travel and other costs related to training, reduce time for program completion, increase employees' accessibility to training across the business, and provide administrative capabilities to track program completion and course enrollments. An LMS allows companies to track all of the learning activity in the business. Consider how the LMS at Ferguson Enterprises and Gukenheimer support the business by helping to manage human capital and tracking training.[74] As a planning tool the LMS helps track how many training courses were accessed, course enrollment and completion, training hours completed, and differences in managers and nonmanagers involvement in training. The data is used to help determine how training supports the business. Data from the LMS was also used to determine which days and times employees participated in training. This helped ensure that training

**Learning management system (LMS)**
Technology platform that automates the administration, development, and delivery of a company's training program.

### Artificial Intelligence Helps Customize Training to the Learner

As their availability and sophistication increases, companies are using artificial intelligence to customize training for employees and increase its effectiveness. Artificial intelligence (AI) refers to the development of a system, such as a computer, a computer-controlled robot, or software, that can think intelligently like humans. AI is developed by studying how we think, learn, decide, and work while trying to solve a problem and then using this information to build intelligent software and systems.

Machine learning refers to artificial intelligence systems that learn. The systems learn by applying algorithms to data to identify user trends and patterns that inform future suggestions and data searches. Software can monitor what trainees do and how they engage with online training content and then "learn" what types of other training courses it should suggest, when to provide training content, and provide training in the format (audio, video) that trainees prefer. Also, machine learning can

be used to create a more personalized and customized learning experience for trainees similar to how Netflix works for television and Spotify for music.

For example, Aristocrat Technologies, a gaming machine manufacturer, replaced online learning courses for its repair technicians with adaptable microlearning modules. The modules are sent to their phones so they can review the content between their jobs and answer short quiz questions. The system uses their quiz scores to learn what they know (and don't know) and uses this information to choose what content to send them next. Technicians have to master each module twice before they can move on to another module.

Air Methods, a company that provides medical transportation using helicopters, implemented a cloud-based learning system that uses artificial intelligence to adapt to each helicopter pilot's topic knowledge based on how that pilot performs on quizzes and games. If the pilot is not scoring well on the quizzes for a particular

training module, the system will present information in a new way and retest before the pilot can move to the next training module. The use of adaptive training has saved training costs by eliminating 50% of the company's in-person, instructor-led training courses and reduced the time it takes for the training that new pilots have to complete as part of the onboarding process.

**DISCUSSION QUESTION**

1. How can adaptable training using AI improve the effectiveness of training?

SOURCE: Based on "What Is Artificial Intelligence?" from https://www.tutorialspoint.com/artificial_intelligence/artificial_intelligence_overview.htm, accessed March 19, 2018; R. High, "3 Terms All Business Professionals Need to Understand", *VentureBeat*, February 24, 2018, from https://venturebeat.com, accessed March 7, 2018; S. Gale, "Ready or Not, the Guture Is Now," *Chief Learning Officer*, March 2017, pp. 20–21; McKinsey Global Institute, "Jobs Lost, Jobs Gained: Workforce Transitions in a Time of Automation," December 2017, from www.mckinsey.com/mgi accessed March 19, 2018; S. Gale, "Learning on the Fly," *Chief Learning Officer*, September 2017, pp. 32–36; K. Rockwood, "The University of You," *HR Magazine*, May 2017, pp. 39–42; A. Sharma and B. Szostak, "Adapting to Adaptive Learning," *Chief Learning Officer*, January/February 2018, pp. 32–35.

---

**Group- or team-building methods** Training methods that help trainees share ideas and experiences, build group identity, understand the dynamics of interpersonal relationships, and get to know their own strengths and weaknesses and those of their co-workers.

supporting a new customer service initiative was available during the times employees were available to complete it. Guckenheimer uses its LMS to track assignments, completions, and compliance. Automatic assignments are available in the LMS to ensure training is accessible the day an employee is hired or promoted to a position. The LMS allows the company to track which employees have completed assignments and required compliance training and renewal of certifications.

### Group- or Team-Building Methods

**Group- or team-building methods** are training methods designed to improve team or group effectiveness. Training is directed at improving the trainees' skills as well as team effectiveness.

In group-building methods, trainees share ideas and experiences, build group identity, understand the dynamics of interpersonal relationships, and get to know their own strengths and weaknesses and those of their co-workers. Group techniques focus on helping teams increase their skills for effective teamwork. All involve examination of feelings, perceptions, and beliefs about the functioning of the team; discussion; and development of plans to apply what was learned in training to the team's performance in the work setting. Group-building methods fall into three categories: experiential programs, team training, and action learning.

*Experiential Programs.* **Experiential programs** involve gaining conceptual knowledge and theory; taking part in a behavioral simulation or activity; analyzing the activity; and connecting the theory and activity with on-the-job or real-life situations.[75]

For experiential training programs to be successful, several guidelines should be followed. The program needs to tie in to a specific business problem. The trainees need to be moved outside their personal comfort zones but within limits so as not to reduce trainee motivation or ability to understand the purpose of the program. Multiple learning modes should be used, including audio, visual, and kinesthetic. When preparing activities for an experiential training program, trainers should ask trainees for input on the program goals. Clear expectations about the purpose, expected outcomes, and trainees' roles in the program are important. Finally, training programs that include experiential learning should be linked to changes in employee attitudes, behaviors, and other business results.

DaVita HealthCare Partners provides kidney-related health care services such as dialysis.[76] DaVita contracted with a training provider to develop a three-hour experiential learning activity that would be collaborative; have a sense of purpose; and reinforce the company's values of teamwork, fulfillment, and fun. The goals of the program were to understand the importance of their work, understand how team members relate to patients and to each other, and how to address challenges. The activity started with a discussion of the importance of communicating and collaborating for successful teamwork on the job. Employees were divided into three member teams and given the task of building prosthetic hands that would be donated to organizations serving amputees. Building the prostheses provided an opportunity for the achievement of the program's goals. The employees built more than 14,000 prostheses during the three-hour activity. The activity concluded with a discussion of ways to apply what they learned to their jobs at DaVita.

**Adventure learning**, a type of experiential program, develops teamwork and leadership skills using structured outdoor activities.[77] Adventure learning appears to be best suited for developing skills related to group effectiveness, such as self-awareness, problem solving, conflict management, and risk taking. Adventure learning may involve strenuous, challenging physical activities such as dogsledding or mountain climbing. It can also use structured individual and group outdoor activities such as climbing walls, going through rope courses, making trust falls, climbing ladders, and traveling from one tower to another using a device attached to a wire that connects the two towers.

For example, 20 coders, marketing executives, and product team members from RealScout left their office and spent a day in the California mountains learning survival skills such as constructing shelters, purifying water, and starting a fire without matches.[78] The program cost $2,000, in addition to the $7,000–$10,000 lost by shutting down the business for the day. RealScout executives believed the benefits of the adventure would outweigh its costs. They believed it helps develop stronger teams, allows employees to better know each other even if they don't work together on a daily basis, and gives employees a fun experience that will aid in retention.

Adventure learning can also include demanding activities that require coordination and place less of a physical strain on team members. For example, Cookin' Up Change is one of

**Experiential programs**
Training programs in which trainees gain knowledge and theory, participate in behavioral simulations, analyze the activity, and connect the theory and activity with on-the-job situations.

**Adventure learning**
Learning focused on the development of teamwork and leadership skills by using structured outdoor activities.

many team-building courses offered around the United States by chefs, caterers, hotels, and cooking schools.[79] These courses have been used by companies such as Honda and Microsoft. The underlying idea is that cooking classes help strengthen communication and networking skills by requiring team members to work together to create a multiple-course meal. Each team has to decide who does what kitchen tasks (e.g., cooking, cutting, cleaning) and who prepares the main course, salads, or dessert. Often team members are required to switch assignments in the middle of preparation to see how the team reacts to change.

For adventure learning programs to succeed, the exercises should be related to the types of skills that participants are expected to develop. Also, after the exercises, a skilled facilitator should lead a discussion about what happened in the exercise, what was learned, how the exercise relates to the job situation, and how to set goals and apply what was learned on the job.[80]

Does adventure learning work? Participants often report that they gained a greater understanding of themselves and the ways they interact with their co-workers. One key to the success of an adventure learning program may be the insistence that whole work groups participate together so that group dynamics that inhibit effectiveness can emerge and be discussed.

The physically demanding nature of adventure learning and the requirement that trainees often have to touch each other in the exercises may increase the company's risk for negligence claims due to personal injury, intentional infliction of emotional distress, and invasion of privacy. Also, the Americans with Disabilities Act (discussed in Chapter 3) raises questions about requiring employees with disabilities to participate in physically demanding training experiences.

*Team Training.* Team training coordinates the performance of individuals who work together to achieve a common goal. Such training is an important issue when information must be shared and individuals affect the overall performance of the group. For example, in the military as well as the private sector (think of nuclear power plants or commercial airlines), much work is performed by crews, groups, or teams. Success depends on team performance, coordination of individual activities to make decisions, and readiness to deal with potentially dangerous situations (like an overheating nuclear reactor).

**Cross-training**
Training in which team members understand and practice each other's skills so that members are prepared to step in and take another member's place should he or she temporarily or permanently leave the team.

**Coordination training**
Training a team in how to share information and decision-making responsibilities to maximize team performance.

**Team leader training**
Training of the team manager or facilitator.

Team training strategies include cross-training and coordination training.[81] In **cross-training**, team members understand and practice each other's skills so that members are prepared to step in and take another member's place. **Coordination training** trains the team in how to share information and decisions to maximize team performance. Coordination training is especially important for commercial aviation and surgical teams, who monitor different aspects of equipment and the environment but must share information to make the most effective decisions regarding patient care or aircraft safety and performance. **Team leader training** refers to training of the team manager or facilitator. This may involve training the manager on how to resolve conflict within the team or how to help the team coordinate activities or other team skills.

For example, United Airlines had its supervisors "lead" ramp employees in attending Pit Instruction & Training (Pit Crew U), which focuses on the preparation, practice, and teamwork of NASCAR pit crews. United used the training to develop standardized methods to safely and efficiently unload, load, and send off its airplanes.[82] Pit Instruction & Training, located outside of Charlotte, North Carolina, has a quarter-mile race track and a pit road with places for six cars. The school offers programs to train new racing pit crews, but most of its business comes from companies interested in having their teams work as safely, efficiently, and effectively as NASCAR pit crews. The training was part of a multimillion-dollar investment that includes updating equipment and providing luggage scanners.

The purpose of the training is to reinforce the need for ramp teams to be orderly and communicate, to help standardize tasks of ramp team members, to help shorten the time an airplane is serviced at the gate, and to improve morale.

The keys for safety, speed, and efficiency for NASCAR pit crews is that each member knows what tasks to do (change tires, use an air gun, add gasoline, clean up spills) and, when the crew has finished servicing the race car, moves new equipment into position anticipating the next pit stop. The training involved the ramp workers actually working as pit crews. They learn how to handle jacks, change tires, and fill fuel tanks on race cars. They are video-recorded and timed just like real pit crews. They receive feedback from professional pit crew members who work on NASCAR teams and trainers. Also, the training requires them to deal with circumstances they might encounter on the job. For one pit stop, lug nuts had been sprinkled intentionally in the area where the car stops to see if the United employees would notice them and clean them up. On their jobs, ramp employees are responsible for removing debris from the tarmac so that it doesn't get sucked into jet engines or harm equipment. For another pit stop, teams had to work with fewer members, as sometimes occurs when ramp crews are understaffed due to absences.

*Action Learning.* In **action learning**, teams or work groups get an actual business problem, work on solving it and commit to an action plan, and are accountable for carrying out the plan.[83] Typically, action learning involves between 6 and 30 employees; it may also include customers and vendors. There are several variations on the composition of the group. In one variation, the group includes a single customer for the problem being dealt with. Sometimes the groups include cross-functional team members (members from different company departments) who all have a stake in the problem. Or the group may involve employees from multiple functions who all focus on their own functional problems, each contributing to helping solve the problems identified. Action learning is often part of quality improvement processes such as Six Sigma training and Kaizen. *Kaizen*, the Japanese word for improvement, is one of the underlying principles of lean manufacturing and total quality management (lean thinking is discussed in Chapter 1).

> **Action learning**
> Training in which teams work on an actual business problem, commit to an action plan, and are accountable for carrying out the plan.

Consider how University Health System and PepsiCo used action learning to solve important and complex business problems.[84] At University Health System, nine cross-functional teams of managers who otherwise would not work together worked on separate business problems. These problems included how to increase patient satisfaction, reduce billing errors, and enhance inventory control. Each team was asked to present its solution to what was called the Shark Tank—three senior executives and the CEO for pediatric services, who served as "sharks." As each team presented their ideas, the sharks provided coaching and feedback. The problem solutions helped University Health System save millions of dollars and improved patient satisfaction. PepsiCo employed action learning when it wanted to train managers to take a global perspective on the company's strategy. Leslie Teichgraeber, who led the training programs, observed that most managers were familiar only with their local or national markets. So she assembled teams of managers from various locations and assigned each team to solve problems related to business needs that had been identified by the heads of their units. At the end of nine months, they presented their ideas to PepsiCo executives.

## ADVICE FOR SELECTING A TRAINING METHOD

Given the large number of available training methods, the task of choosing one may seem difficult. One way to choose a training method is to compare methods. The first step in choosing a method is to identify the type of learning outcome the training is to influence. These outcomes include verbal information, intellectual skills, cognitive strategies,

> **LO 7-7**
> Design a training session to maximize learning.

attitudes, motor skills, or some combination. Training methods may influence one or several learning outcomes.

There is considerable overlap between learning outcomes across the training methods. Group-building methods are unique because they focus on individual as well as team learning (e.g., improving group processes). One of the group-building methods (e.g., experiential learning, team training, action learning) would be appropriate if the goal is to improve the effectiveness of groups or teams. Second, comparing the presentation methods to the hands-on methods illustrates that most hands-on methods provide a better learning environment and transfer of training than do the presentation methods.

E-learning or blended learning can be an effective training method for geographically dispersed trainees. E-learning and other technology-driven training methods have higher development costs, but travel and housing cost savings will likely offset development costs over time. A blended learning approach can take advantage of the positive features of both face-to-face and technology-based instruction. For example, Bankers Life, an insurance company, revised its new sales agents training program to appeal to the way Millennials want to learn and use new technology. It segments learning into small modules that build on each other.[85] Each module includes online coursework, debrief, role-play, and training in the field. Intermedia Inc., a business services company, uses virtual instructor-led training including video, e-learning modules, lab activities, and role plays to train its agents.[86] Agents are able to access any of the training content after they are back in the field, which helps them review what they have learned and keep their skills updated.

A final but important consideration is the training budget. If the budget for developing new training methods is limited, then structured on-the-job training is a good choice. It is a relatively inexpensive yet effective hands-on method. Hands-on methods that facilitate transfer of training, such as simulators, are feasible with a larger budget.

# Evaluating Training Programs

**LO 7-8**
Choose appropriate evaluation design and training outcomes based on the training objectives and evaluation purpose.

**Training outcomes**
A way to evaluate the effectiveness of a training program based on cognitive, skill-based, affective, and results outcomes.

Training evaluation can provide useful information, including the program's strengths and weaknesses, identifying which learners benefited most and least from participating, determining the program's financial benefits and costs, and allowing the comparison of the benefits and costs of different programs.

Examining the outcomes of a program helps in evaluating its effectiveness. These outcomes should be related to the program objectives, which help trainees understand the purpose of the program. **Training outcomes** can be categorized as cognitive outcomes, skill-based outcomes, affective outcomes, results, and return on investment.[87] Table 7.7 shows the types of outcomes used in evaluating training programs and what is measured and how it is measured.

Verizon created Sales Leadership Academy (SLA) for all of the company's over 6,000 Verizon Wireless Retail Sales leaders.[88] The objective of SLA was to engage, enable, and empower the retail leaders to deliver strong financial results while providing the leadership needed to change the retail business over the next three years. Verizon uses several outcomes to evaluate the effectiveness of SLA. The outcomes included participants confidence they could apply the knowledge and skills emphasized in the program on the job (affective outcomes), actual knowledge gained (cognitive outcomes), survey results of leadership behaviors such as engaging and empowering their direct reports (skill-based outcomes), and key retail performance indicators, including average transaction time and average credits per sales transaction (results outcomes).

Which training outcomes measure is best? The answer depends on the training objectives. For example, if the instructional objectives identified business-related outcomes

| OUTCOME | WHAT IS MEASURED | HOW IT IS MEASURED | EXAMPLE |
|---|---|---|---|
| Cognitive outcomes | • Acquisition of knowledge | • Pencil-and-paper tests<br>• Work sample | • Safety rules<br>• Electrical principles<br>• Steps in appraisal interview |
| Skill-based outcomes | • Behavior<br>• Skills | • Observation<br>• Work sample<br>• Ratings | • Jigsaw use<br>• Listening skills<br>• Coaching skills<br>• Airplane landings |
| Affective outcomes | • Motivation<br>• Reaction to program<br>• Attitudes | • Interviews<br>• Focus groups<br>• Attitude surveys | • Satisfaction with training<br>• Beliefs regarding other cultures |
| Results | • Company payoff | • Observation<br>• Data from information system or performance records | • Absenteeism<br>• Accidents<br>• Patents |
| Return on investment | • Economic value of training | • Identification and comparison of costs and benefits of the program | • Dollars |

**Table 7.7**

Outcomes Used in Evaluating Training Programs

such as increased customer service or product quality, then results outcomes should be included in the evaluation. Both reaction and cognitive outcomes are usually collected before the trainees leave the training site. As a result, these measures do not help determine the extent to which trainees actually use the training content in their jobs (transfer of training). Skill-based, affective, and results outcomes measured following training can be used to determine transfer of training—that is, the extent to which training has changed behavior, skills, or attitudes or directly influenced objective measures related to company effectiveness (such as sales).

## Evaluation Designs

As shown in Table 7.8, a number of different evaluation designs can be applied to training programs. Table 7.8 compares each evaluation design on the basis of who is involved (trainees and/or a comparison group that does not receive training), when outcome measures are collected (pretraining, posttraining), the costs, the time needed to conduct the evaluation, and the strength of the design for ruling out alternative explanations for the results (e.g., are improvements due to factors other than the training?). In general, designs that use pretraining and posttraining measures of outcomes and include a comparison group reduce the risk that factors other than training itself are responsible for the evaluation results. This builds confidence to use the results to make decisions. The trade-off is that evaluations using these designs are more costly and time consuming to conduct than evaluations not using pretraining or posttraining measures or comparison groups.

For example, if a manager is interested in comparing the effectiveness of two programs—that is, determining how much outcomes (knowledge, affect, skills, behavior, results)

**Table 7.8**

Comparison of Evaluation Designs

| DESIGN | GROUPS | MEASURES | | | | |
| --- | --- | --- | --- | --- | --- | --- |
| | | PRETRAINING | POSTTRAINING | COST | TIME | STRENGTH |
| Posttest only | Trainees | No | Yes | Low | Low | Low |
| Pretest/posttest | Trainees | Yes | Yes | Low | Low | Medium |
| Posttest only with comparison group | Trainees and comparison | No | Yes | Medium | Medium | Medium |
| Pretest/posttest with comparison group | Trainees and comparison | Yes | Yes | Medium | Medium | High |
| Time series | Trainees | Yes | Yes, several | Medium | Medium | Medium |

have changed as a result of one program compared to another—then a pretest/posttest design is necessary. Consider how Mountain America Credit Union evaluated the effectiveness of a revised sales training program.[89] Mountain America tracked the average monthly sales of 30 new employees during their first two months of employment. Ten of the thirty employees attended training before it was revised (they called this the Traditional Group). Twenty employees attended the program after it was revised (the Express Group). The revised program included more interactions with a variety of customers with different needs. Monthly sales were compared between the Express Group and the Traditional Group. The average number of sales in the Express Group exceeded the average number of sales in the Traditional Group in both the first (11.4 versus 3.5 average) and second months (34.83 versus 5.5) of employment. The Evidence-Based HR box highlights Edwards Jones' use of a pretest/posttest design for training evaluation.

# EVIDENCE-BASED HR

Edward Jones Insurance Partnership program brings together branch teams including one financial advisor, an office administrator, and insurance consultants. The training, which lasts two days, trains the teams in how to design and present insurance solutions and identify clients who need insurance. An evaluation compared the pretraining and posttraining results 15 months after training for over 500 branches. They found that after training the branches placed on average one more insurance policy, the top 50 branches increased the average of permanent policies to eight, and insurance-related gross revenue increased resulting in more than a 600% return on investment.

SOURCE: Based on "Training Top 125, Best Practices & Outstanding Training Initiatives, Edward Jones: Insurance Partnership," *Training*, January/February 2018, p. 87.

Many companies are interested in determining the financial benefits of learning, including training courses and programs, and development activities (see Chapter 9). One way to do this is by determining return on investment (ROI). **Return on investment (ROI)** refers to the estimated dollar return from each dollar invested in learning. Keep in mind that ROI is not a substitute for outcomes that also provide an indication of the success or usefulness of learning, such as trainees' reactions, knowledge acquisition, or behavior change. Also, ROI is best suited for outcomes that can be quantified, such as quality, accidents, or turnover. Otherwise, you will have to make an educated guess about the value of the outcome. For example, how do you value increased leadership skills?

**Return on investment (ROI)**
Refers to the estimated dollar return from each dollar invested in learning.

### Determining the Financial Benefits of Learning
To make an ROI analysis, follow these steps:[90]

1. Identify outcomes (e.g., quality, accidents).
2. Place a value on the outcomes.
3. Determine the change in performance after eliminating other potential influences on training results.
4. Obtain an annual amount of benefits (operational results) from training by comparing results after training to results before training (in dollars).
5. Determine the training costs (direct costs + indirect costs + development costs + overhead costs + compensation for trainees).
6. Calculate the total savings by subtracting the training costs from benefits (operational results).
7. Calculate the ROI by dividing benefits (operational results) by costs. The ROI gives an estimate of the dollar return expected from each dollar invested in training.

ROI can be measured and communicated based on a percentage or a ratio. For example, assume that a new safety training program results in a decline of 5% in a company's accident rate. This provides a total annual savings (the benefit) of $150,000 in terms of lost workdays, material and equipment damage, and workers' compensation costs. The training program costs $50,000 to implement (including both direct and indirect costs). To calculate the ROI, you need to subtract the training costs from the benefits, divide by the costs, and multiply by 100. That is, $\text{ROI} = [(150,000 - 50,000) \div 50,000] \times 100\% = 200\%$. The ROI for this program is 200%. Another way to think about ROI is to consider it as a ratio based on the return for every dollar spent. In this example, the company gained a net benefit of $2 for every dollar spent. This means the ROI is 2:1. Verizon compared a group of customer service representatives who had the opportunity to watch customer service scenarios, practice and record their responses, and receive feedback (the training group) with another group who only watched the videos but did not practice (comparison group).[91] They found that the training group had a 71% increase in acquiring new customers compared to the comparison group. To calculate the ROI, Verizon considered development costs, compensation costs, and costs for materials, instructors, and coaches. They found that the training resulted in a $1.4 million increase in revenue over three months.

# Special Training Issues

To meet the competitive challenges of sustainability, globalization, and technology discussed in Chapter 1, companies must successfully deal with several special training issues. The special training issues include preparing employees to work in different cultures abroad, managing workforce diversity, and orienting and socializing new employees.

**LO 7-9**
Design a cross-cultural preparation program.

## CROSS-CULTURAL PREPARATION

**Expatriate**
Employee sent by his or her company to manage operations in a different country.

As we mentioned in Chapter 1, companies today are challenged to expand globally. Because of the increase in global operations, employees often work outside their country of origin or work with employees from other countries. An **expatriate** works in a country other than his or her country of origin. The most frequently selected locations for expatriate assignments include the United States, China, Africa, and India.[92] At Ernst & Young, about 2,600 of over 167,000 employees are on an international assignment at any one time, including 270 Americans in 30 countries (e.g., Brazil, China, India, Russia, and South Africa).[93] Many U.S. companies are using expatriate assignments as a training tool. For example, employees who want top management positions, such as chief financial officer, need to understand how cultural norms and the political environment influence the movements in currencies and commodities in order to build effective global financial plans.[94]

**Cross-cultural preparation**
The process of educating employees (and their families) who are given an assignment in a foreign country.

We discuss international human resource management in detail in Chapter 15. Here the focus is on understanding how to prepare employees for expatriate assignments. **Cross-cultural preparation** educates employees (expatriates) and their families who are to be sent to a foreign country. To successfully conduct business in the global marketplace, employees must understand the business practices and the cultural norms of different countries.

### Steps in Cross-Cultural Preparation

To succeed overseas, expatriates (employees on foreign assignments) need to be

1. Competent in their areas of expertise.
2. Able to communicate verbally and nonverbally in the host country.
3. Flexible, tolerant of ambiguity, and sensitive to cultural differences.
4. Motivated to succeed; able to enjoy the challenge of working in other countries; and willing to learn about the host country's culture, language, and customs.
5. Supported by their families.[95]

One reason U.S. expatriates often fail is that companies place more emphasis on developing employees' technical skills than on preparing them to work in other cultures. This has resulted in failed overseas assignments, which means companies don't fully capitalize on business opportunities and incur costs for replacing employees who leave the company after returning to the United States.[96] Research suggests that the comfort of an expatriate's spouse and family is the most important determinant of whether the employee will complete the assignment.[97] Studies have also found that personality characteristics are related to expatriates' desire to terminate the assignment and performance in the assignment.[98] Expatriates who were extroverted (outgoing), agreeable (cooperative and tolerant), and conscientious (dependable, achievement oriented) were more likely to want to stay on the assignment and perform well. This suggests that cross-cultural training may be effective only when expatriates' personalities predispose them to be successful in assignments in other cultures. The key to a successful foreign assignment is a combination of training and career management for the employee and family.

### Predeparture Phase

Before departure, employees need to receive language training and an orientation to the new country's culture and customs. It is critical that the family be included in orientation programs.[99] Expatriates and their families need information about housing, schools, recreation, shopping, and health care facilities in the areas where they will live. Expatriates also must discuss with their managers how the foreign assignment fits into their career plans and what types of positions they can expect upon return.

Cross-cultural training methods include presentational techniques, such as lectures that expatriates and their families attend on the customs and culture of the host country, immersion experiences, or actual experiences in the home country in culturally diverse communities.[100] Sodexo provides instructor-led courses for its global leaders on how to build a globally competent workforce and how to develop trust, collaborate, and communicate effectively across cultures.[101] Sodexo also provides research summaries, TED Talks, and articles on topics such as managing global virtual teams and communication across culture that company leaders can access from the company's intranet. Experiential exercises allow expatriates to spend time with a family from the ethnic group of the host country while still in the United States. At Advanced Micro Devices, an Indian trainer took 20 managers on a two-week immersion trip, during which the group traveled to New Delhi, Bangalore, and Mumbai, meeting with business persons and government officials.[102] The program required six months of planning, including providing the executives with information on foods to eat, potential security issues, and how to interact in business meetings. For example, Indians prefer a relatively indirect way into business discussions, so the managers were advised to discuss current events and other subjects before talking business.

Research suggests that the degree of difference between the United States and the host country (cultural novelty), the amount of interaction with host country citizens and host nationals (interaction), and the familiarity with new job tasks and work environment (job novelty) all influence the "rigor" of the cross-cultural training method used.[103] Hands-on and group-building methods are most effective (and most needed) in assignments with a high level of cultural and job novelty that require a good deal of interpersonal interaction with host nationals.

## On-Site Phase

On-site training involves continued orientation to the host country and its customs and cultures through formal programs or through a mentoring relationship. Expatriates should be encouraged to develop social relationships both inside and outside of the workplace.[104] Expatriates and their families may be paired with an employee from the host country who helps them understand the new, unfamiliar work environment and community.[105] Companies are also using the Web to help employees on expatriate assignments get answers to questions.[106] Expatriates can use a website to get answers to questions such as, How do I conduct a meeting here? or What religious philosophy might have influenced today's negotiation behavior? Knowledge management software allows employees to contribute, organize, and access knowledge specific to their expatriate assignment.

A major reason employees refuse expatriate assignments is that they can't afford to lose their spouse's income or are concerned that their spouse's career could be derailed by being out of the workforce for a few years.[107] Some "trailing" spouses decide to use the time to pursue educational activities that could contribute to their long-term career goals. But it is difficult to find these opportunities in an unfamiliar place. To avoid these problems, companies are introducing more flexible expatriate assignments. This can include reducing the amount of time on the assignment, commuting between the parent country and host country assignment, and rotational assignments in which employees alternate between working at home and living back home.[108] Also, to help reduce the stress expatriate assignments can place on spouses and families who are living apart, companies are supporting more frequent family visits to the expatriate in their host country and expatriate visits to home. GlaxoSmithKline's International Service Center, which handles all of its relocations from or to the United States, offers a buddy system for spouses to connect with others who have lived in the area for the past several years.[109] General Motors offers career continuation services, which reimburse spouses $2,500 each year during the expatriate assignment for maintaining professional licenses or certifications. The World Bank manages a dedicated Internet site for expatriates where spouses can post résumés and ask for job leads.

### Repatriation Phase

**Repatriation**

The preparation of expatriates for return to the parent company and country from a foreign assignment.

**Repatriation** prepares expatriates for return to the parent company and country from the foreign assignment. Expatriates and their families are likely to experience high levels of stress and anxiety when they return because of the changes that have occurred since their departure. Employees should be encouraged to self-manage the repatriation process.[110] Before they go on the assignment, they need to consider what skills they want to develop and the types of jobs that might be available in the company for an employee with those skills. Because the company changes and colleagues, peers, and managers may leave while the expatriate is on assignment, they need to maintain contact with key company and industry contacts. Otherwise, on return the employees' reentry shock will be heightened when they have to deal with new colleagues, a new job, and a company culture that may have changed. This includes providing expatriates with company newsletters and community newspapers and ensuring that they receive personal and work-related mail from the United States while they are on foreign assignment. Employees and their families sometimes have to readjust to a lower standard of living in the United States than they had in the foreign country, where they may have enjoyed maid service, a limousine, private schools, and clubs. Salary and other compensation arrangements should be worked out well before employees return from overseas assignments.

Aside from reentry shock, many expatriates decide to leave the company because the assignments they are given upon returning to the United States have less responsibility, challenge, and status than their foreign assignments.[111] For example, consider how Monsanto Company, Asurion, and L'Oreal help employees with repatriation.[112] Monsanto identifies potential return positions before employees even begin their overseas assignment. Asurion, the phone, electronics, and appliance insurer, assigns expatriates to higher level managers who are responsible for finding them a new position when they return. To help expatriates integrate back into the company and feel welcome when they return, L'Oreal invites them to attend orientation and socialization programs as if they were new employees. This is especially important for expatriates on long assignments who are likely not familiar with changes in processes, products, and services and new employees who joined the company.

Visit your instructor's Connect® course and access your eBook to view this video.

"Diversity is when you're invited to the party. Inclusion is when someone actually asks you to dance."

—Mirian M. Graddick-Weir
Executive Vice President, Human Resources, Merck

Source: Video produced for the Center for Executive Succession in the Darla Moore School of Business at the University of South Carolina by Coal Powered Filmworks

## MANAGING WORKFORCE DIVERSITY AND INCLUSION

Diversity can be considered to be any dimension that differentiates one person from another.[113] For example, at Verizon, diversity means embracing differences and variety including age, ethnicity, education, sexual orientation, work style, race, gender, and more. **Inclusion** refers to creating an environment in which employees share a sense of belonging, mutual respect, and commitment from others so that they can perform their best work.[114] Inclusion allows companies to capitalize not only on the diversity of their employees but also on their customers, suppliers, and community partners.

**Diversity training** refers to learning efforts designed to change employee attitudes about diversity or to develop skills needed to work with a diverse workforce. Recently, many diversity training programs have focused on reducing unconscious bias.

Research has shown that men and women's performance can be evaluated very differently because of unconscious bias. **Unconscious bias** is a judgment outside of our consciousness that affects decisions based on background, culture, and personal experience. We are all subject to unconscious bias. For example, one way unconscious bias can affect us is through the attributions or reasons we use to explain another person's behavior. For example, compared to men women receive two and one-half times more feedback about having an aggressive communication style. Many companies such as Microsoft, Google, Facebook, and Dow Chemical are requiring employees to participate in unconscious bias training programs to reduce its negative influence on performance evaluations, promotion decisions, and access to development opportunities.[115] These training programs are designed to make employees aware of unconscious bias and reduce its impact by slowing down decision making and carefully considering reasons behind and language used in judgments.

It is important to realize that training alone is insufficient to capitalize on the strengths of a diverse workforce.[116] **Managing diversity and inclusion** involves creating an environment that allows all employees to contribute to organizational goals and experience personal growth. This environment includes access to jobs as well as fair and positive treatment of all employees. The company must develop employees who are comfortable working with people from a wide variety of ethnic, racial, and religious backgrounds. Managing diversity may require changing the company culture. It includes the company's standards and norms about how employees are treated, competitiveness, results orientation, innovation, and risk taking. The value placed on diversity is grounded in the company culture.

Consider the actions Rockwell Automation, National Life Group, and Blackstone Group are taking to manage diversity.[117] At Rockwell Automation, an automation and software company, diversity is evaluated as part of manager's performance reviews. Whereas males are coached to understand and change attitudes and behaviors that make women and minority employees uncomfortable, unwelcome, and prevent them from advancing in their careers, all employees receive unconscious bias training, potential new hires are interviewed by employee teams that include women and minorities, and customer and staff meetings go beyond golf outings to include wine tasting and cooking classes. Rockwell's efforts have resulted in significant increases in women and minorities in professional positions such as management and engineering. The CEO of National Life Group doesn't believe in diversity quotas. But the company does ask peers and direct reports to evaluate their manager each year on several different diversity principles such as the extent to which they value a diverse and inclusive culture and encourage others to speak out. These evaluations do not influence the manager's bonus so that they don't view the evaluations as punishment. Rather, managers are encouraged to meet with their teams to get feedback about what they are doing well and to discuss plans for improvement. To help increase the number of women in entry-level analysts positions, Blackstone Group LP actively seeks out female recruits in their sophomore year of college to acquaint them with the company and help them improve their résumé writing and interviewing skills.

Diversity may enhance performance when organizations have an environment that promotes learning from diversity. Research shows that diversity training can impact cognitive (acquiring knowledge), affective (attitudes), and behavioral outcomes.[118] Diversity training is most effective when it is part of a larger effort to manage diversity and inclusion rather than a standalone program. This means that a company will see the success of its diversity efforts only if it makes a long-term commitment to managing diversity. Successful diversity requires that it be viewed as an opportunity for employees to (1) learn from each other how to better accomplish their work, (2) be provided with a supportive

**LO 7-10**
Develop a program for effectively managing diversity.

**Inclusion**
Creating an environment in which employees share a sense of belonging, mutual respect, and commitment with others so that they can perform their best work.

**Diversity training**
Refers to learning efforts that are designed to change employees' attitudes about diversity and/or develop skills needed to work with a diverse workforce.

**Unconscious bias**
A judgment outside of our consciousness that affects decisions based on background, culture, and personal experience.

**Managing diversity and inclusion**
The process of creating an environment that allows all employees to contribute to organizational goals and experience personal growth.

and cooperative organizational culture, and (3) be taught leadership and process skills that can facilitate effective team functioning. Diversity is a reality in labor and customer markets and is a social expectation and value. Managers should focus on building an organizational environment, on human resource practices, and on managerial and team skills that capitalize on diversity. As you will see in the discussion that follows, managing diversity requires difficult cultural change, not just slogans on the wall.

Consider Sodexo's diversity effort.[119] Sodexo is the leading food and facilities management company in the United States, Canada, and Mexico, daily serving 10 million customers. Employees in 80 countries representing 128 nationalities connect with customers on a daily basis. A policy of inclusion is not an option or a choice—it is a business necessity. Sodexo is focused on gender representation, generational opportunities in the workplace, people with disabilities, and ethnic minority representation. As a result, diversity and inclusion are core elements of the business strategy. Sodexo believes that diversity and inclusion is a fundamental business objective focused on employees (e.g., work culture, recruitment, talent development, work–life effectiveness), customers, clients, shareholders (e.g., supplier diversity, cross-market diversity council, diversity consulting), and communities (e.g., Sodexo Foundation, Community Partners). For example, some of the company's objectives include understanding and living the business case for diversity and inclusion; increasing awareness of how diversity relates to business challenges; creating and fostering a diverse work environment by developing management practices that drive hiring, promotion, and retention of talent; engaging in relationship management and customer service to attract and retain diverse clients and customers; and partnering with women and minority businesses to deliver food and facility management services. Diversity and inclusion are core competencies at Sodexo. Diversity and inclusion are part of employees' training and managers' annual performance review. The new employee orientation emphasizes Sodexo's values and expectations regarding diversity and inclusion.

Sodexo separates equal employment opportunity (EEO) and legal compliance training from diversity training. At Sodexo, diversity training is part of the managing diversity strategy. Every three years, employees are required to take EEO and affirmative action refresher courses. Top management is also involved in and committed to managing diversity. The Cross-Market Diversity Council (CMDC) is comprised of managers and leaders who want to foster a more diverse and inclusive Sodexo. The objective of this group is to collaborate and operationalize the diversity plan within each business line, serve as thought leaders to advance the diversity and inclusion strategy, implement diversity and inclusion at a regional level, and align with employee network groups (discussed later). Also, senior executives participate in ongoing classroom training that is reinforced with community involvement, sponsoring employee groups, and mentoring diverse employees. Executives are engaged in learning the business case for diversity and are personally held accountable for the company's diversity agenda. The one-day Spirit of Inclusion session, mandatory for all managers, focuses on building awareness and skills around diversity and inclusion. Sodexo's diversity training involves learning labs focused on skill building and diversity awareness. Examples of these learning labs include Generations in the Workplace, Disability Awareness Training, Cross-Cultural Communications, and Improving Team Effectiveness through Inclusion. The company's learning and development team develops customized learning solutions for different functions and work teams. For example, a course related to selling to a diverse client base was developed and offered to the sales force, and a cross-cultural communication program was provided for recruiters.

In addition to diversity training activities, Sodexo has six employee network groups (called Employee Resource Business Groups)—such as the African American Leadership Forum; People Respecting Individuality, Diversity, and Equality (PRIDE); Honoring Our Nation's Finest with Opportunity and Respect (HONOR); the Intergenerational Network

Group (i-Gen); and Sodexo Organization for disAbilities Resources (SOAR). These network groups provide forums for employees to build a sense of community, learn from each other, develop their careers, and share input and ideas to support the company's diversity efforts. Sodexo's Champions of Diversity program rewards and recognizes employees who advance diversity and inclusion. Further, employees can recognize their peers who demonstrate diversity and inclusion behaviors that help to attract and retain diverse talent or increase brand recognition in the community. Employees who receive this recognition are entered into a monthly raffle in which they might win $50 reward cards.

To emphasize the importance of diversity for the company, at Sodexo each manager has a diversity scorecard that evaluates his or her success in recruitment, retention, promotion, and development of all employees. The scorecard includes both quantitative goals as well as evaluation of behaviors such as participating in training, mentoring, and doing community outreach. A proportion of a manager's pay bonus is determined by success in these areas.

Sodexo has found that its diversity training and efforts to manage diversity are positively affecting the business in several different ways. Its mentoring program has led to increased productivity, engagement, and retention of women and people of color. There was an estimated return on investment of $19 for every dollar spent on the program. Sodexo has found that gender-balanced teams—those with 40–60% women in management—outperform nonbalanced teams on measures of global engagement, brand awareness, client retention, and positive profit and growth. Sodexo also has been awarded several new business contracts and retained clients because of its involvement in managing diversity. Sodexo has been recognized for its diversity and inclusion efforts, which helps attract talented employees by signaling that the company cares about the well-being of all of its employees. Sodexo continues to receive recognition for its efforts. For example, in 2017 it earned a top ranking on the *DiversityInc* 2017 Top 50 Companies for Diversity, marking its ninth consecutive year being recognized as a top 10 company. Sodexo is also recognized as a top company for executive women and ranked among the top 10 companies for Latinos, blacks, global diversity, and people with disabilities. Most effective programs to manage diversity, such as Sodexo's, include the key components shown in Table 7.9.

As should be apparent from this discussion, successful diversity programs involve more than just an effective training program. They require an ongoing process of culture change that includes top management support, a position in charge of managing diversity (chief diversity officer), as well as diversity policies and practices in the areas of recruitment and hiring, training and development, and administrative structures, such as conducting diversity surveys and evaluating managers' progress on diversity goals.[120] They also focus on enhancing diversity and inclusion with suppliers, vendors, and in the communities where the company conducts business. For example, ABB North America recently created a chief diversity and inclusion officer position reporting directly to the CEO.[121] This sends a message that diversity is supported and creates a position responsible for managing diversity and inclusion and establishing metrics to track progress.

## ONBOARDING OR SOCIALIZATION

**Onboarding**, or socialization, refers to the process of helping new hires adjust to social and performance aspects of their new jobs.[122] This process is important to help employees adjust to their jobs by establishing relationships to increase satisfaction; clarifying goals and expectations to improve performance; and providing feedback, coaching, and follow-up activities to reduce turnover. Effective onboarding is a process that takes several days, weeks, or even months. As you probably have experienced, employee orientation is an event in which employees receive information about their job, the company, work rules, travel reimbursement;

**Onboarding**
Refers to the process of helping new hires adjust to social and performance aspects of their new jobs.

**Table 7.9**
Key Components of
Effective Diversity
Management
Programs

**Top Management Support**
- Make the business case for diversity.
- Include diversity as part of the business strategy and corporate goals.
- Participate in diversity programs, and encourage all managers to attend.
- Ensure that the composition of the executive management team mirrors the diversity of the workforce.

**Recruitment and Hiring**
- Ask search firms to identify wider arrays of candidates.
- Enhance the interviewing, selection, and hiring skills of managers.
- Expand college recruitment at historically minority colleges.

**Talent Identification and Development**
- Form a partnership with internship programs that target minority students for management careers.
- Establish a mentoring process.
- Refine the company's global succession planning system to improve identification of talent.
- Improve the selection and development of managers and leaders to help ensure that they are capable of maximizing team performance.
- Ensure that all employees, especially women and minorities, have access to management development and leadership programs.

**Employee Support**
- Form resource groups or employee network groups, including employees with common interests, and use them to help the company develop business goals and understand the issues they are concerned with (e.g., Asian Pacific employees, women, gays, lesbians, transgender employees, Native Americans, veterans, Hispanics).
- Celebrate cultural traditions, festivities, and holidays.
- Make work–life balance initiatives (such as flextime, telecommuting, and eldercare) available to all employees.

**Fair Treatment**
- Conduct extensive diversity training.
- Implement an alternative dispute resolution process.
- Include women and minorities on all human resources committees throughout the company.

**Manager Accountability**
- Link managers' compensation to their success in meeting diversity goals and creating openness and inclusion in the workplace.
- Use employee attitude or engagement surveys to track employees' attitudes on inclusion, fairness, opportunities for development, work–life balance, and perceptions of the company culture.
- Implement 360-degree feedback for all managers and supervisors.

**Relationships with External Stakeholders**
- Increase marketing to diverse communities.
- Provide customer service in different languages.
- Broaden the company's base of suppliers and vendors to include businesses owned by minorities and women.
- Provide scholarships and educational and neighborhood grants to diverse communities and their members.

SOURCES: Based on F. Dobbins and A. Kalev, "Why Diversity Programs Fail," *Harvard Business Review*, July/August 2016, pp. 52–60; B. Groysberg and K. Connolly, "Great Leaders Who Make the Mix Work," *Harvard Business Review*, September 2013, pp. 68–76; K. Bezrvkova, K. Jehn, and C. Spell, "Reviewing Diversity Training: Where Have We Been and Where Should We Go?" *Academy of Management Learning & Education* 11 (2012), pp. 207–227; R. Anand and M. Winters, "A Retrospective View of Corporate Diversity Training from 1964 to the Present," *Academy of Management Learning & Education* 7 (2008), pp. 356–72; C. Chavez and J. Weisinger, "Beyond Diversity Training: A Social Infusion for Cultural Inclusion," *Human Resource Management* 47 (2008), pp. 331–50.

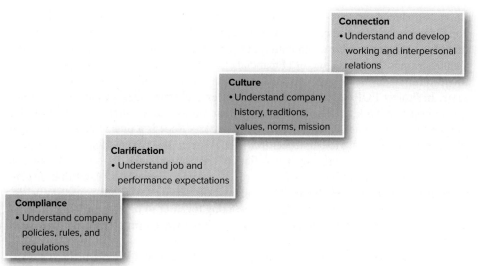

**Figure 7.6**
The Four Steps in Onboarding

SOURCE: Based on T. Bauer, *Onboarding New Employees: Maximizing Success* (Alexandria, VA: SHRM Foundation, 2010); G. Chao, A. O'Leary-Kelly, S. Wolf, H. Klein, and P. Gardner, "Organizational Socialization: Its Content and Consequences," *Journal of Applied Psychology* 79 (1994), pp. 730–43.

complete tax forms; and learn how to complete time sheets. Although onboarding programs vary widely across companies, effective onboarding involves the four steps shown in Figure 7.6. Effective onboarding does include understanding mundane tasks such as completing tax forms and knowing how to complete time sheets or travel reimbursement forms, but it includes much more. Effective socialization includes enhancing new hires' self-confidence and their feeling socially comfortable and accepted by their peers and manager; ensuring that new hires understand their role and job expectations, responsibilities, and performance requirements; and helping them "fit in" to and understand the company culture. Effective onboarding is related to many important outcomes for the employee and the company, including higher job satisfaction, organizational commitment, lower turnover, higher performance, reduced stress, and career effectiveness.[123]

Table 7.10 shows the characteristics of effective onboarding programs. In particular, effective onboarding programs actively involve the new employee. Several companies offer onboarding programs that include these characteristics. For example, Forum Credit

**Table 7.10**
Characteristics of Effective Onboarding Programs

- Employees are encouraged to ask questions.

- Program includes information on both technical and social aspects of the job.

- The employee manager has some onboarding responsibility.

- Debasing or embarrassing new employees is avoided.

- Employees learn about the company culture, history, language, products, services, and customers.

- Follow-up of employee progress occurs at different points up to one year after joining the company.

- Program involves participation, active involvement, and formal and informal interaction between new hires and current employees.

- Relocation assistance is provided (such as house hunting or information sessions on the community for employees and their significant others).

Union, a financial services company with 350 employees, used to have the typical orientation involving lectures and completing paperwork.[124] To help new employees better understand the company products and culture, Forum created a new orientation program that includes games. In The Game of (Financial) Life, teams of new hires compete to learn about the company's products and services by playing a fun and interactive life-size board game. In Project FORUMway, new hires are given a clothing rack and are asked to pick out appropriate work outfits. They present their choices to a panel of judges from HR who give them feedback. The Amazing Headquarters Race is a one-hour scavenger hunt where teams have to talk to employees throughout the company's building. Onboarding at Bazaarvoice, a software company with offices in the United States, Europe, and Australia, emphasizes relationship building. New hires take part in a scavenger hunt that involves completing tasks such as shadowing a client call, setting up a video meeting with a co-worker, answering trivia questions, and working together to organize a snack break for the entire office. The program also includes a global video conference call where new employees introduce themselves to the rest of the company.

Shape Corp. designs, engineers, manufactures, and tests metal and plastic products that absorb impact energy and protect vehicles, their occupants, and pedestrians.[125] Shape's employees work with cutting torches, welders, grinders, and other machinery. This makes it critical that Shape's orientation program focuses on safety as well as onboarding. Based on a needs assessment using employee focus groups, Shape found that many new employees had little experience working in manufacturing and had begun working prior to any training or orientation. As result, the orientation was changed from one day to four days for all new employees, followed by a six-day manufacturing technician training course for employees working in manufacturing. The new orientation includes speakers, plant tours, an introduction to the company's mentoring program and the employee's mentor, Web-based training, and instructor-led safety training. If employees fail the manufacturing technology training course, they are not allowed to work in manufacturing and may be terminated. The orientation program has been implemented globally with 1,800 employees in their native languages. Shape continually revises the program content based on focus groups that meet semiannually. As a result of the orientation program, injury rates have decreased 75% among employees who have worked one year or less at Shape. The program provides employees with the knowledge they need to perform their jobs, improves their safety awareness, and helps them develop relationships at work that enhance their socialization.

## A LOOK BACK

### AT&T

AT&T has made a sizable monetary investment in training employees in the skills they need for emerging roles, which is necessary to keep the company competitive. This investment includes face-to-face training and MOOCs. Also, AT&T is providing employees with tools they can use to understand today's career options.

#### QUESTIONS

1. Do you think AT&T's training investment is motivating employees to engage in continuous learning? Why or Why not?
2. Does replacing traditional career paths with career lattices influence training? Explain.
3. What other steps should AT&T consider to help employees gain technical skills and apply them in their jobs?

# SUMMARY

Technological innovations, new product markets, and a diverse workforce have increased the need for companies to reexamine how their training practices contribute to learning. In this chapter, we discussed a systematic approach to training, including needs assessment, design of the learning environment, consideration of employee readiness for training, and transfer-of-training issues. We reviewed numerous training methods and stressed that the key to successful training was to choose a method that would best accomplish the objectives of training. We also emphasized how training can contribute to effectiveness by establishing a link with the company's strategic direction and demonstrating through cost–benefit analysis how training contributes to profitability. Cross-cultural preparation and managing diversity are two relevant training issues, given companies' needs to capitalize on global markets and a diverse workforce. Onboarding or socialization is critical for helping new hires feel comfortable and connected in their new job.

# KEY TERMS

Continuous learning, 279
Training, 279
Formal training, 279
Informal learning, 279
Explicit knowledge, 280
Tacit knowledge, 280
Knowledge management, 280
Training design process, 281
Needs assessment, 283
Organizational analysis, 284
Person analysis, 284
Task analysis, 284
Readiness for training, 289
Motivation to learn, 289
Microlearning, 289
Transfer of training, 292
Manager support, 292
Action plan, 292
Support network, 293

Opportunity to perform, 293
Performance support systems, 294
Communities of practice, 294
Presentation methods, 295
Teleconferencing, 297
Webcasting, 297
Hands-on methods, 298
On-the-job training (OJT), 298
Apprenticeship, 298
Internship, 299
Simulation, 300
Virtual reality, 301
Augmented reality (AR), 301
Serious games, 302
E-learning, 303
Repurposing, 303
Massive open online courses
    (MOOCs), 304
Blended learning, 305

Learning management system
    (LMS), 305
Group- or team-building methods, 306
Experiential programs, 307
Adventure learning, 307
Cross-training, 308
Coordination training, 308
Team leader training, 308
Action learning, 309
Training outcomes, 310
Return on investment (ROI), 313
Expatriate, 314
Cross-cultural preparation, 314
Repatriation, 316
Inclusion, 317
Diversity training, 317
Unconscious bias, 317
Managing diversity and inclusion, 317
Onboarding, 319

# DISCUSSION QUESTIONS

1. Noetron, a retail electronics store, recently invested a large amount of money to train sales staff to improve customer service. The skills emphasized in the program include how to greet customers, determine their needs, and demonstrate product convenience. The company wants to know whether the program is effective. What outcomes should it collect? What type of evaluation design should it use?

2. "Melinda," bellowed Toran, "I've got a problem, and you've got to solve it. I can't get people in this plant to work together as a team. As if I don't have enough trouble with the competition and delinquent accounts, now I have to put up with running a zoo. It's your responsibility to see that the staff gets along with each other. I want a human relations training proposal on my desk by Monday." How would you determine the need for human relations training? How would you determine whether you actually had a training problem? What else could be responsible for the situation?

3. Assume you are the general manager of a small seafood company. Most training is unstructured and occurs on the job. Currently, senior fish cleaners are responsible for

teaching new employees how to perform the job. Your company has been profitable, but recently wholesale fish dealers that buy your product have been complaining about the poor quality of your fresh fish. For example, some fillets have not had all the scales removed and abdomen parts remain attached to the fillets. You have decided to change the on-the-job training received by the fish cleaners. How will you modify the training to improve the quality of the product delivered to the wholesalers?

4. A training needs analysis indicates that managers' productivity is inhibited because they are reluctant to delegate tasks to their subordinates. Suppose you had to decide between using adventure learning and a lecture using a virtual classroom for your training program. What are the strengths and weaknesses of each technique? Which would you choose? Why? What factors would influence your decision?

5. To improve product quality, a company is introducing a computer-assisted manufacturing process into one of its assembly plants. The new technology is likely to modify jobs substantially. Employees will also be required to learn statistical process control techniques. The new technology and push for quality will require employees to attend numerous training sessions. More than 50% of the employees who will be affected by the new technology completed their formal education more than 10 years ago. Only about 5% of the company's employees have used the tuition reimbursement benefit. How should management maximize employees' readiness for training?

6. A training course was offered for maintenance employees in which trainees were supposed to learn how to repair and operate a new, complex electronics system. On the job, maintenance employees were typically told about a symptom experienced by the machine operator and were asked to locate the trouble. During training, the trainer would pose various problems for the maintenance employees to solve. He would point out a component on an electrical diagram and ask, "What would happen if this component was faulty?" Trainees would then trace the circuitry on a blueprint to uncover the symptoms that would appear as a result of the problem. You are receiving complaints about poor troubleshooting from maintenance supervisors of employees who have completed the program. The trainees are highly motivated and have the necessary prerequisites. What is the problem with the training course? What recommendations do you have for fixing this course?

7. What factors contribute to the effectiveness of e-learning training programs?

8. Choose a job you are familiar with. Design a new employee onboarding program for that job. Explain how your program contributes to effective socialization.

9. What features of games motivate learning, especially for Millennials?

10. Why might employees prefer blended learning to training using only iPads?

11. Are augmented reality (AR) and virtual reality (VR) the same training method? Why or why not?

12. What learning condition do you think is most necessary for learning to occur? Which is least critical? Why?

13. What can companies do to encourage informal learning?

14. List and discuss the steps in cross-cultural preparation.

## SELF-ASSESSMENT EXERCISE

Also assignable in Connect.

In this chapter, we discussed the need for learners to be motivated so that training will be effective. What is your motivation to learn? Find out by answering the following questions.

Read each statement and indicate how much you agree with it, using the following scale:

1. I try to learn as much as I can from the courses I take.    5  4  3  2  1
2. I believe I tend to learn more from my courses than other students do.    5  4  3  2  1
3. When I'm involved in courses and can't understand something, I consider    5  4  3  2  1
   it a challenge and try harder to learn.

5 = Strongly agree
4 = Somewhat agree
3 = Neutral
2 = Somewhat disagree
1 = Strongly disagree

Add up your points across the three statements. Your points could range from 3 to 15. What's your score? The higher your score the greater your motivation to learn.

## EXERCISING STRATEGY

### Social Media and MOOCs at PayPal

PayPal's digital payment platform gives its over 200 million active account holders in markets around the world the confidence to connect and transact in new ways online, on a mobile device, using an app, or in person. The PayPal platform, including Braintree, Venmo, and Xoom, allows consumers and businesses to receive money, withdraw funds, and hold balances in many different monetary currencies. Although PayPal is considered state-of-the art when it comes to using technology to digitize how we pay for products and services, it was not considered cutting edge in using technology for training. However, that has changed as PayPal has infused learning technology into its employee training programs. PayPal decided to incorporate social media into its training because it is easy to use and its over 5,000 employees are familiar with it. PayPal created a private Facebook group where employees can connect with each other and invited experts to ask questions and gain (and share) knowledge. PayPal also encourages workers to use Twitter's video service to watch short training modules. PayPal provides employees with access to Udemy for Business, a supplier of massive open online courses (MOOCs). Employees can access 1,600 courses on a variety of topics and have complete control over when to complete them. They can bookmark important tutorials or save the lecture for future reference. As a result of incorporating technology into its training, PayPal has found that the number of employees who complete two training courses every six months (or who they refer to as "active learners") has doubled. Also, the company realized a 25% savings in training costs.

### QUESTIONS

1. Is PayPal's approach to training strategic? Why or why not?
2. What are the advantages and disadvantages of PayPal's use of social media and MOOCs for its training programs?

SOURCES: Based on H. Clancy, "A New Mind-Set," *Fortune*, January 1, 2017, p. 30; "About PayPal" from www.paypal.com, accessed February 1, 2019; E. Wiechers, "PayPal Invests in Workplace Skills Development with Roll Out of Udemy for Business," April 12, 2016, from https://about.udemy.com/udemy-for-business/paypal-invests-in-workplace-skills-development-with-rollout-of-udemy-for-business/ accessed February 1, 2019.

## MANAGING PEOPLE

### Learning through Gaming at GameStop

GameStop, a retailer of new and used video games, consumer electronics, and wireless services, has over 53,000 employees in more than 5,800 locations worldwide. GameStop customers can get games there that aren't available anywhere else, and the company allows customers to buy, sell, or trade old games and electronics, unlike many of its competitors. GameStop serves a variety of customers, from five year olds and their parents who are looking for Nintendo games, to adult gamers who want to buy the latest gaming equipment. Most GameStop employees (called game-associates) hold part-time, entry-level jobs that require them to work several shifts during the week. Most new employees who join GameStop are expert gamers, have expertise about the technology and trends influencing the gaming market, and were loyal customers themselves. GameStop believes the gaming experience and gaming passion of its employees differentiate it from big-box retailers that also sell games.

Training is especially important for GameStop because of the business realities of normal turnover and seasonal hiring. Game-associates often leave for other jobs or opportunities such as going back to school. During the holiday season, the company hires and needs to train up to 25,000 temporary employees. Although only approximately 15% of these temporary employees become full-time employees, even if they never work for GameStop again, they are still potential customers. Training helps ensure new employees provide consistent customer service, which translates into satisfied customers and return business. As a result, GameStop's training doesn't focus on teaching employees about video games but instead emphasizes how to interact with customers and understand their gaming needs. Also, the training helps employees become ambassadors for the company by sharing their knowledge and passion for gaming with customers.

The Level Up program is an online game-based training program that enables employees to complete training on their own time and at their own pace, scoring points and earning badges based on achieving different skills and advancing to the next level. Learning missions require trainees to read documents, watch videos, and take quizzes. No mission is longer than 30 minutes. Training content varies based on the employees' needs, allows them to log in and out of training at any time, and allows them to skip content they already know. As they earn points to complete levels, the next level of learning is unlocked, giving them access to new badges and learning missions. In addition to preparing new game-associates, the Level Up program provides training for more experienced game-associates who may be more interested in a retail career and want to gain the knowledge and skills necessary to become assistant managers and store managers. To support online learning, all managers complete a train-the-trainer program designed to help them mentor and coach all employees, but especially seasonal hires. Managers learn how to explain the customer service process, create opportunities for new hires to "shadow" them, and provide feedback when trainees make mistakes.

The results for Level Up have been positive. Customer surveys show high levels of satisfaction, employees feel prepared to do their jobs, and managers like having the ability to easily track employees' training progress.

### QUESTIONS

1. Does Level Up support GameStop's business? Explain.
2. Do you think that online game-based learning like Level Up needs to be supplemented with some type of face-to-face training or coaching? Why or why not?
3. What features of game-based learning such as Level Up contribute to its effectiveness as a training method? Explain why.

SOURCES: Based on S. Gale, "'Tis the Season to Be Training," *Chief Learning Officer*, April 2016, pp. 58, 60, 65; M. McGraw, "Staying Power," *Human Resource Executive*, January/February 2015, pp. 39–41; "About GameStop," www.gamestop.com, accessed February 1, 2019.

## HR IN SMALL BUSINESS

### Zeigler Automotive Group Drives Growth by Training Its People

In 2004, the Zeigler Auto Group was four dealerships and a president, Aaron Zeigler, with a desire to expand. Along with aggressive hiring, Zeigler's plan would require a training program to build skills and alignment with the company's values. A solid training program is a lure for ambitious salespeople because recruiters can show that it will help them develop their selling skills and perhaps move into management. Furthermore, the largest dealership networks have formal training programs, and Zeigler wanted to compete for talent with them.

The company built training that combines classroom instruction with videos. Today all the salespeople and service advisers are expected to watch three training videos every day from an online library of more than 2,000, which are categorized by level of complexity. Each video runs five to seven minutes and features a presentation by Aaron Zeigler, the director of talent development Mike Van Ryn, or an outside training specialist. After watching each one, the employees take a quiz to check their understanding. Van Ryn and Zeigler employ video instruction because the format is flexible, allowing employees to learn as their schedule permits. When they meet for classroom training, which happens every month or two, they drill down deeper into topics. Usually, this involves a guest speaker at headquarters, with the presentation shared in other locations via videoconferencing.

In addition to the daily training, new hires participate in an orientation program. The main feature of this training is a six-hour class, which covers teamwork, customer service, and the company's history. Other training brings together selected teams of employees targeted for promotion to management positions. They meet every other month at headquarters in Kalamazoo, Michigan, to study financial statements and learn other management skills.

One measure of the training's success is the low rate of employee turnover in recent years. Previously the turnover rate was nearly 25%. In addition, sales per employee on a monthly basis are much higher than they had been before the company started using the high-frequency video approach to learning. Furthermore, the company continues to meet Zeigler's ambition to expand. Currently, the auto group has more than 23 dealerships in four states. Recently, Zeigler and Van Ryn opened the Elevate Leadership and Team Building Academy, which offers professional team building and leadership training to organizations of all sizes. Zeigler says the company's successful growth can be attributed to developing its employees: "We've always been a big believer in training and development."

### QUESTIONS

1. Imagine you were helping Zeigler and Van Ryn prepare a needs assessment for training. Using examples from the information provided, what information would you include in the needs assessment?
2. What training methods are Zeigler Automotive Group using? What other methods would you recommend it use? Give reasons for your recommendations.

SOURCES: "The History of Zeigler Auto Group," www.zeigler.com, accessed April 28, 2018; Andrea Pratt, "Rev Up Your Team's Engine," *269 Magazine*, http://269mag.com, accessed April 28, 2018; Al Jones, "Kalamazoo-Based Zeigler Buys More Car Dealerships in Chicago Area," *MLive*, January 21, 2016, http://mlive.com; Jon McKenna, "Training Helps Sustain Michigan Dealership Group's Evolution into a Substantial Corporate Player," *CBT Automotive Network*, December 1, 2015, http://cbtnews.com; Arlena Sawyers, "Getting Schooled in the Car Dealership Business," *Automotive News*, June 1, 2015, https://www.autonews.com.

# NOTES

1. E. Salas and J. A. Cannon-Bowers, "The Science of Training: A Decade of Progress," *Annual Review of Psychology* 52 (2002), pp. 471-99; R. Noe, *Employee Training and Development,* 7th ed. (New York: McGraw-Hill Irwin, 2015); H. Aguinis and K. Kraiger, "Benefits of Training and Development for Individuals, Teams, Organizations, and Society," *Annual Review of Psychology* 60 (2009), pp. 451-74.

2. R. Noe, A. Clarke, and H. Klein, "Learning in the Twenty-First Century Workplace," *Annual. Review of Organizational Psychology & Organizational Behavior* 1 (2014), pp. 245-75; U. Sessa and M. London, *Continuous Learning in Organizations* (Mahwah, NJ: Lawrence Erlbaum, 2006); M. London, "Lifelong Learning: Introduction," in M. London (ed.), *The Oxford Handbook of Lifelong Learning* (New York: Oxford University Press, 2011), pp. 3-11.

3. "2016 Training Industry Report," *Training,* November/December 2016, pp. 28-41.

4. J. Roy, "Transforming Informal Learning into a Competitive Advantage," *T + D*, October 2010, pp. 23-25; P. Galagan, "Unformal, the New Normal," *T + D*, September 2010, pp. 29-31.

5. S. I. Tannenbaum, R. Beard, L. A. McNall, and E. Salas, "Informal Learning and Development in Organizations," in S. W. J. Kozlowski and E. Salas (eds.), *Learning, Training, and Development in Organizations* (New York: Routledge, 2010), pp. 303-32; D. J. Bear, H. B. Tompson, C. L. Morrison, M. Vickers, A. Paradise, M. Czarnowsky, M. Soyars, and K. King, *Tapping the Potential of Informal Learning. An ASTD Research Study* (Alexandria, VA: American Society for Training and Development, 2008).

6. T. Bingham and M. Conner, *The New Social Learning* (Alexandria, VA: ASTD Press, 2010).

7. J. Quinn, P. Andersen, and S. Finkelstein, "Leveraging Intellect," *Academy of Management Executive* 10 (1996), pp. 7-39; R. Ployhart and T. Moliterno, "Emergence of the Human Capital Resource: A Multilevel Model," *Academy of Management Review* 36 (2011), pp. 127-50; B. Campbell, R. Coff, and D. Kryscynski, "Rethinking Sustained Competitive Advantage from Human Capital," *Academy of Management Review* 37 (2012), pp. 376-95; T. Crook, S. Todd, J. Combs, D. Woehr, and D. Ketchen, Jr., "Does Human Capital Matter? A Meta-Analysis of the Relationship between Human Capital and Firm Performance," *Journal of Applied Psychology* 96 (2011), pp. 443-56.

8. I. Nonaka and H. Takeuchi, *The Knowledge-Creating Company: How Japanese Companies Create the Dynamics of Innovation* (New York: Oxford University Press, 1995).

9. S. E. Jackson, M. A. Hitt, and A. S. Denisi, eds., *Managing Knowledge for Sustained Competitive Advantage: Designing Strategies for Effective Human Resource Management* (San Francisco: Jossey-Bass, 2003); A. Rossett, "Knowledge Management Meets Analysis," *Training and Development,* May 1999, pp. 63-68; R. Davenport, "Why Does Knowledge Management Still Matter?" *T + D* 59 (2005), pp. 19-23.

10. P. Harris, "Learning in a Minute," *T + D,* October 2017, pp. 56-58.

11. M. Weinstein, "Long-Range Learning Plans," *Training,* November/December 2010, pp. 38-41; L. Miller, *2014 State of the Industry* (Alexandria, VA: American Society for Training & Development, 2014); "2014's Very Best Learning Organizations," *T + D,* October 2014, pp. 34-98.

12. "Training Top 125 2017 Top 10 Hall of Fame: Jiffy Lube International, Inc.," *Training,* January/February 2017, p. 54; L. Freifeld, "Jiffy Lube's Training Drive," *Training,* January/February 2013, pp. 34-37; M. Weinstein, "Jiffy-Lube Greases the Wheels of Success," *Training,* January/February 2015, pp. 36-38; L. Freifeld, "Jiffy-Lube Revs Up to No. 1," *Training,* January/February 2014, pp. 30-38.

13. R. Noe, *Employee Training and Development,* 7th ed. (New York: Irwin/McGraw-Hill, 2015).

14. R. Noe, *Employee Training and Development,* 7th ed. (New York: Irwin/McGraw-Hill, 2015); E. A. Surface, "Training Needs Assessment: Aligning Learning and Capability with Performance Requirements and Organizational Objectives," in *The Handbook of Work Analysis: Methods, Systems, Applications and Science of Work Measurement in Organizations,* ed. M. A. Wilson, W. Bennett, S. G. Gibson, & G. M. Alliger (New York: Routledge Academic, 2012), pp. 437-62.

15. A. Kuzel, "How to Conduct a Learning Audit," *Chief Learning Officer,* November/December 2016, pp. 23-25, 66.

16. J. B. Tracey, S. I. Tannenbaum, and M. J. Kavanaugh, "Applying Trained Skills on the Job: The Importance of the Work Environment," *Journal of Applied Psychology* 80 (1995), pp. 239-52; E. Holton, R. Bates, and W. Ruona, "Development of a Generalized Learning Transfer System Inventory," *Human Resource Development Quarterly* 11 (2001), pp. 333-60; E. Helton III and T. Baldwin, eds., *Improving Learning Transfer in Organizations* (San Francisco: Jossey-Bass, 2003); J. S. Russell, J. R. Terborg, and M. L. Powers, "Organizational Performance and Organizational Level Training and Support," *Personnel Psychology* 38 (1985), pp. 849-63.

17. S. Gale, "Speak Your CEOs Language," *Chief Learning Officer,* February 2016, pp. 26-29; S. Tannenbaum, "A Strategic View of Organizational Training and Learning," in *Creating, Implementing, and Managing Effective Training and Development,* ed. K. Kraiger (San Francisco: Jossey-Bass, 2002), pp. 10-52.

18. "Building Talent: The Very Best of 2017, Genpact," *TD,* October 2017, p. 51.

19. C. Reinhart, "How to Leap over Barrier to Performance," *Training and Development,* January 2000, pp. 20-29; G. Rummter and K. Morrill, "The Results Chain," *T + D,* February 2005, pp. 27-35; O. Rummter, "In Search of the Holy Performance Grail," *Training and Development,* April 1996, pp. 26-31.

20. C. E. Schneier, J. P. Guthrie, and J. D. Olian, "A Practical Approach to Conducting and Using Training Needs Assessment," *Public Personnel Management,* Summer 1988, pp. 191-205; I. Goldstein, "Training in Organizations," in *Handbook of Industrial/Organizational Psychology,* 2nd ed., ed. M. D. Dunnette and L. M. Hough (Palo Alto, CA: Consulting Psychologists Press, 1991), vol. 2, pp. 507-619.

21. L. Freifeld, "All Eyes on Safety Training," *Training,* January/February 2018, p. 8; Company website, "Careers: About Us," www.kla-tencor.com, accessed February 25, 2015; "KLA-Tencor Corporation: Right People, Right Knowledge," *Training,* January/February 2015, pp. 56-57.

22. R. A. Noe, "Trainees' Attributes and Attitudes: Neglected Influences on Training Effectiveness," *Academy of Management Review* 11 (1986), pp. 736-49.

23. T. T. Baldwin, R. T. Magjuka, and B. T. Loher, "The Perils of Participation: Effects of Choice on Trainee Motivation and

Learning," *Personnel Psychology* 44 (1991), pp. 51–66; S. I. Tannenbaum, J. E. Mathieu, E. Salas, and J. A. Cannon-Bowers, "Meeting Trainees' Expectations: The Influence of Training Fulfillment on the Development of Commitment, Self-Efficacy, and Motivation," *Journal of Applied Psychology* 76 (1991), pp. 759–69.

24. D. Rock, "Your Brain on Learning," *Chief Learning Officer,* May 2015, pp. 30–48; A. Beninghof, "Pathways to Retention," *TD,* June 2015, pp. 21–22; C. E. Schneier, "Training and Development Programs: What Learning Theory and Research Have to Offer," *Personnel Journal,* April 1974, pp. 288–93; M. Knowles, "Adult Learning," in *Training and Development Handbook,* 3rd ed., ed. R. L. Craig (New York: McGraw-Hill, 1987), pp. 168–79; R. Zemke and S. Zemke, "30 Things We Know for Sure about Adult Learning," *Training,* June 1981, pp. 45–52; B. J. Smith and B. L. Delahaye, *How to Be an Effective Trainer,* 2nd ed. (New York: Wiley, 1987).

25. A. Fox, "Microlearning for Effective Performance Management," *TD,* April 2016, pp. 116–117.

26. M. Cole, "Microlearning: Delivering Bite-Sized Knowledge" (Alexandria, VA: Association for Talent Development, 2017); L. Kolodny, "One Way to Train Workers One Small Bite at a Time," *Wall Street Journal,* March 14, 2016, p. R6.

27. "Training Top 125, Best Practices & Outstanding Training Initiatives, Nationwide Mutual Insurance Company: Cohort Learning," *Training,* January/February 2017, p. 98; A. Shatto and J. Ruiz, "Zooming in on Purpose-Driven Microlearning," *Chief Learning Officer,* January/February 2018, pp. 45–47, 57.

28. S. Bailey, "The Answer to Transfer," *Chief Learning Officer,* November 2014, pp. 33–41; R. Hewes, "Step by Step," *T + D,* February 2014, pp. 56–61; E. Holton III and T. Baldwin, eds, *Improving Learning Transfer in Organizations* (San Francisco: Jossey-Bass, 2003); J. M. Cusimano, "Managers as Facilitators," *Training and Development* 50 (1996), pp. 31–33.

29. S. Gale, "Taking Leadership in a New Direction at Western Union," *Chief Learning Officer,* March 2017, pp. 54, 56.

30. M. Weinstein, "Sonic Automotive Revs Its Leadership Engine," *Training,* January/February 2017, pp. 46–50.

31. C. M. Petrini, ed., "Bringing It Back to Work," *Training and Development Journal,* December 1990, pp. 15–21.

32. M. Weinstein, "New York Community Bancorp, Inc., Invests in Future-Focused Training," *training,* January/February 2018, pp. 30–32.

33. J. Ford, M. Quinones, D. Sego, and J. Sorra, "Factors Affecting the Opportunity to Perform Trained Tasks on the Job." *Personnel Psychology* 45 (1992): 511-527.

34. M. A. Quinones, J. K. Ford, D. J. Sego, and E. M. Smith, "The Effects of Individual and Transfer Environment Characteristics on the Opportunity to Perform Trained Tasks," *Training Research Journal* 1 (1995/96), pp. 29–48.

35. G. Stevens and E. Stevens, "The Truth about EPSS," *Training and Development* 50 (1996), pp. 59–61; J. Ford and T. Meyer, "Advances in Training Technology: Meeting the Workplace Challenges of Talent Development, Deep Specialization, and Collaborative Learning," in M. Coovert and L. Thompson, eds., *The Psychology of Workplace Technology* (New York: Routledge, 2014), pp. 43–76.

36. A. Rio, "Learning in Practice Awards: Mbinette Chan, Director of Learning Solutions, Synaptics," *Chief Learning Officer,* December 2017, p. 39.

37. S. Prokesch, "Reinventing Talent Management," *Harvard Business Review,* September/October 2017, pp. 54–55.

38. "Tata Consultancy Services," *TD,* October 2016, p. 47.

39. R. D. Marx, "Relapse Prevention for Managerial Training: A Model for Maintenance of Behavior Change," *Academy of Management Review* 7 (1982), pp. 433–41; G. P. Latham and C. A. Frayne, "Self-Management Training for Increasing Job Attendance: A Follow-up and Replication," *Journal of Applied Psychology* 74 (1989), pp. 411–16.

40. "Training Top 125 2018 Rankings 26-35, CVS Health," *training,* January/February 2018, pp. 56–57; "Training Top 125 2018 Rankings 26-35, Gables Residential," *Training,* January/February 2018, pp. 56–57.

41. B. Mirza, "Social Media Tools Redefine Learning," *HR Magazine,* December 2010, p. 74; L. Patel, "The Rise of Social Media," *T + D,* July 2010, pp. 60–61; J. Meister, E. Kaganer, and R. Von Feldt, "2011: The Year of the Media Tablet as a Learning Tool," *T + D,* April 2011, pp. 28–31.

42. "Putting the Distance into Distance Learning," *Training,* October 1995, pp. 111–18.

43. D. Picard, "The Future Is Distance Training," *Training,* November 1996, pp. s3–s10.

44. A. F. Maydas, "On-Line Networks Build the Savings into Employee Education," *HR Magazine,* October 1997, pp. 31–35.

45. "EY: Tax 1 Blended Program," *Training,* January/February 2016, p. 57.

46. T. Byham and A. Lang, "Avoid These 10 Pitfalls of Virtual Classrooms," *Chief Learning Officer,* May 2014, pp. 18–21; C. Huggett, "Make Virtual Training a Success," *T + D,* January 2014, pp. 40–45.

47. "Farmers Insurance: CE–It's Up to Me!" *Training,* January/February 2017, pp. 58–59.

48. W. Davis, "A Mobile-Powered Learning Makeover," *Chief Learning Officer,* July/August 2018, pp. 60–61.

49. R. B. Cohn, "How to Choose a Video Producer," *Training,* July 1996, pp. 58–61.

50. K. Rockwood, "The University of You," *HR Magazine,* May 2017, pp. 39–42.

51. Commerce Clearing House, Inc., *Orientation-Training* (Chicago, IL: Personnel Practices Communications, Commerce Clearing House, 1981), pp. 501–905; K. Tyler, "The American Apprentice," *HR Magazine,* November 2013, pp. 33–36; S. Wartenberg, "No Snow Days," *The Columbus Dispatch,* February 22, 2015, pp. D1, D3; L. Weber, "Here's One Way to Solve the Skills Gap," *Wall Street Journal,* April 28, 2014, p. R3.

52. A. H. Howard III, "Apprenticeships," in *The ASTD Training and Development Handbook,* pp. 803–13; K. Tyler, "The American Apprentice," *HR Magazine,* November 2013, pp. 33–36.

53. M. Riley, "Training Companies to Handle a Hack," *Bloomberg Businessweek,* November 23, 2016, from www.bloomberg.com, accessed March 17, 2017.

54. N. Adams, "Lessons from the Virtual World," *Training,* June 1995, pp. 45–48.

55. N. Adams, "Lessons from the Virtual World," *Training,* June 1995, pp. 45–48.

56. J. Vanian, "Farmers Insurance Is Using the Oculus Rift to Train Workers in Virtual Reality," *Fortune,* October 25, 2017, from www.fortune.com, accessed January 29, 2018.

57. Cornell, "Better than the Real Thing?"; E. Frauenheim, "Can Video Games Win Points as Teaching Tools?" *Workforce Management,* April 10, 2006, pp. 12–14; S. Boehle, "Simulations: The Next Generation of e-Learning," *Training,* January 2005, pp. 22–31; J. Borzo, "Almost Human," *Wall Street Journal,* May 24, 2004; T. Sitzmann, "A Meta-Analytic Examination of the Instructional Effectiveness of Computer-Based Simulation Games," *Personnel Psychology* 64 (2011), pp. 489–528.

58. L. Freifeld, "Solid Sims," *Training*, October 2007, p. 48.

59. J. Keebler, B. Patzer, T. Wiltshire, and S. Fiore, "Augmented Reality Systems in Training," in *The Cambridge Handbook of Workplace Training and Employee Development*, eds. K. Brown (New York: Cambridge University Press, 2018, pp. 278–92.

60. N. Kroc, "Reality Reboot," *HR Magazine,* October 2017, pp. 46–51; D. Zielinski, "Get Intelligent on AI," *HR Magazine,* November 2017, pp. 60–61.; A. Moore, "2017 Trends," *TD,* November 2017, pp. 28–32.

61. B. Roberts, "Gamification: Win, Lose or Draw," *HR Magazine,* May 2014, pp. 28–35; T. Sitzmann, "A Meta-Analytic Investigation of the Instructional Effectiveness of Computer-Based Simulation Games," *Personnel Psychology* 64 (2011), pp. 489–528.

62. D. Schimmoeller, "Everyone Learns with Deloitte's DLearn," *Training,* November/December 2017, pp. 56–57; L. Baughman, "Rx for Rural Health Care: Friday Night at the ER," *Training,* September/October 2017, p. 42.

63. G. P. Latham and L. M. Saari, "Application of Social Learning Theory to Training Supervisors through Behavior Modeling," *Journal of Applied Psychology* 64 (1979), pp. 239–46.

64. M. Rosenberg, *E-Learning Strategies for Delivering Knowledge in the Digital Age* (New York: McGraw-Hill, 2001); "What Is Web-Based Training?" from www.clark.net/pub/nractive/ft.html; R. Johnson and H. Gueutal, *Transforming HR through Technology* (Alexandria, VA: SHRM Foundation, 2010).

65. L. Harris and E. Squire, "Bedside Manners," *T + D*, December 2015, pp. 48–52.

66. S. Herring, "MOOCs Come of Age," *T + D*, January 2014, pp. 46–49.

67. S. Gale, "Teaching the World," *Chief Learning Officer,* October 2018, pp. 30–33.

68. M. Weinstein, "Managing MOOCs," *Training*, September/October 2014, pp. 26–28; R. Grossman, "Are Massive Open Online Courses in Your Future?" *HR* Magazine, August 2013, pp. 30–36; J. Meister, "How MOOCs Will Revolutionize Corporate Learning and Development," *Forbes*, August 20, 2013; C. Straumsheim, "Confirming the MOOC Myth," *Inside Higher Ed,* December 6, 2013, www.insidehighered.com; K. Jordan, "MOOC Completion Rates: The Data," http://www.katyjordan.com/MOOCproject.html; M. Chafkin, "Uphill Climb," *Fast Company*, December 2013/January 2014, pp. 146–56.

69. M. Hamori, "Can MOOCs Solve Your Training Problem?" *Harvard Business Review,* January/February 2018, pp. 70–77.

70. G. Dutton, "There's an App for That!" *Training*, September/October 2011, pp. 36–37.

71. S. Sipek, "Learning Is Doing at PwC," *Chief Learning Officer,* June 2016, pp. 38–39.

72. "Training Top 125 Best Practices & Outstanding Training Initiatives, Anthem Inc.: Flipped Classroom Strategy," *Training,* January/February 2018, pp. 86–87.

73. "Learning Management Systems: An Executive Summary," *Training*, March 2002, p. 4; S. Castellano, "The Evolution of the LMS," *T + D*, November 2014, p. 14.

74. M. Weinstein, "LMS Data Deep Dive," *Training,* September/October 2017, pp. 30–33.

75. D. Brown and D. Harvey, *An Experiential Approach to Organizational Development* (Englewood Cliffs, NJ: Prentice Hall, 2000); J. Schettler, "Learning by Doing," *Training*, April 2002, pp. 38–43; G. Kranz, "From Fire Drills to Funny Skills," *Workforce Management*, May 2011, pp. 28–32.

76. "Lending a Hand," *T + D*, December 2013, p. 72.

77. R. J. Wagner, T. T. Baldwin, and C. C. Rowland, "Outdoor Training: Revolution or Fad?" *Training and Development Journal,* March 1991, pp. 51–57; C. J. Cantoni, "Learning the Ropes of Teamwork," *Wall Street Journal*, October 2, 1995, p. A14.

78. R. Greenfield, "Startup vs. Wild," *Bloomberg Businessweek*, December 3, 2015.

79. D. Mishev, "Cooking for the Company," *Cooking Light*, August 2004, pp. 142–47.

80. P. F. Buller, J. R. Cragun, and G. M. McEvoy, "Getting the Most Out of Outdoor Training," *Training and Development Journal*, March 1991, pp. 58–61.

81. E. Dierdorff and J. Ellington, "Team Training," in *The Cambridge Handbook of Workplace Training and Employee Development*, ed. K. Brown (New York: Cambridge University Press, 2018), pp. 383–406; J. Cannon-Bowers and C. Bowers, "Team Development and Functioning," in *APA Handbook of Industrial and Organizational Psychology*, ed. S. Zedeck (Washington, DC: American Psychological Association, 2011), vol. 1, pp. 597–650; L. Delise, C. Gorman, A. Brooks, J. Rentsch, and D. Steele-Johnson, "The Effects of Team Training on Team Outcomes: A Meta-Analysis," *Performance Improvement Quarterly* 22 (2010), pp. 53–80.

82. S. Carey, "Racing to Improve," *Wall Street Journal*, March 24, 2006, pp. B1, B6.

83. P. Froiland, "Action Learning," *Training*, January 1994, pp. 27–34.

84. "University Health System," *TD,* October 2016, p. 77; Sarah Sipek, "A Global Vision: Leading PepsiCo's Learning Evolution," *Chief Learning Officer,* March 2015, pp. 22–25.

85. "Top 125 2018 Rankings 46-55, Bankers Life," *Training,* January/February 2018, pp. 60–61.

86. "Training Top 125 2018 Rankings 111-115, Intermedia Inc.," *Training,* January/February 2018, pp. 80–81.

87. K. Kraiger, J. K. Ford, and E. Salas, "Application of Cognitive, Skill-Based, and Affective Theories of Learning Outcomes to New Methods of Training Evaluation," *Journal of Applied Psychology* 78 (1993), pp. 311–28; J. J. Phillips, "ROI: The Search for Best Practices," *Training and Development*, February 1996, pp. 42–47; D. L. Kirkpatrick, "Evaluation of Training," in *Training and Development Handbook*, 2nd ed., ed. R. L. Craig (New York: McGraw-Hill, 1976), pp. 18-1–18-27.

88. "Training Top 10 Hall of Fame Outstanding Training Initiatives, Verizon: Sales Leadership Academy (SLA)," *Training,* January/February 2018, pp. 94–95.

89. "Mountain America Credit Union: Flow Philosophy Training," *Training*, January/February 2015, p. 103.

90. J. Phillips, P. Phillips, and R. Ray, "Derive Hard Numbers from Soft Skills," *TD*, September 2015, pp. 54–59; J. J. Phillips, *Handbook of Training Evaluation and Measurement Methods,* 2nd ed. (Houston, TX: Gulf Publishing, 1991); J. Phillips and P. Phillips, "Moving from Evidence to Proof," *T + D*, August 2001, pp. 34–39.

91. P. Leone and R. Pinkston, "Practice Makes Perfect," *TD,* March 2017, pp. 62–63.

92. I. Speizer, "Rolling through the Downturn," *Workforce Management*, August 11, 2008, pp. 31–37.

93. S. Ladika, "Lost in Translation," *Workforce Management*, May 2013, pp. 30–33.

94. K. Johnson, "Career Booster for CFOs: A Stint Abroad," *Wall Street Journal*, February 10, 2015, p. B7.

95. J. Zhu, C. Wanberg, D. Harrison, and E. Diehn, "Ups and Downs of the Expatriate Experience? Understanding Work Adjustment Trajectories and Career Outcomes," *Journal of Applied Psychology* 101 (2016), pp. 549–68; W. A. Arthur Jr. and W. Bennett Jr., "The International Assignee: The Relative Importance of Factors Perceived to Contribute to Success,"

*Personnel Psychology* 48 (1995), pp. 99–114; G. M. Spreitzer, M. W. McCall Jr., and Joan D. Mahoney, "Early Identification of International Executive Potential," *Journal of Applied Psychology* 82 (1997), pp. 6–29.

96. J. Robinson, "Coming Home," *Human Resource Executive*, September 2, 2016, pp. 39–40, 42; R. Feintzeig, "After Stints Abroad, Re-entry Can Be Hard," *Wall Street Journal*, September 18, 2013, p. B6.

97. J. S. Black and J. K. Stephens, "The Influence of the Spouse on American Expatriate Adjustment and Intent to Stay in Pacific Rim Overseas Assignments," *Journal of Management* 15 (1989), pp. 529–44; M. Shaffer and D. A. Harrison, "Forgotten Partners of International Assignments: Development and Test of a Model of Spouse Adjustment," *Journal of Applied Psychology* 86 (2001), pp. 238–54.

98. M. Shaffer, D. A. Harrison, H. Gregersen, J. S. Black, and L. A. Ferzandi, "You Can Take It with You: Individual Differences and Expatriate Effectiveness," *Journal of Applied Psychology* 91 (2006), pp. 109–25; P. Caligiuri, "The Big Five Personality Characteristics as Predictors of Expatriate's Desire to Terminate the Assignment and Supervisor-Rated Performance," *Personnel Psychology* 53 (2000), pp. 67–88.

99. E. Dunbar and A. Katcher, "Preparing Managers for Foreign Assignments," *Training and Development Journal*, September 1990, pp. 45–47.

100. J. S. Black and M. Mendenhall, "A Practical but Theory-Based Framework for Selecting Cross-Cultural Training Methods," in *Readings and Cases in International Human Resource Management*, ed. M. Mendenhall and G. Oddou (Boston: PWS-Kent, 1991), pp. 177–204.

101. Sodexo, "2016 Global Diversity and Inclusion Report," www.sodexousa.com, accessed March 14, 2017.

102. P. Tam, "Culture Course," *Wall Street Journal*, May 25, 2004, pp. B1, B12.

103. S. Ronen, "Training the International Assignee," in *Training and Development in Organizations*, ed. I. L. Goldstein (San Francisco: Jossey-Bass, 1989), pp. 417–53.

104. H. Ren, M. Shaffer, D. Harrison, C. Fu, and K. Fodchuk, "Reactive Adjustment or Proactive Embedding? Multistudy, Multiwave Evidence for Dual Pathways to Expatriate Retention," *Personnel Psychology* 67 (2014), pp. 203–39.

105. P. R. Harris and R. T. Moran, *Managing Cultural Differences* (Houston, TX: Gulf, 1991).

106. J. Carter, "Globe Trotters," *Training*, August 2005, pp. 22–28.

107. C. Solomon, "Unhappy Trails," *Workforce*, August 2000, pp. 36–41.

108. T. Micner, "For Expats, Life and Love Abroad and Apart at Times," *Wall Street Journal*, April 13, 2016, p. D2.

109. C. Patton, "Coming to America," *Human Resource Executive*, January/February 2012, pp. 22, 26–29.

110. H. Lancaster, "Before Going Overseas, Smart Managers Plan Their Homecoming," *Wall Street Journal*, September 28, 1999, p. B1; A. Halcrow, "Expats: The Squandered Resource," *Workforce*, April 1999, pp. 42–48.

111. Harris and Moran, *Managing Cultural Differences*.

112. J. Robinson, "Coming Home," *Human Resource Executive*, September 2, 2016, pp. 39–40, 42; J. Lublin, "Send Abroad? Plan Your Return Now," *Wall Street Journal*, September 6, 2017, p. B8.

113. H. Dolezalek, "The Path to Inclusion," *Training*, May 2008, pp. 52–54.

114. E. McKeown, "Quantifiable Inclusion Strategies," *T + D*, October 2010, p. 16.

115. R. Silverman, "Managers: Watch Your Language," *Wall Street Journal*, September 20, 2015, p. R9; The Royal Society, "Understanding Unconscious Bias," from https://www.youtube.com/watch?v=dVp9Z5k0dEE, accessed November 1, 2018; Google, "Making the Unconscious Conscious," from https://www.youtube.com/watch?v=NW5s_-Nl3JE, accessed November 1, 2018; S. Leibowitz, "Stanford University Researchers Analyzed the Language in 125 Performance Reviews from a Tech Company and Found Something Disturbing," *Business Insider*, October 1, 2015, www.businessinsider.com, accessed November 1, 2018.

116. Q. Roberson, "Diversity in the Workplace: A Review, Synthesis, and Future Research Agenda," *Annual Review of Organizational Psychology and Organizational Behavior* 6 (2019), pp. 69–88; F. Dobbins and A. Kalev, "Why Diversity Programs Fail," *Harvard Business Review*, July/August (2016), pp. 52–60.

117. C. Hymowitz, "White Men Can Change at Rockwell Automation," *Bloomberg Businessweek*, April 27, 2017, from www.bloomberg.com, accessed February 8, 2018; V. Fuhrmans, "The Hidden Battle of the Sexes at Work," *Wall Street Journal*, October 10, 2017, pp. R1, R2; C. Gregory, "Why Doesn't Silicon Valley Hire Black Coders," *Bloomberg Businessweek*, January 21, 2016, from www.bloomberg.com, accessed February 8, 2018.

118. K. Bezrukova, C. Spell, J. Perry, and K. Jehn, "A Meta-Analytical Integration of over 40 Years of Research on Diversity Training Evaluation," *Psychological Bulletin* 142 (2016), pp. 1227–74.

119. "Corporate Responsibility," from www.sodexousa.com, accessed March 14, 2017; "Report Highlights Diversity and Inclusion as a Core Component of Sodexo Business Growth Strategy," February 6, 2017 news release, from www.sodexousa.com, accessed March 14, 2017; "2016 Global Diversity and Inclusion Report," from www.sodexousa.com, accessed March 14, 2017; "The 2017 DiversityInc Top 50 Companies for Diversity," from www.diversityinc.com, accessed March 21, 2018; M. Landel, "How We Did It . . . SODEXO's CEO on Smart Diversification," *Harvard Business Review*, March 2015, pp. 41–44; R. Emelo, "Peer Collaboration Enhances Diversity and Inclusion," *T + D*, December 2014, pp. 48–52. R. Anand and M. Winters, "A Retrospective View of Corporate Diversity Training from 1964 to the Present," *Academy of Management Learning & Education* 7 (2008), pp. 356–72; Dolezalek, "The Path to Inclusion."

120. C. T. Schreiber, K. F. Price, and A. Morrison, "Workforce Diversity and the Glass Ceiling: Practices, Barriers, Possibilities," *Human Resource Planning* 16 (1994), pp. 51–69; K. Bezrvkova, K. Jehn, and C. Spell, "Reviewing Diversity Training: Where Have We Been and Where Should We Go?" *Academy of Management Learning and Education* 11 (2012), pp. 207–227; B. Groysberg and K. Connolly, "Great Leaders Who Make the Mix Work," *Harvard Business Review*, September 2013, pp. 68–76.

121. Groysberg and Connolly, "Great Leaders Who Make the Mix Work."

122. T. Bauer, *Onboarding New Employees: Maximizing Success* (Alexandria, VA: SHRM Foundation, 2010); T. Bauer and B. Erdogan, "Delineating and Reviewing the Role of Newcomer Capital in Organizational Socialization," *Annual Review of Organizational Psychology and Organizational Behavior* 1 (2014), pp. 439–57.

123. T. Allen, L. Eby, G. Chao, and T. Bauer, "Taking Stock of Two Relational Aspects of Organizational Life: Tracing the History and Shaping the Future of Socialization and Mentoring Research," *Journal of Applied Psychology* 102 (2017), pp. 324–337; H. Klein and N. Weaver, "The Effectiveness of Organizational-Level

Orientation Program in the Socialization of New Hires," *Personnel Psychology* 23 (2000), pp. 47–66; C. Wanberg, J. Kammeyer-Mueller, "Predictors and Outcomes of Proactivity in the Socialization Process," *Journal of Applied Psychology* 85 (2000), pp. 373–85; T. Bauer, T. Bodner, B. Erdogan, D. Truxillo, and J. Tucker, "Newcomer Adjustment during Organizational Socialization: A Meta-analytic Review of Antecedents, Outcomes, and Methods," *Journal of Applied Psychology* 92 (2007), pp. 707–21; D. Allen, "Do Organizational Socialization Tactics Influence Newcomer Embeddedness and Turnover?" *Journal of Management* 32 (2006), pp. 237–56; J. Kammeyer-Mueller, C. Wanberg, A. Rubenstein, and Z. Song, "Support, Undermining, and Newcomer Socialization: Fitting in During the First 90 Days," *Academy of Management Journal* 56 (2013), pp. 1104–24.

124. D. Bortz, "All Onboard," *HR Magazine,* December 2017, pp. 44–49.

125. R. Weiss, "Inside Story: A New Orientation Program for New Employees," Association for Talent Development, www.astd.org.

CHAPTER

# 8 Performance Management

## ⌐ LEARNING OBJECTIVES ¬

*After reading this chapter, you should be able to:*

## Moving Toward Continuous Performance Management at Patagonia

Patagonia makes outdoor clothing for climbing, skiing, snowboarding, surfing, fly fishing, mountain biking, and trail running. Patagonia is known for using innovative fabrics and vivid colors in its clothing as well as using environmentally conscious materials such as recycled polyester and organic rather than man-made cotton. The company culture encourages employees to treat work as play and consider themselves the ultimate customers for the products they produce. Patagonia places a high emphasis on transparency and working collaboratively to come up with innovative problems and solutions to problems. To help facilitate collaboration, Patagonia tends to recruit and hire employees based on current employees' informal network of friends, colleagues, and business associates.

When Dean Carter joined Patagonia as vice president of human resources, he was surprised that the company still used only the traditional annual performance review and didn't supplement it with a continuous feedback system. Carter made the case for adding a continuous feedback system to Patagonia's CEO, arguing that this type of system represented the future of performance management and aligned with Patagonia's emphasis on transparency and collaboration. He was so convinced that Patagonia's traditional performance management system needed to be revised that he told the CEO she could replace him if his recommended approach didn't work out.

The additions to Patagonia's performance management system that Carter helped implement included an emphasis on both annual and quarterly goals, continuous feedback, and quarterly manager–employee check-in meetings. Annual goals focused on targets such as sales, expenses, and cost reduction are used for traditional end-of-year formal performance reviews linked to compensation and bonus decisions. Quarterly stretch goals are developmentally focused yet designed to help employees make progress toward their annual goals. Patagonia encourages employees to set truly challenging stretch goals to encourage them to seek out feedback at any time from mangers and peers on their progress toward these goals, which in turn, can help them improve their progress toward their annual goal in the subsequent quarter. Feedback can be requested and provided through an app that employees and managers can access on their notebook computers, tablets, or smartphone. This gives employees the opportunity to receive highly motivating and rewarding social recognition from the people they work with. At quarterly employee–manager check-in meetings, discussions focus on quarterly goal progress, potential changes in goals for the next quarter, and what the employee learned from the feedback they received and how it will change their behavior during the next quarterly performance period.

The changes to the performance management system were implemented in steps starting with encouraging quarterly employee-led conversations with managers and then adding a focus on the importance of continuous feedback and understanding how to give and receive it. At first, the feedback employees provided to each other tended to be positive but gradually it included areas that could be improved. The emphasis on providing feedback helped start a reinforcing cycle in which the employee who was asked to provide feedback felt comfortable asking others for feedback on their performance.

Setting stretch goals and participating in the continuous feedback process using the app is optional. But many employees are motivated to use the continuous feedback approach after considering data showing that those who do are more likely to achieve their annual goals and receive 6% higher bonuses than those who do not participate. Further, since the

*CONTINUED*

new system was implemented Patagonia's employees report that they have a greater understanding of what is expected of them and have greater trust in their manager. The more frequent conversations have also increased managers beliefs that employees have the abilities to take on additional job responsibilities. Also, when Carter asks employees at Town Hall meetings how many of them have changed their behavior as a result of the feedback they received, over 70% raise their hands.

SOURCES: Based on J. Ramirez, "Future of Feedback," *Human Resource Executive*, March 2018, pp. 23–24; "Culture & Life at Patagonia," "Company Information," and "Company History," from www.patagonia.com, accessed January 9, 2019; Dean Carter, "Patagonia's Unconventional HR." from http://leaphr-retail.com/wp-content/uploads/sites/206/2018/01/Patagonia_Unconventional_HR_Dean_Carter.pdf, accessed January 10, 2019; "Research Report: Continuous Performance Management," Deloitte Development LLC (2017), from http://marketing.bersin.com/rs/976-LMP-699/images/Continuous_Performance_Management.pdf, accessed January 10, 2019; "Patagonia Uses HighGround to Align Its Performance Management to Business Values," from https://www.highground.com/resources/patagonia-case-study, accessed January 10, 2019.

# Introduction

Companies that seek competitive advantage through employees must be able to manage the behavior and results of all employees. Traditionally, the formal performance appraisal system was viewed as the primary means for managing employee performance. Performance appraisal was an administrative duty performed by managers and was primarily the responsibility of the human resource function. Managers now view performance appraisal as an annual ritual—they quickly complete the form and use it to catalog all the negative information they have collected on an employee over the previous year. Because they may dislike confrontation and feel that they don't know how to give effective evaluations, some managers spend as little time as possible giving employees feedback. Not surprisingly, most managers and employees dislike performance appraisals. "Time-consuming," "frustrating," "dread," "burden," and "pain" are some of the words that come to employees' minds when giving or receiving performance reviews.[1] Reasons for these reactions include the lack of consistency of use of performance appraisals across the company; the inability to differentiate among performance levels; the inability of the appraisal system to help employees build their skills and competencies; excessive time burdens on managers to complete evaluations; and performance discussions that were limited to only once or twice a year and tended to be backward rather than future focused.[2]

Some people have argued that all performance appraisal systems are flawed to the point that they are manipulative, abusive, autocratic, and counterproductive. However, doing away with performance reviews entirely has been found to lead to lower-quality performance conversations between managers and employees and a decrease in employee engagement. This occurs because, without reviews, managers have difficulty explaining to employees how they have performed and what they need to do to improve.[3] It is important to realize that the criticisms voiced about annual performance appraisals shown in Table 8.1 are not the result of evaluating employee performance. Rather, they result from how the performance management system is developed and used. If done correctly, performance management can provide valuable benefits to both employees and the company. As a result, many companies, including Patagonia (discussed in the chapter opener), Eli Lilly, Adobe, Dell, New York Life, Microsoft, Intel, and Gap, have changed their performance management systems. In fact, one estimate is that more than one-third of U.S. companies are now using performance management systems that encourage more frequent manager–employee performance conversations, reducing or eliminating formal evaluation meetings, and moving away from overall performance ratings. These new systems help meet all employees' need for feedback, coaching, and development opportunities, but especially Millennials, who represent a significant part of the workforce.

**Table 8.1**
Examples of
Problems with
Traditional Annual
Performance
Reviews

"The annual performance review is dead. Progressive HR leaders are realizing they need continuous real time feedback and solutions"
—CEO of Glint

"Over time the rating system has become a huge obstacle. The employee would see their rating first and then the whole review evolved into a discussion of Why this? Why not that? It was no longer driving performance."
—Executive VP for Global HR at Expedia

"There is a lot of pain in performance management."
—Senior Consultant for Towers Watson

"We all know the annual review does not work to improve performance, nor does it deliver needed business outcomes of the development of top talent."
—Doug Dennerline, CEO of BetterWorks

"In a traditional performance review, the employee listens until he hears the rating and then tunes out because he's doing the calculation in his head about how that will affect his bonus."
—Senior VP of Human Resources for Motorola Solutions

SOURCES: "Fixing the Broken Annual Review Process," *Human Resource Executive*, December 2018, p. 10; D. Wilkie, "Is the Annual Performance Review Dead," *HR Magazine*, October 2015, pp. 11–12; E. Goldberg, "Performance Management Gets Social," *HR Magazine*, August 2014, pp. 35–38; J. Ramirez, "Rethinking the Review," *Human Resource Executive*, July/August 2013, pp. 16–19; V. Liberman, "Performance Management: To Get Results Stop Measuring People by Them," *The Conference Board Review*, Summer 2013, pp. 57–63.

We believe that performance appraisal is only one part of the broader process of performance management. We define **performance management** as the process through which managers ensure that employees' activities and outputs are congruent with the organization's goals. Performance management is central to gaining competitive advantage.

Our performance management system has three parts: defining performance, measuring performance, and feeding back performance information. First, a performance management system specifies which aspects of performance are relevant to the organization, primarily through job analysis (discussed in Chapter 4). Second, it measures those aspects of performance through **performance appraisal**, which is only one method for managing employee performance. Third, it provides feedback to employees through **performance feedback** sessions so that they can adjust their performance to the organization's goals. Performance feedback is also fulfilled through tying rewards to performance via the compensation system (such as through merit increases or bonuses), a topic to be covered in Chapters 11 and 12.

In this chapter, we examine a variety of approaches to performance management. First, we provide a brief summary of current performance management practices. Next, we present a model of performance that helps us examine the system's purposes. Then we discuss specific approaches to performance management and the strengths and weaknesses of each. We also look at various sources of performance information. The errors resulting from subjective assessments of performance are presented, as well as the means for reducing those errors. Then we discuss some effective components to performance feedback. Finally, we address components of a legally defensible performance management system.

**Performance management**
The means through which managers ensure that employees' activities and outcomes are congruent with the organization's goals.

**Performance appraisal**
The process through which an organization gets information on how well an employee is doing his or her job.

**Performance feedback**
The process of providing employees information regarding their performance effectiveness.

# The Performance Management Process

Although performance management does include the once- or twice-a-year formal appraisal or evaluation meeting, effective performance management is a process, not an event. Figure 8.1 shows the traditional performance management process. As shown in the process model, providing feedback and the formal performance evaluation are

**LO 8-1**
Identify the major parts and limitations of the traditional performance management process.

**Figure 8.1**

Traditional Performance Management Process

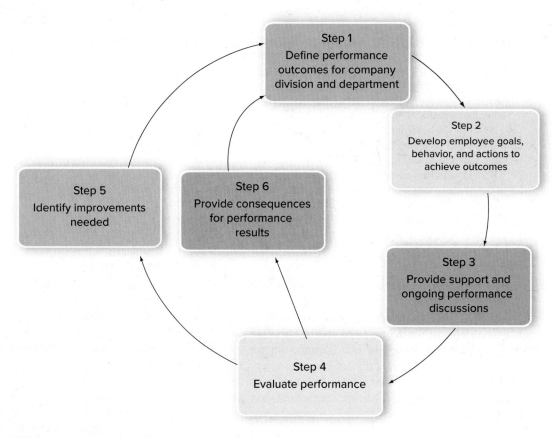

SOURCES: Based on E. Pulakos, R. Hanson, S. Arad, and N. Moye, "Performance Management Can Be Fixed: An On-the-Job Experiential Learning Approach for Complex Behavior Change," *Industrial and Organizational Psychology*, March 2015, pp. 51–76; E. Pulakos, R. Mueller-Hanson, R. O'Leary, and M. Meyrowitz, *Building a High-Performance Culture: A Fresh Look at Performance Management* (Alexandria, VA: SHRM Foundation, 2012); H. Aguinis, "An Expanded View of Performance Management," in J. W. Smith and M. London (eds.), *Performance Management* (San Francisco: Jossey-Bass, 2009), pp. 1–43; J. Russell and L. Russell, "Talk Me through It: The Next Level of Performance Management," *T + D*, April 2010, pp. 42–48.

important, but they are not the only important parts of an effective performance management process that contributes to the company's competitive advantage.[4] Also, visible CEO and senior management support for the system are necessary. This ensures that the system is used consistently across the company, appraisals are completed on time, and giving and receiving performance feedback is an accepted part of the company culture.

The traditional performance management process involves the six steps shown in Figure 8.1. The first two steps of the performance management process involve identifying what the company is trying to accomplish (goals or objectives) and a set of key performance dimensions that represent critical factors or drivers that influence the goals or objectives, and then developing performance measures for the key performance dimensions.[5] The first step in the performance management process starts with understanding and identifying important performance outcomes or results. Typically, these outcomes or results benefit customers, the employee's peers or team, and the organization itself. The company's and department's or team's strategy, mission, and values play an important part in determining these outcomes. Chapter 2 pointed out that most companies pursue some type of strategy to reach revenue, profit, and market share goals. Divisions, departments, teams, and employees must align their goals and behaviors, and choose to engage in activities that help achieve the organization's strategy and goals. The second step of the process involves understanding the process (or how) to achieve the goals established in the first step. This includes identifying measurable goals, behaviors, and activities that will help employees achieve the performance results. The goals, behaviors, and activities should be measurable so that the manager and the employee can determine if they have been achieved. The goals, activities, and behaviors should be part of the employee's job description.

The third step in the process, organizational support, involves providing employees with training, necessary resources and tools, and frequent feedback communication between employees and managers focusing on accomplishments as well as issues and challenges influencing performance. For effective performance management, managers and employees have to value feedback and regularly exchange it. Managers need to make time to provide feedback as well as train in how to give and receive it. The fourth step involves performance evaluation, that is, when the manager and the employee discuss and compare the targeted performance goals and supporting behaviors with the actual results. This typically involves the annual or biannual formal performance review.

The final steps of the performance management cycle involve the employee and the manager identifying what the employee (with help from the manager) can do to capitalize on performance strengths and address weaknesses (step 5) and providing consequences for achieving (or failing to achieve) performance outcomes (step 6). This includes identifying training needs; adjusting the type or frequency of feedback the manager provides to the employee; clarifying, adjusting, or modifying performance outcomes; and discussing behaviors or activities that need improvement or relate to new priorities based on changes or new areas of emphasis in organizational or department goals. Achieving performance results may relate to compensation (salary increases, cash bonuses), recognition, promotion, development opportunities, and continued employment. This depends on the purposes the company decides on for the performance management system (see the section Purposes of Performance Management).

What employees accomplish (or fail to accomplish) and the consequences of those accomplishments (or lack thereof) help shape changes in the organizational business strategy and performance goals and the ongoing performance management process. Evaluating the effectiveness of the performance management system is necessary to determine needed changes. This could include gathering comments about managers' and employees' concerns about the system, analyzing rating data to determine if they are being affected by rating errors, reviewing objectives for their quality, and studying the relationship between employees meeting objectives and department and organizational results.

Today, many companies are moving away from the traditional performance management process and adopting a continuous performance management process. A **continuous performance management process** refers to an approach that encourages ongoing conversations between managers, their direct reports, and teams focused on work progress, providing feedback, accomplishment and necessary adjustment of goals, and development needs.[6] It includes collecting performance

**Continuous performance management process** An approach that encourages ongoing conversations between managers, their direct reports, and teams focused on work progress, providing feedback, accomplishment and necessary adjustment of goals, and development needs.

Mc Graw Hill **connect**

Visit your instructor's Connect® course and access your eBook to view this video.

"Overwhelmingly, our people said, 'we want ratings. We don't want you to eliminate ratings [in performance assessments], we think it's important to know where we stand.'"

—Mirian M. Graddick-Weir
Executive Vice President, Human Resources, Merck

Source: Video produced for the Center for Executive Succession in the Darla Moore School of Business at the University of South Carolina by Coal Powered Filmworks

LO 8-2
Discuss the features of a continuous performance management process and why companies are adopting this approach.

feedback data from members of the employees social network, including managers, peers, customers, and direct reports, who observe their work. Performance feedback is easily provided and accessible for review using apps and websites.

Companies are moving to a continuous performance management process for several reasons.[7] One reason is that employees, especially Millennials, want more regular feedback and transparency, clarity, and responsibility for work. That is, they want to know how they are performing, decide what work needs to be completed and how to do it, and make adjustments when needed. Second, work is increasingly being performed in teams, meaning that peers, and not managers, are in the best position to provide feedback and evaluate and recognize work. Further, apps are available that easily allow employees to provide feedback and recognition to each other using smartphones, tablets, or notebook computers. Third, managers are becoming more responsible for developing and coaching employees. Fourth, business needs to become more agile to successfully deal with economic and competitive forces. This means that biannually or even quarterly or weekly new business, team, and individual performance goals need to be adopted or current goals need to be changed to adapt to current conditions. Also, in the traditional performance management process by the time business goals cascade down to employees they are often outdated, and employees have difficulty identifying what they need to do to help achieve them. Fifth, companies want better data to make talent management decisions about promotions, pay raises, and development opportunities. Finally, several recent surveys conclude that traditional performance management practices are ineffective.[8] For example, more than 50% of managers believe that their performance management process has not had a positive effect on either employee or company performance (and 70% of companies believe they need to improve their performance management practices!). Fifty percent of employees are surprised by the evaluations they receive, and 90% of those are unhappy because they expected a more positive evaluation.

Table 8.2 compares the features of traditional performance management and continuous performance management. Consider some of the differences between traditional performance management and continuous performance management.[9] Performance management is not just based on formal scheduled performance appraisal sessions that occur once or twice per year (midyear, and end-of-year) but includes ongoing performance conversations and feedback as well as more frequent, formal check-ins that can occur weekly, monthly, or quarterly. Managers, peers, direct reports, and even customers can provide feedback. Traditional performance management is considered "backward focused" because relying on only a once or twice a year formal performance appraisal means that the focus tends to be on the manager evaluating how the employee has performed in the prior evaluation periods. Continuous performance management is "forward-facing" because employees receive performance feedback more frequently, and if necessary, gives them the opportunity to adjust performance goals and change their behavior. The performance management process becomes more developmental and managers take on the role of coaching employees to improve.

It is important to consider that, like Patagonia featured in the chapter opener, many companies are moving away from a traditional performance management system emphasizing only the traditional midyear and formal end-of-year evaluation to continuous performance management. One estimate is that over 75% of company executives feel that redesigning their performance management system is a high priority.[10] Keep in mind that as we discuss this evolution many companies have adopted some, but not all of the features of continuous performance management. Also, making this change requires several years because it takes time for managers and employees to understand how to give and receive positive and negative feedback and feel comfortable doing so.

**Table 8.2**

Comparison of the Features of Traditional and Continuous Performance Management Process

| FEATURE | TRADITIONAL | CONTINUOUS |
|---|---|---|
| **When does it occur?** | Midyear and annual review. | Ongoing combined with more formal quarterly, midyear, and/or annual reviews. |
| **Who is involved?** | Manager. | Manager, peers, direct reports. |
| **What is the focus?** | Backward-focused (focus on goals/behavior set at beginning of previous appraisal period). | Forward-facing (focus on helping to achieve goals/change behavior). Goals are fluid, adjusted as necessary. |
| **How is it conducted?** | Ratings and results measured on a formal performance appraisal form. | Emphasizes face-to-face performance conversations. Can include ratings and feedback provided using social media. |
| **What is the level of transparency?** | Goal setting and goal progress is based on private conversation between manager and employee. | Feedback, recognition, goal setting, progress, and achievement is public and transparent. Goals are fluid, adjusted as necessary. |

SOURCE: Based on Deloitte Development LLC, "Continuous Performance Management," 2017, accessed from N. Sloan, D. Agarwal, S. Garr, and K. Pastakia, "Performance Management: Playing a Winning Hand," December 28, 2017, from https://www2.deloitte.com/insights/us/en/focus/human-capital-trends/2017/redesigning-performance-management.html, accessed January 22, 2019; E. Pulakos, R. Mueller-Hanson, and S. Arad, "The Evolution of Performance Management: Searching for Value," *Annual Review of Organizational Psychology and Organizational Behavior* 6 (2019), pp. 249–271; A. Colquitt, *Next Generation Performance Management* (Charlotte, North Carolina: Information Age Publishing, 2017).

For example, consider the changes that Facebook and Proctor & Gamble made to their performance management systems.[11] Facebook is keeping its traditional performance management system but with some important changes. Facebook now conducts performance reviews every six months based on self-evaluations and insights provided by an employee's manager and peers. The reviews are conducted every six months to account for the quickly changing nature of the business.

Facebook took several steps to ensure that its system is fair and transparent, and that it focuses on development. Evaluators are asked to provide ratings on specific performance dimensions, such as technical contributions, before they make their overall performance rating. Peers' evaluations are shared with each other and their managers. Managers are trained to stay up to date on employees' projects and provide employees with feedback and help, if necessary. Managers attend meetings and discuss their direct reports, defending and advocating for them and considering their peer evaluations. The goal of these meetings is to reduce the effect of individual managers being hard or easy evaluators. After the managers write their performance reviews, they examine them for bias (e.g., if words such as *aggressive* or *abrasive* are used more often to describe women and result in lower evaluations). The overall performance ratings are then converted directly into compensation decisions using a formula. This allows managers to focus on making accurate performance evaluations rather than on having to painstakingly deliberate about compensation. Facebook has eliminated the problem of employees being categorized as excellent, good, or poor employees from one year to the next, whether they deserve it or not by using stretch goals (what they call 50–50 goals). These goals are challenging: There is an equal chance that employees will or will not reach these goals. As a result, employees have a chance of just one in three that they will receive the same overall performance rating each year.

Procter & Gamble changed its performance management approach to make it more of an ongoing process emphasizing performance conversations and employee development. There are four phases in the performance management process. The first phase, Prioritize, focuses on setting challenging and achieving goals based on the employees' most meaningful work. The next phase, Evaluation, involves managers and employees discussing what and how results were achieved during the year. In the third phase, Assess, managers consider employees' growth potential. The final stage, Know and Grow, emphasizes discussing and determining employees' development plans. The conversations that managers and employees need to have are critical for the success of performance management. As a result, Procter & Gamble developed coaching videos and workshops to help managers learn how to conduct effective performance conversations and serve as coaches to help employees develop.

# Purposes of Performance Management

**LO 8-3**
Discuss the six purposes of performance management.

Table 8.3 shows the six purposes of performance management: strategic, administrative, developmental, communication, organizational maintenance, and documentation.[12] Despite the importance of these purposes it is difficult for the performance management system to fulfill all of them. One reason is that many managers are reluctant to properly perform their role in them. For example, managers can feel uncomfortable evaluating others and giving feedback. As a result, they tend to evaluate everyone high or the same, making the appraisal information relatively useless. Another reason is that performance management users may have differing and sometimes conflicting expectations. Employees want performance management to give them feedback, recognize their performance, and earn appropriate pay and promotions. But managers and company leaders want a system that enables them to differentiate performance to distribute rewards. This can lead to employees who don't receive rewards and recognition feeling they were treated unfairly

**Table 8.3**
Purposes of Performance Management

| PURPOSE | DESCRIPTION |
| --- | --- |
| Strategic | Link employee behavior and expected results with organizational goals. |
| Administrative | Used in salary administration (pay raises), promotions, retention–termination, layoffs, recognition of employee performance. |
| Developmental | Identify employee strengths and weaknesses for managers to use in providing feedback and coaching and development and career planning. |
| Communication | Emphasize what employees are expected to do, how they are performing, and what they need to improve. Indicate important company values and principles. |
| Organization Maintenance | Show workforce performance, training, and development and talent acquisition needs. |
| Documentation | Record for administrative decisions and information for litigation and investigations. |

SOURCE: Based on A. Colquitt, *Next Generation Performance Management* (Charlotte, North Carolina: Information Age Publishing, 2017); H. Aguinis, *Performance Management* (4th ed.), (Chicago: Chicago, University Press, 2019); J. Cleveland, K. Murphy, and R. Williams, "Multiple Uses of Performance Appraisal: Prevalence and Correlates," *Journal of Applied Psychology* 74 (1989, pp. 130–135).

(and managers gaming the system by inflating performance ratings to provide pay increase). This is why in many new continuous performance management systems providing daily feedback is stressed, ratings that are difficult to understand and justify are being eliminated, and instead, goals are used as the basis for compensation and other administrative decisions (for example, see the Patagonia chapter opener).

GE's new performance management system supports the company's culture change to become more customer-centric.[13] Managers evaluate employees on their understanding of customers' needs and how quickly they test and confirm their assumptions about new products and solutions. Each employee has a series of short-term performance goals or priorities. Managers and employees have performance conversations throughout the year (known as "touchpoints") to review progress toward these goals, and they have a brief summary meeting at the end of the year. Employees are encouraged to give and seek performance feedback from their peers (and their managers) at any time. To help facilitate the feedback process, GE developed a mobile app that allows constructive messages and

Stockbyte/Getty Images

Performance management is critical for executing a talent management system and involves one-on-one contact with managers to ensure that proper training and development are taking place.

praise to be provided under separate categories. Employees are encouraged to attend team meetings that include a facilitator to provide feedback to their managers. The team is expected to hold the manager accountable for changing their behavior through regular progress meetings. The performance management continues to evolve. Employees are becoming less reluctant about providing constructive messages to their managers. Managers are still trying to get employees to adopt new behaviors and be more comfortable testing underdeveloped ideas and product prototypes with customers. One of the key issues GE is debating is how to make promotion and pay decisions without basing them on ranking employees or an overall performance rating.

An important step in performance management is to develop the measures by which performance will be evaluated. We next discuss the issues involved in developing and using different measures of performance.

# Performance Measures Criteria

In Chapter 4 we discussed how, through job analysis, one can analyze a job to determine exactly what constitutes effective performance. Once the company has determined, through job analysis and design, what kind of performance it expects from its employees, it needs to develop ways to measure that performance. This section presents the criteria underlying job performance measures. Later sections discuss approaches to performance measurement, sources of information, and errors.

Although people differ about the criteria to use to evaluate performance management systems, we believe that five stand out: strategic congruence, validity, reliability, acceptability, and specificity.

## STRATEGIC CONGRUENCE

**Strategic congruence** is the extent to which a performance management system elicits job performance that is congruent with the organization's strategy, goals, and culture. If a company emphasizes customer service, then its performance management system should

**LO 8-4**

Identify the five criteria for effective performance management systems.

**Strategic congruence**
The extent to which the performance management system elicits job performance that is consistent with the organization's strategy, goals, and culture.

assess how well its employees are serving the company's customers. Strategic congruence emphasizes the need for the performance management system to guide employees in contributing to the organization's success. This requires systems flexible enough to adapt to changes in the company's strategic posture.

Many companies use critical success factors (CSFs) or key performance indicators (KPIs) in their performance management systems.[14] CSFs are factors in a company's business strategy that give it a competitive edge. Companies measure employee behavior that relates to attainment of CSFs, which increases the importance of these behaviors for employees. Employees can be held accountable and rewarded for behaviors that directly relate to the company attaining the CSFs.

Google's performance management system includes objectives and key results (OKRs) for the entire company, as well as at the team, managerial, and employee levels.[15] The idea is that everyone has a short list of clear, relevant, and challenging objectives to achieve. Employees have four to five OKRs. OKRs are determined on an annual and quarterly bases. The annual OKRs can change but the quarterly ones do not. At the end of each quarter, key results are rated using a 0–1 scale. Employees are not expected to achieve 1s because they likely indicate the expected results were too easy to reach. All objectives and key results are public. Employees can see the objectives and key results for the CEO as well as their peers.

One challenge that companies face is how to measure customer loyalty, employee satisfaction, and other nonfinancial performance areas that affect profitability. To effectively use nonfinancial performance measures managers need to do the following:[16]

- Develop a model of how nonfinancial performance measures link to the company's strategic goals. Identify the performance areas that are critical to success.
- Identify data that exist on key performance measures (e.g., customer satisfaction, employee satisfaction surveys) using already existing databases. If data are not available, identify a performance area that affects the company's strategy and performance. Develop measures for those performance areas.
- Use statistical and qualitative methods for testing the relationship between the performance measures and financial outcomes. Regression and correlation analysis as well as focus groups and interviews can be used. For example, studies show that employees' involvement, satisfaction, and enthusiasm for work are significantly related to business performance, including customer satisfaction, productivity, and profitability.[17]
- Revisit the model to ensure that the nonfinancial performance measures are appropriate and determine whether new measures should be added. This is important to understand the drivers of financial performance and to ensure that the model is appropriate as the business strategy and economic conditions change.
- Act on conclusions that the model demonstrates. For example, Sears found that employee attitudes about the supervision they received and the work environment had a significant impact on customer satisfaction and shareholder results. As a result, Sears invested in managerial training to help managers do a better job of holding employees accountable for their jobs while giving them autonomy to perform their roles.[18]
- Audit whether the actions taken and the investments made produced the desired result.

Most companies' appraisal systems remain constant over a long time and through a variety of strategic emphases. However, when a company's strategy changes, its employees' behavior needs to change, too.[19] The fact that appraisal systems often do not change may account for why many managers see performance appraisal systems as having little impact on a firm's effectiveness.

**Figure 8.2**

Contamination and Deficiency of a Job Performance Measure

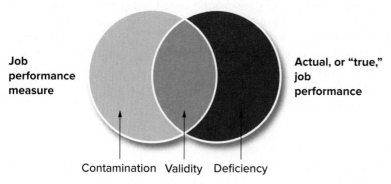

Job performance measure

Actual, or "true," job performance

Contamination  Validity  Deficiency

## VALIDITY

**Validity** is the extent to which a performance measure assesses all the relevant—and only the relevant—aspects of performance. This is often referred to as *content validity*. For a performance measure to be valid, it must not be deficient or contaminated. As you can see in Figure 8.2, one of the circles represents "true" job performance—all the aspects of performance relevant to success in the job. On the other hand, companies must use some measure of performance, such as a supervisory rating of performance on a set of dimensions or measures of the objective results on the job. Validity is concerned with maximizing the overlap between actual job performance and the measure of job performance (the green portion in the figure).

A performance measure is deficient if it does not measure all aspects of performance (the brown portion in the figure). An example is a system at a large university that assesses faculty members based more on research than teaching, thereby relatively ignoring a relevant aspect of performance.

A contaminated measure evaluates irrelevant aspects of performance or aspects that are not job related (the gold portion in the figure). The performance measure should seek to minimize contamination, but its complete elimination is seldom possible. An example of a contaminated measure is the use of actual sales figures for evaluating salespeople across very different regional territories. Often sales are highly dependent upon the territory (number of potential customers, number of competitors, economic conditions) rather than the actual performance of the salesperson. A salesperson who works harder and better than others might not have the highest sales totals because the territory simply does not have as much sales potential as others. Thus, these figures alone would be a measure that is strongly affected by things beyond the control of the individual employee.

## RELIABILITY

**Reliability** refers to the consistency of a performance measure. One important type of reliability is *interrater reliability*: the consistency among the individuals who evaluate the employee's performance. A performance measure has interrater reliability if two individuals give the same (or close to the same) evaluations of a person's job performance. Evidence seems to indicate that most subjective supervisory measures of job performance exhibit low reliability.[20] With some measures, the extent to which all the items rated are internally consistent is important (*internal consistency reliability*).

**Validity**
The extent to which a performance measure assesses all the relevant—and only the relevant—aspects of job performance.

**Reliability**
The consistency of a performance measure; the degree to which a performance measure is free from random error.

In addition, the measure should be reliable over time (*test-retest reliability*). A measure that results in drastically different ratings depending on when the measures are taken lacks test-retest reliability. For example, if salespeople are evaluated based on their actual sales volume during a given month, it would be important to consider their consistency of monthly sales across time. What if an evaluator in a department store examined sales only during May? Employees in the lawn and garden department would have high sales volumes, but those in the men's clothing department would have somewhat low sales volumes. Clothing sales in May are traditionally lower than in other months. One needs to measure performance consistently across time.

## ACCEPTABILITY

**Acceptability**
The extent to which a performance measure is deemed to be satisfactory or adequate by those who use it.

**Acceptability** refers to whether the people who use a performance measure accept it. Many elaborate performance measures are extremely valid and reliable, but they consume so much of managers' time that they refuse to use it. Alternatively, those being evaluated by a measure may not accept it.

Acceptability is affected by the extent to which employees believe the performance management system is fair. As Table 8.4 shows, there are three categories of perceived

**Table 8.4**
Categories of Perceived Fairness and Implications for Performance Management Systems

| FAIRNESS CATEGORY | IMPORTANCE FOR PERFORMANCE MANAGEMENT SYSTEM | IMPLICATIONS |
|---|---|---|
| Procedural fairness | Development | • Give managers and employees opportunity to participate in development of system<br>• Ensure consistent standards when evaluating different employees<br>• Minimize rating errors and biases<br>• Managers should collaborate with employees to set goals and key performance indicators |
| Interpersonal fairness | Use | • Give timely and complete feedback<br>• Allow employees to challenge the evaluation<br>• Provide feedback in an atmosphere of respect and courtesy<br>• Individual, team, and company goals and key performance indicators should be transparent to all employees |
| Outcome fairness | Outcomes | • Communicate expectations regarding performance evaluations and standards<br>• Communicate expectations regarding rewards<br>• The rationale for compensation and development decisions should be communicated and understood |

SOURCE: Based on B. Hancock, E. Hioe, and B. Schaninger, "The Fairness Factor in Performance Management," April 2018, from https://www.mcvkinsey.com, accessed January 10, 2019; *HBR Guide to Performance Management* (Boston MA: Harvard Business Review Press, 2017); S. W. Gilliland and J. C. Langdon, "Creating Performance Management Systems That Promote Perceptions of Fairness," in *Performance Appraisal: State of the Art in Practice*, ed. J. W. Smither (San Francisco: Jossey-Bass, 1998).

fairness: procedural, interpersonal, and outcome fairness. The table also shows specifically how the performance management system's development, use, and outcomes affect perceptions of fairness. In developing and using a performance management system, managers should take the steps shown in the column labeled "Implications" in Table 8.4 to ensure that the system is perceived as fair. Research suggests that performance management systems that are perceived as unfair are likely to be legally challenged, be used incorrectly, and decrease employee motivation to improve.[21]

## SPECIFICITY

**Specificity** is the extent to which a performance measure tells employees what is expected of them and how they can meet these expectations. Specificity is relevant to both the strategic and developmental purposes of performance management. If a measure does not specify what an employee must do to help the company achieve its strategic goals, then it does not achieve its strategic purpose. Additionally, if the measure fails to point out employees' performance problems, it is almost impossible for the employees to correct their performance.

Deloitte's performance management system for its project teams meets most of the criteria for a good performance management system.[22] Deloitte's goals are to recognize, observe, and motivate performance through the annual compensation decision, the project performance snapshot, and the weekly performance conversations. Deloitte's client needs tend to involve both short- and long-term projects that are too complex for any one employee to have the expertise needed to carry them out. So to meet its clients' needs Deloitte relies on employee teams. These teams include a team leader and employees who each bring a different skill set. To evaluate each team member's performance, Deloitte asks team leaders to answer four questions. These questions ask if the leader would award the person the highest possible compensation increase and bonus (measures overall performance and unique value to the organization), always want them on their team (measures ability to work well with others), if the person is a risk for low performance (identifies problems that might harm the customer), and is ready for promotion today (measures potential). These four questions each represent a specific performance dimension (pay, teamwork, poor performance, promotion) that is relevant to Deloitte's project teams. The team leaders were chosen as the raters because they were in the best position to see the performance of team members and in their role must make subjective judgments. The questions were used after they were tested to see if they differentiated ineffective from effective team members and were correlated with other performance outcomes measured in other ways such as engagement surveys.

For short-term projects, team member evaluations occur at the end of each project, and longer-term project evaluations occur quarterly. To ensure that the evaluations are driving team performance and are accepted by team members, every team leader has to check in with each team member once each week. During these conversations, team leaders discuss expectations, review priorities, and provide feedback on recent work. Team members are encouraged to initiate check-ins with team leaders who may otherwise forget to have the discussions because they have many demands on their time. Once each quarter, Deloitte's business leaders use the evaluations to review a group of employees, such as those with critical skills or who are eligible for promotion, to discuss the actions that need to be taken to develop that group. The questions provide input into compensation decisions made at the end of the year by business leaders who also consider the difficulty of project assignments and other contributions team members have made to Deloitte.

**Specificity**
The extent to which a performance measure gives detailed guidance to employees about what is expected of them and how they can meet these expectations.

# Approaches to Measuring Performance

An important part of effective performance management is establishing how we evaluate performance. This is difficult to do because performance is complex—it includes how employees perform their individual work tasks as well as contribute to teams and behave in ways that support their peers and the company.[23] What is considered effective performance and when, what, and how it is measured likely varies across positions. For example, what is measured often differs depending on if employees are in management or professional jobs (called "exempt") or not ("nonexempt").[24] The top measure for non-exempt employees is quality of work, whereas measures of the work quality of management and professional employees more often apply categories such as communication, decision making, leadership, and problem solving. Job knowledge, which formerly was the top measure for all jobs, more recently shows up only as a measure for exempt employees.

In this section, we explore different ways to evaluate performance: the comparative approach, the attribute approach, the behavioral approach, the results approach, and the quality approach. We also evaluate these approaches against the criteria of strategic congruence, validity, reliability, acceptability, and specificity. As you will see, all of these approaches have strengths and weaknesses. As a result, many companies' performance evaluations use a combination of approaches.

There is no one best approach to measuring performance. But to effectively contribute to organizational business strategy and goals and motivate employees, effective performance evaluation systems should measure both what gets accomplished (objectives) and how it gets accomplished (behaviors). Regardless of the approach used, the key is to provide employees with accurate and timely feedback about their performance, emphasize frequent performance discussions between managers and employees rather than one-way manager-led conversations, and simplify appraisal forms. For example, Gables Residential has found that encouraging managers and employees to have informal performance conversations (rather than manager-driven one-way communications about performance) throughout the year in combination with an annual formal performance review improves employee engagement and development.[25] Gables changed its appraisal form so that it focuses more on highlighting employees' achievements and development needs and less on evaluating past performance. The form is used in the annual formal performance review to facilitate performance discussions and to encourage managers to coach employees on how to better capitalize on their strengths. Employees are also encouraged to ask their managers to help them develop in areas they want they to improve.

Figure 8.3 shows an example of a performance management system that evaluates behavior and results. The results (project development) are linked to the goals of the business. The performance standards include behaviors that the employee must demonstrate to reach the results. The system provides feedback to the employee and holds both the employee and the manager accountable for changing behavior.

## THE COMPARATIVE APPROACH

The comparative approach to performance measurement requires the rater to compare an individual's performance with that of others. This approach usually uses some overall assessment of an individual's performance or worth and seeks to develop some ranking of the individuals within a work group. At least three techniques fall under the comparative approach: ranking, forced distribution, and paired comparison.

**Figure 8.3**

Example of a Performance Management System That Includes Behavior and Results

| Accountabilities and Key Results | Performance Standards | Interim Feedback | Actual Results | Performance Rating | Areas for Development | Action |
|---|---|---|---|---|---|---|
| Key result areas that the employee will accomplish during the review period. Should align with company values, business goals, and job description. | How the key result area will be measured (quality, cost, quantity). Focus on work methods and accomplishments. | Employee and manager discuss performance on an ongoing basis. | Review actual performance for each key result. | Evaluate performance on each key result.<br><br>1 = Outstanding<br>2 = Highly effective<br>3 = Acceptable<br>4 = Unsatisfactory | Specific knowledge, skills, and behaviors to be developed that will help employee achieve key results. | What employee and manager will do to address development needs. |
| <u>Project Development</u> Manage the development of project scope, cost estimate studies, and schedules for approval. | Develop preliminary project material for approval within four weeks after receiving project scope. Eighty percent of new projects receive approval. Initial cost estimates are within 5% of final estimates. | Preliminary project materials are developed on time. | By end of year, approvals were at 75%, 5% less than standard. | 3 | Increase knowledge of project management software. | Read articles, research, and meet with software vendors. |

## Ranking

*Simple ranking* requires managers to rank employees within their departments from highest performer to poorest performer (or best to worst). *Alternation ranking*, by contrast, consists of a manager looking at a list of employees, deciding who is the best employee, and crossing that person's name off the list. From the remaining names, the manager decides who the worst employee is and crosses that name off the list—and so forth.

Ranking has received specific attention in the courts. As discussed in Chapter 3, in the *Albemarle Paper v. Moody* case, the validation of the selection system was conducted using employee rankings as the measure of performance. The Court stated, "There is no way of knowing precisely what criteria of job performance that supervisors were considering, whether each supervisor was considering the same criteria—or whether, indeed, any of the supervisors actually applied a focused and stable body of criteria of any kind."[26]

## Forced Distribution

The *forced distribution* method also uses a ranking format, but employees are ranked in groups. This technique requires the manager to put certain percentages of employees into predetermined categories. Most commonly, employees are grouped into three, four, or five categories, usually of unequal size, indicating the best workers, the worst workers, and one or more categories in between. The insurance company American International Group (AIG) uses a forced distribution system in which AIG employees are ranked on a scale from 1 to 4.[27] Based on this system, only 10% of employees receive the top ranking of "1," 20% of employees receive a ranking of "2," 50% of employees receive a ranking of "3," and 20% receive the lowest ranking of "4." Employees with higher rankings receive much more year-end incentive pay such as bonuses than those with lower rankings (employees ranked in the top 10% will get much greater bonuses compared to their peers). The CEO advocated the implementation of the forced distribution system to ensure that the company is paying the best people for their performance and to better differentiate poor from high performers. The company had previously used ranking systems but found that over half of employees were evaluated as high performers.

Advocates of these systems say that they are the best way to identify high-potential employees who should be given training, promotions, and financial rewards and to identify the poorest performers who should be helped or asked to leave. Top-level managers at many companies have observed that despite corporate performance and return to shareholders being flat or decreasing, compensation costs have continued to spiral upward and performance ratings continue to be high. They question how there can be such a disconnect between corporate performance and employees' evaluations and compensation. Forced distribution systems provide a mechanism to help align company performance and employee performance and compensation. These managers argue that employees ranked in in the bottom 10% cause performance standards to be lowered, influence good employees to leave, and keep good employees from joining the company.

A forced distribution system helps managers tailor development activities to employees based on their performance. For example, as shown in Table 8.5, poor performers are given specific feedback about what they need to improve in their job and a timetable is set for their improvement. If they do not improve their performance, they are dismissed. Top performers are encouraged to participate in development activities such as job experiences, mentoring, and completion of leadership programs, which will help prepare them for top-management positions. The use of a forced distribution system is seen as a way for companies to increase performance, motivate employees, and open the door for new talent to join the company to replace poor performers.[28]

Table 8.5
Performance and
Development Based
on Forced
Distribution and
Ranking

| RANKING OR DISTRIBUTION CATEGORY | PERFORMANCE AND DEVELOPMENT PLAN |
|---|---|
| **A** Above average<br>Exceptional<br>A1 performer | • Accelerate development through challenging job assignments<br>• Provide mentor from leadership team<br>• Recognize and reward contributions<br>• Praise employee for strengths<br>• Consider leadership potential<br>• Nominate for leadership development programs |
| **B** Average<br>Meets expectations<br>Steady performer | • Offer feedback on how B can become a high performer<br>• Encourage development of strengths and improvement of weaknesses<br>• Recognize and reward employee contributions<br>• Consider enlarging job |
| **C** Below expectations<br>Poor performance | • Give feedback and agree upon what specific skills, behavior, and/or results need to be improved, with timetable for accomplishment<br>• Move to job that better matches skills<br>• Ask to leave the company |

SOURCES: Based on B. Axelrod, H. Handfield-Jones, and E. Michaels, "A New Game Plan for C Players," *HBR*, January 2002, pp. 80–88; A. Walker, "Is Performance Management as Simple as ABC?" *T + D*, February 2007, pp. 54–57; T. De Long and V. Vijayaraghavan, "Let's Hear It for B Players," *HBR*, June 2003, pp. 96–102.

Advocates say these systems force managers to make hard decisions about employee performance based on job-related criteria, rather than to be lenient in evaluating employees. Critics, by contrast, say the systems in practice are arbitrary, erroneously assume that employees' performance can be best summarized by a normal distribution, may be illegal, and cause poor morale.[29] For example, one work group might have 20% poor performers while another might have only high performers, but the process mandates that 10% of employees be eliminated from both groups. Also, in many forced distribution systems, an unintended consequence is that the bottom category tends to consist of minorities, women, and people over 40 years of age, causing discrimination lawsuits (we discuss legal issues affecting performance management later in the chapter). Finally, it is difficult to rank employees into distinctive categories when criteria are subjective or when it is difficult to differentiate employees on the criteria (such as teamwork or communications skills).

Research simulating different features of a forced system and other factors that influence company performance (e.g., voluntary turnover rate, validity of selection methods) suggests that forced distribution rating systems can improve the potential performance of a company's workforce.[30] The majority of improvement appears to occur during the first several years the system is used, mainly because of the large number of poorly performing employees who are identified and fired. Forced ranking is ethical as long as the system is clearly communicated, the system is part of a positive dimension of the organization's culture (innovation, continuous improvement), and the employees have the chance to appeal decisions.

Despite the potential advantages of forced choice systems, the potential negative side effects on morale, teamwork, recruiting, and shareholder perceptions should be considered before adopting such a system. Many companies are emphasizing the linkage between employees' performance and their development plan without using a forced distribution or ranking system. For example, Microsoft is no longer requiring its managers to evaluate its employees against one another and rank them on a scale from 1 to 5.[31] The system was abandoned because many employees complained that it resulted in unfair rankings, power struggles between managers over which of their employees could receive the more favorable rankings, and aggressive competition between employees. Also, the system was inconsistent with Microsoft's strategic emphasis on teamwork.

### Paired Comparison

The *paired comparison* method requires managers to compare every employee with every other employee in the work group, giving an employee a score of 1 every time he or she is considered the higher performer. Once all the pairs have been compared, the manager computes the number of times each employee received the favorable decision (i.e., counts up the points), and this becomes the employee's performance score.

The paired comparison method tends to be time consuming for managers and will become more so as organizations become flatter with an increased span of control. For example, a manager with 10 employees must make 45 ($10 \times {}^9/_2$) comparisons. However, if the group increases to 15 employees, 105 comparisons must be made.

### Evaluating the Comparative Approach

The comparative approach to performance measurement is an effective tool in differentiating employee performance; it virtually eliminates problems of leniency, central tendency, and strictness. This is especially valuable if the results of the measures are to be used in making administrative decisions such as pay raises and promotions. In addition, such systems are relatively easy to develop and in most cases easy to use; thus, they are often accepted by users.

One problem with these techniques, however, is their common failure to be linked to the strategic goals of the organization. Although raters can evaluate the extent to which individuals' performances support the strategy, this link is seldom made explicit. In addition, because of the subjective nature of the ratings, their validity and reliability depend on the raters themselves. Some firms use multiple evaluators to reduce the biases of any individual, but most do not. At best, we could conclude that their validity and reliability are modest.

These techniques lack specificity for feedback purposes. Based only on their relative rankings, individuals are completely unaware of what they must do differently to improve their ranking. This puts a heavy burden on the manager to provide specific feedback beyond that of the rating instrument itself. Finally, many employees and managers are less likely to accept evaluations based on comparative approaches. Evaluations depend on how employees' performance relates to that of other employees in a group, team, or department (normative standard) rather than on absolute standards of excellent, good, fair, and poor performance.

## THE ATTRIBUTE APPROACH

The attribute approach to performance management focuses on the extent to which individuals have certain attributes (characteristics or traits) believed desirable for the company's success. The techniques that use this approach define a set of traits—such as initiative, leadership, and competitiveness—and evaluate individuals on them.

**Table 8.6**
Example of a Graphic Rating Scale

The following areas of performance are significant to most positions. Indicate your assessment of performance on each dimension by circling the appropriate rating.

| PERFORMANCE DIMENSION | RATING | | | | |
| --- | --- | --- | --- | --- | --- |
| | DISTINGUISHED | EXCELLENT | COMMENDABLE | ADEQUATE | POOR |
| Knowledge | 5 | 4 | 3 | 2 | 1 |
| Communication | 5 | 4 | 3 | 2 | 1 |
| Judgment | 5 | 4 | 3 | 2 | 1 |
| Managerial skill | 5 | 4 | 3 | 2 | 1 |
| Quality performance | 5 | 4 | 3 | 2 | 1 |
| Teamwork | 5 | 4 | 3 | 2 | 1 |
| Interpersonal skills | 5 | 4 | 3 | 2 | 1 |
| Initiative | 5 | 4 | 3 | 2 | 1 |
| Creativity | 5 | 4 | 3 | 2 | 1 |
| Problem solving | 5 | 4 | 3 | 2 | 1 |

## Graphic Rating Scales

The most common form that the attribute approach to performance management takes is the *graphic rating scale*. Table 8.6 shows a graphic rating scale used in a manufacturing company. As you can see, a list of traits is evaluated by a five-point (or some other number of points) rating scale. The manager considers one employee at a time, circling the number that signifies how much of that trait the individual has. Graphic rating scales can provide a number of different points (a discrete scale) or a continuum along which the rater simply places a check mark (a continuous scale).

## Mixed-Standard Scales

*Mixed-standard scales* were developed to get around some of the problems with graphic rating scales. To create a mixed-standard scale, we define the relevant performance dimensions and then develop statements representing good, average, and poor performance along each dimension. These statements are then mixed with the statements from other dimensions on the actual rating instrument. An example of a mixed-standard scale is presented in Table 8.7.

As we see in the table, the rater is asked to complete the rating instrument by indicating whether the employee's performance is above (+), at (0), or below (–) the statement. A special scoring key is then used to score the employee's performance for each dimension. Thus, for example, an employee performing above all three statements receives a 7. If the employee is below the good statement, at the average statement, and above the poor statement, a score of 4 is assessed. An employee below all three statements is given a rating of 1. This scoring is applied to all the dimensions to determine an overall performance score.

Note that mixed-standard scales were originally developed as trait-oriented scales. However, this same technique has been applied to instruments using behavioral rather than trait-oriented statements as a means of reducing rating errors in performance appraisal.[32]

**Table 8.7**
An Example of a
Mixed-Standard
Scale

| Three traits being assessed: | Levels of performance in statements: |
|---|---|
| Initiative (INTV) | High (H) |
| Intelligence (INTG) | Medium (M) |
| Relations with others (RWO) | Low (L) |

Instructions: Please indicate next to each statement whether the employee's performance is above (+), equal to (0), or below (−) the statement.

| | | | | |
|---|---|---|---|---|
| INTV | H | 1. | This employee is a real self-starter. The employee always takes the initiative and his/her superior never has to prod this individual. | + |
| INTG | M | 2. | While perhaps this employee is not a genius, s/he is a lot more intelligent than many people I know. | + |
| RWO | L | 3. | This employee has a tendency to get into unnecessary conflicts with other people. | 0 |
| INTV | M | 4. | While generally this employee shows initiative, occasionally his/her superior must prod him/her to complete work. | + |
| INTG | L | 5. | Although this employee is slower than some in understanding things, and may take a bit longer in learning new things, s/he is of average intelligence. | + |
| RWO | H | 6. | This employee is on good terms with everyone. S/he can get along with people even when s/he does not agree with them. | − |
| INTV | L | 7. | This employee has a bit of a tendency to sit around and wait for directions. | + |
| INTG | H | 8. | This employee is extremely intelligent, and s/he learns very rapidly. | − |
| RWO | M | 9. | This employee gets along with most people. Only very occasionally does s/he have conflicts with others on the job, and these are likely to be minor. | − |

Scoring Key:

| STATEMENTS | | | SCORE |
|---|---|---|---|
| HIGH | MEDIUM | LOW | |
| + | + | + | 7 |
| + | + | + | 6 |
| + | + | + | 5 |
| − | 0 | + | 4 |
| − | − | + | 3 |
| − | − | 0 | 2 |
| − | − | − | 1 |

Example score from preceding ratings:

| | STATEMENTS | | | SCORE |
|---|---|---|---|---|
| | HIGH | MEDIUM | LOW | |
| Initiative | + | + | + | 7 |
| Intelligence | 0 | + | + | 6 |
| Relations with others | − | − | 0 | 2 |

## Evaluating the Attribute Approach

Attribute-based performance methods are quite easy to develop and are generalizable across a variety of jobs, strategies, and organizations. In addition, if much attention is devoted to identifying those attributes relevant to job performance and carefully defining them on the rating instrument, they can be as reliable and valid as more elaborate measurement techniques.

However, these techniques fall short on several of the criteria for effective performance management. There is usually little congruence between the techniques and the company's strategy. These methods are used because of the ease in developing them and because the same method (list of traits, comparisons) is generalizable across any organization and any strategy. In addition, these methods usually have vague performance standards that are open to different interpretations by different raters. Because of this, different raters often provide extremely different ratings and rankings. The result is that both the validity and reliability of these methods are usually low. This can lead to legal challenges. For example, the validity of graphic rating scales was questioned in the *Brito v. Zia* case.[33] In this case, Spanish-speaking employees had been terminated as a result of their performance appraisals. These appraisals consisted of supervisors' rating subordinates on a number of undefined dimensions such as volume of work, quantity of work, job knowledge, dependability, and cooperation. The court criticized the subjective appraisals and stated that the company should have presented empirical data demonstrating that the appraisal was significantly related to actual work behavior.

Virtually none of these techniques provides any specific guidance on how an employee can support the company's goals or correct performance deficiencies. In addition, when raters give feedback, these techniques tend to elicit defensiveness from employees. For example, how would you feel if you were told that on a five-point scale, you were rated a "2" in maturity? Certainly you might feel somewhat defensive and unwilling to accept that judgment, as well as any additional feedback. Also, being told you were rated a "2" in maturity doesn't tell you how to improve your rating.

## THE BEHAVIORAL APPROACH

The behavioral approach to performance management attempts to define the behaviors an employee must exhibit to be effective in the job. The various techniques define those behaviors and then require managers to assess the extent to which employees exhibit them. We discuss three techniques that rely on the behavioral approach.

### Behaviorally Anchored Rating Scales

A *behaviorally anchored rating scale (BARS)* is designed to specifically define performance dimensions by developing behavioral anchors associated with different levels of performance.[34] An example of a BARS is presented in Figure 8.4. As you can see, the performance dimension has a number of examples of behaviors that indicate specific levels of performance along the dimension.

To develop a BARS, we first gather a large number of critical incidents that represent effective and ineffective performance on the job. These incidents are classified into performance dimensions, and the ones that experts agree clearly represent a particular level of performance are used as behavioral examples (or anchors) to guide the rater. The manager's task is to consider an employee's performance along each dimension and determine where on the dimension the employee's performance fits using the behavioral anchors as guides. This rating becomes the employee's score for that dimension.

**Figure 8.4**
Task-BARS Rating
Dimension: Patrol
Officer

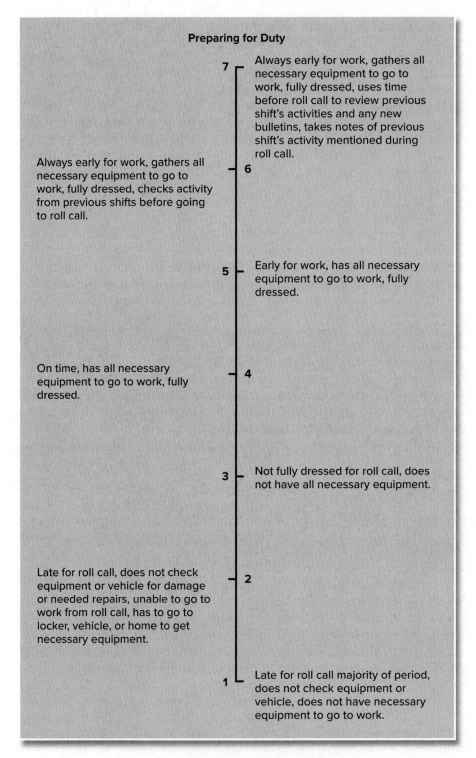

**Preparing for Duty**

7 — Always early for work, gathers all necessary equipment to go to work, fully dressed, uses time before roll call to review previous shift's activities and any new bulletins, takes notes of previous shift's activity mentioned during roll call.

Always early for work, gathers all necessary equipment to go to work, fully dressed, checks activity from previous shifts before going to roll call. — 6

5 — Early for work, has all necessary equipment to go to work, fully dressed.

On time, has all necessary equipment to go to work, fully dressed. — 4

3 — Not fully dressed for roll call, does not have all necessary equipment.

Late for roll call, does not check equipment or vehicle for damage or needed repairs, unable to go to work from roll call, has to go to locker, vehicle, or home to get necessary equipment. — 2

1 — Late for roll call majority of period, does not check equipment or vehicle, does not have necessary equipment to go to work.

SOURCE: Adapted from R. Harvey, "Job Analysis," in *Handbook of Industrial & Organizational Psychology*, 2nd ed., ed. M. Dunnette and L. Hough (Palo Alto, CA: Consulting Psychologists Press, 1991), p. 138.

Behavioral anchors have advantages and disadvantages. They can increase interrater reliability by providing a precise and complete definition of the performance dimension. A disadvantage is that they can bias information recall—that is, behavior that closely approximates the anchor is more easily recalled than other behavior.[35] Research has also demonstrated that managers and their subordinates do not make much of a distinction between BARS and trait scales.[36]

### Behavioral Observation Scales

A *behavioral observation scale (BOS)* is a variation of a BARS. Like a BARS, a BOS is developed from critical incidents.[37] However, a BOS differs from a BARS in two basic ways. First, rather than discarding a large number of the behaviors that exemplify effective or ineffective performance, a BOS uses many of them to more specifically define all the behaviors that are necessary for effective performance (or that would be considered ineffective performance). Instead of using, say, 4 behaviors to define 4 levels of performance on a particular dimension, a BOS may use 15 behaviors. An example of a BOS is presented in Table 8.8.

A second difference is that rather than assessing which behavior best reflects an individual's performance, a BOS requires managers to rate the frequency with which the employee has exhibited each behavior during the rating period. These ratings are then averaged to compute an overall performance rating.

The major drawback of a BOS is that it may require more information than most managers can process or remember. A BOS can have 80 or more behaviors, and the manager must remember how frequently an employee exhibited each of these behaviors over a 6- or 12-month rating period. This is taxing enough for one employee, but managers often must rate 10 or more employees.

A direct comparison of BOS, BARS, and graphic rating scales found that both managers and employees prefer BOS for differentiating good from poor performers, maintaining objectivity, providing feedback, suggesting training needs, and being easy to use among managers and subordinates.[38]

**Table 8.8**
An Example of a Behavioral Observation Scale (BOS) for Evaluating Job Performance

| Teamwork | | | | | | |
|---|---|---|---|---|---|---|
| (1) Works with team members to achieve common goals. | | | | | | |
| Almost Never | 1 | 2 | 3 | 4 | 5 | Almost Always |
| (2) Seeks input from team members. | | | | | | |
| Almost Never | 1 | 2 | 3 | 4 | 5 | Almost Always |
| (3) Communicates work due date changes to team members. | | | | | | |
| Almost Never | 1 | 2 | 3 | 4 | 5 | Almost Always |
| (4) Listens to team members concerns. | | | | | | |
| Almost Never | 1 | 2 | 3 | 4 | 5 | Almost Always |
| (5) Participates in team meetings. | | | | | | |
| Almost Never | 1 | 2 | 3 | 4 | 5 | Almost Always |
| (6) Helps team members with their work | | | | | | |
| Almost Never | 1 | 2 | 3 | 4 | 5 | Almost Always |
| | | | Total = _____ | | | |

| Below Adequate | Adequate | Full | Excellent | Superior |
|---|---|---|---|---|
| 6–10 | 11–15 | 16–20 | 21–25 | 26–30 |

Scores are set by management.

## Competency Models

**Competencies**
Sets of skills,
knowledge, and
abilities and personal
characteristics that
enable employees to
perform their jobs.

**Competency model**
Identifies and provides
a description of
competencies that are
common for an entire
occupation,
organization, job family,
or specific job.

**Competencies** are sets of skills, knowledge, abilities, and personal characteristics that enable employees to successfully perform their jobs.[39] A **competency model** identifies and provides descriptions of competencies that are common for an entire occupation, organization, job family, or a specific job. Competency models can be used for performance management. However, one of the strengths of competency models is that they are useful for a variety of HR practices including recruiting, selection, training, and development. Competency models can be used to help identify the best employees to fill open positions, and as the foundation for development plans that allow the employee and the manager to target specific strengths and development areas.

Table 8.9 shows the competency model that Luxottica Retail, known for premium, luxury, and sports eyewear sold through LensCrafters, Sunglass Hut, and Pearle Vision, developed for its associates in field and store positions.[40] The competency model includes leadership and managerial, functional, and foundational competencies. The goal was to define and identify competencies that managers could use for hiring, performance management, and training. Also, competencies would help associates identify and develop the skills they need to apply for different jobs.

To effectively use competency models for performance evaluation they must be up-to-date, drive business performance, be job related (valid), be relevant (or customized) for all of the company's business units, and provide sufficient detail to make an accurate assessment of employees' performance. At Luxottica Retail, developing competencies started with meetings with business leaders to understand their current and future business strategies. Business drivers were identified and questionnaires, focus groups, and meetings with managers and associates were used to identify important competencies and examples of behaviors related to each. To ensure they are relevant, competencies across business units and brands are reviewed every four or five years or whenever a major

**Table 8.9**
Luxottica Retail's
Competency Model

**Leadership and Managerial**
Leadership
Coach and develop others
Motivate others
Foster teamwork
Think strategically

**Functional**
Global perspective
Financial acumen
Business key performance indicators

**Foundational**
Critical thinking
Foster open communications
Build relationships and interpersonal skills
Develop and manage oneself
Adaptability and flexibility
Customer focus
Act with integrity
Diversity and multiculturalism
Drive and commitment

SOURCE: From C. Spicer, "Building a Competency Model," *HR Magazine*, April 2009, pp. 34–36.

change in jobs or business strategy occurs. Also, the weighting given to each set of competencies in the performance evaluation is reviewed to ensure that they are appropriate (e.g., what weights should be given to the functional skills). Depending on their relevance for a specific job, various combinations of these competencies are used for evaluating associates' performances. Associates are rated for each competency on a scale from 1 to 5, with "5" meaning the employee far exceeds expectations. HR, training and development, and operations teams worked together to define the levels of each competency, that is, what does it mean and what does the competency look like when an employee is rated "meets expectations" versus "below expectations"? This was necessary to ensure that managers are using a similar frame of reference when they evaluate associates using the competencies.

### Evaluation of the Behavioral Approach

The behavioral approach can be very effective. It can link the company's strategy to the specific behavior necessary for implementing that strategy. It provides specific guidance and feedback for employees about the performance expected of them. Most of the techniques rely on in-depth job analysis, so the behaviors that are identified and measured are valid. Because those who will use the system develop the measures, the acceptability is also often high. Finally, with a substantial investment in training raters, the techniques are reasonably reliable.

The major weaknesses have to do with the organizational context of the system. Although the behavioral approach can be closely tied to a company's strategy, the behaviors and measures must be continually monitored and revised to ensure that they are still linked to the strategic focus. This approach also assumes that there is "one best way" to do the job and that the behaviors that constitute this best way can be identified. One study found that managers seek to control behaviors when they perceive a clear relationship between behaviors and results. When this link is not clear, they tend to rely on managing results.[41] The behavioral approach might be best suited to less complex jobs (where the best way to achieve results is somewhat clear) and least suited to complex jobs (where there are multiple ways, or behaviors, to achieve success).

## THE RESULTS APPROACH

The results approach focuses on managing the objective, measurable results of a job or work group. This approach assumes that subjectivity can be eliminated from the measurement process and that results are the closest indicator of one's contribution to organizational effectiveness.[42] We examine three performance management systems that use results: the use of objectives, the balanced scorecard, and the productivity measurement and evaluation system.

### The Use of Objectives

The use of objectives is popular in both private and public organizations.[43] In a results-based system, the top-management team first defines the company's strategic goals for the coming year. These goals are passed on to the next layer of management, and these managers define the goals they must achieve for the company to reach its goals. This goal-setting process cascades down the organization so that all managers set goals that help the company achieve its goals.[44] These goals are used as the standards by which an individual's performance is evaluated.[45]

**Table 8.10**
An Example of an
Objectives Measure
of Job Performance

| KEY RESULT AREA | OBJECTIVE | % COMPLETE | ACTUAL PERFORMANCE |
|---|---|---|---|
| Loan portfolio management | Increase portfolio value by 10% over the next 12 months | 90 | Increased portfolio value by 9% over the past 12 months |
| Sales | Generate fee income of $30,000 over the next 12 months | 150 | Generated fee income of $45,000 over the past 12 months |

For example, a company goal might be to increase sales by 6% in the next year. This goal is linked to the sales team goal of achieving $500,000 in new sales. As a result of the team goal, the individual salesperson's goal is to achieve $100,000 in new sales this year, which represents a 10% improvement in sales over the previous year.

Results-based systems have three common components.[46] They require setting effective goals. The most effective goals are SMART goals. That is, the goals are specific (clearly stated, defining the result to be achieved), measurable (compared to a standard), attainable (difficult but achievable), relevant (linked to organizational success factors or goals), and timely (measured in deadlines, due dates, cycles, or schedules). Different types of measurements can be used for goals or objectives, including timeliness (e.g., responds to requests within 12 hours), quality (report provided clear information with no revisions necessary), quantity (increased sales by 25%), or financial metrics (e.g., reduced purchasing costs by 10%). An example of objectives used in a financial services firm is presented in Table 8.10. Goals are not usually set unilaterally by management but with the managers' and subordinates' participation. And the manager gives objective feedback throughout the rating period to monitor progress toward the goals.

Research on objectives has revealed two important findings regarding their effectiveness.[47] Of 70 studies examined, 68 showed productivity gains, while only 2 showed productivity losses, suggesting that objectives usually increase productivity. Also, productivity gains tend to be highest when there is substantial commitment to the objectives program from top management: an average increase of 56% when commitment was high, 33% when commitment was moderate, and 6% when commitment was low.

Clearly, use of an objectives system can have a positive effect on an organization's performance. Considering the process through which goals are set (involvement of staff in setting objectives), it is also likely that use of an objectives system effectively links individual employee performance with the firm's strategic goals. Evaluation of objectives, based on results or business-based metrics, removes the subjectivity from the evaluation process—employees either meet the objectives or they do not.

Table 8.11 shows how to best use objectives or goals in performance management. Waiting for goals to cascade down from company leaders, to division, function, and their team, takes too much time and employees have a difficult time understanding how their goals are related to company goals (line of sight). As a result, employees should set goals that as much as possible are linked to organizational goals. Goals should be SMART but also meaningful.[48] Rewards and incentives are best for motivating employees to achieve performance goals in jobs in which the results are easily measured and under employees' control. Goals typically focus just on results, not on behaviors, values, or how things get done. If you want employees to behave in certain ways (or avoid behaving in certain ways)

**Table 8.11**
Best Practices in
Goal Setting

1. Employees and managers should discuss and set no more than three to five goals.
2. Goals should be brief, meaningful, challenging, and include the results the employee is expected to achieve.
3. The time frame for goal achievement should be related to when they are expected to be accomplished.
4. The relationship between goals and rewards should be appropriate.
5. Goals should be "linked up" rather than "cascaded down." This means that functions, teams, and employees should set their own goals that are related to company goals.

SOURCES: Based on R. Hanson and E. Pulakos, *Putting the "Performance" Back in Performance Management* (Alexandria, VA: Society for Human Resource Management, 2015); R. Noe and L. Inks, *It's about People: How Performance Management Helps Middle Market Companies Grow Faster* (Columbus, OH: National Center for the Middle Market, Ohio State University Fisher College of Business, GE Capital, 2014): D. Grote, *How to Be Good at Performance Appraisals* (Boston, MA: Harvard University Press, 2011); A. Fox, "Put Plans into Action," *HR Magazine*, April 2013, pp. 27–31.

in achieving goals, you need to ensure that your performance management system includes evaluation of behaviors. Otherwise, for example, a goal emphasis on sales might cause employees to mislead customers and treat their peers poorly. The Competing through Environmental, Social, and Governance Practices box shows how the use of objectives can result in undesirable outcomes for a company's stakeholders.

## Balanced Scorecard

Some companies use the balanced scorecard to measure performance (we discussed the use of the balanced scorecard in Chapter 1). The balanced scorecard includes four perspectives of performance, including financial, customer, internal or operations, and learning and growth (see Table 1.8 in Chapter 1). The financial perspective focuses on creating sustainable growth in shareholder value, the customer perspective defines value for customers (e.g., service, quality), the internal or operations perspective focuses on processes that influence customer satisfaction, and the learning and growth perspective focuses on the company's capacity to innovate and continuously improve. Each of these perspectives is used to translate the business strategy into organizational, managerial, and employee objectives. Employee performance is linked with the business strategy through communicating and educating employees on the elements of the balanced scorecard, translating strategic objectives into measures for departments and employees, and linking rewards to performance measures.[49] Employees need to know the corporate objectives and how they translate into objectives for each business unit, and then develop their own and team objectives that are consistent with the business unit and company objectives. Effective balanced scorecards allow employees to understand the business strategy by looking only at the scorecard and the strategy map (the cause-and-effect relationships among the measures).

For example, for the customer perspective of the balanced scorecard, an airline might have on-time performance as a critical success factor.[50] Gate agents, ground crews, maintenance, and scheduling represent groups of employees who affect on-time performance. Gate agents have four roles that can influence boarding speed including check-in timeliness, effectively dealing with connections, flight documentation, and the boarding process. Gate agents' performance in these four roles should be evaluated because they influence key performance indicators related to on-time performance including cost savings, customer satisfaction, customer losses, and operational costs.

# COMPETING THROUGH ENVIRONMENTAL, SOCIAL, AND GOVERNANCE PRACTICES

## Wells Fargo: Boosting Sales Damages Stakeholders

Wells Fargo has historically been admired by its customers as a solid financial lender that avoided the problems that plagued other banks during the financial crisis of 2007–2009. But regulators found that employees opened as many as 2 million deposit and credit card accounts without customers' knowledge. Employees created fake accounts, invented personal identification numbers, and moved funds between customers' accounts without authorization. Wells Fargo also forced several hundred thousand customers who had auto loans to pay for insurance coverages they didn't need, making some customers default on their loans, which resulted in having their cars repossessed. To make things worse, Wells Fargo terminated employees because they either refused to participate in such aggressive cross-selling practices or reported these activities to the company's ethics hotline or human resources.

The aggressive cross-selling practices were motivated by extremely challenging performance objectives linked to incentives that rewarded employees and their managers for sales of products like checking accounts and credit cards. These objectives were based on Wells Fargo's business model, which depended on selling additional products to its customers who had checking and savings accounts. Many bank branch managers monitored employees' progress toward meeting sales goals hourly, and sales numbers from bank branches were reported to higher-level managers as frequently as seven times each day. Managers asked employees who failed to meet their sales objectives if they could get closer to hitting their goals by opening accounts for their family members or friends. Cross-selling benefits the bank because customers who have more products are not likely to change banks.

As a result of this scandal, Wells Fargo's reputation was tarnished, it likely lost potential customers, and senior management and employees responsible were fired. The company had to pay billions in fines and over $600 million to settle legal claims. Timothy Sloan, Wells Fargo's CEO, is working hard to rebuild customers' trust and the company's culture, which is strongly influenced by how it motivates employees. To do so, Wells Fargo shifted away from objectives and incentives based on cross-selling products to objectives based on customer service, customer usage, and growth in account balances. But some employees feel they are still being pressured to meet aggressive performance goals that they are unable to meet and fear retaliation if they speak out.

### DISCUSSION QUESTION

1. How can Wells Fargo prevent the use of objectives in its performance management system from having a negative impact on its employees and customers?

SOURCES: Based on E. Flitter and S. Cowley, "Wells Fargo Says Culture Better; Some Employees Disagree," *Columbus Dispatch*, March 10, 2019, p. A16; E. Glazer, "Wells Settles with 50 States," *Wall Street Journal*, December 29/30, 2018, pp. A1–A2; G. Colvin, "Can Wells Fargo Get Well?" *Fortune*, June 15, 2017, pp. 138–46; E. Glazer, "Wells Fargo Shakes Up Retail Unit," *Wall Street Journal*, March 10, 2017, p. B9; E. Glazer, "Wells Revamps Pay after Scandal," *Wall Street Journal*, January 7–8, 2016, pp. B1–B2; E. Glazer, C. Rexrode, and A. Andriotis, "Wells Fargo's Next Job: Fixing Its Mess," *Wall Street Journal*, December 28, 2016, pp. A1, A8; E. Glazer, "Wells Chief Quits under Attack," *Wall Street Journal*, October 13, 2016, pp. A1, A2; E. Glazer, "Customers Continue Pullback from Wells," *Wall Street Journal*, December 17–18, 2016, p. B4; E. Glazer, "Wells Fargo Tripped By Its Sales Culture," *Wall Street Journal*, September 16–17, 2016, pp. A1, A8; A. Beck, "Wells's Questionable Cross-Sales," *Wall Street Journal*, September 10–11, 2016, p. B12.

---

### Productivity Measurement and Evaluation System (ProMES)

The main goal of the Productivity Measurement and Evaluation System (ProMES) is to motivate employees to improve team or company-level productivity.[51] It is a means of measuring and feeding back productivity information to employees.

Team members try to map the relationship between specific outcomes and productivity and the relationships between effect and performance, performance and outcomes, and outcomes relationship to satisfaction of employee needs. ProMES consists of four steps. First, people in an organization identify the products, or the set of activities or objectives, the organization expects to accomplish. The organization's productivity depends on how well it produces these products. At a repair shop, for example, a product might be something like "quality of repair." Second, the staff defines indicators of the products. Indicators are measures of how well the products are being generated by the organization. Quality of repair could be indicated by (1) return rate (percentage of items returned that did not function immediately after repair) and (2) percentage of quality-control inspections passed. Third, the staff establishes the contingencies between the amount of the indicators and the level of evaluation associated with that amount. Fourth, a feedback system is developed that provides employees and work groups with information about their specific level of performance on each of the indicators. An overall productivity score can be computed by summing the effectiveness scores across the various indicators.

Research thus far strongly suggests that ProMES is effective in increasing productivity. (Figure 8.5 illustrates the productivity gains in the repair shop described previously.) The research also suggests the system is an effective feedback mechanism. However, users found it time consuming to develop the initial system.

## Evaluation of the Results Approach

The results approach minimizes subjectivity, relying on objective, quantifiable indicators of performance. Thus, it is usually highly acceptable to both managers and employees.

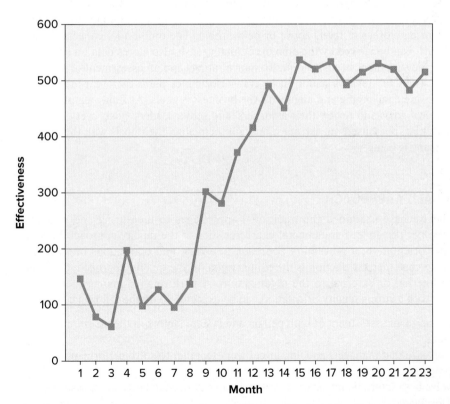

**Figure 8.5**

Increases in Productivity for a Repair Shop Using ProMES Measures

SOURCE: P. Pritchard, S. Jones, P. Roth, K. Stuebing, and S. Ekeberg, "The Evaluation of an Integrated Approach to Measuring Organizational Productivity," *Personnel Psychology*, 42, (1989), pp. 69–115.

Another advantage is that it links an individual's results with the organization's strategies and goals.

However, there are a number of challenges in using objective performance measures. Objective measurements can be both contaminated and deficient—contaminated because they are affected by things that are not under the employee's control and deficient because not all the important aspects of job performance are amenable to objective measurement. For example, consider how an economic recession can influence sales goals or, for a teacher, parental support for studying can influence student's achievement test scores. Another disadvantage is that individuals may focus only on aspects of their performance that are measured, neglecting those that are not. For example, if the large majority of employees' goals relate to productivity, it is unlikely they will be concerned with customer service. One study found that objective performance goals led to higher performance but that they also led to helping co-workers less.[52] It is important to identify if goals should be set at the individual, team, or department level. Setting employees' objectives may not be appropriate if work is team based. Individual objectives may undermine behaviors related to team success such as sharing information and collaboration. A final disadvantage is that, although results measures provide objective feedback, the feedback may not help employees learn how they need to change their behavior to increase their performance. If baseball players are in a hitting slump, simply telling them that their batting average is 0.190 may not motivate them to raise it. Feedback focusing on the exact behavior that needs to be changed (like taking one's eye off the ball or dropping one's shoulder) would be more helpful.[53]

Kimberly-Clark and Zulily take specific actions to deal with the challenges in using objectives.[54] At Kimberly-Clark, salaried employees use an online tool to set goals and report their progress, record accomplishments or mistakes, and ask for and give feedback to peers or employees at levels above or below them. The online tool collects the feedback, which can be viewed by the employee's manager. It also stores data on employees' strengths, development needs, and performance ratings and an assessment of their turnover risk. The CEO reviews senior managers' performance plans each year to make sure their goals are challenging and align with the businesses goals. At Zulily, employees can set their own goals and review their managers' and senior leaders' goals every quarter to see what they are focused on, ask questions, and help align their goals with the direction the company is going.

## THE QUALITY APPROACH

Thus far we have examined the traditional approaches to measuring and evaluating employee performance. Fundamental characteristics of the quality approach include a customer orientation, a prevention approach to errors, and continuous improvement. Improving customer satisfaction is the primary goal of the quality approach. Customers can be internal or external to the organization. A performance management system designed with a strong quality orientation can be expected to do the following:

- Emphasize an assessment of both person and system factors in the measurement system.
- Emphasize that managers and employees work together to solve performance problems.
- Involve both internal and external customers in setting standards and measuring performance.
- Use multiple sources to evaluate person and system factors.[55]

Based on this chapter's earlier discussion of the characteristics of an effective performance management system, it should be apparent to you that these characteristics are not just unique to the quality approach but are characteristics of an effective appraisal system.

Advocates of the quality approach believe that most U.S. companies' performance management systems are incompatible with the quality philosophy for a number of reasons:

1. Most existing systems measure performance in terms of quantity, not quality.
2. Employees are held accountable for good or bad results to which they contribute but do not completely control.
3. Companies do not share the financial rewards of successes with employees according to how much they have contributed to them.
4. Rewards are not connected to business results.[56]

Sales, profit margins, and behavioral ratings are often collected by managers to evaluate employees' performance. These are person-based outcomes. An assumption of using these types of outcomes is that the employee completely controls them. However, according to the quality approach, these types of outcomes should not be used to evaluate employees' performance because they do not have complete control over them (i.e., they are contaminated). For example, for salespeople, performance evaluations (and salary increases) are often based on attainment of a sales quota. Salespeople's abilities and motivations are assumed to be directly responsible for their performance. However, quality-approach advocates argue that better determinants of whether a salesperson reaches the quota are "systems factors" (such as competitors' product price changes) and economic conditions (which are not under the salesperson's control).[57] Holding employees accountable for outcomes affected by systems factors is believed to result in dysfunctional behavior, such as falsifying sales reports, budgets, expense accounts, and other performance measures, as well as lowering employees' motivation for continuous improvement.

Quality advocates suggest that the major focus of performance evaluations should be to provide employees with feedback about areas in which they can improve. Two types of feedback are necessary: (1) subjective feedback from managers, peers, and customers about the personal qualities of the employee and (2) objective feedback based on the work process itself using statistical process control methods.

At Just Born, the company that makes Peeps and Mike and Ike candy, the performance management process is designed with a strong quality orientation.[58] The performance management system is designed to facilitate employee improvement (a forward-looking approach) rather than focus entirely on what the employee has accomplished during the past year. Also, managers and employees are encouraged to work together to solve performance problems.

The performance management system is part of the company's broader people development system (PDS), which is designed to ensure that learning and development align with business strategy and drive business results while ensuring employees have the skills needed to succeed in their current and future jobs. The PDS includes the performance management process, learning and career development processes, and a succession planning process. Information from each of these systems is shared to ensure that employees are developing the skills needed for their current jobs through training and on-the-job experiences, as well as preparing for their future career interests. Just Born's performance management system starts with a planning meeting between the employee and his or her manager. At this meeting, the employee's role and strategic goals of the department are discussed. The manager and the employee agree on up to four personal objectives that will help the department meet its objectives and the employee achieve the specific deliverables described in the job description. Two competencies that the employee needs to deliver or improve on are identified. The manager and the employee work together to develop a learning plan to help the employee gain the competencies. During the year, the employee and the manager meet to discuss the progress in meeting the deliverables and improving the competencies. Pay decisions made at the end of each fiscal year are based on the achievement of performance objectives and learning goals.

Just Born also uses the Wow . . . Now improvement process, a customized Kaizen process to improve business processes and results. The Wow . . . Now improvement process includes teaching employees how to identify improvement opportunities, collect data, make improvements, measure results, and, based on the results, refine practices. Kaizen, the Japanese word for improvement, is one of the underlying principles of lean manufacturing and total quality management (we discussed lean thinking in Chapter 1). **Kaizen** refers to practices participated in by employees from all levels of the company that focus on continuous improvement of business processes.[59] As the Wow . . . Now improvement process illustrates, Kaizen involves considering a continuous cycle of activities including planning, doing, checking, and acting (PDCA).

**Kaizen**
Practices participated in by employees from all levels of the company that focus on continuous improvement of business processes.

Statistical process control techniques are important in the quality approach. These techniques provide employees with an objective tool to identify causes of problems and potential solutions. These techniques include process-flow analysis, cause-and-effect diagrams, Pareto charts, control charts, histograms, and scattergrams. *Process-flow analysis* identifies each action and decision necessary to complete work, such as waiting on a customer or assembling a television set. Process-flow analysis is useful for identifying redundancy in processes that increase manufacturing or service time. In *cause-and-effect diagrams*, events or causes that result in undesirable outcomes are identified. Employees try to identify all possible causes of a problem. The feasibility of the causes is not evaluated, and as a result, cause-and-effect diagrams produce a large list of possible causes. A *Pareto chart* highlights the most important cause of a problem. In a Pareto chart, causes are listed in decreasing order of importance, where *importance* is usually defined as the frequency with which that cause resulted in a problem. The assumption of Pareto analysis is that the majority of problems are the result of a small number of causes. Figure 8.6 shows a Pareto chart listing the reasons managers give for not selecting current employees for a job vacancy. *Control charts* involve collecting data at multiple points in time. By collecting data at different times, employees can identify what factors contribute to an outcome and when they tend to occur. Figure 8.7 shows the percentage of employees hired internally for a company for each quarter between 2013 and 2015. Internal hiring increased dramatically during the third quarter of 2014. The use of control charts helps employees understand the number of internal candidates who can be expected to be hired each year. Also, the control chart shows that the amount of internal hiring conducted during the third quarter of 2014 was much larger than normal. *Histograms* display distributions of large sets of data. Data are grouped into a smaller number of categories or classes. Histograms are useful for understanding the amount of variance between an outcome and the expected value or average outcome.

*Scattergrams* show the relationship between two variables, events, or different pieces of data. Scattergrams help employees determine whether the relationship between two variables or events is positive, negative, or zero.

**Figure 8.6**
Pareto Chart

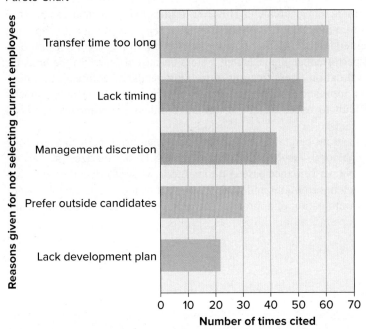

SOURCE: From Clara Carter, *HR Magazine*. Copyright 1992. Reprinted with permission of Society for Human Resource Management.

**Figure 8.7**
Control Chart

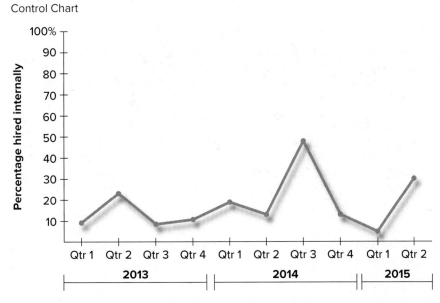

SOURCE: Based on Clara Carter, *HR Magazine*. Copyright 1992.

**LO 8-6**

Choose the most effective approach to performance measurement for a given situation.

## Evaluation of the Quality Approach

The quality approach relies primarily on a combination of the attribute and results approaches to performance measurement. However, traditional performance appraisal systems focus more on individual employee performance, whereas the quality approach adopts a systems-oriented focus.[60] Many companies may be unwilling to completely abandon their traditional performance management system because it serves as the basis for personnel selection validation, identification of training needs, or compensation decisions. Also, the quality approach advocates evaluation of personal traits (such as cooperation), which are difficult to relate to job performance unless the company has been structured into work teams.

In summary, organizations can take five approaches to measuring performance: comparative, attribute, behavioral, results, and quality. Table 8.12 summarizes the various approaches to measuring performance based on the criteria we set forth earlier and illustrates that each approach has strengths and weaknesses. As a result, effective performance evaluations involve a combination of approaches including assessment of objectives and behaviors.

**Table 8.12**

Evaluation of Approaches to Performance Measurement

| | | CRITERIA | | | |
|---|---|---|---|---|---|
| **APPROACH** | **STRATEGIC CONGRUENCE** | **VALIDITY** | **RELIABILITY** | **ACCEPTABILITY** | **SPECIFICITY** |
| Comparative | Poor, unless manager takes time to make link | Can be high if ratings are done carefully | Depends on rater, but usually no measure of agreement used | Moderate; easy to develop and use but resistant to normative standard | Very low |
| Attribute | Usually low; requires manager to make link | Usually low; can be fine if developed carefully | Usually low; can be improved by specific definitions of attributes | High; easy to develop and use | Very low |
| Behavioral | Can be quite high | Usually high; minimizes contamination and deficiency | Usually high | Moderate; difficult to develop, but accepted well for use | Very high |
| Results | Very high | Usually high; can be both contaminated and deficient | High; main problem can be test–retest—depends on timing of measure | High; usually developed with input from those to be evaluated | High regarding results, but low regarding behaviors necessary to achieve them |
| Quality | Very high | High, but can be both contaminated and deficient | High | High; usually developed with input from those to be evaluated | High regarding results, but low regarding behaviors necessary to achieve them |

# Choosing a Source for Performance Information

Whatever approach to performance management is used, it is necessary to decide whom to use as the source of the performance measures. Each source has specific strengths and weaknesses. We discuss five primary sources: managers, peers, direct reports, self, and customers. Many companies include manager and self-assessment of performance. This helps facilitate a conversation about performance during the appraisal meeting and on a more frequent basis.

**LO 8-7**
Discuss the advantages and disadvantages of the different sources of performance information.

## MANAGERS

Managers are the most frequently used source of performance information. It is usually safe to assume that supervisors have extensive knowledge of the job requirements and that they have had adequate opportunity to observe their employees—in other words, that they have the ability to rate their employees. In addition, because supervisors have something to gain from the employees' high performance and something to lose from low performance, they are motivated to make accurate ratings.[61] Finally, feedback from supervisors is strongly related to performance and to employee perceptions of the accuracy of the appraisal if managers attempt to observe employee behavior or discuss performance issues in the feedback session.[62]

**LO 8-8**
Choose the most effective source(s) for performance information for any situation.

Whirlpool's performance management system involves setting and aligning goals with the business strategy, providing feedback and engaging in performance conversations, and evaluating progress toward the goals.[63] Whirlpool found that its managers were spending too much time on evaluating goal progress, which took time away from aligning goals and providing feedback and having performance conversations, the most important parts of the performance management process. To help managers reallocate their time, Whirlpool provided them with coaching and development resources. The "Manager Minute" consisted of videos, blogs, and discussion forums provided by Whirlpool's leaders that offered tips, advice, and stories to inspire managers to become great at managing their employees' performance. Seventy-three percent of the managers reported they were using the Manager Minute for advice and were acting on it.

Problems with using supervisors as the source of performance information can occur in particular situations. In some jobs, for example, the supervisor does not have an adequate opportunity to observe the employee performing his job duties. For example, in outside sales jobs, the supervisor does not have the opportunity to see the salesperson at work most of the time. This usually requires that the manager occasionally spend a day accompanying the salesperson on sales calls. However, on those occasions, the employee will be on his or her best behavior, so there is no assurance that performance that day accurately reflects performance when the manager is not around.

Also, some supervisors may be so biased against a particular employee that to use the supervisor as the sole source of information would result in less-than-accurate measures for that individual. Favoritism is a fact of organizational life, but it is one that must be minimized as much as possible in performance management.[64] Thus, the performance evaluation system should seek to minimize the opportunities for favoritism to affect ratings. One way to do this is not to rely on only a supervisor's evaluation of an employee's performance.

## PEERS

Another source of performance information is the employee's co-workers. Peers are an excellent source of information in a job such as law enforcement, where the supervisor does not always observe the employee. Peers have expert knowledge of job requirements, and they often have the most opportunity to observe the employee in day-to-day activities. Also, peers are often in the best position to praise and recognize each other's performance on a daily basis. Peer evaluations can be even more motivating than managers' evaluations because, unlike managers, peers are not expected to provide feedback.

For example, at Etsy, employees can request feedback from their peers and direct reports.[65] Feedback providers can choose to give their comments anonymously, and feedback receivers have the choice to seek training or coaching from an HR business partner or manager. Technology has made it easier for employees to seek feedback from their peers and managers (and to provide it). See the Competing through Technology box later in the chapter for more on some apps that fill this role.

Peers also bring a different perspective to the evaluation process, which can be valuable in gaining an overall picture of the individual's performance. In fact, peers have been found to provide extremely valid assessments of performance in several different settings.[66]

One disadvantage of using peer ratings is the potential for friendship to bias ratings.[67] Little empirical evidence suggests that this is often a problem, however. Another disadvantage is that when the evaluations are made for administrative decisions, peers often find the situation of being both rater and ratee uncomfortable. When these ratings are used only for developmental purposes, however, peers react favorably.[68]

## DIRECT REPORTS

**Upward feedback**
A performance appraisal process for managers that includes subordinates' evaluations.

Direct reports are employees who report to a manager. Direct reports are an especially valuable source of performance information when managers are evaluated. Direct reports often have the best opportunity to evaluate how well a manager treats employees. **Upward feedback** refers to appraisals that involve collecting subordinates' evaluations of a manager's behavior or skills. To attract and keep talented employees, Dell Inc., the Texas-based computer company, recently took steps to focus not only on financial goals but also on making the company a great place to work.[69] Dell uses upward feedback to help sustain its "culture code" and develop its leaders. To be a successful leader at Dell requires humility: having confidence in your ability, being willing to take on challenges, but always welcoming feedback. Managers are rated by their employees on semiannual "Tell Dell" surveys. Managers who receive less than 50% favorable scores on five statements receive less favorable compensation, bonus, and promotion opportunities and are required to take additional training. Table 8.13 shows the five statements. Managers are

**Table 8.13**
Example of Upward Feedback Survey Statements from "Tell Dell" Surveys

- Even if I were offered a comparable position with similar pay and benefits at another company, I would stay at Dell.
- I receive ongoing feedback that helps me to improve my performance.
- My manager/supervisor supports my efforts to balance my work and personal life.
- My manager/supervisor is effective at managing people.
- I can be successful at Dell and still retain my individuality.

SOURCE: Based on A. Pomeroy, "Agent of Change," *HR Magazine*, May 2005, pp. 52–56.

expected to work continuously to improve their scores. Their goal is to receive at least 75% favorable ratings from employees on the five statements. The Evidence-Based HR box shows the relationship between employee turnover and evaluations of their managers' behavior. One study found that managers viewed receiving upward feedback more positively when receiving feedback from subordinates who were identified, but subordinates preferred to provide anonymous feedback. When subordinates were identified, they inflated their ratings of the manager.[70]

## EVIDENCE-BASED HR

Twice each year Kronos asks its 5,300 employees to provide upward feedback to their managers. That is, employees rate their managers on their behaviors such as whether they talked with them about career development in the past six months. Kronos found that for managers whose ratings were in the bottom 25%, 73% of employees planned to stay with the company in the next year. For managers who scored in the top 25%, 94% of their employees planned to stay.

SOURCE: V. Fuhrmans, "These Employees Rate Their Bosses Twice Each Year," *Wall Street Journal*, January 4, 2018, p. B7.

One problem with subordinate evaluations is that they give subordinates power over their managers, thus putting the manager in a difficult situation.[71] This can lead to managers' emphasizing employee satisfaction over productivity. However, this happens only when administrative decisions are based on these evaluations. As with peer evaluations, it is a good idea to use subordinate evaluations only for developmental purposes. To assure subordinates that they need not fear retribution from their managers, it is necessary to use anonymous evaluations and at least three subordinates for each manager.

### SELF

Although self-ratings are not often used as the sole source of performance information, they can still be valuable.[72] Obviously, individuals have extensive opportunities to observe their own behavior, and they usually have access to information regarding their results on the job. An important aspect of performance management at Analysis Group, a firm that provides economic, financial, and strategy consulting to law firms, corporations, and government agencies, is the self-evaluation that every partner completes.[73] The self-evaluation summarizes each partner's accomplishments for the year, including business sold and who they hired and mentored. This reflects a performance emphasis on both how the partner is contributing to the firm's financial health as well as what the partner is doing to ensure the future health and growth of the business. Meetings are held throughout the year to discuss each person's contributions and identify their development objectives.

One problem with self-ratings, however, is a tendency toward inflated assessments. Research has found that self-ratings for personal traits as well as overall performance ratings tend to be lenient, compared to ratings from other sources.[74] This stems from two sources. If the ratings are going to be used for administrative decisions (e.g., for pay raises), it is in the employees' interests to inflate their ratings. Ample evidence in the social psychology literature indicates that individuals attribute their poor performance to external causes, such as a co-worker who they think has not provided them with timely information. Although self-ratings are less inflated when supervisors provide frequent performance feedback, it is not advisable to use them for administrative purposes.[75] The best use of self-ratings is as a prelude to the performance feedback session to get employees thinking about their performance and to focus discussion on areas of disagreement.

## CUSTOMERS

Many companies are involving customers in their evaluation systems. One writer has defined *services* this way: "Services is something which can be bought and sold but which you cannot drop on your foot."[76] Because of the unique nature of services—the product is often produced and consumed on the spot—supervisors, peers, and subordinates often do not have the opportunity to observe employee behavior. Instead, the customer is often the only person present to observe the employee's performance and thus is the best source of performance information.

Most companies in service industries use customer evaluations of employee performance. Marriott Corporation provides a customer satisfaction card in every room and mails surveys to a random sample of customers after their stay in a Marriott hotel. Whirlpool's Consumer Services Division requires service technicians to ask customers to use their notebook computer to complete a survey immediately after they have serviced their appliances. Umami Burger restaurants provide three jars for customers to evaluate their experience: happiness with service (green), average feelings (yellow), and below expectations (red).[77] Customers are asked to toss a chip in the jar that best matches their experience. This provides Umami's managers with immediate feedback every time a customer places a chip in a jar, as well as cumulative feedback on customer experiences during the day. They can use this feedback to discuss with the restaurant team what's working and what needs to be fixed.

Using customer evaluations of employee performance is appropriate in two situations.[78] The first is when an employee's job requires direct service to the customer or linking the customer to other services within the company. Second, customer evaluations are appropriate when the company is interested in gathering information to determine what products and services the customer wants. That is, customer evaluations serve a strategic goal by integrating marketing strategies with human resource activities and policies. Customer evaluations collected for this purpose are useful for both evaluating the employee and helping to determine whether changes in other HRM activities (such as training or the compensation system) are needed to improve customer service.

The weakness of customer surveys is their expense, particularly if printing, postage, telephone, and labor are involved. On-site surveys completed using handheld computers help eliminate these expenses.

In conclusion, the best source of performance information often depends on the particular job. One should choose the source or sources that provide the best opportunity to observe employee behavior and results. Often, eliciting performance information from a

### Global Work Teams Require Going beyond Managerial Appraisals

BlueJeans is a leading provider of cloud-based video communications services. Its mission is to make online meetings easy to join and use so employees can work productively. Although BlueJeans has its corporate headquarters in California, its over 500 employees are globally distributed in places such as Bengaluru and London.

To build the most innovative and effective technology aides, face-to-face video communications require that employees collaborate with each other in teams regardless of where they are located. BlueJeans uses 360-degree performance reviews for employees to get feedback on their performance from their peers and feedback on their strengths and areas of improvement from their managers. The 360-degree feedback system also gives employees the opportunity to give feedback to their boss about what they can do to help improve teamwork.

The results of the 360-degree performance reviews have been positive. Ninety-nine percent of employees completed peer reviews. Managers find the system helpful for providing information they can use to have performance and development conversations with employees who work for them, but not on a daily or even weekly basis because they are located around the world. Employees like the system because it provides insight into what competencies they need to develop and has made it easier to have conversations about their career with their managers. From BlueJeans perspective, the 360-degree feedback system has helped create a culture of feedback that recognizes and develops talent within the company.

**DISCUSSION QUESTION**

1. Why are 360-degree appraisals particularly useful for global teams?

SOURCES: Based on "BlueJeans Turns Up Worldwide Collaboration with Reflektive," from www.reflektive.com, accessed January 8, 2019; www.bluejeans.com.

---

variety of sources results in a performance management process that is accurate and effective. In fact, one recent popular trend in organizations is called **360-degree appraisal**.[79] This technique consists of having multiple raters (boss, peers, subordinates, customers) provide input into a manager's evaluation. The major advantage of the technique is that it provides a means for minimizing bias in an otherwise subjective evaluation technique. It has been used primarily for strategic and developmental purposes and is discussed in greater detail in Chapter 9.[80] The Competing through Globalization box shows how 360-degree appraisals are especially useful for companies such as BlueJeans that have employees located around the world working as project teams.

## Use of Technology in Performance Management

Technology is influencing performance management systems in three ways. First, many companies are moving to Web-based online paperless performance management systems. These systems help companies ensure that performance goals across all levels of the organization are aligned, they provide managers and employees with greater access to performance information, and they provide tools for understanding and using the performance management process.[81]

**360-degree appraisal**
A performance appraisal process for managers that includes evaluations from a wide range of persons who interact with the manager. The process includes self-evaluations as well as evaluations from the manager's boss, subordinates, peers, and customers.

**LO 8-9**
Discuss the potential advantages of social performance management and electronic monitoring for performance management.

### Want to Give Feedback? There's an App for That

As companies move toward continuous performance management, they are offering homegrown apps or apps from companies like Impraise, Reflektive, and Engagedly to enable peers and managers to quickly provide feedback and recognition. IBM's Checkpoint app allows employees to set short-term performance goals and managers to provide feedback on their progress. Employees and managers at Mozilla can use an app to send each other colorful "badges" to recognize good performance. The badges include slogans such as "you rock" or "kicking butt." Also, employees can receive feedback and coaching from peers and managers by posting short questions about their performance, such as "What did you think about my speech?"

Goldman Sachs uses an app, Ongoing Feedback 360+, that lets an employee's manager and colleagues deliver informal feedback at any time. The idea is that when an employee completes a big transaction, presentation, or product launch, others can praise wins or offer ideas for doing better next time. The employee can view a summary of the year's feedback on a dashboard display. The Ongoing Feedback app is intended to support Goldman's efforts to empower employees and create a high-performance work system where they will want to stay.

Uber uses an app that includes sensors in a driver's smartphone to detect when the driver moves or touches his or her phone, such as during texting. The app also tracks when drivers speed, cut corners, or brake severely. The purpose of the app is to help drivers improve by providing them with more detailed data than the ratings they receive from customers. The data also provide a record that can protect them from groundless customer complaints.

**DISCUSSION QUESTION**

1. What would you do to ensure that employees are willing to use apps to provide feedback and recognition to their peers and act on the feedback they receive?

SOURCE: Based on H. Clancy, "How Am I Doing?" *Fortune*, March 1, 2017, p. 34; D. MacMillan, "Uber to Monitor Actions by Drivers in Safety Push," *Wall Street Journal*, June 30, 2016; M. Weinstein, "Annual Review under Review," *Training*, July/August 2016, pp. 22–29; C. Zillman, "IBM Is Blowing Up Its Annual Performance Review," *Fortune*, February 1, 2016; B. Hassell, "IBM's New Checkpoint Reflects Employee Preferences," *Workforce*, April 2016, p. 12; Goldman Sachs, "Human Capital Management," http://www.goldmansachs.com, accessed May 23, 2018; "A New Era for Goldman Sachs and Performance Appraisals," *Impraise* blog, https://blog.impraise.com, accessed May 23, 2018; Jenny Surane, "Goldman Sachs Introduces Real-Time Employee Performance Reviews," *Bloomberg Quint*, April 23, 2017, https://www.bloombergquint.com; Liz Hoffman, "Goldman Goes beyond Annual Review with Real-Time Employee Feedback," *Wall Street Journal*, April 21, 2017, https://www.wsj.com.

---

**Social performance management**
Social media and microblogs similar to Facebook, LinkedIn, and Yammer that allow employees to quickly exchange information, talk to each other, provide coaching, and receive feedback and recognition in the form of electronic badges.

Second, social media tools similar to Facebook and Twitter are increasingly being used to deliver timely feedback. **Social performance management** refers to systems similar to Facebook, LinkedIn, and Yammer and apps that allow employees to quickly exchange information, talk to each other, provide coaching, and receive recognition. Social performance management is especially valued by Millennials and Generation Z employees, who want more frequent feedback about their performance. This preference has been reinforced by their having grown up connecting to others through social networking via smartphones and computers.[82] Baby Boomers may be more likely to believe that feedback involves judgment, compared to younger generations, who see feedback as an opportunity to learn, but high performers of all ages are likely to seek and value feedback. As emphasized earlier in the chapter, performance feedback is a critical part of the performance management process that should not be limited to quarterly, midyear, or annual formal performance evaluations. Also, peers and co-workers can often give more timely and accurate feedback and recognition than busy managers. The Competing through Technology box describes how apps are being used to make it easier to give and receive performance feedback.

Third, companies are relying on electronic tracking and monitoring systems to ensure that employees are working when and how they should be and to block access to certain websites (such as those containing pornographic images). These systems include hand-print and fingerprint recognition systems, global positioning systems (GPS), software that can track employees using smartphones and notebook computers, and wearables.

For example, at the New York law firm Akin & Smith LLC, paralegals, receptionists, and clerks clock in by placing their finger on a sensor kept at a secretary's desk. The managing partners believe the system improves productivity and keeps everyone honest, holding them to their lunch times.[83]

In the trucking industry, drivers are monitored continually.[84] An onboard computer records whether the driver is on or off duty, documents the driver's gas mileage, and tells him or her where to get gas. If the truck stops while the driver is on duty, he or she is asked to provide an explanation. The electronic monitoring system built in to the computer tells the driver which route to follow and records even slight deviations from the route due to traffic or accidents. UPS uses a computer analysis program to monitor its delivery drivers. This helps them avoid wasting time and fuel on left-hand turns on their routes. It also helps promote driver safety by documenting seat-belt usage and how many feet a driver backs up, which is a dangerous maneuver. Shuttle Express company vans are equipped with cameras, which allows the company to determine if accidents are the driver's fault.

Some hospitals are experimenting with the use of computer vision using monitors that are placed in hallways, next to patient's beds, and in operating rooms.[85] The video images detected by these monitors can be analyzed by a computer using an algorithm to identify certain movements. The idea is to improve patient care by monitoring behavior such as whether a doctor stopped at a soap dispenser to wash their hands after they entered a patient's room (hand-washing is key to stop the spread of preventable infections in hospitals). The data can be digitally stored to track compliance over time allowing incentives and training programs to be implemented in units with low levels of handwashing. Another possible intervention is creating hand sanitizers with a light that will flash to alert doctors to wash their hands if computer vision detects they haven't done so within a short time after entering a patient's room.

Companies are using software that analyzes employees' computers and creates a profile.[86] Over time the software is able to create a baseline of normal behavior, including where they log in, what programs and databases they use, and which external websites they browse. It also provides a score for users (a risk score) based on what dangers they may pose to the company, such as stealing data or new product designs or viewing pornography. Software called Scout can be used to evaluate the content of employees' e-mail and other communications. The software scans for variations in language usage in the e-mails such as an increase in the use of phrases such as "medical bills" or "missed payments," which may mean the employee is at an increased risk for stealing.

Wearables allow us to track our sleep, steps, and exercise levels. Companies offer health-tracking wearables to employees as part of wellness programs designed to reduce health care costs. For example, IBM and Appirio distribute Fitbits to employees to encourage them to exercise and maintain a healthy lifestyle.[87] Appirio used data from the Fitbits to negotiate a reduction in premiums from the company's health insurance provider. Wearables can also be used to track our movements and personal interactions.[88] For example, at Florida Hospital Celebration Health, nurses and patient care technicians wear badges with sensors that allow tracking of their visits to patients' rooms and nurses' stations. The tracking helped the hospital determine that nurses were spending more time finding medicines that were understocked at certain nursing stations. The monitoring helped the hospital improve its supply procedures.

Despite the potential increased productivity and efficiency benefits that can result from these systems, they still present concerns.[89] Critics argue that these systems threaten to reduce the workplace to an electronic sweatshop in which employees are treated as robots that are monitored to maximize productivity for every second they are at work. Electronic monitoring systems threaten employees' right to privacy and dignity to work without being monitored. Also, time-tracking software may be inaccurate. Federal and state lawsuits have been filed against several companies who use time-tracking software, including American Airlines and Kroger.[90] These lawsuits allege that employees work hours are not correctly counted, and as a result, they are being paid less wages than they earned for the amount of time they are working. For example, an employee may work 7 hours and 15 minutes each day but the tracking software rounds their hours worked to 7 hours. This means for every five-day workweek, they are not receiving wages for one and a quarter hours of work. Over several years this can result in employees losing thousands of dollars from their pay!

Some critics argue that electronic tracking systems are needlessly surveilling and tracking employees when there is no reason to believe that anything is wrong. Good managers know what their employees are doing, and electronic systems should not be a substitute for good management. Critics also argue that such systems result in less productivity and motivation, demoralize employees, and create unnecessary stress. A mentality is created that employees always have to be at their desks to be productive. Wearable devices have the potential to gather a much broader range of information than other types of monitoring technology. But most employees don't know what data are being collected, and health and personal data collected by a wearable are not necessarily private or secure. The EEOC requires participation in company wellness programs linked to health insurance plans to be voluntary. But, even if the adoption of wearables is optional, employees may feel pressure to participate and resent the need to do so.

However, electronic monitoring can ensure that time is not abused, it can improve scheduling, and it can help motivate workers and improve performance.[91] To avoid the potential negative effects of electronic monitoring, managers must communicate to employees why they are being monitored. Monitoring can also be used as a way for more experienced employees to coach less experienced employees.

## REDUCING RATER ERRORS, POLITICS, AND INCREASING RELIABILITY AND VALIDITY OF RATINGS

**LO 8-10**
Distinguish types of rating errors, and explain how to minimize each in a performance evaluation.

Research consistently reveals that humans have tremendous limitations in processing information. Because we are so limited, we often use *heuristics*, or simplifying mechanisms, to make judgments, whether about investments or about people.[92] These heuristics, which appear often in subjective measures of performance, cause unconscious bias, which can lead to rater errors and incorrect attributions or reasons we use to explain an employee's performance. As we discussed in Chapter 7, unconscious bias is a judgment outside of our consciousness that affects decisions based on background, culture, and personal experience. We are all subject to unconscious bias. For example, research has found that men tend to receive more feedback linked to a business outcome than do women. It doesn't matter whether the manager conducting the performance evaluation was a man or a woman.[93]

Table 8.14 shows the different types of rating errors. The "similar to me" error is based on stereotypes the rater has about how individuals with certain characteristics are expected to perform.[94] Leniency, strictness, and central tendency are known as distributional errors because the rater tends to use only one part of the rating scale.

**Appraisal politics**
A situation in which evaluators purposefully distort a rating to achieve personal or company goals.

**Appraisal politics** refer to evaluators purposefully distorting a rating to achieve personal or company goals. Research suggests that several factors promote appraisal politics. These factors are inherent in the appraisal system and the company culture. Appraisal politics are most likely to occur when raters are accountable to the employee being rated,

| RATER ERROR | DESCRIPTION |
|---|---|
| Similar to me | Individuals who are similar to us in race, gender, background, interest, beliefs, and the like receive higher ratings than those who are not. |
| Contrast | Ratings are influenced by comparison between individuals instead of an objective standard (e.g., employee receives lower-than-deserved ratings because he or she is compared to outstanding peers). |
| Leniency | Rater gives high ratings to all employees regardless of their performance. |
| Strictness | Rater gives low ratings to all employees regardless of their performance. |
| Central tendency | Rater gives middle or average ratings to all employees despite their performance. |
| Halo | Rater gives employee high ratings on all aspects of performance because of an overall positive impression of the employee. |
| Horns | Rater gives employee low ratings on all aspects of performance because of an overall negative impression of the employee. |

**Table 8.14**
Typical Rater Errors

there are competing rating goals, and a direct link exists between performance appraisal and highly desirable rewards. Also, appraisal politics are likely to occur if top executives tolerate distortion or are complacent toward it, and if distortion strategies are part of "company folklore" and are passed down from senior employees to new employees.

There are four approaches to reducing rating errors.[95] They include rater error training, frame-of-reference training, unconscious bias training, and calibration meetings. *Rater error training* attempts to make managers aware of rating errors and helps them develop strategies for minimizing those errors.[96] These programs consist of having the participants view video-recorded vignettes designed to elicit rating errors such as "contrast." They then make their ratings and discuss how the error influenced the ratings. Finally, they get tips to avoid committing those errors. This approach has been shown to be effective for reducing errors, but there is evidence that reducing rating errors can also reduce accuracy.[97]

*Rater accuracy training*, also called *frame-of-reference training*, attempts to emphasize the multidimensional nature of performance and to get raters to understand and use the same idea of high, medium, and low performance when making evaluations. This involves providing examples of performance for each dimension and then discussing the actual or "correct" level of performance that the example represents.[98] Accuracy training seems to increase accuracy, provided that the raters are held accountable for ratings, job-related rating scales are used, and raters keep records of the behavior they observe.[99]

In addition to these approaches (as we discussed in Chapter 7), many companies, such as Microsoft, Google, Facebook, and Dow Chemical, are requiring employees to participate in unconscious bias training programs to reduce the potential influence of unconscious bias in performance evaluations and other work-related decisions (e.g., promotions).[100] These training programs focus on making employees aware of unconscious bias and reducing its impact by slowing down decision making and carefully considering reasons behind and language used in judgments.

An important way to help ensure that performance is evaluated consistently across managers and to reduce the influence of unconscious bias, rating errors, and appraisal politics is to hold calibration meetings.[101] **Calibration meetings** provide a way to discuss employees'

**Calibration meetings**
A way to discuss employees' performance with the goal of ensuring that similar standards are applied to their evaluations.

performance with the goal of ensuring that similar standards are applied to their evaluations. These meetings include managers responsible for conducting performance appraisals and their managers; they are facilitated by an internal HR representative or an external consultant. In the meetings, each employee's performance rating and the manager's reasons for the ratings are discussed. Managers have the opportunity to discuss the definition of each performance rating and ask questions. The calibration meetings help managers identify if their ratings are too positive or negative or tend to be based on employees' most recent performance. Managers are more likely to provide accurate evaluations that are well documented when they know they may have to justify them in a calibration meeting. Research shows that calibration meetings result in changes in about one-quarter of performance ratings, mostly those that varied significantly from the average.[102] The meeting resulted in performance ratings lowered four times as often as they were increased. As a result of calibration meetings, over time managers ratings became less extremely positive or negative. Also, employees viewed the calibration process as fair but managers saw it as increasing the demands on their time.

Calibration meetings can also help eliminate politics by discussing how performance ratings relate to business results. To minimize appraisal politics, managers also should keep in mind the characteristics of a fair appraisal system, shown in Table 8.4. Thus, managers should also do the following:

- Build top-management support for the appraisal system and actively discourage distortion.
- Give raters some latitude to customize performance objectives and criteria for their ratees.
- Recognize employee accomplishments that are not self-promoted.
- Provide employees with access to information regarding which behaviors are desired and acceptable at work.
- Encourage employees to actively seek and use feedback to improve performance.
- Make sure that constraints such as the budget do not drive the process.
- Make sure that appraisal processes are consistent across the company.
- Foster a climate of openness to encourage employees to be honest about weaknesses.[103]

# Performance Feedback

Once the expected performance has been defined and employees' performances have been measured, it is necessary to feed that performance information back to the employees so that they can correct any deficiencies. The performance feedback process is complex and provokes anxiety for both the manager and the employee.

Few of us feel comfortable sitting in judgment of others. The thought of confronting others with what we perceive to be their deficiencies causes most of us to shake in our shoes. If giving negative feedback is painful, receiving it can be excruciating—thus the importance of the performance feedback process.

### THE MANAGER'S ROLE IN AN EFFECTIVE PERFORMANCE FEEDBACK PROCESS

If employees are not made aware of how their performance is not meeting expectations, their performance will almost certainly not improve. In fact, it may get worse. Effective managers provide specific performance feedback to employees in a way that elicits positive behavioral responses. Because of the importance of performance feedback for an effective performance management system, many companies are training managers on how to provide feedback. For example, Lubrizol Corporation, a chemical manufacturer based in Wickliffe, Ohio, requires that managers enroll in a two-day training course designed to help them provide meaningful feedback.[104] The company's goal is to become recognized as the best developer of people. The training course focuses on how managers give feedback, who they need help from, and how they can hold themselves accountable. To contribute to the effectiveness of a performance management system through providing effective feedback, managers should consider the recommendations in this section.[105]

## Feedback Should Be Given Frequently, Not Once a Year

There are three reasons for this. First, managers have a responsibility to correct performance deficiencies immediately on becoming aware of them. If performance is subpar in January, waiting until December to appraise the performance could mean an 11-month productivity loss. Second, a major determinant of the effectiveness of a feedback session is the degree to which the subordinate is not surprised by the evaluation. An easy rule to follow is that employees should receive such frequent performance feedback that they already know almost exactly what their formal evaluation will be. Third, many employees, especially Millennials, want more frequent and candid performance feedback from managers beyond what is provided once or twice a year during their formal performance review.[106]

Consider how FORUM Credit Union encourages employees to seek feedback and managers to provide it.[107] FORUM Credit Union uses formal check-ins to help managers provide and employees receive more frequent feedback. Each quarter, employees are sent a questionnaire that asks them to respond to four or five questions. The completed questionnaire is sent to the employee's manager, who reviews it and schedules a meeting to discuss the answers. Some managers have monthly meetings with employees, but at a minimum quarterly manager–employee conversations are required.

## Create the Right Context for the Discussion

Managers should choose a neutral location for the feedback session. The manager's office may not be the best place for a constructive feedback session because the employee may associate the office with unpleasant conversations. Managers should describe the meeting as an opportunity to discuss the role of the employee, the role of the manager, and the relationship between them. Managers should also acknowledge that they would like the meeting to be an open dialogue.

## Ask the Employee to Rate His or Her Performance before the Session

Having employees complete a self-assessment before the feedback session can be very productive. It requires employees to think about their performance over the past rating period, and it encourages them to think about their weaknesses. Although self-ratings used for administrative decisions are often inflated, there is evidence that they may actually be lower than supervisors' ratings when done for developmental purposes. Another reason a self-assessment can be productive is that it can make the session go more smoothly by focusing discussion on areas where disagreement exists, resulting in a more efficient session. Finally, employees who have thought about past performance are more able to participate fully in the feedback session.

## Have Ongoing, Collaborative Performance Conversations

Managers should use a "problem-solving" or collaborative approach to work with employees to solve performance problems in an atmosphere of respect and encouragement. When employees participate in the feedback session, they are consistently satisfied with the process. (Recall the discussion of fairness earlier in this chapter.) Participation includes allowing employees to voice their opinions of the evaluation, as well as to discuss performance goals and development needs.

**Table 8.15**

Examples of
Questions That Start
a Collaborative,
Ongoing
Performance
Conversation

- What's working?
- Where did you get stuck?
- How can I help?
- What have you learned?
- What would you do differently next time?
- What skills would you like to develop?
- What would you like to discuss today?
- What do you think the next steps are?
- When can I check-in with you next?

SOURCE: Based on M. Buckingham, "Out with the Old in with ...," *TD*, August 2016, pp. 44–48; "Goodyear
Performance Management Optimization Case Study," presented on September 6, 2016, to MHR 4328 Performance
Management class, The Ohio State University.

Moving to an ongoing collaborative performance conversation is necessary to reduce
the anxiety, uncertainty, and feelings of lack of fairness and control that employees typically experience in a manager-driven "tell-and-sell" or "tell-and-listen" approach.[108] One
study found that, other than satisfaction with one's supervisor, participation was the single most important predictor of satisfaction with the feedback session.[109] Table 8.15 provides examples of questions that managers can use to start a collaborative ongoing
performance conversation with their employees.

### Recognize Effective Performance through Praise
One usually thinks of performance feedback sessions as focusing on the employee's performance problems. This should never be the case. The purpose of the session is to give
accurate performance feedback, which entails recognizing effective performance as well
as poor performance. Praising effective performance provides reinforcement for that
behavior. It also adds credibility to the feedback by making it clear that the manager is not
just identifying performance problems.

### Focus on Solving Problems
A common mistake that managers make in providing performance feedback is to try to
use the session as a chance to punish poorly performing employees by telling them how
utterly lousy their performance is. This only reduces the employees' self-esteem and
increases defensiveness, neither of which will improve performance.

To improve poor performance, a manager must attempt to solve the problems causing
it. This entails working with the employee to determine the actual cause and then agreeing
on how to solve it. For example, a salesperson's failure to meet a sales goal may be the
result of lack of a proper sales pitch, lack of product knowledge, or stolen sales by another
salesperson. Each of these causes requires a different solution. Without a problem-solving
approach, however, the correct solution might never be identified.

### Focus Feedback on Behavior or Results, Not on the Person
One of the most important things to do when giving negative feedback is to avoid questioning the employee's worth as a person. This is best accomplished by focusing the discussion on the employee's behaviors or results, not on the employee. Saying, "You're
screwing up! You're just not motivated!" will bring about more defensiveness and ill feelings than saying, "You did not meet the deadline that you agreed to because you spent too
much time on another project."

### At Penn Station East Coast Subs, STEAKS Are Not Just for Eating

Penn State East Coast Subs specializes in grilled submarine sandwiches, hand-cut fries, and hand-squeezed lemonade. Penn Station East Coast Subs is not only encouraging managers to have more frequent performance conversations but helping ensure they are effective. To do so, Penn Station East Coast Subs provides its managers with a feedback model that uses the STEAKS acronym.

Setting up the conversation (S) emphasizes that the manager needs to communicate the purpose of the conversation to the employees so they know what to expect. Take turns evaluating behavior (T) means that the manager should give the employees the opportunity to provide their opinion of their work behavior. Letting the employees provide their opinion helps prevent employees from becoming defensive, thus avoiding conflict and creating conditions for a productive performance conversation. Communicate the effect of the performance (E) means the manager has to let the employees know how their behavior affects customers, their peers, or the overall business. To align with standards (A), managers need to explain work policies, why they are necessary, and highlight differences between employees' performance and the policies. In addition, the feedback needs to focus on specific improvements or key behaviors (K) that the employees need to change. Last, managers need to summarize the conversation, making sure there is agreement on what was discussed, necessary changes, and next steps (S). They need to follow up with the employees at a later date to determine their progress in changing their behavior and provide help and assistance if necessary.

To ensure STEAKS is adopted, general managers use the model in their performance conversations with assistant managers. This helps reinforce the importance of assistant managers adopting it for their performance conversations with line employees. Preliminary evaluation of the STEAKS model has shown that the number of internal promotions has increased in those store locations that have adopted the model, and franchisees believe the model helps ensure consistency in the quality of sandwiches and customer service across stores.

**DISCUSSION QUESTION**

1. If you were a manager, which of the steps in the STEAKS model do you think would be most difficult to adopt when providing feedback? Explain why.

SOURCE: Based on L. Vaught, "Providing Meaningful Feedback at Penn Station," *Training*, July/August 2017, pp. 51–52; "Our Product," from www.penn-station.com, accessed January 10, 2019.

### Minimize Criticism

One way to avoid personalizing poor performance is to focus on the situation (where the problem behavior occurred), specific behaviors that occurred in the situation, and the results of the behavior for peers, customers, and if appropriate, for themselves.[110] Having been confronted with a performance, a change is in order. However, if the manager personalizes poor performance the employee may get defensive, fail to listen to the feedback, and as a result not change their performance.

### Agree to Specific Goals and Set a Date to Review Progress

The importance of goal setting cannot be overemphasized. It is one of the most effective motivators of performance.[111] Research has demonstrated that it results in increased satisfaction, motivation to improve, and performance improvement.[112] Besides setting goals, the manager must also set a specific follow-up date to review the employee's performance toward the goal. This provides an added incentive for the employee to take the goal seriously and work toward achieving it.

The Integrity in Action box shows how Penn Station East Coast Subs is helping managers have more effective performance conversations.

# What Managers Can Do to Diagnose Performance Problems and Manage Employees' Performance

**LO 8-12**

Identify the cause of a performance problem.

As we emphasized in the previous section, employees need performance feedback to improve their current job performance. As we discuss in Chapter 9, performance feedback is also needed for employees to develop their knowledge and skills for the future. In addition to understanding how to effectively give employees performance feedback, managers need to be able to diagnose the causes of performance problems and take actions to improve and maintain employee performance. For example, giving performance feedback to marginal employees may not be sufficient to improve their performance.

## DIAGNOSING THE CAUSES OF POOR PERFORMANCE

Many different reasons can cause an employee's poor performance. For example, poor performance can be due to lack of employee ability, misunderstanding of performance expectations, lack of feedback, or the need for training an employee who does not have the knowledge and skills needed to meet the performance standards. When diagnosing the causes of poor performance, it is important to consider whether the poor performance is detrimental to the business. That is, is poor performance critical to completing the job, and does it affect business results? If it is detrimental, then the next step is to conduct a performance analysis to determine the cause of poor performance. The different factors that should be considered in analyzing poor performance are shown in Figure 8.8. For example, if an employee understands the expected level of performance, has been given sufficient feedback, understands the consequences, but lacks the knowledge and skills needed to meet the performance standard, this suggests that the manager may want to consider training the employee to improve performance, moving the employee to a different job that better fits that person's skills, or discharging the employee and making sure that selection methods to find a new employee measure the level of knowledge and skills needed to perform the job.

After conducting the performance analysis, the manager should meet with the employee to discuss the results, agree to the next steps that the manager and employee will take to improve performance (e.g., training, providing resources, giving more feedback), discuss the consequences of failing to improve performance, and set a time line for improvement. This type of discussion is most beneficial if it occurs more frequently than the quarterly or yearly performance review, so that performance issues can be dealt with quickly, before they have adverse consequences for the company (and the employee). In the next section, we discuss the actions that should be considered for different types of employees.

## ACTIONS FOR MANAGING EMPLOYEES' PERFORMANCE

Table 8.16 shows actions for the manager to take with four different types of employees. As the table highlights, managers need to take into account employees' ability, motivation, or both in considering ways to improve performance. To determine an employee's level of ability, a manager should consider if he or she has the knowledge, skills, and abilities needed to perform effectively. Lack of ability may be an issue if an employee is new or the job has changed recently. To determine employees' level of motivation, managers need to consider if employees are doing a job they want to do and if they feel they are being

## Input

Does the employee recognize what he or she is supposed to do?

Are the job flow and procedures logical?

Do employees have the resources (tools, equipment, technology, time) needed for successful performance?

Are other job demands interfering with good performance in this area?

## Employee Characteristics

Does the employee have the necessary skills and knowledge?

Does the employee know why the desired performance level is important?

Is the employee mentally, physically, and emotionally able to perform at the expected level?

## Feedback

Has the employee been given information about his or her performance?

Is performance feedback relevant, timely, accurate, specific, and understandable?

## Performance Standard/Goals

Do performance standards exist?

Does the employee know the desired level of expected performance?

Does the employee believe she or he can reach the performance standard?

## Consequences

Are consequences (rewards, incentives) aligned with good performance?

Are the consequences of performance valuable to the employee?

Are performance consequences given in a timely manner?

Do work-group or team norms encourage employees not to meet performance standards?

**Figure 8.8**

Factors to Consider in Analyzing Poor Performance

SOURCES: Based on G. Rummler, "In Search of the Holy Performance Grail," *Training and Development*, April 1996, pp. 26–31; C. Reinhart, "How to Leap over Barriers to Performance," *Training and Development*, January 2000, pp. 20–24; F. Wilmouth, C. Prigmore, and M. Bray, "HPT Models: An Overview of the Major Models in the Field," *Performance Improvement* 41 (2002), pp. 14–21.

appropriately paid or rewarded. A sudden negative change in an employee's performance may indicate personal problems.

Employees with high ability and motivation include likely good and outstanding performers (*solid performers*). Table 8.16 emphasizes that managers should not ignore employees with high ability and high motivation. Managers should provide development opportunities to keep them satisfied and effective. Some individuals who are outstanding or good performers may be candidates for leadership positions within the company. They will need challenging development experiences and exposure to different aspects of the

**Table 8.16**
Ways to Manage
Employees'
Performance

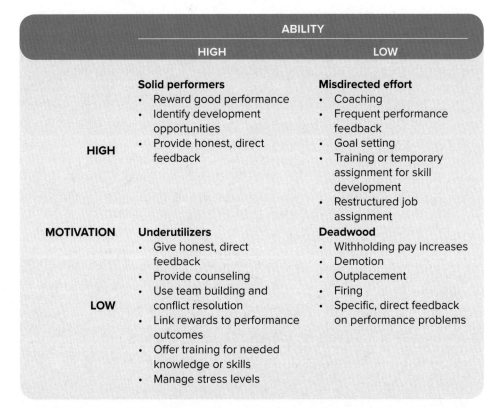

| | ABILITY | |
|---|---|---|
| | **HIGH** | **LOW** |
| **HIGH** | **Solid performers**<br>• Reward good performance<br>• Identify development opportunities<br>• Provide honest, direct feedback | **Misdirected effort**<br>• Coaching<br>• Frequent performance feedback<br>• Goal setting<br>• Training or temporary assignment for skill development<br>• Restructured job assignment |
| **LOW** | **Underutilizers**<br>• Give honest, direct feedback<br>• Provide counseling<br>• Use team building and conflict resolution<br>• Link rewards to performance outcomes<br>• Offer training for needed knowledge or skills<br>• Manage stress levels | **Deadwood**<br>• Withholding pay increases<br>• Demotion<br>• Outplacement<br>• Firing<br>• Specific, direct feedback on performance problems |

MOTIVATION

SOURCES: Based on M. London, *Job Feedback* (Mahwah, NJ: Lawrence Erlbaum Associates, 1997), pp. 96–97; H. Aguinis and E. O'Boyle, Jr., "Star Performers in the Twenty-First Century," *Personnel Psychology* 67 (2014), pp. 313–50; D. Grote, *How to Be Good at Performance Appraisals* (Boston: Harvard University Press, 2011); J. Conger and A. Church, "The 3 Types of C Players and What to Do About Them," February 1, 2018, from https://hbr.org accessed January 10, 2019.

business. We discuss development experiences in Chapter 9. Other employees may not desire positions with managerial responsibility. These employees need development opportunities to help keep them engaged in their work and to avoid obsolescence.

Finally, there are different reasons why employees are considered poor performers (see Table 8.16). Poor performance resulting from lack of ability but not motivation (*misdirected effort*) may be improved by skill development activities such as training or temporary assignments. Managers with employees who have the ability but lack motivation (*underutilizers*) need to consider actions that focus on interpersonal problems or incentives. These actions include making sure that incentives or rewards that the employee values are linked to performance and making counseling available to help employees deal with personal problems or career or job dissatisfaction. Chronic poor performance by employees with low ability and motivation (*deadwood*) indicates that outplacement or firing may be the best solution.

**Performance improvement plan (PIP)**
A plan that describes the performance changes that a poorly performing employee needs to make in a specified time period or face termination.

Many companies use a performance improvement plan to try to improve poorly performing employees.[113] A **performance improvement plan (PIP)** refers to a plan that describes the performance changes that a poorly performing employee needs to make in a specified time period or face termination. In a PIP, a manager needs to be specific about both the changes the employee is expected to make and the time frame for doing so. The manager is expected to try to help the employee improve his or her performance through coaching, training, and feedback. If the desired changes are not made in the expected time frame, the employee is notified that he or she will be fired if job performance does not improve in another time period, typically 30–60 days.

Performance tends to vary over time due to changes in tasks, assignments, and business goals.[114] As a result, managers should consider the categories shown in Table 8.16 but give employees the chance to change. One way to do this is to have frequent performance conversations with employees, which helps them recognize the need to either change or maintain their performance. Actively managing employees by setting expectations, making project assignments based on their skills and interests, and holding employees accountable for their performance makes a difference.

# Developing and Implementing a System That Follows Legal Guidelines

We now discuss the legal issues and constraints affecting performance management. Because performance measures play a central role in administrative decisions such as promotions, pay raises, and discipline, employees who sue an organization over these decisions ultimately attack the measurement systems on which the decisions were made. Two types of cases have dominated: discrimination and unjust dismissal.

In discrimination suits, the plaintiff often alleges that the performance measurement system unjustly discriminated against the plaintiff because of age, race, gender, or national origin. Many performance measures are subjective, and we have seen that individual biases can affect them, especially when those doing the measuring harbor racial or gender stereotypes.

In *Brito v. Zia*, the Supreme Court essentially equated performance measures with selection tests.[115] It ruled that the *Uniform Guidelines on Employee Selection Procedures* apply to evaluating the adequacy of a performance appraisal instrument. This ruling presents a challenge to those involved in developing performance measures because a substantial body of research on race discrimination in performance rating has demonstrated that both white and black raters give higher ratings to members of their own racial group, even after rater training.[116] There is also evidence that the discriminatory biases in performance rating are worse when one group makes up a small percentage of the work group. When the vast majority of the group is male, females receive lower ratings; when the minority is male, males receive lower ratings.[117]

In the second type of suit, an unjust dismissal suit, the plaintiff claims that the dismissal was for reasons other than those the employer claims. For example, an employee who works for a defense contractor might blow the whistle on the company for defrauding the government. If the company fires the employee, claiming poor performance, the employee may argue that the firing was, in fact, because of blowing the whistle on the employer—in other words, that the dismissal was unjust. The court case will likely focus on the performance measurement system used as the basis for claiming the employee's performance was poor. Unjust dismissal also can result from terminating for poor performance an employee who has a history of favorable reviews and raises. This may occur especially when a new evaluation system is introduced that results in more experienced older employees receiving unsatisfactory reviews. Rewarding poor performers or giving poor performers positive evaluations because of an unwillingness to confront a performance issue undermines the credibility of any performance management system. This makes it difficult to defend termination decisions based on a performance appraisal system.

For example, Baltimore-based MRA Systems Inc., a subsidiary of General Electric, paid $130,000 to settle an age discrimination lawsuit.[118] An employee received a lower performance rating, despite his successful job performance, because of his age, which was 61. In addition, MRA Systems had to provide at least two hours of mandatory training on federal laws prohibiting employment discrimination to all managers, supervisors, and other employees who participate in the performance evaluation process or assignment decisions. The EEOC sued Wisconsin Plastics Inc. (WPI), a metal and plastic products manufacturer, for violating federal law by firing several Hmong and Hispanic employees because of their national origin.[119] WPI fired the Hmong and Hispanic employees based on 10-minute observations that marked them down for their English skills even though those skills were not needed to perform their jobs. The fired employees had received satisfactory ratings on their annual performance evaluations.

Because of the potential costs of discrimination and unjust dismissal suits, an organization needs to determine exactly what the courts consider a legally defensible performance management system. Based on reviews of such court decisions, we offer the following characteristics of a system that will withstand legal scrutiny:[120]

1. The system should be developed by conducting a valid job analysis that ascertains the important aspects of job performance. The requirements for job success should be clearly communicated to employees.
2. The system should be based on either behaviors or results; evaluations of ambiguous traits should be avoided. Also, performance discussions should focus on work behavior and results other than questioning potential underlying reasons for behavior and results, such as a physical or mental disability.
3. Raters should be trained in how to use the system rather than simply given the materials and left to interpret how to conduct the appraisal.
4. There should be some form of review by upper-level managers of all the performance ratings, and there should be a system for employees to appeal what they consider to be an unfair evaluation.
5. The organization should provide some form of performance counseling or corrective guidance to help poor performers improve their performance before being dismissed. Both short- and long-term performance goals should be included.
6. Multiple raters should be used, particularly if an employee's performance is unlikely to be seen by only one rating source such as a manager or customer. At a minimum, employees should be asked to comment on their appraisals. There should be a dialogue between the manager and the employee.
7. Performance evaluations need to be documented.

## A LOOK BACK

### Patagonia's Revised Performance Management System

Patagonia's new performance management system includes both annual goals, quarterly stretch goals, and manager–employee check-in meetings, and an emphasis on continuous feedback. Feedback can be requested and provided through an app that employees and their peers as well as managers can access on their notebook computers, tablets, or smartphones.

## QUESTIONS

1. Do the changes Patagonia's made in the performance management system support the company culture? Explain why or why not?
2. What are the advantages and disadvantages of encouraging peers to provide feedback using an app?
3. What characteristics does feedback need to have so that it is useful for changing behavior, and in turn, performance?

# SUMMARY

Measuring and managing performance is a challenging enterprise and one of the keys to gaining competitive advantage. Companies are moving toward a continuous feedback approach for performance management that encourages ongoing performance conversations between managers, their direct reports and teams, adjustment of goals, if necessary, and a developmental focus. Performance management serves several purposes—strategic, administrative, developmental, communication, organizational maintenance, and documentation purposes—their importance cannot be overstated. A performance measurement system should be evaluated against the criteria of strategic congruence, validity, reliability, acceptability, and specificity. Measured against these criteria, the comparative, attribute, behavioral, results, and quality approaches have different strengths and weaknesses. Thus, deciding which approach and which source of performance information are best depends on the job in question. Effective managers need to be aware of the issues involved in determining the best method or combination of methods for their particular situations. In addition, once performance has been measured, a major component of a manager's job is to provide frequent informal as well as formal feedback during performance evaluations in a way that results in improved performance rather than defensiveness and decreased motivation. Technologies can be potentially useful in streamlining the performance management process and providing employees with feedback and other information, which can motivate them to perform effectively. Managers should take action based on the causes for poor performance: ability, motivation, or both. Managers must be sure that their performance management system can meet legal scrutiny, especially if it is used to discipline or fire poor performers.

# KEY TERMS

Performance management, 335
Performance appraisal, 335
Performance feedback, 335
Continuous performance management
   process, 337
Strategic congruence, 341
Validity, 343

Reliability, 343
Acceptability, 344
Specificity, 345
Competencies, 356
Competency model, 356
Kaizen, 364
Upward feedback, 368

360-degree appraisal, 371
Social performance management, 372
Appraisal politics, 374
Calibration meetings, 375
Performance improvement
   plan (PIP), 382

# DISCUSSION QUESTIONS

1. What are examples of administrative decisions that might be made in managing the performance of professors? Developmental decisions?
2. What would you consider the strategy of your university (e.g., research, undergraduate teaching, graduate teaching, a combination)? How might the performance management system for faculty members fulfill its strategic purpose of eliciting the types of behaviors and results required by this strategy?
3. Explain the differences between the traditional and continuous performance management process.
4. What sources of performance information would you use to evaluate faculty members' performance?
5. Why are companies changing their performance management systems? Is this a good idea?
6. Think of the last time you had a conflict with another person, either at work or at school. Using the guidelines for performance feedback, how would you provide effective performance feedback to that person?

7. Explain what fairness has to do with performance management.
8. Why might a manager unintentionally distort performance ratings or the reasons used to explain an employee's performance? What would you recommend to minimize this problem?
9. Can electronic monitoring of performance ever be acceptable to employees? Explain.

10. Customer satisfaction surveys completed after a service call show that a call center representative is having difficulty answering customers' questions about their cell phone bills. How would you diagnose the cause of this performance problem? Explain.
11. How can the use of apps benefit the performance management process? How can they detract from it?
12. What would you do to ensure that a results or objective focus of performance management is effective?

# SELF-ASSESSMENT EXERCISE

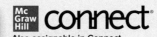

Also assignable in Connect.

How do you like getting feedback? To test your attitudes toward feedback, take the following quiz. Read each statement, and write A next to each statement you agree with. If you disagree with the statement, write D.

_____ 1. I like being told how well I am doing on a project.
_____ 2. Even though I may think I have done a good job, I feel a lot more confident when someone else tells me so.
_____ 3. Even when I think I could have done something better, I feel good when other people think well of me for what I have done.
_____ 4. It is important for me to know what people think of my work.
_____ 5. I think my instructor would think worse of me if I asked him or her for feedback.
_____ 6. I would be nervous about asking my instructor how she or he evaluates my behavior in class.
_____ 7. It is not a good idea to ask my fellow students for feedback; they might think I am incompetent.
_____ 8. It is embarrassing to ask other students for their impression of how I am doing in class.
_____ 9. It would bother me to ask the instructor for feedback.

_____ 10. It is not a good idea to ask the instructor for feedback because he or she might think I am incompetent.
_____ 11. It is embarrassing to ask the instructor for feedback.
_____ 12. It is better to try to figure out how I am doing on my own, rather than to ask other students for feedback.

For statements 1–4, add the total number of As: _____
For statements 5–12, add the total number of As: _____
For statements 1–4, the greater the number of As, the greater your preference for and trust in feedback from others. For statements 5–12, the greater the number of As, the greater the risk you believe there is in asking for feedback.

How might this information be useful in understanding how you react to feedback in school or on the job?

SOURCES: Based on D. B. Fedor, R. B. Rensvold, and S. M. Adams, "An Investigation of Factors Expected to Affect Feedback Seeking: A Longitudinal Field Study," *Personnel Psychology* 45 (1992), pp. 779–805; S. J. Asford, "Feedback Seeking in Inpidual Adaptation: A Resource Perspective," *Academy of Management Journal* 29 (1986), pp. 465–87.

# EXERCISING STRATEGY

## Performance Management Aligns with Asana's Culture

Asana (the Sanskrit word for a pose in yoga) provides software for enabling teamwork. The company's vision is to apply Eastern wisdom traditions to create a culture of clarity, authenticity, and mindfulness. That vision influences how performance management is practiced resulting in a workplace in which key stakeholders—employees in Silicon Valley's highly competitive market for high-tech workers—feel valued and empowered.

At Asana, everyone has clear goals and responsibilities, coupled with a high degree of authority. This exists within an environment of constant observation, learning, and improvement. In this context, performance management is not so much about checking up on employees to find out what they have been doing; Asana's own teamwork software takes care of that. Rather, performance management is about enabling employees to continue improving along with the entire company.

Goal setting applies the principle of clarity. Asana presents the company's purpose as a pyramid. At the top is the mission, to "help humanity thrive by enabling all teams to work together effortlessly." Below that is an easily understood three-part strategy of making a product that enables effortless teamwork, getting the product to all teams, and making Asana the company that does both of these better than any other. To carry out the strategy, the company sets roughly a dozen business, product, and internal objectives for the year. Every team has key results to achieve some of these objectives, and every employee works at projects aimed at the key results. Cross-functional teams define the higher-level goals in twice-yearly meetings to review the previous six months' performance. And once a year, each employee defines personal goals that align with the objectives in the pyramid.

The degree of empowerment is a striking feature of work at Asana. The planning process identifies every task and piece of work, with a deadline for each. Each one is called an area of responsibility (AOR), and each is assigned to one person, the AOR holder, based on the person's expertise. AOR holders are encouraged to discuss issues with their colleagues, but they have the full authority to make decisions within their area. To enable wise use of this authority, all employees receive leadership training that includes listening, giving and receiving feedback nondefensively, and "holding beliefs lightly," that is, being open to new ideas.

This degree of empowerment would make it difficult for a manager to offer performance feedback in the form of directions to improve. Rather, the emphasis is on mentoring and coaching. Employees complete annual self-reviews, and regular peer reviews provide another source of performance data. Managers meet frequently one-on-one with their direct reports. Because the Asana software is already telling managers

what their people have accomplished and whether they are on track toward goals, the meetings focus on employees' needs and goals. When problems arise at any level of the organization—including when an employee leaves—the response is to conduct an analysis of the underlying reasons so that processes can be improved.

So far, this approach is delivering exceptional performance, including high sales growth and employee satisfaction. Maintaining a culture in a fast-growing company is difficult, but the founders point out that change is built into Asana's method of operating. The owners promise to adapt the culture if it becomes necessary.

## QUESTIONS

1. How well do you think Asana's approach to performance management seems to meet the (a) strategic, (b) administrative, (c) developmental, (d) communication, (e) organizational maintenance, and (f) documentation purposes of performance management? Use evidence from the case to support your opinions.
2. Like other high-tech companies, Asana is struggling to build a more diverse workforce. Identify two ways the company is or could be ensuring that its performance management system does not discriminate.
3. Which part of Asana's performance management process contributes most to its effectiveness? Explain.

SOURCE: J. Bercovici, "Two Facebook Alums Seek a New Corporate Zen," *Inc.*, June 2018, pp. 76–78; S. Lewis-Kulin, "The Secret to Asana's Company Culture," *Fortune*, March 1, 2018, http://fortune.com; J. Courtney, "How Does Asana Do Performance Management," PerformYard Talent Management Blog, November 21, 2017, http://blog.performyard.com; R. Zurer, "How Asana Designs Its Successful, Authentic Company Culture," *Conscious Company*, November 1, 2017, https://consciouscompanymedia.com; D. Ongchoco, "Asana's Head of People Ops Shares What Goes into One of Tech's Best Company Cultures," *Huffington Post*, July 17, 2017, https://www.huffingtonpost.com.

# MANAGING PEOPLE

## Helping to Encourage Frequent and Productive Performance Conversations

Adobe Systems Inc. provides multimedia and creativity software products including Photoshop, Adobe Acrobat, and Adobe Acrobat Reader. Adobe was experiencing an increase in turnover, which it discovered was related to employees' dissatisfaction with the performance review process, a lack of recognition, and the lack of regular feedback about their performance. Like other companies, Adobe used a performance review system in which managers provided an overall rating of each employee on a scale from 1 to 4, based on how the employee's performance compared to that of other employees. This created a competitive work environment, rather than the collaborative one that Adobe values. Each year after employees received their reviews, HR saw a spike in voluntary

turnover, which was especially concerning because Adobe was losing good employees.

To improve performance management, Adobe decided to abandon annual ratings and introduced a new system called the Check-In. The Check-In emphasizes ongoing feedback. Instead of managers discussing performance with employees only during the formal performance review, as tended to occur in the old system, Check-In encourages managers and employees to have informal performance discussions at least every other month. Managers are asked to focus performance discussions around employees' performance objectives or goals and what resources they need to succeed. Also, employees' career development needs are part of the conversations.

Managers are given complete freedom to decide how often and in what ways they want to set goals and provide feedback. The discussion is future focused. That is, both the employee and the manager consider what to change to increase the likelihood that performance will be effective. Employees are evaluated on the basis of how they have performed against their goals rather than how they compare to other employees. More frequent performance feedback is especially important to Millennial employees, who are used to real-time communications through texting and postings.

Managers no longer have to complete lengthy performance evaluation forms and submit them to HR. HR's role is to provide managers with consulting and tools to help with performance discussions rather than policing to see if reviews are completed or discussions have occurred. Both managers and employees can access a resource center that provides materials about coaching, giving feedback, and personal and professional development. For example, managers might use the resource center to help them with tough performance conversations such as those involving giving employees difficult feedback. HR relies on what is known as a skip-level process to ensure that performance discussions are occurring throughout the year. This means that the manager's own boss holds the manager accountable for having performance discussions. The boss asks employees if discussions are occurring and if they have a development plan.

There are several indications that Check-In is effective. HR includes questions about performance management on its annual employee survey. Survey results show that 80% of employees responded that they had regular performance meetings with their managers and felt supported by them. Since Check-In was introduced, voluntary turnover has decreased by 25%. Also, it is estimated that Check-In saves Adobe managers 80,000 hours each year that were previously spent completing employee performance evaluation forms.

## QUESTIONS

1. What steps should managers take to ensure that performance discussions are effective?
2. What are the benefits and potential disadvantages of more frequent performance discussions between managers and employees?
3. Which purpose of performance management will be more difficult to achieve for companies like Adobe that decide to abandon ranking or rating employee performance?

SOURCES: Based on R. Feintzeig, "The Trouble with Grading Employees," *Wall Street Journal*, April 22, 2015, pp. B1, B7; D. Meinert, "Reinventing Reviews," *HR Magazine*, April 2015, pp. 36–40; J. Ramirez, "Rethinking the Review," *Human Resource Executive*, July/August 2013, pp. 16–19.

# HR IN SMALL BUSINESS

## Retrofit's Mobile Performance Management

Retrofit offers a combination of a mobile app and personal coaching to help people achieve and maintain a healthy weight. It serves companies looking to improve the health of their workforces and health care organizations seeking to promote healthy lifestyles in their patient populations. Individuals also can sign up for Retrofit's service. Participants use the mobile app to track their food consumption, physical activity, hours of sleep, and weight. They and their coach monitor their progress on a dashboard, and the coach uses the performance data to provide personalized coaching via online video connections.

As an employer of almost 50 people, Chicago-based Retrofit applies similar features—ease of use, mobile technology, and frequent feedback—to its performance management system. Originally, the company started out requiring twice-yearly performance appraisals, but it recently replaced that system by introducing an app called TINYpulse Perform.

Employees work with their managers to enter goals into Perform. When a manager observes goal-related performance to rate, he or she simply opens the app and swipes right for meeting expectations, up for exceeding expectations, or down for falling short. Employees and managers also can enter comments and post supporting documents such as e-mails in praise of an employee's work. At the end of the year, the performance data are available on the app to represent a year's worth of efforts and outcomes for each employee.

According to Catalina Andrade, director of employee happiness at Retrofit, the app supports a goal of making reviews "instantaneous." Managers and employees are less likely to forget about achievements or problems they want to discuss because they quickly record the information right after these events occur. That efficiency supports Retrofit's expectation that managers will discuss performance with their employees at least twice a month. The expectation of frequent feedback, in turn, aims to support employee engagement and what the company's vice president of human resources calls Retrofit's "culture of health and happiness."

## QUESTIONS

1. What methods for measuring performance would be most suitable for the system Retrofit is using? Why?
2. What advice would you give managers at Retrofit to help them deliver performance feedback effectively when they meet with their employees?

SOURCES: Company website, https://www.retrofitme.com, accessed May 23, 2018; John Pletz, "Livongo Buys Chicago Weight-Loss Firm Retrofit," *Crain's Chicago Business*, April 17, 2018, http://www.chicagobusiness.com; Alexia Elajalde-Ruiz, "Annual Reviews Scrapped for Real-Time Feedback," *Chicago Tribune*, April 24, 2016, http://www.chicagotribune.com; "Retrofit Signals Growth: Corporate Weight Management Company Announces Talent Acquisition," news release, March 3, 2015, http://www.prweb.com.

# NOTES

1. A. Bradley, "Taking the Formality out of Performance Reviews," *T + D*, June 2010, p. 18; R. Pyrillis, "The Reviews Are In," *Workforce Management*, May 2011, pp. 20-25.

2. P. Cappelli and A. Tavis, "The Performance Management Evolution," *Harvard Business Review*, October 2016, pp. 58-67; M. Laff, "Performance Management Gives a Shaky Performance," *T + D*, September 2007, p. 18; A. Fox, "Curing What Ails Performance Reviews," *HR Magazine*, January 2009, pp. 52-56.

3. J. Wolper, "The Ever Evolving Workplace," *TD,* December 2016, pp. 40-44; CEB, "The Real Impact of Removing Performance Ratings on Employee Performance," May 12, 2016, from www.cebglobal.com, accessed March 8, 2017.

4. L. Goler, G. Gale, and A. Grant, "Let's Not Kill Performance Evaluations," *Harvard Business Review*, November 2016, pp. 90-94; E. Pulakos, R. Hanson, S. Arad, and N. Moye, "Performance Management Can Be Fixed: An On-the-Job Experiential Learning Approach for Complex Behavior Change," *Industrial and Organizational Psychology*, March 2015, pp. 51-76; E. Pulakos, *Performance Management* (Oxford, U.K.: Wiley-Blackwell, 2009); H. Aguinis, "An Expanded View of Performance Management," in J. W. Smith and M. London (eds.), *Performance Management* (San Francisco: Jossey-Bass, 2009), pp. 1-43; J. Russell and L. Russell, "Talk Me through It: The Next Level of Performance Management," *T + D*, April 2010, pp. 42-48; J. Dahling and A. O'Malley, "Supportive Feedback Environments Can Mend Broken Performance Management Systems," *Industrial and Organizational Psychology* 4 (2011), pp. 201-3; E. Pulakos and R. O'Leary, "Why Is Performance Management Broken?" *Industrial and Organizational Psychology* 4 (2011), pp. 146-64; E. Mone, C. Eisinger, K. Guggenheim, B. Price, and C. Stine, "Performance Management at the Wheel: Driving Employee Engagement in Organizations," *Journal of Business & Psychology* 26 (2011), pp. 205-12.

5. J. Harbour, "The Three 'Ds' of Successful Performance Measurement: Design, Data, and Display," *Performance Improvement* 50 (February 2011), pp. 5-12.

6. E. Pulakos, R. Mueller-Hanson, and S. Arad, "The Evolution of Performance Management: Searching for Value," *Annual Review of Organizational Psychology and Organizational Behavior* 6 (2019), pp. 249-271; A. Colquitt, *Next Generation Performance Management* (Charlotte, NC: Information Age Publishing, 2017); Deloitte Development LLC, "Continuous Performance Management," 2017, from http://marketing.bersin.com, accessed January 22, 2019.

7. E. Pulakos, R. Mueller-Hanson, and S. Arad, "The Evolution of Performance Management: Searching for Value," *Annual Review of Organizational Psychology and Organizational Behavior* 6 (2019), pp. 249-71; A. Colquitt, *Next Generation Performance Management* (Charlotte, NC: Information Age Publishing, 2017); Deloitte Development LLC, "Continuous Performance Management," 2017, from http://marketing.bersin.com, accessed January 22, 2019.

8. S. Chowdury, E. Hioe, and B. Shaninger "Harnessing the Power of Performance Management," April 2018, from www.mckinsey.com, accessed January 22, 2019; V. Fludd, "Performance Management for Managers," *TD,* March 2016, p. 12; "Performance Reviews: Love 'em or Hate 'em," *TD,* February 2016, p. 18; C. Schoenberger, "The Risk of Reviews," *Wall Street Journal,* October 28, 2015, p. R5; M. Weinstein, "Annual Review Under Review," *Training,* July/August 2016, pp. 22-29; D. Wilke, "Is the Annual Performance Review Dead?" *HR Magazine,* October 2015, pp. 11-12.

9. A. Colquitt, *Next Generation Performance Management* (Charlotte, NC: Information Age Publishing, 2017); Deloitte Development LLC, "Continuous Performance Management," 2017, accessed from http://marketing.bersin.com, accessed January 22, 2019; *HBR Guide to Performance Management* (Boston MA: Harvard Business Review Press, 2017)

10. Deloitte Development LLC, "Continuous Performance Management," 2017, accessed from http://marketing.bersin.com, accessed January 22, 2019; N. Sloan, D. Agarwal, S. Garr, and K. Pastakia, "Performance Management: Playing a Winning Hand," December 28, 2017, from https://www2.deloitte.com/insights/us/en/focus/human-capital-trends/2017/redesigning-performance-management.html, accessed January 22, 2019.

11. L. Goler, G. Gale, and A. Grant, "Let's Not Kill Performance Evaluations," *Harvard Business Review,* November 2016, pp. 90-94; R. Feloni, "Facebook's HR Chief Explains How the Company Does Performance Reviews," *Business Insider,* February 5, 2016, from www.businessinsider.com, accessed March 7, 2017; M. McGraw, "Creating Coaches," *Human Resource Executive,* September 2015, pp. 52-53.

12. A. Colquitt, *Next Generation Performance Management* (Charlotte, NC: Information Age Publishing, 2017); H. Aguinis, *Performance Management* (4th ed.), (Chicago: Chicago, University Press, 2019); J. Cleveland, K. Murphy, and R. Williams, "Multiple Uses of Performance Appraisal: Prevalence and Correlates," *Journal of Applied Psychology* 74 (1989), pp. 130-135.

13. R. Silverman, "GE Tries to Reinvent the Employee Review, Encouraging Risks," *Wall Street Journal,* June 8, 2016, pp. B1, B6; R. Silverman, "GE Scraps Staff Ratings to Spur Feedback," *Wall Street Journal,* July 27, 2016, p. B8; GE 2016 Annual Report, www.ge.com, accessed March 2, 2017; M. Weinstein, "Annual Review Under Review," *Training,* July/August 2016, pp. 22-29; M. Schoenberger, "The Risk of Reviews," *Wall Street Journal,* October 28, 2015, p. R5; "How GE Renews Performance Management from Stack Rankings

to Continuous Feedback," from http://blog.impraise.com, accessed March 2, 2017; P. Cappelli and A. Tavis, "The Performance Management Evolution," *Harvard Business Review,* October 2016, pp. 58–67.

14. C. G. Banks and K. E. May, "Performance Management: The Real Glue in Organizations," in *Evolving Practices in Human Resource Management*, ed. A. Kraut and A. Korman (San Francisco: Jossey-Bass, 1999), pp. 118–45; R. Connors and T. Smith, "Want Results? Fix Accountability," *Chief Learning Officer*, February 2015, pp. 44–46.

15. S. Maier, "Companies That Boost Success by Improving Performance Management," October 11, 2017, from https://workology.com, accessed January 8, 2019; J. Yarrow, "This Is the Internal Grading System Google Uses for Its Employees—And You Should Use It Too," January 6, 2014, from https://www.businessinsider.com, accessed January 8, 2019.

16. C. D. Ittner and D. F. Larcker, "Coming Up Short on Nonfinancial Performance Measurement," *Harvard Business Review*, December 2003, pp. 88–95.

17. J. K. Harter, F. Schmidt, and T. L. Hayes, "Business-Unit-Level Relationships between Employee Satisfaction, Employee Engagement, and Business Outcomes: A Meta-analysis," *Journal of Applied Psychology* 87 (2002), pp. 268–79.

18. A. J. Rucci, S. P. Kim, and R. T. Quinn, "The Employee-Customer-Profit Chain at Sears," *Harvard Business Review*, January/February 1998, pp. 82–97.

19. R. Schuler and S. Jackson, "Linking Competitive Strategies with Human Resource Practices," *Academy of Management Executive* 1 (1987), pp. 207–19.

20. L. King, J. Hunter, and F. Schmidt, "Halo in a Multidimensional Forced-Choice Performance Evaluation Scale," *Journal of Applied Psychology* 65 (1980), pp. 507–16.

21. B. R. Nathan, A. M. Mohrman, and J. Millman, "Interpersonal Relations as a Context for the Effects of Appraisal Interviews on Performance and Satisfaction: A Longitudinal Study," *Academy of Management Journal* 34 (1991), pp. 352–69; M. S. Taylor, K. B. Tracy, M. K. Renard, J. K. Harrison, and S. J. Carroll, "Due Process in Performance Appraisal: A Quasi-Experiment in Procedural Justice," *Administrative Science Quarterly* 40 (1995), pp. 495–523; J. M. Werner and M. C. Bolino, "Explaining U.S. Courts of Appeals Decisions Involving Performance Appraisal: Accuracy, Fairness, and Validation," *Personnel Psychology* 50 (1997), pp. 1–24.

22. M. Buckingham and A. Goodall, "Reinventing Performance Management," *Harvard Business Review*, April 2015, pp. 40–50.

23. A. DeNisi and K. Murphy, "Performance Appraisal and Performance Management: 100 Years of Progress?" *Journal of Applied Psychology*, January 26, 2017; J. Campbell and B. Wiernik, "The Modeling and Assessment of Work Performance," *Annual Review of Organizational Psychology and Organizational Behavior* 2 (2015), pp. 47–74.

24. "Training Can Help Facilitate Effective Performance Management Process," *HR Daily Advisor*, March 31, 2017, https://hrdailyadvisor.blr.com; *Talent and Performance Management Survey*, BLR, March 2016, http://catalog.blr.com; S. Bruce, "The 2015 Performance Management Survey Is In!" *HR Daily Advisor*, July 15, 2015, http://hrdailyadvisor.blr.com.

25. Weinstein, "Annual Review under Review."

26. *Albemarle Paper Company v. Moody*, 10 FEP 1181 (1975).

27. S. Ng and J. Lublin, "AIG Pay Plan: Rank and Rile," *Wall Street Journal*, February 11, 2010, p. R8.

28. S. Bates, "Forced Ranking," *HR Magazine*, June 2003, pp. 63–68; A. Meisler, "Deadman's Curve," *Workforce*

*Management*, July 2003, pp. 44–49; M. Lowery, "Forcing the Issue," *Human Resource Executive,* October 16, 2003, pp. 26–29; J. Welch, "Rank and Yank, That's Not How It's Done," *Wall Street Journal*, November 15, 2013, p. A15.

29. J. Welch, "Rank and Yank, That's Not How It's Done," *Wall Street Journal*, November 15, 2013, p. A15; P. Cappelli, "Why Managers Should Stop Thinking of A, B, and C Players," *Wall Street Journal*, February 21, 2017, pp. R5, R7; E. O'Boyle, Jr. and H. Aguinis, "The Best and the Rest: Revisiting the Norm of Normality of Individual Performance," *Personnel Psychology* 65 (2010), pp. 79–119.

30. S. Scullen, P. Bergey, and L. Aiman-Smith, "Forced Choice Distribution Systems and the Improvement of Workforce Potential: A Baseline Simulation," *Personnel Psychology* 58 (2005), pp. 1–32.

31. S. Ovide and R. Feintzeig, "Microsoft Abandons Dreaded 'Stack,'" *Wall Street Journal*, November 13, 2013, pp. B1, B5.

32. F. Blanz and E. Ghiselli, "The Mixed Standard Scale: A New Rating System," *Personnel Psychology* 25 (1973), pp. 185–99; K. Murphy and J. Constans, "Behavioral Anchors as a Source of Bias in Rating," *Journal of Applied Psychology* 72 (1987), pp. 573–77.

33. *Brito v. Zia Co.*, 478 F.2nd 1200 (10th Cir 1973).

34. P. Smith and L. Kendall, "Retranslation of Expectations: An Approach to the Construction of Unambiguous Anchors for Rating Scales," *Journal of Applied Psychology* 47 (1963), pp. 149–55.

35. Murphy and Constans, "Behavioral Anchors"; M. Piotrowski, J. Barnes-Farrel, and F. Esrig, "Behaviorally Anchored Bias: A Replication and Extension of Murphy and Constans," *Journal of Applied Psychology* 74 (1989), pp. 823–26.

36. U. Wiersma and G. Latham, "The Practicality of Behavioral Observation Scales, Behavioral Expectation Scales, and Trait Scales," *Personnel Psychology* 39 (1986), pp. 619–28.

37. G. Latham and K. Wexley, *Increasing Productivity through Performance Appraisal* (Boston: Addison-Wesley, 1981).

38. Wiersma and Latham, "The Practicality of Behavioral Observation Scales, Behavioral Expectation Scales, and Trait Scales."

39. M. Campion, A. Fink, B. Ruggeberg, L. Carr, G. Phillips, and R. Odman, "Doing Competencies Well: Best Practices in Competency Modeling," *Personnel Psychology* 64 (2011), pp. 225–62; J. Shippmann, R. Ash, M. Battista, L. Carr, L. Eyde, B. Hesketh, J. Kehow, K. Pearlman, and J. Sanchez, "The Practice of Competency Modeling," *Personnel Psychology* 53 (2000), pp. 703–40; A. Lucia and R. Lepsinger, *The Art and Science of Competency Models* (San Francisco: Jossey-Bass, 1999).

40. C. Spicer, "Building a Competency Model," *HR Magazine*, April 2009, pp. 34–36.

41. S. Snell, "Control Theory in Strategic Human Resource Management: The Mediating Effect of Administrative Information," *Academy of Management Journal* 35 (1992), pp. 292–327.

42. T. Patten Jr., *A Manager's Guide to Performance Appraisal* (New York: Free Press, 1982).

43. M. O'Donnell and R. O'Donnell, "MBO—Is It Passe?" *Hospital and Health Services Administration* 28, no. 5 (1983), pp. 46–58; T. Poister and G. Streib, "Management Tools in Government: Trends over the Past Decade," *Public Administration Review* 49 (1989), pp. 240–48.

44. E. Locke and G. Latham, *A Theory of Goal Setting and Task Performance* (Englewood Cliffs, NJ: Prentice Hall, 1990).

45. S. Carroll and H. Tosi, *Management by Objectives* (New York: Macmillan, 1973).

46. G. Odiorne, *MBO II: A System of Managerial Leadership for the 80's* (Belmont, CA: Pitman, 1986); E. Pulakos, *Performance Management* (Oxford, England: Wiley-Blackwell, 2009).

47. R. Rodgers and J. Hunter, "Impact of Management by Objectives on Organizational Productivity," *Journal of Applied Psychology* 76 (1991), pp. 322-26.

48. V. Liberman, "Performance Management: To Get Results Stop Measuring People by Them," *Conference Board Review*, Summer 2013, pp. 57-63.

49. R. S. Kaplan and D. P. Norton, "Using the Balanced Scorecard as a Strategic Management System," *Harvard Business Review*, July/August 2007, pp. 150-161.

50. W. Schiemann, "Aligning Performance Management with Organizational Strategy, Values, and Goals," in J. W. Smither and M. London (eds.), *Performance Management* (San Francisco: Jossey-Bass, 2009), pp. 45-87.

51. R. Pritchard, S. Jones, P. Roth, K. Stuebing, and S. Ekeberg, "The Evaluation of an Integrated Approach to Measuring Organizational Productivity," *Personnel Psychology* 42 (1989), pp. 69-115; R. Pritchard, M. Harrell, D. DiazGranados, and M. Guzman, "The Productivity Measurement and Enhancement System: A Meta-Analysis," *Journal of Applied Psychology* 93 (2008), pp. 340-67.

52. P. Wright, J. George, S. Farnsworth, and G. McMahan, "Productivity and Extra-Role Behavior: The Effects of Goals and Incentives on Spontaneous Helping," *Journal of Applied Psychology* 78, no. 3 (1993), pp. 374-81.

53. Latham and Wexley, *Increasing Productivity through Performance Appraisal*.

54. L. Weber, "At Kimberly-Clark, 'Dead Wood' Workers Have Nowhere to Hide," *Wall Street Journal*, August 22, 2016, pp. A1, A10; G. Tucker, "HR in the Age of Disruption," *HR Magazine*, September 2016, pp. 69-73.

55. R. L. Cardy, "Performance Appraisal in a Quality Context: A New Look at an Old Problem," in *Performance Appraisal: State of the Art in Practice*, ed. J. W. Smither (San Francisco: Jossey-Bass, 1998), pp. 132-62.

56. E. C. Huge, *Total Quality: An Executive's Guide for the 1990s* (Homewood, IL: Richard D. Irwin, 1990): see Chapter 5, "Measuring and Rewarding Performance," pp. 70-88; W. E. Deming, *Out of Crisis* (Cambridge, MA: MIT Center for Advanced Engineering Study, 1986).

57. M. Caroselli, *Total Quality Transformations* (Amherst, MA: Human Resource Development Press, 1991); Huge, *Total Quality*.

58. M. Sallie-Dosunmu, "Born to Grow," *T + D*, May 2006, pp. 33-37.

59. A. Brunet and S. New, "Kaizen in Japan: An Empirical Study," *International Journal of Production and Operations Management* 23 (2003), pp. 1426-46.

60. D. E. Bowen and E. E. Lawler III, "Total Quality-Oriented Human Resource Management," *Organizational Dynamics* 21 (1992), pp. 29-41.

61. R. Heneman, K. Wexley, and M. Moore, "Performance Rating Accuracy: A Critical Review," *Journal of Business Research* 15 (1987), pp. 431-48.

62. T. Becker and R. Klimoski, "A Field Study of the Relationship between the Organizational Feedback Environment and Performance," *Personnel Psychology* 42 (1989), pp. 343-58; H. M. Findley, W. F. Giles, and K. W. Mossholder, "Performance Appraisal and Systems Facets: Relationships with Contextual Performance," *Journal of Applied Psychology* 85 (2000), pp. 634-40.

63. WorldatWork, "Performance Management at Whirlpool," www.youtube.com/user/WorldatWorkTV, accessed March 6, 2017.

64. L. Axline, "Performance Biased Evaluations," *Supervisory Management*, November 1991, p. 3.

65. G. Tucker, "HR in the Age of Disruption," *HR Magazine*, September 2016, pp. 69-73.

66. K. Wexley and R. Klimoski, "Performance Appraisal: An Update," in *Research in Personnel and Human Resource Management* (vol. 2), ed. K. Rowland and G. Ferris (Greenwich, CT: JAI Press, 1984).

67. F. Landy and J. Farr, *The Measurement of Work Performance: Methods, Theory, and Applications* (New York: Academic Press, 1983).

68. G. McEvoy and P. Buller, "User Acceptance of Peer Appraisals in an Industrial Setting," *Personnel Psychology* 40 (1987), pp. 785-97.

69. "Our Culture Code" and "How We Lead Matters," www.dell.com, accessed March 8, 2017; C. A. Pomeroy, "Agent of Change," *HR Magazine*, May 2005, pp. 52-56.

70. D. Antonioni, "The Effects of Feedback Accountability on Upward Appraisal Ratings," *Personnel Psychology* 47 (1994), pp. 349-56.

71. K. Murphy and J. Cleveland, *Performance Appraisal: An Organizational Perspective* (Boston: Allyn & Bacon, 1991).

72. J. Bernardin and L. Klatt, "Managerial Appraisal Systems: Has Practice Caught Up with the State of the Art?" *Public Personnel Administrator*, November 1985, pp. 79-86.

73. M. Samuelson, "How I Did It...Analysis Group's CEO on Managing with Soft Metrics," *Harvard Business Review*, November 2015, pp. 43-45; Analysis Group website, www.analysisgroup.com, accessed February 4, 2019.

74. H. Heidemeier and K. Moser, "Self-Other Agreement in Job Performance Rating: A Meta-analytic Test of a Process Model," *Journal of Applied Psychology* 94 (2008), pp. 353-70.

75. R. Steel and N. Ovalle, "Self-Appraisal Based on Supervisor Feedback," *Personnel Psychology* 37 (1984), pp. 667-85; L. E. Atwater, "The Advantages and Pitfalls of Self-Assessment in Organizations," in J. Smither (ed.) *Performance Appraisal: State of the Art in Practice* (San Francisco: Jossey-Bass, 1998) pp. 331-65.

76. E. Gummerson, "Lip Services—A Neglected Area of Service Marketing," *Journal of Services Marketing* 1 (1987), pp. 1-29.

77. Weinstein, "Annual Review under Review."

78. J. Bernardin, B. Hagan, J. Kane, and P. Villanova, "Effective Performance Management: A Focus on Precision, Customers, and Situational Constraints," in *Performance Appraisal: State of the Art in Practice*, ed. J. W. Smither (San Francisco: Jossey-Bass, 1998), pp. 3-48.

79. R. Hoffman, "Ten Reasons You Should Be Using 360-Degree Feedback," *HR Magazine*, April 1995, pp. 82-84.

80. S. Sherman, "How Tomorrow's Best Leaders Are Learning Their Stuff," *Fortune*, November 27, 1995, pp. 90-104; W. W. Tornow, M. London, and Associates, *Maximizing the Value of 360-Degree Feedback* (San Francisco: Jossey-Bass, 1998); D. A. Waldman, L. E. Atwater, and D. Antonioni, "Has 360-Degree Feedback Gone Amok?" *Academy of Management Executive* 12 (1988), pp. 86-94.

81. J. Farr, J. Fairchild, and S. Cassidy, "Technology and Performance Appraisal," in *The Psychology of Workplace Technology,* ed. M. Coovert and L. Thompson (New York: Routledge, 2014), pp. 77-98.

82. A. Adkins, "What Millennials Want from Work and Life," www.gallup.com, May 11, 2016; A. Williams, "Move over Millennials: Here Comes Generation Z," *New York Times,* September 18, 2015, p. ST1.

83. K. Maher, "Big Employer Is Watching," *Wall Street Journal*, November 4, 2003, pp. B1, B6.

84. B. Morris, "Meet the Truck Driver of 2013," *Wall Street Journal*, November 14, 2013, pp. B1, B6; L. Katz, "Big Employer Is Watching," *HR Magazine*, June 2015, pp. 67-74.

85. L. Ward, "Doctors, Beware: You're Being Watched," *Wall Street Journal*, May 29, 2018, p. R10.

86. D. Lawrence, "Tracking the Enemy Within," *Bloomberg Businessweek*, March 16-March 22, 2015, pp. 39-41.

87. C. Farr, "Fitbit At Work," *FastCompany*, May 2016, pp. 27-30.

88. D. Brin, "Wearable Worries," *HR Magazine*, June 2016, pp. 138-40.

89. Katz, "Big Employer Is Watching"; Brin, "Wearable Worries"; "Should Companies Monitor Their Employees Social Media," *Wall Street Journal*, May 12, 2014, pp. R1, R2.

90. R. Feintzeig, "Workers Challenge Time Trackers," *Wall Street Journal,* May 21, 2018, p. B3.

91. D. Bhave, "The Invisible Eye? Electronic Performance Monitoring and Employee Job Performance," *Personnel Psychology* 67 (2014), pp. 605-35.

92. R. Silverman, "Managers: Watch Your Language," *Wall Street Journal*, September 20, 2015, p. R9; The Royal Society, "Understanding Unconscious Bias," https://www.youtube.com/watch?v=dVp9Z5k0dEE, accessed November 1, 2016; A. Tversky and D. Kahneman, "Availability: A Heuristic for Judging Frequency and Probability," *Cognitive Psychology* 5 (1973), pp. 207-32.

93. S. Leibowitz, "Stanford University Researchers Analyzed the Language in 125 Performance Reviews from a Tech Company and Found Something Disturbing," *Business Insider*, October 1, 2015.

94. K. Wexley and W. Nemeroff, "Effects of Racial Prejudice, Race of Applicant, and Biographical Similarity on Interviewer Evaluations of Job Applicants," *Journal of Social and Behavioral Sciences* 20 (1974), pp. 66-78.

95. D. Smith, "Training Programs for Performance Appraisal: A Review," *Academy of Management Review* 11 (1986), pp. 22-40.

96. G. Latham, K. Wexley, and E. Pursell, "Training Managers to Minimize Rating Errors in the Observation of Behavior," *Journal of Applied Psychology* 60 (1975), pp. 550-55.

97. J. Bernardin and E. Pence, "Effects of Rater Training: Creating New Response Sets and Decreasing Accuracy," *Journal of Applied Psychology* 65 (1980), pp. 60-66.

98. E. Pulakos, "A Comparison of Rater Training Programs: Error Training and Accuracy Training," *Journal of Applied Psychology* 69 (1984), pp. 581-88; E. Dierdorff, E. Surface, and K. Brown, "Frame-of-Reference Training Effectiveness: Effects of Goal Orientation and Self-Efficacy on Affective, Cognitive, Skill-Based and Transfer Outcomes," *Journal of Applied Psychology* 95 (2010), pp. 1181-91.

99. H. J. Bernardin, M. R. Buckley, C. L. Tyler, and D. S. Wiese, "A Reconsideration of Strategies in Rater Training," in G. R. Ferris (ed.), *Research in Personnel and Human Resource Management* (Greenwich, CT: JAI Press, 2000), vol. 18, pp. 221-74.

100. K. Dykstra, "Defeat Unconscious Bias through Manager Training," *TD,* July 2018, pp. 70-71; A. Moore, "What Bias?" *TD,* August 2018, pp. 23-25; Silverman, "Managers: Watch Your Language"; Google, "Making the Unconscious Conscious," https://www.youtube.com/watch?v=NW5s_-Nl3JE, accessed January 4, 2019.

101. J. Sammer, "Calibrating Consistency," *HR Magazine*, January 2008, pp. 73-75.

102. B. Demere, K. Sedatole, and A. Woods, "The Role of Calibration Committees in Subjective Performance Evaluation Systems," *Management Science* from https://pubsonline.informs.org/doi/10.1287/mnsc.2017.3025, accessed January 10, 2019.

103. S. W. J. Kozlowski, G. T. Chao, and R. F. Morrison, "Games Raters Play: Politics, Strategies, and Impression Management in Performance Appraisal," in *Performance Appraisal: State of the Art in Practice*, pp. 163-205; C. Rosen, P. Levy, and R. Hall, "Placing Perceptions of Politics in the Context of the Feedback Environment, Employee Attitudes, and Job Performance," *Journal of Applied Psychology* 91 (2006), pp. 211-20.

104. R. Pyrillis, "The Reviews Are In," *Workforce Management*, May 2011, pp. 20-25.

105. K. Wexley, V. Singh, and G. Yukl, "Subordinate Participation in Three Types of Appraisal Interviews," *Journal of Applied Psychology* 58 (1973), pp. 54-57; K. Wexley, "Appraisal Interview," in *Performance Assessment*, ed. R. A. Berk (Baltimore: Johns Hopkins University Press, 1986), pp. 167-85; D. Cederblom, "The Performance Appraisal Interview: A Review, Implications, and Suggestions," *Academy of Management Review* 7 (1982), pp. 219-27; B. D. Cawley, L. M. Keeping, and P. E. Levy, "Participation in the Performance Appraisal Process and Employee Reactions: A Meta-analytic Review of Field Investigations," *Journal of Applied Psychology* 83, no. 3 (1998), pp. 615-63; H. Aguinis, *Performance Management* (Upper Saddle River, NJ: Pearson Prentice Hall, 2007); C. Lee, "Feedback, Not Appraisal," *HR Magazine*, November 2006, pp. 111-14; R. Hanson and E. Pulakos, *Putting the "Performance" Back in Performance Management* (Alexandria, VA: Society for Human Resource Management, 2015); M. Budworth, G. Latham, and L. Manroop, "Looking Forward to Performance Improvement: A Field Test of the Feedforward Interview for Performance Management," *Human Resource Management* 54 (2014), pp. 45-54; A. Kinicki, K. Jacobson, S. Peterson, and G. Prussia, "Development and Validation of the Performance Management Behavior Questionnaire," *Personnel Psychology* 66 (2013), pp. 1-45.

106. B. Hite, "Employers Rethink How They Give Feedback," *Wall Street Journal*, October 13, 2008, p. B5.

107. Weinstein, "Annual Review under Review."

108. R. Feintzeig, "Everything Is Awesome! Why You Can't Tell Employees They're Doing a Bad Job," *Wall Street Journal*, February 10, 2015, p. B1; A. Bryant, "A Boss's Challenge: Have Everyone Join the 'In' Group," *New York Times*, March 23, 2013, p. BU2.

109. W. Giles and K. Mossholder, "Employee Reactions to Contextual and Session Components of Performance Appraisal," *Journal of Applied Psychology* 75 (1990), pp. 371-77.

110. S. Shellenbarger, "Tell the Hard Truth at Work," *Wall Street Journal,* October 11, 2017, p. A15; *HBR Guide to Performance Management* (Boston MA: Harvard Business Review Press, 2017).

111. E. Locke and G. Latham, *A Theory of Goal Setting and Task Performance* (Englewood Cliffs, NJ: Prentice Hall, 1990).

112. H. Klein, S. Snell, and K. Wexley, "A Systems Model of the Performance Appraisal Interview Process," *Industrial Relations* 26 (1987), pp. 267-80; C. Crossley, C. Cooper, and T. Wernsing, "Making Things Happen Through Challenging Goals: Leader Proactivity, Trust, and Business-Unit Performance," *Journal of Applied Psychology* 98 (2103), pp. 540-49.

113. E. Kasson, "Plan Your Exits," *HR Magazine,* June 2016, pp. 111-17.

114. Cappelli, "Why Managers Should Stop Thinking of A, B, and C Players."

115. *Brito v. Zia Co.*, 478 F.2d 1200 (10th Cir 1973).

116. K. Kraiger and J. Ford, "A Meta-Analysis of Ratee Race Effects in Performance Rating," *Journal of Applied Psychology* 70 (1985), pp. 56-65; S. Needleman, "Monitoring the Monitors: Small Firms Increasingly Are Keeping Tabs on Their Workers, Keystroke by Keystroke," *Wall Street Journal*, August 16, 2010, p. R8.

117. P. Sackett, C. DuBois, and A. Noe, "Tokenism in Performance Evaluation: The Effects of Work Groups Representation on Male-Female and White-Black Differences in Performance Ratings," *Journal of Applied Psychology* 76 (1991), pp. 263-67.

118. "GE Subsidiary MRA Systems to Pay $130,000 to Settle EEOC Age Discrimination Suit," June 3, 2010, news release from www.eeoc.gov, accessed April 29, 2015.

119. "EEOC Sues Wisconsin Plastics for Discrimination against Hmong and Hispanic Employees," June 9, 2014, news release from www.eeoc.gov, accessed April 29, 2015.

120. J. Segal, "That Difficult Conversation," *HR Magazine*, April 2016, pp. 74-75; E. Kasson, "Plan Your Exits," *HR Magazine*, June 2016, pp. 111-17; G. Barrett and M. Kernan, "Performance Appraisal and Terminations: A Review of Court Decisions since *Brito v. Zia* with Implications for Personnel Practices," *Personnel Psychology* 40 (1987), pp. 489-503; H. Field and W. Holley, "The Relationship of Performance Appraisal System Characteristics to Verdicts in Selected Employment Discrimination Cases," *Academy of Management Journal* 25 (1982), pp. 392-406; J. M. Werner and M. C. Bolino, "Explaining U.S. Courts of Appeals Decisions Involving Performance Appraisal: Accuracy, Fairness, and Validation," *Personnel Psychology* 50 (1997), pp. 1-24; J. Segal, "Performance Management Blunders," *HR Magazine*, November 2010, pp. 75-77.

# 9 Employee Development

## ⌐ LEARNING OBJECTIVES ¬

*After reading this chapter, you should be able to:*

**LO 9-1** Explain how employee development contributes to strategies related to employee retention, development of intellectual capital, and business growth. *page 396*

**LO 9-2** Discuss the steps in the development planning process. *page 399*

**LO 9-3** Explain the employees' and company's responsibilities in planning development. *page 399*

**LO 9-4** Discuss current trends in using formal education for development. *page 403*

**LO 9-5** Relate how assessment of personality type, work behaviors, and job performance can be used for employee development. *page 406*

**LO 9-6** Explain how job experiences can be used for skill development. *page 411*

**LO 9-7** Develop successful mentoring programs. *page 418*

**LO 9-8** Describe how to train managers to coach employees. *page 422*

**LO 9-9** Discuss what companies are doing to melt the glass ceiling. *page 422*

**LO 9-10** Use the 9-box grid for identifying where employees fit in a succession plan and construct appropriate development plans for them. *page 425*

## Development at Vi Inspires Retention and Services to Seniors

Vi, a company with over 2,800 employees, owns and operates 10 continuing care residential communities for older adults across the United States. As the U.S. population ages, there will be increased demand for senior living facilities, which in turn creates a need to attract and retain new employees. Vi believes that investing in employee development is key for attracting and retaining talented employees who in turn provide high-quality services to residents. Satisfied residents are more likely to want to stay in Vi's communities and are more likely to give positive recommendations to their friends and relatives who are potential residents.

One way that Vi invests in employees is through its leadership development programs. Vi believes that making an investment in its potential leaders not only helps to retain top talent but motivates them to manage their staffs in a way that enhances their engagement. In fact, many of Vi's current leaders, who joined the company in high school, have participated in the leadership development programs to advance their careers. Vi has several different leadership development programs. The purpose of the Breakthrough Leadership Program (BLP) is to increase the competencies and effectiveness of high-potential leaders. BLP prepares them to take on additional responsibilities or move into higher-level positions. The program content covers building results and accountability, employee and personal development, and improving communications and influencing others. The one-year program includes classroom, virtual learning, and online learning. Program participants also receive coaching to help them develop and execute an action plan tailored to their personal development needs. The Management Development program focuses on developing future leaders from employees currently working as servers and housekeepers and in engineering, dining, and administrative positions. This year-long program includes courses, experiential learning, and mentoring. In Vi's Emerging Leaders Program, employees participate in a six-month virtual learning program focused on developing the knowledge and skills they need to help them grow as leaders.

In addition to the leadership development programs, Vi has invested in developing career paths for culinary and entry-level nursing positions. In particular, Vi competes with hospitals for nurses and with culinary services and restaurants for dining service employees. To help attract and retain nurses and dining service employees, Vi developed new career paths. These career paths allow employees to take the initiative to advance in their careers by developing skills through training provided by Vi; taking courses outside of Vi at technical schools, colleges, and universities (with tuition reimbursed by Vi); and mentoring opportunities.

Preliminary evaluation of the impact of Vi's development investment have been positive. In the first four months after introduction of the new career paths, 15% of Vi's culinary employees took advantage of training opportunities needed to advance in their careers. Turnover of nurse assistants has decreased 6%.

SOURCES: Based on J. Whitcomb, "Help Wanted: Cultivating Talent Outside Your Organization," *Training*, January/February 2019, pp. 40–41; B. Hassell, "At Vi, Business Is All about Living and Learning," *Chief Learning Officer*, June 2017, pp. 32–33; R. Bell, "Dedicated to Employee Development at Vi," *Chief Learning Officer*, June 2018, pp. 24–25; and "What Is Vi," from www .viliving.com, and "Training Programs," from https://jobs.viliving.com/training-programs, accessed January 3, 2019.

# Introduction

As the Vi example illustrates, development is important for all employees, not just managers. Employee development is a key contributor to a company's competitive advantage by helping employees advance in their careers to meet their personal growth needs and gain the necessary skills for management roles that they might want to pursue. This helps attract and retain valuable employees who might otherwise leave to join clients or competitors. Employee development is a necessary component of a company's efforts to compete in the new economy, to meet the challenges of global competition and social change, and to incorporate technological advances and changes in work design. Employee development is key to ensuring that employees have the competencies necessary to serve customers and create new products and customer solutions. Regardless of the business strategy, development is important for retaining talented employees. Also, because companies (and their employees) must continually learn and change to meet customer needs and compete in new markets, the emphasis placed on both training and development has increased. As we noted in Chapter 1, employee commitment and retention are directly related to how employees are treated by their managers.

This chapter begins by discussing the relationship among development, training, and careers. Choosing an approach is one part of development planning. Before employees choose development activities, the employee and the company must have an idea of the employee's development needs and the purpose of development. Identifying the needs and purpose of development is part of the planning process, which this chapter describes in detail. Employee and company responsibilities at each step of the process are emphasized. The chapter also looks at development approaches, including formal education, assessment, job experiences, and interpersonal relationships, with a focus on the types of skills, knowledge, and behaviors that are strengthened by each development method. The chapter concludes with a discussion of special issues in employee development, including succession planning and using development to help women and minorities move into upper-level management positions (referred to as "melting the glass ceiling").

**Development**
The acquisition of knowledge, skills, and behaviors that improve an employee's ability to meet changes in job requirements and in client and customer demands.

**LO 9-1**
Explain how employee development contributes to strategies related to employee retention, development of intellectual capital, and business growth.

# The Relationship among Development, Training, and Careers

## DEVELOPMENT AND TRAINING

**Development** refers to formal education, job experiences, relationships, and assessment of personality and abilities that help employees prepare for the future. The 3M example illustrates that although development can occur through participation in planned programs, it often results from performing different types of work. Because it is future-oriented, it involves learning that is not necessarily related to the employee's current job.[1] Table 9.1 shows the differences between training and development. Traditionally, training focuses on helping employees' performance in their current jobs. Development prepares them for other positions in the company and increases their ability to move into jobs that may not yet exist.[2] Development also helps employees prepare for changes in their current jobs that may result from new technology, work designs, new customers, or new product markets.

**Table 9.1**
Comparison between Training and Development

|  | TRAINING | DEVELOPMENT |
|---|---|---|
| **Focus** | Current | Future |
| **Use of work experiences** | Low | High |
| **Goal** | Preparation for current job | Preparation for changes |
| **Participation** | Required | Voluntary |

Development is especially critical for talent management, particularly for senior managers and employees with leadership potential (recall our discussion of attracting and retaining talent in Chapter 1). Development is necessary for ensuring that Millennial employees are prepared to take Baby Boomers' leadership roles as they retire. Companies report that the most important talent management challenges they face include developing existing talent and attracting and retaining existing leadership talent.[3] Also, development provides opportunities for all employees to grow their skills and use them in different ways, which has been shown to contribute to high levels of engagement and satisfaction.[4]

Chapter 7 emphasized the strategic role of training. As training continues to become more strategic (i.e., related to business goals), the distinction between training and development will blur. Both training and development will be required and will focus on current and future personal and company needs.

## DEVELOPMENT AND CAREERS

Today's careers are known as *protean careers*.[5] A **protean career** is based on self-direction with the goal of psychological success in one's work. Employees take major responsibility for managing their careers. For example, an engineer may decide to take a sabbatical from her position to work in management at the United Way for a year. The purpose of this assignment could be to develop her managerial skills as well as help her personally evaluate if she likes managerial work more than engineering.

The protean career has several implications for employee development. The goal of the new career is **psychological success**: the feeling of pride and accomplishment that comes from achieving life goals that are not limited to achievements at work (such as raising a family and having good physical health). Psychological success is self-determined rather than determined solely through signals the employee receives from the company (like salary increases and promotions). For example,when Kat Cole was in her teens, she started working as a waitress at Hooters.[6] She balanced that with college courses for two years, then focused solely on her job. The company was growing fast, so it offered opportunities to those who were willing to tackle challenges, and Cole was one of those people. At 20, she was offered a post in the HR department at Hooters' headquarters. The job would involve less pay, but Cole saw an opportunity to learn the business and accepted the offer. The job required her to travel overseas to open new franchises—a big stretch for a young woman who had almost never left her home state of Florida. She volunteered for assignments and took the initiative to research the business. Coupled with her firsthand experience of working in a restaurant, she soon had significant insight into the operations. A few years later, she worked her way up to vice president of training and development.

Cole determined that for her to succeed in management, she would need more formal education. Even while she continued working, she returned to school, completed college, and earned a master's in business administration from Georgia State University. In 2010, she left Hooters to become president of Cinnabon, part of a restaurant group called FOCUS Brands. Five years later, the company made her group president of FOCUS, which includes Cinnabon, Auntie Anne's Pretzels, Carvel, Schlotzky's, and other food-service operations.

Employees need to develop new skills rather than rely on a static knowledge base. This has resulted from companies' need to be more responsive to customers' service and product demands. As we emphasized in Chapter 7, learning is continuous, often informal, and involves creating and sharing knowledge.

**Protean career**
A career that is changing frequently due to both changes in the person's interests, abilities, and values and changes in the work environment.

**Psychological success**
The feeling of pride and accomplishment that comes from achieving life goals.

The emphasis on continuous learning has altered the direction and frequency of movement within careers (known as a *career pattern*).[7] Traditional career patterns consisted of a series of steps arranged in a linear hierarchy, with higher steps related to increased authority, responsibility, and compensation. Expert career patterns involve a lifelong commitment to a field or specialization (such as law, medicine, or management). These types of career patterns will not disappear. Rather, career patterns involving movement across specializations or disciplines (a spiral career pattern) will become more prevalent. These new career patterns mean that developing employees (as well as employees taking control of their own careers) will require providing them with the opportunity to (1) determine their interests, skill strengths, and weaknesses and (2) based on this information, seek appropriate development experiences that will likely involve job experiences and relationships as well as formal courses.

The most appropriate view of today's careers are that they are "boundaryless and often change."[8] A career may include movement across several employers (job hopping) or even different occupations. Studies have found that by age 35, 25% of employees have held five jobs or more, and for employees 55 and older, 20% have held 10 jobs or more.[9] One-third of employers expect job hopping to occur, especially among new college graduates, but 40% believe it becomes less acceptable when employees are in their mid-30s. The reality is that employees will be unlikely to stay at one company for their entire or even a significant part of their career. This means that companies and employees should add value to each other.[10] That is, regardless of how long employees stay, developing them can help the company adapt to changing business conditions and strategies by providing new skill sets and managerial talent. It can help reduce employees' job hopping because they feel less need to change employers to build their skill sets or gain valuable job experiences.

For example, to develop and retain millennial employees Miami Children's Health System are assigned projects that expose them to senior leaders.[11] One of the projects involved having clinical staff members work with the learning and development team to create short videos showing operating procedures. The staff members received a financial reward for their work and were recognized in an internal newsletter. Millennials are also asked to attend town hall meetings and small discussion groups where they can interact with the chief operations officer, vice presidents, and other senior leaders.

*Boundaryless* means that careers may involve identifying more with a job or profession than with the present employer. A career can also be considered boundaryless in the sense that career plans or goals are influenced by personal or family demands and values. One way that employees cope with changes in their personal lives as well as in employment relationships is to rearrange and shift their roles and responsibilities. Employees can change their careers throughout their lives based on awareness of strengths and weaknesses, perceived need to balance work and life, and the need to find stimulating and exciting work.[12] Career success may not be tied to promotions but to achieving goals that are personally meaningful to the employee rather than those set by parents, peers, or the company. As we discuss later in the chapter, careers are best managed through partnerships between employees and their company that create a positive relationship through which employees are committed to the organization but can take personal control for managing their own careers to benefit themselves and the company.

**Development planning system**
A system to retain and motivate employees by identifying and meeting their development needs (also called *career management systems*).

As this discussion shows, to retain and motivate employees, companies need to provide a system to identify and meet employees' development needs. This is especially important to retain good performers and employees who have potential for managerial positions. Such systems are often known as **development planning systems** or career management systems. We discuss these systems in the next section.

# Development Planning Systems

Companies' development planning systems vary in the level of sophistication and the emphasis they place on different components of the process. Steps and responsibilities in the development planning system are shown in Figure 9.1.

**LO 9-2**
Discuss the steps in the development planning process.

## SELF-ASSESSMENT

*Self-assessment* refers to the use of information by employees to determine their career interests, values, aptitudes, and behavioral tendencies. It often involves psychological tests such as the Myers-Briggs Type Indicator (described later in the chapter), the Strong Interest Inventory, and the Self-Directed Search. The Strong Interest Inventory helps employees identify their occupational and job interests; the Self-Directed Search identifies employees' preferences for working in different types of environments (like sales, counseling, landscaping, and so on). Tests may also help employees identify the relative values they place on work and leisure activities.

**LO 9-3**
Explain the employees' and company's responsibilities in planning development.

Through the assessment, a development need can be identified. This need can result from gaps between current skills and/or interests and the type of work or position the employee wants. CarMax, the automobile retailer, makes available to its associates a Career Conversation Guide that helps them take ownership of their own development by assessing the competencies and behaviors they need to be successful in an entry-level management position.[13] After completing the guide associates are encouraged to initiate a career conversation with their manager. Eighty-three percent of associates who completed the assessment had a career conversation with their manager. The guide provides the basis for an informed discussion about the associates development needs and possible career paths.

## REALITY CHECK

*Reality check* refers to the information employees receive about how the company evaluates their skills and knowledge and where they fit into the company's plans (potential promotion opportunities, lateral moves). Usually this information is provided by the

**Figure 9.1**

Steps and Responsibilities in the Development Planning Process

| | Self-assessment | Reality check | Goal setting | Action planning |
|---|---|---|---|---|
| **Employee responsibility** | Identify opportunities and needs to improve. | Identify what needs are realistic to develop. | Identify goal and method to determine goal progress. | Identify steps and timetable to reach goal. |
| **Company responsibility** | Provide assessment information to identify strengths, weaknesses, interests, and values. | Communicate performance evaluation; where employee fits in long-range plans of the company; and changes in industry, profession, and workplace. | Ensure that goal is SMART (specific, measurable, attainable, relevant, and timely); commit to help employee reach the goal. | Identify resources employee needs to reach goal, including additional assesment, courses, work experiences, and relationships. |

employee's manager as part of performance appraisal. Some companies also use the 360-degree feedback assessment, which involves employees completing a self-evaluation of their behaviors or competencies while managers, peers, direct reports, and even customers provide smaller evaluations. (360-degree feedback is discussed later in the chapter.) It is not uncommon in well-developed systems for the manager to hold separate performance appraisals and development discussions. In the development discussions the manager focuses on discussing the employees values and career interests, the strengths and weaknesses of their skills or competencies, and how to capitalize on their strengths and develop their weaknesses.[14]

For example, IBM provides employees with access to Blue Matching, an algorithm that makes personalized recommendations about job openings based on data from their résumé, assessments of what kind of work excites them and their abilities.[15] In its first two years, Blue Matching has helped more than 1,000 employees find jobs, and its users are three times more likely to apply for internal job openings than those who haven't used the system. GE is developing an app to help increase the effectiveness of development conversations between employees and their managers.[16] The app uses data on the historical movement of GE employees and how the relationship between job descriptions to help employees identify potential positions across the company.

## GOAL SETTING

*Goal setting* refers to the process of employees developing short- and long-term development objectives. These goals usually relate to desired positions (e.g., becoming sales manager within three years), level of skill application (using one's budgeting skills to improve the unit's cash flow problems), work setting (moving to corporate marketing within two years), or skill acquisition (learning how to use the company's human resource information system). These goals are usually discussed with the manager and written into a development plan. A sample development plan for a product manager is shown in Figure 9.2. Development plans usually include descriptions of strengths and weaknesses, career goals, and development activities for reaching the career goal. An effective development plan is simple, clear, and realistic, and it focuses on developmental needs that are most relevant to both the individual's career and the organization's strategic objectives.[17]

Procter & Gamble's promotion-from-within policy is supported by the development plans completed by every employee.[18] These plans identify what type of experience the employee needs for their next job as well as future jobs they might hold. Employees post their résumés online to show managers the skills they are building as well as communicating whether they are willing to take a different job. At monthly meetings for each business unit, employee career paths and résumés are reviewed.

## ACTION PLANNING

**Action plan**
A document summarizing what the trainee and manager will do to ensure that training transfers to the job.

During this phase, employees complete an action plan. An **action plan** is a written strategy that employees use to determine how they will achieve their short- and long-term career goals. Action plans may involve any one or a combination of development approaches such as enrolling in courses and seminars, getting additional assessment, obtaining new job experiences, or finding a mentor or coach (see the section Approaches to Employee Development).[19] The development approach used depends on the needs and developmental goal. Wells Fargo's online iDevelop site helps employees prioritize their development needs and create development plans.[20] Employees use the site to identify their competencies. They use the competencies they consider as strengths to choose development activities including training programs and online resources.

**Figure 9.2**
Sample Development Plan

---

**Name:** _____    **Title:** Project Manager    **Immediate Manager:** _____

---

**Competencies**
*Please identify your three greatest strengths and areas for improvement.*
**Strengths**
• Strategic thinking and execution (confidence, command skills, action orientation)
• Results orientation (competence, motivating others, perseverance)
• Spirit for winning (building team spirit, customer focus, respect colleagues)

---

**Areas for Improvement**
• Patience (tolerance of people or processes and sensitivity to pacing)
• Written communications (ability to write clearly and succinctly)
• Overly ambitious (too much focus on successful completion of projects rather than developing relationships with individuals involved in the projects)

---

**Development Goals**
*Please describe your overall career goals.*
• **Long-term:** Accept positions of increased responsibility to a level of general manager (or beyond). The areas of specific interest include but are not limited to product and brand management, technology and development, strategic planning, and marketing.
• **Short-term:** Continue to improve my skills in marketing and brand management while utilizing my skills in product management, strategic planning, and global relations.

---

**Next Assignments**
*Identify potential next assignments (including timing) that would help you develop toward your goals.*
• Manager or director level in planning, development, product, or brand management. Timing estimated to be Fall 2021.

---

**Training and Development Needs**
*List both training and development activities that will either help you develop in your current assignment or provide overall development.*
• Master's degree classes will allow me to practice and improve my written communications skills. The dynamics of my current position, teamwork, and reliance on other individuals allow me to practice patience and to focus on individual team members' needs along with the success of the projects.

---

**Employee** _____    **Date** _____
**Immediate Manager** _____    **Date** _____
**Mentor** _____    **Date** _____

## EXAMPLES OF DEVELOPMENT PLANNING AND CAREER MANAGEMENT SYSTEMS

Effective development planning systems include several important features (see Table 9.2). For example, consider the career management and development systems at Penn Station and Genentech.[21] Penn Station, a restaurant chain that specializes in sub sandwiches, provides employees with My Penn Path Development Tool. Employees use My Penn Path Development to see the skills needed for each level of employment at the company and

**Table 9.2**
Design Features
of Effective
Development
Systems

1. System is positioned as a response to a business need or supports the business strategy.
2. Employees and managers participate in development of the system.
3. Employees are encouraged to take an active role in career management and development.
4. Evaluation is ongoing and used to improve the system.
5. Business units can customize the system for their own purposes (with some constraints).
6. Employees have access to development and career information sources (including advisors and positions available).
7. Senior management and the company culture support the development system.
8. The development system is linked to other human resource practices such as performance management, training, and recruiting systems.
9. A large, diverse talent pool is created.
10. Development plans and talent evaluation information are available and accessible to all managers.

SOURCE: Based on B. Kaye and C. Smith, "Career Development: Shifting from Nicety to Necessity," *T + D*, January 2012, pp. 52–55; M. Weinstein, "Paths to Success: Responsibility vs. Promotion," *Training*, July/August 2014, pp. 52–54; D. Hall, *Careers in and out of Organizations* (Thousand Oaks, CA: Sage, 2002).

identifies how the employee can learn them. Print media, video and online learning, and experiences on the job are used in programs that develop the skills employees need. The biotechnology company Genentech Inc. developed CareerLab to help employees perform well in their current job and provide opportunities for job enrichment and lateral career moves. CareerLab is a physical and virtual place where employees can consider their skill strengths and weaknesses, their interests, and take ownership of their development. CareerLab includes the opportunity to get career advice from consultants, participate in LearningLabs (webinars and class sessions that cover different topics such as networking for career growth and managing your personal brand), receive mentoring, and attend career workshops. CareerLab also provides access to online career resources including assessments that cover personal style, values, skills, strengths, and interests. Genentech has found that employee who use CareerLab have a high level of engagement with their work, improved productivity, better career conversations with their managers, and a greater likelihood of staying with the company.

## Approaches to Employee Development

Four approaches are used to develop employees: formal education, assessment, job experiences, and interpersonal relationships.[22] Many companies use a combination of these approaches. Telus International has several development programs for employees at different career stages.[23] IEvolve is for all new employees, IAspire is for emerging leaders, IExcel is for managers and supervisors, and ILead is for senior leaders. The development programs include online and instructor-led courses, mentoring and coaching, and 360-degree assessment. Figure 9.3 shows the frequency of use of different employee development practices. Both high-visibility assignment and stretch opportunities are considered developmental job experiences.

Although much development activity is targeted at managers, all levels of employees may be involved in development. For example, most employees typically receive performance

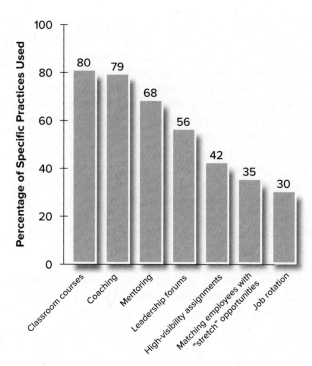

**Figure 9.3**
Frequency of Use
of Employee
Development
Practices

SOURCE: EFMD, Network of Corporate Academies, Society for Human Resource Management, "Leadership
Development: The Path to Greater Effectiveness," 2016, www.shrm.org.

appraisal feedback (a development activity related to assessment) at least once per year. As
part of the appraisal process (see Chapter 8), employees are typically asked to complete
individual development plans outlining (1) how they plan to change their weaknesses and
(2) their future plans (including positions or locations desired and education or experience
needed). Next we explore each type of development approach.

## FORMAL EDUCATION

**Formal education programs** include off-site and on-site programs designed specifically for
the company's employees, short courses offered by consultants or universities, executive
MBA programs, and university programs in which participants live at the university while
taking classes. These programs may involve lectures by business experts, business games
and simulations, adventure learning, and meetings with customers.

Many companies, such as McDonald's and General Electric, rely primarily on in-house
development programs offered by training and development centers or corporate universities, rather than sending employees to programs offered by universities.[24] Companies rely
on in-house programs because they can be tied directly to business needs, can be easily
evaluated using company metrics, and can get senior-level management involved.

The thousands of restaurant managers and owner-operators who attend McDonald's
Hamburger University each year in Chicago, Illinois, get classroom training and participate in simulations on how to run a business that delivers consistent service, quality, and
cleanliness. They also receive coaching and peer support face-to-face and online. The
company's highest-performing executives participate in a nine-month leadership institute
at Hamburger U, where they tackle major issues facing the company.

**LO 9-4**
Discuss current trends
in using formal
education for
development.

**Formal education
programs**
Employee development
programs, including
short courses offered
by consultants or
universities, executive
MBA programs, and
university programs.

General Electric (GE) has one of the oldest and most widely known management development centers in the world. GE invests approximately $1 billion each year in training and education programs for its employees.[25] Since 2000, the 189 most senior executives in the company spent at least 12 months in training and professional development. GE develops managers at the John F. Welch Leadership Development Center at Crotonville, New York, offering over 1,800 instructor-led and virtual courses and programs.[26] The facility has residence buildings where participants stay while attending programs, as well as classrooms for courses, programs, and seminars. Each year, GE employees—chosen by their managers based on their performance and potential—attend management development programs. The programs include professional skills development and specialized courses in areas such as risk analysis and loan structuring. All of the programs emphasize theory and practical application. Course time is spent discussing business issues facing GE. The programs are taught by in-house instructors, university faculty members, and even CEO Jeff Immelt. GE also offers courses through its global learning centers in Rio de Janeiro, Abu Dhabi, Shanghai, and Bengaluru (in fact, over 70% of in-person sessions are delivered outside the United States).

Examples of management development programs available at GE are shown in Table 9.3. As you can see, GE uses a combination of coursework and job experiences to develop entry-level and top levels of management. Other programs such as the Business Manager Course and the Executive Development Course involve action learning. GE also holds seminars on better understanding customer expectations and leadership

**Table 9.3**

Examples of Leadership Development Programs at General Electric

| PROGRAM | SUMMARY | QUALIFICATIONS TO ATTEND |
|---|---|---|
| Commercial Leadership Program | Two-year rotational program focused on development through three or four rotational assignments, education that develops sales competencies, and exposure to and coaching from leaders. The program prepares individuals for a successful career in sales or sales support. The rotational assignments include projects driven by business priorities. Commercial skills development occurs through business-specific training, coursework, and global training summits. | Bachelor's degree in engineering, or relevant business or science degree. Prior intern or co-op experience, or up to three years' work experience in sales, sales support, or marketing. Strong analytical, communication, interpersonal, and leadership skills. Willingness to relocate. |
| Experienced Commercial Leadership Program (ECLP): Sales and Marketing | Two-year program includes international training in a variety of locations and leadership opportunities, including change initiatives. Committee participation is encouraged to improve ability to interact with senior business leaders. Every four months, employees complete a self-assessment and review it with managers to identify development needs, career interests, and accomplishments. | An MBA/postgraduate degree with sales and/or marketing experience; demonstrated leadership, and communication and analytical skills; willingness to travel; fluency in English; expertise that is aligned with a particular GE business. |

SOURCES: Based on "Commercial Leadership Program Summary," https://www.ge.com/careers/working-at-ge/commercial-leadership-program accessed January 31, 2019; "Experienced Commercial Leadership Program," http://www.ge.com/au/careers/our-programs/eclp/what-you-need-to-know, and http://www.ge.com/au/careers/our-programs/eclp/about-eclp, accessed January 31, 2019.

conferences designed specifically for African Americans, women, or Hispanic managers to discuss leading and learning.

A number of institutions offer executive education in the United States and abroad, including Harvard University, the Wharton School, the University of Michigan, INSEAD, the International Institute for Management Development (IMD), and the Center for Creative Leadership. At the University of Virginia, the Darden School of Business offers an executive MBA program in which students attend classes on campus once a month (Thursday through Saturday). The on-campus time provides opportunities for students to collaborate on presentations, simulations, and case studies. The school also brings executive MBA students to campus four times for leadership residencies. During each week-long residency, the students use workshops, coaching, and reflection to get better at handling their everyday management challenges. Between the times on campus, the students continue their education with independent study, online classes, and tools for virtual meetings and online exams.[27]

Another trend in executive education is for employers and the education provider to create programs with content and experiences designed specifically for the audience. For example, the National Basketball Association (NBA) has several different leadership development programs, each focusing on managers at different levels. About one-third of all NBA managers and 50 high-potential leaders participate in the program each year. The curriculum focuses on new managers, directors, vice presidents, and advanced leaders who participate in 70 hours of development over five to seven months. The Rising Talent program is designed for midcareer leaders. The Veteran Track is for vice presidents. Most course modules are taught by the NBA's own leaders and business school professors. The courses include experiential learning activities and case studies based on actual NBA issues and problems. In addition to attending the course modules, program participants work in small teams to propose solutions to current strategic business issues and challenges facing their team and the NBA.[28] TELUS partnered with the University of Victoria's Peter B. Gustavson School of Business to create a customized MBA program tailored specifically to the company's and the telecommunication industry leadership and strategy issues. The program includes face-to-face instruction on campus, video lectures, virtual interactions, and team projects. TELUS senior leaders participated in the program as guest lecturers, mentors, and project sponsors. High performing managers with at least three years of experience were eligible to apply. The payoffs from the first cohort of 20 managers has been positive. Forty percent of the managers have been promoted to new roles. The project recommendations that the managers provided saved TELUS $27 million.[29]

Managers who attend the Center for Creative Leadership development program take psychological tests; receive feedback from managers, peers, and direct reports; participate in group-building activities (like adventure learning, discussed in Chapter 7); receive counseling; and set improvement goals and write development plans.[30]

Enrollment in executive education programs or MBA programs may be limited to managers or employees identified to have management potential. As a result, many companies also provide tuition reimbursement as a benefit for all employees to encourage them to develop. **Tuition reimbursement** refers to the practice of reimbursing employees' costs for college and university courses and degree programs. Companies that have evaluated tuition reimbursement programs have found that the programs increase employee retention rates, readiness for promotion, and improve job performance.[31]

The Integrity in Action box highlights how several companies are paying for employees education expenses to help them get the formal education they need to succeed in their careers.

**Tuition reimbursement** The practice of reimbursing employees' costs for college and university courses and degree programs.

# INTEGRITY IN ACTION

## Footing the Bill for Employee Development

Typically, companies require employees to complete the required formal education they need for obtaining their job. To advance in their careers to higher paying jobs, employees often need additional education but lack the financial resources necessary to pay for it. To help employees reach their career goals, Verizon Wireless, Discover Financial Services, Taco Bell, and Disney are paying the cost of employees tuition, fees, books, and other educational expenses.

Verizon Wireless invests $26 million annually in its tuition reimbursement program. Employees are eligible for tuition reimbursement the first day of hire and have to make no commitment to stay employed with the company. Expenses are limited to $8,000 per year for full-time employees but this exceeds the $5,250 annual reimbursement limit that most

companies use based on the tax-free minimum established by the IRS.

At Discover Financial Services, 80% of call center and field staff lack a college degree. So the company introduced a program that pays employees expenses to attend the University of Florida, Brandman University, and Wilmington University to pursue degrees in areas where the company needs talent such as in cybersecurity, computer engineering, and business. Taco Bell covers employees education expenses up to $5,000 per year and negotiate deals for textbooks and other services.

Disney expects to spend $50 million on employee education by mid-2019 and $25 million in subsequent years. Bob Iger, chief executive of Disney, believes the cost is worthwhile because it helps give employees more career opportunities, and

even if they end up leaving Disney, it enhances employees engagement and confidence.

### DISCUSSION QUESTIONS

1. Is development planning necessary for employees and companies to fully recognize the benefits of education expense programs described? Explain.
2. How might the benefits of educational expense programs vary depending on the labor market?
3. What do educational expense programs say to you about the values of these companies?

SOURCES: Based on K. Gee, "Employers Offer to Pay for College," *Wall Street Journal*, January 3, 2019, p. B5; "Disney Allocates $25 Million Yearly for Staff Tuition," *T+D*, December 2018, p. 13; Verizon, "Frequently Asked Questions: Do You Offer Tuition Reimbursement/Assistance?" from www.verizon.com, accessed January 3, 2019; "Top 125 Hall of Fame: Verizon," *Training*, January/February 2014, pp. 58–59.

## ASSESSMENT

**LO 9-5**

Relate how assessment of personality type, work behaviors, and job performance can be used for employee development.

**Assessment**

Collecting information and providing feedback to employees about their behavior, communication style, or skills.

**Assessment** involves collecting information and providing feedback to employees about their behavior, communication style, or skills.[32] The employees, their peers, managers, and customers may provide information. Assessments are used for several reasons. First, assessment is used most frequently to identify employees with managerial potential and to measure current managers' strengths and weaknesses. Assessment is also used to identify managers with the potential to move into higher-level executive positions, and it can be used with work teams to identify the strengths and weaknesses of individual team members and the decision processes or communication styles that inhibit the team's productivity. Assessments can help employees understand their tendencies, their needs, the type of work environment they prefer, and the type of work they might prefer to do.[33] This information, along with the performance evaluations they receive from the company, can help employees decide what type of development goals might be most appropriate for them (e.g., leadership position, increased scope of their current position).

Companies vary in the methods and the sources of information they use in developmental assessment. Many companies use employee performance evaluations. Companies with sophisticated development systems use psychological tests to measure employees' skills, interests, personality types, and communication styles. Self, peer, and managers' ratings of employees' interpersonal styles and behaviors may also be collected. Popular assessment tools include personality tests, assessment center performance appraisal, and 360-degree feedback.

## Personality Tests and Inventories

Tests are used to determine if employees have the personality characteristics necessary to be successful in specific managerial jobs or jobs involving international assignments. Personality tests typically measure five major dimensions: extraversion, adjustment, agreeableness, conscientiousness, and openness to experience (see Table 6.3 in Chapter 6).

The **Myers-Briggs Type Inventory (MBTI)** refers to an assessment that is based on Carl Jung's personality type theory. This theory emphasizes that we have a fundamental personality type that shapes and influences how we understand the world, process information, and socialize. The assessment determines which one of 16 personality types fits best. The 16 unique personality types are based on preferences for introversion (I) or extraversion (E), sensing (S) or intuition (N), thinking (T) or feeling (F), and judging (J) or perceiving (P). The assessment tool identifies individuals' preferences for energy (introversion versus extraversion), information gathering (sensing versus intuition), decision making (thinking versus feeling), and lifestyle (judging versus perceiving).[34] Each personality type has implications for work habits and interpersonal relationships. For example, individuals who are introverted, sensing, thinking, and judging (known as ISTJs) tend to be serious, quiet, practical, orderly, and logical. These persons can organize tasks, be decisive, and follow through on plans and goals. ISTJs have several weaknesses because they do not tend to use the opposite preferences: extraversion, intuition, feeling, and perceiving. These weaknesses include problems dealing with unexpected opportunities, appearing too task-oriented or impersonal to colleagues, and making overly quick decisions. Visit the website www.cpp.com for more information on the personality types.

**Myers-Briggs Type Inventory (MBTI)**
A psychological test used for team building and leadership development that identifies employees' preferences for energy, information gathering, decision making, and lifestyle.

The DiSC assessment measures personality and behavioral style, including dominance (direct, strong-willed, forceful), influence (sociable, talkative), steadiness (gentle accommodating), and conscientiousness (private, analytical).[35] See www.discprofile.com for more information on DiSC.

For example, consider how Guckenheimer and CareSource use personality tests and inventories.[36] Guckenheimer, a corporate restaurant management and catering company, has its managers complete DiSC to understand their communication style. Then, managers complete training to develop their skill in adjusting their communication style to improve their interactions with their employees. CareSource, a Medicaid-managed care provider in Dayton, Ohio, has a defined process for identifying and developing employees who have the potential to be strong leaders and effective managers. Assessment of fit with the organization's values and culture, which emphasize serving the underserved, begins with the recruiting process. The company uses multiple assessment tools to evaluate managers' competencies (recall the discussion of competencies in Chapter 8). These assessments include the Myers-Briggs Type Indicator; Gallup's StrengthsFinder, to identify managers' strengths and develop plans for using their strengths with their employee team; and the Leadership Practices Inventory, which provides managers with an idea of their leadership skills as evaluated by peers, their boss, and their own self-assessment, and is used to build a personal leadership development plan. Also, twice a year, managers are evaluated on competencies and behavior that CareSource believes are characteristics of an effective leader and manager: a service orientation, organizational awareness, teamwork, communications, and organizational leadership. Based on the assessment results, managers with high leadership potential are encouraged to participate in a variety of development activities.

## Assessment Center

At an **assessment center**, multiple raters or evaluators (assessors) evaluate employees' performance on a number of exercises.[37] An assessment center is usually at an off-site location such as a conference center. Between 6 and 12 employees usually participate at one time. Assessment centers are used primarily to identify if employees have the personality characteristics, administrative skills, and interpersonal skills needed for managerial jobs. They are also increasingly being used to determine if employees have the necessary skills to work in teams.

The types of exercises used in assessment centers include leaderless group discussions, interviews, in-baskets, and role-plays.[38] In a **leaderless group discussion**, a team of five to seven employees is assigned a problem and must work together to solve it within a certain time period. The problem may involve buying and selling supplies, nominating a subordinate for an award, or assembling a product. In the **interview**, employees answer questions about their work and personal experiences, skill strengths and weaknesses, and career plans. An **in-basket** is a simulation of the administrative tasks of the manager's job. The exercise includes a variety of documents that may appear in the in-basket on a manager's desk. The participants read the materials and decide how to respond to them. Responses might include delegating tasks, scheduling meetings, writing replies, or even ignoring a memo. In a **role-play**, the participant takes the part or role of a manager or another employee. For example, an assessment center participant may be asked to take the role of a manager who has to give a negative performance review to a subordinate. The participant is told about the subordinate's performance and is asked to prepare for and actually hold a 45-minute meeting with the subordinate to discuss the performance problems. The role of the subordinate is played by a manager or other member of the assessment center design team or company. The assessment center might also include interest and aptitude tests to evaluate an employee's vocabulary, general mental ability, and reasoning skills. Personality tests may be used to determine if employees can get along with others, their tolerance for ambiguity, and other traits related to success as a manager.

Assessment center exercises are designed to measure employees' administrative and interpersonal skills. Skills typically measured include leadership, oral and written communication, judgment, organizational ability, and stress tolerance. Table 9.4 shows an example of the skills measured by the assessment center. Each exercise gives participating employees the opportunity to demonstrate several different skills. For example, the exercise requiring scheduling to meet production demands evaluates employees' administrative and problem-solving ability. The leaderless group discussion measures interpersonal skills such as sensitivity toward others, stress tolerance, and oral communication skills.

Managers are usually used as assessors. The managers are trained to look for employee behaviors that are related to the skills that will be assessed. Typically, each assessor observes and records one or two employees' behaviors in each exercise. The assessors review their notes and rate each employee's level of skills (e.g., 5 = high level of leadership skills, 1 = low level of leadership skills). After all employees have completed the exercises, the assessors discuss their observations of each employee. They compare their ratings and try to agree on each employee's rating for each of the skills.

As we mentioned in Chapter 6, research suggests that assessment center ratings are related to performance, salary level, and career advancement.[39] Assessment centers may also be useful for development because employees who participate in the process receive feedback regarding their attitudes and skill strengths and weaknesses.[40] For example, Steelcase, the office furniture manufacturer based in Grand Rapids, Michigan, has used assessment centers for first-level managers.[41] The assessment center exercises include in-basket, interview simulation, and a timed scheduling exercise requiring participants to fill

**Table 9.4**

Examples of Skills Measured by Assessment Center Exercises

| | IN-BASKET | SCHEDULING EXERCISE | LEADERLESS GROUP DISCUSSION | PERSONALITY TEST | ROLE-PLAY |
|---|---|---|---|---|---|
| EXERCISES | | | | | |
| **SKILLS** | | | | | |
| Leadership (dominance, coaching, influence, resourcefulness) | X | | X | X | X |
| Problem solving (judgment) | X | X | X | | X |
| Interpersonal (sensitivity, conflict resolution, cooperation, oral communication) | | | X | X | X |
| Administrative (organizing, planning, written communications) | X | X | X | | |
| Personal (stress tolerance, confidence) | | | X | X | X |

NOTE: X indicates skill measured by exercise.

positions created by absences. Managers are also required to confront an employee on a performance issue, getting the employee to commit to improve. Because the exercises relate closely to what managers are required to do at work, feedback given to managers based on their performance in the assessment center can target specific skills or competencies that they need to become successful managers.

## Performance Appraisals and 360-Degree Feedback Systems

As we described in Chapter 8, *performance appraisal* is the process of measuring employees' performance. Performance appraisal information can be useful for employee development under certain conditions.[42] The appraisal system must tell employees specifically about their performance problems and how they can improve their performance. This includes providing a clear understanding of the differences between current performance and expected performance, identifying causes of the performance discrepancy, and developing action plans to improve performance. Managers must be trained in frequent performance feedback. Managers also need to monitor employees' progress in carrying out action plans.

Nordstrom's performance management system, known as Grow@Nordstrom, emphasizes a quarterly informal employee-led conversation with their managers in which they discuss progress toward performance and career objectives. The performance management process at LoyaltyOne requires managers to to meet with employees every 90 days to discuss progress, share feedback, and provide coaching on performance and development.[43]

A recent trend in performance appraisals for management development is the use of upward feedback and 360-degree feedback. **Upward feedback** refers to appraisal that involves collecting subordinates' evaluations of managers' behaviors or skills.

**Upward feedback**
A performance appraisal process for managers that includes subordinates' evaluations.

**Table 9.5**
Skills Related to Managerial Success

| | |
|---|---|
| Resourcefulness | Can think strategically, engage in flexible problem solving, and work effectively with higher-level management |
| Doing whatever it takes | Has perseverance and focus in the face of obstacles |
| Being a quick study | Quickly masters new technical and business knowledge |
| Building and mending relationships | Knows how to build and maintain working relationships with co-workers and external parties |
| Leading subordinates | Delegates to subordinates effectively, broadens their opportunities, and acts with fairness toward them |
| Compassion and sensitivity | Shows genuine interest in others and sensitivity to subordinates' needs |
| Straightforwardness and composure | Is honorable and steadfast |
| Setting a developmental climate | Provides a challenging climate to encourage subordinates' development |
| Confronting problem subordinates | Acts decisively and fairly when dealing with problem subordinates |
| Team orientation | Accomplishes tasks through managing others |
| Balance between personal life and work | Balances work priorities with personal life so that neither is neglected |
| Decisiveness | Prefers quick and approximate actions to slow and precise ones in many management situations |
| Self-awareness | Has an accurate picture of strengths and weaknesses and is willing to improve |
| Hiring talented staff | Hires talented people for the team |
| Putting people at ease | Displays warmth and a good sense of humor |
| Acting with flexibility | Can behave in ways that are often seen as opposites |

SOURCE: Based on C. D. McCauley, M. M. Lombardo, and C. J. Usher, "Diagnosing Management Development Needs: An Instrument Based on How Managers Develop," *Journal of Management* 15 (1989), pp. 389–403.

**360-degree feedback systems**
A performance appraisal process for managers that includes evaluations from a wide range of persons who interact with the manager. The process includes self-evaluations as well as evaluations from the manager's boss, subordinates, peers, and customers.

The 360-degree feedback process is a special case of upward feedback. In **360-degree feedback systems**, employees' behaviors or skills are evaluated not only by subordinates but also by peers, customers, their bosses, and the employees themselves. The raters complete a questionnaire asking them to rate the person on a number of different dimensions. Table 9.5 illustrates the types of skills related to management success that are rated in a 360-degree feedback questionnaire. Typically, raters are asked to assess the manager's strength in a particular area or whether development is needed. Raters may also be asked to identify how frequently they observe a competency or skill (e.g., always, sometimes, seldom, never). For example, at CHG Healthcare Services any employees who is interested in a leadership position is required to complete a 360-degree feedback survey that assesses behaviors related to the company's culture and core values.[44]

The results of a 360-degree feedback system show how the manager was rated on each item. The results also show how self-evaluations differ from evaluations from the other raters. Typically managers review their results, seek clarification from the raters, and set specific development goals based on the identified strengths and weaknesses.[45] Table 9.6 shows the type of activities involved in using 360-degree feedback for development.[46]

The benefits of 360-degree feedback include collecting multiple perspectives of managers' performance, allowing employees to compare their own personal evaluations with the views of others, and formalizing communications about behaviors and skills ratings

**Table 9.6**
Activities Involved in
Using 360-Degree
Feedback for
Development

1. **Understand strengths and weaknesses**
   Review ratings for strengths and weaknesses
   Identify skills or behaviors where self and others' (manager's, peers', customers')
   ratings agree and disagree
2. **Identify a development goal**
   Choose a skill or behavior to develop
   Set a clear, specific goal with a specified outcome
3. **Identify a process for recognizing goal accomplishment**
4. **Identify strategies for reaching the development goal**
   Establish strategies such as reading, job experiences, courses, and relationships
   Establish strategies for receiving feedback on progress
   Establish strategies for reinforcing the new skill or behavior

between employees and their internal and external customers. Several studies have shown that performance improves and behavior changes as a result of participating in upward feedback and 360-degree feedback systems.[47] The most change occurs in individuals who receive lower ratings from others than they gave themselves (overraters).

Potential limitations of 360-degree feedback include the time demands placed on the raters to complete the evaluations, managers seeking to identify and punish raters who provided negative information, the need to have a facilitator help interpret results, and companies' failure to provide ways that managers can act on the feedback they receive (development planning, meeting with raters, taking courses).

In effective 360-degree feedback systems, reliable or consistent ratings are provided, raters' confidentiality is maintained, the behaviors or skills assessed are job related (valid), the system is easy to use, and managers receive and act on the feedback.[48]

Technology allows 360-degree questionnaires to be delivered online to the raters. This increases the number of completed questionnaires returned, makes it easier to process the information, and speeds feedback reports to managers.

Regardless of the assessment method used, the information must be shared with the employee for development to occur. Along with assessment information, the employee needs suggestions for correcting skill weaknesses and using skills already learned. Suggestions might include participating in training courses or developing skills through new job experiences. Based on the assessment information and available development opportunities, employees should develop action plans to guide their self-improvement efforts.

At Lupin Limited, 360-degree feedback is used to develop company leaders.[49] Leaders behavior and how well they follow the company's six values (integrity, passion for excellence, teamwork, entrepreneurial spirit, respect and care, and customer focus) are included in the assessment. Leaders are expected to identify development areas and personal development plans using the results of the 360-degree feedback that are shared with them.

## JOB EXPERIENCES

Most employee development occurs through **job experiences**:[50] relationships, problems, demands, tasks, or other features that employees face in their jobs. A major assumption of using job experiences for employee development is that development is most likely to occur when employees are given stretch assignments. **Stretch assignments** refer to assignments in which there is a mismatch between the employee's skills and past experiences and the skills required for success on the job. To succeed in their jobs, employees must stretch their skills—that is, they are forced to learn new skills, apply their skills and

**Job experience**
The relationships, problems, demands, tasks, and other features that employees face in their jobs.

**Stretch assignments**
Job assignments in which there is a mismatch between an employee's skills and past experiences and the skills required for success on the job.

**LO 9-6**
Explain how job experiences can be used for skill development.

Mc Graw Hill **Connect**®

Visit your instructor's Connect® course and access your eBook to view this video.

"We believe everybody, in HR or in any other function, should be in a situation or a job in which they are stretched—I would almost use the word 'uncomfortable'— because learning happens when people are outside of their comfort zones."

—Susan P. Peters, Senior Vice President, Human Resources, GE

Source: Video produced for the Center for Executive Succession in the Darla Moore School of Business at the University of South Carolina by Coal Powered Filmworks

knowledge in a new way, and master new experiences.[51] New job assignments help take advantage of employees' existing skills, experiences, and contacts, while helping them develop new ones.[52] For example, Jennifer Rosemann's boss asked her to take over financial management of the area where she was supervising client-service staff.[53] Trained as a social worker she had no interest or skills in accounting. Her boss trusted Ms. Rosemann to learn the job and expected her to be successful. After a few months of managing revenue and expenses she realized that she enjoyed the sense of teamwork and accomplishment from meeting financial targets. She has since been promoted to an executive vice president. For job experiences to be effective development activities, they should be tailored to employees' development needs and goals.

Most of what we know about development through job experiences comes from a series of studies conducted by the Center for Creative Leadership.[54] Executives were asked to identify key career events that made a difference in their managerial styles and the lessons they learned from these experiences. The key events included those involving the job assignment (such as fixing a failing operation), those involving interpersonal relationships (getting along with supervisors), and the specific type of transition required (situations in which the executive did not have the necessary background). The job demands and what employees can learn from them are described in Table 9.7.

**Table 9.7**
Job Demands and What Employees Can Learn from Them

| Job Demands | What Employees Can Learn |
|---|---|
| Transitions | Handling responsibilities that are new, different, or broader than those in previous job |
| Change | Developing new strategic direction, reorganizing, growing or reducing staff, or responding to rapid change; dealing with poorly performing employees |
| High Level of Responsibility | Making highly visible and important decisions that impact the business; managing multiple groups, functions, products, or departments; dealing with external stakeholders such as unions, government agencies, local politicians |
| Nonauthority Relationships | Getting work done by influencing persons over whom you have no direct authority, such as peers, boss, and external stakeholders |
| Obstacles | Coping and succeeding despite adverse business conditions, a lack of top management or peer support and encouragement, or working with a boss who has poor management skills or a different management style |

SOURCES: Based on C. McCauley and M. McCall Jr. (eds.), *Using Experience to Develop Leadership Talent* (San Francisco: Jossey-Bass, 2014); C. D. McCauley, L. J. Eastman, and J. Ohlott, "Linking Management Selection and Development through Stretch Assignments," *Human Resource Management* 84 (1995), pp. 93–115; W. Macaux, "Making the Most of Stretch Assignments," *TD*, June 14, 2010; G. Morris and K. Rogers, "High Potentials Are Still Your Best Bet," *T + D*, February 2013, pp. 58–62.

One concern regarding the use of demanding job experiences for employee development is whether they are viewed as positive or negative stressors. Job experiences that are seen as positive stressors challenge employees to stimulate learning. Job challenges viewed as negative stressors create high levels of harmful stress for employees exposed to them. Recent research findings suggest that all of the job demands, with the exception of obstacles, are related to learning.[55] Managers reported that obstacles and job demands related to creating change were more likely to lead to negative stress than the other job demands. This suggests that companies should carefully weigh the potential negative consequences before placing employees in development assignments that involve obstacles or create change.

Although the research on development through job experiences has focused on executives and managers, line employees can also learn from job experiences. As we noted earlier, for a work team to be successful, its members now need the kinds of skills that only managers were once thought to need (such as dealing directly with customers, analyzing data to determine product quality, and resolving conflict among team members). Besides the development that occurs when a team is formed, employees can further develop their skills by switching work roles within the team.

Figure 9.4 shows the various ways that job experiences can be used for employee development. These include enlarging the current job, job rotation, transfers, promotions, downward moves, and temporary assignments. For companies with global operations (multinationals), employee development sometimes involves international assignments that require frequent travel or relocation. The Competing through Globalization box shows how Mondelēz International is using global job experiences for employee development.

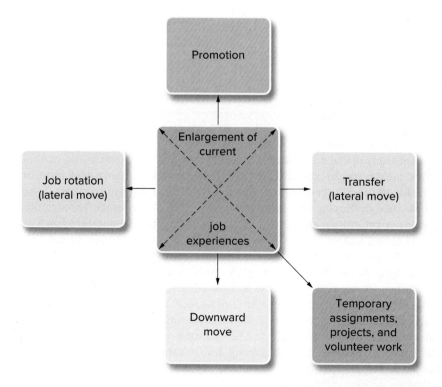

**Figure 9.4**
How Job Experiences Are Used for Employee Development

### Developing Employees through Worldwide Job Experiences

Mondelēz International is one of the largest snack companies in the world. Its corporate name might be unfamiliar, but some of its brands will ring a bell: Oreo cookies, Ritz crackers, Toblerone chocolate bars, Trident gum, and Halls cough drops, to name a few. With famous brands and customers in 160 countries, the company needs a continuing supply of management talent to keep the business growing. The leaders' recognition of this is evident in the company's strategy statement, which includes "grow our people" through building world-class capabilities and empowering courageous leaders and world-class teams.

For employees across functions, Mondelēz International offers challenging job experiences to those who participate in the company's social-impact program. The program, building on the company's purpose statement to "create more moments of joy,"

sends Joy Ambassadors—teams of about 15 employees—to cocoa-farming communities in Ghana. These "ambassadors" work alongside farmers and visit processing plants and schools to learn about the challenges and opportunities facing the communities. Applying their own knowledge and skills to what they observe, the teams develop and teach ideas for building a more successful farming economy. The experience develops teamwork and problem-solving skills and inspires employees by giving them a meaningful way to contribute. At the same time, it strengthens the supply chain that Mondelēz depends on for a key ingredient and brings sustainable agriculture to a part of the world where the need is great.

**DISCUSSION QUESTIONS**
1. What kinds of value does Mondelēz International

receive from the Joy Ambassador program?
2. Would you consider participating in the Joy Ambassador program to be a stretch assignment? Why or Why not?
3. What would be your potential concerns about using the Joy Ambassador program for employee development?

SOURCES: Based on "Mondelez International Employees Journey to Cocoa Life Communities for Skills-Exchange Mission," September 19, 2018, from https://ir .mondelezinternational.com/news-releases/, accessed January 3, 2019; Mondelēz International, "Strategy Globe" from https:// www.mondelezinternational.com/about-us/ our-purpose-strategy "accessed January 3, 2019; Mondelēz International, "2018 Fact Sheet," http://www.mondelezinternational.com, accessed January 3, 2019; K. France, "How a 'Skills-Exchange' Program Can Improve Your Workplace," *Daily Herald* (Arlington Heights, IL), March 16, 2018, http://www.dailyherald.com; Greg Trotter, "More Companies Find Spending on Corporate Responsibility Increases the Bottom Line," *Chicago Tribune*, December 8, 2017, http://www.chicagotribune.com; David McCann, "Training Aims to Unify Far-Flung Finance Staff," *Chief Financial Officer*, October 4, 2017, http://ww2.cfo.com, accessed January 9, 2019.

### Enlarging the Current Job

**Job enlargement**
Adding challenges or new responsibilities to an employee's current job.

**Job enlargement** refers to adding challenges or new responsibilities to employees' current jobs. This could include special project assignments, switching roles within a work team, or researching new ways to serve clients and customers. For example, an engineering employee may join a task force developing new career paths for technical employees. Through this project work, the engineer may lead certain aspects of career path development (such as reviewing the company's career development process). As a result, the engineer not only learns about the company's career development system but also uses leadership and organizational skills to help the task force reach its goals. Some companies are enlarging jobs by giving two managers the same responsibilities and job title and allowing them to divide the work (two-in-a-box).[56] This helps managers learn from a more experienced employee; helps companies fill jobs that require multiple skills; and, for positions requiring extensive travel, ensures that one employee is always on site to deal with work-related issues. For example, at Cisco Systems, the head of the Cisco routing group, who was trained as an engineer but now works in business development, shared a job with an engineer. Each employee was exposed to the other's skills, which has helped both perform their jobs better.

## Job Rotation and Lateral Moves

**Job rotation** gives employees a series of job assignments in various functional areas of the company or movement among jobs in a single functional area or department. Job rotation involves a planned sequence of jobs that the employee is expected to hold, whereas lateral moves may not necessarily involve a predetermined sequence of jobs or positions. Job rotation helps employees gain an overall appreciation of the company's goals, increases their understanding of different company functions, develops a network of contacts, and increases employees' skills.[57]

Clothing retailer H&M makes job rotation part of the employee development process for all its office and warehouse employees, even executives.[58] When the company hires a new employee, that person begins by spending up to 13 weeks working in a store. The employee first staffs the fitting rooms, then tries sales positions, and for management jobs, works on store and cash management. That way, employees who work behind the scenes understand the challenges of the store workers, as well as how customer service, store environment, and other factors contribute to the company's performance. Haskell provides job rotation opportunities at its Packaging Center of Excellence in Atlanta for design engineers to work with a design team.[59] They also provide the opportunity to rotate into the Systems Analytics group whose responsibilities include process improvement and simulation testing for manufacturing systems. This helped engineers understand the importance of data-driven decisions based on complex testing. The rotation has resulted in fewer manufacturing errors, improved designs, and the reduction of time and costs for project installations. The job rotations also helped identify engineers who were ready for promotion. Two thirds of the promotions at the Atlanta location occurred because of job rotation.

Despite the advantages of job rotation, there are several potential problems for both the employee and the work unit. The rotation may cause employees to adopt a short-term perspective when problem solving. Employees' satisfaction and motivation may be adversely affected because they find it difficult to develop functional specialties and they don't spend enough time in one position to receive a challenging assignment. Productivity losses and workload increases may be experienced by both the department gaining a rotating employee and the department losing the employee due to training demands and loss of a resource.

**Job rotation**
The process of systematically moving a single individual from one job to another over the course of time. The job assignments may be in various functional areas of the company, or movement may be between jobs in a single functional area or department.

## Transfers, Promotions, and Downward Moves

Upward, lateral, and downward mobility is available for development purposes in most companies.[60] In a **transfer**, an employee is assigned a job in a different area of the company. Transfers do not necessarily increase job responsibilities or compensation. They are likely lateral moves (a move to a job with similar responsibilities). **Promotions** are advancements into positions with greater challenges, more responsibility, and more authority than in the previous job. Promotions usually include pay increases. For example, PepsiCo Inc.'s former chief executive Indra Nooyi promoted the head of the company's Europe and sub-Saharan Africa business to president, which covers global operations, corporate strategy, public policy, and government affairs.[61] This position stretched his skill set as he took on responsibility to increase sales and productivity to fund investments.

A **downward move** occurs when an employee is given less responsibility and authority.[62] This may involve a move to another position at the same level (lateral demotion), a temporary cross-functional move, or a demotion because of poor performance. Temporary cross-functional moves to lower-level positions, which give employees experience working in different functional areas, are most frequently used for employee development. For example, engineers who want to move into management often take lower-level positions (like shift supervisor) to develop their management skills.

**Transfer**
The movement of an employee to a different job assignment in a different area of the company.

**Promotions**
Advances into positions with greater challenge, more responsibility, and more authority than the employee's previous job.

**Downward move**
A job change involving a reduction in an employee's level of responsibility and authority.

Because of the psychological and tangible rewards of promotions (such as increased feelings of self-worth, salary, and status in the company), employees are more willing to accept promotions than lateral or downward moves. Promotions are more readily available when a company is profitable and growing. When a company is restructuring or experiencing stable or declining profits—especially if numerous employees are interested in promotions and the company tends to rely on the external labor market to staff higher-level positions—promotion opportunities may be limited.[63]

Transfers, job rotation, promotions, lateral moves, and downward moves may involve relocation within the United States or to another country. This can be stressful not only because the employee's work role changes, but if the employee is in a two-career family, the spouse also must find new employment. In addition, the family has to join a new community. Transfers disrupt employees' daily lives, interpersonal relationships, and work habits.[64] People have to find new housing, shopping, health care, and leisure facilities, and they may be many miles from the emotional support of friends and family. They also have to learn a new set of work norms and procedures; they must develop interpersonal relationships with their new managers and peers; and they are expected to be as productive in their new jobs as they were in their old jobs even though they may know little about the products, services, processes, or employees for whom they are responsible.

Because transfers can provoke anxiety, many companies have difficulty getting employees to accept them. Research has identified the employee characteristics associated with a willingness to accept transfers:[65] high career ambitions, a belief that one's future with the company is promising, and a belief that accepting a transfer is necessary for success in the company. Employees who are not married and not active in the community are generally most willing to accept transfers. Among married employees, the spouse's willingness to move is the most important influence on whether an employee will accept a transfer.

Unfortunately, many employees have difficulty associating transfers and downward moves with development. They see them as punishments rather than as opportunities to develop skills that will help them achieve long-term success with the company. Many employees decide to leave a company rather than accept a transfer. Companies need to successfully manage transfers not only because of the costs of replacing employees but also because of the costs directly associated with them. For example, one estimate is that a full-service relocation for an employee and his or her family is approximately $70,000.[66] To help encourage employees to reduce relocation costs and to give employees control over how to spend relocation allowances to best meet their needs, many companies are providing lump sums for relocation. That is, employees are given a set amount of money to pay for relocation costs. They are typically not required to submit receipts for expenses. Also, some companies provide employees with a network of recommended service providers so that the employees don't feel burdened by identifying responsible vendors.

To ensure that employees accept transfers, promotions, and downward moves as development opportunities, companies can provide

- Information about the content, challenges, and potential benefits of the new job and location.
- Involvement in the transfer decision by sending the employees to preview the new location and giving them information about the community.
- Clear performance objectives and early feedback about their job performance.
- A host at the new location to help them adjust to the new community and workplace.
- Information about how the job opportunity will affect their income, taxes, mortgage payments, and other expenses.
- Reimbursement and assistance in selling and purchasing or renting a place to live.

- An orientation program for the new location and job.
- Information on how the new job experiences will support the employee's career plans.
- Assistance for dependent family members, including identifying schools and child care and elder care options.
- Help for the spouse in identifying and marketing skills and finding employment.[67]

## Temporary Assignments, Projects, Volunteer Work, and Sabbaticals

**Temporary assignments** refer to job tryouts such as employees taking on a position to help them determine if they are interested in working in a new role, employee exchanges, sabbaticals, and voluntary assignments. All temporary assignments have a predetermined ending date after which the employees return to their permanent position. For example, Mondelēz International, a snack company with 100,000 employees, wanted to help its managers learn about how to market its products using mobile devices. For several days, they sent their managers to nine small mobile-technology companies to help them gain an understanding of their entrepreneurial spirit and how quickly these companies generated ideas and built and tested prototypes of new marketing efforts.[68] An associate brand manager from PepsiCo's New York headquarters spent a week at Airbnb, a San Francisco–based online travel rental business. Managers from the two companies hoped to learn from each other's brand management practices. Both companies have casual, collaborative work environments. But compared to PepsiCo's brand management, Airbnb's brand management is based more on instinct than on data analysis and the ideas of marketing agencies. Marketing managers at Airbnb were interested in learning about how PepsiCo built data sets of market research. To develop a broad understanding of the business, directors at Genentech Inc. spend 10% of their time over six to nine months in a different function working on special projects, participating in task forces, and shadowing business leaders.[69]

*Employee exchange* is another type of temporary assignment. Procter & Gamble (P&G) and Google have swapped employees.[70] Employees from the two companies participated in each other's training programs and attend meetings where business plans are discussed. Both companies hope to benefit from the employee swap. Procter & Gamble was trying to increase its understanding of how to market laundry detergent, toilet paper, and skin cream products to a new generation of consumers who spend more time online than watching television. Google wanted to gain more ad revenue by persuading companies to shift from showcasing their brands on television to video-sharing sites such as YouTube.

Temporary assignments can include a **sabbatical**. A sabbatical refers to a leave of absence from the company for personal reflection, renewal, and skill development. Employees on sabbatical often receive full pay and benefits. Sabbaticals let employees get away from the day-to-day stresses of their jobs and acquire new skills and perspectives. Sabbaticals also allow employees more time for personal pursuits such as writing a book or spending more time with young children. Sabbaticals are common in a variety of industries ranging from consulting firms to the fast-food industry.[71] They typically range from 4 to 10 weeks. Sabbaticals can involve travel, finishing a degree or other learning opportunities, donating time to charity, working on research or new product development, or working on a "green" cause. For example, at Edelman Financial Services, located in Fairfax, Virginia, employees are eligible for four weeks of paid sabbatical after five years with the company.[72] As a motivation to use the time well, the company requires that the employee submit a syllabus outlining their plans for the time away from work. Adviser Rey Roy took a cross-country bike ride, raising money for charity. The time he spent pedaling cleared his mind and gave him a fresh perspective, so that when he returned to work, he had renewed enthusiasm. In addition, Roy saw that other employees were inspired by his experience.

**Temporary assignments**
Job tryouts such as employees taking on a position to help them determine if they are interested in working in a new role.

**Sabbatical**
A leave of absence from the company to renew or develop skills.

*Volunteer assignments* can also be used for development. Volunteer assignments may give employees opportunities to manage change, teach, have a high level of responsibility, and be exposed to other job demands (see Table 9.7). Some companies encourage their employees to donate their expertise without losing pay or vacation time. A research and development engineer at General Mills who develops food products spends some of her work time helping small food companies in Africa. Using teleconferencing, she has helped the African companies understand how to manage food contamination risks when handling raw ingredients. She also traveled to Malawi to visit a food production plant to help them prepare for a government inspection. Her pro bono work was personally rewarding but also helped her use her professional skills in ways that are limited by her current role. At Prudential Financial, teams of up to five employees can work on consulting projects with one of the company's nonprofit partners. These projects are supported by Prudential's founding principle that everyone should have the opportunity to achieve financial security. The partnership builds the capacity of local partners and gives employees the opportunity to develop their business skills and leadership competencies outside of their normal work environments. The Evidence-Based HR box shows the positive outcomes employees and their employer can realize from leadership development programs that include project work.

## EVIDENCE-BASED HR

Associates in the BB&T Corporation's Leadership Excellence Program receive coaching by a leadership consultant, attend workshops focused on different aspects of leadership, and work on a project that will benefit their area of business. BB&T compared associates who participated in the Leadership Excellence Program with their peers who had not yet participated in the program (comparison group). Program participants had over a two times faster promotion rate and a 31% retention rate, which translated into saving $13 million in replacement costs—that is, costs that would have been incurred for hiring and training new associates.

SOURCE: Based on "Training Top 125 Best Practices & Outstanding Training Initiatives, BB&T Corporation: Leadership Excellence Program" *Training*, January/February 2017, p. 97; J. Castaneda, "Bench Strength," *TD*, June 2015, pp. 30–35.

## INTERPERSONAL RELATIONSHIPS

**LO 9-7**
Develop successful mentoring programs.

Employees can also develop skills and increase their knowledge about the company and its customers by interacting with a more experienced organization member. Mentoring and coaching are two types of interpersonal relationships that are used to develop employees.

### Mentoring

**Mentor**
An experienced, productive senior employee who helps develop a less experienced employee.

A **mentor** is an experienced, productive senior employee who helps develop a less experienced employee (the protégé). Because of the lack of potential mentors, and recognizing that employees can benefit from relationships with peers and colleagues, some companies have initiated and supported group and peer mentoring.

Most mentoring relationships develop informally as a result of interests or values shared by the mentor and the protégé. Research suggests that employees with certain

**Table 9.8**
Examples of Mentoring Programs

**Cisco Systems**—To reduce the time it takes new board of director members to be effective, they are paired with a more experienced board director who serves as a mentor. The mentor helps them understand board of directors meeting norms, provides the content for members beliefs, explains terms used in briefing materials, and gives advice on the right place to sit in the board meeting room.

**Microsoft**—The mentoring program includes career development mentoring and peer mentoring. Career development mentoring focuses on career and professional development through structured, year-long cross-group mentoring. Peer mentoring is less structured and focuses on transfer of work-related knowledge among members of the same work team.

**Sodexo**—Peer-to-peer mentoring is a program managed directly by Sodexo's Network Groups. Networks are organized around a common dimension of diversity and are created by employees who want to raise awareness in Sodexo of their identity groups. They include network groups based on national origin, race, sexual orientation, military service, and intergenerations. The Spirit of Mentoring Bridge Programs are informal divisional pairings in which newly hired and front-line managers come together to expand professional development opportunities and increase the depth and diversity of Sodexo's management.

**Mariner Finance**—The company uses technology such as chat functions, video, and specific websites for mentors and protégés to enable more timely communications between themselves as well as between all employees participating in the mentoring program.

**Michigan Medicine**—MicroMentors provides early and midcareer emerging leaders with the opportunity to spend up to 60 minutes of uninterrupted time with a mentor discussing important issues such as salary negotiations, managing disruptive employees, and career development.

**Vistage Worldwide**—Teams of 15–20 employees provide opportunities for advice on personal or professional challenges. A trained peer-group facilitator guides the discussion and helps the team listen, paraphrase, and ask probing questions in order to provide new perspectives on the issue and potential solutions.

SOURCES: Based on J. Lublin, "New in Boardrooms: Buddy System," *Wall Street Journal*, September 20, 2017, p. B7; C. Elton and A. Gostick, "Impact and Learning Span the Generations," *Chief Learning Officer*, December 2018, p. 62; "*Training* Top 125: Aditya Birla Minacs," *Training*, January/February 2014, p. 101; Sodexo, Inc., website, www.sodexousa.com, accessed March 26, 2017; "*Training* Top 125: Vistage Worldwide," *Training*, January/February 2017, p. 69; M. Weinstein, "Mentoring in the Digital Age," *Training*, September/October 2016, pp. 28–31; R. Emelo, "Shift Your Focus with Modern Mentoring," *TD*, September 2015, pp. 36–41; R. Emelo, "Conversations with Mentoring Leaders," *T + D*, June 2011, pp. 32–37.

personality characteristics (like emotional stability, the ability to adapt their behavior based on the situation, and high needs for power and achievement) are most likely to seek a mentor and be an attractive protégé for a mentor.[73] Mentoring relationships can also develop as part of a formal mentoring program, that is, a planned company effort to bring together successful senior employees with less experienced employees. Table 9.8 shows examples of how companies are using formal mentoring programs. Mentoring programs have many important purposes, including socializing new employees, developing managers, and providing opportunities for women and minorities to share experiences and gain the exposure and skills needed to move into management positions.

*Developing Successful Mentoring Programs.* One major advantage of formalized mentoring programs is that they ensure access to mentors for all employees, regardless of gender or race. An additional advantage is that participants in the mentoring relationship know what is expected of them.[74] One limitation of formal mentoring programs is that mentors may not be able to provide counseling and coaching in a relationship that has been created artificially.[75] To overcome this limitation, it is important that mentors and protégés spend time discussing work styles, their personalities, and their backgrounds, which helps build the trust needed for both parties to be comfortable with their relationship.[76]

**Table 9.9**
Characteristics of Successful Formal Mentoring Programs

1. Mentor and protégé participation is voluntary. Relationship can be ended at any time without fear of punishment.
2. The mentor–protégé matching process does not limit the ability of informal relationships to develop. For example, a mentor pool can be established to allow protégés to choose from a variety of qualified mentors.
3. Mentors are chosen on the basis of their past record in developing employees, willingness to serve as a mentor, and evidence of positive coaching, communication, and listening skills.
4. Mentor–protégé matching is based on how the mentor's skills can help meet the protégé's needs.
5. The purpose of the program is clearly understood. Projects and activities that the mentor and protégé are expected to complete are specified.
6. The length of the program is specified. Mentor and protégé are encouraged to pursue the relationship beyond the formal period.
7. A minimum level of contact between the mentor and protégé is specified. Mentors and protégés need to determine when they will meet, how often, and how they will communicate outside the meetings.
8. Protégés are encouraged to contact one another to discuss problems and share successes.
9. The mentor program is evaluated. Interviews with mentors and protégés give immediate feedback regarding specific areas of dissatisfaction. Surveys gather more detailed information regarding benefits received from participating in the program.
10. Employee development is rewarded, which signals to managers that mentoring and other development activities are worth their time and effort.

Toshiba America Medical Systems doesn't have a formal mentoring program. However, Toshiba encourages informal mentoring from the first day employees are hired. Both managers and HR business partners take the time to help new employees meet their colleagues and show them around the workplace.[77]

Table 9.9 presents the characteristics of a successful formal mentoring program. Mentors should be chosen based on interpersonal and technical skills. They also need to be trained.[78] For mentors, protégés, and the company to get the most out of mentoring, tools and support are needed.[79] The U.S. Government Accountability Office (GAO) uses its mentoring program to create a collaborative learning environment, improve employee engagement, and provide development opportunities. Mentors attend an orientation to ensure they understand the purpose of the program and their roles. Additionally, mentors meet quarterly to receive ongoing support and training.[80]

A key to successful mentoring programs is that the mentor and protégé be well matched and can interact with each other face-to-face, virtually, or using social media. Matching systems are available to help match mentors and protégés, track mentors' and protégés' work, help build development plans, and schedule mentor and protégé meetings.[81] The Competing through Technology box shows how companies are relying on algorithms using software to create more effective mentor and protégé matches.

***Benefits of Mentoring Relationships.*** Both mentors and protégés can benefit from a mentoring relationship. Research suggests that mentors provide career and psychosocial support to their protégés. **Career support** includes coaching; protection; sponsorship; and providing challenging assignments, exposure, and visibility. **Psychosocial support** includes serving as a friend and a role model, providing positive regard and acceptance, and creating an outlet for the protégé to talk about anxieties and fears. Additional benefits for the protégé include higher rates of promotion, higher salaries, and greater organizational influence.[82]

**Career support**
Coaching, protection, sponsorship, and providing challenging assignments, exposure, and visibility.

**Psychosocial support**
Serving as a friend and role model, providing positive regard and acceptance, and creating an outlet for a protégé to talk about anxieties and fears.

### Can Formulas Ensure Effective Mentoring Relationships?

Some companies are using software to ensure that mentors and protégés are effectively matched. At General Motors the software considers profiles completed by both prospective protégés and mentors. Mentors are asked about their business expertise, years of professional experience, and what skills they feel they can help a protégé develop. Proteges are asked about the skills they would like to develop and how many years of experience they want their mentor to have. Based on an algorithm that determines the overlap between protégés and mentors profiles, protégés are provided with a list of up to 10 potential mentors. The list includes a percentage showing the degree to which their profiles match. Before they begin their relationship, mentors and protégés are encouraged to review the mentoring resources available on the company's career development website. These resources include webinars for first-time mentors and advice on how to gain the most benefits from a mentoring relationship.

To find mentors outside of work, the creators of the Bumble dating app have created Bumble Bizz, which allows users to search for prospective mentors and network with other professionals. Users create a professional profile, including their career goals, and if they choose, can complete a skills inventory, provide a digital résumé and samples of their work, and a digital photograph. When two users swipe right on each other's profiles they can chat using text.

In contrast to technology-based approaches, at PayPal mentors and protégés are matched based on face-to-face interaction not software. Employees can sign up for small group sessions including six employees who interact with a potential mentor. After a few meetings, if employees feel a connection they can express interest in becoming the mentor's protégé.

#### DISCUSSION QUESTIONS

1. Considering the characteristics of successful formal mentoring relationships shown in Table 9.9, how does a software-based system help ensure the effectiveness of mentoring relationships? Explain.

2. What advantages does a face-to-face protégé–mentor matching process such as the one used at PayPal provide over a technology-based approach using software?

SOURCE: Based on R. Feintzeig, "Employee Mentorship Gets a Reboot," *Wall Street Journal*, December 28, 2017, p. B6; B. Hassell, "Create Mentorships, Not Minions," *Chief Learning Officer*, May 2016, pp. 30–32; K. Gee, "New in Bumble's Dating App: Swipe Right for Business Contacts," November 8, 2017, from www.wsj.com; D. Kuczwara, "The Bumble Bizz App Can Help Businesses Network," from https://www.businessnewsdaily.com/10532-the-buzz-on-bumble-bizz.html, accessed January 3, 2019.

Jose Yanes served as a mentor for several employees at Ford Motor Company.[83] He found that serving as a mentor helped his own personal development by helping him improve his own communication skills and work harder at building trust with other people.

Mentoring relationships provide opportunities for mentors to develop their interpersonal skills and increase their feelings of self-esteem and worth to the organization. For individuals in technical fields, such as engineering or health services, the protégé may help mentors gain knowledge about important new scientific developments in their field (and therefore prevent them from becoming technically obsolete).

**Reverse mentoring** refers to mentoring in which younger employees mentor more senior employees. UnitedHealth Group pairs senior executives with emerging Millennial leaders.[84] UnitedHealth hopes that the program will help executives see the business differently and help create a workplace that will attract, retain, and motivate Millennials. For example, for one high-level leader, quality of care was primarily related to patient outcomes. But as a result of his monthly meetings with his Millennial mentor, he realized that her generation was also concerned with the speed of access to care and customer

**Reverse mentoring**
A business situation in which younger employees mentor more senior employees.

service. Through participating in the program she gained access to a high-level manager that she normally wouldn't have. Also, although she is a younger and less experienced employee, the experience improved her self-confidence by showing that her ideas are important and can benefit the company.

Mentoring can also occur between mentors and protégés from different organizations. Websites such as Everwise are available to help find online mentors. For example, Amy Dobler wanted to enhance her career at Jive Software, so she went online and was matched with Edel Keville, a human resources vice president at Levi Strauss & Company.[85] Using Everwise, Dobler completed an online questionnaire about her personality, education, career path, and personal goals. Both women had similar personalities and career paths in human resources and technology. After the online match, an Everwise relationship manager personally introduced the two women. The advice, guidance, and support that Dobler received from Keville in the mentoring relationship over a few months helped her gain the confidence needed to present to senior managers, lead international training sessions, and improve her delegation skills.

## Coaching

**LO 9-8**

Describe how to train managers to coach employees.

**Coach**

A peer or manager who works with an employee to motivate the employee, help him or her develop skills, and provide reinforcement and feedback.

A **coach** is a peer or manager who works with employees to motivate them, help them develop skills, and provide reinforcement and feedback. There are three roles that a coach can play.[86] Part of coaching may be one-on-one with an employee (such as giving feedback). Another role is to help employees learn for themselves. This involves helping them find experts who can assist them with their concerns and teaching them how to obtain feedback from others. Third, coaching may involve providing resources such as mentors, courses, or job experiences that employees may not be able to gain access to without the coach's help.

Consider the role of coaches at PwC and Procter & Gamble.[87] PwC prepares new employees by combining classroom training with one-on-one coaching by trained coaches. The employees receive suggested readings and practice exercises, and they receive practice and feedback in meetings with their coach. When they complete the program, PwC offers online support through a "Mobile Coach," which delivers reminders and links to development-related content. Coaching is an expected part of managers' role at Procter & Gamble. The company has trained its managers to give employees positive feedback and to match career goals with business needs, among other coaching skills. P&G's aim is to develop managers who can in turn develop their people, resulting in a highly engaged workforce that thinks creatively.

Research shows that coaching helps employees improve by identifying areas for improvement and setting goals.[88] This is especially the case when an internal coach is used (e.g., a manager who has been trained in coaching). Getting results from a coaching relationship can take at least six months of weekly or monthly meetings. To be effective, a coach generally conducts an assessment, asks questions that challenge the employee to think deeply about his or her goals and motives, helps the employee create an action plan, and follows up regularly to help the employee stay on track. Employees contribute to the success of coaching when they persevere in practicing the behaviors identified in the action plan.[89]

# Special Issues in Employee Development
## MELTING THE GLASS CEILING

**LO 9-9**

Discuss what companies are doing to melt the glass ceiling.

A major development issue facing companies today is how to get women and minorities into upper-level management positions—how to melt the **glass ceiling**.

At the large companies of the S&P 500, just over one-quarter of executive positions are held by women, and 4.8% of CEOs are female.[90] Interestingly, the share of female chief operating officers, considered the number-two position in an organization, has been growing, so observers are curious whether more women will start to move to the CEO spot—or whether the COO job will come to be seen as a new glass ceiling. Men are promoted at much higher rates than women during their early career stages, and entry-level women are significantly more likely than men to have spent five or more years in the same job.

From a leadership development perspective, companies may be reluctant to treat women differently than men despite acknowledging that women lack executive sponsors or mentors, have insufficient experience, and need better work–life balance. This barrier may be due to stereotypes or company systems that adversely affect the development of women or minorities.[91] The glass ceiling is likely caused by lack of access to training programs, appropriate developmental job experiences, and developmental relationships (such as mentoring).[92] The Competing through Environmental, Social, and Governance Practices box describes West Monroe Partners' commitment to social responsibility including supporting an inclusive and diverse culture that cultivates leadership development.

For example, Mary Barra made history when she became the first woman CEO of global automobile maker General Motors.[93] Prior to becoming CEO, Barra was in a product development job, an operational job critical to the company's success. But 55% of women are in functional roles such as lawyers, chief of finance, or human resources, which may not put them in the career path needed to become a CEO. Women and minorities often have trouble finding mentors because of their lack of access to the "old boy network"; managers' preference to interact with other managers of similar status rather than with line employees; and intentional exclusion by managers who have negative stereotypes about women's and minorities' abilities, motivation, and job preferences.[94]

Research has found no gender differences in access to job experiences involving transitions or creating change.[95] However, male managers receive significantly more assignments involving high levels of responsibility (high stakes, managing business diversity, handling external pressure) and appreciation for their contributions than female managers of similar ability and managerial level. Also, compared to male managers, female managers report experiencing more challenge due to lack of personal support (a type of job demand considered to be an obstacle and related to harmful stress) and lack of appreciation for their contributions.

In their quest for diversity and inclusion, organizations are engaging managers to consider their role in maintaining a workplace that draws fully upon the contributions of female as well as male employees.[96] For example, career encouragement from peers and senior managers can help women advance to higher management levels. Managers making developmental assignments need to carefully consider whether gender biases or stereotypes are influencing the types of assignments given to women versus men. Also, managers need to identify the kinds of behavior that may be well intentioned but create awkwardness on teams and in mentoring relationships. Going further to draw out women's talents more fully, some managers are implementing tactics like imposing a rule against interruptions in meetings and making a conscious practice of ensuring that every person in the room has had a chance to speak and be heard. Of course, this kind of management practice not only draws out the ideas of women, who on average are interrupted more often than men, but it also gathers ideas from any employees who tend to be quieter than others.

Many companies are making efforts to melt the glass ceiling.[97] General Electric has emphasized placing women in more powerful roles and including them in leadership meetings. For example, women hold positions leading GE's China health care and

**Glass ceiling**
A barrier to advancement to higher-level jobs in the company that adversely affects women and minorities. The barrier may be due to lack of access to training programs, development experiences, or relationships (e.g., mentoring).

# COMPETING THROUGH ENVIRONMENTAL, SOCIAL, AND GOVERNANCE PRACTICES

## Maximizing Stakeholder Value through Skill Development and an Inclusive and Diverse Culture

West Monroe Partners, a technology consulting firm, helps employees develop while also demonstrating social responsibility to its stakeholders. One way is through West Monroe's 1 + 1 + 1 program that budgets for giving 1% of employees' time in volunteer hours, 1% of its employees to work for nonprofits at no charge, and 1% of its profits in charitable contributions. The firm has established the Fischer Fellowship, which pays several employees a year to do volunteer work for three to six months anywhere in the world. Employees selected for the fellowship tackle difficult problems and may collaborate with their colleagues in the firm. For example, an employee who taught computer and technology skills in Ghana worked with experts in the company to get the dilapidated equipment up and running and got ideas for sustainable energy from consultants in the energy and utilities practice. Another consultant, Tricia Anklan, worked on improving water quality in rural Nicaragua. She credits the program with making her a more inspirational leader, motivating people in the community to act,

because it was obvious she would not be able to solve the problem on her own. Employees have also provided pro bono work to a variety of organizations in the United States, including community health services, furniture banks, abused deaf women advocacy, and theater groups.

Another way that West Monroe Partners demonstrates social responsibility to its stakeholders is through recognizing that inclusion and diversity in addition to skill development is necessary to build and support the next generation of company leaders. West Monroe Partners has taken several steps to create a more inclusive and diverse culture and provide all employees regardless of background the opportunity to become leaders. These steps have included celebrating LGBT+ employees and supporters; supporting The Women's Leadership Network, an employee resource group that helps women learn and grow through education, mentorship, collaboration, and communication; and stimulating regular dialogue on topics that aren't easy to discuss (e.g., how it can be uncomfortable for men and women to network out of the

office, which leads to perceptions of unequal mentoring opportunities and lack of inclusion). West Monroe also challenged its more than 80 directors to take ownership for an inclusive workforce by drafting a personal list of actions for making the people around them feel more included.

### DISCUSSION QUESTIONS

1. Is developing women's skills alone sufficient for melting the glass ceiling? Explain your position.
2. How could development plans and mentors be useful in supporting employees skill development from volunteer opportunities?

SOURCE: Based on West Monroe Partners, "About Us," https://www.westmonroepartners.com, accessed January 3, 2019; K. Gurchiek, "'Chief of Anything' Program Develops Skills, Workplace Community," Society for Human Resource Management, April 12, 2018, https://www.shrm.org; Andie Burjek, "Workforce 100: It Feels Like the First Time," *Workforce*, April 26, 2017, http://www.workforce.com; B. Paulen, "Important Steps to Achieving a Diverse Workforce" from https://www.seattlebusinessmag.com, accessed January 3, 2019; Inclusion & Diversity, from https://www.acceptthechallenge.com/Values-and-Rewards/Inclusion-and-Diversity, accessed January 3, 2019; "The 1+1+1 Program" from https://www.acceptthechallenge.com/Values-and-Rewards/Doing-Good, accessed January 3, 2019.

transportation businesses and sit on the company's highest management committee. Women account for approximately 25% of GE's executives, an increase of 16% since 2001. The software company SAP SE set a goal for women to hold 25% of all managerial roles by the end of 2017. SAP's Leadership Excellence Acceleration Program (LEAP) includes high-performing women whom managers have identified as ready for promotion. In the

**Table 9.10**
Recommendations
for Melting the Glass
Ceiling

- Make sure senior management supports and is involved in the program.
- Make a business case for change.
- Make the change public.
- Gather data on problems causing the glass ceiling using task forces, focus groups, and questionnaires.
- Create awareness of how gender attitudes and management practices affect the company culture and behavioral expectations of employees.
- Force accountability through reviews of promotion rates and assignment decisions.
- Promote development for all employees.

SOURCES: Based on R. Gunther McGrath, "Eight Simple Ways to Keep More Women in the Executive Pipeline," *Wall Street Journal*, February 22, 2018, https://blogs.wsj.com; B. Groysberg and K. Connolly, "Great Leaders Who Make the Mix Work," *Harvard Business Review*, September 2013, pp. 68–76; D. McCracken, "Winning the Talent War for Women," *Harvard Business Review*, November/December 2000, pp. 159–67.

program's virtual course, they meet monthly to listen to guest speakers, they complete action assignments, and by the end of the course they are expected to have increased their personal network. So far, the first group of LEAP graduates have become first-level managers and 11% of current managers have moved into director roles. Adobe, American Express, Cisco Systems, and American Electric Power use executive shadowing and coaching programs to help women enhance their visibility and access to top business leaders.

Table 9.10 provides recommendations for melting the glass ceiling and helping retain talented women.

## SUCCESSION PLANNING

**Succession planning** refers to the process of identifying and tracking high-potential employees who are capable of moving into different positions in the company resulting from planned or unplanned job openings due to turnover, promotion, or business growth. Succession planning is often discussed when considering company's managers or top leaders, but it is an important consideration for any job. Succession planning helps organizations in several different ways.[98] It requires senior management to systematically review leadership talent in the company. It ensures that top-level managerial talent is available. It provides a set of development experiences that managers must complete to be considered for top management positions; this avoids premature promotion of managers who are not ready for upper management ranks. Succession planning systems also help attract and retain managerial employees by providing them with development opportunities that they can complete if upper management is a career goal for them. **High-potential employees** are those the company believes are capable of being successful in higher-level managerial positions such as general manager of a strategic business unit, functional director (such as director of marketing), or CEO.[99] High-potential employees typically complete an individual development program that involves education, executive mentoring and coaching, and rotation through job assignments. Job assignments are based on the successful career paths of the managers whom the high-potential employees are being prepared to replace. High-potential employees may also receive special assignments, such as making presentations and serving on committees and task forces.

Despite the importance of succession planning, many companies do not do it well. A survey of company directors showed that fewer than half believed they were spending enough time on succession planning and 18% did not agree that their company had

**LO 9-10**
Use the 9-box grid for identifying where employees fit in a succession plan and construct appropriate development plans for them.

**Succession planning**
The identification and tracking of high-potential employees capable of filling higher-level managerial positions.

**High-potential employees**
Employees the company believes are capable of being successful in high-level management positions.

**Bench strength**
The business strategy of having a pool of talented employees who are ready when needed to step in to a new position within the organization.

adequate bench strength in its talent pipeline.[100] **Bench strength** refers to having a pool of talented employees who are ready when needed. Companies also find it difficult to follow the succession planning process.[101] One challenge is that today's business environment is changing so fast that succession plans go out of date. Suppose a candidate was selected years before an executive opening occurs. By then, the most important job requirements might have changed. Companies including PepsiCo have addressed this by carrying out succession planning over a shorter timeline. Another issue involves the selection of candidates to label as having high potential. People have sometimes-unconscious ideas of what a "high-potential" person is like, and those ideas might look a certain age, gender, race, or physical appearance. Or a manager might select or reject an employee for reasons other than potential—say, to avoid hurt feelings or to keep a valued staffer on the team, rather than in a development assignment elsewhere.

Table 9.11 shows the process used to develop a succession plan.[102] The first step is to identify what positions are included in the succession plan, such as all management positions or only certain levels of management. The second step is to identify which employees are part of the succession planning system. For example, in some companies only high-potential employees are included in the succession plan. Third, the company needs to identify how positions will be evaluated. For example, will the emphasis be on competencies needed for each position or on the experiences an individual needs to have before moving into the position? Fourth, the company should identify how employee potential will be measured. To the extent possible, measurable criteria are used rather than managers intuition. For example, will employees' performance in their current jobs as well as ratings of potential be used? Will employees' position interests and career goals be considered? Fifth, the succession planning review process needs to be developed. Typically, succession planning reviews first involve employees' managers and human resources. A talent review could also include an overall assessment of leadership talent in the company, an identification of high-potential employees, based on their performance and potential, and a discussion of plans to keep key managers from leaving the company.

Many companies use the 9-box grid for conducting the succession planning review. The **9-box grid** is a three-by-three matrix used by groups of managers and executives to compare employees within one department, function, division, or the entire company.[103]

**9-box grid**
A three-by-three matrix used by groups of managers and executives to compare employees within one department, function, division, or the entire company.

**Table 9.11**
The Process of Developing a Succession Plan

1. Identify what positions are included in the plan.
2. Identify the employees who are included in the plan.
3. Develop standards to evaluate positions (e.g., competencies, desired experiences, desired knowledge, developmental value).
4. Determine how employee potential will be measured (e.g., current performance and potential performance).
5. Develop the succession planning review.
6. Link the succession planning system with other human resource systems, including training and development, compensation, performance management, and staffing systems.
7. Determine what feedback is provided to employees.
8. Measure the effectiveness of the succession plan.

SOURCES: Based on A. Cremo and T. Bux, "Creating a Vibrant Organizational Leadership Pipeline," *TD*, July 2016, pp. 76–77; W. Rothwell, "The Future of Succession Planning," *T + D*, September 2010, pp. 51–54; B. Dowell, "Succession Planning," in *Implementing Organizational Interventions*, ed. J. Hedge and E. Pulaskos (San Francisco: Jossey-Bass, 2002), pp. 78–109; R. Barnett and S. Davis, "Creating Greater Success in Succession Planning," *Advances in Developing Human Resources* 10 (2008), pp. 721–39.

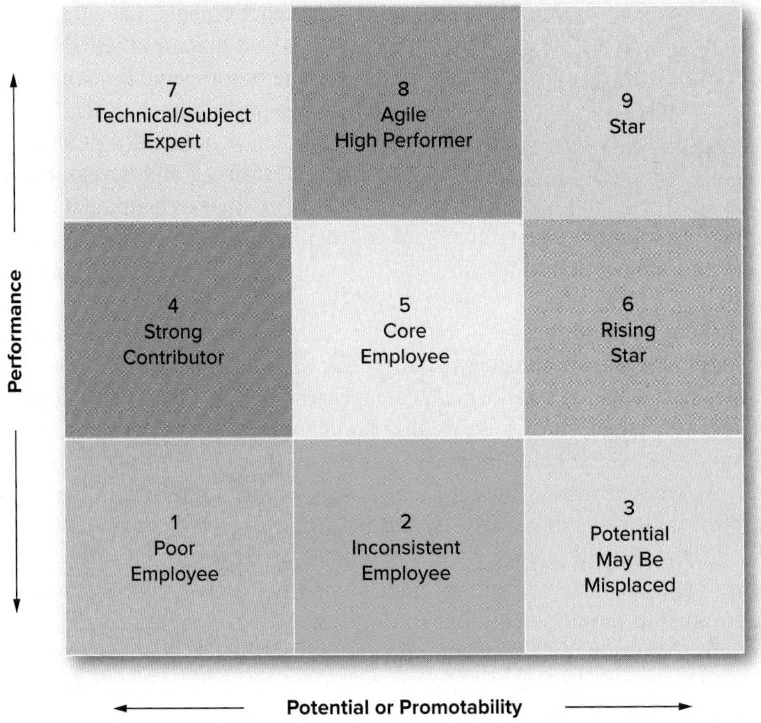

**Figure 9.5**
Example of a 9-Box Grid

The 9-box grid is used for analysis and discussion of talent, to help formulate effective development plans and activities, and to identify talented employees who can be groomed for top-level management positions in the company. As shown in Figure 9.5 one axis of the matrix is based on an assessment of job performance. The other axis is typically labeled "potential" or "promotability." Typically, managers' assessment of performance (based on the company's performance management system) and potential influences employees' development plans. For example, as shown in Figure 9.5, "Stars" should be developed for leadership positions in the company.

For example, CHG Healthcare Services' goal was to increase the number of company leaders by 15% and reduce leaders' turnover.[104] CHG used the 9-box to identify potential leaders and develop leadership bench strength. Employees were evaluated based on their performance and potential. Employees who were identified as high performers with high potential were selected to go through a 360-degree assessment of their skills. This assessment was used in a leadership program designed specifically to develop their potential and skills to ensure they were ready for promotion. The results have been positive. Leadership turnover has decreased by one-third, internal promotion rates for leaders have increased by nearly 50%, and the leader-to-employee ratio has improved by 24%.

Contrast the development plans of "Stars" with employees in the other areas of the grid. The development plans for "Poor Employees" emphasize performance improvement in their current position rather than getting them challenging new job experiences. If they do not improve in their current position, they are likely to be fired. "Technical/Subject Experts" are outstanding performers but have low potential for leadership positions. Their development plans likely emphasize keeping their knowledge, skills, and competencies current and getting them experiences to continue to motivate them and facilitate creativity and innovation. "Potential May Be Misplaced" employees may have just taken a new position and haven't had the time to demonstrate high performance, or these employees' knowledge, skills, or competencies might not match their job requirements. Their development plans might emphasize moving them to a position that best matches their skill set or, if they have just moved to the job, ensuring that they get the training and development opportunities and resources necessary to help them attain high performance levels. "Core Employees" are solid but not outstanding performers who have moderate potential. Development plans for these employees will include a mix of training and development designed to help ensure their solid performance continues. Also, their development plans likely include some development experiences that can help grow their skills and determine their interest and ability to perform in positions requiring different skills and/or more responsibility.

It is important to keep in mind that performance tends to be variable over time due to changes in tasks, assignments, and business goals.[105] The implications of this is when managing employees performance consider the categories shown in Figure 9.5 but give employees the chance to change. One way to do this is to have frequent performance conversations with employees, which helps them recognize the need to change or maintain their performance. Actively managing employees by setting expectations, making project assignments based on their skills and interests, and holding employees accountable for their performance does make a difference.

Sixth, succession planning is dependent on other human resource systems, including compensation, training and development, and staffing. Incentives and bonuses may be linked to completion of development opportunities. Activities such as training courses, job experiences, mentors, and 360-degree feedback should be part of high-potential employees' development plans. Companies need to decide, for example, whether they will fill an open management position internally with a less-experienced employee who will improve in the role over time or hire a manager from outside the company who can deliver results immediately. Seventh, employees need to be provided with feedback on future moves, expected career paths, and development goals and experiences. Finally, the succession planning process needs to be evaluated. This includes identifying and measuring appropriate results outcomes (such as reduced time to fill manager positions, increased use of internal promotions) as well as collecting measures of satisfaction with the process (reaction outcomes) from employees and managers. Also, modifications that will be made to the succession planning process need to be identified, discussed, and implemented.

Turnover is common in Valvoline Instant Oil Change's industry.[106] This means that succession planning and developing bench strength are critical for all employees. Each month managers rate all their employees on their readiness for promotion to their next job level and provide an overall evaluation of when they are ready, such as "today" or "within six months." Managers work with employees on development plans designed to get them to be ready today. The development plans and evaluations are entered into an online system that allows higher-level managers to identify stores and areas where talent is not available in order to improve succession plans. Managers can identify employees, known as "blockers," who are not willing or able to develop further but are in positions that would be considered as a promotion for other employees. Succession planning has initiated a demand for training across the entire career path to ensure that assistant managers are developed as well as senior technicians who might take their jobs and new technicians who need to be ready to take on more responsibilities. Top-level managers use the online system to identify if talent is available to expand stores in a geographic area. Also, the company includes the number of managers available for promotion on their balanced scorecards, which measure company performance.

Blue Cross Blue Shield of Michigan (BCBSM) identifies and develops the company's next generation of leaders as well as talented employees.[107] Members of the executive team have formal succession plans. At the executive level, potential successors' evaluations include an evaluation of their readiness for a new position, for example, ready today or ready in three-to-five years. This has resulted in the development of considerable bench strength for executive positions. All executive positions have at least one successor identified, and 75% of the successors are evaluated as ready today to take the position. But BCBSM also supports succession planning and talent review at all levels of the organization. BCBSM conducts companywide talent reviews to identify current and future skill strengths and weaknesses. BCBSM uses a 9-box grid to assess performance and potential. Management teams meet to discuss the 9-box results for their employees individually and as a group. Part of the meeting is devoted to ensuring that managers are using similar standards for evaluating employee performance and likelihood of future advancement. After the talent reviews are completed, BCBSM holds talent summits to ensure that managers across all divisions understand the company's talent and its development needs, and are aware of cross-division job openings and talent strengths and weaknesses. Supporting this process, BCBSM conducts an annual talent inventory. Employees are asked to identify their career interests and skills. This information is used in manager–employee discussions of BCBSM's talent needs and their individual development plans, career goals, and development activities.

Succession planning at ITU AbsorbTech, a company who provides absorbents used during printing and manufacturing, became a high priority because of its aging workforce.[108] It involves measuring employees performance and potential over a two-year period and identifying high performers. Employees complete a career development plan that helps them identify the potential positions they could hold in the short and long term. Also, development activities such as mentoring that could help employees prepare for the positions are identified. Each position is reviewed to determine if a potential opening may occur because the employee plans to retire or is slated to move to a new position.

One of the important issues in succession planning is deciding whether to tell employees if they are on or off the list of potential candidates for higher-level manager positions.[109] There are several advantages and disadvantages that companies need to consider. One advantage of making a succession planning list public or telling employees who are on the list is that they are more likely to stay with the company because they understand they likely will have new career opportunities. Another is that high-potential employees who are not interested in other positions can communicate their intentions. This helps the company avoid investing costly development resources in them and allows the company to have a more accurate idea of its high-potential managerial talent. The disadvantages of identifying high-potential employees are that those not on the list may become discouraged and leave the company or changes in business strategy or the employees' performance could take them off the list. Also, employees might not believe they have had a fair chance to compete for leadership positions if they already know that a list of potential candidates has been established. One way to avoid these problems is to let employees know they are on the list but not discuss a specific position they will likely reach. Another is to frequently review the list of candidates and clearly communicate plans and expectations. Managers at Midmark Corporation, a medical equipment manufacturer based in Versailles, Ohio, identify successors every six months as part of the company's performance review process and produce a potential list of candidates. Some employees are also labeled as high potential and others are identified as having high potential for leadership positions. Employees with high potential for leadership positions are considered for challenging development assignments involving overseas relocation. Using interviews, the company determines if employees on the succession list are interested in and qualified for leadership positions.

## A LOOK BACK

### Vi's Employee Development Programs

The chapter opener described how Vi uses leadership development programs, tuition reimbursement, mentoring, and career paths to enhance employees skill and career development in order to attract and retain talented employees.

#### QUESTIONS

1. What other development activities might Vi want to consider to develop its leaders? Identify an activity and explain why Vi should consider it.
2. What data or outcomes should Vi's learning and development team collect to monitor the effectiveness of the leadership programs? Explain the business reason for your choice of data.

## SUMMARY

Companies use various employee development methods, including formal education, assessment, job experiences, and interpersonal relationships. Most companies use one or more of these approaches to develop employees. Formal education involves enrolling employees in courses or seminars offered by the company or educational institutions. Assessment involves measuring the employee's performance, behavior, skills, or personality characteristics. Job experiences include job enlargement, rotating to a new job, promotions, transfers, or temporary assignments. A more experienced, senior employee (a mentor) can help employees better understand the company and gain exposure and visibility to key persons in the organization. Part of a manager's job responsibility may be to coach employees. Regardless of the development approaches used, employees should have a development plan to identify (1) the type of development needed, (2) development goals, (3) the best approach for development, and (4) whether development goals have been reached. For development plans to be effective, both the employee and the company have responsibilities that need to be fulfilled.

## KEY TERMS

Development, 396
Protean career, 397
Psychological success, 397
Development planning system, 398
Action plan, 400
Formal education programs, 403
Tuition reimbursement, 405
Assessment, 406
Myers-Briggs Type Inventory (MBTI), 407
Assessment center, 408
Leaderless group discussion, 408

Interview, 408
In-basket, 408
Role-plays, 408
Upward feedback, 409
360-degree feedback systems, 410
Job experiences, 411
Stretch assignments, 411
Job enlargement, 414
Job rotation, 415
Transfer, 415
Promotions, 415
Downward move, 415

Temporary assignment, 417
Sabbatical, 417
Mentor, 418
Career support, 420
Psychosocial support, 420
Reverse mentoring, 421
Coach, 422
Glass ceiling, 423
Succession planning, 425
High-potential employees, 425
Bench strength, 426
9-box grid, 426

## DISCUSSION QUESTIONS

1. How could assessment be used to create a productive work team?
2. List and explain the characteristics of effective 360-degree feedback systems.
3. Why do companies develop formal mentoring programs? What are the potential benefits for the mentor? For the protégé?

4. Your boss is interested in hiring a consultant to help identify potential managers among current employees of a fast-food restaurant. The manager's job is to help wait on customers and prepare food during busy times, oversee all aspects of restaurant operations (including scheduling, maintenance, on-the-job training, and food purchase), and help motivate employees to provide high-quality service. The manager is also responsible for resolving disputes that might occur between employees. The position involves working under stress and coordinating several activities at one time. She asks you to outline the type of assessment program you believe would do the best job of identifying employees who will be successful managers. What will you tell her?
5. Many employees are unwilling to relocate because they like their current community, and spouses and children prefer not to move. Yet employees need to develop new skills, strengthen skill weaknesses, and be exposed to new aspects of the business to prepare for management positions. How could an employee's current job be changed to develop management skills?
6. Can experiences that managers have outside of the company be beneficial for development? Identify the types of experiences and explain why they are beneficial.

7. What are some examples of sabbaticals, and why are they beneficial?
8. What is coaching? Is there one type of coaching? Explain.
9. Why are many managers reluctant to coach their employees?
10. Why should companies be interested in helping employees plan their development? What benefits can companies gain? What are the risks?
11. What are the manager's roles in a development system? Which role do you think is most difficult for the typical manager? Which is the easiest role? List the reasons why managers might resist involvement in career management.
12. Draw the 9-box grid. How is it useful for succession planning?
13. Nationwide Financial, a 5,000-employee life insurance company based in Columbus, Ohio, found that its management development program contained four types of managers. One type, unknown leaders, have the right skills but their talents are unknown to top managers in the company. Another group, arrogant leaders, believe they have all the skills they need. What types of development program would you recommend for each of these types of managers?

## SELF-ASSESSMENT EXERCISE

Also assignable in Connect.

Go to www.keirsey.com. Complete the Keirsey Temperament Sorter. What did you learn about yourself? How could the instrument you completed be useful for employee development? What might be some disadvantages of using this instrument?

## EXERCISING STRATEGY

### New Manager Development at Valvoline Instant Oil Change

Like other quick-service oil change businesses, Valvoline hires multitudes of entry-level workers. That means it is competing with many other retail businesses to sort through a flood of applicants who need work but do not necessarily hope to stay in this type of job for very long. Valvoline's strategy for meeting this challenge is to select candidates with leadership potential and give them opportunities to participate in its voluntary employee development program. This results in a workforce that is above average in employee retention and provides a supply of qualified candidates to promote to management positions.

The development program, called Super-Pro 10, is structured around certificates. The talent development team identified the knowledge and skills necessary to succeed in jobs at various levels, and it prepared a training process to meet those requirements. Training sessions focus on hands-on learning, supplemented with readings and online interactive lessons.

Every time an employee completes a level of training by demonstrating all the skills on the checklist for that level, the employee receives a certificate that identifies him or her as qualified for a promotion (and an increase in pay). This sets up employees to begin practicing supervisory skills within their first year on the job, even as they continue to add to their technical skills.

Employees also receive performance feedback at least every four months, with performance measures including how well employees develop whomever they supervise. The automated review system asks managers to indicate whether the employee is ready for promotion. The company's performance management system uses the data to indicate to management where the level of talent indicates opportunities to expand the business.

This approach is creating increasing numbers of management talent to meet Valvoline's present needs and future growth.

A succession planning system keeps tracks of employees progress toward meeting the requirements for promotion to service manager, a key position where talent has to be available in order for Valvoline to grow the business through opening new stores. Over the past few years, all of Valvoline's service center managers have been promoted to that position from hourly jobs with the company. In addition, 100% of its area manager positions and more than 90% of its market manager positions (responsible for 25 or more stores) have been filled through promotions. Many headquarters managers also started out in Valvoline's stores.

## QUESTIONS

1.  Does Valvoline's development practices contribute to its competitive advantage in the quick-change oil business? Why or why not?

2.  What advantages does Valvoline's investment in developing entry-level employees to fill management positions give the company compared to a strategy of hiring managers externally?

3.  What other types of development activities should Valvoline consider for developing employees for management positions? Explain your choice(s).

SOURCES: Based on "Best Winners at a Glance: #28 Valvoline Instant Oil Change," *TD*, October 2018, p. 76; Ave Rio, "The Future of the Corporate University," *Chief Learning Officer*, May 3, 2018, http://www.clomedia.com; Kelsey Gee, "Who Deserves a Promotion? One Company Has It Figured Out," *Wall Street Journal*, January 31, 2018, https://www.wsj.com; Stephanie Castellano, "A Well-Oiled Machine," *TD*, October 2017, pp. 32–34; Lorri Freifeld, "Training Top 125 Best Practice: Super-Pro 10 Certification at Valvoline Instant Oil Change," *Training*, May 31, 2016, https://www.trainingmag.com.

# MANAGING PEOPLE

## Development at 3M

3M has been around for more than 100 years, using science and innovation to provide consumer products including tape, Post-It notes, bandages, sandpaper, and business products such as various types of films, filters, and wound care dressings. 3M considers all employees as leaders, and so it provides development opportunities at each stage of their careers. 3M strives to engage all employees by focusing on their career and development desires. In fact, one of 3M's sustainability objectives is that all of its global workforce (90,000 employees in 70 countries) will be actively involved in development opportunities by 2025.

Each year, all employees create or update their development plan, which includes short- and long-term career goals. All employees are encouraged to continuously learn and improve their skills. 3M's tuition reimbursement program encourages employees to seek education in order to meet current job responsibilities and help prepare for career changes or to advance on their chosen career paths. For many functional areas, competency models are available that provide links to relevant training opportunities and development recommendations that can be discussed and agreed upon with the employee's supervisor. Options include growing the competency through on-the-job activities or social learning through a coach or mentor.

Because 3M believes leadership development provides a competitive advantage, it has invested in multiple leadership development programs offered at different stages in an employee's career. Business and leadership courses are available to employees at any level, including online programs available to all of 3M's global employees. 3M emphasizes diversity, collaboration, and inclusion in all of its leadership programs. Leadership programs are based on key leadership behaviors, which are linked to leaders' performance evaluations.

For example, one leadership development program, 3M Leadership Way, has four levels: Spark, Ignite, Amplify, and Catalyst. Spark is targeted to junior 3M leaders who have been identified as having high potential. Ignite participants are new managers who are learning their roles. Training on how to build effective teams is provided using gamification and virtual technology. Managers complete a project to show the impact of learning and applications in their daily work. In Amplify, leaders of multiple teams work on projects, visit customers, and work on their skills for nine months. Catalyst is a year-long program in which leaders attend leadership meetings; gain exposure to customer and other perspectives outside of 3M; and work on a project that focuses on a challenge issued by top management, a customer-based project to help solve the customer's needs, or a community-based project. All of the levels include self-assessment of competencies as well as 360-degree feedback and coaching.

## QUESTIONS

1.  How does development at 3M help the company gain a competitive advantage?

2.  Why does 3M emphasize development for all employees rather than just focus on employees with the greatest potential to be company leaders?

3.  Which of the development activities provided by 3M is most beneficial for employees and the company? Why?

SOURCES: Based on B. Hassell, "The Best of Both Worlds: Learning through a Marketer's Lens," *Chief Learning Officer*, September 2016, pp. 26, 28, 30; "About" from www.3M.com and "Education and Career Growth," from http://www.3m.com/3M/en_US/sustainability-report/global-challenges/education-and-development/#EducationCareerGrowth, accessed May 22, 2017.

# HR IN SMALL BUSINESS

## How Service Express Serves Employees First

Service Express Inc. (SEI), headquartered in Grand Rapids, Michigan, provides maintenance for critical computer hardware, such as the servers that run companies' data processing and the storage units that keep data secure but accessible. Its customers include hospitals, universities, banks, manufacturing companies, and other organizations in more than a dozen states, and employees travel to the customers' work sites. This type of work requires people who are dependable, technically skilled, and committed to responsive, fast service.

SEI attracts, equips, and keeps such employees with a vision that is unusual for a business: to "work with our employees to help them achieve their personal, professional, and financial goals." What is unusual is that the company puts the employees' goals first. The perspective goes back to the company's founder, who realized that the value placed on helping employees achieve their goals attracted people with similar values, and they in turn focused on helping customers achieve their goals.

To put the vision into practice, SEI managers hold twice-yearly Vision Talks with each of their employees, starting with the employee's first day on the job. During these meetings, the employee shares or updates his or her goals, working with the manager to identify how the company can enable the employee to achieve the goals. The company trains managers in how to conduct the Vision Talks effectively, recognizing that employees will need to build trust before they start sharing personal goals.

During the talks, managers help the employees shape general ideas into measurable and attainable goals. These become

part of a personal development plan, updated quarterly, which also includes objectives for training, project completion, and so on. Occasionally, managers identify goals that can be tied to a business opportunity. For example, an employee who wants to move to another state can be part of a business expansion into that state, or an employee who wants to build something from the ground up can lead a new business line. A dramatic example involves a salesperson who had no interest in management, so he focused on developing sales skills. At one point, the salesperson's manager asked him to help train and coach a newer employee, and the salesperson discovered that he found it satisfying to help another person succeed. He set a new goal to become a manager—and eventually became vice president of sales.

### QUESTIONS

1. How does the description of careers at Service Express fit the chapter's description of a protean career? What is the role of employee development in this context?
2. Suppose SEI continues growing and asks you to advise management on how to maintain its focus on employee development. Suggest two or three development methods from the chapter, and explain why you recommend each.

SOURCES: Company website, "About SEI," www.serviceexpress.com, accessed May 7, 2018; "Best Workplaces in Technology by Great Place to Work® and FORTUNE," www.serviceexpress.com, accessed May 7, 2018; Bo Burlingham, "The Best Small Companies in America: 2016," *Forbes*, January 27, 2016, http://www.forbes.com; Service Express, *The SEI Way: Values and Practices of a Growing Company* (2009), available at http://www.seiservice.com.

# NOTES

1. D. Day, *Developing Leadership Talent* (Alexandria, VA: SHRM Foundation, 2007); M. London, *Managing the Training Enterprise* (San Francisco: Jossey-Bass, 1989); C. McCauley and S. Heslett, "Individual Development in the Workplace," in *Handbook of Industrial, Work, and Organizational Psychology*, vol. 1, ed. N. Anderson, D. Ones, H. Sinangil, and C. Viswesveran (London: Sage Publications, 2001), pp. 313–35.
2. R. W. Pace, P. C. Smith, and G. E. Mills, *Human Resource Development* (Englewood Cliffs, NJ: Prentice Hall, 1991); W. Fitzgerald, "Training versus Development," *Training and Development Journal*, May 1992, pp. 81–84; R. A. Noe, S. L. Wilk, E. J. Mullen, and J. E. Wanek, "Employee Development: Issues in Construct Definition and Investigation of Antecedents," in *Improving Training Effectiveness in Work Organizations*, ed. J. K. Ford (Mahwah, NJ: Lawrence Erlbaum, 1997), pp. 153–89.
3. PricewaterhouseCoopers, "Good to Grow: 2014 US CEO Survey," www.pwc.com, accessed February 20, 2015; J. Green, "Chowing Down on Boomers' Brains," *Bloomberg Businessweek*, January 25–31, 2016, pp. 19–20.
4. ATD Staff, "All the Happy People," *TD*, July 2016, p. 15.
5. M. Gubler, J. Arnold, and C. Coombs, "Reassessing the Protean Career Concept: Empirical Findings, Conceptual Components, and Measurement," *Journal of Organizational Behavior* 35 (2014), pp. 23–40; D. T. Hall, "Protean Careers of the 21st Century," *Academy of Management Executive* 11 (1996), pp. 8–16; D. Hall, *Careers in and out of Organizations* (Thousand Oaks, CA: Sage, 2002); J. Greenhaus, G. Callahan, and V. Godshalk, *Career Management*, 4th ed. (Thousand Oaks, CA: Sage, 2010).
6. David Ward, "Risky Business," interview of Kat Cole, *HR Magazine*, May 2017, pp. 18–19.

7. K. R. Brousseau, M. J. Driver, K. Eneroth, and R. Larsson, "Career Pandemonium: Realigning Organizations and Individuals," *Academy of Management Executive* 11 (1996), pp. 52–66.

8. M. Wang and C. Wanberg, "100 Years of Applied Psychology Research on Individual Careers: From Career Management to Retirement," *Journal of Applied Psychology* 102 (2017), pp. 546–63; W. Inn and B. Crowell, "Organizations and Managers Must Reassess How They View Career Development," *TD,* September 2015, pp. 42–46; M. B. Arthur, "The Boundaryless Career: A New Perspective of Organizational Inquiry," *Journal of Organization Behavior* 15 (1994), pp. 295–309; P. H. Mirvis and D. T. Hall, "Psychological Success and the Boundaryless Career," *Journal of Organization Behavior* 15 (1994), pp. 365–80; M. Lazarova and S. Taylor, "Boundaryless Careers, Social Capital, and Knowledge Management: Implications for Organizational Performance," *Journal of Organizational Behavior* 30 (2009), pp. 119–39; D. Feldman and T. Ng, "Careers: Mobility, Embeddedness, and Success," *Journal of Management* 33 (2007), pp. 350–77.

9. "Nearly One-Third of Employers Expect Workers to Job-Hop," *Career Builder,* www.careerbuilder.com, accessed April 2, 2015; "Is Job Hopping the New Normal?" *T + D,* August 2014, p. 20.

10. J. Lublin, "Job Hopping Is Losing Its Stigma," *Wall Street Journal,* July 27, 2016, p. B8; R. Hoffman, B. Casnocha, and C. Yeh, "Tours of Duty: The New Employer-Employee Compact," *Harvard Business Review,* June 2013, pp. 48–58.

11. S. Castellano, "Internal Care, Miami Children's Health System," *TD,* October 2017, pp. 60–62.

12. L. Mainiero and S. Sullivan, "Kaleidoscope Careers: An Alternative Explanation for the 'Opt-Out' Revolution," *Academy of Management Executive* 19 (2005), pp. 106–23; S. Sullivan and L. Mainiero, "Benchmarking Ideas for Fostering Family-Friendly Workplaces," *Organizational Dynamics* 36 (2007), pp. 45–62.

13. "Training Top 125 2018 Rankings 46-55, Carmax, Inc.," *Training,* January/February 2018, pp. 60–61.

14. M. Derven, "From Career Conversations to Deliberate Action," *TD,* February 2015, pp. 63–67.

15. Derven, "From Career Conversations to Deliberate Action."

16. S. Prokesch, "Reinventing Talent Management," *Harvard Business Review,* September/October 2017, pp. 54–55.

17. P. Asinof, "IDPs: Talent Development's Superglue," *TD,* January 2016, pp. 42–47.

18. W. Bunch, "No Place Like Home," *Human Resource Executive,* November 2017, pp. 12–14.

19. D. T. Jaffe and C. D. Scott, "Career Development for Empowerment in a Changing Work World," in *New Directions in Career Planning and the Workplace,* ed. J. M. Kummerow (Palo Alto, CA: Consulting Psychologists Press, 1991), pp. 33–60; L. Summers, "A Logical Approach to Development Planning," *Training and Development* 48 (1994), pp. 22–31; D. B. Peterson and M. D. Hicks, *Development First* (Minneapolis, MN: Personnel Decisions, 1995).

20. M. McGraw, "Millennials Take Up the Mantle," *Human Resource Executive,* December 2015, pp. 16–20.

21. "Training Top 125 2018 Rankings 76-80, Penn Station Inc.," *Training,* January/February 2018, pp. 66–67; "Training Top 125, Genentech, Inc.," *Training,* January/February 2016, p. 67; R. Emlo, "The Power of Discovery," *Chief Learning Officer,* January 2015, pp. 38–48; "Genentech, Inc.: Career Lab," *Training,* January/February 2015, pp. 102–03.

22. R. Noe, *Employee Training and Development,* 7th ed. (New York: McGraw-Hill, Irwin, 2015); K. O'Leonard and L. Loew, "Investing in the Future," *Human Resource Executive,* July/August 2012, pp. 30–34.

23. A. Bordonaro, "Telus About Your Global Learning," *Chief Learning Officer* (November 2018): 30-33.

24. C. Waxer, "Course Review," *Human Resource Executive,* December 2005, pp. 46–48; Pat Galagan, "90,000 Served: Hamburger University Turns 50," *T + D,* April 2011, pp. 46–51; Beth Kowitt, "Why McDonald's Wins in Any Economy," *Fortune,* September 5, 2011.

25. General Electric, "GE Crotonville: The Future of Leadership," https://www.ge.com/sites/default/files/GE_Crotonville_Future_of_Leadership.pdf, accessed March 24, 2017.

26. R. Knight, "GE's Corporate Boot Camp cum Talent Spotting Venue," *Financial Times Business Education,* March 20, 2006, p. 2; J. Durett, "GE Hones Its Leaders at Crotonville," *Training,* May 2006, pp. 25–27.

27. University of Virginia Darden School of Business, "MBA for Executives," www.darden.virginia.edu, accessed March 30, 2012.

28. S. Gale, "The NBA's New MVP," *Chief Learning Officer,* October 2017, pp. 22–24, 26.

29. "Best of the Best: TELUS," *TD,* October 2018, p. 66.

30. Center for Creative Leadership, "Leadership Development Programs," https://www.ccl.org/open-enrollment-programs/leadership-development-program/, accessed March 24, 2017.

31. R. Johnson, "The Learning Curve: The Value of Tuition Reimbursement," *Training,* November 2005, pp. 30–33; G. Benson, D. Finegold, and S. Mohrman, "You Paid for the Skills, Now Keep Them: Tuition Reimbursement and Voluntary Turnover," *Academy of Management Journal* 47 (2004), pp. 315–31.

32. Day, *Developing Leadership Talent.*

33. E. Harrell, "A Brief History of Personality Tests," *Harvard Business Review,* March/April 2017, 63; M. Weinstein, "Personalities & Performance," *Training,* July/August 2008, pp. 36–40.

34. S. K. Hirsch, *MBTI Team Member's Guide* (Palo Alto, CA: Consulting Psychologists Press, 1992); A. L. Hammer, *Introduction to Type and Careers* (Palo Alto, CA: Consulting Psychologists Press, 1993); J. Llorens, "Taking Inventory of Myers-Briggs," *T + D,* April 2010, pp. 18–19.

35. From www.discprofile.com, website for DiSC, accessed February 1, 2012.

36. "Training Top 125 2018 Rankings 111-115, Guckenheimer," *Training,* January/February 2018, pp. 80–81; M. Weinstein, "The X Factor," *Training,* May/June 2011, pp. 65–67.

37. G. C. Thornton III and W. C. Byham, *Assessment Centers and Managerial Performance* (New York: Academic Press, 1982); L. F. Schoenfeldt and J. A. Steger, "Identification and Development of Management Talent," in *Research in Personnel and Human Resource Management,* ed. K. N. Rowland and G. Ferris (Greenwich, CT: JAI Press, 1989), vol. 7, pp. 151–81.

38. Thornton and Byham, *Assessment Centers and Managerial Performance.*

39. B. B. Gaugler, D. B. Rosenthal, G. C. Thornton III, and C. Bentson, "Metaanalysis of Assessment Center Validity," *Journal of Applied Psychology* 72 (1987), pp. 493–511; D. W. Bray, R. J. Campbell, and D. L. Grant, *Formative Years in Business: A Long-Term AT&T Study of Managerial Lives* (New York: Wiley, 1974).

40. R. G. Jones and M. D. Whitmore, "Evaluating Developmental Assessment Centers as Interventions," *Personnel Psychology* 48 (1995), pp. 377–88.

41. J. Schettler, "Building Bench Strength," *Training*, June 2002, pp. 55-58.
42. S. B. Silverman, "Individual Development through Performance Appraisal," in *Developing Human Resources* 5 (1991), pp. 120-151.
43. "BEST Winners at a Glance: #16 LoyaltyOne," *TD,* October 2018, p. 57; A. Bordonaro, "The Business of Development," *Chief Learning Officer,* September 2018, pp. 22-25.
44. "Training Top Ten Hall of Fame, CHG Healthcare Services," *Training,* January/February 2017, p. 53.
45. J. S. Lublin, "Turning the Tables: Underlings Evaluate Bosses," *Wall Street Journal*, October 4, 1994, pp. B1, B14; D. O'Reilly, "360-Degree Feedback Can Change Your Life," *Fortune*, October 17, 1994, pp. 93-100; J. F. Milliman, R. A. Zawacki, C. Norman, L. Powell, and J. Kirksey, "Companies Evaluate Employees from All Perspectives," *Personnel Journal*, November 1994, pp. 99-103.
46. Center for Creative Leadership, *Skillscope for Managers: Development Planning Guide* (Greensboro, NC: Center for Creative Leadership, 1992); G. Yukl and R. Lepsinger, "360-Degree Feedback," *Training*, December 1995, pp. 45-50.
47. K. Kim, L. Atwater, P. Patel, and J. Smither, "Multisource Feedback, Human Capital, and the Financial Performance of Organizations," *Journal of Applied Psychology* 101 (2016), pp. 1569-84; L. Atwater, P. Roush, and A. Fischthal, "The Influence of Upward Feedback on Self- and Follower Ratings of Leadership," *Personnel Psychology* 48 (1995), pp. 35-59; J. F. Hazucha, S. A. Hezlett, and R. J. Schneider, "The Impact of 360-Degree Feedback on Management Skill Development," *Human Resource Management* 32 (1993), pp. 325-51; J. W. Smither, M. London, N. Vasilopoulos, R. R. Reilly, R. E. Millsap, and N. Salvemini, "An Examination of the Effects of an Upward Feedback Program over Time," *Personnel Psychology* 48 (1995), pp. 1-34; J. Smither and A. Walker, "Are the Characteristics of Narrative Comments Related to Improvements in Multirater Feedback Ratings over Time?" *Journal of Applied Psychology* 89 (2004), pp. 575-81; J. Smither, M. London, and R. Reilly, "Does Performance Improve Following Multisource Feedback? A Theoretical Model, Meta-analysis, and Review of Empirical Findings," *Personnel Psychology* 58 (2005), pp. 33-66.
48. D. Bracken, "Straight Talk about Multirater Feedback," *Training and Development*, September 1994, pp. 44-51; K. Nowack, J. Hartley, and W. Bradley, "How to Evaluate Your 360-Feedback Efforts," *Training and Development*, April 1999, pp. 48-52; M. Levine, "Taking the Burn out of the 360-Degree Hot Seat," *T + D*, August 2010, pp. 40-45.
49. P. Harris, "Adopting Values to Live By," *TD,* October 2018, pp. 42-44.
50. S. Seibert, L. Sargent, M. Kraimer, and K. Kiazad, "Linking Developmental Experiences to Leader Effectiveness and Promotability: The Mediating Role of Leadership Self-Efficacy and Mentoring Network," *Personnel Psychology*, 70 (2017), pp. 357-97; M. W. McCall Jr., M. M. Lombardo, and A. M. Morrison, *Lessons of Experience* (Lexington, MA: Lexington Books, 1988); L. Dragoni, P. Tesluk, J. Russell, and I. Oh, "Understanding Managerial Development: Integrating Developmental Assignments, Learning Orientation, and Access to Developmental Opportunities in Predicting Managerial Competencies," *Academy of Management Journal* 52 (2009), pp. 731-43.
51. M. Paese, "Permission to Fail," *TD,* July 2017, pp. 57-61; R. S. Snell, "Congenial Ways of Learning: So Near Yet So Far," *Journal of Management Development* 9 (1990), pp. 17-23.
52. R. Morrison, T. Erickson, and K. Dychtwald, "Managing Middlescence," *Harvard Business Review*, March 2006, pp. 78-86.
53. S. Shellenbarger, "How to Land a Job That's a Stretch," *Wall Street Journal*, September 27, 2017, p. A11.
54. McCall et al., *Lessons of Experience*; M. W. McCall, "Developing Executives through Work Experiences," *Human Resource Planning* 11 (1988), pp. 1-11; M. N. Ruderman, P. J. Ohlott, and C. D. McCauley, "Assessing Opportunities for Leadership Development," in *Measures of Leadership*, pp. 547-62; C. D. McCauley, L. J. Estman, and P. J. Ohlott, "Linking Management Selection and Development through Stretch Assignments," *Human Resource Management* 34 (1995), pp. 93-115.
55. S. Courtright, A. Colbert, and D. Choi, "Fired Up or Burned Out? How Developmental Challenge Differentially Impacts Leader Behavior," *Journal of Applied Psychology* 99 (2014), pp. 681-96; C. D. McCauley, M. N. Ruderman, P. J. Ohlott, and J. E. Morrow, "Assessing the Developmental Components of Managerial Jobs," *Journal of Applied Psychology* 79 (1994), pp. 544-60; J. LePine, M. LePine, and C. Jackson, "Challenge and Hindrance Stress: Relationships with Exhaustion, Motivation to Learn, and Learning Performance," *Journal of Applied Psychology* 89 (2004) pp. 883-91.
56. S. Thurm, "Power-Sharing Prepares Managers," *Wall Street Journal*, December 5, 2005, p. B4.
57. M. London, *Developing Managers* (San Francisco: Jossey-Bass, 1985); M. A. Campion, L. Cheraskin, and M. J. Stevens, "Career-Related Antecedents and Outcomes of Job Rotation," *Academy of Management Journal* 37 (1994), pp. 1518-42; M. London, *Managing the Training Enterprise* (San Francisco: Jossey-Bass, 1989).
58. M. Porado, "Try This Job on for Size," *Benefits Canada*, January/February 2018, pp. 8-9.
59. "Training Top 125 2017 Rankings, Haskell," *Training,* January/February 2017, pp. 66-67; "Training Top 125 2018 Rankings 16-25, Haskell," *Training,* January/February 2018, pp. 54-55.
60. D. C. Feldman, *Managing Careers in Organizations* (Glenview, IL: Scott Foresman, 1988); D. Hall, *Careers In and Out of Organizations* (Thousand Oaks, CA: Sage, 2002).
61. J. Maloney, "PepsiCo 'Stretches' Managers at Top," *Wall Street Journal,* July 21, 2017, pp. B1, B2.
62. D. T. Hall and L. A. Isabella, "Downward Moves and Career Development," *Organizational Dynamics* 14 (1985), pp. 5-23.
63. H. D. Dewirst, "Career Patterns: Mobility, Specialization, and Related Career Issues," in *Contemporary Career Development Issues*, ed. R. F. Morrison and J. Adams (Hillsdale, NJ: Lawrence Erlbaum, 1991), pp. 73-108.
64. J. M. Brett, L. K. Stroh, and A. H. Reilly, "Job Transfer," in *International Review of Industrial and Organizational Psychology: 1992*, ed. C. L. Cooper and I. T. Robinson (Chichester, England: Wiley, 1992); D. C. Feldman and J. M. Brett, "Coping with New Jobs: A Comparative Study of New Hires and Job Changers," *Academy of Management Journal* 26 (1983), pp. 258-72.
65. R. A. Noe, B. D. Steffy, and A. E. Barber, "An Investigation of the Factors Influencing Employees' Willingness to Accept Mobility Opportunities," *Personnel Psychology* 41 (1988), pp. 559-80; S. Gould and L. E. Penley, "A Study of the Correlates of Willingness to Relocate," *Academy of Management Journal* 28 (1984), pp. 472-78; J. Landau and T. H. Hammer, "Clerical Employees' Perceptions of Intra-organizational Career Opportunities," *Academy of Management Journal* 29 (1986), pp. 385-405; R. P. Duncan and C. C. Perruci, "Dual Occupation Families and Migration," *American Sociological Review* 41

(1976), pp. 252–61; J. M. Brett and A. H. Reilly, "On the Road Again: Predicting the Job Transfer Decision," *Journal of Applied Psychology* 73 (1988), pp. 614–620.

66. J. Ramirez, "Smart Money," *Human Resource Executive*, January/February 2015, pp. 22–27.

67. J. M. Brett, "Job Transfer and Well-Being," *Journal of Applied Psychology* 67 (1992), pp. 450–63; F. J. Minor, L. A. Slade, and R. A. Myers, "Career Transitions in Changing Times," in *Contemporary Career Development Issues*, pp. 109–20; C. C. Pinder and K. G. Schroeder, "Time to Proficiency Following Job Transfers," *Academy of Management Journal* 30 (1987), pp. 336–53; G. Flynn, "Heck No—We Won't Go!" *Personnel Journal*, March 1996, pp. 37–43.

68. R. Silverman, "Field Trip: Learning from Startups," *Wall Street Journal*, March 27, 2013, p. B8.

69. C. McCauley, "Make Experience Count," *Chief Learning Officer*, May 2014, p. 50.

70. E. Byron, "A New Odd Couple: Google, P&G Swap Workers to Spur Innovation," *Wall Street Journal*, November 19, 2008, pp. A1, A18.

71. C. J. Bachler, "Workers Take Leave of Job Stress," *Personnel Journal*, January 1995, pp. 38–48; "Types of Sabbaticals," www.yoursabbatical.com, accessed April 17, 2013.

72. S. Sataline, "Breaking Away," *Washingtonian*, August 2016, pp. 105–08.

73. D. B. Turban and T. W. Dougherty, "Role of Protégé Personality in Receipt of Mentoring and Career Success," *Academy of Management Journal* 37 (1994), pp. 688–702; E. A. Fagenson, "Mentoring: Who Needs It? A Comparison of Protégés' and Nonprotégés' Needs for Power, Achievement, Affiliation, and Autonomy," *Journal of Vocational Behavior* 41 (1992), pp. 48–60.

74. A. H. Geiger, "Measures for Mentors," *Training and Development Journal*, February 1992, pp. 65–67.

75. K. E. Kram, *Mentoring at Work: Developmental Relationships in Organizational Life* (Glenview, IL: Scott Foresman, 1985); K. Kram, "Phases of the Mentoring Relationship," *Academy of Management Journal* 26 (1983), pp. 608–25; G. T. Chao, P. M. Walz, and P. D. Gardner, "Formal and Informal Mentorships: A Comparison of Mentoring Functions and Contrasts with Nonmentored Counterparts," *Personnel Psychology* 45 (1992), pp. 619–36; C. Wanberg, E. Welsh, and S. Hezlett, "Mentoring Research: A Review and Dynamic Process Model," in *Research in Personnel and Human Resources Management*, ed. J. Martocchio and G. Ferris (New York: Elsevier Science, 2003), pp. 39–124.

76. E. White, "Making Mentorships Work," *Wall Street Journal*, October 23, 2007, p. B11; E. Holmes, "Career Mentors Today Seem Short on Advice but Give a Mean Tour," *Wall Street Journal*, August 28, 2007, p. B1; J. Sandberg, "With Bad Mentors It's Better to Break Up Than to Make Up," *Wall Street Journal*, March 18, 2008, p. B1.

77. M. Weinstein, "Please Don't Go," *Training*, May/June 2011, pp. 28–34.

78. L. Eby, M. Butts, A. Lockwood, and A. Simon, "Protégés' Negative Mentoring Experiences: Construct Development and Nomo-logical Validation," *Personnel Psychology* 57 (2004), pp. 411–47; M. Boyle, "Most Mentoring Programs Stink—but Yours Doesn't Have To," *Training*, August 2005, pp. 12–15.

79. R. Emelo, "Conversations with Mentoring Leaders," *T + D*, June 2011, pp. 32–37.

80. R. Emelo, "Black Belt Mentors," *Chief Learning Officer*, September 2017, pp. 18–21.

81. "Training Top 125: Cartus," *Training*, January/February 2015, p. 87; J. Alsever, "Looking for a Career Mentor You Love? Let Cold Data Be Your Guide, *Fast Company*, www.fastcompany.com, accessed July 22, 2014; M. Weinstein, "Tech Connects," *Training*, September 2008, pp. 58–59.

82. T. Allen, L. Eby, G. Chao, and T. Bauer, "Taking Stock of Two Relational Aspects of Organizational Life: Tracing the History and Shaping the Future of Socialization and Mentoring Research," *Journal of Applied Psychology*, 102 (2017), pp. 324–37; G. F. Dreher and R. A. Ash, "A Comparative Study of Mentoring among Men and Women in Managerial, Professional, and Technical Positions," *Journal of Applied Psychology* 75 (1990), pp. 539–46; T. D. Allen, L. T. Eby, M. L. Poteet, E. Lentz, and L. Lima, "Career Benefits Associated with Mentoring for Protégés: A Meta-Analysis," *Journal of Applied Psychology* 89 (2004), pp. 127–36; R. A. Noe, D. B. Greenberger, and S. Wang, "Mentoring: What We Know and Where We Might Go," in *Research in Personnel and Human Resources Management*, ed. G. Ferris and J. Martucchio (New York: Elsevier Science, 2002), pp. 129–74; R. A. Noe, "An Investigation of the Determinants of Successful Assigned Mentoring Relationships," *Personnel Psychology* 41 (1988), pp. 457–79; B. J. Tepper, "Upward Maintenance Tactics in Supervisory Mentoring and Nonmentoring Relationships," *Academy of Management Journal* 38 (1995), pp. 1191–205; B. R. Ragins and T. A. Scandura, "Gender Differences in Expected Outcomes of Mentoring Relationships," *Academy of Management Journal* 37 (1994), pp. 957–71.

83. S. Gale, "Mentoring Is a Two-Way Street at Ford," *Chief Learning Officer,* August 2016, pp. 48–49.

84. T. Lytle, "Putting Mentoring in Reverse," *HR Magazine,* May 2017, pp. 46–51; J. Crosby, "Target, UnitedHealth, and Other Companies Turning to Reverse Mentoring to Tap Millennials Knowledge," *Star Tribune*, July 25, 2016, from www.startribune.com accessed March 24, 2017.

85. Alsever, "Looking for a Career Mentor You Love? Let Cold Data Be Your Guide."

86. D. B. Peterson and M. D. Hicks, *Leader as Coach* (Minneapolis, MN: Personnel Decisions, 1996).

87. "Outstanding Training Initiatives," *Training*, May/June 2017, pp. 50–52; Cappelli and Tavis, "HR Goes Agile."

88. R. Jones, S. Woods, and Y. Guillaume, "The Effectiveness of Workplace Coaching: A Meta-Analysis of Learning and Performance Outcomes from Coaching," *Journal of Occupational and Organizational Psychology*, 89 (2016), pp. 249–77; J. Dahling, S. Taylor, S. Chau, and S. Dwight, "Does Coaching Matter? A Multilevel Model Linking Managerial Coaching Skill and Frequency to Sales Goal Attainment," *Personnel Psychology*, 69 (2016), pp. 863–94; J. Smither, M. London, R. Flautt, Y. Vargas, and L. Kucine, "Can Working with an Executive Coach Improve Multisource Ratings over Time? A Quasiexperimental Field Study," *Personnel Psychology* 56 (2003), pp. 23–44.

89. A. Vorro, "Coaching Counsel," *Inside Counsel*, February 2012, Business & Company Resource Center, http://galenet.galegroup.com.

90. Catalyst, "Women in the Workforce: United States," http://www.catalyst.org, accessed May 3, 2018; Renee Morad, "Are Women COOs Facing a New Kind of Glass Ceiling?" *NBC News*, March 29, 2018, http://www.nbcnews.com; LeanIn.Org and McKinsey & Company, "Women in the Workplace 2016," https://womenintheworkplace.com/, accessed March 24, 2017.

91. U.S. Department of Labor, *A Report on the Glass Ceiling Initiative* (Washington, DC: U.S. Department of Labor, 1991).

92. B. Groysberg and K. Connolly, "Great Leaders Who Make the Mix Work," *Harvard Business Review*, September 2013, pp. 68–76; P. J. Ohlott, M. N. Ruderman, and C. D. McCauley, "Gender Differences in Managers' Developmental Job Experiences," *Academy of Management Journal* 37 (1994), pp. 46–67; D. Mattioli, "Programs to Promote Female Managers Win Citations," *Wall Street Journal*, January 30, 2007, p. B7.

93. J. Green, "This Is Not a Trend," *Bloomberg Businessweek*, September 1–September 7, 2014, pp. 19–20.

94. U.S. Department of Labor, *A Report on the Glass Ceiling Initiative*; R. A. Noe, "Women and Mentoring: A Review and Research Agenda," *Academy of Management Review* 13 (1988), pp. 65–78; B. R. Ragins and J. L. Cotton, "Easier Said Than Done: Gender Differences in Perceived Barriers to Gaining a Mentor," *Academy of Management Journal* 34 (1991), pp. 939–51.

95. L. A. Mainiero, "Getting Anointed for Advancement: The Case of Executive Women," *Academy of Management Executive* 8 (1994), pp. 53–67; J. S. Lublin, "Women at Top Still Are Distant from CEO Jobs," *Wall Street Journal*, February 28, 1995, pp. B1, B5; P. Tharenov, S. Latimer, and D. Conroy, "How Do You Make It to the Top? An Examination of Influences on Women's and Men's Managerial Advancement," *Academy of Management Journal* 37 (1994), pp. 899–931.

96. "Men and Equality," http://www.catalyst.org, accessed May 3, 2018; John Simons, "Men Learn How to Be 'Allies,' without Fear, to Female Colleagues," *The Wall Street Journal*, April 4, 2018, https://www.wsj.com; Rita Gunther McGrath, "Eight Simple Ways to Keep More Women in the Executive Pipeline," *The Wall Street Journal*, February 22, 2018, https://blogs.wsj.com; P. Tharenou, "Going Up? Do Traits and Informal Social Processes Predict Advancement in Management?" *Academy of Management Journal* 44 (2001), pp. 1005–17.

97. N. Waller, "How Men and Women See the Workplace Differently," *Wall Street Journal*, September 27, 2016, pp. B1, B2; J. Lublin, "Group Vows to Advance More Women at Work," *Wall Street Journal*, December 6, 2016; J. Lublin, "GE Engineers New Paths to Promote Women," *Wall Street Journal*, December 14, 2016, p. B5.

98. W. J. Rothwell, *Effective Succession Planning*, 4th ed. (New York: AMACOM, 2010).

99. C. B. Derr, C. Jones, and E. L. Toomey, "Managing High-Potential Employees: Current Practices in Thirty-Three U.S. Corporations," *Human Resource Management* 27 (1988), pp. 273–90.

100. J. Lublin and T. Francis, "Boards Often Fumble CEO Changes," *Wall Street Journal*, June 9, 2016, pp. B1–B2.

101. Cappelli and Tavis, "HR Goes Agile"; T. Chamorro-Premuzic and A. Bhaduri, "How Office Politics Corrupts the Search for High-Potential Employees," *Society for Human Resource Management*, October 25, 2017, https://www.shrm.org.

102. D. Sims, "Five Ways to Increase Success in Succession Planning," *T + D*, August 2014, pp. 60–63; Rothwell, *Effective Succession Planning*; N. Davis and W. Pina-Ramirez, "Essential Continuity," *T + D*, March 2015, pp. 45–47.

103. K. Tyler, "On the Grid," *HR Magazine*, August 2011, pp. 67–69; D. Day, *Developing Leadership Talent* (Alexandria, VA: SHRM Foundation, 2007).

104. M. Weinstein, "The Heart of CHG Healthcare Services," *Training*, January/February 2015, pp. 44–48.

105. P. Cappelli, "Why Managers Should Stop Thinking of A,B, and C Players," *Wall Street Journal*, February 21, 2017, pp. R5, R7.

106. "Valvoline Instant Oil Change: Bench Planning," *Training*, January/February 2014, p. 108.

107. M. Weinstein, "BCBSM's Big Picture Focus," *Training*, January/February 2016, pp. 46–50; M. Weinstein, "BCBSM Empowers Employees," *Training*, January/February 2015, pp. 50–53.

108. S. Castellano, "A Marathon, Not a Sprint," *TD*, October 2017, pp. 70–72.

109. "Should You Tell Employees They're Part of a Succession Plan?" *HR Magazine*, January/February 2015, pp. 26–27; M. Steen, "Where to Draw the Line on Revealing Who's Next in Line," *Workforce Management*, June 2011, pp. 16–18.

# 10 Employee Separation and Retention

## ⌐ LEARNING OBJECTIVES ¬

*After reading this chapter, you should be able to:*

**LO 10-1** Distinguish between involuntary and voluntary turnover, and discuss how each of these forms of turnover can be leveraged for competitive advantage. *page 441*

**LO 10-2** List the major elements that contribute to perceptions of justice and how to apply these in organizational contexts involving discipline and dismissal. *page 445*

**LO 10-3** Specify the relationship between job satisfaction and various forms of job withdrawal, and identify the major sources of job satisfaction in work contexts. *page 459*

**LO 10-4** Design a survey feedback intervention program, and use this to promote retention of key organizational personnel. *page 467*

## Google Employees Protest "Pass the Trash" Sexual Harassment Practices

One industry analyst has noted that when it comes to its business model, Google's is "built on human capital and not much else." The company's motto is "Do No Evil," and it promotes its culture as a great place to work in order to attract and retain the best talent—most of whom could easily find work at other employers at the drop of the hat. Thus, when 20,000 Google employees across the globe staged a walkout to protest how the company responded to sexual misconduct allegations, this definitely caught the attention of senior leaders.

The specific trigger for the protest was the revelation that Google had paid large sums of cover-up money to senior executives who seemed to be guilty of sexual harassment. One of the executives, Andy Rubin was given $90 million to leave and, on top of this, was sent off with a celebration where he was treated as a hero. Larry Page, the chief executive at the time hailed Rubin as the "father of Android" and its "billion-plus happy users." Page wished him "all the best with what comes next."

Many of the protesting employees thought that what should come next was a criminal charge, not a lucrative buyout. Moreover, rather than being solely a result of this one revelation, the underlying belief among many workers was that Google condoned a subculture that was antagonistic to women in general, not just in terms of condoning a hostile environment, but also in terms of pay and promotion opportunities. In fact, at the same time Google was showering purported harassers with money, it was under investigation by the U.S. Department of Labor for alleged systematic pay discrimination against female employees.

Google's practice of "passing the trash" is hardly unique, however. Since the inception of the #MeToo movement, the number of sexual harassment claims filed with the EEOC has more than doubled, and since most incidents are not reported at this level, this is just the tip of the iceberg. Rather than going to federal agencies, most complaints are filed with HR departments that, all too often, like Google, seek to settle the claims quietly by working jointly with alleged perpetrators to get them to leave the company voluntarily. This practice is an attempt to avoid costly litigation and reputational damage to the firm, but it fails to meet the victim's need for justice and shifts the threat posed by the predator to some other hapless employer.

Back at Google, senior leaders reacted quickly to the employee walkout. Current chief executive Sundar Pichai and vice president of "People Operations" (HR) Eileen Naughton met with employees and offered a public apology. They also noted that in just the last two years, 48 executives—13 of which were at high levels—were discharged *without compensation* in response to credible harassment claims. This seemed like an odd boast to employees, many of whom wondered why there were so many perpetrators at high levels. The company also announced an end to the practice of "mandatory arbitration" for such cases as a condition of employment. Mandatory arbitration tends to hide the problem in a context where transparency is desperately needed. Indeed, in an effort to increase transparency, an anonymous, grassroots e-mail list called "Yes, at Google" was created where any employee could post complaints about abusive behavior at the company. Although not a program launched by HR professionals of the company, those same HR professionals now monitor the site closely. Clearly, this is a "playing from behind" HR strategy necessitated by the fact that employees don't feel free to come to HR in the first place.

SOURCES: D. Wakabayashi and K. Benner, "Google Workers Fume Over Executives' Payout After Sexual Harassment Claims," *The New York Times Online*, October 26, 2018; D. Wakabayashi and K. Benner, "How Google Protected Andy Rubin, the 'Father of Android,'" *The New York Times Online*, October 25, 2018; "K. Conger and D. Wakabayashi, "Google Overhauls Sexual Misconduct Policy After Employee Walkout," *The New York Times Online*, November 8, 2018; E. Huet and M. Bergen "A Spotlight on Harassment at Google," *Bloomberg Businessweek*, June 2, 2017.

# Introduction

Every executive recognizes the need for satisfied, loyal customers. If the firm is publicly held, it is also safe to assume that every executive appreciates the need to have satisfied, loyal investors. Customers and investors provide the financial resources that allow the organization to survive. However, it seems that not every executive understands the need to generate satisfaction and loyalty among employees. Yet there is a strong link between employee satisfaction and retention, on the one hand, and critical organizational outcomes, on the other hand.[1] This may even be the deciding factor when it comes to who wins and who loses in the competitive market. Research has established a direct link between employee retention rates and sales growth, and companies that are cited as one of the "100 Best Companies to Work For" routinely outperform their competition on many other financial indicators of performance.[2] This is especially the case in the service industry, where the direct contact between employees and customers enhances the relationship between employee satisfaction and customer satisfaction.

In addition to holding on to key personnel, another hallmark of successful firms is their ability and willingness to dismiss employees who are engaging in counterproductive behavior or behavior that threatens other employees. One could argue that the organizations HR department should be at the forefront of supporting employees along these lines, but as the opening vignette on Google shows, this has not always been the case. The #MeToo movement has clearly revealed that many companies have failed to protect lower level employees who have been victimized by supervisors or colleagues, and instead of punishing the perpetrators, HR actually helped these perpetrators cover their tracks.[3] In fact, beyond this, as part of the cover-up process, many companies, like Google, have rewarded perpetrators with lavish exit packages. For example, CBS offered a $120 million severance package to former CEO Les Moonves, who was also found to have been the subject of a large number of credible sexual harassment claims.[4]

In order to get the attention of their HR units, like we see in the "Yes at Google" movement, victims often had to bypass HR. For example, at Nike, there were scores of complaints registered with HR regarding sex bias and sexual harassment issues, but HR was apparently the place where these complaints went to die. Frustrated with the lack of effectiveness of following the chain of command, a large number of women got together and forwarded the huge sum total of their complaints—all with highly detailed documentation—directly to CEO Mark Parker. The sheer volume of the accusations finally led to the termination of close to a dozen top-level executives in 2018.[5] In fact, even worse than ignoring complaints and not protecting employees at all, the HR staff at several tech companies have been implicated in actually retaliating against people who came forward with complaints about harassment and gender discrimination.[6] This makes HR complicit and worthy of punishment itself.

As we saw in the vignette that opened this chapter, Google was reluctant to terminate the employment of many individuals who were engaging in sexual harassment, and in the end, this resulted in a widespread employee revolt. If the 20,000 employees who walked out for a day ever walked out for good, that might very well be the beginning of the end for Google. These are talented people, and people like that always have other options.

Thus, to compete effectively, organizations must take steps to ensure that good performers are motivated to stay with the organization, whereas chronically low performers or employees engaged in misdeeds are allowed, encouraged, or—if necessary—forced to leave. Those who work in HR need to be at the front line of the "attrition–termination" battle in the war for talent. Perhaps, spurred on by the #MeToo movement, HR departments need to refocus their efforts on protecting and supporting employees at all levels of the organization, even if this includes safeguarding employees from other employees who have higher status.

Thus, this chapter focuses on employee separation and retention. The material presented in Chapters 8 and 9 can be used to help establish who are the current effective performers as well as who is likely to respond well to future developmental opportunities. This chapter completes Part Three by discussing what can be done to retain high-performing employees who warrant further development as well as how to manage the separation process for low-performing employees who have not responded well to developmental opportunities.

Since much of what needs to be done to retain employees involves compensation and benefits, this chapter also serves as a bridge to Part Four, which addresses these issues in more detail. The chapter is divided into two sections. The first examines **involuntary turnover**, that is, turnover initiated by the organization (often among people who would prefer to stay). The second deals with **voluntary turnover**, that is, turnover initiated by employees (who the company often would prefer to keep). Although both types of turnover reflect employee separation, they are clearly different phenomena that need to be examined separately.

**Involuntary turnover**
Turnover initiated by the organization (often among people who would prefer to stay).

**Voluntary turnover**
Turnover initiated by employees (who the company often would prefer to keep).

# Managing Involuntary Turnover

Despite a company's best efforts in the area of personnel selection, training, and design of compensation systems, some employees will occasionally fail to meet performance requirements or will violate company policies while on the job. For example, in 2012, Secret Service members responsible for protecting the president of the United States on an upcoming trip to Colombia were caught bringing prostitutes to their hotel rooms. Secret Service work rules forbid bringing *any* foreign national, let alone prostitutes, to a security zone prior to a presidential visit; hence, these employees had to be terminated.[7] However, problems at this agency persisted, and in 2015, the terminations climbed higher into the organizational ranks when four top Secret Service officers were also removed from their jobs following an incident in which a man carrying a knife jumped the White House fence and managed to run all the way into the mansion before being caught. The new top official noted that "change is necessary to gain a fresh perspective on how we conduct business," and this is the rationale behind most such terminations.[8]

In another recent case, in 2018, several employees at Amazon were found to have accepted bribes in order to leak data on sellers and customers to disreputable merchants and scam artists. The companies that offered the bribes used the information to sell counterfeit products, violate trademarks, sabotage other sellers, and place fake orders using customer data. This is such an existential threat to Amazon's business model that the firm had to move quickly and decisively. The head of HR at Amazon emphasized this stating that "if bad actors abuse our systems, we take swift action, including terminating employment, seller accounts, deleting reviews, withholding funds, taking legal action and working with law enforcement."[9]

Despite the need for taking decisive action, however, terminating someone's employment can be a difficult task that needs to be handled with the utmost care and attention to detail. The increased willingness of people to sue their employers, combined with an unprecedented level of violence in the workplace, has made discharging employees personally dangerous and legally complicated.

With respect to danger, recent data indicate that more than 25,000 occupational assault injuries occur each year at the hands of employees who claim their stress levels pushed them over the edge.[10] For example, in 2019, an employee who was terminated after 15 years of working at a factory in Aurora, Illinois, shot and killed five co-workers and wounded five police officers in retaliation for what he felt was unfair treatment.

**LO 10-1**
Distinguish between involuntary and voluntary turnover, and discuss how each of these forms of turnover can be leveraged for competitive advantage.

Police Chief Kristen Ziman, noted that "I hate to use the term classic workplace shooting, it pains me to do that, but that is exactly what it was."[11] Attaching the word *classic* to a type of murder is sad, but does reveal how common the problem is.[12]

With respect to being legally complicated, the legal aspects of this decision can have important repercussions for the organization. Historically, in the absence of a specified contract, either the employer or the employee could sever the employment relationship at any time. The severing of this relationship could be for "good cause," "no cause," or even "bad cause." Over time, this policy has been referred to as the **employment-at-will doctrine**. This employment-at-will doctrine has eroded significantly over time, however. Today employees who are fired sometimes sue their employers for wrongful discharge.

A *wrongful discharge suit* typically attempts to establish that the discharge either (1) violated an implied contract or covenant (i.e., the employer acted unfairly) or (2) violated public policy (i.e., the employee was terminated because he or she refused to do something illegal, unethical, or unsafe). For example, in July 2014, a United Airlines flight from San Francisco to Hong Kong was close to departing when a team of flight attendants found threatening graffiti scrawled on the plane. The attendant crew refused to allow the plane to take off unless it was given a new, full security check, but company authorities who did not want to delay the flight balked and said the plane had already been cleared once and they were not going to do it twice. The flight attendants stood their ground and the flight was eventually cancelled, but the entire crew was then fired for insubordination. This was deemed a wrongful discharge, however, because the crew was obviously refusing to do something that was potentially unsafe.[13]

In another very publicized case, a large number of contract workers who worked for Lionbridge Software—a subcontractor for Microsoft—filed a wrongful discharge suit when their jobs were all eliminated after the group formed a union. The employees argued that the firm was retaliating against them for creating a legal collective bargaining unit, but the employer argued that the layoffs were due to a reduced demand for labor. The evidence showed, however, that the amount of billable hours that Lionbridge charged to Microsoft had not changed prior to or after the terminations, and the company eventually decided to settle out of court for an undisclosed amount of money in 2018.[14]

Wrongful discharge suits can also be filed as a civil rights infringement if the person discharged is a member of a protected group. For example, in 2015, 10 African American employees at McDonald's sued the company, alleging that they were fired because of their race. In fact, the manager at the franchise was quoted as saying that he "needed to get the ghetto out of the store." McDonald's Corporation had no intention of defending this manager but tried to argue that this was an issue between the employees and the "franchisee" (i.e., the local manager) not the "franchiser" (i.e., the corporate entity). The National Labor Relations Board did not see it that way and ruled against the corporation.[15]

The number of such protected groups is large and includes racial minorities, women, older workers (over 40 years of age), members of the LGBTQ community, disabled workers (including the obese), whistle-blowers, people who have filed workers compensation claims, and—if one counts reverse discrimination claims—Caucasians. As noted by Lisa Cassilly, a defense attorney for the firm Alston and Bird, "It's difficult to find someone who doesn't have some capacity to claim protected status."[16] This means that in almost any instance when someone is fired for poor performance, the alternative possibility that this person was a victim of discrimination can be raised.

Not surprisingly, this has led to an increase in litigation. Although the research suggests that a plaintiff usually loses a wrongful termination case, the high cost of litigating the case makes some employers reluctant to fire employees, even when they are low performers. When this happens, the employer's short-term emphasis on staying out of court has come into

**Employment-at-will doctrine**
The doctrine that, in the absence of a specific contract, either an employer or an employee could sever the employment relationship at any time.

conflict with the long-term need to develop a competitive workforce and grow. As an extreme example of this, due to past failures monitoring the legal and ethical practices of employees who were committing fraud against their customers, Wells Fargo Bank was punished by government regulators who put a solid cap on the size of the company. This resulted in the closure of over 5,000 bank branches, as well as strict limits regarding future growth. Indeed, years after the initial report of fraud, the company is still in the process of terminating regional managers who were supposedly overseeing the employees who were engaged in illegal activity.[17]

One reaction to this dilemma is to endure long stretches of poor performance in order to create the extensive "paper trail" that would support a negative action. Whereas HR professionals often point the finger of blame at supervisors who have not done a diligent job documenting past performance problems, supervisors often turn around and accuse HR of being cowards who never seem satisfied with the amount of evidence provided by supervisors. Moreover, keeping poor performers in their roles does not directly affect HR professionals every day, as it does supervisors, who have to watch helplessly as the morale of the rest of the workforce erodes. There is nothing more corrosive to team-based structures than wide variability in effort and performance between different members.

For example, Kimberly-Clark was once considered a paternalistic organization that hired people for life. However, increasingly, performance problems associated with certain individuals were seriously harming bottom-line results. One 30-year veteran at the company noted, "We all talk about how having the best team is the most important difference maker in your results, but we didn't have the supporting processes to make that sustainable." In 2015, a new emphasis on performance management helped Kimberly-Clark retain 95% of its top performers while shedding 45% of workers whose performance was rated unacceptable or inconsistent.[18]

Another questionable reaction is to initiate punitive actions short of termination in an effort to get the employee to quit on his or her own. This reaction is often a result of frustrated supervisors, who, unable to fire someone because of HR, resort to punishing the employee in other ways. This might include giving the person a low-level work assignment, a downsized office, or some other form of undesirable treatment. The problem with this approach, however, is that it might be construed as "retaliation," and the employer could be sued for this, even if the original discrimination suit is dismissed.

Finally, a third unsustainable reaction is to pay off the employee with thousands of dollars in excess severance pay in return for waiving the right to sue for wrongful dismissal. That is, even if the employer feels the case is unwarranted, in order to avoid litigation, the employer may offer the terminated employee $20,000 or more to waive the right to sue. The problem with this strategy is that it sets the expectation that all poor performers or people who engage in misdeeds are entitled to compensation on their way out the door, which eventually increases the amount of potential future litigation by rewarding frivolous charges. As defense attorney Mark Dichter notes, "I can design HR policies that can virtually eliminate your risk of facing employment claims, but you'll have a pretty lousy workforce. At the end of the day, you have to run your business."[19]

In some cases, the problem of having "a lousy workforce" eventually gets solved by outside forces. For example, when Warren Buffet teamed up 3G Capital, a private equity firm, to buy ketchup maker Heinz, 90% of the executive management team at the company was ousted in less than one month. 3G eventually cut 20% of the workforce, and one year later, adjusted earnings at Heinz rose by 40%. Although this may seem harsh, Warren Buffet stated bluntly that "efficiency is required over time in capitalism and I really tip my hat to what the 3G people have done.[20]

This drastic overhaul of the workforce is easier to accomplish in some cultures than others. As you can see from the Competing through Globalization box, recent

## Flexicurity: Translating the French Labor Code into Swedish

The term *flexicurity* is an awkward combination of the words *flexible security*. It also embodies a contradiction in the sense that "flexible" is the opposite of stable, and if one's job security is not stable, then in what sense is it still secure? Regardless of whether or not this is an oxymoron, for the French, the term *flexible security* translates into fighting words where the battle is increasingly waged in the streets of Paris. Although the most recent violent protest in Paris in December 2018 was triggered by an increase in the fuel tax, these protests were really a continuation of protests that erupted in September 2017, when French President Emmanuel Macron announced major changes to the *Code de Travail*—France's centuries old labor code.

The French code is a 3,000-page tome that spells out the security provisions that are legally mandated to French employees. The regulations constrain employers from terminating employment and limit the number of non-full-time employees, and many employers believe this is the major obstacle to economic growth experience in France relative to many of its European neighbors. For example, the unemployment rate in France has been mired at the 10% level for decades, twice that experienced by other members of European Union. Macron ran for the presidency based on a promise to rein back the code and make France more "employer friendly" and "growth oriented," and the model he relied on to

accomplish this was based upon the Scandinavian-style system. This system, also emulated by Germany, has successfully balanced the needs for flexibility and security by trading off increased employer freedom to react to changes in product markets for increased worker training efforts to ensure that the skills of the labor force will always be in tune with changing markets.

Under this model, on the employer side of the equation, rather than having to negotiate working conditions and employment levels with national unions, the employer can work directly with its own workforce in order to jointly arrive at compromises between two sides. As noted by Muriel Penicaud, "the company itself is the space where the creation of social standards most efficiently fulfills the specific needs of workers and companies in the construction of the best compromises—closest to the ground." The new rules also limit the potential fines associated with any "wrongful discharge" cases that can be levied by courts. Both of these new rules are aimed at increasing motivation of French employers to hire more workers—especially small companies that are adamant about staying under the 50-worker ceiling where the *Code de Travail* kicks in. Many of these small companies would rather stay small, even in the face of increased demand for their products, than grow.

On the employee side, however, the changes in the rules were enacted prior to the

installation of the promised €15 billion in training support for workers. This triggered the perception that Macron, a former investment banker, was selling out the workers and stealing from the poor to give to the rich. This triggered the riots of 2017 which, until the riots of 2018, were the most violent in over 30 years. Notably, Macron eventually blinked in 2018 and repealed the fuel tax, and many now feel that there may also be a chance to revisit the changes in work rules instituted in 2017. As noted by Jean-Paul Fitoussi, an economics professor at the Institut d'Etudes Politiques de Paris, "Right now, it is flexibility without security."

### DISCUSSION QUESTIONS

1. Compare and contrast how the French balance worker rights and business growth versus the United States or China.
2. How does the process of bending over backward to support incumbents of full-time jobs restrict the opportunities for those who are out of work or new to the labor force?
3. Given the negative impact of worker protections on the French economy, why might government officials still stick by these policies?

SOURCES: A. Nossiter, "Macron Takes on France's Labor Code, 100 Years in the Making," *The Wall Street Journal Online*, August 4, 2017; J. McAuley, "French Opposition Protests Macron's New Labor Laws," *The Wall Street Journal Online*, September 23, 2017; L. Alderman, "French Companies Have Newfound Freedom . . . to Fire," *The Wall Street Journal Online*, January 23, 2018; N. Nossiter, "France Suspends Fuel Tax Increase That Spurred Violent Protests," *The Wall Street Journal Online*, December 4, 2018.

moves in France aimed at increasing the flexibility of their workforce has met the kind of resistance that has never been seen in the United States.

Zero tolerance for poor performers is a critical element of success, especially for new and small firms when there is a great deal on the line. For example, new start-ups are notorious for terminating workers ruthlessly in the early stages of their development, and firing people after just three days is not uncommon. Yammer, a social networking site for businesses, fired over 30% of its employees in its first few years of doing business. Adam Pisoni, the senior technical chief at Yammer, boasts, "We are just really good about eliminating people whose skills were lacking and brutally honest when it comes to evaluating newcomers."[21]

Within this industry, where "failing fast" is considered a virtue, helping an employee move on from a situation where the fit is bad may result in that person moving on to a place where the fit is better. For example, Paul English was fired from one start-up, NetCentric Corporation, and this experience led him back to his roots as a coder. He eventually started his own business, which he later sold for millions of dollars. English's strategy with newcomers at his own start-up—not surprisingly—was equally tough. When it comes to poor performers, English notes, "You've got to cut that tumor out. If you can't fix it, you've got to get rid of it."[22]

WIN-Initiative/Getty Images

Start-up companies are notorious for terminating employees in a ruthless manner in the early days of their development.

The costs associated with letting poor performers stay on within the organization cannot be discounted. Organizations that introduce forced distribution rating systems—where low performers are systematically identified and, where necessary, eliminated from payrolls—often experience quick improvement gains in the range of 40%.[23] These gains often decrease over time, but illustrate how many organizations lose the discipline needed to hold each and every employee to high standards.[24] Given the critical financial and personal risks associated with employee dismissal, it is easy to see why the development of a standardized, systematic approach to discipline and discharge is critical to all organizations. These decisions should not be left solely to the discretion of individual managers or supervisors. In the next section, we explore aspects of an effective discipline and discharge policy.

## PRINCIPLES OF JUSTICE

The key to an effective discipline system is that all employees, including the individual who is being punished, view the system as "fair." There are three specific types of justice or fairness perceptions that need to be managed in this context. The first type of justice is outcome justice, sometimes referred to as "distributive justice," which considers (1) the outcomes one receives relative to one's inputs and (2) the comparison of that ratio to some ratio for some other reference person. This type of justice does not require that everyone gets treated equally, but only that the person's outcomes relative to the other person are proportionate with their inputs. Indeed, as the Competing through Environmental, Social, and Governance Practices box shows, there can be highly unequal outcomes for individuals that might still not generate widespread feelings of injustice.

**LO 10-2**
List the major elements that contribute to perceptions of justice and how to apply these in organizational contexts involving discipline and dismissal.

## Equity, Equality, and Executive Pay: What Ratio Is "Fair"?

Many have raised concerns about the shrinking middle class in the United States, as well as the growing inequality in wealth between those in the top 1% and the rest of the distribution. How much inequality can the country withstand, and at some point, will the imbalance become unsustainable for the tenuous social contract holding the country's various factions together? For people who had this concern, 2018 was an eye-opening year, because for the first time, large corporations had to report the ratio of their CEO's pay to the median worker pay in a public format. This requirement grew out of the 2010 Dodd-Frank Act, which was passed in the wake of the financial crisis back in 2008. The goal was to help shareholders understand and challenge executive-compensation practices at major U.S. companies that came to light during the crisis. Many in corporate America believed that this day would never come and that the new Congress elected in 2016 would repeal the act. But it didn't.

In some ways, the results were a confirmation of what everyone feared. The average ratio turned out to be close to 360 to 1, where the median employee salary was roughly $40,000. Of course, there was wild variability between firms and across industries. Toy maker Mattel had the highest pay gap of all of the S&P 500 companies at roughly

5,000 to 1. At the other extreme, Berkshire Hathaway Inc. had the lowest pay ratio of all S&P 500 companies at just 2 to 1, adding to the legendary status of its CEO, Warren Buffett. Ironically, some companies where the CEO performed so poorly that he or she had to be terminated turned out to be some of the most disparate on the metric. And this does even include the average 50 million golden parachute awarded to such executives.

On the other hand, comparing the ratios across companies is a little bit like comparing apples to oranges. Mattel is a very large manufacturing company that off-shores most of its labor to third world countries, where wages are low. Berkshire Hathaway, on the other hand, is a holding company that does not really manufacture anything. Moreover, HR strategy matters a great deal. Companies that outsource low-wage work to other U.S. companies can lift employee median pay for their own workers and make a company's ratio lower. On the other hand, offshoring operations in low-wage countries can drive the pay figure for the median employee lower and result in a ratio that is significantly higher.

Regardless, although some expected the kind of widespread negative reaction to the release of this data—something akin to the Occupy Wall Street Movement in 2011—in fact, the public

response was muted. Perhaps, in the future, the side-by-side comparisons of these the two numbers may lead to outcries from the public for one to get smaller and one to get bigger. Indeed, Rich Clayton, the research director for a large investment company, notes that in the future, "Americans will eventually be frustrated when they see a company's profits grow year after year along with CEO pay, while the median wage isn't moving. That will galvanize the point that something is broken." Given the way capitalism is fused into the DNA of American culture, that future may be a long way off.

### DISCUSSION QUESTIONS

1. Although the ratio of executive pay to the median worker captures inequality, in what ways does it not fully capture outcome justice, procedural justice, and interactive justice as discussed in the text?

2. How might the failures to capture these aspects of fairness judgments explain the muted response of many people when it comes to shrugging off highly disparate ratios?

SOURCES: J. McGregor, "As Companies Reveal Gigantic CEO-to-Worker Pay Ratios, Some Worry How Low-Paid Workers Might Take the News," *The Washington Post*, February 1, 2018; T. Francis and V. Furhmans, "Are You Underpaid? In a First, U.S. Firms Reveal How Much They Pay Workers," *Wall Street Journal*, March 12, 2018; D. Hembree, "CEO Pay Skyrockets To 361 Times That of the Average Worker," *Forbes.com*, May 22, 2018; A. Melin, "Workers of the World Shrug," *Bloomberg Businessweek*, August 27, 2018, pp. 28–29.

When it comes to termination decisions, outcome justice is critical because the terrible outcome received by the individual who is terminated must (1) be justified by their actions (inputs) and (2) be consistent with how other individuals who engaged in the same offense were treated. Thus, if the employee feels they did nothing wrong or if the employee perceives they did do something wrong but other people who did the same thing did not get terminated, then this will generate perceptions of outcome unfairness.

This perception is likely to be especially pronounced when, in addition to losing one's current job, one might then be prevented from seeking a similar job elsewhere. For example, employers are increasingly asking would-be hires to sign noncompete clauses in their hiring paperwork. A noncompete clause means that if the employee is terminated or voluntarily leaves the job, this person cannot seek new employment at a firm in the same industry. Traditionally, these kinds of clauses were aimed at high-paid jobs such as top-level executives or senior technical personnel who, due to their positions, had access to critical proprietary knowledge about the company's strategy or technology. These contracts were traditionally jointly negotiated between two powerful parties and were generally considered "fair."

Today, however, these contracts have trickled down to low-paid, entry-level employees where there is little negotiation and wide power asymmetries. For example, Jimmy John's, the ubiquitous sandwich-making franchise, makes all employees sign a noncompete clause as a matter of standard business practice. Although the company has never tried to stop minimum-wage employees from taking all their knowledge to Blimpie or another chain, the mere fact that they have the clause strikes many observers as unbalanced and unfair.[25]

In general, if one is sued, courts rarely support noncompete contracts that are not aimed at protecting proprietary information, trade secrets, or copyrighted formulas. As one legal expert notes, "You are not allowed to get a noncompete just because you don't want the person to quit."[26] In fact, some states have recently passed laws that make noncompete contracts unenforceable. For example, lawmakers in California believe that the ability of workers in places like Silicon Valley to hop from one employer to another actually spurs creativity and adds to the competitive advantage of the state as a whole. Thus, the belief is that it is in the state's best interest to set these employees free.[27]

Whereas outcome justice focuses on the ends, procedural and interactional justice focus on means. If methods and procedures used to arrive at and implement decisions that impact the employee negatively are seen as fair, the reaction is likely to be much more positive than if this is not the case. **Procedural justice** focuses specifically on the *methods used to determine the outcomes received*. Table 10.1 details six key principles that determine

**Procedural justice**
A concept of justice focusing on the methods used to determine the outcomes received.

**Table 10.1**
Six Determinants of Procedural Justice

1. **Consistency.** The procedures are applied consistently across time and other persons.
2. **Bias suppression.** The procedures are applied by a person who has no vested interest in the outcome and no prior prejudices regarding the individual.
3. **Information accuracy.** The procedure is based on information that is perceived to be true.
4. **Correctability.** The procedure has built-in safeguards that allow one to appeal mistakes or bad decisions.
5. **Representativeness.** The procedure is informed by the concerns of all groups or stakeholders (co-workers, customers, owners) affected by the decision, including the individual being dismissed.
6. **Ethicality.** The procedure is consistent with prevailing moral standards as they pertain to issues like invasion of privacy or deception.

whether people perceive procedures as being fair. Even given all the negative ramifications of being dismissed from one's job, the person being dismissed may accept the decision with minimum anger if the procedures used to arrive at the decision are consistent, unbiased, accurate, correctable, representative, and ethical. When the procedures that led to the decision are perceived in this fashion, the individual does not feel unfairly singled out. This helps someone maintain faith in the system as a whole, even if one is unhappy with the specific decision that was triggered by the system.

Lack of bias and informational accuracy are the most critical features of the six, and the potential for subjective judgments to be biased means that employers often have to go beyond simple supervisor evaluations in most cases.[28] In an effort to ensure that they have an airtight case, many employers have turned to private investigators to collect objective evidence where necessary. For example, when a Florida hospital suspected that a worker who claimed she was out with the flu for three days was instead completely healthy, it hired a private investigator to look into the case. In fact, the woman had gone to Universal Studio theme parks those days, and the investigation uncovered photos of her from three different roller coaster rides (which routinely photograph riders and then try to sell the pictures to them), as well as a video showing her volunteering as part of an animal act—all time-stamped and dated. Needless to say, this led to a termination that the worker was not interested in challenging.[29]

**Interactional justice**
A concept of justice referring to the interpersonal nature of how the outcomes were implemented.

Whereas procedural justice deals with how a decision was made, **interactional justice** refers to the *interpersonal nature of how the outcomes were implemented.* For example, in many documented cases, after giving employees the news of their termination, employers immediately have security guards whisk them out of the building with their various personal items haphazardly thrown together in cardboard boxes. This strips people of their dignity, as well as their job, and employees who witness this happen to a co-worker show a drastically lower level of organizational commitment from that day forward. Table 10.2 lists the four key determinants of interactional justice. When the decision is explained well and implemented in a fashion that is socially sensitive, considerate, and empathetic, this helps defuse some of the resentment that might come about from a decision to discharge an employee.

Although all termination decisions should pass the tests of outcome, procedural, and interactive justice, this is especially true when employers engage in this practice routinely, and actually advertise it when recruiting new workers. For example, Netflix states publicly that its culture is one that is characterized by frequent firings, and that employees at all levels are encouraged to give each other frank (some would say brutal) feedback when they have failed to perform well or live up to the company's standards.

The value statement of Netflix refers to the "keeper test," which asks every person to be able to defend why they would keep some employee. Then, when employees are discharged, there is a group intervention where everyone who worked with that individual gets together and discusses why they felt the termination was fair or unfair, as well as what everyone needs to learn from the incident. Clearly, this is not a culture that would be right for everyone, but Netflix is very up front and transparent when it comes to its values.[30] This was also the case at Uber, but as you can see from the Integrity in Action box the cultural values espoused by Uber ultimately got them into trouble and were eventually revoked.

**Table 10.2**
Four Determinants of Interactional Justice

1. **Explanation.** Emphasize aspects of procedural fairness that justify the decision.
2. **Social sensitivity.** Treat the person with dignity and respect.
3. **Consideration.** Listen to the person's concerns.
4. **Empathy.** Identify with the person's feelings.

# INTEGRITY IN ACTION

## Culture Change at Uber: Changing Values (and Personnel)

Travis Kalanick, the founder and former CEO of Uber, helped build a $75 billion company that operates in more than 400 cities. The company employs 11,000 corporate employees as well millions of drivers scattered all over the world. Moreover, the basic idea behind its ride-sharing platform literally changed the transportation industry, inspiring countless imitators and competitors. Kalanick attributed much of this success to the company's four core values that included (1) Let Builders Build, (2) Always Be Hustlin', (3) Meritocracy and Toe Stepping, and (4) Principled Confrontation. Those values were believed to have served the company well. Until they didn't.

The downfall at Uber started with a female engineer and blogger who worked for the company named Sarah Fowler. Fowler detailed a series of sexual harassment incidents she had endured at Uber, including one she reported to HR but was rebuffed because the perpetrator was "a high performer." This was the drop that turned into a trickle and then a deluge, as scores of other employers reported their own horror stories. This included a video post of Kalanick verbally abusing a driver, a written description of the "Greyball" program aimed at avoiding riders who were government officials, excessive alcohol consumption at work, out-of-control off-site parties,

romantic relationships between supervisors and women who reported to them, and even the cover-up of a rape incident in India. One industry analyst summed it all up noting that "no other company can come close to matching Uber when it comes to lawsuits, headaches, and embarrassing exposes chronicling the maltreatment of its employees, contract drivers and competitors, and deceiving local law enforcement, tax collection and other government agencies."

The situation got so bad that in 2017, the company's board of directors hired former U.S. Attorney General Eric Holder to conduct an examination of all that was wrong at Uber. The Holder investigation took 14 weeks, analyzing over 200 complaints filed with HR (many of which were never acted upon), as well as interviews with current and former employees and drivers. The report prompted the firing of 20 senior officials, and Kalanick himself stepped down as the CEO. The report listed 40 specific practices that had to be either eliminated or instituted at the company in order to promote a more ethical and inclusive climate. Most pointedly, the report recommended throwing away the four core value statements because, in Holder's opinion, the "values were being used to justify misbehavior."

The recommendations were presented at a June 13th meeting,

where the vice president of HR, Lisa Hornsy, introduced the new value statement—"Do the Right Thing Period." She stated that "while change does not happen overnight, we're committed to rebuilding trust with our employees, riders and drivers." Regrettably, at this very same meeting, a member of the board of directors made a sexist statement that forced his resignation as well, several hours later. Hornsy herself was ousted in September 2018 for making "racially charged comments" and covering up racial discrimination charges at the company. Clearly, culture change at the ride-sharing company is still a journey in progress.

### DISCUSSION QUESTIONS

1. How much impact do you believe value statements have on day-to-day employee behavior?

2. Do you believe that it is possible to have major cultural change without separating current employees from the organization, and if not, what percentage is required to install lasting substantive change?

SOURCES: M. Isaac, "Uber Embraces Major Reforms as Travis Kalanick, the CEO Step's Away," *The New York Times Online*, June 13, 2017; R. Stross, "Why Companies Like Uber Get Away with Bad Behavior," *The New York Times Online*, June 13, 2017; M. Isaac and S. Chira, "David Bonderman Resigns from Uber after Sexist Remark," *The New York Times Online*, June 13, 2017; G. Bensinger, "How Uber's Cultural Overhaul Was Tested by Complaints Against Top Deal Maker," *The Wall Street Journal Online*, September 26, 2018.

## PROGRESSIVE DISCIPLINE AND ALTERNATIVE DISPUTE RESOLUTION

Except in the most extreme cases, employees should generally not be terminated for a first offense. Rather, termination should come about at the end of a systematic discipline program. Effective discipline programs have two central components: documentation (which includes specific publication of work rules and job descriptions that should be in place prior to administering discipline) and progressive punitive measures. Thus, as shown in Table 10.3, punitive measures should be taken in steps of increasing magnitude, and only after having been clearly documented.

This may start with an unofficial warning for the first offense, followed by a written reprimand for additional offenses. At some point, later offenses may lead to a temporary suspension. Before a company suspends an employee, it may even want to issue a "last chance notification," indicating that the next offense will result in termination. Such procedures may seem exasperatingly slow, and they may fail to meet one's emotional need for quick and satisfying retribution. In the end, however, when problem employees are discharged, the chance that they can prove they were discharged for poor cause has been minimized.

**Alternative dispute resolution (ADR)**
A method of resolving disputes that does not rely on the legal system, often proceeding through the four stages of open-door policy, peer review, mediation, and arbitration.

At various points in the discipline process, the individual or the organization might want to bring in outside parties to help resolve discrepancies or conflicts. As a last resort, the individual might invoke the legal system to resolve these types of conflicts, but to avoid this, more and more companies are turning to **alternative dispute resolution (ADR)**. Alternative dispute resolution can take on many different forms, but in general, ADR proceeds through the four stages shown in Table 10.4. Each stage reflects a somewhat broader involvement of different people, and the hope is that the conflict will be resolved at earlier steps. However, the last step may include binding arbitration, in which an agreed-upon neutral party resolves the conflict unilaterally if necessary.

The use of ADR has grown rapidly among employers. In 2012, only 16% of employers required workers to sign away their legal rights to sue the employer in exchange for ADR procedures, but by 2014 this figure was up to 43%. Part of this trend is attributable to a 2011 Supreme Court ruling that upheld the legal status of pre-employment-required ADR sign-offs. Prior to this ruling, many lower courts were vacating or striking down ADR judgments, which meant that rather than keeping disputes out of court, ADR just added another layer to the process. The Supreme Court removed this layer and ruled that employees voluntarily signed the agreements. Thus, they were bound to them, even though

**Table 10.3**
An Example of a Progressive Discipline Program

| OFFENSE FREQUENCY | ORGANIZATIONAL RESPONSE | DOCUMENTATION |
|---|---|---|
| First offense | Unofficial verbal warning | Witness present |
| Second offense | Official written warning | Document filed |
| Third offense | Second official warning, with threat of temporary suspension | Document filed |
| Fourth offense | Temporary suspension and "last chance notification" | Document filed |
| Fifth offense | Termination (with right to go to arbitration) | Document filed |

| |
|---|
| **Stage 1: Open-door policy** |
| The two people in conflict (e.g., supervisor and subordinate) attempt to arrive at a settlement together. If none can be reached, they proceed to |
| **Stage 2: Peer review** |
| A panel composed of representatives from the organization that are at the same level of those people in the dispute hears the case and attempts to help the parties arrive at a settlement. If none can be reached, they proceed to |
| **Stage 3: Mediation** |
| A neutral third party from outside the organization hears the case and, via a nonbinding process, tries to help the disputants arrive at a settlement. If none can be reached, the parties proceed to |
| **Stage 4: Arbitration** |
| A professional arbitrator from outside the organization hears the case and resolves it unilaterally by rendering a specific decision or award. Most arbitrators are experienced employment attorneys or retired judges. |

**Table 10.4**
Stages in Alternative Dispute Resolution

they could not have been hired had they not signed. This makes ADR very attractive to employers. Litigation costs associated with class action suits dropped by roughly $150 million between 2011 and 2014.[31]

However, jump ahead to 2018, and the popularity of ADR's started to wane due to the #MeToo movement. In case after case, employers used mandatory ADR, in conjunction with nondisclosure agreements (NDA), to silence victims and protect predators—exactly as we saw in our opening vignette regarding Google. Thus, some have questioned the future of mandatory ADR as a process because of its lack of transparency and the way it was used by the powerful (and HR working as an accomplice) to separate victims from their legal rights.[32]

## EMPLOYEE ASSISTANCE AND WELLNESS PROGRAMS

Many of the problems that lead an organization to consider terminating an individual's employment relate to drug or alcohol abuse. In these cases, the organization's discipline and dismissal program should also incorporate an employee assistance program. Due to the increased prevalence of these programs in organizations, we describe them in detail here.

An **employee assistance program (EAP)** is a referral service that supervisors or employees can use to seek professional treatment for various problems. EAPs vary widely, but most share some basic elements. First, the programs are usually identified in official documents published by the employer (such as employee handbooks). Supervisors (and union representatives, where relevant) are trained to use the referral service for employees whom they suspect of having health-related problems. Employees are also trained to use the system to make self-referrals when necessary.

**Employee assistance program (EAP)**
Employer program that attempts to ameliorate problems encountered by workers who are drug dependent, alcoholic, or psychologically troubled.

Although originally targeted at the use of illegal drugs, many EAPs increasingly have had to deal with employees who have problems attributable to prescription drugs, especially painkillers. The percentage of workers who have tested positive for illegal drugs has decreased steadily from 14% in 1988 to just 3% in 2013. However, positive tests for painkillers such as Oxycontin and Vicodin rose 175% between 2005 and 2013 alone.[33]

This problem is particularly acute for white working-class men. A recent study suggests that 11% of this group is unemployed and not seeking work, and that nearly half of them are taking pain medication on a daily basis. Worse yet, those who do work report similar levels of pain medication use as those who do not work.

Obviously, a worker taking a prescription drug may still pose a safety threat to other workers or customers when under the drug's influence. Thus, many organizations have zero-tolerance policies for many prescription drugs that are just as strict as their policies for illegal drugs.[34] Moreover, even if a painkiller is legal in one country where the firm operates, it may not be legal in another country. For example, in 2015, Julie Hamp, the most senior female executive at Toyota, was forced to resign when she was arrested for being in possession of oxycodone—another powerful painkiller—that just happened to be illegal in Japan.[35]

In addition to considering both illegal drugs and prescription drugs, in some states, employee assistance programs also have to address legal, nonprescription drugs. As we noted in Chapter 6, many states in the United States allow for the recreational use of marijuana. However, even though it may be fine for the state government to ignore someone's drug use, this is much more difficult for employers who may be liable for any accidents or crimes when an employee in a safety sensitive occupation tests positive for marijuana. Moreover, unlike alcohol, where a breathalyzer can detect if you have been drinking very recently, a drug test for marijuana can come back positive weeks later. Thus, this is an issue that has to be addressed by an EAP program.[36]

The key to the effectiveness of an EAP is striking the right balance between collecting information that can be used to promote employee health, on the one hand, and the employee's right to privacy, on the other. Many employees are afraid to come forward with information that they think may damage their careers, and so it is in the employer's best interest to support people who do self-refer by keeping their information confidential, and then supporting them through counseling and rehabilitation.[37] However, rehabilitation rates for workers with alcohol or drug addiction are far from 100%, so the employer still has an obligation to monitor progress to make sure that these workers are not a safety threat to others. For example, the EEOC ruled in 2014 that if a worker is part of an EAP and is being treated for alcoholism, a manager who knows this and sees this person drinking alcohol at an office party is obligated to report this to the EAP. Again, this may seem a violation of privacy, but this right has to be weighed against other employees' right to a safe workplace.[38]

Whereas EAPs deal with employees who have developed problems at work because of health-related issues, employee wellness programs take a proactive and preemptive focus on trying to prevent health-related problems in the first place. The cost of employer provided health care in 2018 was roughly $20,000 per employee, and costs have been going up 5% per year.[39] Hence, it is clearly in the employer's interest to have healthy workers, and this is where employee wellness programs come in.

Employee wellness programs come in many different sizes and varieties, so it is difficult to make general statements about their cost and effectiveness. Some companies just hand out pamphlets on how to maintain better health and call that a wellness program.[40] Other programs have employees use wearable sensors like Fitbits, monitor their health status continuously, provide company-sponsored facilities and medical staff to support better health, and then reward employees financially for accomplishing health-related goals.[41] Although these kinds of voluntary programs are popular, as the Evidence-Based HR box shows, the effectiveness of voluntary programs has been questioned.

# EVIDENCE-BASED HR

There was some evidence from early evaluations of company wellness programs that suggested that voluntary interventions were achieving their goals when it comes to moving the needle on employee health-related metrics. However, all of the early research was characterized by studies that were not true experiments where people were randomly assigned to conditions. Instead, the evaluations just compared employees who volunteered for the programs versus those who did not volunteer when tracked over time. This is called a quasi-experiment, and this design is considered inferior to a true experiment because people who volunteer could differ from those who fail to volunteer for any number of reasons, all of which might serve as alternative explanations for the apparent success of the program.

The first large-scale true experiment on this topic was conducted in the State of Illinois in 2018, and the results cast some doubt on previous claims. In the Illinois study, 5,000 employees were tracked, with 1,500 assigned to a control group and 3,500 assigned to a wellness program that featured classes on weight loss, tai chi, smoking cessation, and alcohol consumption, along with financial incentives for improvement on key metrics. Only a portion of the 3,500 employees actually took advantage of the program, however, which allowed for a comparison of (1) the control group, (2) the group that voluntarily took advantage of the intervention, and (3) the nonvolunteers who failed to enter into the program.

The results were a confirmation of many people's worst fears, in the sense that, when it came to outcomes such as (1) trips to the gym, (2) running outside the gym, (3) heart rate and blood pressure, (4) health care spending, and (5) employee retention, the volunteer group outperformed the control group who in turn outperformed the nonvolunteer group. Regrettably, when the volunteer and nonvolunteer groups were combined, there was no effect for the combined group versus the control group. Thus, this study suggests that whereas wellness programs can help some people, past studies that compared only volunteers to nonvolunteers greatly overestimated their positive effects.

SOURCE: A. Fradera, "First Randomised-Controlled Trial of an Employee 'Wellness Program' Suggests They Are a Waste of Money," *Research Digest Online*, August 23, 2018.

Because of the questionable effectiveness of voluntary wellness programs, employers sometimes turn to more controversial programs that are less voluntary. For example, the Michelin Tire Company not only collects health-related data from employees, but also punishes employees who fail to meet health goals. Michelin employees who have high blood pressure or whose waistlines exceed a certain limit (40 inches for men and 35 inches for women) are forced to pay an extra $1,000 for health care coverage. This might seem unfair for a company whose mascot is the "spare-tired" Michelin Man, but similar penalties have been levied by Miracle-Gro, CVS/Caremark, Honeywell, and General Electric.

All of these companies have found that people react more strongly to threats of losses than promises of gains. Reward programs at these companies that offered incentives to get healthier simply did not seem to work. By contrast, punishment-based programs definitely get people's attention. These companies have also found that roughly 80% of health care costs are generated by just 20% of workers, and a staggering 1% of workers generate

33% of the costs. Targeting these specific individuals has proven to be an efficient way to get costs under control, but there are legal limits to how far employers can go with these sorts of penalties.[42]

One of the major determinants of how far employee wellness programs can push their employees is how central health is to effectively performing the work. In general, if one defines obesity as having a body mass index (BMI) of 30 or higher, then there is an obesity epidemic in the United States.[43] The obesity rate for Americans doubled between 1993 and 2012, and for some organizations, this is a threat to their ability to accomplish their mission. For example, the Federal Aviation Authority (FAA) passed a new rule in 2013 that any commercial or private pilot with a BMI of 40 or more has to be examined by a sleep specialist to confirm that they do not have sleep apnea. Sleep apnea is highly related to obesity, and the FAA identified over a half-dozen incidents in 2012 where a pilot fell asleep in the cockpit. This included a well-publicized case in which a Bombardier regional jet traveling to Hawaii overflew the airport where it was supposed to land by 30 miles after a 20-minute lapse in radio communication with the tower.[44]

Another organization that is highly concerned about obesity is the U.S. Federal Bureau of Investigation (FBI). In 2015, the director of the agency issued a new requirement that its agents pass a fitness test once a year and that failure to do so will be part of their annual performance evaluation and raise process. At one time, almost all members of the FBI worked in highly active jobs in the field where they were chasing and arresting criminals. However, the threats of terrorism, cybersecurity, and large-scale fraud have pushed many employees into offices, where they sit at computers for long stretches of time. This has had a predictable effect on obesity rates in the agency. To counter the problem, the agency now requires agents to be able to do 24 push-ups without stopping and 35 sit-ups in a minute. It also requires that agents be able to sprint 300 yards in less than a minute and run a mile in under 12 minutes.[45]

## OUTPLACEMENT COUNSELING

Outplacement counseling
Counseling to help displaced employees manage the transition from one job to another.

The permanent nature of an employee termination not only leaves the person angry, but it also leads to confusion as to how to react and in a quandary regarding what happens next. If the person feels there is nothing to lose and nowhere else to turn, the potential for violence or litigation is higher than most organizations are willing to tolerate. Therefore, many organizations provide **outplacement counseling**, which tries to help dismissed employees manage the transition from one job to another. There is a great deal of variability in the services offered via outplacement programs, typically including career counseling, job search support, résumé critiques, job interviewing training, and provision of networking opportunities. Increasingly, these programs are moving online both to reduce costs and in recognition that most job search activity now takes place online. Face-to-face meetings between counselors and clients are largely becoming a thing of the past, being replaced by Web-based tools.[46]

Many observers have criticized the effectiveness of outplacement programs, charging that the companies that offer the services care more about avoiding litigation and bad public relations than about getting former employees new jobs. Many programs take a "one-size-fits-all" approach with standardized training programs not tailored to the specific needs of clients and industries, as well as boilerplate résumé services that send out almost identical documents for different workers. The evidence suggests that 40% of workers offered such services never show up, and another 30% quit using them after one or two sessions.[47] Many employers remain committed to these programs, however, and evidence supports the business case for this activity.

Specifically, when it comes to employee lawsuits, employers that offer outplacement activities have a 10% reduced likelihood of litigation by former employees, relative to companies that fail to provide such services. In addition, roughly 20% of employers that engaged in outplacement activities reported that turnover decreased among employees who remained after the initiation of such programs. Recruitment costs for new employees were also reported to be 24% lower for firms that provided this sort of employee assistance. Finally, 38% of employers that offered outplacement saw an increase in employee satisfaction one year after the downsizing event, compared to just 14% for employers that did not offer services.[48] For all of these reasons, some companies actually boast about their ability to place workers who lost their jobs in even better jobs at other companies. For example, Oracle advertises the fact that over a dozen former executives who ran out of room to grow at Oracle went on to become CEOs at other companies, burnishing the firm's reputation as a great place to launch a career.[49]

At the very least, outplacement counseling can help people realize that losing a job is not the end of the world and that other opportunities exist. For example, when John Morgridge was fired from his job as branch manager at Honeywell, it made him realize that his own assertiveness and need for independence were never going to cut it in a large, bureaucratic institution like Honeywell. Morgridge took his skills and went on to build computer network maker Cisco Systems, which is now worth more than $1 billion.[50] This is a success story for Morgridge, but the fact that a major corporation like Honeywell let his talent go certainly reflects a lost opportunity for the company. Retaining people who can make such contributions is key to gaining and maintaining competitive advantage. The second half of this chapter is devoted to issues related to retention.

# Managing Voluntary Turnover

Earlier in this chapter, our focus was on how to help employees who were not contributing to the organization's goal in a manner that protected the firm's ability to compete and how to support former employees' transition into alternative employment. In this section, we focus on the other side of the separation equation—preventing employees who are highly valued by the organization from leaving (and perhaps even joining the competition). Research suggests that the average economic cost to a company of turning over a skilled job is over 200% of the cost of one year's compensation for that role. This is attributable to the costs of hiring, onboarding, training, learning curve losses, higher error rates, and the general negative impacts on the employees left behind in terms of their own workloads.[51] Indeed, the loss of certain individuals would be so costly to some small businesses that the companies take out life insurance policies on the employee.[52] Although this does not do much good if the employee just leaves on his or her own, it does reinforce the point that some human capital is almost irreplaceable.

Moreover, an organization that has a reputation for being successful becomes an especially attractive target to external forces that may look to steal talent. For example, because of its positive reputation, Apple has always been a company that has had to work hard to hold on to its valued employees. Tesla Motors has hired over 150 former Apple executives, designers, and engineers in the past few years alone. Part of Tesla's competitive strategy is to exploit the fact that software has gone from providing 10% of the value of a car to 60%; thus, the skills and orientation of former Apple employees are a great fit for Tesla's business model.[53] Although this hiring pattern might be good news for Tesla, it is bad news for Apple who may wish that employees were more attached to their jobs.

For example, Costco Wholesale is well known throughout the retail industry for treating its employees better than most of its competitors. Costco pays many of its its hourly workers over $20/hour, compared to the industry average of $12/hour. Costco also provides company-sponsored health insurance to all employees, as well as tuition reimbursement programs that allow employees who start out at the lowest level of the shop floor to climb the corporate ladder. The result is that voluntary turnover within the organization is very low for the retail industry. The turnover rate among employees is less than 5% in a cutthroat industry where the average is closer to 30%. This feeds directly into Costco's business model and strategic plan. Due to Costco's emphasis on low prices, 80% of its profit comes from membership fees. Even though Costco's membership fees are 20% higher than Sam's Club's, over 90% of customers renew each year, providing a stable and predictable source of income. CEO Craig Jelinek notes, "We know it's a lot more profitable in the long term to minimize employee turnover and maximize employee productivity, commitment and loyalty. If you treat consumers with respect and treat employees with respect, good things are going to happen to you."[54]

Employees may be attached to their jobs for any of a number of reasons, and employers need to recognize this in their efforts to retain workers. For example, pay and job security used to be the primary drivers of retention for older generations of workers, but this is not always the case today. Evidence seems to suggest that younger employees prefer benefits to cash, and they generally want to work in an environment that is fun and collaborative and that provides a great deal of immediate feedback and opportunities for development. This generation of employees has a lot to offer employers, including the fact that they are technically skilled, racially diverse, socially interconnected, and willing to collaborate.

However, the annual rate of voluntary turnover among Millennials tends to be higher than that associated with other generations, which has led some observers to conclude that they are impatient and entitled. For example, according to one recent survey, Millennial employees working in the investment banking industry left their positions after just 17 months on the job.[55] However, as one experienced manager notes, "If they don't feel like they're making a contribution to a company quickly, they don't stay, but if you provide them with the right environment, they'll work forever—around the clock."[56] In this section of the chapter, we examine the job withdrawal process that characterizes voluntary employee turnover, and we illustrate the central role that job satisfaction plays in this process.

## PROCESS OF JOB WITHDRAWAL

Job withdrawal is a set of behaviors that dissatisfied individuals enact to avoid the work situation. The right side of Figure 10.1 shows a model grouping the overall set of behaviors into three categories: behavior change, physical job withdrawal, and psychological job withdrawal.

**Progression of withdrawal**
The theory that dissatisfied individuals enact a set of behaviors to avoid the work situation.

We present the various forms of withdrawal in a progression, as if individuals try the next category only if the preceding is either unsuccessful or impossible to implement. This theory of **progression of withdrawal** has a long history and many adherents.[57] For example, someone who is dissatisfied with the job or organization might not be able to just jump to another job right away but will instead either disengage temporarily (through absenteeism or tardiness) or psychologically (through lower job involvement and organizational commitment) until the right opportunity comes along.

Indeed, a good predictor at this stage of the turnover process is whether the employee is assimilating into the organization's culture, as evidenced by the language the employee uses.

**Figure 10.1**

An Overall Model of the Job Dissatisfaction–Job Withdrawal Process

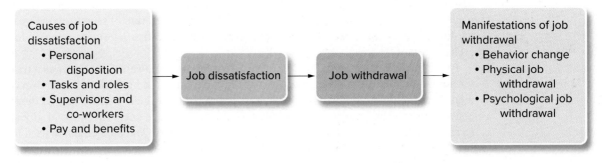

A study that examined 10 million e-mail traces of new employees found that newcomers who eventually thrived and stayed with the company were quick to adopt the language patterns of veteran employees when it came to practices like cursing, expressions of positive emotions, and imagery. Employees who were more likely to leave for either voluntary or involuntary reasons tended to maintain the linguistic style they had prior to joining the company.[58]

Others theories have suggested that there is no tight progression in that any one of the categories can compensate for another, and people choose the category that is most likely to redress the specific source of dissatisfaction. Still other theories maintain that turnover is set up by a general level of persistent dissatisfaction that then is triggered abruptly by some single disruptive event at work that either pushes the employee away (such as a dispute with a supervisor or co-worker) or pulls the employee away (an alternative employment opportunity).[59] This model focuses on "the straw that breaks the camel's back" but shares with all the other theories an emphasis on job dissatisfaction as the necessary but insufficient cause of turnover. Regardless of what specific theory one endorses, there is a general consensus that withdrawal behaviors are clearly related to one another, and they are all at least partially caused by job dissatisfaction.[60]

## Behavior Change

One might expect that an employee's first response to dissatisfaction would be to try to change the conditions that generate the dissatisfaction. This can lead to supervisor–subordinate confrontation, perhaps even conflict, as dissatisfied workers try to bring about changes in policy or upper-level personnel. Although at first this type of conflict can feel threatening to the manager, on closer inspection, this is really an opportunity for the manager to learn about and perhaps solve an important problem. When properly channeled by a secure and supportive leader, "voicing opportunities" for lower-level employees can often result in substantial organizational improvements and prevent turnover among highly engaged employees.[61]

Less constructively, employees can initiate change through **whistle-blowing** (making grievances public by going to the media). Whistle-blowers are often dissatisfied individuals who cannot bring about internal change and, out of a sense of commitment or frustration, take their concerns to external constituencies. For example, regardless of what others thought of him, in his own mind, Edward Snowden was doing the right thing. Concerned that the National Security Agency was increasingly spying on U.S. citizens by collecting information on over 10 million telephone calls, he went public with this

**Whistle-blowing**
Making grievances public by going to the media or government.

information in June 2013. He felt he was doing his civic duty in trying to inspire a national debate on the "security–privacy" trade-off that seemed to be taking place in the United States at that time. He also knew the severity of his actions, noting, "I understand I will be made to suffer for my actions, but I will be satisfied if the federation of secret law, unequal pardon and irresistible executive powers that rule the world that I love are revealed for even an instant."[62]

In the eyes of many people within the U.S. government, Edward Snowden was a traitor. In the effort to thwart global terrorism, the program at the heart of this controversy merely captured data on who was talking to whom, and not the content of any of those conversations. The program was simply trying to lay out the social network of global terrorists, part of which resides within the country's borders. The data could be used to secure a legal warrant for tapping a phone, but no phone was ever tapped illegally. However, by making the program public, Snowden tipped off potential terrorists to heretofore unknown dangers and thus aided and abetted them in the goal of avoiding detection.[63] Whether or not Edward Snowden is a whistle-blower or traitor will be for history to decide, but for ethicists, this example illustrates how the employee has to balance two central trusts: the trust of his employer, who pays him to do specific work under a specific contract he willingly signed, and the trust of the larger society in which he resides to protect its citizens from rogue companies or overreaching branches of government.[64]

Although this type of whistle-blowing activity has always taken place, the advent of websites like Wikileaks has provided a more obvious and convenient outlet for this activity. Wikileaks is most famous for collecting and publishing information provided by government and military sources, but it has also threatened private companies such as Bank of America.[65] This type of whistle-blowing is also on the rise because of a provision of the 2010 Dodd-Frank regulatory overhaul that encourages this behavior by offering 30% of penalties collected by the government to individuals who help unearth illegal actions, in an effort to compensate them for the risks they take.[66]

### Physical Job Withdrawal

If the job conditions cannot be changed, a dissatisfied worker may be able to solve the problem by leaving the job. This could take the form of an internal transfer if the dissatisfaction is job specific (i.e., the result of an unfair supervisor or unpleasant working conditions). However, if the source of the dissatisfaction relates to organization-wide policies (lack of job security or below-market pay levels), then organizational turnover is likely. As we indicated earlier, there is a negative relationship between turnover rates and organizational performance, and it is generally costly to replace workers—especially high performers in skilled jobs.[67]

Another way of physically removing oneself from the dissatisfying work, short of quitting altogether, is to be absent. Although less financially disruptive relative to having an employee quit his or her job, absenteeism is still costly for many employers, especially small companies, where it is often harder to make up for a single person's absence. The direct cost of employee absenteeism has been estimated to represent roughly 2% of payroll; however, there are also indirect costs of absenteeism. For example, the employer may need to pay a replacement worker or pay other workers overtime to make up for the person who failed to show up. In addition, production might be reduced and customers might have to wait longer for services. When these indirect costs are added to the equation, absenteeism costs closer to 4% of payroll.[68]

### Psychological Withdrawal

When dissatisfied employees are unable to change their situation or remove themselves physically from their jobs, they may psychologically disengage themselves from their jobs. Although they are physically on the job, their minds may be somewhere else.

This psychological disengagement can take several forms. First, if the primary dissatisfaction has to do with the job itself, the employee may display a very low level of job involvement. **Job involvement** is the degree to which people identify themselves with their jobs. People who are uninvolved with their jobs consider their work an unimportant aspect of their lives. A second form of psychological disengagement, which can occur when the dissatisfaction is with the employer as a whole, is a low level of organizational commitment. **Organizational commitment** is the degree to which an employee identifies with the organization and is willing to put forth effort on its behalf. Individuals who feel they have been treated unjustly by their employer often respond by reducing their level of commitment and are often looking for the first good chance to quit their jobs. In contrast, employees who are involved in their job and committed to their employer are much more likely to respond to problems by speaking up, voicing their concerns, and trying to change what they may consider a bad situation. Most whistle-blowers tend to be people committed to their jobs and organizations, not people who forget about their jobs the moment they leave the workplace.[69]

**Job involvement**
The degree to which people identify themselves with their jobs.

**Organizational commitment**
The degree to which an employee identifies with the organization and is willing to put forth effort on its behalf.

## JOB SATISFACTION AND JOB WITHDRAWAL

As we saw in Figure 10.1, the key driving force behind all the different forms of job withdrawal is **job satisfaction**, which we define as a pleasurable feeling that results from the perception that one's job fulfills or allows for the fulfillment of one's important job values.[70] This definition reflects three important aspects of job satisfaction. First, job satisfaction is a function of *values*, defined as "what a person consciously or unconsciously desires to obtain." Second, this definition emphasizes that different employees have different views of which values are important, and this is critical in determining the nature and degree of their job satisfaction. The third important aspect of job satisfaction is *perception*. An individual's perceptions may not be a completely accurate reflection of reality, and different people may view the same situation differently.

In particular, people's perceptions are often strongly influenced by their frame of reference. A **frame of reference** is a standard point that serves as a comparison for other points and thus provides meaning. For example, a nurse might compare her salary to the salaries of other nurses and her overall satisfaction with pay depends on this comparison as much as the absolute value of pay itself. A female nurse makes, on average, a little over $55,000 a year in salary. This is a healthy salary, and she might be satisfied with this salary until she learns that, on average, a male nurse doing the same work made slightly over $65,000 a year.[71]

A similar "pay gap" between men and women also exists for people who have obtained MBA degrees. According to a survey of over 12,000 individuals who received MBAs within the last eight years, the evidence suggests that both men and women degree holders start out at close to the same rate of pay—roughly $98,000 for women and $105,000 for men. After eight years, however, that gap widens with men earning $175,000 compared to $140,000 for women. Because men and women differ on the industries where they work (men tend to work more in finance) and the nature of the work they do (e.g., the survey suggests that men supervise five people on average versus women who supervise

**LO 10-3**
Specify the relationship between job satisfaction and various forms of job withdrawal, and identify the major sources of job satisfaction in work contexts.

**Job satisfaction**
A pleasurable feeling that results from the perception that one's job fulfills or allows for the fulfillment of one's important job values.

**Frame of reference**
A standard point that serves as a comparison for other points and thus provides meaning.

three), it is hard to know if this reflects bias; but it is still a hard social comparison for some women to take.[72]

These kinds of frame-of-reference effects are powerful, and many companies try to reduce the impact of social comparisons by making pay levels secret. However, as work becomes more collaborative and team oriented, there is increasing demand for transparency about pay and even for team member input into pay decisions. Balancing team members' need-to-know with privacy concerns, as well as the need to mitigate conflict between team members who disagree about their relative worth, is increasingly a struggle in many business contexts.[73]

## SOURCES OF JOB DISSATISFACTION

Many aspects of people and organizations can cause dissatisfaction among employees. Managers and HR professionals need to be aware of these because they are the levers that can raise job satisfaction and reduce employee withdrawal.

### Unsafe Working Conditions

Earlier in this chapter, we discussed the employer's role in helping employees stay healthy via employee assistance programs for specific problems like drug addiction and alcohol dependency. Obviously, if employers care this much about the risk employees are exposed to off the job, then there needs to be an even stronger emphasis on risk exposure that occurs on the job.

Of course, each employee has a right to safe working conditions. In Chapter 3, we reviewed the Occupational Safety and Health Act of 1970 (OSHA), which spells out those rights in detail. We also discussed in that chapter how to develop safety awareness programs that identify and communicate job hazards, as well as how to reinforce safe work practices that would allow one to pass an OSHA inspection. Although in that chapter we primarily emphasized legal compliance, we need to revisit the topic because OSHA is not the only audience likely to evaluate the safety of jobs. The perception and reaction of the organization's own employees to working conditions has implications for satisfaction, retention, and competitive advantage that go well beyond merely meeting the legal requirements. That is, if applicants or job incumbents conclude that their health or lives are at risk because of the job, then attracting and retaining workers will be impossible.

Not all jobs pose safety risks, but the nature of the work in a whole host of jobs makes managing safety-related perceptions critical.[74] This includes jobs such as fishing boat operators, timber cutters, airline pilots/flight attendants, structural metal workers, garbage collectors, and taxi drivers/chauffeurs, all of which have been identified as jobs where people are most likely to be involved in fatal accidents. In fact, in these job categories alone, close to 1,000 people die annually. Other jobs that rate low in terms of fatal accidents rate higher in nonfatal accidents, and this includes many jobs in eating establishments, hospitals, nursing homes, convenience stores, and the long-haul trucking industry. Still other jobs pose risks in terms of contracting occupational diseases due to exposure to chemicals.

Finally, some jobs create health risks simply because of the long hours and high stress associated with them. This was highlighted recently by several cases in the aviation industry, in which air traffic controllers who were working at night were found to be sleeping on the job because of extended hours. For example, in one case, a lone controller was working on less than 2 hours' sleep in the previous 24 hours, and this was a contributing factor in the crash of Comair Flight 191 in Lexington, Kentucky.[75] In general, working at night runs counter to the basic physiology of the human body and disrupts one's natural circadian rhythm, which in turn causes a whole host of physical problems. Thus, working at night has to be considered a safety issue in any job for which this is a task requirement.[76]

Protecting workers and ensuring their safety is particularly challenging when trying to manage overseas operations. For example, in 2013, companies in the fashion industry, such as H&M, Gap, and Zara, were blamed for the deaths of over 1,000 garment workers who perished when the old and dilapidated building they worked in collapsed in Bangladesh. In the wake of that disaster, Western companies vowed to help Bangladesh upgrade the safety of its facilities. Yet three years later, 80% of the 1,600 buildings identified as unsafe had not been touched. Kohl Gill, a labor activist notes, "There's been so much attention put on this, it's kind of surprising so little progress has been made."[77]

## Personal Dispositions

Because dissatisfaction is an emotion that ultimately resides within the person, it is not surprising that many researchers who have studied these outcomes have focused on individual differences. For example, **Negative affectivity** is a term used to describe a dispositional dimension that reflects pervasive individual differences in satisfaction with any and all aspects of life. Individuals who are high in negative affectivity report higher levels of aversive mood states, including anger, contempt, disgust, guilt, fear, and nervousness across all contexts (work and nonwork). People who are high in negative affectivity tend to focus extensively on the negative aspects of themselves and others. They also tend to persist in their negative attitudes even in the face of organizational interventions, such as increased pay levels, that generally increase the levels of satisfaction of other people.

> **Negative affectivity**
> A dispositional dimension that reflects pervasive individual differences in satisfaction with any and all aspects of life.

All of this implies that some individuals tend to bring low satisfaction with them to work. Thus, these people may be relatively dissatisfied regardless of what steps the organization or the manager takes. By contrast, research suggests that people who are positive tend to work harder, are more likely to be committed to the organization, are paid more, and are promoted more often.[78] Like anything, however, one can get too much of a good thing, and if a work group is made up of people who are all high in positive affect, they are often overly optimistic and fail to engage in a sufficient level of critical thinking regarding what might go wrong with plans or projects. Thus, when it comes to team composition, a built-in "devil's advocate" can be a highly valuable member.[79]

The evidence on the linkage between these kinds of traits and job satisfaction suggests the importance of personnel selection as a way of raising overall levels of employee satisfaction. If job satisfaction remains relatively stable across time and jobs because of characteristics like negative affectivity, this suggests that transient changes in job satisfaction will be difficult to sustain in these individuals, who will typically revert to their "dispositional" or adaptation level over time. Thus, some employers try to screen for this when selecting job candidates.

## Tasks and Roles

As a predictor of job dissatisfaction, nothing surpasses the nature of the task itself. Many aspects of a task have been linked to dissatisfaction. Several elaborate theories relating task characteristics to worker reactions have been formulated and extensively tested. We discussed several of these in Chapter 4. In this section, we focus on three primary aspects of tasks that affect job satisfaction: the complexity of the task, the amount of flexibility in where and when the work is done, and, finally, the value the employee puts on the task.

With a few exceptions, there is a strong positive relationship between task complexity and job satisfaction. That is, the boredom generated by simple, repetitive jobs that do not mentally challenge the worker leads to frustration and dissatisfaction.[80] Many observers have attributed much of the recent labor unrest in China to this specific aspect of the work. For example, the Han Hoi riot started as a minor fracas between two young workers but soon escalated into a pitched battle that involved over 2,000 employees and 5,000 paramilitary forces. The two workers, who everyone agrees started the riot, were from different regions and had just finished a stressful 12-hour shift at the factory that makes iPods and iPads. The work was boring and low paid, and frustrations boiled over when a small argument turned into a shoving and pushing match.

Witnesses claim that security workers at the plant overreacted to the incident and began brutally beating the two young people. At that point, hundreds of workers rushed the security personnel and returned the favor. Soon, more and more security personnel were called to the scene, followed by more and more restive workers. A major revolt was under way, and when it was over, 40 people were hospitalized and the facility had to be shut down for days after fires and looting gutted many stretches of the campus that housed close to 80,000 workers.[81] This riot was just one of many that put a spotlight on the tension between Chinese factories that base their business model on low-cost strategies that create low-scope jobs and unpleasant working conditions, and a new generation of Chinese workers who seem less willing to tolerate those conditions.

One of the major interventions aimed at reducing job dissatisfaction by increasing job complexity is *job enrichment*. As the term suggests, this intervention is directed at jobs that are "impoverished" or boring because of their repetitive nature or low scope. Many job enrichment programs are based on the job characteristics theory discussed earlier in Chapter 4. Another task-based intervention is **job rotation**. This is a process of systematically moving a single individual from one job to another over the course of time. Although employees may not feel capable of putting up with the dissatisfying aspects of a particular job indefinitely, they often feel they can do so temporarily.

Job rotation can do more than simply spread out the dissatisfying aspects of a particular job. It can increase work complexity for employees and provide valuable cross-training in jobs so that employees eventually understand many different jobs. This makes for a more flexible workforce and increases workers' appreciation of the other tasks that have to be accomplished for the organization to complete its mission. For example, Walmart recently introduced a new program, called Upskilling, that is a combination of job rotation and job enrichment aimed at developing low-level workers into middle-level managers.[82]

Because of the degree to which nonwork roles often spill over and affect work roles, and vice versa, a second critical aspect of work that affects satisfaction and retention is the degree to which scheduling is flexible. For example, some companies allow workers to work from home, at least for a percentage of time. This helps improve efficiency for workers facing long commutes and also cuts down on real estate costs. Due to needs for creativity and collaboration at work, however, many firms have reined in these polices recently because they believe face-to-face interaction is critical for innovation. Ironically, IBM was one of the first movers when it came to having their employees work off site, but in a dramatic reversal, they are now building a $750 million facility where the emphasis is on real teamwork rather than virtual collaboration.[83]

**Job rotation**
The process of systematically moving a single individual from one job to another over the course of time. The job assignments may be in various functional areas of the company, or movement may be between jobs in a single functional area or department.

Of course, even worse that inflexible scheduling is scheduling unpredictability, and this is a major source of dissatisfaction at work for many in the retail or hospitality sectors of the economy.[84] Workers hate to be called in at the last minute, especially on weekends. Indeed, one of the core values at Chick-fil-A, the fast-food restaurant, is that they are closed on Sunday so that workers are guaranteed to have that day off to share with their family and friends. This helps the company maintain a turnover rate of just 4% a year compared to an industry average of 150%.[85] Although one might fear that the loss of revenue on Sundays might offset the value of retaining workers, HR staff at the company note that they have highly loyal customers that have grown accustomed to meeting their needs at Chick-fil-A on all the other days of the week—hence avoiding any real loss.[86] Although not all businesses have the luxury of shutting down on Sundays, as the Competing through Technology box shows, there are new apps that can help provide employees with some degree of scheduling predictability.

Companies can also help employees manage their multiple roles via family-friendly policies. These policies may include provisions for child care, elder care, job sharing, telecommuting, and extended maternal and paternal leaves. When it comes to maternity and paternity leave, however, most employers in the United States do far less than what one sees in the rest of the world. Although the Family and Medical Leave Act requires employers to give parents 12 weeks of leave after having a child, this is an unpaid leave, and many employees cannot afford to go that long without pay—especially after having a baby. In terms of international rankings, the United States ranks last, tied with Liberia, Papua New Guinea, and Suriname, as one of only four countries that does not offer paid leave for new parents.[87]

Many U.S. companies do not necessarily need prodding by the government to improve the work–life balance of their employees.[88] Especially in the field of investment banking, employers are responding to the demands of the Millennial labor force, which seems less willing to work 80 hours a week in the hope of some big payoff down the line.[89] Indeed, the percentage of business school graduates going into investment banking dropped from 13% to 4% between 2007 and 2015, whereas the percentage going into Silicon Valley–type jobs increased from 7% to 17% over the same period.[90]

By far, the most important aspect of work in terms of generating satisfaction is the degree to which it is meaningfully related to core values of the worker. The term **prosocial motivation** is often used explicitly to capture the degree to which people are motivated to help other people. When people believe that their work has an important impact on other people, they are much more willing to work longer hours. This form of motivation can also be triggered by recognizing that one's work has a positive impact on those who benefit from one's service, such as customers or clients. In contrast, when one's social needs are thwarted, they often react negatively and in self-defeating ways that drive people away from them.[91]

**Prosocial motivation** The degree to which people are motivated to help other people.

In addition to prosocial motivation, work may have meaning for people because they see it as a calling that gives their lives purpose. In this case, the exact tasks that go into the work may not even matter. Rather, everything depends on the outcome that results from the work. For example, Michael Pratt, a researcher who has studied meaning at work extensively, often recounts a fable of bricklayers all working at the same site who are asked what they are doing. One sighs and states sadly, "I am putting one brick on top of another." A second says with indifference that he is "making six pence an hour." The third responds excitedly, exclaiming, "I am building a cathedral!" All three workers are doing the same work, but one person finds meaning in it whereas the others do not, and this makes all the difference when it comes to job satisfaction.[92]

# COMPETING THROUGH TECHNOLOGY

## Technology Solves Predictable Problems with Predictive Scheduling

From an employer's point of view, the only thing worse than not having enough workers on hand to meet a spike in demand is to pay a large number of employees to stand around and do nothing when there is a dip in demand. Thus, employers would like to have the flexibility to call workers in to work on a moment's notice or send them home, also at a moment's notice. Of course, the only thing worse from an employee's point of view than being sent home early because there is no work to do is to get called into work at the last minute, disrupting all of one's plans. In the past, when there were labor surpluses, employer's tended to have the upper hand in this battle for scheduling flexibility, but that is changing for two reasons.

First, widespread labor shortages, especially in industries like retail or hospitality, have shifted the balance of power to workers. For example, according to the Bureau of Labor Statistics, there were over 750,000 unfilled job openings in the retail sector in 2017, up 100,000 from the previous year and 100,000 less than what was being projected for 2018. Adam Challenger, vice president of the outplacement firm Challenger, Gray & Christmas, noted that, "there's going to be a war for retail talent" and firms that fail to meet workers' needs for scheduling

predictability are very unlikely to win that war.

Second, there is wave of new legislation being passed that makes it illegal for employers to schedule outside rigidly defined parameters. For example, the cities of New York City, San Francisco, and Seattle have passed new laws that guarantee workers more predictability when it comes to their work schedules. These laws state that employers must post schedules between 7 to 14 days in advance and then give some bonus pay to any worker impacted when an employer changes the schedule after it was posted. The laws also set fixed rest periods between shifts and limits "clopening," that is, scheduling one person to both open and close the operation sequentially.

Fortunately, new technology is being introduced in many companies to help optimize the joint needs of employers and employees when it comes to scheduling. For example, in 2018, Walmart launched a new program in 4,500 of its U.S. stores that guarantees workers the exact same schedule for 13 weeks. The technology uses big data analytics to determine the precise level of staffing required for each store based upon past historical data. It then matches this set of staffing requirements to the results of a survey that asks employees to list the hours that they

will be available to work each week. The program generates the schedule and distributes it to employees, along with access to a mobile app that allows employees to directly trade with each other if their needs change over the course of the 13 weeks. The program makes it easy for workers who want to expand their hours to increase their share of the available schedule while others pull back. It also helps Walmart accurately predict labor costs by eliminating unplanned, last-minute changes. Although the program is still under evaluation, the early results have been positive both in terms of employee satisfaction and turnover rates, which have been reduced by 10% in the stores that employed the technology.

### DISCUSSION QUESTIONS

1. In what ways can the development of new technologies be stimulated by changes in labor supply and labor demand?

2. What other industries other than retail might be interested in the technology described here and why?

SOURCES: M. Hanbury, "People Don't Want to Work at Stores like Target and Macy's and Its Creating a Huge Problem for the Industry," *Business Insider*, September 23, 2018; C. Blanchard, "Predictive Scheduling: What to Expect," *Workforce*, April, 2018; S. Nassauer, "In the Battle for Workers, WalMart Promises Steadier Schedules," *The Wall Street Journal Online*, November 13, 2018.

## Supervisors and Co-Workers

The two primary sets of people in an organization who affect job satisfaction are co-workers and supervisors. Workers may be satisfied with their supervisors for one of two reasons.

First, job incumbents may see their supervisors as having "warmth," that is, genuinely caring about the workers and respecting them as people. Thus, being in a culture where people are generally civil and polite makes people feel their own dignity and worth above and beyond their contributions to the work itself. Incivility causes stress, and research shows that people who are treated rudely have a hard time focusing on the task and, instead, ruminate about their poor treatment and ways to perhaps get even.[93] They also are highly likely to leave, and in some cases leave in large groups. For example, at the software company Tanium Inc., over a dozen senior officials resigned at once in retaliation for alleged abusive supervision at the hands of CEO Orion Hindawi. This group included the president, as well as the chief officers of marketing, accounting, operations, and finance—basically shutting down the company at the strategic level.[94]

Second, people may be satisfied with their supervisors because the supervisors provide support that helps them achieve their own goals. That is, although it is nice to have a supervisor and co-workers who are warm, it is also critical that these people be "competent" in terms of helping workers and their teams get the mission accomplished. In fact, when given a choice between a leader who was warm but incompetent or a leader who was cold but competent, 70% opted for the cold and competent leader.[95] Still, nothing beats the combination of high warmth and high competence in a leader, and employees led by a supervisor who is viewed as both supportive and competent will work longer hours and delay gratification in terms of rewards, trusting that something good will eventually come to them from all their hard work.

Supervisors are not the only potential source of social warmth and support, and in many cases, abuse by co-workers can have an even more profound negative influence on one's job satisfaction. For example, a 2017 survey indicated that 20% of respondents reported being bullied by co-workers on the job.[96] *Workplace bullying* is defined as repeated health-harming mistreatment by one or more perpetrators at work that takes the form of verbal abuse and offensive conduct that is threatening, humiliating, or intimidating to the point where it prevents work from getting done. Unlike abusive bosses, who often let up once a specific task is accomplished, bullying by co-workers tends to be a constant, unrelenting process. Although it is common for high schools to adopt non-bullying rules, this has not been the case among employers, even though bullies rarely stop being bullies simply because they graduated from high school.[97]

Because a supportive environment reduces dissatisfaction, many organizations foster team building both on and off the job (such as via softball or bowling leagues). The idea is that group cohesiveness and support for individual group members will be increased through exposure and joint efforts. Although management certainly cannot ensure that each stressed employee develops friends, it can make it easier for employees to interact—a necessary condition for developing friendship and rapport.

Visit your instructor's Connect® course and access your eBook to view this video.

"It means that we have to be in the core business. That we have to be fully integrated into everything that's going on within the business."
—Jose Tomas, Former Executive Vice President and Chief Human Resources Officer, Anthem Inc.

Source: Video produced for the Center for Executive Succession in the Darla Moore School of Business at the University of South Carolina by Coal Powered Filmworks

### Pay and Benefits

We should not discount the influence of the job incumbent, the job itself, and the surrounding people in terms of influencing job satisfaction, but for most people, work is their primary source of income and financial security. Pay is also seen as an indicator of status within the organization as well as in society at large. Thus, for many individuals, the standing of their pay relative to those within their organization, or the standing of their pay relative to others doing similar work for other employers, becomes even more important than the level of pay itself. For example, a class action suit organized by a large group of women was filed against Microsoft when the data indicated that female workers were paid roughly 10% less than men doing the exact same job.[98]

For many people, beyond a means of financial support, pay is a reflection of self-worth, so pay satisfaction takes on critical significance when it comes to retention.[99] The role of pay and benefits is so large that we devote the entire next part of this book to these topics. Within this chapter, we focus primarily on satisfaction with two aspects of pay (pay levels and benefits) and how these are assessed within the organization. Methods for addressing these issues are discussed in Part Four of this book.

One of the main dimensions of pay satisfaction deals with pay levels relative to market wages. When it comes to retention, employees recruited away from one organization by another are often lured with promises of higher pay levels. In fact, exit surveys of high-performing employees who have left their organization indicate "better pay" as the reason in over 70% of the cases, compared to only 33% who indicate "better opportunity." Ironically, when the managers of those same workers are polled, 68% cite "better opportunity" versus the 45% who indicate it was "better pay," suggesting quite a difference of opinion.[100]

As labor markets started tightening up in recent years, many employers recognized the need to raise pay levels in order to stop attrition.[101] Even Walmart, which bases its entire business model on cutting costs, boosted the pay of many of its employees to $10/hour in 2015, well above the minimum wage, in order to retain its most experienced personnel and reduce the need to hire and train new workers. Walmart also initiated a program that would allow workers to access a portion of their earned wages prior to payday.[102] CEO Doug McMillon, who initiated the raises, noted, "We want associates who care about the company and are highly engaged about the business."[103] This was not an isolated case, and national data showed that wages rose roughly 3% between 2016 and 2017.[104]

Satisfaction with benefits is another important dimension of overall pay satisfaction. Because many individuals have a difficult time ascertaining the true dollar value of their benefits package, however, this dimension may not always be as salient to people as pay itself. To derive competitive advantage from benefits' expenditures, it is critical not only to make them highly salient to employees but also to link them to the organization's strategic direction.

For example, Starbucks wanted to attract workers who were smart and valued education but could not necessarily afford to hire people with college educations. So, Starbucks started a tuition reimbursement program that would pay for employees who pursued their bachelor's degree at Arizona State University. The cost of the program was roughly $45,000 per employee over the course of the four years, but the company saw this as a great way of attracting and retaining the kind of employee that fit its business model.[105] Another increasingly popular benefit is to help new employees pay off student debt already accrued.[106]

## MEASURING AND MONITORING JOB SATISFACTION

Most attempts to measure job satisfaction rely on workers' self-reports. There is a vast amount of data on the reliability and validity of many existing scales as well as a wealth of data from companies that have used these scales, allowing for comparisons across firms.

Table 10.5
Sample Items from a
Standardized Job
Satisfaction Scale
(the JDI)

**Instructions:** Think of your present work. What is it like most of the time? In the blank beside each word given below, write

  __Y__  for "Yes" if it describes your work

  __N__  for "No" if it does NOT describe your work

  __?__  if you cannot decide

| Work Itself | | Pay | | Promotion Opportunities | |
|---|---|---|---|---|---|
| ? | Routine | ? | Less than I deserve | ? | Dead-end job |
| ? | Satisfying | ? | Highly paid | ? | Unfair policies |
| ? | Good | ? | Insecure | ? | Based on ability |
| Supervision | | | | Co-Workers | |
| ? | Impolite | | | ? | Intelligent |
| ? | Praises good work | | | ? | Responsible |
| ? | Doesn't supervise enough | | | ? | Boring |

SOURCE: W. K. Balzar, D. C. Smith, D. E. Kravitz, S. E. Lovell, K. B. Paul, B. A. Reilly, and C. E. Reilly, *User's Manual for the Job Descriptive Index (JDI)* (Bowling Green, OH: Bowling Green State University, 1990).

Established scales are excellent places to begin if employers wish to assess the satisfaction levels of their employees. An employer would be foolish to "reinvent the wheel" by generating its own versions of measures of these broad constructs. Of course, in some cases, organizations want to measure their employees' satisfaction with aspects of their work that are specific to that organization (such as satisfaction with one particular health plan versus another). In these situations the organization may need to create its own scales, but this will be the exception rather than the rule.

One standardized, widely used measure of job satisfaction is the Job Descriptive Index (JDI). The JDI emphasizes various facets of satisfaction: pay, the work itself, supervision, co-workers, and promotions. Table 10.5 presents several items from the JDI scale. Other scales exist for those who want to get even more specific about different facets of satisfaction. For example, although the JDI assesses satisfaction with pay, it does not break up pay into different dimensions.[107] The Pay Satisfaction Questionnaire (PSQ) focuses on these more specific dimensions (pay levels, benefits, pay structure, and pay raises); thus, this measure gives a more detailed view of exactly what aspects of pay are most or least satisfying.[108]

Although satisfaction surveys used to be a once-a-year affair, increasingly technology is creating opportunities for firms and managers to get more rapid feedback. Pulse surveys are very short questionnaires that go out every day or once a week that focus on a small set of specific questions—perhaps even just one question—that the company wants to keep track of over time.[109] The idea behind these quick-fire polls is to uncover issues faster and as they develop rather than wait until the end of the year when the issue may have festered. Also, these surveys tend to avoid long-term memory problems that reduce the value ofonce-a-year questionnaires. Usually these surveys are anonymous in order to reduce employees' fear of voicing opinions, and organizations try to show demonstrable actions taken soon after issues are raised.[110]

## SURVEY FEEDBACK INTERVENTIONS

Regardless of what measures are used or how many facets of satisfaction are assessed, a systematic, ongoing program of *employee survey research* should be a prominent part of any HRM strategy for a number of reasons. First, it allows the company to monitor trends over time and thus prevent problems in the area of voluntary turnover before they happen.

**LO 10-4**
Design a survey feedback intervention program, and use this to promote retention of key organizational personnel.

**Figure 10.2**

Average Profile for Different Facets of Satisfaction over Time

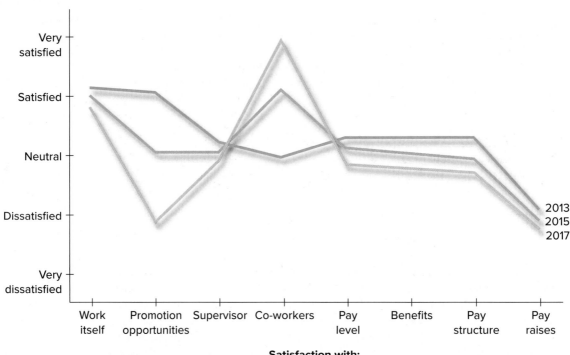

Nationwide, data from this type of longitudinal examination of trends showed the job satisfaction among U.S. workers in 2017 was at the highest level since 2005. According to this survey, 51% of U.S. workers reported being satisfied with their job overall. However, there was a great deal of variation when it came to specific elements of work, and only 30% reported satisfaction with promotion opportunities.[111]

With this kind of question in mind, Figure 10.2 shows a hypothetical example of the average profile for different facets of satisfaction for a hypothetical company in 2013, 2015, and 2017. As the figure makes clear, the level of satisfaction with promotion opportunities in this company has eroded over time, whereas the satisfaction with co-workers has improved. If there was a strong relationship between satisfaction with promotion opportunities and voluntary turnover among high performers, this would constitute a threat that the organization might need to address via some of the employee development techniques discussed in Chapter 9.

A second reason for engaging in an ongoing program of employee satisfaction surveys is that it provides a means of empirically assessing the impact of changes in policy (e.g., introduction of a new performance appraisal system) or personnel (e.g., introduction of a new CEO) on worker attitudes. Figure 10.3 shows the average profile for different satisfaction facets for a hypothetical organization one year before and one year after a merger. An examination of the profile makes it clear that since the merger, satisfaction with supervision and pay structure has decreased dramatically, and this has not been offset by any increase in satisfaction along other dimensions. Again, this might point to the need for training programs for supervisors (like those discussed in Chapter 7) or changes in the pay system (like those discussed in Chapter 11).

A real-world example of this type of effect can be found in the experience of workers at Whole Foods. Job satisfaction at Whole Foods dropped significantly after the retailer was

**Figure 10.3**

Average Profile for Different Facets of Satisfaction before and after a Major Event

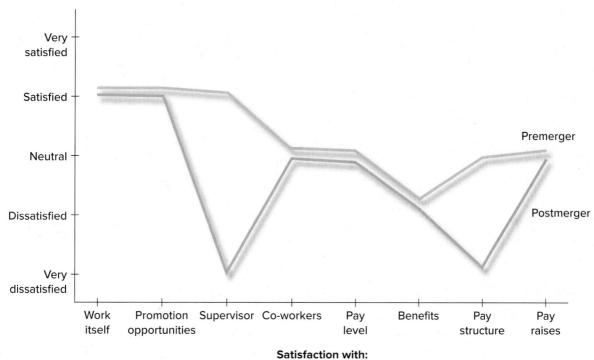

Satisfaction with:

taken over by Amazon, and this drop was particularly pronounced when it came to satisfaction with pay. Amazon eliminated the profit sharing arrangement that had been in place for everyone at Whole Foods and introduced a new program that was available only to executives. This prompted a drive by workers to form a collective bargaining unit in 2018 and illustrates the general principle that workers are highly sensitive to any changes in pay that result in a loss relative to what they experienced before.[112]

Third, when these surveys incorporate standardized scales like the JDI, they often allow the company to compare itself with others in the same industry along these dimensions. For example, Figure 10.4 shows the average profile for different satisfaction facets for a hypothetical organization and compares this to the industry average. Again, if we detect major differences between one organization and the industry as a whole (on overall pay levels, for example), this might allow the company to react and change its policies before there is a mass exodus of people moving to the competition.

According to Figure 10.4, the satisfaction with pay levels is low relative to the industry, but this is offset by higher-than-industry-average satisfaction with benefits and the work itself. As we showed in Chapter 6, the organization might want to use this information to systematically screen people. That is, the fit between the person and the organization would be best if the company selected applicants who reported being most interested in the nature of the work itself and benefits, and rejected those applicants whose sole concern was with pay levels.

Within the organization, a systematic survey program also allows the company to check for differences between units and, hence, to benchmark "best practices" that might be generalized across units. For example, Figure 10.5 shows the average profile for five different regional divisions of a hypothetical company. The figure shows that satisfaction with pay raises is much higher in one of the regions relative to the others. If the overall

**Figure 10.4**

Average Profile for Different Facets of Satisfaction versus the Industry Average

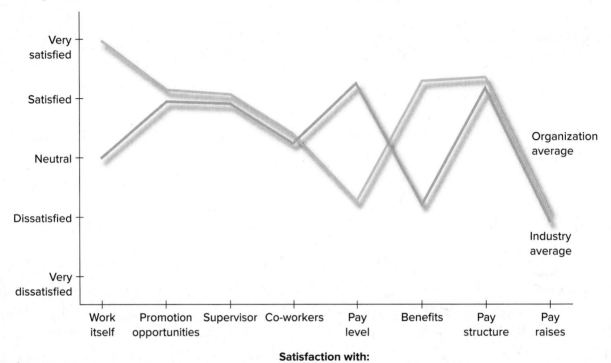

**Figure 10.5**

Average Profile for Different Facets of Satisfaction for Different Regional Divisions

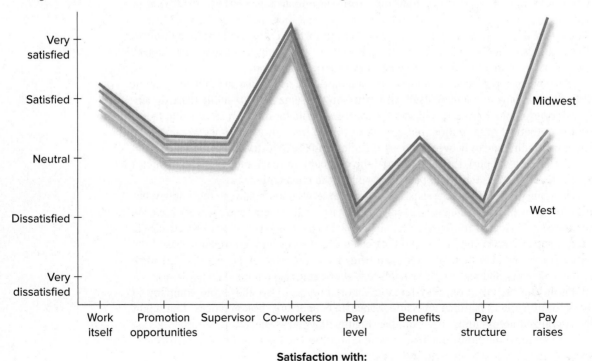

amount of money allocated to raises was equal through the entire company, this implies that the manner in which raises are allocated or communicated in the Midwest region might be something that the other regions should look in to.

Finally, although the focus in this section has been on surveys of current employees, any strategic retention policy also has to consider surveying people who are about to become ex-employees. Exit interviews with departing workers can be a valuable tool for uncovering systematic concerns that are driving retention problems. If conducted properly, an exit interview can reveal the reasons why people are leaving. For example, results from recent exit interviews among employees show that there are two distinct groups of people who are leaving their jobs—one set of workers who cannot get enough hours and a second set of workers who are working too many hours. This may seem ironic and counter-intuitive, but in some ways it makes sense, given the way work is increasingly structured around two distinct classes of workers—hourly and salaried. That is, because they are being paid by the hour, it makes sense for employers to limit the amount of time hourly workers spend on the job. They want to avoid paying any overtime hours (valued at time and a half), but beyond that, they may even try to limit the number of hours to 30 in order to avoid having to pay for mandated health care.[113] Thus, many hourly workers cannot get enough work.[114] In contrast, salaried employees represent a fixed rather than variable cost; hence, there is pressure to make these individuals work very long hours, including nights and weekends. Many of these workers forgo taking vacation days that are provided to them or work while on vacation.[115] Obviously, it would benefit everyone in the workforce to help smooth out some of this over- and under-demand for labor, but this shows the pervasive power of rules regarding pay and pay structure—the topic of Part Four.

# A LOOK BACK

## Employee Separation and Retention: Lessons From Google

A key factor influencing the ability of any organization to accomplish its mission is who is leaving and who is staying when it comes to turnover. In the vignette that opened this chapter about Google, we saw that how an organization manages employees who engage in misdeeds affects all the remaining employees, and not just the victim of those misdeeds. Organizations need to have policies in place that make it easy and advantageous for low performers or unethical employees to leave (involuntary turnover), but make it difficult and costly for valued contributors to leave (voluntary turnover). Managing the "flow" of employees thus becomes a critical source of competitive advantage that can be drawn from HR, and is often the difference between survival and bankruptcy for many companies.

### QUESTIONS

1. In what ways does an organizational crisis like that faced by Google, in some cases, make it easier for firms to manage involuntary turnover? In what ways does an organizational crisis like that faced by Google make it more difficult for firms to manage voluntary turnover?
2. What role can employee attitude surveys play in maintaining a loyal and engaged workforce? What are some of the challenges associated with getting accurate information from employee surveys, and how can a survey process "backfire" in terms of harming, rather than helping, a firm's efforts?

# SUMMARY

This chapter examined issues related to employee separation and retention. Involuntary turnover reflects a separation initiated by the organization, often when the individual would prefer to stay a member of the organization. Voluntary turnover reflects a separation initiated by the individual, often when the organization would prefer that the person stay a member. Organizations can gain competitive advantage by strategically managing the separation process so that involuntary turnover is implemented in a fashion that does not invite retaliation, and voluntary turnover among high performers is kept to a minimum. Retaliatory reactions to organizational discipline and dismissal decisions can be minimized by implementing these decisions in a manner that promotes feelings of procedural and interactional justice. Voluntary turnover can be minimized by using surveys to measure and monitor employee levels of satisfaction with critical facets of the job and the organization, and then addressing any problems identified by such surveys.

# KEY TERMS

Involuntary turnover, 441
Voluntary turnover, 441
Employment-at-will doctrine, 442
Procedural justice, 447
Interactional justice, 448
Alternative dispute resolution (ADR), 450

Employee assistance program
(EAP), 451
Outplacement counseling, 454
Progression of withdrawal, 456
Whistle-blowing, 457
Job involvement, 459

Organizational commitment, 459
Job satisfaction, 459
Frame of reference, 459
Negative affectivity, 461
Job rotation, 462
Prosocial motivation, 463

# DISCUSSION QUESTIONS

1. The discipline and discharge procedures described in this chapter are systematic but rather slow. In your opinion, should some offenses lead to immediate dismissal? If so, how would you justify this to a court if you were sued for wrongful discharge?

2. Organizational turnover is generally considered a negative outcome, and many organizations spend a great deal of time and money trying to reduce it. What situations would indicate that an increase in turnover might be just what an organization needs? Given the difficulty of terminating employees, what organizational policies might be used to retain high-performing workers and, at the same time, increase attrition among low-performing workers?

3. Three popular interventions for enhancing worker satisfaction are job enrichment, job rotation, and role analysis. What are the critical differences among these interventions, and under what conditions might one be preferable to the others?

4. If off-the-job stress and dissatisfaction begin to create on-the-job problems, what are the rights and responsibilities of the human resource manager in helping the employee to overcome these problems? Are intrusions into such areas an invasion of privacy, a benevolent and altruistic employer practice, or simply a prudent financial step taken to protect the firm's investment?

5. Discuss the advantages of using published, standardized measures in employee attitude surveys. Do employers ever need to develop their own measures for such surveys? Where would one turn to learn how to do this?

# SELF-ASSESSMENT EXERCISE

Also assignable in Connect.

The characteristics of your job influence your overall satisfaction with the job. One way to be satisfied at work is to find a job with the characteristics that you find desirable. The following assessment is a look at what kind of job is likely to satisfy you.

The following phrases describe different job characteristics. Read each phrase, then circle a number to indicate how much of the job characteristic you would like. Use the following scale: 1 = very little; 2 = little; 3 = a moderate amount; 4 = much; 5 = very much.

1. The opportunity to perform a number of different activities each day   1 2 3 4 5
2. Contributing something significant to the company   1 2 3 4 5
3. The freedom to determine how to do my job   1 2 3 4 5
4. The ability to see projects or jobs through to completion, rather than performing only one piece of the job   1 2 3 4 5
5. Seeing the results of my work, so I can get an idea of how well I am doing the job   1 2 3 4 5
6. A feeling that the quality of my work is important to others in the company   1 2 3 4 5
7. The need to use a variety of complex skills   1 2 3 4 5
8. Responsibility to act and make decisions independently of managers or supervisors   1 2 3 4 5
9. Time and resources to do an entire piece of work from beginning to end   1 2 3 4 5
10. Getting feedback about my performance from the work itself   1 2 3 4 5

Add the scores for the pairs of items that measure each job characteristic. A higher score for a characteristic means that characteristic is more important to you.

*Skill Variety:* The degree to which a job requires you to use a variety of skills.

Item 1: _____ + Item 7: _____ = _____

*Task Identity:* The degree to which a job requires completion of a whole and identifiable piece of work.

Item 4: _____ + Item 9: _____ = _____

*Task Significance:* The degree to which a job has an impact on the lives or work of others.

Item 2: _____ + Item 6: _____ = _____

*Autonomy:* The degree to which a job provides freedom, empowerment, and discretion in scheduling the work and determining processes and procedures for completing the work.

Item 3: _____ + Item 8: _____ = _____

*Feedback:* The degree to which carrying out job-related tasks and activities provides you with direct and clear information about your effectiveness.

Item 5 _____ + Item 10: _____ = _____

SOURCE: Adapted from R. Daft and R. Noe, *Organizational Behavior* (New York: Harcourt, 2001).

# EXERCISING STRATEGY

## Tales of Amazon Warriors

"This is the greatest place I hate to work." These are the words John Rossman, a former Amazon executive, uses in attempting to describe how people working at Amazon feel about the culture. This mixed message seems to perfectly capture the positive and negative sentiments that exist side by side among employees at the company. Certainly, one cannot argue with Amazon's success. In 2015 Amazon surpassed Walmart as the most valuable retailer in the country with a market valuation of over $250 billion. The company's CEO, Jeff Bezos was ranked by *Forbes* magazine as the fifth-wealthiest person in the world and he notes, "My main job today? I work hard at helping to maintain the culture."

There are several aspects of Amazon's culture that makes it unique. Bezos believes that there are several forces that sap businesses over time after they become successful, including bureaucracy, excessive spending, and lack of discipline. Employees are empowered to be creative and given wide-ranging autonomy to pursue revolutionary ideas, like "package delivering drones." At the same time, they are held to incredibly high standards of accountability, but these are the very factors that explain

why some people absolutely thrive and love working for the company.

Above and beyond the three demons of bureaucracy, spending, and discipline, however, what really makes Amazon most unique is its stance toward conflict. Whereas most organizations try to minimize conflict, Bezos believes that "harmony" is totally overvalued at most work organizations and employees are encouraged to disagree, debate, and tear one another's ideas to pieces. Instead of polite praise and compromise, the goal is to see whose ideas can survive in Darwinian battle for the one best solution or innovation. The internal phone directory even provides instructions on how to send anonymous feedback to one another's supervisors. Many employees cannot stand up to this kind of scrutiny, however. Bo Olson, who spent two years in the book marketing branch at Amazon, noted that "You walk out of a conference room and you'll see a grown man covering his face—nearly every person I worked with I saw cry at their desk." Still, although many individuals cannot seem to endure the culture for long, Amazon seems to sustain the culture with a never-ending stream of new recruits ready to do battle.

## QUESTIONS

1.  If you were working in HR for Amazon, what kinds of individuals would you look for and avoid when it comes to making hiring decisions?
2.  Although debate can bring about more refined ideas, can you envision any situations where public confrontation might escalate in a way that ultimately harms an organization?

SOURCES: J. Kantor and D. Streitfeld, "Inside Amazon: Wrestling Big Ideas in a Bruising Workplace," *The New York Times Online*, August 15, 2015; J. Kantor and D. Streitfeld, "Jeff Bezos and Amazon Employees Join Debate Over Its Culture," *The New York Times Online*, August 17, 2015; D. Streitfeld and J. Kantor, "Depiction of Amazon Stirs Debate about Work Culture," *The New York Times Online*, August 18, 2015.

# MANAGING PEOPLE

## There Is Really No Good Answer to the Question: "Rogue Employees or Toxic Culture?"

One of the key strategic pillars to the success and growth of Wells Fargo bank was the idea of cross-selling. Cross-selling refers to the practice of taking a person who is already a customer with one account, for example, a checking account, and then getting them to open a new account, such as a credit card. Since customers get charged for each account, the more accounts the merrier in terms of revenue streams. The organization set aggressive cross-selling goals for employees where meeting goals was rewarded with bonuses and failing to meet goals led to terminations. The goal was eight accounts per customer and on average, Wells Fargo customers had 6.3 products—far more than customers at other banks. Unfortunately, the only way these goals could be met, however, was by selling customer products without their consent. Indeed, in one of the largest cases of bank fraud in history, the Los Angeles City Attorney's Office proved that Wells Fargo opened over 2 million deposit and credit accounts without customers' knowledge.

The bank tried to attribute this crime to rogue employees who, against the bank's wishes, engaged in this unlawful behavior of their own free volition. The bank was able to point to internal documents that explicitly stated that "customer consent for each specific solution or service is required every time," and that "splitting a customer deposit and opening multiple accounts for the purpose of increasing potential incentive compensation is sales integrity violation." The company was also able to point to routine purges where employees were fired for this practice, one of which netted over 5,000 employees in less than one year.

However, the practice of cross-selling without customer consent was so recurrent and widespread, that the focus quickly shifted to the organizational culture and leadership as the source of the problem. Employees were told by their supervisors to ignore the ethics guidelines and that they would wind up being terminated anyway if they did not meet their sales goals. The goals were very unrealistic, and apparently, according to CEO John Stumpf, the number eight was chosen "because it rhymed with great." Although one might hope that the company's human resources department might have helped workers deal with this system, instead, it was revealed that people who called the HR Ethics Hotline were fired quickly after those calls.

Stumpf was eventually called into a congressional hearing on the topic and was accused by Senator Elizabeth Warren as exhibiting "gutless leadership." The bank agreed to pay over $185 million in fines for the operations in California alone, with similar fines issued in other states like Arizona. Although the "gutless leadership" charge may have hurt the CEO, he could take solace in the fact that he did not have to pay back any of his own pay and bonuses—which amounted to over $20 million—the highest pay for any CEO in the banking industry.

### QUESTIONS

1.  How does the culture within a company often outweigh its explicit written rules and procedures?
2.  Although it is good to have specific and difficult goals, in what ways can unrealistic or uninformed goals backfire when it comes to a company's culture?

SOURCES: E. Glazer, "How Wells Fargo's High-Pressure Sales Culture Spiraled Out of Control," *The Wall Street Journal Online*, September 16, 2016; M. Corkery and S. Cowley, "Wells Fargo Warned Workers Against Sham Accounts, But 'They Needed a Paycheck,'" *The New York Times Online*, September 16, 2016; M. Egan, "I Called the Wells Fargo Ethics Line and Was Fired," *CNN.Money Online*, September 21, 2016; M. Corkery, "Elizabeth Warren Accuses Wells Fargo Chief of Gutless Leadership," *The New York Times Online*, September 20, 2016.

# HR IN SMALL BUSINESS

## Learning to Show Appreciation at Datotel

Datotel is a St. Louis company whose name explains what it does. The name combines the word *data* with the word *hotel*, and it uses its computers to safely store backups of its client companies' data. It's a fast-growing business, and for founder David Brown, one important challenge has been making sure employees know the company appreciates them even as everyone is scrambling to keep up with the demands of expanding a small business.

With about three dozen people to think about, Brown first tried a methodical approach: He created an employee-of-the-month program in which the lucky recipient would receive a thank-you e-mail message, a $25 gift card, and recognition for all employees to see on the company's intranet. Brown saw this program as one he could readily find the time to implement, and he hoped the reward and recognition would inspire high levels of job involvement and organizational commitment.

One advantage of a small company is that you can quickly see people's reactions to your efforts. Unfortunately, what Brown saw on people's faces and heard in their conversations was that recipients of the employee-of-the-month rewards were not exactly excited. The program was just too formulaic and impersonal. If Datotel was to keep employees engaged, it needed a different way to show that their efforts mattered.

So Brown tried a different approach, even though it required more effort. He committed his eight managers to noticing and reporting employee accomplishments. To implement this, he sets aside part of regular management meetings—part of each daily phone meeting and 15 minutes of each weekly in-person meeting—to discuss employee accomplishments. Whenever a manager notes that an employee has done something extraordinary, Brown asks for one of the managers besides the person's direct supervisor to thank the employee in person. Brown has also made a personal commitment to write thank-you notes. In fact, with e-mail the norm at his technology company, he makes some of the notes stand out by writing them by hand and mailing them to the employees at home.

One employee who thinks the extra effort matters is engineer Stephanie Lewis. One day Lewis returned home to find a note from Brown, observing that he had heard during management meetings that Lewis had done exceptionally well in working with a customer. Brown thanked her for the effort. Lewis's reaction: "It made me feel important to get something so personal and unique" from her company's busy leader.

Just as communicating "thank you" has helped with motivation, going the extra mile to communicate has helped Datotel's managers stay connected with one another and the company's mission. As the company grew and jobs became more specialized, Brown recognized that he would have to bring people together formally to share information about what was happening. He began to call meetings once a quarter, and so that the environment will be positive, he establishes a theme he thinks will get employees thinking and generate some fun. When the theme was "Rumble in the Jungle," the company leaders dressed as boxers, and when the theme was "Top Gun," they dressed as aviators and met in an airplane hangar.

The effort to allow for fun is interwoven with the company's core values: passion, integrity, fun, teamwork, "superior business value," and "improving the community in which we work." These values aim to unite the employees in a commitment to customer service that gives the company an edge in its industry. The values are also meant to be an advantage for recruiting and retaining the best people. On Datotel's website, the "Inside Datotel" page lists 10 reasons for wanting to work at the company, and the top reason is the core values: "Our Core Values represent everything that we stand for, and we take pride in them."

## QUESTIONS

1. Based on the information given, which sources of job satisfaction has Datotel addressed? What other sources might the company address, and how?
2. Suggest several measures Datotel could use to evaluate the success of its employee retention efforts. Be sure these are practical for a company of a few dozen employees.
3. In a company as small as Datotel, losing even one employee can present real difficulties. Suppose one of Datotel's managers begins to have performance problems and seems unwilling or unable to improve. Suggest how you, as an HR consultant, could help David Brown resolve this problem in a way that is fair to everyone involved and that keeps the company moving forward.

SOURCES: Datotel corporate website, www.datotel.com, accessed July 8, 2015; Nadine Heintz, "Building a Culture of Employee Appreciation," *Inc.*, September 2009; Jeremy Nulik, "Never Stop Being a Student of Business," *Small Business Monthly (St. Louis)*, July 2009, www.sbmon.com; Christopher Boyce, "Engineer Finds Solution to Business Problem," *St. Louis Post-Dispatch*, June 12, 2009.

## NOTES

1. A. Bryson, J. Forth, and L.Stokes, "Does Employees' Subjective Well-Being Affect Workplace Performance?" *Human Relations*, May 9, 2017.
2. P. Schrodt, "The 100 Best Places to Work in 2018 and the Jobs they Have Open Right Now," *Money.com*, December 6, 2017.
3. K. Benner, "Women in Tech Speak Frankly on Culture of Harassment," *The New York Times Online*, June 30, 2017.
4. J. Koblin, "The Year of Reckoning at CBS: Sexual Harassment Allegations and Attempts to Cover Them Up," *The New York Times Online*, December 17, 2018.
5. J. Creswell, K. Draper, and R. Adams, "At Nike, Revolt Led by Women Leads to Exodus of Male Executives," *The New York Times Online*, April 28, 2018.

6. L. Weber, "After #MeToo, Those Who Report Harassment Still Risk Retaliation," *The Wall Street Journal Online*, December 12, 2018.

7. E. Perez and D. Molinski, "More Firings at Secret Service," *Wall Street Journal*, April 19, 2012.

8. A. Grossman, "Four Top Secret Service Officials to Be Removed from Posts," *Wall Street Journal*, January 14, 2015.

9. J. Emont, "Amazon, Amid Crackdown on Seller Scams, Fires Employees Over Data Leak," *The Wall Street Journal Online*, December 10, 2018.

10. B. Haskins, "OSHA Updates Guidance on Preventing Workplace Violence in Health Care, Social Services," *Safety and Health*, April 15, 2017.

11. J. Barrett, "Gunman Kills Five In Illinois Factory Shooting," *The Wall Street Journal Online*, February 15, 2019.

12. A. Campos-Flores and L. Stevens, "Ex-UPS Employee in Alabama Kills Two; Self," *Wall Street Journal*, September 23, 2014.

13. D. Bennet, "United's Quest to Be Less Awful," *Bloomberg Businessweek*, January 14, 2016, pp. 50-56.

14. J. Eidelson and H. Kanu, "Microsoft Bug Testers Unionized, Then They Got Terminated," *Bloomberg Businessweek*, August 27, 2018, pp. 23-24.

15. J. Gershman, "McDonald's Wrongful Termination Lawsuit to Test NLRB Ruling," *Wall Street Journal*, January 22, 2015.

16. M. Orey, "Fear of Firing," *Bloomberg Businessweek*, April 23, 2007, pp. 52-62.

17. E. Glazer, "Wells Fargo Firing Dozens of Regional Managers in Retail-Bank Cleanup," *The Wall Street Journal Online*, December 5, 2018.

18. L. Weber, "At Kimberly Clark, 'Dead Wood' Workers have No Place to Hide," *Wall Street Journal*, August 21, 2016.

19. Orey, "Fear of Firing."

20. S. Berfield, "Things Are about to Get Ugly at Kraft," *Bloomberg Businessweek*, August 24, 2015, p. 20.

21. S. Gleason and R. Feintzeig, "Startups Are Quick to Fire," *Wall Street Journal*, December 12, 2013, www.wsj.com.

22. R. Feintzeig, "Once Fired, Now a Founder: How a Tech Leader Rebuilt His Career," *Wall Street Journal*, December 13, 2013.

23. S. E. Scullen, P. K. Bergey, and L. Aimon-Smith, "Forced Distribution Rating Systems and the Improvement of Workforce Potential: A Baseline Simulation," *Personnel Psychology* 58 (2005), pp. 1-32.

24. G. Gupta, "Are You Still Using Force Rankings? Please Stop," *Forbes Online*, March 23, 2018

25. N. Irwin, "When the Guy Making Your Sandwich Has a No-Compete Clause," *New York Times*, October 14, 2014.

26. A. Viswanatha, "Noncompete Agreements Hobble Junior Employees," *Wall Street Journal*, February 2, 2016.

27. The Editorial Board, "Agreements That Lock Up Workers Legally," *The New York Times Online*, May 16, 2017.

28. E. J. Castilla and S. Bernard, "The Paradox of Meritocracy in Organizations," *Administrative Science Quarterly* 55 (2010), pp. 543-76.

29. E. Spitznagel, "The Sick Day Bounty Hunters," *Bloomberg Businessweek*, December 6, 2010, pp. 93-95.

30. S. Ramachandron, "At Netflix, Radical Transparency and Blunt Firings Unsettle the Ranks," *The Wall Street Journal Online*, October 25, 2018.

31. L. Weber, "More Companies Block Employees from Filing Suits," *Wall Street Journal*, March 31, 2015.

32. C. Alter, "What's Changed since 2016, *Time*, October 15, 2018, p. 25.

33. L. Weber, "Drug Use on Decline at Work, Except Rx," *Wall Street Journal*, November 18, 2014.

34. A. Campo-Flores, "Drug Use at Work Roils Firms," *Wall Street Journal*, October 12, 2014.

35. Y. Kubota and E. Pfanner, "Arrested Toyota Managing Officer Resigns," *Wall Street Journal*, July 1, 2015.

36. K. Nagl, "Marijuana Legalization—What It Means for Employers," *Crain's Detroit Business Online*, November 07, 2018.

37. R. Pyrillis, "A Monumental Problem," *Workforce*, September 2014, pp. 45-47.

38. K. Everson, "Dealing with Demons and Deadlines," *Workforce*, April 2015, pp. 29-31.

39. A. W. Mathews, "Employer Provided Health Insurance Approaches $20,000 a Year," *The Wall Street Journal Online*, October 3, 2018.

40. S. Sipek, "Wondering about Wellness," *Workforce*, July 2014.

41. L. Weber, "Wellness Programs Get a Health Check," *Wall Street Journal*, October 7, 2014.

42. L. Kwoh, "When Your Boss Makes You Pay for Being Fat," *Wall Street Journal*, April 5, 2013.

43. S. Sipek, "Observations on Obesity in the Workforce," *Workforce*, September 2014, p. 18.

44. A. Pasztor, "FAA to Evaluate Obese Pilots for Sleep Disorder," *Wall Street Journal*, November 20, 2013.

45. M. S. Schmidt, "Battling Crime and Calories at the FBI," *New York Times*, April 5, 2015.

46. L. Weber and R. Feintzeig, "Assistance to Laid off Workers Gets Downsized," *Wall Street Journal*, February 18, 2014.

47. P. Dvorack and J. S. Lublin, "Outplacement Firms Struggle to Do Job," *Wall Street Journal*, August 20, 2009.

48. B. Lowsky, "Inside Outplacement," *Workforce*, July 2014, pp. 37-38.

49. V. Furhmans, "The Case for Letting Your Best People Go," *The Wall Street Journal Online*, April 18, 2017.

50. J. Jones, "How to Bounce Back if You're Bounced Out," *Bloomberg Businessweek*, January 27, 1998, pp. 22-23.

51. J. Altman, "How Much Does Employee Turnover Really Cost," *Huffington Post Online*, January 17, 2017.

52. L. Braham, "How to Prepare for Your Star's Exit," *Bloomberg Businessweek*, March 31, 2017, pp. 46-47.

53. T. Higgins and D. Hull, "Apple Induction," *Bloomberg Businessweek*, February 15, 2015, pp. 36-37.

54. B. Stone, "How Cheap Is Craig Jelinek," *Bloomberg Businessweek*, June 6, 2013, pp. 55-60.

55. D. Huang and L. Gellman, "Millennial Employees Confound Big Banks," *Wall Street Journal*, April 8, 2016.

56. L. Kwoh, "More Firms Bow to Generation Y's Demands," *Wall Street Journal*, August 21, 2012.

57. P. Hom, T. W. Lee, J. D. Shaw, and J. Hausknecht, "One Hundred Years of Employee Turnover Theory and Research," *Journal of Applied Psychology*, 102 (2017), pp. 530-45.

58. J. Lublin, "The Telltale Sign a New Hire Isn't Fitting In," *Wall Street Journal*, June 10, 2017.

59. T. W. Lee, T. C. Burch, T. R. Mitchell, "The Story of Why We Stay: A Review of Job Embeddedness," *Annual Review of Organizational Psychology and Organizational Behavior*, 1 (2014), pp. 199-216.

60. T. A. Judge, H. M. Weiss, J. D. Kammeyer-Mueller, and C. L. Hulin, "Job Attitudes, Job Satisfaction, and Job Affect: A Century of Continuity and of Change," *Journal of Applied Psychology*, 102 (2017), pp. 356-74.

61. E. J. McClean, E. R. Burris, and J. R. Detert, "When Does Voice Lead to Exit? It Depends on Leadership," *Academy of Management Review*, 56 (2013), pp. 525-48.

62. D. Barrett and D. Yadron, "Contractor Says He Is Source of NSA Leak," *Wall Street Journal*, June 10, 2013.

63. M. Mukasey, "Leaking Secrets to Terrorists," *Wall Street Journal*, June 9, 2013.

64. D. E. Wittkower, "Are You a Whistleblower or a Snitch?" *Wall Street Journal*, June 17, 2013.

65. H. Son and A. Lee, "B of A Was Unprepared for Wikileaks, Chief Moynihan Says," *Bloomberg Businessweek*, March 23, 2011, p. 23.

66. S. Patterson and J. Strasburg, "Source's Cover Blown by SEC," *Wall Street Journal*, April 25, 2012.

67. T. Y. Park and J. D. Shaw, "Turnover Rates and Organizational Performance: A Meta-analysis," *Journal of Applied Psychology*, 98 (2013), pp. 268–309.

68. S. E. Needleman, "Sick Time Rules Re-Emerge," *Wall Street Journal*, March 1, 2012.

69. S. Shellenbarger, "When It Comes to Work, Can You Care Too Much?" *Wall Street Journal*, April 29, 2014.

70. E. A. Locke, "The Nature and Causes of Job Dissatisfaction," in *The Handbook of Industrial & Organizational Psychology*, ed. M. D. Dunnette (Chicago: Rand McNally, 1976), pp. 901–69.

71. B. Casselman, "Male Nurses Make More Money," *Wall Street Journal*, February 25, 2013.

72. N. Kitroef and J. Rodkin, "The Pay Gap that Haunts MBAs," *Bloomberg Businessweek*, October 26, 2016, pp. 38–42.

73. R. E. Silverman, "Psst . . . This Is What Your Co-Worker Is Paid," *Wall Street Journal*, January 29, 2013.

74. S. Stebbins, E. Comen, and C. Stockdale "Workplace Fatalities: The 25 Most Dangerous Jobs in America," *USA Today Online*, January 9, 2018.

75. J. Jacoby, "Air Traffic Control Staffing under Scrutiny," *CNN .com*, March 25, 2011.

76. M. Price, "The Risks of Night Work," *Monitor on Psychology*, January 2011, pp. 39–41.

77. V. Vara, "The Toll of Cheap Clothing." *Bloomberg Businessweek*, October 31, 2016.

78. C. Kenny, "The Economic Power of Positive Thinking," *Bloomberg Businessweek*, January 10, 2015, pp. 8–9.

79. M. McCardle, "Why Negativity Is Really Awesome," *Bloomberg Businessweek*, February 20, 2014, pp. 6–7.

80. L. W. Porter and R. M. Steers, "Organizational, Work and Personal Factors in Employee Absenteeism and Turnover," *Psychological Bulletin* 80 (1973), pp. 151–76.

81. P. Mozur and T. Orlink, "Hon Hoi Riot Undermines Squeeze on Chinese Manufacturers," *Wall Street Journal*, September 24, 2012.

82. T. Jacoby, "Walmart Tests Upskilling," *Wall Street Journal*, September 4, 2015.

83. J. Simons, "The Boss Wants You Back in the Office," *The Wall Street Journal Online*, July 25, 2017.

84. R. Premack, "The Fast Food Industry Is Facing a Growing Crisis," *Business Insider Online*, May 1, 2018.

85. Premack, "The Fast Food Industry Is Facing a Growing Crisis."

86. A. Househ, "Home Cooked HR," *Workforce*, June 2018, pp. 28–31.

87. L. Sandler, "How to Love Paid Family Leave," *Wall Street Journal*, July 27, 2014.

88. R. E. Silverman, "High Finance and Family Friendly? KKR Is Trying," *Wall Street Journal*, September, 26, 2016.

89. C. Cain Miller, "More Than Their Mothers, Young Women Plan Career Pauses," *New York Times*, July 22, 2015.

90. J. Surane, "The MBA Dilemma," *Bloomberg Businessweek*, August 10, 2015, pp. 41–42.

91. A. M. Grant, E. M. Campbell, G. Chen, K. Cottone, D. Lapedia, and K. Lee, "Impact and Art of Motivation Maintenance: The Effects of Contact with Beneficiaries on Persistance Behavior," *Organizational Behavior and Human Decision Processes* 103 (2007), pp. 53–67.

92. K. Weir, "More Than Job Satisfaction," *Monitor on Psychology*, December 2013, pp. 39–43.

93. C. Porath, "No Time to Be Nice at Work," *New York Times*, June 19, 2015.

94. L. Chapman and S. McBride, "Security Software, Insecurity Culture," *Bloomberg Businessweek,* April 21, 2017, pp. 38–39.

95. S. Shellenbarger, "When the Boss Works Long Hours, Must We All?" *Wall Street Journal*, February 9, 2014.

96. M. Townsend and E. E. Deprez, "Is the Corporate Bully the Next Workplace Pariah?" *Bloomberg Businessweek*, May 14, 2018, pp. 22–23.

97. D. Wescot, "Field Guide to Office Bullies," *Bloomberg Businessweek*, November 26, 2012, pp. 94–95.

98. J. Nocera, "The Pay Gap, Microsoft, and the Limits of Class Actions," *Bloomberg Businessweek*, October 5, 2018, p. 80.

99. S. C. Currall, A. J. Towler, T. A. Judge, and L. Kohn, "Pay Satisfaction and Organizational Outcomes," *Personnel Psychology* 58 (2005), pp. 613–40.

100. E. White, "Opportunity Knocks, and It Pays a Lot Better," *Wall Street Journal*, November 13, 2006, p. B3.

101. L. Stevens, "Amazon to Raise Its Minimum U.S. Wage to $15 an Hour," *The Wall Street Journal Online,* October 2, 2018.

102. M. Corkery, "Walmart Will Let Its 1.4 Million Workers Take Their Pay Before Payday," *The New York Times Online,* December 13, 2017.

103. P. Ziobro and E. Morath, "Wal-Mart Raising Wages as Market Gets Tighter," *Wall Street Journal*, February 19, 2015.

104. N. Schwartz, "Recovery Finally Yields Big Gains for Average Worker's Pay," *The New York Times Online,* January 6, 2017.

105. F. Wilkinson, "Starbucks, Magna Cum Grande," *Bloomberg Businessweek*, June 19, 2014, p. 14.

106. R. Pyriliss, "Benefits Providing an Edge in the War for Young Talent," *Workforce*, August 2017, p 14.

107. H. G. Heneman and D. S. Schwab, "Pay Satisfaction: Its Multidimensional Nature and Measurement," *International Journal of Applied Psychology* 20 (1985), pp. 129–41.

108. T. Judge and T. Welbourne, "A Confirmatory Investigation of the Dimensionality of the Pay Satisfaction Questionnaire," *Journal of Applied Psychology* 79 (1994), pp. 461–66.

109. R. E. Silverman, "Are You Happy at Work? Bosses Push Weekly Polls," *Wall Street Journal*, December 2, 2014.

110. C. Mims, "Bosses Use Anonymous Networks to Learn What Workers Really Think," *Wall Street Journal*, June 21, 2015.

111. L. Weber, "U.S. Workers Report Highest Level of Job Satisfaction since 2005," *The Wall Street Journal Online,* August 29, 2018.

112. H. Haddan, "Whole Foods Workers Push to Unionize," *The Wall Street Journal Online,* September 6, 2018.

113. E. Maltby and S. E. Needleman, "Some Small Businesses Opt for the Health-Care Penalty," *Wall Street Journal*, April 7, 2013.

114. S. J. Lambert, "When Flexibility Hurts," *New York Times*, September 19, 2012.

115. P. Coy, "The Leisure Gap," *Bloomberg Businessweek*, July 23, 2012, pp. 8–9.

CHAPTER

# 11 Pay Structure Decisions

## ┌─ LEARNING OBJECTIVES ─┐

*After reading this chapter, you should be able to:*

**LO 11-1**   List the main decision areas and concepts in employee compensation management. *page 480*

**LO 11-2**   Describe the major administrative tools used to manage employee compensation. *page 484*

**LO 11-3**   Explain the importance of competitive labor market and product market forces in compensation decisions. *page 496*

**LO 11-4**   Discuss the significance of process issues such as communication in compensation management. *page 499*

**LO 11-5**   Describe new developments in the design of pay structures. *page 501*

**LO 11-6**   Explain where the United States stands on pay issues from an international perspective. *page 503*

**LO 11-7**   Explain the reasons for the controversy over executive pay. *page 506*

**LO 11-8**   Describe the regulatory framework for employee compensation. *page 510*

## Unemployment Rates Down, Employee Compensation Up: Competing for Employees to Execute Strategy

What do Walmart, Amazon, Starbucks, CVS, and many other retailers have in common? All have increased compensation in response to increased competition for employees in the face of a national unemployment rate of 3.9%, the lowest since 1969 and which compares to a national unemployment rate of 9.6% as recently as 2010. To see how much more employees change jobs when the unemployment rate is this low, consider that in 2010 (unemployment rate = 9.6%) there were 47.3 million total hires by employers in the United States and employers lost 46.3 million employees. By comparison, in 2018 (unemployment rate = 3.9%), employers hired 68.0 million employees and lost 65.6 million employees. In other words, employees left employers at a 65.6/46.3 = 42% faster rate and thus compelled employers to increase hiring by a similar rate. The increases in compensation needed to compete in this sort of "heated up" labor market have included hourly wage increases. For example, CVS raised its minimum hourly wage to $11, up from $9. Costco raised its minimum to $14/hour. Target's minimum wage is now $12, and it plans to increase that to $15 within the year. Walmart's minimum has been raised to $11, and a Walmart executive also noted that he and his team are "reviewing store worker wages every two weeks to make sure the retailer is competitive in each market" where stores operate. But, employers are also increasing benefits to increase attractiveness of their jobs. For example, Walmart is increasing paid maternity leave for full-time employees from 6 to 8 weeks at half pay to 10 weeks at full pay. Also, Walmart will, for the first time, offer paid leave (of six weeks at full pay) to full-time employees who are new fathers or nonbirthing mothers. CVS, which competes with Walmart for employees,

will offer four weeks of paid parental leave to full-time employees and will freeze health care premiums for the coming year. CVS estimates that its wage and benefits increases together will cost it an additional $425 million per year. Although the current competition for employees makes it more difficult, employers continue to make an effort to the degree possible to keep compensation increases from becoming fixed costs. Thus, for example, Walmart will pay bonuses of a few hundred up to $1,000 per employee this year, which it estimates will cost the company roughly $400 million. However, unlike wage and benefits increases, these bonus payments do not become part of base compensation going forward, and such payments can be scaled back or ended in future years when competition in hiring and retaining employees becomes less fierce. As an executive from staffing firm Robert Half puts it: "Companies are still reluctant to move base wages up too much. It's a lot harder to take that away than bonuses." Finally, employers are seeking to gain efficiencies. Those can come in the form of more or better quality work expectations that go with higher compensation. In the case of Walmart, an earlier impetus for increases in compensation was that compensation had not been high enough to attract and retain the quality of workers needed to provide the type of customer experience Walmart felt was necessary to execute its strategy to be successful. Another employer response to rising employee compensation is to substitute technology for employees (i.e., to automate some work). Walmart is using more automation and fewer employees on its docks to unload trucks and for related inventory control. Starbucks and McDonald's are replacing cashiers with kiosks.

*CONTINUED*

SOURCES: C. Rugaber and A. D'Innocenzio, "U.S. Retailers Hope Higher Pay Will Buy More Efficient Workers," *AP News*, December 29, 2018, www.apnews.com; T.-P. Chen and E. Morath, "Firms Choose Bonuses over Raises," *Wall Street Journal*, September 19, 2018; S. Terlep, "CVS to Raise Starting Wage," *Wall Street Journal*, February 9, 2018; N. Irwin, "How Did Walmart Get Cleaner Stores and Higher Sales? It Paid Its People More," *New York Times*, October 15, 2016; N. Bomey, "Walmart Boosts Minimum Wage to $11, Hands out Bonuses up to $1,000 for Hourly Workers," *USA Today*, January 11, 2018; E. Morath, "Wages Rise as Hiring Accelerates," *Wall Street Journal*, November 3/4, 2018; S. Nassauer, "Costco to Raise Starting Wage to $14 an Hour: Retail Chain Is Latest to Boost Pay in Attempt to Attract and Maintain Workers," *Wall Street Journal*, January 11, 2019.

# Introduction

**LO 11-1**

List the main decision areas and concepts in employee compensation management.

From the employer's point of view, pay is a powerful tool for furthering the organization's strategic goals. First, pay has a large impact on employee attitudes and behaviors. It influences the kind of employees who are attracted to (and remain with) the organization. In the chapter opener, we saw that several retailers raised wages to compete for employees in the low unemployment rate labor market. Some, like Walmart, have also increased benefits (e.g., paid parental leave) in another effort to attract and retain employees. Walmart also decided a few years ago that it needed to increase its compensation in an effort to attract a workforce more in line with what it needed to execute its business strategy (including creating the desired customer experience). Pay can also be a powerful motivational tool for aligning current employees' interests with those of the broader organization (an issue we address more fully in Chapter 12). Second, employee compensation is typically a significant organizational cost and thus requires close scrutiny. As Table 11.1 shows, the cost of total compensation (cash and benefits) is 18% to 44% of revenues, depending on the industry and 30% across industries. Table 11.1 also

**Table 11.1**

Total Compensation as a Percentage of Revenues, Industry and Company Examples

| | TOTAL COMPENSATION/REVENUES |
|---|---|
| **Industries** | |
| Health care | 44%[a] |
| Manufacturing/engineering | 21[a] |
| Utilities | 18[a] |
| All industries | 30[b] |
| **Organizations** | |
| HCA HealthCare Inc. | 46 |
| Southwest Airlines | 35 |
| United Airlines | 28 |
| Goldman Sachs | 38 |
| Milwaukee Brewers | 49 |
| Boston Red Sox | 55 |
| New York Yankees | 33 |
| University of Wisconsin–Madison | 42 |

SOURCE: Southwest Airlines. Form 10-Q. October 30, 2018; HCA Healthcare, Inc. Form 10-K. February 23, 2018. www.SEC.gov; Goldman Sachs. 10-Q. November 2, 2018. www.SEC.gov; United Airlines. 10-Q. October 17, 2018. www.sec.gov; Data Digest FY 2018. University of Wisconsin-Madison 2017–2018 Data Digest, p. 75 and p. 78; Spotrac. MLB Team Cash Tracker. www.spotrac.com; The Business of Baseball. Forbes. www.Forbes.com; PwC, *Trends in HR Effectiveness: With Excerpts from 2016 PwC Saratoga Benchmarks*, November 2016, http://www.pwc.com/us/en/hr-management/publications/assets/pwc-trends-in-hr-effectiveness-final.pdf; PwC, *Trends in HR Effectiveness: With Excerpts from 2015 PwC Saratoga Benchmarks*, November 2015, http://www.pwc.com/us/en/hr-management/publications/assets/pwc-trends-in-the-workforce-2015.pdf.

[a]Based on November 2016 report.

[b]Based on November 2015 report.

provides examples of individual organizations. HCA HealthCare Inc., at 46%, is similar to the health care industry overall, which is 44%. Goldman Sachs, financial services, is at 38%. We also see that there are differences within industries. Southwest has a higher total compensation/revenues percentage than does United. The Boston Red Sox are higher than the New York Yankees and the Milwaukee Brewers. Finally, the University of Wisconsin–Madison is 42%. Most of the organization examples are cases where valuable human capital is core to the product and how the organization competes, whether it be doctors and nurses, investment bankers, pitchers and shortstops, or professors and scientists. Compensation costs are a lower share of revenues in airlines, where there is a large investment in capital (e.g., planes).

For Walmart and other companies (e.g., airlines like Southwest, and to a degree, United), competing by keeping prices low for customers has traditionally translated into paying low wages and raising them only when pressure from labor market competition (and perhaps from other sources, as we saw in the chapter opener) becomes sufficiently strong, such as now, with growth in the economy and lower unemployment rates. However, as Walmart realized, keeping wages and employee headcount too low to control costs can get in the way of executing the business strategy (e.g., by undermining the customer experience), resulting in decreased revenues and profits.[1] The economic cycle means economic activity and labor market competition will eventually slow. When things slow down for companies, they often cut labor costs by reducing headcount or reducing variable aspects of compensation [e.g., profit sharing bonuses or 401(k) retirement plan contributions]. But every company should plan ahead for how it will have an efficient workforce in place and ready to go when the demand for their products picks up again. For example, when Toyota paused automobile assembly at U.S. plants due to slow sales, it did not lay off workers. It did offer a voluntary buyout plan under which workers signing up received 10 weeks of salary plus 2 weeks' salary for every year worked. Employees who remained worked 36-hour, rather than 40-hour, weeks and reallocated their time to receive increased training and look for new ways to reduce costs.

From the employees' point of view, policies having to do with wages, salaries, and other earnings affect their overall income and thus their standard of living. Both the level of pay and its seeming fairness compared with others' pay are important. Pay is also often considered a sign of status and success. Employees attach great importance to pay decisions when they evaluate their relationship with the organization. Therefore, pay decisions must be carefully managed and communicated.

Total compensation, as noted, consists of cash compensation (salary, merit increases, bonuses, stock options, and other incentives) and benefits (e.g., health insurance, paid vacation, unemployment compensation). In this chapter, we focus on salary levels. In Chapter 12, we address merit increases and incentive issues. In Chapter 13, we examine benefits decisions. Total rewards, total returns, and inducements are concepts that include not only total compensation but also any other (nonmonetary) rewards (interesting or fulfilling work, good co-workers, development opportunities, recognition) that are associated with the employment relationship. These nonmonetary rewards are discussed in Chapters 4, 5, and 10. An organization must choose to what degree its total rewards strategy depends on monetary rewards (compensation) and what mix of compensation components will be used.

Salary level decisions can be broken into two areas: pay structure and individual pay. In this chapter, we focus on **pay structure**, which in turn entails a consideration of pay level and job structure. **Pay level** is defined here as the average pay (including wages, salaries, and bonuses) of jobs in an organization. (Benefits also matter, but these are discussed separately in Chapter 13.) **Job structure** refers to the relative pay of jobs in an

**Pay structure**
The relative pay of different jobs (job structure) and how much they are paid (pay level).

**Pay level**
The average pay, including wages, salaries, and bonuses, of jobs in an organization.

**Job structure**
The relative pay of jobs in an organization.

organization. Consider the same two jobs in two different organizations. In Organization 1, jobs A and B are paid an annual average compensation of $40,000 and $60,000, respectively. In Organization 2, the pay rates are $45,000 and $55,000, respectively. Organizations 1 and 2 have the same pay level ($50,000), but the job structures (relative rates of pay) differ.

Both pay level and job structure are characteristics of organizations and reflect decisions about jobs rather than about individual employees. This chapter's focus is on why and how organizations attach pay policies to jobs. In Chapter 12, we look within jobs to discuss the different approaches that can determine the pay of individual employees as well as the advantages and disadvantages of these different approaches.

Why is the focus on jobs in developing a pay structure? As the number of employees in an organization increases, so too does the number of human resource management decisions. In determining compensation, for example, each employee must be assigned a rate of pay that is acceptable in terms of external, internal, and individual equity (defined later) and in terms of the employer's cost. Although each employee is unique and thus requires some degree of individualized treatment, standardizing the treatment of similar employees (those with similar jobs) can help greatly to make compensation administration and decision making more manageable and more equitable. Thus, pay policies are often attached to particular jobs rather than tailored entirely to individual employees.

## Equity Theory and Fairness

In discussing the consequences of pay decisions, it is useful to keep in mind that employees often evaluate their pay relative to that of other employees. Equity theory suggests that people evaluate the fairness of their situations by comparing them with those of other people.[2] Equity is not equality. Equal pay for two workers with unequal contributions (*inputs* in equity theory) would likely be perceived as unfair if this information is known, especially by the worker making the stronger contributions to the organization. According to equity theory, a person (p) compares her own ratio of perceived outcomes ($O$) (pay, benefits, working conditions) to perceived inputs ($I$) (effort, ability, experience) to the ratio of a comparison other (o).

$$O_p/I_p <, >, \text{ or } = O_o/I_o?$$

If p's ratio ($O_p/I_p$) is smaller than the comparison other's ratio ($O_o/I_o$), then *underreward inequity* results. If p's ratio is larger, then *overreward inequity* results, although evidence suggests that this type of inequity is less likely to occur and less likely to be sustained because p may rationalize the situation by reevaluating her outcomes less favorably or inputs (self-worth) more favorably.[3]

The consequences of p's comparisons depend on whether equity is perceived. If equity is perceived, no change is expected in p's attitudes or behavior. In contrast, perceived inequity may cause p to restore equity. Some ways of restoring equity are counterproductive, including (1) reducing one's own inputs (not working as hard), (2) increasing one's outcomes (such as by

"But you know you have a successful organization when the people who work for you and work with you will openly and with a great deal of comfort say, 'I'm looking for another job.'"

—Jerrold Williams,
Chief HR Officer, Daymon Worldwide

theft), or (3) leaving the situation that generates perceived inequity (leaving the organization or refusing to work or cooperate with employees who are perceived as overrewarded).

Equity theory's main implication for managing employee compensation is that, to an important extent, employees evaluate their pay by comparing it with what others get paid, and their work attitudes and behaviors are influenced by such comparisons. For example, consider one provision of the contract that former Texas Ranger and New York Yankee shortstop Alex Rodriguez signed years ago. It stated that during the first several years of his contract, his base compensation had to be at least $2 million higher than any other shortstop in major league baseball. A second provision permitted Rodriguez to void seasons in the latter years of his contract unless his base compensation was at least $1 million higher than any position player in major league baseball. Otherwise, Rodriguez would be free to leave his current team. These provisions that pegged Rodriguez's pay to other players' pay provide a compelling example of the importance of being paid well in *relative* terms.

Another implication is that employee perceptions are what determine their evaluation. The fact that management believes its employees are paid well compared with those of other companies does not necessarily translate into employees' beliefs. Employees may have different information or make different comparisons than management. For example, Toyota recently set a goal to move from using wages in the U.S. auto industry as the standard of comparison to using the (lower) prevailing wages in the state where each plant is located. To do so, however, Toyota recognizes its challenge is to educate team members (employees) and managers to help them understand and accept the change.

Two types of employee social comparisons of pay are especially relevant in making pay level and job structure decisions. (See Table 11.2.) First, *external equity* pay comparisons focus on what employees in other organizations are paid for doing the same general job. Such comparisons are likely to influence the decisions of applicants to accept job offers as well as the attitudes and decisions of employees about whether to stay with an organization or take a job elsewhere. (See Chapters 5 and 10.) The organization's choice of pay level influences its employees' external pay comparisons and their consequences. A market pay survey is the primary administrative tool organizations use in choosing a pay level.

Second, *internal equity* pay comparisons focus on what employees within the same organization are paid. Employees make comparisons with lower-level jobs, jobs at the same level (but perhaps in different skill areas or product divisions), and jobs at higher levels. These comparisons may influence general attitudes of employees; their willingness to

**Table 11.2**

Pay Structure Concepts and Consequences

| PAY STRUCTURE DECISION AREA | ADMINISTRATIVE TOOL | FOCUS OF EMPLOYEE PAY COMPARISONS | CONSEQUENCES OF EQUITY PERCEPTIONS |
|---|---|---|---|
| Pay level | Market pay surveys | External equity | External employee movement (attraction and retention of quality employees); labor costs; employee attitudes |
| Job structure | Job evaluation | Internal equity | Internal employee movement (promotion, transfer, job rotation); cooperation among employees; employee attitudes |

transfer to other jobs within the organization; their willingness to pursue and accept promotions to higher level jobs; their inclination to cooperate across jobs, functional areas, or product groups; and their commitment to the organization. The organization's choice of job structure influences its employees' internal comparisons and their consequences.[4] Job evaluation is the administrative tool organizations use to design job structures.

In addition, employees make internal equity pay comparisons with others performing the same job. Such comparisons are most relevant to Chapter 12, which focuses on using pay to recognize individual contributions and differences.

We now turn to ways to choose and develop pay levels and pay structures, the consequences of such choices, and the ways two administrative tools—market pay surveys and job evaluation—help in making pay decisions.

# Developing Pay Levels
## MARKET PRESSURES

**LO 11-2**
Describe the major administrative tools used to manage employee compensation.

Any organization faces two important competitive market challenges in deciding what to pay its employees: product market competition and labor market competition.[5]

### Product Market Competition

First, organizations must compete effectively in the product market. In other words, they must be able to sell their goods and services at a quantity and price that will bring a sufficient return on their investment. Organizations compete on multiple dimensions (quality, service, and so on), and price is one of the most important dimensions. An important influence on price is the cost of production.

An organization that has higher labor costs than its product market competitors will have to charge higher average prices for products of similar quality. Thus, for example, if labor costs are 30% of revenues at Company A and Company B, but Company A has labor costs that are 20% higher than those of Company B, we would expect Company A to have product prices that are higher by $(0.30 \times 0.20) = 6\%$. At some point, the higher price charged by Company A will contribute to a loss of its business to competing companies with lower prices (like Company B). Until recently, in the automobile industry, hourly labor cost (including not only wages but also retiree and active worker benefits such as health care) in assembly plants averaged $75 for the U.S. Big Three (Chrysler, General Motors, Ford), compared to $52 for Toyota and Honda plants in the United States. On average, it takes roughly 30 hours to assemble a car. So, the labor cost to assemble for the Big Three was $30 \times \$75 = \$2,250$, compared to $30 \times \$52 = \$1,560$ for Toyota and Honda. That labor cost disadvantage had to have been offset by superior vehicle quality, performance, and so forth for the Big Three to make a profit. The bankruptcies at Chrysler and General Motors indicate that was not possible. More recently, the Big Three have reduced their labor costs to $47/hour at Chrysler, $55/hour at General Motors, and $57/hour at Ford, primarily by hiring new workers at lower wages and by reducing benefits costs.[6] That is a major change, now putting them much closer to the (current) roughly $52/hour labor cost at Honda and Toyota. As a result, the Big Three have become much more competitive and their financial performance has improved dramatically. Toyota's labor costs have risen over time in the United States due to the inevitable aging of its workforce and the associated increased health care and retiree benefits. In a sense, it is going through the same life cycle as the Big Three did.

In contrast, a newly opened plant, such as the Volkswagen plant in Chattanooga, Tennessee, is estimated to have hourly labor costs of $27 initially.[7] That $27/hour cost to build Volkswagen Passats in Tennessee is much lower than Volkswagen's hourly labor cost to build cars in Germany, which had been estimated as high as nearly $100 (when the euro was at its strongest against the U.S. dollar). A more recent estimate of Volkswagen's hourly labor cost in Chattanooga is $38/hour.[8] Due to this labor cost saving (and due to lower costs for parts, transportation, and so forth), Volkswagen expected to be able to reduce the price of a Passat from $28,000 (when it was built in Germany) to $20,000 when it was first built in Tennessee. Lower labor costs can be found in Mexico (and even lower labor costs than in Mexico in other parts of the world). Thus, although Audi, Honda, Mazda, and Nissan have all announced plans to open new North American plants, all will be built in Mexico. Only recently, for the first time in many years, did an automobile company (Chinese-owned Volvo) announce plans to build a new plant in the United States, specifically in South Carolina, which has the lowest rate of unionization of any U.S. state.[9]

The cost of labor is directly reflected in the price of the car. Therefore, *product market competition* places an *upper bound* on labor costs and compensation. This upper bound is more constrictive when labor costs are a larger share of total costs and when demand for the product is affected by changes in price (i.e., when demand is *elastic*). Unless higher labor costs are offset by higher worker productivity or desirable product features that allow a higher product price, it will be difficult to sustain these relatively high costs in a competitive product market. As we have noted, Volkswagen will be able to lower the price of its Passat by producing it in the United States, where its labor costs will be lower than in Germany and lower than those of U.S. competitors. The search for lower labor costs is a continuous process. As companies move production to low-wage countries, wages there eventually rise, sometimes causing companies to move production to countries with still lower wages.

What components make up labor costs? A major component is the average cost per employee. This is made up of both direct payments (such as wages, salaries, and bonuses) and indirect payments (such as health insurance, Social Security, and unemployment compensation). A second component of labor costs is the staffing level (number of employees). Not surprisingly, financially troubled organizations often seek to cut costs by focusing on one or both components. Staff reductions, hiring freezes, wage and salary freezes, and sharing benefits costs with employees are several ways of making the organization's labor costs more competitive in the product market. Another way to control labor costs is to substitute capital for labor (i.e., replace employees with automation/technology), as the Amazon example in the Competing through Technology box indicates.

## Labor Market Competition

A second important competitive market challenge is *labor market competition*, which reflects the number of workers available relative to the number of jobs available. Shortages and surpluses influence pay levels. For example, as we saw in the chapter-opening story, a shortage of workers will put upward pressure on wages and salaries, as organizations must pay to compete against other companies that hire similar employees. These labor market competitors typically include not only companies that have similar products but also those in different product markets that hire similar types of employees. If an organization is not competitive in the labor market, it will fail to attract and retain employees of sufficient numbers and quality. For example, even if a computer manufacturer offers newly graduated electrical engineers the same pay as other computer manufacturers, if automobile manufacturers and other labor market competitors offer salaries $5,000 higher, the computer company may not be able to hire enough qualified electrical engineers. Labor market competition places a *lower bound* on pay levels.

## Automation, Technology, and the Demand for Employees

Labor cost, which is a function of cost per employee (wages and benefits) × number of employees, is a major expense for many firms. Thus, firms must decide on an ongoing basis not only how much to pay employees but also how many employees to have. One factor involved in these decisions is the availability of technology. Labor (employees) and capital (e.g., technology such as computers, machinery, robots, and automation) can be complements or substitutes in production. If complements, use of more capital requires use of more labor in production. If substitutes, use of more capital requires less use of labor in production (i.e., fewer employees).

When labor and capital are substitutes, an increase in the price of labor and/or a decrease in the cost of capital will generally result in the use of fewer employees in production. A caveat is that as production becomes more efficient, allowing lower prices for the product, resulting increases in demand for the product may result in an increase in the number of at least some types of employees (called the scale effect), even as the role of labor in production declines relative to the role of capital. Some firms are expanding production in countries with high labor costs but are controlling costs by using more robots and automation to reduce the number of employees they need.

Consider the case of Amazon. Amazon hires many seasonal workers every year for the big holiday shopping season that kicks off after Thanksgiving Day—but not as many as it used to hire. Amazon hired about 80,000 seasonal workers for the 2014 holiday shopping season and even more (100,000) for the 2015 holiday shopping season as its year-to-year sales grew by 20%. However, even though Amazon has continued to grow its sales (by roughly 32% per year since 2015) and even though its annual sales for 2018 ($221 billion) were more than double those for 2015 ($107 billion), guess how many seasonal workers it hired for the 2018 holiday season? Twice as many as in 2015, or about 200,000? Nope. Amazon hired 100,000 seasonal workers for the 2018 holiday seasons, the same number it hired for the 2015 holiday season, despite its 2018 sales being more than twice as high as in 2015. What happened?

Part of the answer is that automation "happened." Consider that in the United States alone, Amazon has 250,000 year-round workers and 100,000 seasonal workers. It just increased its minimum wage to $15/hour. If the average year-round worker works 1,500 hours per year and the average seasonal worker works 180 hours per year, and even if each employee earns only the minimum of $15/hour (which we

know is not the case, so this is a very lower bound estimate), the cost of wages would be $15 × (1,500 × 250,000 + 180 × 100,000) = $5.90 billion (that's with a "b"). Of course, as we will see, benefits (health insurance, etc.) adds another roughly $0.40 on top of every dollar of wages, at least for year-round workers. That would bring total labor cost to $8.25 billion. Amazon has decided that it does not want its labor costs to increase in proportion to either increases in its wage level or in proportion to increases in its sales.

Automation is a strategy to break both of these connections. (And, of course, robots do not pose labor relations problems—at least not yet!) Amazon purchased Kiva Systems, a robotics company, for $775 million in 2012. By late 2014, it was using its robots in its warehouses. These robots do the traditional warehouse tasks of sorting, picking, packing, and shipping items and are said to be able to do in 15 minutes what it takes a human employee 60 minutes to do. As Amazon implements these robotic systems in more of its warehouses, it needs to hire fewer employees to meet increased sales demand for its products.

Other retailers too are moving to automate jobs in an effort to reduce labor costs and increase efficiency. Without doing this, competitors will have lower costs and thus will

*CONTINUED*

be able to provide goods and services at lower prices. In the digital economy, where products can be compared efficiently by customers on quality and price, companies that cannot compete on price are increasingly in trouble. There is often little to stand in the way of efficient price discovery and purchase by customers.

A key Amazon competitor, and the other "800-pound gorilla" of retail is Walmart, which is also seeking to automate to be more efficient and better able to compete for customers. It has made major technology and related investments to build its e-commerce capability, but it is also using robotics to automate jobs and reduce labor costs. For example, its investments in its stores include, similar to Amazon, self-scanning robots, but also cashier-less checkout for customers ("Scan & Go").

Walmart recently acquired Amazon competitor Jet.com, which is part of its broad strategy to remake itself as a digital company, which is said to include a plan to drop use of the word "stores."

## DISCUSSION QUESTIONS

1. What factors make it more likely that employers will substitute technology for employees?

2. Does technology inevitably result in a lower demand for employees? Can you think of examples where demand for employees was not reduced or was even increased? (*Hint:* How did people get around before the automobile? Or, how did computations get done before computers? Or, how did people shop before there was Amazon? How did these technology changes affect employment, both at

particular companies and in the economy overall?)

3. What about from the point of view of the consumer? Can you provide examples of technology that has made your life better (or worse)? How do you feel about shopping via Amazon?

4. Is automation good or bad for employees? In thinking about this, think about the relationships between efficiency and revenue growth and between revenue growth and employment growth.

SOURCES: S. Salinas, "Amazon Raises Minimum Wage to $15 for All US Employees," *CNBC.com*, October 2, 2018; A. Griswold, "Amazon Is Hiring Fewer Workers This Holiday Season, a Sign That Robots Are Replacing Them," *Quartz*, November 2, 2018; J. Dastin and A. Panchadar, "Amazon's Holiday Season Sales Outlook Misses Views; Shares Sink," *Reuters.com*, October 25, 2018; S. Nassauer, "Walmart Trims Management Jobs," *Wall Street Journal*, February 14, 2018; L. Hirsch, "Walmart Is Reportedly Planning to Cut over 1,000 Corporate Jobs," *CNBC.com*, January 12, 2018.

## EMPLOYEES AS A RESOURCE

Because organizations have to compete in the labor market, they should consider their employees not just as a cost but also as a resource in which the organization has invested and from which it expects valuable returns.[10] Although controlling costs directly affects an organization's ability to compete in the product market, the organization's competitive position can be compromised if costs are kept low at the expense of employee productivity and quality. Having higher labor costs than your competitors is not necessarily a concern if you also have the best and most effective workforce, one that produces products more efficiently and with better quality (see our earlier example of Walmart). Recently, some companies have recognized the importance of helping employees, especially those whose wages are low, avoid financial insecurity (or "financial precarity"). The Competing through Environmental, Social, and Governance Practices box explains the social and business case for helping employees better deal with financial precarity.

Pay policies and programs are one of the most important human resource tools for encouraging desired employee behaviors and discouraging undesired behaviors. Therefore, they must be evaluated not just in terms of costs but also in terms of the returns they generate—how they attract, retain, and motivate a high-quality workforce. For example, if the average revenue per employee in Company A is 20% higher than in Company B, it may not be important that the average pay in Company A is 10% higher than in Company B.

# COMPETING THROUGH ENVIRONMENTAL, SOCIAL, AND GOVERNANCE PRACTICES

## Reducing Employee Financial Precarity

Over 50 million working Americans face a challenge in making ends meet each month. As long as nothing unexpected happens, things are mostly fine. However, they have no financial cushion to handle the unexpected, whether it be medical, home, auto, or other unforeseen and out of the ordinary expenses. Most lack access to anything but very expensive credit and/or high interest "payday loans," which can lock them into a financial crisis from which they may not be able to escape. As such, in the United States, it has been reported that "money-related concerns are a more prevalent source of distress than those related to health, work, or family" and that "most people . . . do not have $400 in savings to cover an emergency." There is also evidence that such "financial precarity" can adversely affect employee performance at the workplace.

What can employers do? Higher wages, of course, is one solution. However, employers can also encourage/incentivize employees to save enough money for an emergency (e.g., by cooperating with banks) through programs that help with balancing work and family and through programs that encourage wellness.

One example of a product that employers can offer in cooperation with banks is a short-term installment loan program from SalaryFinance. A borrower with a 500 U.S. FICO credit score would pay an annual interest rate of 12%. That compares to interest rates on payday loans as high as 200% for someone with such a low credit score. Another product in this area is PayActiv. It provides advance access to wages that have been earned but not yet paid. It costs employees $5/month to enroll, and a payday loan typically costs $35, regardless of credit score. The business model works for PayActiv because repayment of the paycheck advance is automatically deducted from future paychecks, thus minimizing the risk that the loan will not be repaid to PayActiv.

Researchers from the Harvard Kennedy School estimate that such programs reduce employee turnover by 19% or more, presumably because an employee would be reluctant to move to an employer that did not provide such a program to reduce financial precarity. They note that at a company like Target, estimated employee turnover is $567 million per year, or $3,300 per turnover. They note that even a 5% reduction in turnover would thus save $28 million per year.

Walmart is one of the major users of PayActiv. Within a recent four-month period, 80,000 Walmart employees used PayActiv to access over $30 million in advances on their paychecks. The hope is that these employer-sponsored programs will not only reduce turnover costs for employers, but also significantly improve the quality of life for low-income workers and help them avoid the risk of falling into a bad financial situation that can be all but impossible to escape.

### DISCUSSION QUESTIONS

1. How common is financial precarity? What effects, especially over time, can financial precarity have on an individual?

2. If you have experienced financial precarity and if you are willing to share your experience, describe the effects you experienced.

3. From the point of view of an organization, why take steps to reduce employee financial precarity?

SOURCES: T. Baker and S. Kumar, "A Better Alternative to Payday Loans," *Wall Street Journal*, May 14, 2018; J. Meuris and C. Leana, "The Price of Financial Precarity: Organizational Costs of Employees' Financial Concerns," *Organization Science*, 29, (2018), pp. 398–417; J. Meuris and C. R. Leana, "The High Cost of Low Wages: Economic Scarcity Effects in Organizations," *Research in Organizational Behavior*, 35 (2015), pp. 143–158; A. Tergensen, "Workers School in Money: More Firms Pay Workers to Shore Up Their finances through Education, Cutting Debt," *Wall Street Journal*, February 21, 2018.

## DECIDING WHAT TO PAY

Although organizations face important external labor and product market pressures in setting their pay levels, a range of discretion remains.[11] How large the range is depends on the particular competitive environment the organization faces. Where the range is broad, an important strategic decision is whether to pay above, at, or below the market average. The advantage of paying above the market average is the ability to attract and retain the top talent available and help generate positive job attitudes (e.g., satisfaction), all of which can translate into a highly effective and productive workforce. The disadvantage, of course, is the added cost.[12] See the Evidence-Based HR comparison of Costco (higher wages) with Walmart (lower wages).

# EVIDENCE-BASED HR

Walmart is legendary for its attention to (some would say, obsession with) cost control so that it can pass lower prices on to customers, making it difficult for other retailers to compete. However, as alluded to in the chapter opener, Walmart seems to have metrics-based evidence that, in the past, it perhaps has pushed labor cost control too far, reducing workforce quality and motivation, to the detriment of the customer experience, sales, and profits. That evidence was based on the company's own internal data. External benchmarking data suggest a similar story. Although Walmart continues in last place (out of 20 companies) in its category (department and discount stores) on the American Customer Satisfaction Index, it has improved from a score of 66 a few years ago to 71 most recently. As we also saw in the chapter opener, Walmart has recently taken steps to increase employee compensation in hopes of being able to better compete for employees in the face of a low unemployment rate, which is critical to executing its business strategy, which continues to focus on controlling costs, but also improving the customer experience.

In contrast to Walmart, Costco is first in the same category, department and discount stores, on the American Customer Satisfaction Index, and since 2006 there have been only two years when another company (it was Nordstrom) in its category ranked higher. That difference may be due in part to Costco traditionally following a different strategy than Walmart, paying higher wages and covering more of its employees with health insurance, requiring them to pay smaller health insurance premiums, and contributing more to their retirement plans. As we saw, Walmart recently raised its lowest wage to $11/hour. Costco's lowest wage is $14.00/hour.

Some major retailers experience as high as 100% turnover each year, and the associated costs (for hiring, orienting, training, and replacing employees) can add up. Over the years, Walmart has been known as one such high employee turnover company. In contrast, Costco has traditionally had much lower turnover. James Sinegal, who founded Costco in 1983, states that Costco's strategy is to "pay the highest wages in all of retail," which he says helps contribute to an employee turnover rate at Costco of 7%, compared to what he states is "60 to 70 percent at other retailers." Costco's high compensation approach translates into it regularly being among the Top 5 on *Forbes*'s list of America's Best Employers. We know that

*CONTINUED*

satisfied and happy employees in customer-facing jobs help make for satisfied and happy customers. It also makes for lower employee turnover, which lowers costs of hiring, replacement, training, and loss of customer service.

In summary, Walmart competes primarily on product cost, whereas Costco, which offers products at a higher price point, competes primarily on customer service. In these two cases, the different business strategies translate into different strategies for human resources, including in compensation strategy. That, in turn, leads to different metrics/evidence being emphasized in assessing the effectiveness of their human resource and compensation strategies.

SOURCES: S. Nassauer, "Costco to Raise Starting Wage to $14 an Hour: Retail Chain Is Latest to Boost Pay in Attempt to Attract and Maintain Workers," *Wall Street Journal*, January 11, 2019; J. Calfas, "This Company Has the Best Pay and Benefits, According to Employees," *Money Magazine*, February 27, 2018, Time.com/money, http://time.com/money/5177506/best-company-to-work-indeed/; D. Brown, "Costco, Google and T-Mobile Ranked as Best Large Companies to Work for This Year," *USA Today*, December 10, 2018; T. Relihan, "How Costco's Obsession with Culture Drove Success. Ideas Made to Matter," *MIT Management Sloan School*, May 11, 2018, https://mitsloan.mit.edu/ideas-made-to-matter/how-costcos-obsession-culture-drove-success; *American Customer Satisfaction Index*, http://www.theacsi.org.

**Efficiency wage theory**
A theory stating that wages influence worker productivity.

Under what circumstances do the benefits of higher pay outweigh the higher costs? According to **efficiency wage theory**, one circumstance is when organizations have technologies or structures that depend on highly skilled employees. For example, organizations that emphasize decentralized decision making may need higher-caliber employees. Another circumstance in which higher pay may be warranted is when an organization has difficulties observing and monitoring its employees' performance. It may therefore wish to provide an above-market pay rate to ensure the incentive to put forth maximum effort. The theory is that employees who are paid more than they would be paid elsewhere will be reluctant to shirk because they wish to retain their good jobs.[13] Interestingly, some companies (e.g., Zappos, Amazon) have decided that it sometimes makes sense to pay employees to leave if they are staying only because of the money and despite being a better fit elsewhere.[14]

## MARKET PAY SURVEYS

**Benchmarking**
Comparing an organization's practices against those of the competition.

To compete for talent, organizations use **benchmarking**, a procedure in which an organization compares its own practices against those of the competition. In compensation management, benchmarking against product market and labor market competitors is typically accomplished through the use of one or more pay surveys, which provide information on going rates of pay among competing organizations.

The use of pay surveys requires answers to several important questions:[15]

1. Which employers should be included in the survey? Ideally, they would be the key labor market and product market competitors.
2. Which jobs are included in the survey? Because only a sample of jobs is ordinarily used, care must be taken that the jobs are representative in terms of level, functional area, and product market. Also, the job content must be sufficiently similar.
3. If multiple surveys are used, how are all the rates of pay weighted and combined? Organizations often have to weight and combine pay rates because different surveys are often tailored toward particular employee groups (labor markets) or product markets. The organization must decide how much relative weight to give to its labor market and product market competitors in setting pay.

Several factors affect decisions on how to combine surveys.[16] Product market comparisons that focus on labor costs are likely to deserve greater weight when (1) labor costs represent a large share of total costs, (2) product demand is elastic (it changes in response to product price changes), (3) the supply of labor is inelastic, and (4) employee skills are specific to the product market (and will remain so). In contrast, labor market comparisons may be more important when (1) attracting and retaining qualified employees is difficult and (2) the costs (administrative, disruption, and so on) of recruiting replacements are high.

As this discussion suggests, knowing what other organizations are paying is only one part of the story. It is also necessary to know what those organizations are getting in return for their investment in employees. To find that out, some organizations examine ratios such as revenues/employees and revenues/labor costs. The first ratio includes the staffing component of employee cost but not the average cost per employee. The second ratio, however, includes both. Note that comparing these ratios across organizations requires caution. For example, different industries rely on different labor and capital resources. So comparing the ratio of revenues to labor costs of a petroleum company (capital intensive, high ratio) to a hospital (labor intensive, low ratio) would be like comparing apples and oranges. But within industries, such comparisons can be useful. Besides revenues, other return-on-investment data might include product quality, customer satisfaction, and potential workforce quality (such as average education and skill levels).

### Rate Ranges (Pay Grades)

As the preceding discussion suggests, obtaining a single "going rate" of market pay is a complex task that involves a number of subjective decisions; it is both an art and a science. Once a market rate has been chosen, how is it incorporated into the pay structure? Typically—especially for white-collar jobs—it is used for setting the midpoint of pay ranges for either jobs or pay grades (discussed next). Market survey data are also often collected on minimum and maximum rates of pay as well. The use of **rate ranges** permits a company to recognize differences in employee performance, seniority, training, and so forth in setting individual pay (discussed in Chapter 12). For some blue-collar jobs, however, particularly those covered by collective bargaining contracts, there may be a single rate of pay for all employees within the job.

**Rate ranges**
Different employees in the same job may have different pay rates.

### Key Jobs and Nonkey Jobs

In using pay surveys, it is necessary to make a distinction between two general types of jobs: key jobs and nonkey jobs. **Key jobs** (also known as benchmark jobs) have relatively stable content and—perhaps most important—are common to many organizations. Therefore, it is possible to obtain market pay survey data on them. Note, however, that to avoid too much of an administrative burden, organizations may not gather market pay data on all such jobs. In contrast to key jobs, **nonkey jobs** are, to an important extent, unique to organizations (and/or have content different from jobs in other organizations having the same title). Thus, by definition, they cannot be directly valued or compared through the use of market surveys. Therefore, they are treated differently in the pay-setting process.

**Key jobs**
Benchmark jobs, used in pay surveys, that have relatively stable content and are common to many organizations.

**Nonkey jobs**
Jobs that are unique to organizations and that cannot be directly valued or compared through the use of market surveys.

## DEVELOPING A JOB STRUCTURE

Although external comparisons of the sort we have been discussing are important, employees also evaluate their pay using internal comparisons. So, for example, a vice president of marketing may expect to be paid roughly the same amount as a vice president of information systems because they are at the same organizational level, with similar levels of responsibility and similar impacts on the organization's performance. A job structure can be defined as the relative worth of various jobs in the organization, based on these types of internal comparisons. We now discuss how such decisions are made.

## Job Evaluation

**Job evaluation**
An administrative procedure used to measure internal job worth.

**Compensable factor**
The characteristics of jobs that an organization values and chooses to pay for.

One typical way of measuring internal job worth is to use an administrative procedure called **job evaluation**. A job evaluation system is composed of compensable factors and a weighting scheme based on the importance of each **compensable factor** to the organization. Simply stated, compensable factors are the characteristics of jobs that an organization values and chooses to pay for. These characteristics may include job complexity, working conditions, required education, required experience, and responsibility. Most job evaluation systems use several compensable factors. Job analysis (discussed in Chapter 4) provides basic descriptive information on job attributes, and the job evaluation process that assigns values to these compensable factors.

Scores can be generated in a variety of ways, but they typically include input from a number of people. A job evaluation committee commonly generates ratings. Although there are numerous ways to evaluate jobs, the most widely used is the point-factor system, which yields job evaluation points for each compensable factor.[17]

## The Point-Factor System

After generating scores for each compensable factor on each job, job evaluators often apply a weighting scheme to account for the differing importance of the compensable factors to the organization. Weights can be generated in two ways. First, *a priori* weights can be assigned, which means factors are weighted using expert judgments about the importance of each compensable factor. Second, weights can be derived empirically based on how important each factor seems in determining pay in the labor market. (Statistical methods such as multiple regression can be used for this purpose.) For the sake of simplicity, we assume in the following example that equal *a priori* weights are chosen, which means that the scores on the compensable factors can simply be summed.

Table 11.3 shows an example of a three-factor job evaluation system applied to three jobs. Note that the jobs differ in the levels of experience, education, and complexity required. Summing the scores on the three compensable factors provides an internally oriented assessment of relative job worth in the organization. In a sense, the programmer analyst job is worth 41% ($155/110 - 1$) more than the computer tech job, and the systems analyst job is worth 91% ($210/110 - 1$) more than the computer tech job. Whatever pay level is chosen (based on benchmarking and competitive strategy), we would expect the pay differentials to be somewhat similar to these percentages. The internal job evaluation and external survey-based measures of worth can, however, diverge.

**Table 11.3**
Example of a Three-Factor Job Evaluation System

| JOB TITLE | COMPENSABLE FACTORS | | | |
| | EXPERIENCE | EDUCATION | COMPLEXITY | TOTAL |
| --- | --- | --- | --- | --- |
| Computer tech | 40 | 30 | 40 | 110 |
| Programmer analyst | 40 | 50 | 65 | 155 |
| Systems analyst | 65 | 60 | 85 | 210 |

**Table 11.4**
Job Evaluation and Pay Survey Data

| JOB | KEY JOB? | JOB TITLE | JOB EVALUATION | SURVEY 1 (S1) | SURVEY 2 (S2) | SURVEY COMPOSITE (2/3*S1 + 1/3*S2) |
|-----|----------|-----------|----------------|---------------|---------------|-------------------------------------|
| A | y | Computer tech | 110 | $3,219 | $2,770 | $3,070 |
| B | y | Engineering tech I | 115 | 3,530 | 3,053 | 3,370 |
| C | y | Programmer analyst | 155 | 4,666 | 4,142 | 4,491 |
| D | n | Industrial engineer | 165 | — | — | — |
| E | n | Compensation analyst | 170 | — | — | — |
| F | y | Accountant | 190 | 5,781 | 4,958 | 5,507 |
| G | y | Systems analyst | 210 | 6,840 | 6,166 | 6,614 |
| H | n | Director of personal | 225 | — | — | — |
| I | y | Software engineer | 245 | 7,971 | 7,210 | 7,717 |
| J | y | Systems analyst—senior | 255 | 8,328 | 6,832 | 7,829 |
| K | y | Accounting manager | 270 | 9,389 | 9,043 | 9,274 |
| L | y | Electrical engineer—senior | 275 | 8,794 | 7,670 | 8,419 |
| M | n | Accounting director | 315 | — | — | — |
| N | y | Director of engineering | 320 | 11,242 | 10,515 | 11,000 |
| O | n | Chief scientist | 330 | — | — | — |

SOURCES: Adapted from S. Rynes, B. Gerhart, G. T. Milkovich, and J. Boudreau, *Current Compensation Professional Institute* (Scottsdale, AZ: American Compensation Association, 1988); G. T. Milkovich and B. Gerhart, *Cases in Compensation*, Version 11.1e (2013). Reprinted with permission.

## DEVELOPING A PAY STRUCTURE

In the example provided in Table 11.4, there are 15 jobs, 10 of which are key jobs. For these key (also known as benchmark) jobs, both pay survey and job evaluation data are available. For the five nonkey jobs, by definition, no survey data are available, only job evaluation information. Note that, for simplicity's sake, we work with data from only two pay surveys and we use a weighted average that gives twice as much weight to survey 1. Also, our example works with a single structure. Many organizations have multiple structures that correspond to different job families (like clerical, technical, and professional) or product divisions.

How are the data in Table 11.4 combined to develop a pay structure? First, it is important to note that both internal and external comparisons must be considered in making compensation decisions. However, because the pay structures suggested by internal and external comparisons do not necessarily converge, employers must balance them carefully. Studies suggest that employers may differ significantly in the degree to which they place priority on internal- or external-comparison data in developing pay structures.[18]

At least three pay-setting approaches, which differ according to their relative emphasis on external or internal comparisons, can be identified: (1) using market survey data, (2) using the pay policy line, and (3) using pay grades.[19]

### Market Survey Data

The approach with the greatest emphasis on external comparisons (market survey data) is achieved by basing pay directly on market surveys that cover as many key jobs as possible.

**Table 11.5**
Pay Midpoints under Different Approaches

| JOB | KEY JOB? | JOB TITLE | JOB EVALUATION | (1) SURVEY + POLICY | (2) PAY POLICY | (3) GRADES |
|---|---|---|---|---|---|---|
| A | y | Computer tech | 110 | $3,070 | $2,936 | $3,480 |
| B | y | Engineering tech I | 115 | 3,370 | 3,117 | 3,480 |
| C | y | Programmer analyst | 155 | 4,491 | 4,570 | 5,296 |
| D | n | Industrial engineer | 165 | 4,933 | 4,933 | 5,296 |
| E | n | Compensation analyst | 170 | 5,114 | 5,114 | 5,296 |
| F | y | Accountant | 190 | 5,507 | 5,840 | 5,296 |
| G | y | Systems analyst | 210 | 6,614 | 6,566 | 7,110 |
| H | n | Director of personnel | 225 | 7,110 | 7,110 | 7,110 |
| I | y | Software engineer | 245 | 7,717 | 7,837 | 7,110 |
| J | y | Systems analyst—senior | 255 | 7,828 | 8,200 | 8,926 |
| K | y | Accounting manager | 270 | 9,274 | 8,744 | 8,926 |
| L | y | Electrical engineer—senior | 275 | 8,419 | 8,926 | 8,926 |
| M | n | Accounting director | 315 | 10,377 | 10,377 | 10,741 |
| N | y | Director of engineering | 320 | 11,000 | 10,560 | 10,741 |
| O | n | Chief scientist | 330 | 10,922 | 10,922 | 10,741 |

SOURCES: Adapted from S. Rynes, B. Gerhart, G. T. Milkovich, and J. Boudreau, *Current Compensation Professional Institute* (Scottsdale, AZ: American Compensation Association, 1988); G. T. Milkovich and B. Gerhart, *Cases in Compensation*, Version 11.1e (2013). Reprinted with permission.

**Pay policy line**
A mathematical expression that describes the relationship between a job's pay and its job evaluation points.

For example, the rate of pay for job A in Table 11.5 would be $3,070; for job B, $3,370; and for job C, $4,491. For nonkey jobs (jobs D, E, H, M, and O), however, pay survey information is not available, and we must proceed differently. Basically, we develop a market **pay policy line** based on the key jobs (for which both job evaluation and market pay survey data are available). As Figure 11.1 shows, the data can be plotted with a line of best

**Figure 11.1**
Pay Policy Lines, Linear and Natural Logarithmic Functions

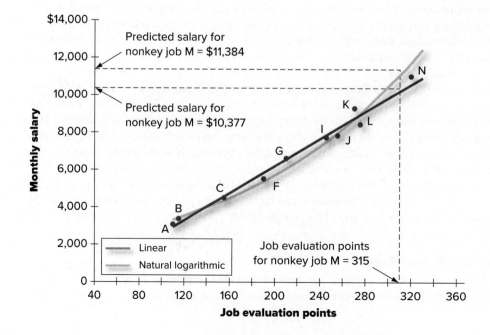

fit estimated. This line can be generated using a statistical procedure (regression analysis). Regressing the data from the "Survey Composite" column in Table 11.4 on the data from the "Job Evaluation" column in Table 11.4 (using only rows without missing data) yields the following equation:

$$-\$1,058 + \$36.30 \times \text{job evaluation points}$$

In other words, the predicted monthly salary (based on fitting a line to the key job data) is obtained by plugging the number of job evaluation points into this equation. Thus, for example, job M, a nonkey job, would have a predicted monthly salary of $-\$1,058 + \$36.30 \times 315 = \$10,377$.

As Figure 11.1 also indicates, it is not necessary to fit a straight line to the job evaluation and pay survey data. In some cases, a pay structure that provides increasing monetary rewards to higher-level jobs may be more consistent with the organization's goals or with the external market. For example, nonlinearity may be more appropriate if higher-level jobs are especially valuable to organizations and the talent to perform such jobs is rare. The curvilinear function in Figure 11.1 is obtained in the same way as above, except that the salary survey data are first transformed using the natural logarithm before being regressed on job evaluation points. The predicted monthly salaries are then transformed back into dollars (e.g., using the EXP function in Excel). The resulting equation using this approach is as follows:

$$\text{Natural logarithm of pay} = \$7.446 + (0.006 \times \text{job evaluation points})$$

## Pay Policy Line
A second pay-setting approach that combines information from external and internal comparisons is to use the pay policy line to derive pay rates for both key and nonkey jobs. This approach differs from the first approach in that actual market rates are no longer used for key jobs. This approach introduces a greater degree of internal consistency into the structure because the pay of all the jobs is linked directly to the number of job evaluation points.

## Pay Grades
A third approach is to group jobs into a smaller number of pay classes, pay ranges, or **pay grades**. Table 11.6 (see also Table 11.5, last column), for example, demonstrates one possibility: a five-grade structure. Each job within a grade would have the same rate

**Pay grades**
Jobs of similar worth or content grouped together for pay administration purposes.

**Table 11.6**
Sample Pay Grade Structure

| PAY GRADE | JOB EVALUATION POINTS RANGE | | MONTHLY PAY RATE RANGE | | |
|---|---|---|---|---|---|
| | MINIMUM | MAXIMUM | MINIMUM | MIDPOINT | MAXIMUM |
| 1 | 100 | 150 | $2,784 | $3,480 | $4,176 |
| 2 | 150 | 200 | 4,237 | 5,296 | 6,354 |
| 3 | 200 | 250 | 5,688 | 7,110 | 8,533 |
| 4 | 250 | 300 | 7,141 | 8,926 | 10,710 |
| 5 | 300 | 350 | 8,592 | 10,741 | 12,906 |

**Figure 11.2**

Sample Pay Grade
Structure

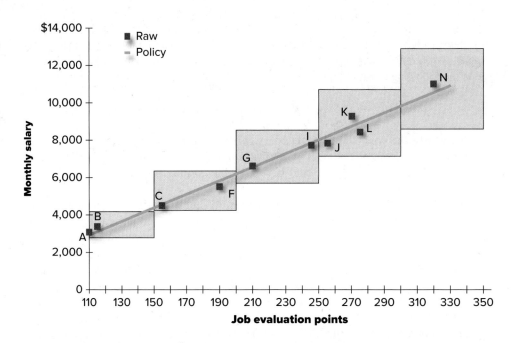

**Range spread**
The distance between
the minimum and
maximum amounts in a
pay grade.

range (i.e., would be assigned the same midpoint, minimum, and maximum). The advantage of this approach is that the administrative burden of setting separate rates of pay for hundreds (even thousands) of different jobs is reduced. It also permits greater flexibility in moving employees from job to job without raising concerns about, for example, going from a job having 230 job evaluation points to a job with 215 job evaluation points. What might look like a demotion in a completely job-based system is often a nonissue in a grade-based system. Note that the **range spread** (the distance between the minimum and maximum) is larger at higher levels, in recognition of the fact that performance differences are likely to have more impact on the organization at higher job levels. (See Figure 11.2.)

The disadvantage of using grades is that some jobs will be underpaid and others overpaid. For example, job C and job F both fall within the same grade (Pay Grade 2). The midpoint for job C under a grade system is $5,296 per month, or about $700 to $800 or so more than under the two alternative pay-setting approaches in Table 11.5. Obviously, this will contribute to higher labor costs and potential difficulties in competing in the product market. Unless there is an expected return to this increased cost, the approach is questionable. Job F, by contrast, is paid roughly $200 to $500 less per month under the grades system than it would be otherwise. Therefore, the company may find it more difficult to compete in the labor market.

## CONFLICTS BETWEEN MARKET PAY SURVEYS AND JOB EVALUATION

**LO 11-3**
Explain the importance
of competitive labor
market and product
market forces in
compensation
decisions.

An examination of Table 11.5 suggests that the relative worth of jobs is quite similar overall, whether based on job evaluation or pay survey data. However, some inconsistencies typically arise, and these are usually indicated by jobs whose average survey pay is significantly below or above the pay policy line. The closest case in Table 11.5 is job L, for which the average pay falls significantly below the policy line. One possible explanation is that a relatively plentiful supply of people in the labor market are capable of performing this job, so the pay needed to attract and retain them is lower than would be expected given the job evaluation points. Another kind of inconsistency occurs when market surveys show that a job is paid higher than the policy line (like job K). Again, this may reflect relative supply and demand, in this case driving pay higher.

How are conflicts between external and internal equity resolved, and what are the consequences? The example of the vice presidents of marketing and information technology may help illustrate the type of choice faced. The marketing VP job may receive the same number of job evaluation points, but market survey data may indicate that it typically pays less than the information technology VP job, perhaps because of tighter supply for the latter. Does the organization pay based on the market survey (external comparison) or on the job evaluation points (internal comparison)?

Emphasizing the internal comparison would suggest paying the two VPs the same. In doing so, however, either the VP of marketing would be "overpaid" or the VP of information technology would be "underpaid." The former drives up labor costs (product market problems); the latter may make it difficult to attract and retain a quality VP of information technology (labor market problems).

Another consideration has to do with the strategy of the organization. In some organizations (like Pepsi and Nike), the marketing function is critical to success. Thus, even though the market for marketing VPs is lower than that for information technology VPs, an organization may choose to be a pay leader for the marketing position (pay at the 90th percentile, for example) but only meet the market for the information technology position (perhaps pay at the 50th percentile). In other words, designing a pay structure requires careful consideration of which positions are most central to dealing with critical environmental challenges and opportunities in reaching the organization's goals.[20]

What about emphasizing external comparisons? Two potential problems arise. First, the marketing VP may be dissatisfied because she expects a job of similar rank and responsibility to that of the information technology VP to be paid similarly. Second, it becomes difficult to rotate people through different VP positions (for training and development) because going to the marketing VP position might appear as a demotion to the VP of information technology.

There is no one right solution to such dilemmas. Each organization must decide which objectives are most essential and choose the appropriate strategy. However, there has been a shift over time such that most organizations now emphasize external comparisons/market pricing, perhaps because of increasing competitive pressures over time.[21]

## MONITORING COMPENSATION COSTS

Pay structure influences compensation costs in a number of ways. Most obviously, the pay level at which the structure is pegged influences these costs. However, this is only part of the story. The pay structure represents the organization's intended policy, but actual practice may not coincide with it. Take, for example, the pay grade structure presented earlier. The midpoint for grade 1 is $3,480, and the midpoint for grade 2 is $5,296. Now, consider the data on a group example of individual employees in Table 11.7. One frequently used index of the correspondence between actual and intended pay is the **compa-ratio**, computed as follows:

**Compa-ratio**
An index of the correspondence between actual and intended pay.

$$\text{Grade compa-ratio} = \text{actual average pay for grade/pay midpoint for grade}$$

The compa-ratio directly assesses the degree to which actual pay is consistent with the pay policy. A compa-ratio less than 1.00 suggests that actual pay is lagging behind the policy, whereas a compa-ratio greater than 1.00 indicates that pay (and costs) exceeds that of the policy. Although there may be good reasons for compa-ratios to differ from 1.00, managers should also consider whether the pay structure is allowing costs to get out of control.

**Table 11.7**
Compa-Ratios for
Two Grades

| EMPLOYEE | JOB | PAY | MIDPOINT | EMPLOYEE COMPA-RATIOS |
|---|---|---|---|---|
| **Grade 1** | | | | |
| 1 | Engineering tech I | $3,690 | $3,480 | 1.06 |
| 2 | Computer tech | 3,306 | 3,480 | .95 |
| 3 | Engineering tech I | 4,037 | 3,480 | 1.16 |
| 4 | Engineering tech I | 3,862 | 3,480 | 1.11 |
| | | | Mean | **1.07** |
| **Grade 2** | | | | |
| 5 | Programmer analyst | 6,250 | 5,296 | 1.18 |
| 6 | Accountant | 6,037 | 5,296 | 1.14 |
| 7 | Accountant | 5,878 | 5,296 | 1.11 |
| | | | Mean | **1.15** |

## GLOBALIZATION, GEOGRAPHIC REGION, AND PAY STRUCTURES

As Figure 11.3 shows, market pay structures can differ substantially across countries both in terms of their level and in terms of the relative worth of jobs. Compared with cities in China, India, and Mexico, the labor markets in U.S. and German cities provide much higher levels of pay overall and also different payoffs to skill, education, and advancement. These differences create a dilemma for global companies. For example, should a German manager posted to Beijing be paid according to the standard in Germany or China? If the Germany standard is used, a sense of inequity is likely to exist among local Chinese peers in Beijing. If the China market standard is used, it may be all but impossible to find a German engineer willing to accept an assignment in Beijing. Typically,

**Figure 11.3**
Earnings in Selected Occupations, Six World Cities

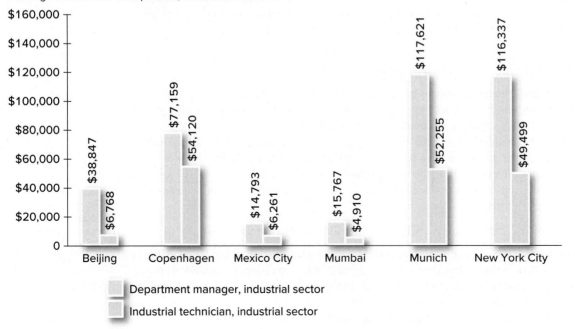

- Department manager, industrial sector
- Industrial technician, industrial sector

SOURCE: UBS, "Prices and Earnings 2018," Zurich, Switzerland.

expatriate pay and benefits (like housing allowance and tax equalization) continue to be linked more closely to the home country. However, this link appears to be slowly weakening and now depends more on the nature and length of the assignment.[22]

Grant V. Faint/Photodisc/Getty Images

Geographic location is an important factor for HR departments to consider when establishing a pay structure. Living in New York City is more expensive than other places, and employers need to factor in living costs when deciding on salaries so that they can hire a strong workforce.

Within the United States, companies often have either a formal or an informal policy that provides for pay differentials based on geographic location.[23] These differentials are intended to prevent inequitable treatment of employees who work in more expensive parts of the country. For example, according to Salary.com, the cost of living index for New York City is roughly 83% higher than in Madison, Wisconsin. Therefore, an employee receiving annual pay of $50,000 in Madison would require annual pay of $91,500 in New York City to retain the same purchasing power. The most common company approach is to move an employee higher in the pay structure to compensate for higher living costs. However, the drawback of this approach is that it may be difficult to adjust the salary downward if costs in that location fall or if the employee moves to a lower-cost area. Thus, some companies choose to pay an ongoing supplement that changes or disappears in the event of such changes.

# The Importance of Process: Participation and Communication

Compensation management has been criticized for following the simplistic belief that "if the right technology can be developed, the right answers will be found."[24] In reality, however, any given pay decision is rarely obvious to the diverse groups that make up organizations, regardless of the decision's technical merit or basis in theory. Of course, it is important when changing pay practices to decide which program or combination of programs makes the most sense, but how such decisions are made and how they are communicated also matter.[25]

**LO 11-4**
Discuss the significance of process issues such as communication in compensation management.

## PARTICIPATION

Employee participation in compensation decision making can take many forms. For example, employees may serve on task forces charged with recommending and designing a pay program. They may also be asked to help communicate and explain its rationale. This is particularly true in the case of job evaluation as well as many of the programs discussed in Chapter 12. To date, for what are perhaps obvious reasons, employee participation in pay-level decisions remains fairly rare.

It is important to distinguish between participation by those affected by policies and those who must actually implement the policies. Managers are in the latter group (and often in the former group at the same time). As in other areas of human resource management, line managers are typically responsible for making policies work. Their intimate involvement in any change to existing pay practices is, of course, necessary.

## COMMUNICATION

A dramatic example of the importance of communication was found in a study of how an organization communicated pay cuts to its employees and the effects on theft rates and perceived equity.[26] Two organization units received 15% across-the-board pay cuts. A third unit received no pay cut and served as a control group. The reasons for the pay cuts were communicated in different ways to the two pay-cut groups. In the "adequate explanation" pay-cut group, management provided a significant amount of information to explain its reasons for the pay cut and also expressed significant remorse. In contrast, the "inadequate explanation" group received much less information and no indication of remorse. The control group received no pay cut (and thus no explanation).

The control group and the two pay-cut groups began with the same theft rates and equity perceptions. After the pay cut, the theft rate was 54% higher in the "adequate explanation" group than in the control group. But in the "inadequate explanation" condition, the theft rate was 141% higher than in the control group. In this case, communication had a large, independent effect on employees' attitudes and behaviors.

Communication is likely to have other important effects. We know, for example, as emphasized by equity theory, that not only actual pay but also the comparison standard influence employee attitudes.[27] Under two-tier wage plans, employees doing the same jobs are paid two different rates, depending on when they were hired. Moreover, the lower-paid employees do not necessarily move into the higher-paying tier. Common sense might suggest that the lower-paid employees would be less satisfied, but this is not necessarily true. In fact, a study by Peter Cappelli and Peter Sherer found that the lower-paid employees were more satisfied on average.[28] Apparently, those in the lower tier used different (lower) comparison standards than those in the higher tier. The lower-tier employees compared their jobs with unemployment or lower-paying jobs they had managed to avoid. As a result, they were more satisfied, despite being paid less money for the same work. This finding does not mean that two-tier wage plans are likely to be embraced by an organization's workforce. It does, however, support equity theory through its focus on the way employees compare their pay with other jobs and the need for managers to take this into consideration. Employees increasingly have access to salary survey information, which is likely to result in more comparisons and thus a greater need for effective communication.

Managers play the most crucial communication role because of their day-to-day interactions with their employees.[29] Therefore, they must be prepared to explain why the pay structure is designed as it is and to judge whether employee concerns about the structure need to be addressed with changes to the structure. One common issue is deciding when a job needs to be reclassified because of substantial changes in its content. If an employee takes on more responsibility, he or she will often ask the manager for assistance in making the case for increased pay for the job.

# Challenges
## PROBLEMS WITH JOB-BASED PAY STRUCTURES

The approach taken in this chapter, that of defining pay structures in terms of jobs and their associated responsibilities, remains the most widely used in practice. However, job-based pay structures have a number of potential limitations.[30] First, they may encourage bureaucracy. The job description sets out specific tasks and activities for which the incumbent is responsible and, by implication, those for which the incumbent is not responsible. Although this facilitates performance evaluation and control by the manager, it can also encourage a lack of flexibility and a lack of initiative on the part of employees: "Why should I do that? It's not in my job description." Second, the structure's hierarchical nature reinforces top-down decision making and information flow as well as status differentials, which do not lend themselves to taking advantage of the skills and knowledge of those closest to production. Third, the bureaucracy required to generate and update job descriptions and job evaluations can become a barrier to change because wholesale changes to job descriptions can involve a tremendous amount of time and cost. Fourth, the job-based pay structure may not reward desired behaviors, particularly in a rapidly changing environment where the knowledge, skills, and abilities needed yesterday may not be very helpful today and tomorrow. Fifth, the emphasis on job levels and status differentials encourages promotion-seeking behavior but may discourage lateral employee movement because employees are reluctant to accept jobs that are not promotions or that appear to be steps down.

**LO 11-5**
Describe new developments in the design of pay structures.

## RESPONSES TO PROBLEMS WITH JOB-BASED PAY STRUCTURES
### Delayering and Banding

In response to the problems caused by job-based pay structures, some organizations have implemented **delayering**, or reducing the number of job levels to achieve more flexibility in job assignments and in assigning merit increases. Pratt & Whitney, for example, changed from 11 pay grades and 3,000 job descriptions for entry-level through middle-management positions to 6 pay grades and several hundred job descriptions.[31] These broader groupings of jobs are also known as *broad bands*. Table 11.8 shows how banding might work for a small sample of jobs.

**Delayering**
Reducing the number of job levels within an organization.

IBM greatly reduced the bureaucratic nature of the system, going from 5,000 job titles and 24 salary grades to a simpler 1,200 jobs and 10 bands. Within their broad bands, managers were given more discretion to reward high performers and to choose pay levels that were competitive in the market for talent.

One possible disadvantage of delayering and banding is a reduced opportunity for promotion. Therefore, organizations need to consider what they will offer employees instead. In addition, to the extent that there are separate ranges within bands, the new structure may not represent as dramatic a change as it might appear. These distinctions can easily become just as entrenched as they were under the old system. Broad bands, with their

| TRADITIONAL STRUCTURE | | BANDED STRUCTURE | |
|---|---|---|---|
| GRADE | TITLE | BAND | TITLE |
| 10 | Senior engineer | 5 | Senior engineer |
| 8 | Engineer II | 4 | Engineer |
| 6 | Engineer I | | |

**Table 11.8**
Example of Pay Bands

greater spread between pay minimums and maximums, can also lead to weaker budgetary control and rising labor costs. Alternatively, the greater spread can permit managers to better recognize high performers with high pay. It can also permit the organization to reward employees for learning.

### Paying the Person: Pay for Skill, Knowledge, and Competency

A second, related response to job-based pay structure problems has been to move away from linking pay to jobs and toward building structures based on individual characteristics such as skills or knowledge.[32] Competency-based pay is similar but usually refers to a plan that covers exempt employees (such as managers). The basic idea is that if you want employees to learn more skills and become more flexible in the jobs they perform, you should pay them to do it. (See Chapter 7 for a discussion of the implications of skill-based pay systems on training.) According to Gerald Ledford, however, it is "a fundamental departure" because employees are now "paid for the skills they are capable of using, not for the job they are performing at a particular point in time."[33]

**Skill-based pay**
Pay based on the skills employees acquire and are capable of using.

**Skill-based pay** systems seem to fit well with the increased breadth and depth of skill that changing technology continues to bring.[34] Indeed, research demonstrates that workforce flexibility is significantly increased under skill-based pay.[35] For example, in a production environment, workers might be expected not only to operate machines but also to take responsibility for maintenance and troubleshooting, quality control, and even modifying computer programs.[36] Toyota concluded years ago that "none of the specialists [e.g., quality inspectors, many managers, and foremen] beyond the assembly worker was actually adding any value to the car. What's more . . . assembly workers could probably do most of the functions of specialists much better because of their direct acquaintance with conditions on the line."[37]

In other words, an important potential advantage of skill-based pay is its contribution to increased worker flexibility, which in turn facilitates the decentralization of decision making to those who are most knowledgeable. It also provides the opportunity for leaner staffing levels because employee turnover or absenteeism can now be covered by current employees who are multiskilled.[38] In addition, multiskilled employees are important in cases where different products require different manufacturing processes or where supply shortages or other problems call for adaptive or flexible responses—characteristics typical, for example, of many newer so-called advanced manufacturing environments (like flexible manufacturing and just-in-time systems).[39] More generally, it has been suggested that skill-based plans also contribute to a climate of learning and adaptability and give employees a broader view of how the organization functions. Both changes should contribute to better use of employees' know-how and ideas. Consistent with the advantages just noted, a field study found that a change to a skill-based plan led to better quality and lower labor costs in a manufacturing plant.[40]

Of course, skill-based and competency-based approaches also have potential disadvantages.[41] First, although the plan will likely enhance skill acquisition, the organization may find it a challenge to use the new skills effectively. Without careful planning, it may find itself with large new labor costs but little payoff. In other words, if skills change, work design must change as quickly to take full advantage. Second, if pay growth is based entirely on skills, problems may arise if employees "top out" by acquiring all the skills too quickly, leaving no room for further pay growth. (Of course, this problem can also afflict job-based systems.) Third, and somewhat ironically, skill-based plans may generate a large bureaucracy—usually a criticism of job-based systems. Training programs need to be developed. Skills must be described, measured, and assigned monetary values. Certification tests must be developed to determine whether an employee has acquired a certain skill.

Finally, as if the challenges in obtaining market rates under a job-based system were not enough, there is almost no body of knowledge regarding how to price combinations of skills (versus jobs) in the marketplace. Obtaining comparison data from other organizations will be difficult until skill-based plans become more widely used.

## CAN THE U.S. LABOR FORCE COMPETE?

We often hear that U.S. labor costs are simply too high to allow U.S. companies to compete effectively with companies in other countries. The average hourly labor costs (cash and benefits) for manufacturing production workers in the United States and in other advanced industrialized and newly industrialized countries are given in Table 11.9 in U.S. dollars. The Competing through Globalization box provides some examples of recent production location decisions by companies that appear to have been significantly influenced by labor cost considerations.

**LO 11-6**
Explain where the United States stands on pay issues from an international perspective.

As we saw in Chapter 5 and in this chapter, companies continue to monitor labor costs and other factors in deciding where to locate production. Based solely on a cost approach, it would perhaps make sense to try to shift many types of production from a country like Germany to other countries, particularly the newly industrialized countries. Would this be a good idea? Not necessarily. There are several factors to consider.

### Instability of Country Differences in Labor Costs

First, note that relative labor costs are very unstable over time. For example, Table 11.9 shows that in 1985, U.S. labor costs were 36% greater than those of (West) Germany. But by 1990, the situation was reversed, with (West) German labor costs exceeding those of the United States by 44%, and remaining higher. Did German employers suddenly become

**Table 11.9**

Average Hourly Labor Cost (Cash and Benefits) for Production Workers in Manufacturing by Country and Year, in U.S. Dollars

| | 1985 | 1990 | 1995 | 2000 | 2005 | 2010 | 2015 | 2016 |
|---|---|---|---|---|---|---|---|---|
| **Industrialized** | | | | | | | | |
| Canada | $10.95 | $15.95 | $16.10 | $16.04 | $26.81 | $34.60 | $30.94 | $30.08 |
| Czech Republic | | | | 2.83 | 7.28 | 11.61 | 10.29 | 10.71 |
| Germany[a] | 9.57 | 21.53 | 30.26 | 23.38 | 38.18 | 43.83 | 42.42 | 43.18 |
| Japan | 6.43 | 12.64 | 23.82 | 22.27 | 25.56 | 31.75 | 23.60 | 26.46 |
| United States | 13.01 | 14.91 | 17.19 | 19.76 | 29.74 | 34.81 | 37.71 | 39.03 |
| **Newly industrialized** | | | | | | | | |
| Brazil | | | | 4.38 | 5.05 | 11.08 | 7.97 | 7.98 |
| China | | | | | 0.83 | 1.98 | 4.93[b] | 5.37[b] |
| Korea, Republic of | 1.25 | 3.82 | 7.29 | 8.19 | 15.13 | 17.73 | 22.68 | 22.98 |
| Mexico | 1.60 | 1.80 | 1.51 | 2.08 | 5.36 | 6.14 | 5.90 | 3.91 |
| Taiwan | 1.49 | 3.90 | 5.85 | 7.30 | 7.93 | 8.37 | 9.51 | 9.82 |

[a] West Germany for 1985 and 1990 data.

[b] Most recent Conference Board data for China were from 2014. The 2015 and 2016 estimates for China were obtained by inflating the 2014 Conference Board estimate based on wage inflation data from the National Bureau of Statistics of China.

SOURCES: Data from 1985–2010 are from the Bureau of Labor Statistics, U.S. Department of Labor, "International Comparisons of Hourly Compensation Costs in Manufacturing," various years. Data from post-2010 are from the Conference Board, "International Comparisons of Hourly Compensation Costs in Manufacturing, 2016," February 16, 2018.

more generous while U.S. employers clamped down on pay growth? Not exactly. Because our figures are expressed in U.S. dollars, currency exchange rates influence such comparisons, and these exchange rates often fluctuate significantly from year to year. For example, in 1985, when German labor costs were 74% of those in the United States, the U.S. dollar was worth 2.94 German marks. But in 1990 the U.S. dollar was worth 1.62 German marks. If the exchange rate in 1990 were still 1 to 2.94, the average German hourly wage in U.S. dollars would have been $11.80, or about 80% of the U.S. average in 1990 rather than the actual $21.53, or 144% of the U.S. average.

In any event, relative to countries like Germany, U.S. labor costs during many of the years shown in Table 11.9 have been lower. This explains, in part, decisions by German companies like BMW, Mercedes-Benz, and Volkswagen to locate production facilities in South Carolina, Alabama, and Tennessee, respectively, where labor costs are substantially lower than in Germany. Proximity to the large U.S. market and currency exchange hedging are other factors. More recently, as noted earlier, German automakers (and those from other countries) have been building new North American plants in Mexico for these reasons and because of Mexico's low labor costs. Finally, we see in Table 11.9 that from 2010 to 2015 labor costs have seemingly declined in a number of countries. Again, however, that is a function in many cases of the costs being expressed in U.S. dollars and fluctuating currency exchange rates, not a decline in labor costs in local currency. For example, in 2010, one Canadian dollar was worth 0.97 U.S. dollars, but by 2015, one Canadian dollar was worth only 0.78 U.S. dollars, a decline in value of roughly 20%. As such, when expressed in Canadian dollars (using Conference Board data not shown in the table), labor costs in the local currency grew in Canada from 35.46 in 2010 to 39.58 in 2015, an increase of roughly 12%.[42]

On the other side of the world, Foxconn (Hon Hai Precision) is a Taiwanese company that assembles Apple products such as the iPhone, mostly in plants in China, where it has roughly 1 million employees, including over 200,000 employees on its Longhua and Guanlan campuses in Shenzhen. Foxconn is said to be considering building a $7 billion facility (to provide display panels for Sharp) in the United States that would create a significant number of jobs.[43] (It turned out that Foxconn chose Wisconsin for this new investment.) However, by one estimate, the labor cost component of an iPhone assembled in Shenzhen, China, is less than one-quarter of what it would cost if assembled at a U.S. facility.[44] Some estimates are that the labor cost difference would be much larger, more consistent with the difference shown in Table 11.9.[45] Additionally, the supply chain (with suppliers having similarly lower labor costs) for Apple products is well established in Asia. Thus, moving any significant part of the production of Apple products to the United States would be a challenge. It is perhaps most likely in the case where shipping costs are high (e.g., display panels versus iPhones) and where political pressures and/or tariffs point to locating at least some production in such markets.

### Skill Levels

Second, the quality and productivity of national labor forces can vary dramatically. This is an especially important consideration in comparisons between labor costs in industrialized countries like the United States and developing countries like Mexico. For example, the high school graduation rate in the United States is 77% versus 44% in Mexico.[46] Thus, lower labor costs may reflect the lower average skill level of the workforce; certain types of skilled labor may be less available in low-labor-cost countries. By contrast, any given company needs only enough skilled employees for its own operations. Some companies have found that low labor costs do not necessarily preclude high quality.

As we have seen, many automakers have chosen Mexico for new plants to serve markets in North America. In Europe, countries such as Poland, Slovakia, and the Czech Republic have many skilled workers and lower labor costs than countries such as Germany, which has resulted in the expansion of production there and is also used as a bargaining chip when seeking more productive work rules at home.

## Productivity

Third, and most directly relevant, are data on comparative productivity and unit labor costs, essentially meaning labor cost per hour divided by productivity per hour worked. One indicator of productivity is gross domestic product (or total output of the economy) per person. On this measure, the United States fares well. (See Figure 11.4.) The combination of lower labor costs and higher productivity translates, at least on average, into lower unit labor costs in the United States than in Japan and western Europe.

## Considerations Other Than Labor Cost

Fourth, any consideration of where to locate production cannot be based on labor cost considerations alone. For example, although the average hourly labor cost in Country A may be $15 versus $10 in Country B, if labor costs are 30% of total operating costs and

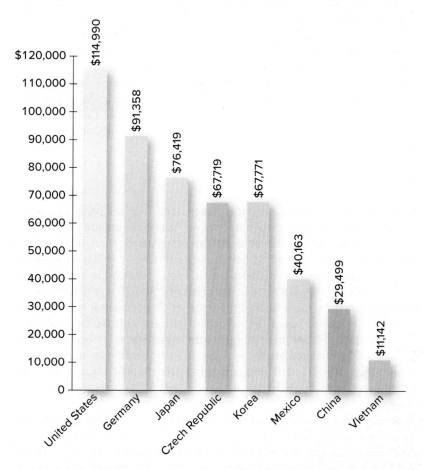

**Figure 11.4**

Gross Domestic Product per Worker, Adjusted for Purchasing Power Differences, U.S. Dollars

SOURCE: International Labor Organization, "Output per Worker (GDP constant 2011 international $ in PPP)," March 27, 2019, www.ilo.org/ilostat.

nonlabor operating costs are roughly the same, then the total operating costs might be $65 ($50 + $15) in Country A and $60 ($50 + $10) in Country B. Although labor costs in Country B are 33% less, total operating costs are only 7.7% less. This may not be enough to compensate for differences in skills and productivity, customer wait time, transportation costs, taxes, and so on. Further, the direct labor component of many products, particularly high-tech products (such as electronic components), may often be 5% or less. Therefore, the effect on product price-competitiveness may be less significant.[47]

Thus, the decision on where to locate production depends on labor costs but also on other factors. Being close to where customers are matters a great deal. Product development speed may be greater when manufacturing is physically close to the design group. Quick response to customers (as when making a custom replacement product) is difficult when production facilities are on the other side of the world. Inventory levels can be reduced dramatically through the use of manufacturing methods such as just-in-time production, but suppliers need to be in close physical proximity. The Competing through Globalization box provides an example of how these considerations, including labor costs, affect even a company like Tesla that does not see itself as being like other companies.

On the other hand, some firms are aggressively offshoring jobs (including professional or knowledge worker jobs) primarily to reduce labor costs. For example, financial services firms like Goldman Sachs and Citigroup now have significant numbers of employees in India doing statistical and research work at much lower pay levels.[48] As another example, IBM began to move thousands of programmer jobs overseas to countries such as China, where the hourly cost at the time was $12.50/hour versus $56/hour in the United States, potentially saving more than $100 million per year.[49] In some cases, companies using low-cost labor overseas have decided that those workers are paid too little and pay more than would be necessary simply to attract and retain enough workers. For example, a few years ago, European garment retailers including H&M and Zara wrote to the prime minister of Cambodia "pledging" to pay owners of Cambodian garment suppliers more so that they could pay their workers more. Subsequently, the garment industry wage increased by over 50%.[50]

## EXECUTIVE PAY

**LO 11-7**
Explain the reasons for the controversy over executive pay.

The issue of executive pay has been given widespread attention in the press. In a sense, the topic has received more coverage than it deserves because there are very few top executives and their compensation often accounts for a small share of an organization's total labor costs. However, top executives have a disproportionate ability to influence organization performance, so decisions about their compensation are critical. They can also be symbolic. During the global financial crisis of 2007–2008, the U.S. government, as part of the Troubled Asset Relief Program (TARP), decided it was appropriate to further regulate executive pay in firms receiving government "bailout" money.

Top executives also help set the tone or culture of the organization. If, for example, the top executive's pay seems unrelated to the organization's performance, with pay staying high even when business is poor, employees may not understand why some of their own pay is at risk and fluctuates (not only up, but also down), depending on how the organization is performing.

How much do executives make? Table 11.10 provides some data. Long-term compensation, typically in the form of stock plans, is the major component of CEO pay, which means that CEO pay varies with the performance of the stock market (see the "Annual Change in S&P 500" column). Table 11.11 shows that some CEOs are paid well above the medians/averages shown in Table 11.10.

## Where to Manufacture? Labor Costs and the Automobile Industry (including Tesla)

As Table 11.9 shows, average hourly labor cost (wages and benefits) vary greatly across countries. Car producers operate in competitive product markets, especially as product markets have globalized. Gone are the days when, for example, a customer in the United States could only buy a car sold by a U.S. company and made in the United States. Now, cars produced by U.S. companies are increasingly made elsewhere (e.g., Mexico), and cars sold in the United States may be sold by foreign companies but made in the United States (e.g., Toyotas built in Georgetown, Kentucky). Indeed, more cars are produced in the United States by foreign producers than by U.S. producers.

How do automobile companies decide where to produce cars? As we discussed in this section of the chapter, there are many factors, including workforce education/skills and productivity, proximity to customer, and so forth. However, labor cost continues to be a major consideration. If you take a look at the following exhibit, you can compare Labor Cost (per hour) across countries, including within three parts of the world: Europe, North America, and Asia. In each region, there are low-labor-cost and high-labor-cost countries.

| | LABOR COST (PER HOUR) | PRODUCTION (MILLIONS) | PRODUCTION (MILLIONS) | PRODUCTION % CHANGE |
|---|---|---|---|---|
| | 2005 | 2005 | 2017 | 2005 to 2017 |
| **Europe** | | | | |
| Germany | $38.18 | 5.76 | 5.65 | –2% |
| Czech Republic | $7.28 | 0.60 | 1.42 | 137 |
| **North America** | | | | |
| United States | $29.74 | 11.95 | 11.19 | –6 |
| Canada | $26.81 | 2.69 | 2.67 | –1 |
| Mexico | $5.36 | 1.68 | 4.07 | 142 |
| **Asia** | | | | |
| Japan | $25.56 | 10.80 | 9.69 | –10 |
| China | $0.83 | 5.72 | 29.02 | 407 |

SOURCE: International Organization of Motor Vehicle Manufacturers, http://www.oica.net/.

Can you guess where production grew and where it did not going forward from 2005? That's right: Production grew in low-labor-cost countries like the Czech Republic (137%), Mexico (142%), and China (407%). In contrast, production did not grow and indeed shrank somewhat in the high-labor-cost countries such as Germany (–2%), United States (–6%), Canada (–1%), and Japan (–10%). Similarly, many new automobile plants built or announced for North America in recent memory are in Mexico. (The NAFTA trade deal and its new incarnation, USMCA, play a role here.) Even when new plants are located within the United States, they are, with one recent exception, located in the southern part of the United States (e.g., BMW and Volvo in South Carolina, Daimler Benz in Alabama, Toyota in Kentucky and Alabama, Volkswagen in Tennessee), where not only are labor costs generally lower, but they are also lower because no plant in the southern United States has been successfully organized by a labor union, which brings higher wages and benefits costs.

Some expansion of production has occurred at union-organized

*CONTINUED*

automobile plants in the United States, in part because of success in recent contract negotiations (most recently in 2015) in which union-organized workers agreed (under the pressure of production continuing to relocate to lower-labor-cost locations) to lower wage and benefit costs. In summary, although the decision of where to locate production is not just about labor costs, it continues to be a dominant factor in such decisions.

Finally, consider a car company that many would say is unique: Tesla. Tesla is unique, but like the traditional automobile companies, it faces international competition and must control/reduce its labor costs, or otherwise risk not being able to sell its cars at a competitive price. As such, Tesla recently announced that it would reduce its workforce by 7%, or roughly 3,150 employees. One estimate is that Tesla production employees receive about $21 in wages per hour, which would imply an annual wage of about $44,000. Another estimate is considerably higher and says that employees most closely related to car production receive annual cash compensation of roughly $80,000. This estimate is higher for a number of reasons: It includes not only production workers, but also other employees, such as engineers, who are more highly paid. It also includes bonus payments and overtime hours.

Let's use $60,000 as the cost per worker. That does not include the cost of benefits such as health insurance. As we will see in Chapter 13, benefits add on average another $0.40 per dollar of wages. So, that brings us to $60,000 × 1.40 = $84,000/ employee. Once upfront costs of

the workforce reduction are considered (e.g., any severance pay, unemployment insurance tax increases that are based on number of former workers drawing unemployment insurance from the government), the projected savings per year would be 3,150 × $84,000 = $264.6 million. Consider that in the most recent 12-month period, according to Tesla's 10-Q report, its operating income was negative: It lost $535.5 million. So, the question is whether Tesla can continue to generate the same or greater revenue, while substantially reducing its costs through employment reductions. Its head, Elon Musk, described the challenge in an e-mail (also posted to the Tesla company blog) to employees: "Looking ahead at our mission of accelerating the advent of sustainable transport and energy, which is important for all life on Earth, we face an extremely difficult challenge: making our cars, batteries and solar products cost-competitive with fossil fuels. . . . we need to reach more customers who can afford our vehicles. Moreover, we need to continue making progress towards lower priced variants of Model 3." He continues: "As a result of the above, we unfortunately have no choice but to reduce full-time employee headcount by approximately 7% (we grew by 30% last year, which is more than we can support) and retain only the most critical temps and contractors. Tesla will need to make these cuts while increasing the Model 3 production rate and making many manufacturing engineering improvements in the coming months. Higher volume and manufacturing design improvements are crucial for

Tesla to achieve the economies of scale required to manufacture the standard range (220 mile), standard interior Model 3 at $35k and still be a viable company. There isn't any other way."

**DISCUSSION QUESTIONS**

1. How important do labor costs appear to be in determining where companies manufacture automobiles?

2. What factors other than labor costs do firms consider when making production location decisions. Are there differences across companies? If so, what factors explain these differences? For example, do General Motors and Tesla make these decisions the same or differently?

3. Under what circumstances is a firm most likely to emphasize low labor costs versus other factors in locating production? Is one factor the nature of the product? Do firms have some products that are more mass market and some that are more customized?

SOURCES: A. Roberts and J. J. Stoll, "Toyota Plant Puts Foreign Car Makers on Path to Pass Detroit in U.S. Production," *Wall Street Journal*, January 11, 2018; J. Kirby, "USMCA, the New Trade Deal between the US, Canada, and Mexico, Explained: NAFTA Gets an Upgrade with New Provisions on Autos, Dairy, and More," *VOX*, October 2, 2018, VOX.com; P. W. Howard, "UAW Grows Strike Fund, Membership as Workers Head into Wage Talks," *Detroit Free Press*, December 10, 2018; E. Musk, "Company Update," *Tesla Blog*, January 18, 2019, https://www.tesla.com/blog/tesla-company-update?redirect=no; E. Kosak, "Peeking behind Tesla's Labor Curtain," *CleanTechnical*, July 11, 2018, cleantechnical.com; L. Hansen, "Tesla Worker: Long Hours, Low Pay and Unsafe Conditions," *The Mercury News*, February 9, 2017, www.mercurynews.com; M. Snider, "Tesla to Cut Workforce by 7 percent, Increase Model 3 Production at Lower Prices," *USA TODAY*, January 18, 2019; U.S. Securities and Exchange Commission, "Form 10-Q, Tesla Inc.," November 2, 2018, www.sec.com.

**Table 11.10**

Realized CEO Compensation

| YEAR | CEO PAY | | | | | | ANNUAL CHANGE IN CEO PAY | ANNUAL CHANGE IN S&P 500 | WORKER PAY* | CEO PAY/ WORKER PAY** |
|---|---|---|---|---|---|---|---|---|---|---|
| | SALARY | BONUS | SALARY PLUS BONUS | STOCK OPTIONS | STOCK GRANTS*** | TOTAL PAY | | | | |
| 2017 | $1.1 million | $2.0 million | $3.1 million | $1.1 million | $5.6 million | $11.9 million | 3% | 19% | $40,393 | 295 |
| 2016 | 1.1 million | 2.0 million | 3.1 million | 1.1 million | 5.5 million | 11.5 million | 11 | 12 | 38,088 | 302 |
| 2015 | 1.1 million | 2.0 million | 3.1 million | 1.1 million | 5.1 million | 10.4 million | 1 | 1 | 37,186 | 280 |
| 2014 | 1.1 million | 2.1 million | 3.2 million | 1.2 million | 4.7 million | 10.3 million | 1 | 14 | 36,455 | 283 |
| 2013 | 1.1 million | 2.0 million | 3.1 million | 1.4 million | 4.2 million | 10.2 million | 11 | 32 | 35,555 | 287 |
| 2012 | 1.0 million | 1.9 million | 2.9 million | 1.3 million | 3.8 million | 9.2 million | 4 | 16 | 34,519 | 269 |
| 2011 | 1.0 million | 2.0 million | 3.0 million | 1.7 million | 3.3 million | 8.9 million | **** | 2 | 33,800 | 263 |
| 2010 | | | 3.0 million | 3.0 million | 2.5 million | 8.5 million | −29 | 15 | 33,119 | 258 |
| 2009 | | | 3.0 million | 3.3 million | 5.8 million | 12.1 million | −14 | 26 | 32,093 | 377 |
| 2008 | | | 3.6 million | 3.6 million | 6.9 million | 14.1 million | −18 | −37 | 31,617 | 446 |
| 2007 | | | 4.0 million | 4.9 million | 8.2 million | 17.1 million | 34 | 5 | 30,682 | 558 |
| 2006 | | | 3.8 million | 2.4 million | 6.5 million | 12.7 million | 3 | 16 | 29,529 | 431 |
| 2005 | | | 3.7 million | 2.1 million | 6.6 million | 12.4 million | — | — | 28,305 | 438 |
| 2000 | | | 2.9 million | 4.5 million | 7.0 million | 14.3 million | — | — | 25,013 | 573 |
| 1995 | | | 2.0 million | 0.7 million | 0.7 million | 3.3 million | — | — | 20,804 | 160 |
| 1990 | | | 1.6 million | 0.3 million | 0.7 million | 2.6 million | — | — | 18,187 | 144 |

*Worker pay (annual) is based on establishment survey data on earnings of production and nonsupervisory workers on private nonfarm payrolls, U.S. Bureau of Labor Statistics, *Employment & Earnings Online, Establishment Data from the Current Employment Statistics Survey* (CES), National, Table B-8a, https://www.bls.gov/opub/ee/archive.htm. The December average weekly earnings number is multiplied by 52 to obtain worker pay (annual).

**Ratio of CEO pay to hourly employee pay.

***Through 2010, "other" compensation is included in this category. In most cases, the value of stock grants accounts for most of pay in this category.

****Not computed due to change in definition of total compensation from a mean to a median.

NOTE: Through 2010, the three pay category averages of salary plus bonus, stock awards, and stock options add up to equal average total pay. Beginning in 2011, the pay categories do not add up to total pay because some compensation categories (non-equity incentive plan compensation, change in pension value and nonqualified deferred compensation earnings, all other compensation) reported in the Summary Compensation Table of company proxy statements are excluded and because medians are used.

SOURCES: Through 2010, CEO pay data are *averages* from *Forbes* magazine. Through 1999 (1995 here), *Forbes* data pertain to the 800 largest companies. Beginning with year 2000 through 2010, *Forbes* data pertain to the 500 largest U.S. companies (S&P 500). Beginning in 2011, CEO pay data pertain to the 500 largest U.S. companies (S&P 500) and are *medians* (versus averages) from Equilar, *CEO Pay Trends (multiple years)*, https://www.meridiancp.com/wp-content/uploads/Equilar-CEO-Pay-Trends-Report.pdf.

**Table 11.11**
Highest-Paid
Executives

| | TOTAL COMPENSATION |
|---|---|
| Hock E. Tan (Broadcom) | $103 million |
| Frank J. Bisignano (First Data) | 102 million |
| Michael Rapino (Live Nation Entertainment) | 71 million |

SOURCE: Grant Suneson. The Highest Paid CEOs of 2018. 24/7 Wall St. December 7, 2018. https://247wallst.com.

As Table 11.10 shows, the ratio of top-executive pay to that of an average worker has been around 300 recently. (The ratio is much higher in some earlier years, usually because in those years average rather than median CEO pay was measured. Average pay is always higher than median pay for CEOs.) The ratio in the United States is higher than in the other largest world economies (China, Japan, Germany, United Kingdom).[51] Such comparisons, however, typically do not adjust for the fact that U.S. CEOs lead larger companies than those in comparison countries. Large companies pay more.

This ratio (or differential) has been described as creating a "trust gap"—that is, in employees' minds, a "frame of mind that mistrusts senior management's intentions, doubts its competence, and resents its self-congratulatory pay." The issue becomes more salient when many of the same companies with high executive pay simultaneously engage in layoffs or other forms of employment reduction. Employees might ask, "If the company needs to cut costs, why not cut executive pay rather than our jobs?"[52] The issue is one of perceived fairness. One study, in fact, reported that business units with higher pay differentials between executives and rank-and-file employees had lower customer satisfaction, which was speculated to result from employees' perceptions of inequity coming through in customer relations.[53] An important factor to consider in assessing how much executives are paid is how they are paid (i.e., whether their pay is performance based). This is an issue we return to in Chapter 12.

# Government Regulation of Employee Compensation

We discuss equal employment opportunity, as well as minimum wage, overtime, and prevailing wage laws here. We also discuss regulation of executive compensation in Chapter 12.

### EQUAL EMPLOYMENT OPPORTUNITY

**LO 11-8**
Describe the
regulatory framework
for employee
compensation.

Equal employment opportunity (EEO) regulation (such as Title VII of the Civil Rights Act) prohibits sex- and race-based differences in employment outcomes such as pay, unless justified by business necessity (like pay differences stemming from differences in job performance). In addition to regulatory pressures, organizations must deal with changing labor market and demographic realities. At least two trends are directly relevant in discussing EEO.[54] First, whereas women represented 33% of all employees in 1960, they now make up 47% of all employees. Second, since 1960, the percentage of whites among all employees has dropped from 90% to 78%. White men now account for 43% of all U.S. employment, and that percentage will probably continue to decline, making attention to EEO issues in compensation even more important.

Is there equality of treatment in pay determination? Typically, the popular press focuses on raw earnings ratios. For example, among full-time workers, the ratio of female-to-male weekly median earnings is 0.80, the ratio of black-to-white earnings is 0.80, and the ratio of Hispanic/Latino-to-white earnings is 0.75.[55] These percentages have generally risen over the past two to three decades, but significant differences in pay clearly remain.[56] In contrast, Asian Americans earn 17% more than whites. Among executives, women appear to have lower pay than men, partly due to women being less likely to receive performance-based (e.g., stock and bonus-related) pay.[57]

The usefulness of raw percentages is limited, however, because some portion of earnings differences arises from differences in legitimate factors: education, labor market experience, and occupation. Adjusting for such factors reduces earnings differences based on sex and race or ethnicity, but significant differences remain. With few exceptions, such adjustments rarely account for more than half of the earnings differential.[58]

What aspects of pay determination are responsible for such differences? In the case of women, it is suggested that their work is undervalued. Another explanation rests on the "crowding" hypothesis, which argues that women were historically restricted to entering a small number of occupations. As a result, the supply of workers far exceeded demand, resulting in lower pay for such occupations. If so, market surveys would only perpetuate the situation.

**Comparable worth** (or pay equity) is a public policy that advocates remedies for any undervaluation of women's jobs. The idea is to obtain equal pay, not just for jobs of equal content (already mandated by the Equal Pay Act of 1963) but also for jobs of equal value or worth, on the basis of Title VII of the Civil Rights Act. Typically, job evaluation is used to measure worth. Table 11.12, which is based on Washington state data from one of the first comparable worth cases years ago, compares measures of worth based on internal comparisons (job evaluation) and external comparisons (market surveys).[59] Disagreements between the two measures are apparent. Internal comparisons suggest that women's jobs are underpaid, whereas external comparisons are less supportive of this argument. For example, although the licensed practical nurse job receives 173 job evaluation points and the truck driver position receives 97 points, the market rate (and thus the state of Washington employer rate) for the truck driver position was $1,493 per month versus only $1,030 per month for the nurse. The truck driver was paid 26.6% more than the pay policy line would predict, whereas the nurse is paid only 75.3% of the pay policy line prediction.

**Comparable worth**
A public policy that advocates remedies for any undervaluation of women's jobs (also called *pay equity*).

**Table 11.12**
Job Evaluation Points, Monthly Prevailing Market Pay Rates, and Proportion of Incumbents in Job Who Are Female

| BENCHMARK JOB TITLE | JOB EVALUATION POINTS | MARKET PAY | MARKET PAY AS PERCENTAGE OF PREDICTED PAY | PERCENT FEMALE IN JOB |
|---|---|---|---|---|
| Warehouse worker | 97 | $1,286 | 109.1% | 15.4% |
| Truck driver | 97 | 1,493 | 126.6 | 13.6 |
| Licensed practical nurse | 173 | 1,030 | 75.3 | 89.5 |
| Maintenance carpenter | 197 | 1,707 | 118.9 | 2.3 |
| Civil engineer | 287 | 1,885 | 116.0 | 0.0 |
| Registered nurse | 348 | 1,368 | 76.3 | 92.2 |
| Senior computer systems analyst | 384 | 2,080 | 113.1 | 17.8 |

NOTE: Predicted salary is based on regression of prevailing market rate on job evaluation points $2.43 \times$ job evaluation points $+ 936.19$, $r = 0.77$.

Based on job evaluation points, the value of the nurse is 78.3% (173/97 − 1) higher, not 31.0% (1 − $1,030/$1,493) lower as is seen in the market pay.

One potential problem with using job evaluation to establish worth independent of the market is that job evaluation procedures were never designed for this purpose.[60] Rather, as demonstrated earlier, their major use is in helping to capture the market pay policy and then applying that to nonkey jobs for which market data are not available. In other words, job evaluation has typically been used to help apply the market pay policy, quite the opposite of replacing the market in pay setting.

As with any regulation, there are also concerns that EEO regulation obstructs market forces, which, according to economic theory, provide the most efficient means of pricing and allocating people to jobs. In theory, moving away from a reliance on market forces would result in some jobs being paid too much and others too little, leading to an oversupply of workers for the former and an undersupply for the latter. In addition, some empirical evidence suggests that a comparable worth policy would not have much impact on the relative earnings of women in the private sector.[61] One limitation of such a policy is that it targets single employers, ignoring that men and women tend to work for different employers.[62] To the extent that segregation by employer contributes to pay differences between men and women, comparable worth would not be effective. In other words, to the extent that sex-based pay differences are the result of men and women working in different organizations with different pay levels, such policies will have little impact.

Perhaps most important, despite potential problems with market rates, the courts have consistently ruled that using the going market rates of pay is an acceptable defense in comparable worth litigation suits.[63] The rationale is that organizations face competitive labor and product markets. Paying less or more than the market rate will put the organization at a competitive disadvantage. Thus, there is no comparable worth legal mandate in the U.S. private sector.

However, by the early 1990s, almost half of the states had begun or completed comparable worth adjustments to public-sector employees' pay. In addition, in 1988 the Canadian province of Ontario mandated comparable worth in both the private and public sectors. Further, although comparable worth is not mandated in the U.S. private sector, the Department of Labor (Office of Federal Contracts Compliance), which enforces Executive Order 11246, put into place enforcement standards and guidelines in 2006 that prohibit race- or sex-based "systemic compensation discrimination," which it defines as a situation "where there are statistically significant compensation disparities (as established by a regression analysis) between similarly situated employees, after taking into account the legitimate factors which influence compensation, such as: education, prior work experience, performance, productivity, and time in the job."[64] Further, passage of the 2009 Lilly Ledbetter Fair Pay Act means that employers may face claims in situations where a discriminatory decision (e.g., too small of a pay raise) was made many years earlier, but the effect (lower pay) continues into the more current period.

Some work has focused on pinpointing where women's pay falls behind that of men. One finding is that the pay gap is wider where bonus and incentive payments (not just base salary) are examined. Other evidence indicates that women lose ground at the time they are hired and, in some cases, actually do better once they are employed for some time.[65] One interpretation is that when actual job performance (rather than the limited general qualification information available on applicants) is used in decisions, women may be less likely to encounter unequal treatment. If so, more attention needs to be devoted to ensuring fair treatment of applicants and new employees.[66] However, a "glass ceiling" is believed to exist in some organizations that allows women (and minorities) to come within sight of the top echelons of management, but not advance to them (see Melting the Glass Ceiling in Chapter 9). In many cases, however, women's lower salaries in previous jobs are perpetuated through the common employer practice of asking applicants what they earned on their previous jobs. Thus, as the Integrity in Action box describes, some companies have directed their recruiters to stop asking applicants about their salary histories and some states and locales now prohibit such questions.

It is likely, however, that organizations will differ in terms of where women's earnings disadvantages arise. For example, advancement opportunities for women and other protected groups may be hindered by unequal access to the "old boy" or informal network. This, in turn, may be reflected in lower rates of pay. Mentoring programs have been suggested as one means of improving access. Indeed, one study found that mentoring was successful, having a significant positive effect on the pay of both men and women, with women receiving a greater payoff in percentage terms than men.[67]

## MINIMUM WAGE, OVERTIME, AND PREVAILING WAGE LAWS

For covered ("nonexempt") employees, the 1938 **Fair Labor Standards Act (FLSA)** establishes a **minimum wage** for jobs, which now stands at $7.25/hour. State and local laws can (and often do) specify higher minimum wages. The FLSA also permits a subminimum training wage that is approximately 85% of the minimum wage, which employers are permitted to pay most employees under the age of 20 for a period of up to 90 days.

The FLSA also requires that nonexempt employees be paid at a rate of one and a half times their hourly rate for each hour of overtime worked beyond 40 hours in a week. The hourly rate includes not only the base wage but also other components such as bonuses and piece-rate payments. The FLSA requires overtime pay for any hours beyond 40 in a week that an employer "suffers or permits" the employee to perform, regardless of whether the work is done at the workplace or whether the employer explicitly asked or expected the employee to do it. If the employer knows the employee is working overtime but neither moves to stop it nor pays time and a half, a violation of the FLSA may have occurred. A department store was the target of a lawsuit that claimed employees were "encouraged" to, among other things, write thank-you notes to customers outside of scheduled work hours but were not compensated for this work. Although the company denied encouraging this off-the-clock work, it reached an out-of-court settlement to pay between $15 million and $30 million in back pay (plus legal fees of $7.5 million) to approximately 85,000 sales representatives it employed over a three-year period.[68]

Technology has helped create a sharing economy. With a touch of your smartphone, you can hail a car from Uber or schedule a housekeeper from Handy to clean your home or fix something in it. However, technology has also exposed gaps in employment law and raised challenges for workers and companies. Because these workers are often independent contractors, rather than employees, they are not covered by standard employment laws. Several sharing-economy companies have faced lawsuits by workers contending they should be treated as employees and thus be covered by FLSA requirements such as for overtime and a minimum wage. Although Uber's own study reported that its drivers make an average of $19/hour, that is before expenses. Drivers, especially those making less than $19/hour (gross), may not have a net wage that reaches the (federal) minimum wage of $7.25/hour, given that they supply their own vehicles and thus pay for expenses, including depreciation of their vehicles.[69]

Executive, professional, administrative, outside sales, and certain "computer employees" occupations are **exempt** from FLSA coverage. *Nonexempt* occupations are covered and include most hourly jobs. Exempt status depends on job responsibilities and salary.

**Fair Labor Standards Act (FLSA)**
The 1938 law that established the minimum wage and overtime pay.

**Minimum wage**
The lowest amount that employers are legally allowed to pay; the 1990 amendment of the Fair Labor Standards Act permits a subminimum wage to workers under the age of 20 for a period of up to 90 days.

**Exempt**
Employees who are not covered by the Fair Labor Standards Act. Exempt employees are not eligible for overtime pay.

## Making Questions about Salary History Off Limits

Companies such as Amazon and Bank of America say they have directed their recruiters not to ask candidates about the salary or benefits they receive(d) in current or previous jobs. At Bank of America, for example, recruiters have gone through training that includes focusing on the salary ranges/grades the bank has established for each job. If an applicant meets the requirements of a job, then he or she is to be paid accordingly.

There are also an increasing number of state and local laws that prohibit asking applicants about their salary histories. By one count, there are 12 state-wide bans and 10 local bans in place across the country. As one example, the state of California, as of January 1, 2018, prohibits private and public employers from seeking an applicant's salary history, and if the applicant volunteers his/her salary history, the employer is prohibited from using the information to set the pay level for the person if hired. On the other hand, the employer is required to provide applicants with salary information for the job.

What is the rationale for not asking about salary history? To the extent that current salaries reflect discrimination against certain demographic groups

(e.g., women), then deciding future salary based on past salary is likely to perpetuate such discrimination. Instead, the suggested alternative to achieving better pay equity is to assess applicant qualifications as objectively as possible and slot the new hire into the correct salary range and at the correct place in the salary range based on those qualifications, not on what a previous employer decided to pay for those qualifications.

Of course, not everyone agrees with the idea of not asking about salary histories. For example, a survey of chief human resource officers found that 65% believe it will do little to improve pay equity. However, 65% of these respondents also report that their organizations will be affected by new legislation (see above) on this issue. It is important to note that some states have gone in a different legislative direction. For example, Michigan and Wisconsin have a ban on salary history bans. In other words, employers may not be restricted from asking about salary history in those states. Still, as noted, some employers have chosen to voluntarily ban their recruiters from asking about salary history, in

hopes of not only achieving better pay equity, but also to demonstrate their commitment to pay equity to prospective employees, which may make them more attractive employers for some of those prospective employees and may also help retain current employees.

### DISCUSSION QUESTIONS

1. From the point of view of someone looking for a job, would you prefer that questions about your salary history be prohibited? Compare your thoughts to those of others in your class.

2. From the point of view of an employer, what are the pros and cons of a prohibition on asking questions about salary history? Are there steps that can be taken to replace salary history information in the pay-setting process? What are these?

SOURCES: "Salary History Bans: A Running List of States and Localities That Have Outlawed Pay History Questions," *HRDive*, January 10, 2019, www.hrdive.com; K. Gee, "Salary History Loses Impact on Hiring," *Wall Street Journal*, April 19, 2018; S. Milligan, "Salary History Bans Could Reshape Pay Negotiations," *HR News*, February 16, 2018, www.shrm.org; Korn Ferry, "Korn Ferry Executive Survey: New Laws Forbidding Questions on Salary History Likely Changes the Game for Most Employers," November 14, 2017, www.kornferry.com.

All exemptions (except for outside sales) require that an employee be paid no less than $684/week (or $35,568/year).[70]

The job responsibility criteria vary. For example, the executive exemption is based on whether two or more people are supervised; whether there is authority to hire and fire (or whether particular weight is given to the employee's recommendations); and whether the employee's primary duty is managing the enterprise, recognized department, or subdivision of the enterprise. The Wage and Hour Division (www.dol.gov/whd/), U.S. Department of Labor, and its local offices can provide further information on these definitions. (The exemptions do *not* apply to police, firefighters, paramedics, and other first responders.)

Two pieces of legislation—the Davis-Bacon Act of 1931 and the Walsh-Healey Public Contracts Act of 1936—require federal contractors to pay employees no less than the prevailing wages in the area. Davis-Bacon covers construction contractors receiving federal money of more than $2,000. Typically, prevailing wages have been based on relevant union contracts, partly because only 30% of the local labor force is required to be used in establishing the prevailing rate. Walsh-Healey covers all government contractors receiving $10,000 or more in federal funds.

Finally, employers must take care in deciding whether a person working on their premises is classified as an employee or an independent contractor. We return to this issue in Chapter 13.

## A LOOK BACK

### Pay Levels, Labor Costs, and Pay Strategy

We began this chapter with a look at some companies that have recently increased their pay levels and/or benefits. Although controlling compensation costs is important, it is especially important for some of these companies (e.g., Walmart) to be able to compete on price in their product markets. They also need to pay more to compete in their labor markets, which have become more competitive in recent years as the economy has recovered and grown and the unemployment rate has dropped. Not increasing compensation would make it more difficult to recruit and retain the quality of workforce needed. In the case of Walmart, contributing to its decision to increase pay levels was labor market competition as well as the need to better execute its business strategy, including improving the customer experience, which required better workforce quality. We also saw in this chapter how companies such as automobile makers continue to use relative labor cost as an important decision in where they locate production plants. Thus, pay level and pay structure decisions influence the success of strategy execution by influencing not only labor costs but also workforce quality, as well as employee perceptions of equity. Different pay structures can also vary in the degree to which they provide flexibility and incentives for employees to learn and be productive.

#### QUESTIONS

1. What types of changes have the companies discussed in this chapter made to their pay levels and pay structures to support execution of their business strategies?
2. Would other companies seeking to better align their pay structures with their business strategies benefit from imitating the changes made at these companies?

# SUMMARY

Equity theory suggests that social comparisons are an important influence on how employees evaluate their pay. Employees make external comparisons between their pay and the pay they believe is received by employees in other organizations. Such comparisons may have consequences for employee attitudes and retention. Employees also make internal comparisons between what they receive and what they perceive others within the organization are paid. These types of comparisons may have consequences for internal movement, cooperation, and attitudes (like organization commitment). Such comparisons play an important role in the controversy over executive pay, as illustrated by the focus of critics on the ratio of executive pay to that of lower-paid workers.

Pay benchmarking surveys and job evaluation are two administrative tools widely used in managing the pay level

and job structure components of the pay structure, which influence employee social comparisons. Pay surveys also permit organizations to benchmark their labor costs against other organizations. Globalization is increasing the need for organizations to be competitive in both their labor costs and productivity. The nature of pay structures is undergoing fundamental changes in many organizations, including the move to fewer pay levels to reduce labor costs and bureaucracy, and a shift by some employers from paying employees for narrow jobs to giving them broader responsibilities and paying them to learn the necessary skills. How a new compensation program is decided on, designed, implemented, and communicated is perhaps just as important as its core characteristics.

# KEY TERMS

Pay structure, 481
Pay level, 481
Job structure, 481
Efficiency wage theory, 490
Benchmarking, 490
Rate ranges, 491
Key jobs, 491

Nonkey jobs, 491
Job evaluation, 492
Compensable factors, 492
Pay policy line, 494
Pay grades, 495
Range spread, 496
Compa-ratio, 497

Delayering, 501
Skill-based pay, 502
Comparable worth, 511
Fair Labor Standards
    Act (FLSA), 513
Minimum wage, 513
Exempt, 513

# DISCUSSION QUESTIONS

1. You have been asked to evaluate whether your organization's current pay structure makes sense in view of what competing organizations are paying. How would you identify the organizations with which to compare your organization? Why might your organization's pay structure differ from those in competing organizations? What are the potential consequences of having a pay structure that is out of line relative to those of your competitors?

2. Top management has decided that the organization is too bureaucratic and has too many layers of jobs to compete effectively. You have been asked to suggest innovative alternatives to the traditional "job-based" approach to employee compensation and to list the advantages and disadvantages of these new approaches.

3. If major changes of the type mentioned in Question 2 are to be made, what types of so-called process issues need to be considered? Of what relevance is equity theory in helping to understand how employees might react to changes in the pay structure?

4. Are executive pay levels unreasonable? Why or why not?

5. Your company plans to build a new manufacturing plant but is undecided where to locate it. What factors would you consider in choosing in which country (or state) to build the plant?

6. You have been asked to evaluate whether a company's pay structure is fair to women and minorities. How would you go about answering this question?

# SELF-ASSESSMENT EXERCISE

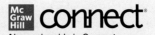

Also assignable in Connect.

Consider your current job or a job you had in the past. For each of the following pay characteristics, indicate your level of satisfaction by using the following scale: 1 = very dissatisfied; 2 = somewhat dissatisfied; 3 = neither satisfied nor dissatisfied; 4 = somewhat satisfied; 5 = very satisfied.

____ 1. My take-home pay
____ 2. My current pay
____ 3. My overall level of pay
____ 4. Size of my current salary
____ 5. My benefit package
____ 6. Amount the company pays toward my benefits
____ 7. The value of my benefits
____ 8. The number of benefits I receive
____ 9. My most recent raise
____ 10. Influence my manager has over my pay
____ 11. The raises I have typically received in the past
____ 12. The company's pay structure
____ 13. Information the company gives about pay issues of concern to me
____ 14. Pay of other jobs in the company
____ 15. Consistency of the company's pay policies
____ 16. How my raises are determined
____ 17. Differences in pay among jobs in the company
____ 18. The way the company administers pay

These 18 items measure four dimensions of pay satisfaction. Find your total score for each set of item numbers to measure your satisfaction with each dimension.

*Pay Level*
Total of items 1, 2, 3, 4, 9: _____
*Benefits*
Total of items 5, 6, 7, 8: _____
*Pay Structure and Administration*
Total of items 12, 13, 14, 15, 17, 18: _____
*Pay Raises*
Total of items 10, 11, 16: _____

Considering the principles discussed in this chapter, how could your company improve (or how could it have improved) your satisfaction on each dimension?

SOURCE: Based on H. G. Heneman III and D. P. Schwab, "Pay Satisfaction: Its Multidimensional Nature and Measurement," *International Journal of Psychology* 20 (1985), pp. 129–41.

# EXERCISING STRATEGY

## The Wealth Management Industry and the Drive to Lower Costs (and Increase Revenues)

Earlier, we saw that retailers such as Amazon and Walmart continually look for ways to control or reduce labor costs. In the examples we discussed, it was through automation. We also saw earlier that automobile companies share a similar focus on labor costs. Although they too have focused on automation, we highlighted their focus on increasingly locating automobile production in lower-labor-cost countries. Of course, white-collar jobs are not immune to the efficiency imperative driven by product market competition. Here, we focus on financial services and specifically wealth management. At a macro level, we focus on the advent of the index fund, a type of mutual fund whose creation is usually credited to Vanguard's John Bogle, who recently died. An index fund uses "passive" investment management rather than "active" management of investments on behalf of clients. For example, the original Vanguard index fund he created in 1975 sought to simply have its holdings mirror those of the S&P 500, rather than invest in significant research on each individual company and conducting related trades. As Bogle put it: "Don't look for the needle in the haystack. Just buy the haystack!" (The passive index fund was initially derided as "Bogle's folly.") The passive approach of an index fund requires fewer financial professionals to manage fund investments, thus allowing that investment firm to reduce its labor costs and thus charge clients lower fees to manage their investments. As the *Wall Street Journal* put it, "His campaign to cut fees put Mr. Bogle squarely into an American tradition of iconoclastic discounters like Henry Ford of Ford Motor, Sam Walton of Walmart and Michael Dell of Dell Inc.—men who built giant companies by selling directly to the consumer at rock-bottom prices." Before John Bogle, mutual funds charged an average annual feel of 0.5% per year, with some as high as 2.0%. They also charged "sales loads" (commissions) on transactions, of up to 8.5%. Soon, Vanguard had fees of 0.27% with no commissions and it became the largest mutual fund firm. (The creation in the tax code in 1978 of a new retirement vehicle, the 401(k), which went on to generate trillions in retirement assets to be invested, was also helpful.) Today, Vanguard's average fee is 0.10% and it is the second largest in the industry with $4.9 trillion in assets under management.

The search for lower costs and new revenue sources continues. For example, Merrill Lynch announced that it will reduce broker pay to reduce its costs. With 17,000 brokers, any savings adds up. Traditionally, brokers (also called financial advisers) were paid on the basis of "production," which refers to the fees they generate for managing clients' wealth and investments. In 2018, an adviser producing $1 million in fees would "keep" (earn) 42% of that, or $420,000. Going forward, that adviser would receive the same 42%, but on 97% of the $420,000, resulting in earnings of $0.97 \times \$420,000 = \$407,400$, a reduction of $12,600 or 3%. To re-capture that lost $12,600 and to earn more than what was lost, they will need to "cross-sell," which means persuading their wealth management clients to purchase other Merrill Lynch (or Bank of America, which acquired Merrill Lynch several years ago) products, such as mortgages, money market funds, checking accounts, and loans. This cross-selling strategy has been in the news of late as we will see when we come to the Exercising Strategy portion of Chapter 12, which includes a description of problems Wells Fargo encountered with its emphasis on cross-selling.) Some brokers say they feel "cheated out of pay they have earned" and are resistant to having to sell their customers, with whom they have often built close relationships, a slew of Bank of America products. Company executives, in contrast, see the change to the incentive structure for brokers as a strategy to "cut costs and juice growth."

## QUESTIONS

1. Describe the nature of the innovation in investing introduced by John Bogle and Vanguard. If need be, search for more information on the Web using terms like *active investing* and *passive investing*.
2. What happened to Vanguard's revenues in response to Vanguard driving its costs down?
3. Was John Bogle seen as an innovator when his idea was first introduced? What about now?
4. How is the change that has taken place in the wealth management industry currently playing out at Merrill Lynch?

SOURCES: L. Beilfuss, "Merrill Lynch Reduces Its Broker's Pay," *Wall Street Journal*, November 5, 2018; J. Zweig and S. Krouse, "John C. Bogle, Founder of Vanguard Group, Dies at 89," *Wall Street Journal*, January 17, 2019; J. Zweig, "What Drove Jack Bogle to Upend Investing," *Wall Street Journal*, January 18, 2019; No author, "Jack Bogle, the Financial Revolutionary," *Pensions & Investments*, January 21, 2019. www.pionline.com.

# MANAGING PEOPLE

## Reporting the Ratio of Executive Pay to Worker Pay: Is It Worth the Trouble?

Section 953(b) of the 2010 Dodd-Frank Wall Street Reform and Consumer Protection Act requires covered companies to report the ratio of annual total compensation of the chief executive officer (or any equivalent position) to the median of the annual total compensation of all other employees. In August 2015, the Securities and Exchange Commission (SEC) provided rules for companies to follow in computing and reporting the ratio.[71] However, following President Trump's election, on February 6, 2017, the acting chairman of the SEC stated "I have ... directed the staff to reconsider the implementation of the rule" until the SEC receives further public input. As such, the future of the rule is uncertain.

Supporters of the rule, such as the AFL-CIO labor organization, argue that reporting the ratio will help rein in what it sees as exorbitant (and growing) levels of executive pay, especially when compared to what has happened to worker pay. According to an analysis of S&P 500 firms by the AFL-CIO, the ratio of CEO pay to typical U.S. worker pay rose from 42 in 1980 to 380 more recently.

The AFL-CIO and other supporters of the rule hope it will also encourage boards of directors to consider whether worker pay, which has grown more slowly than inflation (and as indicated above, much more slowly than CEO pay), should be higher. The AFL-CIO also argues that research shows that larger pay differentials between CEOs and rank-and-file workers lead to poorer firm performance due to perceptions of inequity and the negative effects that has on worker morale and productivity. There is also a feeling that when CEOs get paid as much as they do, too much credit goes to them for a firm's success and not enough to other employees.

Many companies see things differently. David Hirschmann, head of the U.S. Chamber of Commerce's Center for Capital Markets, says the ratio is not meaningful or helpful to investors and will instead be used as "a political tool to attack companies." Companies argue that with a global workforce and different payroll systems in different countries, computing the ratio is much more difficult than it would seem. For example, the consulting firm Accenture has 246,000 employees in 120 countries and a variety of payroll systems (and definitions of pay in different countries). Jill Smart, head of human resources at Accenture, says that the work required to compute the ratio of CEO to worker pay would be "quite incredible."

Other companies, however, are already doing it and have done so for years. They say it is not that difficult or costly. Whole Foods, for example, capped the ratio of executive to front-line worker pay at 19 about a decade ago. Mark Ehrnstein, a vice president there, says that it does not take months, but rather a few days, and that it does not cost "millions of dollars" to calculate the ratio.

## QUESTIONS

1. Do you believe it is an undue burden on companies to compute and report the ratio of chief executive compensation to employee compensation? Why or why not?
2. Do you believe reporting this ratio will result in changes that benefit companies, employees, or society? Explain.

SOURCES: U.S. Securities and Exchange Commission, "SEC Adopts Rule for Pay Ratio Disclosure," Press Release 2015-160 (Washington, DC: Author, August 5, 2015), http://www.sec.gov/news/pressrelease/2015-160.html; G. Morgenson, "Despite Federal Regulation, C.E.O.–Worker Pay Gap Data Remains Hidden," *New York Times*, April 10, 2015; L. Kwoh, "Firms Resist New Pay-Equity Rules," *Wall Street Journal*, June 26, 2012; E. B. Smith and P. Kuntz, "CEO Pay 1,795-to-1 Multiple of Wages Skirts U.S. Law," www.bloomberg.com, April 29, 2013.

# HR IN SMALL BUSINESS

## Changing the Pay Level at Eight Crossings

Based in Sacramento, California, Eight Crossings provides transcription services for physicians, lawyers, hospitals, and authors. Its employees also answer phones, edit documents, and transcribe legal documents. The company's employees work either at the service center in Sacramento or in their homes, where they receive audio or text files via the Internet. In this way, Eight Crossings' employees can work in their specialty as needed without tying up a doctor's or attorney's office space.

Initially, the ease of sending files electronically was an advantage that enabled Eight Crossings to grow at a tremendous pace. But it has also opened up the company to competition from similar services provided from low-wage locations such as India. In addition, as voice recognition software has improved, automation could take over some of the processes that have been handled by skilled, experienced transcribers.

In that situation, Eight Crossings CEO Patrick Maher felt the pressure when clients began to ask him for a lower rate. Most of the costs of running Eight Crossings are related to labor. Overhead and materials are minimal for this type of work. Consequently, for Maher to offer his clients a better price, he would have to cut what he paid employees or stop earning a profit.

The pay level at Eight Crossings had been about 5% above the average for the industry. Maher believed that this pay strategy gave his company an advantage in recruiting and keeping the best transcribers. Pay was calculated per line of text at a rate that varied according to the complexity of the material being transcribed. Depending on how many hours they worked and how complex the jobs they took, each transcriber earned between $20,000 and $70,000 a year.

In looking for ways to trim expenses, Maher considered that part of most documents included sections of boilerplate text. These are generated automatically by transcribers' software but were included in the number of lines for which the transcribers were paid. Maher concluded these amounted to a 5% bonus paid for each assignment. Maher decided he could cut transcribers' pay by 5% and in effect still pay them the same rate for what they were actually transcribing (but without the "bonus").

That pay cut would bring pay levels at Eight Crossings down to the market rate. Would that mean employees would leave for greener pastures? Maher guessed not, considering that his company was receiving résumés from experienced transcribers looking for work.

Maher's next challenge was how to communicate the pay cut to employees working in 22 locations, many working from home and communicating with the office electronically. He began by discussing the situation with the company's eight supervisors, who check the transcribers' work for quality. This prepared them to address employees' concerns. Next, he sent an e-mail to the transcribers, explaining the reasons for the change and inviting questions.

Maher's fears about the pay cut were not realized. Employees expressed understanding of the move and appreciation for his commitment to continue sending work to U.S. workers. And because Eight Crossings is paying the market rate, moving to another company would not offer employees an advantage in terms of pay.

## QUESTIONS

1. How did the change in pay level at Eight Crossings affect its ability to attract and retain a high-quality workforce?
2. Do you think the company's pay structure was better suited to its objectives before or after the reduction in pay level? Why?
3. How would you evaluate the company's method of communicating the change in pay level? What improvements to that process can you suggest?

SOURCES: D. Dahl, "Special Financial Report: Employee Compensation," *Inc.*, July 2009; Eight Crossings, corporate website, www.eightcrossings.com, accessed May 30, 2015, and "Company Profile: No. 609, Eight Crossings," Inc. 500/5000 (2000), www.inc.com.

# NOTES

1. N. Irwin, "How Did Walmart Get Cleaner Stores and Higher Sales? It Paid Its People More," *New York Times*, October 15, 2016.

2. J. S. Adams, "Inequity in Social Exchange," in *Advances in Experimental Social Psychology*, ed. L. Berkowitz (New York: Academic Press, 1965); P. S. Goodman, "An Examination of Referents Used in the Evaluation of Pay," *Organizational Behavior and Human Performance* 12 (1974), pp. 170-95; C. O. Trevor and D. L. Wazeter, "A Contingent View of Reactions to Objective Pay Conditions: Interdependence among Pay Structure Characteristics and Pay Relative to Internal and External Referents," *Journal of Applied Psychology* 91 (2006), pp. 1260-1275; M. M. Harris, F. Anseel, and F. Lievens, "Keeping Up with the Joneses: A Field Study of the Relationships among Upward, Lateral, and Downward Comparisons and Pay Level Satisfaction," *Journal of Applied Psychology* 93, no. 3 (May 2008), pp. 665-73; Gordon D. A. Brown, Jonathan Gardner, Andrew J. Oswald, Jing Qian, "Does Wage Rank Affect Employees' Well-being?" *Industrial Relations* 47, no. 3 (July 2008), p. 355; D. Card, M. Alexandre, E. Moretti, and E. Saez, "Inequality at Work: The Effect of Peer Salaries on Job Satisfaction," *American Economic Review* 102 (2012), pp. 2981-3003; E. Della Torre, M. Pelagatti, and L. Solari, "Internal and External Equity in Compensation Systems, Organizational Absenteeism, and the Role of the Explained Inequalities," *Human Relations* 68 (2015), pp. 409-40. D. E. Rupp, D. L. Shapiro, R. Folger, D. P. Skarlicki, and R. Shao, "A Critical Analysis of the Conceptualization and Measurement of Organizational Justice: Is It Time for Reassessment?" *Academy of Management Annals* 11, 2 (2017), pp. 919-59.

3. J. B. Miner, *Theories of Organizational Behavior* (Hinsdale, IL: Dryden Press, 1980); B. Gerhart and S. L. Rynes, *Compensation: Theory, Evidence, and Strategic Implications* (Thousand Oaks, CA: Sage, 2003).

4. J. R. Keller, "Posting and Slotting: How Hiring Processes Shape the Quality of Hire and Compensation in Internal Labor Markets," *Administrative Science Quarterly*, 63 (2018), p. 848-78; A. Kacperczyk and C. Balachandran, "Vertical and Horizontal Wage Dispersion and Mobility Outcomes: Evidence from the Swedish Microdata," *Organization Science* 29, no. 1 (2018), pp. 17-38; M. J. Bidwell, "Paying More to Get Less: The Effects of External Hiring versus Internal Mobility," *Administrative Science Quarterly,* 56 (2011),pp. 369-407; E. P. Lazear and S. Rosen, "Rank-Order Tournaments as Optimum Labor Contracts," *Journal of Political Economy* 89, no. 5 (1981), pp. 841-64; T. Y. Park, S. Kim, and L. K. Sung, "Fair Pay Dispersion: A Regulatory Focus Theory View," *Organizational Behavior and Human Decision Processes* 142 (2017), pp. 1-11.

5. B. Gerhart and G. T. Milkovich, "Employee Compensation: Research and Practice," in *Handbook of Industrial and Organizational Psychology*, 2nd ed., ed. M. D. Dunnette and L. M. Hough (Palo Alto, CA: Consulting Psychologists Press, 1992); G. T. Milkovich, J. M. Newman, and B. Gerhart, *Compensation*, 11th ed. (New York: McGraw-Hill/Irwin, 2014).

6. M. Martinez, "Ford: Labor Costs Up about 1.5% Yearly after UAW Deal," *Detroit News*, November 30, 2015; B. Snavely, "Chrysler Has Lowest per Worker Labor Costs," *Detroit Free Press*, March 23, 2015; D. Barkholz, "Can UAW Fix Tier 2 Disparity? Return to Pattern Bargaining Unlikely," *Automotive News*, March 8, 2015;

K. Naughton, "Detroit Worker Bonuses Approach Records on Rising Profits," *Bloomberg Businessweek*, February 13, 2015.

7. Mike Ramsey, "VW Chops Labor Costs in U.S.," *Wall Street Journal*, May 23, 2011, http://online.wsj.com/article/SB10001424 052748704083904576335501132396440.html; Mark Guarino, "Lower Wages Now at Big Three Automakers, But New Hires Aren't Whining," *Christian Science Monitor*, May 7, 2013.

8. Snavely, "Chrysler Has Lowest per Worker Labor Costs"; J. D. Stoll, "Volvo to Open Plant in U.S., State to Be Chosen in a Month; Car Maker Says Labor Rates Are Just Part of It," *Wall Street Journal*, March 30, 2015.

9. J. D. Stoll, "Volvo to Open Plant in U.S., State to Be Chosen in a Month; Car Maker Says Labor Rates Are Just Part of It," *Wall Street Journal*, March 30, 2015; Diana T. Kurylko, "Volvo's Catch-Up Game: South Carolina's European Supply Base Makes Things Easier for Automaker," *Automotive News*, August 1, 2016.

10. C. Chadwick, "Towards a More Comprehensive Model of Firms' Human Capital Rents," *Academy of Management Review*, November 12, 2015, doi:10.5465/amr.2013.0385; W. F. Cascio and J. W. Boudreau, *Investing in People: Financial Impact of Human Resource Initiatives*, 2nd ed. (Upper Saddle River, NJ: Pearson Financial Times Press, 2010); I. S. Fulmer and R. E. Ployhart, "Our Most Important Asset: A Multidisciplinary/Multilevel Review of Human Capital Valuation for Research and Practice," *Journal of Management*, November 12, 2013; I. S. Fulmer, B. Gerhart, and K. S. Scott, "Are the 100 Best Better? An Empirical Investigation of the Relationship between Being a 'Great Place to Work' and Firm Performance," *Personnel Psychology* 56 (2003), pp. 965-93; A. Edmans, "Does the Stock Market Fully Value Intangibles? Employee Satisfaction and Equity Prices," *Journal of Financial Economics* 101 (3), pp. 621-40.

11. B. Gerhart and G. T. Milkovich, "Organizational Differences in Managerial Compensation and Financial Performance," *Academy of Management Journal* 33 (1990), pp. 663-91; E. L. Groshen, "Why Do Wages Vary among Employers?" *Economic Review* 24 (1988), pp. 19-38; Gerhart and Rynes, *Compensation*.

12. J. D. Shaw, "Pay Levels and Pay Changes," in *Handbook of Industrial, Work and Organizational Psychology* (2014), Thousand Oaks, CA: Sage; A. L. Heavey, J. A. Holwerda, and J. P. Hausknecht, "Causes and Consequences of Collective Turnover: A Meta-Analytic Review," *Journal of Applied Psychology* 98, no. 3 (2013), p. 412; M. L. Williams, M. A. McDaniel, N. T. Nguyen, "A Meta-Analysis of the Antecedents and Consequences of Pay Level Satisfaction," *Journal of Applied Psychology* 91 (2006), pp. 392-413; M. C. Sturman, C. O. Trevor, J. W. Boudreau, and B. Gerhart, "Is It Worth It to Win the Talent War? Evaluating the Utility of Performance-Based Pay," *Personnel Psychology* 56 (2003), pp. 997-1035; B. Klaas and J. A. McClendon, "To Lead, Lag or Match: Estimating the Financial Impact of Pay Level Policies," *Personnel Psychology* 49 (1996), pp. 121-41; S. C. Currall, A. J. Towler, T. A. Judge, and L. Kohn, "Pay Satisfaction and Organizational Outcomes," *Personnel Psychology* 58 (2005), pp. 613-40; M. P. Brown, M. C. Sturman, and M. J. Simmering, "Compensation Policy and Organizational Performance: The Efficiency, Operational, and Financial Implications of Pay Levels and Pay Structures," *Academy of Management Journal* 46 (2003), pp. 752-62; Eric A. Verhoogen, Stephen V. Burks, and Jeffrey P. Carpenter, "Fairness and Freight-Handlers: Local Labor Market Conditions and Wage-Fairness Perceptions in a Trucking Firm,"

*Industrial & Labor Relations Review* 60, no. 4 (July 2007), p. 477; T. A. Judge, R. F. Piccolo, N. P. Podsakoff, J. C. Shaw, and B. L. Rich, "The Relationship between Pay and Job Satisfaction: A Meta-Analysis of the Literature," *Journal of Vocational Behavior* 77 (2010), pp. 157–67; M. Subramony, N. Krause, J. Norton, and G. N. Burns, "The Relationship between Human Resource Investments and Organizational Performance: A Firm-Level Examination of Equilibrium Theory," *Journal of Applied Psychology* 93 (2008), pp. 778–88; J. P. Hausknecht and C. O. Trevor, "Collective Turnover at the Group, Unit, and Organizational Levels: Evidence, Issues, and Implications," *Journal of Management* 37 (2011), pp. 352–88; A. L. Heavey, J. A. Holwerda, and J. P. Hausknecht, "Causes and Consequences of Collective Turnover: A Meta-Analytic Review," *Journal of Applied Psychology* 98 (2013), pp. 412–53.

13. G. A. Akerlof, "Gift Exchange and Efficiency-Wage Theory: Four Views," *American Economic Review* 74 (1984), pp. 79–83; J. L. Yellen, "Efficiency Wage Models of Unemployment," *American Economic Review* 74 (1984), pp. 200–5.

14. J. McGregor, "Zappos to Employees: Get Behind Our 'No Bosses' Approach, or Leave with Severance," *Washington Post*, March 31, 2015; K. Peterson, "Why Amazon Pays Employees $5,000 to Quit," *CBS Moneywatch*, April 11, 2014, http://www.cbsnews.com/news/amazon-pays-employees-5000-to-quit/.

15. S. L. Rynes and G. T. Milkovich, "Wage Surveys: Dispelling Some Myths about the Market Wage," *Personnel Psychology* 39 (1986), pp. 71–90; R. J. Greene, "Compensation Surveys: The Rosetta Stones of Market Pricing," *World at Work*, 2014, 1st Quarter, pp. 23–31.

16. B. Gerhart and G. T. Milkovich, "Employee Compensation: Research and Practice," in *Handbook of Industrial and Organizational Psychology*, 2nd ed., ed. M. D. Dunnette and L. M. Hough (Palo Alto, CA: Consulting Psychologists Press, 1992).

17. Milkovich, Newman, and Gerhart, *Compensation*, 11th ed.

18. B. Gerhart, G. T. Milkovich, and B. Murray, "Pay, Performance, and Participation," in *Research Frontiers in Industrial Relations and Human Resources*, ed. D. Lewin, O. S. Mitchell, and P. D. Sherer (Madison, WI: IRRA, 1992).

19. C. H. Fay, "External Pay Relationships," in *Compensation and Benefits*, ed. L. R. Gomez-Mejia (Washington, DC: Bureau of National Affairs, 1989).

20. J. P. Pfeffer and A. Davis-Blake, "Understanding Organizational Wage Structures: A Resource Dependence Approach," *Academy of Management Journal* 30 (1987), pp. 437–55; M. A. Carpenter and J. B. Wade, "Micro-level Opportunity Structures as Determinants of Non-CEO Executive Pay," *Academy of Management Journal* 45 (2002), pp. 1085–103.

21. M. Bidwell, F. Briscoe, I. Fernandez-Mateo, and A. Sterling, "The Employment Relationship and Inequality: How and Why Changes in Employment Practices Are Reshaping Rewards in Organizations," *Academy of Management Annals* 7, no. 1 (2013), pp. 61–121; G. E. Ledford, "The Changing Landscape of Employee Rewards: Observations and Prescriptions," *Organizational Dynamics* 43, no. 3 (2014), pp. 168–79; Milkovich, Newman, and Gerhart, *Compensation*, 11th ed.

22. C. M. Solomon, "Global Compensation: Learn the ABCs," *Personnel Journal*, July 1995, p. 70; R. A. Swaak, "Expatriate Management: The Search for Best Practices," *Compensation and Benefits Review*, March/April 1995, p. 21.

23. *1997-1998 Survey of Geographic Pay Differential Policies and Practices* (Rochester, WI: Runzeimer International); M. C. Sturman, A. D. Ukhov, and S. Park, "The Effect of Cost of Living on Employee Wages in the Hospitality Industry," *Cornell Hospitality Quarterly*, 58(2) (2017), pp. 179–89.

24. E. E. Lawler III, *Pay and Organizational Development* (Reading, MA: Addison-Wesley, 1981).

25. R. Folger and M. A. Konovsky, "Effects of Procedural and Distributive Justice on Reactions to Pay Raise Decisions," *Academy of Management Journal* 32 (1989), pp. 115–30; H. G. Heneman III and T. A. Judge, "Compensation Attitudes," in S. L. Rynes and B. Gerhart, eds., *Compensation in Organizations* (San Francisco: Jossey-Bass, 2002), pp. 61–103; J. Greenberg, "Determinants of Perceived Fairness of Performance Evaluations," *Journal of Applied Psychology* 71 (1986), pp. 340–42; H. G. Heneman III, "Pay Satisfaction," *Research in Personnel and Human Resource Management* 3 (1985), pp. 115–39.

26. J. Greenberg, "Employee Theft as a Reaction to Underpayment of Inequity: The Hidden Cost of Pay Cuts," *Journal of Applied Psychology* 75 (1990), pp. 561–68.

27. Adams, "Inequity in Social Exchange"; C. J. Berger, C. A. Olson, and J. W. Boudreau, "The Effect of Unionism on Job Satisfaction: The Role of Work-Related Values and Perceived Rewards," *Organizational Behavior and Human Performance* 32 (1983), pp. 284–324; P. Cappelli and P. D. Sherer, "Assessing Worker Attitudes under a Two-Tier Wage Plan," *Industrial and Labor Relations Review* 43 (1990), pp. 225–44; R. W. Rice, S. M. Phillips, and D. B. McFarlin, "Multiple Discrepancies and Pay Satisfaction," *Journal of Applied Psychology* 75 (1990), pp. 386–93.

28. Cappelli and Sherer, "Assessing Worker Attitudes."

29. S. Marasi and R. J. Bennett, "Pay Communication: Where Do We Go from Here?" *Human Resource Management Review* 26 (2016), pp. 50–58; I. S. Fulmer and Y. Chen, "How Communication Affects Employee Knowledge of and Reactions to Compensation Systems," in V. Miller and M. Gordon, eds., *Meeting the Challenge of Human Resource Management: A Communication Perspective* (New York: Routledge/Taylor & Francis, 2014), pp. 167–78; I. Caron, A. K. Ben-Ayed, and C. Vandenberghe, "Collective Incentive Plans, Organizational Justice and Commitment," *Relations Industrielles/Industrial Relations* 68, no. 1 (2013).

30. R. M. Kanter, *When Giants Learn to Dance* (New York: Simon & Schuster, 1989); E. E. Lawler III, *Strategic Pay* (San Francisco: Jossey-Bass, 1990); "Farewell, Fast Track," *Bloomberg Businessweek*, December 10, 1990, pp. 192–200; R. L. Heneman, G. E. Ledford, Jr., and M. T. Gresham, "The Changing Nature of Work and Its Effects on Compensation Design and Delivery," in S. L. Rynes and B. Gerhart, eds., *Compensation in Organizations*.

31. P. R. Eyers, "Realignment Ties Pay to Performance," *Personnel Journal*, January 1993, p. 74.

32. Lawler, *Strategic Pay*; G. Ledford, "3 Cases on Skill-Based Pay: An Overview," *Compensation and Benefits Review*, March/April 1991, pp. 11–23; G. E. Ledford, "Paying for the Skills, Knowledge, Competencies of Knowledge Workers," *Compensation and Benefits Review*, July/August 1995, p. 55; Heneman et al., "The Changing Nature of Work"; G. Ledford, "Factors Affecting the Long-Term Success of Skill-Based Pay," *WorldatWork Journal*, First Quarter (2008), pp. 6–18; J. Canavan, "Overcoming the Challenge of Aligning Skill-Based Pay Levels to the External Market," *WorldatWork Journal*, First Quarter (2008), pp. 18–24; E. C. Dierdorff and E. A. Surface, "If You Pay for Skills, Will They Learn? Skill Change and Maintenance Under a Skill-Based Pay System," *Journal of Management* 34 (2008), pp. 721–43.

33. Ledford, "3 Cases."

34. Heneman et al., "The Changing Nature of Work."

35. A. Mitra, N. Gupta, and J. D. Shaw. "A Comparative Examination of Traditional and Skill-Based Pay Plans," *Journal of Managerial Psychology* 26 (2011), pp. 278–96.

36. T. D. Wall, J. M. Corbett, R. Martin, C. W. Clegg, and P. R. Jackson, "Advanced Manufacturing Technology, Work Design, and Performance: A Change Study," *Journal of Applied Psychology* 75 (1990), pp. 691–97.

37. J. P. Womack, D. T. Jones, D. Roos, and D. S. Carpenter, *The Machine That Changed the World: Based on the Massachusetts Institute of Technology 5-Million Dollar 5-Year Study on the Future of the Automobile* (New York: Rawson Assoc., 1990), p. 56.

38. Lawler, *Strategic Pay.*

39. Lawler, *Strategic Pay*; Gerhart and Milkovich, "Employee Compensation."

40. B. C. Murray and B. Gerhart, "An Empirical Analysis of a Skill-Based Pay Program and Plant Performance Outcomes," *Academy of Management Journal* 41, no. 1 (1998), pp. 68–78.

41. B. C. Murray and B. Gerhart, "An Empirical Analysis of a Skill-Based Pay Program and Plant Performance Outcomes," *Academy of Management Journal* 41, no. 1 (1998), pp. 68–78; N. Gupta, D. Jenkins, and W. Curington, "Paying for Knowledge: Myths and Realities," *National Productivity Review*, Spring 1986, pp. 107–23; J. D. Shaw, N. Gupta, A. Mitra, and G. E. Ledford, "Success and Survival of Skill-Based Pay Plans," *Journal of Management* 31 (2005), pp. 28–49.

42. *The Conference Board International Labor Comparisons, Manufacturing Hourly Compensation Costs, Data 1996–2015*, https://www.conference-board.org/ilcprogram/index.cfm?id=18777.

43. M. Snider, "Foxconn May Build $7B Plant in U.S.," *USA Today*, January 23, 2017, https://www.usatoday.com/story/tech/news/2017/01/23/foxconn-may-build-7b-plant-us/96945414/.

44. M. Lau, "Would US Workers Really Want the Jobs That Have Gone to China?" *South China Morning Post*, January 29, 2017, http://www.scmp.com/news/china/policies-politics/article/2059590/would-us-workers-really-want-jobs-have-gone-china.

45. R. Jennings, "Foxconn May Follow, If Trump Pulls US Tech Companies Back to America," *South China Morning Post*, December 29, 2016, http://www.scmp.com/business/article/2057959/foxconn-may-follow-if-trump-pulls-us-tech-companies-back-america.

46. *Education at a Glance—OECD Indicators* 2010, www.OECD.org.

47. M. Hayes, "Precious Connection: Companies Thinking about Using Offshore Outsourcing Need to Consider More than Just Cost Savings," *Information Week*, October 20, 2003; Harold L. Sirkin et al., "Made in America Again," Boston Consulting Group, August 2011; K. Chu, "Not Made in China," *Wall Street Journal*, May 1, 2013; Y. Zhang, "China Begins to Lose Edge as World's Factory Floor," *Wall Street Journal*, January 17, 2013; A. Fox, "America, Inc.: More U.S. Manufacturers Are Making a U-turn on Offshoring," *HR Magazine*, May 2013, pp. 45–48.

48. Heather Timmons, "Cost-Cutting in New York, but a Boom in India," *New York Times*, August 12, 2008, p. C1. Reprinted with permission of PARS International.

49. W. Bulkeley, "IBM Documents Give Rare Look at Sensitive Plans on 'Offshoring,'" *Wall Street Journal*, January 19, 2004; D. Wessel, "Big U.S. Firms Shift Hiring Abroad," *Wall Street Journal*, April 19, 2011.

50. C. Larson, "Cambodia's Wages Rise, Orders Don't. A Year after Garment Worker Strikes, Pay Is up 63 Percent," *Bloomberg Businessweek*, February 5, 2015; T. Wright, "Stores Propose Higher Wages in Asia," *Wall Street Journal*, October 15, 2014, p. B8; J. Hookway and S. Narin, "Cambodia Sets Minimum Wage below Union Demands," *Wall Street Journal*, November 12, 2014.

51. W. Liu and A. Melin, "The Best and Worst Countries to Be a Rich CEO," *Bloomberg Businessweek*, November 16, 2016.

52. A. Farnham, "The Trust Gap," *Fortune*, December 4, 1989, pp. 56ff; Scott McCartney, "AMR Unions Express Fury," *Wall Street Journal*, April 17, 2003; AFL-CIO, "Dodd-Frank Section 953(b): Why CEO-to-Worker Pay Ratios Matter For Investors," www.aflcio.org/content/download/1090/9807/version/1/file/Why-CEO-to-Worker-Pay-Ratios-Matter-For-Investors.pdf, accessed May 16, 2013.

53. D. M. Cowherd and D. I. Levine, "Product Quality and Pay Equity between Lower-Level Employees and Top Management: An Investigation of Distributive Justice Theory," *Administrative Science Quarterly* 37 (1992), pp. 302–20.

54. U.S. Bureau of Labor Statistics, "The Employment Situation–December 2018," January 4, 2019. USDL-19-0002; U.S. Bureau of Labor Statistics, "Women in the Labor Force: A Databook, April 2017," Report 1065.

55. U.S. Bureau of Labor Statistics, *Highlights of Women's Earnings in 2015*, Report No. 1064. Washington, DC: Author, November 2016.

56. U.S. Bureau of Labor Statistics, *Highlights of Women's Earnings in 2015*, Report No. 1064. Washington, DC: Author, November 2016.

57. C. Kulich, G. Trojanowski, M. K. Ryan, S. A. Haslam, and L. D. R. Renneboog, "Who Gets the Carrot and Who Gets the Stick? Evidence of Gender Disparities in Executive Remuneration," *Strategic Management Journal* 32 (2011), pp. 301–21; F. Munôz-Bullón, "Gender-Level Differences among High-Level Executives," *Industrial Relations* 49 (2010), pp. 346–70.

58. B. Gerhart, "Gender Differences in Current and Starting Salaries: The Role of Performance, College Major, and Job Title," *Industrial and Labor Relations Review* 43 (1990), pp. 418–33; G. G. Cain, "The Economic Analysis of Labor-Market Discrimination: A Survey," in *Handbook of Labor Economics*, ed. O. Ashenfelter and R. Layard (New York: North-Holland, 1986), pp. 694–785; F. D. Blau and L. M. Kahn, "The Gender Pay Gap: Have Women Gone as Far as They Can?" *Academy of Management Perspectives*, February 2007, pp. 7–23.

59. H. Remick, "The Comparable Worth Debate," *Public Personnel Management*, Winter 1981.

60. D. P. Schwab, "Job Evaluation and Pay-Setting: Concepts and Practices," in *Comparable Worth: Issues and Alternatives*, ed. E. R. Livemash (Washington, DC: Equal Employment Advisory Council, 1980).

61. B. Gerhart and N. El Cheikh, "Earnings and Percentage Female: A Longitudinal Study," *Industrial Relations* 30 (1991), pp. 62–78; R. S. Smith, "Comparable Worth: Limited Coverage and the Exacerbation of Inequality," *Industrial and Labor Relations Review* 61 (1988), pp. 227–39.

62. W. T. Bielby and J. N. Baron, "Men and Women at Work: Sex Segregation and Statistical Discrimination," *American Journal of Sociology* 91 (1986), pp. 759–99.

63. Rynes and Milkovich, "Wage Surveys"; and G. T. Milkovich, J. M. Newman, and B. Gerhart, *Compensation*, 10th ed. (New York: McGraw-Hill/Irwin, 2010).

64. U.S. Department of Labor website, at www.dol.gov/esa/regs/compliance/ofccp/faqs/comstrds.htm.

65. Gerhart, "Gender Differences in Current and Starting Salaries"; B. Gerhart and G. T. Milkovich, "Salaries, Salary Growth, and Promotions of Men and Women in a Large, Private Firm," in *Pay Equity: Empirical Inquiries*, ed. R. Michael, H. Hartmann, and B. O'Farrell (Washington, DC: National Academy Press, 1989); K. W. Chauvin and R. A. Ash, "Gender Earnings Differentials in Total Pay, Base Pay, and Contingent Pay," *Industrial and Labor Relations Review* 47 (1994), pp. 634–49; M. M. Elvira and M. E. Graham, "Not Just a Formality: Pay System Formalization and Sex-Related Earnings Effects," *Organization Science* 13

(2002), pp. 601–17; A. D. Sterling and R. M. Fernandez, "Once in the Door: Gender, Tryouts, and the Initial Salaries of Managers," *Management Science*, 64 (2018), pp. 5444–60.

66. Gerhart, "Gender Differences in Current and Starting Salaries"; B. Gerhart and S. Rynes, "Determinants and Consequences of Salary Negotiations by Graduating Male and Female MBAs," *Journal of Applied Psychology* 76 (1991), pp. 256–62.

67. G. F. Dreher and R. A. Ash, "A Comparative Study of Mentoring among Men and Women in Managerial, Professional, and Technical Positions," *Journal of Applied Psychology* 75 (1990), pp. 539–46.

68. G. A. Patterson, "Nordstrom Inc. Sets Back-Pay Accord on Suit Alleging 'Off-the-Clock' Work," *Wall Street Journal*, January 12, 1993, p. A2; for additional information on overtime legal issues, see A. Weintraub and J. Kerstetter, "Revenge of the Overworked Nerds," *Bloomberg Businessweek*, www.businessweek.com, December 8, 2003.

69. L. Weber and R. E. Silverman, "On-Demand Workers: 'We Are Not Robots'," *Wall Street Journal*, January 28, 2015, p. B1.

70. U.S. Department of Labor, "U.S. Department of Labor Issues Final Overtime Rule," News Release 19-1715-NAT, https://www .dol.gov/newsroom/releases/whd/whd20190924.

71. After waiting several years to issue a proposed rule and then providing time for groups to comment, the U.S. Securities and Exchange Commission (SEC) issued its final rule in August 2015. Rule details are provided in SEC press release 2015-160 available at www.sec.gov.

# 12 Recognizing Employee Contributions with Pay

## LEARNING OBJECTIVES

*After reading this chapter, you should be able to:*

**LO 12-1** Discuss how pay influences individual employees, and describe three theories that explain the effect of compensation on individuals. *page 527*

**LO 12-2** Describe the fundamental pay programs for recognizing employees' contributions to the organization's success. *page 534*

**LO 12-3** List the advantages and disadvantages of the pay programs. *page 536*

**LO 12-4** Describe how organizations combine incentive plans in a balanced scorecard. *page 546*

**LO 12-5** Discuss issues related to performance-based pay for executives. *page 547*

**LO 12-6** Explain the importance of process issues such as communication in compensation management. *page 551*

**LO 12-7** List the major factors to consider in matching the pay strategy to the organization's strategy. *page 552*

## Employers Raise Pay but Try to Keep an Eye on Fixed Costs—A Challenge in a Tight Labor Market

According to the Employment Cost Index, U.S. Bureau of Labor Statistics, employer costs (per employee) for wages and benefits combined grew 2.9% last year in private industry. In recent years, it has hovered around 2.0%, up from a low of 1.3% in 2009, the year in which the unemployment rate peaked at a 25-year high of 10%. By contrast, the unemployment rate for 2019 averaged under 4%, a 49-year low, and the unemployment rate has remained low in entering 2020. The growth in pay, albeit modest, reflects the tightening of labor markets that we discussed in Chapter 11 and just saw in the form of a 3.9% unemployment rate. Breaking out costs indicates that wages and salaries grew 3.1% and benefits grew 2.5%. Prior to 2017 and 2018, the last time compensation costs grew as much as 3.0% was in 2007.

Aon reports, based on a survey of larger companies, that merit pay increases are expected to average close to 3% this year. Many companies also award bonuses, especially to employees at higher pay levels, such as white-collar managers and professionals. These are expected to be almost 13% of salary. Ken Abosch of Aon observes that the lack of larger increases to base pay is "a little counterintuitive" given how the economy has strengthened and how competition for workers has intensified. In his opinion, "it's indicative of the pressure organizations are under to keep the lid on fixed costs." Using bonuses, a form of variable pay, makes cost containment more possible in future years if business turns downward. Or, as Barry Gerhart of the University of Wisconsin–Madison notes, "If you put the money into salary, it's there forever. If you give out money in terms of a bonus, people get it that

year and have to re-earn it the following year." As we saw in Chapter 11, even companies that are growing are focused on controlling and sometimes reducing their labor costs, both now and looking toward the future. Sometimes that is by automating. Sometimes it is by reducing the workforce. Sometimes (e.g., in the case of automobile companies) it has been shifting compensation to profit sharing over the years, which means some of labor costs only have to be paid when profits are strong. Across companies, as Abosch observes, this often takes the related form of bonuses, which may be linked to profits, but also to other factors (such as individual performance).

However, as we saw in Chapter 11, the tight labor market does seem to have caused at least some companies to do something that Abosch might describe as "more intuitive": they have increased the fixed parts (i.e., wages and salaries) of employee compensation. As we will see in this chapter, agency theory and perhaps logic tell us that employees prefer certain income (e.g., wages, salaries) to uncertain income (e.g., variable forms of pay such as bonuses, which may depend on profits or other variable outcomes). Amazon, for example, as part of raising its minimum wage to $15 (again, see Chapter 11), eliminated monthly bonuses and stock awards, forms of variable pay, for its warehouse and other hourly workers. Amazon gave as a reason that "because [compensation is] no longer incentive-based, the compensation will be more immediate and predictable." (Again, keep this in mind when you come to agency theory.) Another commentator noted that the "higher [fixed] hourly wage that new workers

*CONTINUED*

immediately receive is a better recruiting tool in a tight labor market than stock options that take years to materialize, especially in the warehouse industry that sees high turnover." Another similarly noted: "They probably realized people weren't applying for warehouse jobs for the stock options."

To summarize, a long-term structural change in the U.S. labor market is an effort by employers to control fixed labor costs and avoid being stuck with them in the future when at some point their profits and thus ability to pay high compensation decrease. However, there is a countervailing cyclical (short-term) pressure from the historically tight current labor market situation that makes competition for employees intense. Different employers, perhaps depending on their own business situation, are making different decisions on how to balance these pressures.

SOURCES: U.S. Bureau of Labor Statistics, U.S. Department of Labor, *Employment Cost Index Summary*, October 31, 2018; www.bls.gov; S. Soper, "Amazon Warehouse Workers Lose Bonuses, Stock Awards for Raises," *Bloomberg*, October 3, 2018, Bloomberg.com; J. McGregor, "Holding Out Hope for a Bigger Raise or Bonus in 2017?" *Washington Post*, September 27, 2016; J. McGregor, "Why Many Companies Are Giving Bonuses—not Raises—after the New Tax Cuts," *Washington Post*, January 18, 2018; T.-P. Chen and E. Morath, "Firms Choose Bonuses over Raises," *Wall Street Journal*, September 19, 2018.

# Introduction

As the chapter opening illustrates, organizations must pay competitive salaries and benefits to compete in the labor market, which has tightened recently with unemployment rates dropping. At the same time, however, organizations must control labor costs (which influence product price) to compete in the product market. Employers have also learned to be especially careful about taking on fixed labor costs, although some (e.g., Amazon) have decided that objective must be put on hold given the current labor market situation.

Chapter 11 discussed setting pay for jobs. In this chapter we focus on setting pay for individual employees. We examine how to use pay to recognize and reward employees' contributions to the organization's success. Employees' pay does not depend solely on the jobs they hold. Instead, differences in performance (individual, group, or organization), seniority, skills, and so forth are used as a basis for differentiating pay among employees.[1] In some cases, large amounts of compensation can be at stake.

Several key questions arise in evaluating different pay programs for recognizing contributions. First, what are the costs of the program? Second, what is the expected return (in terms of influences on attitudes and behaviors) from such investments? Third, does the program fit with the organization's human resource strategy and its overall business strategy? Fourth, what might go wrong with the plan in terms of unintended consequences? For example, will the plan encourage managers and employees to pay more attention to some objectives (e.g., short-term sales) than to some others (e.g., customer service, long-term customer satisfaction, and long-term sales)?

Organizations have a relatively large degree of discretion in deciding how to pay, especially compared with the pay level decisions discussed in Chapter 11. The same organizational pay level (or "compensation pie") can be distributed (shared) among employees in many ways. Whether each employee's share is based on individual performance, profits, seniority, or other factors (the "how" to pay decision), the size of the pie (and thus the cost to the organization, the "how much" to pay decision) can remain the same.

Regardless of cost differences, different pay programs can have very different consequences for productivity and return on investment. Indeed, a study of 150 organizations found not only that the largest differences between organizations had to do with how (rather than how much) they paid but also that these differences resulted in different levels of profitability.[2]

# How Does Pay Influence Individual Employees?

Pay plans are typically used to energize, direct, sustain, or control the behavior of current employees. We refer to the effect of pay plans (often with a focus on pay for performance plans) on current employees as an **incentive effect**.[3] (Later, we will introduce the concept of a sorting effect, which is how pay influences employee behaviors by how pay shapes the composition of the workforce.) Equity theory, described in Chapter 11, is relevant here as well. Most employees compare their own pay with that of others, especially those in the same job. Perceptions of inequity may cause employees to take actions to restore equity. Unfortunately, some of these actions (like quitting, reduced effort, or lack of cooperation) may not help the organization.

Three additional, more detailed theories also help explain the effects of compensation: reinforcement, expectancy, and agency theories.

## REINFORCEMENT THEORY

E. L. Thorndike's law of effect states that a response followed by a reward is more likely to recur in the future. The implication for compensation management is that high employee performance followed by a monetary reward will make future high performance more likely. By the same token, high performance not followed by a reward will make it less likely in the future. The theory emphasizes the importance of a person's actual experience of a reward.

## EXPECTANCY THEORY

Although **expectancy theory** also focuses on the link between rewards and behaviors, it emphasizes expected (rather than experienced) rewards. In other words, it focuses on the effects of incentives. Behaviors (job performance) can be described as a function of ability and motivation. In turn, motivation is hypothesized to be a function of expectancy, instrumentality, and valence perceptions. Compensation systems differ according to their impact on these motivational components. Generally speaking, the main influence of compensation is on instrumentality: the perceived link between behaviors and pay. In other words, as an employee, will my outcomes be better (e.g., higher pay, faster promotions, more autonomy) if I perform well or is performance simply not very relevant to my outcomes? Valence of pay outcomes should remain the same under different pay systems. Expectancy perceptions (the perceived link between effort and performance) often have more to do with employee selection, job design, and training than with pay systems. (A possible exception would be skill-based pay, which directly influences employee training and thus expectancy perceptions.)

### Intrinsic and Extrinsic Motivation

Although expectancy theory implies that linking an increased amount of rewards to performance will increase motivation and performance, some authors have used cognitive evaluation theory (and later, social determination theory) to question this

**LO 12-1**
Discuss how pay influences individual employees, and describe three theories that explain the effect of compensation on individuals.

**Incentive effect**
The effect a pay plan has on the behaviors of current employees.

**Expectancy theory**
The theory that says motivation is a function of valence, instrumentality, and expectancy.

Visit your instructor's Connect® course and access your eBook to view this video.

"People want to know that their hard work and their results are going to be rewarded appropriately, and that ultimately we don't want to pay our lower performers the same as we pay our higher performers."
—Timothy J. Richmond,
Senior Vice President, Human Resources, AbbVie

Source: Video produced for the Center for Executive Succession in the Darla Moore School of Business at the University of South Carolina by Coal Powered Filmworks

assumption, arguing that monetary rewards may increase extrinsic motivation but decrease intrinsic motivation. Extrinsic motivation depends on rewards (such as pay and benefits) controlled by an external source, whereas intrinsic motivation depends on rewards that flow naturally from work itself (like performing interesting work).[4] In other words, the concern would be that paying a child to read books may diminish the child's natural interest (intrinsic motivation) in reading, and the child may in the future be less likely to read books in the absence of monetary incentives.

Although monetary incentives may reduce intrinsic motivation in some settings (such as education), the evidence suggests that such effects are small and probably not very relevant to most work settings, where monetary payment is the norm.[5] A meta-analytic review of field research found that intrinsic motivation was actually higher, not lower, when extrinsic incentives were in place. One reason that extrinsic incentives may not have an adverse effect on intrinsic motivation in the workplace is the sorting process (discussed shortly) in the labor market, which matches people, over time, to jobs that fit their preferences, including reward preferences (e.g., for intrinsic and/or extrinsic motivators).[6] Further, evidence indicates that incentive pay has significant positive effects on performance, which is a function of both intrinsic and extrinsic motivation.[7] Scholars in the study of creativity (thought to be an increasingly important organization capability) in organizations have proposed a revised model in which pay for performance can have positive synergistic effects with intrinsic motivation on creativity.[8] Therefore, although money is not the only effective way to motivate behavior and monetary rewards will not always solve motivation problems, monetary rewards do not appear to run much risk of compromising intrinsic motivation in most work settings.[9] And, as we will see, although pay for performance has its risks, there may be more risk in not using it in terms of foregone performance.

## AGENCY THEORY

Agency theory focuses on the divergent interests and goals of the organization's stakeholders and the ways that employee compensation can be used to align these interests and goals. We cover agency theory in some depth because it provides especially relevant implications for compensation design.

An important characteristic of the modern corporation is the separation of ownership from management (or control). Unlike the early stages of capitalism, in which owner and manager were often the same, today, with some important exceptions (mostly smaller companies), most stockholders are far removed from the day-to-day operation of companies. Although this separation has important advantages (like mobility of financial capital and diversification of investment risk), it also creates agency costs—the interests of the **principals** (owners) and their **agents** (managers) may no longer converge. What is best for the agent, or manager, may not be best for the owner.

Agency costs can arise from two factors. First, principals and agents may have different goals (goal incongruence). Second, principals may have less than perfect information about the degree to which the agent is pursuing and achieving the principal's goals (information asymmetry).

Consider three examples of agency costs that can occur in managerial compensation.[10] First, although shareholders seek to maximize their wealth, management may spend money on things such as perquisites (e.g., corporate jets) or "empire building" (making acquisitions that do not add value to the company but may enhance the manager's prestige or pay). Second, managers and shareholders may differ in their attitudes toward risk. Shareholders can diversify their investments (and thus their risks) more easily than managers (whose only major source of income may be their jobs), so managers are typically more averse to risk. They may be less likely to pursue projects or acquisitions with high

**Principal**
In agency theory, a person (e.g., the owner) who seeks to direct another person's behavior.

**Agent**
In agency theory, a person (e.g., a manager) who is expected to act on behalf of a principal (e.g., an owner).

potential payoff. It also suggests a preference on the part of managers for relatively little risk in their pay (high emphasis on base salary, low emphasis on uncertain bonuses or incentives). Indeed, research shows that managerial compensation in manager-controlled firms is more often designed in this manner.[11] Third, decision-making horizons may differ. For example, if managers change companies more than owners change ownership, managers may be more likely to maximize short-run performance (and pay), perhaps at the expense of long-term success.

Agency theory is also of value in the analysis and design of nonmanagers' compensation. In this case, interests may diverge between managers (now in the role of principals) and their employees (who take on the role of agents).

In designing either managerial or nonmanagerial compensation, the key question is: How can such agency costs be minimized? Agency theory says that the principal must choose a contracting scheme that helps align the interests of the agent with the principal's own interests (that is, it reduces agency costs). These contracts can be classified as either behavior oriented (such as merit pay) or outcome oriented (stock options, profit sharing, commissions, and so on).[12] The "performance" in pay for performance programs, including in outcome-based contracts, can take many forms besides the most common that rely on financial outcomes (e.g., stock, profit, and sales outcomes). For example, in the Competing through Environmental, Social, and Governance Practices box, the performance to be incentivized is (lower) carbon-emissions to support climate initiatives.

At first blush, outcome-oriented contracts using financial outcomes seem to be the obvious solution. For example, if profits are high, compensation goes up. If profits drop, compensation goes down. The interests of "the company" and employees are aligned. An important drawback, however, is that such contracts also increase the agent's risk. And because agents are averse to risk, they may require higher pay (a compensating wage differential) to make up for it.[13] Thus, a trade-off between risk and incentives must be considered. Outcome-oriented contracts are, for example, typically a major component of executive compensation.[14]

Behavior-based contracts, on the other hand, do not transfer risk to the agent and thus do not require a compensating wage differential. However, the principal must be able to overcome the information asymmetry issue. To do so the principal must either invest in monitoring (e.g., add more supervisors) and information or else revert, at least in part, to structuring the contract so that pay is linked at least partly to outcomes.[15]

Which type of contract should an organization use? It depends partly on the following factors:[16]

- *Risk aversion.* Risk aversion among agents makes outcome-oriented contracts less likely.
- *Outcome uncertainty.* Profit is an example of an outcome. Agents are less willing to have their pay linked to profits to the extent that there is a risk of low profits. They would therefore prefer a behavior-oriented contract.
- *Job programmability.* As jobs become less programmable (less routine), outcome-oriented contracts become more likely because monitoring becomes more difficult.[17]
- *Measurable job outcomes.* When outcomes are more measurable, outcome-oriented contracts are more likely.[18]
- *Ability to pay.* Outcome-oriented contracts contribute to higher compensation costs because of the risk premium.
- *Tradition.* A tradition or custom of using (or not using) outcome-oriented contracts will make such contracts more (or less) likely.

In summary, the reinforcement, expectancy, and agency theories all focus on the fact that behavior–reward contingencies in pay for performance programs can shape behaviors.

# COMPETING THROUGH ENVIRONMENTAL, SOCIAL, AND GOVERNANCE PRACTICES

## Carbon-Emissions Targets (and Incentives) at Royal Dutch Shell

Royal Dutch Shell announced that it plans to set detailed, short-term (three- to five-year) carbon-emissions targets that will be revised each year to stay on track to achieve its longer-term target. Shell will use emissions control success as a factor in determining executive compensation payouts. Although the Norwegian Oil company Equinor ASA (formerly Statoil) already does so, Shell will be the first of the largest oil companies to link emissions control with executive compensation.

Last year, investors were critical of Shell for only having long-term "ambitions" to cut its emissions of carbon dioxide in half by 2050, with no actual binding targets. Shell's new plan includes signing a joint statement with a group of over 300 investors with more than $30 trillion of assets under management, called Climate Action 100+. David Cumming of Aviva Investors described this result as "evidence of the growing power of what they call ESG—environmental, social and governance—investing."

The agreement came as (many) governments met in Poland for talks on how to complete rules for the Paris Climate Agreement. A spokesman for the Church of England, another investor that was at the forefront of the initiative, stated that the agreement with Shell shows "the benefit of engagement—aligning institutional investors' long-term interests with Shell's desire to be at the forefront of the energy transition." It has also been observed that investors are increasingly concerned with the risks associated with their investments in fossil-fuel companies, as governments take steps to reduce carbon emissions.

For example, China is among nine countries that have indicated they may ban internal combustion engines. California, which would be the fifth largest economy in the world if it was a separate country, has stricter emissions standards than other states, and there is a bill in the legislature that would end

manufacturing and registration of new gasoline cars in the state by 2040. Of course, some bills pass and some do not. However, broadly speaking, investors seem to foresee a number of important risks unless companies like Shell change.

**DISCUSSION QUESTIONS**

1. Why did Royal Dutch Shell decide to incentivize achievement of carbon-emissions target? Because they care about the environment, because it is good for business, and/or because of stakheholder pressure? (Is it necessary to pick one?)

2. Do you think other companies will make similar decisions? Which companies and why? Would you recommend they use incentives in a way similar to how Royal Dutch Shell is using them? Do you have other suggestions for how to encourage these behaviors?

SOURCE: A. Stewart, "More Firms Move to Reprice Options," *Wall Street Journal*, September 13, 2016.

However, agency theory is of particular value in compensation management because of its emphasis on the risk–reward trade-off, an issue that needs close attention when companies consider variable pay plans, which can carry significant risk.

# How Do Pay Sorting Effects Influence Labor Force Composition?

Traditionally, using pay to recognize employee contributions has been thought of as a way to influence the behaviors and attitudes of current employees, whereas pay level and benefits have been seen as a way to influence so-called membership behaviors: decisions about whether to join or remain with the organization. However, it is now recognized that individual pay programs may also affect the nature and composition of an organization's workforce.[19] For example, it is possible that an organization that links pay to performance may attract more high performers than an organization that does not link the two. There may be a similar effect with respect to job retention.[20] This effect on workforce composition is sometimes referred to as a **sorting effect**.

Continuing the analysis, different pay systems appear to attract people with different personality traits and values.[21] Organizations that link pay to individual performance may be more likely to attract individualistic and risk-oriented employees, whereas organizations relying more heavily on team rewards are more likely to attract team-oriented employees. The implication is that the design of compensation programs needs to be carefully coordinated with the organization and human resource strategy. Increasingly, both in the United States and abroad, employers are seeking to establish stronger links between pay and performance.

**Sorting effect**
The effect a pay plan has on the composition of the current workforce (the types of employees attracted and retained).

# Pay-for-Performance Programs
## DIFFERENTIATION IN PERFORMANCE AND PAY

Many organizations seek to use pay to differentiate between employees (i.e., create pay dispersion) based on their performance, especially in jobs (e.g., higher job levels) where the consequences of good versus average versus poor performance become more important to organization performance.[22] Some evidence suggests that high performers can generate a disproportionate amount of value.[23] If so, paying high performers an amount they feel is equitable (see Chapter 11) to motivate them (i.e., achieve positive incentive effects), as well as to attract and retain them (i.e., achieve positive sorting effects), becomes increasingly important. Conventional wisdom sometimes says that differentiation among individuals is ill advised in certain contexts (e.g., teams, collectivistic cultures, where creativity/innovation are critical), but the evidence does not support such simple claims and, indeed, differentiation/pay for individual performance can be important for success in these contexts also.[24] What we can say is that employees will pay close attention to why different employees get paid differently and how fair those differences are, and their perceptions of fairness will drive their behaviors. Here, it is important to remember that equity and equality are not the same thing. Higher performers will expect higher pay and believe that is more fair than being paid equal to lower performers.[25] The amount of differentiation that makes sense will depend on the level of interdependence and cooperation desired in a particular context.[26] Another consideration is how to employee technology effectively in using pay for performance, as the Competing through Technology box demonstrates.

### DIFFERENTIATION STRENGTH/INCENTIVE INTENSITY: PROMISE AND PERIL

A key decision in designing pay-for-performance plans concerns *incentive intensity*, the strength of the relationship between performance and pay (i.e., how strongly we differentiate in performance and pay). For example, if I increase (decrease) my performance by 20%, by what percent will my pay increase (decrease)? The larger the change in pay, the stronger the incentive intensity. For jobs in which objective, results-based measures of performance are available (e.g., sales, executives, stock brokers, investment bankers, investment portfolio managers, loan officers), incentive intensity tends to be higher, compared to jobs in which more subjective, behavior-based (e.g., performance ratings) must be used (e.g., staff jobs in human resources, accounting). It is generally more of a challenge to credibly link big differences in pay to subjective measures.

## Financial Services Firms Turn to Social Media and Automation

At the end of Chapter 11, we learned about what turned out to be a revolution in wealth or asset management: the "invention" of the passive (versus actively managed) mutual fund and investment strategy in the 1970s by John Bogle at Vanguard. It resulted in a huge reduction in fees paid by investors to have their wealth/investments managed and led to Vanguard becoming, for many years, the largest firm in the industry.

The development of passive mutual funds is still causing change. Just recently, Heidi Messer, a director at the wealth management firm, AllianceBernstein Holding LLP, advised its CEO, Peter Kraus, that passive investing continued to be "a low-cost disrupter." Her experience included seeing a variety of industries disrupted by "technology-savvy" new firms that often were able undercut traditional firms on price. Now, CEO Kraus has moved to a new firm, Aperture, and is following her advice by pursuing a new concept at the firm: Its asset managers should charge their clients higher fees than charged by competitors that instead use a passive asset management strategy only if Aperture asset managers achieve higher returns for their clients than they would have realized at competitors. An important implication is that the pay received by Aperture asset managers will also thus depend on their performance— the investment returns they achieve for their clients.

Its plan then goes a step further. Aperture will look not just at short-term asset manager performance, but also performance over a five-year timeframe. If asset managers receive bonuses that, after this longer time period, turn out to be unwarranted given long-term performance, the plan is to "claw back" some of that bonus money from the asset manager. Thus, both short-term and long-term performance will determine asset manager pay. Asset managers who do not perform well will experience a pay reduction and may choose to leave. The technology part of the plan is to use social media and mobile platforms to turn its top performing asset managers into stars who are visible and easily accessible to investors, including small investors. Technology will serve not only to advertise the opportunity to invest with such stars, but will also make it more efficient and profitable than in the past to take on clients with less money to invest.

As another example of how technology has affected another part of the financial services industry, banking, consider that Bank of America had 305,000 employees as of about 2007, but only about 200,000 today, even though (nominal) revenues have remained about the same. Much of this was due to the shift to artificial intelligence and robotic process automation, as well as consolidating data centers, which is enabled by being able to store data and applications in the cloud. Its CEO, Brian Moynihan notes that an effort has been made to avoid layoffs and that a key to that strategy is realizing that the operation of attrition alone, which in its experience is about 10% of its workforce each year, can play a large role in workforce reduction.

BlackRock Inc., the world's largest asset manager, has begun to rely more heavily on "robots" (computer models) and less on human money managers to choose investments. The reason is that there is increasingly slim evidence that asset managers can generate better returns than computer models. Yet the cost of employing asset managers is significant. BlackRock's customers are increasingly pushing back on paying investment fees that they feel may be out of line with investment returns. So, like Aperture, they feel they must respond. Low-cost, passive investing (e.g., index-based mutual funds) is a competing investment model that appeals to many customers, and BlackRock can offer this model using more technology and fewer people.

### DISCUSSION QUESTIONS

1. How does social media offer the opportunity for a firm to capitalize on the performance of its star employees in this case? Also, what are its implications for pricing of services for customers?

2. How does the move over recent decades to low-cost, passive investing help explain the growth of automation in these financial services firms?

SOURCES: J. Baer, "Fund to Cut Pay for Market Laggards," *Wall Street Journal*, September 21, 2018, www.wsj.com; S. Krouse, "BlackRock Shake-Up Favors Computers over Humans," *Wall Street Journal*, March 29, 2017; H. Son, "Bank of America CEO Moynihan Says He Cut Jobs Equal to the Workforce of Delta Air Lines," *CNBC*, October 16, 2018. CNBC.com.

An important principle is that the stronger the incentive intensity, the stronger the motivation but also the greater the chance for unintended, undesirable consequences.[27] For instance, we can link the pay of an automobile repair shop manager to sales and that will likely drive higher sales. We hope the higher sales result from efficiency and innovation in customer service, but we have to acknowledge the risk that higher sales may be driven by fixing things on customers' cars that do not need fixing. Likewise, paying mortgage loan officers based on the mortgage revenue they create can generate more revenue, it is hoped again through outstanding customer service, but the risk is that loans will be given to people who cannot afford them, which can become a problem for the bank in the future. Similarly, we can pay teachers based in part on how well their students perform on standardized tests. But we need to safeguard against the possibility that some teachers may look for ways to increase scores through means other than better teaching. Finally, if a financial institution's top executives believe the government will decide the institution is "too big to fail," they may be likely to take larger investment risks ("excessive risk taking" to the government that subsequently decides it must bail out the firm if the risks go bad and to the shareholders who lose if bankruptcy ensues). This is especially a risk if the executives do not have the same downside risk faced by shareholders. We will see other risks of pay for performance in this chapter as well and also steps that companies and regulators have taken to avoid such risks (e.g., caps on bonuses, clawback provisions, balanced scorecards).

We will see another example of incentives gone wrong at Wells Fargo at the end of the chapter. One last example is Volkswagen. Volkswagen was discovered to have installed software that sensed when an engine was being tested for emissions and (temporarily) reduced emissions to a level that would pass the test. In actual driving conditions, however, VW diesel engines emitted emissions up to 40 times the legal limit. VW's marketing campaign had emphasized the wonder of the diesel engine's performance combined with environmental benefits, even though it was not true. That campaign in turn was a vital part of VW's Strategy 2018 growth plan to bypass General Motors and Toyota to become the world's largest automaker. Employees were subjected to tremendous pressure and intimidation from the top, cascading down to every level, to do whatever was necessary to achieve this growth goal (and keep their jobs). This apparently included engineers "willing to commit crimes to defraud the public." As a result of this scandal, multiple legal actions have been brought against the company. VW has entered into settlements of civil lawsuits brought by drivers who found themselves stuck with noncompliant vehicles. This includes the largest U.S. class action settlement ever. To date, its cost has been many billions of dollars. In an effort to avoid such problems in the future and to "quell investor ire" that executives earned large bonuses (despite their role in the scandal and large VW losses), the company is changing the way it pays. No bonuses will be paid in the future if certain financial objectives are not met. Base salary will be increased 30%, but the total amount of base salary plus bonus that an executive can receive will now be capped at $10 million for the CEO and $5.5 million for other board members. Also, for the first time, executives will be given company stock, presumably in an effort to better align their interests with those of shareholders. It appears that this stock-based compensation is not subject to the caps. Thus, if shareholders do well, executives can still do quite well.[28]

As another example, the Integrity in Action box provides another example. Novartis has revised the way it pays its salesforce such that achieving sales objectives alone is not sufficient. Now, pay also depends on how those objectives are obtained. When one hears stories of what can go wrong with pay for performance, it may be tempting to choose a weaker incentive intensity to avoid such problems. That may be wise in some cases. However, one must be careful not to weaken incentive intensity too much, else the reward for high performance can become too weak to motivate employees. And if a competitor provides a

## INTEGRITY IN ACTION

### Novartis Changes the Way It Pays: Now, Not Just Whether, but also How, You Achieve Your Objectives Matters

Novartis has an integrity problem having to do with unethical sales practices. Novartis, a health care solutions company that includes medicines, pharmaceuticals, and eye care, is changing how its salesforce is compensated. Under the revamped compensation system, which has been in place for two years, bonuses (also called variable pay) will be limited to no more than 35% of total compensation.

The Novartis General Counsel indicated that the change is intended to discourage unethical sales practices. This follows bribery scandals or legal settlements in China, South Korea, and the United States. In China, for example, it entered a settlement to address charges that it had bribed Chinese health care professionals in an effort to increase Novartis sales in China. Novartis was also in the news from $1.2 million in payments to U.S. President Donald Trump's ex-attorney, Michael Cohen, allegedly in hopes of gaining influence on policies and laws affecting Novartis.

Going forward, employees will be rated on a three-point scale on "their values and behavior." A rating of 3 indicates "role model" behavior and a rating of 2 indicates meeting expectations. A rating of 2 or 3 is required to receive any bonus. An employee falling short will face additional action, including the possibility of dismissal. Thus, strong sales performance will continue to be incentivized and rewarded (up to a point), but the sales must be achieved in the "right" way. The Novartis General Counsel reports that there has been a decline of 39% in reports of unethical conduct since the new compensation plan was implemented.

Novartis has also taken other steps to improve ethical conduct, including creating a new position, chief ethics and compliance officer, and this officer serves on the executive committee of the company. It has also revised its five strategic priorities, which now include "Trust & Reputation" and "Culture Transformation." It has implemented new data analytics to help monitor compliance with ethical standards (and investigative procedures), and it has taken steps to change the culture to encourage more upward feedback from employees.

#### DISCUSSION QUESTIONS

1. What caused the Novartis scandals? What can you infer about the nature of its former pay strategy and the role it may have played?

2. Consider Novartis's revised pay strategy. How well do you think it will succeed going forward? Do you have suggestions for other changes? Explain.

SOURCES: Novartis AG Investor Relations, "ESG Investor Call, Investor Presentation," September 17, 2018, www.novartis.com; A. Kanski, "Novartis Revises Bonus Structure to Promote Ethical Behavior," *MM&M*, September 21, 2018; J. Miller, "Novartis Links Bonuses to Ethics in Bid to Rebuild Reputation," *Reuters*, September 17, 2018, www.reuters.com.

pay-for-performance environment with stronger incentive intensity, your strong performers may decide to work there instead (i.e., a negative sorting result). So, as we have noted, there is also a risk to weakening incentive intensity/pay for performance too much.

### TYPES OF PAY FOR PERFORMANCE: AN OVERVIEW

**LO 12-2**
Describe the fundamental pay programs for recognizing employees' contributions to the organization's success.

Table 12.1 classifies pay programs for recognizing employee contributions on the basis of three dimensions. First, programs differ depending on whether payouts become part of base pay (merit pay, skill-based pay), are a fixed cost, or are variable. Second, some programs (merit pay and merit bonuses) measure performance using primarily subjective measures, whereas others (e.g., incentive pay) rely on more objective performance measures. Third, performance can be measured at the individual level (e.g., merit pay) or at the unit (gainsharing) or organization level (profit sharing, ownership).

**Table 12.1**
Programs for Recognizing Employee Contributions

| | MERIT PAY | MERIT BONUS | INCENTIVE PAY | PROFIT SHARING | STOCK OWNERSHIP/ STOCK OPTIONS | GAINSHARING | SKILL BASED |
|---|---|---|---|---|---|---|---|
| **Design features** | | | | | | | |
| Fixed (becomes part of base salary) or variable | Fixed | Variable (bonus) | Variable (bonus) | Variable (bonus) | Variable (equity changes) | Variable (bonus) | Fixed |
| Performance measure (subjective or objective) | Subjective (usually supervisor rating) | Subjective (usually supervisor rating), but higher-level jobs may include objective components also | Objective (e.g., productivity) | Objective (profit) | Objective (stock price/returns) | Objective (e.g., productivity, safety, rework, customer satisfaction) | Objective and/or subjective (certifying which skills are acquired) |
| Performance measure (individual or collective) | Individual | Individual, but higher-level jobs may include unit and/or organization outcomes. | Individual | Collective (organization) | Collective (organization) | Collective (unit) | Individual |

**Table 12.2**
Sample Performance
Dimensions

1. Knows job
2. Takes initiative
3. Exercises good judgment
4. Inspires and develops others
5. Demonstrates interpersonal and teaming skills
6. Produces results

In compensating employees, an organization does not have to choose one program over another. Instead, a combination of programs is often the best solution.[29] For example, one program may foster teamwork and cooperation but not enough individual initiative. Another may do the opposite. Used in conjunction, a balance may be attained. Such balancing of objectives, combined with careful alignment with the organization and human resource strategy, may help increase the probability that a pay-for-performance program has its intended effects and reduce the probability of unintended consequences and problems.[30] The balanced scorecard, which we discuss later in this chapter, is an example of a structured approach to balancing objectives. The fundamental principle is that we care about financial results, but we also care about *how* they are achieved and also how nonfinancial measures can be used, tracked, and influenced to achieve better future financial results. So, it also helps avoid too much short-term focus.[31]

**Merit pay**
Traditional form of pay
in which base pay is
increased permanently.

### Merit Pay (and Merit Bonuses)

**LO 12-3**
List the advantages and
disadvantages of the
pay programs.

In traditional **merit pay** programs, annual base pay increases are usually linked to performance appraisal ratings. (See Chapter 8.) Some type of merit pay program exists in almost all organizations.[32] In some cases, employers have moved toward a form of merit pay that relies on bonuses rather than increases to base pay. One reason for the widespread use of merit pay, or **merit bonuses**, a form of variable pay, is its ability to define and reward a broad range of performance dimensions. (See Table 12.2 for an example.) Indeed, given the pervasiveness of merit pay programs, we devote a good deal of attention to them here.[33]

**Merit bonus**
Merit pay paid in the
form of a bonus, instead
of a salary increase.

*Basic Features.* Many merit pay programs work off of a **merit increase grid**. As Table 12.3 indicates, the size and frequency of pay increases are determined by two factors. The first factor is the individual's performance rating (better performers receive higher pay). The second factor is position in range (that is, an individual's compa-ratio). So, for example, an employee with a performance rating that exceeds expectations and a compa-ratio of 120 would receive a pay increase of roughly 3%. By comparison, an employee with a performance rating of exceeds expectations and a compa-ratio of 85 would receive an increase of around 7%. (Note that the

**Merit increase grid**
A grid that combines an
employee's performance
rating with his or her
position in a pay range to
determine the size and
frequency of his or her
pay increases.

**Table 12.3**
Merit Increase Grid

| RECOMMENDED SALARY INCREASES BY PERFORMANCE RATING AND COMPA-RATIO | | |
|---|---|---|
| **COMPA-RATIO**[a] | | |
| 80–90% | 91–110% | 111–120% |
| Performance rating | | |
| Exceeds expectations    7% | 5% | 3% |
| Meets expectations    4 | 3 | 2 |
| Below expectations    2 | 0 | 0 |

[a]Employee salary/midpoint of their salary range.

| PERFORMANCE RATING | COMPA-RATIO TARGET |
| --- | --- |
| Exceeds expectations | 111–120 |
| Meets expectations | 91–110 |
| Below expectations | Below 91 |

**Table 12.4**
Performance Ratings
and Compa-Ratio
Targets

general magnitude of increases in such a table is influenced by inflation rates.) One reason for factoring in the compa-ratio is to control compensation costs and maintain the integrity of the pay structure. If a person with a compa-ratio of 120 received a merit increase of 7%, she would soon exceed the pay range maximum. Not factoring in the compa-ratio would also result in uncontrolled growth of compensation costs for employees who continue to perform the same job year after year. Instead, some organizations think in terms of assessing where the employee's pay is now and where it should be, given a particular performance level. Consider Table 12.4. An employee who consistently performs at the highest level is targeted to be paid at 111–120% of the market (i.e., a compa-ratio of 111–120). To the extent that the employee is far from that pay level, larger and more frequent pay increases are necessary to move the employee to the correct position. However, if the employee is already at that pay level, smaller pay increases will be needed. The main objective in the latter case would be to provide pay increases that are sufficient to maintain the employee at the targeted compa-ratio.

In controlling compensation costs, another factor that requires close attention is the distribution of performance ratings. (See Chapter 8.) In many organizations, 60–70% of employees fall into the top two (out of four to five) performance rating categories.[34] This means tremendous growth in compensation costs because most employees will eventually be above the midpoint of the pay range, resulting in compa-ratios well over 100. To avoid this, some organizations provide guidelines regarding the percentage of employees who should fall into each performance category, usually limiting the percentage that can be placed in the top two categories. These guidelines are enforced differently, ranging from true guidelines to strict forced-distribution requirements.[35]

In general, merit pay programs have the following characteristics. First, they identify individual differences in performance, which are assumed to reflect differences in ability or motivation. By implication, system constraints on performance are not seen as significant. Second, the majority of information on individual performance is collected from the immediate supervisor. Peer and subordinate ratings are rare, and where they exist, they tend to receive less weight than supervisory ratings.[36] Third, there is a policy of linking pay increases to performance appraisal results.[37] Fourth, the feedback under such systems tends to occur infrequently, often once per year at the formal performance review session. Fifth, the flow of feedback tends to be largely unidirectional, from supervisor to subordinate.

***Criticisms of Traditional Merit Pay Programs.*** Criticisms of this process have been raised. For example, W. Edwards Deming, a leader of the total quality management movement, argued that it is unfair to rate individual performance because "apparent differences between people arise almost entirely from the system that they work in, not from the people themselves."[38] Examples of system factors include co-workers, the job, materials, equipment, customers, management, supervision, and environmental conditions. These are believed to be largely outside the worker's control, instead falling under management's responsibility. Deming argued that the performance rating is essentially "the result of a lottery."[39] Although that may be true for some jobs, for others (attorneys, consultants, investment bankers, athletes, salespeople, managers), there can be major differences in individual performance.[40]

Deming also argued that the individual focus of merit pay discourages teamwork: "Everyone propels himself forward, or tries to, for his own good, on his own life preserver. The organization is the loser."[41] As an example, if people in the purchasing department are evaluated based on the number of contracts negotiated, they may have little interest in materials quality, even though manufacturing is having quality problems.

Deming's solution was to eliminate the link between individual performance and pay. This approach reflects a desire to move away from recognizing individual contributions. What are the consequences of such a move? It is possible that fewer employees with individual-achievement orientations would be attracted to and remain with the organization. One study of job retention found that the relationship between pay growth and individual performance over time was weaker at higher performance levels. As a consequence, the organization lost a disproportionate share of its top performers.[42] In other words, too little emphasis on individual performance may leave the organization with average and poor performers.[43]

Thus, although Deming's concerns about too much emphasis on individual performance are well taken, one must be careful not to replace one set of problems with another. Instead, there needs to be an appropriate balance between individual and group objectives. At the very least, ranking and forced-distribution performance-rating systems need to be considered with caution, lest they contribute to behavior that is too individualistic and competitive.[44]

Another criticism of merit pay programs is the way they measure performance. If the performance measure is not perceived as being fair and accurate, the entire merit pay program can break down. One potential impediment to accuracy is the almost exclusive reliance on the supervisor for providing performance ratings, even though peers, subordinates, and customers (internal and external) often have information on a person's performance that is as good as or better than that of the supervisor. A 360-degree performance feedback approach (discussed in Chapter 9) gathers feedback from each of these sources. To date, however, organizations have mainly used such data for development purposes and have been reluctant to use these multisource data for making pay decisions.[45]

In general, process issues, including communication, expectation setting, and credibility/fairness, are important in administering merit pay and pay for performance.[46] In any situation where rewards are distributed, employees appear to assess fairness along two dimensions: distributive (based on how much they receive) and procedural (what process was used to decide how much).[47] Some of the most important aspects of procedural fairness, or justice, appear in Table 12.5. These items suggest that employees desire clear and consistent performance standards, as well as opportunities to provide input, discuss their performance, and appeal any decision they believe to be incorrect.

**Table 12.5**
Examples of Procedural Justice in Merit Pay Decisions

**Employees' Belief That in Evaluating Their Performance, Their Supervisor...**
- Was honest and ethical and tried to be fair
- Considered your input
- Used consistent standards
- Provided feedback
- Took the time to become familiar with your role and performance, including factors beyond your control
- After a merit pay decision was made, was receptive to discussion of how the decision was made (and/or an appeal) and working together to develop an action plan going forward

SOURCE: Adapted from R. Folger and M. A. Konovsky, "Effects of Procedural and Distributive Justice on Reactions to Pay Raise Decisions," *Academy of Management Journal* 32 (1989), p. 115.

| | PERCENT OF WORKFORCE | AVERAGE BASE PAY INCREASE |
|---|---|---|
| Highest-rated | 8% | 4.8% |
| Next highest-rated | 28 | 3.7 |
| Middle-rated | 57 | 2.6 |
| Low-rated | 6 | 1.1 |
| Lowest-rated | 2 | 0.2 |

**Table 12.6**
Distribution of Performance Rating and Average Base Pay Increase as a Function of Performance (United States)

Note: Based on companies with a five-point rating scale.
SOURCE: Mercer, *2017/2018 US Compensation Planning Survey*, www.mercer.com.

| | % WHO AGREE |
|---|---|
| When I do a good job, my performance is rewarded. | 40% |
| My organization does an adequate job of matching pay to performance. | 46 |

**Table 12.7**
Pay and Performance, Employee Perceptions

SOURCE: Mercer, *What's Working*™ *Survey, United States*, www.mercer.com.

Perhaps the most basic criticism is that merit pay does not really exist. High performers, it is argued, are not paid significantly more than mediocre or even poor performers in most cases.[48] For example, consider the data in Table 12.6 from a *WorldatWork* survey. It shows that high performers received an average merit increase of 4.8%, compared to 2.6% for average performers. On a salary of $50,000 per year, that is a difference of $1,100 per year, or $21.15 per week (before taxes). Critics of merit pay point out that this difference is probably not significant enough to influence employee behaviors or attitudes. Indeed, as Table 12.7 indicates, the majority of employees do not believe there is much payoff to higher levels of performance in their organizations. Unless employees perceive such payoffs to be meaningful, their impact too is not likely to be meaningful.[49] Whether that view varies among high, average, and low performers is not known.

In fact, however, small differences in pay can accumulate into large differences over time. Consistently receiving 4.8% increases (versus 2.6%) over 30 years with a starting salary of $50,000 would translate into a career salary advantage (before taxes) of roughly $1,000,000 (net present value of roughly $600,000, assuming a discount rate of 2.5%).[50] Whether employees think in these terms is open to question. But even if they do not, nothing prevents an organization from explaining to employees that what may appear to be small differences in pay can add up to large differences over time.

Of course, the accumulation effect just described can also be seen as a drawback if it contributes to an entitlement mentality. Here the concern is that a big merit increase given early in an employee's career remains part of base salary "forever." It does not have to be re-earned each year, and the cost to the organization grows over time, perhaps more than either the employee's performance or the organization's profitability would always warrant. Merit bonuses (payouts that do not become part of base salary, a form of variable pay), are thus increasingly used by organizations in lieu of or in addition to merit increases. In fact, merit bonuses (see Table 12.8), in the companies that use them and for the employee groups they use them for, are now larger than traditional pay increases. Preliminary evidence suggests that merit bonuses may have a larger positive impact (compared to traditional merit

**Table 12.8**
Merit Bonus as a
Percentage of Salary,
by Employee Group

| HOURLY UNION NONEXEMPT | SALARIED NONEXEMPT | SALARIED EXEMPT |
|---|---|---|
| 6.2% | 7.1% | 13.0% |

SOURCE: K. Abosch, "The Shifting Landscape of Variable Pay," *Workspan*, April 2017, pp. 6042–47.

increases) on future performance.[51] If that result proves to be robust across organizations, it, together with the merit bonus advantage in terms of controlling fixed costs, likely goes far toward explaining the greater use of merit bonuses. The payoff to high performance that comes from merit bonuses adds to the payoff from merit increases.

Finally, high-performing employees are also more likely to be promoted (into higher-paying jobs) and are also more likely to have higher-paying opportunities at alternative employers. Indeed, these are the major pathways through which employees increase their salaries (and earnings overall, including through bonus and stock plans) over the course of their careers, not through pay increases received within the same jobs.[52] Unless one believes that employees rise to higher job and pay levels over time primarily due to some other factor (chance, seniority), it seems likely that performance differences are largely responsible and determinative over time. All these factors can be communicated to employees to help them see the payoff to high performance. And the higher the performance, the more likely it is one can keep the job (and salary).[53]

### Individual Incentives

Like merit pay, individual incentives reward individual performance, but with two important differences. First, payments are not rolled into base pay. They must be continuously earned and re-earned. Second, performance is usually measured as physical output (such as number of water faucets produced) rather than by subjective ratings. Individual incentives have the potential to significantly increase performance. Ed Locke and his colleagues found that monetary incentives increased production output by a median of 30%—more than any other motivational device studied.[54]

Nevertheless, individual incentives, at least in their purest form, are relatively rare, covering roughly 7% of all U.S. workers and less than 4% of those outside of sales occupations. In fact, the amount of attention received by individual incentives in research (and the popular press) is arguably out of proportion with their (limited) presence in the workplace, especially relative to merit pay.[55] Why is that the case? First, most jobs (like those of many managers and professionals) have, strictly speaking, no physical output measure. Instead, they involve what might be described as "knowledge work." There may or may not be alternative objective measures of performance available (e.g., financial and/or operational), which are needed to use individual incentives. The balanced scorecard gives a good flavor of what objective performance outcomes for managers often look like when they are available. Second, even in jobs where physical output measures are available, potential administrative problems (such as setting and maintaining acceptable standards) often prove intractable.[56] Third, individual incentives may do such a good job of motivating employees that they do whatever they get paid for and nothing else. (For example, one *Dilbert* cartoon showed employees celebrating when told they would be paid for every software error they found and fixed. The implication was that they would deliberately write errors into the software and then fix them to earn as much money as possible.) Fourth, as the name implies, individual incentives, again if used in their purest/simplest form, typically do not fit well with a team approach. Fifth, they may be inconsistent with the goals of acquiring multiple skills and proactive problem solving. Learning new skills often requires employees to slow or stop production. If the employees are paid based on production volume, they may not want to slow down or stop. Sixth, some incentive plans, if not designed carefully, reward output volume at the expense of quality or customer service. Seventh, especially for lower-paid employees, the risk of a variable pay plan like incentive pay not paying off, perhaps because of factors beyond the employee's control, is difficult to manage and/or may undermine motivation or cause unintended consequences such as gaming the system to protect income.

Therefore, although individual incentives carry potential advantages and, in fact, can have large positive effects, they are not likely to contribute to a flexible, proactive, quality-conscious, problem-solving workforce unless they can be designed to avoid the potential pitfalls described here.[57] Incorporating a broader range of objectives beyond physical output alone is one common step toward that end.

### Profit Sharing and Ownership

***Profit Sharing.*** At the other end of the individual–group continuum are profit sharing and stock ownership plans. Under **profit sharing**, payments are based on a measure of organization performance (profits), and the payments do not become part of the base salary. Profit sharing has two potential advantages. First, it may encourage employees to think more like owners, taking a broad view of what needs to be done to make the organization more effective. Thus, the sort of narrow self-interest encouraged by individual incentive plans (and perhaps also by merit pay) is presumably less of an issue. Instead, increased cooperation and citizenship are expected. Second, because payments do not become part of base pay, but instead are variable pay, labor costs are automatically reduced during difficult economic times, and wealth is shared during good times. Consequently, organizations may not need to rely on layoffs as much to reduce costs during tough times.[58]

Does profit sharing contribute to better organization performance? The evidence is not clear. Although there is consistent support for a correlation between profit sharing payments and profits, questions have been raised about the direction of causality.[59] For example, Ford, Chrysler, and GM all have profit sharing plans in their contracts with the United Auto Workers (UAW). (See Table 12.9 for provisions of the GM–UAW plan.) Years ago, under an older profit sharing plan, the average profit sharing payment at Ford one year was $4,000 per worker versus an average of $550 per worker at GM and $8,000 at Chrysler. Given that the profit sharing plans used were very similar, it seems unlikely that the profit sharing plans (through their effects on worker motivation) caused Ford and Chrysler to be more profitable. Rather, it would appear that profits were higher at Ford for other reasons (e.g., better cars), resulting in higher profit sharing payments.

This example also helps illustrate the fundamental drawback of profit sharing. Why should automobile workers at GM receive profit sharing payments that are only 1/15 the size received by those doing the same type of work at Chrysler? Is it because Chrysler UAW members performed 15 times better than their counterparts at GM that year? Probably not. Rather, workers are likely to view top-management decisions regarding products, engineering, pricing, and marketing as more important. As a result, with the exception of top (and perhaps some middle) managers or plans that cover a small number of employees (i.e., in small companies), most employees are unlikely to see a strong connection between what they do and what they earn under profit sharing. This means that performance motivation is likely to change very little under profit sharing. Consistent

**Profit sharing**
A compensation plan in which payments are based on a measure of organization performance (profits) and do not become part of the employees' base salary.

**Table 12.9**
Profit Sharing in the
General Motors—
United Auto Workers
Contract

| PROFITS $BILLIONS | | | MAXIMUM $PAYOUT | PROFITS $BILLIONS | | | MAXIMUM $PAYOUT |
|---|---|---|---|---|---|---|---|
| – | < | 1.25 | 0 | 6.50 | < | 6.75 | 6,500 |
| 1.25 | < | 1.50 | 1,250 | 6.75 | < | 7.00 | 6,750 |
| 1.50 | < | 1.75 | 1,500 | 7.00 | < | 7.25 | 7,000 |
| 1.75 | < | 2.00 | 1,750 | 7.25 | < | 7.50 | 7,250 |
| 2.00 | < | 2.25 | 2,000 | 7.50 | < | 7.75 | 7,500 |
| 2.25 | < | 2.50 | 2,250 | 7.75 | < | 8.00 | 7,750 |
| 2.50 | < | 2.75 | 2,500 | 8.00 | < | 8.25 | 8,000 |
| 2.75 | < | 3.00 | 2,750 | 8.25 | < | 8.50 | 8,250 |
| 3.00 | < | 3.25 | 3,000 | 8.50 | < | 8.75 | 8,500 |
| 3.25 | < | 3.50 | 3,250 | 8.75 | < | 9.00 | 8,750 |
| 3.50 | < | 3.75 | 3,500 | 9.00 | < | 9.25 | 9,000 |
| 3.75 | < | 4.00 | 3,750 | 9.25 | < | 9.50 | 9,250 |
| 4.00 | < | 4.25 | 4,000 | 9.50 | < | 9.75 | 9,500 |
| 4.25 | < | 4.50 | 4,250 | 9.75 | < | 10.00 | 9,750 |
| 4.50 | < | 4.75 | 4,500 | 10.00 | < | 10.25 | 10,000 |
| 4.75 | < | 5.00 | 4,750 | 10.25 | < | 10.50 | 10,250 |
| 5.00 | < | 5.25 | 5,000 | 10.50 | < | 10.75 | 10,500 |
| 5.25 | < | 5.50 | 5,250 | 10.75 | < | 11.00 | 10,750 |
| 5.50 | < | 5.75 | 5,500 | 11.00 | < | 11.25 | 11,000 |
| 5.75 | < | 6.00 | 5,750 | 11.25 | < | 11.50 | 11,250 |
| 6.00 | < | 6.25 | 6,000 | 11.50 | < | 11.75 | 11,500 |
| 6.25 | < | 6.50 | 6,250 | 11.75 | < | 12.00 | 11,750 |
| | | | | | > | = 12.0 | Continues[a] |

Note: Employees working 1,850 or more hours per year receive the maximum payout. Those working fewer hours receive a prorated payout based on their hours worked. Profits are defined as operating income (earnings before interest and taxes) for North America (only).

[a]Effective 2019, each additional $1 billion in profits beyond $12 billion continues to increase profit sharing payout by $1,000. Prior to 2019, profit sharing payouts were capped at $12,000.

SOURCE: Contract Summary: Hourly Workers, *UAW*, 2015, 2019, https://uaw.org/app/uploads/2015/10/64171_UAW-GM-Hourly-Highlights-Revp-11-final.pdf

with expectancy theory, motivation depends on a strong link between behaviors and valued consequences such as pay (instrumentality perceptions).

Another factor that reduces the motivational impact of profit sharing plans is that most plans are of the deferred type. Roughly 16% of full-time employees in medium-size and large private establishments participate in profit sharing plans, but only 1% of employees overall (about 6% of those in profit sharing plans) are in cash plans where profits are paid to employees during the current time period.[60]

Not only may profit sharing fail to increase performance motivation, but employees may also react very negatively when they learn that such plans do not pay out during business downturns.[61] First, they may not feel they are to blame because they have been performing their jobs well. Other factors are beyond their control, so why should they be penalized? Second, what seems like a small amount of at-risk pay for a manager earning $80,000 per year can be very painful to someone earning $15,000 or $20,000. As such, one theoretical advantage of profit sharing—that it makes labor costs variable and more in line with ability to pay—may not always be realized. A caveat is that making labor costs more variable (including downward) may be more feasible in companies that have been under financial duress and face serious long-term competitive challenges. An example would be the automobile industry.

Their recent performance has been strong, which has translated into high profit sharing payments for employees. However, as we have also seen, salary increases (which become fixed costs) at the automobile companies have been rare in recent years.

Consider the case of the Du Pont Fibers Division, which had a plan that linked a portion of employees' pay to division profits.[62] After the plan's implementation, employees' base salary was about 4% lower than similar employees in other divisions unless 100% of the profit goal (a 4% increase over the previous year's profits) was reached. Thus, there was what might be called downside risk. However, there was also considerable upside opportunity: If 100% of the profit goal was exceeded, employees would earn more than similar employees in other divisions. For example, if the division reached 150% of the profit goal (6% growth in profits), employees would receive 12% more than comparable employees in other divisions.

Initially, the plan worked fine. The profit goal was exceeded, and employees earned slightly more than employees in other divisions. In the following year, however, profits were down 26%, and the profit goal was not met. Employees received no profit sharing bonus; instead, they earned 4% less than comparable employees in other divisions. Profit sharing was no longer seen as a very good idea. Du Pont management responded to employee concerns by eliminating the plan and returning to a system of fixed base salaries with no variable (or risk) component. This outcome is perhaps not surprising from an agency theory perspective, which suggests that employees must somehow be compensated to assume increased risk.

One solution some organizations choose is to design plans that have upside but not downside risk. In such cases, when a profit sharing plan is introduced, base pay is not reduced. Thus, when profits are high, employees share in the gain, but when profits are low, they are not penalized. Such plans largely eliminate what is purported to be a major advantage of profit sharing: reducing labor costs during business downturns. During business upturns, labor costs will increase. Given that the performance benefits of such plans are not assured, an organization runs the risk under such plans of increasing its labor costs with little return on its investment.

In summary, although profit sharing may be useful as one component of a compensation system (to enhance identification with broad organizational goals), it may need to be complemented with other pay programs that more closely link pay to outcomes that individuals or teams can control (or "own"), particularly in larger companies. In addition, profit sharing runs the risk of contributing to employee dissatisfaction or higher labor costs, depending on how it is designed. However, moving beyond concerns about its motivation impact, profit sharing does have the major advantage of making labor costs more variable, a major advantage when sales and profits decline.

***Ownership (Including Stock Options).*** Recent data show that in the neighborhood of 20 million Americans own stock in the companies for which they work.[63] Employee ownership is similar to profit sharing in some key respects, such as encouraging employees to focus on the success of the organization as a whole. In fact, with ownership, this focus may be even stronger. Like profit sharing, ownership may be less motivational the larger the organization. And because employees may not realize any financial gain until they actually sell their stock (typically upon leaving the organization), the link between pay and performance may be even less obvious than under profit sharing. Thus, from a reinforcement theory standpoint (with its emphasis on actually experiencing rewards), the effect on performance motivation may be limited.[64]

One way of achieving employee ownership is through **stock options**, which give employees the opportunity to buy stock at a fixed price. Say the employees receive options to purchase stock at $10 per share in 2016, and the stock price reaches $30 per share in 2021. They have the option of purchasing stock ("exercising" their stock options) at $10 per share in 2021, thus making a tidy return on investment if the shares are then sold. If the stock

**Stock options** An employee ownership plan that gives employees the opportunity to buy the company's stock at a previously fixed price.

price goes down to $8 per share in the year 2021, however, there will be no financial gain. Therefore, employees are encouraged to act in ways that will benefit the organization.

For many years, stock options had typically been reserved for executives in larger, established companies. Then, there was a trend for some years toward pushing eligibility farther down in the organization.[65] In fact, many companies, including PepsiCo, Merck, McDonald's, Walmart, and Procter & Gamble, began granting stock options to employees at all levels. Among start-up companies like those in the technology sector, these broad-based stock option programs have long been popular and companies like Microsoft and Cisco Systems attribute much of their growth and success to these option plans. Some studies suggest that organization performance is higher when a large percentage of top and mid-level managers are eligible for long-term incentives such as stock options, which is consistent with agency theory's focus on the problem of encouraging managers to think like owners.[66] However, it is not clear whether these findings would hold up for lower-level employees, particularly in larger companies, who may see much less opportunity to influence overall organization performance. Another issue with options is whether executives and employees place sufficient value on them, given their cost.[67]

The Golden Age of stock options has faded some. Investors have long questioned the historically favorable tax treatment of employee stock options. In 2004, the Financial Accounting Standards Board (FASB) issued FAS 123R, a landmark change, requiring companies to expense options on their financial statements, which reduces reported net income, dramatically in some cases. Microsoft decided to eliminate stock options in favor of actual stock grants. This is partly in response to the new accounting standards and partly in recognition of the fact that Microsoft's stock price is not likely to grow as rapidly as it once did, making options less effective in recruiting, retaining, and motivating its employees. It appears that many companies are cutting back on stock options overall, and especially for nonexecutive employees.

Those companies that continue to use broad-based stock options have encountered difficulties in keeping employees motivated during years when there has been a steep decline in stock prices. For example, in 2009 Google's stock price dropped to $306, down from $741 in 2007, putting many employee stock options "underwater" (i.e., the stock price was under the option/exercise price), meaning that employees were not able to make any gain from exercising their options. Google's answer to this situation was an option exchange where employees turned in their underwater options in return for options having an exercise price equal to the current (lower) stock price. The hope was that employee motivation and retention would be reinvigorated.[68] As another example of the challenge in using stock-based compensation, one estimate was that (nonexecutive) employees of Facebook and of Zynga experienced declines in the value of their company stock and stock options of $7.2 billion and $1.4 billion, respectively, after initial public offerings of stock.[69] (Now, some years later, it seems like things have worked out OK for them!)

**Employee stock ownership plans (ESOPs)**
An employee ownership plan that provides employers certain tax and financial advantages when stock is granted to employees.

**Employee stock ownership plans (ESOPs)**, under which employers give employees stock in the company, are the most common form of employee ownership, with the number of employees in such plans increasing from 4 million in 1980 to about 14 million in 2017 in the United States.[70] Including non-ESOP stock option, stock purchase, and stock-based retirement plans, it is estimated that about 28 million U.S. employees own some portion of the companies for which they work, controlling about 8% of U.S. corporate equity. In Japan, most companies listed on Japanese stock markets have an ESOP, and these companies appear to have higher average productivity than non-ESOP companies.[71] ESOPs raise a number of unique issues. On the negative side, they can carry significant risk for employees. An ESOP must, by law, invest at least 51% of assets in its company's stock, resulting in less diversification of investment risk (in some cases, no diversification). Consequently, when employees buy out companies in poor financial condition to save their jobs, or when the ESOP is used to fund pensions, employees risk serious financial difficulties if the company does poorly.[72] This is not just a concern for employees, because, as agency theory suggests, employees may require higher pay to offset increased risks of this sort.

ESOPs can be attractive to organizations because they have tax and financing advantages and can serve as a takeover defense (under the assumption that employee owners will be "friendly" to management). ESOPs give employees the right to vote their securities (if registered on a national exchange).[73] As such, some degree of participation in a select number of decisions is mandatory, but overall participation in decision making appears to vary significantly across organizations with ESOPs. Some studies suggest that the positive effects of ownership are larger in cases where employees have greater participation,[74] perhaps because the "employee–owner comes to psychologically experience his/her ownership in the organization."[75]

Overall, however, meta-analytic evidence finds a small, positive relationship of employee ownership with firm performance.[76]

## Gainsharing, Group Incentives, and Team Awards

*Gainsharing.* **Gainsharing** programs offer a means of sharing productivity gains with employees. Although sometimes confused with profit sharing plans, gainsharing differs in two key respects. First, instead of using an organization-level performance measure (profits), the programs measure group or plant performance, which is likely to be seen as more controllable by employees. Second, payouts are distributed more frequently and not deferred. In a sense, gainsharing programs represent an effort to combine the best features of organization-oriented plans like profit sharing and individual-oriented plans like merit pay and individual incentives. Like profit sharing, gainsharing encourages pursuit of broader goals than individual-oriented plans do. But, unlike profit sharing, gainsharing can motivate employees much as individual plans do because of the more controllable nature of the performance measure and the frequency of payouts. Studies indicate that gainsharing improves performance.[77]

> **Gainsharing**
> A form of group compensation based on group or plant performance (rather than organization-wide profits) that does not become part of the employee's base salary.

One type of gainsharing, the Scanlon plan (developed in the 1930s by Joseph N. Scanlon, president of a local union at Empire Steel and Tin Plant in Mansfield, Ohio), provides a monetary bonus to employees (and the organization) if the ratio of labor costs to the sales value of production is kept below a certain standard. Table 12.10 shows a modified (i.e., costs in addition to labor are included) Scanlon plan. Because actual costs ($850,000) were less than allowable costs ($907,500) in the first and second periods, there is a gain of $57,500. The organization receives 45% of the savings, and the employees receive the other 55%, although part of the employees' share is set aside in the event that actual costs exceed the standard in upcoming months (as Table 12.10 shows did occur).

Gainsharing plans like the Scanlon plan and pay-for-performance plans in general often encompass more than just a monetary component. There is often a strong emphasis on taking advantage of employee know-how to improve the production process through problem-solving teams and suggestion systems.[78] A number of recommendations have been made about the organization conditions that should be in place for gainsharing to succeed. Commonly mentioned factors include (1) management commitment; (2) a need to change or a strong commitment to continuous improvement; (3) management's acceptance and encouragement of employee input; (4) high levels of cooperation and interaction; (5) employment security; (6) information sharing on productivity and costs; (7) goal setting; (8) commitment of all involved parties to the process of change and improvement; and (9) agreement on a performance standard and calculation that is understandable, seen as fair, and closely related to managerial objectives.[79]

**Table 12.10**
Example of
Gainsharing
(Modified Scanlon
Plan) Report

| ITEMS | AVERAGE OF 1ST AND 2ND PERIODS | AVERAGE OF 2ND AND 3RD PERIODS |
|---|---|---|
| 1.  Sales in dollars | $2,000,000 | $2,000,000 |
| 2.  Inventory change and work in process | 200,000 | 200,000 |
| 3.  Sales value of production | 2,200,000 | 2,200,000 |
| 4.  Allowable costs (85% × 3 above) | 1,870,000 | 1,870,000 |
| 5.  Actual costs | 1,700,000 | 1,880,000 |
| 6.  Gain (4–5 above) | 170,000 | (10,000) |
| 7.  Employee share (50% of 6 above) | 85,000 | (5,000) |
| 8.  Monthly reserve (20% of 7 above)* | 17,000 | (5,000) |
| 9.  Bonus to be distributed (7–8) | 68,000 | 0 |
| 10.  Company share (50% of 6 above) | 85,000 | (5,000) |
| 11.  Participating payroll | 264,000 | 264,000 |
| 12.  Bonus percentage (9/11) | 26% | 0% |
| 13.  Monthly reserve (8 above) | 17,000 | (5,000) |
| 14.  Reserve at the end of last period | 0 | 17,000 |
| 15.  Year-end reserve to date | 17,000 | 12,000 |

*If no bonus, 100% of 7 above

SOURCE: From *Gainsharing and Goalsharing: Aligning Pay and Strategic Goals*, by K. Mericle and D. O. Kim. Reproduced with permission of Greenwood Publishing Group via Copyright Clearance Center.

***Group Incentives and Team Awards.*** Whereas gainsharing plans are often plant-wide, group incentives and team awards typically pertain to a smaller work group.[80] Group incentives (like individual incentives) tend to measure performance in terms of physical output, whereas team award plans may use a broader range of performance measures (like cost savings, successful completion of product design, or meeting deadlines). As with individual incentive plans, these plans have a number of potential drawbacks. Competition between individuals may be reduced, but it may be replaced by competition between groups or teams. Also, consistent with our earlier discussion of pay effects on workforce composition, any plan that does not adequately recognize differences in individual performance risks demotivating top performers or losing them. Finally, as with any incentive plan, a standard-setting process must be developed that is seen as fair by employees, and these standards must not exclude important dimensions such as quality.

## Balanced Scorecard

**LO 12-4**
Describe how organizations combine incentive plans in a balanced scorecard.

As the preceding discussion indicates, every pay program has advantages and disadvantages. Therefore, rather than choosing one program, some companies find it useful to design a mix of pay programs, one that has just the right chemistry for the situation at hand. Relying exclusively on merit pay or individual incentives may result in high levels of work motivation but unacceptable levels of individualistic and competitive behavior and too little concern for broader plant or organization goals. Relying too heavily on profit sharing and gainsharing plans may increase cooperation and concern for the welfare of

**Table 12.11**
Illustration of Balanced Scorecard Incentive Concept

| PERFORMANCE MEASURE | INCENTIVE SCHEDULE | | | | |
|---|---|---|---|---|---|
| | TARGET INCENTIVE | PERFORMANCE | % TARGET | ACTUAL PERFORMANCE | INCENTIVE EARNED |
| Financial | $100 | 20% + | 150 | 18% | $100 |
| • Return on capital | | 16–20 | 100 | | |
| employed | | 12–16 | 50 | | |
| | | Below 12 | 0 | | |
| Customer | $40 | 1 in: | | 1 in 876 | $20 |
| • Product returns | | 1,000 + | 150 | | |
| | | 900–999 | 100 | | |
| | | 800–899 | 50 | | |
| | | Below 800 | 0 | | |
| Internal | $30 | 9% + | 150 | 11% | $45 |
| • Cycle time reduction (%) | | 6–9 | 100 | | |
| | | 3–6 | 50 | | |
| | | 0–3 | 0 | | |
| Learning and growth | $30 | Below 5% | 150 | 7% | $30 |
| • Voluntary employee | | 5–8 | 100 | | |
| turnover | | 8–12 | 50 | | |
| Total | $200 | | | | $195 |

SOURCE: From F. C. McKenzie and M. P. Shilling, "Avoiding Performance Traps: Ensuring Effective Incentive Design and Implementation," *Compensation and Benefits Review*, July–August 1998, pp. 57–65. *Compensation and Benefits Review by American Management Association*. Reproduced with permission of Sage Publications, Inc. via Copyright Clearance Center.

the entire plant or organization, but it may reduce individual work motivation to unacceptable levels. However, a particular mix of merit pay, gainsharing, and profit sharing could contribute to acceptable performance on all these performance dimensions.

One approach that seeks to balance multiple objectives is the balanced scorecard (see Chapter 1), which Kaplan and Norton describe as a way for companies to "track financial results while simultaneously monitoring progress in building the capabilities and acquiring the intangible assets they would need for future growth."[81]

Table 12.11 shows how a mix of measures might be used by a manufacturing firm to motivate improvements in a balanced set of key business drivers. We will also see shortly a scorecard used by Tenet Healthcare.

# Managerial and Executive Pay

Because of their significant ability to influence organization performance, top managers and executives are a strategically important group whose compensation warrants special attention, including its competitiveness in the labor market.[82] In Chapter 11 we discussed how much this group is paid. Here we focus on the issue of how their pay is determined.

**LO 12-5**
Discuss issues related to performance-based pay for executives.

Business magazines such as *Forbes* and *Bloomberg Businessweek* often publish lists of top executives who did the most for their pay and those who did the least. The latter group has been the impetus for much of the attention to executive pay. The problem seems to be that in some companies, top executive pay is high every year, regardless of profitability or stock market performance. One study, for example, found that CEO pay changes by $3.25 for every $1,000 change in shareholder wealth. Although this relationship was interpreted to mean that "the compensation of top executives is virtually independent of corporate performance," later work demonstrates, to the contrary, that executive pay, in most companies, is significantly aligned with shareholder return.[83]

How can executive pay be linked to organization performance? From an agency theory perspective, the goal of owners (shareholders) is to encourage the agents (managers and executives) to act in the best interests of the owners. This may mean less emphasis on noncontingent pay, such as base salary, and more emphasis on outcome-oriented "contracts" that make some portion of executive pay contingent on the organization's profitability or stock performance.[84] Among mid-level and top managers, it is common to use both short-term bonus and long-term incentive plans to encourage the pursuit of both short- and long-term organization performance objectives. Indeed, the bulk of executive compensation comes from restricted stock, stock options, and other forms of long-term compensation. Putting pay "at risk" in this manner can be a strong incentive. However, agency theory suggests that while too little pay at risk may weaken the incentive effect, too much pay at risk can also be a problem if executives take excessive risks with firm assets.[85] The banking and mortgage industry problems of late provide an example.

Organizations use such pay-for-performance plans, and what are their consequences? Research suggests that organizations vary substantially in the extent to which they use both long-term and short-term incentive programs. Further, greater use of such plans among top and mid-level managers is associated with higher subsequent levels of profitability. As Table 12.12 indicates, greater reliance on short-term bonuses and long-term incentives (relative to base pay) resulted in substantial improvements in return on assets.[86] For top executives, aligning compensation with past shareholder return is associated with his or her future shareholder returns.[87]

Earlier, we saw how the balanced scorecard approach could be applied to paying manufacturing employees. It is also useful in designing executive pay. Table 12.13 shows how the choice of performance measures can be guided by a desire to balance shareholder, customer, and employee objectives. Financial results can be seen as a lagging indicator that tells the company how it has done in the past, whereas customer and employee metrics like those in Table 12.13, used by Tenet Healthcare, are leading indicators that tell the company how its financial results will be in the future. Importantly, empirical research should be conducted in each company to validate these or other hypothesized leading indicators of financial performance.[88]

As we saw in the global financial crisis, a focus on only (aggressive) financial goals, without also considering how those goals are achieved, raises the danger that executives and others will take too great a risk and/or engage in unethical behavior to achieve those objectives.

**Table 12.12**
The Relationship between Managerial Pay and Organization Return on Assets

| | | PREDICTED RETURN ON ASSETS | |
|---|---|---|---|
| BONUS/BASE RATIO | LONG-TERM INCENTIVE ELIGIBILITY | % | $a |
| 10% | 28% | 5.2% | $250 million |
| 20 | 28 | 5.6 | 269 million |
| 10 | 48 | 5.9 | 283 million |
| 20 | 48 | 7.1 | 341 million |

aBased on the assets of the average *Fortune* 500 company in 1990.

SOURCE: B. Gerhart and G. T. Milkovich, "Organizational Differences in Managerial Compensation and Financial Performance," *Academy of Management Journal* 33 (1990), pp. 663–91.

**Table 12.13**
Balanced Scorecard for Executives, Tenet Healthcare

| OBJECTIVES | MEASURES | DESCRIPTION | WEIGHTING |
|---|---|---|---|
| **Financial** | | | |
| Cost | Earnings | | 60% |
| | Free Cash Flow | | 15% |
| Growth | Same-Facility Inpatient Admissions | | 2% |
| | Same-Facility Outpatient Visits | | 2% |
| **Operational** | | | |
| Quality | CMS Overall Star Rating | Quality of care rating assigned to hospitals by Centers for Medicare and Medicaid Services | 2% |
| | AHRQ Culture of Safety Survey | Employees' perception of the climate for patient safety (survey conducted by AHRQ) | 2% |
| | Tenet Quality Composite Index | Hospital Associated Infections Readmissions Morality | 2% |
| Service | Inpatient Satisfaction | Patient satisfaction (survey conducted by Tenet) | 5% |
| | Physician Net Promoter Score | Physician engagement and loyalty (survey conducted by Tenet) | 5% |
| People | Employee Turnover | Percentage of employees who terminate their employment | 5% |

SOURCE: 2018 Notice of Annual Meeting and Proxy Statement, Tenet Healthcare Corporation, www.tenethealth.com.

These behaviors can do great harm to the company over time. A scorecard used by Citigroup for its top 50 executives had a weight of 70% toward financial objectives (profitability, expense management, use of capital, risk) and 30% toward nonfinancial (in the short-term) objectives (setting strategic direction; having strong risk and controls management and strong personnel management; enhancing relations with external stakeholders, including shareholders). The highest possible performance score was 100%, whereas the lowest was minus 40%. The hope is that by linking pay incentives to this broader set of performance objectives, not just to financial goals as in the past, Citigroup will achieve better financial performance over time and achieve it in a less risky manner. Nobody wants to go through another financial industry meltdown, and this is one part of the plan to avoid that. Similarly, as we saw earlier, Volkswagen recently changed the way it pays its executives in response to a major (and costly) scandal that it hopes to avoid repeating in the future. Other examples include Novartis (see the earlier Integrity in Action box) and Wells Fargo (at the end of the chapter).

Finally, there is pressure from regulators and shareholders to better link pay and performance. The U.S. Securities and Exchange Commission (SEC) requires companies to report compensation levels for the five highest-paid executives and the company's performance relative to that of competitors over a five-year period. In 2006, the SEC put additional rules into effect that require better disclosure of the value of executive perquisites and retirement benefits. In 2010, the Dodd-Frank Wall Street Reform and Consumer Protection Act was signed into law in the United States. Although its focus is primarily on financial institutions, Dodd-Frank added Section 14A to the Securities and Exchange, which added new requirements for public companies broadly.[89] For example, it requires that shareholders have a "say on pay," meaning that they have the right to a (nonbinding) vote on executive pay plans. Dodd-Frank also requires that firms disclose the ratio of the pay of the top executive to that of rank-and-file employees. Companies, under pressure from regulators and investors, have also increasingly adopted policies that allow them to claw back (i.e., get back) compensation paid to executives who are later found to have increased their pay by engaging in behaviors detrimental to companies and the economy.

Regulators in a number of countries have also sought to limit the size of bonus payments in hopes of reducing the incentive to engage in behaviors such as excessive risk taking, which have proved detrimental in the past.[90] Large retirement fund investors such as TIAA-CREF and CalPERS have proposed guidelines to better ensure that boards of directors act in shareholders' best interests when making executive pay decisions, rather than being beholden to management. Some of the governance practices believed to be related to director independence from management (Dodd-Frank has similar provisions) are shown in Table 12.14. More detailed analyses of board governance practices are

**Table 12.14**
Guidelines for Board of Directors Independence and Leadership

1. **Majority of independent directors:** At a minimum, a majority of the board consists of directors who are independent. Boards should strive to obtain board composition made up of a substantial majority of independent directors.
2. **Independent executive session:** Independent directors meet periodically (at least once a year) alone in an executive session, without the CEO. The independent board chair or lead (or presiding) independent director should preside over this meeting.
3. **Independent director definition:** Each company should disclose in its annual proxy statement the definition of "independence" relied upon by its board.
4. **Independent board chairperson:** The board should be chaired by an independent director. The CEO and chair roles should only be combined in very limited circumstances; in these situations, the board should provide a written statement in the proxy materials discussing why the combined role is in the best interest of shareowners, and it should name a lead independent director.
5. **Examine separate chair/CEO positions:** When selecting a new chief executive officer, boards should reexamine the traditional combination of the "chief executive" and "chair" positions.
6. **Board role of retiring CEO:** Generally, a company's retiring CEO should not continue to serve as a director on the board and at the very least be prohibited from sitting on any of the board committees.
7. **Board access to management:** The board should have a process in place by which all directors can have access to senior management.
8. **Independent board committees:** Committees that perform the audit, director nomination, and executive compensation functions should consist entirely of independent directors.
9. **Board oversight:** The full board is responsible for the oversight function on behalf of shareowners. Should the board decide to have other committees (e.g., executive committee) in addition to those required by law, the duties and membership of such committees should be fully disclosed.
10. **Board resources:** The board, through its committees, should have access to adequate resources to provide independent counsel advice, or other tools that allow the board to effectively perform its duties on behalf of shareowners.

SOURCE: The California Public Employees Retirement System, "Global Principles of Accountable Corporate Governance," August 18, 2008, updated November 14, 2011, www.iccr.org.

available from Institutional Shareholder Services.[91] In addition, when a firm's future is at risk, the board may well need to demonstrate its independence from management by taking dramatic action, which may include removing the chief executive.

# Process and Context Issues

In Chapter 11 we discussed the importance of process issues such as communication and employee participation. Earlier in the present chapter we discussed the importance of fairness, both distributive and procedural. Significant differences in how such issues are handled can be found both across and within organizations, suggesting that organizations have considerable discretion in this aspect of compensation management.[92] As such, it represents another strategic opportunity to distinguish one's organization from the competition.

**LO 12-6**
Explain the importance of process issues such as communication in compensation management.

## EMPLOYEE PARTICIPATION IN DECISION MAKING

Consider employee participation in decision making and its potential consequences. Involvement in the design and implementation of pay policies has been linked to higher pay satisfaction and job satisfaction, presumably because employees have a better understanding of and greater commitment to the policy when they are involved.[93]

What about the effects on productivity? Agency theory provides some insight. The delegation of decision making by a principal to an agent creates agency costs because employees may not act in the best interests of top management. In addition, the more agents there are, the higher the monitoring costs.[94] Together, these issues suggest that delegation of decision making can be very costly.

However, agency theory suggests that monitoring would be less costly and more effective if performed by employees because they have knowledge about the workplace and behavior of fellow employees that managers do not have. As such, the right compensation system might encourage self-monitoring and peer monitoring.[95] Researchers have suggested that two general factors are critical to encouraging such monitoring: monetary incentives (outcome-oriented contracts in agency theory) and an environment that fosters trust and cooperation. This environment, in turn, is a function of employment security, group cohesiveness, and individual rights for employees—in other words, respect for and commitment to employees.[96]

In any case, a survey of organizations found that only 11% of employees always or often participated in compensation design teams. Participation by managers was better, but still the exception (32%).[97]

## COMMUNICATION

Another important process issue is communication.[98] Earlier, we spoke of its importance in the administration of merit pay, both from the perspective of procedural fairness and as a means of obtaining the maximum impact from a merit pay program.[99] More generally, a change in any part of the compensation system is likely to give rise to employee concerns. Rumors and assumptions based on poor or incomplete information are always an issue in administering compensation, partly because of its importance to employee economic security and well-being. Therefore, in making any changes, it is crucial to determine how best to communicate reasons for the changes to employees. Some organizations rely on video messages from the chief executive officer to communicate the rationale for major changes. Brochures and/or websites that include scenarios for typical employees are sometimes used, as are focus group sessions in which small groups of employees are interviewed to obtain feedback about concerns that can be addressed in later communication programs. Ultimately, however, most pay-related communications come through individual discussions with one's supervisor, still ahead of the company website, e-mail, and discussions with the human resource department.[100]

### PAY AND PROCESS: INTERTWINED EFFECTS

The preceding discussion treats process issues such as participation as factors that may facilitate the success of pay programs. At least one commentator, however, has described an even more important role for process factors in determining employee performance:

> Worker participation apparently helps make alternative compensation plans . . . work better— and also has beneficial effects of its own. . . . It appears that changing the way workers are treated may boost productivity more than changing the way they are paid.[101]

This suggestion raises a broader question: How important are pay decisions, per se, relative to other human resource practices? Although it may not be terribly useful to attempt to disentangle closely intertwined programs, it is important to reinforce the notion that human resource programs, even those as powerful as compensation systems, do not work alone.

Consider gainsharing programs. As described earlier, pay is often only one component of such programs. (See Table 12.10.) How important are the nonpay components?[102] There is ample evidence that gainsharing programs that rely almost exclusively on the monetary component can have substantial effects on productivity.[103] However, a study of an automotive parts plant found that adding a participation component (monthly meetings with management to discuss the gainsharing plan and ways to increase productivity) to a gainsharing pay incentive plan raised productivity. In a related study, employees were asked about the factors that motivated them to engage in active participation (such as suggestion systems). Employees reported that the desire to earn a monetary bonus was much less important than a number of nonpay factors, particularly the desire for influence and control in how their work was done.[104] A third study reported that both productivity and profitability were enhanced by the addition of employee participation in decisions, beyond the improvement derived from monetary incentives such as gainsharing.[105]

# Organization Strategy and Compensation Strategy: A Question of Fit

**LO 12-7**

List the major factors to consider in matching the pay strategy to the organization's strategy.

Although much of our focus has been on the general, or average, (positive) effects of different pay for performance programs,[106] it is also useful to think in terms of matching pay strategies to organization strategies.[107] To take an example from medicine, using the same medical treatment regardless of the symptoms and diagnosis would be odd. Likewise, in choosing a pay strategy, one must consider how effectively it will further the organization's overall business strategy. Consider again the findings reported in Table 12.12. The average effect of moving from a pay strategy with below-average variability in pay to one with above-average variability is an increase in return on assets of almost two percentage points (from 5.2% to 7.1%). But in some organizations, the increase could be smaller. In fact, greater variability in pay could contribute to a lower return on assets in some organizations. In other organizations, greater variability in pay could contribute to increases in return on assets of greater than two percentage points. Obviously, being able to tell where variable pay works and where it does not could have substantial consequences. Conventional wisdom has sometimes argued that choice of management practices, including compensation, depends on the country (and/or national culture). However, each organization must decide how best to compete in a global economy, which will sometimes require deviating from national norms. As an example, see the Competing through Globalization box.

## COMPETING THROUGH GLOBALIZATION

### Japanese Companies Shift Emphasis from Seniority to Performance: Some Japanese Now Even Switch Companies

In the traditional Japanese employment system, seniority is a major determinant of how much an employee is paid. Performance has not been emphasized as strongly in Japan as in countries like the United States. Over the last decade, the rate of economic growth in Japan comes in last among the world's other largest economies (United States, China, Germany, France, United Kingdom). So the idea of looking at how non-Japanese companies in better-performing economies pay their employees and using some of those practices is perhaps overdue. It is also part of Prime Minister Shinzō Abe's plan to improve company efficiency in hopes of larger economic growth and wage growth in Japan.

Further pressure to revisit traditional seniority-based practices comes from the fact that there are now 158 jobs for every 100 applicants, a 44-year high. Unemployment is also quite low at 2.5%. What this means is that even in Japan, where the norm at many companies is still to hire employees right out of college with the expectation of both employer and employee that they will stay for life and be rewarded for doing so by paying for seniority, switching jobs and paying for performance are becoming more common. Companies are increasingly bidding away other companies' employees. For example, a record 30% of job switchers received salary increases of 10% or more with their new employers. Some Japanese companies

have sought in past years to shift to a greater emphasis on performance. A renewed commitment is being made to that effort by some companies, including Toyota, Hitachi, Sony, and Panasonic. The plan is to increase the importance of not only performance but also job responsibility in setting employee pay. The change may start primarily with younger employees, as companies are reluctant to modify the nature of the accepted relationship with older, more senior employees.

In addition to providing stronger performance incentives for current employees, these companies hope to gain an edge in recruiting younger employees, who would welcome working for a company where, rather than wait until they are older to make more money, they would have the opportunity to be paid well now if their contributions to the company prove to be valuable.

Recently, Toyota Motor Corporation placed job posters on a train line whose riders include many engineers working at research facilities owned by companies such as Fujitsu, NEC, and Toshiba to persuade them to switch jobs and come to Toyota. The poster read, "We want engineers from the Nambu Line area, more than from Silicon Valley." Another company that operates the fashion site Zozotown advertised for seven "geniuses" and said they would pay them $1 million each. An executive from its technology unit notes how foreign companies like Google and Apple pay much more for an

employee who can "make a big impact on the business" (i.e., exceptional performance).

To be clear, job switching is still much less common in Japan than in a country like the United Kingdom or the United States. But, at least some Japanese companies are moving in that direction. It also depends on the age group. A survey by Hays Japan reports that while less than 10% of workers aged 40 to 45 have changed employers, over half of those under 35 have already done so. That would seem to suggest that broad change is on its way.

#### DISCUSSION QUESTIONS
1. What is wrong with paying for seniority instead of performance?
2. Why is the prime minister of Japan interested in how companies pay?
3. If you were choosing between a company that paid for seniority and a company that paid for performance, which would you choose? What about 20 years from now? What if you were a native of Japan, working in Japan? Would you make the same choice? Explain.

SOURCES: M. Fujikawa, "Japan's Job-for-Life Culture Fades," *Wall Street Journal*, April 12, 2018; U. Dresser, "Money Motivates in Japan, Too—Hays Salary Guide 2018," *Japan Industry News*, February 22, 2018, www.japanindustrynews.com; M. Oi, "Japan Seeks Alternatives to Its Pay System," *BBC News, Japan*, March 22, 2016; K. Inagaki, "Japan Inc Shuns Seniority in Favour of Merit-Based Pay," *Financial Times*, January 27, 2015; Y. Hagiwara and C. Trudell, "Toyota Plans Overhaul to Seniority-Based Pay," *Bloomberg .com*, January 26, 2015.

**Table 12.15**
Matching Pay
Strategy and
Organization
Strategy

| PAY STRATEGY DIMENSIONS | ORGANIZATION STRATEGY | |
|---|---|---|
| | CONCENTRATION | GROWTH |
| Risk sharing (variable pay) | Low | High |
| Time orientation | Short term | Long term |
| Pay level (short run) | Above market | Below market |
| Pay level (long-run potential) | Below market | Above market |
| Benefits level | Above market | Below market |
| Centralization of pay decisions | Centralized | Decentralized |
| Pay unit of analysis | Job | Skills |

SOURCES: L. R. Gomez-Mejia and D. B. Balkin, *Compensation, Organizational Strategy, and Firm Performance* (Cincinnati, OH: South-Western, 1992), Appendix 4b; and L. R. Gomez-Mejia, P. Berrone, and M. Franco-Santos. *Compensation and Organizational Performance* (Armonk, NY: M.E. Sharpe 2010), Appendix 3.2.

Of course, as this chapter and Chapter 11 suggest, certain best practices may be of benefit to all or at least most organizations. Returning to our medical analogy, scientific consensus seems to be that certain behaviors (e.g., exercise, good nutrition) enhance health, whereas others (e.g., smoking, drugs, alcohol) harm health. So, too, there may be best practices when it comes to compensation strategy. Examples include choosing a pay level that balances the ability to compete in the product market and in the labor market, paying for performance to obtain positive incentive and sorting effects, paying attention to both distributive (e.g., equity theory) and procedural justice issues, and complying with regulatory requirements.

Returning to how to approach the issue of fit, recall that in Chapter 2 we discussed directional business strategies, two of which were growth (internal or external) and concentration ("sticking to the knitting"). How should compensation strategies differ according to whether an organization follows a growth strategy or a concentration strategy? Table 12.15 provides some suggested matches. Basically, a growth strategy's emphasis on innovation, risk taking, and new markets is linked to a pay strategy that shares risk with employees but also gives them the opportunity for high future earnings by having them share in whatever success the organization has.[108] This means relatively low levels of fixed compensation in the short run but the use of bonuses and stock options, for example, that can pay off handsomely in the long run. Stock options have been described as the pay program "that built Silicon Valley," having been used by companies such as Apple, Microsoft, and others.[109] When such companies become successful, everyone from top managers to secretaries can become millionaires if they own stock. Growth organizations are also thought to benefit from a less bureaucratic orientation, in the sense of having more decentralization and flexibility in pay decisions and in recognizing individual skills, rather than being constrained by job or grade classification systems. By contrast, concentration-oriented organizations are thought to require a very different set of pay practices by virtue of their lower rate of growth, more stable workforce, and greater need for consistency and standardization in pay decisions. As noted earlier, Microsoft has eliminated stock options in favor of stock grants to its employees, in part because it is not the growth company it once was.

## A LOOK BACK

### Pay for Performance: Balancing Objectives (and Risks)

In this chapter, we discussed the potential advantages and disadvantages of different types of incentive or pay-for-performance plans. We saw that these pay plans can have both intended and unintended consequences. We also saw that some organizations have paid a big price for not realizing the problems with their pay plans until it was too late and only then did they change them. (See also Exercising Strategy at the end of the chapter.) Designing a pay-for-performance strategy typically seeks to balance the pros and cons of different plans and reduce the chance of unintended consequences. To an important degree, pay strategy will depend on the particular goals and strategy of the organization and its units. At the beginning of this chapter, we saw that many organizations are working to link pay to performance and reduce fixed labor costs.

#### QUESTIONS

1. Does money motivate? Use the theories and examples discussed in this chapter to address this question.
2. Think of a job that you have held. Design an incentive plan. What would be the potential advantages and disadvantages of your plan? If your money was invested in the company, would you adopt the plan?

## SUMMARY

Our focus in this chapter has been on the design and administration of programs that recognize employee contributions to the organization's success. These programs vary as to whether they link pay to individual, group, or organization performance. Often, it is not so much a choice of one program or the other as it is a choice between different combinations of programs that seek to balance individual, group, and organization objectives.

Wages, bonuses, and other types of pay have an important influence on an employee's standard of living. This carries at least two important implications. First, pay can be a powerful motivator. An effective pay strategy can substantially promote an organization's success; conversely, a poorly conceived pay strategy can have detrimental effects. Second, the importance of pay means that employees care a great deal about the fairness of the pay process. A recurring theme is that pay programs must be explained and administered in such a way that employees understand their underlying rationale and believe they are fair.

The fact that organizations differ in their business and human resource strategies suggests that the most effective compensation strategy may differ from one organization to another. Although benchmarking programs against the competition is informative, what succeeds in some organizations may not be a good idea for others. The balanced scorecard suggests the need for organizations to decide what their key objectives are and use pay to support them.

## KEY TERMS

Incentive effect, 527
Expectancy theory, 527
Principal, 528
Agent, 528
Sorting effect, 531

Merit pay, 536
Merit bonus, 536
Merit increase grid, 536
Profit sharing, 541
Stock options, 543

Employee stock ownership plans
   (ESOPs), 544
Gainsharing, 545

## DISCUSSION QUESTIONS

1. To compete more effectively, your organization is considering a profit sharing plan to increase employee effort and to encourage employees to think like owners. What are the potential advantages and disadvantages of such a plan? Would the profit sharing plan have the same impact on all types of employees? Is the size of your organization an important consideration? Why? What alternative pay programs should be considered?

2. Gainsharing plans have often been used in manufacturing settings but can also be applied in service organizations. How could performance standards be developed for gainsharing plans in hospitals, banks, insurance companies, and so forth?

3. Your organization has two business units. One unit is a long-established manufacturer of a product that competes on price and has not been subject to many technological innovations. The other business unit is just being started. It has no products yet, but it is working on developing a new technology for testing the effects of drugs on people via simulation instead of through lengthy clinical trials. Would you recommend that the two business units have the same pay programs for recognizing individual contributions? Why?

4. Throughout the chapter, we have seen many examples of companies making changes to how they pay for performance. Do you believe the changes at these companies make sense? What are the potential payoffs and pitfalls of their new pay strategies?

## SELF-ASSESSMENT EXERCISE

Also assignable in Connect.

Pay is only one type of incentive that can motivate you to perform well and contribute to your satisfaction at work. This survey will help you understand what motivates you at work. Consider each aspect of work and rate its importance to you, using the following scale: 5 = very important, 4 = somewhat important, 3 = neutral, 2 = somewhat unimportant, 1 = very unimportant.

| | | | | | |
|---|---|---|---|---|---|
| Salary or wages | 1 | 2 | 3 | 4 | 5 |
| Cash bonuses | 1 | 2 | 3 | 4 | 5 |
| Boss's management style | 1 | 2 | 3 | 4 | 5 |
| Location of workplace | 1 | 2 | 3 | 4 | 5 |
| Commute | 1 | 2 | 3 | 4 | 5 |
| Job security | 1 | 2 | 3 | 4 | 5 |
| Opportunity for advancement | 1 | 2 | 3 | 4 | 5 |

| | | | | | |
|---|---|---|---|---|---|
| Work environment | 1 | 2 | 3 | 4 | 5 |
| Level of independence in job | 1 | 2 | 3 | 4 | 5 |
| Level of teamwork required for job | 1 | 2 | 3 | 4 | 5 |
| Other (enter your own): | | | | | |
| _____ | 1 | 2 | 3 | 4 | 5 |
| _____ | 1 | 2 | 3 | 4 | 5 |
| _____ | 1 | 2 | 3 | 4 | 5 |

Which aspects of work received a score of 5? A score of 4? These are the ones you believe motivate you to perform well and make you happy in your job. Which aspects of work received a score of 1 or 2? These are least likely to motivate you. Is pay the only way to motivate you?

SOURCE: Based on the "Job Assessor" found at www.salarymonster.com, accessed August 2002.

## EXERCISING STRATEGY

### Pay and Strategy Execution at Wells Fargo and "Down Under" (at ANZ): Incentives Gone Awry

Wells Fargo continues to pay the price for scandals that involved it making money by exploiting customers and opening accounts (as many as 3.5 million bank and credit card accounts without customers' knowledge). Most recently, it agreed to pay $575 million to 50 states and the District of Columbia. Prior to that, it paid a $1 billion fine imposed by federal regulators and $480 million to settle a class action suit brought by investors. It is also restricted by the Federal Reserve from getting larger than $2 trillion assets until the Federal Reserve is convinced it has changed its ways.

Customer exploitation appears to have been a consequence of pressuring employees to meet unrealistic, aggressively high sales targets. They used both "carrots and sticks" to drive employee behavior. Meeting sales targets often meant larger bonuses. Not meeting sales targets could result in losing your job. One way that employees met aggressive sales targets was by cross-selling. Cross-selling refers to the practice of asking existing customers to open another account (e.g., a checking account, a new credit card, a home loan, or a line of credit). However, employees at Wells Fargo went a step further and opened new accounts ("fake" accounts) for customers who did not ask for the accounts. One method, for example, was that if a customer was applying for a home loan, the banker would include a form for a line of credit and hope the customer would not notice when signing all the papers.

According to New York Federal Reserve President Bill Dudley, the "widespread fraud" at Wells Fargo shows the "powerful role—for good or bad—that incentives can play." Wells Fargo reports that it has changed its compensation plan away from a focus on cross-selling as many banking products as possible to a focus on customer service, customer usage, and growth in primary balances.

The problems at Wells Fargo are also a challenge elsewhere. In the Integrity in Action box, we saw that Novartis has limited incentive/bonus payments for high sales performance and now monitors whether the sales were achieved in an appropriate manner. On the other side of the world, the Australia and New Zealand Banking Group (ANZ) recently announced it was taking a more dramatic step and eliminating sales-based bonuses entirely. This comes after customer complaints about wealth management firms alleging that advisers had conflicts of interests, largely due to the incentive system, which led them to give advice that was not in the best interests of the customer (e.g., overextending themselves and/or taking on overly risk investments), but which led to higher adviser pay. ANZ's chief risk officer reported that an audit of past advising indicated that 5% of advice given "failed to meet the requirement that it be in the best interest of the client."

Going forward, ANZ has stated that not only will it end bonuses, but also that advisers will be evaluated and compensated entirely on the basis of customer satisfaction, how consistent the adviser is with the bank's values, and how well the adviser minimizes risks and adheres to compliance standards. Advisers who fail two audits of their behaviors will be dismissed. Advisers must also complete training in these areas.

## QUESTIONS
1. Have you experienced cross-selling as a bank customer? What was your reaction? What would your reaction be if the bank opened a line of credit for you that you did not want (or tell you about)?
2. How is what happened at Wells Fargo similar to what happened at Volkswagen or at Novartis? (See the Integrity in Action box, earlier in this chapter.)
3. What caused the problems at Wells Fargo, and how can they be fixed? How helpful will the new compensation plan be in fixing things? Why?
4. Consider the same questions for ANZ. How would you react as a customer if your adviser did not act in your best interest? If you currently have a financial adviser, how do you know that person is acting in your best interest? Will the changes to AMZ's compensation be effective?

SOURCES: E. Glazer, "Wells Fargo to Roll Out New Compensation Plan to Replace Sales Goals: Bankers Say Previous Lofty Goals Pushed Them to Open Accounts without Customers' Knowledge," *Wall Street Journal*, January 6, 2017; B. Chappell, "Wells Fargo Fined $185 Million over Creation of Fake Accounts for Bonuses," *National Public Radio*, September 8, 2016; M. Egan, "Wells Fargo Customers in $110 Million Settlement over Fake Accounts," *CNNMoney.com*, March 29, 2017; C. Arnold, "Former Wells Fargo Employees Describe Toxic Sales Culture, Even at HQ," *National Public Radio*, October 4, 2016; M. Egan, "Top Fed Official Likens Wells Fargo Fraud to Mortgage Crisis," *CNNMoney.com*, March 21, 2017.

## MANAGING PEOPLE

### ESOPs: Who Benefits?

Mandy Cabot wants to make sure the shoemaking business that she and her husband built over the past 20 years remains in good hands after they're gone. The 58-year-old co-founder of Dansko, a West Grove, Pennsylvania, company with more than $150 million in annual sales, says she fears that selling to a competitor, or a private-equity firm, would result in layoffs or other cost-cutting measures.

So last February, the couple transferred ownership of the business to its 180 employees. By "keeping it in the family" and giving workers a real stake in its future, Ms. Cabot says she hopes the company will keep going strong for years to come. "This is our baby, but at some point we have to cease being parents and become grandparents," she adds.

Ms. Cabot, who launched Dansko in 1990 by selling shoes from the back of a Volvo station wagon, says the tax benefits associated with employee stock ownership enabled the S corporation to manage the long-term debt of buying out the couple's ownership stake. But, she adds, "It's not some tax dodge."

Known as employee stock ownership plans, or ESOPs, the move is being embraced by smaller firms, especially those struggling to find buyers during the weak economy. Under typical plans, an owner's interest in a business is bought out, in part or in whole—often through a bank loan—with the stock being held in trust. Employees then cash in their shares as they retire.

Michael Keeling, president of the ESOP Association, a Washington lobby group, argues, "A company's success isn't just driven by the brilliance of the CEO, but also by its employees, and more owners feel [their employees] deserve something more for that."

This week, a bipartisan group of lawmakers introduced a bill to encourage employee-ownership plans. But critics of the plans say owners who are looking for an easy exit are simply spreading the risks of business ownership by convincing employees to gamble their retirement savings. Andrew Stumpff, University of Michigan, says it's bad enough to risk your retirement savings in a single company. But it's even worse if that company is your employer, he says. "If the company fails, you lose your savings and your job." That risk is very real, he adds, citing Enron, WorldCom, and Lehman Brothers as examples of high-profile failures at shared-ownership companies, especially Enron Corp. where workers lost their savings.

The real attraction for owners, opponents say, is generous tax breaks that shelter capital gains and dividends tied to the plans.

As of 2011, there were an estimated 10,900 employee-owned businesses across the country, a 12% increase from 2007 and a record high dating back to the mid-1970s, when the plans first appeared, according to the National Center for Employee Ownership. Nearly all of the employee-owned businesses have fewer than 500 workers. Some 10 million employees are currently enrolled in these plans, representing more than $860 billion in assets, the group estimates.

Norman Stein, Drexel University, says employee ownership under the ESOP model causes more harm than good. Many of the plans are based on a bloated assessment of the value of the businesses. Many workers who are participating in the plans are left holding overvalued shares, long after the original owner has cashed out: "I'm not against employees owning some stock in their employer, but not if it's tied to a retirement plan," he says. "It's a troubling trend."

Separate studies by Harvard University and Rutgers, as well as by the National Bureau of Economic Research, have found that businesses with shared-ownership plans fared better during the recession than more traditionally structured firms, including fewer layoffs, higher productivity and stronger employee loyalty.

Dawn Huston, 31, started working at Dansko 11 years ago, sorting shoes for delivery. Now a warehouse processor, she says the idea of owning a piece of the company made her nervous at first—though she wasn't worried about her retirement savings, since the company offers a separate 401(k) plan, she adds. Over the past year, she's begun referring to Dansko as "our company." "I feel like they consider us family and it feels like a family," she says of the switch to employee ownership.

Adele Connors, 60, co-founder of Adworkshop, a Lake Placid, New York, marketing agency, says a move to employee ownership "really changed the culture of our company" with workers now being "more engaged." Kelly Frady, 43, an account supervisor at Adworkshop, says the agency's employee-ownership plan has fostered a team spirit among its staff. "Everyone knows that you do well and your stock will rise," she says. "It's a driving factor in making the company succeed in the long term."

Kim Jordan, who co-founded the New Belgium Brewing Co. with her husband in 1991, says employee ownership ensures that the company's values and culture will remain intact—including its commitment to sustainable farming and an environmentally friendly production process. In December, she extended full ownership of the Fort Collins, Colorado, brewery to its 480 employees.

"We've always tried to involve our people in the running of the business," she says. The goal, she says, isn't just to reward employees, but also to foster innovation by creating a company culture where workers think more like entrepreneurs.

### QUESTIONS

1. Is an ESOP good for employees? Why or why not?
2. Does an ESOP motivate employees "better"? Explain the reasons for your answer.
3. What happens to employees' retirement income if they are at an ESOP company that runs into financial problems? What happens to the same employees, if instead, they work at a non-ESOP company that runs into financial problems?

SOURCE: A. Loten, "Founders Cash Out, but Do Workers Gain?" *Wall Street Journal*, April 17, 2013.

## HR IN SMALL BUSINESS

### Employees Own Bob's Red Mill

Headquartered in Portland, Oregon, Bob's Red Mill Natural Foods sells a variety of whole-grain flours and mixes, specializing in gluten-free products. The "Bob" of the company's name is Bob Moore, the founder and president. In 2010, more than 30 years after he started the business, Moore called his 200 employees together and announced that he was giving them the company. As a retirement plan for them, he had set up an employee stock ownership plan, placing the company's stock in a trust fund. All employees who had been with the company at least three years were immediately fully vested in the plan. As employees retire, they will receive cash for their shares.

Watching the company's stock rise in their retirement plan is not the only financial incentive for employees of Bob's Red Mill. In the mid-1990s, the company established a profit sharing plan. The chief financial officer gives employees a weekly sales update, which they can use to estimate profits and determine their share.

The numbers have been mostly good during the past two decades. When John Wagner, chief financial officer, joined the company in 1993, there were just 28 employees generating sales of $3.2 million. Under Wagner's guidance, the company began participating in trade shows, attracting the interest of health food stores, food distributors, and later on, supermarket chains. The company's market expanded from a few states to cover North America and some international markets. The company reports that its revenues have grown at rates between 20% and 30% in the years since 2004.

Along the way, Moore and his employees have been unwavering in their dedication to the company and its mission of providing foods that make America healthier. Ten years after the business started, a fire caused by arson destroyed the mill, but Moore had it rebuilt, and the company now runs a 15-acre production facility, operating in three shifts, six days a week.

Why did Moore give his company to his employees on his 81st birthday rather than selling it to one of the many parties who have expressed an interest in buying? For Moore, the answer is all about his employees and their commitment to the company. He told a reporter, "These people are far too good at their jobs for me to just sell [the business]." Employees return the praise. For example, Bo Thomas, maintenance superintendent, said, "It just shows how much faith and trust Bob has in us. For all of us, it's more than just a job."

## QUESTIONS

1. Which types of incentive pay are described in this case? Are these based on individual, group, or company performance?
2. Would you expect the motivational impact of stock ownership or profit sharing to be different at a small company like Bob's Red Mill than in a large corporation? Explain.
3. Suppose Bob's Red Mill brought you in as a consultant to review the company's total compensation. Explain why you would or would not recommend that the company add other forms of incentive pay, and identify any additional forms of compensation you would recommend for the company's employees.

SOURCES: Corporate website, "About Us," www.bobsredmill.com; K. E. Klein, "ESOPs on the Rise among Small Businesses," *Bloomberg Businessweek*, April 26, 2010; D. Tims, "Founder of Bob's Red Mill Natural Foods Transfers Business to Employees," *Oregon Live*, February 16, 2010, http://blog.oregonlive.com; and C. Brozyna, "American Heart: Owner of Multi-Million Dollar Company Hands Over Business to Employees," *ABC News*, February 18, 2010, http://abcnews.go.com.

## NOTES

1. We draw freely in this chapter on several literature reviews: B. Gerhart and G. T. Milkovich, "Employee Compensation: Research and Practice," in *Handbook of Industrial and Organizational Psychology*, vol. 3, 2nd ed., ed. M. D. Dunnette and L. M. Hough (Palo Alto, CA: Consulting Psychologists Press, 1992); B. Gerhart and S. L. Rynes, *Compensation: Theory, Evidence, and Strategic Implications* (Thousand Oaks, CA: Sage, 2003); B. Gerhart, "Compensation Strategy and Organization Performance," in S. L. Rynes and B. Gerhart, *Compensation in Organizations: Current Research and Practice* (San Francisco: Jossey-Bass, 2000), pp. 151–94; B. Gerhart, S. L. Rynes, and I. S. Fulmer, "Compensation," *Academy of Management Annals* 3 (2009); B. Gerhart and M. Fang, "Pay for (Individual) Performance: Issues, Claims, Evidence and the Role of Sorting Effects," *Human Resource Management Review*, 24 (2014), pp. 41–52.
2. B. Gerhart and G. T. Milkovich, "Organizational Differences in Managerial Compensation and Financial Performance," *Academy of Management Journal* 33 (1990), pp. 663–91.
3. Y. Garbers and U. Konradt, "The Effect of Financial Incentives on Performance: A Quantitative Review of Individual and Team-Based Financial Incentives," *Journal of Occupational and Organizational Psychology* 87 (2014), pp. 102–37; D. G. Jenkins Jr., A. Mitra, N. Gupta, and J. D. Shaw, "Are Financial Incentives Related to Performance? A Meta-Analytic Review of Empirical Research," *Journal of Applied Psychology*, 83 (1998), pp. 777–87; Gerhart and Fang, "Pay for (Individual) Performance: Issues, Claims, Evidence and the Role of Sorting Effects"; J. D. Shaw and A. Mitra, "The Science of Pay-for-Performance Systems: Six Facts That All Managers Should Know," Unpublished manuscript (2017); J. D. Shaw and N. Gupta, "Let the Evidence Speak Again! Financial Incentives Are More Effective Than We Thought," *Human Resource Management Review* 25 no. 3 (2015), pp. 281–93; B. Gerhart, "Incentives and Pay for Performance in the Workplace," in *Advances in Motivation Science*, vol. 4 (Elsevier, 2017), pp. 91–140; J. M. Beus and D. S. Whitman, "Almighty Dollar or Root of All Evil? Testing the Effects of Money on Workplace Behavior," *Journal of Management* 43, no. 7 (2017), pp. 2147–67.
4. E. Deci and R. Ryan, *Intrinsic Motivation and Self-Determination in Human Behavior* (New York: Plenum, 1985); A. Kohn, "Why Incentive Plans Cannot Work," *Harvard Business Review*, September/October 1993.
5. B. Gerhart and M. Fang, "Pay, Intrinsic Motivation, Extrinsic Motivation, Performance, and Creativity in the Workplace: Revisiting Long-Held Beliefs," *Annual Review of Organizational Psychology and Organizational Behavior* 2 (2015), pp. 489–521; R. Eisenberger and J. Cameron, "Detrimental Effects of Reward: Reality or Myth?" *American Psychologist* 51 (1996), pp. 1153–66;

S. L. Rynes, B. Gerhart, and L. Parks, "Personnel Psychology: Performance Evaluation and Compensation," *Annual Review of Psychology,* 56 (2005), pp. 571–600; M. Fang and B. Gerhart, "Does Pay for Performance Diminish Intrinsic Interest? A Workplace Test Using Cognitive Evaluation Theory and the Attraction-Selection-Attrition Model," *International Journal of Human Resource Management* 23 (2012), pp. 1176–96; M. Gagné and E. L. Deci, "Self-Determination Theory and Work Motivation," *Journal of Organizational Behavior* 26, pp. 331–62; G. E. Ledford Jr., M. Fang, and B. Gerhart, "Negative Effects of Extrinsic Rewards on Intrinsic Motivation: More Smoke Than Fire," *World at Work Journal* 16, no. 2 (2013), pp. 17–29; K. Byron, and S. Khazanchi, "Rewards and Creative Performance: A Meta-Analytic Test of Theoretically Derived Hypotheses," *Psychological Bulletin* 138 (2012), pp. 809–30.

6. P. C. Cerasoli, J. M. Nicklin, and M. T. Ford, "Intrinsic Motivation and Extrinsic Incentives Jointly Predict Performance: A 40-Year Meta-Analysis," *Psychological Bulletin* 140 (2014), pp. 980–1008; A. A. Grandey, N. W. Chi, and J. A. Diamond, "Show Me the Money! Do Financial Rewards for Performance Enhance or Undermine the Satisfaction from Emotional Labor?" *Personnel Psychology* 66, no. 3 (2013), pp. 569–612.

7. Y. Garbers and U. Konradt, "The Effect of Financial Incentives on Performance: A Quantitative Review of Individual and Team-Based Financial Incentives," *Journal of Occupational and Organizational Psychology* 87 (2014), pp. 102–37; D. G. Jenkins "Are Financial Incentives Related to Performance? A Meta-Analytic Review of Empirical Research"; Gerhart and Fang, "Pay for (Individual) Performance: Issues, Claims, Evidence and the Role of Sorting Effects."

8. T. M. Amabile and M. G. Pratt, "The Dynamic Componential Model of Creativity and Innovation in Organizations: Making Progress, Making Meaning," *Research in Organizational Behavior* 36 (2016), pp. 157–83.

9. For an alternative view, see E. L. Deci, A. H. Olafsen, and R. M. Ryan, "Self-Determination Theory in Work Organizations: The State of a Science," *Annual Review of Organizational Psychology and Organizational Behavior* 4 (2017), pp. 19–43. For a workplace study that claims to find that financial incentives "crowded out" (reduced) intrinsic motivation, see T. Gubler, I. Larkin, and L. Pierce, "Motivational Spillovers from Awards: Crowding Out in a Multitasking Environment," *Organization Science* 27 (2016), pp. 286–303. A study that concludes that pay for performance has a net negative effect on work effort is B. Kuvaas, R. Buch, M. Gagné, A. Dysvik, and J. Forest, "Do You Get What You Pay For? Sales Incentives and Implications for Motivation and Changes in Turnover Intention and Work Effort," *Motivation and Emotion* 40 (2016), 667–80. However, when I compute total effects of pay for performance on work effort using their Figure 3, I find a positive net effect.

10. D. R. Dalton, M. A. Hitt, S. T. Certo, and C. M. Dalton, "The Fundamental Agency Problem and Its Mitigation: Independence, Equity, and the Market for Corporate Control," *Academy of Management Annals* 1 (2007), pp. 1–64; R. A. Lambert and D. F. Larcker, "Executive Compensation, Corporate Decision Making, and Shareholder Wealth," in *Executive Compensation,* ed. F. Foulkes (Boston: Harvard Business School Press, 1989), pp. 287–309.

11. L. R. Gomez-Mejia, H. Tosi, and T. Hinkin, "Managerial Control, Performance, and Executive Compensation," *Academy of Management Journal* 30 (1987), pp. 51–70; H. L. Tosi Jr. and L. R. Gomez-Mejia, "The Decoupling of CEO Pay and Performance: An Agency Theory Perspective," *Administrative Science Quarterly* 34 (1989), pp. 169–89.

12. K. M. Eisenhardt, "Agency Theory: An Assessment and Review," *Academy of Management Review* 14 (1989), pp. 57–74.

13. R. E. Hoskisson, M. A. Hitt, and C. W. L. Hill, "Managerial Incentives and Investment in R&D in Large Multiproduct Firms," *Organizational Science* 4 (1993), pp. 325–41; M. Bloom and G. T. Milkovich, "Relationships among Risk, Incentive Pay, and Organizational Performance," *Academy of Management Journal* 41 (1998), pp. 283–97.

14. A. J. Nyberg, I. S. Fulmer, B. Gerhart, and M. A. Carpenter, "Agency Theory Revisited: CEO Return and Shareholder Interest Alignment," *Academy of Management Journal* 53 (2010), pp. 1029–49; Douglas A. Bosse and Robert A. Phillips, "Agency Theory and Bounded Self-Interest," *Academy of Management Review* 41, no. 2 (2016), pp. 276–97.

15. Eisenhardt, "Agency Theory."

16. Eisenhardt, "Agency Theory"; E. J. Conlon and J. M. Parks, "Effects of Monitoring and Tradition on Compensation Arrangements: An Experiment with Principal–Agent Dyads," *Academy of Management Journal* 33 (1990), pp. 603–22; K. M. Eisenhardt, "Agency- and Institutional-Theory Explanations: The Case of Retail Sales Compensation," *Academy of Management Journal* 31 (1988), pp. 488–511; Gerhart and Milkovich, "Employee Compensation"; J. Devaro and F. A. Kurtulus, "An Empirical Analysis of Risk, Incentives and the Delegation of Worker Authority," *Industrial and Labor Relations Review* 63 (2010), pp. 641–61.

17. G. T. Milkovich, J. Hannon, and B. Gerhart, "The Effects of Research and Development Intensity on Managerial Compensation in Large Organizations," *Journal of High Technology Management Research* 2 (1991), pp. 133–50; J. Devaro and F. A. Kurtulus, "An Empirical Analysis of Risk, Incentives and the Delegation of Worker Authority," *Industrial and Labor Relations Review,* 63 (2010), pp. 641–61.

18. V. Brenčič and J. B. Norris, "On-the-Job Tasks and Performance Pay: A Vacancy-Level Analysis," *Industrial and Labor Relations Review* 63 (2010), pp. 511–44. See also the discussion of performance reliability in B. Gerhart and S. L. Rynes, *Compensation* (2003).

19. G. T. Milkovich and A. K. Wigdor, *Pay for Performance* (Washington, DC: National Academy Press, 1991); Gerhart and Milkovich, "Employee Compensation"; Gerhart and Rynes, *Compensation: Theory, Evidence, and Strategic Implications*; A. Nyberg, "Retaining Your High Performers: Moderators of the Performance-Job Satisfaction-Voluntary Turnover Relationship," *Journal of Applied Psychology* 95 (2010), pp. 440–53; C. O. Trevor, G. Reilly, and B. Gerhart, "Reconsidering Pay Dispersion's Effect on the Performance of Interdependent Work: Reconciling Sorting and Pay Inequality," *Academy of Management Journal* 55 (2012), pp. 585–610; S. Carnahan, R. Agarwal, and B. A. Campbell, "Heterogeneity in Turnover: The Effect of Relative Compensation Dispersion of Firms on the Mobility and Entrepreneurship of Extreme Performers," *Strategic Management Journal,* 33 (2012), pp. 1411–30; J. D. Shaw, "Pay Dispersion, Sorting, and Organizational Performance," *Academy of Management Discoveries* 1 (2015), pp. 165–79.

20. C. Trevor, B. Gerhart, and J. W. Boudreau, "Voluntary Turnover and Job Performance: Curvilinearity and the Moderating Influences of Salary Growth and Promotions," *Journal of Applied Psychology* 82 (1997), pp. 44–61; C. B. Cadsby, F. Song, and F. Tapon, "Sorting and Incentive Effects of Pay-for-Performance:

An Experimental Investigation," *Academy of Management Journal* 50 (2007), pp. 387–405; A. Salamin and P. W. Hom, "In Search of the Elusive U-Shaped Performance-Turnover Relationship: Are High Performing Swiss Bankers More Liable to Quit?" *Journal of Applied Psychology* 90 (2005), pp. 1204–16; J. D. Shaw, and N. Gupta, "Pay System Characteristics and Quit Patterns of Good, Average, and Poor Performers," *Personnel Psychology* 60 (2007), pp. 903–28; J. D. Shaw, B. R. Dineen, R. Fang, R. F. Vellella, "Employee-Organization Exchange Relationships, HRM practices, and Quit Rates of Good and Poor Performers," *Academy of Management Journal*, 52 (2009), pp. 1016–1033.

21. I. S. Fulmer and J. D. Shaw, "Person-Based Differences in Pay Reactions: A Compensation-Activation Theory and Integrative Conceptual Review," *Journal of Applied Psychology* 103, no. 9 (2018), p. 939; B. D. Blume, R. S. Rubin, and T. T. Baldwin, "Who Is Attracted to an Organization Using a Forced Distribution Performance Management System?" *Human Resource Management Journal* 23, no. 4 (2013), pp. 360–78; T. Dohmen and A. Falk, "Performance Pay and Multidimensional Sorting: Productivity, Preferences, and Gender," *American Economic Review* 101, no. 2 (2011), pp. 556–90; R. D. Bretz, R. A. Ash, and G. F. Dreher, "Do People Make the Place? An Examination of the Attraction-Selection-Attrition Hypothesis," *Personnel Psychology* 42 (1989), pp. 561–81; T. A. Judge and R. D. Bretz, "Effect of Values on Job Choice Decisions," *Journal of Applied Psychology* 77 (1992), pp. 261–71; D. M. Cable and T. A. Judge, "Pay Performances and Job Search Decisions: A Person-Organization Fit Perspective," *Personnel Psychology* 47 (1994), pp. 317–48.

22. G. T. Milkovich, J. M. Newman, and B. Gerhart, *Compensation*, 11th ed. (New York: McGraw-Hill/Irwin, 2014); K. Abosch and B. Gerhart, "The Case for Differentiated Pay for Performance," World at Work Total Rewards Conference & Exhibition, 2013; B. Baik, J. H. Evans III, K. Kim, and Y. Yanadori, "White Collar Incentives," *Accounting, Organizations and Society* 53 (2016), pp. 34–49; Gerhart, "Incentives and Pay for Performance in the Workplace."

23. E. H. O'Boyle and H. Aguinis, "The Best and the Rest: Revisiting the Norm of Normality of Individual Performance," *Personnel Psychology* 65 (2012), pp. 79–119; H. Aguinis and E. O'Boyle, "Star Performers in Twenty-First Century Organizations," *Personnel Psychology* 67, no. 2 (2014), pp. 313–50; H. Aguinis, E. O'Boyle, E. Gonzalez-Mulé, and H. Joo, "Cumulative Advantage: Conductors and Insulators of Heavy-Tailed Productivity Distributions and Productivity Stars," *Personnel Psychology*, 2014; K. F. Hallock, *Pay: Why People Earn What They Earn and What You Can Do Now to Make More* (Cambridge: Cambridge University Press, 2012). A key part of the argument is that performance is not normally distributed. For an alternative view of the evidence questioning whether the performance distribution is nonnormal, see J. W. Beck, A. S. Beatty, and P. R. Sackett, "On the Distribution of Job Performance: The Role of Measurement Characteristics in Observed Departures from Normality," *Personnel Psychology* 67 (2014) pp. 531–66.

24. Gerhart and Fang, "Pay for (Individual) Performance: Issues, Claims, Evidence and the Role of Sorting Effects"; S. Sukanya and Y. Yoon, "Moderating Effect of Pay Dispersion on the Relationship between Employee Share Ownership and Labor Productivity," *Human Resource Management* 57, no. 5 (2018), pp. 1083–96; C. O. Trevor, G. Reilly, and B. Gerhart,

"Reconsidering Pay Dispersion's Effect on the Performance of Interdependent Work: Reconciling Sorting and Pay Inequality," *Academy of Management Journal* 55, no. 3 (2012), pp. 585–610.

25. J. D. Shaw, "Pay Dispersion," *Annual Review of Organizational Psychology and Organizational Behavior* 1, no. 1 (2014), pp. 521–44; P. E. Downes and D. Choi, "Employee Reactions to Pay Dispersion: A Typology of Existing Research," *Human Resource Management Review* 24, no. 1 (2014), pp. 53–66; C. O. Trevor, G. Reilly, and B. Gerhart, "Reconsidering Pay Dispersion's Effect on the Performance of Interdependent Work: Reconciling Sorting and Pay Inequality," *Academy of Management Journal* 55 (2012), pp. 585–610; A. Bucciol, N. J. Foss, and M. Piovesan, "Pay Dispersion and Performance in Teams," *PloS ONE* 9, no. 11 (2014), e112631.

26. W. He, L. R. Long, and B. Kuvaas, "Workgroup Salary Dispersion and Turnover Intention in China: A Contingent Examination of Individual Differences and the Dual Deprivation Path Explanation," *Human Resource Management* 55 (2015), pp. 301–320; S. H. Moon, S. E. Scullen, and G. P. Latham, "Precarious Curve Ahead: The Effects of Forced Distribution Rating Systems on Job Performance," *Human Resource Management Review* 26, no. 2 (2016), pp. 166–79; N. Gupta, S. A. Conroy, and J. E. Delery, "The Many Faces of Pay Variation," *Human Resource Management Review* 22, no. 2 (2012), pp. 100–15; J. D. Shaw, "Pay Dispersion," *Annual Review of Organizational Psychology and Organizational Behavior* 1, no. 1 (2014), pp. 521–44; W. Huang, "Responsible Pay: Managing Compliance, Organizational Efficiency and Fairness in the Choice of Pay Systems in China's Automotive Companies," *International Journal of Human Resource Management* 27, no. 18 (2016), pp. 2161–81; S. Conroy and N. Gupta, "Team Pay-for-Performance: The Devil Is in the Details," *Group & Organization Management* 41, no. 1 (2016), pp. 32–65.

27. B. Gerhart, "Incentives and Pay for Performance in the Workplace," *Advances in Motivation Science* 4 (2017), pp. 91–140; B. Gerhart and M. Fang, "Competence and Pay for Performance," in *Handbook of Competence and Motivation,* 2nd ed., ed. A. J. Elliot, C. S. Dweck, and D. S. Yeager (New York: Guilford, 2017); D. Pohler and J. A. Schmidt, "Does Pay-for-Performance Strain the Employment Relationship? The Effect of Manager Bonus Eligibility on Nonmanagement Employee Turnover," *Personnel Psychology* 69 (2015), pp. 395–429.

28. W. Boston, "VW Revamps Pay, Imposes Caps," *Wall Street Journal,* February 25/26, 2017; S. Randazzo, "U.S. Court Gives Initial Approval to Volkswagen Vehicle Emissions Settlement," *Wall Street Journal,* February 14, 2017; J. Rothfeder, "The Volkswagen Settlement: How Bad Management Leads to Big Punishment," *The New Yorker,* July 1, 2016.

29. A. J. Nyberg, M. A. Maltarich, D. D. Abdulsalam, S. M. Essman, and O. Cragun, "Collective Pay for Performance: A Cross-Disciplinary Review and Meta-Analysis," *Journal of Management* 44, no. 6 (2018), pp. 2433–72; J. J. Gerakos, C. D. Ittner, and F. Moers, "Compensation Objectives and Business Unit Pay Strategy," *Journal of Management Accounting Research* 30, no. 2 (2017), pp. 105–30; C. O. Barry, O. Trevor, and Mary E. Graham, "New Directions in Compensation Research: Synergies, Risk and Survival," *Research in Personnel and Human Resource Management,* ed. G. R. Ferris (London: JAI Press, 1996); S. De Spiegelaere, G. Van Gyes, and G. Van Hootegem, "Innovative Work Behaviour and Performance-Related Pay: Rewarding the Individual or the Collective?" *International Journal of Human Resource Management* 29, no. 12 (2018), pp. 1900–19.

30. E. E. Lawler III, *Strategic Pay* (San Francisco: Jossey-Bass, 1990); Gerhart and Milkovich, "Employee Compensation"; Gerhart and Rynes, *Compensation: Theory, Evidence, and Strategic Implications*; B. Gerhart, C. Trevor, and M. Graham, "New Directions in Employee Compensation Research" in *Research in Personnel and Human Resources Management*, ed. G. R. Ferris (London: JAI Press, 1996), pp. 143–203; M. Beer and M. D. Cannon, "Promise and Peril in Implementing Pay-for-Performance," *Human Resource Management* 43 (2004), pp. 3–20.

31. In some cases, under exceptional circumstances, an organization may, at least temporarily, design an incentive plan to focus everyone's attention on one critical objective. For example, after the oil spill and worker fatalities in the Gulf of Mexico, BP temporarily revised its compensation program to make safety the sole factor in determining pay raises. (See G. Chazan and D. Mattioli, "BP Links Pay to Safety in Fourth Quarter," *Wall Street Journal*, October 19, 2010.) But having a single objective is not typically advisable.

32. R. D. Bretz, G. T. Milkovich, and W. Read, "The Current State of Performance Appraisal Research and Practice," *Journal of Management* 18 (1992), pp. 321–52; R. L. Heneman, "Merit Pay Research," *Research in Personnel and Human Resource Management* 8 (1990), pp. 203–63; Milkovich and Wigdor, *Pay for Performance*; Rynes, Gerhart, and Parks, "Personnel Psychology: Performance Evaluation and Compensation." Some evidence suggests that merit pay may be more effective when reinforced by other aspects of the pay strategy and/or by leadership of supervisors. See J. H. Han, K. M. Bartol, and S. Kim, "Tightening Up the Performance–Pay Linkage: Roles of Contingent Reward Leadership and Profit-Sharing in the Cross-Level Influence of Individual Pay-for-Performance," *Journal of Applied Psychology* 100 (2014), pp. 417–30. Other evidence suggests that merit pay may be more effective with certain employee personality profiles, consistent with our earlier discussion of sorting. See I. S. Fulmer and W. J. Walker, "More Bang for the Buck? Personality Traits as Moderators of Responsiveness to Pay-for-Performance," *Human Performance* 28, no. 1 (2015), pp. 40–65; I. S. Fulmer and J. D. Shaw, "Person-Based Differences in Pay Reactions: A Compensation-Activation Theory and Integrative Conceptual Review," *Journal of Applied Psychology* 103, no. 9 (2018), p. 939.

33. Gerhart ("Incentives and Pay for Performance in the Workplace") states that merit pay is likely used in virtually 100% of private-sector U.S. organizations based on the following: WorldatWork, the professional association for compensation professionals, as one of its activities, conducts surveys of compensation practices in organizations. It reports that 94% have merit pay programs (*Compensation Programs and Practices*; Scottsdale, AZ: WorldatWork, 2016). Given that 22% of responding organizations were in the nonprofit, not-for-profit, or public sectors, where we know that the use of pay for performance is considerably lower, as is its intensity when it is used (WorldatWork, *Compensation Programs and Practices*; Scottsdale, AZ: WorldatWork, 2012), it seems likely that merit pay is used in essentially all private-sector organizations in the United States.

34. Bretz et al., "Current State of Performance Appraisal."

35. B. D. Blume, T. T. Baldwin, and R. S. Rubin, "Reactions to Different Types of Forced Distribution Performance Evaluation Systems," *Journal of Business and Psychology* 24 (2009), pp. 77–91.

36. Bretz et al., "Current State of Performance Appraisal."

37. Bretz et al., "Current State of Performance Appraisal."

38. W. E. Deming, *Out of the Crisis* (Cambridge, MA: Center for Advanced Engineering Study, Massachusetts Institute of Technology, 1986), p. 110.

39. Deming, *Out of the Crisis*, p. 110.

40. E. O'Boyle Jr. and H. Aguinis, "The Best and the Rest: Revisiting the Norm of Normality of Individual Performance," *Personnel Psychology* 65 (2012), pp. 79–119; C. O. Trevor, G. Reilly, and B. Gerhart, "Reconsidering Pay Dispersion's Effect on the Performance of Interdependent Work: Reconciling Sorting and Pay Inequality," *Academy of Management Journal*, 55 (2012), pp. 585–610.

41. Deming, *Out of the Crisis*.

42. Trevor et al., "Voluntary Turnover."

43. Gerhart and Rynes, *Compensation: Theory, Evidence, and Strategic Implications*.

44. S. Scullen, P. Bergey, and L. Aiman-Smith, "Forced Distribution Rating Systems and the Improvement of Workforce Potential: A Baseline Simulation," *Personnel Psychology* 58(1), 2005, pp. 1–33; S. H. Moon, S. E. Scullen, and G. P. Latham, "Precarious Curve Ahead: The Effects of Forced Distribution Rating Systems on Job Performance," *Human Resource Management Review* 26, no. 2 (2016), pp. 166–79.

45. Rynes, Gerhart, and Parks, "Personnel Psychology: Performance Evaluation and Compensation."

46. J. Schaubroeck, J. D. Shaw, and M. K. Duffy, "An Under-Met and Over-Met Expectations Model of Employee Reactions to Merit Raises," *Journal of Applied Psychology* 93 (2008) pp. 424–34; S. Kepes, J. Delery, and N. Gupta, "Contingencies in the Effects of Pay Range on Organizational Effectiveness," *Personnel Psychology* 62 (2009), pp. 497–531; M. S. Chien, J. S. Lawler, and J. F. Uen, "Performance-Based Pay, Procedural Justice and Job Performance for RD Professionals: Evidence from the Taiwanese High-Tech Sector," *International Journal of Human Resource Management* 21 (2010), pp. 2234–48; P. Bamberger and E. Belogolovsky, "The Impact of Pay Secrecy on Individual Task Performance," *Personnel Psychology* 63 (2010), pp. 965–96.

47. R. Folger and M. A. Konovsky, "Effects of Procedural and Distributive Justice on Reactions to Pay Raise Decisions," *Academy of Management Journal* 32 (1989), pp. 115–30; J. Greenberg, "Determinants of Perceived Fairness of Performance Evaluations," *Journal of Applied Psychology* 71 (1986), pp. 340–42.

48. Rynes, Gerhart, and Parks, "Personnel Psychology: Performance Evaluation and Compensation."

49. A. Mitra, A. Tenhiälä, and J. D. Shaw, "Smallest Meaningful Pay Increases: Field Test, Constructive Replication, and Extension," *Human Resource Management* 55, no. 1 (2016), pp. 69–81.

50. B. Gerhart and S. Rynes, "Determinants and Consequences of Salary Negotiations by Graduating Male and Female MBAs," *Journal of Applied Psychology* (1991), pp. 256–62; Gerhart and Rynes, *Compensation: Theory, Evidence, and Strategic Implications*.

51. A. J. Nyberg, J. R. Pieper, and C. O. Trevor, "Pay-for-Performance's Effect on Future Employee Performance: Integrating Psychological and Economic Principles toward a Contingency Perspective," *Journal of Management* 42, no. 7 (2016). However, a different study reports no effect of merit bonuses but does find a positive effect of merit pay on subsequent performance. See S. Park and M. C. Sturman, "Evaluating Form and Functionality of Pay-for-Performance Plans," *Human Resource Management* 55, no. 4 (2016), pp. 697–719. Both the Nyberg et al. and Park and Sturman studies are of single organizations. Different pay-for-performance strategies may work in different organizations.

52. Gerhart and Fang, "Pay for (Individual) Performance"; Gerhart, "Incentives and Pay for Performance in the Workplace."

53. J. C. Dencker, "Why Do Firms Lay Off and Why?" *Industrial Relations*, 51 (2012), pp. 152–69.

54. E. A. Locke, D. B. Feren, V. M. McCaleb, K. N. Shaw, and A. T. Denny, "The Relative Effectiveness of Four Methods of Motivating Employee Performance," in *Changes in Working Life*, ed. K. D. Duncan, M. M. Gruenberg, and D. Wallis (New York: Wiley, 1980), pp. 363–88; Jenkins et al., "Are Financial Incentives Related to Performance? A Meta-Analytic Review of Empirical Research" for a summary of additional evidence, see also Gerhart and Rynes, *Compensation: Theory, Evidence, and Strategic Implications*.

55. Gerhart and Milkovich, "Employee Compensation"; Gerhart, "Incentives and Pay for Performance in the Workplace."

56. D. Roy, "Quota Restriction and Goldbricking in a Machine Shop," *American Journal of Sociology* 57, no. 5 (1952), pp. 427–42.

57. A recent study, for example, found that in using a monthly incentive/commission with health care providers, performance was better if an occasional exception was made to prevent providers' income from dropping as much as the formula would determine in months when their sales were low. M. Maltarich, A. J. Nyberg, G. Reilly, D. Abdulsalam, and M. Martin, "Pay-for-Performance, Sometimes: An Interdisciplinary Approach to Integrating Economic Rationality with Psychological Emotion to Predict Individual Performance," *Academy of Management Journal*, 60 (2017), pp. 2155–74.

58. This idea has been referred to as the "share economy." See M. L. Weitzman, "The Simple Macroeconomics of Profit Sharing," *American Economic Review* 75 (1985), pp. 937–53. For supportive empirical evidence, see the following studies: J. Chelius and R. S. Smith, "Profit Sharing and Employment Stability," *Industrial and Labor Relations Review* 43 (1990), pp. 256S–73S; B. Gerhart and L. O. Trevor, "Employment Stability under Different Managerial Compensation Systems," working paper (Ithaca, NY: Cornell University Center for Advanced Human Resource Studies, 1995); D. L. Kruse, "Profit Sharing and Employment Variability: Microeconomic Evidence on the Weitzman Theory," *Industrial and Labor Relations Review* 44 (1991), pp. 437–53.

59. Gerhart and Milkovich, "Employee Compensation"; M. L. Weitzman and D. L. Kruse, "Profit Sharing and Productivity," in *Paying for Productivity*, ed. A. S. Blinder (Washington, DC: Brookings Institution, 1990); D. L. Kruse, *Profit Sharing: Does It Make a Difference?* (Kalamazoo, MI: Upjohn Institute, 1993); M. Magnan and S. St-Onge, "The Impact of Profit Sharing on the Performance of Financial Services Firms," *Journal of Management Studies* 42 (2005), pp. 761–91.

60. "GM/UAW: The Battle Goes On," *Ward's Auto World*, May 1995, p. 40; E. M. Coates III, "Profit Sharing Today: Plans and Provisions," *Monthly Labor Review*, April 1991, pp. 19–25.

61. Gerhart and Rynes, *Compensation: Theory, Evidence, and Strategic Implications*.

62. American Management Association, *CompFlash*, April 1991, p. 3.

63. "New Data Show Widespread Employee Ownership in U.S.," National Center for Employee Ownership, www.nceo.org/library/widespread.html.

64. Indeed, a recent study found that the correlation between use of broad-based stock and/or stock option plans and firm performance was small (r = .04). E. H. O'Boyle, P. C. Patel, and E. Gonzalez-Mulé, "Employee Ownership and Firm Performance:

A Meta-Analysis," *Human Resource Management Journal* 26, no. 4 (2016), pp. 425–48.

65. "Executive Compensation: Taking Stock," *Personnel* 67 (December 1990), pp. 7–8; "Another Day, Another Dollar Needs Another Look," *Personnel* 68 (January 1991), pp. 9–13; J. Blasi, D. Kruse, and A. Bernstein, *In the Company of Owners* (New York: Basic Books, 2003).

66. Gerhart and Milkovich, "Organizational Differences in Managerial Compensation."

67. K. F. Hallock, *Pay: What People Earn and What They Can Do to Earn More* (Cambridge: Cambridge University Press, 2012).

68. S. Thurm, J. S. Lublin, and J. E. Vascellaro, "Google's 'One-to-One' Exchange Could Prompt Others to Follow," *Wall Street Journal*, January 23, 2009.

69. S. Ovide and S. Thurm, "Silicon Valley's Stock Funk," *Wall Street Journal*, October 6–7, 2012.

70. National Center for Employee Ownership, *ESOP (Employee Stock Ownership Plan) Facts,* www.esop.org, retrieved June 2, 2017.

71. D. Jones and T. Kato, "The Productivity Effects of Employee Stock Ownership Plans and Bonuses: Evidence from Japanese Panel Data," *American Economic Review* 185 (1995), pp. 391–414. At the time of the study, 91% of Japanese companies had an ESOP.

72. "Employees Left Holding the Bag," *Fortune,* May 20, 1991, pp. 83–93; M. A. Conte and J. Svejnar, "The Performance Effects of Employee Ownership Plans," in *Paying for Productivity*, ed. A. S. Blinder (Washington, DC: Brookings Institution, 1990), pp. 245–94.

73. Conte and Svejnar, "Performance Effects of Employee Ownership Plans."

74. Conte and Svejnar, "Performance Effects of Employee Ownership Plans."; T. H. Hammer, "New Developments in Profit Sharing, Gainsharing, and Employee Ownership," in *Productivity in Organizations*, ed. J. P. Campbell, R. J. Campbell and Associates (San Francisco: Jossey-Bass, 1988); K. J. Klein, "Employee Stock Ownership and Employee Attitudes: A Test of Three Models," *Journal of Applied Psychology* 72 (1987), pp. 319–32. A.M. Benson and S. S. Sajjadiani, "Are Bonus Pools Driven by Their Incentive Effects? Evidence from Fluctuations in Gainsharing Incentives," *Industrial and Labor Relations Review*, 71 (2018), pp. 567–99.

75. J. L. Pierce, S. Rubenfeld, and S. Morgan, "Employee Ownership: A Conceptual Model of Process and Effects," *Academy of Management Review* 16 (1991), pp. 121–44.

76. E. H. O'Boyle, P. C. Patel, and E. Gonzalez-Mulé, "Employee Ownership and Firm Performance: A Meta-Analysis," *Human Resource Management Journal* 26(4) (2016), pp. 425–448.

77. D. C. Jones, P. Kalmi, and A. Kauhanen, "Teams, Incentive Pay, and Productive Efficiency: Evidence from a Food-Processing Plant," *Industrial and Labor Relations Review* 63 (2010), pp. 606–26; R. T. Kaufman, "The Effects of Improshare on Productivity," *Industrial and Labor Relations Review* 45 (1992), pp. 311–22; M. H. Schuster, "The Scanlon Plan: A Longitudinal Analysis," *Journal of Applied Behavioral Science* 20 (1984), pp. 23–28; M. M. Petty, B. Singleton, and D. W. Connell, "An Experimental Evaluation of an Organizational Incentive Plan in the Electric Utility Industry," *Journal of Applied Psychology* 77 (1992), pp. 427–36; W. N. Cooke, "Employee Participation Programs, Group-Based Incentives, and Company Performance: A Union-Nonunion Comparison," *Industrial and Labor Relations Review* 47 (1994), pp. 594–609; J. B. Arthur and L. Aiman-Smith, "Gainsharing and Organizational Learning: An Analysis of Employee Suggestions over Time," *Academy of*

*Management Journal* 44 (2001), pp. 737–54; J. B. Arthur and G. S. Jelf, "The Effects of Gainsharing on Grievance Rates and Absenteeism over Time," *Journal of Labor Research* 20 (1999), pp. 133–45.

78. J. L. McAdams, "Design, Implementation, and Results: Employee Involvement and Performance Reward Plans," *Compensation and Benefits Review*, March/April 1995, pp. 45–55.

79. T. L. Ross and R. A. Ross, "Gainsharing: Sharing Improved Performance," in *The Compensation Handbook*, 3rd ed., ed. M. L. Rock and L. A. Berger (New York: McGraw-Hill, 1991).

80. T. M. Welbourne and L. R. Gomez-Mejia, "Optimizing Team Incentives in the Workplace," in *The Compensation Handbook*, 3rd ed., ed. M. L. Rock and L. A. Berger (New York: McGraw-Hill, 2000), pp. 275–290; E. Siemsen, S. Balasubramanian, and A. V. Roth, "Incentives That Induce Task-Related Effort, Helping, and Knowledge Sharing in Workgroups," *Management Science* 10 (2007), pp. 1533–50.

81. R. S. Kaplan and D. P. Norton, "Using the Balanced Scorecard as a Strategic Management System," *Harvard Business Review*, January–February 1996, pp. 75–85.

82. I. S. Fulmer, "The Elephant in the Room: Labor Market Influences on CEO Compensation," *Personnel Psychology* 62 (2009), pp. 659–95.

83. M. C. Jensen and K. J. Murphy, "Performance Pay and Top-Management Incentives," *Journal of Political Economy* 98 (1990), pp. 225–64. A stronger relationship between CEO pay and performance was found by R. K. Aggarwal and A. A. Samwick, "The Other Side of the Trade-off: The Impact of Risk on Executive Compensation," *Journal of Political Economy* 107 (1999), pp. 65–105; A. J. Nyberg, I. S. Fulmer, B. Gerhart, and M. A. Carpenter, "Agency Theory Revisited: CEO Returns and Shareholder Interest Alignment," *Academy of Management Journal* 53 (2010), pp. 1029–49. Also, these observed relationships translate into significant changes in CEO pay in response to modest changes in financial performance of a company, as made clear by Gerhart and Rynes, *Compensation: Theory, Evidence, and Strategic Implications*; B. Gerhart, S. L. Rynes, and I. S. Fulmer, "Pay and Performance: Individuals, Groups, and Executives," *Academy of Management Annals* 3 (2009), pp. 251–315.

84. M. C. Jensen and K. J. Murphy, "CEO Incentives—It's Not How Much You Pay, but How," *Harvard Business Review* 68, May/June 1990, pp. 138–53. The definitive resource on executive pay is B. R. Ellig, *The Complete Guide to Executive Compensation*, 2nd ed. (New York: McGraw-Hill); Gerhart et al., "Pay and Performance: Individuals, Groups, and Executives."

85. C. E. Devers, A. A. Cannella, G. P. Reilly, and M. E. Yoder, "Executive Compensation: A Multidisciplinary Review of Recent Developments," *Journal of Management* 33 (2007), pp. 1016–72; W. G. Sanders and D. C. Hambrick, "Swinging for the Fences: The Effects of CEO Stock Options on Company Risk Taking and Performance," *Academy of Management Journal* 50 (2007), pp. 1055–78; Gerhart, Rynes, and Fulmer, "Pay and Performance."

86. Gerhart and Milkovich, "Organizational Differences in Managerial Compensation."

87. M. Hanlon, S. Rajgopal, and T. Shevlin, "Are Executive Stock Options Associated with Future Earnings?" *Journal of Accounting and Economics* 36 (2003), pp. 3–43; A. J. Nyberg, I. S. Fulmer, B. Gerhart, and M. Carpenter "Agency Theory Revisited: CEO Return and Shareholder Interest Alignment," *Academy of Management Journal* 53 (2010), pp. 1029–49.

88. See A. J. Rucci, S. P. Kirn, and R. T. Quinn, "The Employee-Customer-Profit Chain at Sears," *Harvard Business Review*, January/February 1998, pp. 82–97; C. D. Ittner and D. F. Larcker, "Coming Up Short on Nonfinancial Performance Measurement," *Harvard Business Review*, November 2003, pp. 88–95.

89. J. E. Bachelder III, *New York Law Journal*, March 21, 2014.

90. L. Noonan, "UK's Top 5 Banks Slash Bonus Pools by More Than £1 Billion," *Financial Times*, April 6, 2015; D. Wighton, "Many More EU Firms Face Caps on Bonuses," *Wall Street Journal*, March 5, 2015, p. C3; B. Moshinsky, "Too-Big-to-Fail May Lead to U.S. Bank Pay Rules: Hoenig," *Bloomberg Businessweek*, December 9, 2014.

91. Institutional Shareholder Services, *ISS Governance QuickScore 2.0*, http://www.issgovernance.com/file/files/ISSGovernance QuickScore2.0.pdf.

92. J. Cutcher-Gershenfeld, "The Impact on Economic Performance of a Transformation in Workplace Relations," *Industrial and Labor Relations Review* 44 (1991), pp. 241–60; Irene Goll, "Environment, Corporate Ideology, and Involvement Programs," *Industrial Relations* 30 (1991), pp. 138–49.

93. L. R. Gomez-Mejia and D. B. Balkin, *Compensation, Organizational Strategy, and Firm Performance* (Cincinnati, OH: South-Western, 1992); G. D. Jenkins and E. E. Lawler III, "Impact of Employee Participation in Pay Plan Development," *Organizational Behavior and Human Performance* 28 (1981), pp. 111–28.

94. D. I. Levine and L. D. Tyson, "Participation, Productivity, and the Firm's Environment," in *Paying for Productivity*. ed. A. S. Blinder (Washington, DC: Brookings Institution, 1990).

95. T. Welbourne D. Balkin, and L. Gomez-Mejia, "Gainsharing and Mutual Monitoring: A Combined Agency–Organizational Justice Interpretation," *Academy of Management Journal* 38 (1995), pp. 881–99.

96. T. Welbourne et al., "Gainsharing and Mutual Monitoring: A Combined Agency–Organizational Justice Interpretation."

97. D. Scott and T. McMullen, *The Impact of Rewards Programs on Employee Engagement* (Scottsdale, AZ: WorldatWork, June 2010).

98. I. S. Fulmer and Y. Chen, "How Communication Affects Employee Knowledge of and Reactions to Compensation Systems," in *Meeting the Challenge of Human Resource Management: A Communication Perspective*, ed. V. Miller and M. Gordon (New York: Routledge/Taylor & Francis, 2014).

99. A. Colella, R. L. Paetzold, A. Zardkoohi, and M. J. Wesson, "Exposing Pay Secrecy," *Academy of Management Review* 32 (2007), pp. 55–71; J. Schaubroeck et al., "An Under-Met and Over-Met Expectations Model of Employee Reactions to Merit Raises," *Journal of Applied Psychology* 93 (March 2008), pp. 424–34; S. Marasi and R. J. Bennett, "Pay Communication: Where Do We Go From Here?" *Human Resource Management Review* 26 (2016), pp. 50–58.

100. I. Caron, A. K. Ben-Ayed, and C. Vandenberghe, "Collective Incentive Plans, Organizational Justice and Commitment," *Relations Industrielles/Industrial Relations* 68, no. 1 (March 2013); WorldatWork, *Compensation Programs and Practices* (Scottsdale, AZ: WorldatWork, 2012).

101. A. S. Blinder, *Paying for Productivity* (Washington, DC: Brookings Institution, 1990).

102. Hammer, "New Developments in Profit Sharing"; Milkovich and Wigdor, *Pay for Performance*; D. J. B. Mitchell, D. Lewin, and E. E. Lawler III, "Alternative Pay Systems, Firm Performance and Productivity," in *Paying for Productivity*. ed. A. S. Blinder (Washington, DC: Brookings Institution, 1990).

103. Kaufman, "The Effects of Improshare on Productivity"; M. H. Schuster, "The Scanlon Plan: A Longitudinal Analysis," *Journal of Applied Behavioral Science* 20 (1984), pp. 23–28; J. A. Wagner III, P. Rubin, and T. J. Callahan, "Incentive Payment and Nonmanagerial Productivity: An Interrupted Time Series Analysis of Magnitude and Trend," *Organizational Behavior and Human Decision Processes* 42 (1988), pp. 47–74.

104. C. R. Gowen III and S. A. Jennings, "The Effects of Changes in Participation and Group Size on Gainsharing Success: A Case Study," *Journal of Organizational Behavior Management* 11 (1991), pp. 147–69.

105. L. Hatcher, T. L. Ross, and D. Collins, "Attributions for Participation and Nonparticipation in Gainsharing-Plan Involvement Systems," *Group and Organization Studies* 16 (1991), pp. 25–43; Mitchell et al., "Alternative Pay Systems."

106. B. Gerhart and G. T. Milkovich, "Organizational Differences in Managerial Compensation and Financial Performance," *Academy of Management Journal* 33, no. 4 (1990), pp. 663–91; B. Gerhart, S. L. Rynes, and I. S. Fulmer, "6 Pay and Performance: Individuals, Groups, and Executives," *Academy of Management Annals* 3, no. 1 (2009), pp. 251–315; Jenkins et al., "Are Financial Incentives Related to Performance? A Meta-Analytic Review of Empirical Research," p. 777; C. P. Cerasoli, J. M. Nicklin, and M. T. Ford, "Intrinsic Motivation and Extrinsic Incentives Jointly Predict Performance: A 40-Year Meta-Analysis," *Psychological bulletin 140,* 4 (2014), p. 980; S. Ikäheimo, J.-P. Kallunki, S. Moilanen, and E. Schiehll, "Do White Collar Employee Incentives Improve Firm Profitability?" *Journal of Management Accounting Research* (2017); B. Gerhart, "Incentives and Pay for Performance in the Workplace," in *Advances in Motivation Science,* Vol. 4 (Elsevier 2017), pp. 91–140.

107. L. R. Gomez-Mejia, P. Berrone, and M. Franco-Santos, *Compensation and Organizational Performance* (Armonk, NY: M. E. Sharpe, 2010).

108. B. R. Ellig, "Compensation Elements: Market Phase Determines the Mix," *Compensation and Benefits Review* 13, no. 3 (1981), pp. 30–38; Gomez-Mejia and Balkin, *Compensation, Organizational Strategy, and Firm Performance;* M. K. Kroumova and J. C. Sesis, "Intellectual Capital, Monitoring, and Risk: What Predicts the Adoption of Employee Stock Options?" *Industrial Relations* 45 (2006), pp. 734–52; Y. Yanadori and J. H. Marler, "Compensation Strategy: Does Business Strategy Influence Compensation in High-Technology Firms?" *Strategic Management Journal* 27 (2006), pp. 559–70; B. Gerhart, "Compensation Strategy and Organizational Performance" in *Compensation in Organizations,* ed. S. L. Rynes and B. Gerhart (San Francisco: Jossey-Bass, 2000); A. Tenhiala and T. Laamanen, "Right on the Money? The Contingent Effects of Strategic Orientation and Pay System Design on Firm Performance," *Strategic Management Journal* 39 (2018), pp. 3408–33; M. S. Giarratana, M. Mariani, and I. Weller, "Rewards for Patents and Inventor Behaviors in Industrial Research and Development," *Academy of Management Journal* 61, no. 1 (2018), pp. 264–92.

109. A. J. Baker, "Stock Options—a Perk That Built Silicon Valley," *Wall Street Journal*, June 23, 1993, p. A20.

CHAPTER

# 13 Employee Benefits

┌─ **LEARNING OBJECTIVES** ─┐

*After reading this chapter, you should be able to:*

**LO 13-1**  Discuss the growth in benefits costs and the underlying reasons for that growth. *page 569*

**LO 13-2**  Explain the major provisions of employee benefits programs. *page 572*

**LO 13-3**  Discuss how employee benefits in the United States compare with those in other countries. *page 582*

**LO 13-4**  Describe the effects of benefits management on cost and workforce quality. *page 586*

**LO 13-5**  Explain the importance of effectively communicating the nature and value of benefits to employees. *page 598*

**LO 13-6**  Describe the regulatory constraints that affect the way employee benefits are designed and administered. *page 603*

## Work (and Family?) in Tech, Finance, and Consulting: Millennials Speak Up

Recent statistics from the Organization for Economic Cooperation and Development (OECD) show that the average American works 1,780 hours each year. By comparison, for the two largest economies in Europe, Germany and France, the corresponding numbers are 1,356 and 1,514. In other words, if the workweek is roughly 40 hours, workers in Germany and France work 7 to 11 weeks less per year than do those in the United States. Even in Japan, the largest developed economy in Asia (and second largest overall after China), which has wrestled with the problem of "death by overwork," OECD data show workers work fewer hours per year (1,710) than those in the United States. The United States is sometimes referred to as "the no vacation nation." The United States is also one of the very few advanced economies that does not require employers to provide paid sick leave or paid maternity leave.

A few years ago, as it was recruiting, PwC sensed a change in new college graduates away from the way it had always been: namely, "signing away nights, weekends, and any semblance of a normal family life or social calendar" and in return, the prestige of a blue-chip firm, a big salary to start, and an even bigger paycheck later if they made partner. One PwC executive described the work culture at PwC as: "We sort of pride ourselves on [that] we don't need to have lives." However, that culture is now changing. Millennial employees now account for about two-thirds of PwC's workforce, and they apparently are less willing to pay the price for success if it means "not having a life." Recruiters noticed less enthusiasm at recruiting events, and those that did join PwC seemed more willing to leave when they felt work grew out of balance with family/social time.

It was not necessarily just a concern about hours worked. It was also questioning why the work had to be done at a PwC location. Why couldn't they have the flexibility to do the work from somewhere like home if they got the work done? The tight labor market of recent years meant they had other job opportunities. Actually, it turned out that Millennials and non-Millennials had similar views on work time and flexibility, but Millennials were more willing to speak out and act if their concerns were not addressed. Accordingly, PwC implemented a plan giving employees the ability to request flexibility in forms such as compressed workweeks, telecommuting, and job sharing. PwC reports that 90% of its employees make use of such flexibility options. PwC has also launched a new wellness program called Be Well, Work Well. The focus is on helping employees think about how they manage their time and energy, including whether they need to work such long hours, as PwC cites research that shows productivity drops significantly after 50 hours per week, as does attendance and health (and thus health insurance costs).

The norm of working many hours is also found in the tech sector. Several years ago, Facebook co-founder and chief executive Mark Zuckerberg said, "We may not own a car. We may not have a family. Simplicity in life allows us to focus on what's important." There are different models, however, even in tech. SAS Institute, a software company in North Carolina, has been on the Great Places to Work Institute/*Fortune* list of 100 Best Companies to Work For in each of the 21 years the list has been published. In describing SAS, the 100 Best list states that "the data analytics firm pulls out the stops to make employees stress less" and that is "the key to

*CONTINUED*

innovation" at SAS. For example, SAS has long had a policy of a 35-hour workweek. SAS also provides 90 days of fully paid maternity leave and 20 days of fully paid paternity leave. And, unlike some companies, where employees seem to be reluctant to take the leave, at SAS the average maternity leave is 61 days and the average paternity leave is 9 days. Now, some West Coast tech firms, including Twitter and even Facebook, are moving in this direction. Facebook allows four months of paid parental leave and reports that it "encourages" supervisors to ask "when—not if" both expecting mothers and fathers plan to take the time off. Twitter offers five months of parental leave and reports that its message to fathers, in particular, is "if you don't take it, it's borderline idiotic." American Express has a similar (paid) parental leave program and feels it "gives them an edge in recruiting top talent," especially among Millennials, who they feel place more value on work–life balance (much like the experiences of firms discussed above).

One final example of traditionally working long hours is the finance industry. The career formula on Wall Street has always been "grind out years of marathon workweeks" of up to 100 hours "and marathon tasks in exchange" for later opportunities to do deals and make millions. Here too, however, new hires may be pushing back. For example, in 1995, the average stay of a newly hired associate was 30 months. Now, it is 17 months. Firms are working to stem turnover by redesigning associate work to be less menial and to help associates advance more quickly to jobs with more

responsibility. Another initiative is to reduce work hours, as well as to allow associates some time to pursue other things important to them. For example, JP Morgan began an initiative called "Pencils Down" that encourages investment bankers to take weekends off. But the initiative comes with the caveat that if bankers are doing a deal, putting their pencils down may not be advisable. The bank is also now limiting hours of summer interns, requiring them to stay away from the office between midnight and 7:00 a.m. Of course, not all more senior employees are enthused, especially with the moves to limit workweek hours because the amount of work to be done has not necessarily changed and it is frustrating when a "younger analyst isn't available as they want them to be." On the other hand, one executive opined that "just because other people worked 80 to 100 hours" every week "doesn't mean these people should." Ultimately, if firms want to be able to attract and retain top talent, they may need to adapt to workers' changing preferences in order to be competitive with other firms inside and outside of their industries.

SOURCES: Hours Worked (indicator). https://data.oecd.org/emp/hours-worked.htm, accessed January 22, 2019; C. Purtill, "PWC's Millennial Employees Led a Rebellion—and Their Demands Are Being Met," *Quartz at Work*, March 20, 2018, https://z.com; "World's Best Workplaces 2018," October 15, 2018. www.greatplacestowork.com; "100 Best Companies to Work For 2017," *Fortune*, March 9, 2017. www.fortune.coms; C. C. Miller, "Silicon Valley's Struggle Adapting to Families," *New York Times*, April 8, 2015, p. A3; D. Huang and L. Gellman, "Millennial Employees Confound Big Banks," *Wall Street Journal*, April 8, 2016; E. Glazer and D. Huang, "J.P. Morgan to Workaholics: Knock It off," *Wall Street Journal*, January 21, 2016; V. Fuhrmans, "Firms Push Dads to Take Paternity Leave: Facebook, Twitter, American Express Try to Overcome Reticence about Taking Time Off," *Wall Street Journal*, July 12, 2018.

# Introduction

If we think of benefits as a part of total employee compensation, many of the concepts discussed in Chapters 11 and 12 apply here as well. This means, for example, that both cost and behavioral objectives are important. The cost of benefits adds an average of 46.4% to every dollar of payroll, thus accounting for 31.7% of the total employee compensation package. Controlling labor costs is not possible without controlling benefits costs. Similarly, achieving the objective of labor costs being variable and moving in the same direction of revenues and profits (rather than being fixed costs) is also not possible without careful attention to benefits strategy. On the behavioral side, benefits seem to influence whether potential employees come to work for a company, whether they stay, when they retire—perhaps even how they perform (although the empirical evidence, especially for the latter point, is surprisingly limited).[1] Employers continue to be focused on cost control, which has included shifting health care costs and responsibility for retirement (retiree income, but also retiree health care coverage and costs) to employees. However, different employees look for different types of benefits and, as the chapter opener indicates, cost considerations and traditional views on working hours are giving way in the pursuit of attracting (and retaining) employees, at least for some employers. As we will see, benefits can (also) be used to differentiate an employer from competitors, allowing it to tap in to what in some cases may be a valuable, but underutilized, part of the pool of human capital.

Although it makes sense to think of benefits as part of total compensation, benefits have unique aspects. First, there is the question of legal compliance. Although direct compensation is subject to government regulation, the scope and impact of regulation on benefits is far greater. Some benefits, such as Social Security, are mandated by law. Others, although not mandated, are subject to significant regulation or must meet certain criteria to achieve the most favorable tax treatment; these include pensions and savings plans. The heavy involvement of government in benefits decisions reflects the central role benefits play in maintaining economic security.

A second unique aspect of benefits is that organizations offer them so commonly that they have come to be institutionalized. Providing medical and retirement benefits of some sort remains almost obligatory for many (e.g., large) employers. A large employer that did not offer such benefits to its full-time employees would be highly unusual, and the employer might well have trouble attracting and retaining a quality workforce.

A third unique aspect of benefits, compared with other forms of compensation, is their complexity. It is relatively easy to understand the value of a dollar as part of a salary but not as part of a benefits package. The advantages and disadvantages of different types of medical coverage, pension provisions, disability insurance, and investment options for retirement funds are often difficult to grasp, and their value (beyond a general sense that they are good to have) is rarely as clear as the value of one's salary. Most fundamentally, employees may not even be aware of the benefits available to them; and if they are aware, they may not understand how to use them. When employers spend large sums of money on benefits but employees do not understand the benefits or attach much value to them, the return on employers' benefits investment will be fairly dismal.[2] One reason for giving more responsibility to employees for retirement planning and other benefits is to increase their understanding of the value of such benefits.

# Reasons for Benefits Growth

In thinking about benefits as part of total compensation, a basic question arises: Why do employers choose to channel a significant portion of the compensation dollar away from cash (wages and salaries) into benefits? Economic theory tells us that people prefer a dollar in cash over a dollar's worth of any specific commodity because the cash can be used to purchase the commodity or something else.[3] Cash is less restrictive. Several factors, however, have contributed to less emphasis on cash and more on benefits in compensation. To understand these factors, it is useful to examine the growth in benefits over time and the underlying reasons for that growth.

Figure 13.1 gives an indication of the overall growth in benefits. Note that in 1929, on the eve of the Great Depression, benefits added an average of only 3% to every dollar of

**LO 13-1**
Discuss the growth in benefits costs and the underlying reasons for that growth.

**Figure 13.1**

Growth of Employee Benefits, Percentage of Wages and Salaries and of Total Compensation, 1929–2018, Civilian Workers

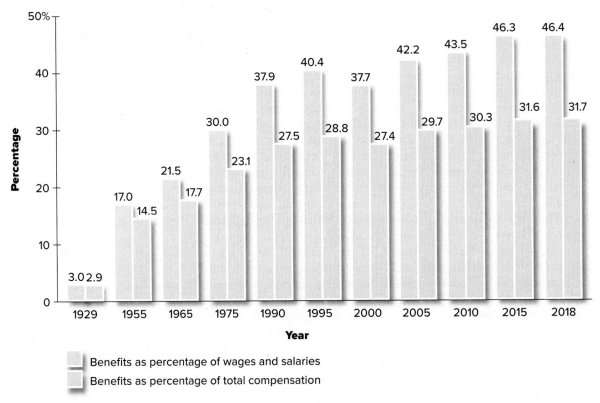

□ Benefits as percentage of wages and salaries
□ Benefits as percentage of total compensation

SOURCES: Data through 1990, U.S. Chamber of Commerce Research Center, *Employee Benefits 1990, Employee Benefits 1997, Employee Benefits 2000* (Washington, DC: U.S. Chamber of Commerce, 1991, 1997, and 2000). Data from 1995 onward, "Employer Costs for Employee Compensation," www.bls.gov.

payroll. By 1955 this figure had grown to 17%, and it has continued to grow, now accounting for 46.3 cents on top of every payroll dollar.

Many factors contributed to this tremendous growth.[4] First, during the 1930s several laws were passed as part of Franklin Roosevelt's New Deal, a legislative program aimed at buffering people from the devastating effects of the Great Depression. The Social Security Act and other legislation established legally required benefits (such as the Social Security retirement system) and modified the tax structure in such a way as to effectively make other benefits—such as workers' compensation (for work-related injuries) and unemployment insurance—mandatory. Second, wage and price controls instituted during World War II, combined with labor market shortages, forced employers to think of new ways to attract and retain employees. Because benefits were not covered by wage controls, employers channeled more resources in this direction. Once institutionalized, such benefits tended to remain even after wage and price controls were lifted.

**Marginal tax rate**
The percentage of an additional dollar of earnings that goes to taxes.

Third, the tax treatment of benefits programs is often more favorable for employees than the tax treatment of wages and salaries, meaning that a dollar spent on benefits has the potential to generate more value for the employees than the same dollar spent on wages and salaries. The **marginal tax rate** is the percentage of additional earnings that

| | NOMINAL TAX RATE | EFFECTIVE TAX RATE |
|---|---|---|
| Federal | 25.00% | 25.00% |
| State (New York) | 6.65 | 4.99 |
| City (New York) | 3.59 | 2.69 |
| Social Security | 6.20 | 6.20 |
| Medicare | 1.45 | 1.45 |
| Total tax rate | 42.89 | 40.33 |

**Table 13.1**
Example of Marginal Tax Rates for an Employee Salary of $80,000

NOTE: State and city taxes are deductible on the federal tax return, reducing their effective tax rate.

goes to taxes. Consider the hypothetical employee in Table 13.1 and the effect on take-home pay of a $1,000 increase in salary. The total effective marginal tax rate is higher for higher-paid employees and also varies according to state and city. (The state of New York and New York City have among the highest marginal tax rates.) A $1,000 annual raise for the employee earning $80,000 per year would increase net pay $596.70 ($1,000 × [1 − 0.4033]). In contrast, an extra $1,000 put into benefits would lead to an increase of $1,000 in "take-home benefits."

Employers, too, realize tax advantages from certain types of benefits. Although both cash compensation and most benefits are deductible as operating expenses, employers (like employees) pay Social Security tax on salaries up to a limit ($132,900 for 2019) and Medicare tax on the entire salary, as well as other taxes like workers' compensation and unemployment compensation. However, no such taxes are paid on most employee benefits. The bottom line is that the employer may be able to provide more value to employees by spending the extra $1,000 on benefits instead of salary.

The tax advantage of benefits also takes another form. Deferring compensation until retirement allows the employee to receive cash, but at a time (retirement) when the employee's tax rate is sometimes lower because of a lower income level. More important, perhaps, is that investment returns on the deferred money typically accumulate tax free, resulting in much faster growth of the investment.

A fourth factor that has influenced benefits growth is the cost advantage that groups typically realize over individuals. Organizations that represent large groups of employees can purchase insurance (or self-insure) at a lower rate because of economies of scale, which spread fixed costs over more employees to reduce the cost per person. Insurance risks can be pooled more easily in large groups, and large groups can also achieve greater bargaining power in dealing with insurance carriers or medical providers.

A fifth factor influencing the growth of benefits was the growth of organized labor from the 1930s through the 1950s. This growth was partly a result of another piece of New Deal legislation, the National Labor Relations Act, which greatly enhanced trade unions' ability to organize workers and negotiate contracts with employers. Benefits were often a key negotiation objective. (Indeed, they still are. Benefits issues continue to be a common reason for work stoppages.) Unions were able to successfully pursue their members' interests in benefits, particularly when tax advantages provided an incentive for employers to shift money from cash to benefits. For unions, a new benefit such as medical coverage was a tangible success that could have more impact on prospective union members than a wage increase of equivalent value, which might have amounted to only a cent or two per hour. Also, many nonunion employers responded to the threat of

**Table 13.2**
Differentiating via Benefits

| | |
|---|---|
| Provides up to one year of parental leave and unlimited vacation | Netflix |
| Reimbursement for mothers to pump and ship breast milk anywhere in world | Twitter, IBM, Zillow, Goldman Sachs |
| Offers up to five free nights each year at any of the company's hotels (plus meals for half-price during those stays) | Four Seasons |
| Gives expectant mothers four weeks of leave at 100% pay *prior* to the birth of a child (and six to eight weeks' leave at 100% pay after giving birth) | Genentech |
| Gives employees an annual stipend of $2,000 to travel and stay in Airbnb lodgings anywhere in the world | Airbnb |
| Provides a 1,200-acre camping and recreational area for employee use | Steelcase |
| Shuts down the entire company for one week in December and one week over the summer | Adobe |
| Offers a free Double-Double burger and fries during each shift | In-N-Out Burger |
| Provides a rooftop dog park | Zynga |

SOURCES: R. Umoh, "5 Companies with Employee Perks that Rival Google's," *CNBC*, April 28, 2018, www.cnbc.com; M. Lansat, "19 of the Best Job Perks and Benefits Millennials Have That Their Parents Didn't," *Business Insider*, September 3, 2018, www.businessinsider.com; P. Mosendz, "These 20 Companies Offer Incredible (and Unusual) Benefits," *Bloomberg*, February 7, 2017, https://www.bloomberg.com/news/articles/2017-02-07/these-20-companies-offer-incredible-and-unusual-benefits; Zynga company website, "Benefits," https://www.zynga.com/careers/benefits; R. Hackett, "5 Great Reasons to Work for Four Seasons," *Fortune*, February 1, 2015, http://fortune.com/2015/02/01/perks-four-seasons/; Great Place to Work Institute, Genentech, http://reviews.greatplacetowork.com/genentech; L. Dishman, "These Are the Best Employee Benefits and Perks," *FastCompany*, February 3, 2016, https://www.fastcompany.com/3056205/these-are-the-best-employee-benefits-and-perks.

unionization by implementing the same benefits for their own employees, thus contributing to benefits growth.

Finally, employers may also provide unique benefits as a means of differentiating themselves in the eyes of current or prospective employees. In this way, employers communicate key aspects of their culture that set them apart from the rest of the pack. Patagonia, an outdoor clothing company, prides itself on its commitment to the "triple bottom line": Do well by shareholders, but also by employees and the community/environment. When it comes to shareholders and employees, Patagonia makes sure its employees get outside and test its gear. (To make that easier, the company allows employees to set their own hours.) That is something its employees enjoy, and it also helps the company design and redesign products so that they are attractive to customers, which makes money for shareholders. It is only fitting for employees located in Ventura, California, that the title of founder Yvon Chouinard's memo is "Let My People Go Surfing."[5] Table 13.2 shows some additional examples.

## Benefits Programs

**LO 13-2**
Explain the major provisions of employee benefits programs.

Most benefits fall into one of the following categories: social insurance, private group insurance, retirement, pay for time not worked, and family-friendly policies.[6] Table 13.3, based on Bureau of Labor Statistics (BLS) data, provides an overview of the prevalence of specific benefits programs. As the table shows, the percentage of employees covered by these benefits programs increases with establishment size. Likewise, as shown

**Table 13.3**
Percentage of Full-Time Workers in U.S. Private Industry with Access to Selected Benefits Programs, by Establishment Size

| | | ESTABLISHMENT SIZE | |
|---|---|---|---|
| | ALL | 1–99 EMPLOYEES | 500 OR MORE EMPLOYEES |
| Medical care | 69% | 55% | 88% |
| Short-term disability insurance | 42 | 31 | 63 |
| Long-term disability insurance | 34 | 24 | 59 |
| All retirement | 68 | 53 | 88 |
| Defined benefit pension | 17 | 7 | 41 |
| Defined contribution plan | 64 | 51 | 82 |
| Life insurance | 57 | 40 | 84 |
| Paid leave | | | |
| Sick | 71 | 62 | 87 |
| Vacation | 77 | 70 | 89 |
| Personal | 43 | 33 | 62 |
| Family | 16 | 12 | 25 |

SOURCE: U.S. Bureau of Labor Statistics, *National Compensation Survey: Employee Benefits in the United States*, March 2018, Bulletin 2789, September 2018, https://www.bls.gov/ncs/ebs/.

**Table 13.4**
Total Hourly Compensation and Benefits Costs, U.S. Private Industry, by Establishment Size

| | | ESTABLISHMENT SIZE | |
|---|---|---|---|
| | ALL | 1–99 EMPLOYEES | 500 OR MORE EMPLOYEES |
| Total compensation | $34.54 | $29.07 | $49.29 |
| Wages and salaries | 24.06 | 21.13 | 32.17 |
| Benefits | 10.48 | 7.94 | 17.11 |

SOURCE: *Employer Costs for Employee Compensation—September 2018. News Release.* December 4, 2018. USDL-18-1941, https://www.bls.gov/news.release/pdf/ecec.pdf.

in Table 13.4, benefits (and total compensation) costs also increase with establishment size.

## SOCIAL INSURANCE (LEGALLY REQUIRED)

### Social Security

Among the most important provisions of the Social Security Act of 1935 was the establishment of old-age insurance and unemployment insurance. The act was later amended to add survivor's insurance (1939), disability insurance (1956), hospital insurance (Medicare Part A, 1965), and supplementary medical insurance (Medicare Part B, 1965) for the elderly. Together these provisions constitute the federal Old Age, Survivors, Disability, and Health Insurance (OASDHI) program. More than 90% of U.S. employees are covered by the program, the main exceptions being railroad and federal, state, and local government employees, who often have their own plans. Note, however, that an individual employee must meet certain eligibility requirements to receive benefits. To be fully insured typically requires 40 quarters of covered employment and minimum earnings ($1,300 in 2017) per quarter. However, the eligibility rules for survivors' and disability benefits are somewhat different.

For those born in 1940, Social Security retirement (old-age insurance) benefits for fully insured workers begin at age 65 years and 6 months (full benefits) or age 62 (at a permanent reduction of 22.5% in benefits). The "full retirement age" now rises with birth year, reaching age 67 for those born in 1960 or later. Although the amount of the benefit depends on one's earnings history, benefits do not go up after reaching a certain earnings level. Thus high earners help subsidize benefit payments to low earners. In 2019, the maximum benefit at full retirement age was $2,861/month ($34,322/year). However, the highest maximum benefit ($3,777/month, $34,222/year for high earners) is, in fact, obtained by waiting beyond the "full retirement age" until age 70 to retire. Cost-of-living increases are provided each year that the consumer price index increases. There is also a spousal benefit of up to 50% of the primary recipient's benefit (if larger than the spouse's own benefit).

An important attribute of the Social Security retirement benefit is that for those at full retirement age, it is free from state tax in about half of the states and free from federal tax if no other income is received or if that other income falls below a certain level (recently, $25,000 for single tax return filers, $32,000 for married/joint filers). At high income levels, a maximum of 85% of benefits are subject to federal tax. Additionally, the federal tax code has an earnings test for those who are still earning wages (and not yet at full retirement age). In 2019, beneficiaries (who must be 62 or older) below the full retirement age were allowed to make $17,640; in the year an individual reaches full retirement age, the earnings test is $46,920. If these amounts are exceeded, the Social Security benefit is reduced $1 for every $2 in excess earnings for those under the full retirement age and $1 for every $3 in the year a worker reaches the full retirement age. These provisions are important because of their effects on the work decisions of those between age 62 and full retirement age. The earnings test increases a person's incentive to retire (otherwise, full Social Security benefits are not received), and if she continues to work, the incentive to work part time rather than full time increases. A major change made in January 2000 is that there is no earnings test once full retirement age is reached. Therefore, these workers no longer incur any earnings penalty (and thus have no tax-related work disincentive).

How are retirement and other benefits financed? Both employers and employees are assessed a payroll tax of 7.65% (a total of 15.3%) on the first $132,900 (as of 2019) of the employee's earnings. Of the 7.65%, 6.2% funds OASDHI and 1.45% funds Medicare (Part A). Unlike the OASDHI tax, the 1.45% Medicare tax continues to be assessed on earnings above $132,900. (The self-employed pay a 12.4% OASDHI tax plus a 2.9% Medicare tax.) In addition, as of 2013, the Affordable Care Act added what the Social Security Administration calls a High Income Tax and what the Internal Revenue Service calls the Additional Medicare Tax, which is 0.9% on adjusted gross income above $200,000 for single filers and $250,000 for married filers. This tax is paid only by individuals. Employers do not pay this tax.

What are the behavioral consequences of Social Security benefits? Because they are legally mandated, employers do not have discretion in designing this aspect of their benefits programs. However, Social Security does affect employees' retirement decisions. The eligibility age for benefits and any tax penalty for earnings influence retirement decisions. The elimination of the tax penalty on earnings for those at full retirement age should mean a larger pool of older workers in the labor force for employers to tap into.

### Unemployment Insurance

Established by the 1935 Social Security Act, this program has four major objectives: (1) to offset lost income during involuntary unemployment, (2) to help unemployed workers find new jobs, (3) to provide an incentive for employers to stabilize employment, and

(4) to preserve investments in worker skills by providing income during short-term layoffs (which allows workers to return to their employer rather than start over with another employer).

The unemployment insurance program is financed largely through federal and state taxes on employers. Although, strictly speaking, the decision to establish the program is left to each state, the Social Security Act created a tax incentive structure that quickly led every state to establish a program. The federal tax rate is currently 0.6% on the first $7,000 of wages. Many states have a higher rate or impose the tax on a greater share of earnings. Currently, Washington state has the maximum covered (taxable) earnings of any state at $47,300.[7]

An important feature of the unemployment insurance program is that no state imposes the same tax on every employer. Instead, the size of the tax depends on the employer's experience rating. Employers that have a history of laying off a large share of their work-forces pay higher taxes than do those that do not. In some states, an employer that has had very few layoffs may pay no state tax. In contrast, an employer with a poor experience rating could pay a tax as high as 5–10%, depending on the state.[8]

Unemployed workers are eligible for benefits if they (1) have a prior attachment to the workforce (often 52 weeks or four quarters of work at a minimum level of pay); (2) are available for work; (3) are actively seeking work (including registering at the local unemployment office); and (4) were not discharged for cause (such as willful misconduct), did not quit voluntarily, and are not out of work because of a labor dispute.

Benefits also vary by state, but they are typically about 50% of a person's earnings and last for 26 weeks. Extended benefits for up to 13 weeks are also available. A state must, for example, pay extended benefits if the insured unemployment rate for the previous 13 weeks is at least 5% and is 120% of the rate for the same 13-week period in the two previous years.[9] Emergency extended (federal) benefits are also sometimes funded by Congress. All states have minimum and maximum weekly benefit levels. In contrast to Social Security retirement benefits, unemployment benefits are taxed as ordinary income.

Because unemployment insurance is, in effect, legally required, management's discretion is limited here, too. Management's main task is to keep its experience rating low by avoiding unnecessary workforce reductions (e.g., by relying on the sorts of actions described in Chapter 5).

## Workers' Compensation

Workers' compensation laws cover job-related injuries and death.[10] Prior to enactment of these laws, workers suffering work-related injuries or diseases could receive compensation only by suing for damages. Moreover, the common-law defenses available to employers meant that such lawsuits were not usually successful. In contrast, these laws operate under a principle of no-fault liability, meaning that an employee does not need to establish gross negligence by the employer. In return, employers receive immunity from lawsuits. (One exception is the employer who intentionally contributes to a dangerous workplace.) Employees are not covered when injuries are self-inflicted or stem from intoxication or "willful disregard of safety rules."[11] Approximately 90% of all U.S. workers are covered by state workers' compensation laws, although again there are differences among states, with coverage ranging from 70% to more than 95%.

Workers' compensation benefits fall into four major categories: (1) disability income, (2) medical care, (3) death benefits, and (4) rehabilitative services.

Disability income is typically two-thirds of predisability earnings, although each state has its own minimum and maximum. In contrast to unemployment insurance benefits, disability benefits are tax free. The system is financed differently by different states, some having a single state fund, most allowing employers to purchase coverage from private insurance companies. Self-funding by employers is also permitted in most states. The cost to the employer is based on three factors. The first factor is the nature of the occupations and the risk attached to each. Premiums for low-risk occupations may be less than 1% of payroll; the cost for some of the most hazardous occupations may be as high as 100% of payroll. The second factor is the state where work is located. For example, in the 50 U.S. states, the maximum compensation a worker can receive for loss of an arm averages $169,878, but it ranges from a minimum of $48,840 in Alabama to a maximum of $859,634 in Nevada.[12] The third factor is the employer's experience rating.

The experience rating system again provides an incentive for employers to make their workplaces safer. Dramatic injuries (like losing a finger or hand) are less prevalent than minor ones, such as sprains and strains. Back strain is the most expensive benign health condition in developed countries. Each year in the United States, 3–4% of the population is temporarily disabled and 1% is permanently and totally disabled.[13] Many actions can be taken to reduce workplace injuries, such as work redesign and training, and to speed the return to health, and thus to work (e.g., exercise).[14] Some changes can be fairly simple (such as permitting workers to sit instead of having them bend over). It is also important to hold managers accountable (in their performance evaluations) for making workplaces safer and getting employees back to work promptly following an injury. With the passage of the Americans with Disabilities Act, employers came under even greater pressure to deal effectively and fairly with workplace injuries. See the discussion in Chapter 3 on safety awareness programs for some of the ways employers and employees are striving to make the workplace safer.

One challenge is managing pain from workplace injuries effectively and efficiently and avoiding prescription painkiller abuse. Some firms and insurers have moved toward using data better to assess high-risk workers. In such cases, employees are assigned a case worker right from the start. The case worker closely monitors the employee's situation. If, for example, a case worker sees that a worker with a broken ankle continues taking opioids longer than two weeks, an alert may be issued. The idea is to intervene so that a broken ankle or a minor lower-back injury does not turn into a lifetime problem with prescription painkiller addiction. Companies can also use analytics from Rising (Rising Medical Solutions) and similar companies to benchmark their workers' compensation cases against those of other companies in the same industry or geographic location as a way to compare the risk of fraud and abuse to that faced by other companies, which can help them decide how much of a problem they have.

## PRIVATE GROUP INSURANCE

As we noted earlier, group insurance rates are typically lower than individual rates because of economies of scale, the ability to pool risks, and the greater bargaining power of a group. This cost advantage, together with tax considerations and a concern for employee security, helps explain the prevalence of employer-sponsored insurance plans. We discuss two major types: medical insurance and disability insurance. Note that these programs are not legally required; rather, they are offered at the discretion of employers.

### Medical Insurance

Not surprisingly, public opinion surveys indicate that medical benefits are by far the most important benefit to the average person.[15] As Table 13.3 indicates, most full-time employees have medical insurance, especially in larger workplaces. Three basic types of medical expenses are typically covered: hospital expenses, surgical expenses, and physicians' visits.

Other benefits that employers may offer include dental care, vision care, birthing centers, and prescription drug programs. Perhaps the most important issue in benefits management is the challenge of providing quality medical benefits while controlling costs, a subject we return to in a later section. We also discuss the Affordable Care Act in a later section.

The **Consolidated Omnibus Budget Reconciliation Act (COBRA)** of 1985 requires employers to permit employees to extend their health insurance coverage at group rates for up to 36 months following a "qualifying event" such as termination (except for gross misconduct), a reduction in hours that leads to the loss of health insurance, death, and other events. The beneficiary (whether the employee, spouse, or dependent) must have access to the same services as employees who have not lost their health insurance. Note that the beneficiaries do not get free coverage. Rather, they receive the advantage of purchasing coverage at the employer rate rather than the individual rate.

**Consolidated Omnibus Budget Reconciliation Act (COBRA)**
The 1985 act that requires employers to permit employees to extend their health insurance coverage at group rates for up to 36 months following a qualifying event, such as a layoff.

### Disability Insurance

Two basic types of disability coverage exist.[16] As Table 13.3 indicates, only in larger workplaces are most employees covered by short-term and long-term disability insurance. Short-term plans typically provide benefits for six months or less, at which point long-term plans take over, potentially covering the person for life. The median and modal salary replacement rate is 60%, although short-term plans sometimes have higher rates. There are typically (in 88% of plans) caps on the amount (median = $8,000) that can be paid each month.[17] Federal income taxation of disability benefits depends on the funding method. Where employee contributions completely fund the plan, there is no federal tax. Benefits based on employer contributions are taxed. Finally, disability benefits, especially long-term ones, need to be coordinated with other programs, such as Social Security disability benefits.

## RETIREMENT

Earlier we discussed the old-age insurance part of Social Security, a legally required source of retirement income. This remains the largest single component of the elderly's overall retirement income (35%). Other sources of income are pensions (17%), earnings from assets (savings and other investments like stocks and bonds, 11%), earnings (34%), and other sources (3%).[18]

Employers have no legal obligation to offer private retirement plans, but many do. As we note later, if a private retirement plan is provided, it must meet certain standards set forth by the Employee Retirement Income Security Act.

### Defined Benefit

A *defined benefit plan* guarantees ("defines") a specified retirement benefit level to employees based typically on a combination of years of service and age as well as on the employee's earnings level (e.g., the three to five highest earnings years). For instance, an organization might guarantee a monthly pension payment of $1,500 to an employee retiring at age 65 with 30 years of service and an average salary over the final 5 years of $40,000. As Table 13.3 indicates, full-time employees in 17% of all workplaces, 41% of large workplaces, are covered by such plans. (Defined benefit coverage has fallen by half since 1980.)[19]

Defined benefit plans insulate employees from investment risk, which is borne by the company. In the event of severe financial difficulties that force the company to

**Pension Benefit
Guaranty
Corporation (PBGC)**
The agency that
guarantees to pay
employees a basic
retirement benefit in
the event that financial
difficulties force a
company to terminate
or reduce employee
pension benefits.

terminate or reduce employee pension benefits, the **Pension Benefit Guaranty Corporation (PBGC)** provides some protection of benefits. Established by the **Employee Retirement Income Security Act (ERISA)** of 1974, the PBGC guarantees a basic benefit, not necessarily complete pension benefit replacement, for employees who were eligible for pensions at the time of termination. It ensures the retirement benefits of 41 million workers in more than 24,000 plans. In fiscal year 2018, PBGC paid benefits of $5.9 billion to 861,000 retirees from more than 4,919 failed single-employer plans.[20] The maximum annual benefit for single-employer plans is limited to the lesser of an employee's annual gross income during a PBGC-defined period or $30,283 at age 55, $43,742 at age 60, $67,295 at age 65, $111,710 at age 70, and $204,578 at age 75 for plans terminated in 2019.[21] Thus, higher-paid employees, who would have received higher pensions under the company plan, can experience major cuts in pensions if the PBGC must take over the plan. Payouts are not adjusted for cost-of-living changes. The PBGC is funded by an annual premium of $80 per (single-employer) plan participant in 2019, plus an additional variable-rate premium of $43 per 1,000 of unfunded vested benefits for underfunded plans.[22] Note that the PBGC does not guarantee retiree health care benefits.

**Employee
Retirement Income
Security Act (ERISA)**
The 1974 act that
increased the fiduciary
responsibilities of
pension plan trustees,
established vesting
rights and portability
provisions, and
established the Pension
Benefit Guaranty
Corporation (PBGC).

### Defined Contribution

Unlike defined benefit plans, *defined contribution plans* do not promise a specific benefit level for employees upon retirement. Rather, an individual account is set up for each employee with a guaranteed size of contribution. The advantage of such plans for employers is that they shift investment risk to employees and present fewer administrative challenges because there is no need to calculate payments based on age and service and no need to make payments to the PBGC. As Table 13.3 indicates, defined contribution plans are especially preferred in smaller companies, perhaps because of small employers' desire to avoid long-term obligations or perhaps because small companies tend to be younger, often being founded since the trend toward defined contribution plans. Some companies have both defined benefit and defined contribution plans.

There is a wide variety of defined contribution plans, a few of which are described briefly here. One of the simplest is a money purchase plan, under which an employer specifies a level of annual contribution (such as 10% of salary). At retirement age, the employee is entitled to the contributions plus the investment returns. The term *money purchase* stems from the fact that employees often use the money to purchase an annuity rather than taking it as a lump sum. Profit sharing plans and employee stock ownership plans are also often used as retirement vehicles. Both permit contributions (cash and stock, respectively) to vary from year to year, thus allowing employers to avoid fixed obligations that may be burdensome in difficult financial times. Section 401(k) plans (named after the tax code section) permit employees to defer compensation on a pretax basis. Annual contributions in 2019 are limited to $19,000.[23] For those age 50 or over, an additional $6,000 per year in catch-up contributions is also permitted. Additionally, many employers (80%) match some portion (mean = 4.7%) of employee contributions.[24] A final incentive is tax based. For example, based on Table 13.1, $10,000 contributed to a 401(k) plan would only be worth $(1 - 0.4333) \times \$10,000 = \$5,667$ if taken in salary.

Defined contribution plans continue to grow in importance, while, as we saw earlier, defined benefit plans have become less common. An important implication is that defined contribution plans put the responsibility for wise investing squarely on the shoulders of the employee. Several factors affect the amount of income that will be available to an

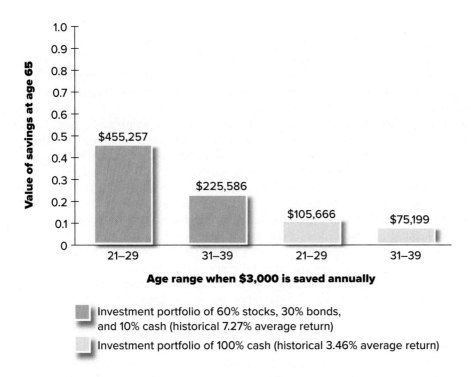

Note: Historical rates of return, geometric averages, 1928–2016: stocks (S&P 500), 9.53%; bonds (10-year U.S. Treasury Bond), 5.18%; cash (3-month U.S. Treasury Bill), 3.46%.

SOURCE: A. Damodaran, "Annual Returns on Stock, T. Bonds and T. Bills: 1928–Current," http://people.stern.nyu.edu/adamodar/New_Home_Page/datafile/histretSP.html.

employee upon retirement. First, the earlier the age at which investments are made, the longer returns can accumulate. As Figure 13.2 shows, an annual investment of $3,000 made between ages 21 and 29 will be worth much more at age 65 than a similar investment made between ages 31 and 39. Second, different investments have different historical rates of return. Between 1928 and 2016 the average annual return was 9.53% for stocks, 5.18% for bonds, and 3.46% for cash (e.g., short-term Treasury bills or bank savings accounts). As Figure 13.2 shows, *if* historical rates of return were to continue, an investment in a mix of 60% stock, 30% bonds, and 10% cash between the ages of 21 and 29 would be worth about four times as much at age 65 as would the same amount kept in the form of cash. A third consideration is the need to counteract investment risk by diversification because stock and bond prices can be volatile in the short run. Although stocks have the greatest historical rate of return, that is no guarantee of future performance, particularly over shorter time periods. (This fact becomes painfully obvious during the dramatic drops in stock market values that are experienced every so often, most recently a drop of 38% in the S&P 500 in 2008.) Thus some investment advisers recommend a mix of stock, bonds, and cash, as shown in Figure 13.2, to reduce investment risk. Younger investors may wish to have more stock, while those closer to retirement age typically have less stock in their portfolios.

It's also important—indeed, extraordinarily important—not to invest too heavily in any single stock.[25] Some Enron employees had 100% of their 401(k) assets in Enron stock. When the price dropped from $90 to less than $1 and Enron entered bankruptcy, their retirement money was gone. Employees at Bear Stearns, a storied Wall Street firm, also learned the hard way what can happen when you put all your eggs in one basket—company stock. When the stock price fell from its peak of $160 to $2 and Bear was purchased by JP Morgan Chase, the value of employee-owned shares fell from $6.3 billion to $79 million, a loss of 99%. Risk is compounded further by risk of job loss when one's employer struggles financially. So, repeat several times: *Always diversify*, and don't put all your retirement eggs in one basket.[26]

The Pension Protection Act (PPA) of 2006 requires defined contribution plans holding publicly traded securities to provide employees with (1) the opportunity to divest employer securities and (2) at least three investment options other than employer securities. The PPA also allows employers to enroll workers in their 401(k) plan automatically and to increase a worker's 401(k) contribution automatically to coincide with a raise or a work anniversary. Workers can decline, but the onus is on them to do so. Since the PPA, automatic enrollment (50% of plans) and automatic escalation (44%) have become common, thus helping increase worker retirement contributions.[27]

According to the U.S. Department of Labor's Employee Benefits Security Administration, ERISA requires that employers "meet fiduciary responsibilities." That includes acting solely in the interest of plan participants in managing the retirement plan, carrying out these management duties prudently, following plan documents, diversifying plan investments, and paying only reasonable plan expenses. Companies can be sued for any breach of these fiduciary responsibility duties. As an example, Lockheed reached a $62 million settlement in 2015 of a lawsuit that alleged its 401(k) plan was not prudently managed (e.g., because it charged excessive fees to participants). Toward the end of Barack Obama's presidency, the Department of Labor issued a new fiduciary rule, which would have required any financial professional working with retirement plans and/or who provides retirement planning advice to meet the fiduciary standard described here. Under Donald Trump's administration, the fiduciary rule has been put on hold and is under review by the Department of Labor. In the meantime, most financial professionals will continue to be held to the lesser "suitability standard," which means they are required to provide investment recommendations suitable for their clients but not necessarily in the best interest of their clients.

### Cash Balance Plans

**Cash balance plan**
A retirement plan in which the employer sets up an individual account for each employee and contributes a percentage of the employee's salary; the account earns interest at a predetermined rate.

One way to combine the advantages of defined benefit plans and defined contribution plans is to use a **cash balance plan**. This type of retirement plan consists of individual accounts, as in a 401(k) plan. But in contrast to a 401(k), all the contributions come from the employer. Usually, the employer contributes a percentage of the employee's salary, say, 4% or 5%. The money in the cash balance plan earns interest according to a predetermined rate, such as the rate paid on U.S. Treasury bills. Employers guarantee this rate as in a defined benefit plan. This arrangement helps employers plan their contributions and helps employees predict their retirement benefits. If employees change jobs, they generally can roll over the balance into an individual retirement account.

Organizations switching from traditional defined benefit plans to cash balance plans should consider the effects on employees as well as on the organization's bottom line. Defined benefit plans are most generous to older employees with many years of service, and cash balance plans are most generous to young employees who will have many years ahead in which to earn interest. For an organization with many experienced employees, switching from a defined benefit plan can produce great savings in pension benefits. In that case, the older workers are the greatest losers, unless the organization adjusts the program to retain their benefits.

## Funding, Communication, and Vesting Requirements

ERISA does not require organizations to have pension plans, but those that are set up must meet certain requirements. In addition to the termination provisions discussed earlier, plans must meet certain guidelines on management and funding. For example, employers are required to make yearly contributions that are sufficient to cover future obligations. (As noted previously, underfunded plans require higher premiums.) ERISA also specifies a number of reporting and disclosure requirements involving the IRS, the Department of Labor, and employees.[28] Employees, for example, must receive within 90 days after entering a plan a **summary plan description (SPD)** that describes the plan's funding, eligibility requirements, risks, and so forth. Upon request, an employer must also make available to an employee an individual benefit statement, which describes the employee's vested and unvested benefits. Obviously, employers may wish to provide such information on a regular basis anyway as a means of increasing employees' understanding and the value employees attach to their benefits.

ERISA guarantees employees that when they become participants in a pension plan and work a specified minimum number of years, they earn a right to a pension upon retirement. These are referred to as *vesting rights.*[29] Vested employees have the right to their pension at retirement age, regardless of whether they remain with the employer until that time. Employee contributions to their own plans are always completely vested. The vesting of employer-funded pension benefits must take place under one of two schedules. Employers may choose to vest employees after five years; until that time, employers can provide zero vesting if they choose. Alternatively, employers may vest employees over a three- to seven-year period, with at least 20% vesting in the third year and each year thereafter. These two schedules represent minimum requirements; employers are free to vest employees more quickly. These are the two choices relevant to the majority of employers. However, so-called top-heavy plans, where pension benefits for "key" employees (like highly paid top managers) exceed a certain share of total pension benefits, require faster vesting for nonkey employees. On the other hand, multiemployer pension plans need not provide vesting until after 10 years of employment.

These requirements were put in place to prevent companies from terminating employees before they reach retirement age or before they reach their length-of-service requirements in order to avoid paying pension benefits. Transferring employees or laying them off as a means of avoiding pension obligations is not legal either, even if such actions are motivated partly by business necessity.[30] Employers are, however, free to choose whichever of the two vesting schedules is most advantageous. For example, an employer that experiences high quit rates during the fourth and fifth years of employment may choose five-year vesting to minimize pension costs.

The traditional defined benefit pension plan discourages employee turnover or delays it until the employer can recoup the training investment in employees.[31] Even if an employee's pension benefit is vested, it is usually smaller if the employee changes employers, mainly because the size of the benefit depends on earnings in the final years with an employer. Consider an employee who earns $30,000 after 20 years and $60,000 after 40 years.[32] The employer pays an annual retirement benefit equal to 1.5% of final earnings times the number of years of service. If the employee stays with the employer for 40 years, the annual benefit level upon retirement would be $36,000 ($0.015 \times \$60,000 \times 40$). If, instead, the employee changes employers after 20 years (and has the same earnings progression), the retirement benefit from the first employer would be $9,000 ($0.015 \times \$30,000 \times 20$). The annual benefit from the second employer would be $18,000 ($0.015 \times \$60,000 \times 20$). Therefore, staying with one

**Summary plan description (SPD)**
A reporting requirement of the Employee Retirement Income Security Act (ERISA) that obligates employers to describe the plan's funding, eligibility requirements, risks, and so forth within 90 days after an employee has entered the plan.

employer for 40 years would yield an annual retirement benefit of $36,000, versus a combined annual retirement benefit of $27,000 ($9,000 + $18,000) if the employee changes employers once. It has also been suggested that pensions are designed to encourage long-service employees, whose earnings growth may eventually exceed their productivity growth, to retire. This is consistent with the fact that retirement benefits reach their maximum at retirement age.[33]

The fact that in recent years many employers have sought to reduce their workforces through early retirement programs is also consistent with the notion that pensions are used to retain certain employees while encouraging others to leave. One early retirement program approach is to adjust years-of-service credit upward for employees willing to retire, resulting in a higher retirement benefit for them (and less monetary incentive to work). These workforce reductions may also be one indication of a broader trend toward employees becoming less likely to spend their entire careers with a single employer.[34] On one hand, if more mobility across employers becomes necessary or desirable, the current pension system's incentives against (or penalties for) mobility may require modification. On the other hand, perhaps increased employee mobility will reinforce the continued trend toward defined contribution plans [like 401(k)s], which have greater portability (ease of transfer of funds) across employers.[35]

## PAY FOR TIME NOT WORKED

**LO 13-3**
Discuss how employee benefits in the United States compare with those in other countries.

At first blush, paid vacation, holidays, sick leave, and so forth may not seem to make economic sense. The employer pays the employee for time not spent working, receiving no tangible production value in return. Therefore, some employers may see little direct advantage. Perhaps for this reason, a minimum number of vacation days (20) is mandated by law in the European Community. As many as 30 days of vacation is not uncommon for relatively new employees in Europe. By contrast, there is no legal minimum in the United States, but 10 days is typical for large companies. U.S. workers must typically be with an employer for 20 to 25 years before they receive as much paid vacation as their western European counterparts.[36]

Sick leave programs in the United States, among employers that provide them, often provide full salary replacement for a limited period of time, usually not exceeding 26 weeks. The amount of sick leave is often based on length of service, accumulating with service (one day per month, for example). Sick leave policies need to be carefully structured to avoid providing employees with the wrong incentives. For example, if sick leave days disappear at the end of the year (rather than accumulate), a "use it or lose it" mentality may develop among employees, contributing to greater absenteeism. Organizations have developed a number of measures to counter this.[37] Some allow sick days to accumulate, then pay employees for the number of sick days when they retire or resign. Employers may also attempt to communicate to their employees that accumulated sick leave is better saved to use as a bridge to long-term disability because the replacement rate (the ratio of sick leave or disability payments to normal salary) for the former is typically higher. Sick leave payments may equal 100% of usual salary, whereas the typical replacement ratio for long-term disability is 60%, so the more sick leave accumulated, the longer an employee can avoid dropping to 60% of usual pay when unable to work. Microsoft recently required its contractors and vendors to provide paid sick leave for their employees.[38] In 2015, President Obama signed an executive order requiring companies that contract with the federal government to provide paid sick leave. Other companies pay for time that employees devote to charity. For example, employees in General Electric's high-potential program can

**Figure 13.3**

Normal Annual
Hours Worked
Relative to United
States

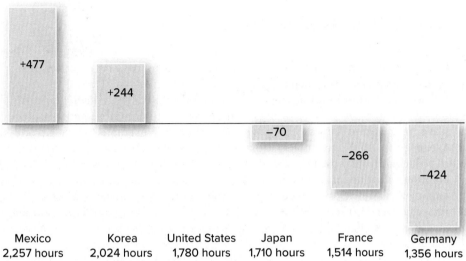

| Mexico | Korea | United States | Japan | France | Germany |
|---|---|---|---|---|---|
| 2,257 hours | 2,024 hours | 1,780 hours | 1,710 hours | 1,514 hours | 1,356 hours |

SOURCE: Organization for Economic Cooperation and Development. Data for 2017. http://stats.oecd.org. Labour, Subsection, Labour Force Statistics. Accessed January 30, 2019.

be paid for a week doing charitable work. One recent example was volunteering with BuildOn, a charity that has built more than 660 schools in impoverished areas of the world.[39]

Although vacation and other paid leave programs help attract and retain employees, there is a cost to providing time off with pay, especially in a global economy. The fact that vacation and other paid leave practices differ across countries contributes to the differences in labor costs described in Chapter 11. Consider that, on average, in manufacturing, German workers work 424 fewer hours per year than their U.S. counterparts. (See Figure 13.3.) In other words, based on a 35 hour workweek, German workers are at work approximately 12 fewer weeks per year than their U.S. counterparts. It is perhaps not surprising then that German manufacturers have looked outside Germany for alternative production sites. (However, you might consider what you could do with the equivalent of an extra 12 plus weeks away from work.) Even in Japan, which is sometimes said to have a death by overwork problem (Karōshi), hours worked per year is less than in the United States.

## FAMILY-FRIENDLY POLICIES

To ease employees' conflicts between work and nonwork, organizations may use *family-friendly policies* (also known as policies that help balance work and family) such as family leave policies, child care, and flexible work arrangements.[40] Although the programs discussed here would seem to be targeted to a particular group of employees, these programs often have "spillover effects" on other employees, who see them as symbolizing a general corporate concern for human resources, thus promoting loyalty even among employee groups that do not use the programs and possibly resulting in improved organizational performance.[41] Evidence suggests that firms using family-friendly policies have better quality management practices overall that are positively associated with organization performance.[42] The Evidence-Based HR box provides some examples of company experiences with improvements to their paid leave programs.

# EVIDENCE-BASED HR

Organizations have implemented and expanded paid family leave practices in an effort to help employees better balance work and family and also to help them be more successful in attracting and retaining employees who place a priority on such balance. A number of organizations report that improvements in paid leave have helped improve employee retention. For example, when Google expanded its paid leave policy from 12 to 18 weeks years ago, the retention of post-maternity women increased by 50%. A Deloitte survey found that 77% of employee respondents said that paid parental leave influenced their choice of employer, and 50% said they would prefer more parental leave over a pay increase. Nestlé offers 26 weeks of leave, 14 of which are paid leave, and all employees are eligible. Nestlé reports that since putting the program into place, there are fewer sick visits for infants, and health care costs for infants are 12% lower when parents participate in the program. Best Buy reports that it decreased turnover by 14 percentage points (from 46% to 32%) over the past four years (even as unemployment rates declined) through introduction of what it calls a paid leave program. In the absence of control groups and random assignment of participants to the "experimental treatment" (paid leave in this case), it is less possible to rule out alternative explanations for these improvements (e.g., an increase in the unemployment rate contributing to higher retention or parents with healthier infants participating in paid leave or improvements in other benefits or compensation areas). Nevertheless, this evidence, such as it is, combined with the logic that parents are less likely to have to choose between work and family when they have paid leave programs, suggests that paid leave is an avenue toward better employee retention, lower health care costs, and better choices for employees. With additional data (on cost), the next step would be to estimate the return on investment of such programs.

SOURCES: T. L. Rhodes, "Paid Family Leave Is Increasing Employee Retention Rates," *Risk & Insurance*, July 18, 2018, https://riskandinsurance.com; A. Van Abbema, "How Best Buy Cut Its Staff Turnover More Than 30 Percent in Four Years," *Minneapolis / St. Paul Business Journal*, December 6, 2018; National Partnership for Women & Families, "Paid Family and Medical Leave: Good for Business," September 2018, www.nationalpartnership.org; K. Mayer, "Major Employers Join Forces to Move the Needle on Paid Leave," *Employee Benefit News*, November 15 2018, www.benefitnews.com.

**Family and Medical Leave Act**
The 1993 act that requires employers with 50 or more employees to provide up to 12 weeks of unpaid leave after childbirth or adoption; to care for a seriously ill child, spouse, or parent; or for an employee's own serious illness.

Since 1993 the **Family and Medical Leave Act** requires organizations with 50 or more employees within a 75-mile radius to provide as much as 12 weeks of unpaid leave after childbirth or adoption; to care for a seriously ill child, spouse, or parent; or for an employee's own serious illness. Employees are guaranteed the same or a comparable job on their return to work. Employees with less than one year of service or who work less than 25 hours per week or who are among the 10% highest paid are not covered.

Many employers had already taken steps to deal with this issue, partly to help attract and retain key employees. Less than 10% of American families fit the image of a husband working outside the home and a wife who stays home to take care of the children.[43]

The United States still offers significantly less unpaid leave than most western European countries and Japan. Moreover, paid family leave remains rare in the United States (16% of employees are eligible, according to Table 13.3), in even sharper contrast to western Europe and Japan, where it is typically mandated by law.[44] Until the passage of the Americans with Disabilities Act, the only applicable law was the Pregnancy Discrimination Act of 1978, which requires employers that offer disability plans to treat pregnancy as they would any other disability.

Sweden-based IKEA is an example of a company that recently began to provide paid family leave in the United States, even for low-paid employees, of 12–16 weeks, depending on how long employees have been with the company.[45] The policy will cover roughly 13,000 of its 15,000 U.S. employees, and the policy will apply to mothers and fathers and to births, adoptions, and foster children. Employees with at least one year of tenure will receive 12 weeks, with 100% of their salary paid for the first 6 weeks and 50% of their salary paid for the remaining 6 weeks. Employees with at least three years of tenure will receive 16 weeks, with 8 weeks of 100% pay and the remaining 8 weeks at 50% of pay. Even employees who work only 10 hours a week would be eligible. IKEA's plan is to use interim assignments to do the work and to encourage managers, one-half of whom are women, to use the program themselves as part of its strategy to make hourly workers comfortable using it. In addition to helping provide a more sustainable approach to balancing work and nonwork spheres, IKEA, like many companies, especially retailers, is also facing a tightening labor market, as we discussed in Chapter 11. As such, IKEA also recently increased its minimum hourly wage to nearly $12/hour.

Experience with the Family and Medical Leave Act suggests that a majority of those opting for this benefit fail to take the full allotment of time. This is especially the case among female executives. Many of these executives find they do not enjoy maternity leave as much as they expected they would and miss the challenges associated with their careers. Others fear that their careers would be damaged in the long run by missing out on opportunities that might arise while they are out on leave.[46]

## Child Care

U.S. companies increasingly provide some form of child care support to their employees. This support comes in several forms that vary in their degree of organizational involvement.[47] The lowest level of involvement, offered by 38% of companies, is when an organization supplies and helps employees collect information about the cost and quality of available child care. At the next level, organizations provide vouchers or discounts for employees to use at existing child care facilities (2% of companies). At the highest level, firms provide child care at or near their work sites (7% of companies). Toyota's Child Development Program provides 24-hour-a-day care for children of workers at its Georgetown, Kentucky, plant. This facility is designed to meet the needs of employees working evening and night shifts who want their children to be on the same schedule. In this facility, the children are kept awake all night.

DAVID Perry/Lexington Herald-Leader/Tribune News Service/Getty Images

Toyota employees check in on their kids at the Georgetown location on-site child care.

At the end of the night shift, the parents pick up their children and the whole family goes home to bed.[48]

An organization's decision to staff its own child care facility should not be taken lightly. It is typically a costly venture with important liability concerns. Moreover, the results, in terms of reducing absenteeism and enhancing productivity, are often mixed.[49] One reason for this is that many organizations are "jumping on the day care bandwagon" without giving much thought to the best form of assistance for their specific employees.

As an alternative example, Memphis-based First Tennessee Bank, which was losing 1,500 days of productivity a year because of child care problems, considered creating its own on-site day care center. Before acting, however, the company surveyed its employees. This survey indicated that the only real problem with day care occurred when the parents' regular day care provisions fell through because of sickness on the part of the child or provider. Based on these findings, the bank opted to establish a sick-child care center, which was less costly and smaller in scope than a full-time center and yet still solved the employees' major problem. As a result, absenteeism dropped so dramatically that the program paid for itself in the first nine months of operation.[50]

# Managing Benefits: Employer Objectives and Strategies

**LO 13-4**
Describe the effects of benefits management on cost and workforce quality.

Although the regulatory environment places some important constraints on benefits decisions, employers retain significant discretion and need to evaluate the payoff of such decisions.[51] As discussed earlier, however, this evaluation needs to recognize that employees have come to expect certain things from employers. Employers who do not meet these expectations run the risk of violating what has been called an "implicit contract" between the employer and its workers. If employees believe their employers feel little commitment to their welfare, they can hardly be expected to commit themselves to the company's success.

Clearly, there is much room for progress in the evaluation of benefits decisions.[52] Despite some of the obvious reasons for benefits—group discounts, regulation, and minimizing compensation-related taxes—organizations do not do as well as they could in spelling out what they want their benefits package to achieve and evaluating how well they are succeeding. Research suggests that most organizations do not have written benefits objectives.[53] Obviously, without clear objectives to measure progress, evaluation is difficult (and less likely to occur). Table 13.5 provides the most highly ranked benefits objectives across U.S. companies.[54]

**Table 13.5**
The Five Most Highly Ranked Benefits Objectives for Employers

Increase employee productivity
Increase employee satisfaction
Increase employee loyalty
Attract employees
Help employees make better financial decisions

SOURCE: *MetLife's 15 Annual U.S. Employee Benefits Trends Study,* 2017, https://benefittrends.metlife.com/media/1382/2017-ebts-report_0320_exp0518_v2.pdf.

**% of Total Compensation**

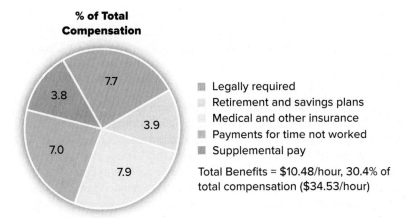

Legally required
Retirement and savings plans
Medical and other insurance
Payments for time not worked
Supplemental pay

Total Benefits = $10.48/hour, 30.4% of total compensation ($34.53/hour)

**Figure 13.4**

Employee Benefits Cost by Category, Private-Sector Workers

SOURCE: U.S. Department of Labor, "Employer Costs for Employee Compensation— September 2018," December 14, 2018, News Release USDL-18-1941.

## SURVEYS AND BENCHMARKING

As with cash compensation, an important element of benefits management is knowing what the competition is doing. Survey information on benefits packages is available from private consultants, the U.S. Chamber of Commerce, and the Bureau of Labor Statistics (BLS).[55] BLS data of the sort in Table 13.3 and the more detailed information on programs and provisions available from consultants are useful in designing competitive benefits packages. To compete effectively in the product market, cost information is also necessary. A good source is again the BLS, which provides information on benefits costs for specific categories as well as breakdowns by industry, occupation, union status, and organization size. (See Figure 13.4.)

## COST CONTROL

In thinking about cost control strategies, it is useful to consider several factors. First, the larger the cost of a benefit category, the greater the opportunity for savings. Second, the growth trajectory of the benefit category is also important: even if costs are currently acceptable, the rate of growth may result in serious costs in the future. Third, cost containment efforts can work only to the extent that the employer has significant discretion in choosing how much to spend in a benefit category. Much of the cost of legally required benefits (like Social Security) is relatively fixed, which constrains cost reduction efforts. Even with legally required benefits, however, employers can take actions to limit costs because of "experience ratings," which, for example, impose higher taxes on employers with high rates of unemployment or workers' compensation claims. When it comes to health care, as the Competing through Environmental, Social, and Governance Practices box shows, some employers are seeking to control costs and improve quality by making medical care more accessible to their employees.

One benefit—medical and other insurance—stands out as a target for cost control for two reasons. Costs are high and growth in costs has typically been high, even in the face of determined efforts to control the growth of costs. Second, employers have many options for attacking costs and improving quality, and the Affordable Care Act makes these issues even more salient for employers.

# COMPETING THROUGH ENVIRONMENTAL, SOCIAL, AND GOVERNANCE PRACTICES

## Employers Become Health Care Providers

Although on average companies continue to pass on more health care costs to employees through higher premiums and deductibles, an increasing number of employers are following a somewhat different strategy. Specifically, one-third of large employers in a recent survey are providing at least some health care directly to their employees, and sometimes, especially in the cases of primary care and other basic care, care is provided for free.

For example, in Kokomo, Indiana, Fiat Chrysler is providing free health care to most employees and their families, about 22,200 people, and it does so through five clinics it operates in the area. The company hopes that by spending more now, it will be able to eventually reduce the $100 million in health care costs each year it incurs just in Indiana. A major part of this is making primary care free or low cost as a means toward better and earlier diagnosis and control of what can be expensive long-term costs of unmanaged chronic conditions related to diabetes or workplace injuries (e.g, back pain). Avoiding unnecessary emergency room visits is another priority. Before opening the clinics, Fiat Chrysler examined data indicating that 40% of its Kokomo employees did not have a primary care doctor and that many used emergency rooms when they could no longer avoid care.

Companies such as Serta Simmons Bedding have also sought to remove barriers and encourage better use of health care by its employees. Serta began using mobile health clinics at its 28 U.S. factories a few years ago. A priority was to "help its largely male workforce get annual physicals." Providing this easy access was one part of it. Making the physicals free was another. United Shore Financial Services opened a clinic at its headquarters outside of Detroit. One employee, an account executive, noted that he goes to the clinic "when back trouble flares up during the day" and that it saves him (and United Shore) "from losing time by driving home for care and then back to work."

There are other strategies being used by employers as well. For example, General Motors recently negotiated a health care agreement with the Henry Ford Health System, eliminating what has traditionally been the "middle man" role played by an insurance company. Walmart has done the same and has plans to require its employees to use certain hospitals for certain costly spine surgeries in an effort to have more control and avoid unnecessary procedures and costs while also aiming to improve quality, which is generally associated with a hospital's experience in conducting a procedure.

In New York City, Stephen Fealy, an orthopedic surgeon, heads downtown on Wednesdays, not to go to his office, but rather to go to Goldman Sachs where he works with other doctors at the Goldman Sachs clinic on the 10th floor of its headquarters. Dr. Fealy reports that "These people work incredibly hard" and come to see him with hip pain and what he calls "investment-banker neck," which is an arthritic condition that people in their late 40s seem especially prone to, especially "ones peering at lots of monitors." Again, going to a different floor in the same building to get treat-ment is much more efficient than having to leave to go elsewhere (especially in cross-town traffic) if you can get an appointment with a traditional provider. If time is money, and it certainly is even more true in the case of investment bankers, this is a big advantage.

### DISCUSSION QUESTIONS

1. What factors have contributed to adoption of these health care delivery strategies by Fiat Chrysler, Serta Simmons, Henry Ford Health System, Goldman Sachs, and other companies?

2. Will both employees and companies from this policy? What about shareholders? Explain.

3. Discuss why these companies use somewhat different health care delivery strategies.

SOURCES: L. Lagnad, "The Doctor Is in—At Work," *Wall Street Journal*, January 9, 2018; A. Wilde Mathews, "New Tactics on Health Costs," *Wall Street Journal*, December 4, 2018; T. Murphy, "Employers Jump into Providing Care as Health Costs Rise," *AP News*, September 30, 2018, www.apnews.com; T. Murphy, "Survey: Companies Keep Passing Health Costs to Workers," *Detroit News*, October 3, 2018.

**Table 13.6**

Health Care Costs and Outcomes in Various Countries

| | LIFE EXPECTANCY AT BIRTH, FEMALE | INFANT MORTALITY RATE (PER 1,000) | HEALTH EXPENDITURES AS A PERCENTAGE OF GDP |
|---|---|---|---|
| Canada | 84 | 5 | 10% |
| France | 86 | 4 | 12 |
| Germany | 84 | 3 | 11 |
| Japan | 87 | 2 | 11 |
| Korea | 85 | 3 | 8 |
| Mexico | 78 | 12 | 5 |
| United Kingdom | 83 | 4 | 10 |
| United States | 81 | 6 | 17 |

SOURCES: Organization for Economic Cooperation and Development, *OECD Health Statistics 2018*, www.OECD.org, Accessed January 30, 2019.

## Health Care: Controlling Costs and Improving Quality

As Table 13.6 indicates, the United States spends more on health care than any other country in the world, which helps explain why there is so much focus on controlling health care costs. U.S. health care expenditures have gone from roughly 5% of gross domestic product (GDP) in 1960 (about $27 billion) to roughly 17% (which works out to well over $3 trillion) more recently. Yet the percentage of full-time workers receiving job-related health benefits had declined over the same period, now standing at 69% and there are nearly 30 million uninsured and now rising (see Table 13.7).[56] As Table 13.6 shows, the United States also trails Japan and western Europe on measures of life expectancy and infant mortality. The United States recently made substantial progress on health insurance coverage between 2013 and 2016 (see Table 13.7), apparently due to the Affordable Care Act. However, Table 13.6 shows that since beginning in 2017, that progress began to be reversed.[57]

Unlike workers in most western European countries, who have nationalized health systems, the majority of Americans receiving health insurance get it through their (or a family member's) employer.[58] Consequently, health insurance, like pensions, discourages employee turnover because not all employers provide health insurance benefits.[59]

One trend in plan design has been to shift costs to employees through the use of (higher) deductibles, co-insurance, exclusions and limitations, and maximum benefits.[60] These costs can be structured such that employees act on incentives to shift to less expensive plans.[61] Another trend has been to focus on reducing, rather than shifting, costs through such activities as preadmission testing and second surgical opinions. The use of

Visit your instructor's Connect® course and access your eBook to view this video.

"We see the HTA triggering a marketplace of competition where buyers of health care challenge providers of health care to compete with each other in a better way."
—Robert Andrews, CEO Health Transformation Alliance

Source: Video produced for the Center for Executive Succession in the Darla Moore School of Business at the University of South Carolina by Coal Powered Filmworks

**Table 13.7**

Number and Percentage of People without Health Insurance, United States

| YEAR | CENTERS FOR DISEASE CONTROL AND PREVENTION, ALL AGES | | GALLUP–HEALTHWAYS, 18 AND OLDER |
| | MILLIONS | % | % |
| --- | --- | --- | --- |
| 2000 | 41.3 | 14.9 | |
| 2005 | 41.2 | 14.2 | |
| 2010 | 48.6 | 16.0 | 16.4 |
| 2011 | 46.3 | 15.1 | 17.0 |
| 2012 | 45.5 | 14.7 | 16.8 |
| 2013 | 44.8 | 14.4 | 17.1[a] |
| 2014 | 36.0 | 11.5 | 12.9[a] |
| 2015 | 28.6 | 9.1 | 11.9[a] |
| 2016 | 28.6 | 9.0 | 10.9[a] |
| 2017 | 29.3 | 9.1 | 12.2[a] |
| 2018 | | | 13.7[a] |

[a]Fourth quarter of year.

SOURCES: D. Witter, "U.S. Uninsured Rate Rises to Four-Year High," *Gallup*, January 23, 2019, https://news.gallup.com; Z. Auter, "US Uninsured Rate Holds at Low of 10.9% in Fourth Quarter," *Gallup*, January 19, 2017, http://www.gallup.com/poll/201641/uninsured-rate-holds-low-fourth-quarter.aspx; J. Levy, "In U.S., Uninsured Rate Dips to 11.9% in First Quarter," http://www.gallup.com/poll/182348/uninsured-rate-dips-first-quarter.aspx; R. A. Cohen et al. "Health Insurance Coverage: Early Release of Estimates from the National Health Interview Survey of 2017," Centers for Disease Control and Prevention, May 2018, www.cdc.gov.

**Health maintenance organization (HMO)**
A health care plan that provides benefits on a prepaid basis for employees who are required to use only HMO medical service providers.

**Preferred provider organization (PPO)**
A group of health care providers who contract with employers, insurance companies, and so forth to provide health care at a reduced fee.

alternative providers like **health maintenance organizations (HMOs)** and **preferred provider organizations (PPOs)** has also increased. HMOs differ from more traditional providers by focusing on preventive care and outpatient treatment, requiring employees to use only HMO services, and providing benefits on a prepaid basis. Many HMOs pay physicians and other health care workers a flat salary instead of using the traditional fee-for-service system, under which a physician's pay may depend on the number of patients seen. Paying on a salary basis is intended to reduce incentives for physicians to schedule more patient visits or medical procedures than might be necessary. (Of course, there is the risk that incentives will be reduced too much, resulting in inadequate access to medical procedures and specialists.) PPOs are essentially groups of health care providers that contract with employers, insurance companies, and so forth to provide health care at a reduced fee. They differ from HMOs in that they do not provide benefits on a prepaid basis and employees often are not required to use the preferred providers. Instead, employers may provide incentives for employees to choose, for example, a physician who participates in the plan. In general, PPOs seem to be less expensive than traditional delivery systems but more expensive than HMOs.[62]

Another trend in employers' attempts to control costs has been to vary required employee contributions based on the employee's health and risk factors rather than charging each employee the same premium. Some companies go further, refusing to employ people with certain risk factors such as smokers.

Some employers now offer a "Medical tourism" benefit, which means sending patients to other countries where medical procedures can sometimes be done much more cheaply. For example, under a program at Hannaford Brothers, a Maine-based grocery chain, the company would pay for an employee (and significant other) to travel to Singapore for a knee or hip replacement. Doing so saved the company roughly $30,000 to $40,000 and saved the employee about $3,000 in out-of-pocket costs (i.e., the deductible). And, the employee and travel companion get to experience another country.[63] Deploying technology, including telemedicine, is another approach to reducing costs (see the Competing through Technology box).

*Employee Wellness Programs.* Employee wellness programs (EWPs) focus on changing behaviors both on and off work time that could eventually lead to future health problems. EWPs are preventive in nature; they attempt to manage health care costs (and workers' compensation costs) by decreasing employees' needs for services. Typically, these programs aim at specific health risks such as high blood pressure, high cholesterol levels, smoking, and obesity. They also try to promote positive health influences such as physical exercise and good nutrition. Johnson & Johnson estimated a return of $2.71 for every $1.00 spent on employee wellness programs.[64] Of course, not all companies have found such positive returns.[65] Thus, each company should bring evidence to bear to evaluate its own return, which will likely depend on the program design, the nature of the workforce, and other contextual factors. However, evidence suggests that "well-designed and well-executed wellness programs that are founded on evidence-based principles can achieve positive health and financial outcomes."[66] One review concluded that wellness programs, on average, return $3.27 in medical expenditure savings for every dollar spent and $2.73 in absenteeism savings for every dollar spent. Another review reported 25% lower medical and absenteeism costs among program participants compared to nonparticipants.[67]

EWPs are either passive or active. Passive programs use little or no outreach to individuals, nor do they provide ongoing support to motivate them to use the resources. Active wellness centers assume that behavior change requires not only awareness and opportunity but also support and reinforcement.

One example of a passive wellness program is a health education program that aims to raise awareness of the importance of good health and how to achieve it. In these programs, a health educator usually conducts classes or lunchtime lectures (or coordinates outside speakers). The program may also have various promotions (like an annual mile run or a "smoke-out") and include a newsletter that reports on current health issues.

Another kind of passive employee wellness program is a fitness facility. In this kind of program, the company sets up a center for physical fitness equipped with aerobic and muscle-building exercise machines and staffed with certified athletic trainers. The facility is publicized within the organization, and employees are free to use it on their own time. Aetna, for example, has created five state-of-the-art health clubs that serve more than 7,500 workers.[68] Northwestern Mutual Life's fitness facilities are open 24 hours a day to its 3,300 employees.[69] Health education classes related to smoking cessation and weight loss may be offered as well.

One kind of active wellness center is the outreach and follow-up model. This type of wellness center contains all the features of a passive model, but it also has counselors who handle one-on-one outreach and provide tailored, individualized programs for employees. Typically, tailored programs obtain baseline measures on various indicators (weight, blood pressure, lung capacity, and so on) and measure individuals' progress relative to these indicators over time. The programs set goals and provide small, symbolic rewards to individuals who meet their goals. Of course, stronger incentives are available and these could be paired with a wellness program.

This encouragement provided under an active wellness center needs to be particularly targeted to employees in high-risk categories (like those who smoke, are overweight, or

## COMPETING THROUGH TECHNOLOGY

### Alliances, Technology, and Virtual Care (Telemedicine)

Amazon, Berkshire Hathaway, and JPMorgan Chase, which have 1.1 million employees, will launch a separate venture whose goal is to leverage technology and other resources to reduce employer health care costs. Since 1990, employer costs for employee health care in the United States have risen from about $250 billion to $665 billion (in inflation-adjusted dollars), or 170%. By comparison, for example, U.S. gross domestic product during that same period rose by about 90%, or roughly about one-half as fast. As Warren Buffett (also known as the "Oracle of Omaha"), CEO of Berkshire, describes it: "The ballooning costs of healthcare act as a hungry tapeworm on the American economy" and the new venture hopes to "check the rise in health care costs while concurrently enhancing patient satisfaction and outcomes."

Amazon may play a key role if it can translate its expertise in deploying technological advances such as artificial intelligence, the cloud, and information sharing platforms to health care. A Notre Dame professor, Idris Adjerid, states research finds that "technology initiatives which facilitated information sharing between disconnected hospitals resulted in significant reductions in healthcare spending." The new venture has also begun to use technology (IBM's Watson software) to "meld member companies' health-claims data" to allow better analysis of whether treatment and drug prescription decisions can be improved, either in terms of efficacy (the patient satisfaction and outcomes emphasized by Warren Buffett) or in terms of cost. For example, the alliance can enter into contracts for how conditions such as diabetes, hip and knee replacements, and lower back pain will be treated and how providers will be compensated (e.g., based not solely on procedures performed, but also on the basis of how well targets such as recovery time are met.)

However, even if patterns are identified that suggest room for improvement (e.g., in cost), it then typically becomes a question of how much leverage health care consumers such as the three companies in the new venture (and perhaps additional companies in the future) can achieve to get health care providers to change and pass some of the cost savings on to the consumers. One challenge, for example, is that a critical mass of employees (individual health care consumers at an employer) has traditionally been necessary to achieve such leverage, but even very large employers will have locations with few employees. The hope is that alliances or ventures like the one undertaken here by these three companies will be able to "pool" in some sense their employee populations and thus gain more leverage in negotiations with providers. However, there are challenges with employers cooperating in such efforts given that they often have different employee populations (e.g., in terms of age, types of health challenges, and income). In any case, the hope is to make strides even in the face of these and other challenges.

Finally, employers continue to move toward greater use of virtual care (or "telemedicine"), which now includes coaching, condition management, remote monitoring, physical therapy, and cognitive behavioral therapy.

### DISCUSSION QUESTIONS

1. What role do you think technology will play in controlling what Warren Buffett calls "the hungry tapeworm of the American economy"? How successful do you believe this initiative will be? Explain.

2. As an employee, how would you feel about using the telemedicine option? Explain.

SOURCES: A. LaVito and J. Cox, "Amazon, Berkshire Hathaway, and JPMorgan Chase to Partner on US Employee Health Care," *CNBC*, January 30, 2018, www.CNBC.com; J. D. McKinnon, "Tech Firms Make Vow on Health Records," *Wall Street Journal*, August 14, 2018; Federal Reserve Bank of St. Louis, "Real Gross Domestic Product (GDPC1)," https://fred.stlouisfed.org/series/GDPC1; "Frustrated with Rising Healthcare Costs, Employers Get Creative in Care Delivery," *Employee Benefit News*, August 8, 2018, www.benefitnews.com.

have high blood pressure) for two reasons. First, a small percentage of employees create a disproportionate amount of health care costs; therefore, targeted interventions are more efficient. Second, research shows that those in high-risk categories are the most likely to perceive barriers (like family problems or work overload)[70] to participating in company-sponsored fitness programs. Thus, untargeted interventions are likely to miss the people that most need to be included.

Research on these different types of wellness centers leads to several conclusions.[71] First, the costs of health education programs are significantly less than those associated with either fitness facility programs or the follow-up model. Second, all three models are effective in reducing the risk factors associated with cardiovascular disease (obesity, high blood pressure, smoking, and lack of exercise). However, the follow-up model is significantly better than the other two in reducing the risk factors.

Somewhat ironically, well-meaning employers sometimes do things that work at cross-purposes—for example, providing employees with easy access to good food, while also wanting employees to be fit. Google decided to keep its good food, but it also decided it needed to change the way it presented food to employees. Its research found that people tend to load up on the first food they see. So, Google changed the cafeteria line so that the first thing employees now see is something healthy: the salad bar. Desserts weren't taken away but were banished to the far corner of the cafeteria (and serving size reduced). Google also focused on communicating to employees which foods were low in calories (green tags) and which ones (those higher in calories) were best taken in smaller portions (red tags).[72]

Another aspect of wellness is financial wellness. In the United States, it has been reported that "money-related concerns are a more prevalent source of distress than those related to health, work, or family" and that "most people . . . do not have $400 in savings to cover an emergency," and there is some evidence that such "financial precarity" can adversely affect employee performance at the workplace.[73] In addition to higher wages, of course, employers can also take steps to encourage/incentivize employees to save enough money for an emergency (e.g., by cooperating with banks), through programs that help with balancing work and family, and, by programs that encourage wellness.[74]

***Health Care Costs and Quality: Ongoing Challenges.*** In 2018, the average annual premium for family coverage was $19,616, up 4.5% from the previous year, with employers paying $13,927 (71%) and employees paying $5,687 (29%) on average. For single coverage, the average premium was $6,896, up 3.1% from the previous year, with employers paying $5,654 (82%) and employees paying $1,241 (18%).[75] (These numbers pertain only to employers that provide health care benefits.) Not included in premium costs are payments made by employees in the form of co-insurance (paying a percentage of the cost of a medical service received, co-payments (paying a flat fee that covers part of the cost of a medical service received), and deductibles (paying the first $x$ dollars of cost for medical services received during a year before insurance coverage, funded by premiums, kicks in to cover the cost). These three costs average an additional $800 annually for employees of large firms. The largest increase over time has been in deductibles.[76]

Two important phenomena are often encountered in cost control efforts. First, piecemeal programs may not work well because steps to control one aspect (such as medical cost shifting) may lead employees to "migrate" to other programs that provide medical treatment at no cost to them (like workers' compensation). Second, there is often a so-called Pareto group, which refers to a small percentage (perhaps 20%) of employees being responsible for generating the majority (often 80%) of health care costs. Obviously, cost control efforts will be more successful to the extent that the costs generated by the Pareto group can be identified and managed effectively.[77]

Although cost control will continue to require a good deal of attention, there is a growing emphasis on monitoring health care quality, which has been described as "the next battlefield." A major focus is on identifying best medical practices by measuring and monitoring the relative success of alternative treatment strategies using large-scale databases and research.[78] "Big data" can be used to move beyond intuition to make better decisions, including helping organizations to provide quality health care coverage for employees, while controlling costs.

At Caesars Entertainment Corporation (which operates casinos), health insurance claim data on its 65,000 employees and their covered family members is analyzed as part of meeting this challenge. Among the thousands of variables that can be tracked are how much different medical services are used, the degree to which employees use name-brand versus (less expensive) generic prescription drugs, and the number of emergency room (ER) visits, which cost over $1,200 on average (for outpatient visits). By contrast, a visit to the doctor's office or to an urgent care facility is much less expensive (e.g., between $100 and $200). As an example, when Caesars looked at its Harrah's property in Philadelphia, it discovered that only about 11% of emergencies were being treated at urgent care facilities versus 34% across all of Caesars. To encourage employees to use the less expensive urgent care option more and emergency rooms less, Harrah's initiated a campaign to remind employees of how expensive ER visits are and provided them with a list of urgent care and alternative facilities that they were encouraged to use. Two years later, 17% of emergencies (up from 11%) were going to urgent care. Further, multiple ER visits by individual employees fell from 40% to 30%. Overall, on a companywide basis, in the first few years since beginning to track ER visits, Caesars employees had 10,000 fewer ER visits, replacing them with less expensive alternatives, resulting in a savings of $4.5 million.[79] In addition, employers increasingly cooperate with one another to develop "report cards" on health care provider organizations to facilitate better choices by the employers and to receive improved health care. General Motors, Ford, and Chrysler, for example, have developed this type of system and made it Web accessible.[80]

When we discuss the Affordable Care Act later in this chapter, we will see that the act allows employers to use larger incentives (and penalties) than previously to encourage employee wellness, and some companies are making changes accordingly. We have provided a number of examples in this chapter of how employers use these tools. We now provide a few more. The state of Maryland will penalize employees as much as $450 per year for not undergoing required screenings or for not following up on treatment plans for chronic conditions. At pharmacy company CVS Health, an employee who does not complete the annual health assessment will have to pay $600 more per year for insurance coverage. (On the incentive side, JetBlue employees can receive as much as $400 per year in their health savings or reimbursement accounts for signing up for a variety of activities including smoking cessation.) Survey evidence indicates that most employees don't approve of such programs. Nevertheless, use seems to be increasing as employers seek to control health care costs.[81]

### Staffing Responses to Control Benefits Cost Growth

Employers may change staffing practices to control benefits costs.

*Overtime.* First, because benefits costs are fixed (in that they do not usually increase with hours worked), the benefits cost per hour can be reduced by having employees work more hours. However, there are drawbacks to having employees work more hours. The Fair Labor Standards Act (FLSA), introduced in Chapter 11, requires that nonexempt employees be paid time-and-a-half for hours in excess of 40 per week. Yet the decline in U.S. work hours tapered off in the late 1940s; work hours have increased since then. Thus, even with the time-and-a-half cost of overtime, employers may prefer employees to work more hours, given the level of fixed benefits costs (and the fact that hiring additional workers would further increase fixed benefits costs in addition to increasing recruiting and training costs).[82]

*Exempt Status.* A second possible effect of FLSA regulations (although this is more speculative) is that organizations will try to have their employees classified as exempt whenever possible (although such attempts may run afoul of FLSA law). The growth in the number of salaried workers (many of whom are exempt) may also reflect an effort by organizations to limit the benefits cost per hour without having to pay overtime.

*Temporary Workers.* A third potential effect is the growth in part-time employment and the use of temporary workers, which may be a response to rising benefits costs. Part-time workers are less likely to receive benefits than full-time workers, although labor market shortages in recent years have reduced this difference.[83] Benefits for temporary workers are also usually quite limited. Temporary workers, workers supplied by contract firms, on-call workers, and/or independent contractors (see next section) are sometimes described as having "alternative work arrangements." Another term, contingent workers, is used to refer to those who expect their jobs to be temporary. Interestingly, according to the Bureau of Labor Statistics, the percentage of of those who are contingent workers or in alternative work arrangements has remained stable over time.[84]

*Independent Contractors versus Employees.* Fourth, employers may be more likely to classify workers as independent contractors rather than employees, which eliminates the employer's obligation to provide legally required employee benefits. One investment banker described the thinking of many companies regarding hiring employees as follows: "Can I automate it? If not, can I outsource it? If not, can I give it to an independent contractor or freelancer?" In other words, adding an employee is "a last resort." Virgin Atlantic's chief executive tells investors that "we will outsource every job that we can that is not customer-facing." So far, that includes baggage delivery, reservations, catering, and heavy maintenance. Google, which is regularly ranked by *Fortune* as one of the best places to work, is thought to have equal numbers of outsourced workers and employees. Uber, of course, relies on independent contractors. Some gig workers prefer this model. However, some do not because of uncertain work and income and the lack of benefits.[85]

However, the Internal Revenue Service (IRS) scrutinizes such decisions carefully, as Microsoft and other companies have discovered. Microsoft (now many years ago) was compelled to reclassify a group of workers as employees (rather than as independent contractors) and to grant them retroactive benefits. Uber, which competes with taxis by providing ride-sharing, is one of many companies that has faced legal action challenging its classification of workers (drivers in the Uber case) as contractors rather than as employees. The IRS looks at several factors, including the permanency of the relationship between employer and worker, how much control the employer exercises in directing the worker, and whether the worker offers services to only that employer. Permanency, control, and dealing with a single employer are viewed by the IRS as suggestive of an employment relationship. The Integrity in Action box provides examples of how gig workers fare in tech companies Google and Microsoft (and their suppliers).

# INTEGRITY IN ACTION

## Being a Contractor versus an Employee

At Google, workers wear red or white name badges. The red name badges are said to outnumber the white name badges. What is the difference? White name badges are worn by Google employees. Red name badges are worn by Google contract workers who are employees of another company that provides workers on a contract basis for Google. Employees and contract workers at Google differ in terms of status, influence, and benefits. A Google spokesman states that they hire "TVCs" (temps, vendors, and contractors) primarily in two cases: (1) when the skills are not available within Google, such as in the case of doctors, quality assurance testers, and shuttle bus drivers, and (2) when positions vacated by employees on leave need to be covered.

Contractors, of course, differ in their satisfaction. Some feel "peripheral" or isolated or like "second class citizens." Contractors do not receive Google stock, some do not have health insurance coverage (or do not have good quality coverage) through their own employers, and some feel their pay is low compared to Google employees. Other contractors are more positive, feeling, for example, that the opportunity to work at Google was a boost to their careers. Some contractors are paid quite well,

with some software designers, for example, earning as much as $150/hour.

One approach that can be taken is for a company to require employers of its contractors to provide certain benefits. For example, a few years ago, Microsoft began to require that its suppliers provide their employees with at least 15 days of paid time off each year. More recently, Microsoft has implemented a new requirement that its suppliers, of which it says it has over 1,000, if they have at least 50 employees and "perform substantial work for Microsoft," must also provide a minimum of 12 weeks of paid parental leave and an additional 8 weeks for birth mothers. One impetus for this new policy is likely a recent law passed in Washington state that takes effect in 2020 and will require employers to provide paid parental leave. Microsoft headquarters is located in Redmond, Washington. However, in its statement, Microsoft said that it "realized that while [the new law] will benefit the employees of our suppliers in Washington State, it will leave thousands of valued contributors outside of Washington behind." Thus they decided to "apply Washington's parental leave policy more broadly, and not to wait until 2020." In its announcement, Microsoft went on to cite research

it says shows that employers providing parental paid leave see "improved productivity, higher morale, and lower turnover rates."

### DISCUSSION QUESTIONS

1. Do you believe that Google should change its use of contractors? Explain.
2. Why did Microsoft take the action it did? Do you feel other companies can and should do the same? Explain.
3. Is doing something that is good for workers and costs money always bad for business (win–lose, zero-sum), or can it be good for business and workers (win–win)?
4. What are the different types of contractors/gig workers? Do the groups have similar or different preferences and leverage? Does one group need more protection than the other group? Explain.
5. Do you feel it is better to leave decisions about the relationship with workers in the hands of employers, or do you see the need for a larger role of government? Explain.

SOURCES: S. Salinas, "Microsoft Will Start Requiring Partners and Suppliers to Offer Paid Family Leave, and It Will Help Cover the Costs," www.cnbc.com, August 30, 2018; M. Bergen and J. Eidelson, "Inside Google's Shadow Workforce of Contract Laborers—Many Don't Have Health Insurance," July 25, 2018, Bloomberg.com; R. Lerman, "Microsoft Requires Contractors to Offer Paid Parental Leave," *The Seattle Times*, August 31, 2018, www.seattletimes.com.

Some companies have re-thought using contractors instead of employees because the cost of acquiring and retaining workers who are not employees is beginning to eat up the theoretical cost savings of the gig model. For example, Managed by Q, which provides office and cleaning services, hires employees. Homer, a food delivery and logistics company in New York, hires its couriers as employees and pays $15 an hour.

### Improving Expatriate Access to Health Care

By one report, there are 66 million expatriate workers (i.e., working in a country different than their home country for varying lengths of time) worldwide. That means there are 66 million people who must learn how to access health care in a foreign country's system, which is almost significantly different than the system they know in their own country.

One part of the solution is for employers to offer what is called either telehealth or telemedicine (typically non-emergency) care. Whether for domestic or expatriate employees, this option can allow access to general medical advice within a few days rather than having to wait potentially weeks for an in-person appointment and then also take the time to travel to and from and potentially wait at the appointment. In the case of an expatriate employee, it offers the additional advantage of eliminating any language barrier, as well as the need to deal with the idiosyncrasies of the foreign health care system. It may also save the employer a significant amount of money.

Mobile apps allow direct access to a doctor who not only speaks the employee's language, but will also be more familiar with any cultural aspects that may come into play. In some cases, a 10 or 15 minute teleconsultation may help avoid a costly and drawn-out visit to an emergency room or doctor's office. There are, of course, challenges and risks in using telemedicine. For example, a virtual exam has limitations compared to an in-person exam. For example, it may be possible to diagnose the concern raised by the patient, but other concerns that might be noticed by a doctor in an in-person exam may be be more likely to go unnoticed. Another challenge is that some countries may ban doctors from providing health care unless they hold a license in that country. And/or they may not permit the doctor to write prescriptions in that country. In such cases, some sort of partnership with a local doctor would be necessary.

#### DISCUSSION QUESTIONS

1. Have you ever had a health problem while overseas and needed care? Describe your experience.
2. How do you feel about using teleconsultation/telemedicine? Explain.

SOURCES: T. Starner, "Improving Access to Healthcare for Expat Workers," *Human Resource Executive*, October 30, 2018, hrexecutive.com; T. Anderson, "The Magic of Telemedicine," *International Travel and Health Insurance Journal*, October 28, 2018, www.itij.com.

Homer believes that this has created a "culture of retention," which saves on recruiting and turnover costs and also makes for consistently better customer service. Similarly, Eden, a company in the Bay Area that helps manage offices, uses "wizards" (employees) to clean and fix things for its clients. It says that the employee model means that its costs are 30% higher, but this approach works for Eden because its employees also "stay 30% longer."[86]

### NATURE OF THE WORKFORCE

Although general considerations such as cost control and "protection against the risks of old age, loss of health, and loss of life" are important, employers must also consider the specific demographic composition and preferences of their current workforces in designing their benefits packages. The Competing through Globalization box provides examples of how some companies have tailored their policies to provide health care to global/expatriate employees.

At a broad level, basic demographic factors such as age and sex can have important consequences for the types of benefits employees want. For example, an older workforce

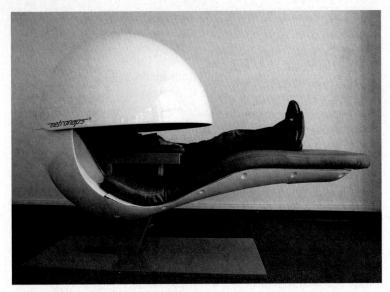

Stan Honda/AFP/Getty Images

is more likely to be concerned about (and use) medical coverage, life insurance, and pensions. A workforce with a high percentage of women of childbearing age may care more about disability leave. Young, unmarried men and women often have less interest in benefits generally, preferring higher wages and salaries.

Although some general conclusions about employee preferences can be drawn based on demographics, more finely tuned assessments of employee benefit preferences need to be done. One approach is to use marketing research methods to assess employees' preferences the same way consumers' demands for products and services are assessed.[87] Methods include personal interviews, focus groups, and questionnaires. Relevant questions might include the following:

- What benefits are most important to you?
- If you could choose one new benefit, what would it be?
- If you were given $x$ dollars for benefits, how would you spend it?

As with surveys generally, care must be taken not to raise employee expectations regarding future changes. If the employer is not prepared to act on the employees' input, surveying may do more harm than good.

The preceding discussion may imply that the current makeup of the workforce is a given, but this is not the case. As discussed earlier, the benefits package may influence the composition of the workforce. For example, a benefits package that has strong medical benefits and pensions may be particularly attractive to older people or those with families. An attractive pension plan may be a way to attract workers who wish to make a long-term commitment to an organization.[88] Where turnover costs are high, this type of strategy may have some appeal. On the other hand, a company that has lucrative health care benefits may attract and retain people with high health care costs. Sick leave provisions may also affect the composition of the workforce. Organizations need to think about the signals their benefits packages send and the implications of these signals for workforce composition. In this vein, Table 13.8 shows the benefits used by Google, a company that regularly tops *Fortune*'s list of "100 Best Companies to Work For," to attract and retain its desired workforce.

## COMMUNICATING WITH EMPLOYEES AND MAXIMIZING BENEFITS VALUE
### Employees Typically Underestimate the Value of Their Benefits

**LO 13-5**
Explain the importance of effectively communicating the nature and value of benefits to employees.

Effective communication of benefits information to employees is critical if employers are to realize sufficient returns on their benefits investments. Research makes it clear that current employees and job applicants often have a very poor idea of what benefits provisions are already in place and the cost or market value of those benefits. One study

Table 13.8
Employee Benefits
at Google

- Google Shuttle to San Francisco
- Sleep pods
- Up to $8,000/year in tuition reimbursement
- On-site perks include medical and dental facilities; oil change and bike repair; valet parking; free washers and dryers; and free breakfast, lunch, and dinner on a daily basis at 11 gourmet restaurants
- Seven-acre sports complex, which includes a roller hockey rink; courts for basketball, bocce, and shuffle ball; and horseshoe pits
- Unlimited sick leave
- 27 days of paid time off after one year of employment
- Global Education Leave program, enabling employees to take a leave of absence to pursue further education for up to five years and $150,000 in reimbursement
- Free shuttles equipped with WiFi from locations around the Bay Area to headquarter offices
- Fuel-efficiency vehicle incentive program ($5,000 incentive to purchase a hybrid car)
- A climbing wall
- Classes on a variety of subjects from estate planning and home purchasing to foreign language lessons in French, Spanish, Japanese, and Mandarin
- The ability to bring your dog to work
- When an employee dies, the spouse receives 50% of salary for 10 years and children each receive $12,000 per year until age 19 (age 23 if full-time students)
- Paid maternity (and paternity) leave: five months for mothers, three months for fathers

SOURCES: E. Jang, "Are Google Employees More Productive Because of Company Perks?" *Forbes*, July 9, 2018, www.forbes.com; "100 Best Companies to Work For 2017," *Fortune*, http://beta.fortune.com/best-companies/; M. Garner, "Google Employees' Favorite Perks—Here's 8 of the Best," *The Street*, January 18, 2016, https://www.thestreet.com/story/13420255/4/google-employees-favorite-perks-here-s-8-of-the-best.html; J. Bort, "These 18 Tech Companies Offer the Best Benefits, According to Employees," *Business Insider*, May 1, 2015; J. D'Onfro and K. Smith, "Google Employees Reveal Their Favorite Perks about Working for the Company," *Business Insider*, July 1, 2014.

asked employees to estimate both the amount contributed by the employer to their medical insurance and what it would cost the employees to provide their own health insurance. Employees significantly underestimated both the cost and market value of their medical benefits. In the case of family coverage, employee estimates of what it costs their employer to provide coverage for them were, on average, 62% below the actual cost.[89] As we saw earlier, the average employer today providing health care benefits spends $13,927 per year for family coverage. In the absence of effective communication, the just-discussed study would imply that a typical employee today might credit employers with providing a benefit worth only $5,292 (i.e., 0.38 × $13,927)—again, a very poor return on the employer's investment.

Research suggests that the situation with job applicants is no better. One study of MBAs found that 46% believed that benefits added 15% or less on top of direct payroll. Not surprisingly, perhaps, benefits were dead last on applicants' priority lists in making job choices.[90] A study of undergraduate business majors found similar results, with benefits ranked 15th (out of 18) in importance in evaluating jobs. These results must be interpreted with caution, however. Some research suggests that job attributes can be ranked low in importance, not because they are unimportant per se, but because all employers are perceived to be about the same on that attribute. If some employers offered noticeably poorer benefits, the importance of benefits could become much greater.

Organizations can help remedy the problem of applicants' and employees' lack of knowledge about benefits. One study found that employees' awareness of benefits information was significantly increased through several media, including memoranda, question-and-answer meetings, and detailed brochures. The increased awareness, in turn, contributed to significant increases in benefits satisfaction. Another study suggests, however, that increased employee knowledge of benefits can have a positive or negative effect, depending on the nature of the benefits package. For example, there was a negative, or inverse, correlation between cost to the employee and benefits satisfaction overall, but the correlation was more strongly negative among employees with greater knowledge of their benefits.[91] The implication is that employees will be least satisfied with their benefits if their cost is high and they are well informed.

One thing an employer should consider with respect to written benefits communication is that it has been estimated that tens of millions of employees in the United States may be functionally illiterate. Of course, there are many alternative ways to communicate benefits information. (See Table 13.9.) Nevertheless, most organizations spend little to communicate information about benefits, and much of this is spent on general written communications. Considering that Bureau of Labor Statistics data cited earlier indicate that U.S. employers spend a large amount of money on

**Table 13.9**

Benefits Communication Methods, Percentage of Organizations Reporting "Very Effective"

| COMMUNICATION METHOD | % VERY EFFECTIVE |
|---|---|
| **Face-to-Face** | |
| One-on-one meetings | 51% |
| Orientation/onboarding | 40 |
| Group communications | 37 |
| Benefits fairs | 26 |
| Lunch-and-learn | 21 |
| **Virtual** | |
| Bulletins to screensavers | 20 |
| Webinars | 15 |
| Social media | 15 |
| Virtual education | 14 |
| **Information Portal** | |
| Online benefits portal | 32 |
| Intranet | 21 |
| **Materials** | |
| Enrollment materials | 35 |
| E-mail | 31 |
| Text messages | 25 |
| Direct mail to residence | 16 |
| Handouts | 15 |
| Newsletters | 13 |

Note: Survey of 447 organizations.

SOURCE: Society for Human Resource Management, "Strategize with Benefits," December 19, 2017, www.shrm.org.

**Table 13.10**

Percentage of
Employees
Preferring Amount
and Types of
Benefits
Communication

**Frequency of Communication Preferred**

Happy with current frequency: 55%

Prefer more frequently: 31%

No opinion: 10%

Prefer less frequently: 4%

**Type of Communication Preferred**

Work e-mail: 47%

Personal e-mail: 28%

Online avatar that recommends benefits to meet individual needs: 19%

Group meetings: 19%

Individual one-on-one meetings: 18%

SOURCES: Frequency preferences: Prudential Group Insurance, *Ninth Study of Employee Benefits: Today & Beyond*, 2016, http://research.prudential.com/documents/rp/benefits_and_beyond_2016.pdf. Based on *N* = 969 employees, ages 22 or older, who work full time for a company with at least 50 employees. Type preferences: Prudential Group Insurance, *Eighth Annual Study of Employee Benefits: Today & Beyond*, 2014, http://research.prudential.com. Based on *N* = 1,000 employees, ages 22 or older, who work full time for a company with at least 25 employees.

benefits ($10.48/hour or about $21,798/year). Large employers spend even more ($17.11/hour or about $35,589/year), together with the complex nature of many benefits and the poor understanding of most employees, the typical communication effort may be inadequate.[92]

On a more positive note, organizations are increasingly using online tools to personalize and tailor communications to individual employees. Online tools have also enabled many organizations to eliminate benefits-related jobs now that employees can get answers to many benefits questions on their own. In addition, effective use of traditional approaches (e.g., enrollment materials) can have a large effect on employee awareness.[93] Survey data (see Table 13.10) indicate that both traditional and online methods are seen as effective by employees, although one suspects that will continue to evolve over time. The table also indicates that although most employees are happy with the current frequency of benefits communication from their employers, a sizable minority would like more. Interestingly, Tables 13.9 and 13.10 seem to differ on what benefits communication methods (e.g., see one-on-one meetings) are most effective/preferred. The most likely reason would seem to be that employers (HR professionals) are responding in Tables 13.9 and employees are responding in Table 13.10. (Take a look at the two tables and see if you have an explanation.)

## Flexible Benefits Plans

Rather than a single standard benefits package for all employees, flexible benefit plans (flex-plans or cafeteria-style plans) permit employees to choose the types and amounts of benefits they want for themselves. The plans vary according to such things as whether minimum levels of certain benefits (such as health care coverage) are prescribed and whether employees can receive money for having chosen a "light" benefits package (or have to pay extra for more benefits). One example is vacation, where some plans permit employees to give up vacation days for more salary or, alternatively, purchase extra vacation days through a salary reduction.

What are the potential advantages of such plans?[94] In the best case, almost all of the objectives discussed previously can be positively influenced. First, employees can gain a greater awareness and appreciation of what the employer provides them, particularly with plans that give employees a lump sum to allocate to benefits. Second, by permitting employee choice, there should be a better match between the benefits package and the employees' preferences. As just one example of heterogeneous employee preferences, one study looked at how much salary employees would be willing to give up to have certain benefits. In the case of work schedule flexibility, females, those above median pay, and those age 57 or older would give up 23%, 30%, and 28% more base pay (compared to other groups), respectively, for greater flexibility.[95] Matching benefits to different employee preferences should improve employee attitudes and retention and perhaps performance.[96] Third, employers may achieve overall cost reductions in their benefits programs. Cafeteria plans can be thought of as similar to defined contribution plans, whereas traditional plans are more like defined benefit plans. The employer can control the size of the contribution under the former, but not under the latter, because the cost and utilization of benefits is beyond the employer's control. Costs can also be controlled by designing the choices so that employees have an incentive to choose more efficient options. For example, in the case of a medical flex-plan, employees who do not wish to take advantage of the (presumably more cost-effective) HMO have to pay significant deductibles and other costs under the alternative plans. Choice and resulting better matches might also lower costs by reducing spending on benefits that few employees value.

One drawback of cafeteria-style plans is their administrative cost, especially in the initial design and start-up stages. However, software packages and standardized flex-plans developed by consultants offer some help in this regard. Another possible drawback to these plans is adverse selection. Employees are most likely to choose benefits that they expect to need the most. Someone in need of dental work would choose as much dental coverage as possible. As a result, employer costs can increase significantly as each employee chooses benefits based on their personal value. Another result of adverse selection is the difficulty in estimating benefits costs under such a plan, especially in small companies. Adverse selection can be controlled, however, by limiting coverage amounts, pricing benefits that are subject to adverse selection higher, or using a limited set of packaged options, which prevents employees from choosing too many benefits options that would be susceptible to adverse selection.

### Flexible Spending Accounts

A flexible spending account permits pretax contributions of up to $2,650 to an employee account that can be drawn on to pay for uncovered health care expenses (like deductibles or co-payments). A separate account of up to $5,000 per year is permitted for pretax contributions to cover dependent care expenses. The federal tax code requires that funds in the health care and dependent care accounts be earmarked in advance and spent during the plan year. Remaining funds revert to the employer. Therefore, the accounts work best to the extent that employees have predictable expenses. The major advantage of such plans is the increase in take-home pay that results from pretax payment of health and dependent care expenses. Consider again the hypothetical employee with an effective total marginal tax rate of 40.33% from Table 13.1. The take-home pay from an additional $10,000 in salary with and without a flexible dependent care account is as follows:

| | NO FLEXIBLE SPENDING CARE ACCOUNT | FLEXIBLE SPENDING CARE ACCOUNT |
|---|---|---|
| Salary portion | $10,000 | $10,000 |
| Pretax dependent care contribution | 0 | −2,600 |
| Taxable salary | 10,000 | 7,400 |
| Tax (40.33%) | −4,033 | −2,984 |
| After-tax cost of dependent care | −2,600 | 0 |
| Take-home pay | $ 3,367 | $ 4,415 |

Therefore, the use of a flexible spending account saves the employee just over $1,000 ($4,415 − $3,367 = $1,048) per year.

# General Regulatory Issues

Although we have already discussed a number of regulatory issues, some additional ones require attention.

**LO 13-6**

Describe the regulatory constraints that affect the way employee benefits are designed and administered.

## AFFORDABLE CARE ACT

The Affordable Care Act (ACA), signed into law in 2010, has several provisions that will have a major impact on employers as they are implemented through the year 2018. As we go to press, the future of the law is not clear. So far, there has been much discussion about the repeal or revision of the ACA, but no legislation has been passed and no executive action has been taken to change the employer mandate, which is the key part of ACA for our purposes. Thus, at present, employers continue to be subject to its provisions, which are summarized in Table 13.11.

## NONDISCRIMINATION RULES, QUALIFIED PLANS, AND TAX TREATMENT

As a general rule, all benefits packages must meet certain rules to be classified as qualified plans. What are the advantages of a qualified plan? Basically, it receives more favorable tax treatment than a nonqualified plan. In the case of a qualified retirement plan, for example, these tax advantages include (1) an immediate tax deduction for employers for their contributions to retirement funds, (2) no tax liability for the employee at the time of the employer deduction, and (3) tax-free investment returns (from stocks, bonds, money markets, or the like) on the retirement funds.[97]

What rules must be satisfied for a plan to obtain qualified status? Each benefit area has different rules. It would be impossible to describe the various rules here, but some general observations are possible. Taking pensions as an example again, vesting requirements must be met. More generally, qualified plans must meet so-called nondiscrimination rules. Basically, this means that a benefit cannot discriminate in favor of "highly compensated employees." One rationale behind such rules is that the tax benefits of qualified benefits

**Table 13.11**
The Affordable Care Act: Impact on Employers

**PENALTIES FOR NOT PROVIDING HEALTH BENEFITS**

The health reform law does not require employers to provide health benefits. However, it does impose penalties in some cases on larger employers (those with 50 or more full-time workers or 50 or more full-time equivalents [FTE]) that do not provide insurance to their workers or that provide coverage that is unaffordable.

Larger employers that do not provide coverage are assessed a penalty if any one of their workers receives a tax credit when buying insurance on their own in a health insurance exchange. Workers with income up to 400% of the poverty level are eligible for tax credits. The employer penalty is equal to $2,000 multiplied by the number of workers in the business in excess of 30 workers (with the penalty amount increasing over time).

In some instances, larger employers that offer coverage could be subject to penalties as well. If the coverage does not have an actuarial value of at least 60%—meaning that on average it covers at least 60% of the cost of covered services for a typical population—or the premium for the coverage would exceed 9.5% of a worker's income, then the worker can obtain coverage in an exchange and be eligible for a tax credit. For each worker receiving a tax credit, the employer will pay a penalty up to a maximum of $2,000 times the number of workers in excess of 30 workers.

Businesses with fewer than 25 FTEs and average annual wages of less than $50,000 that pay at least half of the cost of health insurance for their employees are eligible for a tax credit.

**TAXES***

The law increases the Medicare Hospital Insurance (Part A) payroll tax on earnings for higher-income taxpayers (more than $200,000/individual and $250,000/couple) by 0.9 percentage points, from 1.45% to 2.35%. Employers will be responsible for withholding these taxes.

The law creates a new tax on so-called "Cadillac" insurance plans provided by employers. Beginning in 2018, plans valued at $10,200 or more for individual coverage or $27,500 or more for family policies will be subject to an excise tax of 40% on the value of the plan that exceeds these thresholds. The tax will be levied on insurers and self-insured employers, not directly on employees. The threshold amounts will be increased for inflation beginning in 2020, and may be adjusted upward if health care costs rise more than expected prior to implementation of the tax in 2018. The thresholds are also adjusted upward for retired individuals age 55 and older who are not eligible for Medicare, for employees engaged in high-risk professions, and for firms that may have higher health care costs because of the age or gender of their workers.

**COVERAGE OF DEPENDENTS**

The ACA requires plans and issuers that offer dependent coverage to make the coverage available until a child reaches the age of 26. Both married and unmarried children qualify for this coverage. This rule applies to all plans in the individual market and to new employer plans. It also applies to existing employer plans unless the adult child has another offer of employer-based coverage (such as through his or her job). Children up to age 26 can stay on their parent's employer's plan even if they have another offer of coverage through their own employer.

**WELLNESS PROGRAMS**

Employers can provide rewards to employees of up to 30% of the total plan premium as part of a wellness program incentive, up from the previous limit of 20%. Under the law, the Secretary of Health and Human Services may increase this limit to 50% if deemed appropriate. Wellness programs must be "reasonably designed to promote health or prevent disease." The law also creates a five-year grant program to encourage small employers that do not currently have wellness programs to establish them. The program would offer $200 million in fiscal years 2011–2015 to employers with fewer than 100 employees who work 25 hours or more per week.

*Two new taxes do not directly involve employers. First, there is a 2.3% medical device excise tax on the sale of any taxable medical device by its manufacturer, producer, or importer. (However, a moratorium on this tax has been extended.) Second, there is (another) additional Medicare payroll tax of 0.9% on investment income for singles earning $200,000 or more and couples earning $250,000 or more.

SOURCES: Internal Revenue Service, "Questions and Answers on Employer Shared Responsibility Provisions Under the Affordable Care Act," www.irs.gov, accessed May 5, 2015; The Henry J. Kaiser Family Foundation, http://kff.org/health-reform/faq/health-reform-frequently-asked-questions/and http://kff.org/quiz/health-reform-quiz/, accessed May 22, 2013; UC-Berkeley Labor Center, "Affordable Care Act Summary of Provisions Affecting Employer-Sponsored Insurance," April 2013, http://laborcenter.berkeley.edu/healthpolicy/ppaca12.pdf, accessed May 22, 2013; National Association of Manufacturers, "Affordable Care Act Provisions Affecting Employers, 2013 and Beyond," www.nam.org/media/DB85A8CD0C174B6A8BC9077850FE6AC9/AffordableCareActEmployers_11_2_12.pdf, accessed May 22, 2013; U.S. Department of Labor, Employee Benefits Security Administration, "Young Adults and the Affordable Care Act: Protecting Young Adults and Eliminating Burdens on Businesses and Families," www.dol.gov/ebsa/faqs/faq-dependentcoverage.html.

plans (and the corresponding loss of tax revenues for the U.S. government) should not go disproportionately to the wealthy.[98] Rather, the favorable tax treatment is designed to encourage employers to provide important benefits to a broad spectrum of employees. The nondiscrimination rules discourage owners or top managers from adopting plans that benefit them exclusively.

## SEX, AGE, AND DISABILITY

Beyond the Pregnancy Discrimination Act's requirements discussed earlier in the chapter, a second area of concern for employers in ensuring legal treatment of men and women in the benefits area has to do with pension benefits. Women tend to live longer than men, meaning that pension benefits for women are more costly, all else being equal. However, in its 1978 *Manhart* ruling, the Supreme Court declared it illegal for employers to require women to contribute more to a defined benefit plan than men: Title VII protects individuals, and not all women outlive all men.[99]

Two major age-related issues have received attention under the Age Discrimination in Employment Act (ADEA) and later amendments such as the Older Workers Benefit Protection Act (OWBPA). First, employers must take care not to discriminate against workers over age 40 in the provision of pay or benefits. As one example, employers cannot generally cease accrual (stop the growth) of retirement benefits at some age (like 65) as a way of pressuring older employees to retire.[100] Second, early retirement incentive programs need to meet the following standards to avoid legal liability: (1) The employee is not coerced to accept the incentive and retire, (2) accurate information is provided regarding options, and (3) the employee is given adequate time (is not pressured) to make a decision.

Employers also have to comply with the Americans with Disabilities Act (ADA), which went into effect in 1992. The ADA specifies that employees with disabilities must have "equal access to whatever health insurance coverage the employer provides other employees." However, the act also notes that the terms and conditions of health insurance can be based on risk factors as long as this is not a subterfuge for denying the benefit to those with disabilities. Employers with risk-based programs in place would be in a stronger position, however, than employers who make changes after hiring employees with disabilities.[101]

## MONITORING FUTURE BENEFITS OBLIGATIONS

**Financial Accounting Statement (FAS) 106**, issued by the Financial Accounting Standards Board, became effective in 1993. This rule requires that any benefits (excluding pensions) provided after retirement (the major one being health care) can no longer be funded on a pay-as-you-go basis. Rather, they must be paid on an accrual basis, and companies must enter these future cost obligations on their financial statements. The effect on financial statements can be substantial.

Increasing retiree health care costs (and the change in accounting standards) have also led some companies to require white-collar employees and retirees to pay insurance premiums for the first time in history and to increase co-payments and deductibles. Survey data indicate that some companies are ending retiree health care benefits altogether. GM, for example, recently eliminated retiree health care benefits for white-collar workers. Union contracts prevented GM from eliminating the blue-collar plan.

However, as part of its bankruptcy proceeding, GM reached a settlement with the United Automobile Workers (UAW) union to create a voluntary employee benefit association (VEBA) trust. GM agreed to contribute roughly $35 billion to fund the VEBA. Ford ($13.2 billion) and Chrysler ($7.1 billion) also reached agreements to set up VEBAs.

**Financial Accounting Statement (FAS) 106** The rule issued by the Financial Accounting Standards Board in 1993 requiring companies to fund benefits provided after retirement on an accrual rather than a pay-as-you-go basis and to enter these future cost obligations on their financial statements.

By one estimate, the VEBAs moved $100 billion in retiree health care obligations off the financial statements of the three U.S. automakers, playing a major role in reducing labor cost per vehicle produced. Also, the VEBAs, like defined contribution plans, make the cost for the companies certain. After paying to set up the VEBAs, they have no future obligations to cover retiree health care. It is up to the UAW to administer the VEBA.[102]

Other companies have reduced benefits or increased retiree contributions. Obviously, such changes hit the elderly hard, especially those with relatively fixed incomes. Not surprisingly, legal challenges have arisen. The need to balance the interests of shareholders, current employees, and retirees in this area will be one of the most difficult challenges facing managers in the future.

Although use of defined benefit (pension) plans has declined significantly over time in the United States, tens of millions of people are covered by ongoing plans (and/or frozen plans—those not open to new participants). Two factors, in particular, influence employer costs. First, the Pension Benefit Guaranty Corporation, which insures pensions, regularly increases the premium paid by employers. For example, the PBGC raised its annual premium to $90 per single-employer plan participant 2019, up from $35 per participant in 2010. Second, the Society of Actuaries revised its mortality tables for the first time since 2000. Life expectancy for a 65-year-old has been revised upward from 85.2 to 88.8 for women and from 82.6 to 86.6 for men, again substantially increasing the cost obligation to employers.[103]

## A LOOK BACK

### Employee Benefits: More Responsibility for Workers

We have seen that some organizations, especially those in competition for employees with high human capital, have expanded their benefits offerings and/or are covering more of the costs. Other organizations, however, have become less paternalistic in their employee benefits strategies as they seek to control costs and shift risk to employees. Employees now have more responsibility, and, as noted, sometimes more risk, regarding their benefits choices. ("Gig" workers, who are typically independent contractors, have even more responsibility, because they have no employer and thus no employer-provided benefits.) One change has been in the area of retirement income plans, where employers have moved toward greater reliance on defined contribution plans. Such plans require employees to understand investing; otherwise, their retirement years may not be so happy. The risk to employees is especially great when defined contribution plans invest a substantial portion of their assets in company stock. One reason companies do this is because they wish to move away from an entitlement mentality and instead link benefits to company performance. However, if the company has financial problems, employees risk losing not only their jobs but also their retirement money. Another change has been in the area of health care benefits. Employees are being asked to pay an increased proportion of the costs and also to use data on health care quality to make better choices about health care. Of course, different companies have different benefits strategies. We saw at the beginning and throughout the chapter that some companies (and not just those in the tech industry) are not primarily in the mode of reducing benefits and/or passing on more costs to employees. Rather, they are looking for ways to make their benefits packages more attractive to help them compete in the labor market for valuable human capital.

## QUESTIONS

1. Why do employers offer benefits? Is it because the law requires it, because it makes good business sense, or because it is the right thing to do?
2. How much responsibility should employers have for the health and well-being of their employees? Take the perspective of both a shareholder and an employee in answering this question.
3. If you were advising a new company on how to design its health care plan, what would you recommend?

## SUMMARY

Effective management of employee benefits is an important means by which organizations compete successfully. Benefits costs are substantial and continue to grow rapidly in some areas, most notably health care. Control of such costs is necessary to compete in the product market. At the same time, employers must offer a benefits package that permits them to compete in the labor market. Beyond investing more money in benefits, the attraction and retention of quality employees can be helped by better communication of the value of the benefits package and by allowing employees to tailor benefits to their own needs through flexible benefits plans.

Employers continue to be a major source of economic security for employees, often providing health insurance, retirement benefits, and so forth. Changes to benefits can have a tremendous impact on employees and retirees. Therefore, employers carry a significant social responsibility in making benefits decisions. At the same time, employees need to be aware that they will increasingly become responsible for their own economic security. Health care benefit design is changing to encourage employees to be more informed consumers, and retirement benefits will depend more and more on the financial investment decisions employees make on their own behalf.

## KEY TERMS

Marginal tax rate, 570
Consolidated Omnibus Budget
  Reconciliation Act
  (COBRA), 577
Pension Benefit Guaranty Corporation
  (PBGC), 578

Employee Retirement Income Security
  Act (ERISA), 578
Cash balance plan, 580
Summary plan description
  (SPD), 581
Family and Medical Leave Act, 584

Health maintenance organization
  (HMO), 590
Preferred provider organization
  (PPO), 590
Financial Accounting Statement
  (FAS) 106, 605

## DISCUSSION QUESTIONS

1. The chapter opener described how some companies are reducing their expectations of employees to work long hours each week. Why are these employers changing their expectations? Explain what the consequences are for employers and employees and whether you think such changes are a good idea.
2. Employers are shifting more responsibility to employees in the area of employee benefits. Describe specific examples of this trend. What are the likely consequences of this change? Where does the social responsibility of employers end, and where does the need to operate more efficiently begin?
3. Your company, like many others, is experiencing substantial increases in health care costs. What suggestions can you offer that may reduce the rate of cost increases?

4. Why is communication so important in the employee benefits area? What sorts of programs can a company use to communicate more effectively? What are the potential positive consequences of more effective benefits communication?
5. What are the potential advantages of flexible benefits and flexible spending accounts? Are there any potential drawbacks?
6. Although benefits account for a large share of employee compensation, many people feel there is little evidence on whether an employer receives an adequate return on the benefits investment. One suggestion has been to link benefits to individual, group, or organization performance. Explain why you would or would not recommend this strategy to an organization.

# SELF-ASSESSMENT EXERCISE

Also assignable in Connect.

One way companies determine which types of benefits to provide is to use a survey asking employees which types of benefits are important to them. Read the following list of employee benefits. For each benefit, mark an X in the column that indicates whether it is important to you or not.

| Benefit | Important to Have | Not Important to Have | % Employers Offering |
|---|---|---|---|
| Dependent-care flexible spending account | _____ | _____ | 70% |
| Flextime | _____ | _____ | 64 |
| Ability to bring child to work in case of emergency | _____ | _____ | 30 |
| Elder-care referral services | _____ | _____ | 21 |
| Adoption assistance | _____ | _____ | 21 |
| On-site child care center | _____ | _____ | 6 |
| Gym subsidy | _____ | _____ | 28 |
| Vaccinations on site (e.g., flu shots) | _____ | _____ | 61 |
| On-site fitness center | _____ | _____ | 26 |
| Casual dress days (every day) | _____ | _____ | 53 |
| Organization-sponsored sports teams | _____ | _____ | 39 |
| Food services/subsidized cafeteria | _____ | _____ | 29 |
| Travel-planning services | _____ | _____ | 27 |
| Dry-cleaning services | _____ | _____ | 15 |
| Massage therapy services at work | _____ | _____ | 12 |
| Self-defense training | _____ | _____ | 6 |
| Concierge services | _____ | _____ | 4 |

Compare your importance ratings for each benefit to the corresponding number in the right-hand column that indicates the percentage of employers that offer the benefit. Are you likely to find jobs that provide the benefits you want? Explain.

SOURCE: Based on Figure 2, "Percent of Employers Offering Work/Life Benefits (by Year)," in *Workplace Visions* 4 (2002), p. 3, published by the Society for Human Resource Management.

# EXERCISING STRATEGY

## Different Employers Take Different Approaches to Employee Health Care and Benefits

Health insurance, which accounts for over one-fourth of employer spending on benefits and is thus the single most costly benefit offered by employers, has, as we have also seen, received particular attention by employers. (And, of course, we cannot forget that employees too pay a significant part of their health care costs, especially when not just premium costs, but also co-insurance, co-payment, and deductible costs are included.) As we have also seen in this chapter, different employers have taken different approaches to benefits. Mostly, we have highlighted employers (e.g., Fiat Chrysler) who are moving toward making health care for employees free or as close as possible for at least some types. These employers incur larger costs, at least in the short run. Other employers have created or expanded (either in terms of who is covered or the number of weeks) paid parental leave programs. Again, this means incurring short-term costs. We have also seen examples of employers (e.g., Google) that provide unique benefits (see Table 13.8). Yet again, these cost money. Of course, other employers take a different approach, instead seeking to reduce such benefits costs. We have noted that this trend exists and differs from some of the examples we have highlighted of companies "bucking" the trend by spending more. *Forbes*, for example, had an article entitled "Bait and Switch: The Sneaky Way Your Employer Just Passed Healthcare Costs onto You." The article focuses on high deductible health care plans. They give an example of someone who has walking pneumonia. That patient may require a chest X-ray, blood tests, antibiotics, and a follow-up visit. That could costs thousands of dollars. An employee on a high-deductible plan would have to pay that cost before his/her health insurance kicked in (for which s/he has already paid a premium for such coverage). The Kaiser Family Foundation reports that about 10 years ago, only one in eight employees at large companies were covered by high deductible insurance plans. Now, it is closer to one in two employees. At smaller firms, a still larger percentage are covered by high deductible plans. As we also saw earlier in the chapter, the Affordable Care Act includes an employer mandate that employers with 50 or more employees provide health care coverage to their employees. Finally, we also saw that not all people who work at or on behalf of a company are employees of that company and that different approaches are taken in deciding what benefits they receive.

## QUESTIONS

1. The overarching question is: Why do employers use such different strategies/approaches to employee benefits, especially health care? Are some employers simply more altruistic or are there other factors? (Hint: The next question implies that we think there may be other factors!)
2. What other factors influence employer benefits strategy choice, especially in health care coverage and cost-sharing with employees? Think of how the companies we have seen are similar and different? What are the key ways they differ? (Another hint: Think of how they compete, the types of employees they need to do that, and what they need to do to attract, motivate, and retain these employees.) How and why might these matter in choosing a health care benefits strategy?
3. How do workforce demographics come into play specifically?
4. Are some of the factors that influence employer benefits strategies cyclical? What about the role of the unemployment rate and the labor market?

SOURCES: T. Murphy, "Survey: Companies Keep Passing Health Costs to Workers," *Detroit News*, October 3, 2018; P. Hubel, "Bait and Switch: The Sneaky Way Your Employer Just Passed Healthcare Costs Onto You," *Forbes*, February 28, 2018; www.forbes.com; G. Claxton, L. Levitt, M. Rae, and B. Sawyer, "Increases in Cost-Sharing Payments Continue to Outpace Wage Growth," *Peterson-Kaiser Health System Tracker*, June 15, 2018, www.healthsystemtracker.org; U.S. Bureau of Labor Statistics, U.S. Department of Labor, "Employer Costs for Employee Compensation – September 2018," December 14, 2018, USDL-18-1941, www.bls.gov.

## MANAGING PEOPLE

### Some Companies Want Employees (Back) at the Office

Roughly one in five U.S. workers perform some work from home or some other remote location, and this remote work group averages about three hours of remote work per day. There are a variety of reasons why some companies allow (some) employees to work remotely. In the case of IBM, it reported at one point that about 40% of its employees worked remotely, allowing it to reduce its office space by almost 80 million square feet, saving it about $100 million per year. Giving employees the flexibility to balance work, family, and other nonwork issues, as well as the improvements in technology (and its falling cost), contributed to companies adopting remote work policies. Some employees (and perhaps their supervisors) also felt that they would be more productive if given this flexibility. Other well-known companies that were prominent adopters of remote work included Aetna, Bank of America, Best Buy, Honeywell, IBM, and Yahoo!.

What do these companies and IBM have in common now? The answer is that all have since either ended or curtailed programs that allow employees to work remotely, rather than at the company office. IBM, for example, recently gave remote working employees the choice of returning to work at the office or applying for a new position. Presumably, some will not wish to choose either option and will look for another job and/or retire. Why have these companies changed their view on remote work? The commonly stated reasons are that more work is done by teams and that face-to-face interaction between team members is thought to be more effective in identifying business problems to solve and business opportunities to exploit, developing creative solutions/strategies to do so, and executing them well.

**QUESTIONS**

1. Do these companies that have scaled back or ended remote work have anything in common? For example, are these companies with strong revenue, profit, and market value growth? Are they in similar or different industries/businesses? To the degree they have something in common, are these companies likely representative of what other companies are doing, or will do in terms of how much they permit remote working?

2. Summarize the advantages and disadvantages of remote work. Are there particular types of companies where remote work is more/less likely to be effective?

3. How do you think employees will react to changes (such as those at IBM) in remote work policies? What will be the short-run and long-run consequences?

SOURCE: J. Simons, "The Boss Wants You Back in the Office," *Wall Street Journal*, July 25, 2017, https://www.wsj.com/articles/the-boss-wants-you-back-in-the-office-1500975001?tesla=y?mod=djem_jiewr_HR_domainid; S. Kesler, "IBM, Remote-Work Pioneer, Is Calling Thousands of Employees Back to the Office," *Quartz*, March 21, 2017, https://qz.com/924167/ibm-remote-work-pioneer-is-calling-thousands-of-employees-back-to-the-office/; J. Simons, "IBM, a Pioneer of Remote Work, Calls Workers Back to the Office," *Wall Street Journal*, May 18, 2017, https://www.wsj.com/articles/ibm-a-pioneer-of-remote-work-calls-workers-back-to-the-office-1495108802.

# HR IN SMALL BUSINESS

## Babies Welcomed at T3

T3 is an independent advertising agency launched by Gay Warren Gaddis in Austin, Texas, in 1989. It has grown rapidly, thanks to Gaddis's ability to stay in front of tumultuous change in the advertising and marketing industry. Traditional agencies have approached their work by thinking about ads to be placed on the air or in newspapers and magazines. In contrast, Gaddis and her staff have specialized in developing integrated campaigns that harness all the ways to communicate about a brand, including communication via the Internet.

Innovation continues to be a company value. The company's careers webpage says T3 looks for "Great thinkers. Individuals with curious, open minds. Relentless problem-solvers constantly looking for new, often unconventional, solutions." The company is structured without the boundaries that have traditionally separated functions in the advertising world, so that employees can bring their perspectives together to solve client problems.

That innovative spirit hasn't been limited to advertising. Gaddis also thinks creatively about managing her firm's human resources. Six years after starting T3, Gaddis observed that four of her key employees were all pregnant at about the same time. If they all proceeded in the traditional way, taking a few months' leave, Gaddis would be scrambling to keep her agency running without them. So Gaddis decided to try something unusual: She told the four employees they were welcome to bring their babies to work. While some big companies establish on-site day care, Gaddis simply counted on the employees to work flexibly in the presence of their children.

Many people would assume that babies at work would create a distracting environment, but in fact, the new program was a success. T3 kept the policy in place and even gave it a name: T3 and Under. So far, 80 babies have come to work at one point or another. Gaddis says parents are so appreciative that they try extra hard to make the arrangement work. One such parent, Emily Dalton, feels reassured by being able to just swivel her chair when she wants to check on her baby: "You're not worrying," she told a newspaper reporter, "You're being spit up on, but you're not . . . calling somewhere to check on your child." She admits that she has to be extra flexible when her baby, Annie, is awake but adds, "I powerhouse when she sleeps." When the babies reach nine months or start to crawl, the parents are expected to make arrangements for day care.

Bringing babies to work is, of course, only one employee benefit. T3, which now has offices in New York and San Francisco as well as the one in Austin, offers medical, dental, and vision insurance; various life insurance policies; disability insurance; a 401(k) plan; paid time for vacations, holidays, and sick leave; and discounts on gym memberships and cell phone plans. There are also some other unusual benefits: breakfast on Mondays, candy on Fridays, a book club, and a "bring your dog to work" policy. As for this last policy, the T3 website comments, "While we don't have hard metrics on what [dogs] do for our creativity or productivity, we do believe they play a part in adding balance to what can be a very unbalanced business."

Advertising may be an "unbalanced" business, but so far, T3 seems to be coping well enough. And T3's fearless leader, Gay Warren Gaddis, was named Ernst and Young's Entrepreneur of the Year for central Texas in 2014.

**QUESTIONS**

1. Of the employee benefits mentioned in this case, which do you think are important for keeping a creative workforce engaged at T3?

2. What are some of the advantages of the agency's T3 and Under policy? What are some of the risks? How can the company address those risks?

3. At what other kinds of companies, if any, do you think a "bring your baby to work" policy might be effective as an employee benefit? Why?

SOURCES: J. Spiro, "Where Every Day Is Take Your Baby to Work Day," *Inc.*, December 9, 2009; E. Aasen, "Babies-at-Work Programs Let New Parents Stay Close to Their Kids," *Dallas Morning News*, March 26, 2008; T3, "Careers" and "Company," corporate website, www.t-3.com, accessed July 21, 2014.

# NOTES

1. J. H. Dulebohn, J. C. Molloy, S. M. Pichler, and B. Murray, "Employee Benefits: Literature Review and Emerging Issues," *Human Resource Management Review* 19 (2009), pp. 86–103; J. J. Martocchio, *Employee Benefits*, 2nd ed. (New York: McGraw-Hill, 2006).

2. H. W. Hennessey, "Using Employee Benefits to Gain a Competitive Advantage," *Benefits Quarterly* 5, no. 1 (1989), pp. 51–57; B. Gerhart and G.T. Milkovich, "Employee Compensation: Research and Practice," in *Handbook of Industrial and Organizational Psychology*, vol. 3, 2nd ed., ed. M. D. Dunnette and L. M. Hough (Palo Alto, CA: Consulting Psychologists Press, 1992); J. Swist, "Benefits Communications: Measuring Impact and Value," *Employee Benefit Plan Review*, September 2002, pp. 24–26.

3. R. Ehrenberg and R. S. Smith, *Modern Labor Economics: Theory and Public Policy*, 7th ed. (Upper Saddle River, NJ: Addison Wesley Longman, 2000).

4. B. T. Beam Jr. and J. J. McFadden, *Employee Benefits*, 6th ed. (Chicago: Dearborn Financial Publishing, 2000).

5. J. Murphy, "At Patagonia, Trying New Outdoor Adventures Is a Job Requirement," *Wall Street Journal,* March 9, 2015; B. Schulte, "A Company That Profits as It Pampers Workers," *Washington Post*, October 25, 2014.

6. The organization and description in this section draws heavily on Beam and McFadden, *Employee Benefits*.

7. U.S. Department of Labor, Employment and Training Administration, "Comparison of State Unemployment Laws 2018," oui.doleta.gov.

8. J. A. Penczak, "Unemployment Benefit Plans," in *Employee Benefits Handbook*, 3rd ed., ed. J. D. Mamorsky (Boston: Warren, Gorham & Lamont, 1992).

9. U.S. Department of Labor, "Unemployment Compensation: Federal-State Partnership," Office of Unemployment Insurance, Division of Legislation, April 2013.

10. J. V. Nackley, *Primer on Workers' Compensation* (Washington, DC: Bureau of National Affairs, 1989).

11. Beam and McFadden, *Employee Benefits*, p. 81.

12. L. Groeger, M. Grabell, and C. Cotts, "Workers' Comp Benefits: How Much Is a Limb Worth?" *ProPublica*, accessed May 4, 2015, http://projects.propublica.org; see also: www.dol.gov/esa.

13. A. H. Wheeler, "Pathophysiology of Chronic Back Pain," 2002, www.emedicine.com.

14. J. R. Hollenbeck, D. R. Ilgen, and S. M. Crampton, "Lower Back Disability in Occupational Settings: A Review of the Literature from a Human Resource Management View," *Personnel Psychology* 45 (1992), pp. 247–78; J. J. Martocchio, D. A. Harrison, and H. Berkson, "Connections between Lower Back Pain, Interventions, and Absence from Work: A Time-Based Meta-Analysis," *Personnel Psychology* (2000), p. 595.

15. Employee Benefit Research Institute, "Value of Employee Benefits Constant in a Changing World," March 28, 2002, www.ebri.org.

16. Beam and McFadden, *Employee Benefits*.

17. U. S. Bureau of Labor Statistics, *National Compensation Survey: Employee Benefits in the United States, 2014*, Bulletin 2779, September 2014, USDL-15-0386, www.bls.gov.

18. Social Security Administration, "Fast Facts and Figures about Social Security, 2014," published September 2014, http://www.ssa.gov/policy/docs/chartbooks/fast_facts/2014/fast_facts14.html#page5

19. B. A. Butrica, H. M. Iams, K. E. Smith, and E. J. Toder, "The Disappearing Defined Benefit Pension and Its Potential Impact on the Retirement Incomes of Baby Boomers," *U.S. Social Security Administration, Social Security Bulletin*, Vol. 69, No. 3, 2009.

20. Pension Benefit Guaranty Corporation, www.pbgc.gov.

21. Pension Benefit Guaranty Corporation, Maximum Monthly Guarantee Tables, https://www.pbgc.gov/wr/benefits/guaranteed-benefits/maximum-guarantee.html, accessed January 30, 2019.

22. Pension Benefit Guaranty Corporation, Maximum Monthly Guarantee Tables.

23. www.irs.gov. Those age 50 and over have higher contribution limits.

24. "PSCA Releases Results of 59th Annual Survey of Profit Sharing and 401(k) Plans," https://www.psca.org/psca-releases-results-of-59th-annual-survey-of-profit-sharing-and-401-k-plans; PSCA's *57th Annual Survey of Profit Sharing and 401(k) Plans*, 2014.

25. J. Fierman, "How Secure Is Your Nest Egg?" *Fortune*, August 12, 1991, pp. 50–54.

26. A. R. Sorking, "JP Morgan Pays $2 a Share for Bear Stearns," *New York Times*, March 17, 2008; P. Lattman and J. Strasburg, "We Are All in a Daze, Says One Employee, Life Savings Wiped Out," *Wall Street Journal*, March 18, 2008; D. Maxey, J. L. Pessin, and I. Salisbury, "The Job/Stock Double Whammy: Bear Saga Shows Perils of Loading Up on Employer Equity," *Wall Street Journal*, March 18, 2008.

27. *PSCA's 57th Annual Survey of Profit Sharing and 401(k) Plans.*

28. Beam and McFadden, *Employee Benefits*.

29. B. J. Coleman, *Primer on Employee Retirement Income Security Act*, 3rd ed. (Washington, DC: Bureau of National Affairs, 1989).

30. *Continental Can Company v. Gavalik*, summary in *Daily Labor Report* (December 8, 1987): "Supreme Court Lets Stand Third

Circuit Ruling That Pension Avoidance Scheme Is ERISA Violation," No. 234, p. A-14.

31. A. L. Gustman, O. S. Mitchell, and T. L. Steinmeier, "The Role of Pensions in the Labor Market: A Survey of the Literature," *Industrial and Labor Relations* 47 (1994), pp. 417-38.

32. D. A. DeCenzo and S. J. Holoviak, *Employee Benefits* (Englewood Cliffs, NJ: Prentice Hall, 1990).

33. E. P. Lazear, "Why Is There Early Retirement?" *Journal of Political Economy* 87 (1979), pp. 1261-84; Gustman et al., "The Role of Pensions."

34. P. Cappelli, *The New Deal at Work: Managing the Market-Driven Workforce* (Boston: Harvard Business School Press, 1999).

35. S. Dorsey, "Pension Portability and Labor Market Efficiency," *Industrial and Labor Relations* 48, no. 5 (1995), pp. 276-92.

36. Commission of the European Communities, European Community Directive 93/104/EC, issued November 23, 1993, and amended June 22, 2000, by Directive 2000/34/EC, http://europa/eu.int/comm/index_en.htm.

37. DeCenzo and Holoviak, *Employee Benefits.*

38. C. C. Miller, "Microsoft Tells Its Partners to Provide Paid Sick Leave," *New York Times,* March 26, 2015, p. A3.

39. N. Knox and M. Murphy, "Charity as a Recruiting Tool," *Wall Street Journal,* September 2, 2014, p. B4.

40. Y. Chen and I. Smithey Fulmer, "Fine-Tuning What We Know about Employees' Experience with Flexible Work Arrangements and Their Job Attitudes," *Human Resource Management* 57, no. 1 (2018), pp. 381-95; J. H. Wayne, M. M. Butts, W. J. Casper, and T. D. Allen, "In Search of Balance: A Conceptual and Empirical Integration of Multiple Meanings of Work-Family Balance," *Personnel Psychology* 70 (2016), pp. 167-210; A. Huffman and L. T. Eby, *The Oxford Handbook of Work and Family* (Oxford, UK: Oxford University Press, 2016); T. D. Allen, R. C. Johnson, K. M. Kiburz, and K. M. Shockley, "Work-Family Conflict and Flexible Work Arrangements: Deconstructing Flexibility," *Personnel Psychology* 66 (2013), pp. 345-76; A. Mandeville, J. Halbesleben, and M. Whitman, "Misalignment and Misperception in Preferences to Utilize Family-Friendly Benefits: Implications for Benefit Utilization and Work-Family Conflict," *Personnel Psychology* 69 (2016), pp. 895-929; R. S. Gajendran, D. A. Harrison, and K. Delaney-Klinger, "Are Telecommuters Remotely Good Citizens? Unpacking Telecommuting's Effects on Performance Via I-Deals and Job Resources, *Personnel Psychology* 68 (2015), pp. 353-93; T. L. Dumas and J. Sanchez-Burks, "The Professional, the Personal, and the Ideal Worker: Pressures and Objectives Shaping the Boundary between Life Domains," *Academy of Management Annals* 9 (2015), pp. 803-43; G. M. Spreitzer, L. Cameron, and L. Garrett, "Alternative Work Arrangements: Two Images of the New World of Work," *Annual Review of Organizational Psychology and Organizational Behavior* 4 (2017), pp. 473-99.

41. S. L. Grover and K. J. Crooker, "Who Appreciates Family Responsive Human Resource Policies: The Impact of Family-Friendly Policies on the Organizational Attachment of Parents and Non-parents," *Personnel Psychology* 48 (1995), pp. 271-88; T. J. Rothausen, J. A. Gonzalez, N. E. Clarke, and L. L. O'Dell, "Family-Friendly Backlash: Fact or Fiction? The Case of Organizations' On-Site Child Care Centers," *Personnel Psychology* 51 (1998), p. 685; M. A. Arthur, "Share Price Reactions to Work-Family Initiatives: An Institutional Perspective," *Academy of Management Journal* 46 (2003), p. 497; J. E. Perry-Smith and T. Blum, "Work-Family Human Resource Bundles and Perceived Organizational Performance," *Academy of Management Journal* 43 (2000), pp. 1107-17.

42. N. Bloom, T. Kretschmer, and J. Van Reenen, "Are Family-Friendly Workplace Practices a Valuable Firm Resource?" *Strategic Management Journal* 32 (2011), pp. 343-67.

43. "The Employer's Role in Helping Working Families." For examples of child care arrangements in some well-known companies (e.g., AT&T, Apple, Exxon, IBM, Merck), see "A Look at Child-Care Benefits," *USA Today,* March 14, 1989, p. 4B; U.S. Census Bureau, "America's Families and Living Arrangements," June 2001, www.census.gov.

44. J. Waldfogel, "International Policies toward Parental Leave and Child Care," *Future of Children* 11, no. 1 (2001), pp. 99-111.

45. B. Lam, "IKEA's Leave Policy Actually Includes Most of Its Workers," *The Atlantic,* December 6, 2016; A. D'Innocenzio, "As Workforce Tightens, IKEA Expands Parental Leave," *Milwaukee Journal Sentinel,* December 6, 2016.

46. P. Hardin, "Women Execs Should Feel at Ease about Taking Full Maternity Leave," *Personnel Journal,* September 1995, p. 19.

47. Families and Work Institute, "2012 National Study of Employers," http://familiesandwork.org/site/research/reports/main.html. Nationally representative survey of 1,126 employers with 50 or more employees.

48. J. Fierman, "It's 2 a.m.: Let's Go to Work," *Fortune,* August 21, 1995, pp. 82-88.

49. E. E. Kossek, "Diversity in Child Care Assistance Needs: Employee Problems, Preferences, and Work-Related Outcomes," *Personnel Psychology* 43 (1990), pp. 769-91.

50. "A Bank Profits from Its Work/Life Program," *Workforce,* February 1997, p. 49.

51. R. Broderick and B. Gerhart, "Nonwage Compensation," in *The Human Resource Management Handbook,* ed. D. Lewin, D. J. B. Mitchell, and M. A. Zadi (San Francisco: JAI Press, 1996).

52. J. Dulebohn et al., "Employee Benefits: Literature Review and Emerging Issues," *Human Resource Management Review* 19 (2009), pp. 86-103.

53. Hennessey, "Using Employee Benefits to Gain a Competitive Advantage."

54. One study, conducted in Spain, reports that employee perceptions of benefits level (amount, value, and number of benefits) correlate 0.42 with their organization commitment and - 0.32 with their turnover intention. J. M. de la Torre-Ruiz, M. D. Vidal-Salazar, and E. Cordón-Pozo, "Employees Are Satisfied with Their Benefits, but So What? The Consequences of Benefit Satisfaction on Employees' Organizational Commitment and Turnover Intentions," *International Journal of Human Resource Management,* April 7, 2017, pp. 1-24. In their review of other studies on the correlation between benefits level and turnover intention, the authors state that these studies "have not reached definitive conclusions," but the majority of studies they reviewed reported, consistent with their own findings, that employee intention to leave was reduced when benefits were higher and/or perceived as higher.

55. U.S. Bureau of Labor Statistics, "Employer Cost for Employee Compensation," www.bls.gov; U.S. Chamber of Commerce Research Center, Employee Benefits Study, annual (Washington, D.C.: U.S. Chamber of Commerce).

56. www.census.gov.

57. S. Armour, "Uninsured Rate Down Sharply Since Health Law Was Enacted," *Wall Street Journal,* March 16, 2015, www.wsj.com.

58. Employee Benefit Research Institute, *EBRI's Fundamentals of Employee Benefit Programs,* 6th ed. (Washington, DC: Author, 2009).

59. A. C. Monheit and P. F. Cooper, "Health Insurance and Job Mobility: The Effects of Public Policy on Job-Lock," *Industrial and Labor Relations Review* 48 (1994), pp. 86-102.

60. Tom Murphy. "Survey: Companies Keep Passing Health Costs to Workers," *Detroit News,* October 3, 2018; R. Lieber, "New Way to Curb Medical Costs: Make Employees Feel the Sting," *Wall Street Journal*, June 23, 2004, p. A1.

61. M. Barringer and O. S. Mitchell, "Workers' Preferences among Company-Provided Health Insurance Plans," *Industrial and Labor Relations Review* 48 (1994), pp. 141–52.

62. Beam and McFadden, *Employee Benefits.*

63. J. Shelly, "Transformation Vacation," *Human Resource Executive*, November 1, 2008.

64. L. Berry, A. Mirabito, and W. Baun, "What's the Hard Return on Employee Wellness Programs?" *Harvard Business Review*, December 2010, pp. 104–12.

65. Rand Corporation, *Do Workplace Wellness Programs Save Employers Money?* 2004, http://www.rand.org/content/dam/rand/pubs/research_briefs/RB9700/RB9744/RAND_RB9744.pdf. The return to $1 spent on disease management was estimated as $3.80 for disease management, but only $0.50 for lifestyle management (eating, smoking, exercise).

66. R. Z. Goetzel et al., "Do Workplace Health Promotion (Wellness) Programs Work?" *Journal of Occupational and Environmental Medicine*, 56 (2014), pp. 927–34.

67. K. Baicker, D. Cutler, and Z. Song, "Workplace Wellness Programs Can Generate Savings," *Health Affairs*, 29 (2010), pp. 304–11; L. Chapman, "Meta-Evaluation of Worksite Health Promotion Economic Return Studies: 2012 Update," *American Journal of Health Promotion*, 26 (2012), pp. TAH1–TAH12; We became aware of the two preceding reviews by reading: R. Z. Goetzel et al., "Do Workplace Health Promotion (Wellness) Programs Work?" *Journal of Occupational and Environmental Medicine*, 56 (2014), 927–34.

68. S. Tully, "America's Healthiest Companies," *Fortune*, June 12, 1995, pp. 98–106.

69. G. Flynn, "Companies Make Wellness Work," *Personnel Journal*, February 1995, pp. 63–66.

70. D. A. Harrison and L. Z. Liska, "Promoting Regular Exercise in Organizational Fitness Programs: Health-Related Differences in Motivational Building Blocks," *Personnel Psychology* 47 (1994), pp. 47–71.

71. J. C. Erfurt, A. Foote, and M. A. Heirich, "The Cost-Effectiveness of Worksite Wellness Programs for Hypertension Control, Weight Loss, Smoking Cessation and Exercise," *Personnel Psychology* 45 (1992), pp. 5–27.

72. J. Chang and M. Marsh, "The Google Diet: Search Giant Overhauled Its Eating Options to 'Nudge' Healthy Choices," *ABC News*, January 25, 2013.

73. J. Meuris and C. Leana, "The Price of Financial Precarity: Organizational Costs of Employees' Financial Concerns," *Organization Science*, 29 (2018), pp. 398–417.

74. J. Meuris and C. R. Leana, "The High Cost of Low Wages: Economic Scarcity Effects in Organizations," *Research in Organizational Behavior* 35 (2015), pp. 143–158; A. Tergensen, "Workers Schooled in Money: More Firms Pay Workers to Shore Up Their Finances through Education, Cutting Debt," *Wall Street Journal*, February 21, 2018.

75. Henry J. Kaiser Family Foundation, *2018 Employer Health Benefits Survey,* files.kff.org.

76. G. Claxton, L. Levitt, M. Rae, and B. Sawyer, "Increases in Cost-Sharing Payments Continue to Outpace Wage Growth," *Peterson-Kaiser Health System Tracker,* June 15, 2018, www.healthsystemtracker.org; Murphy, "Survey: Companies Keep Passing Health Costs to Workers"; P. Hubel, "Bait and Switch: The Sneaky Way Your Employer Just Passed Healthcare Costs onto You," *Forbes*, February 28, 2018, www.forbes.com.

77. H. Gardner, unpublished manuscript (Cheyenne, WY: Options & Choices, 1995); The Henry J. Kaiser Family Foundation and Health Research and Educational Trust, http://kff.org/health-costs/slide/concentration-of-health-care-spending-in-the-u-s-population-2010/, accessed May 20, 2013.

78. H. B. Noble, "Quality Is Focus for Health Plans," *New York Times*, July 3, 1995, p. A1; J. D. Klinke, "Medicine's Industrial Revolution," *Wall Street Journal*, August 21, 1995, p. A8.

79. S. Rosenbush and M. Totty, "How Big Data Is Changing the Whole Equation for Business," *Wall Street Journal*, March 8, 2013; S. Kliff, "An Average ER Visit Costs More than an Average Month's Rent," *Washington Post*, March 2, 2013; A. W. Mathews, "Same Doctor Visit, Double the Cost," *Wall Street Journal*, August 27, 2012.

80. J. B. White, "Business Plan," *Wall Street Journal*, October 19, 1998, p. R18.

81. L. Weber, "A Health Check for Wellness Programs," *Wall Street Journal*, October 8, 2014, p. B1.

82. J. Schor, *The Overworked American: The Unexpected Decline of Leisure* (New York: Basic Books, 1991); U.S. Bureau of Labor Statistics, "Workers Are on the Job More Hours over the Course of a Year," *Issues in Labor Statistics*, February 1997.

83. Hewitt Associates, www.hewitt.com.

84. U.S. Bureau of Labor Statistics, *Contingent and Alternative Employment Arrangements Summary*, June 7, 2018. USDL-18-0942, www.bls.gov. As noted in the text, no change was found in the percentages in of contingent and alternative workers over time, specifically since the last detailed survey conducted in 2005.

85. The Editorial Board, "The Gig Economy's False Promise," *New York Times*, April 10, 2017.

86. L. Weber, "The End of Employees," *Wall Street Journal*, February 3, 2017.

87. Beam and McFadden, *Employee Benefits.*

88. One study found that having a supplemental defined contribution retirement plan improved safety among truck drivers and that this effect was larger in smaller companies. One possible explanation provided is that older workers are safer drivers and more likely to be attracted to (and stay with) a company that offers better retirement benefits. S. Werner, C. S. Kuiate, T. R. Noland, and A. J. Francia, "Benefits and Strategic Outcomes: Are Supplemental Retirement Plans and Safer Driving Related in the US Trucking Industry?" *Human Resource Management* 55 (2015), pp. 885–900.

89. M. Wilson, G. B. Northcraft, and M. Neale, "The Perceived Value of Fringe Benefits," *Personnel Psychology* 38 (1985), pp. 309–20.

90. R. Huseman, J. Hatfield, and R. Robinson, "The MBA and Fringe Benefits," *Personnel Administrator* 23, no. 7 (1978), pp. 57–60. See summary in Hennessey, "Using Employee Benefits to Gain a Competitive Advantage."

91. H. Hennessey et al., "Impact of Benefit Awareness on Employee and Organizational Outcomes," *Benefits Quarterly* 8 (1992); the same study found no impact of the increased awareness and benefits satisfaction on overall job satisfaction. G. F. Dreher, R. A. Ash, and R. D. Bretz, "Benefit Coverage and Employee Cost: Critical Factors in Explaining Compensation Satisfaction," *Personnel Psychology* 41 (1988), pp. 237–54.

92. M. C. Giallourakis and G. S. Taylor, "An Evaluation of Benefit Communication Strategy," *Employee Benefits Journal* 15, no. 4 (1991), pp. 14–18; Employee Benefits Research Institute, "How Readable Are Summary Plan Descriptions for Health Care Plans," *EBRI Notes*, October 2006, ebri.org.

93. J. Abraham, R. Feldman, and C. Carlin, "Understanding Employee Awareness of Health Care Quality Information: How Can Employers Benefit?" *Health Services Research* 39 (2004), pp. 1799–1816; J. H. Marler, S. L. Fisher, and W. Ke, "Employee Self-Service Technology Acceptance: A Comparison of Pre-Implementation and Post-Implementation Relationships," *Personal Psychology* 62 (2009), pp. 327–58.

94. Beam and McFadden, *Employee Benefits*; M. W. Barringer and G. T. Milkovich, "A Theoretical Explanation of the Adoption and Design of Flexible Benefit Plans: A Case of Human Resource Innovation," *Academy of Management Review* 23 (1998), pp. 305–24.

95. T. Eriksson and N. Kristensen, "Wages or Fringes? Some Evidence on Trade-Offs and Sorting," *Journal of Labor Economics* 32, no. 4 (2014), pp. 899–928.

96. For supportive evidence, see A. E. Barber, R. B. Dunham, and R. A. Formisano, "The Impact of Flexible Benefits on Employee Satisfaction: A Field Study," *Personnel Psychology* 45 (1992), pp. 55–75; E. E. Lawler, *Pay and Organizational Development* (Reading, MA: Addison-Wesley, 1981); J. C. Dencker, A. Joshi, and J. J. Martocchio, "Employee Benefits as Context for Intergenerational Conflict," *Human Resource Management Review* 17 (2007), pp. 208–20; A. Caza, M. W. McCarter, and G. B. Northcraft, "Performance Benefits of Reward Choice: A Procedural Justice Perspective," *Human Resource Management Journal* 25 (2015), 184–199. Caza et al. also found a positive effect of benefits choice on performance in a library study where performance was measured by how well undergraduate students were able to combine words into compound words.

97. Beam and McFadden, *Employee Benefits*.

98. Beam and McFadden, *Employee Benefits*.

99. *Los Angeles Dept. of Water & Power v. Manhart*, 435 US SCt 702 (1978), 16 EPD, 8250.

100. S. K. Hoffman, "Discrimination Litigation Relating to Employee Benefits," *Labor Law Journal*, June 1992, pp. 362–81.

101. Hoffman, "Discrimination Litigation Relating to Employee Benefits," p. 375.

102. S. J. Sacher and J. Day, "The New VEBAs," *BNA Pension and Benefits* blog, June 1, 2010, http://pblog.bna.com; P. C. Borzi, "Retiree Health VEBAs: A New Twist on an Old Paradigm. Implications for Retirees, Unions, and Employers," The Henry J. Kaiser Family Foundation, March 2009.

103. V. Monga, "Pension Plans Brace for a One-Two Punch," *Wall Street Journal*, March 25, 2014, p. B1.

## PART FIVE

**CHAPTER**

# 14 Collective Bargaining and Labor Relations

## LEARNING OBJECTIVES

*After reading this chapter, you should be able to:*

**LO 14-1**   Describe what is meant by collective bargaining and labor relations. *page 618*

**LO 14-2**   Identify the labor relations goals of society, management, and labor unions. *page 620*

**LO 14-3**   Explain the legal environment's impact on labor relations. *page 631*

**LO 14-4**   Describe the major labor–management interactions: organizing, contract negotiations, and contract administration. *page 635*

**LO 14-5**   Describe new, less adversarial approaches to labor–management relations. *page 652*

**LO 14-6**   Explain how changes in competitive challenges (e.g., product market competition and globalization) are influencing labor–management interactions. *page 660*

**LO 14-7**   Explain how labor relations in the public sector differ from labor relations in the private sector. *page 664*

## Collective Bargaining Comes to JetBlue

Airlines are typically unionized. Even at Southwest, which is known for its strong relationship with employees, almost all eligible employees are unionized and have collective bargaining contracts with Southwest. On the other hand, JetBlue has operated without any labor union presence since its founding about two decades ago. However, that changed recently, as 74% of pilots who voted in an election in 2014 chose to be represented by the Airline Pilots Association union. By one estimate, the first-year cost for JetBlue of the new contract negotiated a few years later with the pilots will be $130 million. But, that may be just the start as 66% of inflight employees (called flight attendants elsewhere) have also voted to be represented by a labor union, in this case, the Transport Workers Union. (A previous vote in 2014 by inflight employees had rejected union representation.) According to its annual report, among JetBlue's 14,870 full-time employees, 3,211 are pilots, 4,251 are inflight, 4,512 are in airport operations, 585 are technicians (knows as mechanics elsewhere), 1,430 are agents, and 3,219 are management and other employees. If the trend continues, all (except management, which is not eligible) could be unionized in the near future and all will seek to negotiate first contracts.

JetBlue described what it saw as the risks of this trend as follows in a recent annual report (10-K filing with the Securities and Exchange Commission): "Our business is labor intensive and the unionization of any of our Crewmembers could result in demands that may increase our operating expenses and adversely affect our financial condition and results of operations. Any of the different crafts or classes of our Crewmembers could unionize at any time, which would require us to negotiate in good faith with the Crewmember group's certified representative concerning a collective bargaining agreement. In addition, we may be subject to disruptions by unions protesting the non-union status of our other Crewmembers. Any of these events would be disruptive to our operations and could harm our business." According to its annual report, JetBlue's revenues from the most recent year were $7.1 billion and its cost for salaries, wages, and benefits was $1.9 billion, or about 27% of revenues. Its operating income was $1.0 billion. If pilots represent about one-quarter of employees eligible for unionization (although we must keep in mind that pilots receive significantly higher pay), we can see that if the one-year cost of a collective bargaining agreement for pilots is $130 million, that cost will be considerably higher as other employee groups follow suit in electing to join a union and successfully negotiate contracts with JetBlue. Unless there are productivity gains from JetBlue employees joining unions, the added cost will come out of the $1.0 billion in operating income. To make up for that, either investors in JetBlue will need to accept a smaller return (and not move their investment elsewhere in response), customers will need to be willing to pay more for their tickets (and not decide to fly another airline instead), or JetBlue will need to somehow find a way to operate more efficiently.

SOURCES: M. Schlangenstein and J. Bachman, "JetBlue Pilots Approve First Labor Deal in Airline's History," *Bloomberg Business*, July 27, 2018, www.bloomberg.com; JetBlue, "Annual Report (10-K)," February 16, 2018, www.sec.gov; T. Reed, "JetBlue 'Disappointed' As 66% of Flight Attendants Vote to Join Transport Workers Union," *Forbes*, April 17, 2018, www.forbes.com.

# Introduction

In the chapter opener, we saw an example of where what was once a start-up company whose culture did not include a role for unions changed and some of its workers are now voting to join unions. As we saw, this will have significant cost implications for JetBlue and thus potentially for stakeholders beyond management and employees. In the end, JetBlue management and employees must balance conflicts against the common interests that bind them together. Worker jobs and income, as well as company profits, depend on the two parties being able to cooperate and effectively resolve conflicts to ensure the company's ability to be competitive and survive, which is also the only sure path to worker job security.

# The Labor Relations Framework

**LO 14-1**
Describe what is meant by collective bargaining and labor relations.

John Dunlop, former secretary of labor and a leading industrial relations scholar, suggested in the book *Industrial Relations Systems* (1958) that a successful industrial relations system consists of four elements: (1) an environmental context (technology, market pressures, and the legal framework, especially as it affects bargaining power); (2) participants, including employees and their unions, management, and the government; (3) a "web of rules" (rules of the game) that describe the process by which labor and management interact and resolve disagreements (such as the steps followed in settling contract grievances); and (4) ideology.[1] For the industrial relations system to operate properly, the three participants must, to some degree, have a common ideology (e.g., acceptance of the capitalist system) and must accept the roles of the other participants. Acceptance does not translate into convergence of interests, however. To the contrary, some degree of worker–management conflict is inevitable because, although the interests of the two parties overlap (e.g., survival of the firm and thus survival of workers' jobs and investors' profits), they also diverge in key respects (such as how to divide the economic profits between workers and investors).[2]

Therefore, according to Dunlop and other U.S. scholars of like mind, an effective industrial relations system does not eliminate conflict. Rather, it provides institutions (and a web of rules) that resolve conflict in a way that minimizes its costs to management, employees, and society. The collective bargaining system is one such institution, as are related mechanisms such as mediation, arbitration, and participation in decision making. These ideas formed the basis for the development in the 1940s of schools and departments of industrial and labor relations to train labor relations professionals who, working in both union and management positions, would have the skills to minimize costly forms of conflict such as strikes (which were reaching record levels at the time) and maximize integrative (win–win) solutions to such disagreements.

A more recent industrial relations model, developed by Harry Katz and Thomas Kochan, is particularly helpful in laying out the types of decisions management and unions make in their interactions and the consequences of such decisions for attainment of goals in areas such as wages and benefits, job security, and the rights and responsibilities of unions and managements.[3] According to Katz and Kochan, these choices occur at three levels.

First, at the strategic level, management makes basic choices such as whether to work with its union(s) or to devote its efforts to developing nonunion operations. Environmental factors (or competitive challenges) offer both constraints and opportunities in implementing strategies. For example, if public opinion toward labor unions becomes negative during a particular time period, some employers may see that as an opportunity to rid themselves of unions, whereas other employers may seek a better working relationship with their unions. Similarly, increased competition may dictate the need to increase productivity or reduce labor costs, but whether this is accomplished by shifting work to nonunion facilities or by working with unions to become more competitive is a strategic choice that management faces.

Although management has often been the initiator of change in recent years, unions face a similar choice between fighting changes to the status quo and being open to new labor–management relationships (like less adversarial forms of participation in decision making, such as labor–management teams).

Katz and Kochan suggest that labor and management choices at the strategic level in turn affect the labor–management interaction at a second level, the functional level, where contract negotiations and union organizing occur, and at the final workplace level, the arena in which the contract is administered. The relationships between labor and management at each of the three levels are somewhat interdependent, but the relationship at the three levels may also differ. For example, whereas management may have a strategy of building an effective relationship with its unions at the strategic level, there may be significant day-to-day conflicts over work rules, grievances, and so forth at any given facility or bargaining unit (workplace level).

The labor relations framework depicted in Figure 14.1 incorporates many of the ideas discussed so far, including the important role of the environment (the competitive challenges); union, management, and societal goals; and a separation of union–management interactions into categories (union organizing, contract negotiation, contract administration) that can have important influences on one another but may also be analyzed somewhat independently. The model also highlights the important role that relative bargaining power plays in influencing

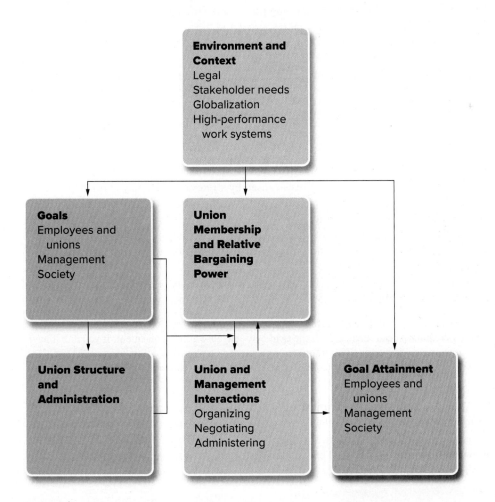

**Figure 14.1**

A Labor Relations Framework

goals, union–management interactions, and the degree to which each party achieves its goals. Relative bargaining power, in turn, is significantly influenced by the competitive environment (legal, social, quality, high-performance work systems, and globalization competitive challenges) and the size and depth of union membership.[4]

We now describe the components of this model in greater depth. The remainder of the chapter is organized into the following sections: the goals and strategies of society, management, and unions; union structure (including union administration and membership); the legal framework, perhaps the key aspect of the competitive environment for labor relations; union and management interactions (organizing, contract negotiation, contract administration); and goal attainment. Environmental factors (other than legal) and bargaining power are discussed in the context of these sections. In addition, two special topics, international comparisons and public-sector labor relations, are discussed.

# Goals and Strategies

## SOCIETY

**LO 14-2**
Identify the labor relations goals of society, management, and labor unions.

In one sense, labor unions, with their emphasis on group action, do not fit well with the individualistic orientation of U.S. capitalism. However, industrial relations scholars such as Beatrice and Sidney Webb and John R. Commons argued in the late 1800s and early 1900s that individual workers' bargaining power was far smaller than that of employers, who were likely to have more financial resources and the ability to easily replace workers.[5] Effective institutions for worker representation (like labor unions) were therefore seen as a way to make bargaining power more equal.

Labor unions' major benefit to society is the institutionalization of industrial conflict, which is therefore resolved in the least costly way. Although disagreements between management and labor continue, it is better to resolve disputes through discussion (collective bargaining) than by battling in the streets. As an influential group of industrial relations scholars put it in describing the future of advanced industrial relations around the world, "Class warfare will be forgotten. The battles will be in the corridors instead of the streets, and memos will flow instead of blood."[6] In this sense, collective bargaining not only has the potential to reduce economic losses caused by strikes but also may contribute to societal stability. For this reason, industrial relations scholars have often viewed labor unions as an essential component of a democratic society.[7] These were some of the beliefs that contributed to the enactment of the National Labor Relations Act (NLRA) in 1935, which sought to provide an environment conducive to collective bargaining and has since regulated labor and management activities and interactions.

Even former Senator Orrin Hatch, described by *Bloomberg Businessweek* as "labor's archrival on Capitol Hill," has spoken of the need for unions:

> There are always going to be people who take advantage of workers. Unions even that out, to their credit. We need them to level the field between labor and management. If you didn't have unions, it would be very difficult for even enlightened employers not to take advantage of workers on wages and working conditions, because of [competition from] rivals. I'm among the first to say I believe in unions.[8]

Although an industrial relations system based on collective bargaining has drawbacks, so too do the alternatives. Unilateral control by management sacrifices workers' rights. Extensive involvement of government and the courts can result in conflict resolution that is expensive, slow, and imposed by someone (a judge) with much less firsthand knowledge of the circumstances than either labor or management.

## MANAGEMENT

One of management's most basic decisions is whether to encourage or discourage the unionization of its employees. It may discourage unions because it fears higher wage and benefit costs, the disruptions caused by strikes, and an adversarial relationship with its employees or, more generally, greater constraints placed on its decision-making flexibility and discretion. Historically, management has used two basic strategies to avoid unionization.[9] It may seek to provide employment terms and conditions that employees will perceive as sufficiently attractive and equitable so that they see little gain from union representation. Or it may aggressively oppose union representation, even when there is significant employee interest. Use of the latter strategy has increased significantly over the past several decades.

If management voluntarily recognizes a union or if employees are already represented by a union, the focus is shifted from dealing with employees as individuals to employees as a group. Still, certain basic management objectives remain: controlling labor costs and increasing productivity (by keeping wages and benefits in check) and maintaining management prerogatives in important areas such as staffing levels and work rules. Of course, management always has the option of trying to decertify a union (i.e., encouraging employees to vote out the union in a decertification election) if it believes that the majority of employees no longer wish to be represented by the union.

## LABOR UNIONS

Labor unions seek, through collective action, to give workers a formal and independent voice in setting the terms and conditions of their work. Table 14.1 shows typical provisions negotiated by unions in collective bargaining contracts. Labor unions attempt to represent their members' interests in these decisions. Without adequate union representation, not only workers' wages, but also their safety and welfare, are more likely to be put at risk. This is particularly true in low-wage economies where regulatory protection may also be lacking.

Just before more than 1,100 workers perished in the Rana Plaza eight-story factory building collapse in Bangladesh in April 2013, workers on the third floor were startled by what sounded like an explosion. They also saw cracks in the walls. An engineer was brought in to examine the cracks, and he found that they were structural. He recommended immediate evacuation of the building. Workers evacuated but were ordered back to work. If they did not go back, they would lose their pay, which, at $38/month, they likely did not feel they could afford.

The question was how could such a tragedy be prevented from happening again? One response has been for companies that buy from garment suppliers in Bangladesh to develop and enforce worker safety and treatment standards. (See the Integrity in Action box for more details on this effort.) Another response is: What if the workers at Rana Plaza had been represented by a labor union? Perhaps the workers, if unionized, could have refused to follow the order to return to work. As one response to the tragedy, the Bangladesh government stated that it would begin to allow the country's 4 million garment workers to form trade unions and do so without first obtaining permission from factory owners. Labor unions can provide protection for workers and also help negotiate higher wages to give workers a better standard of living. Of course, these potential advantages will be weighed against the potential consequence of higher labor costs and/or lost working time due to strikes (and thus less competitive product prices, which could reduce sales and employment). In the best case scenario, an effective labor–management relationship can bring more efficient organization of workers in the production process, and higher wages can allow more selectivity in hiring and a more productive workforce.

**Table 14.1**
Typical Provisions in Collective Bargaining Contracts

**Establishment and administration of the agreement**
- Bargaining unit and plant supplements
- Contract duration and reopening and renegotiation provisions
- Union security and the checkoff
- Special bargaining committees
- Grievance procedures
- Arbitration and mediation
- Strikes and lockouts
- Contract enforcement

**Functions, rights, and responsibilities**
- Management rights clauses
- Plant removal
- Subcontracting
- Union activities on company time and premises
- Union–management cooperation
- Regulation of technological change
- Advance notice and consultation

**Wage determination and administration**
- General provisions
- Rate structure and wage differentials
- Allowances
- Incentive systems and production bonus plans
- Production standards and time studies
- Job classification and job evaluation
- Individual wage adjustments
- General wage adjustments during the contract period

**Job or income security**
- Hiring and transfer arrangements
- Employment and income guarantees
- Reporting and call-in pay
- Supplemental unemployment benefit plans
- Regulation of overtime, shift work, and so on
- Reduction of hours to forestall layoffs
- Layoff procedures; seniority; recall
- Worksharing in lieu of layoff
- Attrition arrangements
- Promotion practices
- Training and retraining
- Relocation allowances
- Severance pay and layoff benefit plans
- Special funds and study committees

**Plant operations**
- Work and shop rules
- Rest periods and other in-plant time allowances
- Safety and health
- Plant committees
- Hours of work and premium pay practices
- Shift operations
- Hazardous work
- Discipline and discharge

**Paid and unpaid leave**
- Vacations and holidays
- Sick leave
- Funeral and personal leave
- Military leave and jury duty

**Employee benefit plans**
- Health and insurance plans
- Pension plans
- Profit sharing, stock purchase, and thrift plans
- Bonus plans

**Special groups**
- Apprentices and learners
- Workers with disabilities and older workers
- Women
- Veterans
- Union representatives
- Nondiscrimination clauses

SOURCE: From H. Katz, T. Kochan, and A. Colvin, *An Introduction to Collective Bargaining and Industrial Relations*, 4th ed (New York: McGraw-Hill, 2008).

A major goal of labor unions is bargaining effectiveness, because with it comes the power and influence to make the employees' voices heard and to effect changes in the workplace.[10] The right to strike is one important component of bargaining power. In turn, the success of a strike (actual or threatened) depends on the relative magnitude of the costs imposed on management versus those imposed on the union. A critical factor is the size of union membership. More members translate into a greater ability to halt or disrupt production and also into greater financial resources for continuing a strike in the face of lost wages.

# INTEGRITY IN ACTION

## The Alliance for Bangladesh Worker Safety

According to the website of the Alliance for Bangladesh Worker Safety, it was established to improve workplace safety in Bangladesh's garment factories in the aftermath of factory tragedies there, such as the collapse of the Rana Plaza building that killed 1,134 people and injured thousands more. Earlier, there had been a deadly fire at the Tazreen Fashions facility. The Alliance reports that its accomplishments in its first year included the following:

- Developed and implemented Bangladesh's first integrated fire safety and structural integrity standard.
- Inspected all 587 factories used by Alliance members as sources for their garments.
- Provided fire safety training to roughly 1 million workers and managers employed in these factories.

The Alliance's first annual report also provided the following case study of its actions at a local company called RSI Apparels Limited. It reported that an inspection revealed a building structural problem that posed an immediate risk to worker safety. Production at the factory was stopped and safety upgrades made. The Alliance paid one-half of the salaries of workers who were not able to work during that time period and the owner of the factory paid the other half.

The Alliance's third report, two years later, includes a comparison of fire safety in Bangladesh garment factories in 2012, prior to establishment of the Alliance, and 2016. There were 250 garment factory fires in Bangladesh in 2012, which claimed 115 lives. In contrast, in 2016, there were 30 fires and no lives lost. Fire safety training is a continued emphasis. The Alliance also reported that 1.2 million workers had been trained and another 800,000 received a refresher course by 2016. The Alliance also reported that it had "suspended" (i.e., removed from the Alliance-compliant list) 97 factories "for failure to make progress on repairs that address safety concerns." That does not prevent such factories from operating, but if there is loss of life in one of those factories, the companies using them will have to answer for their decision.

In the Alliance's fifth (and final) report in 2018, it reports that initial remediation is almost complete at nearly 700 factories, with remediation complete for 93% of them (i.e., their initial Corrective Action Plans (CAPs) have been completed). Remediation involves five steps: (1) a factory receives an initial inspection report and must develop a CAP; (2) the CAP must be approved; (3) factories begin remediation, working with Alliance staff and consultants; (4) Alliance staff conducts up to three visits to audit progress on the CAP; (5) final inspection by a third party. As an example of remediation, one factory replaced locking gates that would not allow exit in case of an emergency with gates that have panic bars to allow easy exit even when locked. As another example, a combustible storage area that was not separated from workers was separated with a newly installed fire-rated door. Not all factories are successful: 178 factories were suspended as a result of this process. Training of 1.6 million workers, security guards, and factory managers in fire safety (and retraining of 1.3 million) has also been completed. There are worker safety committees at a significant number of factories. More than 1.5 million workers in 1,017 factories now have access to the Alliance's 24-hour confidential worker helpline, where they can report safety concerns. Importantly, the result of these efforts has been zero electrical, structural, or fire-related deaths since the Alliance began.

Beginning in 2019, the Alliance reports that most of its 29 member brands "plan to work through a locally-based organization to collectively monitor safety in the factories from which they source."

### DISCUSSION QUESTIONS

1. Why did the companies come together to form the Alliance to address worker safety in Bangladesh factories?
2. How effective has the Alliance been? Explain.
3. What do you think will happen with worker safety in Bangladesh going forward?

SOURCE: Alliance for Bangladesh Worker Safety, *Fifth Annual Report: An Industry Transformed: Leaving a Legacy of Safety in Bangladesh's Garment Sector*, November 2018; Alliance for Bangladesh Worker Safety, *Third Annual Report: Protecting and Empowering Bangladesh Garment Workers*, September 2016; *First Annual Report: Protecting the Lives and Livelihoods of Bangladesh's Garment Workers*, July 2014, www.bangladeshworkersafety.org.

# Union Structure, Administration, and Membership

A necessary step in discussing labor–management interactions is a basic knowledge of how labor and management are organized and how they function. Management has been described throughout this book. We now focus on labor unions.

## NATIONAL AND INTERNATIONAL UNIONS

Most union members belong to a national or international union. In turn, most national unions are composed of multiple local units, and most are affiliated with the American Federation of Labor and Congress of Industrial Organizations (AFL-CIO).

The largest national unions are listed in Table 14.2. The National Education Association, which is not affiliated with the AFL-CIO, is the largest union, with almost 3 million members. An important characteristic of a union is whether it is a craft or industrial union. The electrical workers' and carpenters' unions are craft unions, meaning that the members all have a particular skill or occupation. Craft unions often are responsible for training their members (through apprenticeships) and for supplying craft workers to employers. Requests for carpenters, for example, would come to the union hiring hall, which would decide which carpenters to send out. Thus craft workers may work for many employers over time, their constant link being to the union. A craft union's bargaining power depends greatly on the control it can exercise over the supply of its workers.

In contrast, industrial unions are made up of members who are linked by their work in a particular industry (such as steelworkers and autoworkers). Typically they represent many different occupations. Membership in the union is a result of working for a particular employer in the industry. Changing employers is less common than it is among craft

**Table 14.2**
Largest Labor Unions in the United States

| ORGANIZATION | NUMBER OF MEMBERS |
| --- | --- |
| 1. National Education Association | 3,002,516 |
| 2. Service Employees International Union | 1,919,358 |
| 3. American Federation of Teachers | 1,677,775 |
| 4. American Federation of State, County, and Municipal Employees | 1,299,644 |
| 5. International Brotherhood of Teamsters | 1,279,752 |
| 6. United Food and Commercial Workers International Union | 1,255,743 |
| 7. International Brotherhood of Electrical Workers | 672,551 |
| 8. Communications Workers | 627,373 |
| 9. Laborers | 576,475 |
| 10. Steelworkers | 559,558 |
| 11. United Automobile, Aerospace, and Agricultural Implement Workers of America International Union | 430,871 |
| 12. Carpenters | 424,826 |
| 13. International Union of Operating Engineers | 380,596 |
| 14. United Association of Journeymen and Apprentices of the Plumbing and Pipe Fitting Industry of the United States and Canada | 348,439 |
| 15. Police | 339,476 |
| 16. Firefighters | 314,990 |

SOURCE: U.S. Department of Labor, Office of Labor-Management Standards, Online Public Disclosure Room, Union Search [search on "Membership"], https://www.dol.gov/olms/regs/compliance/rrlo/lmrda.htm. Accessed January 30, 2019.

workers, and employees who change employers remain members of the same union only if they happen to move to other employers covered by that union. Whereas a craft union may restrict the number of, say, carpenters to maintain higher wages, industrial unions try to organize as many employees in as wide a range of skills as possible.

## LOCAL UNIONS

Even when a national union plays the most critical role in negotiating terms of a collective bargaining contract, negotiation occurs at the local level as well as over work rules and other issues that are locally determined. In addition, administration of the contract is carried out largely at the local union level. Consequently, the bulk of day-to-day interaction between labor and management takes place at the local union level.

The local of an industrial-based union may correspond to a single large facility or to a number of small facilities. In a craft-oriented union, the local may cover a city or a region. The local union typically elects officers (like president, vice president, treasurer). Responsibility for contract negotiation may rest with the officers, or a bargaining committee may be formed for this purpose. Typically the national union provides assistance, ranging from background data about other settlements and technical advice to sending a representative to lead the negotiations.

Individual members' participation in local union meetings includes the election of union officials and strike votes. However, most union contact is with the shop steward, who is responsible for ensuring that the terms of the collective bargaining contract are enforced. The shop steward represents employees in contract grievances. Another union position, the business representative, performs some of the same functions, especially where the union deals with multiple employers, as is often the case with craft unions.

## AMERICAN FEDERATION OF LABOR AND CONGRESS OF INDUSTRIAL ORGANIZATIONS (AFL-CIO)

The AFL-CIO is not a labor union but rather an association that seeks to advance the shared interests of its member unions at the national level, much as the Chamber of Commerce and the National Association of Manufacturers do for their member employers. As Figure 14.2 indicates, there are 55 affiliated national and international unions and thousands of locals. An important responsibility of the AFL-CIO is to represent labor's interests in public policy issues such as civil rights, economic policy, safety, and occupational health. It also provides information and analysis that member unions can use in their activities: organizing new members, negotiating new contracts, and administering contracts.

## UNION SECURITY

The survival and security of a union depends on its ability to ensure a regular flow of new members and member dues to support the services it provides. Therefore, unions typically place high priority on negotiating two contract provisions with an employer that are critical to a union's security or viability: checkoff provisions and union membership or contribution. First, under a **checkoff provision**, the employer, on behalf of the union, automatically deducts union dues from employees' paychecks.

A second union security provision focuses on the flow of new members (and their dues). The strongest union security arrangement is a **closed shop**, under which a person must be a union member (and thus pay dues) before being hired. A closed shop is, however, illegal under the NLRA. A **union shop** requires a person to join the union within a certain amount of time after beginning employment (no sooner than the 30th day of employment). An **agency shop** is similar to a union shop but does not require union

**Checkoff provision**
A union contract provision that requires an employer to deduct union dues from employees' paychecks.

**Closed shop**
A union security provision requiring a person to be a union member before being hired. Illegal under NLRA.

**Union shop**
A union security provision that requires a person to join the union within a certain amount of time after being hired.

**Agency shop**
A union security provision that requires an employee to pay union membership dues but not to join the union.

**Figure 14.2**
AFL-CIO
Organization Chart

**55 Affiliated
National Unions**

**Executive Council
55 Vice Presidents**

**President
Secretary-Treasurer
Executive Vice President**

**AFL-CIO Departments**
- Accounting
- Campaigns
- Civil, Human and Women's Rights
- Digital Strategies
- Facilities Management
- Government Affairs
- Human Resources
- Information Technology
- International
- Meetings and Travel
- Office of General Counsel
- Office of Investment
- Organizing
- Policy
- Political
- Public Affairs
- Support Services

**Trade and Industrial
Departments**
- Building and Construction Trades
- Maritime Trades
- Metal Trades
- Professional Employees
- Transportation Trades
- Union Label and Service Trades

Thousands of affiliated local unions and 12.5 million members

51 State Federations

SOURCE: AFL-CIO, https://aflcio.org/about-us/our-unions-and-allies, accessed January 31, 2019.

membership, only that dues be paid. **Maintenance of membership** rules do not require union membership but do require that employees who choose to join must remain members for a certain period of time (such as the length of the contract).

Under the 1947 **Taft-Hartley Act** (an amendment to the NLRA), states may pass so-called **right-to-work laws**, which make union shops, maintenance of membership, and agency shops illegal. The idea behind such laws is that compulsory union membership (or making employees pay union dues) infringes on the employee's right to freedom of association. From the union perspective, a big concern is "free riders," employees who benefit from union activities without belonging to a union. By law, all members of a bargaining unit, whether union members or not, must be represented by the union. If the union is required to offer service to all bargaining unit members, even those who are not union members, it may lose its financial viability.

**Maintenance of membership**
Union rules requiring members to remain members for a certain period of time (e.g., the length of the union contract).

**Taft-Hartley Act**
The 1947 act that outlawed unfair union labor practices.

**Right-to-work laws**
State laws that make union shops, maintenance of membership, and agency shops illegal.

## UNION MEMBERSHIP AND BARGAINING POWER

At the strategic level, management and unions meet head-on over the issue of union organizing. Increasingly, employers are actively resisting unionization in an attempt to control costs and maintain their flexibility. Unions, by contrast, must organize new members and hold on to their current members to have the kind of bargaining power and financial resources needed to achieve their goals in future organizing and to negotiate and administer contracts with management. For this reason we now discuss trends in union membership and possible explanations for those trends.

Since the 1950s, when union membership rose to 35% of employment, membership has consistently declined as a percentage of employment. It now stands at 11.1% of all employment and 6.4% of private-sector employment.[11] As Figure 14.3 indicates, this decline shows no indication of reversing.[12]

### Figure 14.3

Union Membership Density among Employed U.S. Wage and Salary Workers, 1975–2018

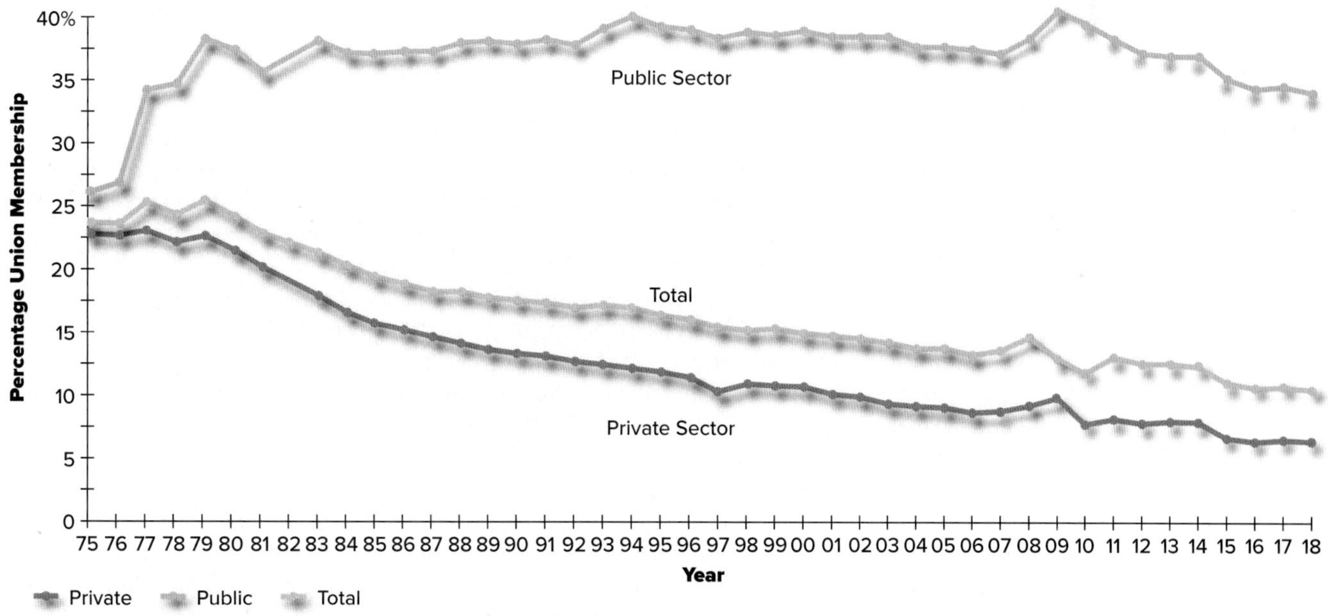

SOURCE: From B. T. Hirsch and D. A. MacPherson, *Union Membership and Earnings Data Book 2001* (Washington, DC: The Bureau of National Affairs, Inc., 2001). Reprinted with permission. Data for 2001 to 2018 obtained from U.S. Bureau of Labor Statistics, www.bls.gov.

What factors explain the decline in union membership? Several have been identified.[13]

## Structural Changes in the Economy

At the risk of oversimplifying, we might say that unions have traditionally been strongest in urban workplaces (especially those outside the South) that employ middle-aged men in blue-collar jobs. However, much recent job growth has occurred among women and youth in the service sector (in contrast to the manufacturing sector) of the economy. Although unionizing such groups is possible, unions have so far not had much success organizing these groups in the private sector. Despite the importance of structural changes in the economy, studies show that they account for no more than one-quarter of the overall union membership decline.[14]

## Increased Employer Resistance

Almost one-half of large employers in a survey reported that their most important labor goal was to be union-free. This contrasts sharply with 60 years ago, when Jack Barbash wrote that "many tough bargainers [among employers] prefer the union to a situation where there is no union. Most of the employers in rubber, basic steel and the automobile industry fall in this category."[15] The idea then was that an effective union could help assess and communicate the interests of employees to management, thus helping management make better decisions. But product-market pressures, such as foreign competition and deregulation (e.g., trucking, airlines, telecommunications), have contributed to increasing employer resistance to unions.[16] These changes in the competitive environment have contributed to a change in management's perspective and goals.[17]

In the absence of significant competition from foreign producers, unions were often able to organize entire industries. For example, the UAW organized all four major producers in the automobile industry (GM, Ford, Chrysler, and American Motors). The UAW usually sought and achieved the same union–management contract at each company. As a consequence, a negotiated wage increase in the industry could be passed on to the consumer in the form of higher prices. No company was undercut by its competitors because the labor cost of all major producers in the industry was determined by the same union–management contract, and the U.S. public had little option but to buy U.S.-made cars. However, the onset of foreign competition in the automobile market changed the competitive situation as well as the UAW's ability to organize the industry.[18] U.S. automakers were slow to recognize and respond to the competitive threat from foreign producers, resulting in a loss of market share and employment.

Competitive threats have contributed to increased employer resistance to union organizing and, in some cases, to an increased emphasis on ridding themselves of existing unions. Unionized workers receive, on average, 26% higher wages, and this advantage is still estimated to be 10–15% when observable characteristics of union and nonunion workers are equated. The compensation advantage is still larger if benefits are also included. Many employers have decided that they can no longer compete with these higher labor costs, and union membership has suffered as a result.[19] One measure of increased employer resistance is the dramatic increase in the late 1960s in the number of unfair employer labor practices (violations of sections of the NLRA such as section 8(a)(3), which prohibits firing employees for union organizing, as we discuss later) even though the number of elections held did not change much. (See Figure 14.4.) The use of remedies such as back pay for workers also grew, but the costs to employers of such penalties does not appear to have been sufficient to prevent the growth in employer unfair labor practices. Not surprisingly, the union victory rate in representation elections decreased from almost 59% in 1960 to below 50% by 1975. Although the union victory rate in recent elections has actually been much higher (e.g., 71% in 2018), the number of elections has

**Figure 14.4**

Employer Resistance to Union Organizing, 1950–2018

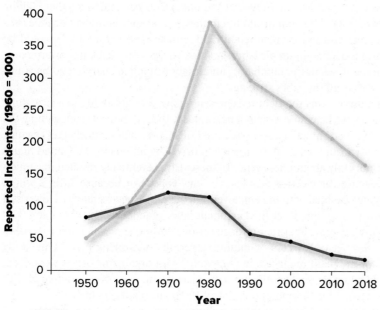

Unfair Labor Practice Charges Filed by Employees

Representation Elections Held

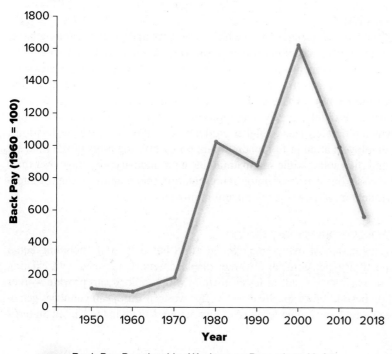

Back Pay Received by Workers as Remedy to Unfair Labor Practices (2016 dollars)

SOURCE: Adapted and updated from R. B. Freeman and J. L. Medoff, *What Do Unions Do*? (New York: Basic Books, 1984). Data for from www.nlrb.gov. Graphs and Data. https://www.nlrb.gov/news-outreach/graphs-data.; accessed January 31, 2019.

declined precipitously, from 7,422 in 1970 to 1,120 in 2018, making union membership gains hard to come by. Decertification elections are another factor, though these have declined (from over 200 per year in 2009–2013 to under 200 per year since then, falling to 159 in fiscal year 2018).[20] It is important to emphasize that the significant decline over time in both elections and union membership percentage (see Figure 14.3) would be expected to result in a decline in unfair labor practice charges and back pay awards over time. As such, the increases in the number of unfair labor practice charges and back pay awards over time is thus all the more striking.

Finally, even if a union wins the right to represent employees, its ability to successfully negotiate a contract with the employer is not guaranteed. Indeed, refusal to bargain by the employer is the unfair labor practice most frequently filed (over half of all charges) against employers. One study examined 22,000 organizing drives by unions in the United States over a six-year period. Only about one-seventh of these drives eventually resulted in a union contract, either because the election was lost (or challenged) or because, after a win, a contract could not be obtained with the employer. Further, this success rate was lower still (by 30%) in cases where the employer filed an unfair labor practice against the union.[21]

At a personal level, some managers may face serious consequences if a union successfully organizes a new set of workers or mounts a serious organizing drive. One study indicated that 8% of the plant managers in companies with organizing drives were fired, and 10% of those in companies where the union was successful were fired (compared with 2% in a control group).[22] Furthermore, only 3% of the plant managers facing an organizing drive were promoted, and none of those ending up with a union contract were promoted (compared with 21% of the managers in the control group). Therefore, managers are often under intense pressure to oppose unionization attempts.

### Substitution with HRM

A major study of the human resource management strategies and practices among large, nonunion employers found that union avoidance was often an important employee relations objective.[23] Top management's values in such companies drive specific policies such as promotion from within, an influential personnel–human resource department, and above-average pay and benefits. These policies, in turn, contribute to a number of desirable outcomes such as flexibility, positive employee attitudes, and responsive and committed employees, which ultimately lead to higher productivity and better employee relations. In other words, employers attempt to remain nonunion by offering most of the things a union can offer, and then some, while still maintaining a productivity advantage over their competitors. Of course, one aspect of union representation that employers cannot duplicate is the independent employee voice that a union provides.

### Substitution by Government Regulation

Since the 1960s, regulation of many employment areas has increased, including equal employment opportunity, pensions, and worker displacement. Combined with existing regulations, this increase may result in fewer areas in which unions can provide worker rights or protection beyond those specified by law. Yet western European countries generally have more regulations and higher levels of union membership than the United States.[24]

### Worker Views

Industrial relations scholars have long argued that the absence in the United States of a history of feudalism and of strong class distinctions found in western Europe have contributed to a more pragmatic, business-oriented (versus class-conscious) unionism.

Although this may help explain the somewhat lower level of union membership in the United States, its relevance in explaining the downward trend is not clear. Further, when U.S. workers are asked about their interest in joining a union, interest is substantial.[25]

### Union Actions and Industry Structure

In some ways, unions have hurt their own cause. First, corruption in some unions may have had a detrimental effect. Second, questions have been raised about how well unions have adapted to recent changes in the economic structure. Employee groups and economic sectors with the fastest growth rates tend to have the lowest rates of unionization.[26] Women are slightly less likely to be in unions (combining private and public sectors) than men (11.1% vs. 12.2%). Focusing on the private sector, nonmanufacturing industries such as finance, insurance, and real estate have a lower union representation (2.1%) than does transportation and utilities (18.3%) or manufacturing (9.7%). Returning to private and public sector combined, the South is also less heavily organized than the rest of the country, with, for example, South Carolina having a unionization rate of 2.7%, compared with 23.1% in New York.[27] Not surprisingly then, none of the foreign-owned automobile assembly plants (e.g., BMW, Mercedes-Benz, Toyota, Volkswagen, Nissan) located in the South are unionized (although they would be in their home countries). One reason for the smaller union presence in southern states is the existence of right-to-work laws (see our earlier discussion) in such states. We should note, however, that since 2012, Indiana, Michigan, and Wisconsin, for example, traditional union strongholds, have all become right-to-work states.

# Legal Framework

Although competitive challenges have a major impact on labor relations, the legal framework of collective bargaining is an especially critical determinant of union membership and relative bargaining power and, therefore, of the degree to which employers, employees, and society are successful in achieving their goals. The legal framework also constrains union structure and administration and the manner in which unions and employers interact. Perhaps the most dramatic example of labor laws' influence is the 1935 passage of the Wagner Act (also known as the National Labor Relations Act or NLRA), which actively supported collective bargaining rather than impeding it. As a result, union membership nearly tripled, from 3 million in 1933 (7.7% of all employment) to 8.8 million (19.2% of employment) by 1939.[28] With increased membership came greater union bargaining power and, consequently, more success in achieving union goals.

Before the 1930s, the legal system was generally hostile to unions. The courts generally viewed unions as coercive organizations that hindered free trade. Unions' focus on collective voice and collective action (strikes, boycotts) did not fit well with the U.S. emphasis on capitalism, individualism, freedom of contract, and property rights.[29]

The Great Depression of the 1930s, however, shifted public attitudes toward business and the free-enterprise system. Unemployment rates as high as 25% and a 30% drop in the gross national product between 1929 and 1933 focused attention on employee rights and on the shortcomings of the system as it existed then. The nation was in a crisis, and President Franklin Roosevelt responded with dramatic action, the New Deal. On the labor front, the 1935 NLRA ushered in a new era of public policy for labor unions, enshrining collective bargaining as the preferred mechanism for settling labor–management disputes.

**LO 14-3**

Explain the legal environment's impact on labor relations.

The introduction to the NLRA states:

> It is in the national interest of the United States to maintain full production in its economy. Industrial strife among employees, employers, and labor organizations interferes with full production and is contrary to our national interest. Experience has shown that labor disputes can be lessened if the parties involved recognize the legitimate rights of each in their relations with one another. To establish these rights under the law, Congress enacted the National Labor Relations Act. Its purpose is to define and protect the rights of employees and employers, to encourage collective bargaining, and to eliminate certain practices on the part of labor and management that are harmful to the general welfare.[30]

The rights of employees are set out in Section 7 of the act, including the "right to self-organization, to form, join, or assist labor organizations, to bargain collectively through representatives of their own choosing, and to engage in other concerted activities for the purpose of collective bargaining. The act also gives employees the right to refrain from any or all of such activities except [in cases] requiring membership in a labor organization as a condition of employment."[31] Examples of protected activities include

- Union organizing
- Joining a union, whether it is recognized by the employer or not
- Going out on strike to secure better working conditions
- Refraining from activity on behalf of the union[32]

Although the NLRA has broad coverage in the private sector, Table 14.3 shows that there are some notable exclusions.

## CONCERTED ACTIVITY

The National Labor Relations Act protects "concerted activity" (taking action on behalf of a group to address work conditions) by workers, whether they are represented by a union or not.[33] As one example, in an effort to create a national movement to raise hourly wages to $15/hour (the "Fight for 15"), a primary target has been McDonald's. In recent years, workers and supporters took part in rallies to pressure McDonald's to increase its lowest wage rates (which it eventually did). The workers who participated in these rallies for a higher wage were protected from discipline for protesting, despite not being members of a union, because their participation constitutes concerted activity.[34]

In another example, three nonunion employees at a Hyundai plant in Alabama were scheduled to work from 6:00 a.m. to 2:00 p.m. on the last day before a holiday break. Two days before that, a supervisor told them they would instead work from 6:30 a.m. to 3:00 p.m. The workers, nevertheless punched out and left at 2:00. They were subsequently informed that they had "voluntarily resigned" by leaving at 2:00 and would no longer be

**Table 14.3**
Are You Excluded from the NLRA's Coverage?

The NLRA specifically excludes from its coverage individuals who are
- Employed as a supervisor
- Employed by a parent or spouse
- Employed as an independent contractor
- Employed in the domestic service of any person or family in a home
- Employed as agricultural laborers
- Employed by an employer subject to the Railway Labor Act
- Employed by a federal, state, or local government
- Employed by any other person who is not an employer as defined in the NLRA

SOURCE: National Labor Relations Board, *Basic Guide to the National Labor Relations Act*, accessed November 6, 2019, www.nlrb.gov.

employed at Hyundai. A National Labor Relations Board (NLRB) judge ruled that the company had violated the employees' rights and ordered it to reinstate the employees, pay them back pay (lost wages) and expenses, and post a notice stating that the NLRB had determined that the company "violated Federal labor law."[35]

Concerted activity among nonunion employees and its legal protections is not something that only large companies need to understand. For example, employees at an urgent care center in Minnesota sent an anonymous letter to the owner, a doctor, who had announced a plan to cut wages by 10%. They suggested alternative ways to save money. Shortly thereafter, two employees who wrote the letter—one, a radiation technologist, and the other, a physician's assistant—were fired. One of the fired employees filed a charge with the NLRB regional office in Minneapolis. After an investigation, a complaint was issued alleging the owner's actions were unlawful. A trial was held before an administrative law judge, who concurred. He ordered the employees reinstated with back pay (for the period of time they missed work due to being fired). The owner appealed the judge's decision to the full NLRB in Washington, DC. A panel of three members of the board unanimously decided to uphold the judge's decision.[36]

## UNFAIR LABOR PRACTICES—EMPLOYERS

The NLRA prohibits certain activities by both employers and labor unions. Unfair labor practices by employers are listed in Section 8(a) of the NLRA. Section 8(a)(1) prohibits employers from interfering with, restraining, or coercing employees in exercising their rights to join or assist a labor organization or to refrain from such activities. Section 8(a)(2) prohibits employer domination of or interference with the formation or activities of a labor union. Section 8(a)(3) prohibits discrimination (e.g., firing employees engaged in union organizing) in any aspect of employment that attempts to encourage or discourage union-related activity. Section 8(a)(4) prohibits discrimination against employees for providing testimony relevant to enforcement of the NLRA. Section 8(a)(5) prohibits employers from refusing to bargain collectively with a labor organization that has standing under the act. Examples of employer unfair labor practices are listed in Table 14.4.

**Table 14.4**
Examples of Employer Unfair Labor Practices

- Threatening employees with loss of their jobs or benefits if they join or vote for a union
- Threatening to close down a plant if organized by a union
- Questioning employees about their union membership or activities in a manner that restrains or coerces them
- Spying or pretending to spy on union meetings
- Granting wage increases that are timed to discourage employees from forming or joining a union
- Taking an active part in organizing a union or committee to represent employees
- Providing preferential treatment or aid to one of several unions trying to organize employees
- Discharging employees for urging other employees to join a union or refusing to hire applicants because they are union members
- Refusing to reinstate workers when job openings occur because the workers participated in a lawful strike
- Ending operation at one plant and opening the same operation at another plant with new employees because employees at the first plant joined a union
- Demoting or firing employees for filing an unfair labor practice or for testifying at an NLRB hearing
- Refusing to meet with employees' representatives because the employees are on strike
- Refusing to supply the employees' representative with cost and other data concerning a group insurance plan covering employees
- Announcing a wage increase without consulting the employees' representative
- Failing to bargain about the effects of a decision to close one of employer's plants

SOURCE: National Labor Relations Board, *Basic Guide to the National Labor Relations Act*, accessed November 6, 2019, www.nlrb.gov.

**Table 14.5**
Examples of Union Unfair Labor Practices

- Mass picketing in such numbers that nonstriking employees are physically barred from entering the plant
- Acts of force or violence on the picket line or in connection with a strike
- Threats to employees of bodily injury or that they will lose their jobs unless they support the union's activities
- Fining or expelling members for crossing a picket line that is unlawful
- Fining or expelling members for filing unfair labor practice charges or testifying before the NLRB
- Insisting during contract negotiations that the employer agree to accept working conditions that will be determined by a group to which it does not belong
- Fining or expelling union members for the way they apply the bargaining contract while carrying out their supervisory responsibilities
- Causing an employer to discharge employees because they spoke out against a contract proposed by the union
- Making a contract that requires an employer to hire only members of the union or employees "satisfactory" to the union
- Insisting on the inclusion of illegal provisions in a contract
- Terminating an existing contract and striking for a new one without notifying the employer, the Federal Mediation and Conciliation Service, and the state mediation service (where one exists)
- Attempting to compel a beer distributor to recognize a union (the union prevents the distributor from obtaining beer at a brewery by inducing the brewery's employees to refuse to fill the distributor's orders)
- Picketing an employer to force it to stop doing business with another employer who has refused to recognize the union (a "secondary boycott")

SOURCE: National Labor Relations Board, *A Guide to Basic Law and Procedures under the National Labor Relations Act*, accessed November 6, 2019, www.nlrb.gov.

## UNFAIR LABOR PRACTICES—LABOR UNIONS

Originally the NLRA did not list any union unfair labor practices. These were added through the 1947 Taft-Hartley Act. The 1959 Landrum-Griffin Act further regulated unions' actions and their internal affairs (like financial disclosure and conduct of elections). Section 8(b)(1)(a) of the NLRA states that a labor organization is not to "restrain or coerce employees in the exercise of the rights guaranteed in Section 7" (described earlier). Table 14.5 provides examples of union unfair labor practices.

## ENFORCEMENT

Enforcement of the NLRA rests with the National Labor Relations Board, which is composed of a five-member board, the general counsel, and 33 regional offices. The basis for the NLRA is the commerce clause of the U.S. Constitution. Therefore, the NLRB's jurisdiction is limited to employers whose operations affect commerce generally and interstate commerce in particular. In practice, only purely local firms are likely to fall outside the NLRB's jurisdiction. Specific jurisdictional standards (nearly 20) that vary by industry are applied. Two examples of businesses that are covered (and the standards) are retail businesses that had more than $500,000 in annual business and newspapers that had more than $200,000 in annual business.

The NLRB's two major functions are to conduct and certify representation elections and prevent unfair labor practices. In both realms, it does not initiate action. Rather, it responds to requests for action. The NLRB's role in representation elections is discussed in the next section. Here we discuss unfair labor practices.

Unfair labor practice cases begin with the filing of a charge, which is investigated by a regional office. A charge must be filed within six months of the alleged unfair practice, and copies must be served on all parties. (Registered mail is recommended.) If the NLRB finds the charge to have merit and issues a complaint, there are two possible actions. It may defer to a grievance procedure agreed on by the employer and union. Otherwise, a hearing is held before an administrative law judge. The judge makes a recommendation, which can be appealed by either party. The NLRB has the authority to issue cease-and-desist orders to halt unfair labor practices. It can also order reinstatement of employees, with or without back pay. In one recent year, for example, $110 million in back pay was awarded. Note, however, that the NLRA is not a criminal statute, and punitive damages are not available. If an employer or union refuses to comply with an NLRB order, the board has the authority to petition the U.S. Court of Appeals. The court can choose to enforce the order, remand it to the NLRB for modification, change it, or set it aside altogether.

# Union and Management Interactions: Organizing

To this point we have discussed macro trends in union membership. Here we shift our focus to the more micro questions of why individual employees join unions and how the organizing process works at the workplace level.

**LO 14-4**
Describe the major labor–management interactions: organizing, contract negotiations, and contract administration.

## WHY DO EMPLOYEES JOIN UNIONS?

Virtually every model of the decision to join a union focuses on two questions.[37] First, is there a gap between the pay, benefits, and other conditions of employment that employees actually receive versus what they believe they should receive? Second, if such a gap exists and is sufficiently large to motivate employees to try to remedy the situation, is union membership seen as the most effective or instrumental means of change? The outcome of an election campaign hinges on how the majority of employees answer these two questions.

## THE PROCESS AND LEGAL FRAMEWORK OF ORGANIZING

The NLRB is responsible for ensuring that the organizing process follows certain steps. At the most general level, the NLRB holds a union representation election if at least 30% of employees in the bargaining unit sign authorization cards (see Figure 14.5). If more than 50% of the employees sign authorization cards, the union may request that the employer voluntarily recognize it. If 50% or fewer of the employees sign, or if the employer refuses to recognize the union voluntarily, the NLRB conducts a secret-ballot election. The union is certified by the NLRB as the exclusive representative of employees if more than 50% of employees vote for the union. If more than one union appears on the ballot and neither gains a simple majority, a runoff election is held. Once a union has been certified as the exclusive representative of a group of employees, no additional elections are permitted for one year. After the negotiation of a contract, an election cannot be held for the contract's duration or for three years, whichever comes first. The parties to the contract may agree not to hold an election for longer than three years, but an outside party cannot be barred for more than three years.

As mentioned previously, union members' right to be represented by leaders of their own choosing was expanded under the Taft-Hartley Act to include the right to vote an existing union out—that is, to decertify it. The process follows the same steps as a

**Figure 14.5**

Authorization Card

# YES, I WANT THE IAM

I, the undersigned employee of

_(Company)_ _____

authorize the International Association of Machinists and Aerospace Workers (IAM) to act as my collective bargaining agent for wages, hours and working conditions. I agree that this card may be used either to support a demand for recognition or an NLRB election, at the discretion of the union.

Name (print) _____ Date _____

Home Address _____ Phone_____

City_____ State _____ Zip_____

Job Title _____ Dept. _____ Shift _____

Sign Here X _____

Note: This authorization to be SIGNED and DATED in employee's own handwriting. YOUR RIGHT TO SIGN THIS CARD IS PROTECTED BY FEDERAL LAW.

RECEIVED BY (Initial) _____

representation election. A decertification election is not permitted when a contract is in effect. Research indicates that when decertification elections are held, unions typically do not fare well, losing the majority of the time.[38]

The NLRB also is responsible for determining the appropriate bargaining unit and the employees who are eligible to participate in organizing activities. A unit may cover employees in one facility or multiple facilities within a single employer, or the unit may cover multiple employers. In general, employees on the payroll just prior to the ordering of an election are eligible to vote, although this rule is modified in some cases where, for example, employment in the industry is irregular. Most employees who are on strike and who have been replaced by other employees are eligible to vote in an election (such as a decertification election) that occurs within 12 months of the onset of the strike.

As shown in Table 14.3, the following types of employees cannot be included in bargaining units: agricultural laborers, independent contractors, supervisors, and managers. Beyond this, the NLRB attempts to group together employees who have a community of interest in their wages, hours, and working conditions. In many cases this grouping will be sharply contested, with management and the union jockeying to include or exclude certain employee subgroups in the hope of influencing the outcome of the election.

During the Obama administration, the NLRB issued a number of important rulings. These rulings will be revisited and perhaps modified or reversed by the NLRB as its five-member board, which acts as a quasi-judicial body and whose members serve five-year terms, begins to change as President Trump's appointees gain influence.[39] One ruling, referred to by the U.S. Chamber of Commerce as the "ambush election rule," was designed to streamline and speed representation elections, presumably in hopes of helping unions be more successful in organizing new workers.[40] Specific changes include allowing unions to file election petitions electronically rather than requiring them to be submitted by mail, requiring businesses to give unions personal e-mail addresses (in addition to telephone numbers) of workers if they have them on file (within two days), and making it more difficult for employers to challenge elections until after they are conducted. The changes are intended to shorten the time between the call for a vote and actual election to 25 days or less, nearly 2 weeks less than the previous median of 38 days and 3.5 weeks less than the median of 59 days in cases where employers contest the holding or other aspects of an election. Evidence suggests that the rules have had the intended effect of shortening time to elections.[41]

A second ruling, Browning-Ferris, makes it more likely that in a case where Company A contracts with a staffing firm (Company B) to provide it with workers, Company A could be held responsible (depending on the amount of control it exercises over workers, directly and/or indirectly) as a joint employer (along with Company B) for employment practices, rather than such responsibility falling exclusively to Company B.[42] As such, a union now has a better chance of being able to negotiate directly with Company A, making it more difficult for Company A to avoid dealing with the union. However, the status of Browning-Ferris is actively being revisited by the NLRB and the Courts.[43]

Another ruling also moves toward making a company responsible for workers who are not its employees, in this case, employees of its franchises. This case involved McDonald's.[44] Some workers brought a complaint against McDonald's for retaliating against workers who went out on strike to join the "Fight for 15" protests for higher wages. Importantly, the NLRB ruled in the case that McDonald's, which owns only 10% of McDonald's stores, is a joint employer with its franchisees, which own and operate, and employ workers in, the other 90% of stores. The NLRB stated that "through its franchise relationship and its use of tools, resources, and technology," McDonald's "engages in sufficient control over its franchisees' operations." The ruling poses a threat to McDonald's and other companies that use a franchise model. McDonald's could become at least partly responsible for (including for the cost of litigation-related expenses) any labor and/or employment law violations committed by its franchisees, and there are many (14,000) of them in far-flung places. The Service Employees International Union (SEIU) hopes the ruling will put pressure on large companies like McDonald's to take more responsibility for the actions of its franchisees, leading to better treatment of workers.[45]

The bigger picture, as implied in the preceding discussion, is that a change in presidential administration will eventually influence how pro-labor versus pro-business the NLRB is, as the terms of current board members expire and the new president has the opportunity to appoint new board members for fixed terms. The expectation is that President Trump's appointees to the NLRB will be more pro-business (or less pro-labor, depending on one's perspective).

A 2016 NLRB ruling, though having a much narrower effect and outside the for-profit business sector, may be of interest to current or future graduate students reading this book. The NLRB ruled that teaching assistants and research assistants at private universities are employees under the NLRA, thus giving them the right to organize and join a union. (At public universities, state laws apply.)[46]

## Organizing Campaigns: Management and Union Strategies and Tactics

Tables 14.6 and 14.7 list common issues that arise during most campaigns.[47] Unions attempt to persuade employees that their wages, benefits, treatment by employers, and opportunity to influence workplace decisions are not sufficient and that the union will be effective in obtaining improvements. Management emphasizes that it has provided a good package of wages, benefits, and so on. It also argues that, whereas a union is unlikely to provide improvements in such areas, it will likely lead to certain costs for employees, such as union dues and the income loss resulting from strikes.

As Table 14.8 indicates, employers use a variety of methods to oppose unions in organizing campaigns in the United States, some of which may go beyond what the law permits, especially in the eyes of union organizers. This perception is supported by our earlier discussion, which noted a significant increase in employer unfair labor practices since the late 1960s. (See Figure 14.4.) Similar information on how employers either support or

**Table 14.6**
Most Common
Issues Raised by
Unions in
Representation
Election Campaigns

| UNION ISSUES | PERCENTAGE OF CAMPAIGNS |
|---|---|
| Union will prevent unfairness and will set up a grievance procedure and seniority system. | 82% |
| Union will improve unsatisfactory wages. | 79 |
| Union strength will give employees voice in wages, working conditions. | 79 |
| Union, not outsider, bargains for what employees want. | 73 |
| Union has obtained gains elsewhere. | 70 |
| Union will improve unsatisfactory sick leave and insurance. | 64 |
| Dues and initiation fees are reasonable. | 64 |
| Union will improve unsatisfactory vacations and holidays. | 61 |
| Union will improve unsatisfactory pensions. | 61 |
| Employer promises and good treatment may not be continued without union. | 61 |
| Employees choose union leaders. | 55 |
| Employer will seek to persuade or frighten employees to vote against union. | 55 |
| No strike without vote. | 55 |
| Union will improve unsatisfactory working conditions. | 52 |
| Employees have legal right to engage in union activity. | 52 |

SOURCE: J. Getman, S. Goldberg, and J. B. Herman, *Union Representation Elections: Law and Reality* (New York: Russell Sage Foundation, 1976), Table 4–3; N = 33 representation election campaigns.

**Table 14.7**
Most Common
Issues Raised by
Companies in
Representation
Election Campaigns

| COMPANY ISSUES | PERCENTAGE OF CAMPAIGNS |
|---|---|
| Improvements not dependent on unionization. | 85% |
| Wages good, equal to, or better than under union contract. | 82 |
| Financial costs of union dues outweigh gains. | 79 |
| Union is outsider. | 79 |
| Get facts before deciding; employer will provide facts and accept employee decision. | 76 |
| If union wins, strike may follow. | 70 |
| Loss of benefits may follow union win. | 67 |
| Strikers will lose wages; lose more than gain. | 67 |
| Unions not concerned with employee welfare. | 67 |
| Strike may lead to loss of jobs. | 64 |
| Employer has treated employees fairly and/or well. | 60 |
| Employees should be certain to vote. | 54 |

SOURCES: J. Fossum, *Labor Relations: Development, Structure and Processes*, 5th ed., 1992. Reprinted with permission of The McGraw-Hill Companies, Inc. Original data from J. Getman, S. Goldberg, and J. B. Herman, *Union Representation Elections: Law and Reality* (New York: Russell Sage Foundation, 1976), Table 4-2; N = 33 representation election campaigns.

resist union organizing attempts and the important effect that has on union organizing success, here based on the United Kingdom experience, appears in Table 14.9.

A number of these practices are aggressive and in the case of the U.S. system, appear to cross the line to be illegal/unfair labor practices. Why would U.S. employers break

**Table 14.8**
Percentage of Firms Using Various Methods to Oppose Union-Organizing Campaigns

| | |
|---|---|
| **Survey of employers** | |
| Consultants used | 41% |
| Unfair labor practice charges filed against employer | 24 |
| **Survey of union organizers** | |
| Consultants and/or lawyers used | 70 |
| Unfair labor practices by employer | |
| Charges filed | 36 |
| Discharges or discriminatory layoffs | 42[a] |
| Company leaflets | 80 |
| Company letters | 91 |
| Captive audience speech | 91[b] |
| Supervisor meetings with small groups of employees | 92 |
| Supervisor intensity in opposing union | |
| Low | 14 |
| Moderate | 34 |
| High | 51 |

[a]This percentage is larger than the figure for charges filed because it includes cases in which no unfair labor practice charge was actually filed against the employer.
[b]Refers to management's requiring employees to attend a session on company time at which the disadvantages of union membership are emphasized.
SOURCE: R. B. Freeman and M. M. Kleiner, "Employer Behavior in the Face of Union Organizing Drives," *Industrial and Labor Relations Review* 43, no. 4 (April 1990), pp. 351–65. © Cornell University.

**Table 14.9**
Employer Actions to Support or Resist Union Organizing Efforts and Organizing Success, United Kingdom

| | UNION ORGANIZING SUCCESS | |
|---|---|---|
| **EMPLOYER ACTIONS** | UNION RECOGNIZED (%) | UNION NOT RECOGNIZED (%) |
| **Employer support** | | |
| Provision of employee list | 63 | 13 |
| Allowing organizers access to the workplace | 94 | 32 |
| Encouraging workers to join the union | 40 | 11 |
| Allowing use of facility time for recruitment | 67 | 16 |
| Providing union with rooms or equipment | 81 | 22 |
| Permitting union presence at induction | 62 | 12 |
| **Employer resistance** | | |
| Threat of legal or police involvement against union | 4 | 21 |
| Denying organizers access to the workplace | 8 | 63 |
| Discouraging employees from joining the union | 11 | 61 |
| Distributing anti-union literature | 4 | 25 |
| Victimization of union activists | 7 | 35 |
| Improving pay and conditions to reduce demand for union membership | 3 | 23 |
| Setting up or strengthening alternative channels of worker participation to substitute for union | 10 | 53 |
| Use of a management consultant to advise on avoiding unionization of the workforce | 0 | 22 |

SOURCE: E. Heery and M. Simms, "Employer Responses to Union Organizing: Patterns and Effects," *Human Resource Management Journal*, 20 (2010), pp. 3–22. N = 97 cases where union recognized and 139 cases where union not recognized.

the law? Fossum suggests that the consequences (like back pay and reinstatement of workers) of doing so are "slight."[48] His review of various studies suggests that discrimination against employees involved in union organizing decreases union-organizing success significantly and that the cost of back pay to union activists reinstated in their jobs is far smaller than the costs that would be incurred if the union managed to organize and gain better wages, benefits, and so forth.

Still, the NLRB attempts to maintain a noncoercive atmosphere under which employees feel they can exercise free choice. It will set aside an election if it believes that either the union or the employer has created "an atmosphere of confusion or fear of reprisals."[49] Examples of conduct that may lead to an election result being set aside include the following:

- Threats of loss of jobs or benefits by an employer or union to influence votes or organizing activities
- A grant of benefits or a promise of benefits as a means of influencing votes or organizing activities
- An employer or union making campaign speeches to assembled groups of employees on company time less than 24 hours before an election
- The actual use or threat of physical force or violence to influence votes or organizing activities[50]

Supervisors have the most direct contact with employees. Thus, as Table 14.10 indicates, it is critical that they be proactive in establishing good relationships with employees

**Table 14.10**
What Supervisors Should and Should Not Do to Stay Union-Free

**WHAT TO DO:**

Report any direct or indirect signs of union activity to a core management group.

Deal with employees by carefully stating the company's response to pro-union arguments. These responses should be coordinated by the company to maintain consistency and to avoid threats or promises.

Take away union issues by following effective management practice all the time:
  Deliver recognition and appreciation.
  Solve employee problems.
  Protect employees from harassment or humiliation.
  Provide business-related information.
  Be consistent in treatment of different employees.
  Accommodate special circumstances where appropriate.
  Ensure due process in performance management.
  Treat all employees with dignity and respect.

**WHAT TO AVOID:**

Threatening employees with harsher terms and conditions of employment or employment loss if they engage in union activity.

Interrogating employees about pro-union or anti-union sentiments that they or others may have or reviewing union authorization cards or pro-union petitions.

Promising employees that they will receive favorable terms or conditions of employment if they forgo union activity.

Spying on employees known to be, or suspected of being, engaged in pro-union activities.

SOURCE: From J. A. Segal, *HR Magazine*. Reproduced with permission of Society for Human Resource Management (www.shrm.org), Alexandria, VA, publisher of *HR Magazine*.

if the company wishes to avoid union-organizing attempts. It is also important for supervisors to know what not to do (Threatening, Interrogating, Promising, Spying—TIPS) should a drive take place.

In response to organizing difficulties, the union movement in the United States has tried alternative approaches. **Associate union membership** is not linked to an employee's workplace and does not provide representation in collective bargaining. Instead the union provides other services, such as discounts on health and life insurance or credit cards.[51] In return, the union receives membership dues and a broader base of support for its activities. Associate membership may be attractive to employees who wish to join a union but cannot because their workplace is not organized by a union. Other types of (nonunion) employee representation models are evolving. The Competing through Environmental, Social, and Governance Practices box provides an example of a model agreed upon by Uber and the International Association of Machinists union.

Supervisors and their employers must also recognize that social media is increasingly used as a tool in union-organizing drives and understand how to effectively and legally respond to such communications. Workers' concerted activity protections under the NLRA apply here.

One challenge is that, unlike the days of discussions around the water cooler, when employees go online to criticize their company or supervisor, such complaints can now reach millions of people, including customers and clients.[52] Companies have sought to prevent such actions by developing policies for use of social media and to protect against disparagement. Such policies are likely to be less subject to challenge to the extent that they are not overly broad (i.e., such that they prohibit almost any topics or any concerted action) and allow discussion of clearly legitimate topics such as wages, hours, and working conditions. Employers may (though it depends on the circumstances) prohibit the use of social media (for any purpose) by employees when they are scheduled to be working. Employers can also prohibit harassment of colleagues.

Employers also need to be aware that the NLRB recently changed its rules on employee use of employer e-mail systems for the purpose of labor organizing. Its new rule states that use of e-mail for union-related communications must be permitted by employers in cases where employers allow employees general access to the employer's e-mail system. Although the board said a total ban was possible, it also stated that "it will be the rare case." As such, in general, the board stated that employees are permitted to use e-mail to engage in "statutorily protected discussions about the terms and conditions of their employment while on nonworking time." The board also stated that employees had the right to use the employer e-mail system for "an initial organizational campaign" when attempting to form a union. Although technically this activity is not to be done during working time, as a practical matter it may be difficult to tell whether an employee was on work time or break time when the e-mail was sent. Finally, it should be noted that an employer is typically permitted to monitor employee e-mail communications as long as it does not increase the intensity of such monitoring in response to union-related activity. Given the power of technology and how it can be used for union-organizing purposes, it is perhaps no surprise that some companies are cautious about encouraging employees to use social media tools and apps and, in some cases, have responded by developing their own. See the Competing through Technology box for more on this point.

**Corporate campaigns** seek to bring public, financial, or political pressure on employers during the organizing (and negotiating) process.[53] For example, the Building and Construction Trades Department of the AFL-CIO successfully lobbied Congress to eliminate $100 million in tax breaks for a Toyota truck plant in Kentucky until Toyota agreed to use union construction workers and pay union wages.[54] The Amalgamated Clothing

**Associate union membership**
A form of union membership by which the union receives dues in exchange for services (e.g., health insurance, credit cards) but does not provide representation in collective bargaining.

**Corporate campaigns**
Union activities designed to exert public, financial, or political pressure on employers during the union-organizing process.

# COMPETING THROUGH ENVIRONMENTAL, SOCIAL, AND GOVERNANCE PRACTICES

## Representing Nonunion Employees in the Gig Economy

A few years ago, Uber entered into an agreement with the International Association of Machinists and Aerospace Workers (IAM) to create an association, the Independent Drivers Guild, for drivers in New York to provide a mechanism for dialogue with the company and to put in place some limited benefits and protections in lieu of forming a traditional union, which is not feasible as long as drivers are independent contractors, not employees.

The Independent Drivers Guild agreement is for five years, and it includes monthly meetings between guild members and Uber management. The agreement also includes an appeal mechanism for drivers who feel they have been treated unfairly. Drivers will also have access to discounted legal services and discounted insurance. However, unlike a traditional union, guild members will not be able to negotiate a contract, which would set fares, benefits, and discipline procedures. Although Uber will receive input from the guild, it will, importantly, retain final say on those matters. Two other differences from a traditional union stand out: The Guild is partially funded by Uber, and it will not be able to ask the NLRB to intervene if it feels the company is violating the agreement. The IAM union has also pledged to refrain from trying to organize drivers and from encouraging them to strike during the term of the agreement.

Uber has been beset by lawsuits and other actions that stem from its model of treating drivers as contractors rather than employees, a model that helps Uber keep costs low and gives it flexibility. As non-employees, drivers are not covered by laws such as the Fair Labor Standards Act, which requires minimum wage and overtime payments or by the NLRA, which provides the right to join and organize a labor union. The agreement with the IAM to deal with the Independent Drivers Guild is perhaps a sign of Uber's desire to find a more sustainable model to manage its relationship with its drivers going forward.

Some people are underwhelmed by the agreement. For example, Abdoul Diallo, who founded a different drivers' association in New York, said the new guild seemed "bogus" and that it would be better to have a real union. Accordingly, he will continue to encourage drivers to sign authorization cards asking that the Amalgamated Transit Union represent them.

More recently, however, the Independent Drivers Guild has run a campaign to get New York City to set a minimum wage for ride-sharing drivers. It argued that most Uber and other rideshare drivers in New York City earned less than the $15 minimum hourly wage. (Again, contractors are not ordinarily covered by minimum wage laws.) The average wage was reported to be $14/hour. The drivers also do not have paid time off, health care, and other benefits that many employees received.

The drivers are also responsible for leasing or purchasing their own vehicle and the upkeep costs. The Independent Drivers Guild recently succeeded in getting New York City to guarantee that drivers receive a minimum wage of $17.22/hour (up from $14/hour). By one estimate, the average annual pay increase for drivers will be $6,300. There are other stipulations that will help the hourly wage. For example, when a driver must drop a rider far outside the city, they will be paid more on the return trip to compensate.

### DISCUSSION QUESTIONS

1. How is the Independent Drivers Guild different from a labor union?
2. Why did Uber agree to work with the guild? Why did the IAM union agree to this model?
3. How well do you think this guild model will work over time? Do you think it will serve as a model for other companies? Explain.
4. How will the new minimum wage guarantee for drivers affect the financial future of companies like Uber? How will it affect drivers?

SOURCES: E. Anzilotti, "Inside New York's Plan to Guarantee Lyft and Uber Drivers a Minimum Wage," *FastCompany*, December 4, 2018, www.fastcompany.com; J. Brustein, "New York Sets Nation's First Minimum Wage for Uber, Lyft Drivers," *Bloomberg Business*, December 4, 2018, www.bloomberg.com; N. Scheiber and M. Isaac, "Uber Recognizes New York Drivers' Group, Short of a Union," *New York Times*, May 10, 2016; J. Cao and E. Newcomer, "Uber and Union Agree to Form Drivers Guild in New York City," Bloomberg.com, May 10, 2016.

### Worker Organizing and Competing Apps at Walmart

The United Food and Commercial Workers (UFCW) union has tried for years without success to organize Walmart employees in hopes of negotiating higher pay and benefits and other standard contractual terms (e.g., a grievance procedure). Recently, a group called OUR Walmart separated from the UFCW union and is now seeking to be an advocate for Walmart employees. Part of its strategy involves using social media, and it recently developed a smartphone app called WorkIt, which it has asked employees to download. The app collects employee-related information, including name, e-mail address, telephone number, and zip code. Of course, such information is essential in any organizing attempt. The app also provides a way for employees to communicate with one another, including comparing notes about working at Walmart. The app uses artificial intelligence, as well as "a peer network of experts," to answer employee questions about working at Walmart, including those having to do with their legal rights.

What was Walmart's response? DON'T—"Don't download" it. The *Wall Street Journal* reports that Walmart has directed store managers to tell employees the app was not developed by Walmart and to describe it as an OUR Walmart "scheme" to get employees to hand over personal information to the union "by using deceptive and slick looking social media and apps."

Clearly, technology allows employees to communicate with one another and for union organizers to communicate with employees. Thus, employers will need to think through their own social media strategies for getting their message across to employees.

Fast forward a few years and we see that Walmart has done just that and has now moved beyond just advising its employees "don't download" WorkIt. Instead, Walmart now has its own app, My Walmart Schedule, a smartphone app that gives employees the ability to view schedules, trade work shifts with co-workers, and pick up additional shifts, all without involving a manager. In other words, it does most everything WorkIt did, which one might infer is exactly what Walmart had in mind. Walmart says the My Walmart Schedule app gives employees more flexibility and also assists managers and frees them up from spending as much time on scheduling.

The app also has a feature called "core hours," which goes well beyond WorkIt and is available in about 2,000 Walmart stores. It allows employees to select a set schedule for a 13-week period. This is a huge improvement over what had been the status quo, where employees would only have 2.5 weeks' notice of what their work schedule would be. That capability helps address employee complaints that such short notice and changing work schedules did not allow them to plan and live their lives. One employee described the new app and the set 13-week schedule ability as "life-changing" because now you can predict your paycheck amount and make a doctor's appointment. That sort of employee reaction is good for Walmart, which as we saw in an earlier chapter, is facing increasing competition for employees given the historically low unemployment rate. As we also saw, this has led to Walmart increasing its wage rate. Giving its employees more stable and predictable work schedules should also help it attract and retain employees. It may also provide further assistance in its effort to stay union-free.

### DISCUSSION QUESTIONS

1. From a union's perspective, what are some advantages of using social media and apps for its communications?
2. From a company's perspective, what are the risks of encouraging employees' use of social media to communicate with one another?
3. Why did Walmart develop its own app?

SOURCES: C. Hroncich, "Walmart Rolls Out New Employee Scheduling App," *Employee Benefit News*, November 21, 2018, www.benefitnews.com; S. Nassauer, "Walmart Vies for Workers with More Stable Shifts," *Wall Street Journal*, November 14, 2018; T. Wiggin, "Labor Organizers Look to Apps to Reach Wider Audiences," *Huffington Post*, August 16, 2018, www.huffingtonpost.com; L. Weber, "Apps Empower Workers, Ease Scheduling," *Wall Street Journal*, January 3, 2017; S. Nassauer, "Wal-Mart Tells Workers: Don't Download Labor Group's Chat App," *Wall Street Journal*, November 15, 2016.

and Textile Workers Union (ACTWU) corporate campaign against J. P. Stevens during the late 1970s was one of the first and best known. The ACTWU organized a boycott of J. P. Stevens products and threatened to withdraw its pension funds from financial institutions where J. P. Stevens officers acted as directors. J. P. Stevens subsequently agreed to a contract with the ACTWU.[55]

Unions also hope to use their financial assets to influence companies. Unions directly control billions in pension funds and share control with employers of billions more. All told, unions may have an influence over about $3 trillion in such investments.[56]

In some success stories, unions have eschewed elections in favor of strikes and negative publicity to pressure corporations to accept a union. Several years ago, the Hotel Employees and Restaurant Employees (HERE) union organized 9,000 workers, with 80% of these memberships resulting from pressure on employers rather than a vote. The Union of Needletrades, Industrial, and Textile Employees (UNITE) also succeeded with this approach. After losing an election by just two votes among employees of Up-to-Date Laundry, which cleans linens for Baltimore hotels and hospitals, UNITE decided to try other tactics, including a corporate campaign. It called a strike to demand that Up-to-Date recognize the union. It also persuaded several major customers of the laundry to threaten to stop using the laundry's services, shared claims of racial and sexual harassment with state agencies and the National Association for the Advancement of Colored People (NAACP), and convinced the Baltimore city council to require testimony from Up-to-Date. Eventually, the company gave in, recognized the union, and negotiated a contract that raised the workers' $6/hour wages and gave them better benefits. A final example would be the "Fight for 15," which involved holding rallies and demonstrations by non-union workers at companies such as McDonald's and Walmart to pressure businesses to raise their minimum hourly wage to $15/hour (and to call for increases in state, local, and federal minimum wages to $15 as well). Although these and other companies did raise their minimum hourly wage, they did not raise it to $15 and it is difficult to know whether it was the "Fight for 15" campaign or a tightening labor market that was the cause (or perhaps both played a role). In any case, by one estimate, the SEIU has spent $19 million in supporting this effort.[57]

Another advantageous union-organizing strategy is to negotiate employer neutrality and card-check provisions into a contract. Under a *neutrality provision*, the employer pledges not to oppose organizing attempts elsewhere in the company. A *card-check provision* is an agreement that if a certain percentage—by law, at least a majority—of employees sign an authorization card, the employer will recognize their union representation. An impartial outside agency, such as the American Arbitration Association, counts the cards. The Communication Workers of America negotiated these provisions in its dispute with Verizon. Evidence suggests that this strategy can be very effective for unions.

However, unions must avoid running afoul of the Racketeer Influenced and Corrupt Organizations Act (RICO). For example, the SEIU waged a corporate campaign beginning in 2009 against Sodexo, a French-owned food service company operating in the United States. The SEIU's campaign, "Clean Up Sodexo," focused on bringing to the public's attention food safety and other concerns at Sodexo, something that could damage its business. Sodexo sued the SEIU, claiming the campaign was an attempt to conspire to extort Sodexo with the threat of financial damage unless Sodexo agreed to a card-check provision for recognizing the union (rather than requiring that workers vote in a secret-ballot election). Sodexo alleged that the SEIU engaged in blackmail, vandalism, and other prohibited actions in an effort to prevent Sodexo from winning food contracts. In 2011, a legal settlement was reached before trial, under which the SEIU agreed to end its campaign against Sodexo.[58]

# Union and Management Interactions: Contract Negotiation

The majority of contract negotiations take place between unions and employers that have been through the process before. In most cases, management has come to accept the union as an organization that it must work with. But when the union has just been certified and is negotiating its first contract, the situation can be very different. In fact, unions are unable to negotiate a first contract in 27-37% of the cases.[59] As noted previously, more than half of all unfair labor practice charges filed against employers pertain to the refusal to negotiate.

Labor-management contracts differ in their bargaining structures—that is, the range of employees and employers that are covered. As Table 14.11 indicates, the contracts differ, first, according to whether narrow (craft) or broad (industrial) employee interests are covered. Second, they differ according to whether they cover multiple employers or multiple plants within a single employer. (A single employer may have multiple plants, some union and some nonunion.) Different structures have different implications for bargaining power and the number of interests that must be incorporated in reaching an agreement.

## THE NEGOTIATION PROCESS

Richard Walton and Robert McKersie suggested that labor-management negotiations could be broken down into four subprocesses: distributive bargaining, integrative bargaining, attitudinal structuring, and intraorganizational bargaining.[60] **Distributive bargaining** focuses on dividing a fixed economic "pie" between the two sides. A wage increase, for example, means that the union gets a larger share of the pie, management a smaller share. It is a win-lose situation. **Integrative bargaining** has a win-win focus; it seeks solutions beneficial to both sides. So if management needs to reduce labor costs, it could reach an

**Distributive bargaining**
The part of the labor–management negotiation process that focuses on dividing a fixed economic "pie."

**Integrative bargaining**
The part of the labor–management negotiation process that seeks solutions beneficial to both sides.

**Table 14.11**
Types and Examples of Bargaining Structures

| EMPLOYEE INTERESTS COVERED | EMPLOYEE INTERESTS COVERED | | |
|---|---|---|---|
| | MULTIEMPLOYER (CENTRALIZED) | SINGLE-EMPLOYER—MULTIPLANT | SINGLE-EMPLOYER—SINGLE PLANT (DECENTRALIZED) |
| **Craft (narrow)** | Construction trades Interstate trucking Longshoring Hospital association | Airline Teacher Police Firefighters Railroad | Craft union in small manufacturing plant Hospital |
| **Industrial or multiskill (broad)** | Coal mining (underground) Basic steel (pre-1986) Hotel association | Automobiles Steel (post-1986) Farm equipment State government Textile | Industrial union in small manufacturing plant |

SOURCE: From H. C. Katz and T. A. Kochan, *An Introduction to Collective Bargaining and Industrial Relations*, 4th ed (New York: McGraw-Hill) 2008.

agreement with the union to avoid layoffs in return for the union agreeing to changes in work rules that might enhance productivity.

**Attitudinal structuring** refers to the relationship and trust between labor and management negotiators. Where the relationship is poor, it may be difficult for the two sides to engage in integrative bargaining because each side hesitates to trust the other side to carry out its part of the deal. For example, the union may be reluctant to agree to productivity-enhancing work-rule changes to enhance job security if, in the past, it has made similar concessions but believes that management did not stick to its assurance of greater job security. Thus the long-term relationship between the two parties can have a very important impact on negotiations and their outcomes.

**Intraorganizational bargaining** reminds us that labor–management negotiations involve more than just two parties. Within management, and to an even greater extent within the union, different factions can have conflicting objectives. High-seniority workers, who are least likely to be laid off, may be more willing to accept a contract that has layoffs (especially if it also offers a significant pay increase for those whose jobs are not at risk). Less senior workers would likely feel very differently. Thus negotiators and union leaders must simultaneously satisfy both the management side and their own internal constituencies. If they do not, they risk the union membership's rejecting the contract, or they risk being voted out of office in the next election. Management, too, is unlikely to be of one mind about how to approach negotiations. Some will focus more on long-term employee relations, others will focus on cost control, and still others will focus on what effect the contract will have on stockholders.

## MANAGEMENT'S PREPARATION FOR NEGOTIATIONS

Clearly, the outcome of contract negotiations can have important consequences for labor costs and labor productivity and, therefore, for the company's ability to compete in the product market. Adapting Fossum's discussion, we can divide management preparation into the following seven areas, most of which have counterparts on the union side:[61]

1. *Establishing interdepartmental contract objectives:* The employer's industrial relations department needs to meet with the accounting, finance, production, marketing, and other departments and set contract goals that will permit each department to meet its responsibilities. As an example, finance may suggest a cost figure above which a contract settlement would seriously damage the company's financial health. The bargaining team needs to be constructed to take into account these various interests.
2. *Reviewing the old contract:* This step focuses on identifying provisions of the contract that might cause difficulties by hindering the company's productivity or flexibility or by leading to significant disagreements between management and the union.
3. *Preparing and analyzing data:* Information on labor costs and the productivity of competitors, as well as data the union may emphasize, needs to be prepared and analyzed. The union data might include cost-of-living changes and agreements reached by other unions that could serve as a target. Data on employee demographics and seniority are relevant for establishing the costs of such benefits as pensions, health insurance, and paid vacations. Finally, management needs to know how much it would be hurt by a strike. How long will its inventory allow it to keep meeting customer orders? To what extent are other companies positioned to step in and offer replacement products? How difficult would it be to find replacement workers if the company decided to continue operations during a strike?
4. *Anticipating union demands:* Recalling grievances over the previous contract, having ongoing discussions with union leaders, and becoming aware of settlements

### Sidebar definitions

**Attitudinal structuring**
The aspect of the labor–management negotiation process that refers to the relationship and level of trust between the negotiators.

**Intraorganizational bargaining**
The part of the labor–management negotiation process that focuses on the conflicting objectives of factions within labor and management.

at other companies are ways of anticipating likely union demands and developing potential counterproposals.

5. *Establishing the cost of possible contract provisions:* Wages have not only a direct influence on labor costs but often an indirect effect on benefit costs (such as Social Security and paid vacation). Recall that benefits add about 46 cents to every dollar's worth of wages. Also, wage or benefit increases that seem manageable in the first year of a contract can accumulate to less manageable levels over time.

6. *Preparing for a strike:* If management intends to operate during a strike, it may need to line up replacement workers, increase its security, and figure out how to deal with incidents on the picket line and elsewhere. If management does not intend to operate during a strike (or if the company will not be operating at normal levels), it needs to alert suppliers and customers and consider possible ways to avoid the loss of their business. This could even entail purchasing a competitor's product in order to have something to sell to customers.

7. *Determining strategy and logistics:* Decisions must be made about the amount of authority the negotiating team will have. What concessions can it make on its own, and which ones require it to check with top management? On which issues can it compromise, and on which can it not? Decisions regarding meeting places and times must also be made.

## NEGOTIATION STAGES AND TACTICS

Negotiations go through various stages.[62] In the early stages, many more people are often present than in later stages. On the union side, this may give all the various internal interest groups a chance to participate and voice their goals. This, in turn, helps send a message to management about what the union feels it must do to satisfy its members, and it may also help the union achieve greater solidarity. Union negotiators often present an extensive list of proposals at this stage, partly to satisfy their constituents and partly to provide themselves with issues on which they can show flexibility later in the process. Management may or may not present proposals of its own; sometimes it prefers to react to the union's proposals.

During the middle stages, each side must make a series of decisions, even though the outcome is uncertain. How important is each issue to the other side? How likely is it that disagreement on particular issues will result in a strike? When and to what extent should one side signal its willingness to compromise on its position?

In the final stage, pressure for an agreement increases as the deadline for a strike approaches. Public negotiations may be only part of the process. Negotiators from each side may have one-on-one meetings or small-group meetings where public relations pressures are reduced. In addition, a neutral third party may become involved, someone who can act as a go-between or facilitator. In some cases, the only way for the parties to convince each other of their resolve (or to convince their own constituents of the other party's resolve) is to allow an impasse to occur.

Various books suggest how to avoid impasses by using mutual gains or integrative bargaining tactics. For example, *Getting to Yes*, by Roger Fisher and William Ury, describes four basic principles:[63]

1. Separate the people from the problem.
2. Focus on interests, not positions.
3. Generate a variety of possibilities before deciding what to do.
4. Insist that the results be based on some objective standard.

## BARGAINING POWER, IMPASSES, AND IMPASSE RESOLUTION

Employers' and unions' conflicting goals are resolved through the negotiation process just described. An important determinant of the outcome of this process is the relative bargaining power of each party, which can be defined as the "ability of one party to achieve its goals when faced with opposition from some other party to the bargaining process."[64] In collective bargaining, an important element of power is the relative ability of each party to withstand a strike. Although strikes in the United States are rare, the threat of a strike often looms large in labor–management negotiations. The relative ability to take a strike, whether one occurs or not, is an important determinant of bargaining power and, therefore, of bargaining outcomes.

## MANAGEMENT'S WILLINGNESS TO TAKE A STRIKE

Management's willingness to take a strike comes down to two questions:

1. *Can the company remain profitable over the long run if it agrees to the union's demands?* The answer is more likely to be yes to the extent that higher labor costs can be passed on to consumers without losing business. This, in turn, is most likely when the price increase is small because labor costs are a small fraction of total costs or there is little price competition in the industry. Low price competition can result from regulated prices, from competition based on quality (rather than price), or from the union's organizing all or most of the employers in the industry, which eliminates labor costs as a price factor. Unions share part of management's concern with long-term competitiveness because a decline in competitiveness can translate into a decline in employment levels. However, the majority of union members may prefer to have higher wages, despite employment declines, particularly if a minority of the members (those with low seniority) suffer more employment loss and the majority keep their employment with higher wages.

2. *Can the company continue to operate in the short run despite a strike?* Although "hanging tough" on its bargaining goals may pay off for management in the long run, the short-run concern is the loss of revenues and profits from production being disrupted. The cost to strikers is a loss of wages and possibly a permanent loss of jobs.

Under what conditions is management most able to take a strike? The following factors are important:[65]

1. *Product demand:* Management is less able to afford a strike when the demand for its product is strong because that is when more revenue and profits are lost.
2. *Product perishability:* A strike by certain kinds of employees (farm workers at harvest time, truckers transporting perishable food, airline employees at peak travel periods) will result in permanent losses of revenue, thus increasing the cost of the strike to management.
3. *Technology:* An organization that is capital intensive (versus labor intensive) is less dependent on its employees and more likely to be able to use supervisors or others as replacements. Telephone companies are typically able to operate through strikes, even though installing new equipment or services and repair work may take significantly longer than usual.
4. *Availability of replacement workers:* When jobs are scarce, replacement workers are more available and perhaps more willing to cross picket lines. Using replacement

workers to operate during a strike raises the stakes considerably for strikers who may be permanently replaced. Most strikers are not entitled to reinstatement until there are job openings for which they qualify. If replacements were hired, such openings may not occur for some time (if at all). In some cases, companies can use managers to temporarily replace striking workers. For example, decades ago, the third author of this text recalls his father, a manager at Ohio Bell in Cleveland, going to New York Bell in New York state to cover for jobs left open by striking workers. (Years before that, he was walking the picket line on strike before he got promoted.) More recently, Caterpillar prepared for a possible strike by "training managerial and support staff for production jobs" at one of its plants.[66]

5. *Multiple production sites and staggered contracts:* Multiple sites and staggered contracts permit employers to shift production from the struck facility to facilities that, even if unionized, have contracts that expire at different times (so they are not able to strike at the same time). For decades, Boeing's production of key aircraft was limited to its unionized Seattle location. It subsequently opened a second production facility in South Carolina, the state with the lowest union membership. Boeing has been successful in its goal of keeping the second production facility nonunion and it can now use it as leverage in negotiations with its unionized workers in Seattle.[67]

6. *Integrated facilities:* When one facility produces something that other facilities need for their products, the employer is less able to take a strike because the disruption to production goes beyond that single facility. The just-in-time production system, which provides very little stockpiling of parts, further weakens management's ability to take a strike.

7. *Lack of substitutes for product:* A strike is more costly to the employer if customers have a readily available alternative source from which to purchase the goods or services the company provides.

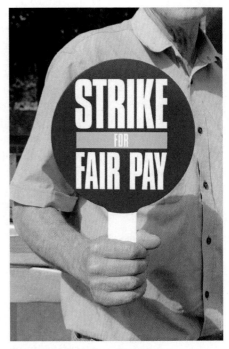

Chris Cooper-Smith/Alamy Stock Photo
Management has several factors to consider before taking on a strike. Most negotiations do not result in a strike since it is often not in the best interests of either party.

Bargaining outcomes also depend on the nature of the bargaining process and relationship, which includes the types of tactics used and the history of labor relations. The vast majority of labor–management negotiations do not result in a strike because a strike is typically not in the best interests of either party. Furthermore, both the union and management usually realize that if they wish to interact effectively in the future, the experience of a strike can be difficult to overcome. When strikes do occur, the conduct of each party during the strike can also have a lasting effect on labor–management relations. Violence by either side or threats of job loss by hiring replacements can make future relations difficult.

## IMPASSE RESOLUTION PROCEDURES: ALTERNATIVES TO STRIKES

Given the substantial costs of strikes to both parties, procedures that resolve conflicts without strikes have arisen in both the private and public sectors. Because many public-sector employees do not have the right to strike, alternatives are particularly important in that arena. In the private sector, alternatives may be used to avoid a strike or to help settle an ongoing dispute and end a strike.

Three often-used impasse resolution procedures are mediation, fact finding, and arbitration. All of them rely on the intervention of a neutral third party, most typically provided by the Federal Mediation and Conciliation Service (FMCS), which must be notified 60 days prior to contract expiration and 30 days prior to a planned change in contract terms (including a strike). Each year, the FMCS's annual report describes its activities in avoiding disputes and in settling ongoing disputes.[68] **Mediation** is the least formal but most widely used of the procedures (in both the public and private sectors). One survey found it was used by nearly 40% of all large private-sector bargaining units.[69] A mediator has no formal authority but, rather, acts as a facilitator and go-between in negotiations.

A **fact finder**, most commonly used in the public sector, typically reports on the reasons for the dispute, the views and arguments of both sides, and (in some cases) a recommended settlement, which the parties are free to decline. That these recommendations are made public may give rise to public pressure for a settlement. Even if a fact finder's settlement is not accepted, the hope is that he or she will identify or frame issues in such a way as to facilitate an agreement. Sometimes, for the simple reason that fact finding takes time, the parties reach a settlement during the interim.

The most formal type of outside intervention is **arbitration**, under which a solution is actually chosen by an arbitrator (or arbitration board). In some instances the arbitrator can fashion a solution (conventional arbitration). In other cases the arbitrator must choose either the management's or union's final offer (final offer arbitration) on either the contract as a whole or on an issue-by-issue basis. Traditionally, arbitrating the enforcement or interpretation of contract terms (rights arbitration) has been widely accepted, whereas arbitrating the actual writing or setting of contract terms (interest arbitration, our focus here) has been reserved for special circumstances. These include some public-sector negotiations, where strikes may be especially costly (such as those by police or firefighters) and a very few private-sector situations, where strikes have been especially debilitating to both sides (the steel industry in the 1970s).[70] One reason for avoiding greater use of interest arbitration is a strong belief that the parties closest to the situation (unions and management, not an arbitrator) are in the best position to effectively resolve their conflicts.

**Mediation**
A procedure for resolving collective bargaining impasses by which a mediator with no formal authority acts as a facilitator and go-between in the negotiations.

**Fact finder**
A person who reports on the reasons for a labor–management dispute, the views and arguments of both sides, and a nonbinding recommendation for settling the dispute.

**Arbitration**
A procedure for resolving collective bargaining impasses by which an arbitrator chooses a solution to the dispute.

# Union and Management Interactions: Contract Administration

## GRIEVANCE PROCEDURE

Although the negotiation process (and the occasional resulting strike) receives the most publicity, the negotiation process typically occurs only about every three years, whereas contract administration goes on day after day, year after year. The two processes—negotiation and administration—are linked, of course. Vague or incomplete contract language developed in the negotiation process can make administration of the contract difficult. Such difficulties can, in turn, create conflict that can spill over into the next negotiation process.[71] Furthermore, events during the negotiation process—strikes, the use of replacement workers, or violence by either side—can lead to management and labor difficulties in working successfully under a contract.

A key influence on successful contract administration is the grievance procedure for resolving labor–management disputes over the interpretation and execution of the contract. During World War II, the War Labor Board helped institutionalize the use of arbitration as an alternative to strikes to settle disputes that arose during the term of the contract. The soon-to-follow Taft-Hartley Act further reinforced this preference. Today the great majority of grievance procedures have binding arbitration as a final step, and only a minority of strikes occur during the term of a contract. (Most occur during the negotiation stage.) Strikes during the term of a contract can be especially disruptive because they are more unpredictable than strikes during the negotiation phase, which occur only at regular intervals.

Beyond its ability to reduce strikes, a grievance procedure can be judged using three criteria.[72] First, how well are day-to-day contract questions resolved? Time delays and heavy use of the procedure may indicate problems. Second, how well does the grievance procedure adapt to changing circumstances? For example, if the company's business turns downward and the company needs to cut costs, how clear are the provisions relating to subcontracting of work, layoffs, and so forth? Third, in multiunit contracts, how well does the grievance procedure permit local contract issues (like work rules) to be included and resolved?[73]

From the employees' perspective, the grievance procedure is the key to fair treatment in the workplace, and its effectiveness rests both on the degree to which employees feel they can use it without fear of recrimination and whether they believe their case will be carried forward strongly enough by their union representative. The **duty of fair representation** is mandated by the NLRA and requires that all bargaining unit members, whether union members or not, have equal access to and representation by the union in the grievance procedure. Too many grievances may indicate a problem, but so may too few. A very low grievance rate may suggest a fear of filing a grievance, a belief that the system is not effective, or a belief that representation is not adequate.

As Table 14.12 suggests, most grievance procedures have several steps prior to arbitration. Moreover, the majority of grievances are settled during the earlier steps of the

**Duty of fair representation**
The National Labor Relations Act requirement that all bargaining unit members have equal access to and representation by the union.

**Table 14.12**
Steps in a Typical Grievance Procedure

**Employee-initiated grievance**

**Step 1**
1. Employee discusses grievance or problem orally with supervisor.
2. Union steward and employee may discuss problem orally with supervisor.
3. Union steward and employee decide (1) whether problem has been resolved or (2) if not resolved, whether a contract violation has occurred.

**Step 2**
1. Grievance is put in writing and submitted to production superintendent or other designated line manager.
2. Steward and management representative meet and discuss grievance. Management's response is put in writing. A member of the industrial relations staff may be consulted at this stage.

**Step 3**
1. Grievance is appealed to top line management and industrial relations staff representatives. Additional local or international union officers may become involved in discussions. Decision is put in writing.

**Step 4**
1. Union decides on whether to appeal unresolved grievance to arbitration according to procedures specified in its constitution and/or bylaws.
2. Grievance is appealed to arbitration for binding decision.

**Discharge grievance**
1. Procedure may begin at step 2 or step 3.
2. Time limits between steps may be shorter to expedite the process.

**Union or group grievance**
1. Union representative initiates grievance at step 1 or step 2 on behalf of affected class of workers or union representatives.

SOURCE: From H. C. Katz, T. A. Kochan, and A. J. S. Colvin, *An Introduction to Collective Bargaining and Industrial Relations*, 4th ed. (New York: McGraw-Hill, 2008). Reprinted with permission of The McGraw-Hill Companies, Inc.

process, which is desirable both to reduce time delays and to avoid the costs of arbitration. If the grievance does reach arbitration, the arbitrator makes the final ruling in the matter. A series of Supreme Court decisions in 1960, commonly known as the Steelworkers' Trilogy, established that the courts should essentially refrain from reviewing the merits of arbitrators' decisions and, instead, limit judicial review to the question of whether the issue was subject to arbitration under the contract.[74] Furthermore, unless the contract explicitly states that an issue is not subject to arbitration, it will be assumed that arbitration is an appropriate means of deciding the issue. Giving further strength to the role of arbitration is the NLRB's general policy of deferring to arbitration.

What types of issues most commonly reach arbitration? Data from the FMCS on a total of 2,473 grievances show that discharge and disciplinary issues topped the list with 913 cases.[75] Other frequent issues include the use of seniority in promotion, layoffs, transfers, work assignments, and scheduling (309 cases); wages (178); and benefits (127).

What criteria do arbitrators use to reach a decision? In the most common case—discharge or discipline—the following due process questions are important:[76]

1. *Did the employee know what the rule or expectation was and what the consequences of not adhering to it were?*
2. *Was the rule applied in a consistent and predictable way?* In other words, are all employees treated the same?
3. *Are facts collected in a fair and systematic manner?* An important element of this principle is detailed record keeping. Both employee actions (such as tardiness) and management's response (verbal or written warnings) should be carefully documented.
4. *Does the employee have the right to question the facts and present a defense?* An example in a union setting is a hearing with a shop steward present.
5. *Does the employee have the right to appeal a decision?* An example is recourse to an impartial third party, such as an arbitrator.
6. *Is there progressive discipline?* Except perhaps for severe cases, an arbitrator will typically look for evidence that an employee was alerted as early as possible that behavior was inappropriate and the employee was given a chance to change prior to some form of severe discipline, such as discharge.
7. *Are there unique mitigating circumstances?* Although discipline must be consistent, individuals differ in terms of their prior service, performance, and discipline record. All of these factors may need to be considered.

## COOPERATIVE LABOR–MANAGEMENT STRATEGIES

**LO 14-5**
Describe new, less adversarial approaches to labor–management relations.

Jack Barbash described the nature of the traditional relationship between labor and management (during both the negotiation and administration phases) as follows:

> Bargaining is a love–hate, cooperation–conflict relationship. The parties have a common interest in maximizing the total revenue which finances their respective returns. But they take on adversarial postures in debating how the revenue shall be divided as between wages and profits. It is the adversarial posture which has historically set the tone of the relationship.[77]

Although there had always been exceptions to the adversarial approach, one reading is that there has been a general trend toward less adversarial workplace relations (at least where the union's role is accepted by management).[78] This transformation has two basic objectives: (1) to increase the involvement of individuals and work groups in overcoming adversarial relations and increasing employee commitment, motivation, and problem solving and (2) to reorganize work so that work rules are minimized and flexibility in managing people is maximized. These objectives are especially important for companies that need to be able to shift production quickly in response to changes in markets and customer demands. The specific programs aimed at achieving these objectives include employee involvement in decision making, self-managing employee teams, labor–management problem-solving teams, broadly defined jobs, and sharing of financial gains and business information with employees. Examples include the labor–management relationships at Ford, Harley-Davidson, and Chrysler's engine plant in Dundee, Michigan.[79]

The Dundee engine plant is not only an example of a new approach to labor relations. It also has the blessing of the UAW. Why? According to the president of the UAW local, "It's a question of survival." Hourly workers at the plant are highly educated and skilled and rotate through different jobs to provide skill flexibility to support production flexibility, engage workers, and reduce repetitive motion injuries. Unlike a traditional plant where there can be scores of hourly job classifications/titles, the Dundee plant has only two: team member and team leader. There are no supervisors. Team leaders, rather than only observing, work alongside teams of six team members. The guiding principles are captured by what are called the "four As": "anyone can do anything anytime, anywhere." That is much different from the more typical idea of "if it's not in my job description, I don't have to do it, I won't do it, and if I did do it, I would probably get in trouble." The UAW was concerned at first with the "four As" approach because without narrow job descriptions, management has more discretion, and workers less discretion, in what workers do each day. As the UAW put it, it could allow management to "pull out anybody, anytime." However, the need for flexibility in production is so central to the success of the plant in a global competitive environment and to Chrysler being willing to make future investments (the key to jobs) in the plant that the UAW leadership agreed. The team approach, job rotation, and flexibility expectations translate into higher skill and education requirements. Hourly workers at the plant must have a two-year technical degree, hold a skilled journeyman's card, or have had several years of experience in advanced manufacturing.[80]

Union resistance to such programs has often been substantial, precisely because the programs seek to change workplace relations and the role that unions play. Without the union's support, these programs are less likely to survive and less likely to be effective if they do survive.[81] Union leaders have often feared that such programs will weaken unions' role as an independent representative of employee interests. Indeed, according to the NLRA, to "dominate or interfere with the formation or administration of any labor organization or contribute financial or other support to it" is an unfair labor practice. An example of a prohibited practice is "taking an active part in organizing a union or committee to represent employees."[82]

One case that has received much attention is that of Electromation, a small electrical parts manufacturer. In 1992 the NLRB ruled that the company had violated Section 8(a)(2) of the NLRA by setting up worker–management committees (typically about six workers and one or two managers) to solve problems having to do with absenteeism and pay scales.[83] The original complaint was filed by the Teamsters union, which was trying to organize the (nonunion) company and felt that the committees were, in effect, illegally competing with them to be workers' representatives. Similarly, Polaroid dissolved an employee committee that had been in existence for over 40 years in response to the U.S. Department of Labor's claim that it violated the NLRA. The primary functions of the employee committee had been to represent employees in grievances and to advise senior management on issues such as pay and company rules and regulations. In a third case, the NLRB ruled in 1993 that seven worker–management safety committees at DuPont were illegal under the NLRA because they were dominated by management. The committee members were chosen by management and their decisions were subject to the approval of the management members of the committees. Finally, the committees made decisions about issues that were mandatory subjects of bargaining with the employees' elected representative—the chemical workers' union.[84] The impact of such cases will be felt both in nonunion companies, as union organizers move to fill the worker representation vacuum, and in unionized companies, as managers find they must deal more directly and effectively with their unions.

Employers must take care that employee involvement meets the legal test, but the NLRB has clearly supported the legality of involvement in important cases. For example, in a 2001 ruling, the NLRB found that the use of seven employee participation committees at a Crown Cork & Seal aluminum can manufacturing plant did not violate federal labor law. The committees in question make and implement decisions regarding a wide range of issues, including production, quality, training, safety, and certain types of worker discipline. The NLRB determined that these committees were not employer-dominated labor organizations, which would have violated federal labor law. Instead of "dealing with" management in a bilateral manner where proposals are made that are either rejected or accepted by management, the teams and committees exercise authority, delegated by management, to operate the plant within certain parameters. Indeed, the NLRB noted that rather than "dealing with management," the evidence indicated that within delegated areas of authority, the teams and committees "are management." This authority was found to be similar to that delegated to a first-line supervisor. Thus the charge that the teams and committees did not have final decision-making authority (and so were not acting in a management capacity) did not weigh heavily with the NLRB, which noted, "Few, if any, supervisors in a conventional plant have authority that is final and absolute." Instead, it was noted that managers typically make recommendations that move up through "the chain of command."[85] Table 14.13 summarizes factors that may indicate a team or committee is in violation of national labor law.

Although there are legal concerns to address, some evidence suggests that these new approaches to labor relations—incorporating greater employee participation in decisions, using employee teams, multiskilling, rotating jobs, and sharing financial gains—can contribute significantly to an organization's effectiveness,[86] as well as to workers' wages and

**Table 14.13**
When Teams or Employee Participation May Be Illegal

| Primary factors to look for that could mean a team violates national labor law: | |
| --- | --- |
| Representation | Does the team address issues affecting nonteam employees? (Does it represent other workers?) |
| Subject matter | Do discussions include "mandatory bargaining subjects" such as wages, grievances, hours of work, and working conditions. (An employee group that only makes recommendations about production and process might not be a risk.) Also, who sets the agenda for meetings? If it is management, that increases the risk. |
| Management involvement | Does the team deal with any supervisors, managers, or executives on any issue? |
| Employer domination | Did the company create the team or decide what it would do and how it would function? Did the company decide which employees would be on the team? (There is less risk if employees initiated and organized the participation program.) |

SOURCE: From *Bloomberg Businessweek*, January 25, 1993; T. Mahoney and A. Drutchas, "Could Your Employee Participation Program Be Illegal?" *Society for Human Resource Management*, June 9, 2016, www.shrm.org.

**Table 14.14**
Patterns in Labor–
Management
Relations Using
Traditional and
Transformational
Approaches

| | PATTERN | |
|---|---|---|
| **DIMENSION** | **TRADITIONAL** | **TRANSFORMATIONAL** |
| **Conflict resolution** | | |
| Frequency of conflicts | High | Low |
| Speed of conflict resolution | Slow | Fast |
| Informal resolution of grievances | Low | High |
| Third- and fourth-step grievances | High | Low |
| **Shop-floor cooperation** | | |
| Formal problem-solving groups (such as quality, reducing scrap, employment security) | Low | High |
| Informal problem-solving activity | Low | High |
| **Worker autonomy and feedback** | | |
| Formal autonomous work groups | Low | High |
| Informal worker autonomous activity | Low | High |
| Worker-initiated changes in work design | Low | High |
| Feedback on cost, quality, and schedule | Low | High |

SOURCE: Adapted from J. Cutcher-Gershenfeld, "The Impact on Economic Performance of a Transformation in Work-Place Relations," *Industrial and Labor Relations Review* 44 (1991), pp. 241–60. Reprinted with permission.

job satisfaction.[87] Indeed, these practices are now often referred to as *high-performance work systems*. One study, for example, compared the features of traditional and transformational approaches to labor relations at Xerox.[88] As Table 14.14 indicates, the transformational approach was characterized by better conflict resolution, more shop-floor cooperation, and greater worker autonomy and feedback in decision making. Furthermore, compared with the traditional approach, transformational labor relations were found to be associated with lower costs, better product quality, and higher productivity. Several years ago, a presidential commission concluded that the evidence is "overwhelming that employee participation and labor–management partnerships are good for workers, firms, and the national economy." National survey data also indicate that most employees want more influence in workplace decisions and believe that such influence leads to more effective organizations.[89] Further evidence (see the Evidence-Based HR box) suggests that these high-performance work systems work well across countries.

# Labor Relations Outcomes

The effectiveness of labor relations can be evaluated from management, labor, and societal perspectives.[90] Management seeks to control costs and enhance productivity and quality. Labor unions seek to raise wages and benefits and exercise control over how employees spend their time at work (such as through work rules). Each of the three parties typically seeks to avoid forms of conflict (like strikes) that impose significant costs on everyone. In this section we examine several outcomes.

# EVIDENCE-BASED HR

A few years ago, a study provided a review of the effect of high-performance work systems (HPWSs) on business performance at the level of the plant and the firm. HPWSs are human resource practices (e.g., selective hiring, strong training/development, worker involvement in decision, pay for performance) that aim to increase worker contributions to business performance. Conventional wisdom is that these practices are best suited to the United States or perhaps a few other countries (e.g., the United Kingdom) whose organizations are seen as having an "Anglo-Saxon" approach to management and are not likely to work as well in other countries due to the greater strength of unions, different legal frameworks, and/or cultural differences. However, many global companies standardize their employment policies despite these differences and feel that they can be successful. That is not to say that policies are executed in the exact same manner in all countries, but the broad policies are consistent. For example, a company may involve workers in decisions, but in Germany it may be mandated in certain sectors of the economy, whereas in the United States it is not but instead is done according to the employer's choice.

So, what does the evidence from the study say? The following table reports the mean correlation, mean $r$, between use of HPWSs and business performance, as well as the number of studies conducted in each country, $K$, and the number of firms/establishments included, $N$, in those $K$ studies in each country. The 95% confidence interval is also reported. Results for the four countries with the largest $K$ outside of the United States are reported separately.

| COUNTRY OR REGION | $K$ | $N$ | MEAN $r$ | 95% CONFIDENCE INTERVAL FOR MEAN $r$ |
|---|---|---|---|---|
| United States | 48 | 11,309 | .23 | .20 to .26 |
| Non–United States | 108 | 24,458 | .22 | .18 to .26 |
| China | 16 | 3,692 | .35 | .26 to .43 |
| Korea | 8 | 1,899 | .26 | .17 to .36 |
| Spain | 13 | 3,430 | .20 | .14 to .26 |
| United Kingdom | 13 | 2,758 | .16 | .06 to .26 |

These countries differ significantly in terms of national culture (see Chapter 15) and in terms of union strength. (For example, in Spain, 70% of employees are covered by collective bargaining agreements versus 13% in the United States.) In looking at this pattern of results, ask yourself the following questions: (1) Is the mean $r$ different in the United States versus outside the United States? (2) Is the mean $r$ negative in any country? (3) Does the confidence interval include .00 for any country? Keeping in mind the caveat that policies can (and sometimes must) be implemented differently in different countries, what do these results say about the claim that policies must be tailored to the country?

SOURCE: T. Rabl, M. Jayasinghe, B. Gerhart, and T. M. Kühlmann, "A Meta-Analysis of Country Differences in the High-Performance Work System–Business Performance Relationship: The Roles of National Culture and Managerial Discretion," *Journal of Applied Psychology* 99, no. 6 (2014), pp. 1011–41.

| YEAR | STOPPAGES | NUMBER OF WORKERS (THOUSANDS) | PERCENTAGE OF TOTAL WORKING TIME LOST |
|------|-----------|-------------------------------|----------------------------------------|
| 1950 | 424 | 1,698 | 0.26% |
| 1955 | 363 | 2,055 | 0.16 |
| 1960 | 222 | 896 | 0.09 |
| 1965 | 268 | 999 | 0.10 |
| 1970 | 381 | 2,468 | 0.29 |
| 1975 | 235 | 965 | 0.09 |
| 1980 | 187 | 795 | 0.09 |
| 1985 | 54 | 324 | 0.03 |
| 1990 | 44 | 185 | 0.02 |
| 1995 | 31 | 192 | 0.02 |
| 2000 | 39 | 394 | 0.06 |
| 2005 | 22 | 100 | 0.01 |
| 2010 | 11 | 45 | <0.005 |
| 2015 | 12 | 47 | <0.005 |
| 2016 | 15 | 99 | <0.005 |
| 2017 | 7 | 25 | <0.005 |

**Table 14.15**
Work Stoppages Involving 1,000 or More Workers

SOURCE: U.S. Bureau of Labor Statistics, *Major Work Stoppages in 2017*. USDL-18-0206, February 9, 2018, https://www.bls.gov.

## STRIKES

Table 14.15 presents data on strikes in the United States that involved 1,000 or more employees. Of the 15 large strikes in 2016, four were in health care (nurses) and three were in education (teachers in two cases, university faculty in the other), and two were among county government employees. The remaining work stoppages were among long-shoremen, cleaners, communication workers (at Verizon and AT&T), painting and decorating employees, and transport workers. So most of the strikes involved white-collar employees. None were in manufacturing. Because strikes are more likely in large units, the lack of data on smaller units is probably not a major concern, although such data would, of course, raise the figure on the estimated time lost to strikes. For example, for the 1960s, this estimate is 0.12% using data on strikes involving 1,000 or more employees versus 0.17% for all strikes. Although strikes impose significant costs on union members, employers, and society, it is clear from Table 14.15 that strikes are the exception rather than the rule. Very little working time is lost to strikes in the United States (with annual work hours of 1,800, less than 6 minutes per worker and less than one hour per unionized worker in 2017) and their frequency in recent years is generally low by historical standards. Does this mean that the industrial relations system is working well? Not necessarily. Those who believe labor should be strong to represent its members would view the low number (by historical standards) of strikes as another sign that labor is too weak to do so.

## WAGES AND BENEFITS

Table 14.16 compares wages and benefits of union members to nonunion members using both a survey of working individuals (CPS) and a survey of employers/establishments (NCS). Unionized and/or union-represented workers almost always receive higher

**Table 14.16**

Compensation, Union versus Nonunion Employees, United States, Worker Survey and Employer Survey

| | | MEDIAN WEEKLY EARNINGS BY UNION REPRESENTATION AND % IN UNION, FULL-TIME WORKERS[a] (WORKER SURVEY) | | |
| --- | --- | --- | --- | --- |
| | | | MEDIAN WEEKLY EARNINGS | |
| | % IN UNION | UNION REPRESENTED | NONUNION | UNION/ NONUNION |
| All | 10.5 | $ 1,042 | $ 860 | 1.21 |
| Men | 12.2 | 1,121 | 948 | 1.18 |
| Women | 11.1 | 958 | 764 | 1.25 |
| Management and professional | 11.2 | 1,222 | 1,250 | 0.98 |
| Service | 9.8 | 781 | 541 | 1.44 |
| Sales and office | 6.5 | 828 | 735 | 1.13 |
| Production, transportation, and material moving | 13.3 | 913 | 680 | 1.34 |
| Private sector | 6.4 | 989 | 848 | 1.17 |
| Public sector | 33.9 | 1,094 | 936 | 1.17 |
| | HOURLY WAGES/SALARIES, BENEFITS, AND TOTAL COMPENSATION (EMPLOYER SURVEY) | | | |
| | | UNION MEMBERS | NONUNION | UNION/ NONUNION |
| Total compensation | | $48.57 | $33.16 | 1.46 |
| Wages and salaries | | $28.85 | $23.59 | 1.22 |
| Benefits | | $19.73 | $ 9.57 | 2.06 |

[a]Part-time workers (6.2%) are less likely than full-time workers (12.8%) to be union members.

SOURCES: Median weekly earnings and percentages in union data based on the Current Population Surveys: U.S. Bureau of Labor Statistics, *Union Members–2018*, USDL-19-0079, January 18, 2019; wages/salaries, benefits, and total compensation data, based on a survey of employers, are from U.S. Bureau of Labor Statistics, National Compensation Survey (NCS), *Employer Costs for Employee Compensation—September 2018*. USDL-18-1941, December 14, 2018; the worker survey includes civilian (private-sector and public-sector) employees. The employer survey includes private-sector employees only.

compensation than their nonunion counterparts, depending on the survey.[91] Based on the employer survey data, the effect of unions on total compensation is especially large because of an even larger effect of unions on benefits than on earnings (wages and salaries).[92] However, these are raw differences. To assess the net effect of unions more accurately, adjustments must be made.[93] We now briefly highlight a few of these.

The union wage effect is likely to be overestimated to the extent that unions can more easily organize workers who are already highly paid or who are more productive. The gap is likely to be underestimated to the extent that nonunion employers raise wages and benefits in response to the perceived "union threat" in the hope that their employees will then have less interest in union representation. When these and other factors are taken into account, the net union advantage in wages, though still substantial, is reduced by as much as one-half. The union benefits advantage is also reduced, but it remains larger than the union wage effect, and the union effect on total compensation is therefore larger than the wage effect alone.[94]

Beyond differences in pay and benefits, unions typically influence the way pay and promotions are determined. Whereas management often seeks to deal with employees as individuals, emphasizing performance differences in pay and promotion decisions, unions seek to build group solidarity and avoid the possibly arbitrary treatment of employees. To do so, unions focus on equal pay for equal work. Any differences among employees in pay or promotions, they say, should be based on seniority (an objective measure) rather than on performance (a subjective measure susceptible to favoritism). It is very common in union settings for there to be a single rate of pay for all employees in a particular job classification.

Although wages and benefits are higher for union members, job satisfaction is lower, on average.[95] Reasons include less positive perceptions of supervision, promotion opportunities, and the interest and discretion in their work. Given that dissatisfaction is an important driver of union activity, it may be that unionization is part consequence (workers in worse jobs are more likely to organize), as well as part cause of job dissatisfaction.

## PRODUCTIVITY

There has been much debate regarding the effects of unions on productivity.[96] Unions are believed to decrease productivity in at least three ways: (1) The union pay advantage causes employers to use less labor and more capital per worker than they would otherwise, which reduces efficiency across society; (2) union contract provisions may limit permissible workloads, restrict the tasks that particular workers are allowed to perform, and require employers to use more employees for certain jobs than they otherwise would; and (3) strikes, slowdowns, and working-to-rule (slowing down production by following every workplace rule to an extreme) result in lost production.[97]

On the other hand, unions can have positive effects on productivity.[98] Employees, whether members of a union or not, communicate to management regarding how good a job it is doing by either the "exit" or "voice" mechanisms. "Exit" refers to simply leaving the company to work for a better employer. "Voice" refers to communicating one's concerns to management without necessarily leaving the employer. Unions are believed to increase the operation and effectiveness of the voice mechanism.[99] This, in turn, is likely to reduce employee turnover and its associated costs. More broadly, voice can be seen as including the union's contribution to the success of labor–management cooperation programs that make use of employee suggestions and increased involvement in decisions. A second way that unions can increase productivity is (perhaps ironically) through their emphasis on the use of seniority in pay, promotion, and layoff decisions. Although management typically prefers to rely more heavily on performance in such decisions, using seniority has a potentially important advantage—namely, it reduces competition among workers. As a result, workers may be less reluctant to share their knowledge with less senior workers because they do not have to worry about less senior workers taking their jobs. Finally, the introduction of a union may have a "shock effect" on management, pressuring it into tightening standards and accountability and paying greater heed to employee input in the design and management of production.[100]

Although there is evidence that unions have both positive and negative effects on productivity, most studies have found that union workers are more productive than nonunion workers. Nevertheless, it is generally recognized that most of the findings on this issue are open to a number of alternative explanations, making any clear conclusions difficult. For example, if unions raise productivity, why has union representation of employees declined over time, even within industries?[101] A related concern is that unionized establishments are more likely to survive where there is some inherent productivity advantage unrelated to unionism that actually offsets a negative impact of unionism. If so, these establishments would be overrepresented, whereas establishments that did not survive the negative impact of unions would be underrepresented. Consequently, any negative impact of unions on productivity would be underestimated.

## PROFITS AND STOCK PERFORMANCE

Even if unions do raise productivity, a company's profits and stock performance may still suffer if unions raise costs (such as wages) or decrease investment by a greater amount. Evidence shows that unions have a large negative effect on profits and that union coverage tends to decline more quickly in firms experiencing lower shareholder returns, suggesting that some firms become more competitive partly by reducing union strength.[102] Similarly, one study found that each dollar of unexpected increase in collectively bargained labor costs resulted in a dollar reduction in shareholder wealth. Another study estimated that if policies were changed to encourage the unionization rate in the United States to double, the value of shareholder equity in newly organized firms would be decreased by 4.3%.[103] Other research suggests that investment in research and development is lower in unionized firms.[104] Strikes, although infrequent, lower shareholder returns in both the struck companies and firms (like suppliers) linked to those companies.[105] These research findings describe the average effects of unions. The consequences of more innovative union-management relationships for profits and stock performance are less clear.

# The International Context

**LO 14-6**
Explain how changes in competitive challenges (e.g., product market competition and globalization) are influencing labor–management interactions.

Except for China, Russia, and Ukraine, the United States has more union members than any other country. (If one were to include only countries where workers can freely elect union leaders of their own choosing, then the United States would arguably rank first in union membership.) Yet, as Table 14.17 indicates, the United States has a low unionization rate (union density) relative to most countries with highly developed economies. Even more striking are differences in union coverage, the percentage of employees whose terms and conditions of employment are governed by a union contract. (See Table 14.17.) In the European Union, for example, the union coverage rate is 60.6%, meaning that the influence of labor unions far outstrips what would be implied by their membership levels

**Table 14.17**
Union Membership and Union Coverage, Selected Countries and Country Groupings

| COUNTRY | MEMBERSHIP PERCENTAGE OF EMPLOYMENT (DENSITY) | COVERAGE PERCENTAGE OF EMPLOYMENT |
|---|---|---|
| United States | 10.3 | 11.7 |
| Japan | 16.8 | 17.3 |
| European Union (28 countries) | 21.7 | 60.6 |
| OECD (36 countries) | 16.3 | 32.0 |

SOURCE: OECD, "Trends in Collective Bargaining Coverage and Trade Union Density", in *Analysis Underpinning the Framework for Policy Action on Inclusive Growth*, OECD Publishing, Paris, 2018 https://doi.org/10.1787/9789264301665-graph24-en.

(21.7%).[106] (In France, the coverage rate has traditionally been above 90%.) Why are the unionization rate and coverage comparatively low in the United States? One explanation is that the United States does not have as strong a history of deep class-based divisions in society as other countries do. For example, labor and social democratic political parties are commonplace in western Europe, and they are major players in the political process. Furthermore, the labor movement in western and northern Europe is broader than that in the United States. It extends not just to the workplace but—through its own or closely related political parties—directly into the national political process.

What is the trend in union membership rates and coverage? In the United States, we saw earlier that the trend is clearly downward, at least in the private sector. Although there have also been declines in membership rates in many other countries, coverage rates have stayed high in many of these countries. In the United States, deregulation and competition from foreign-owned companies have forced companies to become more efficient. Combined with the fact that the union wage premium in the United States is substantially larger than in other advanced industrialized countries, it is not surprising that management opposition would be higher in the United States than elsewhere.[107] This, in turn, may help explain why the decline in union influence has been especially steep in the United States.

It seems likely that—with the growing globalization of markets—labor costs and productivity will continue to be key challenges. The European Union (EU) added 10 new member countries in 2004, 2 more in 2007, and 1 more in 2013, bringing its total to 28 countries and more than 500 million people, or about 63% larger than the United States. The newer EU countries (e.g., Bulgaria, Croatia, the Czech Republic, Poland, Romania, Slovakia) have much lower wages than the existing EU countries. Closer to home, we have the North American Free Trade Agreement among the United States, Canada, and Mexico. These common market agreements mean that goods, services, and production will continue to move more freely across international borders. Where substantial differences in wages, benefits, and other costs of doing business (such as regulation) exist, there will be a tendency to move to areas that are less costly, unless skills are unavailable or productivity is significantly lower there. Unless labor unions can increase their productivity sufficiently or organize new production facilities, union influence is likely to decline.

In addition to membership and coverage, the United States differs from western Europe in the degree of formal worker participation in decision making. Works' councils (joint labor–management decision-making institutions at the enterprise level) and worker representation on supervisory boards of directors (codetermination) are mandated by law in countries such as Germany. The Scandinavian countries, Austria, and Luxembourg have similar legislation. German works' councils make decisions about changes in work or the work environment, discipline, pay systems, safety, and other human resource issues. The degree of codetermination on supervisory boards depends on the size and industry of the company. For example, in German organizations having more than 2,000 employees, half of the board members must be worker representatives. (However, the chairman of the board, a management representative, can cast a tie-breaking vote.) In contrast, worker representation on boards of directors in the United States is still rare.[108]

The works' councils exist in part because collective bargaining agreements in countries such as Germany tend to be oriented toward industrywide or regional issues, with less emphasis on local issues. However, competitive forces have led employers to increasingly opt out of centralized bargaining, even in the countries best known for centralized bargaining, like Sweden and Germany.[109]

What happens when a company from a country with low union strength operates in a country with high union strength? In the case of Amazon, an American company operating in Germany, the answer for now is that it is following its American strategy toward unions in Germany. Amazon has a works council (required by German law), and it deals with worker representatives "directly" (i.e., without the presence of a union). Verdi, a major German labor union, has been trying to change that, saying that Amazon has "a culture that we see as foreign." Amazon similarly says that, "Verdi and Amazon do not go together." Amazon and its "U.S. way of doing business" are sometimes referred to as using a "Wild West" approach to management. (This is not meant as a compliment but rather indicates the belief that there is a lack of concern for worker welfare.) Verdi has called on workers to strike. So far, those actions do not appear to have interrupted Amazon's deliveries to customers in Germany, and Amazon continues to hold to its no-union policy in Germany (as in the United States).[110]

Another interesting example is Volkswagen, a German company operating an automobile production plant in Chattanooga, Tennessee, in the United States. It has a strong, formal relationship with unions in Germany but has no union in the United States. Volkswagen has not actively opposed unionization at its U.S. plant (in contrast to the opposition unions would face from many U.S. companies). The UAW did not receive the necessary 50% + 1 votes in a recent representation election to become the sole representative of workers at VW's Chattanooga plant. Subsequently, Volkswagen, it is said under pressure from its unions in Germany, announced a new labor policy for its Chattanooga plant. Any labor group that receives (based on an independent outside audit) support from at least 15% of workers can have on-site space to post announcements and hold regular meetings with the plant's human resource department. Any group that receives support from at least 45% of workers would additionally be able to meet every two weeks with plant managers. Note that, unlike in Germany, Volkswagen is thought to be unable to use a works council at the Chattanooga plant because under U.S. labor law, it might be deemed an employer-dominated labor organization. (See our earlier discussion of the Electromation case and the closely related Table 14.13.)[111] A more recent development is that the UAW, after losing the plantwide election, did win an organizing vote (108 for, 44 against) to represent a group of skilled tradesmen at Volkswagen's Chattanooga plant. Although the group is a very small portion of the plant's 1,450 manufacturing employees (and 2,500 employees overall), this is the first time any organizing drive at a foreign-owned plant in the U.S. South has been successful. An important caveat, however, is that the UAW has not yet been able to negotiate a first contract with Volkswagen, which, as we have seen, is a step where unions often fail, even after winning an organizing vote.[112]

China is now the world's second largest economy and one of its fastest growing. Workers increasingly want to share in economic growth through higher wages and more purchasing power. That means collective action can be expected to increase. Indeed, recent research finds that the level of strike activity and labor unrest has increased dramatically in China. Moreover, strikes, which were once predominantly defensive or reactive (to protect what workers already had), have become increasingly offensive or proactive (with the aim of achieving new gains for workers, such as higher wages). In some sense, China, on its economic development path, may be now going through what the U.S. economy and labor relations went through many decades ago.[113]

As part of this, Chinese companies are learning how labor relations works differently abroad. An example of a new facility built in the United States by a Chinese company is the new Golden Dragon Precise Copper Tube Group.[114] The $120 million plant created 290 jobs for locals in Wilcox County, Alabama, one of the poorest counties in the country. Golden Dragon makes copper pipes used in air conditioning machinery. State and local governments gave Golden Dragon a variety of incentives such as free land, infrastructure, money to train workers, and a grant of $20 million. Another reason said to

## France and Labor Reforms: President Macron Says He Does Not Plan to End Up as Did Louis XVI and Marie-Antoinette

In late 2017, President Emmanuel Macron of France announced labor law reforms. A key part is making it easier for companies to undertake layoffs and/or dismissals of employees. For example, prior to the reforms, a company had to prove that it was in financial difficulty before carrying out layoffs. Penalties for running afoul of the law were substantial, and a company could be ordered to hire back employees it had dismissed. Under the new reforms, companies can instead negotiate voluntary severance agreements with employees, regardless of the company's financial situation.

Car company Peugeot plans to use the new law to reduce employment in jobs that it has wished to automate or outsource to improve efficiency. As an example, one employee who has worked at Peugeot for a decade would like to retrain to become a teacher. Peugeot will help him achieve this goal. The employee says that he and the company are no longer a good match and that "Better a good divorce than a bad marriage." Société Générale, a bank, will take advantage of the labor law reform to close 300 of its 2,000 branches and automate some of the positions that remain. The net result is a plan to cut over 3,400 jobs over the next few years. Although many of the cuts will be through attrition or redeployment of employees,

the bank also says it will use some layoffs.

More recently, there has been a violent popular revolt in France by those in the "yellow vest" movement. This movement began as a protest against an increase in the gasoline tax, which is a regressive tax that hits lower income people hardest. The protest has morphed to include at least some focus on labor law reforms as well. The yellow-vest protest lasted for about six months in 2019 in Paris and other cities, and images were beamed worldwide of protesters attacking public monuments, boutiques, banks, and police. President Macron told executives that he would stick to the labor reforms and that he would not suffer the same fate of Louis XVI and Marie-Antoinette, who were guillotined exactly 226 years earlier. Indeed, in a speech, he said that "If they met such an end, it is because they had given up on reforming." President Macron's office said that foreign companies, including Mars, Procter & Gamble, and Cisco Systems, would announce investments in France in the sum of more than 600 million euros, with the implication that this would not happen if not for his labor reforms.

Aside from the ferocity and perseverance of the protests, which may indeed seem "foreign" to those of us in the United States,

the labor-related issues may also be a bit of a surprise. For example, protesters are demanding a higher minimum wage. Such protests (e.g., the "Fight for 15" movement, which sought a minimum wage of at least $15/hour) occurred in the States, but without the violence and without lasting as long. But, consider also that the actual national minimum wage in the United States is $7.25/hour. (It is considerably higher in some states and especially some cities.) A U.S. employee working the same 35-hour workweek as a French worker would earn $1,100 per month. Consider that in France the minimum national hourly wage is $11.22, which translates into a monthly minimum of $1,701.70 per month, much higher than in the United States. Yet, the protests went on. (Of course, workers in France do pay higher taxes, reducing their take-home pay advantage, but the difference is not large enough to make a large difference.) In addition, French workers get benefits not found in the United States (e.g., free universal health care and very inexpensive public education, including higher education).

With President Macron's reforms, foreign employers like those mentioned (e.g., Mars) may indeed be more likely to invest in France, which is exactly President Macron's goal. However, there is perhaps

*CONTINUED*

influence Golden Dragon's decision to choose Alabama as the location of its new plant is that it is generally a much less union-friendly environment than in most other states, especially those in the Northeast, Midwest, and Northwest. Thus, Golden Dragon was "taken aback" when workers, who wanted higher pay and reported "difficulties in communicating with Chinese bosses," undertook a union-organizing drive shortly after the plant opened. (One example of a difference in culture might be a banner that hangs inside the factory. It says "One Quality escape erases All the good you have done in the past." Some workers describe its tone as "hectoring.") That was not expected in Alabama. Indeed, Robert Bentley, the governor of Alabama, sent letters to employees urging them to vote against the union. However, by a narrow vote, certified by the NLRB, employees chose to be represented by the United Steelworkers Union. The company is unlikely to have had any experience with union activity of the sort encountered in Alabama, as unions in China work much differently, typically in close coordination with the Communist Party. As a final note, the fact that employees at Golden Dragon in Alabama voted to join a union is only one step toward achieving employee goals. The next step, which is to successfully negotiate a contract with the company, is also necessary. That is far from automatic.

As the Competing through Globalization box demonstrates, reactions to labor-related public policies can be stronger than might often be the case in a country like the United States, even when such policies would seem "normal" from a U.S. point of view.

# The Public Sector

**LO 14-7**

Explain how labor relations in the public sector differ from labor relations in the private sector.

Unlike the private sector, union membership in the public sector grew in the 1960s and 1970s and remained fairly stable through the 1980s. As we saw earlier in Figure 14.3, 34.4% of government employees (versus 6.4% of private-sector employees) are currently union members. Like the NLRA in the private sector, changes in the legal framework contributed significantly to union growth in the public sector. One early step was the enactment in Wisconsin of collective bargaining legislation in 1959 for its state employees.[115] (However, things change. A few years ago, Wisconsin's governor signed a bill that stripped most state and local employees of most of their collective bargaining rights.) Executive Order 10988 provided collective bargaining rights for federal employees in 1962. By the end of the 1960s, most states had passed similar laws. The Civil Service Reform Act of 1978, Title VII, later established the Federal Labor Relations Authority (modeled after the NLRB). Many states have similar administrative agencies to administer their own laws.

An interesting aspect of public-sector union growth is that much of it has occurred in the service industry and among white-collar employees—groups that have traditionally been viewed as difficult to organize. Indeed, as we saw earlier in Table 14.2, of the four currently largest labor unions in the United States, two represent teachers, and the other two represent service workers and public-sector workers.

In contrast to the private sector, strikes are illegal at the federal level of the public sector and in most states. At the local level, all states prohibit strikes by police (Hawaii being a partial exception) and firefighters (Idaho being the exception). Teachers and state employees are somewhat more likely to have the right to strike, depending on the state. In 2016, of the 15 work stoppages involving 1,000 or more workers, 7 were in the public sector (primarily local government, teachers, and health care workers).

# Nonunion Representation Systems

With unions now representing just 11.1% of U.S. workers, the question is to what degree are forms of nonunion representation operating to cover the remaining 88.9% of workers? Table 14.18 indicates that in one survey, about one-third (274 of 823) of nonunion workers were covered by a representation system established by management. In other words, more workers in this survey (274) were covered by nonunion representation systems than were covered by union–management collective bargaining contracts (170). In addition, the perceptions of workers regarding how strongly worker representatives "stand up" for them and how actively they consult with them about their ideas and concerns were remarkably similar under both management-established systems and union collective bargaining agreements. That, of course, does not mean that a nonunion representation system, which ordinarily does not have the same independence and leverage as an elected labor union, is equivalent to having a collective bargaining agreement and union. But, clearly, nonunion representation systems play an important role in the workplace.[116]

**Table 14.18**
Worker Representation Systems, Union and Nonunion

| | COLLECTIVE BARGAINING AGREEMENT (N = 170) | NO COLLECTIVE BARGAINING AGREEMENT (N = 823) | |
| --- | --- | --- | --- |
| | | MANAGEMENT ESTABLISHED SYSTEM[a] (N = 274) | NO SYSTEM (N = 549) |
| Representatives can be counted on to stand up for workers, even if it means disagreeing with management[b] | 84% | 84% | NA |
| Representatives actively consult with workers about their ideas and concerns[b] | 77 | 89 | NA |
| Representatives actively consult with management over wages and benefits | 100[c] | 77 | NA |

N = 993 U.S. workers
[a]Covered by a "nonunion, management established system, where worker representatives meet with management."
[b]Sum of those responding either "To Some Extent" or "To a Great Extent."
[c]Estimated.
SOURCE: J. Godard and C. Frege, "Labor Unions, Alternative Forms of Representation, and the Exercise of Authority Relations in U.S. Workplaces," *Industrial and Labor Relations Review* 66 (2013), pp. 142–68.

# A LOOK BACK

## Labor Union Strength Continues Its Decline in the United States, but Remains a Factor in Certain Sectors

The membership rate, and thus influence, of labor unions in the United States and in many other long-industrialized countries has been on the decline in the private sector. However, even in the United States, there continue to be companies in certain sectors (e.g., automobile manufacturers, health care, education, airlines) where labor unions represent a large share of employees and thus play a major role in the operation and success of those companies. In each of these situations, effective labor relations are crucial for both companies and workers, as well as for society. In nonunion companies, employers that do not have effective employee relations are more likely to face union organizing efforts. Also, as we saw in the chapter opener, workers can take collective action without formal union representation as a possible means of improving their jobs.

### QUESTIONS

1. Many people picture labor union members as being men in blue-collar jobs in manufacturing plants. Is that accurate? Are there certain types of jobs where an employer can be fairly certain that employees will not join a union? Give examples.
2. Why do people join labor unions? Would you be interested in joining a labor union if given the opportunity? Why or why not? As a manager, would you prefer to work with a union, or would you prefer that employees not be represented by a union? Explain.
3. What led to a change in labor relations at Chrysler's Dundee engine plant? What was the nature of the change, and do you think it is an important and sustainable change?
4. What role do (or can) labor unions play in low-wage countries such as Bangladesh?

# SUMMARY

Labor unions seek to represent the interests of their members in the workplace. Although this may further the cause of industrial democracy, management often finds that unions increase labor costs while setting limits on the company's flexibility and discretion in decision making. As a result, the company may witness a diminished ability to compete effectively in a global economy. Not surprisingly, management in nonunion companies often feels compelled to actively resist the unionization of its employees. This, together with a host of economic, legal, and other factors, has contributed to union losses in membership and bargaining power in the private sector. There are some indications, however, that management and unions are seeking new, more effective ways of working together to enhance competitiveness while giving employees a voice in how workplace decisions are made.

# KEY TERMS

Checkoff provision, 625
Closed shop, 625
Union shop, 625
Agency shop 625
Maintenance of membership, 627
Taft-Hartley Act, 627

Right-to-work laws, 627
Associate union membership, 641
Corporate campaigns, 641
Distributive bargaining, 645
Integrative bargaining, 645
Attitudinal structuring, 646

Intraorganizational
   bargaining, 646
Mediation, 650
Fact finder, 650
Arbitration, 650
Duty of fair representation, 651

## DISCUSSION QUESTIONS

1. Why do employees join unions?
2. What has been the trend in union membership in the United States, and what are the underlying reasons for the trend?
3. What are the consequences for management and owners of having a union represent employees?
4. What are the general provisions of the National Labor Relations Act, and how does it affect labor–management interactions?

5. What are the features of traditional and nontraditional labor relations? What are the potential advantages of the "new" nontraditional approaches to labor relations?
6. How does the U.S. industrial and labor relations system compare with systems in other countries, such as those in western Europe?

## SELF-ASSESSMENT EXERCISE

Also assignable in Connect.

Would you join a union? Each of the following phrases expresses an opinion about the effects of a union on employees' jobs. For each phrase, circle a number on the scale to indicate whether you agree that a union would affect your job as described by the phrase.

| Having a union would result in . . . | Strongly Disagree | | | | Strongly Agree |
|---|---|---|---|---|---|
| 1. Increased wages | 1 | 2 | 3 | 4 | 5 |
| 2. Improved benefits | 1 | 2 | 3 | 4 | 5 |
| 3. Protection from being fired | 1 | 2 | 3 | 4 | 5 |
| 4. More promotions | 1 | 2 | 3 | 4 | 5 |
| 5. Better work hours | 1 | 2 | 3 | 4 | 5 |
| 6. Improved productivity | 1 | 2 | 3 | 4 | 5 |
| 7. Better working conditions | 1 | 2 | 3 | 4 | 5 |
| 8. Fewer accidents at work | 1 | 2 | 3 | 4 | 5 |
| 9. More interesting work | 1 | 2 | 3 | 4 | 5 |

| | | | | | |
|---|---|---|---|---|---|
| 10. Easier handling of employee problems | 1 | 2 | 3 | 4 | 5 |
| 11. Increased work disruptions | 5 | 4 | 3 | 2 | 1 |
| 12. More disagreements between employees and management | 5 | 4 | 3 | 2 | 1 |
| 13. Work stoppages | 5 | 4 | 3 | 2 | 1 |

Add up your total score. The highest score possible is 65; the lowest, 13. The higher your score, the more you see value in unions, and the more likely you would be to join a union.

SOURCE: Based on S. A. Youngblood, A. S. DeNisi, J. L. Molleston, and W. H. Mobley, "The Impact of Work Environment, Instrumentality Beliefs, Perceived Union Image, and Subjective Norms on Union Voting Intentions," *Academy of Management Journal* 27 (1984), pp. 576–90.

## EXERCISING STRATEGY

### Different Varieties of Collective Bargaining Contracts and Labor–Management Relations

In the opening to the chapter, we looked at JetBlue's new experience with labor unions and noted it had just negotiated its first collective bargaining contract (with its pilots). Of course, most collective bargaining contracts are negotiated in the context of long-standing unions. For example, Verizon, after a seven-week strike in 2016 by its employees, agreed to a contract in 2016 that expired in August 2019. However, in return for a promise of labor peace, Verizon and its unions (Communication Workers of America and International Brotherhood of Electrical Workers) agreed to extend the contract's terms into 2023. As another example, Kaiser Permanente recently reached a deal on a three-year contract

with its 48,000 employees, who are represented by the Alliance of Health Care Unions in 22 locations (and union locals). In addition to covering standard contract issues such as wages and benefits, the contract further strengthens the labor–management partnership, which includes 3,600 unit-based teams, jointly led by pairs of managers and union-represented employees, which focus on improving quality, affordability, service, and work environment.

Of course, most U.S. workers are not in unions, meaning that union organizing drives often fail, including in "old economy" industries. For example, employees at Boeing's aircraft production plants near Charleston, South Carolina, recently voted against joining the International Association of Machinists (IAM) union. The plants assemble 787 Dreamliner jets and are the sole location where the new 787-10, the largest jet in the Dreamliner family, is assembled. Boeing first purchased existing plants from other companies in 2004, 2008, and 2009. It then built two new aircraft production facilities that began producing planes in 2012 and 2016, respectively. The IAM claimed that Boeing employees in South Carolina make 36% less, on average, than Boeing's unionized employees building 787 aircraft in its main facility in Everett, Washington, just outside of Seattle. An IAM organizer said, "We are disheartened" that employees will continue to work in "a system that suppresses wages, fosters inconsistency and awards only a chosen few." Apparently, however, employees for the most part did not agree, as 74% voted against having the IAM union represent them. The vote perhaps reflects a general discomfort in South Carolina about the likely effect of unions on future economic development. For example, Senator Lindsey Graham and former governor and former United Nations Ambassador, Nikki Haley, both advised Boeing employees not to support a union. Senator Graham said that while he respected the right of employees at Boeing to decide what was in their best interests, he argued that what

was best for South Carolina was if "Boeing stays here and grows" and that "if you destroy the business model that led Boeing to come to South Carolina, we all lose."

## QUESTIONS

1. Why do you think that Verizon and its unions had a work stoppage during their 2016 contract negotiation, but not in their more recent contract negotiation?
2. How is the labor–management relationship at Kaiser Permanente different from some more traditional labor–management relationships? Why do you think that is?
3. Explain Boeing's reasons for wanting to have an alternative (to Seattle) to produce aircraft. Explain why it chose South Carolina.
4. If you were an employee at Boeing in South Carolina, would you have voted for or against the union? Explain.

SOURCES: "Kaiser Permanente Announces Deal with Its Unionized Employees," *NBC News*, October 4, 2018, www.nbcnews.com; A. Pressman, "Exclusive: Verizon Extends Union Contract, Avoiding Possibly Tough Labor Talks Next Year," *Fortune*, July 19, 2018, www.fortune.com; National Labor Relations Board, "Concerted Activity," www.nlrb.gov.; D. Cameron, "Boeing Workers in South Carolina Vote against Joining Union," *Wall Street Journal*, February 15, 2017; M. Ehrenfreund, "Boeing Workers in South Carolina Vote against Union," *Washington Post*, February 15, 2017.

## MANAGING PEOPLE

### Twinkies, HoHos, and Ding Dongs: No Treat for Labor Unions

Let's talk about Twinkies, HoHos and Ding Dongs. They have long been found in the snack food aisle and have even been described as having "a legendary history." One fun fact: The cream inside a Twinkie was banana flavored for many years. But when World War II brought rationing, including of bananas, Hostess changed the flavor of the cream to vanilla. OK, one more fun fact: Although there is an urban legend that Twinkies never go bad, it seems that the reality is they have a shelf life of about 25 days. That is considered quite a long shelf life for a baked good product. What is the secret? It may be that Twinkies lack any dairy products.

Unfortunately, whatever the flavor of the "cream" inside or the shelf life of a Twinkie, the company that makes them, Hostess Brands, recently declared bankruptcy. However, Metropoulos & Co. and Apollo purchased Hostess Brands, which reopened four bakery/plants, coming to the rescue of Twinkie-deprived consumers (Hostess Brands was subsequently sold again to The Gores Group).

One thing Hostess will not do going forward after reopening plants is to use union workers. The 86-year-old company closed down and entered bankruptcy, in part, due to a nationwide strike by one of its unions. Chief executive C. Dean Metropoulos said $60 million in capital investments will be

spent on the plants and that the plan is to hire at least 1,500 workers. But Mr. Metropoulos, in an interview, made his views on the role of unions clear: There will be no role.

Hostess Brands Inc. once employed 19,000 workers. Of those, 15,000 were represented by unions. The Teamsters union, which represented the largest share of Hostess Brands workers, after difficult negotiations agreed to a new collective bargaining contract following the bankruptcy trial in court. In contrast, the second-largest union, the Bakery, Confectionery, Tobacco Workers & Grain Millers International Union, began a nationwide work stoppage after failing to agree on a contract with the company, which led to the company imposing a new, less favorable contract on the union. The resulting strike, according to the company, crippled its operations, ultimately leading the company to shut down.

The company and the bakers union expressed different views on the importance of the unionized bakers. The president of the Bakers union, David Durkee, stated that because only members of the bakers union knew how to run the equipment in the plants used to bake snacks, the bakers union members would be hired back to work. In contrast, the new owners of Hostess have said that they will be able to find capable nonunion workers in the areas where plants are reopening, all located in areas where unemployment is high. Prior to bankruptcy, Hostess plants had been running at less than 50% of capacity. Going forward, the plants are expected to run at 85–90% capacity, making production much more efficient and, presumably, allowing the company to make an adequate profit. Of course, if the nonunion workers to be used going forward are also less costly, that will further bring costs down and profits up. The caveat is that it remains to be seen whether new nonunion bakers can quickly learn how to efficiently do the work in the plants. To avoid hiring Teamsters as drivers, Hostess plans to outsource driving/ delivery and related tasks. It will also outsource sales.

## QUESTIONS

1. Why did Hostess Brands Inc. go into bankruptcy?
2. Did unions act in the best interests of the workers they represented? Did the two unions involved follow the same strategy?
3. Will the new company, Hostess Brands LLC, perform better? Why or why not?

SOURCES: R. Feintzeig, "New Twinkie Maker Shuns Union Labor," *Wall Street Journal*, April 24, 2013; A. Kleinman, "Twinkie Facts: 12 Things You Didn't Know about the Beloved Snack," *Huffington Post*, November 16, 2012, www .huffingtonpost.com/2012/11/16/twinkie-facts-12-things_n_2144143.html; "Twinkies Shelf Life," www.snopes.com/food/ingredient/twinkies.asp.

# HR IN SMALL BUSINESS

## Republic Gets Serious

When Serious Materials acquired Republic Windows and Doors, union–management relations got a much-needed breath of fresh air. Republic had nearly vanished amidst economic meltdown and accusations of mismanagement and corruption. Serious Materials, by contrast, is a firm with a high-minded business strategy and a commitment to fair-mindedness.

The problems became public when workers at Republic staged a six-day sit-in at the Chicago factory, which had been one of the largest window-glass factories in the United States. When orders from construction companies stopped coming in, management, after just three days' warning, closed the plant without granting workers any severance pay or giving the legally required 60 days' notice, and filed for bankruptcy. Bowing to public pressure, the company's lenders, including Bank of America, reached an agreement to give the workers $6,000 apiece in severance pay.

But that wasn't the end. The workers turned to the National Labor Relations Board with another complaint. They said Republic's owner, Richard Gillman, had secretly begun transferring the company's machinery to a (nonunion) window-manufacturing facility he bought in Iowa just before closing the Chicago factory. In fact, all the equipment would have been gone, they said, except that their six-day occupation of the factory interfered with the plan—they wouldn't allow Gillman to enter. Employees also followed trucks carrying machinery to learn where it was being taken. The union demanded that the machinery be returned to the Chicago plant, so a new owner could operate it.

Meanwhile, a hero arrived on the scene: Kevin Surace, founder and chief executive of Serious Materials, a maker of eco-friendly building products, including energy-efficient windows. Surace saw acquisition of the Republic facility as a chance to expand into the Chicago region with a ready-made plant and equipment, not to mention trained people eager to work.

When he decided to make an offer, Surace did something unusual: Instead of talking first to the firms' main creditors, he made his first visit to the employees' union, the United Electrical, Radio, and Machine Workers of America. He met with the union's president, Carl Rosen, as well as several Republic workers. Rosen recalled that Surace's reasoning was that for the deal to work, he needed a skilled workforce. The parties agreed that Serious Materials would make the facility a union shop, and employees would be paid their former salaries and receive credit for their seniority at Republic. Only then did Surace approach Bank of America. The bank initially wasn't interested, so Surace went to General Electric, owner of the lease on the equipment, and bought out the lease, a coup that convinced the bank to sell. Surace announced plans to reopen the plant and rehire the 300 employees who had been laid off when Republic closed its doors. The resulting publicity quickly brought in inquiries and even some paying customers.

Since the acquisition, the Republic story may be nearing its end. County prosecutors brought charges against Gillman for looting the business and stealing machinery for the Iowa enterprise (which also failed, less than two months after it launched). Because Republic had been in bankruptcy, the equipment was not Gillman's but belonged to his creditor, GE. State's Attorney Anita Alvarez said, "Just two weeks before Christmas, in a dire economy, the company shut the doors of their business and deserted their workers and all of their families." Gillman denied the charges.

A sign of Surace's very different attitude toward his workforce came a few months after the acquisition by Serious Materials, when Vice President Joe Biden came to visit the Chicago facility. Biden was there to represent how the Obama administration's economic stimulus plan was supporting "green" initiatives. Surace noticed that onstage for the press conference were various dignitaries but no representatives of the workers. In spite of the Secret Service's reluctance to add last-minute guests, Surace insisted that workers have a face at the press conference. By the time the TV cameras were rolling, the cast of dignitaries included Armando Robles, a maintenance worker and the president of the employees' union.

## QUESTIONS

1. Richard Gillman attempted to stay in business by transferring work to a nonunion facility, and Kevin Surace plans to make the operation profitable as a union shop. Do you think the decision to rely on union or nonunion labor spells the difference between the success and failure of this enterprise? Why or why not?

2. How (if at all) do you think Kevin Surace's initial approach to the union when acquiring the company will influence the business success of the window factory?

3. Imagine that Serious Materials has hired you as an HR consultant for the Chicago window factory. Suggest how the company can build on its initial goodwill with workers to create positive labor relations and a highly motivated workforce for the long run.

SOURCES: R. Mitchum, "Republic Workers File Labor Charges," *Chicago Tribune*, January 7, 2009; R. Mitchum, "Former Republic Workers Find Hope," *Chicago Tribune*, January 15, 2009; A. Sweeney and M. Walberg, "Tables Turn on Man Who Shut Republic Windows," *Chicago Tribune*, September 11, 2009; L. Buchanan, "Entrepreneur of the Year: Kevin Surace of Serious Materials," *Inc.*, December 2009.

## NOTES

1. J. T. Dunlop, *Industrial Relations Systems* (New York: Holt, 1958).
2. C. Kerr, "Industrial Conflict and Its Mediation," *American Journal of Sociology* 60 (1954), pp. 230–45.
3. T. A. Kochan, *Collective Bargaining and Industrial Relations* (Homewood, IL: Richard D. Irwin, 1980), p. 25; H. C. Katz and T. A. Kochan, *An Introduction to Collective Bargaining and Industrial Relations*, 3rd ed. (New York: McGraw-Hill, 2004).
4. Katz and Kochan, *An Introduction to Collective Bargaining*.
5. S. Webb and B. Webb, *Industrial Democracy* (London: Longmans, Green, 1897); J. R. Commons, *Institutional Economics* (New York: Macmillan, 1934).
6. C. Kerr, J. T. Dunlop, F. Harbison, and C. Myers, "Industrialism and World Society," *Harvard Business Review*, February 1961, pp. 113–26.
7. T. A. Kochan and K. R. Wever, "American Unions and the Future of Worker Representation," in *The State of the Unions*, ed. G. Strauss et al. (Madison, WI: Industrial Relations Research Association, 1991).
8. A. Bernstein, "Why America Needs Unions, but Not the Kind It Has Now," *Bloomberg Businessweek*, May 23, 1994, p. 70.
9. Katz and Kochan, *An Introduction to Collective Bargaining*.
10. J. Barbash, *The Elements of Industrial Relations* (Madison: University of Wisconsin Press, 1984).
11. U.S. Bureau of Labor Statistics, www.bls.gov.
12. J. T. Bennett and B. E. Kaufman, *The Future of Private Sector Unionism in the United States* (Armonk, NY: M. E. Sharpe, 2002).
13. Katz and Kochan, *An Introduction to Collective Bargaining*. Katz and Kochan in turn build on work by J. Fiorito and C. L. Maranto, "The Contemporary Decline of Union Strength," *Contemporary Policy Issues* 3 (1987), pp. 12–27.
14. G. N. Chaison and J. Rose, "The Macrodeterminants of Union Growth and Decline," in *The State of the Unions*, ed. George Strauss et al. (Madison, WI: Industrial Relations Research Association, 1991).
15. J. Barbash, *The Practice of Unionism*, (New York: Harper, 1956).
16. D. L. Belman and K. A. Monaco, "The Effects of Deregulation, Deunionization, Technology, and Human Capital on the Work and Work Lives of Truck Drivers," *Industrial and Labor Relations Review* 54 (2001), pp. 502–24.
17. T. A. Kochan, R. B. McKersie, and J. Chalykoff, "The Effects of Corporate Strategy and Workplace Innovations in Union Representation," *Industrial and Labor Relations Review* 39 (1986), pp. 487–501; Chaison and Rose, "The Macrodeterminants of Union Growth"; J. Barbash, *Practice of Unionism* (New York: Harper, 1956), p. 210; W. N. Cooke and D. G. Meyer, "Structural and Market Predictors of Corporate Labor Relations Strategies," *Industrial and Labor Relations Review* 43 (1990), pp. 280–93; T. A. Kochan and P. Cappelli, "The Transformation of the Industrial Relations and Personnel Function," in *Internal Labor Markets*, ed. P. Osterman (Cambridge, MA: MIT Press, 1984); J. Logan, "The Union Avoidance Industry in the United States," *British Journal of Industrial Relations* 44 (2006), pp. 651–75.
18. Kochan and Cappelli, "The Transformation of the Industrial Relations and Personnel Function."
19. The 27% difference is based on 2012 data from www.bls.gov. S. B. Jarrell and T. D. Stanley, "A Meta-Analysis of the Union–Nonunion Wage Gap," *Industrial and Labor Relations Review* 44 (1990), pp. 54–67; P. D. Lineneman, M. L. Wachter, and W. H. Carter, "Evaluating the Evidence on Union Employment and Wages," *Industrial and Labor Relations Review* 44 (1990), pp. 34–53; L. Mischel and M. Walters, "How Unions Help All Workers," Economic Policy Institute Briefing Paper (2003).
20. https://www.nlrb.gov/news-outreach/graphs-data/petitions-and-elections/decertification-petitions-rd, accessed January 31, 2019.
21. J. P. Ferguson, "The Eyes of the Needles: A Sequential Model of Union Organizing Drives, 1999–2004," *Industrial and Labor Relations Review* 62, no. 3 (2008), pp. 3–21.
22. R. B. Freeman and M. M. Kleiner, "Employer Behavior in the Face of Union Organizing Drives," *Industrial and Labor Relations Review* 43 (1990), pp. 351–65.
23. F. K. Foulkes, "Large Nonunionized Employers," in *U.S. Industrial Relations 1950–1980: A Critical Assessment*, ed. J. Steiber et al. (Madison, WI: Industrial Relations Research Association, 1981).
24. Katz and Kochan, *An Introduction to Collective Bargaining*.

25. R. B. Freeman and J. Rogers, *What Workers Want* (Ithaca, NY: Cornell University Press, 1999).

26. E. E. Herman, J. L. Schwarz, and A. Kuhn, *Collective Bargaining and Labor Relations* (Englewood Cliffs, NJ: Prentice Hall, 1992), p. 32.

27. "Union Members—2018," January 18, 2019, USDL-19-0079, www.bls.gov.

28. Herman et al., *Collective Bargaining*, p. 33.

29. Kochan, *Collective Bargaining and Industrial Relations*, p. 61.

30. National Labor Relations Board, *A Guide to Basic Law and Procedures under the National Labor Relations Act* (Washington, DC: U.S. Government Printing Office, 1997).

31. National Labor Relations Board, *A Guide to Basic Law*.

32. National Labor Relations Board, *A Guide to Basic Law*.

33. National Labor Relations Board, "Concerted Activity," www.nlrb.gov.

34. P. Davidson, "Fast-Food Workers Strike, Seeking $15 Wage, Political Muscle," *USA Today*, November 10, 2015; R. L. Swarns, "McDonald's Workers, Vowing a Fight, Say Raises Are Too Little for Too Few," *The New York Times*, April 6, 2015; S. Greenhouse, "A Broader Strategy on Wages," *The New York Times*, March 31, 2015; J. Young and J. Madden, "Hundreds Protest in Downpour at Shut McDonald's Headquarters," *Reuters*, May 26, 2016.

35. B. Harper, "NLRB Rules against Hyundai in Holiday Plant Walkout," *USA Today*, March 10, 2017.

36. National Labor Relations Board, "Protected Concerted Activity," www.nlrb.gov, accessed April 15, 2017.

37. H. N. Wheeler and J. A. McClendon, "The Individual Decision to Unionize," in *The State of the Unions*.

38. National Labor Relations Board annual reports, www.nlrb.gov.

39. K. Johnson, "Under Trump, Labor Protections Stripped Away," *Boston Globe*, September 3, 2018, www.bostonglobe.com.

40. M. Trottman, "New Rules Adopted for Union Elections," *New York Times*, December 13–14, 2014, p. B4.

41. M. Trottman, "New Labor-Board Rule Speeds Union Votes. Average Election Time Has Fallen 40% since NLRB Regulation Took Effect in April," *Wall Street Journal*, August 26, 2015.

42. M. Trottman, "Ruling Clears Way for Unions," *Wall Street Journal*, August 27, 2015; M. Bultman, "One Year after Browning-Ferris, Employers Decry Uncertainty," *Law360*, August 16, 2016, https://www.law360.com/articles/828691/one-year-after-browning-ferris-employers-decry-uncertainty.

43. P. B. Rosen et al., "Joint Employment under NLRA: Interpreting D.C. Circuit Court's Browning-Ferris Decision," *Jackson Lewis*, January 7, 2019, www.jacksonlewis.com.

44. McDonald's USA and Fast Food Workers Committee and Service Employees International Union, CTW, CLC, NLRB Case No. 02-CA-093893; see P. F. Millus, "NLRB and the Joint Employer: Is Franchising on the Ropes?" *Law Journal Newsletters*, May 2016, www.lawjournalnewsletters.com.

45. "Obama's Union McDouble" [editorial], *Wall Street Journal*, December 22, 2014; M. Trottman and J. Jargon, "NLRB Names McDonald's as 'Joint-Employer' at Its Franchisees," *Wall Street Journal*, December 19, 2014.

46. D. Douglas-Gabriel, "Are They Students? Or Are They Employees?" *Washington Post*, August 23, 2016.

47. J. G. Getman, S. B. Goldberg, and J. B. Herman, *Union Representation Elections: Law and Reality* (New York: Russell Sage Foundation, 1976).

48. J. A. Fossum, *Labor Relations*, 8th ed. (New York: McGraw-Hill, 2002), p. 149.

49. National Labor Relations Board, *A Guide to Basic Law*, p. 17.

50. National Labor Relations Board, *A Guide to Basic Law*, p. 17.

51. Herman et al., *Collective Bargaining*; P. Jarley and J. Fiorito, "Associate Membership: Unionism or Consumerism?" *Industrial and Labor Relations Review* 43 (1990), pp. 209–24.

52. W. Welkowitz, "Social Media: The New Big Tool for Union Organizing," Labor and Employment Blog, *Bloomberg BNA*, February 3, 2015, www.bna.com; T. Puckett, "NLRB Rulings Have Far-Reaching Impact on Employers and Policies," *Oklahoma Employment Law Letter*, February 4, 2015, www.hrhero.com.

53. Katz and Kochan, *An Introduction to Collective Bargaining*; R. L. Rose, "Unions Hit Corporate Campaign Trail," *Wall Street Journal*, March 8, 1993, p. B1.

54. P. Jarley and C. L. Maranto, "Union Corporate Campaigns: An Assessment," *Industrial and Labor Relations Review* 44 (1990), pp. 505–24.

55. Katz and Kochan, *An Introduction to Collective Bargaining*.

56. A. McFellin, "Labor Unions in the New Economy," *Common Dreams*, March 24, 2013, www.heartlandnetwork.org/newsroom/10-in-the-news/63-labor-unions-in-the-new-economy-2.

57. T. Devaney, "SEIU Spent $19M on Fight for $15," *The Hill*, April 3, 2017, http://thehill.com/regulation/labor/327011-seiu-spent-19m-on-fight-for-15.

58. K. Maher, "SEIU to End Sodexo Campaign," *Wall Street Journal*, September 15, 2011.

59. Chaison and Rose, "The Macrodeterminants of Union Growth."

60. R. E. Walton and R. B. McKersie, *A Behavioral Theory of Negotiations* (New York: McGraw-Hill, 1965).

61. Fossum, *Labor Relations*. See also C. S. Loughran, *Negotiating a Labor Contract: A Management Handbook*, 2nd ed. (Washington, DC: Bureau of National Affairs, 1990).

62. C. M. Steven, *Strategy and Collective Bargaining Negotiations* (New York: McGraw-Hill, 1963); Katz and Kochan, *An Introduction to Collective Bargaining*.

63. R. Fisher and W. Ury, *Getting to Yes* (New York: Penguin Books, 1991).

64. Kochan, *Collective Bargaining and Industrial Relations*.

65. Fossum, *Labor Relations*.

66. J. R. Haggerty, "Caterpillar Girds for a Strike," *Wall Street Journal*, March 2–3, 2013, p. B3.

67. J. Ostrower, "Union Cancels Boeing Vote," *Wall Street Journal*, April 18–19, 2015, p. B3; J. Ostrower, "New Dreamliner to Be Built at Nonunion Plant," *Wall Street Journal*, July 31, 2014; J. Ostrower, "New Boeing Pact Wins Cost Controls," *Wall Street Journal*, January 5, 2014, p. B3.

68. Federal Mediation and Conciliation Service, *Annual Report for Fiscal Year 2016*, January 13, 2017, https://www.fmcs.gov/wp-content/uploads/2017/01/AnnualReport2017Jan13.pdf.

69. Kochan, *Collective Bargaining and Industrial Relations*, p. 272.

70. Herman et al., *Collective Bargaining*.

71. Katz and Kochan, *An Introduction to Collective Bargaining*.

72. Kochan, *Collective Bargaining and Industrial Relations*, p. 386.

73. Alternative criteria would be efficiency, equity, and worker voice. J. W. Budd and A. J. S. Colvin, "Improved Metrics for Workplace Dispute Resolution Procedures: Efficiency, Equity, and Voice," *Industrial Relations* 47, no. 3 (July 2008), p. 460.

74. *United Steelworkers v. American Manufacturing Co.*, 363 U.S. 564 (1960); *United Steelworkers v. Warrior Gulf and Navigation Co.*, 363 U.S. 574 (1960); *United Steelworkers v. Enterprise Wheel and Car Corp.*, 363 U.S. 593 (1960).

75. Original data from U.S. Federal Mediation and Conciliation Service, *Fiftieth Annual Report, Fiscal Year 2006* (Washington, DC: U.S. Government Printing Office, 2006); www.fmcs.gov.

76. J. R. Redecker, *Employee Discipline: Policies and Practices* (Washington, DC: Bureau of National Affairs, 1989).

77. Barbash, *The Elements of Industrial Relations*, p. 6.

78. T. A. Kochan, H. C. Katz, and R. B. McKersie, *The Transformation of American Industrial Relations* (New York: Basic Books, 1986), chap. 6; J. B. Arthur, "The Link between Business Strategy and Industrial Relations Systems in American Steel Minimills," *Industrial and Labor Relations Review* 45 (1992), pp. 488-506; M. Schuster, "Union Management Cooperation," in *Employee and Labor Relations*, ed. J. A. Fossum (Washington, DC: Bureau of National Affairs, 1990); E. Cohen-Rosenthal and C. Burton, *Mutual Gains: A Guide to Union-Management Cooperation*, 2nd ed. (Ithaca, NY: ILR Press, 1993); T. A. Kochan and P. Osterman, *The Mutual Gains Enterprise* (Boston: Harvard Business School Press, 1994); E. Applebaum and R. Batt, *The New American Workplace* (Ithaca, NY: ILR Press, 1994).

79. J. Marquez, "Streamlined Model: Engine of Change," *Workforce Management*, July 17, 2006, pp. 1, 20-30; B. Visnic, "Harbour–Topping Chrysler JV Engine Plant Attracting Foreign Attention," *Edmunds Auto Observer*, July 20, 2008, www.autoobserver.com; J. McCracken, "Desperate to Cut Costs, Ford Gets Union's Help," *Wall Street Journal*, March 2, 2007, p. A1; M. Oneal, "Model Partnership: Automakers, Labor Could Learn from Harley-Davidson's Kansas City Operation," *Columbus Dispatch*, May 27, 2006 (original article in *Chicago Tribune*).

80. L. P. Vellequette, "FCA's Dundee Engine Plant Achieves Silver Designation for Productivity," *Automotive News*, May 15, 2015.

81. A. E. Eaton, "Factors Contributing to the Survival of Employee Participation Programs in Unionized Settings," *Industrial and Labor Relations Review* 47, no. 3 (1994), pp. 371-89.

82. National Labor Relations Board, *A Guide to Basic Law*.

83. A. Bernstein, "Putting a Damper on That Old Team Spirit," *Bloomberg Businessweek*, May 4, 1992, p. 60.

84. T. Mahoney and A. Drutchas, "Could Your Employee Participation Program Be Illegal?" *Society for Human Resource Management*, June 9, 2016, www.shrm.org; Bureau of National Affairs, "Polaroid Dissolves Employee Committee in Response to Labor Department Ruling," *Daily Labor Report*, June 23, 1992, p. A3; K. G. Salwen, "DuPont Is Told It Must Disband Nonunion Panels," *Wall Street Journal*, June 7, 1993, p. A2.

85. "NLRB 4-0 Approves Crown Cork & Seal's Use of Seven Employee Participation Committees," *HR News*, September 3, 2001.

86. Kochan and Osterman, *Mutual Gains*; J. P. MacDuffie, "Human Resource Bundles and Manufacturing Performance: Organizational Logic and Flexible Production Systems in the World Auto Industry," *Industrial and Labor Relations Review* 48, no. 2 (1995), pp. 197-221; W. N. Cooke, "Employee Participation Programs, Group-Based Incentives, and Company Performance: A Union-Nonunion Comparison," *Industrial and Labor Relations Review* 47, no. 4 (1994), pp. 594-609; C. Doucouliagos, "Worker Participation and Productivity in Labor-Managed and Participatory Capitalist Firms: A Meta-Analysis," *Industrial and Labor Relations Review* 49, no. 1 (1995), pp. 58-77; L. W. Hunter, J. P. MacDuffie, and L. Doucet, "What Makes Teams Take? Employee Reactions to Work Reforms," *Industrial and Labor Relations Review* 55 (2002), pp. 448-72; S. J. Deery and R. D. Iverson, "Labor-Management Cooperation: Antecedents and Impact on Organizational Performance," *Industrial and Labor Relations Review* 58 (2005), pp. 588-609; J. Combs, Y. Liu, A. Hall, and D. Ketchen, "How Much Do High-Performance Work Practices Matter? A Meta-Analysis of Their Effects on Organizational Performance," *Personnel Psychology* 59, no. 3 (2006), pp. 501-28; T. Rabl, M. Jayasinghe,

B. Gerhart, and T. M. Köhlmann, "How Much Does Country Matter? A Meta-Analysis of the HPWP Systems-Business Performance Relationship," *Academy of Management Annual Meeting Proceedings*, August 2011.

87. R. D. Mohr and C. Zoghi, "High-Involvement Work Design and Job Satisfaction," *Industrial and Labor Relations Review* 61, no. 3 (April 2008), pp. 275-96; P. Osterman, "The Wage Effects of High Performance Work Organization in Manufacturing," *Industrial and Labor Relations Review* 59 (2006), pp. 187-204.

88. J. Cutcher-Gershenfeld, "The Impact of Economic Performance of a Transformation in Workplace Relations," *Industrial and Labor Relations Review* 44 (1991), pp. 241-60.

89. R. B. Freeman and J. Rogers, *Proceedings of the Industrial Relations Research Association*, 1995. A survey of workers represented by the United Autoworkers at six Chrysler manufacturing plants found generally positive worker reactions to the implementation of work teams, streamlined job classifications, and skill-based pay. See L. W. Hunter, J. P. MacDuffie, and L. Doucet, "What Makes Teams Take? Employee Reactions to Work Reforms," *Industrial and Labor Relations Review* 55 (2002), p. 448. A study of the airline industry, moreover, concludes that relational factors, such as conflict and workplace culture, also play an important role in firm performance. See J. H. Gittell, A. vonNordenflycht, and T. A. Kochan, "Mutual Gains or Zero Sum? Labor Relations and Firm Performance in the Airline Industry," *Industrial and Labor Relations Review* 57 (2004), p. 163.

90. H. Doucouliagos, R. B. Freeman, and P. Laroche, *The Economics of Trade Unions: A Study of a Research Field and Its Findings* (London: Routledge, 2017).

91. U.S. Bureau of Labor Statistics, *Employer Costs for Employee Compensation (ECEC)*, http://stats.bls.gov.

92. U.S. Bureau of Labor Statistics, *Employer Costs for Employee Compensation (ECEC)*.

93. P. E. Gabriel and S. Schmitz, "A Longitudinal Analysis of the Union Wage Premium for US Workers," *Applied Economics Letters* 21 (2014), pp. 487-89; M. L. Blackburn, "Are Union Wage Differentials in the United States Falling?" *Industrial Relations* 47, no. 3 (July 2008), p. 390.

94. Jarrell and Stanley, "A Meta-Analysis"; R. B. Freeman and J. Medoff, *What Do Unions Do?* (New York: Basic Books, 1984); L. Mishel and M. Walters, "How Unions Help All Workers," *Economic Policy Institute Briefing Paper*, August 2003, www.epinet.org.

95. C. P. Green and J. S. Heywood, "Dissatisfied Union Workers: Sorting Revisited," *British Journal of Industrial Relations* 53, no. 3 (2015), pp. 580-600; T. H. Hammer and A. Augar, "The Impact of Unions on Job Satisfaction, Organizational Commitment, and Turnover," *Journal of Labor Research* 26 (2005), pp. 241-66; B. Artz "The Impact of Union Experience on Job Satisfaction," *Industrial Relations: A Journal of Economy and Society* 49 (2010), pp. 387-405.

96. J. T. Addison and B. T. Hirsch, "Union Effects on Productivity, Profits, and Growth: Has the Long Run Arrived?" *Journal of Labor Economics* 7 (1989), pp. 72-105; H. Doucouliagos and P. Laroche, "Unions and Innovation: New Insights From the Cross–Country Evidence." *Industrial Relations* 52, no. 2 (2013), pp. 467-91.

97. R. B. Freeman and J. L. Medoff, "The Two Faces of Unionism," *Public Interest* 57 (Fall 1979), pp. 69-93.

98. R. B. Freeman and J. L. Medoff, "The Two Faces of Unionism," *Public Interest* 57 (Fall 1979), pp. 69-93; L. Mishel and P. Voos, *Unions and Economic Competitiveness* (Armonk, NY: M. E. Sharpe, 1991); M. Ash and J. A. Seago, "The Effect

of Registered Nurses' Unions on Heart-Attack Mortality," *Industrial and Labor Relations Review* 57 (2004), p. 422; C. Doucouliagos and P. Laroche, "What Do Unions Do to Productivity? A Meta-Analysis," *Industrial Relations* 42 (2003), pp. 650-91.

99. Freeman and Medoff, "Two Faces."

100. S. Slichter, J. Healy, and E. R. Livernash, *The Impact of Collective Bargaining on Management* (Washington, DC: Brookings Institution, 1960); Freeman and Medoff, "Two Faces."

101. R. B. Freeman and J. L. Medoff, *What Do Unions Do?* (New York: Basic Books, 1984); Herman et al., *Collective Bargaining*; Addison and Hirsch, "Union Effects on Productivity"; Katz and Kochan, *An Introduction to Collective Bargaining*; Lineneman et al., "Evaluating the Evidence."

102. B. E. Becker and C. A. Olson, "Unions and Firm Profits," *Industrial Relations* 31, no. 3 (1992), pp. 395-415; B. T. Hirsch and B. A. Morgan, "Shareholder Risks and Returns in Union and Nonunion Firms," *Industrial and Labor Relations Review* 47, no. 2 (1994), pp. 302-18. Hristos Doucouliagos and Partice Laroche, "Unions and Profits: A Meta-Regression Analysis," *Industrial Relations* 48, no. 1 (January 2008), p. 146.

103. D. S. Lee and A. Mas, "Long-Run Impacts of Unions on Firms: New Evidence from Financial Markets, 1961-1999," *Quarterly Journal of Economics*, 127 (2012), pp. 333-78.

104. Addison and Hirsch, "Union Effects on Productivity." See also B. T. Hirsch, *Labor Unions and the Economic Performance of Firms* (Kalamazoo, MI: W. E. Upjohn Institute, 1991); J. M. Abowd, "The Effect of Wage Bargains on the Stock Market Value of the Firm," *American Economic Review* 79 (1989), pp. 774-800; Hirsch, *Labor Unions*.

105. B. E. Becker and C. A. Olson, "The Impact of Strikes on Shareholder Equity," *Industrial and Labor Relations Review* 39, no. 3 (1986), pp. 425-38; O. Persons, "The Effects of Automobile Strikes on the Stock Value of Steel Suppliers," *Industrial and Labor Relations Review* 49, no. 1 (1995), pp. 78-87.

106. C. Brewster, "Levels of Analysis in Strategic HRM: Questions Raised by Comparative Research," Conference on Research and Theory in HRM, Cornell University, October 1997.

107. C. Chang and C. Sorrentino, "Union Membership in 12 Countries," *Monthly Labor Review* 114, no. 12 (1991), pp. 46-53; D. G. Blanchflower and R. B. Freeman, "Going Different Ways: Unionism in the U.S. and Other Advanced O.E.C.D. Countries" (Symposium on the Future Role of Unions, Industry, and Government in Industrial Relations. University of Minnesota),

cited in Chaison and Rose, "The Macrodeterminants of Union Growth," p. 23.

108. J. P. Begin and E. F. Beal, *The Practice of Collective Bargaining* (Homewood, IL: Richard D. Irwin, 1989); T. H. Hammer, S. C. Currall, and R. N. Stern, "Worker Representation on Boards of Directors: A Study of Competing Roles," *Industrial and Labor Relations Review* 44 (1991), pp. 661-80; Katz and Kochan, *An Introduction to Collective Bargaining*; H. Gunter and G. Leminsky, "The Federal Republic of Germany," in *Labor in the Twentieth Century*, ed. J. T. Dunlop and W. Galenson (New York: Academic Press, 1978), pp. 149-96.

109. "Adapt or Die," *The Economist*, July 1, 1995, p. 54; G. Steinmetz, "German Firms Sour on Stem That Keeps Peace with Workers: Centralized Bargaining, a Key to Postwar Gains, Inflates Costs, Companies Fear," *Wall Street Journal*, October 17, 1995, p. A1; H. C. Katz, W. Lee, and J. Lee, *The New Structure of Labor Relations: Tripartism and Decentralization* (Ithaca, NY: ILR Press/Cornell University, 2004).

110. E. Thomasson and M. Potter, "Union Calls New Strikes at Amazon's German Warehouses," *Reuters*, December 21, 2016; N. Wingfield, "Amazon Proves Infertile Soil for Unions, So Far," *New York Times,* May 16, 2016; S. Sloat, "In Germany, Amazon Keeps Unions at Bay," *Wall Street Journal,* September 24, 2014, p. A1.

111. A. Young, "UAW Welcomes Volkswagen Policy Shift After Years of Failing to Gain Traction in Anti-Union South," *International Business Times*, November 12, 2014.

112. C. Brooks, "Chattanooga Auto Workers to Host Strike Meeting," *Labor Notes*, January 6, 2017, www.labornotes.com; M. Ramsey, "UAW Wins Vote at VW Chattanooga Plant as Some Workers Vote to Unionize," *New York Times,* December 7, 2015.

113. M. Elfstrom and S. Kuruvilla, "The Changing Nature of Unrest in China," *Industrial and Labor Relations Review* April 2014, pp. 453-80.

114. J. Haggerty, "A Clash of Cultures at Alabama Factory," *Wall Street Journal*, February 28, 2016.

115. J. F. Burton and T. Thomason, "The Extent of Collective Bargaining in the Public Sector," in *Public Sector Bargaining*, ed. B. Aaron, J. M. Najita, and J. L. Stern (Washington, DC: Bureau of National Affairs, 1988).

116. J. Godard and C. Frege, "Labor Unions, Alternative Forms of Representation, and the Exercise of Authority Relations in U.S. Workplaces," *Industrial and Labor Relations Review* 66 (2013), pp. 142-68; P. J. Gollan and D. Lewin, "Employee Representation in Non-Union Firms: An Overview," *Industrial Relations* 52 (2013), pp. 173-93.

# 15 Managing Human Resources Globally

┌─────────────────────────────────────────────────────────────┐
│ **LEARNING OBJECTIVES**

*After reading this chapter, you should be able to:*

**LO 15-1** Identify the recent changes that have caused companies to expand into international markets. *page 677*

**LO 15-2** Discuss the four factors that most strongly influence HRM in international markets. *page 679*

**LO 15-3** List the different categories of international employees. *page 689*

**LO 15-4** Identify the four levels of global participation and the HRM issues faced within each level. *page 689*

**LO 15-5** Discuss the ways companies attempt to select, train, compensate, and reintegrate expatriate managers. *page 693*
└─────────────────────────────────────────────────────────────┘

# ENTER THE WORLD OF BUSINESS

## Changing the Offshoring Game

For years companies have offshored much of their manufacturing to China because of the low labor costs there. However, such moves, while financially beneficial, had some negative side effects. One of the more important was the loss of intellectual property, as the Chinese government often required companies to partner with Chinese companies forcing them to transfer their technologies. In addition, companies doing business in China often found their intellectual property stolen.

However, with the Trump administration threatening tariffs on a number of goods imported to the United States from China, companies are rethinking their supply chains. Rather than setting up all their operations in China, now companies seek to set up factories in several different countries in order to reduce the political and economic risks that come with concentrating too much in one country.

For instance, Yeti Holdings Inc. (makers of Yeti coolers and mugs) had been modernizing its supply chains by reducing its dependency on China and building more capacity in the Philippines. However, when it discovered that some of its products were on the list of those targeted by the tariffs, it was able to mitigate the negative consequences by simply shifting some of its China production to the Philippines. While long and costly, such shifts are perceived to pay off. Yeti CEO Matt Reintjes says "Sometimes China is the easiest answer, but sometimes it's not the best one for the long term."

As markets have become more globalized, many companies have created global supply chains, sourcing and manufacturing all across the world. With the passage of the North American Free Trade Agreement, Mexico became a prime target for automobile manufacturers to build *maquiladora* plants where Mexican workers

Matthew Busch/Bloomberg/Getty Images

provide a substantial labor cost advantage over U.S.-based United Automobile Workers (UAW) union members. In addition, the products assembled in Mexico are shipped not just to the United States but all around the world. In fact, GM recorded a record profit in its North American market resulting in UAW workers receiving $12,000 in profit sharing. General Motors assembles about 20% of its highly profitable trucks in Mexico and until recently had plans to move much of its sport-utility vehicle production there, as a way to further reduce costs and increase profits.

However, the election of Donald Trump as president of the United States has put a wrinkle in those plans. In an effort to keep companies from moving production outside the United States, Trump has proposed a border tax of as much as 35% on any products coming to the United States from Mexico. However, even a more modest tax of 20% is estimated to wipe out a quarter of GM's profit in the region.

SOURCE: J. Stoll and M. Colias, "Mexico Is Key Cog in GM's Profit Machine," *Wall Street Journal*, February 8, 2017, https://www.wsj.com/articles/gm-says-it-supports-tax-reform-but-border-tax-is-complicated-1486473480.

# Introduction

The environment in which business competes is rapidly becoming globalized. More and more companies are entering international markets by exporting their products overseas, building plants in other countries, and entering into alliances with foreign companies. In the mid-1980s, 61 of the top 100 organizations had their headquarters in the United States. By 2004 that number had dropped to 35, and Table 15.1 shows the world's 25 largest companies in 2018, and of those only 12 were headquartered in the United States, 7 in Asia, and 6 in Europe. As you can see from the table, whereas General Motors used to dominate the globe in market share, Volkswagen, Toyota, and Daimler all had greater sales than GM in 2018.

Most organizations now function in the global economy. U.S. businesses are entering international markets at the same time that foreign companies are entering the U.S. market. In addition, cross-border mergers (e.g., Merck/Schering-Plough, New York Stock Exchange/Deutsche Börse) are increasing. In fact, in the first three quarters of 2018, global mergers had totaled $3.3 trillion, the largest in history.

What is behind the trend toward expansion into global markets? Companies are attempting to gain a competitive advantage, which can be provided by international expansion in a number of ways. First, these countries are new markets with large numbers of potential customers. For companies that are producing below their capacity, expansion provides a means of increasing sales and profits. Second, many companies are

**Table 15.1**
*Fortune* World's Largest Companies, 2018

| RANK | COMPANY | REVENUES ($ MILLIONS) |
|---|---|---|
| 1 | Walmart | 500,343 |
| 2 | State Grid | 348,903 |
| 3 | Sinopec Group | 326,953 |
| 4 | China National Petroleum | 326,008 |
| 5 | Royal Dutch Shell | 311,870 |
| 6 | Toyota Motor | 265,172 |
| 7 | Volkswagen | 260,028 |
| 8 | BP | 244,582 |
| 9 | ExxonMobil | 244,363 |
| 10 | Berkshire Hathaway | 242,137 |
| 11 | Apple | 229,234 |
| 12 | Samsung Electronics | 211,940 |
| 13 | McKesson | 208,357 |
| 14 | Glencore | 205,476 |
| 15 | United Health Group | 201,159 |
| 16 | Daimler | 185,235 |
| 17 | CVS Health | 184,765 |
| 18 | Amazon.com | 184,765 |
| 19 | Exor Group | 177,866 |
| 20 | AT&T | 161,677 |
| 21 | General Motors | 160,546 |
| 22 | Ford Motor | 156,776 |
| 23 | China State Construction Engineering | 156,071 |
| 24 | Hon Hai Precision Industry | 154,699 |
| 25 | AmericanBergen | 153,144 |

SOURCE: From *Fortune*, 2018, Time Inc.

building production facilities in other countries as a means of capitalizing on those countries' lower labor costs for relatively unskilled jobs. For example, many of the Mexican *maquiladora* plants provide low-skilled labor at considerably lower cost than in the United States. In 2016 the average hourly manufacturing wage in Mexico was $3.91, versus $39.03 in the United States.[1] Third, the rapid increase in telecommunications and information technology enables work to be done more rapidly, efficiently, and effectively around the globe. With the best college graduates available for $2.00 an hour in India versus $12–$18 an hour in the United States, companies can hire the best talent (resulting in better work) at a lower cost. And because their day is our night, work done in the United States can be handed off to those in India for a 24/7 work process.[2]

While this process has moved jobs from the United States overseas, technological advances may make the disappearance of jobs a global phenomenon.

Deciding whether to enter foreign markets and whether to develop plants or other facilities in other countries, however, is no simple matter, and many human resource issues surface.

This chapter discusses the human resource issues that must be addressed to gain competitive advantage in a world of global competition. This is not a chapter on international human resource management (the specific HRM policies and programs companies use to manage human resources across international boundaries).[3] The chapter focuses instead on the key factors that must be addressed to strategically manage human resources in an international context. We discuss some of the important events that have increased the global nature of business over the past few years. We then identify some of the factors that are most important to HRM in global environments. Finally, we examine particular issues related to managing expatriate managers. These issues present unique opportunities for firms to gain competitive advantage.

# Current Global Changes

Several recent social and political changes have accelerated the movement toward international competition. The effects of these changes have been profound and far reaching. Many are still evolving. In this section we discuss the major developments that have accentuated the need for organizations to gain a competitive advantage through effectively managing human resources in a global economy.

LO 15-1
Identify the recent changes that have caused companies to expand into international markets.

## EUROPEAN UNION AND "BREXIT"

European countries have managed their economies individually for years. Because of the countries' close geographic proximity, their economies have become intertwined. This created a number of problems for international businesses; for example, the regulations of one country, such as France, might be completely different from those of another country, such as Germany. In response, most of the European countries agreed to participate in the European Union by signing the Maastricht Treaty in 1992. The EU is a confederation of most of the European nations that agree to engage in free trade with one another, with commerce regulated by an overseeing body called the European Commission (EC). Under the EU, legal regulation in the participating countries has become more, although not completely, uniform. Assuming that the EU's trend toward free trade among members continues, Europe has become one of the largest free markets in the world. In addition, as of 1999, all of the members of the EU share a common currency, the euro. This ties the members' economic fates even more closely with one another. In addition to the previous 15 EU states, as of May 1, 2004, 12 EU accession states—Bulgaria, Cyprus, the Czech Republic, Estonia, Hungary, Latvia, Lithuania, Malta, Poland, Romania, Slovakia, and Slovenia—were added to the European Union, expanding the economic zone covered by the European Union. In 2013, Croatia was added to the European Union, and Iceland, Macedonia, Montenegro, Serbia, and Turkey are candidates to be admitted into the European Union.

The European Union has recently been threatened by the exit of the United Kingdom. This "Brexit" stemmed from a slim majority of U.K. voters deciding that they no longer wanted to be governed largely from a bureaucracy located in Brussels, Belgium. Britain and the European Union are currently negotiating the terms of this separation, but many observers predict that, at least in the short term, this exit will have a negative impact on the British economy.

## UNITED STATES–MEXICO–CANADA TRADE AGREEMENT

The North American Free Trade Agreement (NAFTA) was an agreement among Canada, the United States, and Mexico that created a free market even larger than the European Union. The United States and Canada already had a free trade agreement since 1989, but NAFTA brought Mexico into the consortium. The agreement was prompted by Mexico's increasing willingness to open its markets and facilities in an effort to promote economic growth.[4] As previously discussed, the *maquiladora* plants exemplify this trend. In addition, some efforts have been made to expand the membership of NAFTA to other Latin American countries, such as Chile.

NAFTA increased U.S. investment in Mexico because of Mexico's substantially lower labor costs for low-skilled employees. This has had two effects on employment in the United States. First, many low-skilled jobs went south, decreasing employment opportunities for U.S. citizens who lack higher-level skills. Second, it has increased employment opportunities for Americans with higher-level skills.[5]

However, Donald Trump's election changed the nature of this agreement. President Trump believed that the agreement had evolved to favor Canada and Mexico's interests at a cost to U.S. interest. Thus, his team negotiated a new U.S.–Mexico–Canada Trade Agreement (USMCTA). The administration claims that the new agreement will create a more level playing field for U.S. workers; will benefit U.S. farmers; will protect U.S. intellectual property; and will promote digital trade, anti-corruption, and good regulatory practices. However, the agreement has not been in effect long enough to determine the exact outcomes.

## THE GROWTH OF ASIA

An additional global market that is of economic consequence to many firms lies in Asia. Whereas Japan has been a dominant economic force for over 20 years, countries such as Singapore, Hong Kong (SAR), and Malaysia recently have become significant economic forces. More important, China, with its population of more than 1 billion and trend toward opening its markets to foreign investors, presents a tremendous potential market for goods. In fact, some observers predict that China's economy will soon be larger than that of the United States.

## GENERAL AGREEMENT ON TARIFFS AND TRADE

The General Agreement on Tariffs and Trade (GATT) is an international framework of rules and principles for reducing trade barriers across countries around the world. It currently consists of more than 100 member-nations. The most recent round of GATT negotiations resulted in an agreement to cut tariffs (taxes on imports) by 40%, reduce government subsidies to businesses, expand protection of intellectual property such as copyrights and patents, and establish rules for investing and trading in services. It also established the World Trade Organization (WTO) to resolve disputes among GATT members.

These changes—the European Union, Brexit, USMCTA, the growth of Asia, and GATT—all exemplify events that are pushing companies to compete in a global economy. These developments are opening new markets and new sources of technology and labor in a way that has never been seen in history. However, this era of increasing international competition accentuates the need to manage human resources effectively to gain competitive advantage in a global marketplace. This requires understanding some of the factors that can determine the effectiveness of various HRM practices and approaches.

# Factors Affecting HRM in Global Markets

**LO 15-2**
Discuss the four factors that most strongly influence HRM in international markets.

Companies that enter global markets must recognize that these markets are not simply mirror images of their home country. Countries differ along a number of dimensions that influence the attractiveness of direct foreign investment in each country. These differences determine the economic viability of building an operation in a foreign location, and they have a particularly strong impact on HRM in that operation. Researchers in international management have identified a number of factors that can affect HRM in global markets, and we focus on four factors, as depicted in Figure 15.1: culture, education–human capital, the political–legal system, and the economic system.[6] The Competing through Globalization box provides an example of the kinds of challenges firms face when they set up operations in different cultures such as China.

Visit your instructor's Connect® course and access your eBook to view this video.

"Getting that first hire right, we've found, is the key differentiator for how well an operation will evolve over time in a region or not."

—Christine M. Pambianchi,
Senior Vice President of Human Resources, Corning

Source: Video produced for the Center for Executive Succession in the Darla Moore School of Business at the University of South Carolina by Coal Powered Filmworks

## CULTURE

By far the most important factor influencing international HRM is the culture of the country in which a facility is located. Culture is defined as "the set of important assumptions (often unstated) that members of a community share."[7] These assumptions consist of beliefs about the world and how it works and the ideals that are worth striving for.[8]

Culture is important to HRM for two reasons. First, it often determines the other three factors affecting HRM in global markets. Culture can greatly affect a country's laws, in that laws are often the codification of right and wrong as defined by the culture. Culture also affects human capital, because if

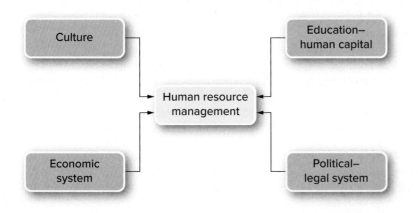

**Figure 15.1**

Factors Affecting Human Resource Management in International Markets

### Amazon Faces Integrity Issues in China

One reason companies expand internationally is to escape the slowing economies of their home country and to capture some of the profits available in rapid-growth regions. An example of this is Amazon, which has risen to be one of the most valuable companies in the world. It has succeeded at getting merchants to sell their products through the Amazon site, such that over 2 million merchants now sell over 550 million products through Amazon. As you probably have experienced if you ever shopped on Amazon, one of the advantages is to see how customers have reviewed the products, and you trust that these reviews provide accurate assessments. In addition, when you search for a product, the order that you see products is based on a number of criteria, including the quality of verified reviews, sales figures, and clicks.

So all of this information is valuable to sellers who want to have their products positioned on the first page.

However, Amazon has recently discovered that a number of employees, especially in China, have been selling data and access to merchants. Some Amazon employees have access to the e-mail addresses of users and also the ability to delete reviews. Brokers seek out Amazon employees and offer them money to delete negative reviews. These brokers charge sellers $300 per review deleted, with a minimum of five reviews, so at least $1,500. Employees can also sell the e-mail addresses of negative reviewers so that the seller can contact them and offer them free or discounted products to revise or delete those reviews. Finally, these brokers also offer information such as the keywords used in searches, sales volumes, and customer buying habits.

Amazon makes clear that it considers such behavior from employees and sellers unacceptable, and it punishes employees caught. It also notes that it will take legal action against sellers that violate its rules. Yet, as competition on the site increases, sellers have more and more justification to work with the brokers. One Chinese seller stated, "If I don't do bad things, I will die."

**DISCUSSION QUESTIONS**
1. How should Amazon deal with any employees who get caught selling information?
2. How should Amazon deal with any sellers who get caught buying information?

SOURCE: J. Emont, L. Stevens, and R. McMillan, "Amazon Investigates Employees Leaking Data for Bribes," *Wall Street Journal*, September 16, 2018, https://www.wsj.com/articles/amazon-investigates-employees-leaking-data-for-bribes-1537106401, (accessed Jan 19, 2019).

education is greatly valued by the culture, then members of the community try to increase their human capital. Finally, as we discuss later, cultures and economic systems are closely intertwined.[9]

However, the most important reason culture is important to HRM is that it often determines the effectiveness of various HRM practices. Practices found to be effective in the United States may not be effective in a culture that has different beliefs and values.[10] For example, U.S. companies rely heavily on individual performance appraisal, and rewards are tied to individual performance. In Japan, however, individuals are expected to subordinate their wishes and desires to those of the larger group. Thus, individual-based evaluation and incentives are not nearly as effective there and, in fact, are seldom observed among Japanese organizations.[11]

In this section we examine a model that attempts to characterize different cultures. This model illustrates why culture can have a profound influence on HRM.

### Hofstede's Cultural Dimensions

In a classic study of culture, Geert Hofstede identified four dimensions on which various cultures could be classified.[12] In a later study he added a fifth dimension that aids in

| | PDᵃ | ID | MA | UA | LT |
|---|---|---|---|---|---|
| United States | 40 Lᵇ | 91 H | 62 H | 46 L | 29 L |
| Germany | 35 L | 67 H | 66 H | 65 M | 31 M |
| Japan | 54 M | 45 M | 95 H | 92 H | 80 H |
| France | 68 H | 71 H | 43 M | 86 H | 30ᶜ L |
| Netherlands | 38 L | 80 H | 14 L | 53 M | 44 M |
| Hong Kong (SAR) | 68 H | 25 L | 57 H | 29 L | 96 H |
| Indonesia | 78 H | 14 L | 46 M | 48 L | 25ᶜ L |
| West Africa | 77 H | 20 L | 46 M | 54 M | 16 L |
| Russia | 95ᶜ H | 50ᶜ M | 40ᶜ L | 90ᶜ H | 10ᶜ L |
| Mainland China | 80ᶜ H | 20ᶜ L | 50ᶜ M | 60ᶜ M | 118 H |

**Table 15.2**
Cultural Dimension Scores for 10 Countries

ᵃPD = power distance; ID = individualism; MA = masculinity; UA = uncertainty avoidance; LT = long-term orientation.
ᵇH = top third; M = medium third; L = bottom third (among 53 countries and regions for the first four dimensions; among 23 countries for the fifth).
ᶜEstimated.
SOURCE: From Geert Hofstede, "Cultural Constraints in Management Theories," *Academy of Management Executive*, February 1993, Vol. 7, No. 1, p. 91. Reproduced with permission of Academy of Management, via Copyright Clearance Center.

characterizing cultures.[13] The relative scores for 10 major countries are provided in Table 15.2. **Individualism–collectivism** describes the strength of the relation between an individual and other individuals in the society—that is, the degree to which people act as individuals rather than as members of a group. In individualist cultures, such as the United States, Great Britain, and the Netherlands, people are expected to look after their own interests and the interests of their immediate families. The individual is expected to stand on her own two feet rather than be protected by the group. In collectivist cultures, such as Colombia, Pakistan, and Taiwan, people are expected to look after the interest of the larger community, which is expected to protect people when they are in trouble.

The second dimension, **power distance**, concerns how a culture deals with hierarchical power relationships—particularly the unequal distribution of power. It describes the degree of inequality among people that is considered to be normal. Cultures with small power distance, such as those of Denmark and Israel, seek to eliminate inequalities in power and wealth as much as possible, whereas countries with large power distances, such as India and the Philippines, seek to maintain those differences.

Differences in power distance often result in miscommunication and conflicts between people from different cultures. For example, in Mexico and Japan individuals are always addressed by their titles (Señor Smith or Smith-san, respectively). Individuals from the United States, however, often believe in minimizing power distances by using first names. Although this is perfectly normal, and possibly even advisable in the United States, it can be offensive and a sign of disrespect in other cultures.

The third dimension, **uncertainty avoidance**, describes how cultures seek to deal with the fact that the future is not perfectly predictable. It is defined as the degree to which people in a culture prefer structured over unstructured situations. Some cultures, such as those of Singapore and Jamaica, have weak uncertainty avoidance. They socialize individuals to accept this uncertainty and take each day as it comes. People from these cultures tend to be rather easygoing and flexible regarding different views. Other cultures, such as those of Greece and Portugal, socialize their people to seek security through technology, law, and religion. Thus, these cultures provide clear rules as to how one should behave.

**Individualism–collectivism**
One of Hofstede's cultural dimensions; describes the strength of the relation between an individual and other individuals in a society.

**Power distance**
One of Hofstede's cultural dimensions; concerns how a culture deals with hierarchical power relationships—particularly the unequal distribution of power.

**Uncertainty avoidance**
One of Hofstede's cultural dimensions; describes how cultures seek to deal with an unpredictable future.

**Masculinity–femininity dimension**
One of Hofstede's cultural dimensions; describes the division of roles between the sexes within a society.

The **masculinity–femininity dimension** describes the division of roles between the sexes within a society. In "masculine" cultures, such as those of Germany and Japan, what are considered traditionally masculine values—showing off, achieving something visible, and making money—permeate the society. These societies stress assertiveness, performance, success, and competition. "Feminine" cultures, such as those of Sweden and Norway, promote values that have been traditionally regarded as feminine, such as putting relationships before money, helping others, and preserving the environment. These cultures stress service, care for the weak, and solidarity.

**Long-term–short-term orientation**
One of Hofstede's cultural dimensions; describes how a culture balances immediate benefits with future rewards.

Finally, the fifth dimension comes from the philosophy of the Far East and is referred to as the **long-term–short-term orientation**. Cultures high on the long-term orientation focus on the future and hold values in the present that will not necessarily provide an immediate benefit, such as thrift (saving) and persistence. Hofstede found that many Far Eastern countries such as Japan and China have a long-term orientation. Short-term orientations, by contrast, are found in the United States, Russia, and West Africa. These cultures are oriented toward the past and present and promote respect for tradition and for fulfilling social obligations.

The current Japanese criticism of management practices in the United States illustrates the differences in long-term–short-term orientation. Japanese managers, traditionally exhibiting a long-term orientation, engage in 5- to 10-year planning. This leads them to criticize U.S. managers, who are traditionally much more short term in orientation because their planning often consists of quarterly to yearly time horizons.

These five dimensions help us understand the potential problems of managing employees from different cultures. Later in this chapter we will explore how these cultural dimensions affect the acceptability and utility of various HRM practices. However, it is important to note that these differences can have a profound influence on whether a company chooses to enter a given country. One interesting finding of Hofstede's research was the impact of culture on a country's economic health. He found that countries with individualist cultures were more wealthy. Collectivist cultures with high power distance were all poor.[14] Cultures seem to affect a country's economy through their promotion of individual work ethics and incentives for individuals to increase their human capital.

## Implications of Culture for HRM

Cultures have an important impact on approaches to managing people. As we discuss later, the culture can strongly affect the education–human capital of a country, the political–legal system, and the economic system. As Hofstede found, culture also has a profound impact on a country's economic health by promoting certain values that either aid or inhibit economic growth.

More important to this discussion, however, is that cultural characteristics influence the ways managers behave in relation to subordinates, as well as the perceptions of the appropriateness of various HRM practices. First, cultures differ strongly on such things as how subordinates expect leaders to lead, how decisions are handled within the hierarchy, and (most important) what motivates individuals. For example, in Germany, managers achieve their status by demonstrating technical skills, so employees look to them to assign their tasks and resolve technical problems. In the Netherlands, by contrast, managers focus on seeking consensus among all parties and must engage in an open-ended exchange of views and balancing of interests.[15] Clearly, these methods have different implications for selecting and training managers in the different countries.

Second, cultures may influence the appropriateness of HRM practices. For example, as discussed previously, the extent to which a culture promotes an individualistic versus a collectivist orientation will impact the effectiveness of individually oriented HRM systems. In the United States, companies often focus selection systems on assessing an individual's technical skill and, to a lesser extent, social skills. In collectivist cultures, by contrast, companies focus more on assessing how well an individual will perform as a member of the work group.

Culture often influences how employees value certain aspects of their work environment. In an interesting study comparing call center workers in India (a collectivist culture) and the United States (an individualistic culture), researchers found that in the United States person–job fit was the stronger predictor of turnover relative to India, where person–organization fit, links to the organization, and links to the community were the stronger predictors of turnover.[16]

Similarly, cultures can influence compensation systems. Individualistic cultures such as those found in the United States often exhibit great differences between the highest- and lowest-paid individuals in an organization, with the highest-paid individual often receiving 200 times the salary of the lowest. Collectivist cultures tend to have much flatter salary structures, with the top-paid individual receiving only about 20 times the overall pay of the lowest-paid one.

Cultural differences can affect the communication and coordination processes in organizations. Collectivist cultures, as well as those with less of an authoritarian orientation, value group decision making and participative management practices more highly than do individualistic cultures. When a person raised in an individualistic culture must work closely with those from a collectivist culture, communication problems and conflicts often appear. Much of the emphasis on "cultural diversity" programs in organizations focuses on understanding the cultures of others in order to better communicate with them. The Evidence-Based HR box discusses the effectiveness of such programs.

# EVIDENCE-BASED HR

## Is National Culture as Important as We Thought?

Although national culture is important, research suggests that its importance may be vastly overstated, particularly with regard to how firms manage people. Researchers reexamining Hofstede's original work found that, in addition to differences across nations, significant cultural differences also existed within nations. They further found that the differences in cultures across organizations within countries was larger than the differences across countries. Their results imply that although one cannot ignore national culture, one must not think that certain HR practices may not be effective simply based on a regard for national culture. People of varying cultural backgrounds within a nation will be drawn to organizations whose cultures better match their individual, as opposed to national, value systems.

In addition, many observers have suggested that the effectiveness of high-performance work systems (HPWS) depends on the cultural or institutional constraints, such that they may be ineffective in cultures that exhibit high power distance or high collectivism. However, a meta-analysis revealed that the effects of HPWS on firm performance were positive in all cultures, and contrary to expectations, if anything, higher in the cultures where the cultural hypothesis suggested they would be lower.

Thus, it seems that the conclusions reached by many regarding how important culture is to determining the effectiveness of HR practices may be at best overstated, and at worst completely wrong.

SOURCES: T. Rable, M. Jayasinghe, B. Gerhart, and T. Kuhlmann, "A Meta-Analysis of Country Differences in the High-Performance Work System–Business Performance Relationship: The Roles of National Culture and Managerial Discretion," *Journal of Applied Psychology* 99, no. 6 (2014), pp. 1011–41; B. Gerhart and M. Fang, "National Culture and Human Resource Management Assumptions and Evidence," *International Journal of Human Resource Management* 16, no. 6 (June 2005), pp. 971–86.

## EDUCATION–HUMAN CAPITAL

A company's potential to find and maintain a qualified workforce is an important consideration in any decision to expand into a foreign market. Thus, a country's human capital resources can be an important HRM issue. *Human capital* refers to the productive capabilities of individuals—that is, the knowledge, skills, and experience that have economic value.[17]

A country's human capital is determined by a number of variables. A major variable is the educational opportunities available to the labor force. In the Netherlands, for instance, government funding of school systems allows students to go all the way through graduate school without paying.[18] Similarly, the free education provided to citizens in the former Soviet bloc resulted in high levels of human capital, in spite of the poor infrastructure and economy that resulted from the socialist economic systems. In contrast, some developing countries, such as Nicaragua and Haiti, have relatively low levels of human capital because of a lack of investment in education.

A country's human capital may profoundly affect a foreign company's desire to locate there or enter that country's market. Countries with low human capital attract facilities that require low skills and low wage levels. This explains why U.S. companies desire to move their currently unionized low-skill–high-wage manufacturing and assembly jobs to Mexico, where they can obtain low-skilled workers for substantially lower wages. Similarly, Japan ships its messy, low-skill work to neighboring countries while maintaining its high-skill work at home.[19] Countries like Mexico, with relatively low levels of human capital, might not be as attractive for operations that consist of more high-skill jobs.

Countries with high human capital are attractive sites for direct foreign investment that creates high-skill jobs. In Ireland, for example, more than 25% of 18 year olds attend college, a rate much higher than in other European countries. In addition, Ireland's economy supports only 1.1 million jobs for a population of 3.5 million. The combination of high education levels, a strong work ethic, and high unemployment makes the country attractive for foreign firms because of the resulting high productivity and low turnover. The Met Life insurance company set up a facility for Irish workers to analyze medical insurance claims. It has found the high levels of human capital and the high work ethic provide such a competitive advantage that the company is currently looking for other work performed in the United States to be shipped to Ireland. Similarly, as already discussed, the skills of newly graduated technology workers in India are as high as or higher than those found among their counterparts in the United States. In addition, because jobs are not as plentiful in India, the worker attitudes are better in many of these locations.[20]

The Competing through Technology box discusses how technology is changing the requirements of jobs such that people will need both technical and creative skills.

## POLITICAL–LEGAL SYSTEM

The regulations imposed by a country's legal system can strongly affect HRM. The political-legal system often dictates the requirements for certain HRM practices, such as training, compensation, hiring, firing, and layoffs. In large part, the legal system is an outgrowth of the culture in which it exists. Thus, the laws of a particular country often reflect societal norms about what constitutes legitimate behavior.[21] Many countries allow (or even expect) that payoffs be made to decision makers, be they procurement employees or politicians. However, the Foreign Corrupt Practices Act prohibits any American companies from doing so, even if they are doing so in another country.

## COMPETING THROUGH TECHNOLOGY

### The Need for Hybrid Skills

Most university students go to college to gain the skills they will need to get a job upon graduation. When doing so, they learn a number of skills, both interpersonal and technical. In the fast-changing technological environment we all live in today, the question is, what skills will be important for tomorrow's jobs?

A new report from labor market analytics firm Burning Glass Technologies suggests that the fastest growing and highest paying jobs in the future will require both creative thinking and technical prowess. The study analyzed millions of job postings to determine what skills employers seek. While, not surprisingly, data analytics or design using digital technology showed up quite a bit, employers also seek employees who can innovatively think about how to use data and creatively develop solutions.

They developed the term "hybrid jobs" to describe ones that required both hard and soft skills and suggested that future jobs might require things like engineering and sales, or data science and marketing. Burning Glass CEO Matt Sigelman said, "The jobs of the future don't involve just one skill. There's a breadth of skills that will be needed."

**DISCUSSION QUESTIONS**

1. What do you think "hybrid jobs" mean for how universities need to education students differently?
2. What do you think "hybrid jobs" mean for how you manage your career?

SOURCE: L. Weber, "The 'Hybrid' Skills That Tomorrow's Jobs Will Require," *Wall Street Journal*, January 22, 2019, https://www.wsj.com/articles/the-hybrid-skills-that-tomorrows-jobs-will-require-11547994266.

The Integrity in Action box describes the recent scandal in South Korea where celebrity, sex, and bribes allegedly intersected.

For example, the United States has led the world in eliminating discrimination in the workplace. Because of the importance this has in our culture, we also have legal safeguards such as equal employment opportunity laws (discussed in Chapter 3) that strongly affect the hiring and firing practices of firms. As a society, we also have strong beliefs regarding the equity of pay systems; thus, the Fair Labor Standards Act (discussed in Chapter 11), among other laws and regulations, sets the minimum wage for a variety of jobs. We have regulations that dictate much of the process for negotiation between unions and management. These regulations profoundly affect how human resources are managed in the United States.

Similarly, the legal regulations regarding HRM in other countries reflect their societal norms. For example, in Germany employees have a legal right to "codetermination" at the company, plant, and individual levels. At the company level, a firm's employees have direct influence on the important decisions that affect them, such as large investments or new strategies. This is brought about through having employee representatives on the supervisory council *(Aufsichtsrat)*. At the plant level, codetermination exists through works councils. These councils have no rights in the economic management of the company, but they can influence HRM policies on such issues as working hours, payment methods, hirings, and transfers. Finally, at the individual level, employees have contractual rights, such as the right to read their personnel files and the right to be informed about how their pay is calculated.[22]

The European Economic Community provides another example of the effects of the political–legal system on HRM. The EEC's Community Charter of December 9, 1989, provides for the fundamental social rights of workers. These rights include freedom of movement, freedom to choose one's occupation and be fairly compensated, guarantee of social protection via social security benefits, freedom of association and collective bargaining, equal treatment for men and women, and a safe and healthful work environment, among others. While not specific to HRM, Google was recently fined $1.7 billion by the European Union. The European Union alleges Google did not allow rivals advertisements to show up on certain websites. This is the third judgement by the European Union against Google since 2017, with the total fines equaling over $7.6 billion.

The legal system often requires that companies do certain things or meet certain guidelines. However, the political system might encourage companies to behave in certain ways, and we see this happening now regarding how companies try to decrease their carbon footprint as described in the Competing through Environmental, Social, and Governance Practices box.

### ECONOMIC SYSTEM

A country's economic system influences HRM in a number of ways. As previously discussed, a country's culture is tied integrally to its economic system, and these systems provide many of the incentives for developing human capital. In socialist economic systems there are ample opportunities for developing human capital because the education system is free. However, under these systems, there is little economic incentive to develop human capital because there are no monetary rewards for increasing human capital. In addition, in former Soviet bloc countries, an individual's investment in human capital did not always result in a promotion. Rather, it was investment in the Communist Party that led to career advancements.

In capitalist systems the opposite situation exists. There is less opportunity to develop human capital without higher costs. (You have probably observed tuition increases at U.S. universities.) However, those who do invest in their individual human capital, particularly through education, are more able to reap monetary rewards, thus providing more incentive

## COMPETING THROUGH ENVIRONMENTAL, SOCIAL, AND GOVERNANCE PRACTICES

### Company Solutions to the Environmental Challenge

Many companies, either driven by a true valuing of the environment or by a public relations ploy, seek to increase their use of renewable energy sources. However, a number of obstacles stand in the way of maximizing the use of green energy such as wind and solar power.

First, energy markets vary by region, particularly in terms of the freedom that firms have to purchase energy. While utilities may produce energy from a variety of sources, it is often impossible for a firm to purchase energy from specific sources, such as a solar project.

Second, technological constraints still exist that make it difficult for firms to completely shift to green energy. For instance, solar and wind power are dependent on other factors (e.g., the sun being out and the wind blowing) that vary. However, companies need energy 24/7.

However, recently companies such as Walmart, General Motors, Google, and Johnson & Johnson have formed a trade association called the "Renewable Energy Buyers Alliance" to help remove the kinds of barriers that complicate the shift from carbon to renewable energy. About 200 companies and public entities (cities and universities) have become part of the alliance. While the alliance will help promote a "demand side" pressure for more renewable energy, some firms have been better able to implement the shift from carbon-based energy.

For instance, Walmart, because of its size advantage, is able to organize multiple sources of renewable power. Steve Chriss, director for energy and strategy analysis at Walmart, says Walmart has "a great desire to operate as cleanly and sustainably as possible. But we also want to operate at the lowest possible cost. With where renewable energy costs have come, we feel that in a number of markets renewable energy is going to be the best cost option. It's not just a specialty play for the interests of a few [companies] who are really into it. It's really about a business play to deliver the lowest-cost resources possible."

#### DISCUSSION QUESTIONS

1. Do you think that the Renewable Energy Buyers Alliance will be successful in creating demand-side pressure for more and better renewable energy sources?

2. Do you think this is a good idea? Why or why not?

SOURCE: C. Domanoske, "Walmart, GM, and Google Among Companies Teaming Up to Buy More Solar and Wind," *National Public Radio*, March 28, 2019, https://www.npr.org/2019/03/28/707007584/companies-organize-to-make-it-easier-to-buy-renewable-energy.

for such investment. In the United States, individuals' salaries usually reflect differences in human capital (high-skill workers receive higher compensation than low-skill workers). In fact, research estimates that an individual's wages increase by between 10% and 16% for each additional year of schooling.[23]

In addition to the effects of an economic system on HRM, the health of the system can have an important impact. For example, we referred earlier to lower labor costs in India. In developed countries with a high level of wealth, labor costs tend to be quite high relative to those in developing countries. Although labor costs are related to the human capital of a country, they are not perfectly related, as shown by Figure 15.2. This chart provides a good example of the different hourly labor costs for manufacturing jobs in various countries.

An economic system also affects HRM directly through its taxes on compensation packages. Thus, the differential labor costs shown in Figure 15.2 do not always reflect the actual take-home pay of employees. Socialist systems are characterized by tax systems that redistribute wealth by taking a higher percentage of a person's income as he or she

**Figure 15.2**

Hourly Compensation Costs in Manufacturing, U.S. Dollars, 2016

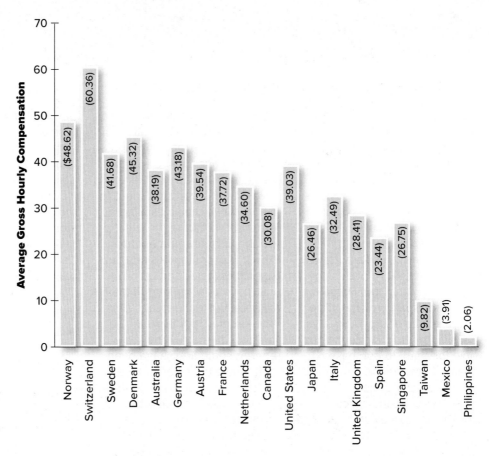

SOURCE: U.S. Bureau of Labor Statistics, www.bls.gov/news.release/pdf/ichcc.pdf.

moves up the economic ladder. Capitalist systems attempt to reward individuals for their efforts by allowing them to keep more of their earnings. Companies that do business in other countries have to present compensation packages to expatriate managers that are competitive in take-home, rather than gross, pay. HRM responses to these issues affecting expatriate managers will be discussed in more detail later in this chapter.

These differences in economies can have a profound impact on pay systems, particularly among global companies seeking to develop an international compensation and reward system that maintains cost controls while enabling local operations to compete in the war for talent. One recent study examining how compensation managers design these systems indicates that they look at a number of factors including the global firm strategy, the local regulatory and political context, institutions and stakeholders, local markets, and national culture. While they try to learn from the best practices that exist globally, they balance these approaches with the constraints imposed by the local environment.[24]

In conclusion, every country varies in terms of its culture, education–human capital, poltical–legal system, and economic system. These variations directly influence the types of HRM systems that must be developed to accommodate the particular situation. The extent to which these differences affect a company depends on how involved the company is in global markets. In the next section we discuss important concepts of global business and various levels of global participation, particularly noting how these factors come into play.

# Managing Employees in a Global Context

## TYPES OF INTERNATIONAL EMPLOYEES

Before discussing the levels of global participation, we need to distinguish between parent countries, host countries, and third countries. A **parent country** is the country in which the company's corporate headquarters is located. For example, the United States is the parent country of General Motors. A **host country** is the country in which the parent country organization seeks to locate (or has already located) a facility. Thus, Great Britain is a host country for General Motors because GM has operations there. A **third country** is a country other than the host country or parent country, and a company may or may not have a facility there.

There are also different categories of employees. The term **expatriate** is generally used for employees sent by a company in one country to manage operations in a different country. With the increasing globalization of business, it is now important to distinguish among different types of expatriates. **Parent-country nationals (PCNs)** are employees who were born and live in the parent country. **Host-country nationals (HCNs)** are those employees who were born and raised in the host, as opposed to the parent, country. Finally, **third-country nationals (TCNs)** are employees born in a country other than the parent country and host country but who work in the host country. Thus, a manager born and raised in Brazil employed by an organization located in the United States and assigned to manage an operation in Thailand would be considered a TCN.

Research shows that countries differ in their use of various types of international employees. One study revealed that Japanese multinational firms have more ethnocentric HRM policies and practices (they tend to use Japanese expatriate managers more than local host-country nationals) than either European or U.S. firms. This study also found that the use of ethnocentric HRM practices is associated with more HRM problems.[25]

## LEVELS OF GLOBAL PARTICIPATION

We often hear companies referred to as "multinational" or "international." However, it is important to understand the different levels of participation in international markets. This is especially important because as a company becomes more involved in international trade, different types of HRM problems arise. In this section we examine Nancy Adler's categorization of the various levels of international participation from which a company may choose.[26] Figure 15.3 depicts these levels of involvement.

### Domestic

Most companies begin by operating within a domestic marketplace. For example, an entrepreneur may have an idea for a product that meets a need in the U.S. marketplace. This individual then obtains capital to build a facility that produces the product or service in a quantity that meets the needs of a small market niche. This requires recruiting, hiring, training, and compensating a number of individuals who will be involved in the production process, and these individuals are usually drawn from the local labor market. The focus of the selection and training programs is often on the employees' technical competence to perform job-related duties and to some extent on interpersonal skills. In addition, because the company is usually involved in only one labor market, determining the market rate of pay for various jobs is relatively easy.

As the product grows in popularity, the owner might choose to build additional facilities in different parts of the country to reduce the costs of transporting the product over

**LO 15-3**

List the different categories of international employees.

**Parent country**
The country in which a company's corporate headquarters is located.

**Host country**
The country in which the parent-country organization seeks to locate or has already located a facility.

**Third country**
A country other than a host or parent country.

**Expatriate**
Employee sent by his or her company to manage operations in a different country.

**Parent-country nationals (PCNs)**
Employees who were born and live in a parent country.

**Host-country nationals (HCNs)**
Employees born and raised in a host, not parent, country.

**Third-country nationals (TCNs)**
Employees born in a country other than a parent or host country.

**LO 15-4**

Identify the four levels of global participation and the HRM issues faced within each level.

**Figure 15.3**

Levels of Global Participation

large distances. In deciding where to locate these facilities, the owner must consider the attractiveness of the local labor markets. Various parts of the country may have different cultures that make those areas more or less attractive according to the work ethics of the potential employees. Similarly, the human capital in the different areas may vary greatly because of differences in educational systems. Finally, local pay rates may differ. It is for these reasons that the U.S. economy in the past 10 years has experienced a movement of jobs from northern states, which are characterized by strong unions and high labor costs, to the Sunbelt states, which have lower labor costs and are less unionized.

Incidentally, even domestic companies face problems with cultural diversity. In the United States, for example, the representation of women and minorities is increasing within the workforce. These groups come to the workplace with worldviews that differ from those of the traditional white male. Thus, we are seeing more and more emphasis on developing systems for managing cultural diversity within single-country organizations, even though the diversity might be on a somewhat smaller scale than the diversity of cultures across national boundaries.[27]

In a meta-analysis of the effects of cultural diversity on the functioning of multicultural work groups, Stahl and colleagues found that cultural diversity leads to process losses through increased task conflict and decreased social integration. At the same time, it leads to process gains through increasing creativity and satisfaction.[28]

It is important to note that companies functioning at the domestic level face an environment with very similar cultural, education–human capital, political–legal, and economic situations, although some variation might be observed across states and geographic areas.

### International

As more competitors enter the domestic market, companies face the possibility of losing market share; thus, they often seek other markets for their products. This usually requires entering international markets, initially by exporting products but ultimately by building production facilities in other countries. The decision to participate in international competition raises a host of human resource issues. All the problems regarding locating facilities are magnified. One must consider whether a particular location provides an environment where human resources can be successfully acquired and managed.

Now the company faces an entirely different situation with regard to culture, education–human capital, the political–legal system, and the economic system. For example, the availability of human capital is of utmost importance, and there is a substantially greater variability in human capital between the United States and other countries than there is among the various states in the United States.

A country's legal system may also present HRM problems. For example, France has a relatively high minimum wage, which drives up labor costs. In addition, regulations make it extremely difficult to fire or lay off an employee. In Germany companies are legally required to offer employees influence in the management of the firm. Companies that develop facilities in other countries have to adapt their HRM practices to conform to the host country's laws. This requires the company to gain expertise in the country's HRM legal requirements and knowledge about how to deal with the country's legal system, and it often requires the company to hire one or more host-country nationals. In fact, some countries legally require companies to hire a certain percentage of HCNs for any foreign-owned subsidiary.

Finally, cultures have to be considered. To the extent that the country's culture is vastly different from that of the parent organization, conflicts, communication problems, and morale problems may occur. Expatriate managers must be trained to identify these cultural differences, and they must be flexible enough to adapt their styles to those of their host country. This requires an extensive selection effort to identify individuals who are capable of adapting to new environments and an extensive training program to ensure that the culture shock is not devastating.

## Multinational

Whereas international companies build one or a few facilities in another country, they become multinational when they build facilities in a number of different countries, attempting to capitalize on lower production and distribution costs in different locations. The lower production costs are gained by shifting production from higher-cost locations to lower-cost locations. For example, some of the major U.S. automakers have plants all over the world. They continue to shift their production from the United States, where labor unions have gained high wages for their members, to *maquiladora* facilities in Mexico, where the wages are substantially lower. Similarly, these companies minimize distribution and labor costs by locating facilities in central and eastern European countries such as Poland, Hungary, and the Slovak Republic for manufacturing and assembling automobiles to sell in the European market.

The HRM problems multinational companies face are similar to those international companies face, only magnified. Instead of having to consider only one or two countries' cultural, education–human capital, political–legal, and economic systems, the multinational company must address these differences for a large number of countries. This accentuates the need to select managers capable of functioning in a variety of settings, give them necessary training, and provide flexible compensation systems that take into account the different market pay rates, tax systems, and costs of living.

Multinational companies now employ many "inpatriates"—managers from different countries who become part of the corporate headquarters staff. This creates a need to integrate managers from different cultures into the culture of the parent company. In addition, multinational companies now take more expatriates from countries other than the parent country and place them in facilities of other countries. For example, a manager from Scotland, working for a U.S. company, might be assigned to run an operation in South Africa. This practice accentuates the need for cross-cultural training to provide managerial skills for interaction with individuals from different cultures.

## Global

Many researchers now propose a fourth level of integration: global organizations. Global organizations compete on state-of-the-art, top-quality products and services and do so with the lowest costs possible. Whereas multinational companies attempt to develop identical products distributed worldwide, global companies increasingly emphasize flexibility and mass customization of products to meet the needs of particular clients. Multinational companies are usually driven to locate facilities in a country as a means of reaching that country's market or lowering production costs, and the company must deal with the differences across the countries. Global firms, by contrast, choose to locate a facility based on the ability to effectively, efficiently, and flexibly produce a product or service and attempt to create synergy through the cultural differences.

This creates the need for HRM systems that encourage flexible production (thus presenting a host of HRM issues). These companies proactively consider the cultures, education–human capital, political–legal systems, and economic systems to determine where production facilities can be located to provide a competitive advantage. Global companies have multiple headquarters spread across the globe, resulting in less hierarchically structured organizations that emphasize decentralized decision making. This results in the need for human resource systems that recruit, develop, retain, and use managers and executives who are competent transnationally.

**Transnational scope**
A company's ability to make HRM decisions from an international perspective.

A transnational HRM system is characterized by three attributes.[29] **Transnational scope** refers to the fact that HRM decisions must be made from a global rather than a national or regional perspective. This creates the need to make decisions that balance the need for uniformity (to ensure fair treatment of all employees) with the need for flexibility (to meet the needs of employees in different countries). **Transnational representation** reflects the multinational composition of a company's managers. Global participation does not necessarily ensure that each country is providing managers to the company's ranks. This is a prerequisite if the company is to achieve the next attribute. **Transnational process** refers to the extent to which the company's planning and decision-making processes include representatives and ideas from a variety of cultures. This attribute allows for diverse viewpoints and knowledge associated with different cultures, increasing the quality of decision making.

**Transnational representation**
Reflects the multinational composition of a company's managers.

**Transnational process**
The extent to which a company's planning and decision-making processes include representatives and ideas from a variety of cultures.

These three characteristics are necessary for global companies to achieve cultural synergy. Rather than simply integrating foreigners into the domestic organization, a successful transnational company needs managers who will treat managers from other cultures as equals. This synergy can be accomplished only by combining selection, training, appraisal, and compensation systems in such a way that managers have a transnational rather than a parochial orientation. However, a survey of 50 companies in the United States and Canada found that global companies' HRM systems are far less transnational in scope, representation, and process than the companies' strategic planning systems and organizational structures.[30]

In conclusion, entry into international markets creates a host of HRM issues that must be addressed if a company is to gain competitive advantage. Once the choice has been made to compete in a global arena, companies must seek to manage employees who are sent to foreign countries (expatriates and third-country nationals). This causes the need to shift from focusing only on the culture, education–human capital, political–legal, and economic influences of the host country to examining ways to manage the expatriate managers who must be located there. Selection systems must be developed that allow the company to identify managers capable of functioning in a new culture. These managers must be trained to identify the important aspects of the new culture in which they will live as well as the relevant legal–political and economic systems. Finally, these managers must be compensated to offset the costs of uprooting themselves and their families to move to a new situation vastly different from their previous lives. In the next section we address issues regarding management of expatriates.

## MANAGING EXPATRIATES IN GLOBAL MARKETS

We have outlined the major macro-level factors that influence HRM in global markets. These factors can affect a company's decision whether to build facilities in a given country. In addition, if a company does develop such facilities, these factors strongly affect the HRM practices used. However, an important issue recognized over the past few years is the set of problems inherent in selecting, training, compensating, and reintegrating expatriate managers.

**LO 15-5**
Discuss the ways companies attempt to select, train, compensate, and reintegrate expatriate managers.

According to a study by the National Foreign Trade Council (NFTC), there were 250,000 Americans on assignments overseas and that number was expected to increase. In addition, the NFTC estimates that the average one-time cost for relocating an expatriate is $60,000.[31] The importance to the company's profitability of making the right expatriate assignments should not be underestimated. Expatriate managers' average compensation package is approximately $250,000,[32] and the cost of an unsuccessful expatriate assignment (i.e., a manager returning early) is approximately $100,000.[33] The failure rate for expatriate assignments among U.S. firms had been estimated at between 15% and 40%. However, more recent research suggests that the current figure is much lower. Some recent studies of European multinationals put the rate at 5% for most firms. Although the failure rate is generally recognized as higher among U.S. multinationals, it is doubtful that the proportion reaches the 15–40% range.[34]

In the final section of the chapter, we discuss the major issues relevant to the management of expatriate managers. These issues cover the selection, training, compensation, and reacculturation of expatriates.

### Selection of Expatriate Managers

One of the major problems in managing expatriate managers is determining which individuals in the organization are most capable of handling an assignment in a different culture. Expatriate managers must have technical competence in the area of operations; otherwise, they will be unable to earn the respect of subordinates. However, technical competence has been almost the sole variable used in deciding who to send on overseas assignments, despite the fact that multiple skills are necessary for successful performance in these assignments.[35]

According to Brookfield Global Relocation Services's 2016 Global Mobility Trends report, almost 80% of companies do not formally assess international assignment candidates in terms of their adaptability, and only 20% use a candidate's self-assessment of their adaptability. Also, 48% are unsure if the attrition rate of their expatriates is higher than the attrition rate in the rest of their workforce.

A successful expatriate manager must be sensitive to the country's cultural norms, flexible enough to adapt to those norms, and strong enough to make it through the inevitable culture shock. In addition, the manager's family must be similarly capable of adapting to the new culture. These adaptive skills have been categorized into three dimensions:[36] (1) *the self dimension* (the skills that enable a manager to maintain a positive self-image and psychological well-being), (2) *the relationship dimension* (the skills required to foster relationships with the host-country nationals), and (3) *the perception dimension* (those skills that enable a manager to accurately perceive and evaluate the host environment). One study of international assignees found that they considered the following five factors to be important, in descending order of importance: family situation, flexibility and adaptability, job knowledge and motivation, relational skills, and extracultural openness.[37] Table 15.3 presents a series of considerations and questions to ask potential expatriate managers to assess their ability to adapt to a new cultural environment.

**Table 15.3**
Select Topics for Assessing Candidates for Overseas Assignments

**Motivation**
- What are the candidate's reasons and degree of interest in wanting an overseas assignment?
- Does the candidate have a realistic understanding of what is required in working and living overseas?
- What is the spouse's attitude toward an overseas assignment?

**Health**
- Are there any health issues with the candidate or family members that might impact the success of the overseas assignment?

**Language ability**
- Does the candidate have the potential to learn a new language?
- Does the candidate's spouse have the ability to learn a new language?

**Family considerations**
- How many moves has the family made among different cities or parts of the United States? What problems were encountered?
- What is the spouse's goal in this move overseas?
- How many children are in the family, and what are their ages? Will all the children move as part of the overseas assignment?
- Has divorce or its potential, or the death of a family member, had a negative effect on the family's cohesiveness?
- Are there any adjustment problems the candidate would expect, should the family move overseas?

**Resourcefulness and initiative**
- Is the candidate independent and capable of standing by his or her decisions?
- Is the candidate able to meet objectives and produce positive results with whatever human resources and facilities are available regardless of challenges that might arise in a foreign business environment?
- Can the candidate operate without a clear definition of responsibility and authority?
- Will the candidate be able to explain the goals of the company and its mission to local managers and workers?
- Does the candidate possess sufficient self-discipline and self-confidence to handle complex problems?
- Can the candidate operate effectively in a foreign country without normal communications and supporting services?

**Adaptability**
- Is the candidate cooperative, open to the opinions of others, and able to compromise?
- How does the candidate react to new situations and efforts to understand and appreciate cultural differences?
- How does the candidate react to criticism, constructive or otherwise?
- Will the candidate be able to make and develop contacts with peers in a foreign country?
- Does the candidate demonstrate patience when dealing with problems? Is he or she resilient and able to move forward after setbacks?

**Career planning**
- Does the candidate consider the assignment more than a temporary overseas trip?
- Is the overseas assignment consistent with the candidate's career development and one that was planned by the company?
- What is the candidate's overall attitude toward the company?
- Is there any history or indication of interpersonal problems with this candidate?

**Financial**
- Are there any current financial and/or legal considerations that might affect the assignment (e.g., house or car purchase, college expenses)?
- Will undue financial pressures be put upon the candidate and his or her family as a result of an overseas assignment?

SOURCES: P. Caligiuri, *Cultural Agility: Building a Pipeline of Successful Global Professionals* (San Francisco: Jossey-Bass, 2012); P. Caligiuri, D. Lepak, and J. Bonache, *Managing the Global Workforce* (West Sussex, United Kingdom: John Wiley & Sons, 2010); M. Shaffer, D. Harrison, H. Gregersen, S. Black, and L. Ferzandi, "You Can Take It with You: Individual Differences and Expatriate Effectiveness," *Journal of Applied Psychology* 91 (2006), pp. 109–25; P. Caligiuri, "Developing Global Leaders," *Human Resource Management Review* 16 (2006), pp. 219–28; P. Caligiuri, M. Hyland, A. Joshi, and A. Bross, "Testing a Theoretical Model for Examining the Relationship between Family Adjustment and Expatriates' Work Adjustment," *Journal of Applied Psychology* 83 (1998), pp. 598–614; David M. Noer, *Multinational People Management: A Guide for Organizations and Employees* (Arlington, VA: Bureau of National Affairs, 1975).

One construct that has been emerging in the expatriate literature is cultural intelligence (CQ). This characteristic refers to an individual's ability to adapt across cultures through sensing the different cues regarding appropriate behavior across cultural settings or in multicultural settings. In fact, one set of researchers found that CQ was related to cultural adjustment and task performance among a sample of international executives.[38]

Little evidence suggests that U.S. companies have invested much effort in attempting to make correct expatriate selections. One researcher found that only 5% of the firms surveyed administered any tests to determine the degree to which expatriate candidates possessed cross-cultural skills.[39] More recent research reveals that only 35% of firms choose expatriates from multiple candidates and that those firms emphasize only technical job-related experience and skills in making these decisions.[40] These findings glaringly demonstrate that U.S. organizations need to improve their success rate in overseas assignments. As discussed in Chapter 6, the technology for assessing individuals' knowledge, skills, and abilities has advanced. The potential for selection testing to decrease the failure rate and productivity problems of U.S. expatriate managers seems promising. For instance, research has examined the "Big Five" personality dimensions as predictors of expatriate success (remember these from Chapter 6). For instance, one study distinguished between expatriate success as measured by not terminating the assignment and success as measured by supervisory evaluations of the expatriate. The researcher found that agreeableness, emotional stability, and extraversion were negatively related to the desire to terminate the assignment (i.e., they wanted to stay on the assignment longer), and conscientiousness was positively related to supervisory evaluations of the expatriate.[41]

A final issue with regard to expatriate selection is the use of women in expatriate assignments. For a long time, U.S. firms believed that women would not be successful managers in countries where women have not traditionally been promoted to management positions (such as in Japan and other Asian countries). However, recent evidence indicates that this is not true. Robin Abrams, an expatriate manager for Apple Computer's Hong Kong office, states that nobody cares whether "you are wearing trousers or a skirt if you have demonstrated core competencies." In fact, some women believe that the novelty of their presence among a group of men increases their credibility with locals. In fact, some research suggests that male and female expatriates can perform equally well in international assignments, regardless of the country's cultural predispositions toward women in management. However, female expatriates self-rate their adjustment lower in countries that have few women in the workforce.[42] Research has shown that female expatriates were perceived as being effective regardless of the cultural toughness of the host country.[43] The fact is that female expatriates feel more strongly than their supervisors that prejudice does not limit women's ability to be successful.[44]

## Training and Development of Expatriates

Once an expatriate manager has been selected, it is necessary to prepare that manager for the upcoming assignment. Because these individuals already have job-related skills, some firms have focused development efforts on cross-cultural training. A review of the cross-cultural training literature found support for the belief that cross-cultural training has an impact on effectiveness.[45] Even so, cross-cultural training is hardly universal. According to one survey, 69% of the 150 respondent companies offered cultural training for their outbound employees.[46]

What exactly is emphasized in cross-cultural training programs? The details regarding these programs were discussed in Chapter 7. Most programs attempt to create an appreciation of the host country's culture so that expatriates can behave appropriately.[47] This entails emphasizing a few aspects of cultural sensitivity. First, expatriates must be clear about their own cultural background, particularly as it is perceived by the host nationals. With an accurate cultural self-awareness, managers can modify their behavior to accentuate the effective characteristics while minimizing those that are dysfunctional.[48]

Second, expatriates must understand the particular aspects of culture in the new work environment. Although culture is an elusive, almost invisible phenomenon, astute expatriate managers must perceive the culture and adapt their behavior to it. This entails identifying the types of behaviors and interpersonal styles that are considered acceptable in both business meetings and social gatherings. For example, Germans value promptness for meetings to a much greater extent than do Latin Americans. Table 15.4 displays some ways body language conveys different messages in different countries.

Finally, expatriates must learn to communicate accurately in the new culture. Some firms attempt to use expatriates who speak the language of the host country, and a few

**Table 15.4**
International Body Language

| COUNTRY | NONVERBAL MESSAGES |
| --- | --- |
| Argentina | If the waiter approaches pointing to the side of his head and making a spinning gesture with his finger, don't think he's lost it—he's trying to say you have a phone call. |
| Bangladesh | Bursting to go to the toilet? Hold it. It is considered very rude to excuse yourself from the table to use the bathroom. |
| Bolivia | Don't make "the sign of the fig" (thumb protruding between index and middle finger), historically a sign that you couldn't care less—it is very insulting. |
| Bulgaria | Bulgarians nod the head up and down to mean no, not yes. To say yes, a Bulgarian nods the head back and forth. |
| Mainland China | In Eastern culture, silence really can be golden. So don't panic if long periods of silence form part of your meeting with Chinese clients. It simply means they are considering your proposal carefully. |
| Egypt | Because across the Arab world the left hand is unclean, use your right to accept business cards and to greet someone. Use only your right hand for eating. |
| Fiji | To show respect to your Fijian hosts when addressing them, stand with your arms folded behind your back. |
| France | The French don't like strong handshakes, preferring a short, light grip or air kissing. If your French colleague is seen to be playing an imaginary flute, however, it means he thinks you are not being truthful. |
| Germany | When Germans meet across a large conference table and it is awkward to reach over and shake hands, they will instead rap their knuckles lightly on the table by way of a greeting. |
| Greece | Beware of making the okay sign to Greek colleagues as it signifies bodily orifices. A safer bet is the thumbs-up sign. The thumbs-down, however, is the kind of gesture reserved for when a Greek motorist cuts you off on the highway. |
| Hong Kong (SAR) | When trying to attract someone's attention, don't use your index finger with palm extended upward. This is how the Cantonese call their dogs. |
| India | Beware of whistling in public—it is the height of rudeness here. |
| Japan | Japan is a real minefield for Western businesspeople, but one that always gets to them is the way the Japanese heartily slurp their noodles at lunch. Far from being rude, it actually shows appreciation of the food in Japanese culture. |
| Jordan | No matter how hungry you are, it is customary to refuse seconds from your host twice before finally accepting a third time. |

*(continued)*

| COUNTRY | NONVERBAL MESSAGES |
|---|---|
| Lebanon | Itchy eyebrow? Don't scratch it. Licking your little finger and brushing it across your eyebrow is provocative. |
| Malaysia | If you find a Malaysian standing with hands on hips before you, you've clearly said something wrong. It means he's livid. |
| Mexico | Mexicans are very tactile and often perform a bizarre handshake whereby, after pressing together the palms, they will slide their hands upward to grasp each other's thumbs. |
| Netherlands | The Dutch may seem open-minded, but if Dutch people tap the underside of their elbow, it means they think you're unreliable. |
| Pakistan | The overt display of a closed fist is an incitement to war. |
| Philippines | The "Roger Moore" is a common greeting here—a quick flash of the eyebrows supersedes the need for handshakes. |
| Russia | The Russians are highly tactile meet and greeters, with bear hugs and kisses directly on the lips commonplace. Don't take this habit to nearby Uzbekistan, however. They'd probably shoot you. |
| Saudi Arabia | If a Saudi man takes another's hand on the street, it's a sign of mutual respect. |
| Samoa | When your new Samoan host offers you a cup of the traditional drink, kava, make sure to deliberately spill a few drops on the ground before taking your first sip. |
| Turkey | Be careful not to lean back on your chair and point the sole of your foot at anyone in a meeting in Istanbul. Pointing with the underside of the foot is highly insulting. |

SOURCES: K. Elkins and M. Nudelman, "The Shocking Differences in Basic Body Language Around the World," *Business Insider*, March 17, 2015, http://www.businessinsider.com/body-language-around-the-world-2015-3; R. Axtell, *Gestures: The Dos and Taboos of Body Language Around the World*, (New York: Wiley, 1991); P. Harris and R. Moran, *Managing Cultural Differences*, 3rd ed. (Houston, TX: Gulf Publishing, 1991); R. Linowes, "The Japanese Manager's Traumatic Entry into the United States: Understanding the American-Japanese Cultural Divide," *Academy of Management Executive* 7, no. 4 (1993), p. 26; D. Doke, "Perfect Strangers," *HR Magazine*, December 2004, pp. 62–68.

provide language training. However, most companies simply assume that the host-country nationals all speak the parent-country's language. Although this assumption might be true, seldom do these nationals speak the parent-country language fluently. Thus, expatriate managers must be trained to communicate with others when language barriers exist.

Recent research has validated some of the most important expatriate adjustment factors. These are listed in Table 15.5.

**Table 15.5**
Expatriate Adjustment Factors

**Work Environment** (the employees, culture, and climate where the expatriate works)
**Language** (the ability of the expatriate to communicate effectively)
**Job or Task Characteristics** (the expatriate's freedom, autonomy and variety in how they work)
**Leisure Time** (opportunities to engage in sports, hobbies and other leisure activities)
**Urbanity** (pollution, traffic, and beauty of the location)
**Work–Life Balance** (ability to balance time spent at work and with family)
**Living Quarters** (size and type of living accommodations)
**Family Life** (family cohesion and harmony with partner)
**Local Friendships** (number and depth of local friendships)
**Contact to Those Left Behind** (ability to maintain relationships with family and friends in the home country)

SOURCE: T. Hippler, P. Caligiuri, J. Johnson, and N. Baytalskaya, "The Development and Validation of a Theory-Based Expatriate Adjustment Scale," *International Journal of Human Resource management* 25, 14 (2014), pp. 1938–59.

Effective cross-cultural training helps ease an expatriate's transition to the new work environment. It can also help avoid costly mistakes, such as the expatriate who attempted to bring two bottles of brandy into the Muslim country of Qatar. The brandy was discovered by customs; not only was the expatriate deported, but the company also was "disinvited" from the country.[49]

### Compensation of Expatriates

One of the more troublesome aspects of managing expatriates is determining the compensation package. As discussed previously, these packages average $250,000, but it is necessary to examine their exact breakdown. Most use a balance sheet approach to determine the total package level. This approach entails developing a total compensation package that equalizes the purchasing power of the expatriate manager with that of employees in similar positions in the home country and provides incentives to offset the inconveniences incurred in the location. Purchasing power includes all of the expenses associated with the expatriate assignment. Expenses include goods and services (food, personal care, clothing, recreation, and transportation), housing (for a principal residence), income taxes (paid to federal and local governments), reserve (savings, payments for benefits, pension contributions), and shipment and storage (costs associated with moving and/or storing personal belongings). A typical balance sheet is shown in Figure 15.4.

**Figure 15.4**

The Balance Sheet for Determining Expatriate Compensation

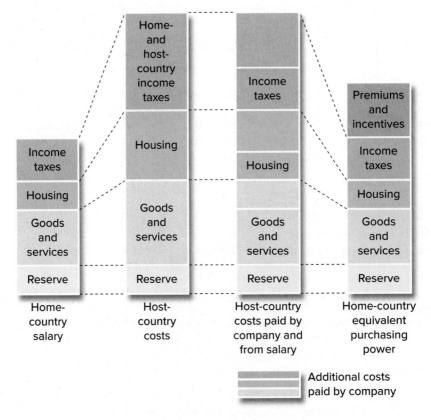

SOURCE: From C. Reynolds, "Compensation of Overseas Personnel," in J. J. Famulari, ed., *Handbook of Human Resource Administration*, 2nd ed., 1986. Copyright © 1986. Reproduced with permission of The McGraw-Hill Companies, Inc.

As you can see from this figure, the employee starts with a set of costs for taxes, housing, goods and services, and reserve. However, in the host country, these costs are significantly higher. Thus, the company must make up the difference between costs in the home and those in the host country, and then provide a premium and/or incentive for the employee to go through the trouble of living in a different environment.

Total pay packages have four components. First, there is the base salary. Determining the base salary is not a simple matter, however. Fluctuating exchange rates between countries may make an offered salary a raise some of the time, a pay cut at other times. In addition, the base salary may be based on comparable pay in the parent country, or it may be based on the prevailing market rates for the job in the host country. Expatriates are often offered a salary premium beyond that of their present salary as an inducement to accept the expatriate assignment.

Tax equalization allowances are a second component. They are necessary because of countries' different taxation systems in high-tax countries.[50] Under most tax equalization plans, the company withholds the amount of tax to be paid in the home country, then pays all of the taxes accrued in the host country.

A third component, benefits, presents additional compensation problems. Most of the problems have to do with the transportability of the benefits. For example, if an expatriate contributing to a pension plan in the United States is moved to a different country, does the individual have a new pension in the host country, or should the individual be allowed to contribute to the existing pension in her home country? What about health care systems located in the United States? How does the company ensure that expatriate employees have equal health care coverage? For example, in one company, the different health care plans available resulted in situations where it might cost significantly less to have the employee fly to the United States to have a procedure performed rather than to have it done in the host country. However, the health plans did not allow this alternative.

Finally, allowances are often offered to make the expatriate assignment less unattractive. Cost-of-living allowances are payments that offset the differences in expenditures on day-to-day necessities between the host country and the parent country. For instance, Table 15.6 shows the differences in cost of living among some of the larger international cities.

**Table 15.6**
The 10 Most Expensive Cities (New York = 100)

| CITY, COUNTRY | WCOL INDEX | RANK | RANK MOVEMENT (SINCE 2016) |
|---|---|---|---|
| Singapore, Singapore | 129 | 1 | 0 |
| Paris, France | 126 | 2 | 0 |
| Oslo, Norway | 124 | 3 | 0 |
| Zurich, Switzerland | 121 | 4 | 0 |
| Sydney, Australia | 120 | 5 | 0 |
| Melbourne, Australia | 118 | 6 | 0 |
| Geneva, Switzerland | 116 | 7 | −1 |
| Copenhagen, Denmark | 115 | 8 | 2 |
| Hong Kong, Hong Kong (SAR) | 113 | 9 | 4 |
| Seoul, South Korea | 113 | 9 | 6 |

SOURCE: Economist Intelligence Unit (2015), "Worldwide Cost of Living 2016." www.eiu.com.

Housing allowances ensure that the expatriate can maintain the same home-country living standard. Education allowances reimburse expatriates for the expense of placing their children in private English-speaking schools. Relocation allowances cover all the expenses of making the actual move to a new country, including transportation to and from the new location, temporary living expenses, and shipping and/or storage of personal possessions. Figure 15.5 illustrates a summary sheet for an expatriate manager's compensation package at Abbvie.

The cost of a U.S. expatriate working in another country is approximately three to four times that of a comparable U.S. employee.[51] In addition, "about 38% of multinational companies surveyed by KPMG LLP for its 2006 Global Assignment Policies and Practices

**Figure 15.5**
International Assignment Allowance Form

### INTERNATIONAL ASSIGNMENT COST ESTIMATE

| | | | |
|---|---|---|---|
| Assignee Name: | John Smith | Home Country: | United States |
| Annual Salary: | USD 165,888.00 | Home City/State/ | Lake County, Illinois |
| Assignment Start Date: | 01-Apr-2019 | Province: | USD |
| Projected End Date: | 31-Mar-2022 | Home Currency: | Mexico |
| Policy: | Developmental Assignment | Host Country: | Mexico City |
| Host Family Size: | 4 | Host City/State/Province: | MXN |
| Home Family Size | | Host Currency | |
| (Tax Family): | 4 | Report Currency: | USD |

| YEAR<br>MONTHS IN YEAR | YEAR 1<br>2019<br>9 | YEAR 2<br>2020<br>12 | YEAR 3<br>2021<br>12 | YEAR 4<br>2022<br>3 | POST YEAR<br>2023<br>12 | TOTAL |
|---|---|---|---|---|---|---|
| **Base Compensation** | | | | | | |
| Base Salary | 124,416 | 174,182 | 182,892 | 48,009 | | 529,499 |
| Annual Incentive Compensation | 31,104 | 43,546 | 45,723 | 12,002 | | 132,375 |
| Fringe Benefits | 25,194 | 35,272 | 37,036 | 9,722 | | 107,224 |
| **Base Compensation Total** | **180,714** | **253,000** | **265,651** | **69,733** | | **769,098** |
| **Allowances** | | | | | | |
| Cost of Living Differential | 511 | 681 | 681 | 170 | | 2,043 |
| Housing Allowance | 45,076 | 60,102 | 60,102 | 15,025 | | 180,305 |
| Host Utilities | 4,109 | 5,478 | 5,478 | 1,370 | | 16,435 |
| Location (Hardship) Allowance | 18,662 | 26,127 | 27,434 | 7,201 | | 79,424 |
| Home Leave Allowance | 7,930 | 7,930 | 7,930 | | | 23,790 |
| Dependent Education | 31,999 | 26,911 | 26,911 | | | 85,821 |
| Home Country Auto Disposal | 20,000 | | | | | 20,000 |
| Miscellaneous Relocation Allowance | 7,500 | | | | | 7,500 |
| **Allowances Total** | **135,787** | **127,229** | **128,536** | **23,766** | | **415,318** |

*(continued)*

| YEAR<br>MONTHS IN YEAR | YEAR 1<br>2019<br>9 | YEAR 2<br>2020<br>12 | YEAR 3<br>2021<br>12 | YEAR 4<br>2022<br>3 | POST YEAR<br>2023<br>12 | TOTAL |
|---|---|---|---|---|---|---|
| **Relocation** | | | | | | |
| Initial Expat Costs | | | | | | |
| Home Finding Trip | 3,648 | | | | | 3,648 |
| Tax Briefing/Orientation | 1,000 | | | | | 1,000 |
| Medical Exams—Employee | 150 | | | | | 150 |
| Medical Exams—Family | 450 | | | | | 450 |
| Visa/Immigration—Employee | 1,958 | 1,230 | 1,230 | | | 4,418 |
| Visa/Immigration—Family | 1,440 | 627 | 627 | | | 2,694 |
| Intercultural Training | 5,150 | | | | | 5,150 |
| Intercultural Training—Children/Dependents | 1,950 | | | | | 1,950 |
| Language Training—Employee | 6,500 | | | | | 6,500 |
| Language Training—Family | 6,500 | | | | | 6,500 |
| Destination Services | 4,180 | | | | | 4,180 |
| Lease Cancellation—Home Country | 5,706 | | | | | 5,706 |
| Household Goods Shipment—Expat | 18,112 | | | | | 18,112 |
| Household Goods Insurance—Expat | 4,620 | | | | | 4,620 |
| Storage in Transit | 1,050 | | | | | 1,050 |
| Travel to Host Location—Employee | 1,167 | | | | | 1,167 |
| Travel to Host Location—Family | 1,701 | | | | | 1,701 |
| Temporary Living—Accommodations | 7,111 | | | | | 7,111 |
| Temporary Living—Car / Meals | 4,804 | | | | | 4,804 |
| **Initial Expat Costs Total** | **77,197** | **1,857** | **1,857** | | | **80,911** |
| Repat Costs | | | | | | |
| Travel to Home Location—Employee | | | | 1,222 | | 1,222 |
| Travel to Home Location—Family | | | | 1,866 | | 1,866 |
| Temporary Accommodations—Repat | | | | 12,499 | | 12,499 |
| Temporary Living—Car/Meals—Repat | | | | 7,628 | | 7,628 |
| Departure Services | | | | 1,155 | | 1,155 |
| Household Goods Transportation—Repat | | | | 19,923 | | 19,923 |

(continued)

## Figure 15.5

International Assignment Allowance Form (*concluded*)

| YEAR<br>MONTHS IN YEAR | YEAR 1<br>2019<br>9 | YEAR 2<br>2020<br>12 | YEAR 3<br>2021<br>12 | YEAR 4<br>2022<br>3 | POST YEAR<br>2023<br>12 | TOTAL |
|---|---|---|---|---|---|---|
| Household Goods<br>Insurance—Repat | | | | 4,620 | | 4,620 |
| Miscellaneous Relocation<br>Allowance—Repat | | | | 7,500 | | 7,500 |
| **Repat Costs Total** | | | | **56,413** | | **56,413** |
| **Relocation Total** | **77,197** | **1,857** | **1,857** | **56,413** | | **137,324** |
| | | | | | | |
| **Service Fees** | | | | | | |
| Relocation Vendor Fees | 3,920 | 3,300 | 3,300 | 2,140 | | 12,660 |
| Tax Provider Fee | 10,000 | 10,000 | 10,000 | 10,000 | 10,000 | 50,000 |
| **Service Fees Total** | **13,920** | **13,300** | **13,300** | **12,140** | **10,000** | **62,660** |
| | | | | | | |
| **Tax Costs** | | | | | | |
| Actual Tax | | | | | | |
| Home Country Income Tax | 6,980 | | 1,951 | 5,491 | | 14,422 |
| Home Country State/<br>Province Tax | 22,944 | 19,867 | 20,801 | 8,073 | 101 | 71,786 |
| Home Country Social Tax | 17,080 | 18,119 | 18,563 | 5,694 | 837 | 60,293 |
| Home Country Employer<br>Portion Social Tax | 12,596 | 15,724 | 15,998 | 3,310 | 837 | 48,465 |
| Host Country Income Tax | 170,598 | 174,010 | 180,617 | 50,606 | | 575,831 |
| Host Country Social Tax | 786 | 1,047 | 1,047 | 261 | | 3,141 |
| Host Country Employer<br>Portion Social Tax | 4,889 | 6,513 | 6,513 | 1,624 | | 19,539 |
| **Actual Tax Total** | **235,873** | **235,280** | **245,490** | **75,059** | **1,775** | **793,477** |
| Hypothetical Tax | | | | | | |
| Home Country Hypothetical<br>Income Tax | −19,328 | −30,748 | −33,305 | −6,808 | | −90,189 |
| Home country Hypothetical<br>State/Province Tax | −6,983 | −10,337 | −10,876 | −2,415 | | −30,611 |
| Home Country Hypothetical<br>Social Tax | −8,322 | −11,397 | −11,555 | −2,800 | | −34,074 |
| **Hypothetical Tax Total** | **−34,633** | **−52,482** | **−55,736** | **−12,023** | | **−154,874** |
| **Tax Costs Total** | **201,240** | **182,798** | **189,754** | **63,036** | **1,775** | **638,603** |
| **Total Costs** | **608,858** | **578,184** | **599,098** | **225,088** | **11,775** | **2,023,003** |
| **Less Base Compensation** | | | | | | |
| Base Compensation | −180,714 | −253,000 | −265,651 | −69,733 | | −769,098 |
| **Base Compensation Total** | **−180,714** | **−253,000** | **−265,651** | **−69,733** | | **−769,098** |
| **Net Incremental Costs** | **428,144** | **325,184** | **333,447** | **155,355** | **11,775** | **1,253,905** |

SOURCE: Courtesy of Tim Richmond, CHRO Abbvie.

say overseas assignment programs are 'more generous than they need to be.' "[52] These two facts combined have put pressure on global organizations to rethink their tax equalization strategy and expatriate packages.

### Reacculturation of Expatriates

A final issue of importance to managing expatriates is dealing with the reacculturation process when the managers reenter their home country. Reentry is no simple feat. Culture shock takes place in reverse. The individual has changed, the company has changed, and the culture has changed while the expatriate was overseas. According to one source, 60–70% of expatriates did not know what their position would be upon their return, and 46% ended up with jobs that gave them reduced autonomy and authority.[53] Twenty percent of workers want to leave the company when they return from an overseas assignment, and this presents potentially serious morale and productivity problems.[54] In fact, the most recent estimates are that 25% of expatriate managers leave the company within one year of returning from their expatriate assignments.[55] If these repatriates leave, the company has virtually no way to recoup its substantial investment in human capital.[56]

Companies are increasingly making efforts to help expatriates through reacculturation. Two characteristics help in this transition process: communication and validation.[57] *Communication* refers to the extent to which the expatriate receives information and recognizes changes while abroad. The closer the contact with the home organization while abroad, the more proactive, effective, and satisfied the expatriate will be upon reentry. *Validation* refers to the amount of recognition received by the expatriate upon return home. Expatriates who receive recognition from their peers and their bosses for their foreign work and their future potential contribution to the company have fewer troubles with reentry compared with those who are treated as if they were "out of the loop." Given the tremendous investment that firms make in expatriate employees, usually aimed at providing global experience that will help the company, firms certainly do not want to lose expatriates after their assignments have concluded.

A research study noted the role of an expatriate manager's expectations about the expatriate assignment in determining repatriation adjustment and job performance. This study found that managers whose job expectations (constraints and demands in terms of volume and performance standards) and nonwork expectations (living and housing conditions) were met exhibited a greater degree of repatriation adjustment and higher levels of job performance.[58] Monsanto has an extensive repatriation program that begins long before the expatriate returns. The program entails providing extensive information regarding the potential culture shock of repatriation and information on how family members, friends, and the office environment might have changed. Then, a few months after returning, expatriate managers hold "debriefing" sessions with several colleagues to help work through difficulties. Monsanto believes that this program provides them with a source of competitive advantage in international assignments.[59]

In sum, a variety of HR practices can support effective expatriation. In general, the selection system must rigorously assess potential expatriates' skills and personalities and even focus on the candidate's spouse. Training should be conducted prior to and during the expatriate assignment, and the assignment itself should be viewed as a career development experience. Effective reward systems must go beyond salary and benefits, and while keeping the employee "whole" and even offering a monetary premium, should also provide access to career development and learning opportunities. Finally, serious efforts should be made to manage the repatriation process.[60] A summary of the key points is provided in Table 15.7.

**Table 15.7**

Human Resource
Practices That
Support Effective
Expatriation

**Staffing and Selection**
- Communicate the value of international assignments for the company's global mission.
- Ensure that those with the highest potential move internationally.
- Provide short-term assignments to increase the pool of employees with international experience.
- Recruit employees who have lived or who were educated abroad.

**Training and Career Development**
- Make international assignment planning a part of the career development process.
- Encourage early international experience.
- Create learning opportunities during the assignment.
- Use international assignments as a leadership development tool.

**Performance Appraisal and Compensation**
- Differentiate performance management based on expatriate roles.
- Align incentives with expatriation objectives.
- Tailor benefits to the expatriate's needs.
- Focus on equality of opportunities, not cash.
- Emphasize rewarding careers rather than short-term outcomes.

**Expatriation and Repatriation Activities**
- Involve the family in the orientation program at the beginning and the end of the assignment.
- Establish mentor relationships between expatriates and executives from the home location.
- Provide support for dual careers.
- Secure opportunities for the returning manager to use knowledge and skills learned while on the international assignment.

SOURCE: From P. Evans, V. Pucik, and J. Barsoux, *The Global Challenge: Framework for International Human Resource Management*, 2002. Reproduced with permission of The McGraw-Hill Companies, Inc.

 # A LOOK BACK

## The Challenges of a Supply Chain

The chapter opening illustrates how companies have to examine a number of factors in determining where to locate manufacturing, sales, and distribution centers across the globe. While for many years firms seemed to focus almost entirely on where they could get the lowest labor costs, increasingly the political turmoil encourages them to potentially trade-off lower costs for higher stability. As the world becomes more complex, firms must also consider a greater variety of factors before deciding where in the world they want to be.

### QUESTIONS

1. While companies used to only consider cost, they now have to consider a number of other factors. What other factors do you think they need to consider?
2. To what extent do you think companies should consider things like a country's stand on human rights or environmental responsibility? How can they do that?

SOURCE: J. Stoll, "'Made in China' Was Once the Easy Answer. Not Anymore," *Wall Street Journal*, January 19, 2019, https://www.wsj.com/articles/made-in-china-was-once-the-easy-answer-not-anymore-11547827204.

## SUMMARY

Today's organizations are more involved in international commerce than ever before, and the trend will continue. Recent historic events such as the development of the European Union, NAFTA, USMCTA, the economic growth of Asia, and GATT have accelerated the movement toward a global market. Companies competing in the global marketplace require top-quality people to compete successfully. This requires that managers be aware of the many factors that significantly affect HRM in a global environment, such as culture, education–human capital, the political–legal system, and the economic system, and that they understand how these factors come into play in the various levels of global participation. Finally, it requires that they be adept at developing HRM systems that maximize the effectiveness of all human resources, particularly with regard to expatriate managers. Managers cannot overestimate the importance of effectively managing human resources to gain competitive advantage in today's global marketplace.

## KEY TERMS

Individualism–collectivism, 681
Power distance, 681
Uncertainty avoidance, 681
Masculinity–femininity dimension, 682
Long-term–short-term orientation, 682

Parent country, 689
Host country, 689
Third country, 689
Expatriate, 689
Parent-country nationals (PCNs), 689

Host-country nationals (HCNs), 689
Third-country nationals (TCNs), 689
Transnational scope, 692
Transnational representation, 692
Transnational process, 692

## DISCUSSION QUESTIONS

1. What current trends and/or events (besides those mentioned at the outset of the chapter) are responsible for the increased internationalization of the marketplace?
2. According to Hofstede (in Table 15.2), the United States is low on power distance, high on individuality, high on masculinity, low on uncertainty avoidance, and low on long-term orientation. Russia, by contrast, is high on power distance, moderate on individuality, low on masculinity, high on uncertainty avoidance, and low on long-term orientation. Many U.S. managers are transplanting their own HRM practices into Russia while companies seek to develop operations there. How acceptable and effective do you think the following practices will be and why? (a) Extensive assessments of individual abilities for selection? (b) Individually based appraisal systems? (c) Suggestion systems? (d) Self-managing work teams?

3. The chapter notes that political–legal and economic systems can reflect a country's culture. The former Eastern bloc countries seem to be changing their political–legal and economic systems. Is this change brought on by their cultures, or will culture have an impact on the ability to change these systems? Why?
4. Think of the different levels of global participation. What companies that you are familiar with exhibit the different levels of participation?
5. Think of a time when you had to function in another culture (on a vacation or job). What were the major obstacles you faced, and how did you deal with them? Was this a stressful experience? Why? How can companies help expatriate employees deal with stress?
6. What types of skills do you need to be able to manage in today's global marketplace? Where do you expect to get those skills? What classes and/or experiences will you need?

## SELF-ASSESSMENT EXERCISE

Also assignable in Connect.

The following list includes a number of qualities that have been identified as being associated with success in an expatriate assignment. Rate the degree to which you possess each quality, using the following scale:

1 = very low
2 = low
3 = moderate
4 = high
5 = very high

_____ Resourcefulness/resilience
_____ Adaptability/flexibility
_____ Emotional stability
_____ Ability to deal with ambiguity/uncertainty/differences
_____ Desire to work with people who are different
_____ Cultural empathy/sensitivity
_____ Tolerance of others' views, especially when they differ from your own
_____ Sensitivity to feelings and attitudes of others
_____ Good health and wellness

Add up your total score for the items. The higher your score, the greater your likelihood of success. Qualities that you rated low would be considered weaknesses for an expatriate assignment. Keep in mind that you will also need to be technically competent for the assignment, and your spouse and family (if applicable) must be adaptable and willing to live abroad.

SOURCE: Based on "Rating Scale on Successful Expatriate Qualities," from P. R. Harris and R. T. Moran, _Managing Cultural Differences_, 3rd ed. (Houston: Gulf, 1991), p. 569.

## EXERCISING STRATEGY

### GM's U.S.–Mexico Challenge

As markets have become more globalized, many companies have created global supply chains, sourcing and manufacturing all across the world. With the passage of the North American Free Trade Agreement, Mexico became a prime target for automobile manufacturers to build _maquiladora_ plants where Mexican workers provide a substantial labor cost advantage over U.S.-based United Automobile Workers (UAW) union members. In addition, the products assembled in Mexico are shipped not just to the United States but all around the world. In fact, GM recorded a record profit in its North American market resulting in UAW workers receiving $12,000 in profit sharing. General Motors assembles about 20% of its highly profitable trucks in Mexico and until recently had plans to move much of its sport-utility vehicle production there, as a way to further reduce costs and increase profits.

However, the election of Donald Trump as president of the United States has put a wrinkle in those plans. In an effort to keep companies from moving production outside the United States, Trump has proposed a border tax of as much as 35% on any products coming to the United States from Mexico. However, even a more modest tax of 20% is estimated to wipe out a quarter of GM's profit in the region.

GM's dilemma resembles that of many other companies seeking to compete in a globalized market. To move more production to Mexico would increase profits and benefit U.S. UAW workers with larger profit-sharing checks but would likely reduce the number of workers receiving those checks. Keeping more production in the United States would maintain or grow the number of workers there but would likely reduce the amount of money they would receive in profit sharing.

### QUESTIONS

1. What do you think is more important: fewer workers with higher pay, or more workers with lower pay?
2. How might the border tax impact Mexican workers and what responsibility does GM have to them? Should a global company care more about its home-country workers than host-country workers?
3. How do you think GM should handle this decision and why?

SOURCE: J. Stoll and M. Colias, "Mexico Is Key Cog in GM's Profit Machine," _Wall Street Journal_, February 8, 2017, https://www.wsj.com/articles/gm-says-it-supports-tax-reform-but-border-tax-is-complicated-1486473480.

## MANAGING PEOPLE

### Huawei's Culture

What is the world's third largest smartphone maker by shipments? Chinese telecommunications company Huawei Technologies Co. has earned that spot over the past five years while doubling revenues to almost $60 billion. But the bigger question is, to what has the company attributed its success? The answer is, its hard-driving culture.

Chief executive officer (CEO) Ren Zhengfei was a former People's Liberation Army engineer, and his military background clearly has influenced the culture. He has been quoted as saying "In victory, we raise glasses to

celebrate together. In defeat, we risk our lives to rescue each other."

That may sound hokey, but in the midst of the Ebola outbreak in 2014, the Chinese workers stayed in the affected areas to maintain production even while other companies were evacuating. In Huawei's 2015 annual report Chairwoman Sun Yafang wrote "When a crisis occurs, you will find Huawei employees heading toward it."

Examples of employee sacrifice have become part of the history of the company. Stories are told of employees in

Siberia building telecom networks in sub-zero temperatures, of expatriates in Germany living in dormitories and sharing bathrooms, and of engineers in Shenzhen keeping mattresses under their desks to pull all-nighters.

But as CEO Zhengfei nears retirement, two questions have emerged. First, can such a sacrificial corporate culture continue to exist, particularly in an industry known for its war for talent? Second, can Mr. Zhengfei's successor lead the company with the same level of authority as he?

## QUESTIONS

1. Would you want to work in a company with a culture like Huawei's? Why or why not?
2. Do you think it is possible to sustain such a culture as leaders change? Why or why not?

SOURCE: J. Osawa, "Huawei's Hard-Charging Workplace Culture Drives Growth, Demands Sacrifice," *Wall Street Journal*, December 4, 2016, https://www.wsj.com/articles/huaweis-founder-casts-a-long-shadow-over-telecom-giant-1480715055.

## HR IN SMALL BUSINESS

### Is Translating a Global Business?

One field in which small businesses have recently enjoyed rapid growth is in the business of providing translations. As barriers to international business continue to fall, more and more people are encountering language differences in the people they work with, sell to, and buy from. At the same time, advances in technology are providing avenues to deliver translations over the phone and over the Internet.

TransPerfect is one of the success stories. The company, based in New York City, started out when founder Steve Iverson, a French teacher, began translating documents for clients. Satisfied customers returned, looking for translations of patents and annual reports—even for court reporting in foreign languages. The company now provides translations in over 170 languages. It has offices in more than 90 cities spread over six continents.

CETRA Language Solutions is headquartered in Elkins Park, Pennsylvania. It started with a lawsuit: While founder Jiri Stejskal was working on his doctorate degree in Slavic languages and literature, a Philadelphia law firm asked him to translate thousands of pages of documents related to a case. Stejskal brought in all the Czech translators he could find, and his company was born. Now CETRA's employees and hundreds of consultants serve the federal government plus companies involved in law, marketing research, and life sciences. The company's freelance translators and interpreters are located throughout the world.

LinguaLinx, based in Troy, New York, handles more than words. It converts documents, websites, and multimedia into almost 150 languages. The company not only has to find qualified translators, but it also needs experts in technology to make state-of-the-art presentations. To recruit employees, LinguaLinx emphasizes interesting work experiences, rather than fancy perks. The company's careers website describes opportunities to work with a diverse, multicultural group, including clients at leading corporations and nonprofit organizations.

### QUESTIONS

1. What kinds of challenges would be involved in recruiting and selecting people to translate documents from Spanish, Polish, and French into English?
2. Would those challenges be easier to meet by recruiting within the United States or by looking for talent overseas? Explain.
3. Suppose a small translation business asked you to advise the company on how to overcome cultural barriers among a staff drawn from three countries. Suggest a few ways the company could use training and performance management to achieve this goal.

SOURCES: T. A. Sykes, "Growth in Translation," *Inc.*, August 4, 2009; J. Dresang, "Iverson Language Associates Acquired by N.Y. Firm," *Milwaukee Journal Sentinel*, December 2, 2008; Business & Company Resource Center, http://galenet.galegroup.com; TransPerfect corporate website, www.transperfect.com, accessed June 19, 2015; CETRA Language Solutions corporate website, www.cetra.com, accessed June 19, 2015; LinguaLinx corporate website, www.lingualinx.com, accessed June 19, 2015.

## NOTES

1. The Conference Board, "International Comparisons of Hourly Compensation Costs in Manufacturing, 2016 - Summary Tables," April 19, 2018, https://www.conference-board.org/ilcprogram/index.cfm?id=38269
2. D. Kirkpatrick, "The Net Makes It All Easier—Including Exporting U.S. Jobs," *Fortune*, May 2003, www.fortune.com/fortune/print/0,15935,450755,00.html.
3. R. Schuler, "An Integrative Framework of Strategic International Human Resource Management," *Journal of Management* (1993), pp. 419-60.
4. L. Rubio, "The Rationale for NAFTA: Mexico's New 'Outward Looking' Strategy," *Business Economics* (1991), pp. 12-16.
5. H. Cooper, "Economic Impact of NAFTA: It's a Wash, Experts Say," *Wall Street Journal*, June 17, 1997.

6. R. Peiper, *Human Resource Management: An International Comparison* (Berlin: Walter de Gruyter, 1990).

7. V. Sathe, *Culture and Related Corporate Realities* (Homewood, IL: Richard D. Irwin, 1985).

8. M. Rokeach, *Beliefs, Attitudes, and Values* (San Francisco: Jossey-Bass, 1968).

9. L. Harrison, *Who Prospers? How Cultural Values Shape Economic and Political Success* (New York: Free Press, 1992).

10. N. Adler, *International Dimensions of Organizational Behavior*, 2nd ed. (Boston: PWS-Kent, 1991).

11. R. Yates, "Japanese Managers Say They're Adopting Some U.S. Ways," *Chicago Tribune*, February 29, 1992, p. B1.

12. G. Hofstede, "Dimensions of National Cultures in Fifty Countries and Three Regions," in *Expectations in Cross-Cultural Psychology*, eds. J. Deregowski, S. Dziurawiec, and R. C. Annis (Lisse, Netherlands: Swets and Zeitlinger, 1983).

13. G. Hofstede, "Cultural Constraints in Management Theories," *Academy of Management Executive* 7 (1993), pp. 81-90.

14. G. Hofstede, "The Cultural Relativity of Organizational Theories," *Journal of International Business Studies* 14 (1983), pp. 75-90.

15. G. Hofstede, "Cultural Constraints in Management Theories."

16. A. Ramesh, and M. Gelfland, "Will They Stay or Will They Go? The Role of Job Embeddedness in Predicting Turnover in Individualistic and Collectivistic Cultures," *Journal of Applied Psychology* 95, no. 5 (2010), pp. 807-23.

17. S. Snell and J. Dean, "Integrated Manufacturing and Human Resource Management: A Human Capital Perspective," *Academy of Management Journal* 35 (1992), pp. 467-504.

18. N. Adler and S. Bartholomew, "Managing Globally Competent People," *The Executive* 6 (1992), pp. 52-65.

19. B. O'Reilly, "Your New Global Workforce," *Fortune*, December 14, 1992, pp. 52-66.

20. A. Hoffman, "Are Technology Jobs Headed Offshore?" Monster.com, http://technology.monster.com/articles/offshore.

21. J. Ledvinka and V. Scardello, *Federal Employment Regulation in Human Resource Management* (Boston: PWS-Kent, 1991).

22. P. Conrad and R. Peiper, "Human Resource Management in the Federal Republic of Germany," in *Human Resource Management: An International Comparison*, ed. R. Peiper (Berlin: Walter de Gruyer, 1990).

23. R. Solow, "Growth with Equity through Investment in Human Capital," The George Seltzer Distinguished Lecture, University of Minnesota.

24. M. Bloom, G. Milkovich, and A. Mitra, "Toward a Model of International Compensation and Rewards: Learning from How Managers Respond to Variations in Local Host Contexts," working paper 00-14 (Ithaca, NY: Cornell University Center for Advanced Human Resource Studies, 2000).

25. R. Kopp, "International Human Resource Policies and Practices in Japanese, European, and United States Multinationals," *Human Resource Management* 33 (1994), pp. 581-99.

26. Adler, *International Dimensions of Organizational Behavior*.

27. S. Jackson and Associates, *Diversity in the Workplace: Human Resource Initiatives* (New York: Guilford Press, 1991).

28. G. Stahl, M. Maznevski, A. Voight, and K. Jonsen, "Unraveling the Effects of Cultural Diversity in Teams: A Meta-Analysis of Research on Multicultural Work Groups," *Journal of International Business Studies* 41 (2010), pp. 690-709.

29. Adler and Bartholomew, "Managing Globally Competent People."

30. Adler and Bartholomew, "Managing Globally Competent People."

31. S. Dolianski, "Are Expats Getting Lost in the Translation?" *Workforce*, February 1997.

32. L. Copeland and L. Griggs, *Going International* (New York: Random House, 1985).

33. K. F. Misa and J. M. Fabriacatore, "Return on Investments of Overseas Personnel," *Financial Executive* 47 (April 1979), pp. 42-46.

34. N. Forster, "The Persistent Myth of High Expatriate Failure Rates: A Reappraisal," *International Journal of Human Resource Management* 8, no. 4 (1997), pp. 414-34.

35. M. Mendenhall, E. Dunbar, and G. R. Oddou, "Expatriate Selection, Training, and Career-Pathing: A Review and Critique," *Human Resource Management* 26 (1987), pp. 331-45.

36. M. Mendenhall and G. Oddou, "The Dimensions of Expatriate Acculturation," *Academy of Management Review* 10 (1985), pp. 39-47.

37. W. Arthur and W. Bennett, "The International Assignee: The Relative Importance of Factors Perceived to Contribute to Success," *Personnel Psychology* 48 (1995), pp. 99-114.

38. K. Ng and C. Earley, "Culture and Intelligence: Old Constructs, New Frontiers," *Group and Organization Management* 31 (2006), pp. 4-19; S. Ang, L. Van Dyne, C. Koh, K. Y. Ng, K. J. Templer, C. Tay, and N. A. Chandrasekar, "Cultural Intelligence: Its Measurement and Effects on Cultural Judgment and Decision Making, Cultural Adaptation, and Task Performance," *Management and Organization Review* 3 (2007), pp. 335-71.

39. R. Tung, "Selecting and Training of Personnel for Overseas Assignments," *Columbia Journal of World Business* 16, no. 2 (1981), pp. 68-78.

40. Moran, Stahl, and Boyer, Inc., *International Human Resource Management* (Boulder, CO: Moran, Stahl, & Boyer, 1987).

41. P. Caligiuri, "The Big Five Personality Characteristics as Predictors of Expatriates' Desire to Terminate the Assignment and Supervisor Rated Performance," *Personnel Psychology* 53 (2000), pp. 67-88.

42. P. Caligiuri and R. Tung, "Comparing the Success of Male and Female Expatriates from a U.S.-based Multinational Company," *International Journal of Human Resource Management* 10, no. 5 (1999), pp. 763-82.

43. L. Stroh, A. Varma, and S. Valy-Durbin, "Why Are Women Left at Home? Are They Unwilling to Go on International Assignments?" *Journal of World Business 35*, no. 3 (2000), pp. 241-55.

44. A. Harzing, *Managing the Multinationals: An International Study of Control Mechanisms* (Cheltenham, UK: Edward Elgar, 1999).

45. J. S. Black and M. Mendenhall, "Cross-Cultural Training Effectiveness: A Review and Theoretical Framework for Future Research," *Academy of Management Review* 15 (1990), pp. 113-36.

46. B. Fitzgerald-Turner, "Myths of Expatriate Life," *HR Magazine* 42, no. 6 (June 1997), pp. 65-74.

47. P. Dowling and R. Schuler, *International Dimensions of Human Resource Management* (Boston: PWS-Kent, 1990).

48. Adler, *International Dimensions of Organizational Behavior*.

49. Dowling and Schuler, *International Dimensions of Human Resource Management*.

50. R. Schuler and P. Dowling, *Survey of ASPA/I Members* (New York: Stern School of Business, New York University, 1988).

51. C. Joinson, "No Returns: Localizing Expats Saves Companies Big Money and Can Be a Smooth Transition with a Little Due Diligence by HR," *HR Magazine* 11, no. 47 (2002), p. 70.

52. J. J. Smith, "Firms Say Expats Getting Too Costly, but Few Willing to Act" 2006, *SHRM*, retrieved March 9, 2007, www.shrm.org/global/library_published/subject/nonIC/CMS_018300.asp.

53. C. Solomon, "Repatriation: Up, Down, or Out?" *Personnel Journal* (1995), pp. 28–37.

54. "Workers Sent Overseas Have Adjustment Problems, a New Study Shows," *Wall Street Journal*, June 19, 1984, p. 1.

55. J. S. Black, "Repatriation: A Comparison of Japanese and American Practices and Results," *Proceedings of the Eastern Academy of Management Bi-annual International Conference* (Hong Kong, 1989), pp. 45–49.

56. J. S. Black, "Coming Home: The Relationship of Expatriate Expectations with Repatriation Adjustment and Job Performance," *Human Relations* 45 (1992), pp. 177–92.

57. Adler, *International Dimensions of Organizational Behavior.*

58. Black, "Coming Home."

59. Solomon, "Repatriation: Up, Down, or Out?"

60. P. Evans, V. Pucik, and J. Barsoux, *The Global Challenge: International Human Resource Management* (New York: McGraw-Hill, 2002), p. 137.

# 16 Strategically Managing the HRM Function

## LEARNING OBJECTIVES

*After reading this chapter, you should be able to:*

**LO 16-1** Describe the roles that HRM plays in firms today and the categories of HRM activities. *page 712*

**LO 16-2** Discuss how the HRM function can define its mission and market. *page 715*

**LO 16-3** Explain the approaches to evaluating the effectiveness of HRM practices. *page 719*

**LO 16-4** Describe the new structures for the HRM function. *page 724*

**LO 16-5** Describe how outsourcing HRM activities can improve service delivery efficiency and effectiveness. *page 727*

**LO 16-6** Relate how process reengineering is used to review and redesign HRM practices. *page 728*

**LO 16-7** Discuss the types of new technologies that can improve the efficiency and effectiveness of HRM. *page 730*

**LO 16-8** List the competencies the HRM executive needs to become a strategic partner in the company. *page 738*

## Rebuilding Wells Fargo

Wells Fargo needs a new CEO and a new culture. The bank had a sterling reputation and had avoided a number of the negative consequences of the financial crisis. However, then the "fake accounts" scandal emerged, where, under pressure to sign up new customers, personal bankers began creating accounts for customers without their knowledge. As a result, the reputation of the firm has been in tatters and former CEO John Stumpf was under pressure to resign. Tim Sloan took over for Stumpf as the CEO of Wells Fargo, but recently resigned after two years in the job. He had been under pressure from regulators in Washington to get the bank's numerous problems under control and was quoted as part of his resignation saying, ". . . it has become apparent to me that our ability to successfully move Wells Fargo forward from here will benefit from a new CEO and fresh perspectives."

Now the bank's board of directors will seek an outsider to fill the CEO role, as Chairman Elizabeth Duke told investors it would be "the most effective way to complete the transformation at Wells Fargo."

The new CEO will have a tremendous challenge ahead. The reward system created pressures for employees to serve themselves rather than the customers. It also created a culture focused on achieving results rather than satisfying customers. Thus, the next CEO will need to have an HR function that can help transform Wells Fargo into a bank that again has the respect of customers and industry competitors.

SOURCES: R. Ensign, "Wells Fargo CEO Tim Sloan Steps Down," *Wall Street Journal*, March 28, 2019, https://www.wsj.com/articles/help-wanted-wells-fargo-board-seeks-ceo-to-charm-washington-fix-bank-11553877969?mod=hp_lead_pos7; R. Ensign, "Help Wanted: Wells Fargo Board Seeks CEO to Charm Washington, Fix Bank," *Wall Street Journal*, March 29, 2019, https://www.wsj.com/articles/help-wanted-wells-fargo-board-seeks-ceo-to-charm-washington-fix-bank-11553877969?mod=hp_lead_pos7.

# Introduction

Throughout this book we have emphasized how human resource management practices can help companies gain a competitive advantage. We identified specific practices related to managing the internal and external environment; designing work and measuring work outcomes; and acquiring, developing, and compensating human resources. We have also discussed the best of current research and practice to show how they may contribute to a company's competitive advantage.

As we said in Chapter 1, the role of the HRM function has been evolving over time. As we see in this chapter's opening story, it has now reached a crossroads. Although it began as a purely administrative function, most HR executives now see the function's major role as being much more strategic. However, this evolution has resulted in a misalignment between the skills and capabilities of members of the function and the new requirements placed on it. Virtually every HRM function in top companies is going through a transformation process to create a function that can play this new strategic role while successfully fulfilling its other roles. This transformation process is also going on globally. Managing this process is the subject of this chapter. First we discuss the various activities of the HRM function. Then we examine how to develop a market- or customer-oriented HRM function. We then describe the current structure of most HRM functions. We discuss some of the software applications used by the HR function. We examine the competencies that will be needed in the future for HR professionals. Finally, we provide a specific analysis of the role that the chief human resources officer plays in making companies more successful.

# Activities of HRM

**LO 16-1**
Describe the roles that HRM plays in firms today and the categories of HRM activities.

To understand the transformation going on in HRM, one must understand HRM activities in terms of their strategic value. One way of classifying these activities is depicted in Figure 16.1. Transactional activities (the day-to-day transactions such as benefits administration, record keeping, and employee services) are low in their strategic value. Traditional activities such as performance management, training, recruiting, selection, compensation, and employee relations are the nuts and bolts of HRM. These activities have moderate strategic value because they often form the practices and systems to ensure strategy execution. For instance, one role of HR is often to set policies regarding the legitimate activities that salespeople can engage in to make sales in foreign countries. Transformational activities create long-term capability and adaptability for the firm.

**Figure 16.1**

Categories of HRM Activities and Percentages of Time Spent on Them

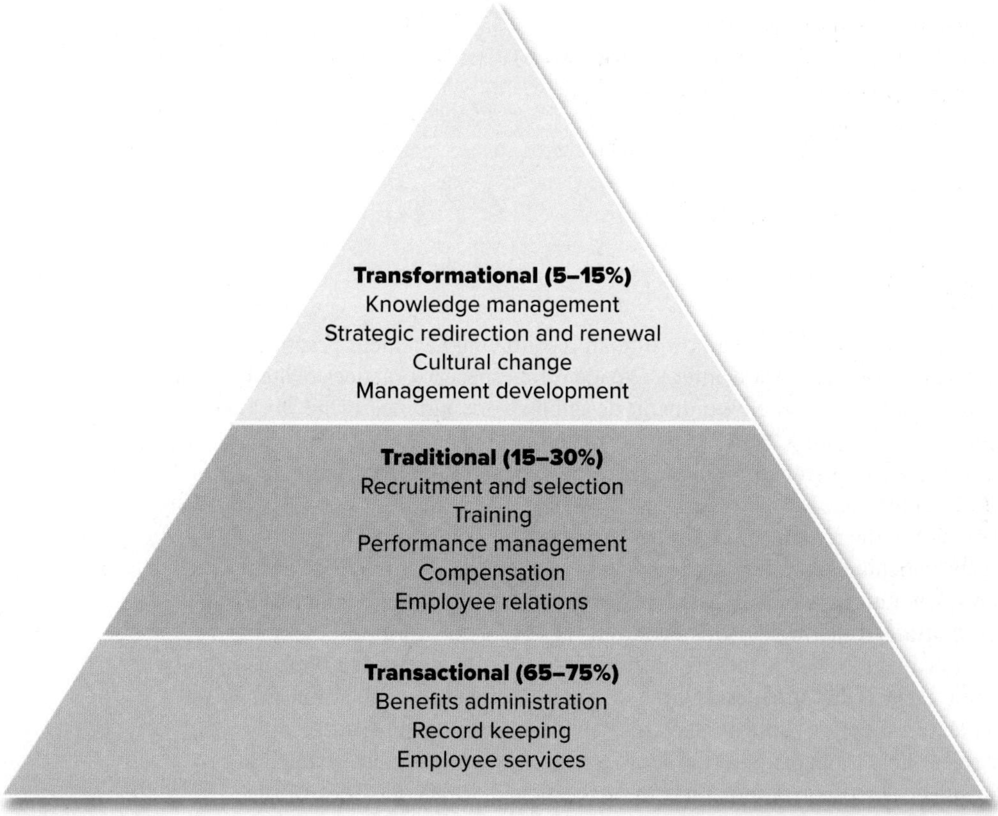

**Transformational (5–15%)**
Knowledge management
Strategic redirection and renewal
Cultural change
Management development

**Traditional (15–30%)**
Recruitment and selection
Training
Performance management
Compensation
Employee relations

**Transactional (65–75%)**
Benefits administration
Record keeping
Employee services

SOURCE: P. Wright, G. McMahan, S. Snell, and B. Gerhart, *Strategic Human Resource Management: Building Human Capital and Organizational Capability*. Technical report. Cornell University, 1998.

These activities include knowledge management, management development, cultural change, and strategic redirection and renewal. Obviously, these activities comprise the greatest strategic value for the firm.

As we see in the figure, historically HRM functions have spent the vast majority of their time on transactional activities, with substantially less on traditional and very little on transformational activities. However, virtually all HRM functions, in order to add value to the firm, must increase their efforts in the traditional and transformational activities. To do this, however, requires that HR executives (1) develop a strategy for the HRM function, (2) assess the current effectiveness of the HRM function, and (3) redesign, reengineer, or outsource HRM processes to improve efficiency and effectiveness. These issues will be discussed in the following sections.

# Strategic Management of the HRM Function

In light of the various roles and activities of the HRM function, it is highly unlikely that any function can (or should) effectively deliver on all roles and all activities. Although this is a laudable goal, resource constraints in terms of time, money, and head count require that the HR executive make strategic choices about where and how to allocate these resources for maximum value to the firm.

Chapter 2 explained the strategic management process that takes place at the organization level and discussed the role of HRM in this process. HRM has been seen as a strategic partner that has input into the formulation of the company's strategy and develops and aligns HRM programs to help implement the strategy. However, for the HRM function to become truly strategic in its orientation, it must view itself as a separate business entity and engage in strategic management in an effort to effectively serve the various internal customers.

In this respect, one recent trend within the field of HRM, consistent with the total quality management philosophy, is for the HR executive to take a customer-oriented approach to implementing the function. In other words, the strategic planning process that takes place at the level of the business can also be performed with the HRM function. HR executives in more progressive U.S. companies have begun to view the HRM function as a strategic business unit and have tried to define that business in terms of their customer base, their customers' needs, and the technologies required to satisfy customers' needs (Figure 16.2). For example, Joe Ruocco, the former chief HR officer at Goodyear, encouraged his HR function to take a customer-centric approach. As you can see in Figure 16.3, Goodyear views the business (line clients) and the employees (associates) as its main customers. The figure provides examples of the different tools and processes at the company's disposal to meet those customer needs.

A customer orientation is one of the most important changes in the HRM function's attempts to become strategic. It entails first identifying customers. The most obvious example of HRM customers are the line managers who require HRM services. In addition, the strategic planning team is a customer in the sense that it requires identification, analysis, and recommendations regarding people-oriented business problems. Employees are also HRM customers because the rewards they receive from the employment relationship are determined or administered by the HRM department.

In addition, the products of the HRM department must be identified. Line managers want to have high-quality employees committed to the organization. The strategic planning team requires information and recommendations for the planning process as well as programs that support the strategic plan once it has been identified. Employees want compensation and benefit programs that are consistent, adequate, and equitable, and they

**Figure 16.2**
Customer-Oriented
Perspective of the
HRM Function

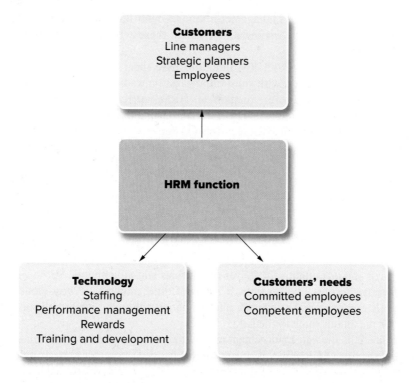

**Figure 16.3**
Goodyear's
Customer-Centric
View of HR

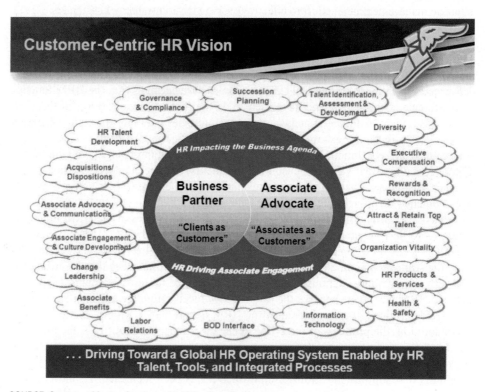

SOURCE: Courtesy of former Goodyear chief HR officer Joe Ruocco.

want fair promotion decisions. At Southwest Airlines, the "People" department administers customer surveys to all clients as they leave the department to measure how well their needs have been satisfied.

Finally, the technologies through which HRM meets customer needs vary depending on the need being satisfied. Selection systems ensure that applicants selected for employment have the necessary knowledge, skills, and abilities to provide value to the organization. Training and development systems meet the needs of both line managers and employees by giving employees development opportunities to ensure they are continually increasing their human capital and, thus, providing increased value to the company. Performance management systems make clear to employees what is expected of them and assure line managers and strategic planners that employee behavior will be in line with the company's goals. Finally, reward systems similarly benefit all customers (line managers, strategic planners, and employees). These systems assure line managers that employees will use their skills for organizational benefit, and they provide strategic planners with ways to ensure that all employees are acting in ways that will support the strategic plan. Obviously, reward systems provide employees with an equitable return for their investment of skills and effort.

# Building an HR Strategy

## THE BASIC PROCESS

How do HR functions build their HR strategies? Research has examined how HR functions go about the process of building their HR strategies that should support the business strategies. Conducting case studies on 20 different companies, Wright and colleagues describe the generic approach as somewhat consistent with the process for developing a business strategy.[1]

As depicted in Figure 16.4, the function first scans the environment to determine the trends or events that might have an impact on the organization (e.g., future talent shortage, increasing immigrant population, aging of the workforce).

It then examines the strategic business issues or needs (e.g., is the company growing, expanding internationally, needing to develop new technologies?). For instance, Figure 16.5 displays Goodyear's major business strategy priorities. As can be seen in this example, a clear strategic priority is the attraction, motivation, and retention of talent.

From these issues, the HR strategy team needs to identify the specific people issues that will be critical to address in order for the business to succeed (a potential leadership vacuum, lack of technological expertise, lack of diversity, etc.). All of this information is used in designing the HR strategy, which provides a detailed plan regarding the major priorities and the programs, policies, and processes that must be developed or executed. Finally, this HR strategy is communicated to the relevant parties, both internal and external to the function. Again, Goodyear's talent management strategy, depicted in Figure 16.6, shows how Goodyear seeks to differentiate itself in the labor market as well as the major priority areas that the HR strategy seeks to address.

**LO 16-2**
Discuss how the HRM function can define its mission and market.

**Figure 16.4**

Basic Process for HR Strategy

| Scan the external environment | → | Identify strategic business issues | → | Identify people issues | → | Develop HR strategy | → | Communicate the HR strategy |

**Figure 16.5**

Goodyear's Strategic Business Priorities

**Figure 16.6**

Goodyear's Global Talent Management Process

Thus, the HR strategy is a framework that guides individuals in HR by helping them understand where and how they will impact the company. At Google this four-pronged People Operations strategy consists of the following elements:

1. "Find them, Grow them, Keep them." The idea is to find great people to work for Google, grow and develop their skills, and do everything possible to keep them at Google.
2. "Put our users first." This goal echoes what Google does as a company, also illustrating how those in HR should think about the users of people operations, which are all the other Google employees.
3. "Put on your own oxygen mask before assisting others." The thinking behind this goal is that in many organizations HR is doing all this work in the company for others and they forget to grow and develop their own people. Eventually this cripples the function's ability to serve the rest of the organization because the very best, most talented people get recruited out of HR to go be heads of HR at other companies.
4. "This space intentionally left blank." In Google's environment, things change very, very quickly and that creates a lot of uncertainty. Uncertainty causes people to put less discretionary effort into their work, to be less satisfied, less collaborative, more competitive with fellow employees as well as making them more likely to leave the company. Hence, this goal is an attempt to explicitly recognize the dynamic nature of Google's internal and external environment.[2]

## INVOLVING LINE EXECUTIVES

This generic process provides for the potential to involve line executives in a number of ways. Because the HR strategy seeks to address business issues, involving those in charge of running the business can increase the quality of information from which the HR strategy is created. This involvement can occur in a few ways. First, line executives could simply provide input, through surveys or interviews about the business challenges and strategy. Second, they could be members of the team that actually develops the HR strategy. Third, once the strategy is developed, they could receive communications with the HR strategy information. Finally, they could have to formally approve the strategy, in essence "signing off" that the HR strategy fully supports the business strategy. The most progressive organizations use all four forms of involvement, asking a large group of executives for input, having one or two executives on the team, communicating the HR strategy broadly to executives, and having the senior executive team formally approve it.

## CHARACTERIZING HR STRATEGIES

As you can see in Figure 16.7, a study of 20 companies revealed the variety of ways that HR strategies can be generated to create a linkage to the business.

First, at the most elementary level, "HR-focused" HR functions articulate people outcomes that stem more from an analysis of what their functions currently do than from an understanding of how those people outcomes relate to the larger business. Second, "people-linked" functions have clearly identified, articulated, and aligned their HR activities around people issues and outcomes, but not business issues and outcomes. Third, "business-linked" HR functions begin with an assessment of what HR is doing, then identify the major people outcomes they should focus on, and, in a few cases, how those might translate into positive business outcomes. Finally, "business-driven" functions have fully developed HR strategies that begin by identifying the major business needs and issues, consider how people fit in and what people outcomes are necessary, and then build HR systems focused on meeting those needs. For example, as Kroger sought to develop a new strategy for competing in the retail grocery store market, it required a different approach to leadership. Figure 16.8 shows the leadership competencies necessary to execute the

**Figure 16.7**

Approaches to
Developing an HR
Strategy

### An Outside-In Perspective

*Business-Driven (5 cases)*

| Business issues/outcomes | → | People issues/outcomes | → | HR Strategy |

### 3 Different Inside-Out Stages

*Business-Linked (5 cases)*

| Business issues/outcomes | ← | People issues/outcomes | ← | HR Strategy |

*People-Linked (7 cases)*

| People issues/outcomes | ← | HR Strategy |

*HR-Focused (3 cases)*

| People issues/outcomes | ← | HR Strategy |

**Figure 16.8**

Kroger's Leadership
Model

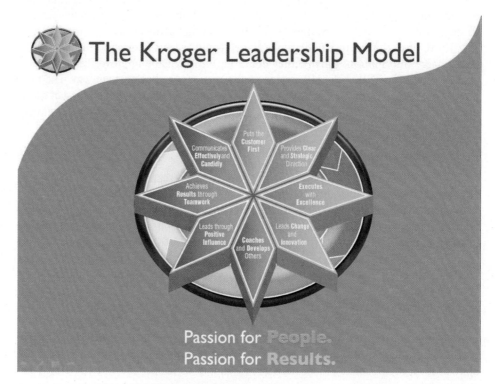

SOURCE: Courtesy of Kroger chief HR officer Katy Barclay.

strategy. The larger focus is on leaders who have a passion for people and a passion for results, with a number of more specific competencies making up each.

The HR strategy must help address the issues the business faces that will determine its success. As finding, attracting, and retaining talent has become a critical issue, virtually every HR function is addressing this as part of the HR strategy.

# Measuring HRM Effectiveness

The strategic decision-making process for the HRM function requires that decision makers have a good sense of the effectiveness of the current HRM function. This information provides the foundation for decisions regarding which processes, systems, and skills of HR employees need improvement. Often HRM functions that have been heavily involved in transactional activities for a long time tend to lack systems, processes, and skills for delivering state-of-the-art traditional activities and are thoroughly unable to contribute in the transformational arena. Thus, diagnosis of the effectiveness of the HRM function provides critical information for its strategic management.

In addition, having good measures of the function's effectiveness provides the following benefits:[3]

- *Marketing the function:* Evaluation is a sign to other managers that the HRM function really cares about the organization as a whole and is trying to support operations, production, marketing, and other functions of the company. Information regarding cost savings and benefits is useful to prove to internal customers that HRM practices contribute to the bottom line. Such information is also useful for gaining additional business for the HRM function.
- *Providing accountability:* Evaluation helps determine whether the HRM function is meeting its objectives and effectively using its budget.

Two approaches are commonly used to evaluate the effectiveness of HRM practices: the audit approach and the analytic approach.

## AUDIT APPROACH

The **audit approach** focuses on reviewing the various outcomes of the HRM functional areas. Both key indicators and customer satisfaction measures are typically collected. Table 16.1 lists examples of key indicators and customer satisfaction measures for staffing, equal employment opportunity, compensation, benefits, training, performance management (employee appraisal and development), succession planning, safety, labor relations, and overall effectiveness. The development of electronic employee databases and information systems has made it much easier to collect, store, and analyze the functional key indicators (more on this later in the chapter) than in the past, when information was kept in file folders.

We previously discussed how HRM functions can become much more customer oriented as part of the strategic management process. If, in fact, the function desires to be more customer focused, then one important source of effectiveness data can be the customers. Just as firms often survey their customers to determine how effectively the customers feel they are being served, the HRM function can survey its internal customers.

One important internal customer is the employees of the firm. Employees often have both direct contact with the HRM function (through activities such as benefits administration and payroll) and indirect contact with the function through their involvement in activities such as performance appraisals, pay raises, and training programs. Many

**LO 16-3**
Explain the approaches to evaluating the effectiveness of HRM practices.

**Audit approach**
Type of assessment of HRM effectiveness that involves review of customer satisfaction or key indicators (e.g., turnover rate, average days to fill a position) related to an HRM functional area (e.g., recruiting, training).

## Table 16.1
Examples of Key Indicators and Customer Satisfaction Measures for HRM Functions

| KEY INDICATORS | CUSTOMER SATISFACTION MEASURES |
|---|---|
| **Staffing** | |
| Average days taken to fill open requisitions | Anticipation of personnel needs |
| Ratio of acceptances to offers made | Timeliness of referring qualified workers to line |
| Ratio of minority/women applicants to representation in local labor market | supervisors |
| Per-capita requirement costs | Treatment of applicants |
| Average years of experience/education of hires per job family | Skill in handling terminations |
| | Adaptability to changing labor market conditions |
| **Equal employment opportunity** | |
| Ratio of EEO grievances to employee population | Resolution of EEO grievances |
| Minority representation by EEO categories | Day-to-day assistance provided by personnel |
| Minority turnover rate | department in implementing affirmative action plan |
| | Aggressive recruitment to identify qualified women and minority applicants |
| **Compensation** | |
| Per-capita (average) merit increases | Fairness of existing job evaluation system in assigning |
| Ratio of recommendations for reclassification to number of employees | grades and salaries |
| Percentage of overtime hours to straight time | Competitiveness in local labor market |
| Ratio of average salary offers to average salary in community | Relationship between pay and performance |
| | Employee satisfaction with pay |
| **Benefits** | |
| Average unemployment compensation payment (UCP) | Promptness in handling claims |
| Average workers' compensation payment (WCP) | Fairness and consistency in the application of benefit policies |
| Benefit cost per payroll dollar | Communication of benefits to employees |
| Percentage of sick leave to total pay | Assistance provided to line managers in reducing potential for unnecessary claims |
| **Training** | |
| Percentage of employees participating in training programs per job family | Extent to which training programs meet the needs of employees and the company |
| Percentage of employees receiving tuition refunds | Communication to employees about available training opportunities |
| Training dollars per employee | Quality of introduction/orientation programs |
| **Employee appraisal and development** | |
| Distribution of performance appraisal ratings | Assistance in identifying management potential |
| Appropriate psychometric properties of appraisal forms | Organizational development activities provided by HRM department |
| **Succession planning** | |
| Ratio of promotions to number of employees | Extent to which promotions are made from within |
| Ratio of open requisitions filled internally to those filled externally | Assistance/counseling provided to employees in career planning |
| **Safety** | |
| Frequency/severity ratio of accidents | Assistance to line managers in organizing safety programs |
| Safety-related expenses per $1,000 of payroll | Assistance to line managers in identifying potential safety hazards |
| Plant security losses per square foot (e.g., fires, burglaries) | Assistance to line managers in providing a good working environment (lighting, cleanliness, heating, etc.) |

*(Continued)*

| KEY INDICATORS | CUSTOMER SATISFACTION MEASURES |
|---|---|
| **Labor relations** | |
| Ratio of grievances by pay plan to number of employees | Assistance provided to line managers in handling grievances |
| Frequency and duration of work stoppages | Efforts to promote a spirit of cooperation in plant |
| Percentage of grievances settled | Efforts to monitor the employee relations climate in plant |
| **Overall effectiveness** | |
| Ratio of personnel staff to employee population | Accuracy and clarity of information provided to managers and employees |
| Turnover rate | |
| Absenteeism rate | Competence and expertise of staff |
| Ratio of per-capita revenues to per-capita cost | Working relationship between organizations and HRM department |
| Net income per employee | |

SOURCE: Reprinted with permission. Excerpts from Chapter 15, "Evaluating Human Resource Effectiveness," pp. 187–222, by Anne S. Tsui and Luis R. Gomez-Mejia, from *Human Resource Management: Evolving Roles and Responsibilities*, edited by Lee Dyer. Copyright © 1988 by The Bureau of National Affairs, Inc., Washington, DC, 20037. To order BNA publications call toll free 1-800-960-1220.

organizations such as AT&T, Motorola, and General Electric use their regular employee attitude survey as a way to assess the employees as users/customers of the HRM programs and practices.[4] However, the problem with assessing effectiveness only from the employees' perspective is that often they are responding not from the standpoint of the good of the firm but rather from their own individual perspective. For example, employees notoriously and consistently express dissatisfaction with pay level (who doesn't want more money?), but to simply ratchet up pay across the board would put the firm at a serious labor cost disadvantage.

Thus, many firms have gone to surveys of top line executives as a better means of assessing the effectiveness of the HRM function. The top-level line executives can see how the systems and practices are impacting both employees and the overall effectiveness of the firm from a strategic standpoint. This can also be useful for determining how well HR employees' perceptions of their function's effectiveness align with the views of their line colleagues. For example, a study of 14 firms revealed that HR executives and line executives agreed on the relative effectiveness of HR's delivery of services such as staffing and training systems (i.e., which were most and least effectively delivered) but not on the absolute level of effectiveness. As Figure 16.9 shows, HR executives' ratings of their effectiveness in different roles also diverged significantly from line executives'. In addition, line executives viewed HRM as being significantly less effective with regard to HRM's actual contributions to the firm's overall effectiveness, as we see in Figure 16.10.[5]

## THE ANALYTIC APPROACH

The **analytic approach** focuses on either (1) determining whether the introduction of a program or practice (like a training program or a new compensation system) has the intended effect, (2) estimating the financial costs and benefits resulting from an HRM practice, or (3) using analytic data to increase organizational effectiveness. For example, in Chapter 7 we discussed how companies can determine a training program's impact on learning, behavior, and results. Evaluating a training program is one strategy for determining whether the program works. Typically, in an overall evaluation of effectiveness, we are interested in determining the degree of change associated with the program.

**Analytic approach**
Type of assessment of HRM effectiveness that involves determining the impact of, or the financial costs and benefits of, a program or practice.

**Figure 16.9**

Comparing HR and Line Executives' Evaluations of the Effectiveness of HRM Roles

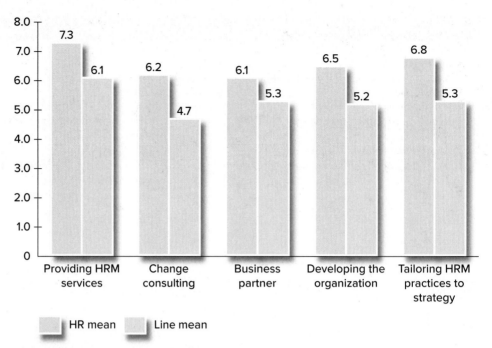

SOURCE: P. Wright, G. McMahan, S. Snell, and B. Gerhart, "Comparing Line and HR Executives' Perceptions of HR Effectiveness: Services, Roles, and Contributions," CAHRS (Center for Advanced Human Resource Studies) working paper 98-29, School of ILR, Cornell University, Ithaca, NY.

**Figure 16.10**

Comparing HR and Line Executives' Evaluations of the Effectiveness of HRM Contributions

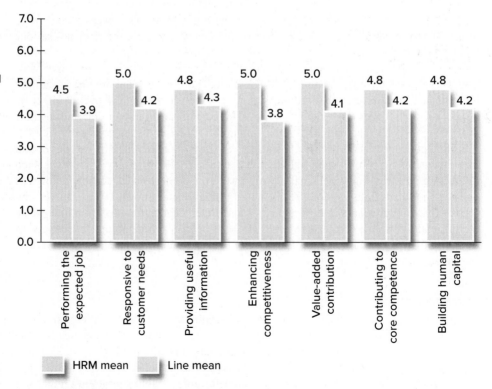

SOURCE: P. Wright, G. McMahan, S. Snell, and B. Gerhart, "Comparing Line and HR Executives' Perceptions of HR Effectiveness: Services, Roles, and Contributions," CAHRS (Center for Advanced Human Resource Studies) working paper 98-29, School of ILR, Cornell University, Ithaca, NY.

**Table 16.2**
Types of Cost–
Benefit Analyses

**Human resource accounting**
- Capitalization of salary
- Net present value of expected wage payments
- Returns on human assets and human investments

**Utility analysis**
- Turnover costs
- Absenteeism and sick leave costs
- Gains from selection programs
- Impact of positive employee attitudes
- Financial gains of training programs

SOURCE: Based on A. S. Tsui and L. R. Gomez-Mejia, "Evaluating HR Effectiveness," in *Human Resource Management: Evolving Roles and Responsibilities*, ed. L. Dyer (Washington, DC: Bureau of National Affairs, 1988), pp. 1–196.

The second strategy involves determining the dollar value of the training program, taking into account all the costs associated with the program. Using this strategy, we are not concerned with how much change occurred but rather with the dollar value (costs versus benefits) of the program. Table 16.2 lists the various types of cost–benefit analyses that are done. The human resource accounting approach attempts to place a dollar value on human resources as if they were physical resources (like plant and equipment) or financial resources (like cash). Utility analysis attempts to estimate the financial impact of employee behaviors (such as absenteeism, turnover, job performance, and substance abuse).

For example, wellness programs are a popular HRM program for reducing health care costs through reducing employees' risk of heart disease and cancer. One study evaluated four different types of wellness programs. Part of the evaluation involved determining the costs and benefits associated with the four programs over a three-year period.[6] A different type of wellness program was implemented at each site. Site A instituted a program involving raising employees' awareness of health risks (distributing news articles, blood pressure testing, health education classes). Site B set up a physical fitness facility for employees. Site C raised awareness of health risks and followed up with employees who had identified health risks. Site D provided health education and follow-up counseling and promoted physical competition and health-related events. Table 16.3 shows the effectiveness and cost-effectiveness of the Site C and Site D wellness models.

The analytic approach is more demanding than the audit approach because it requires the detailed use of statistics and finance. A good example of the level of sophistication

**Table 16.3**
Effectiveness and Cost-Effectiveness of Two Wellness Programs for Four Cardiovascular Disease Risk Factors

|  | SITE C | SITE D |
|---|---|---|
| Annual direct program costs, per employee per year | $30.96 | $38.57 |
| Percentage of cardiovascular disease risks[a] for which risk was moderately reduced or relapse prevented | 48% | 51% |
| Percentage of preceding entry per annual $1 spent per employee | 1.55% | 1.32% |
| Amount spent per 1% of risks reduced or relapse prevented | $0.65 | $0.76 |

[a]High blood pressure, overweight, smoking, and lack of exercise.

SOURCE: J. C. Erfurt, A. Foote, and M. A. Heirich, "The Cost-Effectiveness of Worksite Wellness Programs," *Personnel Psychology* 45 (1992), p. 22.

**Table 16.4**

Example of Analysis Needed to Determine the Dollar Value of a Selection Test

**Cost–benefit information**

| | |
|---|---|
| Current employment | 4,404 |
| Number separating | 618 |
| Number selected | 618 |
| Average tenure | 9.69 years |

**Test information**

| | |
|---|---|
| Number of applicants | 1,236 |
| Testing cost per applicant | $10 |
| Total test cost | $12,360 |
| Average test score | 0.80 SD |
| Test validity | 0.76 |
| $SD_y$ (per year)[a] | $10,413 |

**Computation**

Quantity = Average tenure × Applicants selected
= 9.69 years × 618 applicants
= 5,988 person-years

Quality = Average test score × Test validity × $SD_y$
= 0.80 × 0.76 × $10,413
= $6,331 per year

Utility = (Quantity × Quality) − Costs
= (5,988 person-year × $6,331 per year) − $12,360
= $37.9 million

[a]$SD_y$ = Dollar value of one standard difference in job performance. Approximately 40% of average salary.

SOURCES: From J. W. Boudreau, "Utility Analysis," in *Human Resource Management: Evolving Roles and Responsibilities*, ed. L. Dyer (Washington, DC: Bureau of National Affairs, 1988), p. 150; F. L. Schmidt, J. E. Hunter, R. C. McKenzie, and T. W. Muldrow, "Impact of Valid Selection Procedures on Work-Force Productivity," *Journal of Applied Psychology* 64 (1979), pp. 609–26.

that can be required for cost–benefit analysis is shown in Table 16.4. This table shows the types of information needed to determine the dollar value of a new selection test for entry-level computer programmers.

Finally, HR analytics can be used by the function to increase the effectiveness of the firm. For instance, Google's analytic approach to HR has revealed which backgrounds and capabilities are correlated with high performance as well as the leading cause of attrition—an employee's feeling that he or she is underused at the company. It also discovered that the ideal number of recruiting interviews is 5, down from a previous average of 10.

In addition, Project Oxygen was aimed at developing great managers (named because good management, like oxygen, keeps the company alive). The analytics team poured through performance management scores, employee surveys, and other data on group managers based on two dimensions: their task performance and their people performance. They then conducted a double-blind study focusing on those who were top (or bottom) on both dimensions, in order to identify eight behaviors that characterized good managers.[7]

# Improving HRM Effectiveness

**LO 16-4**

Describe the new structures for the HRM function.

Once a strategic direction has been established and the effectiveness of HRM evaluated, leaders of the HRM function can explore how to improve its effectiveness in contributing to the firm's competitiveness. Returning briefly to Figure 16.1, which depicted the different activities of the HRM function, often the improvement focuses on two aspects of the pyramid. First,

**Figure 16.11**

Improving HRM Effectiveness

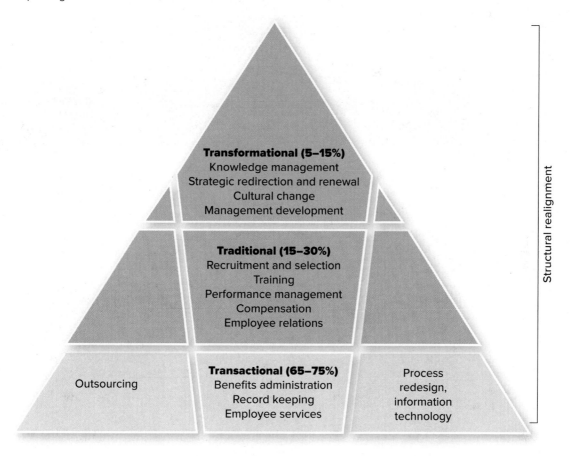

within each activity, HRM needs to improve both the efficiency and effectiveness in perform-ing each of the activities. Second, often there is a push to eliminate as much of the transac-tional work as possible (and some of the traditional work) to free up time and resources to focus more on the higher-value-added transformational work. Redesign of the structure (reporting relationships) and processes (through outsourcing and information technology) enables the function to achieve these goals simultaneously. Figure 16.11 depicts this process.

## RESTRUCTURING TO IMPROVE HRM EFFECTIVENESS

Traditional HRM functions were structured around the basic HRM subfunctions such as staffing, training, compensation, appraisal, and labor relations. Each of these areas had a director who reported to the VP of HRM, who often reported to a VP of finance and administration. However, for the HRM function to truly contribute strategically to firm effectiveness, the senior HR person must be part of the top management team (reporting directly to the chief executive officer), and there must be a different structural arrange-ment within the function itself.

A generic structure for the HRM function is depicted in Figure 16.12. As we see, the HRM function effectively is divided into three divisions: the centers for expertise, the

**Figure 16.12**

Old and New
Structures for the
HRM Organization

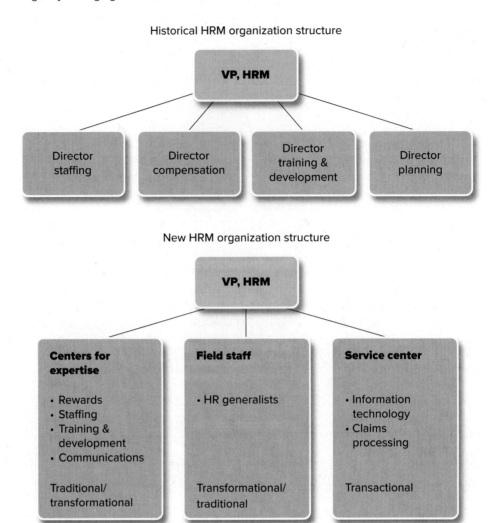

Historical HRM organization structure

Source: P. Wright, G. McMahan, S. Snell, and B. Gerhart, *Strategic Human Resource Management: Building Human Capital and Organizational Capability*, technical report (Ithaca, NY: Cornell University, 1998).

field generalists, and the service center.[8] The centers for expertise usually consist of the functional specialists in the traditional areas of HRM such as recruitment, selection, training, and compensation. These individuals ideally act as consultants in the development of state-of-the-art systems and processes for use in the organization. The field generalists consist of the HRM generalists who are assigned to a business unit within the firm. These individuals usually have dual reporting relationships to both the head of the line business and the head of HRM (although the line business tends to take priority). They ideally take responsibility for helping the line executives in their business to strategically address people issues, and they ensure that the HRM systems enable the business to execute its strategy. Finally, the service center consists of individuals who ensure that the transactional activities are delivered throughout the organization. These service centers often leverage information technology to efficiently deliver employee services. For example, organizations such as Chevron have created call-in service centers where employees can dial a central number where service center employees are available to answer their questions and process their requests and transactions.

Such structural arrangements improve service delivery through specialization. Center for expertise employees can develop current functional skills without being distracted by transactional activities, and generalists can focus on learning the business environment without having to maintain expertise in functional specializations. Finally, service center employees can focus on efficient delivery of basic services across business units.

## OUTSOURCING TO IMPROVE HRM EFFECTIVENESS

Restructuring the internal HRM function and redesigning the processes represent internal approaches to improving HRM effectiveness. However, increasingly HR executives are seeking to improve the effectiveness of the systems, processes, and services the function delivers through outsourcing. **Outsourcing** entails contracting with an outside vendor to provide a product or service to the firm, as opposed to producing the product using employees within the firm.

Why would a firm outsource an HRM activity or service? Usually this is done for one of two reasons: Either the outsourcing partner can provide the service more cheaply than it would cost to do it internally, or the partner can provide it more effectively than it can be performed internally. Early on, firms resorted to outsourcing for efficiency reasons. Why would using an outsourced provider be more efficient than having internal employees provide a service? Usually it is because outsourced providers are specialists who are able to develop extensive expertise that can be leveraged across a number of companies.

For example, consider a relatively small firm that seeks to develop a pension system for employees. To provide this service to employees, the HRM function would need to learn all of the basics of pension law. Then it would need to hire a person with specific expertise in administering a pension system in terms of making sure that employee contributions are withheld and that the correct payouts are made to retired employees. Then the company would have to hire someone with expertise in investing pension funds. If the firm is small, requirements of the pension fund might not fill the time (80 hours per week) of these two new hires. Assume that it takes only 20 total hours a week for these people to do their jobs. The firm would be wasting 60 hours of employee time each week. However, a firm that specializes in providing pension administration services to multiple firms could provide the 20 hours of required time to that firm and three other firms for the same cost as if the firm had performed this activity internally. Thus, the specialist firm could charge the focal firm 50% of what it would cost the small firm to do the pensions internally. Of that 50%, 25% (20 hours) would go to paying direct salaries and the other 25% would be profit. Here the focal firm would save 50% of its expenses while the provider would make money.

Now consider the aspect of effectiveness. Because the outsourced provider works for a number of firms and specializes in pensions, its employees develop state-of-the-art knowledge of running pension plans. They can learn unique innovations from one company and transfer that learning to a new company. In addition, employees can be more easily and efficiently trained because all of them will be trained in the same processes and procedures. Finally, with experience in providing constant pension services, the firm is able to develop a capability to perform these services that could never be developed by two individuals working 25% of the time on these services. This is known as *scale*, which refers to larger companies being better able to allocate human resources efficiently.

What kind of services are being outsourced? Firms primarily outsource transactional activities and services of HRM such as pension and benefits administration as well as payroll. However, a number of traditional and some transformational activities have been outsourced as well.

**LO 16-5**
Describe how outsourcing HRM activities can improve service delivery efficiency and effectiveness.

**Outsourcing**
An organization's use of an outside organization for a broad set of services.

# IMPROVING HRM EFFECTIVENESS THROUGH PROCESS REDESIGN

**LO 16-6**
Relate how process reengineering is used to review and redesign HRM practices.

In addition to structural arrangements, process redesign enables the HRM function to more efficiently and effectively deliver HRM services. Process redesign often uses information technology, but information technology applications are not a requirement. Thus, we will discuss the general issue of process reengineering and then explore information technology applications that have aided HRM in process redesign.

**Reengineering**
Review and redesign of work processes to make them more efficient and improve the quality of the end product or service.

**Reengineering** is a complete review of critical work processes and redesign to make them more efficient and able to deliver higher quality. Reengineering is especially critical to ensuring that the benefits of new technology can be realized. Applying new technology to an inefficient process will not improve efficiency or effectiveness. Instead, it will increase product or service costs related to the introduction of the new technology.

Reengineering can be used to review the HRM department functions and processes, or it can be used to review specific HRM practices such as work design or the performance management system. The reengineering process involves the four steps shown in Figure 16.13: identify the process to be reengineered, understand the process, redesign the process, and implement the new process.[9]

## Identifying the Process

First, the company should identify the process they want to reengineer and the individuals who are part of that process. Managers who control the process or are responsible for functions within the process (sometimes called "process owners") should be identified and asked to be part of the reengineering team. Team members should include employees involved in the process (to provide expertise) and those outside the process, as well as internal or external customers who see the outcome of the process.

## Understanding the Process

Several things need to be considered when evaluating a process:

- Can jobs be combined?
- Can employees be given more autonomy? Can decision making and control be built into the process through streamlining it?
- Are all the steps in the process necessary?
- Are data redundancy, unnecessary checks, and controls built into the process?
- How many special cases and exceptions have to be dealt with?

**Figure 16.13**
The Reengineering Process

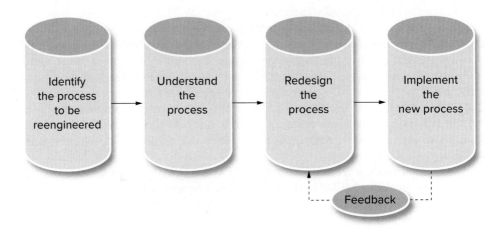

- Are the steps in the process arranged in their natural order?
- What is the desired outcome? Are all of the tasks necessary? What is the value of the process?

Various techniques are used to understand processes. Data-flow diagrams are useful to show the flow of data among departments. Figure 16.14 shows a data-flow diagram for payroll data and the steps in producing a paycheck. Information about the employee and department are sent to the general account. The payroll check is issued based on a payment voucher that is generated from the general accounting ledger. Data-entity relationship diagrams show the types of data used within a business function and the relationship among the different types of data. In scenario analysis, simulations of real-world issues are presented to data end users. The end users are asked to indicate how an information system could help address their particular situations and what data should be maintained to deal with those situations. Surveys and focus groups collect information about the data collected, used, and stored in a functional area, as well as information about time and information-processing requirements. Users may be asked to evaluate the importance, frequency, and criticality of automating specific tasks within a functional area. For example, how critical is it to have an applicant tracking system that maintains data on applicants' previous work experience? Cost–benefit analyses compare the costs of completing tasks with and without an automated system or software application. For example, the analysis should include the costs in terms of people, time, materials, and dollars; the anticipated costs of software and hardware; and labor, time, and material expenses.[10]

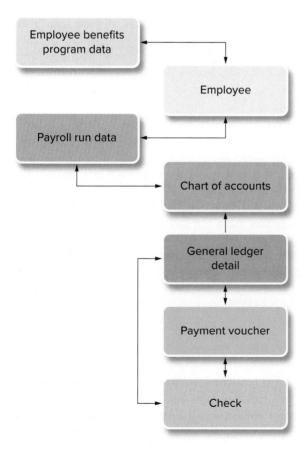

**Figure 16.14**

A Data-Flow Diagram for Payroll Data

### Redesigning the Process

During the redesign phase, the team develops models, tests them, chooses a prototype, and determines how to integrate the prototype into the organization.

### Implementing the Process

**LO 16-7**

Discuss the types of new technologies that can improve the efficiency and effectiveness of HRM.

The company tries out the process by testing it in a limited, controlled setting before expanding companywide. For example, J. M. Huber Corporation, a New Jersey–based conglomerate that has several operating divisions scattered throughout the United States, used reengineering to avoid installing new software onto inefficient processes.[11] HR staff began by documenting and studying the existing work flow and creating a strategy for improving efficiency. Top management, mid-level managers, and HR staff worked together to identify the processes they most wanted to improve. They determined that the most critical issue was to develop a client–server system that could access data more easily than the mainframe computer they were currently using. Also, the client–server system could eliminate many of the requisitions needed to get access to data, which slowed down work. The HRM department's efforts have streamlined record-keeping functions, eliminated redundant steps, and automated manual processes. The fully automated client–server system allows employees to sign up and change benefits information using an interactive voice-response system that is connected to the company's database. In addition, managers have easier access to employees' salary history, job descriptions, and other data. If an employee is eligible for a salary increase and the manager requests a change and it is approved, the system will process it (without entry by a clerical worker), and the changes will be seen on the employee's paycheck. Results of the reengineering effort are impressive. The redesigned processes have reduced the number of problems that HRM has to give to other departments by 42%, cut work steps by 26%, and eliminated 20% of the original work. Although the company is spending more than $1 million to make the technology work, it estimates that the investment should pay for itself in five years.

### Improving HRM Effectiveness through New Technologies—E-HRM

Since the mid-1990s, as HRM functions sought to play a more strategic role in their organizations, the first task was to eliminate transactional tasks in order to free up time to focus on traditional and transformational activities. Part of building a strategic HR function requires moving much of the transactional work away from being done by HR employees so that they can have time available to work on strategic activities. Consequently, the use of technology can make HR more strategic and by doing so increase the value that HR adds to the business.[12] As indicated in Figure 16.11, outsourcing of many of these activities provided one mechanism for reducing this burden. However, more relevant today is the focus on the use of information technology to handle these tasks. Early on this was achieved by the development and implementation of information systems that were run by the HRM function but more recently have evolved into systems that allow employees to serve themselves. As described earlier, employees can access the system and make their benefit enrollment, changes, or claims online. Clearly, technology has freed HRM functions from transactional activities to focus on more strategic actions.

However, the speed requirements of e-business force HRM functions to explore how to leverage technology for the delivery of traditional and transformational HRM activities. This does not imply that over time all of HRM will be executed online, but rather a number of HRM activities currently delivered via paper or face-to-face communications can

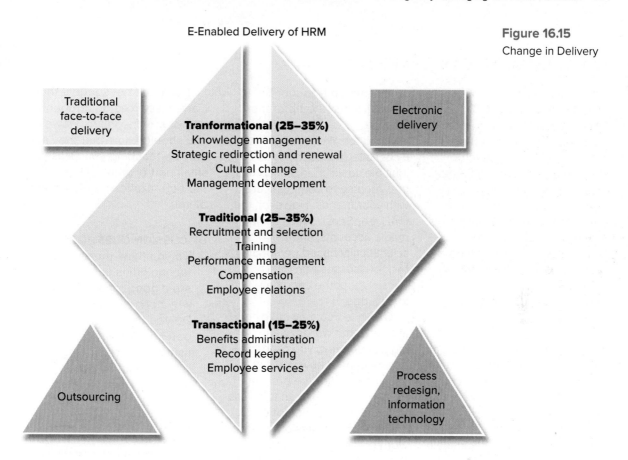

E-Enabled Delivery of HRM

**Figure 16.15**
Change in Delivery

Traditional face-to-face delivery

Electronic delivery

**Tranformational (25–35%)**
Knowledge management
Strategic redirection and renewal
Cultural change
Management development

**Traditional (25–35%)**
Recruitment and selection
Training
Performance management
Compensation
Employee relations

**Transactional (15–25%)**
Benefits administration
Record keeping
Employee services

Outsourcing

Process redesign, information technology

be delivered electronically with no loss (and even gains) in effectiveness and efficiency. This is illustrated by Figure 16.15. We explore some examples next. The Competing through Technology box illustrates how technology has revolutionized the hiring process in many organizations.

In a world dominated by social media, companies like Google are now using it for internal purposes. Google developed "Grow," an internal platform that makes it easy for Googlers to find learning opportunities, jobs, one-on-one advice, and other development resources to suit their needs and interests. Grow unifies myriad learning, development, and job search tools into a one-stop shop for Googlers to manage and act on their development. It suggests courses, opportunities, advisors, and more based on what the company knows about the Googler (e.g., role, level, location) and the data a Googler provides within the tool (e.g., skills he or she wants to develop). Not surprisingly, given Google's search capability, this system allows employees to search for learning resources or jobs of interest.

Grow is an inherently social platform, and every Googler has a customizable profile that is visible to others. Figure 16.16 displays the Grow profile of Sunil Chandra, Google's VP of staffing and operations. As you can see, Googlers can tag skills they have (e.g., consulting, people management, and coaching for Sunil) and those they want to develop (e.g., entrepreneurship and prioritization) in their profile. Skills listed in Grow help the system get to know the user and offer more personalized job recommendations. Googlers can also indicate if they would like to advise others on a particular skill. If Sunil tags

# COMPETING THROUGH TECHNOLOGY

## Robots Are Now in Charge of Hiring

As students you certainly spend time with the Office of Career Services as they provide help for you in getting a job. They help you develop your résumé to highlight your most highlightable aspects. They teach you how to go through interviews to come off as a highly capable and motivated future worker. It is hard to believe, but new development in hiring technologies may make all that help almost obsolete.

Automation has invaded the hiring process to the point that almost all of the *Fortune* 500 companies use some form of it in hiring. For example, computers can weed out potential employees by searching for certain keywords on their résumés. Or robot avatars may actually conduct interviews

applicants go through. But those are just the tip of the iceberg.

If you are like the vast majority of college students, you have multiple social media accounts that you use to communicate with your friends. However, the firm DeepSense scans social media accounts, and using a scientifically based personality test, it assesses personality traits without the candidate's knowledge.

Or, while you may have learned what words to say during an interview, you probably cannot control how you say it. Utah-based HireVue provides AI-based algorithms that assess an interviewee's tone of voice, micro-facial expressions, and word clusters to compare to those who are high performers in the job.

This does not suggest that Career Services departments do not provide value. However, you should know that they may only be teaching you skills in a small part of what will go into the organization's assessment of you.

### DISCUSSION QUESTIONS

1. Do you think these new technologies used in hiring are a good idea? Why or why not?
2. Do you think there is the potential for bias in hiring using these technologies? What should be done about it?

SOURCE: H. Schellmann and J. Bellini, "Artificial Intelligence: The Robots Are Now Hiring," *Wall Street Journal*, September 20, 2018, https://www.wsj.com/articles/artificial-intelligence-the-robots-are-now-hiring-moving-upstream-1537435820.

**Figure 16.16**

Personal Webpage for Sunil Chandra

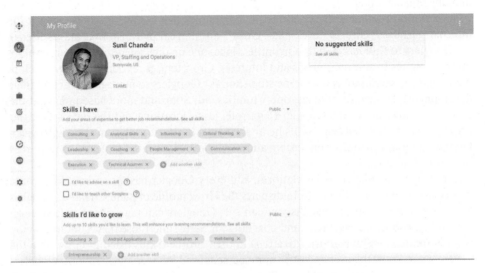

Google, Inc.

himself as a "Skill Advisor" on a topic (e.g., leadership), he will appear in Grow's search results, and other Googlers can view his skills and contact him for advice. He can select the option to "teach other Googlers," as well, which would connect him to Google's g2g (or "Googlers-to-Googlers") program, an internal volunteer teaching network that allows employees to teach their peers on a variety of subjects.

As mentioned earlier, Grow also allows Googlers to list skills they would like to develop. They can add up to 10 skills, and Grow will use these inputs to further customize their learning recommendations. To help Googlers get started, Grow suggests a number of skills on the right-hand side of the page (culled from a multiyear study of the skills that make Googlers effective in their roles). In Sunil's case, he has already added all of his suggested skills directly to his profile, which is why the tool reflects "no suggested skills." Sunil's profile also includes his picture, job title, location, and a link to his internal employee page to help his fellow Googlers get to know him.

In sum, Grow profiles are a great way for Googlers to teach the tool about their skills and development areas, and get better learning and job recommendations in the process. It also helps Googlers connect with their peers as advisors, mentors, or internal teachers, in addition to providing a host of other learning and development resources.

## Recruitment and Selection

Traditional recruitment and selection processes have required considerable face-to-face communications with recruitment firms and potential employees, labor-intensive assessment devices, and significant monitoring of managerial decisions to ensure that hiring patterns and decisions do not run afoul of regulatory requirements. However, technology has transformed these processes.

For example, online recruiting accounts for one of every eight hires according to kforce.com's poll of 300 U.S. companies. IBM employees now fill out forms on the Web to identify contract help they need, and that information is immediately sent to 14 temp agencies. Within an hour, agencies respond with résumés for review, allowing IBM to cut hiring time from 10 days to 3 and to save $3 million per year.

Finally, technology has enabled firms to monitor hiring processes to minimize the potential for discriminatory hiring decisions. For example, Home Depot was accused of forcing female applicants into cashier jobs while reserving the customer service jobs for males. While not admitting guilt, as part of its consent decree Home Depot uses technology to identify people who have skills for jobs they are not applying for based on key words in their résumés. In addition, the technology forces managers to interview diverse candidate sets before making decisions.

## Compensation and Rewards

Compensation systems in organizations probably reflect the most pervasive form of bureaucracy within HRM. In spite of the critical role they play in attracting, motivating, and retaining employees, most systems consist of rigid, time-consuming, and ineffective processes. Managers fill out what they believe to be useless forms, ignore guidelines, and display a general disdain for the entire process.

Leveraging technology may allow firms to better achieve their compensation goals with considerably less effort. For example, one problem many merit or bonus pay plans face is that managers refuse to differentiate among performers, giving everyone similar pay increases. This allows them to spend less time thinking about how to manage (rate and review) performance as well as minimizes the potential conflict they might face. Thus, employees do not see linkages between performance and pay, resulting in lower motivation among all employees and higher turnover among top performers (and possibly lower turnover among bottom performers). To minimize this, Cypress Semiconductors requires managers to distinguish between equity and merit and forces distributions with regard to both concepts.[13] For example, equity means that the top-ranked performer in any group of peers should make 50% more than the lowest-ranked performer, and people with comparable performance should receive comparable salaries. With regard to merit, there must be at least a 7% spread between the lowest and highest pay raises (if the lowest raise is 3%, then the highest must be at least 10%). If ratings and raises are input into a system, the firm can monitor and control the rating process to ensure that adequate differentiations are made consistent with the policy.

## Training and Development

Exploring different vehicles for delivering training (PC, video, and the like) certainly is not a new concept. In addition, a number of firms have begun delivering training via the Web. Their experience suggests that some types of training can be done effectively via the Internet or an intranet, whereas others might not. For example, companies such as IBM and Dell both boast that they have developed Internet-based training for some parts of their workforce.

Interestingly, the challenge of speedy delivery of HRM services brings the concept of Internet-based training to the forefront. In today's competitive environment, firms compete to attract and retain both customers and talented employees. How well a firm develops and treats existing employees largely determines how well it achieves these outcomes. Yet the challenges of speed, project focus, and changing technology create environments that discourage managers from managing their people, resulting in a situation where employees may not feel respected or valued.

This presents a challenge to firms to provide both the incentive and the skills for managers to treat employees as assets rather than commodities. Consider how Internet-based training might facilitate this. Assume that you work for Widget.com, a fast-growing, fast-paced e-business. You arrive at work Monday morning, and your e-mail contains a high-priority message with either an attachment or a link to a URL. It is your Monday morning challenge from the CEO, and you know that the system will track whether you link and complete this challenge. When you link to it, you see a digital video of your CEO telling you how people are Widget.com's competitive advantage, and that when they don't feel valued, they leave. Thus, his challenge to you is to make your employees feel valued today. To do so, you will, in the next 10 minutes, learn how to express appreciation to an employee. You receive six learning points; you observe a digitized video model performing the learning points; you review the learning points again and take a quiz. You then see the CEO giving you the final challenge: that in the next 15 minutes you are to take one of your employees aside and express your appreciation using the skill you just developed.

Notice the advantages of this process. First, it was not time consuming, like most three-day or one-week training programs. The entire process (training and demonstration with a real employee) took less than 30 minutes; you have developed a skill; and an employee now probably feels better about the organization. It communicated a real organizational value or necessary competency. It didn't require any travel expenses to a training facility. It did not overwhelm you with so much information that you would be lucky to remember 10% of what you were exposed to. Finally, it was a push, rather than pull, approach to training. The firm did not wait for you to realize you had a deficiency and then go search and sign up for training. It pushed the training to you.

Technology allows firms to deliver training and development for at least some skills or knowledge faster, more efficiently, and probably more effectively. It can quickly merge training, communication, and immediate response to strategic contingencies.

Creating and nurturing a committed workforce presents a tremendous challenge to firms today. According to a survey conducted by Monster.com, 61% of Americans consider themselves overworked and 86% are not satisfied with their jobs.[14] Such findings suggest that firms need to find ways to monitor commitment levels, identify potential obstacles to commitment, and respond quickly to eliminate those obstacles. In large part, attitude surveys have constituted the platform from which these activities were managed in the past.

Consider the traditional attitude survey. Surveys are administered to employees over a period of four to six weeks. The data are entered and analyzed, requiring another six to eight weeks. A group interprets the results to identify the major problem areas, and task forces are formed to develop recommendations; this process easily takes another four to six months. Finally, decisions must be made about implementing the task force recommendations. In the end, employees might see responses to their concerns at best 12–18 months after the survey—and then the survey administrators cannot understand why employees think that completing the survey is a waste of time.

Now consider how technology can shorten that cycle. E-pulse represents one attempt to create a platform for almost real-time attitude surveys. Developed by Theresa Welbourne at the University of Alabama, E-pulse is a scalable survey device administered online. Normally three questions are asked regarding how employees feel about work, but more questions can be added to get feedback on any specific issue. The survey goes out online, and when employees complete it, the data are immediately entered and analyzed. In essence, the part of the process that took four months in the past has been reduced to a day.

Next the firm can decide how it wants to use the information. For example, it could be broken down by business, site, or work unit, with the relevant information going to the leader of the chosen unit of analysis. In essence, a supervisor could receive almost immediate feedback about the attitudes of his or her work group, or a general manager about his or her business unit. The supervisor or manager can respond immediately, even if only to communicate that she or he realizes a problem exists and will take action soon.

Although technology provides for faster HRM, only a more systemic approach will ensure better and smarter HRM. For example, using technology to disseminate information to supervisors and managers may be faster, but unless those individuals possess good problem-solving and communication skills, they may either ignore the information or, worse yet, exacerbate the problem with inappropriate responses. As we noted with regard to training, this systemic approach requires knocking down traditional functional walls to deliver organizational solutions rather than functional programs. Thus, the challenge is to view the technology not as a panacea or even as a functional tool but rather as a catalyst for transforming the HRM organization.

# Improving HRM Effectiveness through New Technologies—HRM Information Systems

Several new and emerging technologies can help improve the effectiveness of the HRM function. **New technologies** are current applications of knowledge, procedures, and equipment that have not been used previously. New technology usually involves automation—that is, replacing human labor with equipment, information processing, or some combination of the two.

**New technologies** Current applications of knowledge, procedures, and equipment that have not been previously used. Usually involves replacing human labor with equipment, information processing, or some combination of the two.

In HRM, technology has already been used for three broad functions: transaction processing, reporting, and tracking; decision support systems; and expert systems.[15] **Transaction processing** refers to computations and calculations used to review and document HRM decisions and practices. This includes documenting relocation, training expenses, and course enrollments and filling out government reporting requirements (such as EEO-1 reports, which require companies to report information to the government regarding employees' race and gender by job category). **Decision support systems** are designed to help managers solve problems. They usually include a "what if" feature that allows users to see how outcomes change when assumptions or data change. These systems are useful, for example, for helping companies determine the number of new hires needed based on different turnover rates or the availability of employees with a certain skill in the labor market. **Expert systems** are computer systems incorporating the decision rules of people deemed to have expertise in a certain area. The system recommends actions that the user can take based on the information provided by the user. The recommended actions are those that a human expert would take in a similar situation (such as a manager interviewing a job candidate).

The latest trend within HR is the movement toward artificial intelligence (AI) and chatbots. Most HR software systems today (e.g., WorkDay, PeopleSoft, Success Factors) gather significant amounts of information on employees. AI provides a mechanism to mine that information and extract from it what might be optimal decisions. For instance, AI systems can source, screen, and match candidates to positions in a way that eliminates bias.

Chatbots consist of computer-based communications that have traditionally been performed by call center employees. For instance, when employees go through the arduous process of benefits enrollment, a chatbot can lead them through it, answering whatever questions they have.

## Predictive Analytics

The more recent use of technology and data has been in the area of predictive analytics. Earlier in the chapter we discussed how HR functions can analytically evaluate their performance through either tracking certain metrics or surveying internal customers. Although such a backward-looking approach can help the function to pinpoint areas for improvement, more recent effort has been devoted to trying to identify problems before they happen.

Predictive analytics refers to the use of data to make predictions about actions or outcomes in the future. For example, many technology companies hate to see good employees leave because they are so hard to replace. Looking at data to identify indicators that an employee is about to leave would be helpful for organizations if they want to intervene. For instance, Adobe Systems has found that a strong predictor of an employee's desire to leave is when the employee begins to update his or her LinkedIn profile. Google has developed sophisticated algorithms looking at a number of variables and uses these algorithms to identify which employees are likely to leave.

Hershey has recently integrated AI and predictive analytics to create a system that can increase employee retention. Using a compilation of variables predictive of an employee's intention to leave, the system can create a dashboard of which areas or jobs in the organization seem at risk of significant turnover. They can then, within that area or job, create a rank ordering of those employees most likely to turnover in the following six months. Armed with this information, they contact those employees' supervisors with suggestions on how they might better engage and retain those employees. The Evidence-Based HR box describes a measure researchers developed to predict who might leave a company.

---

**Transaction processing**
Computations and calculations used to review and document HRM decisions and practices.

**Decision support systems**
Problem-solving systems that usually include a "what-if" feature that allows users to see how outcomes change when assumptions or data change.

**Expert systems**
Computer systems incorporating the decision rules of people recognized as experts in a certain area.

# EVIDENCE-BASED HR

## The HR Crystal Ball: Predicting Who Might Leave

How can predictive analytics help solve real company problems? No firm wants to lose valued high-performing employees, but often they do not know the employees are thinking about leaving until it is too late. A recent study by Gardner, Van Iddekinge, and Hom found that employees often show behaviors predictive of quitting. The extensive validation study across a number of different employee groups identified the following behaviors as signs that an employee may be thinking about leaving the organization:

1. Their work productivity has decreased more than usual.
2. They have acted less like a team player than usual.
3. They have been doing the minimum amount of work more frequently.
4. They have been less interested in pleasing their manager than usual.
5. They have been less willing to commit to long-term timelines than usual.
6. They have exhibited a negative change in attitude.
7. They have exhibited less effort and work motivation than usual.
8. They have exhibited less focus on job-related matters than usual.
9. They have expressed dissatisfaction with their current job more frequently than usual.
10. They have expressed dissatisfaction with their supervisor more frequently than usual.
11. They have left early from work more frequently than usual.
12. They have lost enthusiasm for the mission of the organization.
13. They have shown less interest in working with customers than usual.

SOURCE: T. M. Garder, C. H. Van Iddekinge, and P. W. Hom, "If You've Got Leavin' on Your Mind: The Identification and Validation of Pre-quitting Behaviors," *Journal of Management*. Published online August 29, 2016.

## Customization

Finally, the vast increases in technological capability and data has a number of companies looking to better customize an employee's experience with the organization. In the past, many companies allowed "cafeteria" benefit plans that allowed employees to choose the benefits they most desired. However, today some firms allow employees to customize their pay mix (e.g., take lesser or greater amounts of fixed versus variable pay, or varying the type of variable pay such as bonuses versus stock). Also, companies can proactively approach employees who may want to think about changing benefits based on changes in life events (e.g, when an employee adds a child as a beneficiary, the company can suggest putting money into life insurance or into educational savings accounts). In all these cases, companies are not forcing changes onto employees but rather are using the information they have about employees to help those employees better manage their work and personal lives.

# The Future for HR Professionals

**LO 16-8**
List the competencies the HRM executive needs to become a strategic partner in the company.

The future for careers in the human resource profession seems brighter than ever. An increasing number of successful companies such as Microsoft have made the top HR job a member of the senior management team, reporting directly to the chief executive officer. CEOs recognize the importance of their workforce in driving competitive success. Firms need to seek the balance between attracting, motivating, and retaining the very best talent and keeping labor and administrative costs as low as possible. Finding such a balance requires HR leaders who have a deep knowledge of the business combined with a deep knowledge of HR issues, tools, processes, and technologies.

For a reader who is just getting a first glimpse of the HRM function, to portray what a vastly different role HRM must play today compared to 20 or even 10 years ago is impossible. As noted earlier, HRM has traditionally played a largely administrative role—simply processing paperwork plus developing and administering hiring, training, appraisal, compensation, and benefits systems—and all of this has been unrelated to the strategic direction of the firm. In the early 1980s, HRM took on more of a one-way linkage role, helping to implement strategy. Now strategic decision makers are realizing the importance of people issues and so are calling for HRM to become the "source of people expertise" in the firm.[16] This requires that HR managers possess and use knowledge of how people can and do play a role in competitive advantage as well as the policies, programs, and practices that can leverage the firm's people as a source of competitive advantage. This leads to an entirely new set of competencies for today's strategic HR executive.[17]

In the future, HR professionals will need four basic competencies to become partners in the strategic management process.[18] First, they will need "business competence"—knowing the company's business and understanding its economic financial capabilities. This calls for making logical decisions that support the company's strategic plan based on the most accurate information possible. Because in almost all companies the effectiveness of decisions must be evaluated in terms of dollar values, the HR executive must be able to calculate the costs and benefits of each alternative in terms of its dollar impact.[19] In addition, the nonmonetary impact needs to be considered. The HR executive must be fully capable of identifying the social and ethical issues attached to HRM practices. HR professionals must often act as the conscience of the organization in all aspects.

Second, HR professionals will need "professional–technical knowledge" of state-of-the-art HRM practices in areas such as staffing, development, rewards, organizational design, and communication. New selection techniques, performance appraisal methods, training programs, and incentive plans are being developed continually. Some of these programs can provide value, whereas others may be no more than the products of today's HRM equivalent of snake oil. HR executives must be able to critically evaluate the new techniques offered as state-of-the-art HRM programs and use only those that will benefit the company. The Competing through Globalization box describes how IKEA is entering India, and highlights the need to have good technical skills in staffing, developing, and rewarding people.

Third, they must be skilled in the "management of change processes," such as diagnosing problems, implementing organizational changes, and evaluating results. Every time a company

Visit your instructor's Connect® course and access your eBook to view this video.

"I don't believe that it's our job in HR just to adminster the change or execute the change. I think our job is to agitate for the change."
— L. Kevin Cox,
Chief Human Resources Officer, American Express

Source: Video produced for the Center for Executive Succession in the Darla Moore School of Business at the University of South Carolina by Coal Powered Filmworks

## IKEA Enters India

IKEA, the global leader in selling affordable furniture, has seen its growth slowing over the past few years. In order to rev up growth, it has decided to go all in trying to build a presence in India. It is the second venture in India, as their first attempt in 2007 failed when the company ran into significant unexpected regulatory obstacles to foreign ownership of retail stores. However, given the fact that India boasts the world's second largest population and a home furnishings market that has increased 90% over the past six years, the company sees it as the growth market it needs.

In preparing for entry into the market, it first needed to understand how India's market for furniture differs from what it is used to. Employees have visited over 1,000 homes to determine how Indians sleep, relax, eat, and entertain. For instance, in India the dining table is a place to discuss as much as eat, and thus, they realized dining room furniture must take on a more prominent role.

Second, it needed to get employees up to speed in serving customers. It sent 75 Indian employees to help open a new IKEA store in Sheffield, England. This enabled them to gain experience in opening a new store. It has also spent significant time training its employees (75 of whom are female) as well as contract workers hired through Bangalore-based online marketplace UrbanClap to assemble furniture.

Finally, because India is spread out and is more used to small retail outlets, IKEA will open a combination of a few big box outlets combined with much smaller satellite stores. It will also jump into the online market much sooner than it has in past efforts to enter new markets.

Notice how people intensive the effort to enter a new market is. This illustrates why HR needs to be effective in ensuring that the organization is able to acquire, train, and motivate the people they need.

### DISCUSSION QUESTIONS

1. Do you think that IKEA will be able to successfully enter the Indian home furnishings market? Why or why not?
2. What skills of HR people do you think are necessary to make sure this is a success?

SOURCE: S. Chaudhuri and C. Abrams, "IKEA's Strategy in India: If We Build It, They Will Come" *Wall Street Journal*, July 23, 2018, https://www.wsj.com/articles/ikea-lets-some-take-diy-off-the-table-1532338200.

changes its strategy in even a minor way, the entire company has to change. These changes result in conflict, resistance, and confusion among the people who must implement the new plans or programs. The HR executive must have the skills to oversee the change in a way that ensures its success. In fact, one survey of *Fortune* 500 companies found that 87% of the companies had their organization development/change function as part of the HR department.[20]

Finally, these professionals must also have "integration competence," meaning the ability to integrate the three other competencies to increase the company's value. This means that, although specialist knowledge is necessary, a generalist perspective must be taken in making decisions. This entails seeing how all the functions within the HRM area fit together to be effective and recognizing that changes in any one part of the HRM package are likely to require changes in other parts of the package.

Google has sought to achieve this integration with what it calls the "three-thirds" staffing model. This consists of the following groups of people with complementary skill sets:

1. *One-third traditional HR people:* subject matter experts in benefits, compensation, employee relations, learning, and recruiting. Their expertise, pattern recognition, and emotional intelligence serve as the foundation for developing services and programs.

2. *One-third consultants:* high-end strategy experts with a background in management consulting who thrive on solving big, amorphous problems and bring a deliberate, business approach to people issues.

3. *One-third analytics professionals:* master's and doctoral-level folks who measure, analyze, and provide insight into all that the people operations function does, and to prove what really works. They have a healthy appetite for the impossible and drive experimentation to ensure that Google is as innovative on the people side as it is on the product side.

This staffing model has enabled Google to build the required skill base and integrate the various people needed to build a world-class HR organization.[21]

# The Role of the Chief Human Resource Officer

Having discussed the increasing importance of HR and the new strategic role of HR professionals, in closing we examine the role of the leader of the HR function. These chief human resource officers (CHROs) bear the responsibility for leading the HR function as well as ensuring that HR systems and processes deliver value to the company. Only recently have researchers attempted to examine what these HR leaders do and how they affect the business.

A recent survey identified seven roles that CHROs have to play to one degree or another, and then asked *Fortune* 150 CHROs to identify how they spend their time across those roles. As can be seen in Figure 16.17, CHROs reported spending the second most time (21%) as a **strategic advisor** to the executive team. This role entails sharing the people expertise as part of the decision-making process, as well as shaping how the firm's human capital fits into its strategy. This also was the role that was most frequently cited as having the greatest impact on the firm. One CHRO described the importance of the strategic advisor role as:

**Strategic advisor**
A role of the CHRO that focuses on the formulation and implementation of the firm's strategy.

> HR is critical, but it's a tool in the firm's portfolio. First, to truly impact the success of the firm, the CHRO needs to have a broad credibility that only comes from understanding every facet of the business at a level deep enough to be able to add business value in discussions with every leader. That means understanding the firm's economics, customer behavior, products,

**Figure 16.17**

Percentage of Time CHROs Spend in Each Role

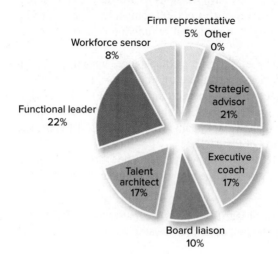

What percent of your time would you say you spend in each of the following roles?

Firm representative 5%
Other 0%
Workforce sensor 8%
Strategic advisor 21%
Functional leader 22%
Executive coach 17%
Talent architect 17%
Board liaison 10%

technology, etc. at a level deep enough to steer and shape decisions in these areas. From that flows the trust and credibility to counter the "conventional wisdom" on how best to manage people and shape the firm's talent agenda. Without this broader credibility, the CHRO can talk about talent, but risks not having sufficient context to make the right decisions. Second, from the CEO's perspective, the most useful thing is the integration of the people strategy with every other part of the firm's operations. The only way to truly integrate these areas is to be actively involved in the broader discussions as well.[22]

The role of **talent architect** also sees a significant portion of time spent (17%) and was also frequently cited as the role in which the CHRO has the greatest impact on the business. Playing the role of talent architect requires that CHROs help the executive team see the importance of talent, identify present and future talent gaps, and come to own the talent agenda. One CHRO described the importance of this role this way:

> Keeping the senior team focused on the strategic talent needs of the business allows proper identification of talent gaps and future needs, thus allowing time to develop best talent and design appropriate experiential assignments.[23]

CHROs report spending as much time in the role of **counselor/confidante/coach** as they do in the talent architect role (17%), and a number of CHROs listed this role as one of the roles with the greatest impact. This role seemingly is a broad one, and it can entail anything from behavioral or performance counseling to being the personal sounding board for the CEO. Perhaps as pressure mounts on CEOs from investors and analysts, the CHRO is the most trusted advisor that can be counted on to give personal advice or simply to listen to the CEO's problems. Sometimes CEOs may tend to behave dysfunctionally, and the CHRO may be the one to help point that out. The Integrity in Action box describes how CBS's CEO may have needed a good CHRO to play this role. Consider the following poignant comment regarding this role:

> If I do my job right, I am the copper wire that connects all the outlets of the firm together effectively. This includes Organization Development work (which some might put in the strategic advisor category), performance counseling and relationship building, business consulting and the strategic elements of talent acquisition and planning.[24]

Often this counselor/confidante/coach role entails coaching senior leaders regarding their communication style, and particularly warning them when their messages might be misinterpreted by those lower in the organizations.

The **leader of the HR function** is the role in which CHROs spent the most time (22%), but it is not seen as one that has the greatest impact. This role deals with ensuring that the HR function is aligning its activities and priorities toward the needs of the business, and it usually entails meeting with direct reports to provide guidance and check on progress. However, CHROs increasingly rely on their direct reports to design and deliver HR services while they shift their attention to advising and counseling the top executive team.

**Liaison to the board of directors** entails all of the activities in which CHROs engage with the board of directors, including discussions of executive compensation, CEO performance, CEO succession, and performance of other members of the executive leadership team. This role is increasing in importance, although it has a long way to go before equaling the strategic advisor, talent architect, and counselor/confidante/coach roles.

Finally, CHROs to some extent become the face of the organization to outside constituents such as labor unions, nongovernmental organizations, and the press. They spend the least amount of time in the **representative of the firm** role (see Table 16.5).

**Talent architect**
A role of the CHRO that focuses on building and identifying the human capital critical to the present and future of the firm.

**Counselor/ confidante/coach**
A role of the CHRO that focuses on counseling or coaching team members or resolving interpersonal or political conflicts among team members.

**Leader of the HR function**
A role of the CHRO that focuses on working with HR team members regarding the development, design, and delivery of HR services.

**Liaison to the board of directors**
A role of the CHRO that focuses on preparation for board meetings, phone calls with board members, and attendance at board meetings.

**Representative of the firm**
A role of the CHRO that focuses on activities with external stakeholders, such as lobbying, speaking to outside groups, and so on.

# INTEGRITY IN ACTION

## CBS's CEO Needed CHRO Help

Television network CBS's former CEO, Leslie Moonves recently became the TV industry's highest ranking casualty of multiple allegations of sexual misconduct. Moonves was an icon in the industry, responsible for such hit shows as *Survivor*, *C.S.I.*, and *The Big Bang Theory* that propelled CBS to being the most-watched network for the past decade.

In a *New Yorker* article, 12 women reported that he had sexually assaulted or harassed them. In response, CBS hired two law firms to investigate the allegations. After having interviewed 11 women, the law firm found their accounts to be credible, although many had occurred years ago. They also reported having received a number of reports that a network employee was constantly "on call" to perform sex acts with Mr. Moonves. They

wrote, "A number of employees were aware of this and believed that the woman was protected from discipline or termination as a result of it." While Moonves admitted to the sex, he and his lawyer described it as consensual.

Charles Elson, an expert on corporate governance stated, "A culture where this behavior could have gone unchecked for so long with so much knowledge is really troubling. The people who kept quiet got rewarded. That sends a powerful message. No amount of ethics or sexual harassment training is going to change that."

This is where a good CHRO can step in and help. Moonves's behavior should have been pretty obvious to many, particularly those close to him such as the CHRO. An effective CHRO would have confronted him with the impropriety or possibly illegality of his behavior. That

CHRO could also have helped coach him to ensure that he did not get into situations where he would be tempted to engage in inappropriate sexual relationships. If Moonves continued to engage in such reckless behavior, the CHRO would have a "badge on the table" moment by going to the board of directors to inform them of the risk, and that might end up risking the CHRO's job.

### DISCUSSION QUESTION

1. In part, because of his leadership deficiencies, Moonves resigned as CEO in 2018. If you had been CBS's CHRO, how would you have tried to counsel him so that his resignation might not have been necessary?

SOURCE: J. Stewart, "CBS Report on Moonves Cites Failure of Oversight," *New York Times*, December 5, 2018, p. B1.

**Table 16.5**
Roles of the CHRO

*Strategic advisor to the executive team:* activities focused specifically on the formulation and implementation of the firm's strategy.

*Counselor/confidante/coach to the executive team:* activities focused on counseling or coaching team members or resolving interpersonal or political conflicts among team members.

*Liaison to the board of directors:* preparation for board meetings, phone calls with board members, attendance at board meetings.

*Talent architect:* activities focused on building and identifying the human capital critical to the present and future of the firm.

*Leader of the HR function:* working with HR team members regarding the development, design, and delivery of HR services.

*Workforce sensor:* activities focused on identifying workforce morale issues or concerns.

*Representative of the firm:* activities with external stakeholders, such as lobbying, speaking to outside groups, and so on.

The Competing through Environmental, Social, and Governance Practices box describes a recent study detailing the roles that CHROs play in company ESG efforts.

The new strategic role for HRM presents both opportunities and challenges. HRM has the chance to profoundly impact the way organizations compete through people. But with this opportunity comes serious responsibility and accountability.[25] HRM functions of the future must consist of individuals who view themselves as businesspeople who happen to work in an HRM function, rather than as HRM people who happen to work in a business.

## A LOOK BACK

### Rebuilding Wells Fargo

Clearly Wells Fargo has a number of challenges to address. Their workforce has lost its pride. The culture needs to change. Its reputation must be repaired. And customer trust must be rebuilt.

The fact that Wells Fargo got to this point suggests that the HR function was lacking in skills, capabilities, and/or credibility. Thus, part of the rebuilding of Wells Fargo will require the rebuilding of the HR function.

### QUESTIONS

1. In light of what you have read in this chapter, what do you think HR needs to be doing to help rebuild Wells Fargo?
2. What will the HR function need to look like to be able to deliver this transformation?

SOURCES: R. Ensign, "Wells Fargo CEO Tim Sloan Steps Down," *Wall Street Journal*, March 28, 2019, https://www.wsj.com/articles/help-wanted-wells-fargo-board-seeks-ceo-to-charm-washington-fix-bank-11553877969?mod=hp_lead_pos7; R. Ensign, "Help Wanted: Wells Fargo Board Seeks CEO to Charm Washington, Fix Bank," *Wall Street Journal*, March 29, 2019, https://www.wsj.com/articles/help-wanted-wells-fargo-board-seeks-ceo-to-charm-washington-fix-bank-11553877969?mod=hp_lead_pos7.

## SUMMARY

The roles required of the HRM function have changed as people have become recognized as a true source of competitive advantage. This has required a transformation of the HRM function from focusing solely on transactional activities to an increasing involvement in strategic activities. In fact, according to one study, 64% of HR executives said that their HRM function is in a process of transformation.[26] The strategic management of the HRM function will determine whether HRM will transform itself to a true strategic partner or simply be blown up.

In this chapter we explored the various changing roles of the HRM function. HRM today includes the roles of administrative expert, employee advocate, change agent, and strategic partner. The function must also deliver transactional, traditional, and transformational services and activities to the firm, and it must be both efficient and effective. HR executives must strategically manage the HRM function just as the firm must be strategically managed. This requires that HRM develop measures of the function's performance through customer surveys and analytic methods. These measures can form the basis for planning ways to improve performance. HRM performance can increase through new structures for the function, through using reengineering and information technology, and through outsourcing.

## KEY TERMS

Audit approach, 719
Analytic approach, 721
Outsourcing, 727
Reengineering, 728
New technologies, 735

Transaction processing, 736
Decision support systems, 736
Expert systems, 736
Strategic advisor, 740
Talent architect, 741

Counselor/confidante/coach, 741
Leader of the HR function, 741
Liaison to the board of
    directors, 741
Representative of the firm, 741

## DISCUSSION QUESTIONS

1. Why have the roles and activities of the HRM function changed over the past 20–30 years? What has been driving this change? How effectively do you think HRM has responded?
2. How can the processes for strategic management discussed in Chapter 2 be transplanted to manage the HRM function?
3. Why do you think that few companies take the time to determine the effectiveness of HRM practices? Should a company be concerned about evaluating HRM practices? Why? What might people working in the HRM function gain by evaluating the function?
4. How might imaging technology be useful for recruitment? For training? For benefits administration? For performance management?
5. Employees in your company currently choose and enroll in benefits programs after reading brochures, completing enrollment forms, and sending them to their HR rep. A temporary staff has to be hired to process the large amount of paperwork that is generated. Enrollment forms need to be checked, sorted, batched, sent to data entry, keypunched, returned, and filed. The process is slow and prone to errors. How could you use process reengineering to make benefits enrollment more efficient and effective?
6. Some observers argue that outsourcing an activity is bad because the activity is no longer a means of distinguishing the firm from competitors. (All competitors can buy the same service from the same provider, so it cannot be a source of competitive advantage.) Is this true? If so, why would a firm outsource any activity?

## SELF-ASSESSMENT EXERCISE

Also assignable in Connect.

How ethical are you? Read each of the following descriptions. For each, circle whether you believe the behavior described is ethical or unethical.

1. A company president found that a competitor had made an important scientific discovery that would sharply reduce the profits of his own company. The president hired a key employee of the competitor in an attempt to learn the details of the discovery.   Ethical / Unethical

2. To increase profits, a general manager used a production process that exceeded legal limits for environmental pollution.   Ethical / Unethical

3. Because of pressure from her brokerage firm, a stockbroker recommended a type of bond that she did not consider to be a good investment.   Ethical / Unethical

4. A small business received one-fourth of its revenues in the form of cash. On the company's income tax forms, the owner reported only one-half of the cash receipts.   Ethical / Unethical

5. A corporate executive promoted a loyal friend and competent manager to the position of divisional vice president in preference to a better qualified manager with whom she had no close ties.   Ethical / Unethical

6. An employer received applications for a supervisor's position from two equally qualified applicants. The employer hired the male applicant because he thought some employees might resent being supervised by a female.   Ethical / Unethical

7. An engineer discovered what he perceived to be a product design flaw that constituted a safety hazard. His company declined to correct the flaw. The engineer decided to keep quiet, rather than taking his complaint outside the company.   Ethical / Unethical

8. A comptroller selected a legal method of financial reporting that concealed some embarrassing financial facts. Otherwise, those facts would have been public knowledge.   Ethical / Unethical

9. A company paid a $350,000 "consulting" fee to an official of a foreign country. In return, the official promised to help the company obtain a contract that should produce a $10 million profit for the company.   Ethical / Unethical

10. A member of a corporation's board of directors learned that her company intended to announce a stock split and increase its dividend. On the basis of this favorable information, the director bought additional shares of the company's stock. Following the announcement of the information, she sold the stock at a gain.   Ethical / Unethical

Now score your results. How many actions did you judge to be unethical?

All of these actions are unethical. The more of the actions you judged to be unethical, the better your understanding of ethical business behavior.

SOURCE: Based on S. Morris et al., "A Test of Environmental, Situational, and Personal Influences on the Ethical Intentions of CEOs," *Business and Society* 34 (1995), pp. 119-47.

## EXERCISING STRATEGY

### Cisco Is Rewiring HR

Fran Katsoudas assumed the chief people officer role at Cisco with the goal of challenging the way that the company had done HR. She called it "breaking HR."

Cisco was there at the creation of the Internet and has become a $49 billion technology company with 70,000 employees working at 372 locations across 92 countries. Managing employees across such a large geographic footprint requires thinking innovatively about processes and rigorously about values and culture.

One innovation in HR process was the decision to eliminate performance ratings. Many firms that have done this studied the elimination of performance ratings, rolled out pilot programs, evaluated them, made changes, and then rolled out a new approach to performance management. Cisco did away with the performance reviews before it had developed the replacement. Katsoudas says, "We announced we were moving away from performance ratings before we knew what we were moving to. We're betting on our managers to have the right type of conversation with their employees." This approach allows them to better involve employees in the design of the new approach.

That leads to the emphasis on values and culture. Based on employee input, Katsoudas developed the "People Manifesto," which lays out how Cisco treats employees and what Cisco expects from employees. This manifesto identifies three foundational principles:

- *Connect everything:* Cisco connects employees with the people, information, and opportunities they need to succeed, and it expects employees to connect with peers to deliver the best outcomes and results.
- *Innovate everywhere:* Cisco provides an open and agile environment to help employees explore ideas, challenge norms, and develop skills, and it expects employees to pursue a better, smarter, and faster tomorrow.
- *Benefit everyone:* Cisco hires the best and the brightest, develops them, and recognizes their contributions, and it expects employees to live the values and believe in winning together.

Fran Katsoudas has made a number of innovative moves with regard to how to manage HR at Cisco. The history of HR at Cisco had been focused on risk and compliance, but the emphasis has shifted to people, culture, and employee experience. In an interview with *Hispanic Executive*, Katsoudas said that her emphasis for 2017 was as follows:

- Creating a culture where employees can experience one company, many careers through job changes, continuous skills development, and stretch assignments
- Building the best teams and creating an environment of safety and trust, which will enable innovation
- Continuing to move to "one size fits one" offerings so that employees can create and experience their own journey

This is what today's HR function works on. Rather than focus on administrative tasks, modern HR functions help to build business success by building the human capabilities firms need to succeed.

## QUESTIONS

1. In light of what you have read in this chapter, do you think that Cisco is innovating? Why or why not?
2. What do you think Katsoudas means by the phrase "one size fits one"?

SOURCE: M. Wylie, "Cisco's Chief People Officer Is 'Breaking HR,'" *BizWomen*, March 10, 2016, http://www.bizjournals.com/bizwomen/news/profiles-strategies/2016/03/san-jose-cisco-s-chief-people-officer-is-breaking.html.

## MANAGING PEOPLE

### Wells Fargo's Recovery?

The power of incentives cannot be underestimated, and if you are looking for an example, look no further than Wells Fargo. The bank recently took a significant reputational and financial hit as illegal and unethical practices on the part of the banks employees came to light. The scandal resulted in a $185 million fine and enforcement action associated with employees opening as many as 2.1 million customer accounts without their knowledge.

The scandal can be traced back to the bank desiring to increase the number of customer accounts. For instance, a customer who has multiple checking and savings accounts, an auto loan, and a mortgage is much more profitable for a bank than someone with just a savings and/or checking account. So, the goal itself made sense as part of the bank's growth strategy.

However, a poorly designed incentive scheme took a legitimate goal but encouraged people to achieve it in ways that were both unethical and illegal. For instance, branch employees who hit their targets for new accounts might earn bonuses from $500 to $2,000 each quarter, and district managers could earn bonuses from $10,000 to $20,000 each year.

The pressure began with a "Jump into January" push where the retail banking head communicated lofty goals for branches and employees. These lofty goals and the associated bonuses with achieving them led many employees to display improper behavior.

When these practices came to light, Wells Fargo fired 5,300 lower level staff who had engaged in improper sales practices over the previous five years. However, remaining staff felt skeptical as the senior level executives had not faced discipline. However, that has begun to change. The board clawed back from the CEO and head of retail banking tens of millions of dollars in equity. Neither was fired, but both left the company shortly thereafter. More recently, the board discussed eliminating bonuses for both the current CEO and CFO. The bank has now fired a number of executives below the c-suite.

## QUESTIONS

1. Do you think Wells Fargo has done enough to punish those responsible for this scandal? Why or why not?
2. Why do you think the board would not fire the CEO and head of retail banking, but rather let them leave voluntarily?

SOURCE: E. Glazer, "Wells Fargo Fires Four Executives Following Probe of Sales-Practices Scandal," *Wall Street Journal*, February 21, 2017, https://www.wsj.com/articles/wells-fargo-fires-four-executives-following-probe-of-sales-practices-scandal-1487704642.

# HR IN SMALL BUSINESS

## Employees Make a Difference at Amy's Ice Creams

One of the bright spots for hungry people in Austin, Texas, is Amy's Ice Creams—its factory on Burnet Road or one of several Amy's stores. Founder Amy Miller, who dropped out of medical school to start the business, figures it is just another way to "make a difference in people's lives," offering customers a fun place to celebrate or cheer up.

Miller had been paying for med school with a job at Steve's Ice Cream, but when the company was sold, she thought the new owners were too stodgy, so she opened her own ice cream shop. Given the motivation to strike out on her own, it's not surprising that her goal is to manage her employees in a different way, one that combines informal fun with care for others.

The spirit of fun is defined by the employee selection process Miller invented. When interviewing candidates, Miller hands them a white paper bag with the instruction to "make something creative" and show her later. One applicant used it to make a hot-air balloon. Another put food in a bag, gave it to a homeless person, took a photo of the gift, and put the photo in the bag to return as the creative offering.

Job design also plays up the fun. Amy's prized employees don't just scoop up ice cream but also come up with ways to create a playful atmosphere. The company encourages workers to juggle shakers or give away a scoop of ice cream to a customer who is willing to sing and dance.

While the two painted concrete cows that sit in front of the Amy's factory are an emblem of the company's commitment to fun, its commitment to caring has a more uplifting sign: Amy's Ice Creams funded the construction of a room in a local children's cancer care center. The room resembles an ice cream shop and includes freezers stocked with ice cream—a treat that patients can share with visiting family members.

Service to the community is also connected to employee engagement. At Amy's, the employees choose the charities the company will support. At a prom hosted by Amy's every year, the company selects a King and Queen to honor based on which employees did the most company-sponsored charitable work. In this way, employee rewards are tied to the company's value.

Fun and community service aren't just a way to be nice; they also have made Amy's Ice Creams a company ice cream lovers care to buy from. The company reaps millions of dollars in sales and has expanded the number of locations to meet growing demand in Austin as well as in Houston and San Antonio. Still, it's not just about the revenues. Co-owner (and Amy's husband) Steve Simmons told a reporter, "We never want to be a mega-company. When we don't know employees' names, there's a problem."

### QUESTIONS

1. Which elements of a customer-oriented HRM perspective does Amy's Ice Creams seem to have? (See Figure 16.2.)
2. Suppose Amy's hired you as a consultant to evaluate whether the company has an effective HRM function. Which outcomes would you look for? How would you measure them?
3. Generally, a small ice cream shop such as Amy's cannot afford to pay store workers very high wages. How well do you think the company can achieve high employee satisfaction without high pay? What can it do to foster satisfaction besides the efforts described here? How could e-HRM support these efforts?

SOURCES: Amy's Ice Creams corporate website, www.amysicecreams.com, accessed June 19, 2015; J. Popick, "GrowCo.: Growth by Involvement at Amy's Ice Creams," *Inc.*, March 16, 2010; R. Rayasam, "Sweet Success," *Austin American-Statesman*, September 29, 2005; Business & Company Resource Center, http://galenet.galegroup.com; M. Malone, "Chain Founder; Amy Miller, Amy's Ice Creams," *Restaurant Business*, March 1, 2003, www.allbusiness.com.

# NOTES

1. P. Wright, S. Snell, and P. Jacobsen, "Current Approaches to HR Strategies: Inside-Out vs. Outside-In," *Human Resource Planning* 27 (2004), pp. 36–46.
2. Personal communication, June 2010.
3. A. S. Tsui and L. R. Gomez-Mejia, "Evaluating HR Effectiveness," in *Human Resource Management: Evolving Roles and Responsibilities*, ed. L. Dyer (Washington, DC: Bureau of National Affairs, 1988), pp. 1-187–1-227.
4. D. Ulrich, "Measuring Human Resources: An Overview of Practice and a Prescription for Results," *Human Resource Management* 36, no. 3 (1997), pp. 303–20.
5. P. Wright, G. McMahan, S. Snell, and B. Gerhart, "Comparing Line and HR Executives' Perceptions of HR Effectiveness: Services, Roles, and Contributions," working paper 98-29 (Ithaca, NY: Cornell University Center for Advanced Human Resource Studies, 1998).
6. J. C. Erfurt, A. Foote, and M. A. Heirich, "The Cost-Effectiveness of Worksite Wellness Programs," *Personnel Psychology* 15 (1992), p. 22.
7. T. H. Davenport, J. Haris, and J. Shapiro, "Competing on Talent Analytics," *Harvard Business Review*, October 2010, pp. 52–59.
8. P. Wright, G. McMahan, S. Snell, and B. Gerhart, *Strategic HRM: Building Human Capital and Organizational Capability*, technical report (Ithaca, NY: Cornell University, 1998).

9. T. B. Kinni, "A Reengineering Primer," *Quality Digest*, January 1994, pp. 26–30; "Reengineering Is Helping Health of Hospitals and Its Patients," *Total Quality Newsletter*, February 1994, p. 5; R. Recardo, "Process Reengineering in a Finance Division," *Journal for Quality and Participation*, June 1994, pp. 70–73.

10. L. Quillen, "Human Resource Computerization: A Dollar and Cents Approach," *Personnel Journal*, July 1989, pp. 74–77.

11. S. Greengard, "New Technology Is HR's Route to Reengineering," *Personnel Journal*, July 1994, pp. 32c–32o.

12. S. Shrivastava and J. Shaw, "Liberating HR through Technology," *Human Resource Management* 42, no. 3 (2003), pp. 201–17.

13. C. O'Reilly and P. Caldwell, *Cypress Semiconductor (A): Vision, Values, and Killer Software* (Stanford University Case Study, HR-8A, 1998).

14. "61 Percent of Americans Consider Themselves Overworked and 86 Percent Are Not Satisfied with Their Job, According to Monster's 2004 Work/Life Balance Survey," *Business Wire*, August 3, 2004.

15. R. Broderick and J. W. Boudreau, "Human Resource Management, Information Technology, and the Competitive Edge," *Academy of Management Executive* 6 (1992), pp. 7–17.

16. G. McMahan and R. Woodman, "The Current Practice of Organization Development within the Firm: A Survey of Large Industrial Corporations," *Group and Organization Studies* 17 (1992), pp. 117–34.

17. B. Becker, M. Huselid, and D. Ulrich, *The HR Scorecard: Linking People, Strategy, and Performance* (Cambridge, MA: HBS Press, 2001).

18. D. Ulrich and A. Yeung, "A Shared Mindset," *Personnel Administrator*, March 1989, pp. 38–45.

19. G. Jones and P. Wright, "An Economic Approach to Conceptualizing the Utility of Human Resource Management Practices," *Research in Personnel/Human Resources* 10 (1992), pp. 271–99.

20. R. Schuler and J. Walker, "Human Resources Strategy: Focusing on Issues and Actions," *Organizational Dynamics*, Summer 1990, pp. 5–19.

21. Company documents.

22. P. Wright, "Strategies and Challenges of the Chief Human Resource Officer: Results of the First Annual Cornell/CAHRS Survey of CHROs," technical report (Ithaca, NY: Cornell University, 2009).

23. Wright, "Strategies and Challenges of the Chief Human Resource Officer."

24. Wright, "Strategies and Challenges of the Chief Human Resource Officer."

25. J. Paauwe, *Human Resource Management and Performance: Unique Approaches for Achieving Long-Term Viability* (Oxford: Oxford University Press, 2004).

26. L. Csoka and B. Hackett, *Transforming the HR Function for Global Business Success* (New York: Conference Board, 1998), Report 1209-19RR.

# GLOSSARY

**360-degree appraisal**   A performance appraisal process for managers that includes evaluations from a wide range of persons who interact with the manager. The process includes self-evaluations as well as evaluations from the manager's boss, subordinates, peers, and customers.

**360-degree feedback systems**   A performance appraisal process for managers that includes evaluations from a wide range of persons who interact with the manager. The process includes self-evaluations as well as evaluations from the manager's boss, subordinates, peers, and customers.

**9-box grid**   A three-by-three matrix used by groups of managers and executives to compare employees within one department, function, division, or the entire company.

**Acceptability**   The extent to which a performance measure is deemed to be satisfactory or adequate by those who use it.

**Action learning**   Training in which teams work on an actual business problem, commit to an action plan, and are accountable for carrying out the plan.

**Action plan**   A document summarizing what the trainee and manager will do to ensure that training transfers to the job.

**Action steps**   The part of a written affirmative action plan that specifies what an employer plans to do to reduce underutilization of protected groups.

**Adventure learning**   Learning focused on the development of teamwork and leadership skills by using structured outdoor activities.

**Agency shop**   A union security provision that requires an employee to pay union membership dues but not to join the union.

**Agent**   In agency theory, a person (e.g., a manager) who is expected to act on behalf of a principal (e.g., an owner).

**Agility**   Companies and their employees ability to anticipate and cause change, adapt to it, and take specific actions to support change.

**Alternative dispute resolution (ADR)**   A method of resolving disputes that does not rely on the legal system, often proceeding through the four stages of open-door policy, peer review, mediation, and arbitration.

**Americans with Disabilities Act (ADA)**   A 1990 act prohibiting individuals with disabilities from being discriminated against in the workplace.

**Analytic approach**   Type of assessment of HRM effectiveness that involves determining the impact of, or the financial costs and benefits of, a program or practice.

**Appraisal politics**   A situation in which evaluators purposefully distort a rating to achieve personal or company goals.

**Apprenticeship**   A work-study training method with both on-the-job and classroom training.

**Arbitration**   A procedure for resolving collective bargaining impasses by which an arbitrator chooses a solution to the dispute.

**Artificial intelligence**   Technology that can think like a human.

**Assessment**   Collecting information and providing feedback to employees about their behavior, communication style, or skills.

**Assessment center**   A process in which multiple raters evaluate employees' performance on a number of exercises.

**Associate union membership**   A form of union membership by which the union receives dues in exchange for services (e.g., health insurance, credit cards) but does not provide representation in collective bargaining.

**Attitudinal structuring**   The aspect of the labor-management negotiation process that refers to the relationship and level of trust between the negotiators.

**Audit approach**   Type of assessment of HRM effectiveness that involves review of customer satisfaction or key indicators (e.g., turnover rate, average days to fill a position) related to an HRM functional area (e.g., recruiting, training).

**Augmented reality (AR)**   A training method in which trainees see the physical world around them but their view includes virtual media.

**Balanced scorecard**   A means of performance measurement that gives managers a chance to look at their company from the perspectives of internal and external customers, employees, and shareholders.

**Bench strength** The business strategy of having a pool of talented employees who are ready when needed to step in to a new position within the organization.

**Benchmarking** Comparing an organization's practices against those of the competition.

**Big data** Information merged from a variety of sources, including HR databases, corporate financial statements, and employee surveys, to make evidence-based HR decisions and show that HR practices can influence the organization's bottom line.

**Blended learning** Delivering content and instruction with a combination of technology-based and face-to-face methods.

**Bona fide occupational qualification (BFOQ)** A job qualification based on race, sex, religion, and so on that an employer asserts is a necessary qualification for the job.

**Calibration meetings** A way to discuss employees' performance with the goal of ensuring that similar standards are applied to their evaluations.

**Career support** Coaching, protection, sponsorship, and providing challenging assignments, exposure, and visibility.

**Cash balance plan** A retirement plan in which the employer sets up an individual account for each employee and contributes a percentage of the employee's salary; the account earns interest at a predetermined rate.

**Centralization** The degree to which decision-making authority resides at the top of the organizational chart.

**Change** The adoption of a new idea or behavior by a company.

**Checkoff provision** A union contract provision that requires an employer to deduct union dues from employees' paychecks.

**Closed shop** A union security provision requiring a person to be a union member before being hired. Illegal under NLRA.

**Cloud computing** A computing system that provides information technology infrastructure over a network in a self-service, modifiable, and on-demand model.

**Coach** A peer or manager who works with an employee to motivate the employee, help him or her develop skills, and provide reinforcement and feedback.

**Cognitive ability tests** Tests that include three dimensions: verbal comprehension, quantitative ability, and reasoning ability.

**Communities of practice** Groups of employees who work together, learn from each other, and develop a common understanding of how to get work accomplished.

**Compa-ratio** An index of the correspondence between actual and intended pay.

**Comparable worth** A public policy that advocates remedies for any undervaluation of women's jobs (also called *pay equity*).

**Compensable factors** The characteristics of jobs that an organization values and chooses to pay for.

**Competencies** Sets of skills, knowledge, and abilities and personal characteristics that enable employees to perform their jobs.

**Competency model** Identifies and provides a description of competencies that are common for an entire occupation, organization, job family, or specific job.

**Competitiveness** A company's ability to maintain and gain market share in its industry.

**Concentration strategy** A strategy focusing on increasing market share, reducing costs, or creating and maintaining a market niche for products and services.

**Concurrent validation** A criterion-related validity study in which a test is administered to all the people currently in a job and then incumbents' scores are correlated with existing measures of their performance on the job.

**Consolidated Omnibus Budget Reconciliation Act (COBRA)** The 1985 act that requires employers to permit employees to extend their health insurance coverage at group rates for up to 36 months following a qualifying event, such as a layoff.

**Content validation** A test-validation strategy performed by demonstrating that the items, questions, or problems posed by a test are a representative sample of the kinds of situations or problems that occur on the job.

**Continuous learning** A learning system that requires employees to understand the entire work process and expects them to acquire new skills, apply them on the job, and share what they have learned with other employees.

**Continuous performance management process** An approach that encourages ongoing conversations between managers, their direct reports, and teams focused on work progress, providing feedback, accomplishment and necessary adjustment of goals, and development needs.

**Coordination training**   Training a team in how to share information and decision-making responsibilities to maximize team performance.

**Corporate campaigns**   Union activities designed to exert public, financial, or political pressure on employers during the union-organizing process.

**Counselor/confidante/coach**   A role of the CHRO that focuses on counseling or coaching team members or resolving interpersonal or political conflicts among team members.

**Criterion-related validity**   A method of establishing the validity of a personnel selection method by showing a substantial correlation between test scores and job-performance scores.

**Cross-cultural preparation**   The process of educating employees (and their families) who are given an assignment in a foreign country.

**Cross-training**   Training in which team members understand and practice each other's skills so that members are prepared to step in and take another member's place should he or she temporarily or permanently leave the team.

**Decision support systems**   Problem-solving systems that usually include a "what-if" feature that allows users to see how outcomes change when assumptions or data change.

**Delayering**   Reducing the number of job levels within an organization.

**Departmentalization**   The degree to which work units are grouped based on functional similarity or similarity of work flow.

**Development**   The acquisition of knowledge, skills, and behaviors that improve an employee's ability to meet changes in job requirements and in client and customer demands.

**Development planning system**   A system to retain and motivate employees by identifying and meeting their development needs (also called *career management systems*).

**Direct applicants**   People who apply for a job vacancy without prompting from the organization.

**Disparate impact**   A theory of discrimination based on facially neutral employment practices that disproportionately exclude a protected group from employment opportunities.

**Disparate treatment**   A theory of discrimination based on different treatment given to individuals because of their race, color, religion, sex, national origin, age, or disability status.

**Distributive bargaining**   The part of the labor–management negotiation process that focuses on dividing a fixed economic "pie."

**Diversity training**   Refers to learning efforts that are designed to change employees' attitudes about diversity and/or develop skills needed to work with a diverse workforce.

**Downsizing**   The planned elimination of large numbers of personnel, designed to enhance organizational effectiveness.

**Downward move**   A job change involving a reduction in an employee's level of responsibility and authority.

**Due process policies**   Policies by which a company formally lays out the steps an employee can take to appeal a termination decision.

**Duty of fair representation**   The National Labor Relations Act requirement that all bargaining unit members have equal access to and representation by the union.

**E-learning**   Instruction and delivery of training by computers through the Internet or company intranet.

**Efficiency wage theory**   A theory stating that wages influence worker productivity.

**Employee assistance program (EAP)**   Employer program that attempts to ameliorate problems encountered by workers who are drug dependent, alcoholic, or psychologically troubled.

**Employee engagement**   The degree to which employees are fully involved in their work and the strength of their job and company commitment.

**Employee experience**   Everything that influences employees daily life both inside and outside of the workplace.

**Employee Retirement Income Security Act (ERISA)**   The 1974 act that increased the fiduciary responsibilities of pension plan trustees, established vesting rights and portability provisions, and established the Pension Benefit Guaranty Corporation (PBGC).

**Employee stock ownership plan (ESOP)**   An employee ownership plan that provides employers certain tax and financial advantages when stock is granted to employees.

**Employee value proposition (EVP)** A strategic statement that communicates the company values, how they affect employees, and how the employee experience reflects the values.

**Employment-at-will doctrine** The doctrine that, in the absence of a specific contract, either an employer or an employee could sever the employment relationship at any time.

**Employment-at-will policies** Policies stating that either an employer or an employee can terminate the employment relationship at any time, regardless of cause.

**Empowering** Giving employees the responsibility and authority to make decisions.

**Equal employment opportunity (EEO)** The government's attempt to ensure that all individuals have an equal opportunity for employment, regardless of race, color, religion, sex, age, disability, or national origin.

**Equal Employment Opportunity Commission (EEOC)** The government commission established to ensure that all individuals have an equal opportunity for employment, regardless of race, color, religion, sex, age, disability, or national origin.

**Ergonomics** The interface between individuals' physiological characteristics and the physical work environment.

**Ethics** The fundamental principles of right and wrong by which employees and companies interact.

**Evidence-based HR** Demonstrating that HR practices have a positive influence on the company's bottom line or key stakeholders (employees, customers, community, shareholders).

**Exempt** Employees who are not covered by the Fair Labor Standards Act. Exempt employees are not eligible for overtime pay.

**Expatriate** Employee sent by his or her company to manage operations in a different country.

**Expectancy theory** The theory that says motivation is a function of valence, instrumentality, and expectancy.

**Experiential programs** Training programs in which trainees gain knowledge and theory, participate in behavioral simulations, analyze the activity, and connect the theory and activity with on-the-job situations.

**Expert systems** Computer systems incorporating the decision rules of people recognized as experts in a certain area.

**Explicit knowledge** Knowledge that is well documented and easily transferred to other persons.

**External analysis** Examining the organization's operating environment to identify strategic opportunities and threats.

**External growth strategy** An emphasis on acquiring vendors and suppliers or buying businesses that allow a company to expand into new markets.

**External labor market** Persons outside the firm who are actively seeking employment.

**Fact finder** A person who reports on the reasons for a labor–management dispute, the views and arguments of both sides, and a nonbinding recommendation for settling the dispute.

**Fair Labor Standards Act (FLSA)** The 1938 law that established the minimum wage and overtime pay.

**Family and Medical Leave Act** The 1993 act that requires employers with 50 or more employees to provide up to 12 weeks of unpaid leave after childbirth or adoption; to care for a seriously ill child, spouse, or parent; or for an employee's own serious illness.

**Financial Accounting Statement (FAS) 106** The rule issued by the Financial Accounting Standards Board in 1993 requiring companies to fund benefits provided after retirement on an accrual rather than a pay-as-you-go basis and to enter these future cost obligations on their financial statements.

**Forecasting** The attempts to determine the supply of and demand for various types of human resources to predict areas within the organization where there will be future labor shortages or surpluses.

**Formal education programs** Employee development programs, including short courses offered by consultants or universities, executive MBA programs, and university programs.

**Formal training** Training and development programs and courses that are developed and organized by the company.

**Four-fifths rule** A rule that states that an employment test has disparate impact if the hiring rate for a minority group is less than four-fifths, or 80%, of the hiring rate for the majority group.

**Frame of reference** A standard point that serves as a comparison for other points and thus provides meaning.

**Gainsharing**  A form of group compensation based on group or plant performance (rather than organization-wide profits) that does not become part of the employee's base salary.

**General duty clause**  The provision of the Occupational Safety and Health Act that states an employer has an overall obligation to furnish employees with a place of employment free from recognized hazards.

**Gig economy**  Companies who rely primarily on nontraditional employment to meet service and product demands

**Glass ceiling**  A barrier to advancement to higher-level jobs in the company that adversely affects women and minorities. The barrier may be due to lack of access to training programs, development experiences, or relationships (e.g., mentoring).

**Goals**  What an organization hopes to achieve in the medium- to long-term future.

**Goals and timetables**  The part of a written affirmative action plan that specifies the percentage of women and minorities that an employer seeks to have in each job group and the date by which that percentage is to be attained.

**Group- or team-building methods**  Training methods that help trainees share ideas and experiences, build group identity, understand the dynamics of interpersonal relationships, and get to know their own strengths and weaknesses and those of their co-workers.

**Hands-on methods**  Training methods that require the trainee to be actively involved in learning.

**Health maintenance organization (HMO)**  A health care plan that provides benefits on a prepaid basis for employees who are required to use only HMO medical service providers.

**High-performance work systems**  Work systems that maximize the fit between employees and technology.

**High-potential employees**  Employees the company believes are capable of being successful in high-level management positions.

**Host country**  The country in which the parent-country organization seeks to locate or has already located a facility.

**Host-country nationals (HCNs)**  Employees born and raised in a host, not parent, country.

**HR dashboard**  HR metrics such as productivity and absenteeism that are accessible by employees and managers through the company intranet or human resource information system.

**HR or workforce analytics**  The practice of using data from HR databases and other data sources to make evidence-based HR decisions.

**Human resource information system (HRIS)**  A system used to acquire, store, manipulate, analyze, retrieve, and distribute information related to human resources.

**Human resource management (HRM)**  The policies, practices, and systems that influence employees' behavior, attitudes, and performances.

**Human resource recruitment**  The practice or activity carried on by the organization with the primary purpose of identifying and attracting potential employees.

**In-basket**  A simulation of the administrative tasks of a manager's job.

**Incentive effect**  The effect a pay plan has on the behaviors of current employees.

**Inclusion**  Creating an environment in which employees share a sense of belonging, mutual respect, and commitment with others so that they can perform their best work.

**Individualism–collectivism**  One of Hofstede's cultural dimensions; describes the strength of the relation between an individual and other individuals in a society.

**Informal learning**  Learning that is learner initiated, involves action and doing, is motivated by an intent to develop, and does not occur in a formal learning setting.

**Intangible assets**  A type of company asset that includes human capital, customer capital, social capital, and intellectual capital.

**Integrative bargaining**  The part of the labor–management negotiation process that seeks solutions beneficial to both sides.

**Interactional justice**  A concept of justice referring to the interpersonal nature of how the outcomes were implemented.

**Internal analysis**  The process of examining an organization's strengths and weaknesses.

**Internal growth strategy**  A focus on new market and product development, innovation, and joint ventures.

**Internal labor force**  Labor force of current employees.

**Internship**  On-the-job learning sponsored by an educational institution, or part of an academic program.

**Interview**  Employees are questioned about their work and personal experiences, skills, and career plans.

**Intraorganizational bargaining**    The part of the labor-management negotiation process that focuses on the conflicting objectives of factions within labor and management.

**Involuntary turnover**    Turnover initiated by the organization (often among people who would prefer to stay).

**ISO 9000:2015**    A family of standards developed by the International Organization for Standardization that includes 20 requirements for dealing with such issues as how to establish quality standards and document work processes.

**Job analysis**    The process of getting detailed information about jobs.

**Job description**    A list of the tasks, duties, and responsibilities (TDRs) that a job entails.

**Job design**    The process of defining the way work will be performed and the tasks that will be required in a given job.

**Job enlargement**    Adding challenges or new responsibilities to an employee's current job.

**Job evaluation**    An administrative procedure used to measure internal job worth.

**Job experience**    The relationships, problems, demands, tasks, and other features that employees face in their jobs.

**Job hazard analysis technique**    A breakdown of each job into basic elements, each of which is rated for its potential for harm or injury.

**Job involvement**    The degree to which people identify themselves with their jobs.

**Job redesign**    The process of changing the tasks or the way work is performed in an existing job.

**Job rotation**    The process of systematically moving a single individual from one job to another over the course of time. The job assignments may be in various functional areas of the company, or movement may be between jobs in a single functional area or department.

**Job satisfaction**    A pleasurable feeling that results from the perception that one's job fulfills or allows for the fulfillment of one's important job values.

**Job specification**    A list of the knowledge, skills, abilities, and other characteristics (KSAOs) that an individual must have to perform a job.

**Job structure**    The relative pay of jobs in an organization.

**Kaizen**    Practices participated in by employees from all levels of the company that focus on continuous improvement of business processes.

**Key jobs**    Benchmark jobs, used in pay surveys, that have relatively stable content and are common to many organizations.

**Knowledge management**    The process of enhancing company performance by designing and using tools, systems, and cultures to improve creation, sharing, and use of knowledge.

**Knowledge workers**    Employees who own the intellectual means of producing a product or service.

**Leader of the HR function**    A role of the CHRO that focuses on working with HR team members regarding the development, design, and delivery of HR services.

**Leaderless group discussion**    Process in which a team of five to seven employees solves an assigned problem within a certain time period.

**Leading indicator**    An objective measure that accurately predicts future labor demand.

**Lean thinking**    A way to do more with less effort, equipment space, and time, but still provide customers what they need and want.

**Learning management system (LMS)**    Technology platform that automates the administration, development, and delivery of a company's training program.

**Learning organization**    An organization whose employees are continuously attempting to learn new things and apply what they have learned to improve product or service quality.

**Liaison to the board of directors**    A role of the CHRO that focuses on preparation for board meetings, phone calls with board members, and attendance at board meetings.

**Long-term–short-term orientation**    One of Hofstede's cultural dimensions; describes how a culture balances immediate benefits with future rewards.

**Maintenance of membership**    Union rules requiring members to remain members for a certain period of time (e.g., the length of the union contract).

**Malcolm Baldrige National Quality Award**    An award established in 1987 to promote quality awareness, to recognize quality achievements of U.S. companies, and to publicize successful quality strategies.

**Manager support**    The degree to which trainees' managers emphasize the importance of attending training programs and stress the application of training content to the job.

**Managing diversity and inclusion** The process of creating an environment that allows all employees to contribute to organizational goals and experience personal growth.

**Marginal tax rate** The percentage of an additional dollar of earnings that goes to taxes.

**Masculinity–femininity dimension** One of Hofstede's cultural dimensions; describes the division of roles between the sexes within a society.

**Massive open online courses (MOOCs)** Online learning designed to enroll large numbers of learners who have access to the Internet and composed of interactive coursework including video lectures, discussion groups, wikis, and assessment quizzes.

**Mediation** A procedure for resolving collective bargaining impasses by which a mediator with no formal authority acts as a facilitator and go-between in the negotiations.

**Mentor** An experienced, productive senior employee who helps develop a less experienced employee.

**Merit bonus** Merit pay paid in the form of a bonus, instead of a salary increase.

**Merit increase grid** A grid that combines an employee's performance rating with his or her position in a pay range to determine the size and frequency of his or her pay increases.

**Merit pay** Traditional form of pay in which base pay is increased permanently.

**Microlearning** Training delivered in small pieces or chunks designed to engage trainees, motivate them to learn, and help facilitate retention.

**Minimum wage** The lowest amount that employers are legally allowed to pay; the 1990 amendment of the Fair Labor Standards Act permits a subminimum wage to workers under the age of 20 for a period of up to 90 days.

**Mobile devices** Equipment such as smartphones and tablet computers that provide employees with anytime, anywhere access to HR applications and other work-related information.

**Motivation to learn** The desire of the trainee to learn the content of a training program.

**Myers Briggs Type Inventory (MBTI)** A psychological test used for team building and leadership development that identifies employees' preferences for energy, information gathering, decision making, and lifestyle.

**Needs assessment** The process used to determine if training is necessary.

**Negative affectivity** A dispositional dimension that reflects pervasive individual differences in satisfaction with any and all aspects of life.

**New technologies** Current applications of knowledge, procedures, and equipment that have not been previously used. Usually involves replacing human labor with equipment, information processing, or some combination of the two.

**Nonkey jobs** Jobs that are unique to organizations and that cannot be directly valued or compared through the use of market surveys.

**Nontraditional employment** Includes the use of independent contractors, freelancers, on-call workers, temporary workers, and contract company workers.

**Occupational Safety and Health Act (OSHA)** The 1970 law that authorizes the federal government to establish and enforce occupational safety and health standards for all places of employment engaging in interstate commerce.

**Offshoring** A special case of outsourcing, in which the jobs that move leave one country and go to another.

**On-the-job training (OJT)** Peers or managers training new or inexperienced employees who learn the job by observation, understanding, and imitation.

**Onboarding** Refers to the process of helping new hires adjust to social and performance aspects of their new jobs.

**Opportunity to perform** The trainee is provided with or actively seeks experience using newly learned knowledge, skills, or behavior.

**Organizational analysis** A process for determining the business appropriateness of training.

**Organizational commitment** The degree to which an employee identifies with the organization and is willing to put forth effort on its behalf.

**Outplacement counseling** Counseling to help displaced employees manage the transition from one job to another.

**Outsourcing** An organization's use of an outside organization for a broad set of services.

**Parent country** The country in which a company's corporate headquarters is located.

**Parent-country nationals (PCNs)** Employees who were born and live in a parent country.

**Pay grades** Jobs of similar worth or content grouped together for pay administration purposes.

**Pay level** The average pay, including wages, salaries, and bonuses, of jobs in an organization.

**Pay policy line** A mathematical expression that describes the relationship between a job's pay and its job evaluation points.

**Pay structure** The relative pay of different jobs (job structure) and how much they are paid (pay level).

**Pension Benefit Guaranty Corporation (PBGC)** The agency that guarantees to pay employees a basic retirement benefit in the event that financial difficulties force a company to terminate or reduce employee pension benefits.

**Performance appraisal** The process through which an organization gets information on how well an employee is doing his or her job.

**Performance feedback** The process of providing employees information regarding their performance effectiveness.

**Performance improvement plan (PIP)** A plan that describes the performance changes that a poorly performing employee needs to make in a specified time period or face termination.

**Performance management** The means through which managers ensure that employees' activities and outcomes are congruent with the organization's goals.

**Performance support systems** Computer applications that can provide (as requested) skills training, information access, and expert advice.

**Person analysis** A process for determining whether employees need training, who needs training, and whether employees are ready for training.

**Power distance** One of Hofstede's cultural dimensions; concerns how a culture deals with hierarchical power relationships—particularly the unequal distribution of power.

**Predictive validation** A criterion-related validity study that seeks to establish an empirical relationship between applicants' test scores and their eventual performance on the job.

**Preferred provider organization (PPO)** A group of health care providers who contract with employers, insurance companies, and so forth to provide health care at a reduced fee.

**Presentation methods** Training methods in which trainees are passive recipients of information.

**Principal** In agency theory, a person (e.g., the owner) who seeks to direct another person's behavior.

**Procedural justice** A concept of justice focusing on the methods used to determine the outcomes received.

**Profit sharing** A compensation plan in which payments are based on a measure of organization performance (profits) and do not become part of the employees' base salary.

**Progression of withdrawal** The theory that dissatisfied individuals enact a set of behaviors to avoid the work situation.

**Promotions** Advances into positions with greater challenge, more responsibility, and more authority than the employee's previous job.

**Prosocial motivation** The degree to which people are motivated to help other people.

**Protean career** A career that is changing frequently due to both changes in the person's interests, abilities, and values and changes in the work environment.

**Psychological success** The feeling of pride and accomplishment that comes from achieving life goals.

**Psychosocial support** Serving as a friend and role model, providing positive regard and acceptance, and creating an outlet for a protégé to talk about anxieties and fears.

**Quantitative ability** Refers to the speed and accuracy with which one can solve arithmetic problems of all kinds.

**Range spread** The distance between the minimum and maximum amounts in a pay grade.

**Rate ranges** Different employees in the same job may have different pay rates.

**Readiness for training** Employee characteristics that provide them with the desire, energy, and focus necessary to learn from training.

**Reasonable accommodation** Making facilities readily accessible to and usable by individuals with disabilities.

**Reasoning ability** Refers to a person's capacity to invent solutions to many diverse problems.

**Recruitment** The process of seeking applicants for potential employment.

**Reengineering** Review and redesign of work processes to make them more efficient and improve the quality of the end product or service.

**Referrals** People who are prompted to apply for a job by someone within the organization.

**Reliability** The consistency of a performance measure; the degree to which a performance measure is free from random error.

**Repatriation**   The preparation of expatriates for return to the parent company and country from a foreign assignment.

**Representative of the firm**   A role of the CHRO that focuses on activities with external stakeholders, such as lobbying, speaking to outside groups, and so on.

**Repurposing**   Directly translating instructor-led training online.

**Reshoring**   Moving jobs from overseas to the United States.

**Return on investment (ROI)**   Refers to the estimated dollar return from each dollar invested in learning.

**Reverse mentoring**   A business situation in which younger employees mentor more senior employees.

**Right-to-work laws**   State laws that make union shops, maintenance of membership, and agency shops illegal.

**Role behaviors**   Behaviors that are required of an individual in his or her role as a jobholder in a social work environment.

**Role-play**   A participant taking the part or role of a manager or other employee.

**Sabbatical**   A leave of absence from the company to renew or develop skills.

**Safety awareness programs**   Employer programs that attempt to instill symbolic and substantive changes in the organization's emphasis on safety.

**Sarbanes-Oxley Act of 2002**   A congressional act passed in response to illegal and unethical behavior by managers and executives. The act sets stricter rules for business, especially related to accounting practices—including requiring more open and consistent disclosure of financial data and the CEO's assurance that the data are completely accurate—and provisions that affect the employee–employer relationship (e.g., development of a code of conduct for senior financial officers).

**Selection**   The process by which an organization attempts to identify applicants with the necessary knowledge, skills, abilities, and other characteristics that will help it achieve its goals.

**Self-service**   Giving employees online access to human resources information.

**Serious games**   Games in which the training content is turned into a game but has business objectives.

**Shared service model**   A way to organize the HR function that includes centers of expertise or excellence, service centers, and business partners.

**Simulation**   A training method that represents a real-life situation, allowing trainees to see the outcomes of their decisions in an artificial environment.

**Situational interview**   An interview procedure where applicants are confronted with specific issues, questions, or problems that are likely to arise on the job.

**Six Sigma process**   A system of measuring, analyzing, improving, and controlling processes once they meet quality standards.

**Skill-based pay**   Pay based on the skills employees acquire and are capable of using.

**Social networking**   Websites and blogs that facilitate interactions between people.

**Social performance management**   Social media and micro-blogs similar to Facebook, LinkedIn, and Yammer that allow employees to quickly exchange information, talk to each other, provide coaching, and receive feedback and recognition in the form of electronic badges.

**Sorting effect**   The effect a pay plan has on the composition of the current workforce (the types of employees attracted and retained).

**Specificity**   The extent to which a performance measure gives detailed guidance to employees about what is expected of them and how they can meet these expectations.

**Stakeholders**   The various interest groups who have relationships with and, consequently, whose interests are tied to the organization (e.g., employees, suppliers, customers, shareholders, community).

**Standard deviation rule**   A rule used to analyze employment tests to determine disparate impact; it uses the difference between the expected representation for minority groups and the actual representation to determine whether the difference between the two is greater than would occur by chance.

**STEM skills**   Science, technology, engineering, and math skills that U.S. employers need and value, but employees lack.

**Stock options**   An employee ownership plan that gives employees the opportunity to buy the company's stock at a previously fixed price.

**Strategic advisor**   A role of the CHRO that focuses on the formulation and implementation of the firm's strategy.

**Strategic choice**   The organization's strategy; the ways an organization will attempt to fulfill its mission and achieve its long-term goals.

**Strategic congruence**   The extent to which the performance management system elicits job performance that is consistent with the organization's strategy, goals, and culture.

**Strategic human resource management (SHRM)**   A pattern of planned human resource deployments and activities intended to enable an organization to achieve its goals.

**Strategy formulation**   The process of deciding on a strategic direction by defining a company's mission and goals, its external opportunities and threats, and its internal strengths and weaknesses.

**Strategy implementation**   The process of devising structures and allocating resources to enact the strategy a company has chosen.

**Stretch assignments**   Job assignments in which there is a mismatch between an employee's skills and past experiences and the skills required for success on the job.

**Succession planning**   The identification and tracking of high-potential employees capable of filling higher-level managerial positions.

**Summary plan description (SPD)**   A reporting requirement of the Employee Retirement Income Security Act (ERISA) that obligates employers to describe the plan's funding, eligibility requirements, risks, and so forth within 90 days after an employee has entered the plan.

**Support network**   Trainees who meet to discuss their progress in using learned capabilities on the job.

**Sustainability**   The ability of a company to make a profit without sacrificing the resources of its employees, the community, or the environment. Based on an approach to organizational decision making that considers the long-term impact of strategies on stakeholders (e.g., employees, shareholders, suppliers, community).

**Tacit knowledge**   Knowledge based on personal experience that is difficult to codify.

**Taft-Hartley Act**   The 1947 act that outlawed unfair union labor practices.

**Talent architect**   A role of the CHRO that focuses on building and identifying the human capital critical to the present and future of the firm.

**Talent management**   Attracting, retaining, developing, and motivating highly skilled employees and managers.

**Task analysis**   The process of identifying the tasks, knowledge, skills, and behaviors that need to be emphasized in training.

**Team leader training**   Training of the team manager or facilitator.

**Technic of operations review (TOR)**   Method of determining safety problems via an analysis of past accidents.

**Teleconferencing**   Synchronous exchange of audio, video, or text between individuals or groups at two or more locations.

**Temporary assignment**   Job tryouts such as employees taking on a position to help them determine if they are interested in working in a new role.

**Third country**   A country other than a host or parent country.

**Third-country nationals (TCNs)**   Employees born in a country other than a parent or host country.

**Total quality management (TQM)**   A cooperative form of doing business that relies on the talents and capabilities of both labor and management to continually improve quality and productivity.

**Training**   A planned effort to facilitate the learning of job-related knowledge, skills, and behavior by employees.

**Training design process**   A systematic approach for developing training programs.

**Training outcomes**   A way to evaluate the effectiveness of a training program based on cognitive, skill-based, affective, and results outcomes.

**Transaction processing**   Computations and calculations used to review and document HRM decisions and practices.

**Transfer**   The movement of an employee to a different job assignment in a different area of the company.

**Transfer of training**   The use of knowledge, skills, and behaviors learned in training on the job.

**Transitional matrix**   A matrix showing the proportion or number of employees in different job categories at different times.

**Transnational process**   The extent to which a company's planning and decision-making processes include representatives and ideas from a variety of cultures.

**Transnational representation**   Reflects the multinational composition of a company's managers.

**Transnational scope**   A company's ability to make HRM decisions from an international perspective.

**Tuition reimbursement**   The practice of reimbursing employees' costs for college and university courses and degree programs.

**Uncertainty avoidance** One of Hofstede's cultural dimensions; describes how cultures seek to deal with an unpredictable future.

**Unconscious bias** A judgment outside of our consciousness that affects decisions based on background, culture, and personal experience.

**Union shop** A union security provision that requires a person to join the union within a certain amount of time after being hired.

**Upward feedback** A performance appraisal process for managers that includes subordinates' evaluations.

**Utility** The degree to which the information provided by selection methods enhances the effectiveness of selecting personnel in real organizations.

**Utilization analysis** A comparison of the race, sex, and ethnic composition of an employer's workforce with that of the available labor supply.

**Validity** The extent to which a performance measure assesses all the relevant—and only the relevant—aspects of job performance.

**Verbal comprehension** Refers to a person's capacity to understand and use written and spoken language.

**Virtual reality** Computer-based technology that provides trainees with a three-dimensional learning experience. Trainees operate in a simulated environment that responds to their behaviors and reactions.

**Virtual teams** Teams that are separated by time, geographic distance, culture, and/or organizational boundaries and rely exclusively on technology for interaction between team members.

**Voluntary turnover** Turnover initiated by employees (who the company often would prefer to keep).

**Webcasting** Classroom instruction provided online via live broadcasts.

**Whistle-blowing** Making grievances public by going to the media or government.

**Workforce utilization review** A comparison of the proportion of workers in protected subgroups with the proportion that each subgroup represents in the relevant labor market.

# NAME AND COMPANY INDEX

# SUBJECT INDEX

job withdrawal process, 456–460
physical job withdrawal, 458
psychological withdrawal, 459
sources of job dissatisfaction, 460–466
Volunteer assignments, 418

Wages. *See* Compensation
Wagner Act. *See* National Labor Relations Act of 1935 (NLRA)
Walsh-Healey Public Contracts Act of 1936, 515
*Wards Cove Packing v. Atonio*, 113, 130
*Wasabi Waiter*, 244
Wearable sensors, 178, 452
Web-based training, 303
Webcasting, 297
Weighting scheme, 492
Wellness programs, 451–454, 604
Whistle-blowing, 457–458
Wisconsin, collective bargaining restrictions and, 664
Women. *See also* Gender

in chip-making facilities, 186
compensation and, 512
glass ceiling for, 422–425
in tech jobs, 264
in workforce, 218
Workerless economy, 157–158
Worker organizing, and competing apps, 643
Workers. *See also* Employees
average annual hours worked, 567
expatriate, access to health care, 597
labor market competition and, 485
part-time, 595
temporary, 595
Workers' compensation, 575–576
Workflow design, 161
Workflow processes, 163–164
Workforce. *See also* Employees
characteristics, 19–21
and economy implications for HRM, 17–21
legacy workforce, 75

multigenerational, 36–38
temporary workers, 208–209
women in, 210, 422–425, 512
Workforce analytics, 11
Workforce changes and diversity, 35–41
aging of workforce, 35–36
mixed gender, race, and nationality, workforce of, 38–41
multigenerational workforce, 36–38
Workforce sensors, 742
Workforce utilization review, 218
Working conditions, job satisfaction and, 460–461
Work redesign, 175
Work samples, 263–265
Work share programs, 217
World Trade Organization (WTO), 678
Wrongful discharge, 442

Yield ratios, 226–227